A
MANUAL OF INDIAN TIMBERS

A
MANUAL OF INDIAN TIMBERS

AN ACCOUNT OF
THE STRUCTURE, GROWTH, DISTRIBUTION, AND
QUALITIES OF INDIAN WOODS

PREPARED BY

J. S. GAMBLE, M.A., F.L.S.
OFFICIATING CONSERVATOR OF FORESTS, BENGAL.

GYAN

Published by

GYAN

Gyan Publishing House
5, Ansari Road
Daryaganj, New Delhi-110002
Phone: 011-47034999, 9811692060
E-mail: books@gyanbooks.com

Distribution Network
gyanbooks.com
India, USA, Canada, UK, Australia, France

ISBN : 978-81-212-2233-4 (HB)
First Published, 1881

2nd Impression 2021

Printed at: Gyan Press, Delhi.

A
Manual of Indian Timbers
Author: J. S. Gamble

A MANUAL OF INDIAN TIMBERS:

AN ACCOUNT OF

THE STRUCTURE, GROWTH, DISTRIBUTION, AND QUALITIES OF INDIAN WOODS.

PREPARED BY

J. S. GAMBLE, M.A., F.L.S.,

OFFICIATING CONSERVATOR OF FORESTS, BENGAL.

Published by Order of the Government of India.

CALCUTTA:

OFFICE OF THE SUPERINTENDENT OF GOVERNMENT PRINTING.

1881.

INTRODUCTION.

In publishing the 'Manual of Indian Timbers,' the compilation of which has, owing to the writer having been at the same time engaged in his ordinary official duties, lasted over three years, it is necessary to make a few remarks on the circumstances which have led to its preparation, the materials by the assistance of which it has been compiled, and the sources from which the information given in its pages has been drawn. It will be remembered that the forests and forest products of India were represented at the Paris Exhibition of 1878 by a collection which was undoubtedly the most complete that has ever been formed in India and sent to Europe for exhibition. This collection, prepared and arranged under the immediate supervision of Dr. Brandis, the Inspector General of Forests, was got together in the winter of 1877-78, by the simple process of inviting from the different Local Governments and their Forest Officers the contribution of rough wood specimens and other products, which were afterwards prepared and arranged in a central workshop, first in Simla and afterwards in Calcutta. During the progress of this work, which lasted from August 1877 to May 1878, a very large and valuable series of wood specimens, of undoubted botanical determination, was received. The pieces of wood (to which class of specimen alone we need now refer) which were then sent, were so large and valuable that it was settled that at the same time as the principal object of the work, the collection for exhibition at Paris, was got ready, a number of duplicate sets should be also prepared, sufficient to supply a good stock to the Royal Gardens at Kew, and to other museums both in Europe and America, as well as type collections to be deposited in the offices of the Forest Conservators in the different Provinces or Circles. It is obvious that such authentic collections are likely to serve as reference collections of great and undoubted value, not only to Forest Officers, but to all persons interested in timber and ornamental woods and their applications to engineering works or industrial manufactures. Chief among these collections was that specially set apart for the Museum of the Forest School of Dehra Dún, and next to it in completeness in India was the collection deposited in the office of the Conservator of Forests in Bengal at Darjeeling, and it is these two collections, and especially the former, which have been chiefly used and consulted in the preparation of this work. But it is necessary here to point out, that the collections prepared in 1877-78 from the contributions to the Paris Exhibition works, would not alone have sufficed for the description of anything like the number of species which find a place herein, and it was owing to the fortunate circumstance that the large private collection of Dr. Brandis was available that it was found possible to make sure of the identification of most of the more ordinary timbers and lay the foundation for the descriptions which are now published. When it is considered that Dr. Brandis' private collection gave no less than 320 specimens, and that the private collection personally formed by the writer in the Darjeeling forests, and that of Burmese and Andaman woods made by the late Mr. S. Kurz and presented by the Superintendent of the Royal Botanical Gardens, Calcutta, gave a further series of 194 specimens, it will be understood that considerable material was available to add to the nucleus formed by the Paris Exhibition sets. But this is not all, for, by the kindness of several Forest Officers, supplementary pieces were received, sometimes spontaneously, sometimes by special request, from time to time; and there have been, even since the work itself was completely printed, several important additions. These were chiefly obtained by the writer's personal collection in various parts of Bengal, such as Darjeeling, the Western Dúars, Chittagong, Chota Nagpore, and Orissa, and have been described, if not in the pages of the work, at any rate in the rather voluminous Adddenda-Corrigenda sheets. In order to explain more definitely the sources from which the original Paris Exhibition woods were obtained, the following extract from Dr. Brandis' Introduction to the Catalogue of specimens of forest produce sent to that Exhibition will be worth quoting:—

"The orders for the preparation of the present collection were received in August 1877; and, as it was necessary to despatch it early in February 1878, so as to be in time for the Exhibition, barely six months were available to bring together specimens from all parts of India, and to prepare and name them. The work was entrusted to the undersigned and to Mr. J. S. Gamble, Assistant Conservator of Forests, who undertook the task of supervising the preparation of the specimens. A workshop was at once established in Simla, and a large number of pieces were collected from the hills in the vicinity of that place. These specimens are numbered from 1 to 115, and from 145 to 159. Early in November the work was transferred to Calcutta, where the specimens from all provinces were collected.

"The bulk of the logs and pieces from which the specimens were prepared arrived in December and January; some, however, were not received until February, after the collection had been prepared, packed, and despatched. It thus happens that a large proportion of the contributions from the southern forests in the Bombay Presidency from Sind, Oudh, and Chittagong, and a portion of those from Madras and Assam could not be utilized for the Exhibition, because they arrived too late.

"The difficulty was, in the short time available, to bring together seasoned pieces of the different species required. Fortunately, a number of pieces collected between 1866 and 1870, from the North-West and Central Provinces, the Punjab and British Burma, which had been kept at Calcutta until they should be required, were available. Some of these pieces had decayed or been eaten by insects, but the remainder yielded a number of excellent and thoroughly seasoned specimens: and it is remarkable how well many of the woods had kept in the damp climate of Calcutta. The specimens yielded by these collections were numbered from 160 to 353.

"From the Punjab a large, varied, carefully named, and selected collection was sent by Mr. Baden-Powell, the Conservator, and the officers under his orders; the main series is numbered from 881 to 947, while those sent from the forests of Kulu, Kangra and Chamba, by Lieutenant-Colonel Stenhouse and Mr. Pengelly, are numbered, respectively, 116 to 132, 602 to 617, and 770 to 782.[1]

"Besides these collections and those made by the undersigned in Simla, and already alluded to, the Rev. Mr. Heyde of the Moravian Mission, Lahoul, sent a number of most interesting specimens from the arid districts of the inner Himalaya (numbered 133 to 144 inclusive): and Mr. F. Halsey of Madhopur sent a small collection of fine, well-seasoned pieces from the district of Gurdaspur (numbered 1190 to 1201).

"The contributions of Ajmere were not large enough to give timber specimens of the size required for the Exhibition; they were numbered from 437 to 472.

"Mr. Greig, the Conservator of Forests in the North-Western Provinces, sent collections made by Messrs. O'Callaghan and Bagshawe and Captain Campbell in the forests of Dehra Dún, Jaunsar, and Kumaun; they are numbered respectively 527 to 544, 420 to 432, and 873 to 875. Larger collections had been made, but, as the logs were unseasoned, they were not sent down to Calcutta. From Oudh a few well-seasoned pieces were early received (Nos. 387 to 394), but the remainder did not arrive till after the Exhibition specimens had left Calcutta.

"The collections sent from Bengal under the orders of the Conservator, Dr. W. Schlich, arrived, with the exception of those from Chittagong, in very good time, and furnished a large number of interesting specimens from parts of the country the forest resources of which are not yet generally known. Mr. Richardson's contributions from the Sundarbans (Nos. 395 to 419) illustrate well the forest growth of the delta of the Ganges and Brahmaputra; and those sent by Mr. Chester from Chittagong (Nos. 708 to 722, and 1951 to 1965) would have been of great interest had not the main series arrived too late. But the chief collections received were sent by Messrs. Johnston and Manson and the late Mr. Bonham Carter from the Darjeeling Hills and Terai, numbering 170 pieces (Nos. 354 to 385, 433 to 436, 473 to 500, 573 to 601, 618 to 627, and 641 to 707), and including several very valuable and interesting kinds of timber. Besides these, a small collection of 14 specimens (Nos. 964 to 976) was obtained by Dr. Schlich from the valley of Chumbi, to the north of Sikkim; which, though to the south of the main Himalayan range, is actually in Thibet territory; and which had not hitherto been explored.

"The collections from Assam sent by Mr. Gustav Mann, the Deputy Conservator, and by the Deputy Commissioners of Cachar and Sylhet, included many fine and well-seasoned pieces. These were numbered from 628 to 641, 783 to 799, 1228 to 1234, 1254 to 1277, 1285 to 1300—the last numbers arriving too late for the Exhibition.

[1] Besides the numbers here given as indicating the specimens received from the Punjab and other provinces, there are a few scattered numbers which it has not been thought necessary to quote.

"From the Central Provinces, the Conservator, Captain Doveton, sent a collection of well-seasoned pieces, numbering 1101 to 1186, procured by Mr. Richard Thompson from the Chanda forests.

"From Berar Mr. Drysdale, the Deputy Conservator, sent fine pieces of timber, numbered 820 to 844, and a valuable series of fibres, numbered 977 to 989.

"The contributions from the Bombay Presidency comprised a few pieces from Guzerat, Poona, and Ahmednagar, too small for cutting up, and a number of large pieces sent by Lieutenant-Colonel Peyton, the Conservator, and Mr. Barrett, the Deputy Conservator, from North Kanara, numbered 992, 993, 1217 to 1227: the latter, as well as the Sind specimens already referred to, and numbered 1379 to 1384, unfortunately arriving too late for the Exhibition.

"The collections sent from Madras were very full and complete. Those from the eastern side of the Presidency were sent by Colonel Beddome, the Conservator, and numbered from 1051 to 1100. Besides this collection a few logs and specimens of minor produce came from Gumsúr—the logs too late for cutting up. From the West Coast were received a large number of specimens, Nos. 723 to 769, 845 to 869, prepared by Mr. Cherry in South Kanara. From Malabar Mr. Ferguson, the officer in charge, sent a most interesting series of sections of young trees, illustrating the rapid growth of teak in the magnificent Conolly plantations at Nilambúr.

"The pieces received from Burma were not very numerous, though they comprised the most useful kinds of trees. Many of them were of very large size. The logs sent by Major Seaton, the Conservator at Moulmein, were numbered 545 to 554 and 1944 to 1950; while those from Mr. Ribbentrop, the Conservator at Rangoon, were from 555 to 572 and from 801 to 819.

"A most important collection was sent from the Andaman Islands by Major General Barwell, the Chief Commissioner. It consisted of 26 large logs (Nos. 501 to 526), besides numerous canes and bamboos."

It must not be supposed that because specimens were too late for the Exhibition that they were not utilized for the other distributed collections and for the descriptions given herein; on the contrary, they proved, several of them, most valuable for description, and especially those from Oudh, Sind, Gumsúr and Chittagong.

After the Exhibition collections had been despatched, by the kindness of the Superintendent of the Royal Botanic Gardens, a series of 100 Andaman Islands woods made in 1866 by Lieutenant Colonel Ford, M.S.C., at that time Superintendent of Port Blair, and which were accompanied by a carefully prepared bound catalogue, giving all the available information regarding quality and uses, was made available. This collection had been received in 1867, and, for better custody, had at that time been deposited in the Calcutta Gardens. Naturally, after ten years' storage in the moist climate of Calcutta, many of the specimens were found to be considerably damaged by decay or by the ravages of white-ants, but it was remarkable that so many species were found to be sound and to have sufficiently resisted those destructive agencies to be capable of furnishing good specimens for description and distribution. They are numbered B 2201 to B 2300, and an examination of the list appended to this work will show what species in particular were fit for use. A small hand collection was also received from the Salem District, Madras; and a small collection of Ceylon woods was available from the Inspector General's Office. These were separately numbered and have been separately quoted.

The chief contributors of further specimens for purposes of description were Colonel Beddome, Captain Bailey, R.E., Messrs. Ribbentrop, Thompson, Dodsworth, Smythies, Vincent, Johnston, Elliot, Oliver, Manson, Fuchs, Wilmot, all Forest Officers; as well as Dr. G. King and Mr. J. F. Duthie, the Superintendents of the Botanic Gardens at Calcutta and Saharunpur.

Taking all these sources together, the number of specimens named, numbered, and described reaches 2,530, belonging to 906 species and 432 genera. All the wood specimens described in this work bear a letter and a number, the numbers having been given in the order of receipt, and each number refers to the particular specimen or series of specimens cut out of one log or piece. In this way there can be no mistake, any numbered specimen can be at once compared with its description in the book by means of its number, the index of numbers, and the list of specimens at the end of the description of each species. It will be noticed that some of the serial numbers from 1 to 3636 are not represented in this work. The reason is that when the Paris Exhibition collections were numbered the specimens of dyes, fibres, manufactured articles, etc., were also included; these, or most of them, have now been omitted, as well as such of the wood specimens as were in too bad a condition for description, or regarding the correct names of which any doubt was felt.

The letter represents the region from which the specimen came. For this purpose eight regions have been established, on the principle that the forests comprised in one region should possess a similar climate and a similar flora.

The regions so established and the letters by which they are designated are—

H. The North-West Himalaya, comprising the mountains of that range above an elevation of 3,000 feet, between the Indus and the Sardah river on the Nepal frontier.

P. The dry and arid region of the plains and lower hills of the Punjab, Rajputana, and Sind.

O. The plains and Sub-Himalayan tract of the North-West Provinces, Oudh and Gorakhpur, ascending to 3,000 feet.

C. Central India, the hilly country lying south of the Jumna and north of the Godavery River, and including the Vindhia and Satpura Hills, as well as Orissa.

E. The North-East comprising the Himalaya from the Nepal frontier eastwards, the Khasia Hills, Assam, Cachar, Chittagong and the Sundarbans.

D. The Dekkan, comprising the country to the south of the Godavery, and chiefly included in Madras and Mysore.

W. The west coast of the peninsula, comprising the Western Ghâts and the country lying between them and the sea.

B. British Burma, including the Andaman Islands.

Exception might, perhaps, be taken to some points in this classification. The flora of Chittagong is, in reality, quite as closely allied to that of Burma as to that of Northern Bengal and Assam; while that of Orissa and Ganjam (Northern Circars) might, perhaps, have more correctly been classed with the flora of the Carnatic than with that of Central India. But the classification adopted is a convenient one, and was established by Dr. Brandis after very careful consideration and discussion. And it will be seen by a reference to the accompanying map, kindly furnished by Mr. H. F. Blanford, F.R.S., Meteorological Reporter to the Government of India, that the regions which we have designated by the eight letters, whose meaning we have just described, are really the regions which represent the different zones of comparative rainfall. The map, it will be seen, is coloured in four shades from white to dark blue, representing:—

1. The *Arid Zone* with a rainfall less than 15 inches.
2. „ *Dry Zone* „ „ of between 15 and 30 inches.
3. „ *Intermediate Zone* „ „ 30 and 70 inches.
4. „ *Moist Zone* „ „ of over 70 inches.

The first or *Arid Zone* covers only the north-western plains of the Punjab, Sind, and Rajputana; this, with a portion of the *Dry Zone*, to the north and east of it, constitute the region marked by the letter 'P'.

The *Dry Zone* has also two further areas in South India, that is in India south of the latitude of 21°; these areas, together with the portion of the *Intermediate Zone* on the east coast of the Peninsula south of the River Godavery and a narrow strip along the east of the range of the Western Ghâts, form the region which we have designated by the letter 'D'. It may, however, be remarked that Berar, from the similarity of its flora to that of the Central Provinces, is classed, though strictly speaking within the *Dry Zone*, under region 'C'.

The rest of the *Intermediate Zone*, forming quite half of the whole country, occupies a band stretching right across the head of the Peninsula, as well as a strip along the foot of the Great Himalayan Range. Though, comparatively speaking, this large area possesses a flora showing a general common likeness and similarity, yet we can easily divide it into two by considering the great sál belt between the foot of the Himalaya and the Ganges as one section; and the great main belt of sál passing into teak between that river and a southern boundary approximately represented by the river Godavery, as a second. These two sections correspond to the regions represented respectively by the letters 'O.' and 'C'.

The *Moist Zone,* shown in the map in dark blue, occupies two main areas: *first,* the great belt of the mountain ranges of northern and north-east India from Kashmir, through Nepal, Sikkim and Assam, to Chittagong and Burma; and, *second,* the narrow belt along the western coast. This latter corresponds to the region we have marked 'W', while the former is divided into 3 sections, each having its characteristic flora: These are—

1. The Himalayan region, from Kashmir to the boundary of Nepal at the Sarda river, in longitude about 81°.
2. The Himalayan region, from the Nepal boundary at the Mechi river, in longitude nearly 88°, the Assam Valley, Khasia Hills, Cachar, and Chittagong, together with the Delta of the Ganges.
3. Burma, including the Andaman Islands.

and are respectively represented by the letters 'H', 'E' and 'B'.

So that, with trifling exceptions, the zones of rainfall and the regions represented by the letters prefixed to the numbers of the specimens agree with each other.

As far as it was published, Bentham and Hooker's "Genera Plantarum" furnished the order in which the families were arranged, as well as the general nomenclature of genera and species. At the time that most of the work was written (1878) the "Genera Plantarum" had only been published as far as the end of *Gamopetalæ.* Since then the *Apetalæ* have been completed, while the *Monocotyledons* may be expected to be published before long. In almost all cases the names given in the "Flora Indica" have been taken, though there are a few exceptions in some of the genera in which it was considered best to use better known names, quoting always the names given in the "Flora Indica" as synonyms. The "Flora Indica" is quoted as far as the end of the second volume, that is, to the end of *Cornaceæ.* The third volume of the 'Genera Plantarum' and the third volume of the 'Flora Indica,' now in course of publication, have very considerably altered the genera and specific names of many of the plants whose woods are here described. To have inserted these alterations either during the course of the printing, or as 'Corrigenda', would have caused considerable delay; and so the text remains as it was written. But when a new edition is published very great alterations will have to be made and especially in some of the large orders like 'Lauraceæ,' which will have to be entirely remodelled. Generally speaking, the only books regularly quoted, are—

1. Hooker's Flora Indica.
2. Roxburgh's Flora Indica.
3. Brandis' Forest Flora of North-West and Central India.
4. Beddome's Flora Sylvatica of the Madras Presidency.
5. Kurz's Forest Flora of British Burma.
6. Gamble's Trees, Shrubs and Large Climbers of the Darjeeling District.

The last-mentioned work being referred to merely as indicating that the tree in question is found in the North-East Himalaya, in the same way as Brandis' Forest Flora shows that the tree is found in North-West and Central India; Beddome's Flora that it occurs in Madras; Kurz's Forest Flora that it is a native of Burma.

A list of other works from which information has been drawn is appended to this introduction, and it must always be borne in mind that, excepting the actual descriptions of the woods, very little of what is here given is new, but has been compiled from all available sources of information. In this way the chief points of information here recorded under each species are—

1. The scientific name—with synonyms, so far as the six books referred to above are concerned.
2. The vernacular names—selected with as much care as possible and with the spelling given according to the most ordinary system and the pronunciation of the word.
3. The description of the wood.
4. The geographical distribution, as shortly as possible.
5. The record of all available information regarding rate of growth.
6. The results of all experiments on weight and strength that it was possible to quote.
7. The uses to which the wood and other products of the tree are generally put.
8. The list of specimens used in identification and description.

To have added also a botanical description of the plant, as is done in Mathieu's "Flore Forestière" would have doubtless increased the value of the work, but it would have at least doubled its size; and, in the present state of our knowledge of the Indian Flora, would have been almost impossible. Besides, as has been already explained, the number of species of which the woods have been described is only a small proportion in reality of the total number of species of woody plants inhabiting India. But some attempt has been made to notice even the species which have not been described. In some important genera, a list of known species and their geographical habitat has been given, in other genera other species of note have been mentioned, and, whenever possible, notes regarding the uses and qualities of the wood and the other products of the trees so referred to have been added. One great object in having thus mentioned other species has been kept in view; *viz.*, to show Forest Officers and others who may have the opportunity, *what we have not got*, and so persuade them to help, by sending to the writer or to the Forest School Museum, specimens that can be described and help at some future time in the publication of a more correct and complete description of the Indian woods than can now be attempted. In a few cases where most of the species are well known, as, for instance, the Maples, an attempt at an analytical key by which the species may be roughly determined in the forests has been given. In the French Forest Flora this has been done for all species, and the different Indian Forest Floras have similar analyses, but they are all dependent on more or less difficult botanical characters, while what we chiefly require is a series of keys which shall enable a non-botanical Forest Officer to ascertain the species of the tree he meets with, by means of the more conspicuous differences in habit, bark, and leaf.

It is now necessary to explain how the descriptions of the woods were made. During the progress of the work of preparation of specimens in Calcutta, and afterwards at more leisure in Simla, the examination of the different woods and their description was made by a committee which consisted of—

1. Dr. D. Brandis, F.R.S., C.I.E., Inspector General of Forests.
2. Mr. J. S. Gamble, M.A., Assistant to the Inspector General of Forests.
3. Mr. A. Smythies, B.A., Assistant Conservator of Forests, Central Provinces.

The descriptions were usually dictated by Dr. Brandis, and written down by one of the others, generally Mr. Smythies, but the wood structure was examined by all three officers and discussed before the description was finally passed. The whole was gone over three or four times, and in the later examinations, when the Committee was more accustomed to the differences of structure, the generic and family characters were discussed and drawn up. Some of the later received specimens, as well as those given in 'Addenda,' were described by the writer, but on the same plan and principle as was originally adopted by the Committee.

In the description of the woods the chief characters of which note has been given are:—

1. Size of tree.
2. Evergreen or deciduous.
3. Description of bark—
    - *a.* Colour.
    - *b.* Thickness.
    - *c.* Appearance and fissures, exfoliation.

4. Description of wood (sapwood and heartwood)—
   a. Colour.
   b. Hardness.
   c. Grain.
5. Annual rings.
6. Pores.
7. Medullary rays.
8. Other characters, such as the presence or absence of concentric markings.

and these characters require a short explanation.

1. *Size.*—The plants are usually described as "shrubs", "large shrubs", "small trees", "trees", "large trees", and "very large trees", according to general size; or as "climbing" or "straggling plants".

2. *Evergreen or Deciduous.*—These characters are given as far as our knowledge of the trees extends, and are easily understood.

3. *Bark.*—Is described according to its colour, which usually presents some shade of grey or brown, varying into white, or red, or black; its thickness represented by the fractions of the inch; its roughness or smoothness, and the fissures and clefts into which it is cut externally; its texture whether hard or soft, papery or corky; and the way in which it exfoliates.

4. *Wood.*—The wood is described whenever possible according to both sapwood and heartwood. The *colour* is given as nearly as possible according to the shades, usually of white or brown, but varying into red, grey, yellow, purple and black. The *hardness* is given according to the different categories as "extremely soft", "very soft", "soft", "moderately hard", "hard", "very hard", and "extremely hard", and in order to give an idea of these different categories we may instance the following among well-known trees:—

Extremely soft	*Cochlospermum Gossypium.*
Very soft	*Sterculia villosa; Bombax malabaricum.*
Soft	*Cedrela Toona; Albizzia stipulata.*
Moderately hard	*Ficus bengalensis; Tectona grandis.*
Hard	*Shorea robusta; Terminalia tomentosa.*
Very hard	*Dalbergia Sissoo; Quercus semecarpifolia.*
Extremely hard	*Pterocarpus santalinus; Hardwickia binata.*

The *grain* is usually recorded as being "close", "even", "open", "rough", "cross", &c., &c., and the relative roughness or smoothness is generally given.

5. *Annual rings.*—In the description of the wood these are only referred to as regards their presence or absence, their being more or less well marked, and the marks which so distinguish them.

6. *Pores.*—As in the case of the hardness, so, too, the pores are described according to a scale of size which varies in those trees which possess them, as "extremely small", "very small", "small", "moderate

sized", "large", "very large", and "extremely large". As examples of these categories may be given—

Extremely small . .	. *Buxus sempervirens.*
Very small . .	. *Acer pictum.*
Small . .	. *Adina cordifolia.*
Moderate-sized . .	. *Bassia latifolia.*
Large . .	. *Albizzia Lebbek.*
Very large . .	. *Erythrina suberosa.*
Extremely large .	. Many climbers,

7. *Medullary rays.*—The classification of the medullary rays has been made upon a similar plan, and they have been divided into "extremely fine", "very fine", "fine", "moderately broad", "broad", "very broad", and "extremely broad", examples of which categories are—

Extremely fine . .	. *Euonymus lacerus.*
Very fine . .	. *Diospyros Melanoxylon.*
Fine . .	. *Albizzia Lebbek.*
Moderately broad .	. *Dillenia pentagyna.*
Broad . .	. *Platanus orientalis.*
Very broad . .	. *Quercus incana.*
Extremely broad .	. *Samara robusta.*

In addition, the distance between the medullary rays is usually given and is compared with the diameter of the pores. The medullary rays are said to be *distant* when they are further apart than twice the diameter of the pores, and in some species they are closer together than that diameter, often bending round the pores which come between them.

8. *Other characters.*—The most noticeable of these are the presence or absence of concentric bars across the rays; and of patches of white tissue and the way they are disposed. These other characters are often valuable accessaries in determining the genera, and even the family to which a wood belongs. The woods of different species of ANONACEÆ are all characterised by regular ladder-like transverse bars, and so far as the experience gained in the preparation of this work goes, the character affords an unmistakeable sign for recognizing the trees of that order.

In SAPOTACEÆ again, the wavy concentric lines and the arrangement of the pores in short wavy lines affords a character which is almost certain; and if any doubt could arise it would be between that order and its neighbour the EBENACEÆ, which, however, almost always differs in having the wood of a white, grey or black colour, while that of SAPOTACEÆ is generally some shade of red.

Concentric lines of soft texture occur in many families and genera. They are very common in the LEGUMINOSÆ, as may be seen from the description of the seven groups which the woods of that family form, as described at pages 115, 116. They occur also in *Garcinia* and *Mesua* among GUTTIFERÆ; in *Elæodendron, Celastrus,* and *Lophopetalum* among CELASTRINEÆ; in *Heynea, Amoora,* and *Walsura* among MELIACEÆ; *Cordia* in BORAGINEÆ, and in other genera. The wood of the trees of the great and important order of CONIFERÆ is always recognizable, at any rate, by the constant character of the absence of pores; that of the CUPULIFERÆ by the arrangement of the pores in wavy, radial lines, and a particular texture; somewhat broad medullary rays often indicate the orders DILLENIACEÆ, RHIZOPHOREÆ, and MYRSINEÆ; a close and even-grained wood, most species of the great order of RUBIACEÆ; while the large genus *Ficus* has its woods extremely uniform in character and recognized by alternate layers of soft and firm tissue.

In this way a little practice enables a very near guess to be made at the scientific name of the tree which gave any wood which it may be necessary to determine, and it may be hoped that, with a rather wider acquaintance with the woods of India, we may be in a position to draw up an analytical table for the woods which are most chiefly in use in India, similar to that given at the end of the French Forest Flora.

Mention has been made of some families and genera which have woods of similar character and structure, but it is also necessary to point out that there is no regular rule for determining orders and genera by means of the wood, for in some cases the structure of the different component genera or species presents characters of a very dissimilar type. In the genus *Dalbergia,* for instance, there is a very great dissimilarity, so that while three species (see p. 124) have hard dark-coloured heavy woods, others have white, often soft, woods without heartwood, and one species has the peculiarity of a wood divided into concentric rings, which are often separable, of alternate layers of wood and bark-like tissue.

But, in general, it may be said that in the same genus the wood structure is usually constant, and in this way the character may often serve as a valuable aid in botanic investigation, as it has constantly done in palæontology.

It is not always easy to give in words an explanation of the reasons which lead one who is tolerably conversant with the structure of woods to pronounce an opinion; there are often characters of appearance, touch, colour, odour, &c., which afford clues, as well as the arrangement and relative size of the pores and medullary rays, and the presence or absence of annual rings; so that it is really only experience and habit that can teach us to recognize, from a mere inspection of a wood, the place which it ought to occupy in the natural system.

As an instance of how the structure of a wood may bear out an opinion on generic distinction the following may be given. When describing the woods of the different species of Olive, one kind was met with which presented a structure entirely dissimilar from the rest. This was our No. E 379 which was sent, accompanied by leaf specimens, from the higher forests of Sikkim. Wishing to ascertain the name, Dr. Brandis took the specimens to the Calcutta Herbarium, and after careful examination pronounced them to belong to a species of *Osmanthus*, a genus closely allied to *Olea*, and it is as *Osmanthus*, nov. sp., that the wood is described at p. 257. A few days ago, in the forest near Darjeeling, the writer found trees of the well known *Osmanthus fragrans*, and on examining the wood, found that it agreed in structure with No. E. 379, having the pretty network of anastomosing bands of pores, and not the more regular and uniform arrangement presented by *Olea*. So that the correctness of Dr. Brandis' determination is borne out by the structure of the wood at any rate.

The examination of specimens to determine the *rate of growth* was chiefly made by Mr. Smythies, assisted at one time by Dr. Warth; and, in writing the account of rate of growth, reference has been made to all the information published, or otherwise obtainable, on the subject. For the principal woods some data have been procured which will doubtless be very valuable; while even the record of the countings made on our small specimens is, though not absolutely reliable, at any rate useful as a commencement. Whenever possible, countings were made on the log, on the whole diameter of the section, but time and leisure were not always available for this during the work in Calcutta, so that many of the results given are merely calculated from an inspection of such pieces as were available, and are necessarily, therefore, not completely reliable. This explanation is necessary, in order that it may be well understood, that our record is not always a record of the results of a series of carefully conducted experiments and examinations, but in many cases is only given as a beginning and as being the best information available.

The discussion of the rate of growth of teak was based on a memorandum which was published by Dr. Brandis on the subject and circulated; that of sál was chiefly drawn up by Mr. Smythies, and appeared first in Vol. IV, page 324, of the *Indian Forester*; the rest were drawn up by the writer. Information regarding the rate of growth of our forest trees is one of the greatest of our desiderata, as such information is essential to the determination of the rotation of forests and the construction of working plans, so that no possible opportunity should be lost of collecting information on the subject.

The rate of growth is recorded as "slow", "moderate", or "fast", according as the number of rings per inch is greater than 12, between 12 and 6, and less than 6. These correspond to ages at 6 feet in girth of 134 years, 67 to 134, and 67 years respectively.

Weight.—As already stated in reference to the annual rings, the experiments made with our specimens in ascertaining the specific gravity of different kinds of woods, are also merely given as being often the only information available. Most of the specimens weighed were of small size, and they were, perhaps, not always cut so as to be capable of very exact measurement, but, nevertheless, the information obtained is of value and can serve until it is supplemented or superseded by more accurate experiments made with a large choice of specimens.

The weighings were done by Mr. Smythies and Dr. H. Warth, and the result is given in the form of the number of pounds per cubic foot, as being a more easily utilized form of information than the figures representing the specific gravity, compared with that of water taken as 1. The weight here recorded is always, unless otherwise stated, that of seasoned timber, and it is given as "light", "moderately heavy", "heavy", and "very heavy" according as the woods give:—

Light, less than 30lbs. per cubic foot.
Moderately heavy, from 30lbs. to 50lbs. per cubic foot.
Heavy, from 50lbs. to 70lbs. per cubic foot.
Very heavy, over 70lbs. per cubic foot.

As in the Forest Flora of North-West and Central India, only the information regarding the *transverse strength* of timber is recorded, though in a few cases the modulus of elasticity is also given.

In regard to *transverse strength*, the value of P is the result obtained by the formula—

$$\frac{W \times L}{B \times D^2}$$

where—

W=The breaking weight, or the weight which when placed on the middle of the bar causes it to break.
L=the length of the bar between supports, in feet.
B=the breadth of the bar, in inches.
D=its thickness, in inches.

A great number of recorded experiments have been brought together, chiefly from those made by Baker, Skinner, Benson, Bennett, Dundas, and others, while in these pages are for the first time published the results of the valuable and careful experiments made in Calcutta by Dr. Brandis in 1864.

In writing the remarks on the *products* of each tree, the uses for which its wood is valuable, and the various economic purposes to which the bark, fibre, gum, fruit, leaves, &c., are put, information has been extracted from a very large series of books and papers, official documents and notes furnished by the officers who contributed to the Paris Exhibition. In fact, almost all available sources of information have been consulted in order to make the remarks as complete as possible. But there is still much to be done, every day adds some new fact to the stores of our information regarding Indian trees: and the Departmental Reports, the *Indian Forester*, and the various publications of Government on the different subjects of economic interest, the dyes, fibres, gums, oils, &c., are constantly still increasing this information, so that before long even the more recently added items will become old in their turn. As our knowledge of Indian trees and their uses and capabilities extends, and as specimens are obtained and wood structures described, so it is hoped that facts may be collected which will enable some future Forest Officer to revise and republish this work, bringing it up to date and making more wide the area of our knowledge of the wonderful productions of the very varied forest flora of India. It may be called ambitious to attempt a description, even in the shape of a 'Prodromus,' of the woods of such a wide field as that of British India; but the difficulty would always be, in attempting to restrict the area, that the various floras of the different regions run so much into one another, and so often contain the same or similar species; so that it may be hoped that the publication of this work, which, except as regards the wood structure alone, is only after all a compilation, will be looked upon chiefly as an attempt to describe the principal woods of India, and in a less degree as a convenient book of reference for the native names and economic uses of Indian trees.

The Addenda-Corrigenda sheets are rather lengthy, but the number of corrected mistakes is not very great, the chief reason for length being the addition of descriptions of woods lately obtained and of native names not before published. The Kól names for instance, it is believed, are herein published for the first time: these, as well as a few Oraon, Bhumij and Kharwar names, were collected by the writer in the winter of 1880-81; and he has also added a number of Uriya names obtained in the forests of Khurda, and Magh and Bengali names obtained in Chittagong. The Mechi and Gáro names attached to Mr. Shakespear's collections in the Bengal Forest Herbarium have also been added, as well as the Mysore names published recently by Major VanSomeren. Some further information regarding the rate of growth has also been given.

J. S. GAMBLE.

DARJEELING:
November, 1881.

LIST OF BOOKS AND PUBLISHED PAPERS REFERRED TO.

Anderson. An Enumeration of the Palms of Sikkim. Journal of the Linnean Society of London, 1868.

——. An Enumeration of the Indian Species of Acanthaceæ. Journal of the Linnean Society of London, 1866.

Atkinson. Economic Products of the North-Western Provinces. 'Gums and Gum-resins,' Allahabad, 1876.

Baden-Powell. Hand-book of the Economic Products of the Punjab, Roorkee, 1868.

Baker. Experiments on the Elasticity and Strength of Different Kinds of Timber. Gleanings in Science, 1829.

Balfour. Timber Trees of India, Madras, 1870.

Beddome. Flora Sylvatica of the Madras Presidency, Madras, 1869-73.

——. Report on the Nilambur Teak Plantations, Madras, 1878.

Bennett. Experiments on Andaman woods. Professional Papers on Indian Engineering, Roorkee.

Bentham and Hooker. Genera Plantarum, Vols. I and II.

Bidie. Report on Neilgherry Loranthaceous Plants, Madras, 1874.

Brandis. Forest Flora of North-West and Central India, London, 1874.

——. List of Specimens of the Woods of British Burma sent to England for the International Exhibition of 1862, Calcutta, 1878.

——. Catalogue of Specimens sent to the Paris Exhibition of 1878, Calcutta, 1878.

Brandis and others. Report on the Deodar Forests of Bussahir, 1865.

——. Working Plan for the Bias Forests, 1871.

——. Working Plan for the Deoban Working Circle, 1875.

——. Preliminary Working Plan of the Sutlej Working Circle, 1875.

——. Suggestions regarding the Demarcation and Management of the Forests of Kulu, 1877.

Brandis. Suggestions regarding Forest Administration in the Central Provinces, 1876.

——. Suggestions regarding Forest Administration in the Hyderabad Assigned Districts, 1877.

——. Suggestions regarding Forest Administration in Assam, 1879.

——. Suggestions regarding Forest Administration in Ajmere and Merwara, 1879.

Cathcart and Hooker. Illustrations of Himalayan Plants, London, 1855.

Clarke. Compositæ Indicæ, Calcutta, 1876.

——. A Revision of the Ferns of Northern India. Transactions of the Linnean Society, 1880.

Cleghorn. The Forests and Gardens of South India, London, 1861.

Clifford. Memorandum on the Timber of Bengal, Calcutta, 1862.

Collins. Report on the Caoutchouc of Commerce, London, 1872.

Cooke. Report on the Gums, Resins, &c., in the India Museum, London, 1874.

Cooke. Report on the Oilseeds and Oils in the India Museum, London, 1874.

Cunningham. On Stone and Timber of the Gwalior Territory, Roorkee Professional Papers, 1854.

De-Candolle. Prodromus Systematis Naturalis Regni Vegetabilis, Paris, 1824-1873.

————. Monographiæ Phanerogamarum, Vol. I, Meliaceæ, Paris, 1878.

Don. Prodromus Floræ Nepalensis, London, 1825.

Drury. The Useful Plants of India, Madras, 1858.

Dundas. Experiments made at Lucknow on the Strength of Sál and Teak Timber. Professional Papers on Indian Engineering, 1879.

Fernandez and Smythies. Report on the Bijeragogarh Reserved Forests, Nagpore, 1875.

Firminger. A Manual of Gardening for India, Calcutta, 1869.

Flückiger and Hanbury. Pharmacographia, London, 1874.

Forsyth. Highlands of Central India, London, 1871.

Gamble. List of the Trees, Shrubs, and Large Climbers of the Darjeeling District, Calcutta, 1878.

Griffith. The Palms of British East India, Calcutta, 1850.

Helfer. The Provinces of Ye, Tavoy, and Mergui on the Tenasserim Coast, Calcutta, 1839.

Hiern. Monograph of the Ebenaceæ. Cambridge Phil. Soc. Transactions, 1873.

Hill and Vincent. Plan of Operations for the Simla Municipal Forests, 1876.

Holtzapffel. Descriptive Catalogue of the Woods commonly employed in the Mechanical and Ornamental Arts, London, 1852.

Home. Report on the Vegetation of the Andaman Islands, Calcutta, 1874.

Hooker. Flora of British India, Vols. I & II.

————. Himalayan Journals, London, 1854.

————. The Rhododendrons of the Sikkim Himalaya, London, 1849.

———— **and Baker.** Synopsis Filicum, London, 1874.

Hunter. Statistical Account of Bengal, London, 1877.

Keay. Scantlings of Timber for Flat Roofs, Roorkee, 1872.

King and Dey. A Glossary of Indian Plants, Calcutta, 1879.

Kurz. Report on the Vegetation of the Andaman Islands, Calcutta, 1870.

————. Preliminary Forest Report of Pegu, Calcutta, 1875.

————. Forest Flora of British Burma, Calcutta, 1877.

Lang. Indian Timber Trees. Professional Papers on Indian Engineering.

Laslett. Timber and Timber Trees, London, 1875.

Lewin. The Hill Tracts of Chittagong, Calcutta, 1869.

Lindley and Moore. Treasury of Botany, London, 1873.

Mathieu. Flore Forestière, Paris, 1877.

Molesworth. Graphic Diagrams for the Strength of Teak Beams. Professional Papers on Indian Engineering, Roorkee.

Munro. A Monograph of the Bambusaceæ. Transactions of the Linnean Society, 1868.

Mueller. Select Plants for Industrial Culture, Melbourne, 1876.

Newbery. Descriptive Catalogue of the Economic Woods of Victoria, Melbourne, 1877.

Ribbentrop. Hints on Arboriculture in the Panjab, Calcutta, 1874.

————. Working Plan of the Kalatop Forest, 1873.

Roxburgh. Flora Indica, Calcutta, 1832, reprint 1874.

Royle. Illustrations of the Botany of the Himalayan Mountains, London, 1839.

———. The Fibrous Plants of India, London, 1855.

Schlich. Report on the Pyinkado Forests of Arakan, Rangoon, 1870.

Sebert. Notice sur les Bois de la Nouvelle Calédonie, Paris.

Skinner. Description and Strength of some Indian Timbers, Madras, 1862.

Stewart. Punjab Plants, Lahore, 1869.

Strettell. Note on Caoutchouc obtained from *Chavannesia esculenta*, Rangoon, 1874.

Thompson. Report on Insects Destructive to Woods and Forests, Allahabad, 1868.

Thwaites. Enumeratio Plantarum Zeylaniæ, London, 1864.

Van Someren. List of the Forest Trees of Mysore and Coorg.

Wallich. Plantæ Asiaticæ Rariores, London, 1830.

———. List of Indian Woods collected by —. By A. Aikin. Transactions of the Society of Arts, 1839.

Waring. Pharmacopœia of India, London, 1868.

Watson. List of Indian Products, London, 1872.

———. Index to Names of Eastern Plants and Products, London, 1868.

Wight. Icones Plantarum Indiæ Orientalis, Madras, 1840-1853.

———. Illustrations of Indian Botany, Madras, 1838—53.

Also numerous papers in the *Indian Agriculturist, Statistical Reporter, Indian Forester* and other periodicals.

ADDENDA AND CORRIGENDA.

Page 1, last line but 6. *For* "H 2850." *read* "H 2820."

" 2, line 7. *After* "Andamans." *add* "It has a red bark, peeling off in hard flakes; light brown, moderately hard wood, with large round pores and broad medullary rays (E 3370. Kasalong Reserve, Chittagong.)"

" 2, *Dillenia indica.* To vernacular names *add* "*Ramphal*, Nep.; *Panpui*, Gáro; *Betta kanagala, kad kanagala*, Kan.; *Chilta*, Monghyr; *Oao*, Uriya;"

" 2, line 6 from the bottom, *after* 'radius.' *add* "A round (E 2310) in the Bengal Forest Museum shews 62 rings for a mean radius of 6½ inches, or nearly 9 rings per inch."

" 3, line 4. *Add* "The leaves are said by Mr. Brownlow of Cachar to be used for feeding the silkworm *Attacus Atlas*."

" 3, *D. pentagyna.* To vernacular names *add* "*Pashkouli*, Rajbanshi; *Agar*, Monghyr; *Uchki*, Gáro; *Korkot*, Oraon; *Korkotta*, Kól; *Kaltega, kad kanagala*, Kan.;"

" 3, *D. pentagyna.* To numbers *add*—

"C 3571. Khurdha Forests, Orissa . . . . . 49 lbs."

" 5, *Talauma Hodgsoni.* To vernacular names *add* "*Luigongron*, Mechi; *Pankakro*, Gáro;"

" 5 *Magnolia Campbellii.* Before vernacular names *add* "Red Magnolia." and to vernacular names *add* "*Patagari*, Bhutia;"

" 6, *Michelia Cathcartii.* To numbers *add*—

"E 3321. Darjeeling, 6,500 ft."

" 6, *M. excelsa.* To vernacular names *add* "*Pendre*, Lepcha;"

" 7, line 2. *After* "specimens." *add* "Young specimens cut in the Park, Darjeeling, shew 4 to 7 rings per inch of radius; while a large round (E 3631) in the Bengal Forest Museum, having a girth of 91 inches, shows 7 rings per inch mean growth."

" 7, *M. excelsa.* To numbers *add*—

"E 3586. Darjeeling, 7,000 ft."

" 7, line 18. *After* "growth moderate" *add* "6 rings per inch of radius."

" 7. *M. lanuginosa.* To numbers *add*—

"E 3331. Darjeeling, 6,000 ft. . . . . . . 36 lbs."

" 9, *Polyalthia cerasoides.* To vernacular names *add* "*San hessare*, Kan;"

" 9. *After* POLYALTHIA *add* "C 3483, from the Kolhán Forests, Singbhúm, Chota Nagpore, is probably *P. suberosa*, Roxb. Vern. *Sandi omé*, Kól. Bark thick, brown. Wood olive grey, hard, close-grained, resembling that of *P. cerasoides*."

" 10, *Saccopetalum tomentosum.* To vernacular names *add* "*Omé, hake húmú* Kól; *Hessare*, Kan.;"

Page 10, *S. tomentosum.* To numbers *add*—

"C 3471. Saranda Forests, Chota Nagpore."

„ 10. *After* SACCOPETALUM above the 12th line from the bottom of the page, *add*—

"C 3536, from the Khurdha Forests, Orissa. Vern. *Patmossu*, Uriya, resembles the wood of *Saccopetalum tomentosum*, but is whiter. Weight, 51 lbs. per cubic foot."

"E 3368, from the Kasalong Reserve, Chittagong, is *Unona longiflora*, Roxb. Fl. Ind. ii. 668; Hook. Fl. Ind. i. 61; Kurz i. 35, a small tree of Assam, the Khasia Hills, and Chittagong. Bark greenish-grey, thin, smooth. Wood yellowish white, moderately hard, close-grained. Pores small, scattered, scanty. Medullary rays moderately broad, joined by numerous white transverse bars.

"B 3380, from the hills to the east of Toungoo, British Burma, is *Mitrephora vandæflora*, Kurz i. 45, a tree of the forests of Chittagong and Pegu, but chiefly found in the Martaban Hills. The wood is grey, moderately hard. Pores small to moderate-sized, not numerous. Medullary rays moderately broad, joined by numerous, regular, white transverse bars.

"E 3300, from Chunbati, Darjeeling, 2,000 ft., is *Goniothalamus sesquipedalis*, Hook. f. and Th.; Hook. Fl. Ind. i. 73; Kurz i. 41; Gamble 3. Vern. *Sané*, Nep.; *Singnok*, Lepcha, a small shrub of the Eastern Himalaya down to Burma. Bark black. Wood dark grey, soft. Pores extremely small. Medullary rays fine to moderately broad, wavy. Transverse bars very numerous, very fine."

„ 11, line 5. *After* "B 273." *add* "B 276."

„ 13, „ 26. *For* "52 lbs." *read* "55 lbs."

„ 13, „ 29. *For* "Naghanda" *read* "Nagkanda"

„ 15. *After* "**2. C. aphylla**" *add*—

"**3. C. horrida**, Linn. f.; Hook. Fl. Ind. i. 178; Brandis 15; Kurz i. 62. *C. zeylanica*, Roxb. Fl. Ind. ii. 567. Vern. *His, karvila*, Pb.; *Karralura*, Oudh; *Adonda*, Tel.; *Katerni*, Gondi; *Gitoran*, Ajmere; *Bagnai*, Monghyr; *Atanday*, Tam.; *Oserwa*, Uriya.

"A climbing thorny shrub. Bark ¼ inch thick, brown, rough. Wood yellowish white, moderately hard. Pores small to moderate-sized, scanty. Medullary rays moderately broad, not numerous, short. Faint, wavy, concentric lines of soft tissue.

"Most parts of India and Burma.

"P 3244. Ajmere . . . . 47 lbs.

"**4. C. multiflora**, Hook. f. and Th.; Hook. Fl. Ind. i. 178; Kurz i. 61; Gamble 5. Vern. *Suntri*, Nep.

"A climbing thorny shrub. Bark smooth, dark. Wood white, moderately hard. Pores small, scanty. Medullary rays short, fine, Faint concentric lines of softer texture.

"Eastern Himalaya, Upper Burma.

"E 3349. Nagri, Darjeeling, 4,000 ft.

"**5. C. olacifolia**, Hook. f. and Th.; Hook. Fl. Ind. i. 178; Gamble 5. Vern. *Naski, kais*, Nep.; *Jhenok*, Lepcha.

"A thorny shrub. Bark ¼ inch thick, brown, rough, corky. Wood white, hard. Pores small, often subdivided, or in radial lines. Medullary rays fine, very numerous.

"Sub-Himalayan tract from Nepal to Assam, chiefly in the undergrowth of Sissú forests, along rivers.

"E 3297. Balasun, Darjeeling Terai . . . . 44 lbs.

"**6. C. sepiaria,** Linn.; Hook. Fl. Ind. i. 177; Brandis 15; Roxb. Fl. Ind. ii. 568; Kurz i. 66. Vern. *Hiún garna*, Pb.; *Kanti kapali*, Uriya.

"A shrub. Bark brown, ⅛th inch thick. Wood white, hard. Pores moderate-sized, scanty. Medullary rays short, fine. Faint, white, concentric bands.

"Dry places in India and Burma.

"P 3242. Ajmere.

"C 3580, from Khurdha, Orissa, is this species. The wood resembles that of the Ajmere specimen, but the medullary rays are moderately broad and longer."

Page 15, *Cratæva religiosa.* To vernacular names *add* "*Tuiladu, bunboronda*, Mechi; *Nirujani*, Coorg;"

„ 16, line 22. *For* "moderately fine" *read* "moderately broad"

„ 16, „ 32. *After* "*Latkan*," *add* "*natkáná*,"

„ 16, „ 33. *After* "*Kuppa-manhala*," *add* "*rangamali*,"

„ 16, „ 13 from the bottom. *Add after* "Nilgiris" "*Sanna solti*, Hassan;"

„ 16, „ 7 from the bottom. *Before* "*Flacourtia*" *add* "*Bixa*,"

„ 16, last line but one. *For* "Kuntto." *read* "Kunth."

„ 17, *Cochlospermum Gossypium.* To vernacular names *add* "*Hupu*, Kól; *Betta tovare*, Kan.; *Konto palás*, Uriya;"

„ 17, line 17. *After* "Burghers," *add* "*Dodda jepalu*, Kan."

„ 18, *Flacourtia Ramontchi.* To vernacular names *add* "*Serali, merlo*, Kól; *Katail*, Palamow; *Bali baincho*, Uriya;" and to numbers *add* "C 3453. Saidope Reserve, Palamow, Chota Nagpore," and "C 3488. Kolhán Forests, Singbhúm, Chota Nagpore."

„ 18, at the end of FLACOURTIA *after* line 18 *add* "C 3519, from the Khurdha Forests, Orissa, is *Flacourtia sepiaria*, Roxb. Vern. *Baincha, bainch koli*, Uriya. Bark yellowish-red, thin. Wood light red, hard, close and even-grained. Pores very small, in radial lines between the very fine, uniform, closely-packed, wavy medullary rays."

„ 18, line 31. *For* "H 2947." *read* "H 2949."

„ 18, line 32. *After* "Assam" *add* "Chota Nagpore"

„ 18, at the bottom of the page, *add* "E 3401 from Julpigori, Bengal, is the wood of *Bixa Orellana*, Linn. Bark brown, ⅛ inch thick. Wood pinkish white, soft, even-grained. Pores moderate-sized, in radial strings of 3 to 6, prominent on a vertical section. Medullary rays fine, closely packed, bent round the pores or groups of pores, so that the distance between the rays is less than the transverse diameter of the pores. Annual rings marked by a line without pores. Growth moderate: 5 rings per inch of radius."

„ 19, Order XI. POLYGALEÆ. At the end *add* "No. E 3393 is *Polygala arillata*, Ham., from Jalapahar, Darjeeling, 7,500 ft. It has a thin grey bark, and white, soft wood. Pores small, arranged in radial, or sometimes oblique, lines or patches. Medullary rays fine, scanty. Annual rings distinct."

„ 20, heading. *For* "*Tamariæ*" *read* "*Tamarix*"

„ 21, line 11 from the bottom. *After* "*Kirballi*," *add* "*ballagi*,"

„ 23, „ 22. *After* "*Mataw*, Burm." *add* "*Divarige*, Kan.;"

„ 24, *Garcinia Cambogia.* To vernacular names *add* "*Manthulli*, Kan."

„ 24, *G. Morella.* To vernacular names *add* "*Kankutake*, Kan.;"

„ 24. *After* "**4. G. Morella**," above line 8 from the bottom, *add*—

"**5. G. stipulata,** T. And.; Hook. Fl. Ind. i. 267; Gamble 7. Vern. *Sanakadan*, Lepcha.

"A tree with brown bark. Wood light orange-yellow, moderately hard, close-grained. Pores moderate-sized, sometimes subdivided. Medullary rays moderately broad, numerous. Numerous wavy concentric bands of soft texture, and of colour lighter than the rest of the wood, across the rays, and often anastomosing.

"Sikkim and Bhutan in damp forests up to 4,000 ft.

"The fruit is yellow and sometimes eaten by Lepchas. It gives a yellow gum, chiefly from the fruit, but it does not seem to be used.

"E 3352. Kalimpung, Bhutan, 4,000 ft.

"E 3365 is a specimen of the wood of a *Garcinia* from Burkhal, Chittagong Hill Tracts. Bark thin, brown. Wood reddish white, moderately hard. Pores large, scanty, often subdivided. Medullary rays fine to broad. Numerous, wavy, concentric bands of soft tissue across the rays."

Page 25, line 16. *For* "are found" *read* "they are found"

„ 25, *Calophyllum inophyllum.* To vernacular names *add* "*Pinekai,* Kan.; *Poonang,* Uriya;"

„ 25, line 10 from the bottom. *Add* "Sebert in 'Les Bois de la Nouvelle Calédonie' says it is a magnificent wood for cabinet-maker's work, and that it gives a yellowish green, pleasantly scented resin. He gives the mean specific gravity as 0·924, equivalent to nearly 59 lbs. per cubic foot. In Orissa it is much cultivated, and an oil extracted from the seeds is used for burning."

„ 26, *C. tomentosum.* To vernacular names *add* "*Kuve, bobbi,* Kan.;"

„ 26, line 15. *After* "per cubic foot." *add* "Molesworth in 'Graphic Diagrams for Strength of Teak Beams' gives: Weight, 37 lbs., P = 640, E = 3,500."

„ 27, *Mesua ferrea.* To vernacular names *add* "*Nahsher,* Mechi; *Kesara,* Kan.;"

„ 27, line 9. *After* "evergreen tree." *add* "Bark ¼ inch thick, reddish brown, peeling off in flat thin flakes, leaving a slightly roughened surface."

„ 27, line 26. *After* "cubic foot in weight." *add* "Molesworth in 'Graphic Diagrams for Strength of Teak Beams' gives: Weight, 71 lbs., P = 1,040, E = 6,000."

„ 27, at the end of MESUA, *add* "C 3513 and C 3524 (55 lbs.), from Kohori, Khurdha, Orissa, where the tree was planted on an area of about 12 acres by a former Raja of Khurdha, are *Ochrocarpus longifolius,* Bth. and Hook. f. Vern. *Chhuriana,* Uriya. Bark reddish brown, ¼ inch thick, exuding a red gum. Wood red, hard, close- and even-grained. Pores moderate-sized. Medullary rays moderately broad, very numerous, the distance between them equal to, or less than, the diameter of the pores. Annual rings marked by a darker line. Lines of soft texture numerous, but indistinct. Numerous resin-ducts in radial long cells, which appear as shining lines on a horizontal, and black points on a vertical transverse section. Growth moderate, 8 rings per inch of radius. Weight, 55 lbs. per cubic foot."

„ 28, line 25. *For* "Bhutan Himalaya." *read* "Sikkim and Bhutan Himalaya."

„ 28, line 10 from the bottom. *Add* "Growth moderate, 7 rings per inch of radius."

„ 29, line 15. *After* "*Ouli gogen,* Nep.;" *add* "*Laidonto,* Mechi;"

„ 29, at the end of **1. S. napaulensis,** *add*—

"**2. S. Roxburghii,** Wall.; Hook. Fl. Ind. i. 287; Kurz i. 103; Gamble 8. *Ternströmia serrata,* Roxb. Fl. Ind. ii. 521. Vern. *Dalúp,* Sylhet; *Ouli gogen,* Nep.; *Dangsipha,* Lepcha; *Laidonto,* Mechi.

"A small tree. Bark thin, reddish brown. Wood reddish brown, soft, with large central pith. Pores small, very numerous. Medullary rays fine, very numerous and closely set.

"Eastern Sub-Himalayan tract, Khasia Hills, Eastern Bengal and Burma.

"E 3271. Borojhar Reserve, Western Dúars . 42 lbs."

Page 29, *Schima Wallichii.* To vernacular names *add* "*Singbrang*, Lepcha; *Gugera*, Gáro; *Gogra*, *phulgogra*, Mechi; *Sangraban*, Magh; *Sambaw*, Arracan;"

" 30, *S. Wallichii.* To numbers *add*—

"E 3602. Sivoke Forests, Darjeeling Terai . . 41 lbs."

" 30, line 9. *After* "demand" *add* "Hooker in Himalayan Journals i. 157, says that it is much prized for ploughshares and other purposes needing a hard wood."

" 30, lines 16 and 17 from the bottom. *For* "Bark thin" *read* "Bark very thin" *and for* "Wood grey, soft, even-grained" *read* "Wood pink, moderately hard, close- and even-grained."

" 30, *Camellia drupifera.* To list of numbers *add*—

"E 3358. Sivoke Hills, Darjeeling, 1,500 ft. . 60 lbs."

" 30, last line. *For* "3142" *read* "3143"

" 32, line 28. *After* "*Guga*," *add* "*walivara*,"

" 32, last line but one. *After* "No. 63," *add* "(marked *D. alatus*, which however is not the 'Eng' tree, as this is)."

" 34, line 13. *For* "Medullary rays fine, broad" *read* "Medullary rays fine to broad."

" 34, *Shorea robusta.* To vernacular names *add* "*Sarjum*, Kól; *Sargi*, Bhumij; *Sakwa*, Kharwar; *Sekwa*, Oraon; *Shal*, Beng;"

" 36, above line 12 from the bottom, *insert* "Recent countings made in the forests of Chota Nagpore shew that the rate of growth in Saranda may be taken at 7 to 9 rings per inch for trees growing in good soil in sheltered localities, and 12 to 15 rings for trees in more exposed conditions. (*Indian Forester*, Vol. VI., p. 318.) Small trees counted in Orissa gave the very good rate of 3 rings per inch. Countings of rings on rounds in the Bengal Forest Museum, cut in the Dulka Jhar Reserve, shew as follows:—

No.	Rings.	Radius.
E 3626	47	8·5 inches.
E 3627	42	8·0 "
E 3628	53	8·5 "
E 3629	70	9·0 "
E 3630	57	8·0 "

or an average of 6·2 rings per inch of radius. No. E 3617 from Sivoke and E 3616 from Bamunpokri, both rounds, give: the first 7, the second 5·7 rings per inch, so that the Sikkim Terai sál seems to have a similar rate of growth to that of Oudh."

" 36, last line but one. *After* "being 790" *add* "Molesworth in 'Graphic Diagrams for Strength of Teak Beams' gives: Weight, 60 lbs., P = 926, E = 4,800."

" 37, in schedule of experiments. *After* "Cunningham" last line but two, *add*—

"Dundas . .	1877	Oudh . .	12	10′×4″×6″	59	551 E=2,500
" . .	"	" . .	12	2′×1″×1″	"	864
Thornhill . .	1846	Terai of N.-W. P. and Oudh.	38	Various	"	710"

" 38, line 13. *After* "now available," *add* "(A tree, measured in the Valley of the Great Rangit, Darjeeling, gave: girth at 4 ft. from the ground 128 inches; height 161 feet; height to first branch, 86 feet.)"

Page 38, in list of numbers. *For* "O 388" *read* "O 386, 387, 388, 390."

„ 38, *After* C1235 *add*—

"C 3434. Kumandi Reserve, Palamow.
"C 3440. Neturhât, Palamow.
"C 3441. Chanpi „
"C 3444. Henar „
"C 3472. } Rongo, Saranda, Singbhúm.
"C 3473. }
"C 3478. } Ankua Hill, Saranda { 2,700 feet.
"C 3479. } { 2,000 „
"C 3480. } { 1,800 „
"C 3490. Kolhán Forests, Singbhúm.
"C 3556. Khurdha Forests, Orissa . . . 48 lbs.
"C 3516. „ „
"E 3385. Berhampore Forest, Rungpore, Bengal 80 lbs.

and *after* "E 2322" *add*—

"E 3616, 3618. Bamunpokri, Darjeeling, 1,000 ft.
"E 3624 to E 3630. Dulka Jhar, Darjeeling Terai 57 lbs. (E3625)
"E 3589. Sivoke Forests, Darjeeling Terai . . 47 lbs.
"E 3617. „ „ „ „
"E 3390. Dhupguri, W. Duars."

„ 39, at the end of 6. **S. siamensis**, *add*—

"7. **S. assamica**, Dyer; Hook. Fl. Ind. i. 307. Vern. *Makai*, Ass.

"A large tree. Wood brown, moderately hard. Pores large, sometimes surrounded by a ring of lighter tissue. Medullary rays fine to moderately broad, short, the distance between them equal to the diameter of the pores.

"Upper Assam.

"The wood, according to Mr. Mann, is used for planking and for making canoes.

"E 3369. Makum, Assam."

„ 40, line 27. *For* "Bennett in 1872, No. 5, Andaman Wood, gave 58 lbs., P = 737" *read* "Bennett in 1872, No. 5, three experiments with Andaman wood 3′×1½″×1½″ gave 58 lbs., P = 711."

„ 42, „ 17 from the bottom. *After* "Beng.;" *add* "*Máoh*, Gáro;"

„ 42, „ 10 from the bottom. *After* "*Juwa, oru*, Beng.;" *add* "*Daswála*, Kan.;"

„ 43, „ 2. *Add* "Sebert in 'Les Bois de la Nouvelle Calédonie' says it is used at Tahiti for planking and building light boats."

„ 43. After line 4 *add* "E 3289, from the Rinkheong Reserve, Chittagong, is the wood of *H. macrophyllus*, Roxb. A small tree. Bark ¼ in. thick, light brown, fibrous, rather smooth. Sapwood white, heartwood light, purplish brown, soft, even-grained. Pores large, somewhat scanty, often subdivided. Medullary rays fine but clearly marked, unequally distributed, short. Annual rings marked by fewer pores in the autumn wood. Growth fast, 3 rings per inch of radius."

„ 43, line 8. *After* "(Wallich);" *add* "*Reké*, Kól;"

„ 43, *Thespesia populnea*. To vernacular names *add* "*Asha, hurvashi*, Kan.; *Bugari*, Hassan;"

„ 43, line 23. *Add* "Sebert in 'Les Bois de la Nouvelle Calédonie' gives the weight at 42 lbs. per cubic ft."

„ 43, *Kydia calycina*. To vernacular names *add* "*Moshungon*, Mechi; *Bitha gonyer*, Kól; *Derhi*, Kharwar; *Kunji*, Gondi; *Bende-náru*, Kan.;"

„ 44, *Bombax malabaricum*. To vernacular names *add*—

"*Panchu*, Gáro; *Dél*, Kól; *Búrga*, Kan.;"

Page 44, *B. malabaricum.* To numbers *add*—

"E 3606. Sivoke Forests, Darjeeling Terai."

„ 44, line 16 from bottom. *After* "cuttings." *add* "C 978 is a fine specimen of the fibre sent from Berar and capable of being used for rough paper."

„ 45, last line but one. *After* "*Dodeli*, Kan.;" *add* "*Bara laiphanzeh*, Mechi;"

„ 46, *Sterculia urens.* To vernacular names *add* "*Keonge*, Manbhúm; *Teley*, Kól; *Mogul, karaunji*, Monghyr;" and to numbers *add*—

"C 3436. Kumandi Reserve, Palamow, Chota Nagpore."

„ 46, *S. villosa.* To vernacular names *add* "*Sisi, walkóm*, Kól; *Pironja*, Mundari; *Sisir*, Oraon;"

„ 47, *S. colorata.* To vernacular names *add* "*Sisi*, Kól; *Lersima*, Kharwar;"

„ 49, *Helicteres Isora.* To vernacular names *add* "*Ainthia dhamin*, Monghyr; *Renta, sakomsing*, Kól; *Aiteni*, Kharwar; *Muri-muri*, Uriya;"

„ 49, *Pterospermum acerifolium.* To vernacular names *add* "*Laider*, Mechi;" and *change* "*Mús*, Beng." *to* "*Mús*, Beng."

„ 49, *P. acerifolium.* To numbers *add*—

"E 3596. Sivoke Forests, Darjeeling Terai . . 46 lbs."

„ 50. *P. suberifolium.* To vernacular names *add* "*Giringa*, Uriya;" and to numbers *add* "C 3523, C 3534. Khurdha Forests, Orissa."

„ 50. *Eriolæna Hookeriana.* To vernacular names *add* "*Búndún, oit bulung*, Kól; *Ponra*, Oraon;"

„ 51, line 8. *For* "C 3791" *read* "C 3191," and *after* it *add* "C 3437. Kumandi Reserve, Palamow, Chota Nagpore."

„ 52, „ 7. *After* "*Chowra*," *add* "*kadu-bende*,"

„ 52, „ 31. *After* "markets." *add* "It is also cut up into thin planking and exported to Assam to make tea-boxes.

„ 52, *Pentace burmanica.* To numbers add "B 2915. Burma."

„ 53. In strength schedule, column 'Year,' last line but one, *after* "A. Mendis, No. 33" *add* "1855"

„ 53, first line after schedule. *After* "probably this." *add* "Molesworth gives: Weight 50 lbs., P = 844, E = 3,000."

„ 53, *Berrya Ammonilla.* To list of numbers *add*—

"No. 33. Ceylon collection . . . . . . 48 lbs."

„ 54, first line. *After* "Tel.;" *add* "*Bolmengo*, Gáro; *Kokúrsida*, Mechi;"

„ 54, *Grewia tiliæfolia.* To vernacular names *add* "*Tarada*, Madura;"

„ 55, *G. salvifolia.* To vernacular names *add* "*Bursu, sita pelu*, Kól" and to numbers *add* "C 3457. Barasand Reserve, Palamow, Chota Nagpore."

„ 55, *G. vestita.* To vernacular names *add* "*Pershuajelah*, Mechi;"

„ 56, *G. pilosa.* To vernacular names *add* '*Bhorkund*, Monghyr;' *Gursikri*, Kharwar;

„ 56, at the end of *G. pilosa.* After line 14 *add* "E 3318 is the wood of a small tree from Pankabari, Darjeeling, 3,000 ft. In structure it resembles the wood of *G. oppositifolia*, but has not the unpleasant odour of the latter. It is probably *G. polygama*, Roxb."

„ 56, „ 18. *After* "*Banj*, Nep.;" *add* "*Saimuladdi*, Mechi;"

„ 57, „ 16. *After* "*Rudrak*, Hind.;" *add* "*Dandla*, Mysore;"

„ 58, *Erythroxylon monogynum.* To vernacular names *add* "*Devadárum*, Kan.;"

„ 58, line 22. *After* "boats." *add* "Dr. Bidie says that 'During the Madras famine the leaves were largely eaten by the starving poor, and as there is nothing in them structurally likely to satisfy the pangs of hunger, it seems probable that they contain some principle like that of *E. Coca*.'"

Page 58, line 21 from the bottom. *After* " Beng.;" *add* " *Boromali*, Uriya;"
" 58, " 9 from the bottom. *After* " Beng.;" *add* " *Kiranelli*, Kan.;"
" 59, " 5. For " *Bönninghau senia* " *read* " *Bönninghausenia* "
" 59, " 7. *For* " *Xanthoxyleæ* " *read* " *Zanthoxyleæ*" and *for* " *Xanthoxylum*" *read* " *Zanthoxylum* "
" 59, " 19. *After* " *Loajam*," *add* " *holholi*"
" 59, " 20. *After* " Burma." *add* " Kyd gives: Weight 36 lbs., P= 267."
" 59, " 22. *After* "Hind.;" *add* "*Chouldua*, Uriya; *Laker-konta*, Monghyr;"
" 59, " 38. *After* " *Kawat*, Mar.;" *add* " *Naibela*, Kan.;"
" 59, " 46. *After* " *Suntala*, Nep.;" *add* " *Shoungpang*, Magh;"
" 60, " 28. *For* " pael " *read* " pale "

Pages 60, 61. For the whole of 2. Xanthoxylum, Linn. *substitute* the following :—

"2. Zanthoxylum, Linn.

"Contains 10 small, rarely large trees or climbing shrubs, usually armed with strong prickles. Besides the species here described *Z. tomentellum*, Hook. Fl. Ind. i. 493, is a small tree of the Eastern Himalaya. *Z. Khasianum*, Hook. f., of the Khasia Hills and *Z. tetraspermum*, W. & A. of the Western Ghâts, are prickly climbing shrubs. *Z. Rhetsa*, DC.; Hook. Fl. Ind. i. 495; Beddome xli (*Fagara Rhetsa*, Roxb. Fl. Ind. i. 417) Vern. *Rhétsa, mán*, Tel.; *Tessal*, Mar.; *Rattu kina*, Cingh., is a large tree of Southern India. *Z. Andamanicum*, Kurz. i. 181, is a straggling shrub of the Andaman Islands.

"1. **Z. alatum**, Roxb. Fl. Ind. iii. 768; Hook. Fl. Ind. i. 493; Beddome xlii.; Brandis 47; Gamble 14. Vern. *Timbúr, timur, tezmal, dúrmúr*, Hind.; *Balay timur*, Nep.; *Gaira*, Monghyr; *Sungrú*, Lepcha.

"A shrub or small tree. Bark corky, young stems with thick conical prickles from a corky base. Wood close-grained, yellow, Pores small, often in radial lines, not uniformly distributed; belts with numerous pores often alternating with belts with scanty pores. Medullary rays fine, short, very numerous.

"Outer Himalaya from the Indus to Bhutan, ascending to 7,000 ft.; Khasia Hills.

"The wood is used for walking-sticks, the branches for making tooth-brushes. The fruit is a remedy for toothache and is also used to purify water and as a condiment. The whole plant has a strong unpleasant aromatic smell.

"H 107. Bhajji, Simla, 4,000 ft. . . . 46 lbs.
"E 2329. Tukdah, Darjeeling, 5,000 ft. . 34 "

"2. **Z. acanthopodium**, DC.; Hook. Fl. Ind. i. 493; Kurz i. 181; Gamble 14. Vern. *Bogay timur*, Nep.

"A small tree. Bark $\frac{1}{8}$ inch thick, greyish brown, shining, studded with the large conical corky bases of the prickles which fall off as the tree grows. Wood yellowish white, soft. Pores small, often in short radial lines. Medullary rays fine, numerous.

"Outer Himalaya from Kumaun to Sikkim, and the Khasia Hills, up to 7,000 ft.

"A common small tree in second growth forest. Growth fast, our specimen (a round) shews 11 rings on a mean radius of $2\frac{1}{2}$ inches, or 4·4 rings per inch of radius.

"E 3415. The Park, Darjeeling, 6,500 ft.

"3. **Z. oxyphyllum**, Edgew.; Hook. Fl. Ind. i. 494; Gamble 14. Vern. *Timur*, Nep.

"A climbing shrub. Bark greyish brown, covered with large corky lenticels, and armed with recurved thorns on a conical corky base, often ¾ inch high. Wood yellowish white, soft, porous. Pores large, usually many times subdivided radially. Medullary rays moderately broad, bent where they pass the pores. Annual rings marked by a white line.

"Himalaya from Garhwal to Bhutan, from 6,000 to 8,000 ft.; Khasia Hills, 4,000 to 6,000 ft.

"E 3375. Darjeeling, 6,500 ft.

"4. **Z. Hamiltonianum,** Wall.; Hook. Fl. Ind. i. 494; Kurz i. 181; Gamble 14. Vern. *Purpuray timur,* Nep.

"A climbing thorny shrub. Bark dark grey with white lenticels, armed with short recurved prickles on a thick, nearly cylindrical corky base, often ¾ inch high. Wood yellowish white, soft. Pores fine, not numerous. Medullary rays fine to moderately broad, numerous, nearly equidistant.

"Sikkim and Assam.

"E 3416. The Park, Darjeeling, 6,500 ft.

"5. **Z. Budrunga,** DC.; Hook. Fl. Ind. i. 495; Kurz i. 182; Vern. *Brojonali,* Ass.; *Mayaning,* Burm.

"A tree with greyish-brown bark; young stems covered with thick conical prickles from a corky base. Wood moderately hard, close-grained, white. Pores small, uniformly distributed, often in short radial lines. Medullary rays fine, short, numerous.

"Eastern Himalaya, Khasia Hills, Eastern Bengal and Burma.

"E 3324. Pankabari, Darjeeling, 2,000 ft.

"6. **Z. ovalifolium,** Wight; Hook. Fl. Ind. i. 492; Beddome xlii.; Gamble 13.

"A shrub. Bark thin, grey-brown, with white vertical streaks. Wood light yellowish-white, very hard, close-grained. Pores very small, rather scanty, evenly distributed. Medullary rays fine, very numerous. Numerous sharp, white, concentric lines, as in *Murraya exotica,* which it much resembles in structure.

"Eastern Himalaya, Khasia Hills, Assam and the Western Ghâts.

"E 3353. Sivoke Hills, Darjeeling, 1,500 ft. . 54 lbs."

Page 61, Heading. *For* "*Xanthoxylum*" *read* "*Zanthoxylum;*"

" 61, *Toddalia aculeata.* To vernacular names *add* "*Tundupara,* Uriya;"

" 61, *Skimmia Laureola.* To numbers *add* "E 3293. Mahalderam, Darjeeling, 7,000 ft."

" 61, line 14 from the bottom. *For* "6" read "5"

" 61, lines 13 to 7 from the bottom. *Strike out* and *add* at the end of *M. exotica* on page 62 the following:

"2. **M. Königii,** Spr.; Hook. Fl. Ind. i. 503; Beddome xliv.; Brandis 48; Kurz i. 190; Gamble 14. *Bergera Königii,* Linn.; Roxb. Fl. Ind. ii. 375. Vern. *Gandla, gandi, bowala,* Pb.; *Harri, katnim,* Hind.; *Barsanga,* Beng.; *Chanangi,* Hyderabad; *Gant,* Banda; *Humwah,* Mechi; *Karsepak, kari-vepa,* Tel.; *Kamwepila,* Tam.; *Kari-bévu,* Kan.

"A small tree. Bark grey with shallow netted fissures. Wood greyish white, hard. Pores small, sometimes subdivided or arranged in short radial lines. Medullary rays fine, very numerous. Concentric white lines less strongly marked than in *M. exotica.*

"Outer Himalaya from the Ravi to Assam, Bengal, South India and Burma. The wood is durable and is used for agricultural implements. The leaves are used to flavour curries.

"O 3265. Saharanpur . . . . . 43 lbs."

Page 62, *Murraya exotica*. To numbers *add* "C 3495. Kolhán Forests, Singbhúm, Chota Nagpore."

„ 62, line 12. *For* "5" *read* "6"

„ 62, *Atalantia monophylla*. To vernacular names *add* "*Narguni*, Uriya;" *and* to numbers *add* "C 3515. Khurdha Forests, Orissa."

„ 62, *Feronia Elephantum*. To vernacular names *add* "*Vellam*, Madura;"

„ 63, *Ægle Marmelos*. To vernacular names *add* "*Maika*, Gondi; *Lohagasi*, Kól; *Auretpang*, Magh;"

„ 63. At the end of 8. **Aegle**. *After* "soft tissue." *add*—

"E 3295 is *Paramignya monophylla*, Wight, from Babookhola, Darjeeling, 4,000 ft. Bark white, corky, vertically cleft. Wood white, hard, close-grained. Pores very small to moderate-sized. Medullary rays very fine, extremely numerous. Prominent, sharp, white, concentric lines at unequal distances and often joining each other.

"E 3371 is the Orange, *Citrus Aurantium*, Linn. from Rajabhatkhawa, W. Dúars. Bark thin, greenish grey. Wood yellowish white, moderately hard, close and even-grained. Pores small, scanty, joined by concentric patches of white colour, which occasionally join, forming concentric circles. Medullary rays fine, very numerous, equidistant.

"E 3348 is the Lime, *Citrus medica*, L., from Darjeeling. Bark yellowish white, thin. Wood white, moderately hard. Pores small, numerous, often subdivided or in short radial lines. Medullary rays fine, very numerous. Concentric white lines distant. Pores often joined by white concentric patches.

"E 3284 is *Glycosmis pentaphylla*, Correa, from Chittagong. Bark light greyish-yellow. Wood white, hard, close-grained. Pores small, sometimes subdivided or arranged in radial lines. Medullary rays fine, wavy, very numerous. Sharp concentric white lines, often running into each other, very prominent.

"E 3355 is *Micromelum pubescens*, Bl., from the Teesta Valley, Darjeeling. Bark thin, white. Wood yellowish white, hard, close-grained. Pores small, scanty, often subdivided. Medullary rays fine, sharply marked. Sharp white concentric lines, often running into each other, prominent.

"E 3354 is *Clausena excavata*, Burm., from Sivoke, Darjeeling Terai. Bark thin, smooth, dark brown. Wood white. Pores small, scanty. Medullary rays very fine, very numerous. White concentric lines often interrupted, but very closely packed radially.

"C 3530 and C 3570 are *Limonia acidissima*, Linn. Vern. *Bhenta*, Uriya, from the Khurdha Forests, Orissa. It has a thin, light-brown bark, and very hard, yellowish-white wood. The pores are small, surrounded by white tissue, solitary or arranged in oblique strings. Medullary rays very fine, numerous, uniform and equidistant. Annual rings marked by a white line. Growth moderate, 8 rings per inch of radius. Weight, 59 lbs. per cubic foot."

„ 64, *Ailanthus malabarica*. To vernacular names *add* "*Mandadúpa*, Hassan;"

„ 64, *A. excelsa*. To vernacular names *add* "*Mahanim*, Uriya; *Ghorkaram*, Palamow;" and to numbers *add* "C 3449. Betlah Reserve, Palamow, Chota Nagpore."

„ 64, line 24. *After* "tree." *add* "Bark light greyish-brown, fibrous, rough."

„ 65, line 12 from the bottom. *For* "*Komari*" *read* "*Koniari*," and at line 5 from the bottom *add*—

"C 3541. Khurdha Forests, Orissa . . 46 lbs."

„ 67, line 3. *For* '*Knkar*' *read* '*Kankar*'

„ 67, *Garuga pinnata*. To vernacular names *add* "*Nia jowa*, Kól; *Kékur*, Khurwar; *Karúr*, Bhumij; *Gharri*, Gondi;"

Page 67, *G. pinnata*. To numbers *add*—

"E 3601. Sukna Forest, Darjeeling Terai."

„ 68, line 3. *After* "Burma." *add* "found by Mr. R. Thompson in Bustar and on the hills of Panabarás."

„ 68, *Canarium bengalense*. To numbers *add*—

"E 3592. Sukna Forest, Darjeeling."

„ 70. *After* line 12 *add* "Molesworth gives in 'Graphic Diagrams for the Strength of Teak Beams': Weight 50 lbs., P = 736, E = 2,900."

„ 71. *After* line 19, to numbers *add*—

"E 3357. Kalimpung, Darjeeling, 4,000 ft.

"E 3360. Rangirúm, Darjeeling, 5,000 ft."

„ 71, at the end of MELIA *add* "E 3499 is *Cipadessa fruticosa*, Bl., from the Khurdha Forests, Orissa, where it is a common shrub or small tree of the dry stony hills and laterite plateaux, and used for fuel. It has a thin reddish-brown bark and a red, moderately hard wood, which has a faint odour resembling that of the Toon wood. Pores very fine, numerous, usually in lines between the very numerous close and fine medullary rays. These latter are slightly wavy and short, and bend where they meet the pores. The pores are prominent as red lines on a vertical section. Annual rings marked by a white line. Growth of our specimen 5 to 6 rings per inch of radius. Weight, about 50 lbs. per cubic foot."

„ 72, *Dysoxylum procerum*. To numbers *add*—

"E 3595. Rungdung Forest, Darjeeling Terai."

„ 72, line 4. *Before* "Assam" *add* "Sikkim and the Western Dúars,"

„ 73, *Amoora Rohituka*. To vernacular names *add* "*Sikru*, Kól;"

„ 73, at the end of "**3. A. spectabilis**" *add*—

"**4. A. decandra**, Hiern; Hook. Fl. Ind. i. 562; Gamble 16. Vern. *Tangarúk*, Lepcha.

"A tree, with thin grey bark. Wood pinkish white, hard. Pores small, scanty, joined by wavy, occasionally concentric, bands of soft tissue. Medullary rays fine, numerous."

"Eastern Himalaya, from 2,000 to 6,000 ft.

"E 3392. Lebong, Darjeeling, 5,500 ft."

„ 74, at the end of "WALSURA" *add* "C 3459, from Bandgaon, Singbhúm, 2,000 ft., is *Heynea trijuga*, Roxb. It has a thin, rough, reddish-brown bark and yellowish-white, moderately hard wood. Pores small, often subdivided, in groups or in short radial strings, surrounded with white tissue and arranged in wavy concentric lines. Medullary rays fine, short, numerous."

„ 74, *Carapa moluccensis*. To vernacular names *add* "*Pussur*, Beng.;"

„ 74, line 22. *After* "the hair." *add* "Capt Baker in May 1829 in 'Gleanings in Science' spoke of *Pussur* or *Pussooah* as being a jungle wood of a deep purple colour, extremely brittle and liable to warp. He said that native boats made of the best species last about 3 years, and that the wood, if of good quality, stands brackish water better than sál.

"The following were Captain Baker's experiments:—

					Weight.	P=
49, 52.	Large tree	1825	.	6′×1½″×2″	51·5	472
47, 48.	Small „	1826	.	„	44	484
95, 101.	Large „	1826	.	„	46	562
104.	Small „	1826	.	„	47	586
334, 335.	Large „	„	.	33″×1½″×1″	...	502"

„ 75, line 31. *After* "wood 546." *add* "Molesworth gives for Honduras wood: Weight 35 lbs., P = 615, E = 3,100."

Page 76, *Soymida febrifuga.* To vernacular names *add* "*Suam,* Uriya;"

„ 76. To numbers *add*—

"C 3566. Khurdha Forests, Orissa . . . 71 lbs."

„ 77, *Chloroxylon Swietenia.* To vernacular names *add* "*Sengel sali,* Kól; *Bharhúl,* Kharwar; *Bhira,* Gondi; *Bhirwa,* Baigas;"

„ 77. Below line 31 *add* "Molesworth in 'Graphic Diagrams for the Strength of Teak Beams' gives: Weight 60 lbs., P = 950, E = 5,200."

„ 77, *C. Swietenia.* To numbers *add*—

		lbs.
"C 3443.	Seemah Reserve, Palamow	...
C 3572.	Khurdha Forests, Orissa . . .	57
D 2926.	Madras	..."

„ 78, *Cedrela Toona.* To vernacular names *add* "*Kujya,* Tippera; *Somso,* Bhutia; *Katangai,* Kól; *Madagiri vembu,* Madura;"

„ 79, *C. Toona.* To numbers *add*—

		lbs.
"C 3476.	Saranda Forests, Chota Nagpore . .	...
"C 3545.	Khurdha Forests, Orissa . . .	31
"E 3599.	Sukna Forests, Darjeeling . . .	39
"E 3619,	Latpanchor, Darjeeling Hills, 4,000 ft. .	...
"E 3623,	Kalingpung, Darjeeling, 2,000 ft. .	35

(The last shews 11 rings on 7 inches radius or 1·6 rings per inch, while No. E 3619 has 31 rings on a radius of 7½, or about 4 per inch, and E 3599 shews 3½ rings per inch.)"

„ 79. After the end of **C. serrata,** above the 6th line from the bottom of the page, *add*—

"In the Monograph of the Meliaceæ published in 1878 by Casimir de Candolle, the species of *Cedrela* formerly grouped under the one head of *Cedrela Toona,* Roxb., have been separately described. They are thus distinguished:—

"Ovary glabrous—

"Leaflets petioled . . . *C. serrata,* Royle.
"Leaflets subsessile . . . *C. glabra,* C. de Cand.

"Ovary hairy—

"Leaflets acute at the base . *C. Toona,* Roxb.
"Leaflets round at the base . *C. microcarpa,* C. de Cand.

"In the 'Trees, Shrubs and Climbers of the Darjeeling District," three varieties were spoken of and separated as follows:—

"'No. 1. Deciduous; flowering March; fruiting June; bark grey-brown, smooth, exfoliating; found in the plains on low land.

"'No. 2. Evergreen; flowering October–November; fruiting February and March; bark dark brown, rough, not exfoliating; found in the lower hills up to 4,000 ft.

"'No. 3, Evergreen; flowering June; fruiting November–December; bark light reddish-brown, exfoliating in long flakes; found in the upper hills from 5,000 to 7,000 ft. and of great size.'

"No. 1 is *C. Toona,* Roxb.; No. 2 probably *C. microcarpa,* C. de Cand.; No. 3, probably *C. glabra,* C. de Cand. It would, however, have probably been better to describe No. 1 as 'deciduous in the cold season' and Nos. 2 and 3 as 'deciduous in the rains.' There is perhaps a fifth species.

"They may also be distinguished as follows by the capsule:—

Capsule smooth . { capsule round . *C. Toona.*
　　　　　　　　 { „ long, pointed . *C. microcarpa.*
Capsule covered with corky tubercles . *C. glabra.*

"Of the Northern Bengal specimens which we have examined, E 360 and E 2333 will be *C. glabra,* while E 655, E 2332, E 3599,

E 3619, and E 3623 will be *C. microcarpa.* Some of the Assam, Chittagong and Burma specimens are probably *C. microcarpa.*

"No. B 3378 from the Salween, 2,000 feet, is probably *C. multijuga*, Kurz i. 229. Vern. *Toungdama.* Burm.; *Nee*, Karen. (Trade name, like the other Toon-woods, *Thitkado.*) It has a light, soft, pink wood, with the usual characteristic scent strongly perceptible, and structure resembling that of the other species of Toon, the pores being perhaps more scantily distributed. Weight, 35·5 lbs. per cubic foot."

At the foot of the page *add*—

"E 3341, from the north-eastern part of Sibságar, Assam, called *Mipak*, is a soft, reddish wood, resembling that of *Melia.* It is evidently a useful wood for the same purposes as Toon is used; it splits well and is used for shingles. Pores moderate-sized to large, often subdivided. Medullary rays moderately broad, short, tapering gradually at the ends. Annual rings distinct, about 7 per inch of radius. Weight, 27 lbs. per cubic foot."

Page 80, line 19. Omit "*Daphniphyllopsis.*"

" 81, *Olax scandens.* To vernacular names *add* "*Arthil*, Monghyr; *Rimmel*, Kól; *Bodobodoria*, Uriya;" To numbers *add* "C 3467. Bandgaon, Singbhúm, Chota Nagpore. *and* C 3494. Kolhán Forests, Singbhúm, Chota Nagpore.

" 81, 2. **Daphniphyllopsis**, Kurz, &c., should be transferred to p. 213 under **CORNACEÆ.** *Nyssa sessiliflora*, Hook. f.; Hook. Fl. Ind. ii. 747.

" 81, *Daphniphyllopsis capitata.* To numbers *add*—

"E 3608. Darjeeling, 6,000 ft."

" 83, line 8. *After* "Weight, 40 lbs." *insert* "Growth: a small tree (E 3407) felled in the Park, Darjeeling, shewed 14 rings with a girth of 18½ inches, or 4·7 rings per inch of radius."

" 85. *After* "5. **E. theæfolius**" *insert*—

"6. **E. frigidus**, Wall.; Hook. Fl. Ind. i. 611; Gamble 18.

A straggling shrub. Wood yellowish white, moderately hard, compact, with extremely small pores, extremely fine medullary rays and annual rings marked by the darker colour of the autumn wood.

"Himalaya, from Kumaun to Bhutan, from 8,000 to 12,000 feet.

"E 3406. Tonglo, Darjeeling, 10,000 feet."

" 86, *Celastrus paniculata.* To vernacular names *add* "*Kujúri*, Kól;"

" 86. *After* line 5 from the bottom *add* "C 3448, from the Barasand Reserve, Palamow, Chota Nagpore, is the same species as E 2334, but it differs in having no corky bark, but a brown thin bark. In the wood the difference is slight and consists merely in smaller pores, and a closer-grained wood. The difference may be only due to climate."

" 87, *Celastrus spinosus.* To numbers *add* "H 2950, Sutlej Valley, Punjab, 3,500 ft."

" 87. *After* "3. **C. senegalensis**" *insert*—

"4. **C. acuminatus**, Wall.; Kurz i. 252. *Gymnosporia acuminata*, Hook. f.; Hook. Fl. Ind. i. 619. *G. Thomsoni*, Kurz; Gamble 19, Vern. *Phugong*, Lepcha.

"A large thorny shrub. Bark thin, greyish white. Wood white, hard, close-grained, with numerous white concentric bands, in structure resembling that of *C. spinosus.*

"Sikkim Himalaya, and Khasia Hills, up to 5,000 feet.

"E 3391. Lebong, Darjeeling, 5,500 feet.

"**5. C. emarginatus,** Willd.; Roxb. Fl. Ind. i. 620; Beddome, lxvi.; *Gymnosporia emarginata,* Roth.; Hook. Fl. Ind. i. 621. Vern. *Bali bhains,* Uriya.

"A thorny shrub. Bark grey, thin; wood white, hard, in structure resembling that of *C. spinosus.*

"Orissa, South India and Ceylon, common shrub on dry laterite soils.

"C 3521. Khurdha, Orissa."

Page 87, *Elæodendron Roxburghii.* To vernacular names *add* "*Miri,* Kól;"

„ 88. Above the first line *add* "P 460. Ajmere."

„ 88. *After* line 7, at the end of CELASTRINEÆ *add* "No. E 3345, from Lebong, Darjeeling, is the wood of *Microtropis discolor,* Wall. Bark very thin, greenish grey. Wood white, soft. Pores very small, rather unevenly distributed in long radial broken strings. Medullary rays very fine, very numerous. Faint, concentric white lines across the rays. Weight, 35 lbs. per cubic foot."

„ 88, *Zizyphus Jujuba.* To vernacular names *add* "*Yellantha,* Madura; *Janumjan,* Kól; *Ringa,* Gondi; *Bor,* Baigas; *Bogri,* Rajhanshi; *Jibang,* Magh;"

„ 89, *Z. Œnoplia.* To vernacular names *add* "*Mahkoa,* Monghyr;"

„ 90, *Z. rugosa.* To vernacular names *add* "*Tshirka,* Kól; *Kataila,* Kharwar; *Bogri,* Rajbanshi;"

„ 90, *Z. xylopyra.* To vernacular names *add* "*Karkata,* Kól; *Goit,* Bhumij; *Kankor,* Kharwar; *Got, gotoboro, kanta bohul,* Uriya; *Ghattól, ghotia,* Gondi;"

„ 90, *Z. xylopyra.* To numbers *add*—

		lbs.
"C 3508.	Sonakalla, Khurdha, Orissa	...
"C 3559.	Khurdha Forests, Orissa	53
"C 3433.	Latihar, Palamow, Chota Nagpore	...

„ 91, line 6. *After* "Kumaun;" *add* "*Bonga sarjum,* Kól; *Kyonti,* Kharwar;"

„ 91. After line 19 *add*—

"C 3484, from the Saranda Forests, Chota Nagpore, is *V. calyculata.* It has a similar bark and structnre of wood to the preceding, but the wood is somewhat closer grained."

„ 92, after "**4. R. procumbens**" *insert*—

"**5. R. nepalensis,** Wall.; Hook. Fl. Ind. i. 640; Gamble 19. Vern. *Achal,* Nep.

"A large shrub. Bark dark brown, rough. Wood brownish grey, moderately hard. Pores very small to small, arranged in obliqu-anastomosing bands, and sometimes in softer whitish tissue. Medullary rays fine and moderately broad, short.

"Eastern Himalaya, ascending to 6,000 ft.; Sub-Himalayan tract; Khasia Hills.

"E 3346. Kalimpung, Darjeeling, 4,000 ft.

"E 3364. Dhupguri, W. Dúars."

„ 93. *After* line 10, at the end of SAGERETIA, *add* "E 3430 is *Gouania leptostachya,* DC. from Darjeeling, 6,500 ft. It has a rough brown bark, ¼ inch thick. Wood soft, with very numerous large pores and broad medullary rays."

„ 93, AMPELIDEÆ, line 5. *After* "*V. lanata,* Roxb." *add* "(E 484. Darjeeling Terai.)"

„ 93, ———, line 6. *After* "*V. repanda,* W. and A." *add* "(E 485. Darjeeling Terai)"

Page 93, AMPELIDEÆ, line 9. *Before* "H 2913" *insert* "H 44."

„ 93, ————, line 10. *After* "flattened stems," *add* "E 486, from the Darjeeling Terai, is *V. elongata.*"

„ 93, ————, line 16. *After* "*L. sambucina*, Willd." *add* "(E 880. Darjeeling Terai)."

„ 93, ————, line 20. *After* "W. Dúars" *add* "Vern. *Ashrah*, Mechi."

„ 95, line 12 from the bottom of the page. *For* "from the Sutlej eastwards," *substitute* "from the Sutlej eastwards to Nepal,"

„ 96, *Schleichera trijuga*. To vernacular names *add* "*Baru*, Kól;" and to numbers *add*—

"C 3533. Khurdha Forests, Orissa . . . . 65 lbs."

„ 97, *Sapindus attenuatus*. To vernacular names *add* "*Tigroht*, Mechi."

„ 97. *After* line 14 *insert* "E 3373, from Kaptai, Chittagong Hill Tracts, is *S. Danura*, Voigt. The wood is white, moderately hard, with scanty moderate-sized pores, very fine, numerous medullary rays, and thin white concentric bands, of soft tissue, intervening between dark bands of firmer texture."

„ 98, line 19. *After* "Kumaun." *add* "The common European Maple is *A. campestre*, Linn.; the Sycamore is *A. pseudoplatanus*, Linn.; the Norway Maple is *A. platanoides*, Linn.; and the Sugar Maple of America is "*A. saccharinum*, Linn."

„ 100, *Acer caudatum*. To vernacular names *add* "*Chetokwa*, Bhutia;"

„ 100, *A. Campbellii*. To vernacular names *add* "*Kilok*, Bhutia;"

„ 101, *A. pictum*. To vernacular names *add* "*Mandar*, Chenab;"

„ 102, line 9. After "*Nagpat*, Nep.;" *add* "*Bundibru*, Mechi;"

„ 103, *Meliosma simplicifolia*. To vernacular names *add* "*Laigongron*, Mechi."

„ 103, line 30. *After* "inch of radius." *add* "It is, however, often fast grown, especially if from coppice shoots: a tree in the Park, Darjeeling, shewed a girth of 22 inches and a height of 32 feet at an age of 22 years, giving thus $6\frac{1}{2}$ rings per inch of radius. Specimens of still faster growth are not uncommon."

„ 107, *Mangifera indica*. To vernacular names *add* "*Bocho*, Gáro; *Uli*, Kól; *Ama*, Baigas; *Tsaratpang*, Magh;"

„ 107, line 30. *After* "P = 471." *add* "Molesworth gives: Weight 42 lbs. P = 592, E = 3,400."

„ 108, *M. sylvatica*. To vernacular names *add* "*Bagnal*, Mechi;"

„ 108, line 30. *After* "are eaten." *add* "The leaves are used in Assam to feed the silkworm *Cricula trifenestrata*."

„ 109, line 20. *For* "D 1066" *read* "D 1065"

„ 109, *Buchanania latifolia*. To vernacular names *add* "*Tarum*, Kól: *Pial*, Bhumij; *Peea*, Kharwar;"

„ 110, *After* line 5, *add*—

"C 3532. Khurdha Forests, Orissa . . . . 34 lbs."

„ 110, *Odina Wodier*. To vernacular names *add* "*Jír, jial*, Monghyr; *Dowka*, Kól; *Dowka gia*, Bhumij; *Moi*, Uriya."

„ 111. *After* line 7 *add* "If this is No. 11 (*Nabhay*) of Bennett's experiments with Andaman woods in 1872 the weight was found to be 59 lbs., and P = 483, in three experiments, with bars $3' \times 1\frac{1}{2}'' \times 1\frac{1}{2}''$.

„ 111. *After* line 24, *below* "C 1103." *add*—

"C 3529. Khurdha Forests, Orissa . . . . 66 lbs."

„ 111, *Semecarpus Anacardium*. To vernacular names *add* "*Soso*, Kól; *Bhilwa*, Baigas;"

Page 113, *Spondias mangifera*. To vernacular names *add* "*Adai*, Gáro;"

„ 113, last line but three. *After* "about Simla." *add* "The silkworm *Actias Silene* is fed upon its leaves."

„ 114, *Moringa pterygosperma*. To vernacular names *add* "*Mulgia*, Kól;"

„ 117, line 1. *For* "Wood white." *read* "Wood white, with an irregular grey heartwood."

„ 117, line 2. *For* "edge" *read* "edges"

„ 117, line 7. *After* "in Europe." *add* "Our Darjeeling specimen shews 12 rings per inch of radius."

„ 117. *After* line 8 *add*—

"E 3405. Sandukpho, Darjeeling, 11,000 ft."

„ 117, line 10. *After* "and Burma." *add* "It has a smooth yellowish bark, white wood and pores rather scanty, solitary or in radial lines between the fine medullary rays. (E 3311. Pankabari, Darjeeling, 3,000 ft.)"

117, at foot of page, *add*—

"3. **Indigofera stachyodes**, Ldl.; Gamble 25. *I. Dosua*, Ham., *var. tomentosa*, Baker; Hook. Fl. Ind. ii, 102. Vern. *Chiringi jhar*, Nep.

"A small tree with thin brown bark. Wood hard, white, with an irregular dark-coloured heartwood. Pores small to moderate-sized, enclosed in patches of white tissue, forming irregular, sometimes concentric, bands. Medullary rays fine, numerous, equidistant.

"Inner Eastern Himalaya, Khasia Hills, Sylhet.

"E 3359. Rhenokh, Sikkim, 3,000 ft.

"C 3447 from Barasand Reserve, Palamow, Chota Nagpore, is *I. pulchella*, Roxb. Vern. *Uterr*, Kól; *Jirhúl*, Kharwar. The wood has a structure similar to that of *I. heterantha*."

„ 118, line 17. *After* "Kumaun;" *insert* "*Hél*, Kól; *Gurar*, Kharwar;"

„ 118, line 18. *For* "No. 3479" *read* "No. E 479."

„ 118, line 19 from the bottom. *After* "Kumaun;" *add* "*Balashoe*, Mechi;"

„ 118, line 8 from the bottom. *After* "fish." *add* "E 3636 from Bamunpokri, Darjeeling Terai, is this species. It has a thin brown bark and white wood with an irregular dark heartwood. Pores moderate-sized, often subdivided, enclosed in, and often joined by, round concentric rings of white tissue. Medullary rays short, fine to very fine, numerous."

„ 119, *Ougeinia dalbergioides*. To vernacular names *add* "*Tinsai*, Gondi; *Ruta*, Kól;" and (p. 120) to numbers *add* "C 3477. Saranda Forests, Chota Nagpore."

„ 121. *After* line 8 *add* "C 3432 is *Desmodium pulchellum*, Roxb., from Amjheria, Lohardugga, Chota Nagpore, with a yellowish-white, hard wood, annual rings marked by a white line, small pores, and fine white medullary rays;"

121, line 10. At the end *add* "*Karzani*, Monghyr; *Kaincho*, Uriya;"

121, *Erythrina suberosa*. To vernacular names *add* "*Farhud*, Kharwar;"

„ 122, *E. indica*. To vernacular names *add* "*Paldua*, Uriya; *Pharad*, Monghyr;"

„ 122, line 12 from the bottom. *For* "F 3106" *read* "E 3106;" and to numbers *add* "E 3330. Darjeeling, 7,000 ft."

„ 122, line 5 from the bottom, *after* "Nep.;" insert "*Moru, múrrd*, Kól; *Bandu, durang*, Kharwar;"

„ 123, line 3. *After* "Gondi;" *add* "*Badúri*, Singrampur; *Chihúnt*, Monghyr;"

Page 123, *Butea frondosa.* To vernacular names *add* "*Palushu,* Mechi; *Murut,* Kól; *Pharsa,* Baigas; *Parás, farás,* Behar;"

" 123, line 26 from bottom. *After* "slow matches." *add* "C 979 is a fine specimen of the fibre sent from Berar."

" 123, last line but three. *After* "Lepcha," *add* "*Dangshukop,* Mechi."

" 123, last line. *Add* "*F. Chappar,* Ham. and *F. strobilifera.,* R. Br., are common shrubs of forest undergrowth. Vern. *Ulu,* Kól."

" 124, line 40. *For* "**4. Dalbergia Sissoo,**" *read* "**4. D. Sissoo,**"

" 126. *After* the schedule *add* "Molesworth gives: Weight, 52 lbs., P. = 760, E. = 3,800," and to numbers "E 3588 Darjeeling Terai."

" 127, *Dalbergia latifolia.* To vernacular names *add* "*Rutė,* Kol; *Ruzerap* Mechi;" and to numbers *add*—

		lbs.
"C 3456.	Saidope Reserve, Palamow	—
"C 3522.	Khurdha Forests, Orissa	61
"D 1476.	Anamalai Hills, Madras	..."

" 128, line 4. *For* "W 720." *read* "W 729."

" 128. *D. lanceolaria.* To vernacular names *add* "*Piri,* Kól;"

" 129, *D. paniculata.* To vernacular names *add* "*Surteli, passi,* Baigas;"

" 130. At the end of DALBERGIA *add* "C 3450 is *Dalbergia volubilis,* Roxb., from Ramundag Reserve, Palamow. Bark thin, brown, peeling off in flakes. Wood light brown, hard. Pores small to very large, scanty. Medullary rays very fine, very numerous. Occasional faint concentric bands."

" 130. In Schedule, last line. *For*—

"Bennett, No. 1	1872	"	49·5	...	827"

read—

"Bennett, No. 1	1872	"	49·5	$3 \times 1\frac{1}{8} \times 1\frac{1}{2}$	830"

" 131, line 12. *For* "B 584" *read* "B 548."

" 132, *Pterocarpus Marsupium.* To vernacular names *add* "*Hitun, híd,* Kól; *Beeya, persar,* Kharwar; *Bijo,* Gondi; *Piasál,* Urya;"

" 133, *P. Marsupium.* To numbers *add*—

"C 3542. Khurdha Forests, Orissa . . . . 54 lbs."

" 133, *Pongamia glabra.* To vernacular names *add* "*Khawári, karmuj,* Sirguja;"

" 133, line 10 from the bottom. *After* "Beng.;" *add* "*Nás-bél,* C. P.;" and *for* "*golari*" *read* "*Golari*"

" 134. *After* line 8 *add* "No. E 3356, from the Sivoke Hills, Darjeeling, 1,500 ft., is probably *Ormosia glauca,* Wall.; Hook. Fl. Ind. ii. 253. Vern. *Chuklein,* Lepcha, a large tree of the Central Himalaya. It has a grey bark, and greyish white, moderately hard wood. The pores are large, scanty, sometimes subdivided; they are joined by irregular, wavy, somewhat anastomosing patches of white, soft tissue. The medullary rays are fine to moderately broad, wavy. The tree bears a woody pod, filled with bright scarlet seeds, which are used by the Lepchas as a bait to catch jungle fowl."

" 135. At the end of CÆSALPINIA *add* "C 3460, from Saranda, Chota Nagpore, is *Cæsalpinia sepiaria,* Roxb. Vern. *Uchay,* Kól; *Gilo,* Uriya. It has a yellowish-white corky bark, with large corky excrescences, bearing strong thorns. The wood is light brown, moderately hard, with masses of reddish-brown harder wood near the centre. The pores are large, often subdivided or in groups, surrounded and connected by anastomosing bands of white tissue. The medullary rays are fine, very numerous, the distance between them much less than the transverse diameter of the pores."

Page 136, line 13, *for* "Manson" *read* 'Mr. Manson" and line 15, *after* "end." *add* "A large tree measured by the Inspector General at Dalingkote was found to have a girth of 121 inches, a height of 181 feet and 110 feet to the first branch."

,, 136, *Cassia Fistula*. To vernacular names *add* "*Hari*, Kól; *Dunrás*, Kharwar; *Jagarúa*, Gondi: *Raella*, Baigas." and *omit* "*persar*, Palamow.", and (p. 137) to numbers *add*—

"C 3544. Khurdha Forests, Orissa . . . 58 lbs."

,, 139, line 8. *For* "*Paur, bela*, Gondi;" *read* "*Paur-bela*, Gondi;" aud then *add* "*Lamma, rúng*, Kól; *Maulan*, Kharwar;"

,, 139, line 17. *After* "Terai." *add* "C 977 is a fine specimen of the fibre sent from Berar. It was examined in 1879 by Mr. Routledge, who reported it to be an excellent, strong fibre, hemp character, and tough, (*Kew Gardens Report, 1879.*)"

,, 139, *Bauhinia malabarica*. To vernacular names *add* "*Laba*, Kól;"

,, 139, *B. racemosa*. To vernacular names *add* "*Kaimu*, Kól; *Ghatonli*, Oraon; *Katmauli*, Kharwar;"

,, 140, *B. purpurea*. To vernacular names *add* "*Buruju*, Kól;"

,, 140, *B. variegata*. To vernacular names *add* "*Kurmang*, Mechi; *Singya*, Kól; *Kundol*, Bhumij;" and at the end of the list of numbers (p. 141) *insert* "H 105 from Bhajji, Punjab, 3,000 ft., is also probably this species."

,, 141, *B. retusa*. To vernacular names *add* "*Laba*, Kól; *Tewar*, Oraon; *Katman*, Kharwar; *Thaur*, Gondi."

,, 142, *Tamarindus indica*. To vernacular names *add* "*Jojo*, Kól; *Chita*, Gondi;"

,, 143, line 15 from the bottom. *After* "line." *add* "At the Dehri workshops on the Sone River, it has been used instead of brass for bearings for machinery, and found to wear well. In the Sone river piles of *anjan* have been found after twenty years as sound as when first put in."

,, 146, lines 12, 11, and 9 from the bottom. *Omit* the words "two of the species now being grown, *viz.*," *and* "*P. pallida* of"

,, 146. *Omit* the last two lines.

,, 147. *Omit* lines 1, 2, 17 to 21.

,, 147, *Prosopis spicigera*. To vernacular names *add* "*Somí*, Monghyr; *Perambai*, Madura;"

,, 148, line 6. *After* "small tree." *add* "Bark brown, fibrous, deeply fissured vertically."

,, 148, *Mimosa rubicaulis*. To vernacular names *add* "*Dandu deta*, Kól; *Arai*, Kharwar;"

,, 148, *Xylia dolabriformis*. To vernacular names *add* "*Kongora*, Uriya;" and (p. 149) to numbers *add*—

"C 3514, 3546. Khurdha Forests, Orissa . . 54 lbs."

,, 149, line 3. *After* "District," *add* "Orissa,"

,, 149, after the schedule *add* "Molesworth gives: Weight 58 lbs., P = 836, E = 4,300."

,, 151, line 34. *After* the words "Skinner gives 884." *add* "Molesworth gives Weight 54 lbs., P = 880, and E = 4,150."

,, 152, *Acacia leucophlœa*. To vernacular names *add* "*Reúnja, rinja*, Gondi; *Goira*, Uriya;" and to numbers *add* "C 3506. Khurdha Forests, Orissa."

,, 154. Above line 19 from the bottom *insert*—

"C 3526. Khurdha Forests, Orissa . . . 62 lbs."

Page 154, line 19 from the bottom. *For* " E 663 " *read* " E 665."

„ 154, „ 7 „ „ „ *For* " locolly " *read* " locally."

„ 154, „ 6 „ „ „ *For* " F 2355 " *read* " E 2355."

„ 154. Below line 4 from the bottom *add* " No. 3420 is a piece of hard, dark-red wood, resembling this last form in appearance and structure. It was obtained from the excavations made at Prince's Dock, Bombay (see Indian Forester, Vol. VI, p 108.)"

„ 155. *A. Intsia.* To vernacular names *add* " *Kundaru*, Kól ;"

„ 155, line 15. *For* " E 2379 " *read* " E 2359. "

„ 155. After line 15 *add* " C 3468, from Bandgaon, Singbhúm, Chota Nagpore, is this species, but the wood is harder and, though recognizable, the angular form of the stem is not so prominent as in the Darjeeling specimens."

„ 155, *A. pennata.* To vernacular names *add* " *Kundaru*, Kól ; *Arar*, Kharwar ;"

„ 156, *Albizzia Lebbek.* To vernacular names *add* " *Tinia*, Uriya." and (p. 157) to numbers *add*—

" C 3560, C 3567. Khurdha Forests, Orissa . 49, 59 lbs."

„ 158, *A. procera.* To vernacular names *add* " *Tinia*, Uriya; *Pandrai*, Kól ; *Garso*, Kharwar ; *Laokri*, Mechi ; "

„ 159, line 2. *For* " between *A. Lebbek* and the woods of *A. procera* " *read* " between the woods of *A. Lebbek* and *A. procera*."

„ 159, line 10. *For* " P = 884 " *read* " P = 695."

„ 160, *A. stipulata.* To vernacular names *add* " *Chapún, kera serum*, Kól ; *Bunsobri*, Mechi ; "

„ 160, *A. amara.* To vernacular names *add* " *Wusel*, Madura ; "

„ 164, line 12. *Add* " Vern. *Lali*, Nep."

„ 164, line 13. *After* " reddish brown " *add* " with a pretty wavy lustre on a radial section."

„ 164, after line 17, *add* " E 3422. Rangirúm, Darjeeling, 6,500 ft."

„ 165, line 10 from the bottom. *After* " Himalaya. " *add* " It has a brown thick, soft bark and porous wood, with large pores and broad medullary rays. (E 3361, Darjeeling, 6,500 ft.)"

„ 166, *Rubus lineatus.* To list of numbers *add* " E 3383. Senchul, Darjeeling, 8,000 feet."

„ 166, line 17 from the bottom. *After* " Roxb. Fl. Ind. ii. 513," *add* " Vern. *Kuá*, Beng."

„ 168. *After* line 6 *add* " E 3335. Rangirúm, Darjeeling, 6,000 feet."

„ 168, at the end of ERIOBOTRYA. *After* line 6 *add* " E 3411, from Darjeeling, is *Docynia indica*, Dcne. The wood closely resembles that of *Pyrus*. Bark ⅓ inch thick, greyish brown, shining, splitting off in irregular flakes and leaving a rough under-surface. Wood light brown with an irregular purple-brown heartwood, hard, close, and even-grained. Pores very small, more numerous in the spring wood. Medullary rays fine, very numerous. Annual rings marked by a line. Our specimen is a round with a mean diameter of 12 inches, and shewing 36 well-marked rings ; the growth, therefore, is 6 rings per inch of radius."

„ 169, last line but two. *Add* " E 3404. Tonglo, Darjeeling, 10,000 feet (has well-marked medullary patches)."

„ 170. *After* line 7 at the end of PYRUS *add*—

" E 3403, from Tonglo, Darjeeling, 9,000 feet, is *P. rhamnoides*, Dcne.; Hook. Fl. Ind. ii. 377. Vern. *Kumbúl*, Lepcha ; *Kangedoc*, Bhutia, a small, often epiphytic tree of the upper forests of the Sikkim Himalaya. It has a hard, yellowish-brown wood, with numerous small, evenly distributed pores and very numerous fine medullary rays. The annual rings are marked by a darker line.

"E 3633, from Goompahar, Darjeeling, 7,000 ft., is *P. Wallichii*, Hook. f. It has a greyish-brown bark; and brown, moderately hard wood. Pores numerous, small to moderate-sized, fewer in the autumn wood and thus marking the annual rings. Medullary rays very fine, very numerous, indistinct. Medullary patches few."

"E 3400, from Darjeeling, 7,000 feet, is *Photinia integrifolia*, Ldl.; Hook. Fl. Ind. ii. 381; Gamble 37. Vern. *Shumbul*, Lepcha, a small tree of the Eastern Himalaya. Bark thin, greyish brown. Wood brown, moderately hard, close-grained. Pores small, uniformly distributed. Medullary rays fine, very numerous, the distance between them about equal to the transverse diameter of the pores. Annual rings marked by a sharp line."

Page 173, line 15 from the bottom. *For* "H 3038." *read* "H 3028."

" 174, line 8. *Omit* "H 2912."

" 177, *Carallia integerrima*. To vernacular names *add* "*Júr*, Kól;" and to numbers *add* "C 3482. Saranda Forests, Chota Nagpore."

" 179, line 6. After "Lepcha;" *add* "*Palandu, koldungi*, Kól; *Kundol*, Bhumij; *Buria, raterr*, Kharwar; *Atundi*, Uriya;"

" 179, *Terminalia belerica*. To vernacular names *add* "*Lupúng, lihúng*, Kól;"

" 180, *T. Chebula*. To vernacular names *add* "*Rola*, Kól; *Hadra*, Oraon;" and (p. 181) to numbers *add*—

"C 3531. Khurdha Forests, Orissa . . . . . 59 lbs."

" 182, *T. tomentosa*. To vernacular names *add* '*Hatana*, Kól;' and to numbers "E 3590. Darjeeling Terai."

" 184, *T. Arjuna*. To vernacular names *add* "*Gara hatana*, Kól;" and (p. 185) to numbers *add*—

"C 3461. Saranda Forests, Chota Nagpore . . 69 lbs."

" 185, *Anogeissus latifolia*. To vernacular names *add* "*Hesel*, Kól;" and (p. 186) to numbers *add*—

"C 3562. Khurdha Forests, Orissa . . . . . 62 lbs."

" 186, *A. acuminata*. To vernacular names *add* "*Gara hesel, pandri, pansi* Kól;" and (p. 187) to numbers *add* "C 3462. Saranda Forests, Chota Nagpore."

" 187, line 23. *After* "A deciduous tree." *add* "Bark thin, greyish white, smooth."

" 187, *Gyrocarpus Jacquini*. To numbers *add* "C 3517. Sonakalla, Khurdha, Orissa."

" 190, line 26. *For* "1095-7" *read* "1095-8" and *for* "2, 3, 4" *read* "2, 3, 4, 5."

" 190, *Psidium Guava*. To vernacular names *add* "*Gaya*, Magh;"

" 193, *Eugenia formosa*. To vernacular names *add* "*Panchidung*, Gáro;"

" 194, *E. operculata*. To vernacular names *add* "*Topa*, Kól;"

" 194, *E. Jambolana*. To vernacular names *add* "*Kuda*, Kól; *Jambún*, Oraon;" and to numbers 'E 3598, Darjeeling Terai.'

" 195. *E. Heyneana*. To vernacular names *add* "*Gara kuda*, Kól; *Jamti*, Kharwar;"

" 195. At the bottom of the page, *add* "E 3430, from the Ramundag Reserve, Palamow, Chota Nagpore, is this species. The white concentric bands are more prominent and enclose the pores."

" 196, after line 5, *add* "No. C 3582, from the Khurdha Forests, Orissa, is probably *E. zeylanica*, Wight. Vern. *Sagarabatna*, Uriya. It is a small myrtle-like shrub of the scrub forests. Bark brown. Wood hard, close-grained, grey. Pores small and extremely small, joined by concentric bands of white tissue, which are closely packed. Medullary rays very fine, very numerous.

Page 196, *Barringtonia acutangula*. To vernacular names *add* "*Ijar*, Monghyr; *Saprung*, Kól; *Hinjara*, Uriya." To numbers *add* "C 3470, Saranda Forests, Chota Nagpore."

„ 197. *Careya arborea*. To vernacular names *add* "*Asunda*, Kól; *Kúm*, Bhumij;"

„ 197, in schedule, line 8 from the bottom, column 5, *omit* the word "Various."

„ 197, in schedule, line 4 from the bottom, column 5, *for* "2 × × 1" *read* "2 × 1 × 1."

„ 198, line 9. *After* "astringent." *add* "C 980 is a fine specimen of the fibre sent from Berar."

„ 199. At the end of MELASTOMA *add*—

"E 3419, from Lebong, Darjeeling, 5,000 feet, is *Oxyspora paniculata*, DC. Bark reddish brown, thin. Wood light reddish-grey, moderately hard, with dark-brown medullary patches. Pores small to moderate-sized, scanty, often in short radial lines. Medullary rays fine, short, numerous, not straight. Concentric bands of soft tissue, often interrupted, prominent.

"C 3561, from the Khurdha Forests, Orissa, is *Memecylon edule*, Roxb. Vern. *Nirása*, Uriya. Wood light brown, very hard, consisting of alternate concentric layers of dark tissue without pores, and lighter tissue in which small but distinct pores are visible. These layers may represent annual rings. Medullary rays of two kinds, the larger fine and short, the smaller extremely fine. Weight, 60 lbs. per cubic foot."

„ 199, line 13 from the bottom. *For* "*Atlacus*" *read* "*Attacus*;"

„ 200, *Woodfordia floribunda*. To vernacular names *add* "*Icha*, Kól; *Dadki*, Bhumij; *Harwari*, Uriya."

„ 200, *Lagerströmia parviflora*. To vernacular names *add* "*Saikre*, Kól; *Sidha* Behar;" and (p. 201) to numbers *add*—

"C 3547. Khurdha Forests, Orissa . . . 58 lbs."

„ 202. *L Reginæ*. To vernacular names *add* "*Gara saikre*, Kól;"

„ 202, line 10 from the bottom. *After* "Ratnagiri." *add* "Saranda forests in Chota Nagpore."

„ 203, *L. Reginæ*. List of Numbers. *For* "E 620" *read* "E 630" and *after* "E 2188. Nowgong, Assam" *add* "E 1433. Assam."

„ 204, *Duabanga sonneratioides*. To vernacular names *add* "*Achúng*, Gáro;" and to numbers "E 3622. Kalimpúng, Darjeeling, 2,000 ft."

„ 204, line 20 from bottom. *After* "radius." *add* "Our specimen No. E 3622 shews only 2 rings per inch."

„ 205. *Sonneratia acida*. To numbers *add*—

"B 3379, from Kyoukphyoo, Arracan . . . . 42 lbs."

„ 206, *Casearia tomentosa*. To vernacular names *add* "*Roré*, Kól; *Béri*, Kharwar;" and to numbers *add*—

"C 3527. Khurdha Forests, Orissa . . . . . 43 lbs."

„ 206, line 23. *For* "O 1393" *read* "O 1363."

„ 206, *C. graveolens*. To vernacular names *add* "*Reri*, Kól; *Béri*, Kharwar;"

„ 208, line 7. *For* "Bark grey-brown, wrinkled." *read* "Bark greyish white, one inch thick, spongy, marked with horizontal wrinkles and small vertical lines of lenticels: peels off in thin papery layers."

„ 209 line 2. *After* "Cachar;" *add* "*Arengi banu*, Kól;"

Page 209, line 6. *After* "H. f and Th.;" *add* "Hook. Fl. Ind. ii. 740."

" 209, line 7. *For* "eastern slopes of the Arracan Yoma." *read* "Khasia Hills and the Eastern, &c."

" 209, at the end of HEPTAPLEURUM *add* "C 3442, from Neturhát, Palamow, 3,000 feet, is *Heptapleurum venulosum*, Seem. Vern. *Sukriruin*, Kól. Bark grey, shining. Wood light brown, soft. Pores small. Medullary rays fine to moderately broad."

"E 3635 from Goompahar Forest, Darjeeling, 7,500 ft., is *H. impressum*, C. B. Clarke. Bark brown, thick, exuding a copious gum. Wood grey, soft. Pores very small, evenly distributed. Medullary rays prominent, moderately broad. Conspicuous concentric white lines which run into each other. Annual rings doubtful.

" 210. At the end of BRASSAIOPSIS *add* "E 3409, from Darjeeling, 6,700 feet, is *Brassaiopsis speciosa*, Dcne. and Plch.; Hook. Fl. Ind. ii. 737 (*B. floribunda*, Seem.; Gamble 44), a moderate-sized tree, with thin grey bark, and soft white wood, in structure resembling that of *B. mitis*. Growth fast, 5 rings per inch of radius."

" 210, line 10. *After* "Miq.;" *add* "Hook. Fl. Ind. ii. 738."

" 210, line 11. *For* "Martaban Hills above 5,000 feet" *add* "Eastern Himalaya, Khasia and Martaban, &c."

" 210, line 12. *After* "Seem.;" *add* "Hook. Fl. Ind. ii. 738."

" 210, line 24. *After* "Linn.;" *add* "Hook. Fl. Ind. ii, 739."

" 210, at the end of HEDERA *add*—

"E 3402, from Tonglo, Darjeeling, 9,000 feet, is *Gamblea ciliata*, C. B. Clarke; Hook. Fl. Ind. ii. 740. Vern. *Rama*, Bhutia, a large tree of the forests of the Senchul and Singalila Ranges above 8,000 feet. Bark grey, smooth. Wood white, shining, moderately hard. Pores extremely small, except on the outer edges of the annual rings, which are very distinctly marked by lines of moderate-sized pores. Medullary rays fine and moderately broad, white, shining, irregularly distributed.

"E 3576, from Darjeeling, 6,000 feet, is *Pentapanax racemosum*, Seem. A large climbing or straggling shrub. Bark silvery grey, thin, peeling off in thin flakes. Wood greyish white, soft. Annual rings very prominently marked by a line of large pores: the pores in the rest of the wood small, scanty. Medullary rays moderately broad."

" 211, line 2. *After* "*Torricellia tiliæfolia*, DC.;" *add* "Hook. Fl. Ind. ii. 748;"

" 211, line 4. *After* "Khasia Hills." *add* "(See p. 81, *Daphniphyllopsis capitata*)."

" 211, line 11. *After* "Thwaites;" *add* "Hook. Fl. Ind. ii. 741;"

" 211. *Alangium Lamarckii*. To vernacular names *add* "*Ankol*, Kól; *Ankula*, *dolanku*, Uriya;" and to numbers *add*—

		lbs.
"C 3466.	Saranda Forests, Chota Nagpore . . .	...
"C 3564.	Khurdha Forests, Orissa	42"

" 211, line 33. *After* "Roxb. Fl. Ind. ii. 261;" *add* "Hook. Fl. Ind. ii. 743;"

" 212, line 5. *After* "Linn.;" *add* "Hook. Fl. Ind. ii. 744;"

" 212, line 9. *After* "Wall.;" *add* "Hook. Fl. Ind. ii. 744;"

" 212, line 24. *After* "Wall.;" *add* "Hook. Fl. Ind. ii. 744;"

" 212, line 36. *After* "Wall.;" *add* "Hook. Fl. Ind. ii. 745;"

" 213, line 11. *After* "Hook. f. and Th.;" *add* "Hook. Fl. Ind. ii. 747;"

Page 215, *Viburnum erubescens.* To vernacular names *add* "*Asari,* Nep.; *Nakouli,* Bhutia;"

„ 217, last line but 8. *For* "E 2866." *read* "E 2856."

„ 219, *Anthocephalus Cadamba.* To vernacular names *add* "*Sanko,* Kól;"

„ 220. *Adina cordifolia.* To vernacular names *add* "*Kúrumba, Komba,* Kól;"

„ 220, last line but 2. *For* "*Hnanbeng*" *read* "*Hnaubeng*"

„ 221, *A. cordifolia.* To numbers, *add*—

"C 3543. Khurdha Forests, Orissa . . . 43 lbs."

„ 222, in page number. *For* "22d" *read* "222"

„ 222. *Stephegyne parvifolia.* To vernacular names *add* "*Gúi, kómba,* Kól; *Guri, guri karam,* Kharwar;" and to list of numbers *add*—

"C 824. Bairagarh Reserve, Berar."

„ 224. *Hymenodictyon excelsum.* To vernacular names *add* "*Sali,* Kól; *Burkunda,* Bhumij; *Konso,* Uriya;"

„ 225. After line 7, *add*—

"C 3565. Khurdha Forests, Orissa . . . 29 lbs."

„ 226, *Webera asiatica.* To numbers *add* "C 3579, C 3520. Khurdha Forests, Orissa. Vern. *Jhaujhauka.*"

„ 226. *Randia uliginosa.* To vernacular names *add* "*Kúmkúm,* Kól;"

„ 227, *R. dumetorum.* To vernacular names *add* "*Portoho,* Kól; *Mohna,* Kharwar;"

„ 227. At the bottom of the page *add* "E 3363, from Dhupguri, W. Dúars, is *R. rigida,* DC. The wood resembles in structure that of *R. uliginosa.*"

„ 228, *Gardenia turgida.* To vernacular names *add* "*Duduri,* Kól; *Kharhar,* Oraon;" and to numbers *add* "C 3435. Kumandi Reserve, Palamow."

„ 228. After G. LUCIDA, at the bottom of the page, *add*: "C 3465, from Bandgaon, Singbhúm, Chota Nagpore, is *G. gummifera,* Linn. Vern. *Bururi, burúi,* Kól; *Bruru,* Bhumij. Bark brown, nearly ¼ inch thick. Wood yellowish white, hard, close-grained. Annual rings indistinct. Pores very small. Medullary rays very fine, very numerous. This wood might serve as a substitute for boxwood."

„ 229. *G. latifolia.* To vernacular names *add* "*Papra, papadar,* Kól; *Popra,* Kharwar;"

„ 229, lines 17, 18. *For* "B" *read* "C"

„ 229. At the end of GARDENIA *add* "E 3286, from the Rinkheong Reserve, Chittagong, is *Hyptianthera stricta,* W. and A. Bark brown, somewhat corky, thin, cleft in long continuous furrows about 2 lines apart. Wood brown, moderately hard, close-grained. Pores small, evenly distributed. Medullary rays of two classes: small ones very fine, very numerous; larger ones few, fine. Our specimen weighs 56 lbs. per cubic foot."

„ 230, *Plectronia didyma.* To vernacular names *add* "*Jór,* Kól;"

„ 230, line 11. *For* "grey" *read* "light brown;"

„ 230, *P didyma.* To numbers *add* "C 3481. Saranda Forests, Chota Nagpore."

„ 230, *Ixora parviflora.* To vernacular names *add* "*Pété,* Kól;" and to numbers *add*—

"C 3464. Saranda Forests, Chota Nagpore."

„ 231, *Pavetta tomentosa.* To vernacular names *add* "*Sikriba, sikérúp,* Kól; *Burhi,* Kharwar;"

„ 231, line 22. *After* "Gamble 49." *insert* "The Coffee plant."

Page 232, *Morinda exserta*. To numbers *add*—

"C 3535. Khurdha Forests, Orissa . . . . 40 lbs."

„ 232. At the end of MORINDA *add* "C 3431 from Amjheria, Lohardugga, is *Hamiltonia suaveolens*, Roxb. Vern. *Kudia*, Kharwar. It has a grey, shining bark, which peels off in short papery flakes. The wood is dark grey, soft, porous, with few small pores often subdivided, and moderately broad to broad medullary rays."

„ 233, line 13. *For* "Weight, 31·5 lbs." *read* "Weight, our specimen gives 27 lbs."

„ 233, last line but one. *For* "*Thibandia*" *read* "*Thibaudia*"

„ 235, line 25. *For* "E 3328" *read* "E 3325"

„ 237, line 9. *After* "*Kégu*," *add* "*kalma*,"

„ 238. At the end of RHODODENDRON *add* "No. E 3394, *Gaultheria Griffithiana*, Wight, from Jalapahar, Darjeeling, 7,500 feet, has a moderately hard, greyish-white wood, with numerous brown medullary spots. Pores extremely small and numerous. Medullary rays fine, scanty. The bark is light brown, peeling off in papery layers."

„ 240. *After* line 25, *add* "C 3438 from Ramundag Reserve, Palamow, and C 3528 from the Khurdha Forests, Orissa, are this species, but the bark is thinner, and the wood differs by having the medullary rays only 'broad' instead of 'extremely broad.'"

„ 241. At the end of ARDISIA *add* "E 3350, from the Sivoke Hills, Darjeeling, 1,500 feet, is *A. involucrata*, Kurz; Gamble 53. Vern. *Denyok*, Lepcha. It has a yellow corky bark and pinkish-white wood; with small, scanty pores, and broad, white, wavy medullary rays.

"E 3367, from the Kasalong Reserve, Chittagong, is *A. paniculata*, Roxb. Fl. Ind. i. 580; Beddome cxxxviii.; Kurz ii. 107, a small tree of Chittagong with handsome pink flowers. The bark is thin, greyish brown; and the wood pinkish white, with small pores radially disposed between the short, broad, wavy medullary rays.

"C 3463, from Bandgaon Ghât, Singbhúm, Chota Nagporê, 2,000 feet, is a species of *Ardisia*, probably *A. solanacea*, Willd. Bark brown, smooth. Wood grey, moderately hard. Pores small and very small, often in short radial lines between the broad, wavy, porous medullary rays."

„ 242. At the end of SARCOSPERMA *add* "C 3504, from the Khurdha Forests, Orissa, is *Sideroxylon tomentosum*, Roxb. Vern. *Kanta bohul*, Uriya. Bark light reddish-brown, thin. Wood light reddish-white, hard. Pores fine to moderate-sized, in short concentric or sometimes oblique lines. Medullary rays very fine, very numerous, equidistant. Concentric bands of rather darker colour having the appearance of annual rings."

„ 243, *Bassia latifolia*. To vernacular names *add* "*Mandukum*, Kól; *Mohúl*, Bhumij;"

„ 246, *Mimusops indica*. To numbers *add*—

"C 3551. Khurdha Forests, Orissa . . . . 72 lbs."

„ 249. *Diospyros Melanoxylon*. To vernacular names *add* "*Tiril*, Kól;"

„ 249, *D. Melanoxylon*. To numbers *add* "C 3493. Kolhán Forests, Singbhúm, Chota Nagpore."

„ 250, last line but 5. *For* "No. 62" *read* "No. 61"

„ 251, *D. Ebenum*. To numbers *add* "W 1207. South Kanara (saplings)."

„ 252, line 18. *For* "white" *read* "grey"

Page 252, *D. Embryopteris.* To numbers *add* "C 3474. Saranda Forests, Chota Nagpore."

" 253. *After* line 9, at the end of EBENACEÆ, *add* "C 3502, from the Khurdh. Forests, Orissa, is *Maba buxifolia*, Pers. Vern. *Guakoli*, Uriya. Bark greyish black, thin. Wood greyish white, moderately hard, Pores small, scanty, in short radial lines. Medullary rays very fine, numerous and equidistant. Concentric lines of white tissue, thin, very numerous and regular. In Orissa it is a very common bush on poor soils."

" 253. *After* line 24 *add* "E 3372, Darjeeling, 6,000 feet, has a similar structure, but the white bands are much less marked. It is probably *S. serrulatum.*"

" 254, at the end of SYMPLOCOS *add*—

"E 3347, Darjeeling, 6,000 feet, is *Symplocos glomerata*, King. It has a thin brown bark and white wood resembling in structure that of *S. lucida.*"

"C 3491, from the Kolhán Forests, Singbhúm, Chota Nagpore, is *S. racemosa*, Roxb. Vern. *Ludum*, Kól; *Lodh*, Oraon. Bark yellow, rough, spongy, ⅜ inch thick. Wood white, soft. Pores small, often in radial lines. Medullary rays short, broad, numerous."

" 254, last line. *After* "Beng.;" *add* "*Samsihar*, Kharwar; *Saparúng*, Kól;"

" 255, *Schrebera swietenioides.* To vernacular names *add* "*Jarjo, sandapsing*, Kól; *Ghato*, Oraon; *Ghanto*, Kharwar;"

" 256, *S. swietenioides.* To numbers *add* "C 3454. Ramundag Reserve, Palamow, Chota Nagpore."

" 256, line 35. *After* "*Shang*, Afg.;" *add* "*Banafsh*, Kandahar;"

" 256, line 40. *After* "good fuel." *add* "Experiments, made at Kandahar by Captain Call, R.E., with pieces 1′ × 1″ × 1″, gave for the average weight 32·2 lbs. and 641 for the value of P. (Indian Forester, Vol. V, p. 480.)"

" 259, after line 17, *add*—

"C 3436 from the Kolhán Forests, Singbhúm, Chota Nagpore, is probably *L. dichotoma*, DC. (*Chionanthus dichotoma*, Roxb. Fl. Ind. i. 108). Vern. *Deorkuda*, Kól. Bark ¼ inch thick, light yellowish-brown. Wood moderately hard, close-grained, white. Pores moderate-sized, often in pairs or threes, scanty. Medullary rays fine, numerous, equidistant, the distance between them equal to, or less than, the diameter of the pores. Fine concentric lines of white tissue, which may be annual rings."

" 259, at the end of LINOCIERA *add*—

"C 3412 from Hazaribagh, and C 3492 from Kolhán, Singbhúm, Chota Nagpore, are *Nyctanthes Arbor-tristis*, Linn. Bark ¼ inch thick, light brown, rough. Wood yellowish-brown, moderately hard, close-grained. Pores small, grouped in short radial lines, but arranged more or less in concentric rings, the annual rings apparently marked by a dark line and a more complete ring of pores. Medullary rays very fine to fine, very numerous, the distance between them equal to the transverse diameter of the pores."

" 261, *Carissa diffusa.* To vernacular names *add* "*Kanuwán*, Oraon; *Anka koli*, Uriya;" and to numbers *add* "C 3518. Khurdha Forests, Orissa."

" 261, at the bottom *add* "C 3511 and C 3569, from the Khurdha Forests, Orissa, are *Carissa Carandas*, Linn., Vern. *Kenda keri, kerendo kuli*, Uriya. Bark yellowish brown, peeling off in square flakes. Wood white, hard, smooth, close-grained. Pores moderate-sized or small, irregularly distributed. Medullary rays fine, short, numerous."

Page 262, *Alstonia scholaris.* To vernacular names *add* "*Chatin, bomudu*, Kól; *Chhatiana*, Uriya;"

„ 263, *Tabernæmontana coronaria.* To vernacular names *add* "*Chameli*, Monghyr;"

„ 263, *Holarrhena antidysenterica.* To vernacular names *add* "*Korkoria*, Oraon; *Kurchi*, Bhumij; *Towa, kuti*, Kól; *Kuria*, Kharwar; *Pita korwa*, Uriya;" and to numbers *add*—

"C 3558. Khurdha Forests, Orissa . . . 39 lbs."

„ 264, *Wrightia tomentosa.* To vernacular names *add* "*Sandikuya*, Kól; *Dudh-koraiya*, Monghyr;"

„ 265. *After* line 2 *add* "C 3496, from Chaibassa, Chota Nagpore, is *Thevetia neriifolia*, Juss. Bark thin, greyish brown, shining. Wood grey, moderately hard. Pores very small and small, numerous. Medullary rays very fine, very numerous, the distance between them less than the transverse diameter of the pores."

„ 265, line 29. *After* "*Auk*, Nep.;" *add* "*Akhwan*, Kharwar; *Palati*, Kól; *Uruk*, Uriya:"

„ 265, at line 17 from the bottom. *After* "purposes." *add* "C 3446, from the Barasand Reserve, Palamow; and C 3512, from Burkool, Khurdha, Orissa, are *Calotropis gigantea*. The bark is light yellowish-white, consisting chiefly of cork, and deeply cleft vertically. Wood white, soft. Pores small to moderate-sized, often subdivided, scanty. Medullary rays extremely fine and numerous."

„ 268, line 20. *For* "Burman" *read* "Burm., an"

„ 268, line 35. *For* "Bark $\frac{1}{10}$ inch thick .... scales" *read* "Bark $\frac{1}{2}$ to $\frac{3}{4}$ inch thick, black or brownish black, corky, very deeply and narrowly cleft vertically, so as to form thin ridges which easily break off."

„ 269, *Strychnos potatorum.* To numbers *add* "C 3500. Khurdha Forests, Orissa."

„ 269, *S. Nux-vomica.* To vernacular names *add* "*Kuchila*, Uriya;" and to numbers, *add* "C 3537 (63 lbs.), C 3538 (54 lbs.). Khurdha Forests, Orissa."

„ 269. At the end of line 11 from the bottom *add* "C3475, from the Koel River, Saranda, Chota Nagpore, is *Rhabdia viminea*, Dalzell. It has a soft white wood, with scanty pores, often subdivided or in short radial lines. Medullary rays extremely fine, very indistinct."

„ 270, *Cordia Myxa.* To vernacular names *add* "*Embrúm*, Kól;'

„ 271, *C. Macleodii.* To vernacular names *add* "*Renta, porponda*, Kól; *Bharwar, belaunan*, Kharwar; and to numbers *add* "C 3455. Betlah Reserve, Palamow."

„ 273. After line 13 *add* "C 3497, from Ghatsila, Dhalbhúm, is *Erycibe paniculata*, Roxb. Vern. *Orumin*, Kól, a climber, with the peculiar structure of climbers: soft porous wood, large pores and moderately broad medullary rays. The woody portions are arranged in wavy concentric masses, separated by lines of cellular tissue. The bark is brown with corky lenticels."

„ 275, *Oroxylum indicum.* To vernacular names *add* "*Sona*, Hazaribagh; *Sanpatti*, Monghyr; *Arengi banu*, Kól; *Sonepatta*, Kharwar; *Phunphuna*, Uriya;"

„ 275, line 31. *For* "E 2396." *read* "E 2395."

„ 277, line 3. *After* "Ceylon Collection" *add* "(marked *Spathodea longifolia*. Vern. *Daanga*, Cingh.)"

„ 278, *Stereospermum chelonoides.* To vernacular names *add* "*Kandior*, Kól;"

278, *S. suaveolens.* To vernacular names *add* "*Kandior*, Kól; *Pandri*, Kharwar;" and (p. 279) to numbers *add* "O 1378. Gonda, Oudh."

Page 279, line 16 from the bottom. *For* "B 2355" *read* "B 2235."

" 280, line 6 from the bottom. *For* "*Ban marua*" *read* "*ban marua*"

" 280, foot-note. *For* "Linn.; Soc." *read* "Linn. Soc."

" 281, *Adhatoda Vasica.* To vernacular names *add* "*Basung*, Uriya;"

" 282, *Callicarpa arborea.* To vernacular names *add* "*Búndún*, Kól; *Bogodi, gogdi*, Kharwar; *Boropatri*, Uriya;" and to numbers *add* "C 3445. Seemah Reserve, Palamow, Chota Nagpore."

" 292. Before line 5 from the bottom *insert* "C 1204. Khandwa, Central Provinces."

" 295. At the end " of PREMNA *add* "C 3578, from the Khurdha Forests, Orissa. Vern. *Agabathu*, Uriya, is a species of *Premna*, near *P. latifolia*, which it resembles in structure. Bark light yellowish-brown, thin."

" 295, *Gmelina arborea.* To vernacular names *add* "*Kasamar*, Kól;" and (p. 296) to numbers *add*—

"C 3549. Khurdha Forests, Orissa . . . 37 lbs.

"E 3605, E 3620. Darjeeling Terai."

" 297, *Vitex Negundo.* To vernacular names *add* "*Ehúri*, Kól; *Sindwar*, Kharwar; *Samálu*, Monghyr;"

" 297, *V. altissima.* To vernacular names *add* "*Simyanga, gua*, Kól;"

" 297, *V. pubescens.* To vernacular names *add* "*Muria*, Uriya;" and to numbers (page 298) *add*—

"C 3550. Khurdha Forests, Orissa . . . 52 lbs."

" 299, line 3. *After* "Mechi;" *add* "*Kula marsal*, Kól; *Anguti*, Uriya;"

" 302, NYCTAGINEÆ. At end *add* "C3507, from the Khurdha Forests, Orissa, is *Pisonia aculeata*, Linn. Vern. *Hati-ankusa*, Uriya. It has a very peculiar structure, consisting of regularly arranged, very large, single or subdivided pores or groups of pores, with 2 or 3 moderate-sized pores radially arranged on the inside of each. The medullary rays are very fine, very numerous, and often pass through and subdivide the pores. Bark light brown, thin."

" 309, *Machilus odoratissima.* To numbers *add* "E 3634. Darjeeling, 7,000 ft."

" 310, line 25. *For* "O 1378," *read* "O 1373"

" 310, *Tetranthera monopetala.* To vernacular names *add* "*Pojo, hajam*, Kól;"

" 311. After line 18 *insert* "C 3581, from the Burnai Forest, Khurdha, Orissa, is *Actinodaphne angustifolia*, Nees. Vern. *Jharchampa*, Uriya. Bark light brown, smooth; wood light brown, moderately hard, even-grained. Pores numerous, moderate-sized, evenly distributed or roughly arranged in oblique lines, often subdivided. Annual rings marked by more numerous pores. Medullary rays uniform, moderately broad."

" 313, line 11. *After* "42 lbs." *add* "This species is not a *Daphnidium*, but *Lindera heterophylla*, Meissn."

" 325, line 23. *For* "E 3377" *read* "E 3317."

" 327, *Streblus asper.* To vernacular names *add* "*Hara saijung*, Kól;" and to numbers *add* "C 3577. Khurdha Forests, Orissa."

" 327, *Plecospermum spinosum.* To vernacular names *add* "*Banabana*, Uriya;"

" 329, line 16. *For* "E 3376" *read* "E 3396."

" 329, *Artocarpus integrifolia.* To vernacular names *add* "*Porós*, Kól;"

" 330, *A. Lakoocha.* To vernacular names *add* "*Dao*, Kól;"

" 331, line 7 from bottom. *For* "W 755" *read* "W 758" and after line 7 from the bottom *insert* "W 1208. South Kanara (*saplings*)."

" 332, line 30. *Omit* "and W 720 from South Kanara;" and *for* "resemble" *read* "resembles"

Page 333, *Ficus bengalensis.* To vernacular names *add* "*Bai,* Kól;"

" 334, *F. infectoria.* To vernacular names *add* "*Baswesa,* Kól;"

" 335, *F. religiosa.* To vernacular names *add* "*Hesar,* Kól; *Jari,* Uriya;"

" 336, *F. retusa.* To vernacular names *add* "*Butisa,* Kól;"

" 338. *F. virgata.* To numbers *add* "H 148. Sainj, Simla, 3,000 feet."

" 339, *F. Cunia.* To vernacular names *add* "*Riu, ain,* Kól; *Poro dumer,* Kharwar;"

" 339, *F. glomerata.* To vernacular names *add* "*Lóa,* Kól; *Dumer,* Kharwar;"

" 340, *F. Roxburghii.* To vernacular names *add* "*Kotang,* Kól;"

" 340, *F. hispida.* To vernacular names *add* "*Kotang, sosokera,* Kól;"

" 341, at the end of FICUS *add*—

"E 3334 from Darjeeling, 7,000 ft., is *F. Fieldingii,* Miq., a common tree of the Hill forests of the N. E. Himalaya, whose leaves are much used for fodder. It has a thin, grey bark; wood white, close-grained, soft. Pores moderate-sized, very scanty. Alternating wavy bands of soft and firmer tissue prominent. Medullary rays short, moderately broad.

"E 3612 from Chenga Forest, Darjeeling, 1,500 ft., is *F. clavata,* Wall. It has a very thin, smooth, greenish-grey bark. Wood white, moderately hard, close-grained, lustrous. Pores moderate-sized, scanty, often subdivided and enclosed in a ring of white tissue. Alternating layers of white, soft, and firmer dark tissue, very regular. Medullary rays fine to moderately broad, very short, white."

" 341, line 12. *For* "2075" *read* "2975."

" 342, *Ulmus integrifolia.* To vernacular names *add* "*Daurango,* Uriya;"

" 344, *Sponia orientalis.* To vernacular names *add* "*Rarunga,* Kól;"

" 347, line 18 from the bottom, *after* "Beng.;" *add* "*Hara sejum,* Kól; *Sikat,* Kharwar; *Mahkoá,* Monghyr;"

" 348, line 27, *after* "Vern." insert "*Simul aloo, simul turúl,* Beng.;"

" 349, *Antidesma Ghæsembilla.* To vernacular names *add* "*Mata suré,* Kól;"

" 352, *Phyllanthus Emblica.* To vernacular names *add* "*Meral,* Kól;" and to numbers *add*—

"C 3539. Khurdha Forests, Orissa . . . 58 lbs."

" 353. At the end of "PHYLLANTHUS," *add* "C 3485, from the Kolhán Forests, Singbhúm, Chota Nagpore, and C 3501 and C 3553, from the Khurdha Forests, Orissa, are *Phyllanthus lanceolarius,* Müll. Arg. Vern. *Marang mata,* Kól; *Kalchua,* Uriya. Bark brown, longitudinally cleft, soft. Wood reddish brown, moderately hard. Pores small and moderate-sized, scanty, in radial lines between the fine medullary rays. The distance between the rays is equal to, or less than, the transverse diameter of the pores. Weight, our specimen 'C 3553' gives 56 lbs. per cubic foot.

"C 3451, from the Betlah Reserve, Palamow, is *Breynia rhamnoides,* Müll. Arg. Bark greyish brown, fibrous. Wood reddish brown, hard, close-grained. Pores small, in radial lines between the numerous, fine medullary rays."

" 353, last line. *For* "E 5469" *read* "E 2469."

" 356, *Briedelia retusa.* To vernacular names *add* "*Kharaka, kaka,* Kól; *Karika,* Bhumij; *Kanj, kaji,* Kharwar; *Káj,* Monghyr;"

" 357, line 8. *After* "Ceylon Collection" *add* "(marked *B. spinosa.* Vern. *Kettekale,* Cingh.)"

" 357. *Briedelia tomentosa.* To numbers *add* "C 3498. Dhalbhúm, Chota Nagpore."

Page 357. At the end of BRIEDELIA *add* "C 3503 from the Khurdha Forests, Orissa, is *Briedelia stipularis*, Bl. Vern. *Gour kassi*, Uriya. Bark brown. Wood greyish brown, moderately hard. Pores scanty, often subdivided or in short radial lines. Medullary rays fine, numerous, uniformly distributed, the distance between them less than the transverse diameter of the pores. Numerous very fine, concentric, transverse bars across the rays."

,, 358, *Lebedieropsis orbicularis*. To vernacular names *add* "*Parasu, pás*, Kól; *Kergaili*, Kharwar;" to numbers *add* "C 3452. Betlah Reserve, Palamow, Chota Nagpore;" and in line 18 after "poisonous," *add* "and in Singbhúm is so used by the Ho Kóls, as also the root, mixed with salt."

,, 359, line 9, *after* "Nep.;" *add* "*Kurti, konya, kuli*, Kól; *Putila*, Bhumij; *Putri*, Kharwar; *Puter*, Monghyr;"

,, 359, *Croton caudatus*. To vernacular names *add* "*Wusta*, Uriya;"

,, 359, line 5 from bottom. *After* "smaller." *add* "C 3458, from Chandwa, Tori, Chota Nagpore, is this. It has a yellow wood, pores moderate-sized, scanty, single or subdivided, or in groups of 3 to 4; and medullary rays fine and very fine, very numerous. Wavy concentric bands of white tissue."

,, 359, *Trewia nudiflora*. To vernacular names *add* "*Kurong*, Nep.; *Gara lohadaru*, Kól; *Gamhár*, Monghyr; *Monda*, Uriya."

,, 363. *Ricinus communis*. To vernacular names *add* "*Bindi*, Kól;"

,, 365, *Jatropha Curcas*. To vernaeular names *add* "*Kulejera, totka bendi*, Kól;"

,, 366. *After* CHÆTOCARPUS *insert* "C 3548, from the Khurdha Forests, Orissa, is *Gelonium lanceolatum*, Willd.; Roxb. Fl. Ind. iii. 831; Beddome ccxiv. Vern. *Kakra*, Uriya; *Suragada*, Tel. It is a pretty evergreen tree of the Eastern Circars and Orissa, and has a yellow, smooth, close and even-grained wood, which weighs 50 lbs. per cubic foot and has a peculiar waxy smell. The pores are moderate-sized, scanty, sometimes subdivided. The medullary rays are very fine, very numerous, and are joined by very faint, fine, white lines. Growth moderate, 6 rings per inch of radius."

,, 369. *After* line 3 *insert* "C 3509, from Khurdha Forests, Orissa, is *Euphorbia Tirucalli*, Linn. Vern. *Séju*. Bark brown or greenish brown. Wood white or grey, moderately hard. Pores small, single or subdiuided, scanty. Medullary rays extremely fine and numerous."

,, 369, line 5. *After* "Baillon." *add* "The Box Tree."

,, 372, line 17 from the bottom. *After* "roofing houses." *add* "(H 130, Rotang Pass, Kulu, 9,000 ft.)"

,, 372, line 10 from the bottom. *For* "E 2404." *read* "E 2403."

,, 373, line 6. *For* "E 2914." *read* "E 2904."; and line 7, *for* "E 2405." *read* "E 2404."

,, 374, line 13. *For* "E 2406." *read* "E 2405."

,, 375, line 12. *For* "*S. serphyllum*" *read* "*S. serpyllum*."

,, 375, *Salix tetrasperma*. To vernacular names *add* "*Nachal*, Kól; *Chéur*, Kharwar;"

,, 379, line 18. *For* "H 3138." *read* "H 3188."

,, 380, line 8. *For* "*Vulgaris*" *read* "*vulgaris*" and line 9, *for* "*Castanea Vesca*" *read* "*Castanea vulgaris*."

,, 384, *Quercus dilatata*. To numbers *add* "H 777. Kalatop Forest, Punjab, 7,000 ft."

,, 386, *Q. acuminata*. To numbers *add* "E 3384, Darjeeling, 6,500 ft."

Page 392, *Juglans regia.* To numbers *add* "H 7. Theog, Simla, 6,000 ft."

„ 392, line 3 from the bottom. *For* "H 41" *read* "H 35."

„ 393, *after* line 4 *add* "E 3587, E 3632, Darjeeling, 7,000 ft. The latter is from a planted tree and shews 15 rings to a radius of 4½ inches, or 3½ rings per inch of radius."

„ 408, line 8. *For* "H 2898." *read* "H 2896."

„ 409, after line 26, *add* "Our No. E 2437 shewed, on the round, a mean diameter of 22 inches corresponding to 134 years or 13 rings per inch of radius. This agrees with several other measurements made in the Singalila Forests in Darjeeling, though at a lower elevation the growth is faster. Twelve rings per inch may be, therefore, taken as an average rate of growth for the Sikkim Silver Fir forests."

„ 410 line 16. *After* "above Ghát." *add* "*C. Lawsoniana*, Murray, is cultivated and grows well at and around Darjeeling."

„ 410, line 6 from the bottom. *After* "Gamble 83." *add* "The Funereal Cypress."

„ 411, line 10. At the beginning *add* "E 3615 from Rangirúm, Darjeeling, 7,000 ft., and" and *for* "is" *write* "are"

„ 411, line 20. *After* "Wood soft," *add* "white, with a brown, often almost black, heartwood,"

„ 412, last line. *For* "H 127." *read* "H 129."

„ 415, line 8, *after* "Cuttack," *add* "*Rengua*, Uriya." and in line 10, *for* "Mid." *read* "Miq."

„ 418, line 11. *For* "talll" *read* "tall"

„ 419, line 6. *After* "Hind.;" *insert* "*Keeta*, Kól;"

„ 421, line 14 from the bottom. *For* "ENTINCKIA" *read* "BENTINCKIA"

„ 423, *Calamus tenuis.* To vernacular names *add* "*Jali*, Cachar;" and to numbers *add* "(E 1298. Cachar)."

„ 424, *C. Mastersianus.* As number *add* "(E 1299. Cachar)."

„ 424, *C. Jenkinsianus.* To vernacular names *add* "*Gallah*, Cachar;" and to numbers "(E 1300. Cachar.)"

„ 426, line 16 from the bottom. *For* "E 1354," *read* "E 1351, 1354,"

„ 427, line 24 from the bottom. *After* "Beng.;" *insert* "*Pepe siman*, Kol;" and *for* "E 1329" *read* "E 1328."

„ 428, line 12. *After* "Hind.;" *insert* "*Katanga*, Kól;"

„ 428, line 16 from the bottom. *After* "E 3428" *add* "E 1327;" and line 15, *for* "E1314" *read* "E1312"

„ 430, line 10. *After* "Beng.;" *insert* "*Mathan, saring, buru mat*, Kól; *Bukhar*, Palamow (the clump);"

„ 430, line 17. *After* "basket work." *add* "(B 1322, Burma. P 1352, Hoshiarpur, Punjab.)"

„ 430, line 12 from the bottom. *After* "E 1341" *add* "E 1466."

„ 431, line 28. *For* "CRYPTOGAMIÆ." *read* "CRYPTOGAMÆ."

„ 432, line 21. *For* "*Braineai nsignis*" *read* "*Brainea insignis*"

Under their proper places *add* E 3593, *Beilschmiedia Roxburghiana*; E 3597, *Ehretia Wallichiana*; E 3600, *Terminalia belerica*; E 3603, *Stereospermum chelonoides*; E 3607, *Quercus pachyphylla*; E 3609, *Quercus annulata*; E 3610, *Echinocarpus dasycarpus*; and E 3611, *Lagerströmia parviflora*,—all from Darjeeling.

MANUAL OF INDIAN TIMBERS.

I. DICOTYLEDONS.

ORDER I. RANUNCULACEÆ.

A family which contains chiefly herbaceous plants. Besides *Clematis* and *Naravelia*, which are genera of climbing shrubs, *Pæonia Emodi*, Wall.; Hook. Fl. Ind i. 30. Vern. *Mamekh*, Pb. is an erect undershrub of the Western Himalaya, whose root is said by Stewart to be used in native medicine, and young shoots as a vegetable in Kumaun.

1. CLEMATIS, Linn.

Of this and the neighbouring genus, *Naravelia*, 22 species occur in India. They are distributed almost all over India: 11 are found in the North-West Himalaya, 14 in the Eastern Himalaya and Khasia Hills, 2 in Central India, 4 in the Dekkan, 4 on the Western Coast and 10 in British Burma.

The commonest kinds in the North-West Himalaya are *C. grata*, Wall., *C. nutans*, Royle, and *C. orientalis*, Linn., with white or yellowish-white panicles of flowers; *C. montana*, Ham., with large white star-shaped flowers, and *C. barbellata*, Edgw., with dull purple ones, common in the hill forests; while *C. Buchananiana*, DC., is conspicuous for its woolly leaves and large soft tomentose bell-shaped flowers. In the Eastern Himalaya this latter species is the most common, with *C. grewiæflora*, DC., covered all over with golden pubescence, and the beautiful pink-flowered *C. smilacifolia*, Wall. *C. gouriana*, Roxb. and *Naravelia zeylanica*, DC., are common in Bengal, Central India, the Dekkan, and in Burma, where the second species of *Naravelia* (*N. laurifolia*, Wall.) is also found.

These climbers are all very ornamental, but they have little or no value, though Kurz says that the "stems of the species from Burma while fresh are often used for ropes and are very strong." Mathieu Fl. For. p. 9 gives the weight at 24 to 36 lbs. per cubic foot for *C. Vitalba*, Linn, the European Clematis, or Traveller's Joy.

1. *C. montana*, Ham.; Hook. Fl. Ind. i. 2; Gamble 1. Vern. *Ghantiáli*, Hind.
   H 2851. Mahasu, Simla, 8,000 ft.
2. *C. barbellata*, Edgw.; Hook. Fl. Ind. i. 3.
   H 2852. Mahasu, Simla, 8,000 ft.
   H 3156. Theog, Simla, 7,000 ft. . . . . . . 40 lbs.
3. *C. grata*, Wall.; Hook. Fl. Ind. i. 3. Vern. *Ghantiáli*, Hind.
   H 2850. Simla, 6,000 ft.
4. *C. Buchananiana*, DC.; Hook. Fl. Ind. i. 6; Kurz i. 17; Gamble 1.
   H 2838. Simla, 6,000 ft.

Woody climbers, with a fibrous bark and a porous yellowish-white wood, with broad or very broad medullary rays and pores which vary from small to very large.

ORDER II. DILLENIACEÆ.

An order of three Indian genera, belonging to two tribes, *viz.*,—

Tribe I.—Delimeæ . . . . *Delima* and *Tetracera*.
„ II.—Dillenieæ . . . . *Dillenia* and *Wormia*.

Delima sarmentosa, Linn.; Hook. Fl. Ind. i. 31; Kurz i. 22; Gamble 2 (*Tetracera sarmentosa*, Roxb. Fl. Ind. ii. 645) Vern. *Monkyourik*, Lepcha, is an evergreen rough-leaved climber of Northern and Eastern Bengal, Burma and the Andamans. *Tetracera* includes two species: *T. lævis*, Vahl.; Hook. Fl. Ind. i. 31 (*T. trigyna*, Roxb. Fl. Ind. ii. 645), a climber of the forests of Malabar; and *T. Assa*, DC.; Hook. Fl. Ind. i. 31; Kurz i. 22, a scandent shrub of Chittagong. *Wormia* is found in Ceylon.

1. DILLENIA, Linn.

Eight species. *D. bracteata*, Wight; Hook. Fl. Ind. i. 37 (*D. repanda*, Roxb. Fl. Ind. ii. 652. *Wormia bracteata*, Beddome t. 115) is a handsome tree of South India. *D. pulcherrima*, Kurz i. 19; Hook. Fl. Ind. i. 37. Vern. *Byoo*, Burm., is a handsome deciduous tree of Pegu and Martaban, chiefly in the Eng forests, which Kurz evidently identifies with No. 2 of Brandis' Burma List of 1862 (*Bjooben*): weight 69 lbs., wood hard and strong, and used for rice-mills. *D. scabrella*, Roxb. Fl. Ind. ii. 653; Hook. Fl. Ind. ii. 38; Kurz i. 21. Vern. *Akachi*, Gáro, is a deciduous tree of Assam, Eastern Bengal and Chittagong. *D. parviflora*, Griff.; Hook. Fl. Ind. ii. 38; Kurz i. 21. Vern. *Lingyau*, Burm., is a deciduous tree of the mixed forests of Burma up to 2,000 feet.

Wood characterized by prominent medullary rays which appear as high, shining plates on a vertical section, giving the wood a remarkably mottled appearance. The rays are generally of two sizes and the pores are small, the distance between the rays being greater than the diameter of the pores.

1. D. indica, Linn.; Hook. Fl. Ind. i. 36; Brandis 1; Kurz i. 19; Gamble 1. *D. speciosa*, Thunb.; Roxb. Fl. Ind. ii. 650; Beddome t. 103. Vern. *Chalta*, Hind.; *Chalta, hargesa*, Beng.; *Phamsikol*, Lepcha; *Otengah*, Ass.; *Rai*, Uriya; *Uva*, Tam.; *Uva, pedda-kalinga*, Tel.; *Syalita*, Mal.; *Mota karmal*, Mar.; *Hondapara*, Cingh.; *Thapru, chauralesi*, Magh; *Thabyoo*, Burm.; *Carllow*, Taleing.

A large evergreen tree. Bark red, peeling off in small hard flakes. Wood red with white specks, close-grained, moderately hard. Pores moderate-sized, numerous, uniformly distributed. Medullary rays of two classes, broad and extremely fine, a large number of fine ones between two broad ones. Two or more lines of pores between each pair of broad rays. The medullary rays are visible on a radial section, giving the wood a mottled appearance, but not to the same extent as in *D. pentagyna*.

Bengal, Central and South India, Burma; often planted for ornament.

Growth moderate, our specimens shew seven rings per inch of radius. The weight and transverse strength have been determined by the following experiments:—

		Weight.		P
Skinner, No. 58, in 1862, in South India	. found	45	lbs.,	721
Kyd in 1831 with Assam wood, bars 2′×1″×1″	. „	45	„	243 (doubtful)
Brandis, in 1862, Burma List, No. 3	. . „	41	„	...
Smythies, in 1878, with our four specimens	. „	44·5	„	...

The wood is used to make helves and gunstocks, and in construction; and is said to be durable under water. It makes good firewood and charcoal. The large fruit is surrounded by the fleshy accrescent calyx which is eaten either raw or cooked. The rough old leaves are used to polish ivory.

		lbs.
E 596.	Khookloong Forest, Darjeeling Terai	40
E 2310.	Sivoke Forests, Darjeeling Terai	41
E 1395.	Chittagong	48
B 2501.	Burma	49

2. D. pentagyna, Roxb. Fl. Ind. ii. 602; Hook. Fl. Ind. i. 38; Beddome t. 104; Brandis 2; Kurz i. 21; Gamble 2. *D. augusta*, Roxb. l. c. Vern. *Aggai*, Oudh; *Kallai*, C.P.; *Karkotta*, Beng.; *Suha-rúk*, Bori, C.P.; *Tatri*, Nep.; *Shukni*, Lepcha; *Akshi*, Ass., Mechi; *Akachi*, Gáro; *Rai*, Uriya; *Rai, pinnai, nai-ték*, Tam.; *Rawadan, chinnakalinga*, Tel.; *Kanagalu*, Mar.; *Mirchi*, Baigas; *Kallei*, Gondi; *Malé geru*, Kúrg; *Machil*, Kan.; *Zambrún*, Magh.; *Zimbyún*, Burm.

A deciduous tree. Bark ½ inch thick, grey or pale-brown, smooth, inner substance red. Wood rough, moderately hard, reddish grey; apt to split, warp and crack; strong, heavy, durable, handsomely marked on a vertical section by the darker-coloured medullary rays which appear as broad plates. Pores small and moderate-sized, many of them filled with a white substance, which is visible both on the horizontal and vertical sections, and is one of the characteristics of the wood. Medullary rays numerous, moderately broad, with a few intermediate, very fine rays. Annual rings marked by a narrow belt in the outer edge (autumn wood) without pores; this is particularly distinct in the wood from Oudh, less so in the specimens from Burma.

Oudh, Bengal, Central and South India, Burma.

Growth moderately fast, our specimens give five to six rings per inch of radius. Saplings grow up very fast, with straight, thick-barked stems, crowned by very large leaves. The weight and transverse strength have been determined by the following experiments:—

		Weight.	P =
Skinner, in 1862, in South India, No. 57 . .	found	70 lbs.	907
Benson, in Burma, with bars 3′×1·4″×1·4″ . .	„	58 „	960
Kyd, in 1831, with Assam wood, in bars 2′×1″×1″ .	„	45 „	593
Brandis, in 1862, Burma List, No. 1	„	48 „	...
„ in 1864, with Burma wood (4 experiments) bars 3′×1″×1″	„	45 „	740
Smythies, in 1878, with our six specimens . .	„	47·5 „	...

The wood is used for construction, ship-building, rice-mills, and for charcoal, which is of good quality. The leaves are very large, often 2 feet long; they are used for plates. The fruit is eaten when green, as also are the flower-buds. The tree is often found with sál.

		lbs.
O 348.	Gorakhpur (1868)	54
E 658.	Rakti Forest, Darjeeling Terai	45
E 2311.	Sivoke, Darjeeling Terai	54
B {302. 303.}	Burma (1867)	47
B 557.	Prome, Burma	38

3. D. aurea, Smith; Hook. Fl. Ind. i. 37; Brandis 2; Kurz i. 20. *D. ornata*, Wall. Vern. *Chamaggai*, Oudh; *Dheugr*, Nep.; *Byooben*, Burm.

A large tree. Bark ½ inch thick, reddish grey. Wood grey, beautiuflly mottled and wainscoted, hard, close-grained. Pores small and very small, often in short radial lines. Medullary rays broad, with a few intermediate very fine rays. Annual rings very indistinct. The wood differs from that of *D. indica* and *D. pentagyna* by smaller pores and narrower medullary rays.

Nepal, Bengal, Burma and Andaman Islands.
Weight: according to Benson, 44 lbs.; Brandis, 45 lbs.; our specimens give 48 to 49 lbs. Benson gives P = 834. Wood not used.

		lbs.
B 2502.	Burma (1862)	49
B 2253.	Andaman Islands (1866)	48

4. D. retusa, Thunb.; Thwaites Enum. 5; Hook. Fl. Ind. i. 37. Vern. *Godapara*, Cingh.

A tree. Wood resembling that of the other species.

Ceylon, up to 2,000 ft.
Weight according to A. Mendis, 51 lbs. per cubic foot. Wood used for building.

	lbs.
No. 29, Ceylon collection	51

Two specimens, B 2245 (52 lbs.) and B 2275 (44 lbs.), sent by Major Ford from the Andaman Islands in 1866 under name of *Lingyau*, have a structure similar to that of *D. aurea*, but the wood is purplish grey and may possibly belong to *D. pilosa*, Roxb. (Kurz i. 20) which, according to Kurz, is a large tree of the Andamans.

2. WORMIA, Rottb.

1. W. triquetra, Rottb.; Thwaites Enum. 4; Hook. Fl. Ind. i. 35. Vern. *Diyapara*, Cingh.

Wood reddish, in structure resembling that of *Dillenia.*

Ceylon, up to 2,000 ft.
Weight 44 lbs. per cubic foot. Wood used for building; the nut gives an oil.

	lbs.
No. 22, Ceylon collection	44

ORDER III. MAGNOLIACEÆ.

Contains 8 genera of Indian trees, shrubs or climbers, which are chiefly found in the Eastern Himalaya and the Eastern moist zone. The order is divided ino 4 tribes, *viz.,*—

Tribe I.—Trochodendreæ	*Euptelea.*
„ II.—Wintereæ	*Illicium.*
„ III.—Magnolieæ	*Talauma, Magnolia, Manglietia* and *Michelia.*
„ IV.—Schizandreæ	*Schizandra* and *Kadsura.*

Four of these genera contain only shrubs or woody climbers: *Euptelea pleiosperma*, Hook. f. and Th.; Hook. Fl. Ind. i. 39, is a shrub of the higher Mishmi Hills; *Illicium* contains two shrubs; *I. Griffithii*, Hook. f. and Th. of the Khasia Hills, and *I. majus*, Hook. f. and Th.; Kurz i. 23, of the Thoungyeen Hills in Tenasserim; *Schizandra*, 4 climbing species of the Eastern Himalaya, of which *S. grandiflora*, Hook. f. and Th.; Hook. Fl. Ind. i. 44; Brandis 571; Gamble 3. Vern. *Klandru, kaljendru*, Simla; *Sillangti*, Kumaun; *Singhata, taksielrik*, Lepcha, with edible fruits, extends as far west as Simla (H. 3,029, Nagkanda, 9,000 ft., with a porous wood and strong resinous smell); and *Kadsura*, two climbers of Assam and Malabar respectively. Of the remaining genera, three are here described, the last, *Manglietia*, containing two large trees;

M. insignis, Bl.; Hook. Fl. Ind. i. 42; Kurz. i. 25, of the Eastern Himalaya, Khasia Hills and Pegu, above 6,000 feet; and *M. Caveana*, Hook. f. and Th. of the Khasia Hills. Nearly all the family are showy plants, with handsome foliage and sweet-scented, large flowers. Many species come from America and are grown in gardens in Europe; among such are *Liriodendron tulipiferum*, the well known Tulip Tree and several handsome Magnolias.

Wood soft, generally rough. Pores generally small, uniformly distributed. Medullary rays sharply marked, fine. The annual rings are generally marked by a clearly defined line, or narrow belt of soft texture. The structure of the different species of this order is so uniform that no attempt has been made to give generic characters.

1. TALAUMA, Juss.

T. Rabaniana, Hook. f. and Th.; Hook. Fl. Ind. i. 40; Kurz i. 24. Vern. *Sappa*, Ass., is a large tree of the Khasia Hills and Burma, whose wood is sometimes used in Assam for furniture and planking; and *T. mutabilis*, Bl.; Hook. Fl. Ind. i. 40 (*T. Candollei*, Bl.; Kurz. i. 24). a shrub of Tenasserim and Tavoy. Most of the species are remarkable for their large fragrant flowers.

1. T. Hodgsoni, Hook. f. and T.; Hook. Fl. Ind. i. 40; Gamble 3. Vern. *Siffoo*, Lepcha; *Harré*, Nep.

An evergreen tree. Bark grey, $\frac{1}{8}$ inch thick, smooth. Wood grey, very soft, even-grained. Annual rings distinct. Pores small. Medullary rays fine and very fine.

Sikkim Himalaya from the Terai up to 6,000 ft.; Khasia Hills.
Growth moderate, 7 rings per inch of radius. Weight 21 lbs. per cubic foot.

		lbs.
E 3100.	Darjeeling 5,000 ft.	21

2. MAGNOLIA, Linn.

Besides the species given below, *M. globosa*, Hook. f. and Th.; Hook. Fl. Ind. i. 41; Gamble 2, is a small tree of the inner ranges of the Sikkim Himalaya; *M. Griffithii*, Hook. f. and Th.; Hook. Fl. Ind. i. 41, an evergreen tree of the forests of Upper Assam; and *M. sphenocarpa*, Roxb.; Hook. Fl. Ind. i. 41; Kurz i. 24. (*Liriodendron grandiflorum*, Roxb. Fl. Ind. ii. 653.) Vern. *Burramtúri*, Ass.; *Duli champa*, Sylhet. is a large evergreen tree of the tropical forests of the base of the Eastern Himalaya, Assam and Eastern Bengal down to Chittagong.

1. M. Campbellii, Hook. f. and Th.; Hook. Fl. Ind. i. 41; Gamble 2. Vern. *Lal champ*, Nep.; *Sigumgrip*, Lepcha; *Pendder*, Bhutia.

A large, tall, deciduous tree. Bark dark coloured, that of the branches black. Wood white, very soft. Annual rings distinctly marked by prominent white lines. Pores small. Medullary rays moderate-sized, prominent.

Sikkim and Bhutan from 7,000 to 10,000 feet. Growth moderate, 11½ rings per inch of radius. Weight 25 lbs. per cubic foot. Wood occasionally used for planking, but now scarce. Chiefly remarkable for its magnificent large pink or white flowers, which appear in April.

		lbs.
E 365.	Rangyrúm Forest, Darjeeling, 7,500 feet	25

3. MICHELIA, Linn.

Besides the 5 species described below, *M. Kisopa*, Ham.; Hook. Fl. Ind. i. 43. Vern. *Banchampa*, Kumaun; *Champ, chobsi*, Nep., is a tall tree of Nepal. A. Aikin, in his Catalogue of Indian woods collected by Wallich, says the wood is yellowish, is used in Nepal for light works, and has 8 to 11 rings per inch of radius. *M. punduana*, Hook.

f. and Th.; Hook. Fl. Ind. i. 43, is found in the Khasia Hills; and *M. nilagirica* Zenk; Hook. Fl. Ind. i. 44; Beddome t. 62. Vern. *Pila champa*, Hind., Mar.; *Shembugha*, Tam.; *Walsapu*, Cingh., with a strong, fine-grained wood, used for building, beams and rafters, in the higher forests of the Western Ghâts and Ceylon.

1. **M. Cathcartii,** Hook. f. and Th.; Hook. Fl. Ind. i. 42; Gamble 2. Vern. *Kala champ*, Nep.; *Atokdúng*, Lepcha.

A large tree, with dark-coloured bark. Sapwood large, white, heartwood dark olive brown, moderately hard. Annual rings distinctly marked by a white line. Pores small. Medullary rays fine, not very prominent.

Sikkim Himalaya, 5,000 to 7,000 feet.

Weight 41 lbs. Wood used for planking, will do well for tea boxes. The flowers are terminal, white, but turn red in drying.

		lbs.
E 2314.	Rangbúl Forest, Darjeeling, 6,500 feet	41

2. **M. Champaca,** Linn.; Hook. Fl. Ind. i. 42; Roxb. Fl. Ind. ii. 656; Beddome vi; Brandis 3; Kurz i. 25; Gamble 3. Vern. *Champa*, Hind.; *Oulia champ*, Nep.; *Titasappa*, Ass.; *Champa, champaka*, Beng.; *Shimbu, sempangam*, Tam.; *Champakamu, sampenga, kanchanamu*, Tel.; *Sampighi*, Kan.; *Champakam*, Mal.; *Tsaga*, Burm.

A tall evergreen tree, with grey bark, ½ inch thick. Wood soft, seasons and polishes well; sapwood white; heartwood light olive brown; annual rings distinctly marked by a white line. Pores small and moderate-sized, equally distributed. Medullary rays short, fine to moderately broad, visible on a radial section.

Cultivated throughout India from the Ravi southwards and up to 5,400 feet in the North-West Himalaya. Wild in Nepal, Bengal, Assam (ascending to 3,000 feet), Burma, and in the forests of the Western Ghâts as far as Kanara.

Growth moderate, our specimens shew seven rings per inch of radius. It often reaches 8 feet girth at an age of 100 to 120 years.

Weight: the mean of 7 experiments made by Brandis in 1864 gave 37 lbs. per cubic foot; Puckle's experiments in Mysore gave 42 lbs.; while Smythies found 38 lbs. per cubic foot as the average of our specimens. In Brandis' experiments of 1864 on Nepal wood, 4 with bars 6′ × 2″ × 2″ gave P = 564, while 3 with bars 6′ × 2″ × 1⅓″ gave P = 561. Puckle's in Mysore with bars 2′ × 1″ × 1″ gave P = 642.

The wood is very durable: *e. g.*, specimen No. 1437 was cut by Griffith in 1836 and has been since then in Calcutta, and is now as sound as if fresh cut. The wood is used for furniture, house-building, carriage work and native drums. It is considered valuable in Northern Bengal for planking, door-panels and furniture; and in Assam for building and canoes. The flowers are prized on account of their sweet scent, and the tree is planted at Hindu shrines.

		lbs.
E 576.	Khookloong Forest, Darjeeling Terai	35
E 2313.	Sukna Forest, Darjeeling Terai	37
E 2195.	Nowgong, Assam	40
E 1049.	Eastern Dúars, Assam	36
E 1437.	Mishmi Hills (Griffith, 1836)	42

3. **M. excelsa,** Blume; Hook. Fl. Ind. i. 43; Gamble 3. Vern. *Bara champ, safed champ*, Nep.; *Sigugrip*, Lepcha; *Gók*, Bhutia.

A lofty deciduous tree. Bark greyish brown, ⅛ inch thick. Wood soft; sapwood small, white; heartwood olive brown, glossy; annual rings distinctly marked by firmer autumn wood with fewer pores. Pores small. Medullary rays short, fine and moderately broad, very numerous, prominent on a radial section. According to Gamble, the wood is yellow when fresh cut.

Eastern Himalaya, from 6,000 to 8,000 feet; Khasia Hills.

Growth rather slow; 13 to 16 rings per inch of radius are shewn by our specimens. Weight, 33 to 34 lbs. per cubic foot. The wood is very durable: *e.g.*, specimen No. 1442 was cut in 1836 and kept since then in Calcutta; the wood is now as sound as if fresh cut.

Used for building, but chiefly for planking, door and window frames, and for furniture. The principal building and furniture wood of the Darjeeling Hills.

		lbs.
E 657.	Chuttockpur Forest, Darjeeling, 6,000 feet	33
E 2312.	Rangbúl Forest, Darjeeling, 7,000 feet	33
E 1442.	Mishmi Hills (Griffith, 1836)	34

4. M. lanuginosa, Wall.; Hook. Fl. Ind. i. 43; Gamble 2. Vern. *Gogay champ*, Nep.

A large deciduous tree. Bark $\frac{1}{8}$ inch thick, greyish brown, smooth. Wood grey, soft, shining. Pores small, scanty. Medullary rays fine and very fine, closely packed. Narrow concentric (annual?) rings of soft texture, often confluent.

Forests of Sikkim and the Khasia Hills from 5,000 to 7,000 feet.

Growth moderate. Weight 27 lbs. per cubic foot.

		lbs.
E 3099.	Darjeeling, 7,000 feet	27

5. M. oblonga, Wall.; Hook. Fl. Ind. i. 43. Vern. *Sappa, phulsappa*, Assam.

A tree. Sapwood white; heartwood dark grey, soft. Annual rings indistinct. Pores moderate-sized, often in short radial lines. Medullary rays fine, uniform, closely packed, equidistant; the distance between two rays less than the transverse diameter of the pores.

Khasia Hills and Assam.

Weight, 40 lbs. per cubic foot. The wood is used in Assam for canoes and rough furniture.

		lbs.
E 1268.	Lakhimpur, Assam	40

ORDER IV. ANONACEÆ.

This order contains 21 Indian genera, the majority of which are South Indian and Burmese.

They belong to 5 tribes, *viz.*,—

Tribe I.—Uvarieæ	*Uvaria* and *Ellipeia.*
„ II.—Unoneæ	*Cyathocalyx, Artabotrys, Cananga, Cyathostemma, Unona, Polyalthia, Anaxagorea* and *Popowia.*
„ III.—Mitrephoreæ	*Oxymitra, Phæanthus, Goniothalamus* and *Mitrephora.*
„ IV.—Xylopieæ	*Anona* and *Melodorum.*
„ V.—Miliuseæ	*Miliusa, Saccopetalum, Alphonsea, Orophea* and *Bocagea.*

One genus, *Anona*, contains introduced fruit trees; five, *Uvaria, Ellipeia, Artabotrys, Oxymitra* and *Melodorum*, chiefly climbing shrubs; fifteen, *Cyathocalyx, Cyathostemma, Unona, Polyalthia, Anaxagorea, Popowia, Phæanthus, Goniothalamus, Mitrephora, Miliusa, Saccopetalum, Orophea, Cananga, Alphonsea* and *Bocagea*, are shrubs or trees. In Northern and Central India the family is represented by 4 species of *Polyalthia*, 3 of *Anona*, 2 of *Saccopetalum* and *Miliusa velutina*. The Eastern Himalaya, Assam and Eastern Bengal, contain trees, shrubs or climbers of the genera *Uvaria*, *Artabotrys*, *Anona*, *Polyalthia*, *Melodorum* and *Miliusa*, while the remaining genera, and the majority of the species of these, are found in South India or Burma.

Of the genera not herein described, the five climbing ones contain about 30 species, the principal of which are: *Uvaria macrophylla*, Roxb. Fl. Ind. ii. 663; Hook. Fl. Ind. ii. 49; Kurz i. 28. Vern. *Bagh-runga*, Beng.; *Thabwot-nway*, Burm., a large evergreen climber common in Eastern Bengal and Burma; *Ellipeia ferruginea*, Hook. f. and Th.; Hook. Fl. Ind. i. 52 (*Uvaria ferruginea*, Ham.; Kurz i. 29), a shrub of the Irrawaddy valley; and *Artabotrys odoratissimus*, R. Br.; Hook. Fl. Ind. i. 54; Kurz i. 31 (*Uvaria odoratissima*, Roxb. Fl. Ind. ii. 666), a large Burmese shrub with fragrant flowers. *Cyathocalyx martabanicus*, Hook, f. and Th.; Hook. Fl. Ind. i. 53; Kurz i. 30, is an evergreen tree of Martaban and Tenasserim. *Cananga odorata*, Hook. f. and Th.; Hook. Fl. Ind. i. 56; Kurz. i. 33 (*Uvaria odorata*, Roxb. Fl. Ind. ii. 661) Vern. *Kadapgnam*, Burm., is a large evergreen tree of Tenasserim. *Unona* contains seven Burmese and three South Indian trees. *Popowia* two, *viz.*: *P. Beddomeana*, Hook. f. and Th.; Hook. Fl. Ind. i. 68 (*P. ramosissima*, Beddome viii.) of the Travancore and Tinnevelly hills; and *P. Helferi*, Hook. f. and Th.; Hook. Fl. Ind. i. 69; Kurz i. 39 of the Andamans and Tenasserim. *Alphonsea* four, *viz.*, *A. madraspatana*, Bedd. t. 92; *A. zeylanica*, Hook. f. and Th., of South India; *A. lutea*, Hook. f. and Th., of Eastern Bengal, South India and Burma; and *A. ventricosa*, Hook. f. and Th., of Assam, Chittagong and the Andamans, all trees of considerable size. *Mitrephora grandiflora*, Beddome t. 91.; Hook. Fl. Ind. i. 78, is a large handsome tree of the South Kanara forests. There are altogether, excluding those of the Malay Peninsula and Ceylon, about 100 Indian species; of these about 60 occur in Burma, 30 in South India and 30 in Eastern Bengal. Further specimens of the wood of the larger species are urgently required for investigation and determination of doubtful woods, such as *Bamau*, &c. (see p. 10).

Wood light-coloured, generally yellowish and soft. Pores small. Medullary rays fine to moderately broad, joined by numerous fine transverse bars. These transverse bars furnish an excellent character for distinguishing the wood of Anonaceæ from that of most other families; they are also found in *Bassia* and *Mimusops*, but in these genera they have more the character of wavy concentric lines. The structure of the different species of this family is so uniform that no attempt has been made to give generic characters.

1. POLYALTHIA, Blume.

Besides the two species here described, *P. simiarum*, Bth. and Hook. f.; Hook. Fl. Ind. i. 63; Kurz i. 37, is a large tree of Eastern Bengal and Burma; *P. Jenkinsii*, Bth. and Hook. f.; Hook. Fl. Ind. i. 64; Kurz i. 37, is a common tree of the Andamans, found also in Assam and Sylhet; *P. coffeoides*, Bth. and Hook. f.; Hook. Fl. Ind. i. 62; Beddome t. 53, is a common tree of the Western Ghâts, where its bark is made into ropes; *P. suberosa*, Bth. and Hook. f.; Hook. Fl. Ind. i. 65; Brandis 5. (*Uvaria suberosa*, Roxb. Fl. Ind. ii. 667.) Vern. *Bara chali*, Beng.; *Banderhola*, Ass.; *Chilka dúdúga*, Tel., is a small tree of Oudh, Bengal and South India, with a corky bark, and close, tough, hard, durable wood, weighing, according to Brandis 40, and Kyd 45 lbs. per cubic foot, and having P = 430. There are also about 8 other species described, from India and Burma.

1. P. longifolia, Benth. and Hook. f.; Hook. Fl. Ind. i. 62; Beddome t. 38; Brandis 4. *Uvaria longifolia*, Lam.; Roxb. Fl. Ind. ii. 664. Vern. *Asok, debdari*, Hind.; *Assothi*, Tam.; *Asoká, devadaru*, Tel.

A large evergreen tree with smooth bark. Wood white. Pores small, often subdivided, uniformly distributed. Medullary rays short, fine to very broad. Numerous, equidistant, very fine transverse bars across the rays.

Wild in Ceylon. Planted as an avenue tree throughout Bengal and South India. Weight: according to Skinner, No. 76, 37 lbs.; Brandis says between 30 and 40; our specimen gives 37 lbs. Skinner's experiments give P = 547.

		lbs.
E 2479.	Calcutta	37

2. P. cerasoides, Benth. and Hook. f.; Hook. Fl. Ind. i. 63; Beddome t. 1.; Brandis 5; Kurz i. 38. *Uvaria cerasoides*, Roxb. Fl. Ind. ii. 666. Vern. *Hoom*, Mar.; *Chilka dúdúgú*, Tel.; *Nakulsi, múlíli*, Tam.

A large evergreen tree. Wood olive grey, moderately hard, close-grained. Pores small. Medullary rays short, broad and moderately fine; the distance between the rays twice or three times as great as the transverse diameter of the pores. Numerous, very distinct, fine, equidistant, tranverse bars between the rays.

Behar, Eastern and Western Gháts, Dekkan, Burma.

Weight, 52 lbs. per cubic foot. The wood is used for carpentry and in boat-building. It is much prized in Bombay.

		lbs.
C 997.	Poona	52

2. ANONA, Linn.

Besides the species given below, the 'Bullock's heart,' *A. reticulata*, Linn.; Vern. *Ramphal*, and the 'Soursop,' *A. muricata*, L., are also cultivated in many parts of India. (Skinner, No. 14, gives for *A. reticulata* W = 40 lbs. P = 640).

1. A. squamosa, Linn.; Hook. Fl. Ind. i. 78; Roxb. Fl. Ind. ii. 657; Brandis 6; Kurz i. 46; Gamble 3. The Custard Apple. Vern. *Sharifa, sitaphal*, Hind.; *Ata, lúna*, Beng.; *Sita*, Tam.; *Sitapundu*, Tel.; *Atta*, Mal., Cingh.; *Auza*, Burm.

A small tree, with an erect, short trunk. Bark thin, grey. Wood soft, close-grained. Pores moderate-sized, scanty. Medullary rays moderate-sized, joined by numerous white transverse bars.

Introduced from the West Indies, and domesticated throughout India and Burma. Cultivated for its fruit, which ripens from July to October. Weight, 46 lbs. per cubic foot.

		lbs.
B 2317.	Myanoung, Burma	46

3. MILIUSA, Lesch.

Besides the two species herein described, *M. indica*, Lesch., *M. Wightiana*, Hook. f. and Th., and *M. nilagirica*, Beddome, are shrubs or small trees of the Western Gháts; *M sclerocarpa*, Kurz, is a small tree, with a rather heavy wood, from Martaban and Tennasserim; and *M. macrocarpa*, Hook. f. and Th., a small tree from Sikkim and the Khasia Hills.

1. M. velutina, Hook. f. and Th.; Hook. Fl. Ind. i. 87; Beddome t. 37; Brandis 6; Kurz i. 47. *Uvaria villosa*, Roxb. Fl. Ind. ii. 664. Vern. *Dom-sál*, Hind.; *Kari*, C. P.; *Kharrei*, Oudh; *Peddachilka dúdúga, nalla dúdúga*, Tel.; *Thabútgyee*, Burm.

A deciduous moderate-sized tree, with a short erect trunk; in Burma a large tree. Bark ½ inch thick, rough. Wood yellow when fresh cut, grey or greyish brown when dry, moderately hard. Annual rings indistinct. Pores small, uniformly distributed, often in short radial lines. Medullary rays fine and moderately broad, the distance between two rays larger than the transverse diameter of the pores. Transverse bars distinct, numerous.

Sub-Himalayan tract from Nepal to the Ganges, Central India, Godaveri districts and Burma.

Brandis says, "The seasoned wood weighs from 40 to 50 lbs. per cubic foot;" Kurz gives the weight at 42 lbs.; Benson's experiments give 60; and Skinner's (No. 93) 50 lbs. Benson's experiments give P = 833, and Skinner's P = 839.

Used for carts and agricultural implements, spear-shafts and oars.

		lbs.
B 3062.	Prome, Burma.	...
B 3122.	Burma (1862)	48
O 3113.	Dehra Dún	53

2. M. Roxburghiana, Hook. f. and Th.; Hook. Fl. Ind. i. 87; Kurz. i. 47; Gamble 4. *Uvaria dioica,* Roxb. Fl. Ind. ii. 659. Vern. *Sungden,* Lepcha; *Tusbi,* Sylhet.

A small tree. Bark thin, grey. Wood greyish white, hard. Pores very small, scanty. Medullary rays short, white, of all sizes, from fine to broad, very numerous, prominent on a radial section. Numerous white parallel wavy transverse bands across the rays.

Terai and valleys of the Bengal Himalaya, Khasia Hills, Chittagong and Burma. Weight 51 lbs.

		lbs.
E 2316.	Chunbati, Darjeeling, 2,000 feet	51

4. SACCOPETALUM, Bennett.

Besides the species here described, *S. longiflorum,* Hook. f. and Th., is a tree of Eastern Bengal found near Purneah.

1. S. tomentosum, Hook. f. and Th.; Hook. Fl. Ind. i. 88.; Beddome t. 39; Brandis, 7. *Uvaria tomentosa,* Roxb. Fl. Ind. ii. 667. Vern. *Kirna, karri,* Hind.; *Hoom,* Bombay; *Chilkadúdú,* Tel.; *Thoska,* Gondi; *Humba,* Kurku.

A large tree with straight stem. Bark ½ inch thick, of various shades, sometimes black, deeply cracked. Wood olive brown, moderately hard, smooth, close-grained; no heartwood. No annual rings. Pores small and moderate-sized, numerous. Medullary rays broad and fine, very numerous, distinctly visible on a radial section as long, narrow plates, giving the wood a mottled appearance. Numerous, regular, fine, white, transverse bars across the medullary rays, the distance between the rays being a little larger than the transverse diameter of the pores.

Oudh, Nepal Terai, Gorakhpur, Behar, Central India, Western Ghâts. Weight, 45 lbs. per cubic foot.

		lbs.
O 342.	Gorakhpur (1868)	...
C 1109.	Ahiri Reserve, Central Provinces	45

The following woods cannot at present be identified, but they probably belong to this family:—

B 1949. (58 lbs.) *Bokenet* from Tavoy. A hard, close-grained, yellow wood; when seasoned it is said to shew black and white stripes, and is then called Zebra Wood. Pores small, scanty. Medullary rays fine and very fine, joined by numerous fine parallel transverse bars. Used for furniture. Scarce in the Mergui Archipelago but plentiful in the Andaman Islands.

B 2281. (32 lbs.) Received from the Andaman Islands in 1866 under the name of *Thanloong.* Pores small, often subdivided. Medullary rays moderately broad, the distance between them many times larger than the transverse diameter of the pores. Numerous faint transverse bars. It may possibly be *Polyalthia Jenkinsii,* Bth. and Hook. f.

B 2251. (33 lbs.) Received from the Andamans in 1866 under the name of *Thitpyoo;* has a white soft wood, with small, scanty pores often in short radial lines. The medullary rays are moderately broad, far apart, joined by innumerable parallel bars, and shew well on a radial section.

B 273. (38 lbs.) Received from Burma in 1867 under the name *Bamau;* has an olive grey wood; it is handsome, even-grained, moderately hard and possesses a certain lustre. Pores small, often subdivided. Medullary rays fine. Numerous faint white transverse bars across the medullary rays. According to Kurz, *Bamau* is *Tetranthera grandis;* but on account of the transverse bars in the wood, we have placed it under Anonaceæ.

B 2236. (53 lbs.) Received from the Andamans in 1866 under the name of *Pan-noo;* has a similar structure to *Bamau.* Wood yellowish grey, hard. Pores small, transverse diameter equal to or one-half the distance between the medullary rays, which are fine and are joined by numerous transverse bars.

ORDER V. MENISPERMACEÆ.

An order which, in India with the single exception of the species described below, contains only climbing plants. Of the 17 genera found in India, many contain only single species. These 17 genera belong to 4 tribes, *viz.,*—

Tribe I.—Tinosporeæ . . . . *Aspidocarya, Parabæna, Tinospora, Fibraurea, Anamirta.*

„ II.—Cocculeæ . . . . *Tiliacora, Limacia, Cocculus, Pericampylus.*

„ III.—Cissampelideæ . . . *Stephania, Cissampelos, Cyclea, Lophopetalum.*

„ IV.—Pachygoneæ . . . . *Pachygone, Pycnarrhena, Hæmatocarpus, Antitaxis.*

Anamirta Cocculus, W. and A.; Hook. Fl. Ind. i. 99; Brandis 8; Kurz i. 53 (*Menispermum Cocculus,* Roxb. Fl. Ind. iii. 807) Vern. *Kakmári,* Hind., a climbing shrub of Southern and Eastern India and Burma, has bitter berries which in India are used to poison fish and crows (whence the native name), and in Europe under the name of 'Cocculus indicus' in the adulteration of beer. *Tinospora cordifolia,* Miers; Hook. Fl. Ind. i. 97; Brandis 8; Kurz i. 52; Gamble 4 (*Menispermum cordifolium,* Willd.; Roxb. Fl. Ind. iii. 811) Vern. *Batindu,* Pb.; *Golancha,* Beng.; *Gurcha,* Kumaun; *Gurjo,* Nep.; *Tippa tiga,* Tel.; *Galwail,* Bombay, is a well known climber which sends down long filiform runners from the branches of the trees over which it climbs; the root is used in native medicine, and elephants are fond of the stem and runners. *Cissampelos Pareira,* Linn. Hook. Fl. Ind. i. 103; Brandis 10; Gamble 4 (*C. convolvulacea,* Roxb. Fl. Ind. iii. 842) Vern. *Katori, parbik, pataki, tikri,* Pb.; *Dakh nirbisi, pári,* N. W. P.; *Harjeuri,* Oudh; *Batúlpati,* Nep.; *Pata,* Tel., a climber common both to the old and new worlds, furnishes the Radix Pareiræ of druggists. *Cocculus Leæba,* DC.; Hook., Fl. Ind. i. 102; Brandis 9. Vern. *Vallúr, illar,* Pb.; and *C. villosus,* DC.; Hook. Fl. Ind. i. 101; Brandis 9 (*Menispermum hirsutum,* Linn.; Roxb. Fl. Ind. iii. 814). Vern. *Hier, dier,* are large climbers of the dry and arid zones, while *Tiliacora racemosa,* Coleb.; Hook. Fl. Ind. i. 99; Brandis 10; Kurz i. 54 (*Menispermum polycarpon,* Roxb. Fl. Ind. iii. 816). Vern. *Tiliakoru,* Beng.; *Karwanth, rangoe,* Hind.; *Tiga mushadi,* Tel., is a large climber of most parts of India, often covering tall trees with its dense dark green foliage. Other genera, such as *Aspidocarya, Stephania* and *Parabæna,* furnish climbing shrubs common in Eastern Bengal and Assam.

"The structure of the wood of Menispermaceæ is remarkable, and differs in several respects from the wood of other Dicotyledons. The vascular bundles of a young branch (which in most Dicotyledons unite and form concentric rings of wood and liber) generally remain distinct in Menispermaceæ, and are separated by broad radial masses of cellular tissue, corresponding to the medullary rays of ordinary wood. After some time these original wood fascicles cease growing, and in the cortical cellular tissue exterior to the liber originates a second circle of bundles similar to the first formed, excepting in the absence of spiral vessels.

After these bundles have attained full development, they in turn cease to grow, and a third circle forms in the cellular tissue of the bark, and so on. There is great variety in the wood structure of the genera of this family."—*Brandis' Forest Flora*, p. 10.

1. COCCULUS, DC.

1. C. laurifolius, DC.; Hook. Fl. Ind. i. 101; Brandis 9. *Menispermum laurifolium*, Roxb. Fl. Ind. iii. 815. Vern. *Tilpara, kakra*, Hind.

A moderate-sized evergreen tree. Bark thin, grey. Wood greyish white, soft, divided by very broad medullary rays and concentric rings of the same substance as the rays, into numerous oblong radial masses, each mass consisting of wood cells and small uniformly distributed pores with a narrow belt of fibres (liber) at the outer edge.

Outer Himalaya from the Ravi to Nepal ascending to 5,000 ft.
Weight 41 lbs. per cubic foot.

		lbs.
H 2939.	Near Suni, Sutlej Valley, 3,000 ft.	42
E 2466.	Calcutta Botanic Gardens	40

ORDER VI. BERBERIDEÆ.

An order containing four Indian genera of woody plants, belonging to two tribes, *viz.*:
Tribe I.—Lardizabaleæ . . . . . . : . *Decaisnea, Parvatia* and *Hollböllia*.
„ II.—Berbereæ . . . . *Berberis*.
Two, each containing one species, are climbers, *viz.*, *Parvatia Brunoniana*, Decaisne; Hook. Fl. Ind. i. 108, from Assam and the Khasia Hills; and *Hollböllia latifolia* Wall.; Hook. Fl. Ind. i. 108; Brandis 13; Gamble 4. Vern. *Gophla*, Kumaun; *Chiriyanangri, bagul*, Nep.; *Pronchadik*, Lepcha; *Domhyem*, Bhutia. The latter is found in the Himalaya from Kumaun eastwards, above 4,000 feet elevation, and in the Khasia Hills. It has a large edible fruit, a soft corky bark and wood with large pores and broad medullary rays (E 2859. Tukdah, Darjeeling, 5,000 feet). *Decaisnea insignis*, Hook. f. and Th.; Hook. Fl. Ind. i. 107. Vern. *Nomorchi*, Lepcha; *Loodooma*, Bhutia, is an erect shrub of the Inner Sikkim Himalaya, growing between 7,000 and 10,000 feet, also with edible fruit.

1. BERBERIS, Linn.

Contains about twelve species, all Himalayan; two only extending southwards to the Nilgiris and the hills of Burma. One species, *B. asiatica*, Roxb. Fl. Ind. ii. 182; Hook. Fl. Ind. i. 110. Vern. *Kilmora*, Kumaun; *Mate-kissi, chitra*, Nep., is also found on Parasnáth in Behar. Besides those here described, *B. umbellata*, Wall., *B. asiatica*, Roxb., *B. Wallichiana*, DC., *B. insignis*, Hook. f., *B. macrosepala*, Hook. f., and *B. concinna*, Hook. f. occur in different parts of the Himalaya, chiefly at elevations above 8,000 ft.

Wood yellow, hard or moderately hard, splits very much in seasoning. Pores small, larger and more numerous on the inner edge of each annual ring, the rest of the pores smaller and arranged in irregular tails or patches. Medullary rays bright yellow, moderately broad, or broad.

The chief North-West Himalayan species may thus be recognized:—
Leaves pinnate . . . . *B. nepalensis*.
Leaves simple—
  Leaves thin with many equal serratures . . . . *B. vulgaris*.
  Leaves coriaceous, serratures few, unequal
    Branches grey
      Leaves large, green beneath . . . . *B. coriacea*.
      Leaves small, glaucous beneath . . . *B. Lycium*.
    Branches reddish . . . . *B. aristata*.

1. B. nepalensis, Spreng.; Hook. Fl. Ind. i. 109; Beddome xi.; Brandis 12; Kurz i. 58; Gamble 5. *B. pinnata,* Roxb. Fl. Ind. ii. 184 (probably). Vern. *Amúdanda, chiror,* Pb.; *Chatri, milkisse, jamnemunda,* Nep.

An evergreen shrub attaining in Bengal a height of 20 feet and occasionally 2 feet in girth. Bark soft, corky. Wood bright yellow, hard. Pores very small, arranged in radial lines or patches. Medullary rays moderately broad, prominent, numerous, well marked on a radial section.

Outer Himalaya from the Ravi to Bhutan, Khasia Hills, Tenasserim, Nilgiris and Western Ghâts, above 5,000 feet elevation.

Weight, 49 lbs. per cubic foot. The wood has a handsome colour and might be useful for inlaying; it is used as a dye by Bhutias.

	lbs.
E 2318. Darjeeling, 7,000 ft.	49

2. B. vulgaris, Linn.; Hook. Fl. Ind. i. 109; Brandis 11. The Barberry. Vern. *Zirishk, kashmal, chochar,* Pb.

A deciduous thorny shrub, with soft brown bark, $\frac{1}{6}$ inch thick. Wood lemon yellow, moderately hard, even-grained. Annual rings marked by an irregular belt of small pores, which are larger than those in the rest of the wood. The pores in the main portion of the annual rings are grouped in short, whitish, irregularly bent lines or tails. Medullary rays fine to moderately broad, well marked on a vertical section.

Himalaya, from Nepal westwards, in shady forests above 8,000 ft. elevation, Afghanistan and Beloochistan, Europe.

Weight, our specimen gives 52 lbs. per cubic foot; Mathieu Fl. For. p. 12, gives 45 to 57 lbs. Fruit edible. The wood is a good firewood.

	lbs.
H 3037. Matiyana, Simla, 9,000 ft.	...
H 3040. Naghanda, Simla, 9,000 ft.	55

3. B. aristata, DC.; Hook. Fl. Ind. i. 110; Beddome xii.; Brandis 12; Gamble 5. *B. angustifolia,* Roxb. Fl. Ind. ii. 183. Vern. *Súmlú, simlu, kasmal, chitra,* Pb.; *Tsema,* Bhutia; *Chitra,* Nep.; *Chotra,* Hind.

An erect spinous shrub. Bark soft, light brown, corky. Wood yellow, hard. Annual rings distinctly marked by a narrow belt of numerous pores. Pores small, in short, narrow, wavy tails of white tissue. Medullary rays moderately broad.

Outer Himalaya from the Sutlej to Bhutan: in the North-West Himalaya 6,000 ft. to 10,000 ft., in Darjeeling above 10,000 ft.; Western Ghâts at high elevations; Ceylon.

Wood used for fuel, the root in native medicine.

	lbs.
H 80. Simla, 7,000 ft.	52
H 2888. Nagkanda, Simla, 8,000 ft.	...
H 3053. Mahasu, Simla, 8,000 ft.	...

4. B. Lycium, Royle; Hook. Fl. Ind. i. 110; Brandis 12. Vern. *Kasmal,* Simla; *Kashmal, chotra,* Hind.

An erect rigid shrub. Bark rough, corky, white or light grey. Wood yellow, moderately hard. Annual rings marked by a narrow porous belt. Pores very small and extremely small, in narrow irregular lines of white tissue. Medullary rays moderately broad, numerous.

North-West Himalaya from 3,000 to 9,000 ft.

		lbs.
H 45.	Simla, 6,500 ft.	...
H 3054.	Mahasu, Simla, 7,500 ft.	52

5. B. coriacea, nov. sp., Brandis. Vern. *Kashmal*, Simla.

A large erect thorny shrub, with soft corky bark. Wood yellow, moderately hard. Annual rings marked by a belt of small or moderately sized pores; in the rest of the wood the pores are very small or extremely small, and arranged in numerous confluent, irregularly shaped tails and patches of whitish tissue. Medullary rays short, fine to broad.

North-West Himalaya above 8,000 ft.; often forming alone or with other shrubs large extents of scrub jungle, *e. g.*, in the valley south of Nagkanda near Simla.

		lbs.
H 48.	Nagkanda, Simla, 9,000 ft.	...
H 2894.	" " "	...
H 3039.	" " "	...
H 3041.	" " "	55
H 3043.	" " "	52
H 3038.	Matiyana, Simla, 8,000 ft.	...
H 3042.	Hattu, Simla, 10,000 ft.	...

6. B. angulosa, Wall.; Hook. Fl. Ind. i. 111; Gamble 5. Vern. *Chutra*, Nep.

A large erect shrub. Bark soft, brown, corky. Wood dark grey or yellowish brown, hard. Annual rings marked by a belt of small pores; in the rest of the wood the pores are very small, arranged in irregular radial tails of whitish tissue. Medullary rays fine, numerous.

Inner ranges of Nepal and Sikkim above 11,000 ft.

E 2862. Suburkum, Darjeeling, 11,000 ft.

ORDER VII. CAPPARIDEÆ.

Six Indian genera are of trees, shrubs or climbers belonging all to one tribe, Cappareæ. The climbing genera are: *Mærua*, one species, *M. arenaria*, Hook. f. and Th.; Hook. Fl. Ind. i. 171 (*Capparis heteroclita*, Roxb. Fl. Ind. ii. 570). Vern. *Patta tiga*, Tel., a large woody climber of the Western Himalaya, Upper Gangetic plain and Central India; and *Roydsia*, two species, *R. suaveolens*, Roxb. Fl. Ind. ii. 643; Hook. Fl. Ind. i. 180; Gamble 5. Vern. *Kasonli*, Nep.; *Tunggor*, Lepcha, in the tropical forests of Sikkim, Bhutan and the Khasia Hills, and *R. obtusifolia*, Hook. f. and Th.; Kurz i. 67. Vern. *Ngaphyoo*, Burm., in the swamp forests of Burma. *Niebuhria linearis*, DC.; Hook. Fl. Ind. i. 171, is a small tree of the hilly parts of the Carnatic; and the species of *Cadaba* are small straggling shrubs chiefly of the arid zone, *C. indica*, Lamk. Vern. *Kali taka*, occurring in Berar and the Dekkan, and *C. heterotricha*, Stocks; Hook. Fl. Ind. ii. 173, being a small tree found in rocks near Cape Monze in Sind.

Wood light-coloured. Pores small to moderate-sized, rarely large; often arranged in radial lines; medullary rays moderately broad, wavy.

1. CAPPARIS, Linn.

A genus of about thirty species of thorny shrubs or climbers. About fifteen occur in Burma, ten in the Dekkan and Carnatic, five on the western coast, eight in Bengal and Assam, two in the Gangetic valley and Central India, and three in the arid zone of the Punjab and Sind. Besides those here described, there are several common species. *C. spinosa*, Linn.; Hook. Fl. Ind. i. 173; Brandis 14. Vern. *Kabawa*, Afg.; *Kábra*, Tibet; *Kaur, keri, kander, kakri, taker, ber, barari, bauri, bussur*, Pb.; *Ulta-kanta*, Kumaun;

Kalvári, Sind, is a small trailing shrub of the Punjab and Sind, whose flower buds give the capers of commerce; they are pickled and eaten in Sind and the Punjab Salt Range. *C. divaricata,* Lamk.; Hook. Fl. Ind. i. 17 (*C. stylosa,* DC.; Beddome xiii) Vern. *Toaratti,* Tam.; *Budareni,* Tel.; *Pachúnda,* Mar., is a shrub or small tree of the Dekkan and Carnatic, with large scarlet fruit. *C. olacifolia,* Hook. f. and Th.; Hook. Fl. Ind. i. 178; Gamble 5. Vern. *Naski, hais,* Nep.; *Jhenok,* Lepcha, is a common thorny shrub of river banks and valleys in Northern Bengal and Assam. *C. horrida,* Linn.; Hook. Fl. Ind. i. 178; Brandis 15 (*C. zeylanica,* Roxb. Fl. Ind. ii. 567). Vern. *Hís, karvila,* Pb.; *Karralura,* Oudh; *Adonda,* Tel.; *Katerni,* Gondi; *Gitoran,* Ajmere; *Atanday,* Tam. is a climbing shrub common in most parts of India.

1. **C. grandis,** Linn. f.; Hook. Fl. Ind. i. 176; Beddome xiii; *C. bisperma,* Roxb. Fl. Ind. ii. 569. Vern. *Guli, regguli, ragota,* Tel.

A small tree. Bark thick, extremely irregular, rough and corky, deeply and irregularly cracked. Wood white, moderately hard. No heartwood, no annual rings. Pores scanty, moderate-sized to large. Medullary rays moderately broad, short.

Chanda district and eastern part of the Dekkan, Eastern Ghâts and Carnatic. Weight, 46 lbs. Wood durable, much used by the natives in the Madras Presidency.

		lbs.
C 1134.	Ahiri, Central Provinces	46

2. **C. aphylla,** Roth; Hook. Fl. Ind. i. 174; Beddome xiii; Brandis 14. Vern. *Karíl,* Pb.; *Kiral,* Sind; *Kari,* Behar.

A small tree with scanty, small, caducous leaves, found only on the young shoots. Bark ½ inch thick, grey, corky, with deep irregular cracks. Wood light yellow, turning brown on exposure, shining, very hard and close-grained. Annual rings doubtful. Pores small, generally in groups or patches between the prominent, very short, numerous, fine medullary rays.

Punjab, Sind, Rajputana and the Dekkan.

Weight, 53 lbs per cubic foot. The wood is used for small beams and rafters in roofs, for the knees of boats, for oilmills and agricultural implements; it is a good firewood, and is not eaten by white ants. The fruit is eaten both raw and preserved, and the young flower buds are preserved as pickle.

		lbs.
P 441.	Ajmere	...
P 892.	Multan	53
P 941.	„	...
P 3056.	„	...

2. CRATÆVA, Linn.

1. **C. religiosa,** Forst.; Hook. Fl. Ind. i. 172; Beddome t. 116 and xiv (*C. Nurvala,* Ham.); Brandis 16; Gamble 5. *C. Roxburghii,* Ham.; Kurz i. 66. *Capparis trifoliata,* Roxb. Fl. Ind. ii. 571. Vern. *Brarna, bilási, bila, biliana,* Hind.; *Barún, tikto-shak,* Beng.; *Purbong,* Lepcha; *Maralingam, marvilinga,* Tam.; *Uskia, usiki, ulimidi, urumatti, tellavoolemara,* Tel.; *Nirvála,* Kan., Mal.; *Kúmla, karwan,* Mar.; *Kadet, katat,* Burm.

A moderate-sized deciduous tree. Bark grey, ½ inch thick, with long horizontal wrinkles. Wood yellowish white, when old turning light brown, moderately hard, even-grained. Pores moderate-sized, numerous and uniformly distributed, often in short radial lines, each pore surrounded by a whitish ring. Medullary rays short, very wavy, fine and moderately broad, the distance between the rays slightly greater than the transverse diameter of the pores.

Sub-Himalayan tract from the Ravi eastwards, Bengal, Assam, Central and South India and Burma.

Weight, 42 lbs. The wood is used for drums, models, writing-boards, combs and in turnery.

		lbs.
P 3217.	Nagpahar, Ajmere	...
O 270.	Garhwal (1868)	33
O 3112.	Dehra Dún	47
C 3115.	Chanda, Central Provinces	45
B 565.	Prome, Burma	43
No. 23.	Salem Collection	44

ORDER VIII. VIOLACEÆ.

This order contains three genera of Indian plants: of these, two, *viz.*, *Viola* and *Ionidium*, are herbaceous; while the third, *Alsodeia*, comprises six shrubs or small trees found in Northern and Eastern Bengal, Burma and Malabar. *A. bengalensis*, Wall.; Hook. Fl. Ind. i. 186; Kurz i. 70; Gamble 6. Vern. *Kalipat*, Nep., occurs in Sikkim, Assam, Burma and the Andamans. *A. Roxburghii*, Wall.; Hook. Fl. Ind. i. 186; Kurz i. 69 (*Vareca heteroclita*, Roxb. Fl. Ind. i. 648), in Sylhet and the Andamans; and *A. racemosa*, Hook. f. and Th.; Hook. Fl. Ind. i. 187 (*A. longiracemosa*, Kurz i. 70), in Assam and Tenasserim, said by Kurz to have a yellowish white close-grained wood.

No. B 3198. (Home, 1874, No. 26, *Kyadoo*). A white scented wood from the Andamans, with scanty, moderately large pores; moderately fine, wavy, medullary rays, and numerous concentric lines of soft tissue, was identified by Kurz from Home's specimens as coming nearest to *Alsodeia* (Brandis' Memorandum on the Forest Resources of the Andamans, dated August 25th, 1874).

ORDER IX. BIXINEÆ.

Seven genera belonging to three tribes:—

Tribe I.—Bixeæ	*Cochlospermum* and *Bixa*.
„ II.—Flacourtieæ	*Scolopia*, *Flacourtia* and *Xylosma*.
„ III.—Pangieæ	*Gynocardia* and *Hydnocarpus*.

Bixa Orellana, Linn.; Roxb. Fl. Ind. ii. 581; Hook. Fl. Ind. i. 190; Beddome t. 79; Brandis 17; Kurz i. 72; Gamble 6. The Arnotto Plant. Vern. *Latkan*, Hind., Beng.; *Jarat*, Ass.; *Jafra*, Tel.; *Kuragúmangjal*, Tam.; *Kuppa-manhala*, Kan.; *Kisri*, Mar.; *Theedin*, Burm., is an American shrub, introduced and cultivated in India for the red dye given by the pulp surrounding the seeds.

Hydnocarpus contains four Indian species. *H. heterophylla*, Bl.; Kurz i. 77. Vern. *Kal-lau-tso*, Burm., is described by Kurz as an evergreen tree with heavy, strong, yellowish white wood, found in the tropical forests of Burma. *H. castanea*, Hook. f. and Th.; Hook. Fl. Ind. i. 197; Kurz i. 79, is a tree of the Andaman Islands. *H. alpina*, Wight; Hook. Fl. Ind. i. 197; Beddome t. 77. Vern. *Maratatti*, Nilgiris, is a tree of the Western Ghâts, whose wood is said by Beddome to be used in the construction of native houses, for packing cases and firewood. *H. Wightiana*, Bl.; Hook. Fl. Ind. i. 196 (*H. Wightiana* and *H. inebrians*, Vahl.; Beddome xvi, xvii). Vern. *Yetti*, *maravetti*, Tam.; *Kowti*, Mar.; *Makúlú*, Cingh., is a common tree of the Western Ghâts and western coast.

The wood of *Flacourtia*, *Xylosma*, *Gynocardia* and *Scolopia* is uniform and remarkably similar to the wood of Euphorbiaceæ; it is hard and close-grained and the pores are small, in short radial lines between fine or very fine, closely packed medullary rays. The wood of *Cochlospermum* has an entirely different structure.

1. COCHLOSPERMUM, Kunth.

1. C. Gossypium, DC.; Hook. Fl. Ind. i. 190; Beddome xiv;

Brandis 17; Kurz i. 72. *Bombax Gossypium*, Roxb. Fl. Ind. iii. 169. Vern. *Kúmbi, gabdi, ganiár, galgal, gangal*, Hind.; *Gangam*, Gondi; *Gúngú, kong, kandu-gogu*, Tel.; *Tanaku, kongillam*, Tam.; *Chima-púnji*, Mal.; *Ganeri*, Bhíl; *Ganeri, gunglay*, Mar.

A small deciduous tree, with short, thick, spreading branches. Bark one inch thick, deeply furrowed; inner substance red. Wood extremely soft, grey; no heartwood. Pores large, scanty, often subdivided into compartments. Medullary rays broad, on a radial section, visible as long rough plates.

Forests at the base of the North-West Himalaya, from the Sutlej eastwards, Central India, Dekkan, Prome District in Burma.

Weight, 17 lbs. per cubic foot. Wood useless. Gives a clear white gum (*Katira*), which, according to Baden-Powell, is used in the trade of shoemaking.

		lbs.
C 1141.	Ahiri Reserve, C. P.	17

2. SCOLOPIA, Schreber.

Three species. *S. crenata*, Clos.; Hook. Fl. Ind. i. 191; Beddome t. 78 (*Phoberos crenatus*, W. and A. Prodr. 29). Vern. *Hitterlú*, Burghers, is a tree of Malabar, Kanara and Mysore, said by Beddome to have a hard, dense, white wood, liable to warp. *S. Roxburghii*, Clos.; Hook. Fl. Ind. i. 190; Kurz i. 73 (*Ludia spinosa*, Roxb. Fl. Ind. ii. 507), is an evergreen tree of Tenasserim, the stem and older branches of which are armed with long, straight or compound spines.

1. S. rhinanthera, Clos.; Hook. Fl. Ind. i. 190. B 1969, collected by Kurz in the Andamans in 1866, bears this name. It has a hard red wood, with a structure similar to that of *Flacourtia*, the pores being small, in short radial lines, between the very fine and closely packed medullary rays. Weight 60 lbs. per cubic foot.

3. FLACOURTIA, Commerson.

Seven Indian species. The following are the names given in the Flora Indica i., 191 to 194:—

1. *F. sumatrana*, Planch.; Kurz i. 74 . . .	Tenasserim.
2. *F. inermis*, Roxb. Fl. Ind. iii. 833; Beddome xvi; Kurz i. 74. Vern. *Tomitomi*, Mal.; *Ubbolu*, Kan. Perhaps introduced. Fruit edible.	Sylhet, S. India, Martaban.
3. *F. montana*, Grah.; Beddome xvi. Vern. *Attak*, Kan., Mar.	Western Coast.
4. *F. mollis*, Hook. f. and Th.; Kurz i. 74 . .	Tenasserim.
5. *F. Cataphracta*, Roxb. Fl. Ind. iii. 834; Beddome xvi; Kurz i. 74. Vern. *Paniala, panizali*, Beng.; *Talispatri, paniala*, Hind.; *Talisapatri*, Tam., Tel.; *Na-yuwai*, Burm.	Bengal, Burma, Bombay, Western Ghâts.
6. *F. Ramontchi*, L'Herit.	India.
7. *F. sepiaria*, Roxb. Fl. Ind. iii. 835 (also *F. obcordata*); Beddome xvi; Brandis 18; Kurz i. 75 (also *F. rotundifolia*). Vern. *Sharawani, dajkar, jidkar*, Hind.; *Kanru*, Tel.	Kumaun, Bengal and South India.

1. F. Ramontchi, L'Herit.; Hook. Fl. Ind. i. 193; Beddome xvi; Brandis 18. *F. sapida*, Roxb. Fl. Ind. iii. 835; Kurz i. 75. Vern. *Kúkai, kukoa, kangú, kandei*, Pb.; *Bilangra, bhauber, kanjú, kandi* *kattár, katti,* Hind.; *Kaikun,* Mhairwarra; *Kánk, kánki, biláti,* C. P.; *Arma-suri, katien,* Gondi; *Gurgoti,* Kurku; *Bincha, katái,* Beng.; *Bonicha,* Uriya; *Pahar, bhekal, kakei, kaker,* Mar.; *Bhutankas,* Hyderabad; *Kanregu, pedda-kanru, kaka, nakka-naregu,* Tel.; *Úgúrassa,* Cingh.; *Na-yuwai,* Burm.

A small thorny deciduous tree. Bark grey. Wood red, hard, close- and even-grained, splits, but does not warp and is durable. Pores small, in radial lines between the fine, uniform, closely-packed and somewhat wavy medullary rays.

Dry hills throughout India, Prome District in Burma.

Weight: Brandis gives 50 lbs. per cubic foot, the average of our specimens is 53 lbs. The wood is used for turning and agricultural implements, and the fruit and leaves are eaten.

		lbs.
P 460.	Ajmere	52
P 3221.	Nagpahar, Ajmere	...
O 260.	Garhwal (1868)	50
C 2739.	Moharli Reserve, C. P.	52
B 3125.	Burma (1862)	59

4. XYLOSMA, Forster.

Three species. *X. controversum,* Clos.; Hook. Fl. Ind. i. 194, is a tree of Nepal and the Khasia Hills, nearly allied to *X. longifolium. X. latifolium,* Hook. f. and Th.; Hook. Fl. Ind. i. 194, is a large thorny tree of the Bababuden Hills in Mysore.

1. X. longifolium, Clos.; Hook. Fl. Ind. i. 194; Brandis 19. Vern. *Chopra, chirúnda, chirndi, drendu,* Pb.; *Kattáwa,* Oudh; *Dandál, katári, kandhára,* Hind.

A small evergreen tree. Bark $\frac{1}{6}$ inch thick, grey. Wood pinkish, moderately hard, even-grained. Pores small, in short radial lines between the wavy, very fine and closely-packed medullary rays.

North-West Himalaya ascending to 5,000 feet, Assam.

Weight, 55 lbs. per cubic foot. The wood is used for fuel and charcoal.

		lbs.
H 2947.	Jander, Sutlej Valley, 3,500 feet	55

5. GYNOCARDIA, R. Br.

1. G. odorata, R. Br.; Hook. Fl. Ind. i. 195; Kurz i. 76; Gamble 6. *Chaulmoogra odorata,* Roxb. Fl. Ind. iii. 835. Vern. *Chaulmúgri, petarkura,* Beng.; *Kadu,* Nep.; *Túk,* Lepcha; *Toungpung,* Magh.

A moderate-sized evergreen tree, readily known by the hard, round fruits which grow on the stem and main branches. Bark $\frac{1}{4}$ inch thick, grey, smooth. Wood hard, close-grained, yellow or light brown. Pores very small, in radial lines between the white, very numerous and prominent medullary rays.

Northern and Eastern Bengal and Assam, Chittagong and Burma.

Weight, 47 lbs. per cubic foot.

The wood is used in Chittagong for planking and for posts, and the pulp of the fruit in Sikkim to poison fish. The seeds give by expression a thick oil, used in the treatment of cutaneous diseases, especially leprosy.

		lbs.
E 708.	Chittagong	47

ORDER X. PITTOSPOREÆ.

An order containing one genus of Indian trees or shrubs, the remaining genera being chiefly Australian. The genus *Pittosporum*, Hook. Fl. Ind. i. 198, contains eight Indian species, two of which, *P. glabratum*, Ldl. and *P. humile*, Hook. f. and Th., grow in the Khasia Hills; three, *P. tetraspermum*, W. and A., *P. nilghirense*, W. and A., and *P. dasycaulon*, Miq., on the Western Ghâts, and one, *P. ferrugineum*, Ait.; Kurz i. 78, in Burma. Of the remaining two: one, *P. eriocarpum*, Royle; Brandis 19, is found in the outer Himalaya of Kumaun and Garhwal (*Meda túmri, gar-silung, garshúna*, Hind.); and the other, *P. floribundum*, W. and A.; Beddome xvii; Brandis 19; Gamble 6 (*Celastrus verticillata*, Roxb. Fl. Ind. i. 624). Vern. *Yekaddi*, Mar.; *Prongzam*, Lepcha, is a common small tree of the outer Himalaya from the Jumna to Bhutan ascending to 8,000 feet, the Khasia Hills and Western Ghâts.

ORDER XI. POLYGALEÆ.

Three Indian genera of woody plants of little forest interest.

· *Polygala arillata*, Ham.; Hook. Fl. Ind. i. 200; Gamble 6 (*Chamæbuxus arillata*, Hassk.; Kurz i. 79). Vern. *Karima*, Nep.; *Michepnor*, Lepcha, is a shrub of Northern Bengal and the Khasia Hills; and *P. Karensium*, Kurz (*C. Karensium*, Kurz i. 79), a shrub of Martaban. *Securidaca tavoyana*, Wall.; Hook. Fl. Ind. i. 208 (*S. inappendiculata*, Hassk.; Kurz i. 80), is a large woody climber of Eastern Bengal, Arracan and Tenasserim. *Xanthophyllum* contains four species: *X. flavescens*, Roxb. Fl. Ind. ii. 222; Hook. Fl. Ind. i. 209; Kurz i. 81 (including, according to Bennett in the "Flora Indica," *X. Arnottianum*, Wight, *X. angustifolium*, Wight, and *X. virens*, Roxb.; Beddome xix). Vern. *Ajensak, gandi*, Beng.; *Thitpyoo*, Burm., is a tree of Bengal, South India, and Burma, said by Kurz to have a heavy, close-grained wood. *X. glaucum*, Wall.; *X. Griffithii*, Hook. f.; and *X. affine*, Korth., are evergreen trees of Burma.

ORDER XII. TAMARISCINEÆ.

A small order containing bushes or small trees with small sessile or scale-like sheathing leaves: two genera, *Tamarix* and *Myricaria*.

Wood white or reddish, sometimes darker in the centre, but no heartwood. Pores small to moderate-sized, often in groups, more numerous and large in the spring wood wherever the annual rings are distinct. Medullary rays generally moderately broad to broad, short, distant.

1. TAMARIX, Linn.

Bushes or small trees, with scale-like leaves and white or pink flowers, chiefly found on the banks of streams and on the lowlands near rivers. There are six species, of which the most important are: *T. articulata*, Vahl., *T. dioica*, Roxb., and *T. gallica*, Linn.; Hook. Fl. Ind. i. 248; Beddome xx; Brandis 20; Kurz i. 83 (*T. indica*, Roxb. Fl. Ind. ii. 100). Vern. *Kóan, rúkh, leinya, ghazlei, pilchi*, Pb.; *Lei, lái, jhau*, Sind; *Yelta*, Tibet; *Jhau*, Beng., the last two species being found along rivers and the sea-coast almost throughout India. Of the remaining species, *T. salina*, Dyer, and *T. stricta*, Boiss, are found in the Punjab and Sind, and *T. ericoides*, Rottb., in Bengal and Central India. Mathieu, Fl. For. p. 23 gives 40 to 48 lbs. as the weight per cubic foot of *T. gallica*.

1. T. dioica, Roxb. Fl. Ind. ii. 101; Hook. Fl. Ind. i. 249; Beddome xx; Brandis 21; Kurz. i. 83; Gamble 6; Vern. *Lei, pilchi, koan, kachlei*, Pb.; *Gaz, láo, jau*, Sind; *Lal jhau*, Beng.; *Jau*, Hind.

A gregarious shrub. Bark grey with reticulate cracks, shewing the red inner bark. Wood moderately hard, red, outer portion white. Pores small to moderate-sized, in groups or short radial lines, more abundant and larger in the spring wood. Medullary rays very prominent, short, fine to very broad, very prominent on a radial section. The distance between the rays is generally three or four times the transverse diameter of the pores.

Throughout India from Sind to Burma. Often planted for ornament.

Of the rate of growth, little is known. Minniken, in his report of 1878 on the Delhi Bela plantation, gives the following measurements of seven trees in the 4th (Jaffar Khan) compartment, 3 years old, 8 to 15 feet high:—

No. 1	25 inches	Average 13 inches or 1·4 rings per inch, which is fast.
„ 2	18 „	
„ 3	15 „	
„ 4	14 „	
„ 5	12 „	
„ 6	6 „	
„ 7	3 „	

Weight, 49 lbs. per cubic foot. The wood is used mainly for fuel, but also for the supporting sticks of roofs.

		lbs.
P 888.	Multan	48
P 1388.	Lahore	51

2. T. articulata, Vahl.; Hook. Fl. Ind. i. 249; Beddome xx; Brandis 22. Vern. *Farâs, farwa, rúkh, ukhan, kharlei, narlei,* Pb.; *Asrelei,* Sind.

A moderate-sized tree, with grey rough bark, coppices well, and is easily reproduced either by seed or by cuttings; wood white, moderately hard; annual rings indistinct. Pores moderate-sized, often in groups, scanty. Medullary rays short, fine to very broad, the distance between the rays somewhat greater than the transverse diameter of the pores; prominent on a radial section as irregularly shaped plates, giving the wood a mottled appearance.

Punjab and Sind.

"Growth rapid, trees 12 years old, on an average attain a girth of 2 to 3 feet, one 15 years old measured 4 ft. 10 in. in girth, and it is stated that at times it attains 5 ft. in 7 years."—*Brandis.* "It grows very rapidly and to a large size, and I have frequently seen trees of 10 to 12 feet girth and 60 or 70 feet high."—*J. L. Stewart, Punjab Plants,* p. 92.

Weight: Brandis says, 40 to 60 lbs. when seasoned; Stewart says, 92 lbs. per cubic foot green and 60 lbs. dry; the specimen received weighed 61 lbs. Wood used for many kinds of ordinary work, for ploughs, Persian wheels and small ornaments, and for charcoal. The bark is used for tanning as well as the galls (*Mái,* Punjab; *Sakun,* Sind) which are also used as a mordant in dyeing.

		lbs.
P 886.	Multan	61

2. MYRICARIA, Desvaux.

The genus contains, besides the species given below, *M. elegans,* Royle, a small bush of the inner Western Himalaya and Tibet, where it is very valuable as fuel.

1. M. germanica, Desv.; Hook. Fl. Ind. i. 250; Brandis 23. Vern. *Bis, shalakát, kathi, humbu,* Pb.; *Ombu,* Lahoul.

A shrub with rough brownish bark. Wood hard, white. Annual rings marked by porous spring wood. Pores small, medullary rays broad, short, very numerous and prominent.

Inner Himalaya from Punjab to Sikkim.

Wood used for fuel, and the branches as fodder for sheep and goats.

		lbs.
H 133.	Lahoul, 10,000 ft.	...
E 974.	Chumbi Valley, Tibet, 10,000 ft.	...

ORDER XIII. HYPERICINEÆ.

A small order with three Indian genera. One, *Ascyrum*, contains only one small plant from Sikkim. *Hypericum*, a number of herbs and small shrubs of the Himalaya, the most common of which are *H. cernuum*, Roxb. Fl. Ind. iii. 400; Hook. Fl. Ind. i. 253, a handsome small shrub with large bright yellow flowers, found in the Western Himalaya especially on rocks; and *H. Hookerianum*, W. and A.; Hook. Fl. Ind. i. 254; Gamble 6. Vern. *Tumbomri*, Lepcha. (E 2861, Darjeeling, 7,000 ft. (43 lbs.)) a very common, rather gregarious, handsome shrub of the Sikkim Himalaya, often used for hedges. This last has a close-grained, moderately hard wood, with annual rings marked by a ring of larger pores than those in the rest of the ring, which are small, scanty. Medullary rays fine, very numerous.

1. CRATOXYLON, Bl.

A genus of five trees from Burma and the Andaman Islands containing besides the one described, *C. formosum*, Bth. and Hook. f., from the Andamans, and *C. pruniflorum*, Kurz, *C. polyanthum*, Korth., and *C. arborescens*, Bl., from Martaban and Tenasserim.

I. C. neriifolium, Kurz i. 85.; Hook. Fl. Ind. i. 257. Vern. *Baibya*, Burm.

A tree. Bark dark coloured, rough. Wood dark grey, hard, close-grained. Pores large, in short narrow wavy irregular patches of softer tissue. Medullary rays not prominent, fine, numerous, on a radial section visible as dark narrow plates.

Chittagong and Burma.

Weight, 47 lbs. per cub. ft. According to Kurz, the wood is used for building purposes, for ploughs, handles of chisels, hammers and other implements.

	lbs.
B 312. Burma (1867)	47

ORDER XIV. GUTTIFERÆ.

An order of tropical trees, containing six genera, belonging to two tribes, *viz.*:—

Tribe I.—Garcinieæ . . . . . *Garcinia* and *Ochrocarpus.*

„ II.—Calophylleæ . . . . . *Calophyllum, Kayea, Mesua* and *Pœciloneuron.*

Of *Ochrocarpus*, there are three species. *O. longifolius*, Bth. and Hook. f.; Hook. Fl. Ind. i. 270; Beddome t. 89. Vern. *Suringi*, Mar.; *Sura-ponna*, Tel.; *Seráya*, Mal.; *Wúndi, taringi* (♂), *poone* (♀), *suringi, gardúndi* (☿), Kan., is a large, usually diœcious tree of the Western Ghâts, whose dried flowers are used for dyeing silk. Skinner, No. 35 (*Calophyllum longifolium*) gives weight 45 lbs. P = 546. *O. siamensis*, T. And.; Hook. Fl. Ind. i. 270; Kurz i. 94. Vern. *Taraphee*, Burm., is an evergreen tree of the Eng forests of Prome and Martaban, and *O. nervosus*, Kurz i. 94, an evergreen tree of the tropical forests of the Arracan Yomah. *Pœciloneuron* includes two species, given by Beddome under Ternströmiaceæ, but referred to this Family by Dyer in "Flora Indica, i. 278." *P. indicum*, Beddome t. 3. Vern. *Kirballi*, Kan., is a large tree of the western slopes of the Ghâts from South Kanara to Malabar, from 3,000 to 4,000 ft., said by Beddome to have a hard wood used for rice-pounders. *P. pauciflorum*, Beddome t. 93. Vern. *Pudangalli*, is a large tree of the Ghâts of Tinnevelly and Travancore with a valuable, hard, reddish timber, used for building, and to make walking-sticks.

Wood red (in *Calophyllum, Mesua* and some species of *Garcinia*), generally with a distinct heartwood. Pores variable in size. Medullary rays generally fine. Numerous concentric lines or bands of soft texture across the rays.

1. GARCINIA, Linn.

A large genus of evergreen, opposite-leaved trees, usually with a yellow juice, generally giving a more or less pure description of gamboge. They chiefly come from the tropical regions of India, none of them extending to Northern and Central India, and only one or two as far as Northern Bengal. There are about 22 Indian species, the synonymy of which is somewhat confused.

The following is Dr. T. Anderson's list, given at pages 259 to 270 of Hooker's Flora Indica, Kurz's species being added in brackets :—

SECTION I.—GARCINIA.

1.	*G. Mangostana*, Linn.; Roxb. Fl. Ind. ii. 618; Kurz i. 87. The Mangosteen. Vern. *Mengkop, youngzalai*, Burm. In Helfer's "Report on the Provinces of Ye, Tavoy and Mergui" of 1839, he says that "a full-grown tree yields 1,000 fruits, which at the lowest can be reckoned at Rs. 3 per 100," and that "the integument of the fruit yields a very strong and valuable tan."	Cultivated in South Tenasserim.
2.	*G. cornea*, Linn.; Roxb. Fl. Ind. ii. 629; Kurz i. 88. "Wood brown, heavy; gives an inferior kind of gamboge."—*Kurz.*	Eastern Bengal and Burma.
3.	*G. speciosa*, Wall.	Tenasserim and Andamans.
4.	*G. indica*, Choisy (*G. purpurea*, Roxb. Fl. Ind. ii. 624; Beddome xxi). *Brindall*, Goa. "The fruit has an agreeable, acid flavour, a syrup is made from it; the seeds furnish a concrete oil called *Kokum* in Bombay."	Ghâts of Concan and Kanara.
5.	*G. Cambogia*, Desrouss.	Western Ghâts.
6.	*G. Cowa*, Roxb.	Assam, Bengal, Burma and Andamans.
7.	*G. lanceæfolia*, Roxb. Fl. Ind. ii. 623; Kurz i. 91. (*G. purpurea* Wall.) Vern. *Kirindur*, Sylhet.	Assam, Sylhet and Chittagong.
8.	*G. loniceroides*, T. And. (*G. succifolia*, Kurz i. 91). "Wood white, perishable; yields little and inferior gamboge."—*Kurz.*	Swamp forests in Pegu.
9.	*G. pedunculata*, Roxb. Fl. Ind. ii. 625; Gamble 7. Vern. *Tikil, tikur*, Beng.; *Borthekra*, Ass.; cultivated for its fruit. "Wood used for planks, beams, and ordinary building."—*Mann.*	Rangpur, Goalpara and Sylhet.
10.	*G. Morella*, Desrouss.	Assam, Eastern Bengal, South India.
11.	*G. heterandra*, Wall. (*G. elliptica*, Wall.; Kurz i. 49). Vern. *Thanat-tau*, Burm. "Wood soft, white; yields a superior quality of gamboge."—*Kurz.*	Hills of Burma up to 3,000 feet.
12.	*G. Wightii*, T. And. . . . . . . "The gamboge of this species is very soluble and yields a good pigment."—*T. And.*	South India.
13.	*G. paniculata*, Roxb. Fl. Ind. ii. 626; Kurz i. 92. Vern. *Búbi-kowa*, Sylhet.	Eastern Himalaya, Khasia Hills, Sylhet and Chittagong.
14.	*G. atro-viridis*, Griff.	Upper Assam.
15.	*G. anomala*, Pl. and Trian.; Kurz i. 89. Vern. *Usaqueng*, Ass.	Khasia Hills, and hills of Martaban, 3,000 to 6,000 feet.

SECTION I.—GARCINIA—*continued.*

16.	*G. stipulata*, T. And.; Gamble 7. Vern. *Sanakadan*, Lepcha. "Fruit yellow, sometimes eaten by Lepchas; the tree and fruit give a yellow gum, but it does not seem to be used."—*Gamble.*	Sikkim and Bhutan, up to 4,000 feet.
17.	*G. merguensis*, Wight; Kurz i. 89 . . .	Tenasserim.
18.	*G. travancorica*, Beddome t. 173 (G. sp. 2. Beddome xxi). Vern. *Malampongu*, Tinnevelly. "Every portion of the tree yields an abundance of bright yellow gamboge, not yet examined."—*Beddome.*	Forests of Travancore and Tinnevelly.
19.	(*G. microstigma*, Kurz i. 91)	Andamans.

SECTION II.—XANTHOCHYMUS.

20.	*G. Xanthochymus*, Hook. f.; Kurz i. 93. *Xanthochymus pictorius*, Roxb. Fl. Ind. ii. 633; Beddome t. 88. Vern. *Tepor*, Ass.; *Maohla*, Phekial; *Dampel*, Hind.; *Iwara memadi, tamalamu, chitakamraku*, Tel.; *Mataw*, Burm. "Yields a large quantity of indifferent gamboge."—*Roxburgh.*	Eastern Himalaya, Eastern Bengal, Burma, South India.
21.	*G. ovalifolia*, Hook. f.; *X. ovalifolius*, Roxb. Fl. Ind. ii. 632; Beddome xxi. Vern. *Kokatie*, Tam.; *Ellagokatu*, Cingh.	Western Gháts.
22.	*G. dulcis*, Kurz i. 92 (*X. dulcis*, Roxb. Fl. Ind. ii. 631).	Andamans.

Wood close-grained, hard. Pores small to large, subdivided. Numerous concentric bands of softer texture. The structure of the wood of the species of *Garcinia* is not uniform. *G. Cowa* and *G. Morella* have similar wood, while *G. speciosa* differs by having fine medullary rays and *G. Cambogia* by the absence of distinct concentric rings. The structure of the *Garcinias* requires further investigation.

1. G. speciosa, Wall.; Hook. Fl. Ind. i. 260; Kurz i. 88. Vern. *Palawa*, Burm.

An evergreen tree. Bark thin, greyish-black. Heartwood red, very hard, cross-, and close-grained. Pores small, very numerous. Numerous short, wavy, transverse bands joining the pores. Medullary rays very fine, uniform, equidistant, not very distinct, the distance between two rays about equal to the transverse diameter of the pores.

Tenasserim and the Andaman Islands.

Weight, according to Major Protheroe, 72 lbs.; our specimens give only 52 lbs. and Wallich (Nos. 73, 74, *Garcinia* sp., *Pullowa*) 45·5 lbs.

Used for house and bridge posts, and other purposes; said to be used by the Andamanese to make bows.

			lbs.
B 504.	Andaman Islands		52
B 2492.	Do.	(Home, 1874, No 18)	52

Two specimens marked B 2493 *Pantagah*, No. 20. (51 lbs.), and B 2,500 *Phungnyet*, No. 19 (62 lbs.), brought by Home from the Andamans in 1874 resemble *G. speciosa*, but the pores are in short radial lines and the medullary rays more distinct.

B 2206 (47 lbs.), received from the Andamans in 1866 under the name of *Thingannee* is similar in structure to B 2493 and 2500, but the pores are larger.

2. G. Cambogia, Desr.; Hook. Fl. Ind. i. 261; Beddome t. 85; Roxb. Fl. Ind. ii. 621. Vern. *Aradal,* Kan.; *Heela,* Burghers.

A small evergreen tree. Wood grey, cross-grained, shining, hard. Pores small and very small, in short radial lines, between the closely packed, uniform, very fine medullary rays. Concentric bands present, but indistinct.

Western Coast and Ceylon.

Weight, 54 lbs. per cubic foot. Beddome says the wood would answer for common furniture.

Thwaites states that this tree yields a yellow insoluble gum, which is consequently valueless as a pigment. It is, however, said to be soluble in spirits of turpentine, and to form a beautiful yellow varnish. Mr. Cherry says it gives an oil which is used in medicine.

		lbs.
W 845.	South Kanara	54

3. G. Cowa, Roxb. Fl. Ind. ii. 622; Hook. Fl. Ind. i. 262; *G. Cowa* and *G. Kydia,* Roxb.; Kurz i. 90. Vern. *Cowa,* Hind.; *Toungthalay,* Burm.

A tall evergreen tree with round stem and dark grey bark. Wood greyish-white, moderately hard. Pores moderate-sized to large, scanty, often subdivided. Medullary rays fine to broad. Numerous, wavy, concentric bands of soft tissue across the rays.

Eastern Bengal, Assam, Chittagong, Burma and the Andaman Islands.

Weight, 42 lbs. per cubic foot (Brandis 1862, No. 19); our specimens give an average of 40 lbs. Kyd gives weight 47 lbs., P = 815. Wood not used. Is said to give a kind of gamboge of a rather different colour to that produced by *G. Morella.*

		lbs.
B 549.	Martaban.	43
B 3148.	Burma (1862)	37

4. G. Morella, Desrouss.; Hook. Fl. Ind. i. 264; Thwaites Enum. 49; Beddome t. 86. *G. pictoria,* Roxb. Fl. Ind. ii. 627; Beddome t. 87. *G. Gutta,* Wight. The Gamboge Tree. Vern. *Aradal, punar puli,* Kan.; *Gokatú, kana-goraka,* Cingh. (The gum resin, *Gota gamba,* Hind.; *Makki,* Tam.; *Revachinni,* Mar.; *Sanatosi,* Burm.; *Gokatu,* Cingh.)

An evergreen tree. Wood yellow, hard, mottled. Pores large, subdivided. Medullary rays moderately broad. Numerous, wavy, concentric bands of soft texture across the rays which are narrower than in *G. Cowa.*

Forests of the Khasia Hills, Eastern Bengal, Western Coast, and Ceylon.

The tree which produces the true gamboge. The gum is, however, not collected in the forests of South India, and the chief trade supply is obtained from Siam. In Ceylon it is usually collected by cutting a thin slice off the bark of the tree here and there of the size of the palm of the hand. On the flat space thus exposed the gum collects and is scraped off when sufficiently dried.

	lbs.
No. 14, Ceylon collection (marked *Cambogia Gutta,* Vern. *Cocatiye*) .	56

2. CALOPHYLLUM, Linn.

A large genus of chiefly tropical trees, of which many species occur in the Malay Peninsula and Ceylon. Six species occur in India, of which four in Burma and the Andamans, three in Southern India and one in Northern and Eastern Bengal. Five species are herein described, and the remaining species is *C. retusum,* Wall.; Hook. Fl. Ind. i. 272 (*C. amœnum,* Wall.; Kurz i. 95), an evergreen tree of Tenasserim. The genus is remarkable for its handsome flowers and beautiful parallel-veined, opposite, coriaceous leaves.

Wood soft and moderately hard, reddish, with a darker coloured heartwood, seasons well, weight moderate. Pores moderate-sized or large, prominent on a vertical section, often arranged in wavy strings or groups. Medullary rays fine or very fine, indistinct on a cross section but prominent as straight narrow lines on a radial section. Interrupted concentric lines of soft tissue.

1. C. spectabile, Willd.; Hook. Fl. Ind. i. 271; Kurz i. 94; *C. Moonii,* Wight, Beddome xxii.; *C. amœnum,* Wall. in Exhibition Catalogue; *C. tetrapetalum,* Roxb. Fl. Ind. ii. 608. Vern. *Panta-ka, kyandoo,* Burm.; *Dakar táladá,* And.; *Lal chuni,* Hind. (from Andamans).

A tall evergreen tree. Wood light red, shining, cross-grained, moderately hard. Pores large, in scattered groups, and wavy lines prominent on a longitudinal section. Medullary rays fine, very numerous, prominent on a radial section as long, straight, dark-coloured narrow plates. Concentric lines of soft tissue divide the wood into what at first sight appear to be annual rings, but on closer examination are found to be interrupted, and cannot be held to be the lines which mark the annual increment; these lines are visible on a vertical section.

Tenasserim and Andaman Islands.

Weight, 38-39 lbs. per cubic foot. No. 13, from the Andaman Islands, of Brandis' experiments of 1866 is probably this: Weight, 39·5 lbs. P = 530—mean of 8 experiments with bars 2′ × 1″ × 1.″

The wood is used for masts and spars; also for planking, for which purpose it has lately been used in building barracks in the Andamans.

		lbs.
B 525.	Andaman Islands	39
B 1992.	„ „ (Kurz, 1866)	38
B 3197.	„ „ (Home, 1874, No. 14, *Teeni*)	39

2. C. inophyllum, Linn.; Hook. Fl. Ind. i. 273; Beddome xxii.; Kurz i. 95; Roxb. Fl. Ind. ii. 606. The Alexandrian Laurel. Vern. *Sultana champa,* Hind., Beng.; *Pinnay,* Tamil; *Púna, púnás,* Tel.; *Wúma,* Kan.; *Undi,* Mar.; *Domba,* Cingh.; *Pongnyet,* Burm.; *Bintangor,* Malay.

An evergreen tree. Bark grey or blackish-brown, smooth. Wood reddish-brown, moderately hard, close-grained. Pores small and moderate-sized, arranged in groups. Medullary rays extremely fine and numerous. Numerous, not very prominent, interrupted concentric lines of soft tissue.

South India, Burma and Andaman Islands, often cultivated for ornament in other parts of India.

Weight: 63 lbs. per cubic foot according to Kurz; the specimens received averaged 42 lbs. omitting the last which was rather decayed. "Used for masts, spars, railway sleepers, machinery, &c."—*Kurz.*

		lbs.
W 733.	South Kanara	38
B 2257.	Andaman Islands (1866)	45
B 2258.	„ „ „	44
B 2263.	„ „ „	26

3. C. polyanthum, Wall.; Hook. Fl. Ind. i. 274; Kurz i. 95; Gamble 7. Vern. *Kandeb,* Beng.; *Kironli,* Nep.; *Sunglyer,* Lepcha.

An evergreen tree. Structure the same as that of *C. spectabile.*

Northern and Eastern Bengal, Khasia Hills, Chittagong and Burma, ascending to 5,000 feet.

Weight, 40 lbs. per cubic foot. Mr. Chester says it is used largely in Chittagong for masts, spars and rafters, and sometimes for small boat building and canoes.

		lbs.
E 1400.	Chittagong	44
E 2490.	Chenga Forest, Darjeeling Terai	38
E 2953.	Chunbati, Darjeeling, 3,000 feet	39

These last two have the same structure as *C. polyanthum*, but the wood has a dark red colour.

4. C. tomentosum, Wight; Hook. Fl. Ind. i. 274; Beddome xxii. *C. elatum,* Beddome t. 2. The Poon Spar Tree. Vern. *Poon, poone,* Mal.; *Pongoo,* Tamil; *Siri poone,* Kan.

A large, tall, evergreen tree. Bark with numerous longitudinal cracks. Structure the same as that of *C. spectabile.*

Evergreen forests of the Western Coast from Kanara southwards.

Weight: Couch's experiments at Plymouth Dockyard gave 36 to 43 lbs. per cubic foot; our specimens give 35 lbs. per cubic foot. Yields the Poon spars of commerce, good spars often fetching large prices. It is also used for building and bridge work. The seeds give an oil.

		lbs.
W 762.	South Kanara	32
D 1279.	Anamalai Hills	38

5. C. Wightianum, Wall.; Hook. Fl. Ind. i. 274; Beddome t. 90. *C. decipiens,* Wight Ic. 106. Vern. *Kalpoon, kull-ponné,* Kan.; *Cheru pinnay,* Tam.

An evergreen tree. Wood hard, red. Pores large and moderate-sized, uniformly distributed. Medullary rays very fine, not very distinct. Numerous interrupted, wavy and anastomozing concentric bands of soft tissue.

Western Ghâts from the Konkan to Travancore.

Weight, 45 lbs. per cubic foot. It is probably No. 36 of Skinner's List (*C. spurium*) W = 39 lbs.; P = 567. Beddome says the timber is much esteemed and valuable for engineering purposes.

		lbs.
W 861.	South Kanara	45

3. KAYEA, Wall.

Two Indian and one Ceylon species. *K. floribunda,* Wall.; Hook. Fl. Ind. i. 276; Kurz i. 96. Vern. *Karram-jowa,* Sylhet, is a tree of the tropical forests of the Eastern Himalaya and of the hills of Martaban, ascending to 3,000 feet. *K. nervosa,* T. And.; Hook. Fl. Ind. i. 277; Kurz i. 97 is an evergreen tree of Tenasserim.

1. K. stylosa, Thwaites Enum. 50; Hook. Fl. Ind. i. 276; Beddome t. 102. Vern. *Súvanda,* Cingh.

A large tree. Bark dark grey. Wood soft, reddish. Pores moderate-sized, numerous. Medullary rays very fine, indistinct, with concentric bands of soft texture across the rays.

A. Mendis gives the weight at 56 lbs. and P = 814.

	lbs.
Ceylon, south of the island. No. 82, Ceylon collection	56

4. MESUA, Linn.

Beddome gives six species of this genus, but all these are included in the Flora Indica by Dr. T. Anderson under one, *Mesua ferrea.* In the "Genera Plantarum" there are said to be three species. These include *M. Thwaitesii,* Pl. and Trian., of Ceylon, and a species from Malacca.

1. M. ferrea, Linn.; Hook. Fl. Ind. i. 277; Roxb. Fl. Ind. ii. 605; Kurz i. 97; Beddome xxiii (with also *M. speciosa,* Choisy; *M. Roxburghii,* Wight; *M. sclerophylla,* Thw.; *M. pulchella,* Pl. and Trian.; and *M. coromandeliana,* Wight; Beddome t. 64); Thwaites Enum. 50. Vern. *Nagesar,* Beng.; *Nahor,* Ass.; *Nageshvoro,* Uriya; *Nangal, mallay nangal,* Tam.; *Naga-kesara,* Tel.; *Nang,* Tinnevelly; *Naga sampigi,* Kan.; *Nag-champa,* Mar.; *Behelta-champagam,* Mal.; *Ná, deya-ná,* Cingh.; *Kaing-go,* Magh; *Gangau,* Burm.

A large evergreen tree. Heartwood dark red, extremely hard. Pores moderate-sized, often in groups, scanty, often filled with yellow resin. Medullary rays extremely fine, uniform, equidistant, very numerous. Numerous fine, wavy, concentric lines of light-coloured tissue.

Eastern Bengal from the Monas eastward (though traces of its having formerly been found west of that river occur sometimes in the names of places, *e. g.,* Nageshwarbari, or Naksarbari, a town in the Sikkim Terai on the Nepal frontier), Assam, South India, Ceylon, Burma and the Andamans, often cultivated.

The weight and transverse strength have been determined by the following experiments:—

		Weight.	Value of P.
A. Mendis	Ceylon No. 59, with bars 2′ × 1″ × 1″ found	72 lbs.	994
Brandis	Burma No. 18, 1862 . . . . „	69 „	...
Bennett	Andamans No. 4, 1872 . . . . „	70 „	1053
Smythies	Assam (4 specimens), 1878 . . „	67·5 „	...
	Kanara (1 „), „ . . . . „	62 „	...
	Burma (6 „), „ . . . . „	70 „	...

Several of our specimens, however, reached 74 to 76 lbs. per cubic foot in weight. It is very durable. It has been found to answer for sleepers equally well with *Pynkado,* but the cost of cutting the hard wood, its weight, and the freight from the Tenasserim forests to Calcutta prevent its being much used, as the total cost is scarcely covered by the price (Rs. 5) per broad-gauge sleeper. It is used for building, for bridges, gunstocks and tool handles; but its more general use is prevented by its great hardness, weight and the difficulty of working it. In Ceylon an oil is obtained from the nut, and the tree is often planted for the sake of its handsome flowers.

			lbs.
E	2309.	E. Dúars, Assam	64
E	793.	Kámrúp „	61
E	2190.	Nowgong „	75
E	1273.	Cachar	70
W	741.	South Kanara	62
B	2504.	Burma (1862)	69
B	554.	Martaban	75
B	2700.	Tavoy (Wallich, 1828)	60
B	2238.	Andamans (Major Ford, 1866)	76
B	2491.	„ (Home, 1874, No. 10)	67
B	520.	„	74
No.	59.	Ceylon Collection (*Mesua Nagaha*)	72

ORDER XV. TERNSTROMIACEÆ.

Twelve genera belonging to three tribes, *viz.*:—

Tribe	I.—Ternströmieæ	*Anneslea, Ternströmia, Adinandra, Cleyera* and *Eurya.*
„	II.—Sauraujeæ	*Actinidia, Saurauja* and *Stachyurus.*
„	III.—Gordonieæ	*Pyrenaria, Schima, Gordonia* and *Camellia.*

Anneslea contains two small trees of Burma: *A. fragrans*, Wall.; Hook. Fl. Ind. i. 280; Kurz i. 98, of the Eng forests, and *A. monticola*, Kurz i. 98, of the hill forests of Martaban at 5,000 to 7,000 feet. *Ternströmia*, two trees of South India and Burma: *T. japonica*, Thunb.; Hook. Fl. Ind. i. 280; Kurz i. 99 (*T. gymnanthera*, Beddome t. 91). Vern. *Kaymone*, Nilgiris, an evergreen tree of the Western Ghâts and the Martaban Hills, said by Beddome to have a pinkish wood, used for house-building; and *T. penangiana*, Choisy; Hook. Fl. Ind. i. 281; Kurz i. 99, an evergreen tree of the Andamans and Tenasserim. *Adinandra villosa*, Choisy; Hook. Fl. Ind. i. 283; Kurz i. 100, is an evergreen tree of Pegu. *Cleyera ochnacea*, DC., and *C. grandiflora*, Hook. f. and Th.; Hook. Fl. Ind. 283, 284, are small trees of the North-Eastern Himalaya and Khasia Hills. *Actinidia* contains two climbing shrubs: *A. callosa*, Ldl. (No. E. 2858, Tukdah Forest, Darjeeling, 5,000 feet, with corky bark and brown, very porous wood) at about 5,000 feet, from Garhwal to Bhutan and the Khasia Hills, and *A. strigosa*, Hook. f. and Th., of the Sikkim Himalaya, at 6,000 to 8,000 feet: both, Hook. Fl. Ind. i. 286; Gamble 8. Vern. *Tikphal*, Nep.; *Taksing*, Lepcha. Fruit edible, of good flavour. *Stachyurus himalaicus*, Hook. f. and Th.; Hook. Fl. Ind. i. 288, is a small glabrous tree of the Eastern Himalaya from 5,000 to 8,000 feet.

In *Pyrenaria* are four evergreen trees: three of which, *P. attenuata*, Seem.; Hook. Fl. Ind. i. 290 (*P. serrata*, Bl.; Kurz i. 105) of Tavoy; *P. diospyricarpa*, Kurz i. 104, and *P. camelliæflora*, Kurz i. 105, of the Martaban Hills, are Burmese: and one, *P. barringtoniæfolia*, Seem.; Hook. Fl. Ind. i. 290, of the Gâro Hills in Assam. *Gordonia obtusa*, Wall.; Hook. Fl. Ind. i. 291; Beddome t. 83. Vern. *Nagetta*, Nilgiris, is a tall grey-barked tree of the Western Ghâts, said by Beddome to have a yellowish-white, even-grained wood, used for house-building, but liable to warp. *G. excelsa*, Bl.; Hook. Fl. Ind. i. 291, is a tree of the Bhutan Himalaya.

Pores small, uniformly distributed between the fine or very fine medullary rays. The species of *Eurya* have a few broader rays alternating with the fine rays.

1. EURYA, Thunb.

A genus of evergreen shrubs or small trees, of the Eastern Himalaya, Assam, Southern India, and Burma. *E. japonica*, Thunb.; Hook. Fl. Ind. i. 284; Beddome t. 92; Brandis 24; Kurz i. 101; Gamble 7. Vern. *Baunra, gonta, deura*, Hind.; *Jhingni*, Nep.; *Tungchong*, Lepcha; *Hoolooni*, Nilgiris; *Toungletpet*, Burm., is found in the Himalaya from the Jumna eastwards, above 3,000 feet in altitude, in the Western Ghâts and in Burma. It grows quickly and often gregariously in the Sikkim hills, and coppices well. *E. trichocarpa*, Korth. is a small tree of Bhutan and the Khasia Hills.

1. E. symplocina, Bl.; Hook. Fl. Ind. i. 284; Kurz i. 102; Gamble 7. Vern. *Bara jhingni, kisi*, Nep.; *Flotungchong*, Lepcha.

A small evergreen tree. Bark brown, thin. Wood reddish-white, soft, close-grained. Annual rings marked by more numerous pores in the spring wood. Pores very small. Medullary rays very fine and moderately broad, the latter short, prominent.

Hills of the North-Eastern Himalaya, from 5,000 to 7,000 feet, Burma.
Weight, 38 lbs. per cubic foot. Used only for firewood.

		lbs.
E 385.	Rangbúl, Darjeeling, 7,000 feet	35
E 2319.		42

2. E. acuminata, DC.; Hook. Fl. Ind. i. 285; Kurz i. 101; Gamble 7. Vern. *Sanu jhingni*, Nep.; *Flotungchong*, Lepcha.

A small evergreen tree. Bark brown, thin, smooth. Wood differs from that of *E. symplocina* in having the larger medullary rays less broad and less prominent.

Hills of the North-Eastern Himalaya, Assam and Martaban, from 5,000 to 8,000 feet.

Weight, according to Kyd 32 lbs.; our specimen, however, weighed 47 lbs. Kyd's experiments on a bar 2′ × 1″ × 1″ gave P = 337, for wood from Goalpara.

E 2320. Rangbúl, Darjeeling, 7,500 ft. . . . . lbs. 47

2. SAURAUJA, Willd.

A genus of trees or shrubs with handsome, parallel-veined, generally scaly and rusty-tomentose leaves, and pink or white flowers. Of the eight Indian species five are found in Burma, and six in the Eastern Himalaya. Besides the species here described, *S. Griffithii*, Dyer; Hook. Fl. Ind. i. 286; Gamble 8. Vern. *Gogen*, Nep.; *Hlosipha*, Lepcha, is an extremely handsome small tree with large leaves bright green above and densely yellow tomentose beneath, found in Sikkim and Assam. *S. fasciculata*, Wall.; Hook. Fl. Ind. i. 287; Gamble 8. Vern. *Gokul, Sare gogen*, Nep.; *Sipha*, Lepcha, from Sikkim; and *S. punduana*, Wall.; Hook. Fl. Ind. i. 287; Kurz i. 103; Gamble 8. Vern. *Rata gogen*, Nep; *Sipha*, Lepcha, from Sikkim, Assam and Burma, are small trees or shrubs; *S. Roxburghii*, Wall.; Hook. Fl. Ind. i. 287; Kurz i. 103; Gamble 287 (*Ternströmia serrata*, Roxb. Fl. Ind. ii. 521). Vern. *Dalúp*, Sylhet; *Ouli gogen*, Nep.; *Dangsipha*, Lepcha, is a small tree of the valleys of Sikkim, the Khasia Hills, and Burma; and *S. tristyla*, DC.; Hook. Fl. Ind. i. 287; Kurz i. 104; (*Ternströmia bilocularis*, Roxb. Fl. Ind. ii. 522) occurs in Tenasserim.

1. S. napaulensis, DC.; Hook. Fl. Ind. i. 286; Brandis 25; Gamble 8. Vern. *Gogina, goganda*, Hind.; *Gogen*, Nep.; *Kasúr*, Lepcha.

A small tree. Bark reddish-brown, thin. Wood light pink, very soft, spongy; shrinks much. Pores small. Medullary rays fine and moderately broad, prominent on a radial section.

Outer Himalaya from the Jumna to Bhutan above 3,000 feet, Khasia Hills. Weight, 25 lbs. per cubic foot. Leaves lopped for cattle fodder.

E 2321. Tukdah, Darjeeling, 5,000 feet. . . . . lbs. 25

3. SCHIMA, Reinw.

Six species. *S. crenata*, Korth.; Hook. Fl. Ind. i. 289; Kurz i. 107. (*Gordonia oblata*, Roxb. Fl. Ind. ii. 572. *G. floribunda*, Wall.) is an evergreen tree of Burma. *S. khasiana*, Dyer; Hook. Fl. Ind. i. 289, is a white-barked tree of the Khasia Hills. *S. monticola*, Kurz i. 107, is a tree of the summits of the Nattoung Range in Martaban, at 6,000 to 7,200 feet; and *S. bancana*, Miq.; Kurz i. 108, is a tree of the Eng forests of Martaban and Tenasserim.

1. S. Wallichii, Choisy; Hook. Fl. Ind. i. 289; Gamble 8. *Gordonia integrifolia*, Roxb. Fl. Ind. ii. 572. Vern. *Chilauni, goechassi*, Nep.; *Makusal*, Hind.; *Sumbrong*, Lepcha; *Gugera*, Goalpara; *Makriah chilauni, makusal*, Ass.; *Dingan*, Khasia; *Boldak*, Gáro; *Jam*, Cachar.

A large evergreen tree. Bark black or dark grey with deep vertical cracks. Wood rough, red, moderately hard, shrinks much in seasoning, but is durable. Pores moderate-sized and small, round, extremely numerous and uniformly distributed. Medullary rays very fine, uniform, equidistant, very numerous: on a radial section visible as narrow, darker coloured plates.

Northern and Eastern Bengal, and Chittagong, ascending to 5,000 ft.

Growth moderately fast, our specimens shew 4 to 8 rings per inch of radius.

The following experiments have been made to determine the weight and transverse strength:—

		Weight.	P =
Kyd with Goalpara wood in 1831, No. 48,	bar 2′ × 1″ × 1″ .	found 43 lbs.	383
Brandis with Sikkim „ in 1864,	bar 6′ × 2″ × 2″ .	„ 45 „	760
Smythies with our four specimens in 1878	. . . . .	„ 45 „	...

The wood is durable; E 1449, brought by Griffith from the Mishmi Hills in 1836, was perfectly sound when cut up in 1878. It is used in Northern Bengal and Assam for many purposes, but chiefly for building. Many of the tea factories in Darjeeling have been built of it, and the Public Works Department have sometimes used it for bridges. Mann states that in Assam it is used for planks and ordinary building purposes and for canoes. In 1875 several sleepers were made over to the Northern Bengal State Railway for experiment, but the result is not yet known. As large quantities of the timber, well grown and straight, are available, it is to be hoped that it may be ere long in more extensive demand.

It seeds profusely every year during the winter; the fruit is a hard capsule which splits open to let fall the flat, slightly winged seeds. In thick forests, however, seedlings are rarely found, but wherever light is admitted and the soil has been slightly stirred, they come up in profusion.

		lbs.
E 491.	Bamunpokri Forest, Darjeeling	43
E 646.	Khooklong Forest, Darjeeling Terai	44
E 636.	Eastern Dúars, Assam	42
E 1449.	Mishmi Hills (Griffith, 1836)	50

2. S. Noronhæ, Rwdt.; Kurz i. 107. Vern. *Panma, thitya*, Burm.

An evergreen tree. Bark brown, irregularly cracked. Wood reddish-brown, moderately hard, close-grained. Pores small, in short radial lines between the very fine and closely-packed medullary rays. There is some doubt about the identification of this number.

Tenasserim and Martaban Hills. Weight 45 lbs. per cubic foot.

		lbs.
B 299.	Burma (1867)	45

4. CAMELLIA, Linn.

Four species. *C. caudata*, Wall.; Hook. Fl. Ind. i. 293; Kurz i. 108, is an evergreen shrub of the forests of the Martaban Hills at 3,000 to 4,000 feet. *C. lutescens*, Dyer; Hook. Fl. Ind. i. 293, is a shrub of the Mishmi Hills.

1. C. drupifera, Lour.; Hook. Fl. Ind. i. 293; Kurz i. 109; Gamble 9. *C. Kissi*, Wall. Vern. *Kissi, hingua*, Nep.; *Chashing*, Bhutia, Lepcha.

A large evergreen shrub. Bark thin, greyish-white. Wood grey, soft, even-grained. Pores very small, uniformly distributed between the very fine, very numerous medullary rays.

Eastern Himalaya, Assam and Khasia Hills, ascending to 8,000 feet, Tenasserim, and Andaman Islands.

E 3111. Kalimpúng, Darjeeling, 4,500 feet.

2. C. Thea, Link.; Brandis 25; Kurz i. 109; Gamble 9, the China Tea Plant. *C. theifera*, Griff.; Hook. Fl. Ind. i. 292, the Assam Tea Plant. Vern. *Cha.*

A shrub with thin grey bark. Wood grey, soft. Pores numerous, very small, uniformly distributed between the numerous fine medullary rays.

Cultivated in many districts in India, especially in Kangra, Kulu, Dehra Dún, Kumaun, Darjeeling, the Western Dúars, Assam, Cachar, Chittagong and Hazáribágh in Northern India, as well as in the Nilgiri Hills and Ceylon.

Weight, 56 lbs. per cubic foot.

		lbs.
O 3142.	Dehra Dún	56

ORDER XVI. DIPTEROCARPEÆ.

An order of great forest importance, containing large resinous trees and a few climbing shrubs, belonging to seven genera, *viz.*, *Dipterocarpus*, *Ancistrocladus*, *Anisoptera*, *Vatica*, *Shorea*, *Hopea* and *Vateria*. *Doona* and *Monoporandra* are found in Ceylon.

Of *Ancistrocladus*, a genus of climbing shrubs, two species are found in India: *A. Wallichii*, Planch; Hook. Fl. Ind. i. 300; Kurz i. 111, in Chittagong, Burma and the Andamans; and *A. Griffithii*, Planch; Hook. Fl. Ind. i. 300; Kurz i. 110. Vern. *Panben-nway*, Burm., in swamp forests in Pegu, Martaban and Tenasserim. *Anisoptera glabra*, Kurz i. 112. Vern. *Thingado*, Burm., is a large evergreen Burmese tree.

The camphor of commerce is obtained from *Dryobalanops Camphora*, a tree of Sumatra. The camphor is often found in the stem in a solid state, but is also procured liquid by incision.

The Dipterocarpeæ here described have a uniform structure. The pores are round, often in groups, small to large, but generally moderate-sized, enclosed in a narrow white ring. The medullary rays are fine and moderately broad, generally equidistant. The heartwood is generally distinct, dark coloured, heavy (from 40 to 70 lbs.) and resinous, exuding wood oils or dammer, which are found, not in separate resinous ducts, but in the pores (vessels) of the wood. The wood of most species is hard, strong and durable, that of several species of *Dipterocarpus* is softer and perishable.

1. DIPTEROCARPUS, Gaertn. f.

Twelve species, all lofty trees, of Eastern Bengal, South India and Burma. These species are:—

1. *D. turbinatus*, Gaertn. f.	Eastern Bengal, Burma and Andamans.
2. *D. lævis*, Ham.	Burma.
3. *D. vestitus*, Wall.; Hook. Fl. Ind. i. 295.	Tavoy.
4. *D. obtusifolius*, Teysm.	Hills of Prome and Martaban.
5. *D. pilosus*, Roxb. Fl. Ind. ii. 615; Hook. Fl. Ind. i. 296; Kurz i. 115. Vern. *Hollong*, Ass.	Arracan, hills of Martaban and Tenasserim.
"Rarely used for canoes, does for planks."—*Mann.*	
6. (*D. Hasseltii*, Bl.; Kurz i. 114)	Tenasserim and Andamans.
7. *D. tuberculatus*, Roxb.	Chittagong and Burma.
8. *D. scaber*, Ham.; Hook. Fl. Ind. i. 297.	Eastern Bengal.
9. *D. alatus*, Roxb.	Chittagong, Burma and Andamans.
10. *D. incanus*, Roxb. Fl. Ind. ii. 614; Hook Fl. Ind. i. 298.	Chittagong.
11. *D. Griffithii*, Miq.; Hook. Fl. Ind. i. 299; Kurz i. 116.	Tenasserim and Andamans.
12. (*D. costatus*, Gaertn.; Kurz i. 117. Under *D. alatus* in Hook. Fl. Ind. i. 298.)	Hills of Chittagong, Martaban and Tenasserim.

This list is chiefly taken from Dyer's description in the "Flora Indica," and Kurz' "Burma Flora," but there is considerable difference in the synomymy given in Kurz, the "Flora Indica" and Alphonse de Candolle's Monograph in the "Prodromus," Vol. xvi. Kurz' species are given in brackets.

The species of *Dipterocarpus* have a reddish, soft or moderately hard heartwood, generally rough. Pores visible on a vertical section, moderate-sized to large. Medullary rays often of two sizes, fine and moderately broad.

1. **D. turbinatus**, Gaertn. f.; Hook. Fl. Ind. i. 295; Roxb. Fl. Ind. ii. 612; Kurz i. 114. The Gurjun-Oil Tree. Vern. *Gurjun*, *tiliyagurjun*, Beng.; *Kanyoung*, Magh; *Kanyin-nee*, *kanyin-wettoung*, Burm.

A lofty evergreen tree. Wood rough, moderately hard; heartwood reddish grey. Pores round, large and moderate-sized, joined by short concentric bands of soft tissue. Medullary rays prominent, broad and very fine, a large number of the latter intervening between a pair of the former; very prominent and shining on a radial section.

Eastern Bengal, Chittagong, Burma and the Andaman Islands.

Skinner, No. 64, gives the weight at 45 lbs. and P = 762; Kurz gives 55 lbs. for the weight, while our specimens average 50 lbs. per cubic foot. The wood is used for house-building and for canoes in Burma; and the wood-oil is used in painting houses and ships.

		lbs.
E 709.	Chittagong	49
B 293.	Burma (1867)	43
B 2216.	Andaman Islands (Major Ford, 1866)	52
B 2555.	Burma (1862)	56

2. D. lævis, Ham.; Kurz i. 114. *D. turbinatus,* Hook. Fl. Ind. i. 295 (in part). Vern. *Kanyin, kanyin-nee,* Burm.

A lofty tree. Sapwood white; heartwood rough, reddish, soft. Pores moderate-sized, numerous. Medullary rays red, fine, moderately broad and broad, visible on a radial section as long bands, the distance between two broader rays equal to two to four times the transverse diameter of the pores.

Tropical forests throughout Burma.

Weight: our specimens give an average of 46 lbs. per cubic foot. The wood is rarely used, but is occasionally employed for planking and rafters. It yields copiously a resin and a wood-oil used for painting.

		lbs.
B 292.	Burma (1867)	43
B 2506.	„ (1862)	49

D. indicus, Beddome t. 94. Vern. *Guga,* Kan., of the Western Ghâts, is referred to this or to *D. turbinatus* by Dyer.

3. D. obtusifolius, Teysm.; Hook. Fl. Ind. i. 295; Kurz i. 115. Vern. *Kanyin-kok,* Burm.

A large deciduous tree. Bark ½ inch thick, ash-grey, longitudinally cracked, rough. Heartwood reddish brown, rough, moderately hard. Pores large and moderate-sized. Medullary rays fine and very fine, numerous.

Eng forests of Prome and Martaban, ascending to 3,000 feet.

Weight, 59 lbs. per cubic foot.

		lbs.
B 3128.	Kya-eng, Attaran Valley, Burma	59

4. D. tuberculatus, Roxb. Fl. Ind. ii. 614; Hook. Fl. Ind. ii. 297; Kurz i. 113. *D. grandiflorus,* Wall. The Eng Tree. Vern. *Eng,* Burm.; *Sooahn,* Taleing.

A large deciduous gregarious tree, with dark grey bark, forming the "Eng forests" of Burma. Wood red, hard. Pores circular, large and moderate-sized, often filled with resin. Medullary rays prominent, moderately broad, with a number of fine rays between each pair of broad ones; distance between broader rays as much as twice transverse diameter of pores.

Chittagong and Burma.

Weight: Brandis in Burma List of 1862, No. 12, gives 55 lbs.; Skinner, No 63, gives 45 and Benson 46 lbs.; while the average of our specimens gives 54 lbs. Benson gives P = 758; Skinner 750. The timber is very largely used in Burma for building, canoes, and house posts. It gives no wood-oil, but a clear yellow resin.

			lbs.
B 2505.	Burma (1862)	. . . .	50
B 306.	„ (1867)	. . . .	52
B 2480.	„	. . . .	59

5. D. alatus, Roxb. Fl. Ind. ii. 614; Hook. Fl. Ind. i. 298; Kurz i. 116. Vern. *Gurjun*, Beng.; *Kanyin*, *kanyin-pyoo*, Burm.

A very large tree with grey bark. Sapwood white; heartwood reddish grey, moderately hard, smooth, mottled. Pores scanty, large, often oval and subdivided. Medullary rays undulating, short, fine and moderately broad, not prominent. Pores prominent on a longitudinal section.

Chittagong, Burma and the Andaman Islands.

Weight: Brandis in Burma List, 1862, No. 11, gives 38 lbs.; our specimen gives 50 lbs.; Bennett, No. 9, Andaman woods, (Kanyin), gives Weight 49 lbs., P = 727. The wood is used for house-building and canoes, but is not durable.

			lbs.
B 818.	Burma	. . . .	50
B 2243.	Andamans (1866) (rather eaten)	. . . .	38

6. D. zeylanicus, Thwaites Enum. 33; Hook. Fl. Ind. i. 297; Beddome xxv. Vern. *Horá*, Cingh.

Heartwood red, moderately hard. Pores moderate-sized to very large. Medullary rays fine and moderately broad, frequently bending.

Ceylon, up to 3,000 feet.

Weight, 45 lbs. per cubic foot. Wood used for building. It gives a wood-oil and gum resin.

			lbs.
No. 37.	Ceylon collection	. . . .	45

E 720 is a wood sent from Chittagong under the name *Michamma*. In structure it resembles *Dipterocarpus*, and differs chiefly by the very numerous, very fine, equidistant medullary rays. The pores are joined by white, wavy concentric lines. The wood is interrupted by concentric belts of fibrous substance resembling liber, about ½ inch thick.

E 1257. (43 lbs.) from Tezpur, Assam, has the structure of *Dipterocarpus*.

E 1960. (37 lbs.) Vern. *Lowa*, Beng.; *Chakyai*, Magh, from Chittagong, is probably a species of *Dipterocarpus*: it is distinguished by numerous broad and fine medullary rays, and moderate-sized, often subdivided pores.

2. VATICA, Linn.

Six species. *V. grandiflora*, Dyer; Hook. Fl. Ind. i. 301 (*Anisoptera odorata*, Kurz i. 112. *Hopea grandiflora*, Wall.) is a deciduous tree of Martaban and Tenasserim, where also are found *V. faginea*, Dyer; Hook. Fl. Ind. i. 301, and *V. Helferi*, Dyer; Hook. Fl. Ind. i. 301 (*Shorea Helferi*, Kurz i. 119). *V. scaphula*, Dyer; Hook. Fl. Ind. i. 301 (*Hopea scaphula*, Roxb. Fl. Ind. ii. 611; Kurz i. 121). Vern. *Boilshura*, Beng., is a tree of Chittagong, especially on Mascal island, whose trunk is used for making canoes. *V. Roxburghiana*, Bl.; Hook. Fl. Ind. i. 302; Beddome t. 95. Vern. *Mendora*, Cingh., is a large tree of the Western Coast and Ceylon, yielding a gum resin.

1. V. lanceæfolia, Bl.; Hook. Fl. Ind. i. 302; Kurz i. 122; Roxb. Fl. Ind. ii. 601. Vern. *Morhal*, Ass.; *Moal*, Sylhet; *Panthitya*, Burm.

A large tree. Heartwood red, rough, hard. Pores small, numerous, uniformly distributed. Medullary rays fine, not distinct.

Eastern Himalaya, Assam, Eastern Bengal, Chittagong and Burma.

If this is Skinner's No. 131 (*Vateria lanceæfolia*, Vern. *Let-touk*, Burm.) the weight is 58 lbs. and P = 931; Wallich gives 54 lbs.; our specimens 35 to 52 lbs. per cubic foot.

The wood is not very good. The tree gives a resin called *ghund*, used in temples.

		lbs.
B 2508.	Burma (1862)	35
B 2282.	Andamans (1866)	52

We identify this last by the structure, though the tree is not given from the Andamans.

3. SHOREA, Roxb.

Nine species. *S. floribunda*, Kurz. i. 119; Hook. Fl. Ind. i. 304, is a deciduous tree of Tavoy. *S. assamica*, Dyer; Hook. Fl. Ind. i. 307, is a tree of Upper Assam discovered by G. Mann on the banks of the Dehing river. *S. gratissima*, Dyer; Hook. Fl. Ind. i. 307 (*Hopea gratissima*, Wall.; Kurz i. 121), is found in Tenasserim.

Wood generally cross-grained. Heartwood brown, hard or very hard. Pores moderate-sized to large, generally filled with resin, in patches of lighter coloured tissue. Medullary rays fine, broad, equidistant.

1. S. stellata, Dyer; Hook. Fl. Ind. i. 304. *Parashorea stellata*, Kurz i. 117. Vern. *Koungmhoo*, Burm.

A very large evergreen tree. Bark ½ inch thick, dark brown, longitudinally fissured. Wood white, hard, rough. Pores round, moderate-sized to large, uniformly distributed, often filled with a white substance; each pore enclosed in a narrow white ring. Medullary rays moderately broad; the distance between two rays generally equal to the transverse diameter of the pores.

Burma.

Weight, 47 to 50 lbs. The wood is a used for canoes and in boat-building.

		lbs.
B 1944.	Tavoy, Burma	47
B 2481.	Tenasserim	50

2. S. Talura, Roxb. Fl. Ind. ii. 618; Hook. Fl. Ind. i. 304. *S. laccifera*, Heyne; Beddome t. 6. *Vatica laccifera*, W. and A. Vern. *Talura, talári*, Tam.; *Jalári*, Tel.; *Jalaranda*, Kan.

A large tree. Bark grey, with longitudinal fissures. Wood grey, very to extremely hard, smooth, with small dark-coloured irregularly-shaped heartwood. Pores small and moderate-sized, often in groups enclosed in patches of white tissue, which are frequently elongated and wavy, forming interrupted concentric bands. No distinct annual rings, but alternating belts, with numerous and with few pores. Medullary rays fine, very numerous, frequently white, bending.

Mysore and the eastern districts of Madras.

Weight: Puckle gives 43 lbs. per cubic foot; our specimens give 65 to 70 lbs. Puckle finds P = 896. The wood is much used for house-building, and is largely sent down to Madras for that purpose.

		lbs.
D 1056.	South Arcot	70
D 1092.	Madura	65

D 1092 has a smooth, yellow, even-grained wood, while D 1056 is grey with a dark brownish-red heartwood, but the structure of the two is identical.

3. S. robusta, Gaertn.; Roxb. Fl. Ind. ii. 615; Beddome t. 4; Brandis 26; Kurz i. 119; Gamble 9. The Sál Tree. Vern. *Sál, sála, salwa, sákhu, sakher*, Hind.; *Sakwa*, Nep.; *Teturl*, Lepcha; *Bolsal*, Gáro; *Salwa, soringhi*, Uriya; *Koroh*, Oudh; *Sarei, rinjal*, C. P.; *Gúgal*, Tel.

A large gregarious tree, never quite leafless. Bark of young trees smooth with a few long, deep, vertical cracks; of old trees 1 to 2 inches thick, dark coloured, rough, with deep longitudinal furrows. Sapwood small, whitish, not durable. Heartwood brown, finely streaked with dark lines, coarse-grained, hard, with a remarkably fibrous and cross-grained structure; the fibres of successive concentric strata in the wood do not run parallel but at oblique angles to each other, so that when the wood is dressed the fibres appear interlaced; does not season well. Annual rings visible. Pores moderate-sized to large, often filled with resin; each pore or group of pores in a patch of whitish tissue. Medullary rays uniform, moderately broad, straight, very prominent, joined by short white transverse lines, clearly visible on a radial section as numerous interrupted bands; the distance between the medullary rays equal to the transverse diameter of the pores.

North-east moist and intermediate zones: Sub-Himalayan tract, from the Bias to Assam, eastern part of Central India, from the Ganges to the Godaveri, extending westward to the longitude of Mandla, with an outlying patch on and around the sandstone hills of the Pachmarhi Range.

The wood of the sál tree has concentric rings, which we at present assume to correspond to one year's growth. There are a few cases on record in which the wood of young trees (up to 15 years) has been found to have a number of rings corresponding to the age of the tree. But sufficient proof to support the assumption has not yet been collected. Assuming, however, that the concentric rings are annual, the following information is available regarding the rate of growth of sál.

In 1873 Mr. Fisher examined 40 sál trees in the Pantan Reserve, Kámrúp district, Assam: 5 trees of 6 feet in girth had, on an average, 10 rings per inch of radius; 20 trees of 4 feet 6 inches girth had an average of 9·7 rings per inch; and 15 trees of 3 feet girth had 11 rings per inch. The rings were counted on lengths of radius, from the centre, of 2·86, 5·73, 8·6 and 11·5 inches respectively, corresponding to a girth of wood only of 18, 36, 54 and 72 inches.

In 1874 he examined 32 trees in the Balipara Reserve, Darrang district, Assam: 10 trees of 1 foot 6 inches girth gave an average of 38 rings, or 13 rings per inch of radius; 10 trees of 3 feet girth gave 61 rings, or 10·6 rings per inch of radius; 10 trees of 4 feet 6 inches girth gave 92 rings, or 10·7 rings per inch; 1 tree of 5 feet 7 inches girth gave 110 rings, or 10·3 rings per inch; and 1 tree of 6 feet girth gave 122 rings, or 10·6 rings per inch of radius.

In 1875 he examined 20 trees in the Sidli forests, Goálpára district, Assam: 3 trees of 4 feet 6 inches girth gave an average of 89 rings, or 10·3 rings per inch radius; and 17 trees of 3 feet girth gave 50 rings, or 8·8 rings per inch radius. The rings were counted in the same manner as in 1873.

In 1876 he examined 11 trees in the same forests: 4 trees of 4 feet 6 inches girth gave 76 rings, or 8·8 rings per inch of radius; 7 trees of 3 feet girth gave 51 rings, or 8·8 rings per inch.

In 1877 he examined 17 trees in the same forests: 1 tree 6 feet in girth gave 103 rings or 9 rings per inch of radius; 1 tree 4 feet 6 inches in girth gave 96 rings, or 11 rings per inch of radius; 13 trees of 3 feet in girth gave 51·5 rings, or 8·9 rings per inch of radius; and 2 trees of 1 foot 6 inches girth gave 26 rings or 9·1 rings per inch.

The rings were counted in the same manner in each case. The result of the detailed counting of the rings was as follows:—

Locality.	Number of trees.	Rings counted on a length of radius from centre, corresponding to a girth (wood only) of			
		18"	36"	54"	72"
Pantan (on the hill)	22	30	56	82	115
„ (in the plains)	18	32	65	96	126
Balipara	32	38	61	92	116
Sidli, 1875	20	28	52	89	...
„ 1876	11	26	51	76	...
„ 1877	17	26	61	72	90
	120	30	56	83	112

On an average the number of rings per inch of radius is 10, and it will be noticed that the annual increments are exceedingly uniform. A tree grows:—

up to 18 inches girth (wood only) in 30 years.				
from 18 to 36	"	"	"	in 26 "
" 36 to 54	"	"	"	in 27 "
" 54 to 72	"	"	"	in 29 "

In the Oudh forests a different result has been obtained. When the first proposals were made in 1863 to regulate the working of the forests of the Kheri division, the following was assumed as the mean rate of growth:—

Girth 18 inches, age 15 years.
" 54 " " 50 "
" 72 " " 80 "

Subsequent data seeming to indicate a somewhat slower rate, it was estimated in 1868, in order to settle the number of trees to be cut over in 1868 and 1869, that a girth of 54 inches would be attained in 65 years, and a girth of 72 inches in 95 years.

In September 1869, Mr. Forrest examined 50 logs cut in the Newal Khar subdivision of the Kheri forests; these logs had a mean girth of 5 feet 3 inches and gave on an average 4·79 rings per inch of radius. Again in 1877 a sál tree about 16 or 17 years old was examined by Captain Wood, and at 1 foot from the base, where the girth was 1 foot 10 inches, it was found that an inch of radius contained 4·80 rings. Thus, supposing we take 5 rings to the inch as indicating the average rate of growth, the trees examined in Oudh would have attained a girth of 6 feet in 57 years, which, it will be seen, is about one-half the time which the trees examined by Mr. Fisher in the Dúars required to attain the same size.

In the Central Provinces the counting of rings has given a mean between Bengal and Oudh. In 1867, Captain Douglas examined 13 stumps in the Bijeragogarh forests; their mean girth at 17 inches from the ground was 5 feet 3 inches, and the average number of rings per inch of radius was 6·5. In 1874 Mr. Fernandez examined a single stump in the same forests, and 7·2 rings were counted per inch of radius. The mean of the results of these countings is 6·85 rings per inch, which would place the age of a tree 6 feet in girth at 78 years. Subsequent observations in the Banjar Valley forest, Mandla district, give a mean of 5 to 8 rings per inch and tend to confirm this rate of growth.

The following cultivated trees of known age were measured by Mr. Brandis in 1863;

Saharanpur, and Eastern Jumna Canal	13 years,	girth 27	inches	(average of 33 trees).
" " "	30 "	" 54½	"	
" " "	35 "	" 79½	"	
Calcutta	25 "	" 69	"	(one tree).

The weight of a cubic foot of seasoned wood is generally found to vary between 50 and 60 lbs. The average of the experiments recorded below is 59 lbs., but while Baker's experiments (85) give an average of 61·6 lbs., Brandis' experiments (114) give only 53·6 lbs. as the average. The average of the 13 specimens weighed in 1878, omitting the last, is 59 lbs., but this includes unseasoned or only partially seasoned wood; the average weight of the Garhwal (O 204) and Mandla (C 173) specimens, which were thoroughly seasoned, is 51 lbs. Clifford gives 55 lbs. as the weight of sál when perfectly dry; 54 to 55 lbs. may therefore be considered as the average weight of seasoned sál.

The transverse strength has been tested by numerous experiments. The value of P as determined by Brandis, Baker and others, ranges from 648 to 939, the mean value being 790. The following abstract shews the results of all the best experiments on this timber.

Experiment by whom conducted.	Year.	Wood whence procured.	No. of experiments.	Size of bar.	Weight.	Value of P.
				Ft. Ins. Ins.		
Brandis	1864	Bengal (Morung) . .	28	6 × 2 × 2	57	806
"	"	" " . . .	8	6 2 1½	56	817
"	"	" " . . .	20	2 1 1	50	745
"	1865-66	" " . . .	11	3 1 1	56	916
"	"	" " . . .	14	3 1 ¾	49	802
"	"	" (Durbhunga). .	13	6 2 2	51	708
"	"	" " . . .	12	6 2 1½	54	791
"	"	" " . . .	8	3 1 1	56	884
Baker	1829	" (Morung) . .	31	7 2 2	59	778
"	"	" " . . .	54	6 2 2	64	792
"	"	" " . . .	24	3 1 1½	...	803
"	"	" " . . .	6	7 2 2	...	829
"	"	Bengal	9	7 2 2	61	717
"	"	"	3	3 1½ 1	...	858
"	"	"	18	2 1 1	...	823
"	"	Gorakhpur . . .	10	6 2 2	62	816
"	"	Pilibhit	6	7 2 2	62	692
Campbell	1831	Morung (seasoned) . .	4	6 2 2	55	870
"	"	" (unseasoned) .	4	6 2 2	66	862
"	"	Gorakhpur " . .	1	6 2 2	65	884
Skinner, No. 132 . . .	1862	Northern India . .	...	......	55	880
Kyd	1831	Morung	1	2 1 1	54	820
Cunningham	1854	Gwalior	3	2 1 1	65	1,007
Wallich	...	India and Nepal . .	3	......	47	...
Smythies	1878	Many localities (See list)	13	......	59	...

The following is a summary of Mr. Clifford's remarks about sál in his Memorandum on the Timber of Bengal:

The inherent qualities of sál render it a very difficult wood to season; it warps and splits in drying, and even when thoroughly seasoned, it absorbs moisture with avidity in wet weather, increasing 1-24th in bulk, and correspondingly in weight. During the process of seasoning it dries with great rapidity on the surface, while beneath it remains as wet as when first cut, and evaporation goes on afterwards with extreme slowness. The effect of this peculiarity is to cover the surface all over with superficial flaws from unequal shrinkage. With proper precautions, however, it can be made to dry slowly, and under these circumstances it has been found by numerous experiments that the ratio of drying is ¾ of an inch annually all round the piece of wood. Sál, when once thoroughly seasoned, stands almost without a rival, as a timber, for strength, elasticity and durability, which qualities it retains without being sensibly affected, for an immense length of time.

Numerous varieties of sál timber are supposed to exist. Mr. Clifford, in the pamphlet above quoted, says: "There are two descriptions of sál brought to Calcutta; they are known as 'Morung' and 'Durbhunga;' one from the forests to the east of the Coosi, the other from the forests to the west. The Morung sál is the best; it is very straight-grained, clean and free from knots; it seasons more kindly, and is stronger than the Durbhungah sál; only a practised eye can distinguish one sál from the other." Many of these supposed varieties, however, exist in imagination only, *e.g.*, the two Buxa pieces E 3137 and E 3138, the Nepalese sawyers say that one is a softer and redder wood than the other, but we can distinguish no such difference between them.

Sál is the timber which in Northern India is the most extensively used. It is in constant request for piles, beams, planking and railing of bridges; for beams, door and window-posts of houses; for gun-carriages; the body of carts (not the wheels, for which it is unsuited and for which sissú or even saj is better); and above all, for railway sleepers, the yearly consumption of which reaches some lakhs of cubic feet. It is used in the hills of Northern Bengal, where it is found, perhaps, of the largest size now available, for making canoes. Owing to its not being floatable, difficulty is experienced in most sál forests in getting the timber out of the forests in log. The difficulty is, however, partially overcome by floating the logs either with the assistance of boats or with floats of bamboos or light woods, such as semul (*Bombax malabaricum*).

When tapped, the tree exudes large quantities of a whitish, aromatic, transparent resin (*lál dhúna*), which is collected and sold. It is used to caulk boats and ships and as incense. "In some places in the Upper Tista forests, large pieces, often 30 to 40 cubic inches in size, are found in the ground at the foot of the trees."—*Gamble.* Large extents of forest, chiefly in Central India, such as Chota Nagpore, the Central Provinces and the country between the Mahanadi and Godavari, are often ruined by this practice of tapping the trees to obtain the resin. The seed is eaten by the Sonthals, especially in time of scarcity, it is roasted and is usually eaten mixed with the flowers of the Mohwa (*Bassia latifolia*).

Scarcely any tree of the Indian forests has such a power of natural reproduction as sál. The seed ripens at the commencement of the rains; and often germinating even while yet on the tree, the heavy seed is scattered around and at once produces a crop of seedlings. Without light, however, these seedlings soon die off, so that cuttings in sál forest where fire protection is assured, might be heavy. But, usually, scarcely have the seedlings reached one year in age when they are destroyed by jungle fires, but so great is the vitality of the plant, that the roots of the stems destroyed again at once put out fresh shoots, and this happens often year after year, so that at the root of the tree a large hard ball of wood and bark is formed. With fire-protection, however, the regeneration of sál forests is almost a certainty; the seedlings in a few years kill down the grass and plants of slower growth which surround them, and form forests, often of very considerable extent, almost to the exclusion of other species of tree. The sál tree coppices, especially when young, but not under all circumstances.

			lbs.
O	204.	Garhwal (1868)	53
O	2990.	„ (1874)	59
O	873.	Ramganga Valley, Kumaun, 1,800 ft.	69
O	388.	Oudh	60
O	1215.	„	59
O	2980.	„ (section of fire-damaged tree)	...
O	{ 1210. 1211. }	„ (sapling sections)	...
O	1213.	„ (sections of shoot)	...
O	1214.	„ (butt ends)	...
C	173.	Mandla, C. P. (1871)	49
C	1235.	Gumsúr, Madras	64
E	497.	Sukna Hills, Darjeeling, 1,500 ft.	58
E	702.	Tista Valley „ „ „	64
E	2322.	Darjeeling Terai	54
E	3137.	Buxa Reserve, Western Dúars	62
E	3138.	„ „ „ „	61
E	635.	Eastern Dúars, Assam	53
E	1440.	Mishmi Hills (Griffith, 1836)	47

(The identification of this last specimen is doubtful; the pores are not filled with resin, and the medullary rays are finer and more numerous than in sál.)

4. S. obtusa, Wall.; Hook. Fl. Ind. i. 306; Kurz i. 118. Vern. *Thitya,* Burm.

A large tree. Bark ½ inch thick, grey, with deep longitudinal fissures. Heartwood the colour of sál, very hard and durable. Pores moderate to large, often filled with resin; each pore surrounded by a narrow white ring. Medullary rays moderately broad to broad, numerous, joined by short irregular transverse bars or lines of lighter coloured tissue. The wood of this tree is more even-grained than that of either sál or *engyin.*

Eng forests of Burma.

Weight: according to Skinner, No. 115, 58 lbs.; Brandis' Burma List of 1862, No. 17, gives 57 lbs.; our specimens vary from 52 to 67 lbs., averaging 60 lbs. Skinner gives P = 730. The wood is much valued on account of its durability; it is used for canoes and in building, and is valuable for tool-handles and planes.

			lbs.
B	555.	Prome, Burma	64
B	556.	" "	67
B	2973.	" "	52
B	283.	Burma (1867)	56

5. S. Tumbuggaiá, Roxb. Fl. Ind. ii. 617; Hook. Fl. Ind. i. 306; Beddome xxvi; t. 5. *Vatica Tumbuggaia,* W. and A. Vern. *Cangú, congo, tambugai, tambagum,* Tam.; *Thambá, googgilapu-karra,* Tel.; *Vanboga,* Mal.

A large tree. Wood smooth, harder than that of sál, but similar in structure. Medullary rays shorter and somewhat unequal. Concentric lines more numerous and more distinctly marked.

Intermediate and south dry zones. Cuddapah and North Arcot Districts.

Weight: Baker gives 68 lbs.; Skinner, No. 133, 58; while our specimens give 67 lbs. Baker gives P varying from 902 to 996; Skinner 980. This is also, probably, Skinner's No. 137 'Congoe'; weight 64 lbs., P = 892. The wood is used for house-building, particularly for door frames and posts and for rafters. It gives a dammer, which is used as a substitute for pitch and for burning in temples.

			lbs.
D	1062.	Cuddapah	66
D	1078.	North Arcot	68

6. S. siamensis, Miq.; Hook. Fl. Ind. i. 304. *Pentacme siamensis,* Kurz i. 119. Vern. *Engyin,* Burm.

A large deciduous tree. Bark ½ inch thick, dark grey, with deep vertical fissures. Heartwood very hard, very heavy and cross-grained; in this respect similar to sál, which it also resembles in colour. Pores moderate-sized, rarely large, sometimes in groups and filled with resin, enclosed in narrow white rings and joined by fine, wavy, concentric lines. Medullary rays fine, numerous, equidistant.

Eng forests of Burma.

Weight: Brandis' Burma List of 1862, No. 16, gives 55 lbs.; our specimens average 54 lbs. The wood is much prized on account of its durability, it is used for house-building, bows and other purposes. It gives a red resin.

			lbs.
B	2507.	Burma (1862)	48
B	3127.	Kya-eng, Attaran Valley, Burma	69
B	2972.	Prome, Burma	46

4. HOPEA, Roxb.

Large, glabrous or hoary tomentose, resinous trees. Eight species, of which 5 are South Indian and 3 Burmese. *H. longifolia,* Dyer; Hook. Fl. Ind. i. 309 (*H. parvi-*

flora, Beddome xxvii., *in part*) is a large tree of Tinnevelly. *H. Wightiana*, Wall.; Hook. Fl. Ind. i. 309; Beddome t. 96. Vern. *Kalbow, kiralboghi*, Kan.; *Kong*, Tinnevelly, is a large tree of the Western Gháts often forming coppice woods and yielding a good timber. *H. glabra*, W. and A.; Hook. Fl. Ind. i. 309 (*H. Wightiana*, Beddome t. 96, *in part*), is a tree of South India; and *H. racophlœa*, Dyer (*Hopea* sp., Beddome xxvii) is a tree of the Wynaad with hard, heavy, durable timber. *H. oblongifolia*, Dyer; Hook. Fl. Ind. i. 309; Kurz i. 121, and *H. Griffithii*, Kurz i. 122; Hook. Fl. Ind. i. 310, are trees of Tenasserim.

Heartwood yellowish brown, hard, smooth, even-grained; seasons well.

1. **H. odorata,** Roxb. Fl. Ind. ii. 609; Hook. Fl. Ind. i. 308; Kurz i. 120. *H. eglandulosa*, Roxb. Fl. Ind. ii. 611. Vern. *Thingan*, Burm.; *Rimdá*, And.

A large evergreen tree. Bark ½ inch thick, dark, with deep longitudinal furrows. Wood yellow or yellowish brown, hard, close and even-grained. Pores moderate-sized and large, less numerous than in sál. Medullary rays short, moderately broad, with a few intermediate fine rays, very prominent, joined by numerous white transverse lines. The rays are visible on a radial section as long straight bands, giving the wood a beautifully mottled appearance.

Eastern moist zone. Scattered in evergreen forests of British Burma and the Andaman Islands.

The weight and transverse strength have been determined by the following experiments:—

				Weight.	Value of P.
Baker	in 1829, 4 experiments with	Tavoy	wood 7′ × 2″ × 2″ gave	51 lbs.	839
Skinner	in 1862, No. 80, ...	Burma	„ ... ... „	45 „	706
Bennett	in 1872, No. 5, „ „	Andaman	„ ... ... „	58 „	737
Wallich	... ... „ „	Martaban	„ ... ... „	30 „	...
Brandis	in 1862, No. 14, „	Burma	„ ... ... „	46 „	...
Smythies	in 1878, 8 „ „	„	and Andaman wood „	50 „	...

Very durable, *e.g.*, the specimens brought by Wallich from Tavoy in 1828, which, though now 50 years old, are perfectly sound and good. Boats made of it are said to last 20 years. It is the chief timber tree of Southern Tenasserim. It is used for house-building and canoes; also considered good for solid cart wheels. It gives a yellow resin, which, according to Major Protheroe, is used by the Andamanese, mixed with beeswax and red ochre, to make a wax used to fasten their spear and arrow-heads.

		lbs.
B 282.	Burma (1867)	44
B 285.	„ „	...
B 546.	Martaban	53
B 2509.	Burma (1862)	43
B 2698.	Tavoy (Wallich, 1828)	52
B 2714.	„ „ „	49
B 2716.	„ „ „	56
B 511.	Andaman Islands	51
B 2201.	„ „ (Major Ford, 1866)	54

2. **H. parviflora,** Beddome t. 7. Hook. Fl. Ind. i. 308. Vern. *Kiral boghi, tirpu*, Kan.; *Irubogam*, Malabar.

A large tree. Wood brown, hard and close-grained. Pores small and moderate-sized, numerous. Medullary rays moderately broad, prominent, generally bent where they touch the pores, uniform and equidistant.

Western moist zone. Malabar and South Kanara, up to 3,500 ft.
Weight, 62 to 63 lbs.

The wood is of good quality, though scarcely known; it is valued in South Kanara for building temples and may be found useful for sleepers.

		lbs.
W 745.	South Kanara	62
W 759.	"	63

5. VATERIA, Linn.

Only one species is indigenous in India, though fourteen are described from Ceylon.

1. V. indica, Linn.; Hook. Fl. Ind. i. 313; Roxb. Fl. Ind. ii. 602. *V. malabarica,* Blume; Beddome t. 84. The Piney Varnish or Indian Copal Tree. Vern. *Piney maram, dhup maram, vallay kungiliam, kondricam,* Tamil; *Dupa maram, dhupa, paini, munda dhup,* Kan.; *Dupada,* Tel.; *Payani, paini mara, vella kondrikam,* Mal.; *Hal,* Cingh.

A large evergreen tree, bark whitish. Sapwood white with a tinge of red; heartwood grey, rough, moderately hard, porous. Pores small and moderate-sized, often in groups. Medullary rays fine and broad, very prominent on all vertical sections, while on a radial section they appear as rough plates with white shining fibres between them. The distance between the broad rays is generally greater than the transverse diameter of the pores.

Western moist zone. Western Ghâts from Kanara to Travancore, ascending to 4,000ft.

Weight 41 lbs. per cubic feet.

Wood not much in request, occasionally used for canoes, for coffins and the masts of native vessels. It gives an excellent varnish resembling copal.

		lbs.
W 747.	South Kanara	41
W 1187.	" "	41

6. DOONA, Thwaites.

A genus of Ceylon trees, 10 species.

1. D. zeylanica, Thwaites Enum. 34; Hook. Fl. Ind. i. 311; Beddome t. 97. Vern. *Doon,* Cingh.

A large tree. Bark rough and cracked. Heartwood the colour of sál, moderately hard. Pores large, often subdivided. Medullary rays fine, uniform and equidistant, the distance between the rays less than the transverse diameter of the pores.

Central Provinces of Ceylon, up to 4,000ft.

Weight, according to A. Mendis, 29 lbs. Wood used for housebuilding. The tree gives a large quantity of colourless gum resin, which, dissolved in spirits of wine or turpentine, makes an excellent varnish.

	lbs.
No. 25, Ceylon Collection	29

ORDER XVII. MALVACEÆ.

An order of which in India about 22 genera are found, mostly herbs or small undershrubs, with ten genera of trees or large shrubs. Few of them are valuable for their timber, though the wood of *Bombax malabaricum* is extensively used for temporary constructions and boxes. Many are valuable for their fibres, and particularly *Adansonia* and *Hibiscus.* The Cotton Plant, *Gossypium,* belongs to this family, only one species of the genus, *G. Stocksii,* Masters, a straggling shrub of the limestone rocks on the coast of Sind, being indigenous in India.

The ten genera belong to two Tribes, *viz.* :—

Tribe I.—Hibisceæ . . . *Decaschistia*, *Dicellostyles*, *Hibiscus* and *Thespesia*.

„ II.—Bombaceæ . . . *Kydia*, *Adansonia*, *Bombax*, *Eriodendron*, *Cullenia* and *Durio*.

Decaschistia contains 2 shrubs of Southern India. *Dicellostyles jujubifolia*' Benth.; Hook. Fl. Ind. i. 333; Gamble 10. Vern. *Kubindé*, Nep.; *Dantaglar*, Lepcha' is a small white-flowered tree of the hills of Sikkim and Bhutan. *Adansonia digitata*, Linn.; Hook. Fl. Ind. i. 348; Roxb. Fl. Ind. iii. 164; Beddome xxix; Brandis 30, the Baobab Tree. Vern. *Gorak imli*, Hind.; *Kalp briksh*, Ajmere, Delhi; *Paparapulia*, Tam., was introduced from tropical Africa and is now cultivated here and there, chiefly in South India and Bengal, but occasionally as far north as Gurgaon (see 'Indian Forester,' Vol. iv. i. p. 102, for description of a tree at Tilpat, measuring 22 feet in girth and rising 50 feet to the first branch). Brandis mentions 3 trees at Deogarh in the Central Provinces, respectively measuring 16, 22 and 40 feet in girth, and there are one or two good-sized trees at Calcutta and Barrackpore. It is being experimentally planted at Calcutta and in the Sundarbans; as, were it capable of easy cultivation, its rapid growth, valuable fibre and fruit would make the extension of its growth desirable; as yet, however, it has not succeeded. *Eriodendron anfractuosum*, DC.; Hook. Fl. Ind. i. 350; Beddome xxx. (*E. orientale*, Steud.; Kurz i. 131. *Bombax pentandrum*, Roxb. Fl. Ind. iii. 165) the White Cotton Tree. Vern. *Safed simal*, *senibal*, *hatian*, *katan*, Hind.; *Shwet simúl*, Beng.; *Ilavam*, Tam.; *Buruga*, *pur*, *kadami*, Tel.; *Shamieula*, Mar.; *Pania*, Mal.; *Imbúl*, Cingh., is a tall deciduous soft-wooded tree of India and Burma, often planted. Skinner, No. 67, gives its weight as 30 lbs., and P = 400. *Cullenia excelsa*, Wight; Hook. Fl. Ind. i. 350; Beddome xxx. Vern. *Malai-konji*, *aini-pillao*, Tam.; *Kattu-bodde*, Cingh., is a tall white-wooded tree of the Western Ghâts and Ceylon, having a large globose, spiny fruit. *Durio Zibethinus*, DC.; Hook. Fl. Ind. i. 351; Roxb. Fl. Ind. iii. 399; Kurz i. 132. Vern. *Duyin*, Burm.; *Durian*, Malay, is the well known and much prized fruit tree, yielding the Durian or Civet-Cat fruit. It is wild in South Tenasserim, but is cultivated as far north as Moulmein.

Wood generally soft, a few species with small dark coloured heartwood. Pores moderate-sized to large. Medullary rays fine or moderately broad. *Kydia calycina* and *Hibiscus syriacus* have transverse bars across the rays.

1. HIBISCUS, Medik.

A genus of herbs, shrubs, climbers or small trees. The 9 Indian woody species consist of 2 small trees, 2 shrubs, 1 climber and 5 introduced garden shrubs. *H. fragrans*, Roxb. Fl. Ind. iii. 195. Vern. *Kinúrlur*, Beng., is a small tree of Assam and Cachar. *H. macrophyllus*, Roxb.; Kurz i. 126 (*H. setosus*, Roxb. Fl. Ind. iii. 194) Vern. *Kachia udal*, *kasyapála* Beng.; *Sho*, *dayban*, Magh; *Yetwoon*, Burm. (Weight, 27 to 28 lbs. per cubic foot, according to Wallich) a small handsome, large-leaved tree of Eastern Bengal, Chittagong and Burma, said by Kurz to have a rather heavy wood, and to give a good rope-making fibre. *H. scandens*, Roxb. Fl. Ind. iii. 200; Kurz i. 127; Gamble 10, is a large climbing shrub of Eastern Bengal from Sikkim to Chittagong; and *H. collinus*, Roxb. Fl. Ind. iii. 198. Vern. *Kandagang*, Tel., a large shrub of the Eastern Madras coast. *H. rosa-sinensis*, Linn., the Shoe Plant. Vern. *Juwa*, *oru*, Beng.; *Khoungyan*, Burm. with brilliant, large, red flowers; *H. tricuspis*, Banks; *H. mutabilis*, Linn.; and *H. syriacus*, Linn. Vern. *Gurhul*, are all shrubs which have been introduced and are now cultivated in gardens.

1. H. tiliaceus, Linn.; Hook Fl. Ind. i. 343; Roxb. Fl. Ind. iii. 192; Beddome xxix; Kurz. i. 126. Vern. *Bola*, *chelwa*, Beng.; *Thengben*, *thimban*, Burm.; *Beligobel*, *bellipatta*, Cingh.

Pores very numerous, small and moderate-sized, often subdivided. Medullary rays fine and moderately broad, not very prominent.

Coasts of India, Burma and Ceylon.
Weight, 35 to 38 lbs. per cubic foot.

The wood is not used, except as fuel. It gives a fibre which is very extensively used in Bengal for rough ropes.

		lbs.
E 405.	Sundarbans	35
No. 7.	Ceylon Collection (marked *Paritium tiliaceum*) . .	38

2. THESPESIA, Corr.

Two species. *T. Lampas*, Dalz. and Gibs.; Hook. Fl. Ind. i. 345; Kurz i. 128; Gamble 10 (*Hibiscus Lampas* and *tetralocularis*, Roxb. Fl. Ind. iii. 197, 198) Vern. *Bonkupash*, Ass. (Wallich); *Kondapatti*, Tel., is a shrub found in most parts of India, whose wood, according to Kyd, weighs 29 lbs. and P = 407.

1. T. populnea, Corr.; Hook. Fl. Ind. i. 345; Beddome t. 63; Kurz i. 128. *Hibiscus populneus*, Willd.; Roxb. Fl. Ind. iii. 190. The Portia Tree or Tulip Tree. Vern. *Parsipu*, Hind.; *Poresh, parash*, Beng.; *Poris, purasa, portia, pursa, pursung, puvarasam*, Tam.; *Gangaraya*, Tel.; *Bendi*, Guz., Mar.; *Sureya*, Cingh.

A moderate-sized evergreen tree. Sapwood soft; wood pale reddish, with small, dark coloured, hard heartwood. Pores moderate-sized, scanty, subdivided, uniformly distributed. Medullary rays fine, uniform, the distance between two rays generally equal to the transverse diameter of the pores.

Coast forests of India, Burma and the Andaman Islands. Planted throughout India.

Weight, Skinner, No. 130, and A. Mendis give 49 lbs.; our specimens give 50 lbs. Skinner gives P = 716, and A. Mendis 708.

Wood durable: it is used in South India for gun stocks, boats, cart and carriage making and for furniture; in Burma for carts and furniture. It yields a good fibre from the bark, and a yellow dye from the capsules.

		lbs.
C 1050.	Guzerat	50
E 2488.	Calcutta	...
B 2470.	Andaman Islands (Kurz, 1866)	...
No. 51.	Salem Collection	53
No. 28.	Salem Collection (marked *Eugenia caryophyllæfolia*) .	48
No. 80.	Ceylon Collection	49

3. KYDIA, Roxb.

Besides the species described below, *K. glabrescens*, Mast.; Hook. Fl. Ind. i. 348, is a tree of Bhutan and Assam.

1. K. calycina, Roxb.; Hook. Fl. Ind. i. 348; Beddome xxviii; Brandis 29; Kurz i. 124; Gamble 10. *K. calycina* and *fraterna*, Roxb. Fl. Ind. iii. 188, 189. Vern. *Pola, púla, púli patha, potári*, Hind.; *Barranga, bhoti*, C. P.; *Kubindé*, Nep.; *Sedangtaglar*, Lepcha; *Mahow*, Mechi; *Boldobak*, Gáro; *Kopásia*, Uriya; *Potri, pandiki, peddapotri, pedda kunji*, Tel.; *Buruk, bosha*, Gondi; *Bendi*, Kan.; *Warung*, Mar.; *Dwabote*, Burm.

A small tree. Bark ¼ inch thick, grey, peels off in irregular flakes. Wood white, soft; no heartwood. Annual rings marked by white concentric lines. Pores scanty, moderate-sized, often oval and subdivided. Medullary rays short, fine to broad, numerous, joined by white transverse bars, and in this respect resembling Anonaceæ; on a radial section distinctly visible as long straight bands.

Common in the forests of all parts of India and Burma, except the arid region. Growth fast, 4 to 8 rings per inch of radius.

Weight, 40 to 45 lbs. per cubic foot according to Brandis; our specimens give 38 lbs. as an average. The wood is used for house-building, ploughs and oars, and for carving. The inner bark gives a fibre.

		lbs.
C 1177.	Ahiri Reserve, Central Provinces	37
C 1163.	" " " "	33
O 3154.	Saharanpur	45

4. BOMBAX, Linn.

1. B. malabaricum, DC.; Hook. Fl. Ind. i. 349; Beddome t. 82; Brandis 31; Kurz i. 130; Gamble 10. *B. heptaphyllum*, Cav.; Roxb. Fl. Ind. iii. 167. The Cotton Tree. Vern. *Simbal*, Hazara; *Shirlan*, Sutlej; *Semul, shembal, semur, pagun, somr*, Hind., Beng.; *Bouro*, Uriya; *Bolchú*, Gáro; *Sunglú*, Lepcha; *Búrga, búgú, buraga*, Tel.; *Illavam, pulá*, Tam.; *Katu-imbúl*, Cingh.; *Wallaiki*, Gondi; *Kalseori*, Bhíl; *Lapaing*, Magh; *Letpan*, Burm.

A very large deciduous tree, with branches in whorls, spreading horizontally, and stem with buttresses at base. Bark grey, when young with conical prickles with corky base, when old with long, irregular, vertical cracks. Wood white when fresh cut, turning dark on exposure, very soft, perishable; no heartwood; no annual rings. Pores scanty, very large, often oval and divided into compartments. Medullary rays fine to broad, numerous, not prominent. Pores prominent on a vertical section.

Throughout India and Burma.

Growth fast. Our specimens shew 3 to 7 rings, averaging 4½ per inch of radius.

Weight: 23 to 24 lbs. according to Brandis, For. Fl., 28 lbs. Burma List of 1862, No. 5; our specimens vary from 17 to 32 lbs. the average being nearly 23 lbs., the Bengal and Assam specimens being lighter than those from the Central Provinces. The value of P is between 642 and 697 (Cunningham). The wood is not durable, except under water, when it lasts tolerably well; it is used for planking, packing cases and tea-boxes, toys, scabbards, fishing floats, coffins, and the lining of wells. In Bengal and Burma the trunk is often hollowed out to make canoes. It gives a brown gum used in native medicine, regarding which Captain Campbell says: "The collection of Semul gum commences in March and is continued till June; it sells in the Kumaun Bhabar at one anna per seer, and is used as a medicine; it is not exported from Kumaun." The cotton which surrounds the seeds is employed to stuff pillows and quilts.

The Semul tree seeds very freely every year, and seedlings come up abundantly and grow very rapidly. It is easily reproduced by cuttings.

		lbs.
P 466.	Ajmere	...
C 201.	Mandla, Central Provinces (1871)	32
C 1117.	Chanda " "	31
E 679.	Bamunpokri, Darjeeling Terai	23
E 2323.	" " "	17
E 1252.	Sibságar, Assam	28
E 1432.	Assam	20
E 1961.	Chittagong	21
B 3117.	Burma (1862)	24
No. 14.	Salem Collection	20

2. B. insigne, Wall.; Hook. Fl Ind. i. 349; Kurz i. 130. Vern. *Semul, thula*, Beng.; *Saitu*, Magh.

A large tree, trunk without prickles. Structure similar to that of *B. malabaricum*, but pores smaller and more scanty.

Chittagong, Burma and the Andaman Islands.

Weight, 31 lbs. per cubic foot. The wood is more durable than that of *B. malabaricum;* the specimen from the Andamans had been 12 years in Calcutta in the rough, and was only slightly discoloured on being cut up.

	lbs.
B 2215. Andaman Islands (Major Ford, 1866)	31

ORDER XVIII. STERCULIACEÆ.

An Order containing 15 Indian genera of herbs, shrubs, climbers or trees. Of these genera, three are herbs or *(Melhania)* undershrubs, and the rest shrubs, erect or climbing, and trees. The Order is divided into 6 Tribes, *viz.:*—

Tribe I.—Sterculieæ	*Sterculia* and *Heritiera.*
„ II.—Helictereæ	*Reevesia, Kleinhovia, Helicteres* and *Pterospermum.*
„ III.—Eriolæneæ	*Eriolæna.*
„ IV.—Dombeyeæ	*Melhania.*
„ V.—Hermannieæ	*Melochia.*
„ VI.—Buettnerieæ	*Abroma, Guazuma, Buettneria* and *Leptonychia.*

Of the genera not here described, *Reevesia* contains two small trees: *R. Wallichii,* Br. and *R pubescens,* Mast.; Hook. Fl. Ind. i. 364; Gamble 11, of Sikkim and the Khasia Hills. *Kleinhovia Hospita,* Linn.; Hook. Fl. Ind. i. 364; Roxb. Fl. Ind. iii. 141; Beddome xxxiii, is a handsome tree commonly cultivated in the hotter regions of India. Fine specimens may be seen in avenues in Calcutta. *Melochia velutina,* Beddome xxxv., is a small tree of Burma and the Malay Archipelago, cultivated elsewhere in India. *Abroma augusta,* Linn.; Hook. Fl. Ind. i. 375; Roxb. Fl. Ind. iii. 156; Gamble 11. Vern. *Ullat kumal,* Beng., is a large shrub or small tree of Sikkim and the Khasia Hills, cultivated in other parts and yielding a strong, white fibre. *Guazuma tomentosa,* Kunth; Hook. Fl. Ind. i. 375; Beddome t. 107; Kurz i. 149. Vern. *Rudraksha,* Tel.; *Thainpuche,* Tam., is an American tree often planted in avenues, having a light brown wood used in Southern India for furniture and packing cases. According to Skinner, No 77, its weight is 32 lbs. per cubic foot, and P = 596. *Buettneria* contains 8 species of small trees and climbers; and *Leptonychia* (under Tiliaceæ in Beddome), two shrubs of Burma and the Western Ghâts. The Cocoa Plant, *Theobroma Cacao,* Linn. belongs to this family, and has been grown in some parts of India and in Ceylon.

The genera of this family have little in common as regards the structure of their wood. The species of *Sterculia* have a very soft and light wood, that of *Heritiera* being very hard and heavy, while the wood of *Eriolæna* and *Pterospermum* is intermediate between the two.

1. STERCULIA, Linn.

In the Flora Indica 22 species of this genus are described. Among these, 13 out of the 14 species described by Kurz occur, and there are also 4 Burmese, chiefly Tavoy, species not occurring in Kurz: total 17 Burmese species. Nine species are described from the north-eastern moist zone, and eight from the western moist zone and Southern India. Three occur in North-West and Central India.

S. fœtida, Linn.; Hook. Fl. Ind. i. 354; Roxb. Fl. Ind. iii. 155; Beddome xxxi; Kurz i. 135. Vern. *Jangli-badam,* Hind.; *Pinári,* Tam.; *Gurapu-badam,* Tel.; *Hlyanpyoo, letkop,* Burma, is a large evergreen tree of South India and Burma, with a light wood and edible seeds According to Skinner, No. 118, the weight is 28 lbs. and P = 464. *S. guttata,* W. and A.; Roxb. Fl. Ind. iii. 148; Hook. Fl. Ind. i. 355 Beddome t. 105; Vern. *Kawili,* Tam.; is a common tree of Southern India whose bark yields a valuable cordage. *S. Roxburghii,* Wall. (*S. lanceæfolia,* Roxb. Fl. Ind. iii. 150), is a tree of the hills of Sikkim and Assam, ascending to 6,000 ft. *S. Balanghas,* Linn.; Beddome xxxii. (*S. angustifolia,* Roxb. Fl. Ind. iii. 148; Kurz i. 138) Vern. *Cavalum,* Mal, is a moderate-sized tree of the western coast. *S. alata,* Roxb. Fl. Ind. iii. 152; Hook. Fl. Ind. i. 360; Beddome xxxii.; Kurz i. 134; Gamble 11. Vern. *Tula,* Beng.; *Muslini,* Nep.; *Dodeli,* Kan.; *Hangkyow,* Magh; *Letkop,* Burm., is a tall tree of Northern and Eastern Bengal, South India and Burma.

The wood is generally light, soft, often spongy, with large pores and moderately broad or broad medullary rays, which are very prominent on a radial section.

1. **S. urens,** Roxb. Fl. Ind. iii. 145; Hook. Fl. Ind. i. 355; Beddome xxxii; Brandis 33; Kurz i. 135. Vern. *Gúlú, kúlú, gular, tabsi, tanuku, karrai,* Hind.; *Odla, hatchanda,* Ass.; *Tabsu,* Tel.; *Vellay pútali,* Tam.; *Hittúm, pinoh,* Gondi; *Takli,* Kurku; *Karai, kandol, gwira,* Mar.; *Kalru,* Ajmere; *Kalauri,* Panch Mehals.

A large deciduous tree. Bark ½ inch thick, very smooth, white or greenish grey, exfoliating in large thin irregular plates. Wood very soft, reddish brown with an unpleasant smell, with lighter coloured sap-wood. Prominent and regular concentric lines, which may possibly be annual rings. Pores large, often oval and subdivided, frequently filled with gum. Medullary rays moderately broad, on a radial section prominent as long, dark, undulating bands, giving the wood a mottled and reticulate appearance; the distance between the rays is larger than the transverse diameter of the pores.

Sub-Himalayan tract from the Ganges eastwards, Southern India and Burma.

Weight, about 42 lbs. per cubic foot; Kyd gives for Assam wood: Weight 18 lbs., P = 103, but it seems probable that Kyd's specimen was not this, but *S. villosa.*

Wood used to make native guitars and toys. It yields a gum called '*Katila*' or '*Katira.*' The seeds are roasted and eaten by Gonds and Kurkus in the Central Provinces. Its bark gives a good fibre, and fine specimens of it from Berar were sent to the Paris Exhibition of 1878 (C. 984 from Bairagarh Reserve, Melghát.)

			lbs.
P	471.	Ajmere	35
P	3220	Nagpahar, Ajmere	...
C	1102.	Ahiri, Central Provinces	39
D	1088.	Madura, Madras	51

2. **S. villosa,** Roxb. Fl. Ind. iii. 153; Hook. Fl. Ind. i. 355; Beddome xxxii; Brandis 32; Kurz i. 136; Gamble 10. Vern. *Poshwa,* Sutlej; *Udal, udar,* Hind.; *Gul-bodla, gul-kandar, massu,* Punjab; *Kanhlyem,* Lepcha; *Kúdar, baringa,* Gondi; *Buti,* Kurku; *Omak, odela, salua,* Ass.; *Udare,* Gáro; *Vake nar, arni, ani-nar,* Tam.; *Sambeing,* Magh.

A moderate-sized tree. Bark grey or brown. Wood grey, very soft, spongy. Annual rings prominent. Pores large, often subdivided. Medullary rays moderately broad, harder than the white spongy tissue between them, joined by numerous transverse bars. On a radial section the pores and medullary rays are distinctly visible, giving the wood a reticulate and mottled appearance.

Sub-Himalayan tract from the Indus eastwards; common in forests throughout India and Burma.

Growth fast, 3 to 6 rings per inch of radius. Weight, 15 to 22 lbs. per cubic foot. Wood not used. The tree is valuable on account of its fibre, which is coarse but strong. It is made into ropes and coarse bags, and in Bengal, Burma and South India into ropes and breastbands for dragging timber. Specimens were sent to the Paris Exhibition of 1878 from many provinces, but especially from Bengal and from Berar (C 986, for Bairagarh Reserve, Melghát). It gives a white pellucid gum which exudes copiously from cuts in the bark. It coppices freely, and is extremely difficult to extirpate in clearings.

			lbs.
E	2324.	Sivoke, Darjeeling Terai	22
E	620.	Bamunpokri, Darjeeling Terai	15
W	847.	South Kanara	20

3. S. coccinea, Roxb. Fl. Ind. iii. 151; Hook. Fl. Ind. i. 357; Kurz i. 137; Gamble 11. Vern. *Sitto uddl*, Nep.; *Katior*, Lepcha.

A small evergreen tree, with smooth, light grey bark. Wood grey, spongy, extremely soft. Structure similar to that of *S. urens*. Transverse bars distinct.

Eastern Himalaya, ascending to 6,000 feet, Assam, Khasia Hills, hills of Burma.

Weight, 17 lbs. per cubic foot.

Bark used for the same purposes as that of *S. villosa*, but less commonly.

		lbs.
E 573.	Khooklong Forest, Darjeeling Terai	17

4. S. colorata, Roxb. Fl. Ind. iii. 146; Hook. Fl. Ind. i. 359; Beddome xxxii; Brandis 34; Kurz i. 138; Gamble 11. Vern. *Bodula, walena, samarri*, Hind.; *Moola*, Beng.; *Sitto udal, phirphiri, omra*, Nep.; *Kanhlyem*, Lepcha; *Bolazong*, Gáro; *Khowsey, pinj*, Berar; *Bhái-koi*, Bombay; *Karaká*, Tel.; *Wet-shaw*, Burm.; *Berdá*, And.

A moderate-sized tree. Bark grey. Wood grey, very soft. Structure similar to that of *S. urens*, but medullary rays broader and shorter, and transverse bars distinct.

Sub-Himalayan tract from the Jumna eastwards, Central and South India, Burma and the Andaman Islands.

Growth fast, 3 to 4 rings per inch of radius. Weight, 24 lbs. per cubic foot.

Bark used in rope-making. Fine specimens of the fibre were sent from Berar to the Paris Exhibition of 1878 (C 985. Bairagarh Reserve, Melghát).

		lbs.
E 1394.	Chittagong	24

2. HERITIERA, Blume.

Contains 3 Indian trees, of which 2 are here described. They have simple leaves, scaly beneath or silvery white. Besides the two here described, *H. Fomes*, Buch.; Hook. Fl. Ind. i. 363. (*H minor*, Roxb. Fl. Ind. iii. 142; Kurz. i. 141) is a tree of Sylhet, Chittagong, Arracan and the deltas of the Ganges and Irrawaddy. It has a red brown, strong wood, weighing 66 lbs. per cubic foot, and used for boats, bridges and house-building.

Heartwood red, very hard. Numerous transverse bars between the medullary rays.

1. H. littoralis, Dryand.; Hook. Fl. Ind. i. 363; Roxb. Fl. Ind. iii. 142; Beddome xxxiii.; Kurz i. 140. Vern. *Sunder, sundri*, Beng.; *Penglai-kanazo*, Burm.; *Mawtdá*, And.

A small gregarious evergreen tree. Bark dark grey, with longitudinal cracks. Sapwood white; heartwood dark red, very hard, close-grained. Pores moderate-sized to large, often oval and subdivided into compartments. Medullary rays uniform, moderately broad, short, wavy, with numerous, very fine, white, transverse bars; the distance between two rays being generally equal to the transverse diameter of the pores.

Coasts and tidal forests of Bengal, the Peninsula, Burma and the Andaman Islands.

Weight, as much as 104 lbs. when wet, according to Schlich. The weight of seasoned wood, as well as the value of P, have been determined by the following experiments which shew that the weight may be tolerably correctly taken at 65 lbs. and the value of P at 850:—

Experiment by whom made.	Year.	Wood whence procured.	Number of experiments.	Size of bar.	Weight.	Value of P.
				Ft. in. in.	lbs.	
Brandis	1864	Bengal	9	6 × 2 × 2	62	860
"	"	"	2	6 × 2 × 1½	63	927
"	1865-6	"	1	6 × 2 × 2	65	783
"	"	"	5	3 × 1 × 1	66	1,288
Skinner, No. 79	1862	Burma	...	......	64	816
Kyd	1831	Assam	1	2 × 1 × 1	67	710
Campbell	"	Bengal (seasoned)	2	6 × 2 × 2	62·5	1,033
"	"	" (unseasoned)	2	6 × 2 × 2	68	744
Baker	1829	" (5 years old)	4	7 × 2 × 2	64	984
"	"	" (4 years old)	1	6 × 2 × 2	62	859
"	"	" "	9	3 × 1½ × 1	...	848
"	"	" "	10	2 × 1 × 1	...	808
"	"	" "	6	7 × 2 × 2	68	883
Wallich	...	India	1	......	59	......
"	...	"	1	......	47	......
Smythies	1878	Different places	6	......	65	......

Sundri wood is durable; it is heavy and does not float, and is extremely tough. It is used for a great variety of purposes, such as beams, buggy shafts, planking, posts, furniture, firewood; but chiefly in boat-building, for which purpose it is very extensively used in Calcutta, and particularly in the Government Dockyard at Kidderpore. It is the chief timber of the Sundarbans forests. Its reproduction is most favourable. On all lands flooded by ordinary flood-tides, a new growth of jungle springs up immediately; but on land ordinarily above high-water mark, it only establishes itself by slow degrees. It soon spreads itself on newly formed islands on the sea edge of the forests. "The roots of the Sundri do not penetrate deep into the ground, but spread laterally 2 to 3 feet below the surface, sending out perpendicular tough shoots, which stand from 3 to 15 inches in height all round the parent stem; and when there are many trees close together, walking through a Sundri forest is very much like finding one's way among a fine growth of inverted tent pegs."—*Home, in "Bengal Forest Report, 1873-74, paragraph 13,"* which, as well as Dr. Schlich's article in the "Indian Forester," Vol. i, p. 6, may be referred to for further details about Sundri.

The Sundri forests are generally very well stocked. Valuations made by Home in 1873-74 gave, for the average amount of material per acre of Sundri forest,—

Seedlings and saplings under 3 feet girth	No. 2,487
Trees above 3 feet girth	" 182

		lbs.
E 401.	Sundarbans	70
E 2916.	"	66
B 3123.	Burma (1862)	69
B 517.	Andaman Islands	63
B 2285.	" " (1866)	68
B 2226.	" " "	53

2. H. Papilio, Beddome t. 218.; Hook. Fl. Ind. i. 363. Vern. *Soundalay únnu*, Tinnevelly.

A very lofty tree. Wood red, very hard, structure similar to that of *H. littoralis*, but pores less numerous and smaller, and transverse bars more numerous and more prominent.

Evergreen forests of the Western Gháts between Travancore and Tinnevelly.

Weight, 63 lbs. per cubic foot. Wood used for building, cart poles and agricultural implements.

		lbs.
D 1066.	Tinnevelly	63

3. HELICTERES, Linn.

The genus contains, besides the common *H. Isora*, Linn., six other species, chiefly small shrubs of Northern and Eastern Bengal and Burma, *H. elongata*, Wall.; Hook. Fl. Ind. i. 365, and *H. spicata*, Colebr.; Hook. Fl. Ind. i. 366, extending as far north as Sikkim.

1. **H. Isora,** Linn.; Hook. Fl. Ind. i. 365; Roxb. Fl. Ind. iii. 143; Beddome xxxiii; Brandis 34; Kurz i. 142. Vern. *Maror-phal, jonkaphal, kapasi, bhendu*, Hind.; *Itah*, Godavari; *Aita*, Gondi; *Kori-buta*, Kurku; *antéri*, Banswara; *Gubadarra, kavanchi*, Tel.; *Kewan, maradsing*, Bombay; *Thoognaychay*, Burm.

A shrub with grey bark, wood white, soft. Pores numerous, small, often in radial lines. Medullary rays fine and very fine.

Sub-Himalayan tract from the Jhelum eastward, Bengal, South and Central India and Burma.

Growth moderate, 10 rings per inch of radius. Weight, 35 lbs. per cubic foot. The branches are used for fuel, fencing and thatching, and the bark yields a strong white fibre made into coarse cordage and canvas for gunny bags (specimens from Berar sent to Paris Exhibition, 1878. C 987. Bairagarh Reserve, Melghát). The fruit is remarkable for its spirally twisted carpels; it is used in native medicine.

		lbs.
C 2804.	Melghát, Berar	35

4. PTEROSPERMUM, Schreb.

Twelve species of this genus occur in India. Of these, two are found in North-West India, three in North-East India, seven in Southern India and five in Burma. They are, most of them, trees with handsome flowers and generally oblique, leathery leaves. Three species are here described. Of the remainder, *P. lanceæfolium*, Roxb. Fl. Ind. iii. 163; Hook. Fl. Ind. i 368; Brandis 35; Kurz i. 146. Vern. *Ban kalla*, Beng., is a large tree of the Sub-Himalayan tract from the Jumna eastwards and of Eastern Bengal down to Chittagong. *P. Heyneanum*, Wall., *P. diversifolium*, Bl., *P. reticulatum*, W. and A., *P. obtusifolium*, Wight, *P. glabrescens*, W. and A., and *P. rubiginosum*, Heyne; Beddome t. 106. Vern. *Kara toveray*, Tinnevelly, are trees of South India; while *P. cinnamomeum*, Kurz i. 147, and *P. javanicum*, Jungh., are trees of Burma.

Wood reddish, moderately hard. Pores small and moderate-sized, often in short radial lines. Medullary rays fine, closely packed.

1. **P. acerifolium,** Willd.; Hook. Fl. Ind. i. 368; Roxb. Fl. Ind. iii, 158; Beddome xxxv; Brandis 35; Kurz i. 145; Gamble 11. Vern. *Kanak-champa, Mûs*, Beng.; *Hattipaila*, Nep.; *Gaik*, Magh; *Toungpetwoon*, Burm.

A tall tree, with thin, grey, smooth bark. Sapwood white; heartwood soft to moderately hard, red. Pores scanty, small, oval or elongated, generally subdivided, visible on a longitudinal section. Medullary rays fine, very numerous, undulating, not prominent, uniform and equidistant. Innumerable very fine transverse lines.

Sub-Himalayan tract from the Jumna eastwards, Bengal, Chittagong and Burma. Often planted for ornament.

Weight, our specimens average 47·5 lbs. per cubic foot. Wood somewhat resembling Thitka, is worthy of notice; it is sometimes used for planking in Bengal. Leaves used as plates and for packing tobacco in Northern Bengal. The down on the leaves is used for tinder and to stop bleeding in wounds.

		lbs.
E 593.	Khookloong Forest, Darjeeling Terai	44
E 3135.	Sukna " " "	48
B 2510.	Burma (1862)	51

2. **P. suberifolium,** Lam.; Hook. Fl. Ind. i. 367; Beddome xxxiv; *P. canescens,* Roxb. Fl. Ind. iii. 162. Vern. *Baelo,* Uriya; *Lolagu,* Tel.; *Taddo,* Tam.; *Velenge,* Cingh.

A moderate-sized tree, wood light red, moderately hard; structure the same as that of *P. acerifolium.* Medullary rays closely packed.

Northern Circars and Carnatic.
Weight, 36 to 40 lbs. Wood tough, used for building, carts and other purposes.

		lbs.
C 1250.	Gumsúr	38
C 1311.	„	40
No. 91.	Ceylon Collection	36

3. **P. semi-sagittatum,** Ham.; Hook. Fl. Ind. i. 368; Roxb. Fl. Ind. iii. 160; Brandis 35; Kurz i. 146. Vern. *Nagyee,* Burm.; *Nwaleinbyeng,* Magh.

A moderate-sized tree with an irregularly shaped, fluted stem and grey bark 1 to 2 inches thick. Wood reddish grey, moderately hard; structure the same as that of *P. acerifolium,* but with more numerous pores and a few broader medullary rays.

Chittagong and Burma; sometimes planted in other parts of India.
Growth moderately fast, 6 rings per inch of radius. Weight, 40 to 50 lbs. per cubic foot. Wood durable.

		lbs.
B 2511.	Burma (1862)	40
B 2706.	Tavoy (Wallich, 1828).	50

Similar in structure to this is B 1418, sent from Burma under the name of *Hman,* the chief difference between its wood and that of *P. semi-sagittatum* being that it is scented, smoother and has much smaller pores.

5. ERIOLÆNA, DC.

Contains six Indian species, one of which comes from Central India, two from the Eastern and Central Himalaya, three from Southern India and one from Burma.

Besides the species here described, there are *E. Stocksii,* Hook. f. and Th.,; Hook. Fl. Ind. i. 370, a shrub; *E. quinquelocularis,* Wight; Beddome xxxv., a tree from Southern India; and *E. spectabilis,* Planch.; Hook. Fl. Ind. i. 371, from the Himalaya.

Heartwood hard, reddish, close-grained, mottled. Pores moderate-sized, in rings of soft tissue often arranged in concentric bands. Medullary rays moderately broad, uniform.

1. **E. Wallichii,** DC.; Hook. Fl. Ind. i. 370. *Eriolæna* sp., Gamble 11. Vern. *Kubindé,* Nep.

A small tree, bark ⅛ inch thick, brown. Sapwood grey; heartwood reddish brown, hard, mottled. Pores moderate-sized, often subdivided, enclosed in irregular patches of soft tissue, and frequently arranged in concentric lines. Medullary rays moderately broad and very fine.

Nepal and Sikkim Himalaya.
Weight, 40 lbs. per cubic foot. Wood much esteemed by Nepalese.

		lbs.
E 2326.	Bamunpokri, Darjeeling	40

2. **E. Hookeriana,** W. and A.; Hook. Fl. Ind. i. 370; Beddome xxxv; Brandis 36. Vern. *Nar-bolku,* Tel.; *Arang,* Berar; *Kútki, bhonder,* Gondi.

A small tree. Bark grey. Wood light red. Annual rings marked by an almost continuous line of pores. Pores small and moderate-sized, often subdivided, enclosed in rings of soft texture. Medullary rays moderate-sized, wavy. Structure similar to that of the wood of *Kydia calycina*, but transverse bars wanting.

Central and Southern India.

Growth moderate; our specimen shews 10 rings per inch of radius. The bark gives a good fibre, and fine specimens were sent to the Paris Exhibition of 1878 from Berar (C 989. Bairagarh Reserve, Melghát).

C 3791. Chanda, Central Provinces . . . .

3. E. Candollei, Wall.; Hook. Fl. Ind. i. 370; Kurz i. 148. Vern. *Dwanee*, Burm.

A deciduous tree, with grey bark. Heartwood brick-red, with orange and brown streaks, old pieces, however, losing their bright colour; hard, close-grained, shining, takes a beautiful polish, seasons well. Pores round, moderate-sized, in narrow rings of white tissue, prominent on a vertical section. Medullary rays numerous, white, prominent, fine and moderately broad. Annual rings marked by sharp concentric lines. Pores frequently arranged in concentric lines, and sometimes joined by narrow, wavy, concentric bands of soft tissue.

Burma.

Weight, according to Kurz 47, according to Brandis' experiments 48 lbs.; our specimens average 51 lbs. According to Brandis' four experiments, made in 1864, with bars $3' \times 1'' \times 1''$ the value of P is = 1020, which shews great transverse strength. Wood used for gunstocks, paddles and rice pounders: it is very handsomely marked and is well worthy of attention.

		lbs.
B 286.	Burma (1867)	41
B 326.	„ „	53
B 1455.	„	54
B 2512.	„ (1862)	55

E 1951 (45 lbs.) is a wood received from Chittagong under the name *Mossé*. It is soft, reddish grey, with a small darker heartwood, splits and warps. Pores moderate-sized, subdivided often in short radial strings. Medullary rays short, moderately broad, joined by innumerable transverse bars. In structure the wood resembles that of *E. Candollei*, but the specimens of leaves which accompanied the wood sent belonged to *Brownlowia elata*, Roxb., a Tiliaceous tree. The wood, however, has no resemblance to that of any of the latter family.

ORDER XIX. TILIACEÆ.

Contains 11 Indian genera. Of these, 9 are trees, shrubs or climbers, and 2, *Corchorus* and *Triumfetta*, herbs or undershrubs. The Order is divided into 4 Tribes, *viz.*:—

Tribe I.—Brownlowieæ	*Brownlowia*, *Pentace* and *Berrya*.
„ II.—Grewieæ	*Grewia*, *Columbia*, *Erinocarpus* and *Triumfetta*.
„ III.—Tilieæ	*Corchorus* and *Plagiopteron*.
„ IV.—Heteropetalæ	*Echinocarpus* and *Elæocarpus*.

Brownlowieæ contains 3 species: *B. elata*, Roxb.; Hook. Fl. Ind. i. 381; Kurz i. 153 (*Humea elata*, Roxb. Fl. Ind. ii. 640.) Vern. *Masjot*, a lofty tree of the tidal forests of Chittagong and Tenasserim (see p. 51, under *Eriolæna* in Sterculiaceæ No. E 1951); *B. lanceolata*, Bth.; Hook. Fl. Ind. i. 381, of the tidal forests of the Sundarbans, Arracan and Tenasserim, and *B. peltata*, Bth.; Kurz i. 153 of Tenasserim. *Columbia* includes two shrubs of Burma. *Erinocarpus Nimmoanus*, Grah.; Hook. Fl. Ind. i. 394; Beddome t. 110. Vern. *Chowra, jangli bendi*, Kan., is a fibrous-barked tree of the western coast, and *Plagiopteron fragrans*, Griff.; Hook. Fl. Ind. i. 399, a climbing shrub of Mergui. To the genus *Corchorus* belongs the Jute Plant, *C. capsularis*, Linn.; Vern. *Pat*, Beng., now extensively grown in and exported from Bengal: and other species, all of which yield fibres. Several species of *Triumfetta* also yield fibres, *e. g.*, *T. angulata*, Lam. (*T. rhomboidea*, Jacq.; Fl. Ind. i. 395) Vern. *Chikti*, Hind., of which fine specimens were sent from Berar to the Paris Exhibition (C. 988. Bairagarh Reserve, Melghát). *Tilia europæa*, L., the Lime Tree or Linden of Europe, belongs to this Order.

The wood of Tiliaceæ is marked by numerous, uniformly distributed, small or moderate-sized pores, and fine, equidistant, medullary rays.

1. PENTACE, Hassk.

1. P. burmanica, Kurz; Hook. Fl. Ind. i. 381; Kurz i. 154. Vern. *Thitka, kathitka*, Burm.

A very large, tall tree. Wood yellowish red, shining, soft, even-grained, takes a good polish. Pores moderate-sized, often oval and subdivided into compartments, numerous, uniformly distributed. Medullary rays moderately broad, wavy, red, visible on a radial section, equidistant; the distance between the rays generally equal to the transverse diameter of the pores. Annual rings visible.

Burma.

Growth rapid, 3 to 4 rings per inch of radius. Weight, 42 lbs. on an average. Now very largely used in Burma for boats, boxes and other purposes for which a light wood is required. Large quantities are annually exported, and though a few years ago the wood was quite unknown, it is now well known, even in European markets.

		lbs.
B 281.	Burma (1867)	42
B 802.	Tharrawaddi, Burma	41
B 815.	Rangoon „	43
B 1386.	Moulmein „	41
B 3119.	Burma (1862)	42

2. BERRYA, Roxb.

1. B. Ammonilla, Roxb. Fl. Ind. ii. 639; Hook. Fl. Ind. i. 383; Beddome t. 58; Kurz i. 155. The Trincomali Wood. Vern. *Petwoon*, Burm.; *Halmillila*, Cingh. (whence the specific name).

A large tree with thin bark. Heartwood dark red, very hard, close-grained, but apt to split; it has, even when old, a smooth, rather damp feel. Pores small, oval, subdivided, enclosed in white patches, which are united by narrow undulating bands of soft tissue. Medullary rays prominent, numerous, uniform and equidistant; the distance between the rays equal to the transverse diameter of the pores.

South India, Burma and Ceylon.

The Weight and Transverse strength have been determined by the following experiments:—

Experiment by whom conducted.	Year.	Wood whence procured.	Number of experiments.	Size of scantling	Weight.	Value of P.
				Ft. in. in.		
Brandis . . .	1864	Burma.	7	{3 × 1 × 1 3 × 1 × 1}	64	825
„ No. 8. . .	1862	„	...	......	56-62	...
Puckle	...	Mysore.	2	2 × 1 × 1	...	971
Skinner No. 28 . .	1862	Ceylon.	...	Various.	60	784
„ No. 31 . .	„	„	...	...	63	1,012
Cat. Exh., 1862 . .	„	„	...	3 × 1½ × 1½	50	622-1028
Baker	1829	„	3	6 × 2 × 2	51	700
A. Mendis, No. 33 .	...	„	...	2 × 1 × 1	48	844
Smythies	1878	Burma.	6	......	61	...

Benson's *Byttneria*, weighing 72 lbs., is probably this. The wood is very durable. No. B 2722 had been 50 years in Calcutta, and was perfectly sound and good on being cut into. It is used for carts, agricultural implements and spear-handles, and in Madras for masúla boats, and is much esteemed for toughness and flexibility.

		lbs.
B 288.	Burma (1867)	52
B 327.	„ (1866)	61
B 1420.	Tharrawaddi, Burma	65
B 1452.	Prome, Burma	65
B 2722.	Tavoy (Wallich, 1828)	63
B 3118.	Burma (1862).	58

3. GREWIA, Linn.

A large genus containing about 30 Indian trees and shrubs, distributed all over India, except in the inner arid Himalaya. *G. oppositifolia* is found as high up as 6,000 feet in the North-West Himalaya. There are 12 species in North-West and Central India, 8 in the North-East, 17 in South India and 10 in Burma.

The genus contains 3 sections, of which the first, *Grewia*, contains the majority of species. The second, *Omphacarpus*, contains only one species *G. calophylla* Kurz i. 157 Vern. *Mayanbo*, Burm., a small evergreen tree of the coast forests of the Andamans. The third *Microcos* contains two species: *G. sinuata*, Wall. Hook. Fl. Ind. i. 392; Kurz i. 158, a large shrub of the swamp forests of Burma; and *G. Microcos*, Linn.; Hook. Fl. Ind. i. 392; Kurz i. 157 (*G. ulmifolia*, Roxb. Fl. Ind. ii. 591). Vern. *Aswar*, Beng.; *Taráh*, Magh; *Myat-ya*, Burm.; *Thayoh*, Arracan—Weight 51 lbs (Brandis, 1862, No. 10), a small tree of Eastern Bengal, Chittagong, Burma and South India. In the section *Grewia*, besides those herein described, may be noticed: *G. villosa*, Willd.; Hook. Fl. Ind. i. 388; Brandis 39 Vern. *Inzarra, pastuwanne*, Pb.; *Dhohan*, Ajmere; *Jalidar, kaskúsri, thamther*, Salt Range, a small shrub of the arid zone in Rajputana, the Punjab and Sind; *G. sapida*, Roxb. Fl. Ind. ii, 590; Hook. Fl. Ind. i. 387; Brandis 41; Gamble 12, a well known, small, yellow flowered undershrub of the Sub-Himalayan forests, sending up yearly numerous shoots from a perennial root-stock; and *G. sclerophylla*, Roxb.; Brandis 39; Kurz i. 162 (*G. scabrophylla*, Roxb. Fl. Ind. ii. 584; Hook. Fl. Ind. i. 387; Gamble 12) Vern. *Pharsia*, Kumaun, a small shrub with white flowers and large leaves, of similar localities; *G. lævigata*, Vahl.; Hook. Fl. Ind. i. 389; Beddome xxxvii; Brandis 42; Kurz i. 150; Gamble 12 (*G. didyma*, Roxb. Fl. Ind. ii. 591) Vern. *Kat bhewal, bhimúl, kakki*, Hind.; *Allpeyar*, Tel.; *Dansagla*, Lepcha, is a small tree of the outer Himalaya, from the Jumna eastwards, Assam, Central and Southern India and Burma, recognized by its long, tapering, glabrescent leaves; while *G. abutilifolia*, Juss.; Hook. Fl. Ind. i. 330; Beddome xxxvii (*G. aspera*, Roxb. Fl. Ind. ii. 591) Vern. *Pedda taraki*, Tel., is a small tree found in Southern India. Some species of *Grewia* have edible fruits, and the wood of some is strong, tough and elastic.

The wood of *Grewia* has small or moderate-sized pores, uniformly distributed, and numerous fine, rarely moderately broad medullary rays. The annual rings are generally marked.

1. G. oppositifolia, Roxb. Fl. Ind. ii. 583; Hook. Fl. Ind. i. 384; Brandis 537. Vern. *Dhamman, pharwa*, Pb.; *Biúl, biúng, bahúl, bhimal, bhengal*, Hind.; *Bieul*, Simla; *Pastuwanne*, Afg.

A moderate-sized tree, with grey bark. Wood white, with a small mass of irregularly-shaped heartwood, hard, giving out an exceedingly unpleasant odour, especially when fresh cut. Annual rings marked by white lines. Pores moderate-sized, very numerous, uniformly distributed. Medullary rays fine, white, wavy, very numerous.

North-West Himalaya, from the Indus to Nepal, ascending to 6,000 feet.

Growth moderate, 7 rings per inch of radius. Weight, 45 to 50 lbs. per cubic foot. The wood is used for oar-shafts, handles, bows, &c., and for most purposes for which elasticity and toughness are required. The bark gives a fibre which is much used in the Punjab for rope and paper-making, but is not durable. The tree is much lopped for feeding cattle during the winter.

		lbs.
H 100.	Bhajji, Simla, 4,000 feet	45
H 154.	Sainj, „ 3,000 „	50

2. G. populifolia, Vahl.; Hook. Fl. Ind. i. 385; Brandis 38. Vern. *Ganger*, Pb.; *Gango*, Sind; *Gangerun*, Rajputana.

A small shrub, with grey bark. Wood yellow, hard, close-grained. Annual rings marked by an almost continuous line of slightly larger pores. Pores small, numerous, uniformly distributed. Medullary rays very fine, white, wavy, very numerous.

Arid zone, in the Punjab, Sind and Rajputana.

Growth very slow. The wood is used for walking sticks and the fruit is eaten.

P 3228. Nagpahar, Ajmere . . . .

3. G. tiliæfolia, Vahl.; Hook. Fl. Ind. i. 386; Roxb. Fl. Ind. ii. 587; Beddome t. 108; Brandis 41; Kurz i. 161. Vern. *Pharsa, dhamin*, Hind.; *Khesla, kasúl*, Gondi; *Dhamni*, Kurku; *Charachi, tharrá*, Tel.; *Dhamono*, Uriya; *Thadsal, batala*, Kan.; *Damnak*, Bhíl; *Daman*, Mar.; *Sadachu*, Mal.; *Daminne*, Cingh.

A moderate-sized tree. Bark $\frac{1}{3}$ inch thick, grey on young trees, dark brown on old trees. Sapwood white; heartwood small, brown, close-grained, hard. Annual rings visible. Pores moderate-sized, numerous, uniformly distributed; a continuous belt of pores in the spring wood; autumn wood harder. Medullary rays fine, prominent on a radial section, giving a handsome silver grain; the distance between the rays equal to the transverse diameter of the pores.

Sub-Himalayan tract from the Jumna to Nepal, ascending to 4,000 feet; Central and South India.

Growth moderate, about 6 rings per inch of radius. Weight, according to Skinner No. 75, 34 lbs.; Brandis says 30 to 40 lbs.; the average of those examined gave 48 lbs. Skinner's experiments in South India gave P = 565. Used for shafts, shoulder poles, masts, oars and all purposes for which elasticity, strength and toughness are required.

The fruit is eaten and the inner bark made into cordage. Fine specimens of this were sent from Berar for the Paris Exhibition of 1878. (C. 983. Bairagarh Reserve, Melghát.)

		lbs.
C 188.	Mandla, Central Provinces (1871)	48
C 1169.	Ahiri Reserve, Central Provinces	46
C 2757.	Moharli Reserve, Central Provinces	53
C 2766.	Melghát, Berar	...
C 1253.	Gumsúr, Madras	49
No. 17.	Ceylon Collection	44

4. **G. salvifolia,** Heyne; Hook. Fl. Ind. i. 386; Beddome xxxvii; Brandis 43. Vern. *Bather, nikki-bekkar, gargas,* Pb.; *Saras,* Ajmere; *Jára,* Circars.

A small tree, with dark-coloured bark. Wood yellow, heartwood orange-brown, hard, close-grained, structure similar to that of *G. tiliæfolia,* but medullary rays more numerous and pores smaller. Annual rings well marked by a line of larger pores.

Punjab, Sind, Central Provinces and Southern India.
Growth slow. Fruit small, edible.

P 3227.	Nagpahar, Ajmere	...
P 3237.	Goran Hills, Ajmere	...

5. **G. vestita,** Wall.; Brandis 40; Gamble 12. *G. elastica,* Royle; Kurz i. 160. *G. asiatica,* Linn. var.; Hook. Fl. Ind. i. 387. Vern. *Farri, phalwa, dhamman,* Pb.; *Pharsia, dhamún, bimla,* Hind.; *Poto dhamun,* Palamow; *Sealposra,* Nep.; *Kúnsúng,* Lepcha; *Pintayan,* Burm.

A small tree, with grey or brown bark. Wood greyish white, hard and close-grained. Annual rings wavy. Pores moderate-sized. Medullary rays fine and moderately broad, numerous, prominently marked on a radial section, and giving the wood a beautiful silver grain.

Sub-Himalayan tract from the Indus eastwards, Bengal, Central India and Burma.

Growth moderately slow, 5 to 7 rings per inch of radius. Weight, our specimens give an average of 48 lbs. per cubic foot; Brandis says 50 lbs. Wood tough and elastic, used for shoulder poles, bows, spear handles, &c. Splits well, and is sometimes used for shingles. The branches are lopped for fodder.

		lbs.
E 651.	Bamunpokri, Darjeeling Terai	43
E 2325.	" " "	51
B 3120.	Burma (1862)	51

6. **G. asiatica,** Linn.; Hook. Fl. Ind. i. 386; Roxb. Fl. Ind. ii. 586; Beddome xxxvii.; Brandis 40; Kurz i. 161. Vern. *Phalsa,* Hind.; *Dhamni,* Ajmere.

A small tree. Bark rough, grey. Wood yellowish white, structure similar to that of *G. vestita.*

Wild in Central India and Rajputana. Cultivated throughout India for its fruit. Bark used in rope-making.

P 470.	Ajmere	...
P 3218.	Nagpahar, Ajmere	...
P 3235.	Goran Hills, Ajmere	...

7. **G. multiflora,** Juss., Hook. Fl. Ind. i. 388; Gamble 12. *G. sepiaria,* Roxb. Fl. Ind. ii. 589.; Brandis 42. Vern. *Pansaura,* Hind., Beng.; *Nilay,* Nep.

A shrub or small tree. Bark brown. Wood white, soft, similar in structure to that of *G. oppositifolia,* but with smaller pores.

Outer Himalaya from Nepal eastwards, ascending to 4,000 feet, Khasia Hills. Used in Bengal for making hedges, for which it is very useful.

		lbs.
E 2327.	Sivoke, Darjeeling Terai	42

8. G. pilosa, Lam.; Hook. Fl. Ind. i. 388; Brandis 39. *G. carpinifolia,* Roxb. Fl. Ind. ii. 587. Vern. *Posangni,* Ajmere.

A shrub with four-angled stem and brown bark. Wood yellowish white, hard, divided into triangular wedges proceeding from the centre towards the four corners and sides, the annual rings in the wedges towards the corners marked by large pores, those towards the sides by a white line and a few moderately large pores. Pores in the rest of the wood small. Medullary rays fine, white, numerous.

Plains of the North-West, Central and South India.

P 3230.	Nagpahar, Ajmere	...
P 3256.	Goran Hills, Ajmere	...

4. ECHINOCARPUS, Blume.

Contains 5 large trees of the forests of the north-east and east moist zone in Sikkim, Bhutan, Assam, the Khasia Hills and Burma. *E. sterculiaceus,* Bth.; Hook. Fl. Ind. i. 400; Gamble 12. Vern. *Banj,* Nep.; *Thabola,* Magh, is a very large tree of the Sikkim Terai, Chittagong and Burma, with a deeply buttressed trunk and large fruit covered with long needle-like spines. *E. tomentosus,* Bth.; Hook. Fl. Ind. i. 400; Gamble 12. Vern. *Kaktay,* Nep.; *Taksor,* Lepcha, is a large tree of the Sikkim Hills from 2,000 to 4,000 feet. *E. Murex,* Bth.; Hook. Fl. Ind. i. 399, is a large tree of the Khasia Hills and Burma (*E. Sigun,* Bl.; Kurz i. 162); and *E. assamicus* Bth.; Hook. Fl. Ind. i. 399. Vern. *Jabba hingori,* Ass., a tree of Upper Assam, whose wood, according to Mr. Mann, is used for planking.

1. E. dasycarpus, Bth.; Hook. Fl. Ind. i. 400; Gamble 12. Vern. *Gobria,* Nep.

A large tree. Bark dark grey. Wood greyish brown, soft. Pores small. Medullary rays fine and moderately broad, closely packed, straight, prominent on a radial section.

Eastern Himalaya, 5,000 to 7,000 feet. (Hooker, in Fl. Ind., says: "Sikkim at 2,000 feet," but I have never seen it below 5,000 feet.—*J. S. G.*)

Weight, 32 lbs. per cubic foot. Used for planking, for tea-boxes and to make charcoal. It is in considerable demand in Darjeeling. The tree is very handsome, as it has showy clusters of yellow-white flowers, capsular fruit, with short close-set spines, black seeds with a red arillus, and drooping branches. It flowers and seeds freely each year, and seedlings come up well.

		lbs.
E. 694.	Chuttockpur, Darjeeling, 6,000 feet	32

E. 1289 sent from Cachar under the name '*Sitarjat*' has a similar structure, but the pores are larger. This is probably *E. tiliaceus* of Mr. G. Mann's Assam Lists (*Phul hingori,* Ass.; *Sitarsauz,* Cachar), Assam Forest Reports, 1874-75 and 1875-76. Said by Mr. Mann to be used for planks and beams where not exposed to changes of weather.

5. ELÆOCARPUS, Linn.

A large genus of trees, chiefly found in the moister parts of India; 25 species are found in India, of which the distribution is:—

North-Western India	1
North-Eastern India	14
Burma	17
Central India	1
Southern India	14

The genus is divided into three sections:

Section I. *Ganitrus* contains *E. Ganitrus*, Roxb. Fl. Ind. ii. 592; Hook. Fl. Ind. i. 400; Beddome xxxvii.; Brandis 43; Kurz i. 168. Vern. *Rudrak*. Hind., a large tree of North-Eastern and Central India, the hard tubercled nuts of which are polished and made into rosaries and bracelets.

Section II. *Dicera* contains, besides the two species described below: *E. serratus*, Linn. Hook. Fl. Ind. i. 401. Beddome xxxviii. Vern. *Jalpai*, Beng.; *Perinkárá*, Kan.; *Wiralu*, Cingh., a tree, with edible fruit, of Bengal, the North-East Himalaya and the Western Coast (Weight, 33 lbs., Wallich); *E. floribundus*, Bl.; Hook. Fl. Ind. i. 401; Kurz i. 167 of Eastern Bengal and Burma; *E. oblongus*, Gaertn.; Beddome xxxviii. Vern. *Bikki*, Nilgiris, of Southern India, with a strong, white, tough wood; and several other less common species.

Section III. *Monocera* contains *E. tuberculatus*, Roxb. Fl. Ind. ii 594; Beddome t. 113; Vern. *Rudrak*, Hind., a large tree of Southern India, whose nuts are used in the same way as those of *E. Ganitrus*; *E. rugosus*, Roxb. Fl. Ind. ii. 596; Hook. Fl. Ind. i. 405; Kurz i. 166; Gamble 13. Vern. *Nandiki*, Nep., of the Eastern Himalaya, Chittagong and Burma; *E. ferrugineus*, Wight; Hook. Fl. Ind. i. 406; Beddome t. 112, a common tree of the Nilgiris; and *E. Varunua*, Ham.; Hook. Fl. Ind. i. 407; Kurz i. 165. Vern. *Tuttcaly*, *saul kuri*, Ass., of the Himalaya from Kumaun to Sikkim, Assam, Sylhet and Chittagong; besides other species.

The species of *Elæocarpus* have usually handsome flowers with laciniate petals, and the fruits of most species resemble an olive and are eaten.

1. **E. robustus**, Bl.; Hook. Fl. Ind. i. 402; Roxb. Fl. Ind. ii. 597; Kurz i. 169; Gamble 13. Vern. *Jalpai*, Sylhet; *Bepari*, *batrachi*, Nep.; *Chekio*, Magh; *Taumagyee*, Burm.

An evergreen tree. Wood white, shining, soft, even-grained. Annual rings marked by a prominent line. Pores moderate-sized, uniformly distributed, generally oval or elongated, subdivided. Medullary rays fine and very fine, closely packed, visible as long narrow bands on a radial section.

Eastern Himalaya ascending to 2,000 feet, Khasia Hills, Eastern Bengal, Chittagong, Burma and Andaman Islands.

Growth moderate. Weight, 38 lbs. per cubic foot.

		lbs.
E 581.	Khookloong Forest, Darjeeling Terai	38

2. **E. lanceæfolius**, Roxb. Fl. Ind. ii. 598; Hook. Fl. Ind. i. 402; Kurz i. 167; Gamble 13. Vern. *Bhadras*, *batrachi*, Nep.; *Shepkyew*, Lepcha; *Sakalang*, Ass.

A large tree. Wood soft, light brown. Pores small, in short strings of 2 to 5. Medullary rays extremely numerous, fine and very fine, appearing as narrow plates on a radial section.

Eastern Himalaya from 6,000 to 8,000 feet, Khasia Hills, Sylhet and Tenasserim.

Growth moderate, 8 rings per inch of radius. Weight 41 lbs. Used for house-building, tea-boxes and charcoal. Fruit edible.

		lbs.
E 358.	Rangbúl, Darjeeling, 7,000 feet	41

ORDER XX. LINEÆ.

A small Order containing 4 genera of Indian trees or shrubs. The only one of any importance is *Erythroxylon*. *Reinwardtia* contains 2 small yellow flowered under-shrubs of the Himalaya, Eastern Bengal and the Western Ghâts; *Hugonia Mystax*,

Linn.; Hook. Fl. Ind. i. 413. is a rambling leafy shrub of Southern India; and *Ixonanthes khasiana*, Hook. f.; Hook. Fl. Ind. i. 416. a small tree of the Khasia Hills. Many species give a strong fibre. *Linum usitatissimum* is the flax plant; cultivated in India for its fibre and oil.

1. ERYTHROXYLON, Linn.

Contains four Indian species. Besides the one described, *E. Kunthianum*, Wall.; Hook. Fl. Ind. i. 414; Kurz i. 171, is a shrub of Eastern Bengal, the Khasia Hills and Burma, above 3,000 feet elevation; and *E. burmanicum*, Griff.; Hook. Fl. Ind. i. 414; Kurz i. 171, a tree of Burma and the Andaman Islands.

The Coca or Spadic Plant of Peru, well known as a powerful stimulant of the nervous system, is the *E. Coca.*

1. E. monogynum, Roxb. Fl. Ind. ii. 449; Hook. Fl. Ind. i. 414; Kurz i. 171. *E. indicum*, Beddome t. 81. *Sethia indica*, DC. Prodr. i. 576. Bastard Sandal. Vern. *Devadarú*, Tam.; *Adivi gerenta*, Tel.

A small tree. Sapwood white; heartwood dark brown, with a pleasant resinous smell, very hard, takes a beautiful polish. Pores very small, very numerous. Medullary rays short, very fine, uniformly distributed.

South India and Ceylon.

Weight, 55 to 67 lbs. per cubic foot.

Used as a substitute for sandalwood. The wood gives an oil used as a preservative for native boats.

		lbs.
D 1083.	North Arcot	55
D 1091.	Madura	66
D 2027.	Mysore	67

ORDER XXI. MALPIGHIACEÆ.

An Order which is represented in India merely by two genera of climbing or straggling shrubs. *Hiptage Madablota*, Gaertn.; Hook. Fl. Ind. i. 418; Brandis 44; Kurz i. 173; Gamble 13. (*Gaertnera racemosa*, Roxb. Fl. Ind. ii. 368) Vern. *Kampti, madmalti*, Hind.; *Endra, chopar, benkar, khumb*, Pb.; *Shempati*, Nep.; *Haladwail*, Mar.; *Madúbúlúta*, Beng., is a common climbing shrub of most parts of India and Burma; *H. candicans*, Hook. f.; Hook. Fl. Ind. i. 419; Kurz i. 174. Vern. *Toungsookapan*, Burm.; and *H. obtusifolia*, DC.; Kurz i. 173 are respectively a large shrub and a climber of Burma; *H. acuminata*, Wall.; Hook. Fl. Ind. i. 419, is a bushy shrub of the Khasia Hills; and *H. parvifolia*, W. and A.; Hook. Fl. Ind. i. 419, a shrub of Southern India and Ceylon: making 5 species. *Aspidopterys* contains 7 climbers, chiefly of the Himalaya, Southern India and Burma, but none of any special interest.

ORDER XXII. GERANIACEÆ.

A large Order, chiefly containing herbaceous plants, such as *Geranium, Oxalis* and *Impatiens*. Only one genus, *Averrhoa*, contains trees, and these introduced: *A. Carambola*, Linn.; Hook. Fl. Ind. i. 439; Roxb. Fl. Ind. ii. 450; Beddome xxxix.; Brandis 45; Kurz i. 177; Gamble 13. Vern. *Kamaranga*, Hind.; *Kamrang*, Beng.; *Soungyah*, Burm., is a small tree which is commonly cultivated in India and Burma for its fruit, which is eaten stewed or made into preserves. Home says it is used in the Sundarbans for building purposes and furniture. Skinner, No. 18, gives its weight as 40 lbs. per cubic foot, and 712 for the value of P; Wallich gives its weight at 39 lbs. *A. Bilimbi*, Linn.; Hook. Fl. Ind. i. 439; Roxb. Fl. Ind. ii. 451; Beddome t. 117. Vern. *Bilimbi, bhimbu, anvalla*, Hind., is a small tree cultivated and often found run wild in India. It has an acid fruit, which is pickled or preserved in sugar, and the juice is used in removing iron stains from linen.

ORDER XXIII. RUTACEÆ.

A large Order, containing however few trees of any size, but generally shrubs or climbers, which are aromatic with gland-dotted leaves.

The Order is divided into 4 Tribes, *viz.*:—

Tribe I.—Ruteæ	Only herbs such as the garden Rue, and the *Bönninghausenia*, so common in Himalayan forests.
„ II.—Xanthoxyleæ . . .	*Evodia*, *Melicope* and *Xanthoxylum*.
„ III.—Toddalieæ	*Toddalia*, *Acronychia* and *Skimmia*.
„ IV.—Aurantieæ	*Glycosmis*, *Micromelum*, *Murraya*, *Clausena*, *Triphasia*, *Limonia* *Luvunga*, *Paramignya*, *Atalantia*, *Citrus*, *Feronia* and *Aegle*.

Melicope contains two shrubs: *M. indica*, Wight; Hook. Fl. Ind. i. 492, Beddome xl., of the higher ranges of the Nilgiri Hills; and *M. Helferi*, Hook. f., of the Andaman Islands and Tenasserim. *Acronychia laurifolia*, Bl.; Hook. Fl. Ind. i. 498; Kurz i. 184; Gamble 14 (*A. pedunculata*, DC.; Beddome xlii.) Vern. *Paowlay*, Nep.; *Loajam*, Ass., is a small tree of the Sikkim Himalaya, Khasia Hills, Assam, Chittagong, South India and Burma. *Glycosmis pentaphylla*, Correa; Hook. Fl. Ind, i. 499; Beddome xliii.; Brandis 49; Kurz i. 186; Gamble 14. Vern. *Ban-nimbu*, *potali*, *pilru potala*, *girgitti*, Hind.; *Kirmira*, Bombay; *Taushouk*, Burm., is a common evergreen shrub, with very variable leaves and fruits, found in most part of India. *Micromelum* contains 2 species: *M. pubescens*, Bl.; Hook. Fl. Ind. i. 501; Beddome xliii.; Kurz i. 186; Gamble 14. Vern. *Lasmani*, Nep.; *Kambrong*, Lepcha; *Tanyenghpo*, Burm., is a small tree of the Eastern Himalaya, Assam, Eastern Bengal, South India and Burma, with a rather heavy, close-grained, yellowish white wood; and *M. hirsutum*, Oliv.; Hook. Fl. Ind. i. 502; Kurz. i. 187., a small Burmese shrub. *Clausena* contains 9 species, chiefly shrubs, the chief of which are *C. pentaphylla*, DC.; Brandis 49. Vern. *Rattanjote*, *surjmukha*, *teyrúr*, Hind., a deciduous shrub of the Sub-Himalayan tract from the Jumna to Nepal; and *C. Willdenovii*, W. and A.; Hook. Fl. Ind. i. 506; Beddome xliv.; Gamble 15. Vern. *Mor kurangi*, Kaders; *Madanay*, Nep.; *Terhilnyok*, *sidemnyok*, Lepcha, a small tree of the Sikkim Himalaya, Western Ghâts and Ceylon. *Triphasia trifoliata*, DC.; Hook. Fl. Ind. i. 507; Kurz i. 192, is a small spinous garden shrub of South India and Burma. *Limonia* contains 4 shrubs of India and Burma, of which *L. acidissima*, Linn.; Hook. Fl Ind. i. 507; Beddome xlv; Brandis 47; Kurz i. 192 (*L. crenulata*, Roxb. Fl. Ind. ii. 381) Vern. *Beli*, Hind.; *Tor-elaga*, Tel.; *Kawat*, Mar.; *Theehaya-za*, Burm. a spinous shrub of dry hills in various parts of India, with a hard close-grained wood, is the most common. *Luvunga* has 2 climbing shrubs, one of Eastern Bengal and Burma, the other of Southern India. *Paramignya*, has 5 shrubs or climbers of Eastern Bengal and Burma, of which the most common is *P. monophylla*, Wight; Hook. Fl. Ind. i. 510; Kurz i. 193; Gamble 15. Vern. *Natkanta*, Nep.; *Jhunok*, Lepcha, an erect or climbing shrub extending from Sikkim down to Tenasserim. *Citrus* contains 3 well-known fruit trees—*C. Aurantium*, Linn. Vern. *Narangi*, *naringi*, Hind.; *Kumla nebu*, Beng.; *Suntala*, Nep.; *Kitchli*, Tam.; *Kittali*, Tel., the Orange, cultivated in most parts of India, but especially in Sikkim and Sylhet (Skinner, No. 48, gives W. = 49, P = 717); *C. medica*, Linn., the Citron, Lemon and Lime, cultivated all over India; and *C. decumana*, Willd., the Shaddock or Pumelo.

The Rutaceæ have a very uniform structure. The wood is close and even-grained, generally white, with a yellowish tinge. The pores are small, uniformly distributed, with a tendency to form radial lines. The medullary rays are fine, uniform and equidistant. The wood of *Skimmia* is anomalous, being distinguished by extremely small pores, arranged in oblique wavy tails, and by very fine, very numerous medullary rays. The wood of most species is marked by white concentric lines, which are generally at unequal distances and often run into each other.

1. EVODIA, Forst.

Contains 6 species of Indian small trees or shrubs. *E. viticina*, Wall.; Hook. Fl. Ind. i. 489; Kurz; i. 179, is a small tree of Tenasserim; *E. rutæcarpa*, Hook. f. and Th., a small tree of the inner valleys of Sikkim, between 7,000 and 10,000 feet; and *E. meliæfolia*, Bth., a small tree of Assam.

1. **E. fraxinifolia,** Hook. f.; Hook. Fl. Ind. i. 490; Gamble 13. Vern. *Kanukpa*, Nep.; *Kanú*, Lepcha.

A small tree. Bark smooth, light grey, $\frac{1}{10}$ inch thick. Wood white, soft. Pores small, often subdivided, numerous near the inner edge of each annual ring. Medullary rays short, moderately broad.

Eastern Himalaya in Sikkim, between 4,000 and 7,000 feet, Khasia Hills from 3,000 to 5,000 feet.

Growth fast, 4 to 6 rings per inch of radius. Weight, 21 lbs. per cubic foot. Wood used only for posts of huts. It comes up commonly in second growth forest, and the leaves, flowers and fruit when bruised, have a disagreeable aromatic smell.

	lbs.
E 3101. Darjeeling, 7,000 feet	21

2. **E. Roxburghiana,** Benth.; Hook. Fl. Ind. i. 487; Kurz i. 180. *E. triphylla*, Beddome xli. *Fagara triphylla*, Roxb. Fl. Ind. i. 416. *Xanthoxylum triphyllum*, Thwaites Enum. 69. Vern. *Nebede, lunuankenda*, Cingh.

A small tree. Wood greyish brown, moderately hard. Pores small, uniformly distributed. Medullary rays short, distant, fine to moderately broad.

Khasia Hills, South India and Ceylon, Tenasserim and the Andaman Islands. Weight, 51 lbs., according to A. Mendis.

	lbs.
No. 60. Ceylon Collection	51

B 1979 collected by Kurz in the Andamans in 1866 and marked *E. triphylla*, DC. (Hook. Fl. Ind. i. 488; Kurz i. 180), has a soft pale red wood, with moderate-sized, oval, elongated and subdivided pores, and very fine and closely packed medullary rays.

2. XANTHOXYLUM, Linn.

A genus containing 10 small, rarely large trees or straggling or climbing shrubs, most of them of very little importance. Besides the one described: *X. acanthopodium*, DC.; Hook. Fl. Ind. i. 493; Kurz i. 181; Gamble 14. Vern. *Bogay timur*, Nep., is a small tree of the outer Himalaya from Kumaun to Sikkim and the Khasia Hills, ascending to 7,000 feet; *X. Rhetsa*, DC.; Hook. Fl. Ind. i. 495, Beddome xli. (*Fagara Rhetsa*; Roxb. Fl. Ind. i. 417) Vern. *Rhetsá mán*, Tel.; *Sessal*, Mar.; *Rattu kina*, Singh. is a large tree of the Western and Eastern Ghâts of South India; and *X. Budrunga*, DC.; Hook. Fl. Ind. i. 495; Kurz i. 182. Vern. *Borjonali*, Ass.; *Mayaning*, Burm., is a tree of Eastern Bengal, Chittagong and Burma, with a rather heavy, soft, yellowish white, close-grained wood. The rest are shrubs or climbers.

1 **X. alatum,** Roxb. Fl. Ind. iii. 768; Hook. Fl. Ind. i. 493; Beddome xlii.; Brandis 47; Gamble 14. Vern. *Timbúr, timur, tezmal, dúrmúr*, Hind.; *Balay timur*, Nep.; *Sungrú*, Lepcha.

A shrub or small tree. Bark corky, young stems with thick conical prickles with a corky base. Wood close-grained, yellow. Pores small, often in radial lines, not uniformly distributed; belts with numerous pores often alternating with belts with scanty pores. Medullary rays fine, short, very numerous.

Outer Himalaya from the Indus to Bhutan, ascending to 7,000 feet, Khasia Hills.

Wood used for walking sticks, the branches for making tooth-brushes. Fruit used as a remedy for tooth-ache, as a condiment and to purify water. The whole plant has a strong aromatic unpleasant smell.

		lbs.
H 107.	Bhajji, Simla, 4,000 feet	46
E 2329.	Tukdah, Darjeeling, 5,000 feet	34

3. TODDALIA, Juss.

Contains two species: one the rambling, sarmentose shrub here described; the other *T. bilocularis*, W. and A.; Hook. Fl. Ind. i. 497 Beddome xliii., a handsome tree of the Western Ghâts, always unarmed and reaching 3 feet in girth.

1. T. aculeata, Pers.; Hook. Fl. Ind. i. 497; Beddome xlii; Brandis 46; Kurz i. 183; Gamble 14. *Scopolia aculeata*, Sm.; Roxb. Fl. Ind. i. 616. Vern. *Kanj*, Hind.; *Dahan, lahan*, Rajputana; *Meinkara* Nep.; *Saphijirik*, Lepcha; *Milkaranai*, Tam.; *Kondakashinda*, Tel.

A large scandent shrub, the branches covered with prickles. Wood porous, yellowish white, soft. Pores moderate-sized, very numerous, often subdivided, uniformly distributed. Medullary rays very fine, uniform and equidistant.

Outer Himalaya from Kumaun eastwards, Khasia Hills and Western Ghâts, ascending to 7,000 feet.

The root bark gives a yellow dye and a bitter and aromatic tonic, used by natives in some parts of the country as a remedy for fever. (*Bidie.*)

E 2855. Tukdah, Darjeeling, 5,000 feet. . . . .

4. SKIMMIA, Thunb.

1. S. Laureola, Hook. f.; Hook. Fl. Ind. i. 499; Brandis 50; Gamble 14. Vern. *Ner, barru*, Pb.; *Nehar, gurl pata*, Kumaun; *Chumlani*, Nep.; *Timburnyok*, Lepcha.

An extremely aromatic shrub. Bark thin, bluish grey. Wood white, soft, with distinct, white, concentric lines which may possibly be annual rings; has an aromatic scent when fresh cut. Pores extremely small, in narrow, irregularly bent lines. Medullary rays fine, numerous.

Himalaya from the Indus to Bhutan, from 5,000 to 11,000 feet, Afghanistan.

Weight, 42 lbs. per cubic foot. The leaves are eaten in the Himalaya in curries.

		lbs.
H 2846.	Mahasu, Simla, 8,000 feet.	...
E 2330.	Tukdah, Darjeeling, 5,000 feet	42

6. MURRAYA, Linn.

Besides the species described, *M. Königii*, Spr.; Hook. Fl. Ind. i. 503; Beddome xliv; Brandis 48; Kurz i. 190; Gamble 14. (*Bergera Königii*, Linn.; Roxb. Fl. Ind. ii. 375) Vern. *Gandla, gandi, bowala*, Pb.; *Harri, katnim*, Hind.; *Barsanga*, Beng.; *Chanangi*, Hyderabad; *Karepak, kari-vepa*, Tel.; *Kamwepila*, Tam., is a small tree of the outer Himalaya from the Ravi to Assam, Bengal, South India and Burma, whose leaves are used for flavouring curries. The wood is close, even-grained, hard and durable, and is used for agricultural implements.

1. M. exotica, Linn.; Hook. Fl. Ind. i. 502; Roxb. Fl. Ind. ii. 374; Beddome xliv.; Brandis 48; Kurz i. 190; Gamble 14. Vern. *Marchula, juti*, Hind.; *Kamini*, Beng.; *Naga golunga*, Tel.; *Raket-berár*, Gondi; *Simali*, Nep.; *Shitzem*, Lepcha; *Makay*, Burm.; *Machalla*, And.

A shrub or small tree, with thin grey bark. Wood light yellow, close-grained, very hard, apt to crack. Pores very small, sometimes in short radial lines. Medullary rays fine, very numerous. Sharp, white, concentric lines, which frequently run into each other.

Outer Himalaya from the Jumna to Assam ascending to 4,500 feet, Behar, South India, Burma and the Andaman Islands.

Weight, 62 lbs. per cubic foot is the average of our specimens; Wallich gives 61 lbs. The wood resembles boxwood and has been tried for wood-engraving, for which it seems suitable if well seasoned; it is also used for handles of implements. It is often planted for ornament, and is sometimes called "Satinwood" at Port Blair.

		lbs.
B 3195.	Andaman Islands (Home, 1874, No. 24)	63
B 519.	Andaman Islands	62
No. 26.	Ceylon Collection	61

5. ATALANTIA, Correa.

Contains 5 small trees of South India and Burma. *A. racemosa*, W. and A.; Hook. Fl. Ind. i. 512; Beddome xlvi, is a small tree of South India and Ceylon; *A. caudata*, Hook. f.; Hook. Fl. Ind. i. 513, a shrub of the Khasia Hills; and *A. macrophylla*, Kurz i. 195, an evergreen tree of the coast forests of the Andamans.

1. A. monophylla, Correa; Hook. Fl. Ind. i. 511; Beddome xlvi.; Kurz i. 195. Vern. *Árawi nim*, Tel.; *Katyalu*, Tam.; *Makhur*, Mar.

Wood yellow, very hard and close-grained. Pores very small; in groups or short radial lines. Medullary rays very fine, numerous; the distance between the rays greater than the transverse diameter of the pores. Numerous white concentric lines at varying distances.

Eastern Bengal, Southern India and Ceylon.

Weight, 65 lbs. per cubic foot. Recommended by Kurz as a substitute for boxwood.

		lbs.
No. 10.	Salem Collection	65

2. A. missionis, Oliv.; Hook. Fl. Ind. i. 513; Beddome xlvi. *Limonia missionis*, Wall.; Thwaites Enum. 45. Vern. *Pambúrú*, Cingh.

Wood yellowish white, moderately hard, close-grained. Annual rings marked by a white line and a belt of more numerous pores. Pores small, uniformly distributed. Medullary rays fine, wavy, very numerous, uniform, not equidistant.

South India and Ceylon.

Weight, 48 lbs. per cubic foot. The wood is used for furniture and cabinet work, it is sometimes variegated.

		lbs.
No. 66.	Ceylon Collection	48

7. FERONIA, Correa.

1. F. Elephantum, Correa; Hook. Fl. Ind. i. 516; Roxb. Fl. Ind. ii. 411; Beddome t. 121; Brandis 56; Kurz i. 198; Gamble 15. The Wood Apple. Vern. *Bilin, kait, kat-bél*, Hind.; *Kath-bel*, Beng.; *Vallanga, velá, kavít*, Tam.; *Velagá, elaka, yellanga*, Tel.; *Bilwar*, Kan.; *Kawat*, Mar.; *Hman*, Burm.

A large tree. Bark dark grey or nearly black. Wood yellowish white, hard. Annual rings distinctly marked by a white line. Pores small, in short radial lines, joined by short, narrow, white, concentric bands. Medullary rays short, white, prominent, fine and moderately broad, very numerous, not straight. Structure similar to that of *Ægle Marmelos* and *Cratæva religiosa*.

Sub-Himalayan forests from the Ravi eastwards, Bengal, South India, Chanda district in the Central Provinces.

Weight, 50 lbs. per cubic foot, according to Skinner, No. 74; 49 according to Cunningham. Value of P. 623 (Cunningham); 645 (Skinner). The wood is used for house-building, naves of wheels, oil-crushers and agricultural implements. It gives a gum similar to gum arabic. The pulp of the fruit is acid and is made into jelly.

E 2487. Calcutta . . . .

8. AEGLE, Correa.

1. A. Marmelos, Correa; Hook. Fl. Ind. i. 516; Roxb. Fl. Ind. 579; Beddome t. 161; Brandis 57; Kurz i. 198; Gamble 15. The Bael Tree. Vern. *Bél*, Hind.; *Bela*, Beng.; *Mahaka*, Gondi; *Bela*, Kurku; *Vilva*, Tam.; *Maredu, patir, marat*, Tel.; *Bilapatri*, Kan.; *Okshit*, Burm.

A small tree, bark ½ inch thick, outer substance soft, grey, exfoliating in irregular flakes. Wood yellowish white, hard, with a strong aromatic scent when fresh cut; no heartwood, not durable, readily eaten by insects. Pores small, uniformly distributed. Medullary rays wavy, fine, short, white, numerous, uniform and equidistant. Annual rings marked by distinct lines, and often by a continuous belt of pores. In some cases the pores are more numerous in the autumn wood.

Sub-Himalayan forests from the Jhelam eastwards, Central and South India, Burma.

Weight, 40 to 50 lbs. (Brandis); Wallich gives 49; our specimens average 57 lbs. The tree is not often cut, as it is chiefly valued for its fruit, the pulp of which is used medicinally in diarrhœa and dysentery, as a sherbet and as a conserve, keeping well when dry. The wood is used in construction, for the pestles of oil and sugar-mills, naves and other parts of carts, and for agricultural implements.

		lbs.
P 441.	Ajmere	...
O 248.	Garhwal (1868)	57
O 268.	" "	60
C 1176.	Ahiri Reserve, Central Provinces	52
C 2785.	Melghát, Berar	62
E 2486.	Calcutta	...
E 638.	Goalpara, Assam	53
B 564.	Prome, Burma	60

The structure of *Cratæva religiosa* is very similar to this, but the wood is much softer, and the pores are enclosed in patches of soft tissue.

ORDER XXIV. SIMARUBEÆ.

Contains eight genera of Indian trees or shrubs, almost always with bitter bark. They belong to 2 Tribes, *viz.*,—

Tribe I.—Simarubeæ . . . . . *Ailanthus, Samadera, Picrasma, Brucea, Eurycoma* and *Suriana*.

" II.—Picramnieæ . . . . . *Harrisonia* and *Balanites*.

Harrisonia Bennettii, Hook.; Hook. Fl. Ind. i. 519; Kurz i. 203. Vern. *Tapooben*, Burm., is a small spinous tree of Burma. *Brucea* contains two bitter shrubs: *B. sumatrana*, Roxb. Fl. Ind. i. 449; Hook. Fl. Ind. i. 521, of Assam, Tenasserim and the Andaman Islands; and *B. mollis*, Wall.; Hook. Fl. Ind. i. 521; Gamble 15, of Sikkim, Bhutan, Sylhet and Burma, ascending to 6,000 feet. *Eurycoma longifolia*, Jack; Hook. Fl. Ind. i. 52; Kurz i. 202, is a small tree of Tenasserim and the Andaman Islands, with a bitter bark which, in the Malay Archipelago, is used as a febrifuge. *Suriana maritima*, Linn.; Hook. Fl. Ind. i. 522; W. and A. Prodr. 361 *(Surianeæ)*, is a sea-side shrub with thick velvety branches and yellow flowers. Quassia wood is the produce of *Quassia amara*, a tree of the West Indies.

Wood white, soft (moderately hard in *Balanites*); no heartwood. Pores moderate-sized. Medullary rays moderately broad to very broad.

1. AILANTHUS, Desf.

Besides the two species described, *A. glandulosa*, Desf., is a lofty tree, indigenous in Japan, but occasionally planted both in Europe and in Northern India. It grows rapidly, throwing up abundant root suckers, and has for that reason been employed in plantations made to clothe barren stony hills in the south of France. It is also often employed as an avenue tree, and is cultivated in gardens.

1. A. malabarica, DC.; Hook. Fl. Ind. i. 518; Beddome t. 122; Brandis 58; Kurz i. 200. Vern. *Peru*, Tam., Tel.; *Dhúp, baga-dhúp, gogul-dhúp*, Kan.; *Matti pál*, Anamalais; *Kambalu, walbiling*, Cingh.

A large deciduous tree, with thick, rough bark. Wood white, very soft and spongy. Pores large, scanty, subdivided. Medullary rays short, moderately broad, the distance between the rays being larger than the transverse diameter of the pores.

Western Ghâts, rare in Pegu. Often planted in South India for ornament.

Weight, 23 lbs. per cubic foot. Wood not used. The tree gives a gum resin which is used medicinally, especially in dysentery. For Mr. Broughton's report on an analysis of it see Beddome t. 122.

		lbs.
W 746.	South Kanara	23

2. A. excelsa, DC.; Hook. Fl. Ind. i. 518; Roxb. Fl. Ind. ii. 450; Beddome xlix; Brandis 58. Vern. *Arúa*, Meywar; *Maha rukh*, Hind., Mar.; *Peru, pee*, Tam.; *Pedu, pey, pedda*, Tel.; *Gormi-kawat*, Uriya.

A large tree. Wood soft, white. Structure similar to that of *A. malabarica*.

Central and Southern India. Often planted.

Weight, 28 lbs. per cubic foot. Wood used to make floats for fishing, sword handles, spear sheaths and catamarans. The bark is aromatic and is used as a febrifuge and tonic.

		lbs.
C 2784.	Melghât, Berar	...
No. 4.	Salem Collection	28

2. SAMADERA, Gaertn.

2. S. indica, Gaertn.; Hook. Fl. Ind. i. 519; Thwaites Enum. 70; Beddome xlix; Kurz i. 200. Vern. *Samadara*, Cingh.; *Kathai*, Burm.

A small tree. Wood light yellow, soft, no heartwood. Pores small; scanty. Medullary rays very fine, uniform, closely packed.

South India and Ceylon.

Weight, 26 lbs. per cubic foot. The bark is used as a febrifuge.

		lbs.
No. 76.	Ceylon Collection	26

3. PICRASMA, Bl.

B 1977. collected by Kurz in the Andamans in 1866 and marked *P. javanica*, Bl. Vern. *Thityooben*, Burm., has a soft, white wood. Pores small, uniformly distributed, joined by fine, concentric lines. Medullary rays short and fine. Weight, 27 lbs. per cubic foot.

Besides this species, *P. nepalensis*, Benn. is a small tree of Nepal and the Khasia Hills, and *P. quassioides*, Benn.; Hook. Fl. Ind. i. 520; Brandis 59, Vern. *Tuthai*, *tithu, hala,* Pb.; *Charangi,* Hind., is a tall shrub of the outer Himalaya from the Chenab to Nepal, occasionally ascending to 8,000 feet, with a bitter bark, which is used as a substitute for quassia.

4. BALANITES, Delile.

1. **B. Roxburghii,** Planch.; Hook. Fl. Ind. i. 522; Brandis 59; Kurz i. 204. *B. ægyptica,* Delile; Beddome l. *Ximenia ægyptiaca,* Roxb. Fl. Ind. ii. 253. Vern. *Hingu, ingua, hingol, hingota,* Hind.; *Garrah,* Gondi; *Gari, ringri,* Tel.; *Nanjunda,* Tam.; *Hingan,* Mar.

A small tree, with grey bark, ¼ inch thick. Wood yellowish white, moderately hard, no heartwood, no annual rings. Pores small or moderate-sized, distributed in irregular bands and groups. Medullary rays short, very broad; on a radial section visible as narrow plates, with a few fine ones intervening.

Drier parts of India and Burma.

Weight, 48 lbs. per cubic foot. Wood used for walking sticks and for fuel. From the seed a fixed oil is expressed. The seeds, bark and leaves are used in native medicine, and the kernel of the fruit, filled with gunpowder, in fireworks.

		lbs.
P 450.	Ajmere	48
C 1171.	Ahiri Reserve, Central Provinces	...

ORDER XXV. OCHNACEÆ.

Contains two genera, *Ochna* and *Gomphia,* comprising glabrous trees and shrubs. *Ochna* is described below. *Gomphia* contains two small trees: *G. angustifolia,* Vahl.: Hook. Fl. Ind. i. 525; Beddome li., a small tree of the Western Ghâts; and *G. sumatrana,* Jack, of the sea-coast of Tenasserim.

Wood red or brown; grain close, but twisted. Pores small or very small, uniformly distributed. Medullary rays moderately broad.

1. OCHNA, Linn.

Besides the three species described, *O. pumila,* Ham., is a small undershrub of the Sub-Himalayan tract, principally in sál forests, with a perennial underground stem throwing up annually, after the jungle fires, stems 2 to 3 feet high, bearing handsome yellow flowers.

1. **O. squarrosa,** Linn.: Hook. Fl. Ind. i. 523; Roxb. Fl. Ind. ii. 643; Beddome l.; Brandis 60. Vern. *Sunari, yerra-juvi,* Tel.; *Narole, mudah,* Kan.; *Komari,* Uriya.

A shrub or small tree. Wood reddish brown, moderately hard, close-grained. Pores very small, very numerous, between the moderately broad, but not very prominent medullary rays, which are clearly visible on a radial section.

Bengal, Burma and South India.

Weight, 51 lbs. per cubic foot.

		lbs.
C 1305.	Gumsúr.	51

2. B. 1978 collected by Kurz in 1866 in the Andaman Islands and marked *O. andamanica,* Kurz, has a red, hard wood, with the medullary rays prominent on a radial section, similar in structure to that of *O. squarrosa.* Weight, 58 lbs. per cubic foot.

3. O. Wallichii, Planch; Hook. Fl. Ind. 524; Kurz i. 205. Vern. *Yodayah*, Burm.

A deciduous tree. Wood light brown, hard, close-grained. Pores small, uniformly distributed. Medullary rays fine and moderately broad, prominent on a radial section.

Burma.

Weight, 54 lbs. per cubic foot.

		lbs.
B 3132.	Burma (1862)	54

ORDER XXVI. BURSERACEÆ.

Contains seven genera of Indian trees, often resinous. They all belong to the Tribe *Bursereæ, viz.*: *Protium, Boswellia, Garuga, Balsamodendron, Bursera, Canarium* and *Filicium*. *Protium* contains two South Indian trees: *P. caudatum*, W. and A.; Hook. Fl. Ind. i. 530; Beddome t. 125. Vern. *Konda mamidi*, Tel.; *Kilevay, niluve*, Tam.; *Konda mávu*, Kan., a deciduous tree with green bark, often used for planting in avenues; and *P. pubescens*, W. and A., a small tree, resembling the former species.

Wood marked by fine distant medullary rays, and small or moderate-sized, uniformly distributed pores.

1. BOSWELLIA, Roxb.

1. B. thurifera, Colebr.; Roxb. Fl. Ind. ii. 383; Beddome lii.; Brandis 61. *B. serrata*, Roxb.; Hook. Fl Ind. i. 528. *B. glabra*, Roxb.; Beddome t. 124. Vern. *Salhe, salei, sálgá*, Hind.; *Gúggar, dúmsal*, Kumaon; *Salla, bor-salei, ganga*, Gondi; *Luban, salai*, Beng.; *Kungli, gúgúlu, kúndrikam, morada*, Tam.; *Anduku, anduga, parangi*, Tel.; *Chittu*, Kan.

A moderate-sized, often gregarious tree. Bark ½ inch thick, yellow, sometimes greenish yellow, exfoliating in small, hard, irregular flakes and thin plates of much larger size. Wood rough, white when fresh-cut, darkening on exposure, moderately hard. Pores moderate-sized, often subdivided. Medullary rays fine and moderate; on a radial section distinctly visible as long narrow plates.

Intermediate, northern and southern dry zones, Sub-Himalayan tract from the Sutlej to Nepal, drier forests of Central and Southern India.

Weight, 30 to 35 lbs. per cubic foot (Brandis); our specimens give 32 lbs. Wood not durable, but it has been reported that 5 sleepers made of it and soaked for some time in a tank filled with the leaves of *Bahera (Terminalia bellerica)* and water and put down in June 1876 on the Holkar and Neemuch State Railway are still perfectly sound and good. (Indore Forest Report, 1876-77, quoted in *Indian Agriculturist* of May 1878.) It is used for fuel and for making charcoal, which in Nimar is used for iron smelting. From wounds and cracks in the bark it gives a transparent, fragrant, green resin, having an agreeable scent when burnt. It is used medicinally as a diaphoretic and astringent, to make ointment for sores, and as incense (*Labanu, kúndúr, kúndúra, kúndrikam*), but is not the true frankincense, which is the produce of a tree of the Somali country and Arabia. (Birdwood in Linn. Trans. xxvii, p. 146. Cooke's Report on the Gums, Resins, Oleo-resins and Resinous Products in the India Museum, p. 81, 1874.)

		lbs.
P 3215.	Nagpahar, Ajmere	...
C 1112.	Ahiri Reserve, Central Provinces	36
C 2780.	Melghát Forest, Berar	28

2. GARUGA, Roxb.

1. G. pinnata, Roxb. Fl. Ind. ii. 400; Hook. Fl. Ind. i. 528;

Beddome t. 118; Brandis 62; Kurz i. 207; Gamble 15. Vern. *Kharpat, katúla, kilmira, sarota*, Pb.; *Ghogar, kaikar*, Hind.; *Gurja*, Banda; *Kukar, kaikra, ghunja, mahárut*, C. P.; *Júm, kharpat, nil bhadi*, Beng.; *Mohi*, Uriya; *Gia*, Mechi; *Dabdabbi*, Nep.; *Mabdit*, Lepcha; *Gendeli poma*, Ass.; *Chitompa*, Gáro; *Mroung-shisha*, Magh; *Garuga, gárgá*, Tel; *Gúpni, kekra*, Gondi; *Kekkeda*, Kurku; *Karre vembu*, Tam.; *Kúrúk*, Mar.; *Chinyok*, Burm.

A large deciduous tree. Bark 1 inch thick, soft, red inside, grey or brown outside, exfoliating in large irregularly shaped scales; sapwood large, heartwood reddish, moderately hard. Pores large, not numerous. Medullary rays short, moderately broad; on a radial section visible as narrow horizontal plates.

Sub-Himalayan forests from the Jumna eastwards, Central and South India, Chittagong, Burma.

Weight, according to Brandis, No. 45, 52 lbs. per cubic foot. The specimens here examined varied from 39 to 46 lbs., giving an average of 40 lbs. This is, very likely, Wallich's *Jeeah*, 36 lbs. The wood is not durable, but it seasons well. It is used occasionally for house-building and for fuel. The bark is used for tanning and the leaves for fodder. It exudes copiously a clear gum of no value. The fruit is sometimes eaten.

			lbs.
O	225.	Garhwal (1868)	39
O	316.	Gorakhpúr (1868)	39
C	1107.	Chanda, Central Provinces	39
E	648.	Darjeeling Terai	39
E	1389.	Chittagong	46
B	812.	Burma	39

3. BALSAMODENDRON, Kunth.

Contains four species of balsamiferous, often spiny shrubs or trees. Besides *B. Mukul*, Hook., described below, it contains *B. pubescens*, Stocks; Hook. Fl. Ind. i. 529; Brandis 65. Vern. *Bayi, bai*, Beluch., a small tree of Beluchistan and the hills separating that country from Sind, as far south as Karachi. It yields a small quantity of tasteless, inodorous, brittle gum, almost entirely soluble in water. *B. Berryi*, Arnott; Hook. Fl. Ind. i. 529; Brandis 65; Beddome t. 126, is a tree of the forests on the east side of the Nilgiris, cultivated as a hedge plant. It is very fragrant and gives a gum-resin. *B. Roxburghii*, Arn. Vern. *Gugala*, Beng., is a small tree of Eastern Bengal and Assam. The drug called 'Myrrh' is the gum-resinous exudation of *Balsamodendron Myrrha*, Ehrenb., a small tree of Arabia and the African coast of the Red Sea.

1. B. Mukul, Hook. Fl. Ind. i. 529; Brandis 64. Vern. *Gúgal*, Sindi.

A small tree, bark greenish yellow, peeling off in long thin, shining paper-like scrolls. Wood soft, white. Pores small. Medullary rays fine, short.

Arid zone, Sind, Kattywar, Rajputana, Khandesh.

Weight, 20lbs. per cubic foot. Wood not used. The tree yields a gum called 'Gugal' or Indian Bdellium, which is obtained from incisions made in the bark, and is used in native medicine and for preparing an ointment for bad ulcers.

			lbs.
P	448.	Ajmere	...
P	2919.	Rajputana	20
P	3238.	Dewair, Ajmere	...

4. BURSERA, Linn.

1. B. serrata, Colebr.; Hook. Fl. Ind. i. 530; Brandis 61; Kurz i. 208. Vern. *Murtenga*, Ass.; *Thadee-ben*, Burm.

A large evergreen tree. Wood hard, sapwood light brown, heartwood red, close-grained. Pores small, uniformly distributed. Medullary rays fine, red; on a radial section distinctly visible as narrow dark bands.

Eastern moist zone, Bengal, Assam, Chittagong and Burma.
Weight, 46 lbs. per cubic foot. Wood good for furniture.

		lbs.
B 313.	Burma (1867)	46
B 2225.	Andamans (similar in structure, but wood lighter and softer)	37

5. CANARIUM, Linn.

Contains 4 large resinous trees of Southern India, Eastern Bengal and Burma. *C. strictum*, Roxb.; Hook. Fl. Ind. i. 534; Beddome t. 128, is the Black Dammer Tree, Vern. *Karapu kongiliam*, Tam.; *Manda dhúp*, Kan.; *Thelli*, Mal., a tall tree of Southern India, giving a brilliant black gum used medicinally and for other purposes (for Mr. Broughton's analysis of it, see Beddome under t. 128). *C. euphyllum*, Kurz, i. 208 and *C. coccineo-bracteatum*, Kurz, i. 209 are large trees of the Andaman Islands.

1. C. bengalense, Roxb. Fl. Ind. iii. 136; Hook. Fl. Ind. i. 534; Kurz i. 209; Gamble 15. Vern. *Goguldhúp,* Nep.; *Narockpa,* Lepcha; *Tekreng,* Gáro; *Bisjang, dhúna,* Ass.

A tall tree with straight cylindrical stem. Bark light coloured, hard, thin, rough with horizontal wrinkles. Wood shining, white when fresh cut, turning grey on exposure, soft, even-grained, does not warp, but decays readily. Pores scanty, large, often oval and subdivided, prominent on a vertical section. Medullary rays fine, white; on a radial section distinctly visible, giving the wood a mottled appearance.

Eastern moist zone, eastern Himalaya, Bengal and Burma.
Weight, 28 lbs. per cubic foot. The wood is much esteemed in Bengal for tea-boxes, and it is also used for shingles. The tree yields a resin which is used as incense; it is clear, amber-coloured and brittle.

		lbs.
E 703.	Great Rangít Valley, Darjeeling, 3,500 feet	28

6. FILICIUM, Thwaites.

1. F. decipiens, Thwaites Enum. 59; Beddome t. 129; Hook. Fl. Ind. i. 539. Vern. *Katu puveras,* Tam.; *Pehimbia,* Cingh.

A tree with elegant fern-like leaves. Heartwood red, moderately hard. Pores small, in groups or short radial lines. Medullary rays fine, numerous, at unequal distances.

Western Ghâts up to 4,500 feet, Ceylon.
Weight, 68 lbs. per cubic foot (A. Mendis). Wood strong, valuable for building.

		lbs.
No. 70.	Ceylon Collection	68

ORDER XXVII. MELIACEÆ.

An Order containing about 20 trees or shrubs, chiefly of the moist zones.
The Order is divided into 4 Tribes, *viz.*:—

Tribe I.—Melieæ	*Turræa, Naregamia, Munronia, Melia* and *Cipadessa.*
„ II.—Trichilieæ	*Dysoxylum, Chisocheton, Sandoricum, Aglaia, Lansium, Amoora, Walsura, Heynea, Beddomea,* and *Carapa.*
III.—Swietenieæ	*Soymida, Chickrassia,* and *Swietenia.*
„ IV.—Cedreleæ	*Chloroxylon* and *Cedrela.*

Of these 20 genera, 10 are described here. The remaining 10 are of much less importance. *Turræa virens*, Linn., *T. villosa*, Benn., and *Naregamia alata*, W. and A., are shrubs of Southern India; *Munronia Wallichii*, Wight, is a shrub of the Eastern Himalaya and the Nilgiris; *Cipadessa fruticosa*, Bl.; Hook. Fl. Ind. i. 545 (*Mallea Rothii*, Adr. Juss.; Beddome liv. *Ekebergia indica*, Roxb. Fl. Ind. ii. 392). Vern. *Nal bilá*, Hind.; *Chendbera, purudona*, Tel., is a small tree of the western coast, used for fuel. *Chisocheton* contains 3 evergreen trees: *C. grandiflorus*, Kurz i. 216. Vern. *Thitkatong*, Burm., with a pale brown, rather heavy, hard and close-grained wood, and *C. dysoxylifolius*, Kurz i. 215, are from Burma; while *C. paniculatus*, Hiern.; Hook. Fl. Ind. i. 552; Kurz i. 216. (*Guarea paniculata*, Roxb. Fl. Ind. ii. 242) Vern. *Kalikoura*, Sylhet, is a tree of the Khasia Hills and Eastern Bengal. *Aglaia* contains about 10 species, chiefly Burmese or East Himalayan trees, among which *A. Roxburghiana*, W. and A.; Hook. Fl. Ind. i. 555; Beddome t. 130, a large tree of the Western Gháts, with a strong useful timber; and *A. edulis*, A. Gray; Hook. Fl. Ind. i. 556; Gamble 16. (*Milnea edulis*, Roxb. Fl. Ind. i. 637.) Vern. *Lali mahwa*, Nep.; *Sinakadang*, Lepcha; *Gúmi*, Sylhet, a tree of Northern and Eastern Bengal with edible fruit, are chiefly noticeable. *Lansium anamallayanum*, Beddome t. 131, is a handsome tree of the Western Gháts. *Heynea trijuga*, Roxb. Fl. Ind. ii. 390; Hook. Fl. Ind. i. 565; Brandis 70; Gamble 16 (*H. affinis*, Juss.; Beddome t. 134. *Walsura trijuga*, Kurz i. 225) Vern. *Yukushi, akhaterwa*, Nep.; *Limbara*, Mar., is a tree of the Outer Himalaya and Sub-Himalayan tract from the Ganges eastwards, the Khasia Hills, South India and Burma. *Beddomea* contains two species: *B. indica*, Hook. f., a large shrub, and *B. simplicifolia*, Beddome t. 135, a tree of the Western Gháts. Most of the Meliaceæ give a good timber, and some of the species are among the most important of Indian forest trees.

Wood red (yellow in *Chloroxylon*, dark reddish brown in *Soymida*). Heartwood generally hard and dark coloured, not distinct in *Cedrela*, in several species of *Melia* and *Dysoxylon*. Pores varying in size, often subdivided, always prominent on a vertical section. Medullary rays fine, numerous and sharply marked in *Chloroxylon*, *Sandoricum* and *Melia*; broader and often less prominent in the other genera. Concentric bands of softer texture in *Amoora Rohituka* and *Walsura robusta*.

1. MELIA, Linn.

Besides the three species, the wood of which is here described, *M. excelsa*, Jack; Hook. Fl. Ind. i. 544; Kurz i. 212; and *M. birmanica*, Kurz i. 213. Vern. *Tau-ta-ma-kha*, Burm., are evergreen trees of Burma.

The wood of *M. dubia* and *M. Azedarach* resembles that of *Cedrela* in structure, but differs in having fine and numerous medullary rays. *M. indica* has a distinct heartwood, which is hard and close-grained, but the pores and medullary rays are similar to those of the two species first named.

1. M. indica, Brandis For. Fl. 67. *M. Azadirachta*, Linn.; Hook. Fl. Ind. i. 544; Roxb. Fl. Ind. ii. 394; Beddome t. 13 (14 by mistake); Kurz i. 212. The Neem or Margosa Tree. Vern. *Azad-darakht, neb*, Pers.; *Ním*, Hind.; *Betain*, Kumaon; *Agas*, Palamow; *Limbo*, C.P.; *Kohumba*, Guz.; *Nimuri*, Sindi; *Veypam*, Tam.; *Yapa, yepa, taruka, vempa*, Tel.; *Limb, nimbay*, Mar.; *Bevina, bévu, heb-bevu*, Kan.; *Thimbau-ta-ma-kha*, Burm.

A large tree. Bark grey, with numerous scattered tubercles. Sapwood grey; heartwood red, very hard. Annual rings doubtful: the wood shews alternating bands with numerous and with fewer pores; also white concentric lines, whether these are annual rings is a matter for further enquiry. Pores moderate-sized and large, often oval and subdivided; visible on a vertical section. Medullary rays fine, numerous white, prominent, bent outwards where they touch the pores; the distance between the rays less than the transverse diameter of the pores.

Planted and self-sown throughout the greater part of India and Burma.

The weight and transverse strength have been determined by the following experiments:—

		Weight.	Value of P.
Puckle in 1859, three experiments, with bars 2′ × 1″ × 1″,	found	49 lbs.	539
Skinner in 1862, No. 19	„	50 „	720
Cunningham in 1854, two experiments, with bars 2′ × 1″ × 1″,	„	52 „	587
Fowke in Catalogue, South Kensington Museum, 1859 .	„	45 „	315
Wallich	„	46 „	...
Smythies in 1878, the mean of our three specimens . .	„	53 „	...

The wood is used for the construction of carts, in ship-building and for making agricultural implements, and in South India for furniture. It is held sacred by Hindus, and idols are made of it. The bark is bitter and is used as a febrifuge. The leaves are made into a poultice for ulcers. The gum is clear, amber-coloured and used as a stimulant. The seeds are employed to kill insects and for washing the hair. The fruit gives a fixed, acrid, bitter, yellow-coloured oil which is used to burn, but smokes badly in burning: it is also used in medicine as an antiseptic and anthelmintic.

		lbs.
P 463.	Ajmere (sapwood)	48
D 1053.	Salem, Madras	53
No. 11.	Salem Collection	59

2. M. Azedarach, Linn.; Hook. Fl. Ind. i. 544; Roxb. Fl. Ind. ii. 395 (also *M. sempervirens*, Sw.); Beddome t. 14 (13 by mistake); Brandis 68; Kurz i. 212; Gamble 16. The Persian Lilac, Bastard Cedar or Bead Tree. Vern. *Chein, kachein*, Sutlej; *Drek, bakain, bakáyan, betain, deikna, bakarja*, Hind.; *Maha limbo, malla ním, muhli*, C. P.; *Bakainú*, Nep.; *Mallay vembu*, Tam.; *Taraka vepa, makáním*, Tel.; *Bévu, chik bévu*, Kan.; *Ta-ma-kha*, Burm.

A tree with smooth grey bark. Sapwood yellowish white; heartwood soft, red. Annual rings marked by a broad belt of large pores, the outer part of each annual ring containing a few smaller-sized pores which are joined by irregular, wavy, concentric bands of soft tissue. Medullary rays moderately broad; visible on a radial section as long rough plates. Pores very prominent on a longitudinal section.

Commonly cultivated throughout India, and believed to be indigenous in the outer Himalaya, Siwalik tract and the hills of Beluchistan.

Growth rapid, 3 to 4 rings per inch of radius; it coppices freely. Weight, 30 lbs. according to Skinner, No. 92; our specimens give an average of 38 lbs. Skinner gives the value of P at 596.

Wood used for furniture. Beddome, Brandis and Kurz all say it warps and splits, but Mr. Halsey of Madhopúr writes to say that it is equally useful either green or seasoned. Our specimens split only very slightly, and we are inclined to think it is better than it has been supposed to be. The wood is very handsomely marked and polishes well. The bark is extremely bitter and is employed as an anthelmintic. The fruit yields an oil, and the nuts are frequently strung as beads. The leaves and pulp of the fruit are used in native medicine.

		lbs.
P 146.	Sainj, Giri Valley, Punjab	38
P 946.	Lahore, Punjab	35
P 1201.	Madhopúr, Punjab	40

3. M. dubia, Cav.; Hook. Fl. Ind. i. 545. *M. composita*, Willd.; Beddome t. 12; Brandis 69; Gamble 16. *M. superba* and *M. robusta*, Roxb. Fl. Ind. ii. 396-7. Vern. *Eisúr, limbarra, nímbarra*, Bombay; *Lapshi*, Nep.; *Dingkurlong*, Khasia Hills; *Mallay vembu*, Tam.; *Bévu, betta bévu, kád bévu*, Kan.

A large deciduous tree, with smooth, dark-brown bark. Sapwood grey; heartwood reddish white, soft. Pores large, generally round, visible on a vertical section. Medullary rays white, fine, scanty, prominent on a radial section. The structure resembles that of Toon, but all the pores are of the same size and the wood is softer. The annual rings are marked by more numerous, but not larger pores.

Eastern Himalaya, South India, Ceylon and Burma.

Growth rapid; 2 to 3 rings per inch of radius in the Madras specimen; that from Bengal was moderate, 7 rings per inch. Roxburgh says that a tree of *M. robusta* grown in the Calcutta Botanic Gardens from Malabar seed produced in 7 years, trees 46 feet high, with a girth of 44 inches at 4 feet from the ground, which is equivalent to about 1 ring per inch of radius. Also that another, of *M. superba*, from seed sent by Dr. Berry from Sunda, reached in 6 years a height of 40 to 50 feet with a girth of 48 inches. Weight, 26 to 33 lbs. per cubic foot; used for building in South India. The wood will probably be found useful for tea-boxes and similar purposes, and the tree should be cultivated on account of its rapid growth.

		lbs.
E 705.	Great Rangít Valley, Darjeeling	33
D 1093.	Madura, Madras	26
No. 49.	Ceylon Collection	26

B 507 (28 lbs.) sent from the Andamans under the name of *Barringtonia speciosa*. Vern. *Kyaigyee*, Burm.; *Doddá*, And., has a wood in every respect similar to that of *M. dubia*, but that tree has not yet been reported from the Andaman Islands.

2. DYSOXYLUM, Blume.

Besides the three species here described, the following occur in India: *D. grande*, Hiern; Hook. Fl. Ind. i. 547, a tree of Sylhet; *D. pallens*, Hiern; Hook. Fl. Ind. i. 548, a tree of Sikkim and the Khasia Hills; *D. malabaricum*, Bedd.; Hook. Fl. Ind. i. 548. (*Dysoxylum* sp., Beddome liv.). Vern. *Porapá*, Kaders; and *D. Beddomei*, Hiern; Hook. Fl. Ind. i. 548, trees of Southern India. The leaves of several species give out a strong odour of garlic; the leaves are compound, with oblique often large leaflets, and the capsules are generally large, containing large brightly coloured seeds.

Wood reddish, rough, moderately hard. Pores prominent on a vertical section, moderate sized to large, often subdivided.

1. D. binectariferum, Hook. f.; Hook. Fl. Ind. i. 546; Kurz i. 215; Gamble 16. *D. macrocarpum*, Bl.; Beddome liv, t. 150. *Guarea binectarifera*, Roxb. Fl. Ind. ii. 240. Vern. *Katongzu*, Lepcha; *Rangirata*, Cachar; *Borogotodhara*, Ass.

A large evergreen tree. Wood reddish-grey, rough and close-grained, hard. Pores large and moderate-sized, often subdivided. Medullary rays moderately broad, red, wavy, irregularly distributed; the distance between the rays generally larger than the transverse diameter of the pores.

Sikkim ascending to 2,000 feet, Assam, Khasia Hills, Chittagong and the Western Gháts.

Weight, our specimens give 44 lbs. per cubic foot. Wood worthy of notice. Kyd (*Guarea Gotodhara*, Ham.) gives 40·5 and P = 290.

		lbs.
E 644.	Khyrbani Forest, Darjeeling Terai	44

2. D. procerum, Hiern; Hook. Fl. Ind. i. 547; Kurz i. 214. Vern. *Dingori, govorpongyota* (Wall.), Ass.

An evergreen tree. Wood bright red, moderately hard. Pores large, often oval and subdivided, prominent on a vertical section. Medullary rays fine, numerous, wavy, not prominent; the distance between the rays generally equal to the transverse diameter of the pores.

Assam, Khasia Hills and Cachar to Pegu and Tenasserim.

Kyd (*Guarea Gobara*, Ham.) gives weight 47 lbs., P = 617; our specimens weigh from 37 to 40 lbs. It is a handsome wood, well deserving of more extensive notice. It is said by Hamilton to be used for canoes.

		lbs.
E 631.	Eastern Dúars	40
E 1434.	Assam	37

B 2484 (44 lbs.), B 2250 (40 lbs.) and B 2255 (31 lbs.) from the Andaman Islands (1866) have been put under this species on account of their structure, although *Dysoxylum* has not been described from the Andamans.

3. D. Hamiltonii, Hiern; Hook. Fl. Ind. i. 548; Gamble 16. Vern. *Bauriphal*, Nep.; *Gendelli poma, bosuniya poma* (Wall.), Ass.; *Bolashin*, Gáro.

A large evergreen tree. Wood red, hard, close-grained. Pores moderate-sized, subdivided. Medullary rays fine, uniform and equidistant; the distance between the rays greater than the transverse diameter of the pores.

Darjeeling Terai, Assam and Sylhet.

Growth moderate, 6 rings per inch of radius. Kyd (*Guarea Alliaria*, Ham.) gives weight 40·5 lbs., P = 523; our specimens average 40 lbs. per cubic foot. Wood used in Assam for boats and planks, said not to be durable.

Hamilton says it is used for canoes.

		lbs.
E 1259.	Tezpur, Assam	47
E 2189.	Nowgong, Assam	36

3. SANDORICUM, Cav.

1. S. indicum, Cav.; Hook. Fl. Ind. i. 553; Roxb. Fl. Ind. ii. 392; Beddome lv.; Kurz i. 217. Vern. *Thitto*, Burm.

An evergreen tree with grey, not very rough, bark. Sapwood grey; heartwood red, moderately hard, close-grained, takes a beautiful polish. Pores small, oval and subdivided. Medullary rays fine, undulating, not prominent; marked on a radial section as long narrow bands, giving the wood a beautifully mottled appearance.

Burma, introduced in Southern India.

Weight, our specimen gives 36 lbs. per cubic foot; Wallich, No. 175, gave 28 lbs. Used for carts and boat-building.

		lbs.
B 804.	Burma	36

4. AMOORA, Roxb.

Besides the three we have described below: *A. Chittagonga*, Hiern; Hook. Fl. Ind. i. 559 (*Aglaia Chittagonga*, Miq.; Kurz i. 218) Vern. *Thitpasaing*, Magh; is a large tree of the North-East Himalaya and Eastern Bengal down to Chittagong and Arracan, whose wood is largely used in Chittagong; *A. Lawii*, Bth. and Hook. f. Beddome t. 133. Vern. *Búrumb*, Bombay, is a tree of the Bombay and Kanara Ghâts; *A. decandra*, Hiern; Hook. Fl. Ind. i. 562; Gamble 16, is a tree of Sikkim and Nepal, from 2,000 to 6,000 ft.; and *A. canarana*, Bth. and Hook. f., a tree of the Western Ghâts.

Wood hard, close-grained, red, with a darker coloured heartwood. Pores small to large, often subdivided, visible or prominent on a vertical section. In *A. Rohituka* the pores are joined by wavy concentric bands of soft texture.

1. **A. Rohituka,** W. and A.; Hook. Fl. Ind. i. 559; Beddome t. 132; Brandis 69; Kurz i. 220; Gamble 16. *Andersonia Rohituka,* Roxb. Fl. Ind. ii. 213. Vern. *Rohituka,* Sans.; *Harin harra, harin khana,* Hind.; *Sohága,* Oudh; *Tikta-raj, pitraj,* Beng.; *Bandriphal,* Nep.; *Tangarúk,* Lepcha; *Lota amari, amora amari,* Ass.; *Okhioungza, okhyang,* Magh.; *Chem-maram* Mal.; *Thitnee,* Burm.

An evergreen tree with thin grey bark. Wood reddish, close and even-grained, hard. Pores small and moderate-sized. Medullary rays moderately broad, uniform and equidistant, distinctly visible on a radial section. Pores joined by reddish, soft, wavy, concentric lines. The concentric bands in this species are remarkable, as they are absent from the two other species here described.

Oudh, Assam, Northern and Eastern Bengal, Western Gháts and Burma.

Average weight, 40·5 lbs. per cubic foot.

Wood good, but little used, in Chittagong canoes are sometimes made of it. In Bengal an oil is expressed from the seeds.

		lbs.
O 1362.	Gonda, Oudh	42
E 2331.	Mangwa, Darjeeling, 6,000 feet	36
E 1261.	Tezpúr, Assam	39
E 711.	Chittagong	45

2. **A. cucullata,** Roxb.; Hook. Fl. Ind. i. 560; Beddome lv.; Kurz i. 221. *Andersonia cucullata,* Roxb. Fl. Ind. ii. 212. Vern. *Amúr, latmi, natmi,* Beng.; *Thitnee,* Burm.

A moderate-sized evergreen tree, with thin grey bark. Wood red, hard, close-grained, but apt to split. Pores small and moderate-sized. Medullary rays very fine, uniform, very numerous.

Coasts of Bengal and Burma.

Weight, 44 lbs. per cubic foot. Wood used for posts and other purposes in Lower Bengal, and for firewood in the Sundarbans.

		lbs.
E 414.	Sundarbans	44

3. **A. spectabilis,** Miq.; Hook. Fl. Ind. i. 561; Kurz i. 221. Vern. *Amari,* Ass.

An evergreen tree. Wood red, hard, close-grained. Pores moderate-sized and large, often oval and subdivided, distinctly visible on a longitudinal section. Medullary rays fine, uniform, equidistant, prominent on a radial section, the distance between them less than the traverse diameter of the pores.

Eastern moist zone. Assam and Burma.

Average weight, 48·5 lbs. Wood durable; takes a good polish. Used for boat-building and furniture in Assam. This is probably Kyd's *Guarea (Amari).* Weight, 47 lbs. P = 792.

		lbs.
E 1255.	Tezpúr, Assam	49
E 2192.	Nowgong, Assam	48

5. WALSURA, Roxb.

B 1986 is a specimen collected by Kurz in the Andaman Islands in 1866, marked *Walsura robusta,* Roxb.; Hook. Fl. Ind. i. 565; Kurz. i. 223. Vern. *Upphing,* Sylhet; *Gyopho, tsoukmayba,* Burm. Wood light red, very hard. Pores small, joined by numerous, prominent, wavy, concentric lines. Medullary rays very fine, numerous. Weight, 63 lbs. per cubic foot.

Six other species of this genus occur in India: *W. tubulata*, Hiern.; Hook. Fl. Ind. i. 563, is a tree of Sikkim and the Khasia Hills; *W. ternata*, Roxb., occurs in the Circars and northern part of Madras; *W. piscidia*, Roxb. Fl. Ind. ii. 389; Hook. Fl. Ind. i. 563; Beddome lvi. Vern. *Walsura*, Tam.; *Wallursi*, Tel., is a small tree of South India with good wood and bark used to poison fish; *W. villosa*, Wall.; Hook. Fl. Ind. i. 564; Kurz. i. 223. Vern. *Gyobo*, Burm. and *W. pubescens*, Kurz, are evergreen trees of Burma; while *W. hypoleuca*, Kurz i. 224 and *W. oxycarpa*, Kurz i. 224 occur in the Andaman Islands.

6. CARAPA, Aubl.

1. C. moluccensis, Lam.; Hook. Fl. Ind. i. 567; Beddome t. 136. *C. obovata*, Bl.; Kurz i. 226. *Xylocarpus Granatum*, Kön. Vern. *Poshúr, dhundul*, Beng.; *Kandalanga*, Tam.; *Pinlayoung*, Burm.

A moderate-sized evergreen tree. Bark thin, grey, peeling off in regular flakes. Wood white, turning red on exposure, hard. Pores small, often in short radial lines. Medullary rays prominent, moderately broad, numerous, uniform and equidistant. Annual rings distinctly marked by a continuous line of pores.

Coasts of Bengal, Malabar, Burma and Ceylon.

Growth moderate, 6·6 rings per inch of radius. Weight, our specimens give 41 lbs.; Brandis, No. 24, Burma List, 1862, gives 47 lbs.; Wallich 47 lbs. Used in Burma for house posts, handles of tools and wheel spokes. Gives a clear, brown, brittle resin. The fruit yields an oil used for burning and for the hair.

		lbs.
E 402.	Sundarbans	41
B 2514.	Burma (1862)	42
B 2239.	Andamans (1866)	41

7. SWIETENIA, Linn.

1. S. Mahagoni, Linn.; Brandis 70. The Mahogany Tree.

A large evergreen tree. Heartwood reddish brown, seasons and works well, hard. Annual rings marked by a continuous line of pores. Pores moderate-sized, scanty, uniformly distributed, subdivided. Medullary rays very short, very numerous, moderately broad, uniform and equidistant.

Jamaica and Central America.

Cultivated in Bengal and as far north as Saharanpur. The tree was introduced into the Botanic Gardens at Calcutta in 1795 (plants from the West Indies), and although it was largely propagated by layers, no further new introductions were probably made until 1865, when about 8,000 seeds were sown in Calcutta by Dr. T. Anderson. A number of these seeds did not succeed, but in the end 460 plants were procured, three-fourths of which were planted in the Mohurgong Forest in the Darjeeling Terai, and the remainder at Calcutta. The plantation at Mohurgong was a failure, but the growth of mahogany at the Calcutta Botanic Gardens, and at other places in Bengal to which it was distributed, has been very satisfactory. The experiment is now being continued, both in Bengal and in Burma, and in time it may be hoped that the tree will be cultivated successfully as an adjunct to teak. In a report submitted to Government by Dr. T. Anderson, of 27th December 1866, he states that 3 trees presumably 73 years of age gave, at 4 feet from the ground, girths of 14 feet 3 inches, 12 feet 3 inches and 13 feet respectively, equivalent to a growth of 3·11 rings per inch of radius. In the great cyclone of 1864 a number of the trees originally introduced in 1795 were blown down; they had then, most of them, attained 12 feet in girth at 4 feet from the ground, and logs cut from them sold at 4½ to 5 annas per superficial foot one inch thick, or at about Rs. 3-6 per cubic foot.

The following measurements of Saharanpur trees are taken from an article in the *Indian Agriculturist*, of the 1st June 1876:—

Trees planted in 1827-28 measured in May 1873, at 3 feet from ground:—

No. 1	90 inches.	Height, 80 to 100 feet. Average girth, 88 inches.
„ 2	77 „	
„ 3	72 „	
„ 4	101 „	
„ 5	101 „	

Trees planted in 1839 measured in May 1873, at 3 feet from ground:—

No. 1	57 inches.	Height, 55 feet.
„ 2	40 „	„ 50 „

Trees planted in 1842-43 measured in May 1873, at 3 feet from ground:—

No. 1	40 inches.	Height, 50 to 70 feet.
„ 2	33 „	
„ 3	24 „	

The first five vary from 3 to 4 rings per inch of radius, averaging 3·41 rings.
„ second pair „ „ 4 to 6 „ „ „ „ 4·78 „
„ third three „ „ 5 to 8 „ „ „ „ 6·09 „

from which it would seem that the growth gets faster as the trees get older. As the 1827-28 and 1839 trees were from plants sent up from Calcutta, the age has been taken at 47 and 36 years respectively, the 1842-43 plants were from seedlings, and were consequently 30 years old. Taking the Calcutta and Saharanpur trees together, we have a mean growth of 4·94 rings per inch of radius as the mean of 13 trees, or an age of 58 years corresponding to a girth of 6 feet. The growth in Calcutta is much faster than this, as the Calcutta average gave 36 years corresponding to a girth of 6 feet.

The weight of Mahogany varies much. Tredgold gives for Honduras wood 35 lbs. and for Spanish Mahogany 53 lbs., and Fowke gives 52 lbs. as the weight of Jamaica mahogany. Our specimen cut from one of the trees destroyed in the 1864 cyclone gave 45 lbs. Tredgold gives for the value of P. for Honduras wood 637, for Spanish Mahogany 425; Fowke gives for Jamaica wood 546. Laslett's experiments give the following results:—

	Weight.	Value of P.
Cuba Mahogany, 6 experiments, bars 7′×2″×2″ (6 feet between supports)	48 lbs.	642
Honduras Mahogany, 6 experiments, bars 7′×2″ ×2″ (6 feet between supports)	41 „	601
Mexican Mahogany, 6 experiments, bars 7′×2″ ×2″ (6 feet between supports)	42 „	587

In Europe the wood is, perhaps, used more extensively than any other for furniture; it is also used in ship-building. On account of its rapid growth and the great value of its wood, the tree should be grown whenever practicable in the tropical regions of India. In the Calcutta market it fetches from 6½ to 8 annas per superficial foot of planking one inch thick; and in London from 4*d*. to 1*s*. 6*d*.

The difficulty in propagating Mahogany in India arises mainly from the want of seeds. In the Saharanpur gardens the trees, as stated above, have never seeded. As far as it is now known, one or two trees in private gardens near Barrackpore, and two or three trees belonging to Government on the Barrackpore road, have been seeding occasionally for many years past. One tree in the Barrackpore Park, and an old damaged and gnarled tree in the Calcutta Botanic Gardens, which, however, was blown down in the cyclone of 1864, have also seeded, but not freely. Whenever these trees did seed, the seeds have been regularly collected and sown.

All attempts to propagate the Mahogany by cuttings have failed. It has, however, been propagated to a considerable extent by means of layers, and trees raised from layers are believed to be much more likely to produce seed early than seedlings; but from their tendency to form low branching bushes, it is feared that they will not yield much valuable timber. It has, therefore, been found necessary to depend upon the West Indies for supplies of seed as yet, and for some years past supplies have been received and the seedlings regularly distributed, chiefly in Bengal.

	lbs.
E 1361. Calcutta Botanic Gardens	45

8. SOYMIDA, Adr. Juss.

1. S. febrifuga, Adr. Juss.; Hook. Fl. Ind. i. 567; Beddome t. 8; Brandis 71; Kurz i. 228. *Swietenia febrifuga,* Willd.; Roxb. Fl. Ind. ii. 398. Indian Red Wood. Vern. *Rohan,* Hind.; *Rohina,* Beng.; *Shem, wond,* Tam.; *Sumi,* Tel.; *Sohan,* Uriya; *Soimi,* Gondi; *Royta,* Bhil.

A large deciduous tree. Bark ⅓ to ½ inch thick, bluish grey or dark brown. Sapwood small, whitish; heartwood extremely hard and close-grained, reddish black, very durable. Pores moderate-sized, scanty. Medullary rays moderately broad, distinctly visible on a radial section as dark, shining, horizontal plates. Numerous fine, concentric lines of lighter colour, often closely packed and forming broader bands.

Central India and Dekkan.

Weight, according to Skinner, No. 117, and Fowke, 66 lbs.; R. Thompson gives 71, and Bombay specimens gave 76; Wallich (*Swietenia febrifuga*) 55 lbs.; our specimens give an average of 73·5 lbs. According to Skinner's experiments, the value of P is 1024, Fowke gives 626. The wood is durable. Skinner says that a piece taken out of the workshop at Fort Saint George, which had been erected in 1803 and pulled down in 1859, stood 1,232 lbs. without breaking a scantling 3' × 1⅛" × 1⅛." It is not much attacked by white ants. It is used for construction, well-work, ploughshares and oil-mills. The bark is bitter, and is used as a febrifuge and in diarrhœa and dysentery.

		lbs.
C 194.	Mandla, Central Provinces, 1871	73
C 1123.	Ahiri Reserve, Central Provinces	72
C 1240.	Gumsúr, Madras	74
D 2113.	Mysore	75

9. CHICKRASSIA, Adr. Juss.

Besides these species, Kurz describes *C. velutina,* Roemer. Vern. *Yimmah,* as occurring in Pegu.

1. C. tabularis, Adr. Juss.; Hook. Fl. Ind. i. 568; Beddome t. 9; Brandis 73; Kurz i. 227. *Swietenia Chickrassa,* Roxb. Fl. Ind. ii. 399. Chittagong Wood. Vern. *Chikrassi,* Beng.; *Boga poma,* Ass.; *Aglay, agal, eleutharay,* Tam.; *Madagari vembu,* Tel.; *Ganti malle,* Salem; *Dalmara,* Kan.; *Pabba,* Mar.; *Main,* Hyderabad; *Saiphra, sey barasi,* Magh; *Chegarasi* Chakma; *Yimmah, yengma,* Burm.; *Arrodah,* And.

A large tree. Bark reddish brown, deeply cracked. Heartwood hard, varying from yellowish brown to reddish brown, with a beautiful satin lustre, seasons and works well; sapwood of a lighter colour. Pores moderate-sized, often oval and subdivided, isolated, uniformly distributed. Medullary rays fine, uniform, mostly equidistant, slightly undulating; the distance between the rays generally equal to the transverse diameter of the pores. Annual rings distinctly marked by a sharp line.

Eastern Bengal, Assam, Chittagong, Burma and South India.

Growth, moderate, 8·6 rings per inch of radius. Weight, according to Skinner, No. 46, 42 lbs.; our specimens give an average of 45·5 lbs. Skinner's experiments give P = 614. The wood is used for furniture and for carving. The bark is a powerful astringent, and the flowers give a red or yellow dye.

		lbs.
E 1260.	Tezpúr, Assam	40
E 2197.	Nowgong, Assam	45
E 1401.	Chittagong	49
W 764.	South Kanara	43
W 1218.	North Kanara	44
B 2516.	Burma (1862)	52

10. CHLOROXYLON, DC.

1. C. Swietenia, DC.; Hook. Fl. Ind. i. 569; Beddome t. 11; Brandis 74. *Swietenia Chloroxylon,* Roxb. Fl. Ind. ii. 400. Satin Wood. Vern. *Behra, girya, behru, bihri,* C. P.; *Múdúdad,* Tam.; *Billu, bilgu,* Tel.; *Burús, purúsh,* Tam.; *Behru,* Uriya; *Halda, bheria,* Mar.; *Huragalu,* Mysore; *Burute, mal burute,* Cingh.

A moderate-sized deciduous tree. Bark $\frac{1}{8}$ inch thick, soft, spongy, light grey or yellow. Wood very hard, yellowish brown, the inner wood of a darker colour, but no distinct heartwood, with a beautiful satiny lustre, seasons well. Annual rings distinct. Pores very small. Medullary rays fine, uniform and equidistant, very numerous, distinctly visible on a radial section as shining irregularly-shaped plates; the distance between the rays is greater than the transverse diameter of the pores.

Central and South India and Ceylon.

Growth slow, 16 rings per inch of radius. The following experiments have been made to determine the weight and transverse strength:—

		Weight.	Value of P.
Baker, in 1829, with Madras wood, 3 experiments, with bars $6' \times 2'' \times 2''$	found	65 lbs.	744
A. Mendis, No. 8, with Ceylon wood, with bars $2' \times 1'' \times 1''$	„	55 „	1,042
A. Mendis, No. 52, with Ceylon wood, with bars $2' \times 1'' \times 1''$	„	57 „	504
Skinner, No. 47, with Madras wood	„	60 „	870
Puckle (Balfour, p. 317) with West Mysore wood, 3 experiments, with bars $2' \times 1'' \times 1''$ . . .	„		812
The Catalogue of the Paris Exhibition, 1862, Central Provinces wood, with bars $3' \times 1\frac{1}{2}'' \times 1\frac{1}{2}''$,	„	61 „	620 to 1,059
Wallich, No. 187, with Ceylon wood	„	51 „	...
Smythies in 1878 found the average of our specimens to give		57 „	...

The wood is used for agricultural implements, cart building, furniture and picture frames. In Madras it is prized for ploughs and oil-mills, and is found to stand well under water. It has been tried as a substitute for boxwood in engraving, but has not been found suitable; it is however good for turning. It is imported into England for cabinet work and the backs of brushes.

		lbs.
C 1153.	Ahiri, Central Provinces	54
C 1412.	Seoni, Central Provinces	49
C 2742.	Jamui, Berar	52
C 1239.	Gumsúr, Madras	56
C 1304.	„ „	56
D 1069.	North Arcot	61
No. 20.	Salem Collection	61
No. 8. No. 52.	Ceylon Collection	56

11. CEDRELA, Linn.

Besides these two species, Kurz gives *C. multijuga,* Kurz i. 228. Vern. *Toung da-ma,* as a large, rather rare, evergreen tree of Pegu.

Wood light, soft, red; no heartwood. Annual rings marked by a continuous belt of larger pores. Pores prominent on a vertical section. Medullary rays distant.

1. C. Toona, Roxb.; Hook. Fl. Ind. i. 568; Roxb. Fl. Ind. i. 635; Beddome t. 10; Brandis 72; Kurz i. 228; Gamble 16. The Toon Tree.

Vern. *Tún, túni, lím, maha ním*, Hind.; *Túni, tún, lúd*, Beng.; *Maha limbu*, Uriya; *Mahlun*, Satpuras; *Drawi*, Pb.; *Túni, bobich, labshi*, Nep.; *Simal*, Lepcha; *Poma, henduri poma*, Ass.; *Súli, máli*, Salem; *Kal kilingi*, Nilgiris; *Sandani vembu*, Tinnevelly; *Tundú, kempú gandagheri*, Kan.; *Nogé, belandi*, Coorg; *Deodari, kúruk*, Mar.; *Chikado, tseetkado*, Magh; *Shurúzbed*, Chakma; *Thitkado*, Burm.

A large tree. Bark thin, dark grey or reddish brown, exfoliating when old in irregular woody scales. Wood brick-red, soft, shining, even but open-grained, fragrant, seasons readily, does not split nor warp. Annual rings distinctly marked by a belt of large and numerous pores. Pores frequently double or subdivided, unequally distributed, scanty in the autumn wood, somewhat unequal in size, prominent on a vertical section; those in the spring wood larger. Medullary rays red, fine and moderately broad, uniform; the distance between the rays generally equal to the transverse diameter of the pores.

Sub-Himalayan forests, Bengal, Burma, South India; ascending in the North-West Himalaya to 3,000 feet, in Sikkim to 7,000 feet.

Growth rapid: Brandis says that in 1863 he measured the following trees on the Eastern Jumna Canal near Saharanpur:—

Age 30 years, girth 58 inches, mean of 6 trees.
„ 35 „ „ 86 „ „ 5 „ .

This would give a growth of 2½ to 3 rings per inch of radius, which is very fast. Our specimens shew a growth varying from 3 to 9 rings per inch of radius, shewing that some have come from fast-grown trees, while others have had only a moderate growth.

The weight and transverse strength have been determined by the following experiments:—

Experiment by whom conducted.	Year.	Wood whence procured.	Number of experiments.	Size of bar.	Weight.	Value of P.
				Ft. in. in.		
Clifford	1862	Bengal	...	6 × 2 × 2	34	369
Campbell	1831	Morung	1	6 × 2 × 2	35	423 (unseasoned).
Kyd	1831	Assam	2	2 × 1 × 1	33	465
Cunningham	1854	Gwalior	2	2 × 1 × 1	34	541
Skinner, No. 45	1862	Travancore	...	...	31	560
Baker	1829	Chittagong	3	6 × 2 × 2	40	550
Fowke	1859	...	...	......	35	420
Brandis, No. 25	1862	Burma	...	......	28	......
R. Thompson	1868	Central Provinces.	...	......	35	......
Wallich, Nos. 39 and 40	...	Assam & India	2	......	34	......
Hamilton	...	...	...	......	36	......
Smythies	1878	Different provinces.	17	......	35	......

The wood is durable and is not eaten by white ants; it is highly valued and universally used for furniture of all kinds, and is also employed for door panels and carving. From Burma it is exported under the name of 'Moulmein Cedar,' and as such is known in the English market. It there fetches about Rs. 65 per ton, the cost of cutting and delivery being Rs. 44, according to Major Seaton. In North-West India it is used for furniture, carvings and other purposes. In Bengal and Assam it is the chief wood for making tea-boxes, but is getting scarce on account of the heavy demand. The Bhutias use it for shingles and for wood carving, they also hollow it out for rice pounders. It is, or rather used to be, for very large trees are now rather scarce, hollowed out for dug-out canoes in Bengal and Assam. In Bengal, Assam and Burma it grows to a very large size, trees 20 feet girth with a height of 80 to 100 feet of clear stem being not uncommon in forests which have been only little worked like those in Dumsong and in some parts of the Chittagong Hill Tracts. At page 91 of the 'Indian Forester,' Vol. i., the cubic contents of 4 trees in the Reyang Valley, Darjeeling, are given as 211, 375, 720 and 400 cubic feet respectively; the third of these had a mean girth of 12 feet and a length of 80 feet, while the second had a girth of 20 feet. It is easily propagated from seed, but the seeds being very small and light, the seed-beds must be sheltered till the seedlings have well come on. It also coppices freely. The leaves are used to feed cattle, and the flowers yield a red or yellow dye (*Gulnari*). The bark is astringent and gives a resinous gum, it is also used as a febrifuge.

		lbs.
P 1191.	Madhopur, Punjab	35
H 8.	Simla, Punjab	37
H 5.	Sirmúr, Punjab	...
O 214.	Garhwal, 1868	36
C 177.	Mandla, Central Provinces, 1871	37
E 360.	Tukdah, Darjeeling, 5,000 ft.	34
E 2333.	Darjeeling, 6,000 ft.	34
E 655.	Bamunpokri, Darjeeling Terai	30
E 2332.	Sukna, Darjeeling, 2,000 ft.	36
E 640.	Kámrúp, Assam	44
E 1266.	Tezpúr, Assam	34
E 1229.	Sibságar, Assam	31
E 712.	Chittagong	...
D 1054.	Salem, Madras	39
W 763.	South Kanara	29
B 272.	Burma, 1867	35
B 803.	Tharrawaddi, Burma	38
No. 18.	Salem Collection	35
No. 19.	„ „ (marked *Chickrassia tabularis*)	37

2. C. serrata, Royle; Brandis 73; Kurz i. 229. *C. Toona*, Roxb.; Hook. Fl. Ind. i. 568 (in part). Vern. *Drawi, dalli, dâl, dauri, khishing, khinam*, N. W. Him.

A tree. Bark dark grey, ½ inch thick, with regular longitudinal furrows. Heartwood light-red, even, but open-grained, fragrant. Annual rings distinctly marked by broad belts of numerous large pores. Pores often double or divided into three compartments, unequal in size, and unequally distributed, very prominent on a vertical section, scanty and small in autumn wood, large and very numerous in spring wood. Medullary rays fine and moderately broad.

North-West Himalaya up to 8,000 ft.

Growth moderate, 10 rings per inch of radius, consequently slower than that of Toon.

Average weight, 31 lbs. per cubic foot. Wood used for many purposes about Simla, also for the hoops of sieves and for bridges. The shoots and leaves are lopped for cattle fodder.

		lbs.
H 3181.	Dúngagalli, Hazara, 6,000 ft.	...
H 920.	Hazara, Punjab, 6,000 ft.	38
H 897.	Murree, Punjab, 7,000 ft.	29
H 782.	Salán, Chamba, 5,000 ft.	28
H 25.	Matiyána, Simla, 7,000 ft.	31
H 430.	Deoban, Jaunsar, 5,500 ft.	30

B 505, sent from the Andaman Islands under the name of *Diospyros undulata*, Vern. *Thikado*, Burm.; *Pádá*, And., has a reddish, moderately hard, even-grained wood which seasons well. Pores large, scanty, often subdivided; very prominent on a vertical section. Medullary rays numerous, fine, uniform; the distance between the rays many times less than the transverse diameter of the pores. It evidently belongs to *Meliaceæ*, but cannot at present be identified.

ORDER XXVIII. CHAILLETIACEÆ.

An Order containing one Indian genus, *Chailletia*, with three species: *C. gelonioides*, Hook. f.; Hook. Fl. Ind. i. 570; Beddome lix.; Kurz i. 230 (*Moacurra gelonioides;* Roxb. Fl. Ind. ii. 69.) Vern. *Moakurra*, Beng., is a small tree of Eastern Bengal, South India and Burma; *C. Helferiana*, Kurz; and *C. longipetala*, Turcz (*C. macropetala*, Turcz; Kurz i. 231), are evergreen shrubs of Tenasserim.

ORDER XXIX. OLACINEÆ.

An Order which contains about 19 or 20 genera of Indian trees, shrubs or climbers, including about 40 species. They are chiefly found in the moist zones of Eastern Bengal, Burma and the Western Ghâts. But little is known of the qualities and uses of their wood.

The Order is divided into 4 Tribes, *viz.*:—

Tribe I.—Olaceæ	*Ximenia, Olax, Erythropalum, Strombosia, Anacolosa* and *Schöpfia.*
„ II.—Opilieæ	*Cansjera, Lepionurus* and *Opilia.*
„ III.—Icacineæ	*Gomphandra, Apodytes, Mappia, Daphniphyllopsis* and *Phlebocalymna.*
„ IV.—Phytocreneæ	*Phytocrene, Miquelia, Sarcostigma, Natsiatum* and *Iodes.*

Ximenia americana, Willd.; Hook. Fl. Ind. i. 574; Roxb. Fl. Ind. ii. 252; Kurz i. 232. Vern. *Uranechra*, Tel.; *Pinlaytsee*, Burm., is a straggling shrub of South India, Tenasserim and the Andamans, with a yellow wood said by Roxburgh to be sometimes used as a substitute for Sandal. Of *Erythropalum*, there are 3 species of climbing shrubs: *E. vagum*, Mast.; Hook. Fl. Ind. i. 578, of the Eastern Himalaya; *E. populifolium*, Mast.; Hook. Fl. Ind. i. 578, of Travancore; and *E. scandens*, Bl.; Hook. Fl. Ind. i. 578; Kurz i. 234; Gamble 18, of the North-East Himalaya, Khasia Hills, Eastern Bengal and Burma. *Strombosia* contains 2 large trees: *S. javanica*, Bl.; Hook. Fl. Ind. i. 579; Kurz i. 235, of Tenasserim, and *S. ceylanica*, Gardn.; Beddome t. 137, of the Western Ghâts. *Anacolosa* includes four trees: *A. densiflora*, Beddome t. 138, of the Anamalai Hills; *A. ilicoides*, Mast.; Hook. Fl. Ind. i. 580, of the Khasia Hills; *A. Griffithii*, Mast.; and *A. puberula*, Kurz i. 235, of Tenasserim and the Andamans. *Schöpfia fragrans*, Wall.; Hook. Fl. Ind. i. 581, is a small tree of Nepal and the Khasia Hills; and *S. acuminata*, Wall., of Assam, the Khasia Hills and Sylhet.

Cansjera Rheedii Gmelin; Hook. Fl. Ind. i. 582; Brandis 75; Beddome clxxix.; Kurz i. 237 (under Thymelæaceæ) (*C. scandens*, Roxb. Fl. Ind. i. 441), is a large evergreen climbing shrub of Oudh, Southern India and Burma. *Lepionurus oblongifolius*, Mast.; Hook. Fl. Ind. i. 583; Gamble 18 [*L. sylvestris*, Kurz ii. 330 (under Santalaceæ)] is a small tree of the North-East Himalaya and Eastern Bengal. *Opilia amentacea*, Roxb. Fl. Ind. ii. 87;. Hook. Fl. Ind. i. 583; Beddome lx.; Kurz i. 238 Vern. *Baleekoma*, Tel., is a scandent shrub or small tree of South India and Burma.

Of *Gomphandra*, there are two South Indian trees: *G. axillaris*, Wall.; and *G. polymorpha*, Wight; Beddome lxi.: while 3 species, *G. penangiana*, Wall.; *G. affinis*, Mast.; and *G. tomentella*, Mast, all under *Stemonurus* in Kurz i. 339,340, occur in Tenasserim. *Apodytes Benthamiana*, Wight; Beddome t. 140, is a tree of the Western Ghâts; and *A. andamanica*, Kurz i. 239, a tree of the Andaman Islands. *Mappia* contains 4 species from South India, *M. fœtida*, Miers; Beddome t. 141, being common on the Nilgiris. *Phlebocalymna* (*Gonocaryum*, Miq. in Kurz i. 240-241) contains 2 Burmese trees.

Phytocrene gigantea, Wall.; Hook. Fl. Ind. i. 591; Kurz i. 241, is a gigantic climber of the forests of Chittagong and Burma, whose stem on being cut gives out a quantity of fresh water good for drinking; the structure of its wood is very curious. Of *Miquelia*, there are two climbing shrubs: *M. Kleinii*, Meissn., of Assam; and *M. dentata*, Beddome, of the Anamalai Hills. *Sarcostigma* and *Iodes* contain also climbing shrubs of little interest. *Natsiatum herpeticum*, Ham.; Hook. Fl. Ind. i. 595; Kurz i. 242; Gamble 18. Vern. *Sungoo*, Lepcha, is a common climber throughout Eastern Bengal and Burma.

1. OLAX, Linn.

Contains six species, of which, besides the one described, one is found in Southern India, *O. Wightiana*, Wall.; Beddome lx.; one, *O. acuminata*, Wall., in Eastern Bengal; two in Chittagong and Tenasserim; and one, *O. nana*, Wall.; Brandis 75, in the valleys of the North-West Himalaya.

1. O. scandens, Roxb. Fl. Ind. i. 163; Hook. Fl. Ind. i. 575; Brandis 75; Kurz i. 233. Vern. *Dheniani*, Hind.; *Koko-aru*, Beng.; *Kurpodur, murki malle, turka-vepa*, Tel.; *Harduli, urchirri*, Mar.; *Lailoo*, Burm.

A large rambling shrub, sometimes a climber. Bark grey, ¼ inch thick. Wood porous, yellowish white, soft. Pores numerous, large and moderately sized, uniformly distributed, often oval. Medullary rays fine, numerous, not prominent.

Sub-Himalayan tract in Kumaun, Behar, Central and South India, Burma.

Weight, 38 lbs. per cubic foot. The fruit is used in Hazáribágh for making sherbet.

		lbs.
C 1184.	Ahiri Reserve, Central Provinces	40
C 2762.	Moharli " " "	36

2. DAPHNIPHYLLOPSIS, Kurz.

1. D. capitata, Kurz in Journal As. Soc. Calc., 1875, p. 201; For. Fl. B. Burma i. 240; Gamble 18. *Ilex daphniphylloides*, Kurz; Hook. Fl. Ind. i. 606. Vern. *Kalay, chilauni*, Nep.; *Tumbrúng*, Lepcha.

A large tree. Wood grey, soft, even-grained. Pores small, often in short radial lines between the fine and very numerous straight medullary rays.

Forests of the Sikkim Himalaya above 5,000 feet, and of Martaban between 4,000 and 6,000 feet.

Weight, 39 lbs. per cubic foot.

Used for house-building and other purposes about Darjeeling.

		lbs.
E 695.	Chuttockpur, Darjeeling, 6,000 feet	39

ORDER XXX. ILICINEÆ.

An Order containing only one Indian genus.

1. ILEX, Linn.

A genus of 21 Indian species, of which 11 are found in the Eastern Himalaya and Khasia Hills, 3 in the North-West Himalaya, 6 in Burma, and 4 in South India.

The following list is taken from the Flora Indica, pp. 598 to 606:—

1. *I. insignis*, Hook. f.	Sikkim, 7,000 feet.
2. *I. dipyrena*, Wall.	Himalaya, Simla to Sikkim.
3. *I. odorata*, Ham.	" Simla to Nepal.
4. *I. malabarica*, Beddome	Western Ghâts.
5. *I. Walkeri*, Wight and Arn.; Beddome lxii. .	" "

6. *I. denticulata*, Wall.	Western Gháts.
7. *I. theæfolia*, Wall.	Sikkim, Khasia, Tenasserim.
8. *I. embelioides*, Hook. f.	Khasia Hills.
9. *I. Griffithii*, Hook. f.	Assam, Sylhet.
10. *I. Thomsoni*, Hook. f.	Eastern Himalaya, Khasia.
11. *I. intricata*, Hook. f.	Eastern Nepal and Sikkim, 10,000 to 11,000 feet.
12. *I. fragilis*, Hook. f.	Eastern Himalaya, Khasia.
13. *I. venulosa*, Hook. f.	Khasia Hills.
14. *I. Gardneriana*, Wight; Beddome lxii.	Nilgiris.
15. *I. Wightiana*, Wall.	"
16. *I. excelsa*, Wall.	Himalaya, Khasia.
17. *I. Godajam*, Colebr.	Eastern Sub-Himalaya, Burma.
18. *I. sulcata*, Wall. (*I. Godajam*, Kurz i. 245, *part*)	Tenasserim.
19. *I. macrophylla*, Wall.; Kurz i. 246	"
20. *I. cymosa*, Bl.; Kurz i. 246	"
21. *I. Wallichii*, Hook. f.; Kurz i. 246	"

I. excelsa, Wall.; Hook. Fl. Ind. i. 603 (*I. exsulca*, Wall.; Brandis 76). Vern. *Túmari*, Hind., is a small evergreen tree of the outer Himalaya and Siwalik tract extending eastwards to Assam and the Khasia Hills. *I. odorata*, Ham.; Brandis 77, is an evergreen tree of the outer Himalaya from the Sutlej to Sikkim, ascending to 6,000 feet. *I. Godajam*, Colebr.; Kurz i. 245; Gamble 18. Vern. *Tirsam*, Ass., is a good-sized tree of the Sub-Himalayan tract from Nepal eastwards. *I. denticulata*, Wall.; Beddome t. 142, with a good timber, which is said not to warp nor crack, is found in the Nilgiris and Anamalai Hills. *I. Wightiana*, Wall. Vern. *Horralu*, Nilgiris, has a pale yellow wood useful for building and for bowls and platters. The European Holly is *I. Aquifolium*, Linn., while the Maté or Paraguay Tea is made from the leaves of *I. paraguayensis*.

Pores small, arranged in radial lines or irregular elongated patches. Medullary rays of two classes, fine and broad, prominent on a vertical section, and generally darker coloured than the fibrous tissue, giving the wood a mottled appearance.

1. I. dipyrena, Wall.; Hook. Fl. Ind. i. 599; Brandis 76; Gamble 18. Vern. *Shangala, kandlar, kalúcho, diúsa, dodru, drúnda*, Pb.; *Kaula, karaput, munasi, gulsima*, Nep.; *Kandara, kadera, kateru*, Simla.

A small evergreen tree. Bark dark, rough. Wood white, hard, close-grained. Pores extremely small, in long irregular wavy radial lines. Medullary rays short, moderately broad to broad, prominent on a radial section, giving the wood a mottled appearance.

Himalaya, from the Indus to Bhutan, above 5,000 feet.
Weight, 46 lbs. per cubic foot.

		lbs.
H 21.	Matiyána, Simla, 7,000 feet	46

2. I. theæfolia, Wall.; Hook. Fl. Ind. i. 601. *I. gaultheriæfolia*, Kurz i. 245.

A moderate-sized evergreen tree. Wood white, soft, close-grained, with white concentric lines, which seem to correspond to annual rings. Pores very small and numerous. Medullary rays very fine and broad; the latter short, scanty, prominent, giving the wood on a vertical section a beautifully reticulate appearance.

Darjeeling and Khasia Hills and Tenasserim.
Weight, 39 lbs. per cubic foot.

		lbs.
E 692.	Chuttockpur, Darjeeling, 6,000 feet	39

3. I. insignis, Hook. f.; Hook. Fl. Ind. i. 599; Gamble 18. Vern. *Lasuni,* Nep.

A small evergreen tree, with smooth grey bark. Wood white, soft, close-grained. Pores very small, numerous, often in radial lines. Medullary rays very fine and broad, the latter longer than in *I. theæfolia,* prominent on a radial section, giving the wood a mottled appearance.

Darjeeling, above 6,000 feet.

Weight, 40 lbs. In winter it has clusters of bright red berries like common holly, and is used for similar purposes of decoration.

	lbs.
E 355. Gumpahar Forest, Darjeeling, 7,000 feet	40

H 256, from the Garhwal Hills, is a specimen sent by Mr. R. Thompson in 1868. It has been much eaten by insects, but shews a structure similar to that of *I. insignis.* We refer it to *I. odorata,* Ham. Weight, 32 lbs. per cubic foot.

ORDER XXXI. CELASTRINEÆ.

An Order of trees, shrubs and climbers, sometimes thorny, and recognised by the flowers having a conspicuous disk. It contains 13 genera, 4 of which are found in North-West India, and the remainder in the Eastern and Western moist zones.

The Order is divided into 2 Tribes, the first being subdivided into 3. These are—

Tribe I.—Celastreæ

Sub-Tribe	I.—Euonymeæ . .	*Euonymus, Glyptopetalum, Microtropis, Lophopetalum* and *Pleurostylia.*
„	II.—Celastreæ . .	*Celastrus, Gymnosporia* and *Kurrimia.*
„	III.—Elæodendreæ . .	*Elæodendron.*

Tribe II.—Hippocrateæ . . . . . . *Hippocratea, Salacia* and *Siphonodon.*

Glyptopetalum contains 3 shrubs or small trees, of which *G. zeylanicum,* Thw. and *G. grandiflorum,* Beddome lxv., are large shrubs of the Western Ghâts; and *G. sclerocarpum* (*Euonymus sclerocarpus,* Kurz i. 250), with a white, close-grained wood, of the Pegu Yoma. *Microtropis* contains 7 species, of which 4 occur in Southern India, 3 in Burma, and 2 in the Eastern Himalaya and Eastern Bengal. The chief species is *M. discolor,* Wall.; Hook. Fl. Ind. i. 614; Kurz i. 251; Gamble 18. (*Euonymus garcinifolia,* Roxb. Fl. Ind. i. 628) Vern. *Suglim,* Lepcha; *Mori,* Sylhet. *Pleurostylia Wightii,* W. and A., Hook. Fl. Ind. i. 617, is a small tree of Southern India. *Kurrimia* contains 3 trees, of which *K. paniculata,* Wall.; Hook. Fl. Ind. i. 622 (*Trochisandra indica,* Beddome t. 120), is a handsome tree of the Anamalai Hills, said to yield a good timber, and *K. pulcherrima,* Wall. (*K. robusta,* Kurz i. 253) Vern. *Kwaydouk,* Burm., an evergreen tree of Burma with a brown, heavy, close-grained wood. *Hippocratea* contains 6 species of climbing shrubs, of which two, *H. indica,* Willd. Vern. *Kurzati,* Bombay; and *H. arborea,* Roxb. Fl. Ind. i. 167; Brandis 83. Vern. *Katha-paharia,* Beng., reach to Northern India. *Salacia* contains also 14 species of climbing shrubs, of which 8 occur in Burma and 6 in South India: while *Siphonodon celastrineus,* Griff., Hook. Fl. Ind. i, 629; Kurz i. 254. Vern. *Myoukopshit,* is an evergreen tree of Burma, with a pale yellowish heavy wood.

Wood even-grained, not very hard; generally without heartwood (except *Elæodendron*). Pores uniformly distributed, very or extremely small. Medullary rays very fine, very numerous.

1. EUONYMUS, Linn.

A genus of about 24 Indian species, of which many are merely small shrubs or climbers. About 11 occur in the Eastern Himalaya, Assam and Eastern Bengal, 5 in the North-West Himalaya, 5 in Burma and 7 in South India. Among them, *E. crenulatus*, Wall.; Hook. Fl. Ind. i. 608; Beddome t. 144, of the Nilgiris, and *E. glaber*, Roxb. Fl. Ind. i. 628; Hook. Fl. Ind. i. 609; Kurz i. 248, of Chittagong and Burma, may be mentioned as most important. *E. echinatus*, Wall.; Hook. Fl. Ind. i. 611; Brandis 80; Gamble 18, is a small climbing or epiphytic shrub of the Himalaya from the Jhelum to Sikkim at 7,000 to 12,000 feet. The wood of some species may be worth trying as a substitute for boxwood.

Wood compact, even-grained, white. Pores very or extremely small. Medullary rays very fine and very numerous.

The first four species here described are common in the North-West Himalaya, and may thus be distinguished:—

Leaves membranous	Leaves deeply cut	. *E. lacerus.*
	„ slightly cut	. *E. Hamiltonianus.*
Leaves coriaceous	Leaves long, sharply serrate .	. *E. pendulus.*
	„ short, obtusely serrate .	. *E. tingens.*

1. E. lacerus, Ham.; Brandis 78. *E. grandiflorus*, Wall.; Hook. Fl. Ind. i. 608. Vern. *Siki, pattali, papar, banchír, dudhapár, hanchu, pásh, mara, chíkan, rangchúl, kioch*, Punjab; *Gule, grui*, Simla.

A small deciduous tree with smooth grey bark. Wood white, moderately hard, exceedingly compact, close and even-grained. Annual rings visible, but not very distinct. Pores extremely small, barely visible under the lens. Medullary rays extremely fine.

Himalaya, from the Indus to Sikkim, between 6,000 and 11,000 feet.

Weight, 48 lbs. per cubic foot. Wood used for carving. The seeds are strung as beads in Bassahir and used for necklaces.

		lbs.
H 67.	Nagkanda, Simla, 9,000 feet	48
H 2883.	„ „ „	46
H 3011.	„ „ „	49
H 3187.	Dungagalli, Hazara, 8,000 feet	...

2. E. Hamiltonianus, Wall.; Hook. Fl. Ind. i. 612; Brandis 78. *E. atropurpureus*, Roxb. Fl. Ind. i. 627. Vern. *Siki, singi, chual, walal, papar, rithu, randi, brahmáni, banchor, karún, skioch, sidhera, naga*, Pb.; *Agniun, agnu*, Kumaun.

A large deciduous shrub, or small or occasionally moderate-sized tree. Bark thick, grey, corky, with deep irregular fissures. Wood white, with a slight yellow tinge, soft, close-grained. Annual rings marked by a narrow belt of firm wood with fewer pores.

Outer Himalaya, from the Indus to Bhutan, Khasia Hills, from 4,000 to 8,000 feet.

Weight, 35 lbs. Wood used for carving into spoons.

		lbs.
H 3173.	Dungagalli, Hazara, 8,000 feet	...
H 919.	Hazára, Punjab, 8,000 feet	36
H 172.	Murree, Punjab (1866), 7,000 feet	...
H 778.	Kalatop Forest, Punjab, 7,000 feet	34
H 2897. H 3012.	Nagkanda, Simla, 9,000 feet	44

3. E. pendulus, Wall.; Hook. Fl. Ind. i. 612; Brandis 79. Vern. *Chopra, pincha, garúr, kúnku*, N.-W. P.

A moderate-sized evergreen tree with grey, rather corky bark, ¼ inch thick. Wood white, moderately hard, compact, with a light red tinge, very close and even-grained. Annual rings marked by an almost continuous line of pores. Pores very small, very numerous. Medullary rays extremely fine, very numerous.

Himalaya, from the Jhelum to Nepal, between 2,500 and 7,500 feet.
Weight, 35 to 41 lbs. per cubic foot.

		lbs.
H 86.	The Glen, Simla, 6,000 feet	35
H 2837.	" " " " "	41

4. E. tingens, Wall.; Hook. Fl. Ind. i. 610; Brandis 79. Vern. *Kungku,* N.-W. P.; *Newar, kasúri,* Nepal; *Chopra, mer mahaul,* Simla.

A small evergreen tree with dark, rather corky outside and yellow inner bark. The structure and appearance of the wood are the same as in *Euonymus lacerus,* except that the wood of this species has a slightly reddish tinge.

Himalaya, from the Sutlej to Nepal, between 6,500 and 10,000 feet.
Weight, 47 lbs. per cubic foot. This is easily recognised from the other 3 species by its large flowers with pretty brown markings on the petals.

		lbs.
H 32.	Madhan, Simla, 7,000 feet	48
H 2844.	Mahasu, Simla, 8,000 feet	46
H 2881.	Nagkauda, Simla, 8,000 feet	...

5. E. theæfolius, Wall.; Hook. Fl. Ind. i. 612; Gamble 18.

A shrub with wood of structure similar to the rest, but the medullary rays are somewhat broader and the annual rings more distinct.

E 3308. Rangbúl, Darjeeling, 7,500 feet.

2. LOPHOPETALUM, Wight.

A genus containing 7 species of Indian trees, of which 6 are Burmese, 1 from Northern and Eastern Bengal, and 1 from South India. *L. fimbriatum,* Wight, is a tall cylindrical-stemmed tree of the valleys of the Sikkim Himalaya, Sylhet and Tenasserim; and *L. floribundum,* Wight, is a tree of Tenasserim.

Wood light, soft to moderately hard, even-grained, somewhat shining. Pores small to moderate-sized. Medullary rays very fine, very numerous, traversed by concentric bands of softer texture.

1. L. littorale, Kurz i. 255. *Kokoona littoralis,* Lawson; Hook. Fl. Ind. i. 617. Vern. *Moondein,* Burm.

A tree. Wood grey, moderately hard, even-grained. Pores small and moderate-sized, often oval and subdivided. Medullary rays very fine, uniform and equidistant, very numerous; the distance between the rays much less than the transverse diameter of the pores. Medullary rays traversed by numerous parallel, concentric, wavy lines, which have the appearance of interrupting the rays, thus forming a succession of wavy, concentric bands.

Pegu and Tenasserim.
Weight, on an average, 35 lbs. per cubic foot.

		lbs.
B 278.	Burma (1867)	27
B 2513.	" (1862)	36
B 2300.	Andaman Islands (1866)	41

2. L. Wightianum, Arn.; Hook. Fl. Ind. i. 615,; Beddome t. 145. Vern. *Bolpalé*, Kan.

A large evergreen tree. Wood reddish grey, moderately hard, close-grained, structure similar to that of *L. littorale.* Pores somewhat larger, and less numerous. Medullary rays prominent on a radial section.

Western coast from the Konkan to Cape Comorin.

Weight, 28 to 29 lbs. per cubic foot. The wood is much esteemed in South Kanara where it is used for house-building.

		lbs.
W 723.	South Kanara	29
W 853.	" "	28

3. L. Wallichii, Kurz i. 255; Hook. Fl. Ind. i. 615. Vern. *Mong-taing, moondein*, Burm.

To this species we refer B 1947 (31 lbs.) sent from Tavoy under the name *Kanazo-ta-loo*, Burm., and B 2248 sent in 1866 from the Andamans under the name of *Toung-hmayo.* The structure is similar to that of *L. littorale*, but the pores are more scanty, moderate-sized and arranged in short radial lines. Medullary rays less numerous, slightly broader, and not of uniform width.

The wood is moderately hard; it is recommended by Kurz for furniture. It is said by Major Ford to be used in the Andamans for writing-boards, and the bark, root and fruit as a febrifuge.

3. CELASTRUS, Linn.

This genus includes 2 of the genera of the Flora Indica, *Celastrus* and *Gymnosporia;* of the former 4, of the latter 15, species are described. The 4 species of the section *Celastrus* contain, besides *C. paniculatus*, common to most parts of India, 3 scandent shrubs of Sikkim, Assam and Eastern Bengal. The species of the section *Gymnosporia* are chiefly erect shrubs, often thorny, chiefly of the Eastern Himalaya and the Western Ghâts. The only species of interest are those here described.

Wood close-and even-grained. Pores small or very small. Medullary rays very fine and very numerous. Most species have concentric bands of soft tissue. This does not include *C. paniculatus*, which has the structure of a climber.

1. C. paniculatus, Willd.; Hook. Fl. Ind. i. 617; Roxb. Fl. Ind. i. 621; Brandis 82; Gamble 18. Vern. *Mál kakni*, Oudh, Kumaun; *Kahundan, rangul, wahrangur*, C. P.; *Kanguni*, Bombay; *Ruglim*, Lepcha.

A scandent shrub, with yellow, corky bark. Wood pinkish yellow, soft. Annual rings distinctly marked by very large pores in the spring wood, which diminish in size, and are small in the autumn wood. Medullary rays very broad.

Outer Himalaya from the Jhelum to Assam ascending to 4,000 feet, Eastern Bengal, Behar, South India and Burma.

The seeds give an oil, which is used medicinally, as are also the leaves.

		lbs.
E 2334.	Tukdah, Darjeeling, 5,000 feet	51

2. C. spinosus, Royle; Brandis 80. *Gymnosporia Royleana*, Wall.; Hook. Fl. Ind. i. 620. Vern. *Dzaral*, Trans-Indus; *Kandu, kandiári, pataki, lei, phulpari, badlo, kadewar*, Pb.; *Kúra, bagriwála darim, gwála darim*, N.-W. P.

A thorny shrub, with thin, grey, corky bark. Wood lemon-coloured, hard and close-grained, with numerous white, concentric bands. Pores very small. Medullary rays very fine, very numerous. It cuts like boxwood, for which it may become a substitute.

Outer North-West Himalaya.
Weight, 49 lbs. The wood deserves attention as possibly suitable for carving and engraving.

		lbs.
P 913.	Salt Range, Punjab	49
P 2932.	Suni, Simla, 3,000 feet	49

3. C. senegalensis, Lam.; Beddome lxvi.; Brandis 81; Kurz i. 252. *C. montana,* Roxb. Fl. Ind. i. 620. *Gymnosporia montana,* Lawson; Hook. Fl. Ind. i. 621. Vern. *Sherawane,* Trans-Indus; *Talkar, dajkar, mareila, kingaro, kharái,* Pb.; *Baikal, gajachinni,* C. P.; *Mál kangoni,* Bombay; *Danta, babur,* Gondi; *Dhatti,* Bhíl; *Bharatti, yekal,* Mar.; *Danti, dantáusi, pedda chintú,* Tel.

A tall spinescent shrub. Bark $\frac{1}{8}$ inch thick, grey, with longitudinal cracks, exfoliating in small scales. Wood pinkish white, soft but close-grained; no heartwood; no annual rings. Pores small, numerous, uniformly distributed. Medullary rays very fine, very numerous. Faint concentric bands.

Northern dry and intermediate zones. North-West India, ascending to 4,000 feet, Central India and the drier parts of the Peninsula.
Weight, 46 lbs. per cubic foot. Wood durable, but not used. The leaves are used for fodder, and the branches as dunnage for the roofs of houses.

		lbs.
C 1162.	Ahiri Reserve, Central Provinces	...
C 2752.	Mohârli " " "	46

4. ELÆODENDRON, Jacq. fil.

1. E. Roxburghii, W. and A.; Beddome t. 148; Brandis 82; Gamble 19. *E. glaucum,* Pers.; Hook. Fl. Ind. i. 623; Roxb. Fl. Ind. i. 638. *Neerija dichotoma,* Roxb. Fl. Ind. i. 646. Vern. *Mirandu, padriún, bakra, janwa,* Pb.; *Bakra, shauria, chauli, daberi, mámri,* N.-W. P.; *Chauri, metkúr,* Oudh; *Chikyeng,* Lepcha; *Jamrási, kala mukha, rohi,* C. P.; *Dhakka, nisur,* Gondi; *Niru,* Kurku; *Aran, tamruj,* Mar.; *Bata karas,* Bhíl; *Karkava, irkuli, selupa, siri,* Tam.; *Nirija, neradi, botanskam, kanemis, bootigi,* Tel.; *Bhutrakshi,* Hyderabad; *Nerrelu,* Cingh.

A tree. Bark $\frac{1}{8}$ inch thick, grey, often blackish, exfoliating in 4-sided very small scales. Wood moderately hard, even- and close-grained, works and polishes well, light brown, often with a red tinge; the outer wood white, but no distinct sapwood; no annual rings. Numerous, wavy, concentric, lighter-coloured bands. Pores small, numerous. Medullary rays fine, very numerous, visible on a radial section.

Sub-Himalayan tract from the Ravi eastwards, Central and South India.
Weight, 40 to 50 lbs. (Brandis); 46 (Skinner and Fowke); 53 (R. Thompson); 40 (C. P. List); our specimens give an average of 53 lbs. Skinner, No. 65, gives P = 513; Fowke P = 511.
The wood is often beautifully curled and flaked; it is used for cabinet work, combs and picture frames. The root is said to be a specific against snake-bite, and the bark is used in native medicine, said to be a virulent poison.

		lbs.
O 235.	Garhwal (1868)	56
O 2991.	„ (1874)	48
C 183.	Mandla, Central Provinces (1870)	50
C 1182.	Abiri Reserve, Central Provinces	55
C 2781.	Melghát, Berar	49
E 2335.	Bamunpokri, Darjeeling Terai	57
No. 63.	Ceylon Collection	56

ORDER XXXII. RHAMNEÆ.

Contains twelve Indian genera, of which six are climbing or straggling shrubs and the remainder shrubs or small trees. The Order is subdivided into four Tribes:—

Tribe I.—Ventilagineæ . . . . *Ventilago* and *Smythea*.
„ II.—Zizypheæ . . . . *Zizyphus* and *Berchemia*.
„ III.—Rhamneæ . . . . *Rhamnus*, *Hovenia*, *Scutia*, *Sageretia*, and *Colubrina*.
„ IV.—Gouanieæ . . . . *Apteron*, *Gouania*, and *Helinus*.

Of the genera not here described, *Smythea* and *Apteron* are scandent shrubs of Tenasserim. *Hovenia dulcis*, Thunb.; Hook. Fl. Ind. i. 640; Roxb. Fl. Ind. i. 630; Brandis 94. Vern. *Chamhún*, Punjab, is a tree commonly cultivated throughout the Himalaya, with a light-coloured, coarse and open-grained wood, and an edible fruit with a flavour like that of the Bergamot Pear. *Scutia indica*, Brongn.; Hook. Fl. Ind. i. 640; Kurz i. 268, is a straggling shrub of Burma and South India. *Colubrina* contains three species, of which *Colubrina asiatica*, Brongn.; Hook. Fl. Ind. i. 642; Beddome lxix.; Kurz i. 268. (*Ceanothus asiaticus*, Roxb. Fl. Ind. i. 615.) Vern. *Kway-nway*, Burm., is a large shrub of the coast forests of Burma and Malabar. *Gouania* contains three climbing shrubs, commonest among which is *G. leptostachya*, DC.; Hook. Fl. Ind. i. 643; Kurz i. 269; Gamble 19. Vern. *Kalalag*, Kumaun; *Batwasi*, Nep.; *Khauta*, Orissa; *Tayounyonway*, Burm., a large climber of the Eastern Himalaya, Burma and South India. *Helinus lanceolatus*, Brandis 574, is a slender twining shrub of the outer North-West Himalaya, ascending to 4,000 feet.

Wood hard or moderately hard. Pores small or moderate-sized. Medullary rays fine or very fine, numerous, equidistant.

1. ZIZYPHUS, Juss.

A genus containing 13 Indian species, 7 of which come from Northern and Central India, about 6 from South India, 4 from Burma, and 6 from the North-East Himalaya and Assam. Six species are here described. Of the remainder, the chief is *Z. vulgaris*, Lamk.; Hook. Fl. Ind. i. 633; Roxb. Fl. Ind. i. 609; Brandis 85. Vern. *Sinjli*, *simli*, *ban*, *ber*, *kandika*, *kandiári*, Hind., a small tree of the arid and northern dry zones. It is found in the outer Himalaya from the Indus to the Ravi, ascending to 6,500 feet, cultivated in the Punjab, Beluchistan, and Bengal, and semi-wild as far as Italy and the south of France—*Mathieu Fl. For.* p. 60. Its fruit is eaten.

Wood reddish, moderately hard or hard; no heartwood. Pores small to moderate-sized, often subdivided, between numerous fine or very fine medullary rays, the distance between the rays being less than the diameter of the pores.

1. Z. Jujuba, Lam.; Hook. Fl. Ind. i. 632; Roxb. Fl. Ind. i. 608; Beddome t. 149; Brandis 86; Kurz i. 266; Gamble 19. Vern. *Bér*, *baer*, *beri*, Hind.; *Kúl*, *bér*, Beng.; *Zeeben*, Burm.; *Rengha*, *regi*, Tel.; *Yellande*, Tam.; *Bhor*, Mar.; *Renga*, Bhíl; *Elentha*, Mal.; *Yelchi*, Kan.

A moderate-sized deciduous tree, almost evergreen. Bark ⅓ inch thick, dark grey, nearly black, with long, deep, irregular cracks. Wood hard, reddish; no heartwood; no annual rings. Pores small or moderate-sized, scanty, often oval and subdivided. Medullary rays fine and very numerous, uniform and equidistant; the distance between two rays much less than the transverse diameter of the pores. Pores frequently joined by very fine, wavy, interrupted, concentric lines.

Cultivated throughout India and Burma. Its original habitat doubtful.

Weight, according to Skinner, No. 135, 58 lbs.; Cunningham, 57 lbs.; our specimens give from 43 to 52 lbs. Cunningham gives the value of P as 495; Skinner 672.

Wood used for saddletrees and agricultural implements, oil-mills, and other purposes. The fruit is commonly eaten and is much improved by cultivation.

		lbs.
O 265.	Garhwal (1868)	...
C 2815.	Melghát, Berar	...
C 1128.	Ahiri Reserve, Central Provinces	43
D 1071.	North Arcot, Madras	52

P 885, from Multán, sent under the name of *Z. flexuosa*, has the same structure as *Z. Jujuba*, but the pores are round and moderate-sized. Weight, 48 lbs.

2. **Z. nummularia**, W. and A.; Hook. Fl. Ind. i. 633; Beddome lxix.; Brandis 88. *Z. microphylla*, Roxb. Fl. Ind. i, 613. Vern. *Karkanna*, Afgh.; *Malla, bér, birár, jhari, kanta*, N.-W. P.; *Gangr, jangra*, Sind; *Parpaili gidda*, Kan.

A thorny shrub with grey bark. Wood yellow, hard, compact. Structure similar to that of *Z. Jujuba*, except that the pores are larger and the medullary rays are somewhat further apart; the distance between the rays is less than the transverse diameter of the pores.

Drier parts of North-West India and the Dekkan.

Growth: No. P 2931 shews well-marked annual rings and a fast growth of 2 to 3 rings per inch of radius. Weight, 43 lbs. per cubic foot on an average. It is used to make fences round fields and gardens. The leaves are threshed out and used as fodder for sheep and goats. The fruit is eaten.

		lbs.
P 2931.	Bhajji, Simla, 3,000 feet	41
P 3077. P 3093.	Sabathu, Punjab, 3,000 feet	42
P 442.	Ajmere	46

3. **Z. oxyphylla**, Edgw.; Hook. Fl. Ind. i. 634; Brandis 86. Vern. *Kúrkun bér*, Afgh.; *Pilni, Kokan ber, amlái, amnia, beri, shamor*, Pb.; *Giggar*, N.-W. P.

A thorny shrub with thin brown bark. Wood white, moderately hard. Pores small, somewhat larger and more numerous on the inner edge of each annual ring. Medullary rays equidistant, very fine; the distance between the rays equal to the diameter of the pores.

Outer Himalaya from the Indus to the Ganges from 2,000 to 6,000 feet.

H 2947. Suni, Sutlej Valley, 3,000 feet.

4. **Z. Œnoplia**, Mill.; Hook. Fl. Ind. i. 634; Beddome lxix.; Brandis 86; Kurz i. 266. *Z. Napeca*, Roxb. Fl. Ind. i. 612. Vern. *Makai*, Hind.; *Shyakúl*, Beng.; *Barokoli*, Uriya; *Irún*, C. P.; *Paranu, paramie, porki*, Tel.; *Tauzeenway*, Burm.

A straggling or climbing shrub with rough, dark-grey bark. Wood reddish with the structure of a climber. Concentric bands consisting of a great mass of moderate-sized to large pores, often subdivided, between closely packed medullary rays, which bend outwards where they touch the pores, presenting a reticulate appearance.

Bengal, Burma, Central and Southern India.
Used for hedges. The fruit is eaten.
C 2753. Moharli Reserve, Central Provinces.

5. Z. xylopyra, Willd.; Hook. Fl. Ind. i. 634; Roxb. Fl. Ind. i. 611; Beddome lxviii.; Brandis 90. Vern. *Kat-ber, béri, goti, gotaha, kakor, chittania, sitabér, ghónt,* Hind.; *Goti,* Tel.; *Goti, bhorgoli,* Mar.; *Challe,* Kan.

A large scrambling shrub. Bark grey or reddish brown. Wood yellowish brown, hard. Pores small and moderate-sized, in patches of soft tissue which are often confluent, forming oblique bands. Medullary rays fine, equidistant, very numerous, the distance between the rays being less than the transverse diameter of the pores.

Sub-Himalayan tract from the Ganges to Nepal, Central and Southern India.

Weight, 60 lbs. per cubic foot (Skinner, No. 136); our specimen gives 49 lbs. Skinner gives P = 800. Used for carts and agricultural implements. The bark is used for tanning; the shoots and leaves for fodder. The fruit is not edible, but is used to give a black dye to leather.

		lbs.
C 2736.	Moharli Reserve, Central Provinces	49
C 2764.	Melghát, Berar	...

6. Z. rugosa, Lam.; Hook. Fl. Ind. i. 636; Beddome lxvii.; Brandis 89; Kurz i. 265; Gamble 19. *Z. latifolia,* Roxb. Fl. Ind. i. 607. Vern. *Dhaura, dhauri,* Oudh; *Suran, churna,* C. P.; *Suran,* Mar.; *Rukh baer, harray baer,* Nep.

A large scrambling shrub or small evergreen tree, with rough, dark bark. Wood reddish, moderately hard, warps. Pores large and moderate-sized, oval and subdivided. Medullary rays fine, extremely numerous, uniform and equidistant, the distance between the rays much less than the transverse diameter of the pores. Pores frequently joined by very faint, wavy, concentric lines.

Sub-Himalayan tract from the Ganges eastwards, Burma, Central and Southern India.

Weight, 45 lbs. per cubic foot. Wood only used as fuel; often attacked by insects. Fruit eaten.

		lbs.
E 2336.	Bamunpokri, Darjeeling Terai	45

2. BERCHEMIA, Neck.

A genus which besides this species contains several erect or climbing shrubs, of which the chief is *B. lineata,* DC.; Hook. Fl. Ind. i. 638; Brandis 91, of the North-West Himalaya.

1. B. floribunda, Brongn.; Hook. Fl. Ind. i. 637; Brandis 91; Kurz i. 264; Gamble 19. Vern. *Kala lag,* Kumaun; *Chiaduk,* Nep.; *Rungyeong rik,* Lepcha.

A large erect or climbing shrub or small tree. Bark whitish, exfoliating and shewing a purple inner layer. Wood yellow, turning grey on exposure, porous. Pores large, oval, subdivided, between undulating moderately broad medullary rays.

Himalaya from the Jhelum to Bhutan, Khasia Hills.
E 2864. Tukdah, Darjeeling, 5,000 feet.

3. VENTILAGO, Gaertn.

Contains 5 species of scandent shrubs. Besides the one described, 2 species occur in Northern and Central India, 4 in Burma, 2 in Southern India and 1 in the Eastern Himalaya and Bengal. *V. calyculata.* Tul.; Hook. Fl. Ind. i. 631; Brandis 96. (V. *madraspatana*, Roxb. Fl. Ind. i. 629.) Vern. *Papri*, C. P.; *Raktapita, kala lag*, Kumaun; *Sakal yel*, Mar., is a large climber of the outer Himalaya from Kumaun eastwards, Southern India and Burma.

1. V. maderaspatana, Gaertn.; Hook. Fl. Ind. i. 631; Beddome lxviii.; Brandis 96; Kurz i. 262. Vern. *Raktapita*, Beng.; *Yerra chicatli*, Tel.; *Papli*, Tam., Kan.; *Lokandi, kanwail*, Bombay; *Chorgu*, Hyderabad.

A large climbing shrub. Bark dark grey with vertical cracks, exposing the inner surface which has a vermillion colour. Wood greyish yellow, porous, soft; structure similar to that of *Berchemia floribunda.*

Central and Southern India and Burma.

The bark is made into cordage, and a red dye is extracted from the root. It is said also to give a gum.

C 2920. Central Provinces.

4. RHAMNUS.

Contains 7 Indian species, indigenous to the Himalaya and the mountains of the Western coast. Besides those here described, *R. persicus*, Boissier; Hook. Fl. Ind. i. 638; Brandis 93. Vern. *Sherawane, wurak*, Afgh.; *Kukei, nar, nikki kunder, jalidar, kuchni*, Pb., is a small tree of the Suliman and Salt Ranges, and the Himalaya from the Jhelum to Garhwal; *R. nepalensis*, Wall.; Hook. Fl. Ind. i. 640, Gamble 19. Vern. *Achal*, Nep., is a large shrub of the Central and Eastern Himalaya and Khasia Hills; while *R. Wightii*, W. and A., is a large shrub of the higher hills of the Western Ghâts.

Wood generally with a brown heartwood, close-grained. Pores very small, arranged in oblique tails and bands which generally anastomose. Medullary rays fine, numerous.

1. R. virgatus, Roxb. Fl. Ind. i. 604; Brandis 92; Gamble 19. *R. dahuricus*, Pall.; Hook. Fl. Ind. i. 639. *R. hirsutus*, W. and A.; Beddome lxx. Vern. *Phipai, dádúr, tadru, seta pajja, kánji, mamrál, shomfol, reteon, gogsa, sindrol, mútni, nior, chatr, romúsk*, Pb.; *Thalot, chetain*, Simla; *Tsápo, mail*, Tibet, Spiti; *Chato, chedwala, chadua*, Hind.

A shrub or small tree, deciduous. Bark thin, grey, smooth. Sapwood whitish; heartwood brown, very hard and close-grained. Annual rings distinctly marked. Pores very small, arranged in oblique anastomosing irregular bands of soft texture, forming an irregular net-work. Medullary rays fine, very numerous, prominent in the meshes of the net-work. The structure of the wood is the same as that of *Rhamnus catharticus*, Linn.

Throughout the Himalaya and Western Ghâts.

Weight, 56 lbs. per cubic foot. Wood not used, except as firewood. The fruit is bitter, emetic and purgative, and is given in affections of the spleen.

			lbs.
H 79.	Mashobra, Simla,	7,000 feet	57
H 2877.	Nagkanda, Simla,	8,000 „	55
H 3168.	Dungagalli, Hazara,	7,000 „	...

2. R. purpureus, Edgew.; Hook. Fl. Ind. i. 639; Brandis 91. Vern. *Bat sinjal, tunani zanani, tadra, tundhi, mimarari, kunji, chaterni,* Pb.

A large deciduous shrub, with thin smooth bark. Wood brownish grey, close-grained. Annual rings marked by an interrupted belt of pores. Pores very small, in narrow irregular radial belts of softer tissue, which often anastomose and have a reticulate appearance. Medullary rays fine, numerous, straight, prominent.

North-west Himalaya from the Indus to Nepal, between 4,500 and 10,000 feet. Weight, 41 lbs. Fruit used as a purgative.

			lbs.
H	70.	Mashobra, Simla, 7,000 feet	41
H	2848.	Mahasu, Simla, 8,000 „	...

3. R. triquetrus, Wall.; Hook. Fl. Ind. i. 639; Brandis 92. Vern. *Gudlei,* Simla; *Fagora, gardhan, phulla,* Pb.; *Gogsa, ghant,* N.-W. P.

A shrub or small tree, deciduous, with thin grey bark. Wood yellowish white, moderately hard, close-grained. Annual rings distinctly marked by an interrupted belt of larger pores. Pores very small to small, arranged in irregular branching bands of softer tissue, which form fantastic patterns. Medullary rays fine and moderately broad, short.

North-West Himalaya from the Jhelum to Nepal, between 3,000 and 6,000 feet.

H 75. Mashobra, Simla, 7,000 feet.
H 2903. Nagkanda, Simla, 8,000 „

4. R. procumbens, Edgew.; Hook. Fl. Ind. i. 640; Brandis 93.

A small procumbent shrub. Wood yellowish, with the same structure as that of *R. virgatus.*

Western Himalaya from Simla to Kumaun, between 7,000 and 8,000 feet.

H 2952. Naldehra, Simla, 7,000 feet.

5. SAGERETIA, Brongniart.

Besides the two species described, *S. oppositifolia,* Brongn.; Hook. Fl. Ind. i. 641; Brandis 95. Vern. *Kanak, gidurdák, drange, girthan,* Pb.; *Aglaia,* Kumaun, is a large shrub of the N.-W. Himalaya.

Wood close-grained, hard. Pores small, round. Medullary rays fine and very fine.

1. S. theezans, Brongn.; Hook. Fl. Ind. i. 641; Brandis 95. Vern. *Dargola,* Simla; *Drangu, ankol, kauli, karúr, phomphli, kánda, brinkol, chaunsh, katráin, thúm, kúm,* Pb.

A large spinescent shrub. Bark thin, grey. Wood very hard, white, with irregular dark-coloured heartwood. Annual rings (?) marked by white lines. Pores round, small, in rings of softer texture, uniformly distributed. Medullary rays fine and very fine, numerous.

Salt Range and Suliman Range. Western Himalaya from Kashmir to Simla, from 3,000 to 8,000 feet. Fruit eaten.

			lbs.
H	2946.	Suni, Sutlej Valley, 3,500 feet	...
H	2951.	Naldehra, Simla, 7,000 „	...
H	3129.	Koti, Simla, 6,000 „	56

2. S. Brandrethiana, Aitch.; Hook. Fl. Ind. i. 642; Brandis 95. Vern. *Ganger, goher,* Pb.; *Maimúna,* Afg.

A small deciduous shrub. Bark grey, with long wrinkles. Wood yellow, very hard, close-grained. Annual rings distinctly marked by white lines and by an interrupted belt of pores. Pores small, round, numerous, between the white, fine, short, very numerous medullary rays; the distance between the rays equal to the transverse diameter of the pores.

Suliman Range and Salt Range, and North-West Himalaya between the Indus and the Jhelum.

The fruit is sweet and much eaten by Afghans and in the frontier districts.

P 914. Salt Range, Punjab.

ORDER XXXIII. AMPELIDEÆ.

The Vines. A large Family containing two genera: *Vitis*, climbing shrubs, often of large size; and *Leea*, large perennial herbs or shrubs, with large pith. The Vines are found in most parts of India, but especially in the moist zones, some of them climbing extensively over lofty trees; they have a soft porous wood, with very large vessels often filled with water, which runs out on their being cut. *V. lanata*, Roxb.; *V. repanda*, W. and A., and *V. latifolia*, Roxb., are the chief species of the forests of the plains of Northern India, while *V. himalayana*, Brandis. Vern. *Phlankur*, Simla; *Zemardachan, zemaro*, Sutlej; *Chappar tang*, Kumaun, is a well-known large climber of the forests of the Himalaya (H 2913, Simla, 7,000 feet, 33 lbs.). Many have curiously twisted or flattened stems. The Grape Vine, *V. vinifera*, Linn., Vern. *Dákh, dakki, drákska, angúr*, Hind.; *Lanang*, Kanawar, has been introduced and successfully cultivated in Kashmir and other parts of India.

The species of *Leea* are found in the undergrowth of the forests of the Himalaya, Eastern Bengal, Burma and the West coast. Some species have fluted stems and very large pith, such are, *L. macrophylla*, Roxb.; *L. aspera*, Wall.; *L. robusta*, Roxb.; *L. crispa*, Willd.; *L. sumatrana*, Kurz; and *L. sambucina*, Willd. *L. robusta*, Roxb. Vern. *Galeni*, Nep.; *Pantóm*, Lepcha (Nos. E 879 and E 2860, Darjeeling), has a moderately hard wood, with broad medullary rays, and is used for fencing and temporary huts: *L. hirta*, Roxb., is a small tree of valleys in the Eastern Himalaya; and *L. gigantea*, Griff.; Kurz; i. 280 (No. E 3278 Múraghát, W. Dúars), is a small tree with moderately hard wood, pores small, radially distributed, and medullary rays of two kinds, very broad and fine.

ORDER XXXIV. SAPINDACEÆ.

Contains about 20 genera of Indian trees or shrubs. Most of these come from Burma or Southern India, but the largest genus *Acer*, the Maple, is almost exclusively found in the Himalaya.

The Order is divided into 4 Tribes, *viz.*—

Tribe I.—Sapindeæ	. .	*Hemigyrosa, Dittelasma, Erioglossum, Allophyllus, Æsculus, Scyphopetalum, Cupania, Lepisanthes, Schleichera, Sapindus, Xerospermum, Nephelium, Pometia, Harpullia, Zollingeria.*
„ II.—Acerineæ	. .	*Acer* and *Dobinæa.*
„ III.—Dodonæeæ	. .	*Dodonæa.*
„ IV.—Staphyleæ	. .	*Staphylea* and *Turpinia.*

Hemigyrosa contains two species: *H. canescens*, Thwaites Enum. 56, 408; Hook. Fl. Ind. i. 671; Beddome t. 151; Kurz i. 290 (*Molinæa canescens*, Roxb. Fl. Ind. ii. 243). Vern. *Nekota, karadipongan*, Tam.; *Korivi*, Tel.; *Kalú yette*, Kan.; *Lokaneli, kurpa*, Mar., is a tree of Southern India, especially the Coromandel Coast and Tenasserim; and *H. deficiens*, Beddome t. 231; Hook. Fl. Ind. i. 671, is a tree of the

Anamalai Hills. *Dittelasma Rarak*, Hook. f.; Hook. Fl. Ind. i. 672; Kurz i. 297, is an evergreen tree of the Pegu Yomas and Tenasserim. *Erioglossum edule*, Blume; Hook. Fl. Ind. i. 672 (*E. rubiginosum*, Bl.; Brandis 108. *Sapindus rubiginosa*, Bl.; Beddome lxxiii.; Roxb. Fl. Ind. ii. 282. *Pancovia rubiginosa*, Baill.; Kurz i. 296) Vern. *Ritha*, Hind.; *Ishi rashi*, Tel.; *Manipangam*, Tam.; *Tseikchay*, Burm. (No. 23 Brandis' Burma List, 1862, marked *Sapindus*, 66 lbs. ex Kurz' MSS.), is a large tree of Sikkim, Assam, South India and Burma, said by Roxburgh to have a strong durable wood with a chocolate-coloured heartwood. *Scyphopetalum ramiflorum*, Hiern.; Hook. Fl. Ind. i. 676, and *Zollingeria macrocarpa*, Kurz i. 288. Vern. *Wetkyotbeng*, Burm., are trees of Burma. *Cupania* contains 9 species, the chief of which are *C. glabrata*, Kurz i. 284; Hook. Fl. Ind. i. 676 (*Sapindus squamosus*, Roxb. Fl. Ind. ii. 282) of Burma and *C. pentapetala*, W. and A.; Hook. Fl. Ind. i. 678. (*Schleichera pentapetala*, Roxb. Fl. Ind. ii. 275) Vern. *Koiki-púra* ♂; *Púrakoi* ♀. Sylhet, a large tree of Sylhet; the rest are small Burmese trees. Of *Lepisanthes* there are two Burmese species; *Xerospermum Noronhianum*, Bl.; Hook. Fl. Ind. i. 686; Kurz i. 295, is a tree of the Khasia Hills, E. Bengal and Burma, while *Harpullia cupanioides*, Roxb.; Hook. Fl. Ind. i. 692 (*H. imbricata*, Bl.; Beddome t. 158), is a large tree of the Western Gháts. *Dobinæa vulgaris*, Ham.; Hook. Fl. Ind. i. 696; Gamble 23. Vern. *Samli*, Nep., is a large shrub of the Eastern Himalaya.

Wood generally soft or moderately soft, even grained; no distinct heartwood except in *Schleichera*. Pores small, or very small, generally uniform and uniformly distributed. Medullary rays very fine or fine rarely moderately broad, often closely packed. Apart from the annual rings, no concentric bands except in *Allophyllus* and *Sapindus*.

1. ALLOPHYLLUS, Linn.

A genus containing 2 large shrubs: that here described, which has trifoliolate leaves, and *A. zeylanicus*, Linn.; Hook. Fl. Ind. i. 673; Gamble 22, a shrub or small tree of the Eastern Himalaya and Assam, with unifoliolate leaves.

1. A Cobbe, Bl.; Hook. Fl. Ind. i. 673; Kurz i. 299. *Ornitrophe Cobbe*, Willd.; Roxb. Fl. Ind. ii. 268. *Schmidelia Cobbe*, Beddome lxxiii. Vern. *Thaukjot*, Burm.

A deciduous shrub. Wood grey, soft. Pores small, scanty, medullary rays moderately broad, short, joined by numerous white parallel and equidistant concentric lines; prominent on a radial section.

Eastern Bengal, South India, Burma and Andaman Islands.

	lbs.
B 1988. Andaman Islands (Kurz 1866)	40

2. ÆSCULUS, Linn.

A genus containing two Indian species. The Horse-chestnut, commonly planted in Europe, is the *Æ. Hippocastanum*, Linn.

Wood white, soft to moderately hard. Annual rings distinct. Pores numerous, small or very small, generally abundant in the spring wood. Medullary rays uniform, equidistant, very fine, very numerous.

1. Æ. indica, Colebr.; Hook. Fl. Ind. i. 675; Brandis 103. The Indian Horse-chestnut. Vern. *Torjaga*, Trans-Indus; *Háne, hanúdún*, Kashmir; *Baukhor, gugu, kanor, pánkar*, Hind.

A large deciduous tree. Bark grey, with long horizontal cracks, exfoliating in long flakes. Wood white, with a pinkish tinge, soft, close-grained. Annual rings marked by a line and sometimes by fewer pores in the autumn wood. Pores very small. Medullary rays very fine, very numerous.

North-West Himalaya between 4,000 and 10,000 feet, from the Indus to Nepal. Weight, 34 lbs. per cubic foot. Wood used for building, water troughs, platters, packing cases and tea boxes. The Tibet drinking cups are sometimes made of it. The twigs and leaves are lopped for fodder. The fruit is given as food to cattle and goats, and in times of scarcity is soaked in water and then ground and eaten mixed with flour, by the hill people.

		lbs.
H 31.	Matiyána, Simla, 7,000 feet	34
H 166.	Kangra, Punjab (1866)	...
H 936.	Hazara, Punjab	35
H 776.	Kalatop, Punjab, 7,000 feet.	34

2. Æ. punduana, Wall.; Hook. Fl. Ind. i. 675; Gamble 22. *Æ. assamica,* Griff.; Kurz i. 286. Vern. *Cherinangri,* Nep.; *Kunkirkola, ekuhea,* As.; *Dingri,* Dúars; *Bolnawak,* Gáro.

A moderate-sized, deciduous tree. Wood white, soft, close-grained. Pores small, in short radial lines between the very fine, closely packed, medullary rays. Annual rings marked by a faint white line.

Northern Bengal, Khasia Hills, Assam and Burma, ascending to 4,000 feet. Growth moderate, 10 rings per inch of radius. Weight, 36 lbs. per cubic foot. Wood rarely used.

		lbs.
E 3139.	Buxa Reserve, Western Dúars	36

3. SCHLEICHERA, Willd.

1. S. trijuga, Willd.; Hook. Fl. Ind. i. 681; Roxb. Fl. Ind. ii. 277; Beddome t. 119; Brandis 105; Kurz i. 289. Vern. *Kosum, gausam,* Hind.; *Rusam,* Uriya; *Púskú, may, roatanga,* Tel.; *Pává, pú, pulachi, zolim-buriki,* Tam.; *Sagdi, sagade, chakota, akota,* Kan.; *Chendala,* Coorg; *Puvatti,* Kaders; *Kassumar, koham, kocham,* Panch Mehals; *Kusumb, peduman,* Mar.; *Komur, púskú,* Gondi; *Baru,* Kurku; *Gyoben,* Burm.; *Cóng, conghas,* Cingh.

A large deciduous tree. Bark ⅓ inch thick, grey, exfoliating in small rounded plates of irregular shape and size. Wood very hard. Sapwood whitish; heartwood light, reddish brown. Pores scanty, moderate-sized, often oval and subdivided. White, wavy, concentric lines, which may possibly indicate the annual rings. Medullary rays very fine, very numerous, wavy, uniform and equidistant, closely packed; the distance between the rays less than the transverse diameter of the pores.

Sub-Himalayan tract from the Sutlej eastwards, Central and South India and Burma.

The weight and transverse strength have been determined by the following experiments:—

		Weight.	Value of P.
Brandis, 1862, No. 22. Burma	found .	70 lbs.	...
„ 1864, 8 experiments with bars 3′ × 1″ × 1″	„ .	68 „	1160
Baker, 4 experiments, 1829 „ „ 7′ × 2″ × 2″	„ .	68 „	618
Wallich, No. 179 (*Scytalia trijuga*)	„ .	60 „	...
Smythies, 1878, with our 8 specimens	„ .	67·5 „	...
A. Mendis, Ceylon Collection, No. 47	„ .	57 „	...

The wood is very strong and durable; it is used for oil, rice and sugar mills, and for agricultural implements and carts. The lac produced on this tree is highly prized. The fruit is often eaten, and the seeds give an oil used for burning in Malabar.

		lbs.
O 206.	Garhwal (1868)	65
O 536.	Dehra Dún	65
C 191.	Mandla, Central Provinces (1870)	66
C 1110.	Ahiri Reserve, Central Provinces	66
C 2769.	Melghát, Berar	62
W 732.	South Kanara	70
B 319.	Burma (1867)	75
B 2515.	„ (1862)	72
No. 47.	Ceylon Collection	57

4. SAPINDUS, Plum.

Four species according to the Flora Indica, but the nomenclature of Beddome and Brandis has been altered by Hiern; it will be convenient to use Brandis' names instead of those given in the Flora Indica. *S. Danura,* Voigt; Hook. Fl. Ind. i. 684; Kurz i. 298 (*Scytalia Danura,* Roxb. Fl. Ind. ii. 274). Vern. *Nancha, danúra,* Beng., is a small tree of Northern India, Northern and Eastern Bengal, Burma and the Andamans, chiefly in the tidal forests. The wood is said by Home (Sundarbans List, 1872-73) to be white, and to be used in Lower Bengal for boat and house building.

1. S. emarginatus, Vahl.; Beddome t. 154; Brandis 107; Roxb. Fl. Ind. ii. 279. *S. trifoliatus,* Linn.; Hook. Fl. Ind. i. 682. The Soapnut Tree. Vern. *Ritha,* Hind.; *Bara-ritha,* Beng.; *Mukta maya,* Uriya; *Konkúdú,* Tel.; *Pounanga, puvandi,* Tam.; *Thalay marathu, antawála,* Kan.; *Areeta,* Mal.; *Puvella,* Cingh.

A large tree. Wood yellow, hard. Pores large, joined by concentric bands of soft tissue, which contain numerous extremely small pores; intervening are darker coloured bands of firmer tissue, in which the very fine, numerous medullary rays are prominent.

Bengal, South India and Ceylon, often cultivated.

Skinner, No. 114, gives the weight of the wood at 64 lbs., and P=682; it is sometimes used for building and carts, but the chief use of the tree is on account of its saponaceous berries, which are largely used as a substitute for soap. The root, bark and fruit are used in native medicine, and a semi-solid oil is extracted from the seed.

D 3209. Cuddapah, Madras.

B 2259 (51 lbs.) is a white, moderately hard wood sent by Major Ford from the Andamans in 1866; it perhaps belongs to this species.

2. S. detergens, Roxb. Fl. Ind. ii. 280; Brandis 107. *S. Mukorossi,* Gaertn.; Hook. Fl. Ind. i. 683. The Soapnut of North India. Vern. *Ritha, dodan, kanmar,* Hind.

A handsome deciduous tree with grey bark. Wood light yellow, rough, moderately hard, compact and close-grained; annual rings distinctly marked by a band of white tissue, containing large pores; the pores in the outer portion of each annual ring are very small and unite by narrow, concentric, often interrupted bands of white tissue. Medullary rays not straight, short, fine, numerous, lighter coloured than the intervening tissue. Pores and medullary rays distinctly visible on a vertical section.

Cultivated throughout North-West India and Bengal.

Growth slow, 13 to 15 rings per inch of radius. Weight, 44 lbs. Wood not used.

The fruit is very largely used and exported as a substitute for soap; the leaves are given as fodder to cattle, and the seeds used in medicine.

		lbs.
H 117.	Waziri Rupi, Kulu, 4,000 feet	44
H 3050.	Kepu, Sutlej Valley, 2,000 „	...

3. S. attenuatus, Wall.; Hook. Fl. Ind., i. 684; Gamble 22. *Sapindus ruber,* Kurz i. 298. *Scytalia rubra,* Roxb. Fl. Ind. ii. 272. Vern. *Achatta,* Nep; *Sirhootúngchir,* Lepcha; *Lal koi-púra,* Sylhet.

A shrub or small tree with thin grey bark. Wood white, moderately hard. Annual rings marked by darker lines. Pores moderately large, scanty, often in short radial or wavy lines. Medullary rays short, white, very fine, numerous.

Eastern Himalaya, Assam and Eastern Bengal, down to Chittagong. Flowers red. Fruit eaten in Sylhet.

E 3272. Western Dúars.

5. NEPHELIUM, Linn.

Four indigenous and two introduced Indian species. The *Rambutan* fruit is the produce of *N. lappaceum,* Linn., a tree of the Malay Archipelago. Of indigenous trees *N. stipulaceum,* Beddome t. 135, is found in the forests of the Western Ghâts; *N. hypoleucum,* Kurz i. 293; and *N. rubescens,* Hiern; Hook. Fl. Ind. i. 688, in Burma.

Wood red, hard; prominent wavy concentric bands.

1. N. Longana, Camb.; Hook. Fl. Ind. i. 688; Kurz i. 294. *Euphoria Longana,* Lamk.; Beddome t. 156. *Scytalia Longana,* Roxb. Fl. Ind. ii. 270. The Longan. Vern. *Ashphal,* Beng.; *Poovati,* Tam.; *Puná,* Courtallum; *Wumb,* Bombay; *Mal ahcotá,* Kan.; *Kyetmouk,* Burm. *Morre,* Cingh.

A moderate-sized evergreen tree. Wood red, moderately hard. Pores small, numerous, uniformly distributed; the transverse diameter equal to the distance between the fine and very fine medullary rays. Prominent, wavy bands, broader than the rays, divide the wood into a succession of concentric strata which may possibly indicate the annual growth.

Mysore, Western Ghâts and Burma. It is also found in China, where it is called *Longan.*

Weight, 44 lbs., Wallich, No. 179; 62 lbs., A. Mendis; our specimens give 51 lbs. per cubic foot. The wood is not used, though Kurz says it is good for furniture; but it deserves notice. The fruit (the Longan) is eaten.

		lbs.
D 1278.	Anamalai Hills, Madras	51
No. 57.	Ceylon Collection	62

2. N. Litchi, Camb.; Hook. Fl. Ind. i. 687; Kurz i. 283. *Scytalia Litchi,* Roxb. Fl. Ind. ii. 269. The Litchi. Vern. *Litchi,* Hind. (originally Chinese); *Kyetmouk,* Burm.

A handsome evergeen tree with thin grey bark. Wood red, hard, heavy. Pores small to moderate-sized, the transverse diameter usually greater than the distance between the rays. Medullary rays very fine, very numerous. Prominent wavy bands, as in *N. Longana.*

Introduced from South China, and now cultivated largely in India for its delicious fruit. Weight, about 55 lbs. per cubic foot.

O 3260. Saharanpur.

6. POMETIA, Forst.

1. P. tomentosa, Bth. and Hook. f.; Hook. Fl. Ind. i. 691; Kurz i. 295. *Pometia eximia*, Beddome t. 157. Vern. *Thabyay*, Burm.; *Badoh*, And.

Under this name was collected by Kurz, in 1866, in the Andaman Islands, No. B 1973. It has a red heartwood, large, scanty, uniformly distributed pores, prominent on a vertical section; and closely packed, very fine medullary rays; the wood is traversed by prominent concentric lines, which may possibly be annual rings. Weight, 48 lbs. per cubic foot.

7. ACER, Tournef.

A large genus of European, Asiatic and American trees, which counts about 14 Indian species. The species not here described are *A. niveum*, Bl.; Hook. Fl. Ind., i. 693; Kurz i. 289, a very large tree of Assam and Burma; *A. stachyophyllum*, Hiern; Hook. Fl. Ind. i. 694, a small tree of Independent Sikkim; *A. isolobum*, Kurz; Hook. Fl. Ind. i. 694; Kurz i. 289, an evergreen tree of the Martaban Hills from 5,000 to 7,000 feet elevation; and *A. pentapomicum*, J. L. Stewart; Hook. Fl. Ind. i. 694; Brandis 111. Vern. *Teekan, kakkri, kitla, tian, kilpattai, serán*, Pb., a tree of hot dry places in the inner ranges of the North-West Himalaya from Kashmir to Kumaun.

The species may thus be distinguished by characters taken almost exclusively from the leaves:—

Leaves undivided—	
Basal nerves 3—	
Leaves white beneath—	
Cymes pubescent	*A. oblongum.*
,, glabrous	*A. niveum.*
Leaves green beneath	*A. lævigatum.*
Basal nerves 5—	
Leaves glabrous beneath—	
Branches green, serratures of leaves none or very indistinct	*A. sikkimense.*
Branches red, leaves finely duplicate-serrate	*A. Hookeri.*
Leaves pubescent beneath	*A. stachyophyllum.*
Leaves 3-lobed—	
Lobes less than half the length of the leaves	*A. Thomsoni.*
Lobes deeper than half the length of the leaves—	
Lobes lanceolate, acutely serrulate	*A. isolobum.*
Lobes ovate, obtusely serrate	*A. pentapomicum.*
Leaves 5-lobed and nerved—	
Leaves pale beneath	*A. cæsium.*
Leaves green beneath—	
Leaves large, serratures distant, simple	*A. villosum.*
Leaves small, serratures close, sharp	*A. caudatum.*
Leaves 5- to 7-lobed and usually 7-nerved—	
Leaves serrulate	*A. Campbellii.*
Leaves entire	*A. pictum.*

The wood of *Acer* is generally shining and mottled by the medullary rays being prominent on a radial section. It is soft and close-grained. There is no heartwood, and the annual rings are generally well marked. The pores are small and very small, uniformly distributed; the medullary rays fine and very fine, often of two sizes. Concentric medullary patches are found in most species. The structure of the wood of the different species of Maple, European, Indian and American, is so similar that it is very difficult and perhaps impossible to distinguish the different species by the structure of their wood.

1. A. oblongum, Wall.; Hook. Fl. Ind. i. 693; Brandis 110; Gamble 22. Vern. *Mark*, Pb.; *Pharengala, patangalia, kirmoli*, N.-W. P.; *Mugila, buzimpála*, Nep.

A moderate-sized deciduous tree. Bark dark grey, smooth, with horizontal wrinkles. Wood light-reddish brown, moderately hard, close-grained. Annual rings faintly marked. Pores small, uniformly distributed. Medullary rays fine, red, distinctly visible on a radial section, giving the wood an elegantly mottled appearance.

Himalaya from the Jhelum eastwards to Bhutan, up to 6,000 feet.

Growth moderate, 7 rings per inch of radius. Weight, 45 lbs. per cubic foot. Wood used for agricultural implements and drinking cups.

		lbs.
H 221.	Garhwal (1868)	45
H 2944.	Sutlej Valley, near Suni, 3,000 feet	...

2. A. lævigatum, Wall.; Hook. Fl. Ind. i. 693; Brandis 110; Kurz i. 289; Gamble 22. Vern. *Saslendi, cherauni, thali kabashi*, Nep.; *Tungnyok*, Lepcha.

A deciduous tree, with thick, smooth, grey bark. Wood white, shining, hard, close-grained. Pores small, scanty. Medullary rays short, not straight, fine and moderately broad, prominent.

Himalaya from the Jumna eastwards to Bhutan, between 5,000 and 9,000 feet, Khasia Hills, Tenasserim.

Weight, 43 lbs. per cubic foot. Used for planking and tea boxes.

		lbs.
E 684.	Sepoydura, Darjeeling, 5,500 feet	43

3. A. sikkimense, Miq.; Hook. Fl. Ind. i. 694; Gamble 22. Vern. *Palegnyok*, Lepcha.

A small tree, with thin grey bark. Wood shining, grey, annual rings distinct. Pores small, very numerous. Medullary rays fine, numerous.

Hills of Sikkim and Bhutan, from 7,000 to 9,000 feet. Mishmi Hills.

Growth slow, 10 to 15 rings per inch of radius.

		lbs.
E 3102.	Darjeeling, 7,000 feet	37

4. A. Hookeri, Miq.; Hook. Fl. Ind. i. 694; Gamble 22. Vern. *Lal kabashi*, Nep.; *Palé*, Lepcha.

A deciduous tree with brown bark, ⅓ inch thick, deeply cracked. Wood grey. Pores small. Medullary rays fine, red, very numerous.

Sikkim and Bhutan, above 7,000 feet.

Growth moderate, 8 rings per inch of radius. Weight, 37 lbs. per cubic foot. Plants with copper-coloured foliage are not uncommon about Darjeeling.

		lbs.
E 2338.	Rangbúl, Darjeeling, 7,500 feet	37

5. A. Thomsoni, Miq.; Gamble 22. *A. villosum*, Wall. var.; Hook Fl. Ind. i. 695. Vern. *Kabashi*, Nep.

A large tree, bark thin, grey. Wood greyish white, soft. Pores small. Medullary rays fine and moderately broad, numerous.

Hills of Sikkim and Bhutan above 4,000 feet.

Growth slow, 16 rings per inch of radius. Weight, 44 lbs. per cubic foot.

		lbs.
E 3103.	Darjeeling, 5,000 feet	44

6. A. cæsium, Wall.; Hook. Fl. Ind. i. 695; Brandis 111. Vern. *Trekhan, tarkhana, tilpattar, mandar, kauri, kalindra, salíma, kanzal,* Pb.; *Kanshin,* Tibet; *Jerimu, shumanjra,* Simla; *Kilu,* Kumaun.

A large deciduous tree. Bark grey, exfoliating in long vertical strips. Wood white, close-grained, less mottled than that of *A. caudatum,* soft to moderately hard; annual rings distinct. Pores small, numerous, uniform, between the fine, very numerous medullary rays.

North-West Himalaya from the Indus to Nepal, between 7,000 and 11,000 feet. Growth slow, 9 to 31 rings per inch of radius, giving an average of 18. Weight, 40 lbs. per cubic foot. Wood scarcely used; drinking cups are sometimes made of it by the Tibetans.

		lbs.
H 33.	Matiyána, Simla, 7,000 feet	40
H 915.	Hazara, Punjab, 7,000 „	41
H 3009. H 2901.	Nagkanda, Simla, 9,000 „	...
H 431.	Deoban, Jaunsar, 8,000 „	40

7. A. villosum, Wall.; Hook. Fl. Ind. i. 695; Brandis 111. Vern. *Karendera,* Simla.

A large deciduous tree, with thin grey bark. Wood white, moderately hard, close-grained, beautifully mottled and shining, annual rings distinct. Pores scanty, small, uniform, uniformly distributed. Medullary rays short, fine and moderately broad.

North-West Himalaya from the Jhelum to Nepal, between 7,000 and 9,000 feet. Growth slow, 16 rings per inch of radius. Weight, 38 lbs. per cubic foot. Wood not used. Leaves lopped for fodder.

		lbs.
H 62.	Nagkanda, Simla, 8,000 feet	38
H 3006. H 2899.	„ „ „	...
H 167.	Kangra (1866)	...

8. A. caudatum, Wall.; Hook. Fl. Ind. i. 695; Brandis 112; Gamble 22. Vern. *Kanzla, kandaru, kanjara,* Simla; *Khansing, kabashi,* Nep.; *Yalishin,* Bhutia.

A moderate-sized deciduous tree, with dark-grey bark. Wood white, with a faint pink tinge, shiny, compact, moderately hard, sometimes with small masses of heartwood near the centre. Annual rings distinct. Pores small, uniform and uniformly distributed. Medullary rays moderately broad, short, giving on a radial section a beautifully mottled appearance.

Himalaya, from the Chenab to Bhutan between 7,000 to 11,000 feet. Growth slow, 26 rings per inch of radius. Weight, 43 lbs. per cubic foot.

		lbs.
H 27.	Matiyána, Simla, 7,000 feet	45
H 41.	Mahasu, „ 8,000 „	44
H 74.	Kalashi, „ 6,000 „	41
H 3007.	Nagkanda, „ 9,000 „	...

9. A. Campbellii, Hook. f. and Th.; Hook. Fl. Ind. i. 696; Gamble 23. Vern. *Kabashi,* Nep.; *Daom, yatli,* Lepcha.

A large deciduous tree, with smooth grey bark. Wood greyish white, moderately hard, shining, close-grained. Annual rings marked by a thin line. Pores small, uniformly distributed. Medullary rays numerous, fine and moderately broad.

Sikkim Himalaya, above 7,000 feet.

Growth moderate, 8 to 15 rings per inch of radius, but rather faster when young. Weight, 38 lbs. per cubic foot. The chief Maple of the North-East Himalaya. The wood is extensively used for planking and for tea boxes. It reproduces freely either by seed or by coppice, and plays an important part in the regeneration of the hill forests.

		lbs.
E 436.	Rangbúl, Darjeeling, 7,000 feet	37
E 2337.	„ „ „	40
E 686.	Sepoydura, Darjeeling, 5,500 feet	37

10. A. pictum, Thunb.; Hook. Fl. Ind. i. 696; Brandis 112. Vern. *Kilpattar, trekhan, tarkhana, kakru, kanzal, kanjar, jerimu, laur,* Pb.; *Kancheli,* N.-W. P.; *Dhadonjra,* Simla.

A moderate-sized tree, with thin grey bark. Wood white, soft to moderately hard, close-grained. Pores very small. Medullary rays fine and very fine.

Outer and Middle Himalaya from the Indus to Assam, between 4,000 and 9,000 feet.

Growth moderate, 12 rings per inch of radius. Weight, 41 lbs. per cubic foot. The commonest Maple of the North-West Himalaya. The wood is used for construction, ploughs, bedsteads, and poles to carry loads. Tibetan drinking cups are made of the knotty excrescences. The branches are lopped for fodder.

		lbs.
H 931.	Hazara, Punjab, 8,000 feet	41
H 3008.	Nagkanda, Simla, 9,000 „	43
H 432.	Deoban, Jaunsar, 7,000 „	38

8. DODONÆA, Linn.

1. D. viscosa, Linn.; Hook. Fl. Ind. i. 697; Beddome lxxv.; Brandis 113; Kurz i. 287; Gamble 23. *D. dioica,* Roxb. and *D. angustifolia,* Linn. f.; Roxb. Fl. Ind. ii. 256. Vern. *Sanatta, mendru, ban mendu,* Pb.; *Banderu,* C. P.; *Bandurgi, bandrike,* Kan.

An evergreen shrub, with thin grey bark exfoliating in long thin strips. Sapwood white; heartwood extremely hard and close-grained, dark brown, with an irregular outline; annual rings (?) distinctly marked by fine white lines. Pores very small, in short radial lines. Medullary rays fine, white, very numerous.

North-West Himalaya from the plains up to 4,500 feet, Punjab, Sindh, South India ascending to 8,000 feet and attaining here the size of a small tree, Burma, planted throughout India for hedges.

Growth slow, 11 to 12 rings per inch of radius. The wood is used for engraving, turning, tool-handles and walking-sticks, and the branches to support the earth of flat roofs. It is likely to be important in re-clothing denuded tracts like the Siwalik Hill of Hoshiarpur.

P 894. Salt Range, Punjab.

9. STAPHYLEA, Linn.

1. S. Emodi, Wall.; Hook. Fl. Ind. i. 698; Brandis 114. Vern. *Marchob* (Serpent Stick), Afg.; *Nagdaun, chitra, chúal, ban-bakhru, ban-shagali, gúldar, kághania,* Hind.

A large shrub or small tree. Bark grey, with darker longitudinal, anastomosing streaks. Wood soft, grey. Pores very small between the fine, closely packed, medullary rays.

North-West Himalaya, above 6,000 feet.

Sticks are made of the wood which are sold in the hill bazars. They are supposed by the Afghans and frontier tribes to have the property of keeping off snakes. Weight, 44 lbs. per cubic foot.

		lbs.
H 2900.	Nagkanda, Simla, 8,000 feet	41
H 3189.	Dungagalli, Hazara, 7,000 feet	47

10. TURPINIA, Vent.

Contains 2 Indian species, which in the Flora Indica are described as one. *T. pomifera*, DC., Kurz i. 292; Gamble 23. Vern. *Nagpat*, Nep.; *Singnok*, Lepcha; *Toukshama*, Burm., is a tree of the tropical forests of Bengal and Burma: while *T. nepalensis* comes from the hills.

1. T. nepalensis, Wall.; Beddome t. 159; Kurz i. 292; Gamble 23. *T. pomifera*, DC.; Hook. Fl. Ind. i. 698. Vern. *Thali*, Nep.; *Murgut*, Lepcha; *Nila*, Nilgiris.

A moderate-sized deciduous tree. Bark $\frac{1}{10}$ inch thick, grey, smooth. Wood grey, soft, even-grained. Pores small, very numerous, uniformly distributed. Medullary rays of two classes, the first being moderately broad, scanty, short, and the second fine, very numerous.

Himalaya from the Nepal Frontier eastwards, between 4,000 and 7,000 feet, Assam, Cachar, Chittagong and Burma.

Weight, 30 lbs per cubic foot. Wood not used, leaves given as fodder to cattle.

		lbs.
E 649.	Sepoydura Forest, Darjeeling, 5,500 feet	30
E 3108.	Darjeeling, 6,000 feet	...

ORDER XXXV. SABIACEÆ.

Contains 2 Indian genera, *viz.*: *Meliosma*, which is here described, and comprises trees or shrubs; and *Sabia*, a genus of about 10 climbing or sarmentose shrubs. Among these latter *S. campanulata*, Wall.; Hook. Fl. Ind. ii. 1; Brandis 116. Vern. *Bakalpata*, Kumaun, of the Himalaya from Simla to Sikkim, above 5,000 ft. (H 3030, Nagkanda, 9,000 ft.; H 3193, Theog. 7,000 ft.); *S. paniculata*, Edgew.; Hook. Fl. Ind. ii. 3; Brandis 117; Gamble 23 of the Sub-Himalayan tract from the Jumna to Sikkim and *S. leptandra*, Hook. f. and Th.; Hook. Fl. Ind. ii. 2; Gamble 23. Vern. *Simali*, Nep.; *Payongrik*, Lepcha, of the Sikkim Hills, are the most noticeable. They have a soft wood, with large pores and broad medullary rays.

1. MELIOSMA, Blume.

A genus containing 7 species of Indian trees. Two are found in North-West India, four in the Eastern Himalaya, one in Burma and three in South India. Of those not here described, *M. pungens*, Wall.; Brandis 116. Vern. *Gardar, kharas*, Kumaun, is a tree of the North-West Himalaya from the Indus to Nepal, but rare west of the Sutlej; *M. Wightii*, Planch. (*M. pungens*, Bedd. lxxvii). Vern. *Tode*, Nilgiris, is a tree of the Western Ghâts often called Hill Mango by Europeans, but not used; *M. Arnottiana*, Wight; Beddome t. 160. Vern. *Huli makay*, Nilgiris; *Massivâra*, Mysore, is a large tree of the hills of South India, above 4,000 ft. elevation. Beddome says the heartwood of old trees is striped red and white, but that the timber is worthless. *M. pinnata*, Roxb. Fl. Ind. i. 104; Gamble 23. Vern. *Bolay*, Nep.; *Batiwa*, Sylhet, is a large tree of the outer Eastern Himalaya and Khasia Hills, whose wood is used for house-building.

Pores small, arranged in groups, or in short radial lines.

1. **M. dilleniæfolia,** Bl.; Hook. Fl. Ind. ii. 4; Brandis 115; Gamble 23. Vern. *Porda, parenga, philli,* Simla; *Gwep,* N.-W. P.

A small deciduous tree, with dark-grey bark. Wood white, soft, even-grained. Annual rings marked by a continuous line of pores. Pores small, in rounded groups of from ten to twenty, except along the annual rings. Medullary rays wavy, moderately broad and fine, distinctly marked on a radial section.

Throughout the Himalaya, from 4,000 to 11,000 feet, from the Sutlej to Bhutan. Growth moderate, 4 to 6 rings per inch of radius; weight, 35 to 38 lbs. per cubic foot.

		lbs.
H 60.	Nagkanda, Simla, 8,000 feet	38
H 2892.	" " "	35

2. **M. simplicifolia,** Roxb. Fl. Ind. i. 103; Hook. Fl. Ind. ii. 5; Beddome lxxvii.; Brandis 116; Kurz i. 301; Gamble 23. *Millingtonia,* Roxb. Vern. *Kosrú,* Nep.; *Hingman,* Lepcha; *Koko,* Mechi; *Dibrú,* Ass.; *Dantrungi,* Sylhet; *Rong,* Chittagong; *Gokpak,* Magh.

An evergreen tree. Wood reddish, moderately hard, warps. Pores small and moderate-sized, single or in short radial lines, numerous, uniformly distributed. Medullary rays moderately broad, very numerous.

Eastern Himalaya, Assam, Chittagong, Burma, South India and Ceylon. Weight, 36 lbs. per cubic foot.

		lbs.
E 2339.	Sivoke, Darjeeling Terai	36

3. **M. Wallichii,** Planch.; Hook. Fl. Ind. ii. 6; Gamble 24. Vern. *Dabdabbi, nunewalai,* Nep.; *Himan,* Lepcha.

A large deciduous tree. Wood white, very soft, spongy. Pores large, in scattered groups of five to ten. Medullary rays broad and fine, distinctly marked on a radial section.

Eastern Himalaya and Khasia Hills, above 5,000 feet.
Growth moderate, 8 to 10 rings per inch of radius. Weight, 18 lbs. per cubic foot. Wood used only for firewood and occasionally for boxes.

		lbs.
E 361.	Rangbúl, Darjeeling, 7,000 ft.	18

Order XXXVI. ANACARDIACEÆ.

Contains 19 Indian genera of trees, rarely shrubs or climbers. Many of the species are very important forest trees, and they are dispersed over the whole of India, but most particularly in Madras and Burma. They have often an acrid, milky juice, and several species give a varnish. Some species have only a soft wood, while others have a hard, often brightly coloured heartwood. The Order is divided into two Tribes, *viz.*—

Tribe I.—Anacardieæ . . . . *Rhus, Pistacia, Mangifera, Anacardium, Bouea, Gluta, Buchanania, Melanorrhœa, Swintonia, Solenocarpus, Tapiria, Odina, Parishia, Semecarpus, Drimycarpus, Holigarna* and *Nothopegia.*

" II.—Spondieæ . . . . *Spondias* and *Dracontomelum.*

Twelve of the genera are here described, while of the rest *Tapiria* contains only one climbing shrub of the Eastern Himalaya and Eastern Bengal down to Chittagong, *T. hirsuta,* Hook. f.; Kurz i. 320; Gamble 24. Vern. *Mashul-lara,* Nep.; *Renchilingrik,* Lepcha. *Swintonia* contains three species, two of which are found in Tenasserim;

while of the third, *S. Schwenckii*, Teysm. and Binnend.; Hook. Fl. Ind. ii. 26; Kurz i. 316, herbarium specimens were sent from Chittagong accompanying E 1964. Vern. *Boilam, boilsur*, Beng.; *Sambúng, sanginphroo*, Magh; *Shibika*, Chakma; *Thayet san*, Burm., which has unfortunately been mislaid. It is a very large tree of the Eastern Peninsula from Chittagong southward and, especially in Chittagong, is remarkable by its tall straight, white stem and handsome foliage, which is tinged with red in the cold season. The wood is sometimes used for boats and is said by Major Lewin to last better than other woods in salt water. *Solenocarpus indica*, W. and A.; Beddome t. 233, is a tree of the Western Gháts. *Parishia insignis*, Hook. f. is a large handsome evergreen tree of Tenasserim and the Andaman Islands. *Nothopegia* contains three small trees of the Western Gháts; and *Dracontomelum mangiferum*, Bl. Vern. *Gunradah*, And., is a large evergreen tree of the Andaman Islands.

According to the structure of the wood the genera of this family may be divided into two series. The first series which comprises *Melanorrhœa, Gluta, Bouea* and *Mangifera* is characterized by closely packed medullary rays and somewhat scanty pores, of these the first three genera have hard and dark-coloured heartwood. The second series comprises *Rhus, Pistacia, Anacardium, Semecarpus, Odina, Buchanania, Spondias*, and *Drimycarpus*, and is marked by numerous fine, medullary rays, which are not closely packed, and numerous small or moderate-sized pores. The wood of the genera of this group is soft, and except that of *Pistacia, Rhus* and *Odina*, has no heartwood. The heartwood of *Pistacia* is hard and that of *Odina* moderately hard.

1. RHUS, Linn.

Contains 11 species, chiefly Himalayan. *Rhus parviflora*, Roxb. Fl. Ind. ii. 100; Brandis 119. Vern. *Túnga, rai túng, dungla, túmra, ranel*, Hind., is a shrub of dry slopes of the N.-W. Himalaya and of the hills of Central India, with a yellowish, close-grained wood. *R. khasiana*, Hook. f. and *R. Griffithii*, Hook. f. are small trees of the Khasia Hills and Chittagong, while *R. paniculata*, Wall., is found in Bhutan and in Burma. *R. Coriaria*, Linn., is the Sumach tree of Europe, whose leaves are used in tanning in the preparation of Morocco leather.

Wood grey, soft except in *R. mysorensis*, often streaked, with a yellow or brown heartwood. Pores small, often large and in continuous porous belts in the spring wood. Medullary rays fine and moderately broad.

1. R. Cotinus, Linn.; Hook. Fl. Ind. ii. 9; Brandis 118. Vern. *Paán, bhán, manu, banthra, túng, titri*, Pb.; *Túnga, tung, chaniát, ámi*, N.-W. P.

A shrub or small tree, deciduous. Bark thin, reddish brown, rough. Wood moderately hard; sapwood small, white; heartwood mottled, of a rich dark yellow colour. Annual rings marked by a belt of moderate-sized and large pores, the pores in the autumn wood very small, arranged in long, irregular, radial groups. Medullary rays fine, short.

Suliman Range, North-West Himalaya to Kumaun, ascending to 6,000 feet.

Growth slow, 32 rings per inch of radius. Weight, 56 lbs. per cubic foot. Used in South Europe for inlaid and cabinet work. In the Himalaya the twigs are used for basket-making, and the bark and leaves for tanning.

			lbs.
H	85.	Bhajji, Simla, 6,000 feet	56
H	3182.	Dungagalli, Hazara	...

2. R. mysorensis, Heyne; Hook. Fl. Ind. ii. 9; Beddome lxxviii.; Brandis 119. Vern. *Dasarni*, Ajmere.

A small shrub with thin brown bark. Wood hard, pinkish yellow, close-grained, heavy. Pores moderate-sized, evenly distributed. Medullary rays fine, very numerous, wavy, bent where they touch the pores.

Suliman Range, Sind, Punjab, Rajputana and the Dekkan. Wood used only for fuel.

P 3231. Nagpahar Forest, Ajmere.
P 3248. Ajmere.

3. R. semialata, Murray; Hook. Fl. Ind. ii. 10; Brandis 119; Gamble 24. *R. buckiamela*, Roxb. Fl. Ind. ii. 99. *R. javanica*, Linn.; Kurz i. 319. Vern. *Tatri, titri, chechar, arkhar, arkol, kakri, dúdla, kakkeran, wánsh, hulashing*, Pb.; *Rashtu*, Sutlej; *Dakhmila, dáswila*, N.-W. P.; *Bakhiamela, bhagmili*, Nep.; *Takhril*, Lepcha.

A moderate-sized deciduous tree. Bark ½ inch thick, rough, with deep vertical furrows. Wood soft, shining, grey with darker streaks. Annual rings marked by a broad belt of closely packed large pores, the outer belt of each annual ring being often very narrow, with patches of very small pores. Medullary rays fine.

Outer Himalaya from the Indus to Assam, ascending to 7,000 feet; Khasia Hills.

Growth variable: the Simla specimens had a slow growth of 16 rings per inch, while the Darjeeling specimens had grown very fast, 2-3 rings per inch of radius. Weight, 26 to 27 lbs. per cubic foot. Wood not used. Fruit eaten by Nepalese and Lepchas, who make a wax of it called *Omlu*, Nep.

			lbs.
H	89.	Bhajji, Simla, 5,000 feet	26
H	2942.	Suni, Sutlej Valley, 3,000 feet	27
H	3079.	Annandale, Simla, 6,000 feet	...
E	2340.	Tukdah, Darjeeling, 5,000 feet	27

4. R. punjabensis, J. L. Stewart; Hook. Fl. Ind. ii. 10; Brandis 120. Vern. *Titri, arkhar, palai, choklu, kangar, kakkrein, dor, rashtu*, Punjab.

A moderate-sized deciduous tree, with rough dark-grey bark and scented aromatic leaves. Wood consisting of alternate layers of soft, porous spring wood and hard autumn wood. Heartwood yellowish grey, with dark longitudinal streaks, moderately hard. Annual rings marked by a broad belt of closely packed large pores; the pores in the rest of the annual rings scattered, small or very small, in groups or patches of soft tissue.

North-West Himalaya, ascending to 8,500 feet.

Growth slow, 14 rings per inch of radius. Weight, 34 lbs. per cubic foot.

			lbs.
H	19.	Matiyána, Simla, 8,000 feet	33
H	3051.	Kotgarh, Simla, 7,000 feet	35
H	3170.	Dungagalli, Hazara	...

5. R. insignis, Hook. f.; Hook. Fl. Ind. ii. 11; Gamble 24. Vern. *Kagphulai*, Nep.; *Serh*, Lepcha.

A moderate-sized tree, with thin grey bark. Wood grey, soft heartwood yellowish brown. Pores small and moderate-sized, uniformly distributed. Medullary rays fine, numerous.

Sikkim and the Khasia Hills, above 4,000 feet.

Growth fast, 3 to 4 rings per inch of radius.

			lbs.
E	3104.	Darjeeling, 7,000 feet	26
E	3105.	Darjeeling, 7,000 feet	27

6. **R. Wallichii,** Hook. f.; Hook. Fl. Ind. ii. 11. *R. vernicifera,* DC.; Brandis 120. Vern. *Kambal, gadúmbal, rikhali, arkhar, arkol, lohása, harkú,* Punjab; *Akoria, kaunki, bhaliún,* N.-W. P.; *Bhálaio, chosi,* Nep.

A small or moderate-sized tree, exuding, from between the bark and the wood, a black acrid varnish, which draws blisters. Sapwood white, soft; heartwood reddish brown, yellow when dry (*Brandis*). Structure similar to that of *R. semialata.*

N.-W. Himalaya, from 2,000 to 7,000 feet.

The wood is used in the Sutlej Valley for saw frames and axe handles. The juice of the leaves is corrosive and blisters the skin.

H 3078. Annandale, Simla, 6,000 feet.

7. **R. succedanea,** Linn.; Hook. Fl. Ind. ii. 12; Roxb. Fl. Ind. ii. 98; Brandis 131. *R. acuminata,* DC.; Gamble 24. Vern. *Tatri, arkol, titar, lakhar, rikhúl, shash, hurku,* Pb.; *Raniwalai,* Nep.; *Serhnyok,* Lepcha; *Dingkain,* Khasia.

A small deciduous tree, with thin bark. Wood white, shining, soft, with a small darker-coloured heartwood. Structure similar to that of *R. semialata.*

Himalaya, from the Jhelum to Assam, Khasia Hills, from 2,000 to 8,000 feet.

The wood is not used. The juice is acrid and causes blisters, the seeds give a good wax, and the tree is planted in Japan along roads and regularly worked for this wax, which is of a snow-white colour and is made into candles.

		lbs.
H 2907.	Nagkanda, Simla, 7,000 feet	32
H 3167.	Dungagalli, Hazára	...

2. PISTACIA, Linn.

Contains only one Indian species. The pistachio nuts (*pista*), which are imported into India from Afghanistan, are the produce of *Pistacia vera,* Linn., a small tree of Western Asia, cultivated in South Europe. *P. Lentiscus,* Linn., a shrub of the Mediterranean region, is the true Mastic of Chios. *P. Terebinthus,* Linn., the Terebinth Tree, gives the Chio or Cyprus turpentine, and the galls found on it are used in tanning.

1. **P. integerrima,** J. L. Stewart; Hook. Fl. Ind. ii. 13; Brandis 122. Vern. *Kaka, kakkar, kakrangche, kakring, kangar, tungu,* Pb.; *Kakar singi,* Kumaon; *Shué, sarawan, masua,* Afg.

A deciduous tree, with rough grey bark. Sapwood white; heartwood yellowish brown, beautifully mottled with yellow and dark veins, very hard. Annual rings marked by a belt of closely packed pores. Pores of two classes: those in the spring wood moderate-sized, while those in the greater portion of the wood are very small, forming interrupted, wavy lines, and grouped in irregular, narrow patches, which are frequently arranged in zigzag lines. Medullary rays fine, very numerous.

Suliman and Salt Ranges, outer North-West Himalaya, ascending to 6,500 feet and extending east as far as Kumaon.

Growth moderate, 8 to 9 rings per inch of radius. Weight, 54 lbs. per cubic foot. The wood is used for furniture, carvings and all kinds of ornamental work. It is usually sold in the hill bazars and particularly at Simla, in the form of thick short planks. The leaves are lopped for fodder for buffaloes and camels, and the galls are used in native medicine.

			lbs.
H	6.	Julung, Simla, 4,000 feet	...
H	11.	Komharsen, Simla, 6,000 feet	50
H	160.	Hazara, Punjab (1866)	52
H	926.	Hazara, Punjab	46
H	898.	Murree, Punjab, 7,000 feet	56
H	227.	Garhwal (1868)	60
H	2930.	Simla, 6,000 feet	63

3. MANGIFERA, Linn.

Besides the 3 species here described: *M. longipes*, Griff.; Kurz i. 303. Vern. *Thayet-thee-nee*, Burm., is an evergreen tree of the swamp forests of Burma; and *M. fœtida*, Lour. Vern. *Lamote*, Burm., a large tree cultivated in Southern Tenasserim for its fruit.

No heartwood. Wood soft, somewhat spongy. Pores large, prominent on a vertical section. Medullary rays fine, generally closely packed. Numerous, fine, wavy, concentric lines.

1. M. indica, Linn.; Hook. Fl. Ind. ii. 13; Roxb. Fl. Ind. i. 641; Beddome t. 162; Brandis 125; Kurz i. 304; Gamble 24. The Mango Tree. Vern. *Am*, Hind.; *Ghari am*, Ass.; *Jegachu*, Garo; *Marka*, Gondi; *Ambe*, Kurku; *Amba*, Mar.; *Maá*, *mangas*, Tam.; *Mamadi*, *mamíd*, Tel.; *Movena*, *mávu*, Kan.; *Mava*, Mal.; *Thayet*, Burm.

A large evergreen tree. Bark thick, dark grey, nearly black, rough with numerous small fissures and exfoliating scales. Wood grey, coarse-grained, soft. Pores scanty, moderate-sized and large, distinctly marked on a longitudinal section. Medullary rays fine, wavy, closely packed.

Wild on the Western Gháts, cultivated all over India.

Weight, 41 lbs. per cubic foot (our specimens); 37 (Puckle); 42 (Skinner, No. 90); 44 (Cunningham); 41 (Baker): the average giving about 41 lbs.

Puckle's three Mysore experiments with bars $2' \times 1'' \times 1''$ gave P = 587; Cunningham's two experiments with similar bars gave P = 650; Skinner's P = 632; and Baker's with bars $6' \times 2'' \times 2''$; P = 471. The wood is used for planking, doors and window frames, in Calcutta for packing cases, and in Behar for indigo boxes; canoes and Masúla boats are made of it. The tree is, however, chiefly grown for the sake of its fruit; its bark gives a gum, and its seed contains gallic acid, is used in medicine and is sometimes eaten. It is generally propagated by layers and grafts; plants raised from seed will sometimes produce good fruit, but there is no dependence to be placed on the quality of the fruit of such trees. The seeds do not retain their vitality long, but germinate well if sown when quite fresh.

			lbs.
E	637.	Goalpara, Assam	48
B	2302.	Assam	38
E	3131.	Calcutta	41
E	1957.	Chittagong	39
D	2053.	Mysore	39

2. M. caloneura, Kurz i. 305; Hook. Fl. Ind. ii. 14. Vern. *Tau-thayet*, Burm.

An evergreen tree. Wood light brown, moderately hard. Pores large, scanty, prominent on a vertical section. Medullary rays fine, very numerous. Fine, wavy, concentric lines.

Burma.

Weight, 35 lbs. per cubic foot.

			lbs.
B	294.	Burma (1867)	38
B	2519.	„ (1862)	32

3. M. sylvatica, Roxb. Fl. Ind. i. 644; Hook. Fl. Ind. ii. 15; Kurz i. 304; Gamble 24. Vern. *Bun am,* Ass.; *Lakshmi am,* Sylhet; *Chuchi am,* Nep.; *Katúr,* Lepcha; *Hseng neng thayet,* Burm.

A large evergreen tree with a thick grey bark. Wood grey, moderately hard. Structure the same as that of *M. caloneura,* but the medullary rays are less distinct and less numerous. Numerous wavy, concentric lines.

Nepal, Eastern Bengal and the Andamans; rare in Burma.

Weight, 34 to 41 lbs. Wood not used, but worth trial for tea boxes. The fruit is sometimes eaten fresh or dried. It is also used medicinally. (*Roxb.*)

		lbs.
E 594.	Kookloong Forest, Darjeeling Terai	41
E 952.	Golaghát, Assam	34

4. ANACARDIUM, Rottb.

1. A. occidentale, Linn.; Hook. Fl. Ind. ii. 20; Roxb. Fl. Ind. ii. 312; Beddome t. 163; Kurz i. 310. The Cashew Nut Tree. Vern. *Kajú,* Hind.; *Hijuli,* Beng.; *Kola mava, mundiri,* Tam.; *Jidi mamidi,* Tel.; *Jidi, Kempu géru,* Kan.; *Thee-hoh thayet,* Burm.

A small evergreen tree, with rough bark. Wood red, moderately hard, close-grained. Pores large, prominent on a vertical section. Medullary rays indistinct.

Originally from South America, now established in the coast forests of Chittagong, Tenasserim, the Andaman Islands and South India.

Growth moderate, 8 to 11 rings per inch of radius. Weight, 38 to 39 lbs. per cubic foot. The wood is used for packing cases in Burma, for boat-building and charcoal. The nuts are roasted and eaten as dessert, they also give, by expression, a yellow oil similar to almond oil. The pericarp of the fruit gives a black acrid oil which is called 'cardol' and gives an acid called 'anacardic acid.' The oil is very caustic, raises blisters and is used for warts, corns, and ulcers; it is also used to prevent the attacks of white ants to wood-work and of insects to the binding of books, and in the Andamans to colour and preserve fishing lines; the enlarged pedicels of the fruit are eaten.

		lbs.
B 2227	. . . .	38
B 2229.	Andamans (1866)	39

5. BOUEA, Meissner.

1. B. burmanica, Griff.; Hook. Fl. Ind. ii. 21. *B. oppositifolia,* Meissn.; Kurz i. 306. *Mangifera oppositifolia,* Roxb. Fl. Ind. i. 640. Vern. *Meriam, mayan,* Burm.

A moderate-sized evergreen tree with dark-grey bark. Wood grey, hard, with a dark reddish brown heartwood. Pores scanty, moderate-sized, prominent on a vertical section. Medullary rays fine, numerous, undulating. Wavy concentric lines dividing the wood into a succession of concentric bands, which may possibly be annual rings.

Burma and Andaman Islands.

Weight, 55 lbs. per cubic foot. The wood is not specially used, but is said by Roxburgh to be very durable. The tree has an edible fruit, for which it is often cultivated.

		lbs.
B 2213.	Andamans (1866)	55

6. GLUTA, Linn.

Contains 3 species: one (that here described) from South India, and two from Burma, *viz.*: *G. tavoyana*, Wall.; Hook. Fl. Ind. ii. 22; Kurz i. 309. Vern. *Thayetthitsay*, Burm., and *G. elegans*, Wall.; Kurz i. 309, small trees of the Tenasserim coast. Kurz says that the wood when steeped in ferruginous mud turns jet black, looking like ebony, and that it is used for building, for boxes and for dyeing.

1. G. travancorica, Beddome t. 60; Hook. Fl. Ind. ii. 22. Vern. *Shencurungi*, Tinnevelly.

A very large evergreen tree, bark ⅓ inch thick, grey. Sapwood light-reddish grey; heartwood dark red, very hard and close-grained, beautifully mottled with dark and light streaks. Pores moderate-sized, scanty, filled with resin. Medullary rays very fine, very numerous, prominent, visible on a radial section as narrow bands. Numerous white, undulating, concentric lines and bands, of lighter colour in the wood.

Ghâts of Tinnevelly and Travancore.

Growth moderate, 12 rings per inch of radius. Weight, according to Beddome, 40 lbs. per cubic foot; our specimens give 46 and 58 lbs. The wood is little used, but its splendid colour and markings should rapidly bring it to notice as a valuable wood for furniture. It seems to season very well, and works and polishes admirably.

		lbs.
D 1066.	Tinnevelly (some sapwood)	46
D 3155.	„ (heartwood only)	58

7. BUCHANANIA, Roxb.

A genus of 7 Indian species, most of which are trees from Tenasserim and the Andaman Islands. *B. angustifolia*, Roxb. Fl. Ind. ii. 386; Hook. Fl. Ind. ii. 23; Beddome lxxix. Vern. *Sara, chara, pedda morali*, Tel., is a small tree of South India.

1. B. latifolia, Roxb. Fl. Ind. ii. 385; Hook. Fl. Ind. ii. 23; Beddome t. 165; Brandis 127; Kurz i. 307. Vern. *Chirauli*, Pb.; *Piál, payála, muriá, katbhilawa*, Garhwal; *Piár, peirah*, Oudh; *Achár, char, chironji*, C. P.; *Saraka, herka*, Gondi; *Taro*, Kurku; *Charu*, Uriya; *Kat maá, aima*, Tam.; *Chara, chinna moral, morli*, Tel.; *Charwari*, Hyderabad; *Nuskul, murkalu*, Kan.; *Sir*, Bhíl; *Pyal, charoli*, Bombay; *Lamboben, lonepho*, Burm.

A tree, leafless only for a very short time. Bark ¼ inch thick, dark grey, sometimes black, rough, tesselated with deep irregular cracks. Wood greyish brown, moderately hard, with a small dark-coloured heartwood. Pores large, round or oval, frequently subdivided, uniform and equidistant, prominent on a longitudinal section. Medullary rays very numerous, fine, reddish, uniform and equidistant, bent outwards where they touch the pores; marked on a radial section as long, narrow, dark-coloured plates, the distance between the rays being less than the transverse diameter of the pores.

Sub-Himalayan tract from the Sutlej eastwards, ascending to 3,000 feet. Throughout India and Burma.

Weight, 36 lbs. (Brandis' Burma List, 1862, No. 108); the average of our specimens gives 33 lbs. The wood seasons well and is fairly durable if kept dry; it is used for boxes, bedsteads, bullock-yokes, doors, window frames, tables and the like. The bark is used for tanning. The fruit is eaten by the hill tribes of Central India, its kernels resemble pistachio nuts; they are largely used in native sweetmeats, and an oil is extracted from them.

		lbs.
O 245.	Garhwal (1868)	35
C 1124.	Ahíri Reserve, Central Provinces	29
C 2751.	Moharli „ „	36
C 2763.	Melghát, Berar	...
C 1249.	Gumsúr, Madras	32

8. MELANORRHŒA, Wall.

Contains 2 species: that here described and *M. glabra,* Wall.; Hook. Fl. Ind. ii. 25; Kurz i. 317. Vern. *Thitseeben,* Burm., a tree of Tenasserim.

1. M. usitata, Wall.; Hook. Fl. Ind. ii. 25; Kurz i. 318. The Varnish Tree of Burma. Vern. *Kheu,* Manipur; *Thitseeben,* Burm.; *Soothan,* Taleing; *Kiahong,* Karen.

A deciduous tree, with dark-grey bark. Wood dark red with yellowish streaks, turning very dark after long exposure; very hard. Pores moderate-sized, not numerous, often subdivided. Each pore or group of pores enclosed in a small patch of light tissue. Medullary rays very fine, wavy, numerous. Numerous white, undulating, concentric lines of softer tissue, unequally distributed in the wood.

Munipur and Burma.

The following experiments have been made to determine the weight and transverse strength:

	Weight.	Value of P.
Benson, in Burma, with bars 3′ × 1·4″ × 1·4″.	found 61 lbs.	526
Skinner, in 1862, No. 91,	„ 61 „	514
Brandis' Burma List, 1862, No. 44	„ 54 „	...
Smythies found the average of our two specimens	. 59 „	...

The wood is used for tool handles, anchor stocks, and has lately been recommended for building, railway sleepers, gun-stocks and other purposes. It gives a black varnish, used to cover buckets to make them watertight. This varnish is used by the Burmese in lacquer work, as size in gilding, for writing in palm-leaf books, and for many other purposes. It has been used in medicine as an anthelmintic with great success.

		lbs.
B 551.	Moulmein, Burma	56
B 2518.	Burma (1862)	62

9. ODINA, Roxb.

1. O. Wodier, Roxb. Fl. Ind. ii. 293; Hook. Fl. Ind. ii. 29; Beddome t. 123; Brandis 123; Kurz i. 321; Gamble 24. Vern. *Kiamil, kimúl, kamlái, kashmala, jhingan, mowen, mohin, moyen, ginyan,* Hind.; *Garja,* Bijeragogarh; *Bara dabdabbi, halloray,* Nep.; *Jiyal, lohar bhadi,* Beng.; *Gob,* Ajmere; *Wodier, wude,* Tam.; *Gumpini, gumpna, dumpini, dumpri, dumper,* Tel.; *Kaikra, gumpri, gharri,* Gondi; *Kekeda,* Kurku; *Shimti, púnil, gojal,* Kan.; *Moi, moja, moye,* Mar.; *Hneingpyoing,* Magh; *Nabhay,* Burm.

A moderate-sized or large deciduous tree with few branches. Bark ½ inch thick, compact, grey, smooth, exfoliating in small irregular plates. Sapwood large; heartwood light red when fresh cut, turning reddish brown on exposure, moderately hard, close-grained, seasons well and does not warp, not very durable. Pores moderate-sized, uniformly distributed, often subdivided. Medullary rays fine, numerous, short, bent where they touch the pores.

Sub-Himalayan tract from the Indus eastwards, ascending to 4,000 feet. Forests of India and Burma.

The following experiments have been made to determine the weight and transverse strength:—

		Weight.	Value of P.
Skinner, No. 101, 1862	found	50	821
Benson, Burma wood, bars 3′ × 1·4″ × 1·4″ . . .	„	60	281
Brandis, No. 46, Burma List, 1862	„	65	...
Smythies, 1878, our specimens (omitting the very old pieces and sapwood)	„	50·5	...

The wood is used for spear-shafts, scabbards, wheel-spokes, cattle-yokes, oil-presses and rice-pounders; it might be good for cabinet work. It has been tried for sleepers both in Madras and in the Oudh and Rohilkhand Line, but has not succeeded. The tree is pollarded for fodder, especially for elephants; its bark is used for tanning; it gives a brown, clear, brittle gum used by the Nepalese as paper-sizing, by weavers in cloth-printing, and in native medicine. With regard to this gum, Captain Campbell, writing from Kumaun, says: "It sells at Rs. 2 per maund, and is used in mixing with lime when white-washing; it is also used for pasting, and is exported annually to the amount of about 100 maunds from Garibolchand forest in the Kumaon Bhabar."

			lbs.
H	3049.	Kumharsen, Sutlej Valley, 2,500 feet (sapwood)	35
P	447.	Ajmere	43
P	3225.	Nagpahar, Ajmere	...
O	226.	Garhwal (1868)	38
O	2992.	„ (1874)	41
C	202.	Mandla, C. P. (1870)	38
C	1103.	Ahiri Reserve, C. P.	48
E	661.	Bamunpokri, Darjeeling Terai	46
E	2342.	„ „ „	48
E	1399.	Chittagong	44
E	1965.	„	61
B	1414.	Tharrawaddy, Burma	64
B	2517.	Burma (1862)	35
B	516.	Andaman Islands	60

10. SEMECARPUS, Linn. fil.

Contains about 6 Indian species, mostly Burmese. Amongst them, besides the species described, the most important are: *S. travancorica*, Beddome t. 232; Hook. Fl. Ind. ii. 31. Vern. *Natu shengote*, Tam.; and *S. auriculata*, Bedd., large handsome trees of the Tinnevelly and Travancore hills.

1. S. Anacardium, Linn. f.; Hook. Fl. Ind. ii. 30; Roxb. Fl. Ind. ii. 83.; Beddome t. 166; Brandis 124; Kurz i. 312; Gamble 25. The Marking-nut Tree. Vern. *Bhilawa, bheyla*, Hind.; *Bhalai*, Nep.; *Bhela, bhelatuki*, Beng.; *Bhallia*, Uriya; *Kongki*, Lepcha; *Bawaræ*, Gáro; *kohka, biba*, Gondi; *Shaing, Shayrang*, Tam.; *Jiri, jidi, nella-jedi*, Tel.; *Gheru, Kari gheru*, Kan.; *Bibwa, bibú*, Mar.; *Chyai beng*, Burm.

A deciduous tree, bark ⅛ inch thick, dark brown, rough, exfoliating in very irregular inner patches; inner bark fibrous. Wood greyish brown, often with yellow streaks, soft, no annual rings. Pores scanty, moderate-sized, frequently subdivided, well marked on a vertical section. Medullary rays numerous, moderately broad, reddish; prominent on a radial section as long, narrow, dark-coloured plates.

Sub-Himalayan tract from the Sutlej eastwards, ascending to 3,500 feet; forests of India, extending to Chittagong but not to Burma.

Weight, 42 lbs. per cubic foot (Brandis); 37 lbs. (Wallich, *Anacardium latifolium*, No. 4); 27 lbs. (Kyd); the average of our specimens gave 37 lbs. Kyd's experiments with bars of Assam wood 2′ × 1″ × 1″ gave P = 197. The wood contains an acrid juice which causes swelling and irritation, and timber-cutters object to felling it; it is not used. The ripe fruit is much used; the fleshy cup is eaten, but is best either dry or roasted. The pericarp contains an acrid juice which is universally used in India for marking ink and in medicine. The ink is improved by the addition of lime water. The green fruit is pounded and made into bird-lime.

		lbs.
C 1157.	Ahiri Reserve, Central Provinces	44
C 2746.	Moharli „ „	40
E 578.	Kookloong Forest, Darjeeling Terai	39
E 627.	Bamunpokri „ „	30
E 2341.	„ „ „	33

The Ahiri specimen, C 1157, has pores joined by irregularly-shaped soft tissue across the medullary rays, and has a harder and closer-grained wood than the Darjeeling specimens; the bark is, however, that of *S. Anacardium*, and there is no reason to doubt its identity. The specimens from Darjeeling are marked by the absence of the lines of softer tissue joining the pores, and it may be suggested for investigation whether they do not come from a different species of *Semecarpus*.

11. DRIMYCARPUS, Hook. f.

1. D. racemosus, Hook. f.; Hook. Fl. Ind. ii. 36; Kurz i. 314; Gamble 26. *Holigarna racemosa*, Roxb. Fl. Ind. ii. 82. Vern. *Kagi*, Nep.; *Brong*, Lepcha; *Telsur*, Beng.; *Amdali*, Ass.; *Chengane, sangaipru, sangryn*, Magh; *Amjour*, Sylhet.

A large evergreen tree. Wood greyish yellow, hard, close-grained. Pores large and moderate-sized, sometimes subdivided, each pore in a narrow white ring. Medullary rays short, moderately broad, uniform and equidistant, joined by innumerable faint, transverse lines.

Eastern Himalaya from 2,000 to 6,000 feet, Khasia hills and Sylhet to Chittagong, Pegu.

Weight, 61 lbs. per cubic foot. Wood used occasionally in Assam for canoes and planking; in Chittagong for boats, for which it is one of the woods most employed. Major Lewin says that boats 50 feet long and 9 feet in girth are sometimes cut.

		lbs.
E 722.	Chittagong	61

12. HOLIGARNA, Ham.

Seven species. *H. Arnottiana*, Hook. f.; Hook. Fl. Ind. ii. 36. (*H. longifolia*, Wt. and Arn.; Beddome t. 167). Vern. *Kagira, kutugeri*, Kan.; *Húlgeri*, Bombay, is a large tree of the Western Gháts, where also are found *H. ferruginea*, Marchand. *H. Grahamii*, Hook. f. (*Semecarpus Grahami*, Wight; Beddome lxxix.) and *H. Beddomei*, Hook. f.; *H. Helferi*, Hook. f.; Kurz i. 315 and *H. albicans*, Hook. f., are trees of Burma.

1. H. longifolia, Roxb. Fl. Ind. ii. 80; Hook. Fl. Ind. ii. 37. Vern. *Barola*, Beng.; *Khreik*, Magh.

Wood grey with yellowish streaks, soft. Pores moderately large, sometimes subdivided, uniform, scanty, prominent as dark lines on a vertical section. Medullary rays fine, white, short, equidistant.

Chittagong and Burma.

Wood not used. It, like all the other species, gives a black acrid exudation which raises blisters and is much dreaded by the hill people.

E 3287. Rinkheong Forest, Chittagong.

13. SPONDIAS, Linn.

Contains 3 species, including, besides the one described, *S. acuminata*, Roxb. Fl. Ind. ii. 453, of South India; and *S. axillaris*, Roxb. Fl. Ind. ii. 453, of Nepal.

1. S. mangifera, Pers.; Hook. Fl. Ind. ii. 42; Roxb. Fl. Ind. ii. 451; Beddome t. 169; Brandis 128; Kurz i. 322; Gamble 25. The Hog Plum. Vern. *Amra, amara, ambodha,* Hind.; *Amara,* Nep., Ass.; *Amna,* Beng.; *Ronchiling,* Lepcha; *Tongrong,* Gáro; *Kat máa,* Tam.; *Aravi mamádi, amatum,* Tel.; *Kat ambolam,* Mal.; *Amb,* Mar.; *Amte,* Kan.; *Hamára,* Gondi; *Ambera,* Kurku; *Puli ille,* Kaders; *Gway,* Burm.

A deciduous tree, with smooth, grey bark. Wood soft, light grey. Pores large, numerous, often subdivided. Medullary rays fine and moderately broad, at unequal distances, white, prominent, distinctly marked on a radial section as long narrow plates.

Sub-Himalayan tract, ascending to 3,000 feet in Sikkim; dry forests of South India and Burma; rare in Central India.

Weight, 43 lbs. (Skinner, No. 116); our specimens gave an average of 26 lbs.; Skinner gives P = 614. Wood soft, of no value. It gives a gum somewhat like gum arabic. The fruit is eaten, and is pickled and is preserved or made into curries; the leaves are acid.

		lbs.
C 2800.	Melghát, Berar	...
E 499.	Kookloong Forest, Darjeeling Terai	30
E 1296.	Cachar (Vern. *Túndúr*)	21
E 1497.	Sylhet (Vern. *Sutrung*)	25
B 560.	Burma	29

ORDER XXXVII. CORIARIEÆ.

An Order containing one Indian genus of a single species.

1. CORIARIA, Linn.

C. myrtifolia, Linn., a shrub of South Europe (*Corroyère,* French), has leaves which are used for tanning and dyeing leather; its fruit is poisonous. *C. sarmentosa* is a New Zealand shrub the fruit of which is made into wine by the settlers.

1. C. nepalensis, Wall.; Hook. Fl. Ind. ii. 44; Brandis 128. Vern. *Masúri, makola,* Hind.; *Raselwa, archarru, pajerra,* Simla; *Bhojinsi* Nep.

A deciduous shrub or small tree. Bark reddish brown, rough. Wood grey, hard, beautifully mottled; no heartwood. Annual rings distinct, marked by a belt of numerous moderate-sized pores; the pores of the outer portion of the annual rings are small and often joined by interrupted concentric bands of whitish tissue. Medullary rays very broad, short.

Outer Himalaya from the Indus to Bhutan, ascending to 8,000 feet in the North-West, and to 11,000 feet in Sikkim.

Growth moderate, 5 to 6 rings per inch of radius. Weight, 47 lbs. per cubic foot. The wood takes a good polish, and is very handsomely marked, so it might be used for boxes and small articles. At present it is only used for firewood, and is often used as such about Simla.

		lbs.
H 68.	Mashobra, Simla, 7,000 feet	48
H 2853.	Mahasu, „ 7,500 „	53
H 2885.	Nagkanda, „ 8,000 „	41

ORDER XXXVIII. MORINGEÆ.

1. MORINGA, Juss.

Wood soft, white. Pores large, scanty, usually in groups of two or three. Medullary rays short, moderately broad.

1. M. pterygosperma, Gaertn.; Hook. Fl. Ind. ii. 45; Beddome t. 80; Brandis 129; Kurz i. 68. *Hyperanthera Moringa*, Roxb. Fl. Ind. ii. 368. The Horse Radish Tree. Vern. *Soanjna, sanjna, senjna, sejna, sohajna, sainjan,* Hind.; *Sujuna,* Beng.; *Swanjera,* Sind.; *Munigha,* Uriya; *Morunga,* Tam.; *Saihan, sejan, múnga, mulaka,* Tel.; *Nuggee,* Kan.; *Daintha, dan-tha-lone,* Burm.

A tree. Bark one inch thick, grey, corky, with longitudinal cracks. Wood soft, white, spongy, perishable. Wood cells large, prominent. Pores large, scanty, often in groups or short radial lines of two or three. Medullary rays short, fine to moderately broad; the distance between them less than the transverse diameter of the pores.

Wild in the Sub-Himalayan tract from the Chenab to Oudh; commonly cultivated in India and Burma.

The tree is pretty; it is generally grown on account of its fruit, which is eaten as a vegetable and is pickled. The root has a strong flavour of horse radish, and is used in medicine as a vesicant. It yields an oil similar to the *Ben oil* of watch-makers, which is not the produce of this but of another species, *M. aptera*, Gaertn., of Africa. It also gives a reddish gum used in native medicine. The leaves and flowers are eaten as well as the fruit, and the branches are lopped for cattle fodder.

E 3214. Calcutta.

2. M. concanensis, Nimmo; Hook. Fl. Ind. ii. 45; Brandis 130. Vern. *Sainjna,* Rajputana.

A tree, bark thick, soft, corky. Wood white, soft, in structure resembling that of *M. pterygosperma,* except that the pores are more variable in size and the medullary rays rather finer.

Rajputana, Sind, Konkan.

Wood apparently not used. The unripe fruit is eaten.

E 3226. Nagpahar, Ajmere.

ORDER XXXIX. CONNARACEÆ.

An Order of little importance, containing 4 genera of Indian trees and shrubs, found in Eastern Bengal, South India and Burma. *Rourea* contains 5 species, four being scandent shrubs from Eastern Bengal, Tenasserim, and the Andamans; and one, *R. santaloides*, Vahl.; Hook. Fl. Ind. ii. 47; Beddome lxxxi. from South India. *Connarus* contains 6 Burmese and two South Indian species: one, *C. paniculatus*, Roxb. Fl. Ind. iii. 139; Hook. Fl. Ind. ii. 52, extending to Chittagong, Sylhet and the Khasia Hills. *Cnestis ramiflora*, Griff.; Hook. Fl. Ind. ii. 54. (*C. platantha*, Griff.; Kurz i. 328.) Vern. *Tankyet louk*, Burm., is a large climbing shrub of Burma; and *Ellipanthus* contains three Burmese shrubs or small trees.

ORDER XL. LEGUMINOSÆ.

The largest Order of Indian trees, shrubs or climbers. It contains about 70 genera containing species distributed over the whole of India, equally in the arid regions of the Inner Himalaya and in the tropical forests of Malabar and Tenasserim. Many of the largest and most important of our forest trees belong to this Order, and with few exceptions they produce valuable timbers. It is divided into three Sub-Orders, *viz.*—

I. Papilionaceæ.
II. Cæsalpinieæ.
III. Mimoseæ.

With the exception of the following genera, *Sesbania, Butea, Erythrina, Pongamia,* and a few species of *Dalbergia* (*D. lanceolaria* and *paniculata*), the wood of the Leguminosæ is characterised by a distinct, hard, dark-coloured heartwood. The pores vary in size, but are generally moderate-sized, large or very large, and enclosed in rings or patches of soft texture, which frequently are confluent, so as to form concentric bands. The medullary rays are generally sharply defined, moderately broad and equidistant (exceptions are *Erythrina* and *Albizzia*).

As regards the structure of their wood, leguminous trees may be most conveniently divided into the following groups, which it will be seen do not correspond with the established division of the Order into genera :—

A. Ougeinia Group.

Pores enclosed in elongated patches of soft tissue, which are arranged in more or less concentric lines. Exceedingly prominent and straight medullary rays. To this group belong *Ougeinia dalbergioides, Afzelia bijuga, Tamarindus indica, Cassia Fistula, marginata* and the new *Cassia* from the Andaman Islands.

B. Prosopis Group.

Pores enclosed in irregularly shaped patches of soft tissue, which are more or less united in concentric bands. To this group belong *Prosopis spicigera,* and the following species of *Acacia,* viz.: *Farnesiana, Catechu, leucophlœa, eburnea* and *pennata. Indigofera, Piptanthus* and *Desmodium* are nearly allied to this group, but differ by having the patches of soft tissue more oblique and less concentric.

To this group also belongs *Hæmatoxylon campeachianum* or "Logwood."

C. Dalbergia Group.

Numerous, narrow, wavy, concentric bands of soft tissue, sometimes interrupted. To this belong all species of *Dalbergia,* except *D. nigrescens,* the identification of which is doubtful, all species of *Pterocarpus, Derris robusta, Cæsalpinia crista* or "Redwood," and *Baphia nitida,* the "Camwood" or "Barwood" of the West African Coast.

D. Bauhinia Group.

Numerous, regularly distributed, concentric bands of soft tissue, which are broader than those in the *Dalbergia* group. To this belong *Pongamia glabra,* all species of *Bauhinia, Cynometra, Cassia Siamea* and *Millettia pendula.*

E. Hardwickia Group.

Pores isolated, not enclosed in patches of soft tissue, though they are generally surrounded by narrow rings. Concentric bands of soft tissue are either wanting entirely, or very scanty. The medullary rays are generally undulating. To this group belong *Xylia dolabriformis, Hardwickia, Adenanthera, Piptadenia, Mimosa, Acacia arabica, modesta* and *ferruginea, Cæsalpinia Sappan* and *echinata* (Brazil or Pernambuco wood).

F. Albizzia Group.

Pores isolated, generally large, not enclosed in patches of soft tissue. None or very few concentric lines of soft tissue. To this group belong all species of *Albizzia, Acacia dealbata* and *Melanoxylon, Acrocarpus, Sesbania,* and *Dalbergia nigrescens.*

G. Erythrina Group.

Pores large. Distinguished by broad medullary rays and broad bands of soft tissue which do not always enclose the large pores. To this group belong all species of *Erythrina,* and *Butea frondosa.*

Sub-order I. PAPILIONACEÆ.

Contains 35 genera, divided into 8 tribes, *viz*:—

Tribe	I.—Podalyrieæ	*Piptanthus.*
„	II.—Genisteæ	*Priotropis* and *Crotalaria.*
„	III.—Galegeæ	*Indigofera, Colutea, Millettia, Mundulea, Tephrosia, Sesbania* and *Caragana.*
„	IV.—Hedysareæ	*Lespedeza, Alhagi, Æschynomene, Ormocarpum, Ougeinia* and *Desmodium.*
„	V.—Viceæ	*Abrus.*
„	VI.—Phaseoleæ	*Mucuna, Erythrina, Spatholobus, Butea, Dioclea, Pueraria, Cajanus, Cylista* and *Flemingia.*
„	VII.—Dalbergieæ	*Dalbergia, Pterocarpus, Pongamia* and *Derris.*
„	VIII.—Sophoreæ	*Dalhousiea, Calpurnia, Sophora, Euchresta* and *Ormosia.*

Many of these, however, contain only small shrubs; such are *Priotropis, Crotalaria, Colutea, Mundulea, Tephrosia, Caragana, Lespedeza, Alhagi, Æschynomene, Ormocarpum, Cajanus, Flemingia, Dalhousiea,* and *Calpurnia*: others only climbing shrubs; such are *Abrus, Mucuna, Spatholobus, Dioclea, Pueraria* and *Cylista.*

Of the genera not here described, *Sophora* contains about six species of which *S. mollis,* Wall.; Brandis 132. Vern. *Arghawán,* Afg.; *Gojár, kún, málan, tilún, kathi, brisari,* Punjab; *Pahar gúngri,* Kumaun, is a yellow-flowered handsome shrub of the Punjab and North-West Himalaya; and *Ormosia travancorica,* Beddome t. 45, is a tree of the Tinnevelly and Travancore Hills.

1. PIPTANTHUS, D. Don.

1. P. nepalensis, D. Don; Hook. Fl. Ind. ii. 62; Brandis 132; Gamble 25. Vern. *Bankaru,* Sutlej; *Shalgari,* Kumaun.

A shrub with greenish-grey bark. Wood white. Pores small, in wavy, oblique and concentric bands, except at the inner edge of the annual rings, which are marked by a continuous line of pores. Medullary rays fine, equidistant.

Himalaya from the Sutlej to Bhutan, above 7,000 feet.

Has handsome, large, yellow flowers, and is sometimes planted for ornament in the hills and in Europe.

		lbs.
H 3024.	Nagkanda, Simla, 9,000 feet	40

Priotropis cytisoides, W. and A.; Kurz i. 363; Gamble 25, is a yellow-flowered branching shrub of the Eastern Himalaya and Burma. *Crotalaria* contains numerous shrubs, of which the most important is *C. juncea,* Linn., the "*Sunn* Hemp Plant," commonly cultivated in India.

2. INDIGOFERA, Linn.

Contains a number of Indian species, about 16 of which are shrubs. Few of them are of any importance except the Indigo Plant, *I. tinctoria,* Linn.; Roxb. Fl. Ind. iii. 379; Brandis 135. Vern. *Nil,* Hind, which is extensively cultivated in Bengal, the North-Western Provinces, the Punjab, Sind and South India. *I. pulchella,* Roxb. Fl. Ind. iii. 382; Hook. Fl. Ind. ii. 101; Beddome lxxxv.; Brandis 136; Kurz i. 361; Gamble 25. Vern. *Sakena, sakna hakna,* Hind.; *Baroli,* Mar.; *Togri,* Bhfl; *Balori,* Kurku; *Hikpi,* Lepcha; *Tau maiyain,* Burm., is a large, handsome, pink-flowered shrub of the forests of the Sub-Himalayan tract, South India and Burma; its flowers are sometimes eaten as a vegetable in Central India.

1. **I. heterantha,** Wall.; Brandis 135. *I. Gerardiana,* Wall.; Hook. Fl. Ind. ii. 100 (*var.*). Vern. *Kati, khenti, mattu, kats, shágali,* Pb.; *Kathi, theot,* Simla.

A small shrub. Bark ⅛ inch thick, brown, with longitudinal anastomosing lines. Wood hard, white, with an irregular heartwood of dark colour. Annual rings distinctly marked by a white line and by a continuous belt of pores. Pores small, enclosed in patches of softer texture, which frequently join, forming short, interrupted, concentric bands. Medullary rays fine, numerous, almost equidistant.

North-West Himalaya and eastern skirts of the Suliman Range, ascending to 8,000 feet.

Growth slow, 20 rings per inch of radius. Weight, 56 lbs. per cubic foot. The twigs are used for basket work and often form part of the twig bridges of the North-West Himalaya.

		lbs.
H 2825.	Fagu, Simla, 8,000 feet	...
H 2870.	Nagkanda, Simla, 8,000 feet	...
H 2935.	Mahasu, Simla, 7,000 feet	56

2. **I. atropurpurea,** Ham.; Brandis 136; Hook. Fl. Ind. ii. 101; Roxb. Fl. Ind. iii. 381. Vern. *Bankati, kala sakena, sakna,* Hind.; *Khenti, jand,* Kaghan; *Kathi, gorkatri,* Kashmir.

A shrub of smaller size, but with wood of structure similar to that of *I. heterantha.*

Salt Range from 2,500 to 5,000 feet. Outer Himalaya from the Jhelum to Nepal, ascending to 9,000 feet, but found as low as 1,200 feet on the Siwalik Hills.

The twigs are used for basket work and twig bridges.

H 2824. Cheog Forest, Simla, 7,000 feet.

Colutea nepalensis, Sims.; Brandis 136. (*C. arborescens*, Linn.; Hook. Fl. Ind. ii. 103). The Bladder Senna. Vern. *Bráa*, Ladak, is a shrub of the arid valleys of the Inner Himalaya.

3. MILLETTIA, Wight and Arn.

Contains about 22 species of trees, shrubs or climbers chiefly from Eastern Bengal and Burma, The genus may be divided into 2 sections:—

1. Trees, containing 7 Burmese and 1 Eastern Bengal species.

2. Climbers, containing 8 species from Burma, 7 from Northern and Eastern Bengal, 3 from Southern India, and 1 from North-West and Central India.

M. pulchra, Bth.; Hook. Fl. Ind. ii. 104; Kurz i. 355. Vern. *Thitpagan*, Burm., is an erect tree of the forests of the Khasia Hills and Eastern Bengal ascending to 4,000 feet. *M. pendula*, Bth.; *M. tetraptera*, Kurz; *M. pubinervis*, Kurz; *M. ovalifolia*, Kurz; *M. Brandisiana*, Kurz; and *M. atropurpurea*, Bth.; Kurz i. 358. Vern. *Kway tanyeng, tanyengnee*, Burm., are all trees of Burma. Among the climbers, *M. auriculata*, Baker; Hook. Fl. Ind. ii. 108; Brandis 138; Gamble 26. (*Robinia macrophylla*, Roxb. Fl. Ind. iii. 329, *Otosemma macrophylla*, Bth.) Vern. *Maudh*, Oudh; *Gonjha, ganj*, Kumaun; *Gurúr*, Gondi; *Murari*, Kurku; *Gonjo*, Nep.; *Brúrik*, Lepcha. (No. 3479, Sukna Forest, Darjeeling Terai) is a very common large climber of the Sub-Himalayan tract, from the Sutlej to Bhutan, ascending to 3,500 feet. *M. cinerea*, Bth. and *M. pachycarpa*, Bth., with 3 other species, are common in the forests of Sikkim and the Khasia Hills; while *M. monticola*, Kurz, is only found in the forests of Sikkim above 6,000 feet and at Nattoung in Martaban, between 6,500 and 7,200 feet.

1. M. pendula, Bth.; Hook. Fl. Ind. ii. 105. *M. leucantha*, Kurz i. 356. Vern. *Thinwin*, Burm.

A deciduous tree, with small purplish black heartwood, beautifully streaked, very hard. Pores few, moderate-sized, joined by narrow concentric bands of soft tissue. Medullary rays fine, uniform and equally distributed.

Savannah forests and dry lower hill forests of Burma, up to 2,000 feet.

Weight, Brandis' Burma List of 1862, No. 41, gives 60 lbs.; our specimens 66 lbs. per cubic foot. The wood is used for cross pieces of harrows, and is worthy of attention for its beautiful grain and dark colour.

		lbs.
B 2520.	Myodwin, Burma (1862)	66

B 2249 (73 lbs.) from the Andamans and B 3141 (67 lbs.) from Myodwin, Burma (1862). Vern. *Chloani*, Burm.; have a dark, reddish brown, very hard heartwood, in structure resembling that of *M. pendula*. It is doubtless a species of *Millettia*.

Mundulea suberosa, Bth.; Hook. Fl. Ind. ii. 110; Beddome lxxxv. is an ornamental small tree of South India, and *Tephrosia* contains several shrubs, among which may be noticed *T. candida*, DC.; Hook. Fl. Ind. ii. 111; Brandis 138; Gamble 26. Vern. *Lehtia*, Kumaun; *Bodle*, Nep., a handsome white-flowered shrub of the Sub-Himalyan tract, Eastern Bengal and Burma. Its leaves are used to poison fish.

4. SESBANIA, Pers.

Soft-wooded shrubs or trees. Wood white, soft. Medullary rays fine and closely packed.

1. S. ægpytiaca, Pers.; Hook. Fl. Ind. ii. 114; Beddome lxxxvi.; Brandis 137; Kurz i. 362; Gamble 26. *Æschynomene Sesban*, Roxb. Fl. Ind. iii. 332. Vern. *Jait, jhijan, janjhan, dhandiáin*, Hind.; *Jayanti*, Beng.; *Saori, sewri*, Berar; *Shewari*, Dekkan; *Suiminta*, Tel.; *Yaythagyee*, Burm.

A soft-wooded tree, 10 to 12 feet high. Wood white, extremely soft. Pores small, in short, linear, radial groups, between the very fine and very numerous medullary rays; the distance between rays being less than the transverse diameter of the pores.

Cultivated in many parts of India and Burma, wild in tropical Africa.

Weight, 27 lbs. per cubic foot. Not durable.

Grown in Berar and the Dekkan to furnish poles as a substitute for bamboo; the bark is made into rope, the wood is used to boil jaggery, and the leaves and branches are cut for cattle fodder. It is commonly planted in Bengal as a hedge-plant, for which purpose its very quick growth renders it suitable. It is also sometimes grown to support the plantations of the betel pepper. Roxburgh says the wood is said to make the best gunpowder charcoal, and Kurz that it is good for children's toys.

	lbs.
C 870. Amraoti, Berar	27

2. **S. grandiflora,** Pers.; Hook. Fl. Ind. ii. 115; Beddome lxxxvi.; Brandis 137; Kurz i. 362. *Æschynomene grandiflora*, Roxb. Fl. Ind. iii. 530. *Agati grandiflora*, Desv.; W. and A. Prodr. 215. Vern. *Basna*, Hind.; *Buka, bak, agasta*, Beng.; *Bagfal*, Sundarbans; *Hadga, heta*, Berar; *Agati*, Tam.; *Avesi*, Tel.; *Agase*, Kan.; *Poukpan, poukpyoo*, Burm.

A short-lived, soft-wooded tree, with large handsome flowers, attaining 20 to 30 feet in height. Wood white, soft. Pores small and moderate-sized, often in radial groups of 3 to 5 between the numerous, fine, white medullary rays.

Cultivated in Southern India, Burma, and in the Ganges Doab.

Weight, 32 lbs. per cubic foot. The wood is not durable; in Lower Bengal it is used for posts for native houses and for firewood (Home); in Berar and the Dekkan it is grown as a substitute for bamboo. The tender leaves, pods and flowers are eaten as a vegetable, and the tree is grown as a support for the betel pepper vine; it is easily known by its very large, handsome, pink flowers and long narrow pods.

	lbs.
C 871. Amraoti, Berar	32

Caragana, Brandis, 133 contains several low spinescent shrubs of the arid region of the Punjab, Sind and Beluchistan, and the inner valleys of the Punjab Himalaya. *Lespedeza* contains a number of undershrubs of Northern India and Burma. Among these, *L. eriocarpa*, DC.; Hook. Fl. Ind. ii. 144, is a shrub of the Himalaya between 3,000 and 9,000 feet, with handsome purple flowers and a hard red wood. Pores moderate-sized, scattered or in short concentric lines. Medullary rays fine. Few concentric lines of soft tissue. (H. 3192. Nowti Valley, Simla, 4,000 feet). *Alhagi Maurorum*, Desv.; Brandis 144. (*Hedysarum Alhagi*, Roxb. Fl. Ind. iii. 344.) The Camel Thorn. Vern. *Jawása*, Hind., is a widely-spread shrub of the Ganges Valley and the arid and northern dry zones, whose leaves are used as fodder for camels. *Æschynomene aspera*, Linn.; Hook. Fl. Ind. ii. 152; Brandis 147; (*Hedysarum lagenarium*, Roxb. Fl. Ind. iii. 365.) Vern. *Sola, phúl-sola*, Hind., Beng.; *Nírjilúza*, Tel., is the *Solah* plant of tanks and marshes in Bengal, from whose stems the well-known white pith is obtained which is used for making hats, toys, and for other purposes. *Ormocarpum sennoides*, Kurz i. 390, is an evergreen shrub of the plains of Central and South India.

5. OUGEINIA, Bth.

1. **O. dalbergioides,** Benth.; Hook. Fl. Ind. ii. 161; Beddome t. 36; Brandis 146. *Dalbergia Oojeinensis*, Roxb. Fl. Ind. iii. 220. Vern. *Sandan, asainda, tinnas, timsa*, Hind.; *Shánjan, pánan*, Oudh; *Sandan pipli*, Nep.; *Bandhona*, Uriya; *Kala palás, tewas*, Mar.; *Sér, shermana*, Gondi; *Dargu, tella motku*, Tel.; *Kari mutal*, Kan.; *Tewsa*, Bhíl; *Rutok*, Kurku; *Tunnia*, Banswara; *Telus*, Khandeish.

A moderate-sized deciduous tree, under certain circumstances gregarious. Bark ⅛ inch thick, light brown, sometimes with bluish patches, with regular longitudinal and horizontal cracks. Sapwood small; heartwood mottled, light brown, sometimes reddish brown, hard, close-grained; annual rings indistinct. Pores moderate-sized, enclosed in irregularly-shaped, more or less concentric but interrupted patches and bands of white soft tissue. These patches, which are tapering and pointed at the ends, are separated by irregularly-shaped belts of firm and darker-coloured shining tissue, in which the fine and numerous, white, uniform and equidistant medullary rays are distinctly visible. Pores marked on a longitudinal section.

Chiefly in the intermediate zone. Sub-Himalayan tract from the Sutlej to the Tista, ascending to 5,000 feet; Central India and the Western Coast.

Weight, 57 to 60 lbs. (*Brandis*); R. Thompson gives 58; our specimens give an average of 55 lbs. The wood is tough and durable, and takes a beautiful polish. It is used for agricultural implements, carriage poles, wheels and furniture; also for building. The tree gives an astringent red gum; the bark is pounded and used to intoxicate fish; and the branches are lopped for cattle fodder. A crystalline substance, probably magnesia, is sometimes found in the wood (see specimen E 601).

		lbs.
P 102.	Sutlej Valley, Punjab	...
O 212.	Garhwal (1868)	52
C 185.	Mandla, Central Provinces (1870)	53
C 1152.	Ahiri Reserve, Central Provinces	54
C 2767.	Melghát, Berar	55
C 1242.	Gumsúr, Madras	52
E 601.	Lohagarhi, Darjeeling Terai	67
W 1226.	North Kanara	53

6. DESMODIUM, Desv.

Contains a number of shrubs found in the forests in almost all parts of India. *D. pulchellum*, Bth.; Hook. Fl. Ind. ii. 162; Brandis 145; Kurz i. 383; Gamble 26 (*Hedysarum pulchellum*, Roxb. Fl. Ind. iii. 361) Vern. *Juta-salpani*, Beng.; *Set krishnapani*, Cuttack; *Tbungtamin*, Burm., is a common erect shrub with the flowers in the axils of bifoliolate bracts. *D. gyroides*, DC.; Hook. Fl. Ind. ii. 175; Kurz i. 388; Gamble 27. Vern. *Bolú*, Nep., is an erect, blue-flowered shrub of the Himalayas, Eastern Bengal and Burma; and *D. gyrans*, DC.; Hook. Fl. Ind. ii. 174; Brandis 146; Gamble 27 (*Hedysarum gyrans*, Roxb. Fl. Ind. iii. 351) Vern. *Gorachand*, Beng., is common in India and Burma, and generally known as the "Telegraph Plant" from its small, sensitive, rotating, lateral leaflets.

1. D. tiliæfolium, G. Don.; Hook. Fl. Ind. ii. 168; Brandis 145. Vern. *Sambar, shamru, chamra, chamyár, chamkat, chamkúl, martan, motha, gurshagal, prí, marára, múss, múrt, laber*, Hind.

A large deciduous shrub, with thin, grey bark. Wood yellowish brown, with a darker centre. Pores small. Annual rings distinctly marked by a belt of small pores; in the outer part of each annual ring the pores are very small, and generally arranged in short, linear, wavy, concentric lines. Medullary rays white, fine to very fine.

Himalaya, from the Indus to Nepal, between 3,000 and 9,000 feet.

Growth slow, 14 rings per inch of radius. Weight, 53 lbs. per cubic foot. The bark is extensively us d for rope-making and paper.

		lbs.
H 3184.	Dung.galli, Hazara, 8,000 feet	...
H 51.	Nagkanda, Simla, 7,000 feet	...
H 2934.	Mahasu, Simla 7,000 feet	53
H 3019.	Kotgarh, Simla, 7,000 feet (var. *argenteum*, Wall.)	...

2. D. Cephalotes, Wall.; Hook. Fl. Ind. ii. 161; Beddome lxxxvii.; Kurz i. 386; Gamble 26. *Hedysarum Cephalotes* and *umbellatum*, Roxb. Fl. Ind. iii. 360. Vern. *Bodle kúrú*, Nep.; *Maniphlyol*, Lepcha; *Cheleuta*, Tel.

A shrub with grey bark and yellowish wood, which in structure resembles that of *D. tiliæfolium*.

Eastern Himalaya, South India and Burma.

E 3281. Dainah Reserve, Western Dúars.

Abrus contains 3 species, of which *A. precatorius*, Linn.; Hook. Fl. Ind. ii. 175; Roxb. Fl. Ind. iii. 258; Brandis 139. Vern. *Gunchi, rakti*, Hind.; *Masputi*, Nep., is a wiry climber, whose seeds (*rakti*) are used as weights by jewellers; they weigh 1½ to 2 grains each.

Mucuna contains several large climbers of Bengal and Burma, among which the chief are *M. imbricata*, DC. Vern. *Kasi*, Beng., with large plaited pod, covered with stinging hairs (No E 483 Darjeeling Terai), and soft, very porous wood; *M. macrocarpa*, Wall.; Gamble 28. Vern. *Balenqra*, Nep., an enormous climber of the hills of Sikkim, Khasia, Sylhet and Burma up to 7,000 feet; and *M. pruriens*, DC. The Cowhage Plant. Vern. *Alkusá*, Beng.; *Kiwach, goncha*, Hind.; *Kouatch*, Nep., which is an annual climber, well known in the forests from its golden brown, velvety pod, covered with irritating hairs, which are used as a vermifuge.

7. ERYTHRINA, Linn.

Contains 7 species of Indian soft-wooded, handsome-flowered, deciduous trees. *E. ovalifolia*, Roxb. Fl. Ind. iii. 254; Hook. Fl. Ind. ii. 189; Beddome lxxxviii.; Kurz i. 367. Vern. *Hari-kekra*, Beng.; *Kone kathit*, Burm., is a tree of the coast forests of Chittagong, Arracan and Pegu, extending northwards to Sylhet and Assam. *E. lithosperma*, Miq. Vern. *Yea-kathit*, Burm. and *E. holosericea*, Kurz i. 367, are trees of Burma, while *E. resupinata*, Roxb. Fl. Ind. iii. 257; Brandis 141, is a herbaceous plant from a perennial root-stock found in the grass lands of the Himalayan Terai.

Wood soft; no heartwood. Pores large, medullary rays broad. Numerous concentric bands of soft texture, which, as a rule, have no connection with the pores.

1. E. suberosa, Roxb. Fl. Ind. iii. 253; Hook. Fl. Ind. ii. 189; Beddome lxxxvii.; Brandis 140; Kurz i. 369; Gamble 27. Vern. *Pangra, dauldhák, rúngra, rowaura, nasút, madára*, Hind.; *Gúlnashtar, pariára, thab*, Pb.; *Fullidha*, Nep.; *Mandal*, Gáro; *Katiang*, Lepcha; *Muni, madnga*, Tam.; *Mulu modugu*, Tel.; *Phangera*, Gondi; *Gada phassa*, Kurku.

A moderate-sized deciduous tree. Outer bark corky, light grey, with deep, irregular, vertical cracks, varying in thickness up to 1 inch; inner bark fibrous, ⅛ inch thick. Wood very soft, spongy, white, fibrous but tough; that near the centre of darker colour, but no regular heartwood. Annual rings visible. Pores very large, scanty, often subdivided. Medullary rays short, broad; the tissue between the rays consisting of narrow, hard, wavy and often interrupted, concentric bands of a darker colour, separated by alternate bands of white, spongy tissue. The tangential section presents the appearance of anastomosing fibres. On the radial section the medullary rays appear as long, wavy, shining bands, giving the wood a handsome mottled appearance. Pores prominent on a vertical section.

Himalaya from the Ravi to Bhutan, ascending to 3,000 feet. Oudh, Central and South India, Burma.

Growth fast, 4 rings per inch of radius. Weight, 13 to 20 lbs. per cubic foot. The wood is used for scabbards, sieve frames, and occasionally for planking. The tree is readily grown from cuttings.

		lbs.
O 530.	Dehra Dún	20
C 1145.	Ahiri Reserve, Central Provinces	...
E 668.	Bamunpokri, Darjeeling Terai	13

E. indica, Lam.; Hook. Fl. Ind. ii. 188; Beddome lxxxvii.; Brandis 139; Kurz i. 368; Roxb. Fl. Ind. iii. 249. The Indian Coral Tree. Vern. *Pangra, panjira, pangara, farad,* Hind.; *Palita mandar,* Beng.; *Muruká,* Tam.; *Modugu,* Tel.; *Pangara, phandra,* Mar.; *Háliwára, páliwára,* Kan.; *Chaldua,* Uriya; *Madar,* Cachar; *Katheik,* Magh; *Penlaykathit,* Burm.; *Dudap,* Malay; *Errabadu,* Cingh. (*Mochi* wood of Madras).

A deciduous tree. Bark yellowish, smooth and shining, peeling off in thin papery flakes, young stems and branchlets armed with prickles. Structure the same as that of *E. suberosa.*

Cultivated throughout India and Burma; wild in Oudh, Bengal, South India and Burma.

Weight, 17 to 26 lbs. per cubic foot according to our specimens, but 18 lbs. is nearest the true weight. Wood rather durable, though it is so light and open-grained it does not warp or split, and it varnishes well. It is used for light boxes, toys, scabbards, trays, and is often grown as a support for and to give shade to the betel pepper vine. It grows readily from cuttings and is used for hedges. It gives a dark-brown gum of no value.

		lbs.
C 820.	Bairagarh Reserve, Berar	17
B 2343.	Myanoung, Burma	18
B 2223.	Andaman Islands (1866)	26

3. E. arborescens, Roxb. Fl. Ind. iii. 256; Brandis 140; Gamble 27. Vern. *Rungara,* Kumaun; *Rodinga, fullidha,* Nep.; *Gyesa,* Lepcha; *Dingsong,* Khasia.

The wood has a similar structure to that of *E. suberosa* and *Indica,* but it is more compact, less spongy, and has more numerous concentric bands of soft texture.

Outer Himalaya from the Ganges to Bhutan, up to 7,000 feet; Khasia Hills.

It is very handsome when covered with its bright scarlet flowers; it grows easily from cuttings, and is often planted for ornament, as in the avenues at Darjeeling.

F 3106. Darjeeling, 7,000 feet.

E 2344 (16 lbs. per cubic foot) from Bamunpokri, Darjeeling Terai, has been identified as *E. stricta,* Roxb.; Beddome t. 175; Kurz i. 369; Gamble 27. Vern. *Mouricou, kichige,* Kan.; *Toung kathit,* Burm., described from Western India and Burma. The structure is the same as that of *E. suberosa.*

Spatholobus Roxburghii, Bth.; Brandis 143; Gamble 27. (*Butea parviflora,* Roxb. Fl. Ind. iii. 248; Kurz i. 365) Vern. *Mala, mula, maula,* Hindi.; *Debrelara,* Nep.; *Terolrik,* Lepcha; *Pouknway,* Burm., is a very common gigantic creeper of the forests of the Sub-Himalayan tract from the Jumna eastwards, Bengal and Burma, with trifoliolate leaves, white flowers and a soft porous wood in concentric layers separated by a ring of soft tissue exuding a red gum resembling "kino" (E 480, Darjeeling; O 2027, Garhwal, 1874).

8. BUTEA, Roxb.

Besides the species described below, *B. superba*, Roxb. Fl. Ind. iii. 247; Brandis 143; Kurz i. 365. Vern. *Yĕl parás*, Mar.; *Tige motku*, Tel.; *Samur*, Gondi; *Tunang*, Kurku; *Pouknway*, Burm., is a large scarlet-flowered climber of India and Burma, giving a gum like that of *B. frondosa*; and *B. minor*, Ham.; Hook. Fl. Ind. ii. 195; Gamble 27, is a shrub or climber of the Eastern Himalaya.

1. B. frondosa, Roxb. Fl. Ind. iii. 244; Hook. Fl. Ind. ii. 194; Beddome t. 176; Brandis 142; Kurz i. 364; Gamble 27. Vern. *Dhák, palás, kakria, kankrei, Chichra*, Hind.; *chalcha*, Bandelkhand; *Chiúla, puroha*, C. P.; *Palás*, Beng.; *Palási, bulyettra*, Nep.; *Lahokúng*, Lepcha; *Porásu*, Uriya; *Murr*, Gondi; *Pharsa*, Kurku; *Porasan*, Tam.; *Modugu, mohtu*, Tel.; *Muttuga, thorás*, Kan.; *Parás*, Mar.; *Gasskeala, calukeale*, Cingh.; *Pouk*, Burm.

A moderate-sized deciduous tree. Bark ¼ inch thick, fibrous, grey, exfoliating in small irregular pieces; exuding from cuts and fissures a red juice which hardens into a ruby-coloured gum similar to *kino*. Wood dirty white, soft, not durable; no annual rings. Pores large, scanty. Medullary rays broad and moderately broad, white; the darker tissue between the rays is broken up into oblong patches by broad concentric bands of white tissue similar in appearance to the medullary rays; the latter distinctly visible on a radial section as long, irregular bands.

Throughout India and Burma, extending in the North-West Himalaya as far as the Jhelum.

The weight is given by Kyd as 32 lbs. per cubic foot; by Adrian Mendis, Ceylon Collection, No. 11, 38 lbs.; the average of our specimens is 36 lbs. Kyd gives P = 335. The wood is not durable, but is said to be better under water, and so is used in North-West India for well curbs and piles. The bark of the root yields a good fibre which is used for coarse cordage, for caulking boats and to make slow matches. The gum is sold as "Bengal Kino" and has the same properties as that obtained from the *Pterocarpus Marsupium*; it is said to be used to purify indigo. The seeds are used as a purgative and vermifuge. In Oudh and Central India lac is collected on its branches. The leaves are used as plates and as fodder for buffaloes. The tree is well known from its handsome scarlet flowers, appearing in the hot season before the leaves; they give a yellow dye, which treated with alum is used at the Holi festival.

		lbs.
O 237.	Garhwal (1868)	...
C 1119.	Ahiri Reserve, Central Provinces	...
C 2759.	Moharli Reserve, Central Provinces	36
E 674.	Rakti Forest, Darjeeling Terai	31
E 2345.	Sivoke „ „ „	40

Dioclea reflexa, Hook. Fl. Ind. ii. 196, is a climbing shrub of the Andamans. *Pueraria tuberosa*, DC.; Hook. Fl. Ind. ii. 197; Brandis 141; Gamble 28. (*Hedysarum tuberosum*, Roxb. Fl. Ind. iii. 363) Vern. *Siáli, badár, bilei kand, billi, pona*, Hind; *Dari, gumodi*, Tel., is a large tuberous-rooted, deciduous climber with bright blue flowers and soft, spongy wood. *Cajanus indicus*, Spreng., is a shrub cultivated in most parts of India for its seed (*Arhar*, Beng.; *Paisigong*, Burm.) and for its leaves which are given as fodder to cattle. *Cylista scariosa*, Ait., is a climbing shrub of South India and Burma. *Flemingia* contains a number of shrubs found in the forests of India, and Burma, among which one of the most common is *F. semialata*, Roxb. Fl. Ind. iii. 341; Kurz i. 374; Gamble 28 (*F. congesta*, Roxb. *var.*; Hook. Fl. Ind. ii. 228.) Vern. *Bhalia*, Hind.; *Batwási*, Nep.; *Mipitmúk*, Lepcha, a tall handsome-flowered shrub of Northern India with a white wood having rather broad medullary rays, scanty pores and concentric lines of white tissue like that of *Erythrina* (E 3279, Dainah Forest, W. Dúars).

9. DALBERGIA, Linn. fil.

Contains about 28 Indian species, of which one-half are trees and the other half climbing shrubs. About 8 species are found in North-West and Central India, 13 in the Eastern Himalaya, Assam and Eastern Bengal, 8 in South India, and 18 in Burma. The Genus is divided into sections as follows:—

Pod flattened, winged at the edges—
  Staminal bundle split on one side only . *Sissoa.*
  „ „ „ two sides . . *Dalbergaria.*
Pod thickened, not winged, falcate . . . *Selenolobium* (*Drepanocarpus* Kurz).

To the section Sissoa belong the trees *D. Sissoo, latifolia, rimosa* and *cultrata* and nine climbing shrubs. To the section Dalbergaria belong the trees *D. lanceolaria, purpurea, paniculata, glomeriflora* and *hircina* and five climbing shrubs. To the section Selenolobium belong *D. spinosa* and *reniformis*, trees or erect shrubs and two climbers.

D. rimosa, Roxb. Fl. Ind. iii. 233; Hook. Fl. Ind. ii. 232; Brandis 148, Vern. *Kaogrúm*, Sylhet and *D. hircina*, Ham.; Brandis 151. Vern. *Saras, bandír, tantia, gogera*, Hind., are trees found in the Sub-Himalayan tract from the Ganges eastwards. *D. reniformis* Roxb. Fl. Ind. iii. 226; Hook. Fl. Ind. ii. 238. (*Drepanocarpus reniformis*, Kurz i. 336). Vern. *Kures*, Sylhet; *Htoukma*, Burm.; and *D. spinosa*, Roxb. Fl. Ind. iii. 233. Vern. *Yaychinya*, Burm., are small trees of the tidal forests of Burma, the latter species, according to Kurz i. 337, having: "Wood soft, beautifully silvery white, close and straight grained. The roots powdered absorb alcohol, and a spoonful of the powder in a tumblerful of water is said to be sufficient to destroy in less than half an hour the effects of alcohol, even in cases bordering on delirium tremens." *D. glomeriflora*, Kurz, is a tree of the upper forests of the Pegu Yomas.

Among the climbers, which have mostly a hard wood, the chief are *D. volubilis*, Roxb.; Brandis 152. Vern. *Bhatia, bankhara*, Hind., found in the Sub-Himalayan tract; and *D. tamarindifolia*, Roxb.; Gamble 29. Vern. *Damar*, Nep.; *Keti*, Sylhet, of the outer Eastern Himalaya, Eastern Bengal, Burma and the Andamans. *D. monosperma*, Dalz. (*Drepanocarpus monospermus*, Kurz i. 337), is a scandent shrub of tidal forests in Upper Tenasserim. *D. Cumingii*, Bth., is a scandent shrub said by Kurz to give a dyewood, the *Kayu-lakka* of commerce. *D. congesta*, Grah.; and *D. sympathetica*, Nimmo, are climbing shrubs of the hills of South India.

D. Sissoo, latifolia and *cultrata* have a hard, dark-coloured, heavy heartwood; while *D. stipulacea, lanceolaria* and *paniculata* have white wood without heartwood. All Dalbergias, with the exception of *nigrescens* (the identification of which is doubtful), have scanty, moderate-sized pores, joined by narrow bands or lines of soft texture. Medullary rays fine, uniform and equidistant.

1. Dalbergia Sissoo, Roxb. Fl. Ind. iii. 223; Hook. Fl. Ind. ii. 231; Beddome t. 25; Brandis 149; Gamble 28. The Sissoo. Vern. *Shisham, sissu, sissai*, Hind.; *Shewa*, Pushtu; *Táli, safedar, shín, nelkar*, Pb.; *Sissái*, Oudh; *Yette*, Tam.

A large deciduous tree. Bark between ⅓ and ½ inch thick, grey, exfoliating in narrow longitudinal strips. Sapwood small, white; heartwood brown with darker longitudinal veins, close and even grained, seasons well, very hard. Annual rings not distinctly marked, alternating dark and light-coloured bands, which run into each other. Pores large and moderate-sized, uniformly distributed, joined by irregular, narrow, wavy, white, concentric bands. Medullary rays white, very fine, uniform and equidistant, numerous. Pores well defined on a longitudinal section.

Sub-Himalayan tract from the Indus to Assam, ascending to 3,000 feet. Van Someren, in his "List of Forest Trees of Mysore and Coorg," gives it as occurring under the Kanarese name *biridi*, but it is probably not indigenous in those provinces.

The amount of data available regarding the rate of growth of Sissú is as yet very small. In the "Forest Flora of the North-West and Central India," Brandis says that it attains under favourable circumstances, on an average, 2½ feet girth in 12, and 4½ feet in 30 years. Since then a few data have been collected, principally from the specimen saplings sent from the Punjab for the Paris Exhibition of 1878.

The annual rings in the sapwood are, as a rule, fairly distinct; those in the heartwood are generally ill-defined: in either case a lens is required to make them out. The following statement exhibits the rings counted on sections from the Changa-Manga plantation, which were cut in 1877:—

Known age.	Number of rings visible.	Average diameter of section.	Average diameter of heartwood.	Rings per inch.
		Inches.	Inches.	
5 years	4	6·75	0·75	1·2
6 "	6	8	2	1·5
7 "	6	9	3	1·3
8 "	6	12	4·5	1
9 "	9	10·75	3·2	1·7
10 "	6	11	5	1·1
Average rings per inch of average radius				1·3

The calculation has, however, been based on the number of rings counted; if we take the known age, the number of rings will be respectively 1·5, 1·5, 1·5, 1·3, 1·7, 1·8, giving an average of 1·55 year per inch of average radius. But these data refer to trees up to 10 years of age only, and grown in favourable conditions on irrigated land, so that no further calculation can be derived from them, the measurements of older trees being much wanted. But, assuming this rate of increase of 1·55 ring per inch, we should have at 12 years of age about 4 feet girth, which is a much faster growth than Brandis' estimate.

The specimens from the Jhelum Sailaba plantations on non-irrigated land gave 4 rings per inch of radius average. This would make 30 years to a girth of 4 feet, which is nearly Brandis' estimate.

The Punjab plantations also give the following information:—

Changa-Manga plantation (*Punjab Forest Report*, 1876-77. *p.* 22).

	Age.	Average height.	Average girth.
	Years.	Ft.	Inches.
Vhankara Circle Compartments 6, 5, 8, Block I . . .	6	35	28
Manjoki " " 77, to 87 & 99 to 111, Block I .	4	20	9

Delhi Bela plantation (*Mr. Minnikin's Report*, 1878).

	Age.	Average height.	Average girth.
Chandrawál, Compartment I 3 trees	7½	25 to 30	15
Kudsia, " III	6	20	15
" " "	2	12	6
Jáffar Khan, " IV 6 trees	6	...	15·5

This gives for the Changa-Manga plantation 1·35 to 2·8 rings per inch of radius, and for Delhi Bela 2 to 3·14, or an average of 2·5 rings per inch. This gives a girth of 30 inches at 12 years of age, which is Brandis' estimate.

A specimen from the Darjeeling Terai, in the Bengal Forest Museum, gives 35 rings on a mean diameter of 11 inches, 27 rings being heartwood.

The weight and transverse strength have been calculated by the following experiments :—

Experiment by whom conducted.	Year.	Wood whence procured.	Weight.	Number of experiments.	Size of bar used.	Value of P.
					Ft. In. In.	
Cunningham .	1854	Gwalior . . .	48	4	2 × 1 × 1	697
Campbell . .	...	Bengal . . .	56	1	6 × 2 × 2	923
Skinner, No. 56 .	1862	„ . . .	50	...	{3 × 1½ × 1½ {2 × 1 × 1	}870
Russell . .	„	„ . . .	55·5	...	– × 1 × 1	967
Baker . . .	1829	Northern Bengal (Cossipore, 1819).	49	9	7 × 2 × 2	762
„ . . .	„	Northern Bengal (Cossipore factory).	45	6	6 × 2 × 2	734
„ . . .	„	Northern Bengal .	..	8	3 × 1½ × 1	709
„ . . .	„	„ „ .	...	13	2 × 1 × 1	606
Brandis . .	1864	Bengal . . .	49	15	6 × 2 × 2	738
„ . .	„	„ . . .	47	18	6 × 2 × 1⅓	740
„ . .	1865-66	„ . . .	46	9	6 × 2 × 2	787
„ . .	„	„ . . .	47	17	3 × 1 × 1	869
„ . .	„	„ . . .	44	11	2 × 1 × 1	854
„ . .	„	„ . . .	45	14	2 × 1 × 0¾	919
Smythies . .	1878	Northern India, various places.	48	8	......	...

The wood is very durable, seasons well and does not warp or split. It is highly esteemed for all purposes where strength and elasticity are required. Clifford says that "in strength it is only inferior to sâl, while in many other useful qualities it surpasses it, and has the advantage of being lighter. For felloes and naves of wheels and carved work of every description, for framings of carriages and similar work, it is unsurpassed by any other wood, owing to its fine seasoning and standing qualities." It is extensively used for boat-building, carts and carriages, agricultural implements, in construction and especially for furniture.

Formerly, it was more extensively used for gun-carriages than it can be at present, owing to the comparatively small supply. With regard to its durability and strength as a wood for wheels, Clifford says, "The wheels of our ordnance carriages have never failed, however arduous or lengthened the service has been on which they have been employed, of which no more striking example can be furnished than the campaign in Afghanistan, about the most trying country in the world for wheels. Some of our batteries served throughout the campaign, went to Baneean and even to the Hindoo Koosh and came back again to India without a break-down, while Royal Artillery wheels built of the very best materials Woolwich could produce, specially for Indian service, almost fell to pieces after few months' exposure and service on the plains of India."

It has been tried and found to be good for sleepers, and Mr. McMaster in the Proceedings of the Institution of Civil Engineers, vol. xxiii. 1863, says it will be really good for that purpose.

It is much planted as an avenue tree all over India and in forest plantations in the Punjab and Bengal.

			lbs.
P	145.	Giri Valley, Punjab, 3,000 feet	44
P	884.	Multan, „	52
P	1205.	Changa-Manga plantation (9 specimens)	...
P	1347.	Peraghaib and Saila plantations, Jhelum (8 specimens) . . .	...
O	205.	Garhwal (1868)	52
O	537.	Dehra Dún	...
O	1460.	Bahraich, Oudh	49
O	1486.	Kheri, „	52

		lbs.
E 675.	Rakti Forest, Darjeeling Terai	47
E 2347.	Sukna „ „ „	46
E 634.	Eastern Dúars, Assam	42

2. **D. latifolia,** Roxb. Fl. Ind. iii. 221; Hook. Fl. Ind. ii. 231; Beddome t. 24; Brandis 148; Gamble 29. The Blackwood or Rosewood of Southern India. Vern. *Sitsal,* Beng., Nep., Oudh; *Shisham, sisu, kalarukh, bhotbeula, sissúi,* Mar.; *Sissu,* Guz.; *Sirás, sissú, sirsa, sissa,* Mandla; *Sissa,* Uriya; *Iti, eruvadi,* Tam.; *Jitegi, yerugudu, jitangi,* Tel.; *Biti, thodagatti,* Kan.; *Bhotuk,* Bhíl; *Serís,* Gondi; *Serisso,* Kurku.

A deciduous tree attaining a large size in South India. Bark ⅓ inch thick, grey, with irregular short cracks, exfoliating in thin fibrous longitudinal flakes. Sapwood yellow, small; heartwood extremely hard, dark purple, with black longitudinal streaks; no distinct annual rings, but alternating concentric belts of dark and light colour, which, however, run irregularly into each other. Pores moderate-sized, uniformly distributed, generally joined by narrow, white, wavy interrupted, concentric lines. Medullary rays light-coloured, fine, numerous, uniform and equidistant.

Oudh, Eastern Bengal, Central and South India.

Growth moderate when young, 5 to 9 rings per inch of radius (*Brandis*); some of our specimens shew 8 rings.

It coppices well, is easily raised from seed, and reproduces well naturally.

The weight and transverse strength have been determined by the following experiments:—

Experiment by whom conducted.	Year.	Wood whence procured.	Weight.	Number of experiments.	Size of bar.	Value of P.
					Ft. In. In.	
Wallich, No. 52	...	India	66·5	......	......	......
Puckle	1859	Mysore	51	4	2 × 1 × 1	1,052
Maitland	1862	Anamalais	51	......	3 × 1½ × 1½	746 to 996
Skinner, No. 54	1862	„	50	......	Various	912
Baker	1829	Malabar	55	3	6 × 2 × 2	822
R. Thompson	1873	Central Provinces.	66	......	......	......
Smythies	1878	Various provinces.	56	15	......	......

Brandis says the value of P may be taken at 950.

It is a valuable furniture wood, and is exported to Europe from the forests of Kanara and Malabar. Wood sent to London for sale in 1878 fetched £13 10s. per ton. It is also used for cart wheels, agricultural implements and for gun-carriages. It is good for carving and fancy work, and is used for the handles of knives, kukris and other arms. It has been used for sleepers. Nine sleepers which had been down 7 to 8 years on the Mysore State Railway were found to have, when taken up, 5 good, 3 still serviceable, and 1 bad. It has been grown in plantations in Malabar and Kanara.

		lbs.
P {464. 467.}	Ajmere	...
C 187.	Mandla, Central Provinces (1869)	46
C 2984.	Jabalpur (1863)	53
C 1146.	Ahiri Reserve, Central Provinces	58
C 2732.	Moharli Reserve, Central Provinces	52
C 955.	Dangs Forests, Guzerat, Bombay	53
C 1236.	Gumsúr, Madras	64
C 1303.	„ „	64
E 492.	Khookloong Forest, Darjeeling Terai	...

		lbs.
E 672.	Bamunpokri, Darjeeling Terai	50
E 2348.	" " "	60
W 1227.	North Kanara	54
W 720.	South "	55
W 855.	" "	49
D 2044.	Mysore	51
D 1072.	North Arcot	57
No. 24.	Salem Collection	62

3. **D. cultrata,** Grah.; Hook. Fl. Ind. ii. 233; Kurz i. 342. Vern. *Yendike,* Burm.

A moderate-sized tree. Bark ½ inch thick, smooth, with short transverse clefts. Wood purplish black, with darker streaks, with harder wood than, but structure similar to, that of *D. latifolia.*

Burma.

Weight, according to Benson, 83 lbs.; according to Brandis' Burma List, 1862, No. 36, 64 lbs.; our specimens give 69 and 70 lbs. Benson gives, from experiments made with bars 3′ × 1·4″ × 1·4″, P = 1003. It is used for wheels, agricultural implements, handles of dahs and spears, and especially for carvings. The sap-wood is very perishable, but the heartwood extremely durable.

		lbs.
B 2521.	Burma (1862)	70
B 2728.	Nawing Forests, Prome (1858)	69
B 2697.	Tavoy (Wallich, 1828)	...

---

4. Specimens marked *Thitpoke* (B2523), collected in Burma in 1862 (Brandis' Burma List, 862, No. 133), have light yellow wood with numerous concentric bands, scanty, large and moderate sized pores, and very fine, very numerons, uniform and equidistant medullary rays. *Thitpoke* is identified by Kurz as *Dalbergia purpurea,* Wall., Hook. Fl. Ind. ii. 235; Kurz i. 344; which has a small heartwood. To this also belongs B 2230 from the Andaman Islands.

---

5. **D. lanceolaria,** Linn.; Hook. Fl. Ind. ii. 235; Brandis 151; Gamble 29. *D. frondosa,* Roxb. Fl. Ind. iii. 226; Beddome lxxxviii. Vern. *Takoli, bithúa,* Hind.; *Bander siris,* Nep.; *Barbat, parbati,* Banswarra; *Gengri,* Panch Mehals; *Harráni,* Dharwar; *Nal valanga,* Tam.; *Pedda sopara, yerra patsaru, pasarganni,* Tel.; *Dandous, kaurchi,* Mar.

A deciduous tree. Bark ¼ inch thick, compact, grey, smooth, exfoliating in thin rounded patches. Wood white, moderately hard, not durable, no heartwood. Annual rings (?) marked by thin, concentric lines. Pores scanty, large and moderate-sized, larger and somewhat more numerous in the spring wood; often oval and subdivided, very prominent on a longitudinal section. Medullary rays extremely fine, very numerous, very regularly distributed, joined by very fine, short, white bars.

Sub-Himalayan tract from the Jumna eastwards, ascending to 2,500 feet, Central and South India.

Skinner, No. 53, gives for the weight 62 lbs. per cubic foot; Wallich 46 lbs.; our specimens give only 33 to 44 lbs. Skinner also gives P = 1003, but it is probable that he has not described the right wood, for, although he gives the correct Telugu name, yet he calls his specimens (No. 53, p. 75) *Moukshow,* Burm., and "Moulmein lance-wood;" while Kurz, the latest authority, does not give *D. lanceolaria* as occurring in Burma. Skinner says that one log was brought from the western coast, and another by Conductor Bowman from Burma. Beddome says the timber is useful for building purposes.

		lbs.
C 1144.	Ahiri Reserve, Central Provinces	...
E 618.	Champasari Forest, Darjeeling Terai	33
E 2346.	Bamunpokri, Darjeeling Terai	44

6. D. paniculata, Roxb. Fl. Ind. iii. 227; Hook. Fl. Ind. ii. 236; Beddome lxxxviii.; Brandis 150; Kurz i. 345. Vern. *Katsirsa,* Oudh; *Dhobein, dhohein, pássi, satpuria,* Hind.; *Patchalai, valange,* Tam.; *Potrum, porilla, patsuru, toper,* Tel.; *Sondarra, sheodur, topia,* Mar.; *Hasur guniri, pachári,* Kan.; *Piangani,* Mal.; *Tapoukben,* Burm.; *Padri,* Gondi, Bhíl; *Phassi,* Kurku.

A large deciduous tree. Bark ⅛ inch thick, compact, grey, smooth, with occasional horizontal cracks. Wood yellowish or greyish white, soft, perishable; no heartwood. Structure most remarkable, entirely different from that of other species of the genus: broad concentric masses of wood alternate with narrow, dark coloured belts of a fibrous substance, resembling the inner bark. Planks cut out of old trees fall to pieces. Pores small, scanty. Medullary rays very fine, numerous. Wavy, narrow, concentric bands of white tissue alternate with broader bands of harder and darker substance.

North-West Himalaya from the Jumna to Oudh, Central and South India. (Quoted by Kurz from Burma, but identification doubtful.)

Weight, according to Skinner, No. 55, and R. Thompson 48 lbs. per cubic foot; our specimens give an average of 37 lbs. Skinner gives P = 872. Wood not durable and very subject to the attacks of insects. Beddome says it is used for building and other purposes.

		lbs.
C 1115.	Ahiri Reserve, Central Provinces	32
C 2928.	Seoni, Central Provinces	46

7. D. nigrescens, Kurz i. 346. Vern. *Thitsanweng,* Burm.

A moderate-sized deciduous tree. Wood light grey, soft. Pores scanty, large, subdivided. Medullary rays very fine, very numerous.

Dry mixed forests of Upper Burma.

		lbs.
B 291.	Burma (1867)	38
B 2522.	„ (1862)	39

There is some doubt about the identification of this species, owing to the absence of concentric bands.

8. D. stipulacea, Roxb. Fl. Ind. iii. 233; Hook. Fl. Ind. ii. 237; Kurz i. 346; Gamble 29. Vern. *Tatebiri,* Nep.; *Garodosal,* Mechi; *Tón-nyok,* Lepcha.

A large climbing shrub. Wood soft, greenish grey, with a purplish brown heartwood, porous. Pores numerous, of different sizes, small to extremely large, in white, undulating, concentric bands running into each other. Medullary rays white, fine, very numerous.

Eastern Himalaya, ascending to 4,000 feet, Assam, Khasia Hills, Chittagong and Burma.

Weight, 48 lbs. per cubic foot. Growth, about 9 rings per inch of radius.

		lbs.
E 574.	Khookloong Forest, Darjeeling Terai	...
E 2349.	Sivoke „ „ „	48

9. D. foliacea, Wall.; Hook. Fl. Ind. ii. 232; Kurz i. 347; Gamble 29. Vern. *Tatebiri,* Nep.

A large straggling shrub, with white porous wood with a small dark heartwood, in structure ressmbling that of *D. stipulacea*, except that the medullary rays are broader.

Eastern Himalaya and Burma.
E 3274. Múrnghát Reserve, W. Dúars.

10. PTEROCARPUS, Linn.

Contains 4 Indian species. *P. macrocarpus*, Kurz i. 349; Hook. Fl. Ind. ii. 239, is a deciduous tree of the Eng and upper mixed forests of Martaban and Tenasserim, rare in Prome. The "Rosewood" or "Lancewood" of West Africa is produced by *P. erinaceus*, Poir.

The wood of the three species examined is very uniform in structure, though the colours differ. They all have extremely fine, uniform and equidistant medullary rays, large and small pores, and fine, wavy, concentric bands.

1. P. indicus, Willd.; Hook. Fl. Ind. ii. 238; Beddome t. 23; Kurz i. 349. *P. dalbergioides*, Roxb. Fl. Ind. iii. 236. Andaman Redwood. Vern. *Padouk*, Burm.; *Chalanga-dá*, And.

A lofty tree, sometimes evergreen, with grey bark. Sapwood small; heartwood dark red, close-grained, moderately hard to hard, with a slight aromatic scent. Pores scanty, small to large, sometimes oval and subdivided. Very fine, white, wavy, interrupted, concentric lines, irregularly distributed. Medullary rays extremely fine, very numerous, uniform and equidistant. The transverse diameter of the pores much larger than the distance between the rays.

Burma and the Andaman Islands.

The weights of our specimens from Burma differ considerably from those from the Andamans, the latter being much lighter, the wood softer and the colour rather lighter. The weight and transverse strength have been determined from the following experiments:—

Experiment by whom made.	Year.	Wood whence procured.	Weight.	Number of experiments.	Size of bar.	Value of P.
					Ft. in. in.	
Simpson	...	Tenasserim	62	...	3 × 1½ × 1½	781
"	...	"	81	...	3 × 1½ × 1½	1,575
Benson	...	"	71	...	3 × 1·4 × 1·4	1,033
Skinner, No. 110	1862	Burma	56	...	Various	864
Maitland	"	"	57	...	3 × 1½ × 1½	620 to 1,122
Brandis, No. 39	"	"	60	...	......	......
Smythies	1878	"	60	3	......	......
"	"	Andamans	48	4	......	......
Bennett, No. 1	1872	"	49·5	...	......	827

Used for furniture, carts, gun-carriages and other purposes. It is said to be the most useful wood in the Andamans, where it grows to an enormous size. Major Protheroe describes a tree felled in 1876 with a clear stem of 65 feet and a girth of 17 feet, and says that the wood of the root is closer-grained, darker-coloured and more beautifully marked than that of the stem. The plank sent to the Paris Exhibition of 1878 measured nearly 4 feet across. In London, a portion of the same log from which the plank was cut fetched a price of £17-10*s.* per ton, or nearly Rs. 4 per cubic foot, while three logs lately sold in Calcutta fetched Rs. 60 per ton. Furniture made from Padouk wood and exhibited at Paris in 1878 by Messrs. Jackson and Graham was much admired. They reported on it as follows:—

"This is a straight-grown wood, with rather a coarse open grain, but without any strong figure or markings. When first cut it is of a reddish brown colour, but it fades to much the same colour as teak—a wood it resembles very much, and it is about as hard, but much heavier. From the six specimen trees sent us, we imagine that it does not grow to any great size. The largest sent to us measured 16 feet long × 1 foot 7 inches × 1 foot 6 inches. We consider it suitable for all kinds of furniture. We manufactured it into a suite of morning-room furniture, which was exhibited at the Paris Exhibition, and which stood the test of a very hot summer in a most satisfactory manner."

It seasons well, works well and takes a very fine polish. It gives a kind of gum "kino." Home's valuation surveys in the Andamans gave an average of 7 mature trees per acre, which shews what a large quantity of the wood might be made available for export.

		lbs.
B 584.	Martaban	60
B 2524.	Pegu (1862)	60
B 2708.	Tavoy (Wallich, 1828)	62
B 2716.	" (" ")	59
B 526.	Andaman Islands	46
B 2207.	" " (1866)	43
B 2494.	" " (Home, 1874, No. 1)	55

2. P. santalinus, Linn. f.; Hook. Fl. Ind. ii. 239; Roxb. Fl. Ind. iii. 234; Beddome t. 22; Brandis 153. The Red Sanders Tree. Vern. *Lal chandan, rakta chandan, seyapu chandanum,* Tam., Tel.; *Honné,* Kan.

A small tree. Sapwood white; heartwood purplish black, dark-orange red when fresh cut, extremely hard, the shavings giving a blood-red orange colour. Pores moderate-sized, often subdivided, scattered. Medullary rays fine, numerous, equidistant, wavy. The pores are joined by many fine, white, undulating, concentric lines at unequal distances.

South India, chiefly in Cuddapah, North Arcot and the southern portion of the Karnúl district.

Growth, Beddome mentions a tree 5 years old having 18 feet 5 inches in height and 9 inches in girth; this would give 3 rings per inch of radius, which is fast, but the tree was young and the annual growth of old trees is much slower. In Captain Campbell-Walker's Report on the Cuddapah forests of March 1875, he mentions a tree having grown in 14 months to a height of $4\frac{1}{2}$ feet and girth of 3 inches.

Weight, according to Skinner, No. 112, 70 lbs.; our specimens give 76 to 77 lbs. Skinner gives P = 975. Beddome says it is used for building purposes and for turning. It is exported from Madras in billets and root pieces as a dyewood, as it contains a red colouring principle, "santalin," which is soluble in alcohol and ether, but not in water. Dissolved in alcohol, it dyes cloth a beautiful salmon-pink colour. It is used in medicine by the natives as an astringent, but does not seem to have much value.

Regarding the method of planting the "Red Sanders" Tree, the following memorandum by Mr. Yarde was published at page 98 of the Report of the Forest Conference Meeting in 1875:—

"The seeds are gathered in May and sown in July, in small beds about eight feet square, prepared adjacent to where water is to be had. They are thrust into the light soil perpendicularly, or at an inclination, and about an inch deep (just sufficient to cover the winged seed). From 700 to 800 may be put into the nursery beds of the above-mentioned dimensions, and watered every second evening by a watering-can. Seeds soaked for a night in cold water germinate in 20 to 25 days, while those unsoaked take from 30 to 35. After germination has taken place, the beds must be moderately watered by a picotta or other means, with small communicating or distribution channels made between the beds. During the first six months particular care in watering is very necessary. Too much water proves equally destructive as none at all. The condition of the soil where planted must be the best guide, as they seem only to inhabit the country where the rainfall is small.

"The leading shoot at six months has a tendency to drop from the top weight of leaves, and should be supported with a forked stick, which is sufficient to straighten the stem. The nursery must be kept free from weeds, and when the plants in the nursery are about six months old, they may be safely transferred to wicker or bamboo baskets, which must be done during the rains. They must be carefully removed with pointed instruments, so that their tap-roots are not injured or broken. The wicker baskets with the plants should be placed in a shady spot and watered every second or third day, and when it is perceived that the roots have taken firm hold, and the plants quite revived, the baskets should be buried in pits 1′ × 1′ × 2″ at about five or six feet apart, and watered till the rains set in. During the time the plants are in the nursery, as a protection from the sun, I always found Peruvian cotton, planted near or around, very beneficial. Of course any shade will suit the purpose required."

		lbs.
D 2066.	Mysore	76
D 2917.	Madras (Brandis)	...
D 1075.	North Arcot (with sapwood)	66
D 3151.	Cuddapah, Madras	77

3. P. Marsupium, Roxb.; Fl. Ind. iii. 234; Hook. Fl. Ind. ii. 239; Beddome t. 21; Brandis 152. Vern. *Bija, bijasár, bijasál, piasal,* Hind.; *Byasa,* Uriya; *Dhorbeula, ásan,* Mar.; *Peddei,* Gondi; *Peddagi, yeanga, yeggi, yegísa, pedéga, pedéi,* Tel.; *Vengai,* Tam.; *Benga, honné,* Kan.; *Bijaira,* Bijeragogarh; *Radat bera,* Bhíl.

A large deciduous tree. Bark ½ inch thick, grey, with long vertical cracks, exfoliating in small pieces of irregular shape and size. Sapwood small; heartwood brown, with darker streaks, very hard, durable, yielding a red resin. Pores moderate-sized and large, often subdivided, uniformly distributed. Numerous fine, white, wavy, concentric lines at regular intervals. Medullary rays extremely fine and numerous; not visible except under a lens, uniform and equidistant, prominent on a radial section. Pores marked on a vertical section; the transverse diameter of the pores many times larger than the distance between the rays.

Central and South India, extending northwards to the Banda District of the North-Western Provinces.

The weight and transverse strength have been determined by the following experiments:—

Experiment by whom conducted.	Year.	Wood whence procured.	Weight.	No. of experiments.	Size of bar used.	Value of P.
					Ft. in. in.	
Wallich, No. 224 . .	...	Travancore . .	47	...	......	...
Puckle	1859	Mysore	56	...	......	...
"	"	"	51	...	2 × 1 × 1	821
Skinner, No. 111 . .	1862	South India . .	56	...	... ...	868
French	1861	Madras (Erode workshops).	...	3	1 × 1 × 1	511
Baker (Nos. 501 to 504) .	1829	Baggri Forest, Midnapore . .	63	4	7 × 2 × 2	667
Smythies	1878	Different places .	52	10	......	...

The wood is durable, seasons well and takes a fine polish; the heartwood is full of gum resin and stains yellow when damp. It is much used for doors and window frames, posts and beams, furniture, agricultural implements, cart and boat building. It has also been used for sleepers. Out of 25 sleepers which had been down 7 to 8 years on the Mysore State Railway, there were found, when taken up, 9 good, 11 still serviceable and 5 bad. It has also been used to a certain extent on the Holkar and Neemuch and other lines. It yields, from wounds in the bark, a red gum-resin called "kino," a valuable astringent, much used in medicine.

		lbs.
C 175.	Mandla, Central Provinces (1870)	47
C 1105.	Ahiri Reserve, Central Provinces	58
C 2741.	Moharli Reserve, Central Provinces	49
C 2918.	Seoni, Central Provinces	56
C 1238.	Gumsúr, Madras	56
W 742.	South Kanara	48
W 752.	" "	45
W 850.	" "	53
D 1061.	South Arcot	...
D 1086.	Madura	59
No. 39.	Salem Collection	52

11. PONGAMIA, Vent.

1. **P. glabra**, Vent.; Hook. Fl. Ind. ii. 240; Beddome t. 177; Brandis 153; Kurz i. 335. *Galedupa indica*, Lam.; Roxb. Fl. Ind. iii. 239. Vern. *Karanj, papar*, Hind.; *Dalkaramcha, karanja*, Beng.; *Koranjú*, Uriya; *Pongá*, Tam.; *Kanga, pungu, kaniga, ganuga*, Tel.; *Garanji*, Gondi; *Charr*, Ajmere; *Húngay, pong*, Kan.; *Thinwin*, Burm.

A moderate-sized tree, almost evergreen. Bark soft, ⅓ inch thick, greyish brown, covered with small tubercles. Wood moderately hard, white, turning yellow on exposure. Annual rings indistinct. Pores moderate-sized, scanty, included in and joined by white, wavy, concentric anastomosing bands of soft tissue, which alternate with bands of darker colour and firmer texture. In the darker-coloured bands the fine, white, numerous and uniformly distributed medullary rays are distinctly visible.

Sub-Himalayan tract from the Ravi eastwards, ascending to 2,000 feet; Bengal, Burma, Central and South India.

Weight, according to Skinner, No. 107, 40 lbs. per cubic foot; our specimens give an average of 42 lbs. Skinner gives P = 686. The wood is not durable, and is readily eaten by insects, but is improved by seasoning in water. In Lower Bengal it is used for oil-mills and firewood; in South India for solid cart-wheels. The seeds are used in native medicine; they also give a thick, red-brown oil used for burning, and medicinally as an application for skin diseases, for which it is said to be very efficacious. The leaves are used for manure for rice-fields in Mysore. The tree is easily grown from cuttings.

		lbs.
P 457.	Ajmere	45
C 1133.	Ahiri Reserve, Central Provinces	38
E 411.	Sundarbans	43

12. DERRIS, Loureiro.

Contains several climbing shrubs or trees, chiefly Burmese. *D. scandens*, Bth.; Hook. Fl. Ind. ii. 240; Brandis 154; Kurz i. 339 (*Dalbergia scandens*, Roxb. Fl. Ind. iii. 232) Vern. *Gunj*, Pb.; *Noaluta*, Beng.; *golari, potra, nalavail*, Gondi; *Cheratali badu, nala-tige*, Tel.; *Tupail*, Mar.; *Meekyoung-nway*, Burm., is a large climbing shrub, common all over India and Burma; it has a white, hard wood, with regular structure. *D. uliginosa*, Bth.; Hook. Fl. Ind. ii. 241; Kurz i. 339. Vern. *Kelia lota*, Beng., is a large evergreen scandent shrub of the tidal forests of Bengal and Burma, whose stems are used in the Sundarbans for tying logs to boats. Several other species, all climbing, occur in Burma, chiefly in tidal forests.

1. **D. robusta**, Bth.; Hook. Fl. Ind. ii. 241; Brandis 154; Kurz i. 338. *Dalbergia Krowee*, Roxb. Fl. Ind. iii. 229. Vern. *Mowhitta*, Ass.; *Bolkakarú*, Gáro; *Krowee*, Sylhet; *Gumbong*, Magh.

A deciduous tree. Wood light brown, hard. Pores large and moderate-sized. Medullary rays prominent, fine, wavy, equidistant. Numerous narrow, wavy, concentric bands of soft texture frequently joining the pores.

Outer Himalaya from the Ganges eastwards, Assam, Eastern Bengal, down to Pegu.

Weight, 53 lbs. per cubic foot. Roxburgh says it grows quickly to a large size.

		lbs.
E 786.	Kamrúp, Assam	53

Dalhousiea bracteata, Wall.; Hook. Fl. Ind. ii. 248; Wight Ic. t. 265, is a shrub of the Khasia Hills and Eastern Bengal. *Calpurnia aurea,* Lam.; Hook. Fl. Ind. ii. 251; Beddome lxxxix., is a handsome shrub of the hills of South India. *Euchrista Horsfieldii,* Bennett; Hook. Fl. Ind. ii. 248, is an erect shrub of the Khasia Hills.

SUB-ORDER II. CÆSALPINIEÆ.

Contains 17 genera, divided into 5 tribes, *viz.,*—

Tribe I.—Eucæsalpinieæ	*Peltophorum, Mezoneurum, Cæsalpinia, Pterolobium, Acrocarpus, Wagatea, Poinciana* and *Parkinsonia.*
„ II.—Cassieæ	*Cassia.*
„ III.—Bauhinieæ	*Bauhinia.*
„ IV.—Amherstieæ	*Amherstia, Humboldtia, Afzelia, Tamarindus* and *Saraca.*
„ V.—Cynometreæ	*Hardwickia* and *Cynometra.*

Mezoneurum and *Pterolobium* contain only climbing shrubs. The former has three species: *M. cucullatum,* W. and A.; Brandis 155; Kurz i. 409; Gamble 30. (*Cæsalpinia cucullata,* Roxb. Fl. Ind. ii. 358) Vern. *Biskoprah,* Oudh; *Sungray,* Nep.; *Runggong, yangkup,* Lepcha; *Ragi,* Bombay; *Kyoungchet,* Burm., a large climber whose stems and branches are armed with strong hooked prickles with a corky base, with porous wood, and found in the Sub-Himalayan tract from the Sarda eastwards, Western Ghâts and Burma (E. 488, Darjeeling Terai); *M. enneaphyllum,* W. and A.; Hook. Fl. Ind. ii. 258, a climber of Cachar, Chittagong and Burma; and *M. glabrum,* Desf., a large climber of Pegu. The latter has one species, *Pterolobium indicum,* A. Rich.; Hook. Fl. Ind. ii. 259 (*P. macropterum,* Kurz i. 410. *Cæsalpinia lacerans,* Roxb. Fl. Ind. ii. 367) Vern. *Walekadúda,* Tel.; *Kyoungyet-nway,* Burm., a prickly climber of Burma. The remaining genera contain chiefly trees.

Peltophorum ferrugineum, Bth.; Hook. Fl. Ind. ii. 257; Kurz i. 408, is an evergreen tree of the coast forests of the Andamans, said by Kurz to have a blackish heartwood. *Poinciana* contains one indigenous tree, *P. elata,* Linn.; Hook. Fl. Ind. ii. 260; Roxb. Fl. Ind. ii. 355; Beddome t. 178; Brandis 157; Vern. *Padenarayan,* Tam.; *Sunkeswar,* Tel.; *Nirangi,* Kan., found in the forests of South India, but more often seen planted. Skinner, No. 106, says it has wood of a yellow colour, tolerably close and even grained, easily worked, and giving a smooth surface, warping slightly, but not subject to crack, well suited for cabinet work; and that its weight is 45 lbs. per cubic foot, and P = 516. It also contains *P. regia,* Bojer, the well-known ornamental tree with crimson and orange flowers appearing in the hot season. It was introduced from Madagascar, and is now found planted almost all over India. Kurz says the wood is white, soft, light and loose-grained, and that the tree gives a plentiful gum. *Parkinsonia aculeata,* Linn. Hook. Fl. Ind. ii. 260; Beddome xci.; Brandis 158; Kurz i. 403, is an introduced shrub or small tree, now almost naturalised in India, especially in the arid zone, where it is grown as a hedge plant. The wood is whitish, light and soft, but close-grained and polishes fairly. Skinner, No. 102, gives W = 40, P = 565. *Wagatea spicata*, Dalz.; Hook. Fl. Ind. ii. 261, is a climbing shrub of the Western Ghâts. *Amherstia nobilis*, Wall.; Hook. Fl. Ind. ii. 272; Kurz i. 411. Vern. *Thawka, soka*, Burm., perhaps the most beautiful flowering tree in the world, was discovered by Mr. Crawford and Dr. Wallich at Kogun in the Salween Valley; it is now cultivated in gardens round Calcutta and elsewhere, and is usually propagated by layers. *Humboldtia* contains three or four small trees of South India: *H. unijuga*, Beddome t. 183, is a handsome tree of the Travancore Ghâts, said to yield a hard durable timber; *H. Brunonis*, Wall., is found in the forests of Coorg and South Kanara, and *H. Vahliana*, Wight, on the Nilgiris.

Altogether, there is scarcely any class of trees with such a variety of species with handsome flowers and generally, at the same time, valuable wood as the sub-order Cæsalpinieæ. Besides the Indian genera there are numerous others of value such as the Logwood *Hæmatoxylon Campechianum*, Linn., (No. 2966,) of Central America and the West Indies; the Copaiba Balsam Tree, *Copaifera officinalis*, and the Carob Tree, *Ceratonia siliqua*, Linn., now almost naturalised in the Salt Range and other parts of the Punjab.

13. CÆSALPINIA, Linn.

Contains 10 shrubs, chiefly climbing and prickly. *C. Bonducella*, Roxb. Fl. Ind. ii. 357; Hook. Fl. Ind. ii. 254. Brandis 156; Gamble 30. The Fever Nut. Vern. *Katkaranj*, Hind.; *Nata*, Beng.; *Gajkai*, Kan., is a common very prickly climbing shrub of India, often used for hedges. Its seeds are used in medicine, and contain an oil; they are tonic and antiperiodic. *C. sepiaria*, Roxb. Fl. Ind. ii. 360; Hook. Fl. Ind. ii. 256; Brandis 156; Kurz i. 406. The Mysore Thorn. Vern. *Urn, úri, arlu, relu, kando, aila*, Hind.; *Chillar*, Mar.; *Hotsigé*, Kan., is a large prickly climber used for hedges. *C. pulcherrima*, Sw. Vern. *Krishna-chúra*, Beng., is a handsome shrub cultivated in gardens in most parts of India. *C. crista*, "Redwood" or "Brésillet," (No. 2963) comes from the West Indies; *C. echinata*, "Brazil Wood" or "Pernambuco Wood," (No. 2964) from South America, and *C. braziliensis*, "Brazilletto," from the West Indies and Brazil. *C. Coriaria*, Willd., is the American Sumach or Divi-divi. Weight, 56 lbs.; P = 724 (Skinner No. 32).

1. C. Sappan, Linn.; Hook. Fl. Ind. ii. 255; Roxb. Fl. Ind. ii. 357; Beddome xc.; Brandis 156; Kurz i. 405. Vern. *Bakam*, Hind., Guz., Beng.; *Patunga*, Tam.; *Bakamu, bakapu*, Tel.; *Bokmo*, Uriya; *Pattang*, Mar.; *Patanga*, Kan.; *Teing nyet*, Burm.

A small thorny tree. Sapwood white, heartwood red. Pores isolated, enclosed in narrow rings. Medullary rays fine; the distance between the rays equal to, or somewhat larger than, the transverse diameter of the pores.

South India, Bengal and Burma.

Weight, according to Skinner No. 33, 60 lbs. per cubic foot; Wallich gives 61 lbs. Skinner gives P = 1540! The wood takes a fine polish and does not warp or crack; it yields a valuable dye, which is largely exported. It has been grown in plantations at Nilambúr and in the Central Provinces.

		lbs.
C 3136.	Moharli, Central Provinces (cultivated) (sapwood) . . .	52

14. ACROCARPUS, Wight.

A genus placed by Baker in Flora Indica, Vol. ii., under *Mimoseæ*; but by Bentham and Hooker in the Genera Plantarum as here described.

1. A. fraxinifolius, Wight; Hook. Fl. Ind. ii. 292; Beddome t. 41; Brandis 158; Kurz i. 410; Gamble 30. Vern. *Mandania*, Nep.; *Madling*, Lepcha; *Mallay kone*, Tinnevelly; *Kilingi*, Burghers; *Hantige, belanji, kavulige*, Kan.

A lofty deciduous tree, with thin, light-grey bark. Sapwood white; heartwood light red, moderately hard. Pores moderate-sized to very large, often oval and divided into two to five compartments, either isolated or enclosed in narrow interrupted bands of softer tissue prominent on a vertical section. Medullary rays fine and moderately broad.

Hills of the Eastern Himalaya down to Chittagong, ascending to 4,000 feet; South India, and Burma.

Weight, 39 lbs. per cubic foot. The wood is used by planters in Darjeeling for tea-boxes and planking, in the Wynaad for building and furniture, and in Coorg for shingles. It is an extremely handsome tree, growing with a fine tall cylindrical stem, handsome flowers and large bipinnate leaves, which are red when young; it reproduces easily and is fast growing. Beddome mentions a tree 27 feet in girth above the buttresses, and Manson states that a windfall tree in the Lower Darjeeling Hills had a bole 70 feet without a branch and measured 11 feet in girth at the small end.

		lbs.
E 667.	Lama Gumba Forest, Darjeeling	39
D 1085.	Madura, Madras	39

15. CASSIA, Linn.

A large genus containing 18 species of herbs, shrubs and large trees. It is of considerable importance, as the trees produce fine timber and some of the shrubs and herbs the "Senna" leaves used in medicine. *C. auriculata*, Linn.; Hook. Fl. Ind. ii. 263; Brandis 165, Vern. *Tarwar*, *awal*, Hind.; *Turota*, Berar; *Tangedu*, *tangar*, Tel.; *Avarike*, Kan., is a shrub of Central and South India; its bark is used for tanning and dyeing leather, and its seeds as an application for ophthalmia, as are those of *C. Absus*, Linn. *C. obovata*, Colladon, is a shrub common all over India, and is one of the plants furnishing the medicinal senna leaves. *C. alata*, Linn., is an introduced shrub, now run wild, whose leaves are an excellent application for ring-worm.

C. glauca, Lam.; Hook. Fl. Ind. ii. 265; Beddome xci.; Kurz i. 394, (*Senna arborescens*, Roxb. Fl. Ind. ii. 345) is a large shrub or small tree of the eastern part of South India and of Burma. *C. nodosa*, Ham.; Kurz i. 392. Vern. *Gnoothein*, Burm., and *C. renigera*, Wall. Vern. *Gnooshay*, Burm., are large trees of Burma, the former extending to the Eastern Himalaya.

Heartwood hard, heavy, dark-coloured. Pores moderate-sized and large, in patches of soft texture, which in some species are confluent and form continuous concentric bands.

1. C. Fistula, Linn.; Hook. Fl. Ind. ii. 261; Roxb. Fl. Ind. ii. 333; Beddome xci.; Brandis 194; Kurz i. 391; Gamble 30. *Cathartocarpus Fistula*, Pers. The Indian Laburnum. Vern. *Amaltás*, Hind.; *Alash, ali, karangal, kiár, kaniár*, Pb.; *Raj briksh, kitola*, Kumaun; *Chimkani*, Sind.; *Gurmala*, Guz.; *Sundali, bandarlati*, Beng.; *Sandari*, Uriya; *Kitwáli, kitoli, itola, shimarra, sím*, North-Western Provinces; *Warga*, Oudh; *Jaggarwah, raila, hirojah, karkacha*, C. P.; *Jaggra, kambar, rera*, Gondi; *Banag, bangru*, Kurku; *Bahawah, baya, bawa*, Mar.; *Raj birij*, Nep.; *Sonalu*, Gáro; *Bonurlati, bonurlauri, persar*, Palamow; *Sunaru*, Assam; *Bandolat*, Cachar; *Kone, sirikone*, Tam.; *Reylu, rela, suvarnam, konay*, Tel.; *Kaki*, Tam.; *Kakke*, Kan. *Ahalla*, Cingh.; *Gnooshway, gnoogyee*, Burm.

A moderate-sized deciduous tree. Bark ¼ inch thick, compact, greenish grey and smooth when young, dark-reddish brown and rough when old, exfoliating in many-sided patches. Sapwood large, heartwood varying in colour from grey or yellowish red to brick-red, very hard to extremely hard. Sharp, thin, white, concentric lines which may possibly be annual rings. Pores moderate-sized, uniformly distributed, enclosed in, and joined by, white, wavy, irregular and often interrupted concentric bands of soft tissue. Medullary rays very fine, very numerous, uniform and equidistant, slightly bent, prominent in the dark, firm tissue which separates the wavy bands.

Sub-Himalayan tract, ascending to 4,000 feet, and throughout India and Burma Growth moderate, 9 rings per inch of radius.

The weight and transverse strength have been determined by the following experiments:—

Experiment by whom made.	Years.	Wood whence produced.	Weight.	Number of experiments.	Size of bar.	Value of P.
					Ft. In. In.	
Kyd	...	Assam . .	56	...	2 × 1 × 1	588
Skinner, No. 43 . .	1862	South India .	61	...	......	846
R. Thompson . .	1868	Central Provinces.	52	...	......	...
Brandis, Nos. 33 and 34	1862	Burma . .	{ 57 66	...	......	...
Central Provinces List .	1873	Central Provinces.	66	...	......	...
Smythies . . .	1878	Different Provinces.	60	11	......	...

The wood is very durable, but rarely of sufficiently large size for timber. It makes excellent posts, and is good for carts, agricultural implements and rice-pounders. The pulp of the pods is a strong purgative, the bark is used in dyeing and tanning, and the gum as an astringent. It is a very handsome tree, having long pendulous racemes of bright yellow flowers, and a long, straight, cylindrical, indehiscent pod, often one and two feet long. It is often cultivated for ornament.

		lbs.
P 101.	Sutlej Valley, Punjab, 3,000 feet	...
P 437.	Ajmere	...
P 439.	„	61
O 244.	Garhwal (1868)	52
O 333.	Gorakhpur (1868)	52
C 1154.	Ahiri Reserve, Central Provinces	56
E 579.	Lohagarhi Forest, Darjeeling Terai	62
E 2352.	Bamunpokri, Darjeeling Terai	62
E 783.	Kamrúp, Assam	60
W 864.	South Kanara	62
D 2052.	Mysore	58
D 1076.	North Arcot, Madras	73
B 2525.	Burma (1862)	66

The difference between the wood of this tree and that of *Ougeinia dalbergioides* consists in this, that in the former the patches of white soft tissue are continuous, forming belts; whereas in *Ougeinia* they are rhomboidal, pointed at the ends, and form interrupted belts.

2. C. marginata, Roxb. Fl. Ind ii. 338; Hook. Fl. Ind. ii. 262. *C. Roxburghii,* DC.; Beddome t. 180. Vern. *Urimidi, uskiamen,* Tel.; *Ngoomee,* Burm.; *Ratoo-waa,* Cingh.

A small deciduous tree, with deeply cracked, brown bark. Heartwood light brown, very hard. Pores moderate-sized and large, joined by narrow, undulating, irregular, white bands of soft tissue. Medullary rays fine and very numerous, uniform and equidistant, prominent in the dark firm tissue which separates the bands of white soft tissue. Structure similar to that of *C. Fistula.*

Madras, Ceylon and Burma (Thoungyeen forests).

Weight, Skinner, No. 44, gives 63 lbs.; our specimen gives 59 lbs. per cubic foot. Skinner gives P = 880. The wood is well adapted for turning, naves of wheels and handles of tools.

		lbs.
B 301.	Burma (1862)	59

3. C. siamea, Lamk.; Hook. Fl. Ind. ii. 264.; Kurz i. 392. *C. florida,* Vahl; Beddome t. 179. *Senna sumatrana,* Roxb. Fl. Ind. ii. 347. Vern. *Beati, manje konne,* Tam.; *Sime tangadi,* Kan.; *Waa,* Cingh.; *Maizalee,* Burm.

A moderate-sized tree with smooth bark. Sapwood whitish, rather large. Heartwood dark brown, nearly black, very hard. Pores large and moderate-sized, joined by concentric, light-coloured, wavy bands of soft tissue which alternate with black belts of firm texture, in which the fine, light-coloured, uniform and equidistant medullary rays are prominent. Frequently beautifully mottled on a vertical section.

South India, Burma and Ceylon.

Weight, according to Skinner, No. 39, 58 lbs.; our specimens give 54·5. P = 840. Very durable. Used in Burma for mallets, helves and walking-sticks; in South India it is little known, but it is considered one of the best kinds of fuel for locomotives in Ceylon (*Beddome*).

		lbs.
D 1080.	North Arcot	58
B 2526.	Burma (1862)	54
B 2712.	Tavoy (Wallich, 1828)	52

4. C. timoriensis, DC.; Hook. Fl. Ind. ii. 265; Beddome xcii.; Kurz i. 393. Vern. *Arremene,* Cingh.; *Toung maizalee,* Burm.

A handsome, small, evergreen tree. Wood dark brown, nearly black. Structure resembling that of *C. siamea.*

Burma and Ceylon.

Weight, 57 lbs., P = 594, according to Adrian Mendis. Used in Ceylon for building and furniture.

		lbs.
No. 4.	Ceylon Collection	57

B 2260, 45 lbs., and B 2295, 46 lbs., sent by Major Ford from the Andamans in 1866 under the name of *Gnoogyee,* belong to a species of *Cassia.* Wood hard, durable, olive brown, with a structure similar to that of *Ougeinia dalbergioides.* It is evidently a common wood in the Andamans.

16. BAUHINIA, Linn.

Contains about 20 to 30 species, almost equally divided into trees and climbers. Few of the species reach a very large size, but their commonness renders them important. They are easily recognised by their two leaflets being generally joined together for a portion of their length, forming apparently a bilobed, palmately veined leaf.

Tree section. B. acuminata, Linn.; Hook. Fl. Ind. ii. 276; Roxb. Fl. Ind. ii. 324; Brandis 159; Kurz i. 396. Vern. *Kanchan,* Beng.; *Kachnar,* Hind.; *Mahahlayka phyoo,* Burm., is an erect, white-flowered, handsome shrub of South India and Burma. *B. tomentosa,* Linn.; Hook. Fl. Ind. ii. 275; Roxb. Fl. Ind. ii. 323; Beddome xcii.; Brandis 159. Vern. *Kachnar,* Hind.; *Kanchini,* Tam., Tel., is a shrub or small tree of South India with showy, yellow flowers, having a purple eye, and a tough wood, with nearly black heartwood. *B. triandra*, Roxb. Fl. Ind. ii. 320, is a small tree grown in avenues in Bengal. *B. monandra*, Kurz. Vern. *Swaitan*, Burm., *B. polycarpa*, Wall., and *B. elongata*, Korth., are trees of Burma.

The *creepers* contain some of the most important plants found in our forests. *B. Vahlii*, W. and A.; Hook. Fl. Ind. ii. 279; Beddome xciii.; Brandis 161; Kurz i. 401; Gamble 31. (*B. racemosa*, Vahl.; Roxb. Fl. Ind. ii. 325) Vern. *Taur*, Punjab; *Malghan, malján, malu, maurain, jallaur*, Hind.; *Sihár, mahalan, maúl*, C. P.; *Borla*, Nep.; *Chehur*, Beng.; *Sungung rik*, Lepcha; *Shioli*, Uriya; *Paur, bela*, Gondi; *Adda*, Tam.; *Chamboli*, Dekkan, is perhaps the most gigantic of the numerous large climbers of the Indian forests. It is found in the Sub-Himalayan tract from the Chenab eastwards, in Northern and Central India, and in Tenasserim. Its uses are almost more numerous than those of any other forest plant except the bamboo. Its large, flat leaves are sewn together and used as plates, cups, rough table cloths, umbrellas and rain-caps; its pod is roasted and the seeds eaten; its bark is made into rough ropes, and it gives a copious gum, which, however, seems to be of little value. The wood is porous, in broad, irregularly broken concentric layers, alternating with red, juicy, bark-like tissue; the pith is cross-shaped. (P 108, Sutlej; O 544, Dehra Dún; E 474, E 2954, Darjeeling Terai). The foliage is very dense and the stems do great damage to the trees they climb over; it is very prevalent in sál forest, and in many provinces is being systematically cut out. *B. anguina*, Roxb. Fl. Ind. ii. 328; Hook. Fl. Ind. ii. 284; Beddome xciii.; Kurz i. 403; Gamble 31. Vern. *Nagpút*, Sylhet; *Naiwilli*, Nep., is the Snake Climber of the moist forests of Northern and Eastern Bengal, Chittagong, Martaban and South India; its bark is also used in rope-making, and its wood is very soft and porous. The stems are usually very curiously twisted, generally in alternate bends and often with a straight thick margin. (E 482, Darjeeling Terai.)

Wood red or brown, hard; no heartwood; concentric bands of soft tissue alternating with bands of finer texture, in which the numerous fine, uniform and equidistant medullary rays are distinctly visible. The pores are uniform in size.

1. B. malabarica, Roxb. Fl. Ind. ii. 321; Hook. Fl. Ind. ii. 277; Beddome xcii.; Brandis 159; Kurz i. 399; Gamble 31. Vern. *Amli, amlosa*, Hind.; *Karmai*, Beng.; *Amli taki*, Nep.; *Kattra*, Ass.; *Cheppura, Basavana páda*, Kan.; *Amli*, Mar.; *Kundapula, dhondel, kangali*, Gondi; *Ambotha, chapa*, Kurku; *Pulla dondur, puli shinta, pulhari*, Tel.; *Apta*, Berar; *Bwaygyin*, Burm.

A moderate-sized deciduous tree. Bark ⅓ inch thick, rough, brown, exfoliating in linear flakes. Wood light-reddish brown, with irregular masses of black or purplish wood near the centre; moderately hard. Pores moderate-sized, generally oval and subdivided. Numerous narrow, wavy, white, concentric bands of softer tissue alternate with bands of harder and red-coloured wood of equal width, in which the numerous, fine, uniform and equidistant medullary rays are distinctly visible.

Sub-Himalayan tract from the Ganges to Assam, Bengal, Burma, South India.

Weight, the average of our specimens gives 48 lbs.; Brandis, 1862, Burma List, No. 31, 42 lbs. The wood is rarely used. The tree is recognised by its acid leaves which are eaten.

		lbs.
C 1137.	Ahiri Reserve, Central Provinces	...
C 2817.	Melghát, Berar (sapwood)	44
C 821.	Bairagarh Reserve, Berar	47
E 590.	Khookloong Forest, Darjeeling Terai	51
E 2350.	Bamunpokri, Darjeeling Terai	48
B 3203.	Burma (1862)	...

2. B. racemosa, Lam.; Hook. Fl. Ind. ii. 276; Beddome t. 182; Brandis 159; Kurz i. 397. *B. parviflora*, Vahl.; Roxb. Fl. Ind. ii. 323. Vern. *Kosúndra, taur*, Pb.; *Kachnál, gúriál, thaur, ashta, makkúna, maula, dhorára*, Hind.; *Dhondri, dhundera, astra, bosha*, Gondi; *Jhinja*,

Ajmere; *Ari*, *arro*, Tel.; *Ati, archi, areka*, Tam.; *Apta, seyára*, Mar.; *Banraj*, Beng.; *Ambhota*, Uriya; *Aupta*, Kan.; *Hpalan*, Burm.; *Amba bhósa*, Bhíl; *Bossai*, Kurku.

A small deciduous tree. Bark ¼ inch thick, dark brown, very rough, with numerous, deep, vertical cracks. Wood light brown, hard, with irregularly-shaped masses of darker-coloured and harder wood near the centre. Pores moderate-sized, often in radial lines. Narrow, white, irregular bands of softer tissue alternate with darker bands of somewhat greater width, in which the very numerous, fine, uniform and equidistant medullary rays are distinctly visible.

Sub-Himalayan tract from the Ravi eastwards, ascending to 5,000 feet; Oudh, Bengal, Burma, Central and South India.

Weight, Brandis' Burma List, 1862, No. 32, gives 44 lbs.; R. Thompson, 56 lbs.; our specimens give 50 lbs. on an average. The wood is good, but not used. The fibres of the bark are used to make ropes and slow matches.

		lbs.
P 453.	Ajmere	...
P 3216.	Nagpahar, Ajmere	...
O 247.	Garhwal (1868)	53
O 335.	Gorakhpur (1868)	47
C 200.	Mandla, Central Provinces (1869)	56
C 1170.	Ahiri Reserve, Central Provinces	44
C 2770.	Melghât, Berar (sapwood)	41

3. **B. purpurea,** Linn.; Hook. Fl. Ind. ii. 284; Roxb. Fl. Ind. ii. 320; Beddome xcii.; Brandis 160; Kurz i. 398; Gamble 31. Vern. *Koiral, karár, karalli, gray*, Pb.; *Koliár, kaniár, kandan, khairwal, kwillar, koilari, sona*, Hind.; *Khwairalo*, Nep.; *Kachik*, Lepcha; *Deva kanchan, rakta kancha, koiral*, Beng.; *Kodwari*, Gondi; *Koliari*, Kurku; *Atmatti*, Mar.; *Kanchan*, Tel.; *Pedda aré, mandareh*, Tam.; *Sarúl, kanchivála*, Kan.; *Mahalay kani*, Burm.

A moderate-sized deciduous tree. Bark ⅓ to ½ inch thick, ash-coloured to dark brown. Wood pinkish white, turning dark brown on exposure, moderately hard. Pores moderate-sized, mostly oval, subdivided. Wavy, concentric bands of soft tissue alternating with darker-coloured bands of firmer tissue, in which the white, fine, uniform and equidistant medullary rays are distinctly visible.

Sub-Himalayan tract from the Indus eastward, Central and South India and Burma.

Weight, according to Skinner, No. 24, 39 lbs.; our specimens give an average of 49 lbs. Wood used for agricultural implements and in construction. The bark is used for tanning, the leaves for cattle fodder, and the flower buds are pickled and eaten.

		lbs.
P 153.	Sainj, Giri Valley, 3,000 feet	42
O 229.	Garhwal (1868)	55
O 230.	" "	46
C 822.	Bairagarh Reserve, Berar	50
C 2792.	Melghát, Berar (sapwood)	36
E 585.	Khooklong Forest, Darjeeling Terai	50

4. **B. variegata,** Linn.; Hook. Fl. Ind. 284; Roxb. Fl. Ind. ii. 319; Beddome xcii.; Brandis 160; Kurz i. 397; Gamble 31. Vern. *Kachnar, koliár, kurál, padrián, khwairal, guriál, gwiar, bariál*, Hind.; *Taki*, Nep.; *Rha*, Lepcha; *Rakta kanchan*, Beng.; *Borara*, Uriya; *Segapu-munthari*, Tam.; *Kanchivala-do*, Kan.; *Bwaycheng*, Burm.

A moderate-sized deciduous tree. Bark grey, with vertical cracks. Wood grey, moderately hard, with irregular masses of darker and harder wood in the centre. Pores moderate-sized, enclosed in round or elongated and pointed concentric patches of white soft tissue, which often run into each other. The intervening tissue is firm and dark coloured, with very numerous, fine, uniform and equidistant white medullary rays. Distinct, white, concentric lines, which probably are annual rings. Medullary rays distinctly visible on a radial section, giving the wood a handsome mottled appearance.

Sub-Himalayan tract from the Indus eastwards, and throughout the forests of India and Burma. Often planted for ornament.

Weight, according to R. Thompson, 54 lbs.; our specimen gives 42 lbs. Used for agricultural implements. The bark is used for dyeing and tanning, and the leaves and flower buds eaten. The flowers are very handsome, somewhat like those of some of the *Azaleas*, but having four white and one crimson petal.

		lbs.
P 1200.	Madhopur, Punjab.	33
C 823.	Bairagarh Reserve, Berar	48
E 591.	Khooklong Forest, Darjeeling Terai	47
E 2351.	Bamunpokri „ „ „	39

5. B. retusa, Ham.; Hook. Fl. Ind. ii. 279; Roxb. Fl. Ind. ii. 322; Beddome xciii.; Brandis 161. Vern. *Kurál*, Pb.; *Kandla, kanalla, kuayral, gwayral, kanlao, semla*, Hind.; *Nirpa*, Gondi, Tel.; *Tewar*, Palamow.

A moderate-sized deciduous tree. Bark ¼ inch thick, dark brown, with a few vertical cracks. Wood reddish white, with irregularly shaped, darker masses near the centre, hard. Pores moderate-sized and large, scanty, occasionally grouped. Numerous narrow, white, concentric bands of softer tissue, alternating with harder and darker bands of equal width, in which the white, fine, uniform equidistant and very numerous medullary rays are prominent.

North-West Himalaya from the Beas eastwards, ascending to 4,500 feet; Central India.

Weight, 58 lbs. per cubic foot. Wood not used. It gives a clear gum called Semla Gum, almost exactly resembling gum arabic; it is largely collected and exported from the Dehra Dún. Of this gum Capt. Campbell says:—

"The collection of the Semla gum commences in January and is continued throughout February and March. It sells in Dehra at Re. 1-8, Rs. 2 or Rs. 2-8 per maund, according to quality, and is utilised as a medicine and in compound with other medicines. Occasionally too it is eaten in its crude state by the very poorest natives down country. It is also used to waterproof terraced roofs. The annual export from the Dehra Dún is about 2,500 maunds."

		lbs.
O 532.	Dehra Dún	58
C 1160.	Ahiri Reserve, Central Provinces	...

17. AFZELIA, Sm.

Contains 2 trees: *A. retusa*, Kurz, is a small evergreen tree of the coast forests of the Andamans. The *Marabow* wood of Malacca is probably *A. palembanica*, Baker.

1. A. bijuga, A. Gray; Hook. Fl. Ind. ii. 274; Kurz i. 412. Vern. *Shoondul, hinga*, Beng.; *Pynkado*, Burm. in the Andamans; *Pirijdá, dsagundá*, And.

A moderate-sized evergreen tree. Bark thin, grey, peeling off in fine, papery scrolls. Sapwood white, moderately hard, large in young trees, small in old trees; heartwood reddish brown, hard, close-grained.

Pores moderate-sized, frequently oval and subdivided, enclosed in oval patches of soft tissue, prominent on a longitudinal section. Medullary rays fine, numerous, uniform and equidistant, wavy, visible on a radial section as long narrow bands.

Sundarbans of Bengal, Andaman Islands and the Malay Archipelago. It will probably be found on the coasts of Arracan, Pegu and Tenasserim.

Weight, young wood 36 to 42 lbs.; old wood 45 to 49 lbs. Brandis' Memorandum on Andaman woods, 1874, Nos. 12, 13, gives 50 lbs. A valuable wood, used in the Andamans for bridge and house building.

		lbs.
E 403.	Sundarbans	36
E 415.	„	42
B 315.	Burma (1867) (*Kohbeng*)	49
B 524.	Andaman Islands	45
B 2209.	„ „ (1866)	48

18. TAMARINDUS, Linn.

1. T. indica, Linn.; Hook. Fl. Ind. ii. 273; Roxb. Fl. Ind. iii. 215; Beddome t. 184; Brandis 163; Kurz i. 414; Gamble 32. The Tamarind. Vern. *Amli, ambli, imli,* Hind.; *Tintiri, tintil, tintúl,* Beng.; *Titri,* Nep.; *Teteli* Ass.; *Tentúli, koyam,* Uriya; *Púli,* Tam.; *Chinta,* Tel.; *Sitta, hitta,* Gondi; *Chicha,* Kurku; *Karangi, kamal, asam,* Mysore; *Hunase,* Kan.; *Amli, chitz,* Mar.; *Siyembela,* Cingh.; *Magyee,* Burm.

A large evergreen tree. Bark ½ inch thick, dark grey, with longitudinal fissures and horizontal cracks. Wood yellowish white, sometimes with red streaks, hard and close-grained. Heartwood small, near the centre of old trees only, dark purplish brown, with an irregular outline and radiating ramifications, very durable. Annual rings indistinct. Pores moderate-sized, uniformly distributed, each pore or group of pores surrounded by round patches of soft tissue, which are often confluent, forming irregular and oblique bands. Medullary rays very fine, very numerous, uniform and equidistant.

Cultivated throughout India and Burma as far north as the Jhelum.

The weight and transverse strength have been ascertained by the following experiments:—

Experiment by whom conducted.	Year.	Wood whence procured.	Weight.	No. of experiments.	Size of bar.	Value of P.
					Ft. In. In.	
Puckle . . .	......	Mysore . .	83	4	2 × 1 × 1	792
Skinner, No. 121 . .	1862	South India .	79	......	......	804
Cunningham . .	......	Gwalior . .	60	2	2 × 1 × 1	614, sapwood.
„	......	„ . .	79	2	2 × 1 × 1	815, heartwood.
Adrian Mendis, No. 79 .	1855	Ceylon . .	80	......	2 × 1 × 1	780
Smythies . . .	1878	Mysore . .	82	1	......	heartwood.
		Other Provinces . .	62	2	.....	sapwood.

Wood highly prized, though extremely difficult to work. It is used for wheels, mallets, planes, furniture, rice-pounders, oil and sugar mills, and is an excellent wood for turning. The fruit is used in medicine as a laxative; it is made into preserves and exported to Europe. The leaves are also used in curries, and the seed, ground to powder and mixed with gum, gives a strong cement.

It is very largely planted in avenues and topes, and is one of the most beautiful of Indian trees.

			lbs.
C 2811.	Melghát, Berar	sapwood	61
P 451.	Ajmere	sapwood	63
E 2353.	Siliguri, Bengal	sapwood	63
D 2014.	Mysore	heartwood	82
No. 79.	Ceylon Collection	heartwood	80

19. HARDWICKIA, Roxb.

Contains 2 species, both from Central and South India.

Heartwood dark coloured, hard, heavy. Pores moderate-sized, filled with resin. Medullary rays fine, very numerous; the distance between the rays being less than the transverse diameter of the pores.

1. H. binata, Roxb. Fl. Ind. ii. 423; Hook. Fl. Ind. ii. 270; Beddome t. 26; Brandis 162. Vern. *Anjan*, Hind., Mar.; *Acha, alti*, Tam.; *Nar yepi, yapa*, Tel.; *Kamrá, karachi*, Kan.; *Chhota dundhera*, Gondi; *Bone*, Kurku; *Parsíd*, Singrowli.

A deciduous tree. Bark ½ inch thick, dark grey, rough with irregular vertical cracks, exfoliates in narrow flakes. Sapwood small, white; heartwood extremely hard, dark red, often with a purplish tinge, cross and very close grained. Pores moderate-sized, often subdivided, filled with resin, uniformly distributed. Medullary rays fine, numerous, undulating, and frequently bent where they touch the pores, visible on a radial section as straight, narrow, white bands. Scanty, fine, concentric lines.

In dry forests of South and Central India, but not everywhere; generally gregarious in isolated belts or patches of greater or less extent. Most commonly found on sandstone, but also to be met with on trap and granite. Wanting in the western moist-zone, and not found in Northern India, though it occurs as far north as the Banda District of the North-Western Provinces.

Weight, according to Skinner, No. 78, 85 lbs.; R. Thompson gives 67; and the Central Provinces List of 1873, 65 lbs.; our specimens give an average of 82 lbs. Skinner gives P = 942. Perhaps the hardest and heaviest wood in India; it is extremely durable, liable to split, but does not warp. It is used for bridge and house posts and for ornamental work. It has been recommended for sleepers, but is probably too hard, heavy and difficult to work to be much in favour. Out of 9 sleepers laid down on the Mysore State Railway and taken up after 7 to 8 years, 6 were found good, 2 still serviceable, and only 1 bad. About 2,000 have been used on the Holkar and Neemuch line. The bark yields a strong and valuable fibre. The leaves are given as fodder to cattle. It yields a gum.

		lbs.
C 800.	Punassa Reserve, Central Provinces	84
C 1147.	Ahiri " " "	84
C 2986.	Nimar, Central Provinces	83
C 2929.	Palamow, Bengal	82
D 1055.	Salem, Madras	83
D 2025.	Mysore	77
No. 31.	Salem Collection	82

2. H. pinnata, Roxb. Fl. Ind. ii. 425; Hook. Fl. Ind. ii. 270; Beddome t. 255. Vern. *Kolávu*, Tinnevelly; *Matáyen samprâni*, Travancore; *Yenne*, Manjarabad (*VanSomeren*).

A very large tree. Sapwood large; heartwood brown, moderately hard, exuding a red, sticky substance similar to copaiba balsam, which consists of different resins dissolved in an essential oil. Pores moderate-sized and large, often subdivided. Medullary rays fine, nearly equidistant, bending where they touch the pores. Scanty, not very prominent, concentric lines of soft texture.

Western Ghâts from South Kanara to Travancore.

Weight, 47 lbs. per cubic foot. Wood used for building by coffee planters and others. For analysis of the gum resin see Mr. Broughton's Report in Beddome Fl. Sylv. Madr. t. 255.

		lbs.
D. 1064.	Tinnevelly	47

20. CYNOMETRA, Linn.

Contains 4 Indian species. *C. cauliflora*, Linn.; Hook. Fl. Ind. ii. 268; Beddome t. 315, is an evergreen tree cultivated in Burma and South India; *C. travancorica*, Beddome t. 316; Hook. Fl. Ind. ii. 267, is a lofty tree of the hills of Travancore and Tinnevelly, between 2,000 and 4,000 feet.

Wood red, hard, heavy; no heartwood. Numerous, narrow, concentric bands similar to those of *Bauhinia*.

1. **C. ramiflora,** Linn.; Hook. Fl. Ind. ii. 267; Beddome t. 315; Kurz i. 415. *C. bijuga*, Spanoghe. Vern. *Shingr*, Beng.; *Irapú*, Tam.; *Myeng kabeng*, Burm.; *Gal mendora*, Cingh.

A large evergreen tree. Wood red, hard, close-grained. Pores small, uniformly distributed, often oval and subdivided. Numerous wavy bands of soft, light-coloured tissue, alternating with narrower bands of hard and firmer tissue, in which the fine and very numerous medullary rays are distinctly visible.

Sundarbans, South India and Burma in tidal forests.

Weight, 56 lbs.; P = 826, Skinner, No. 52; our specimens give 58 lbs. per cubic foot; Nos. 27, 32, of Adrian Mendis' Ceylon Collection bear the names *Gal mendora* and *Hal mendora*, weight, 56 to 58 lbs.; P = 740. Skinner says that it is used for house-building and carts, and that chips of the wood give in water a purple dye. It is used in the Sundarbans for posts for native huts and for fuel.

		lbs.
E 397.	Sundarbans	58

2. **C. polyandra,** Roxb. Fl. Ind. ii. 372; Hook. Fl. Ind. ii. 268. Vern. *Ping*, Cachar, Sylhet.

A large evergreen tree. Wood light red, hard, close-grained. Pores moderate-sized, joined by narrow concentric bands of soft tissue. Medullary rays moderately broad.

Khasia Hills, Sylhet and Cachar.

Weight, 53 lbs. according to Wallich; our specimens give 60 lbs. Mann says the wood is very useful for scantlings and makes good charcoal.

		lbs.
E 1276.	Cachar	60

21. SARACA, Linn.

Three Indian species are given in the Flora Indica. *S. Lobbiana*, Baker; Hook. Fl. Ind. ii. 272, is a tree of Martaban; and *S. triandra*, Baker; Hook. Fl. Ind. ii. 272 (*Jonesia triandra*, Roxb. Fl. Ind. ii. 220) of Tenasserim.

1. **S. indica,** Linn.; Hook. Fl. Ind. ii. 271; Beddome t. 57; Brandis 166; Kurz ii. 415. *Jonesia Asoca*, Roxb. Fl. Ind. ii. 218. Vern. *Asok*, Hind.; *Asoka*, Beng.; *Aseka*, *ati*, Cuttack; *Diyera tembela*, Cingh.; *Ashunkar*, Kan.; *Jassundi*, Bombay; *Thaw-ka-hpo*, Burm.

Wood light, reddish-brown, soft. Pores moderate-sized in radial and frequently oblique lines. Medullary rays indistinct, crossed by numerous, fine, wavy, concentric lines.

Eastern Bengal, South India, Arracan and Tenasserim.

Weight, 50 lbs. per cubic foot. Often cultivated for its handsome flowers.

	lbs.
No. 23. Ceylon Collection	58

The Carob tree, *Ceratonia siliqua*, has a hard wood, with a pink heartwood. Pores moderately small, often in groups or radial lines. Medullary rays narrow, unequal, irregularly distributed (No. 3266. Saharanpur).

Sub-Order III. MIMOSEÆ.

Contains 13 Genera divided into 5 Tribes, *viz.*,—

Tribe I.—Parkieæ	*Parkia.*
„ II.—Adenanthereæ . . .	*Entada, Piptadenia, Adenanthera, Prosopis* and *Dichrostachys.*
„ III.—Eumimoseæ . . .	*Mimosa, Leucæna* and *Xylia.*
„ IV.—Acacieæ	*Acacia.*
„ V.—Ingeæ	*Calliandra, Albizzia* and *Pithecolobium.*

Parkia contains 3 species from Eastern Bengal and Burma: *P. Roxburghii*, G. Don; Hook. Fl. Ind. ii. 289 (*Mimosa biglobosa*, Roxb. Fl. Ind. ii. 551). Vern. *Sapota*, Sylhet, is a tree of Assam, Eastern Bengal, Chittagong and Burma, with a grey wood with fine medullary rays and large pores joined by concentric bands of white tissue (O 3264, Saharanpur). *P. insignis*, Kurz; and *P. leiophylla*, Kurz i. 418, are large trees, the first of Martaban, the second of Pegu. *Entada scandens*, Bth.; Hook. Fl. Ind. ii. 287; Brandis 167; Kurz i. 416; Gamble 32 (*E. Pursætha*, DC., *Mimosa scandens*, Roxb. Fl. Ind. ii. 554) Vern. *Gilla*, Beng.; *Geredi*, Uriya; *Pangra*, Nep.; *Taktokhyem*, Lepcha; *Gardal*, Bombay; *Kongnyin-nway*, Burm., is a large climber of the forests of Eastern Bengal, South India, Burma and the Andaman Islands, with spirally twisted stems, soft, fibrous, spongy wood (E 477, Darjeeling Terai), and broad, flat pods, often 2 to 4 feet long, and 4 to 5 inches broad, containing large, flat, ovate seeds, which are eaten after roasting and steeping in water. Children play with them, and they may be made into snuff-boxes and other articles. The kernels are used also by the Nepalese for washing their hair, and in Bengal by washermen for crimping linen.

Leucæna glauca, Bth.; Hook. Fl. Ind. ii. 290; Brandis 172, is a small tree found in the outer valleys of Kumaun and Garhwal. *Calliandra Griffithii*, Bth., and *C. umbrosa*, Bth.; Hook. Fl. Ind. ii. 302, are small trees of the Khasia Hills, Eastern Bengal and Chittagong. *Pithecolobium* contains about 9 Indian species. *P. dulce*, Bth.; Hook. Fl. Ind. ii. 302; Beddome t. 188; Brandis 173. (*Inga dulcis*, Willd.; Kurz i. 431; *Mimosa dulcis*, Roxb. Fl. Ind. ii. 556). Vern. *Dakhani babúl*, Hind.; *Karkapilly*, Tam.; *Sime hunase*, Kan.; *Kwaytanyeng*, Burm., is a tree introduced from Mexico, and commonly cultivated in India and Burma. It has a reddish brown heartwood, weighing 40 lbs. per cubic foot (Skinner, No. 82; P = 517); it coppices well, and is grown as a hedge plant and for fuel. *P. bigeminum*, Martius; Hook. Fl. Ind. ii. 303; Beddome xcvi.; Brandis 173; Gamble 34. Vern. *Kachlora*, Hind., is a large tree of the forests of the outer Himalaya from the Ganges eastwards, and of South India, giving a dark-coloured heartwood. *P. anamallayanum*, Beddome t. 189, is a large handsome tree of the higher ranges of the Anamalai Hills, above 5,000 feet. *P. angulatum*, Bth.; Hook. Fl. Ind. ii. 306; Kurz i. 430; Gamble 34, (*Mimosa heterophylla*, Roxb. Fl. Ind. ii. 545.) Vern. *Tukpyit*, Lepcha; *Kawahuruni*, Sylhet, is a large tree of the forests of Northern and Eastern Bengal and Burma; while *P. Saman* has been introduced and is likely to be largely cultivated in India on account of its extremely rapid growth. *Inga cynometroides*, Beddome; Hook. Fl. Ind. ii. 306. (*Calliandra cynometroides*, Beddome t. 317), is a tree of the Tinnevelly and Travancore Hills.

22. PIPTADENIA, Benth.

1. P. oudhensis, Brandis 168; Hook. Fl. Ind. ii. 289. *Adenanthera oudhensis,* J. L. Stewart. Vern. *Gainti,* Oudh.

A moderate-sized tree. Bark ½ inch thick, grey-brown to dusky red, rough with flattish, exfoliating woody scales; inner bark red, fibrous. Wood yellowish or reddish, close-grained, no heartwood, hard, durable. Pores moderate-sized and large, often subdivided in patches of soft tissue, which are sometimes confluent. Medullary rays short, numerous, moderately broad.

Forests at the foot of the Nepal Hills, Gonda division, Oudh, discovered by Mr. R. Thompson.

O 3084. Gonda, Oudh.

23. ADENANTHERA, Linn.

1. A. pavonina, Linn.; Hook. Fl. Ind. ii. 287; Roxb. Fl. Ind. ii. 370; Beddome t. 96; Brandis 168; Kurz i. 417. Vern. *Rakta-chandan, ranjana,* Beng.; *Ani kundamani,* Tam.; *Bandi gurivenda,* Tel.; *Manjati,* Mal.; *Thorlaganj,* Mar.; *Manjádi,* Kan. *Madateya,* Cingh.; *Gung,* Magh; *Ywaygyee,* Burm.; *Rechedá,* And.

A deciduous tree, with grey bark. Heartwood red, hard, close-grained. Pores small, scanty, in short radial lines. Medullary rays very fine, extremely numerous.

Bengal, South India, Burma and Andaman Islands.

Weight, Skinner, No. 12, gives 56 lbs., which is the same as our specimen; Bennett gives 55 lbs. Skinner gives P = 863; and Bennett 942. The wood is used in South India for house-building and cabinet-making purposes, and gives a red dye. The seeds are worn as ornaments, and are used as weights by goldsmiths and jewellers as they are said to be very constant in weight, *viz.*, 4 grains; they give an oil.

	lbs.
B 523. Andaman Islands	56

24. PROSOPIS, Linn.

Contains about 18 species, dispersed over the tropical and sub-tropical regions of Asia, Africa and America. Of the five sections which compose the genus, sections whose characters are based to some extent upon the shape and structure of the fruit, three may be noticed, as they contain species which have lately been introduced into India:—

1. With the pod smooth or slightly thickened at the seeds	Adenopis . .	Contains the two Indian species; *P. spicigera,* the well-known "Jhand" and *P. Stephaniana* of the Northern Punjab plains and Western Asia.
2. With the pod smooth, thickened at the seeds so as to be almost jointed, and generally falcate	Algarobia . .	Contains two of the species now being grown, *viz.*, *P. glandulosa* of the mountains of Western Texas; and *P. pallida* of South America.
3. With the pod spirally twisted	Strombocarpa .	Contains the true "Mesquit" Bean, or *P. pubescens* of Texas and New Mexico.

P. spicigera, Linn., is here described; *P. Stephaniana,* Kunth; Hook. Fl. Ind. ii. 288; Brandis 171. Vern. *Jembút,* Arab., is a small thorny shrub of no economic use.

P. pallida, Kunth, is a native of South America, and has been successfully grown in Ceylon. Its pods are considered of high value as a tanning material, containing, it is said, as much as 90 per cent. of tannic acid. They are known by the name of "Balsamocarpon."

P. glandulosa, Torr., the "Mesquit or Algaroba of Texas," is a native of the mountain regions of Western Texas, where it grows into a small tree from 20 to 40 feet high, and with a diameter of 18 inches. It has straight or curved, rather flattened, almost jointed pods, the interior of which is filled with a sweet pulp. The pods, it is believed, are useful for fodder, and are not injurious. It yields an excessively hard and durable timber, with a beautiful grain, and is used for furniture picket poles and in the manufacture of charcoal. It also affords a large quantity of gum resembling gum arabic, which exudes from the stem and branches, and has been used as mucilage in the making of jujubes, and for other purposes.

P. pubescens, Bth., the "Screw Bean" or "Screw Mesquit," is a small tree of Texas, New Mexico and Arizona. Remarkable for its screw-shaped pods. These pods grow in abundant clusters of 8 or 10 upon the same stem, ripen at all times of the year, and contain much nutritious saccharine matter; but great caution is required in their use as fodder for horses.

Another species, a native of Jamaica, and possibly not distinct from *P. glandulosa*, is the *P. juliflora*, DC., of the section Algarobia. Its fruits have poisonous properties, though, for other purposes, the tree appears to be useful for planting in some localities, as the plants when once established go on sending up shoot after shoot, and are difficult to eradicate.

1. **P. spicigera**, Linn.; Hook. Fl. Ind. ii. 288; Beddome t. 56; Brandis 169. *Adenanthera aculeata*, Roxb. Fl. Ind. ii. 371. Vern. *Jhand, khár*, Pb.; *Kandi, kundi*, Sind.; *Chaunkra*, Agra; *Khejra*, Rajputana; *Sangri*, Pertabgarh; *Semru, hamra*, Guz.; *Shemi, saunder*, Mar.; *Shami*, Beng., Uriya; *Perumbe, vunne, jambu*, Tam.; *Chani*, Tel.

A moderate-sized, deciduous, thorny tree. Bark ¾ to 1 inch thick, grey, rough, with deep longitudinal fissures and horizontal cracks. Sapwood large, perishable; heartwood purplish brown, extremely hard. Pores very small to moderate-sized, generally imbedded in narrow irregular concentric bands of soft tissue, filled with resin. Medullary rays short, extremely numerous, fine, wavy.

Arid, northern and southern dry zones. Punjab, Sindh, Rajputana, Guzerat, Bandelkhand and Dekkan.

Brandis says the growth is probably slow, it having 3 feet girth in 30 years (Saharanpur); this would give about 5 years per inch of radius, which is moderately fast.

Weight, according to Skinner, No. 108, 72 lbs., but the identification of his specimens is doubtful; Dalzell gives 58 lbs.; and J. L. Stewart 51 lbs.; our specimens give 58 lbs. Skinner gives P = 981. The wood is tough, but not durable, liable to dry rot, and readily eaten by insects. It is easily raised from seed and coppices well. It is used for building, carts, well curbs, furniture, and agricultural implements; but is chiefly valuable for fuel, as its heating power is very great. Brandis gives the results of experiment made at Karachi in May 1869, that 1,374 lbs. of its wood were consumed in evaporating 11·8 cubic feet of water per hour during 7 hours, the pressure of steam being kept at 27 lbs. per square inch, while of *Acacia arabica* wood 1,388 lbs., and of *Tamarix gallica* wood 1,627 lbs., were required for the same test. It is largely used for fuel for locomotives and steamers in the Punjab and Sind, and has been planted in the Punjab plantations. The pods are used as fodder for camels, cattle and goats; and the mealy sweetish substance is eaten, raw or cooked, in parts of the Punjab, Guzerat and the Dekkan, and has the flavour of that of the Carob tree. It has an enormously long tap root: one specimen of which pieces were sent to the Paris Exhibition of 1878 had a root 86 feet long, penetrating vertically to a depth of 64 feet. It gives a gum somewhat similar to gum arabic, but which is not used.

		lbs.
P 882.	Multán	57
P 939.	„ (rootwood)	...
P 1380.	Karokpo Forest, Hyderabad, Sind	59
P 459.	Ajmere (young tree)	37

25. DICHROSTACHYS, DC.

1. D. cinerea, W. and A.; Hook. Fl. Ind. ii. 288; Beddome t. 185; Brandis 171. *Mimosa cinerea,* Roxb. Fl. Ind. ii. 561. Vern. *Vurtuli,* Hind.; *Kunlai, kunrat, kheri,* Mhairwarra; *Vadatalla, vadatara,* Tam.; *Velturu, yeltu,* Tel.; *Segum kati,* Mar., Gondi; *Andara,* Cingh.

A thorny shrub or small tree. Heartwood red, extremely hard. Pores moderate-sized, enclosed in rings of soft texture. Medullary rays short, moderately broad, equidistant, the distance between the rays equal to the transverse diameter of the pores.

Dry, stony hills in South and Central India, Rajputana.
Weight, 75 lbs. per cubic foot. Wood used for walking-sticks.

			lbs.
No.	25.	Salem Collection.	79
No.	3.	Ceylon Collection (marked *Vachellia farnesiana*) . .	71
P	3239.	Ajmere	...
P	3229.	Nagpahar, Ajmere	...

26. MIMOSA, Linn.

M. pudica, Linn.; Hook. Fl. Ind. ii. 291. The Sensitive Plant. Vern. *Lajwánti* Kumaun; *Lajuk,* Beng., is now naturalised over the greater part of tropical and subtropical India, where it grows to be a small shrub, and is with difficulty eradicated. *M. hamata,* Willd.; Hook. Fl. Ind. ii. 291, is a prickly shrub of South India.

1. M. rubicaulis, Linn.; Hook. Fl. Ind. ii. 291; Brandis 172; Gamble 32. *M. mutabilis,* Roxb. Fl. Ind. ii. 564. Vern. *Rál, khair, didriár,* Pb.; *Hajeru,* Sind; *Agla, agl, kingli, kacheyta,* Hind.; *Aradi,* Nep.; *Sibriú,* Lepcha; *Chilatti,* Bhíl.

A large, straggling, prickly shrub with grey bark. Sapwood yellowish white; heartwood red, hard. Pores small and moderate-sized, frequently oval and subdivided. Medullary rays fine and very numerous.

Throughout the greater part of India, ascending to 4,000 feet in Kumaun and Sikkim.
Weight, 41 to 52 lbs. Used for gunpowder charcoal.

			lbs.
E	680.	Bamunpokri, Darjeeling Terai	41
E	2354.	Chunbati, Darjeeling, 2,000 feet	52

27. XYLIA, Bth.

1. X. dolabriformis, Benth.; Hook. Fl. Ind. ii. 286; Beddome, t. 186; Brandis 171; Kurz i. 419. *Mimosa xylocarpa,* Roxb. Fl. Ind. ii. 543. *Inga xylocarpa,* DC. The Ironwood Tree of Pegu and Arracan. Vern. *Jambu,* Hind.; *Jamba, suria,* Mar.; *Boja,* Uriya; *Irúl,* Tam.; *Konda tangedu, tangedu, eruvalu, bojeh,* Tel.; *Jambé, tirawa,* Kan.; *Shilve,* Coorg; *Pynkado,* Burm.

A large deciduous tree. Bark ¼ inch thick, grey or reddish brown, with short cracks irregularly distributed. Sapwood small; heartwood dark brown or reddish brown, extremely hard, beautifully mottled, cross-grained, the fibres on a longitudinal section being wavy. Annual rings indistinct, but alternate concentric bands of darker and lighter colour. Pores small and moderate-sized, often subdivided into numerous compartments, and then oval or oblong. Pores or groups of pores in irregular patches of whitish tissue, which are often arranged in zig-zag lines. These patches are separated by hard, dark-coloured tissue in which the very fine and very numerous medullary rays are distinctly visible. Some of the specimens of this wood have an oily touch.

Chanda District, South India, Arracan and Burma.

The weight and transverse strength have been determined by the following experiments:—

Experiment by whom conducted.	Year.	Wood whence procured.	Weight.	No. of experiments.	Size of bar.	Value of P.
					Ft. in. in.	
Puckle	1859	Mysore	58	...	2 × 1 × 1	693
List of woods	1863	„	58	...	...	...
Brandis, No. 37	1862	Burma	60-66	...	...	...
Commissariat Department .	...	Moulmein	83	...	...	1153
Skinner, No. 83	1862	South India	58	...	...	836
Benson	...	Burma	83	...	3 × 1·4 × 1·4	1191
Laslett	1875	„	73·5	6	7 × 2 × 2	955
Smythies	1878	Chanda	59	1	...	...
	„	Kanara	61	4	...	...
	„	Burma	65	3	...	...

The wood is very durable—a property it doubtless owes in great measure to the resinous substance contained in it. This resin is more abundant in Burmese wood than in wood grown in South India. No. B 1451, which was brought by Dr. Wallich from Tavoy in 1828, is still so full of resin that it is quite sticky on the outside, and the resin may be scraped off with a knife. This substance is partially soluble in hot water, to which it imparts a reddish colour.

The wood is used for boat-building and for agricultural implements in Burma; also for carts and tool handles. In South India it is used for railway sleepers, posts, boat-building and carts. In Burma and Bengal it has been largely used for telegraph posts, for which it has answered well. The large forests in Arracan, of which Dr. Schlich in his report on the ironwood forests of Arracan, dated 1st September 1869, says that "a third of the forest vegetation consists of Pynkado," produce large numbers of telegraph poles and railway sleepers. Major Seaton in his report for 1876-77 said that 10,000 such sleepers from Arracan had then lately been sold at Calcutta at Rs. 5 each, and Mr. Ribbentrop's Report states that Pynkado pieces and sleepers are brought out from the forests in Pegu. It is likely, however, to be found too hard, heavy and difficult to cut. It is useful wood for piles and beams of bridges. It exudes a red resin, and the seeds give an oil.

		lbs.
C 1151.	Ahiri Reserve, Central Provinces	59
W 754.	South Kanara	59
W 761.	„ „	61
W 857.	„ „	61
W 1222.	North Kanara	62
B 805.	Tharrawaddi, Burma	67
B 3066.	Burma (1862)	66
B 1451.	Tavoy (Wallich, 1828)	62

28. ACACIA, Willd.

Contains about 18 Indian species, of which four are climbing or straggling thorny shrubs, and the rest trees or erect shrubs. *A. Latronum*, Willd.; Hook. Fl. Ind. ii. 296; Beddome xcv.; Brandis 180. (*Mimosa Latronum*, Roxb. Fl. Ind. ii. 559) Vern. *Bhes*, Hind.; *Paki-túma*, Tel., is a gregarious, very thorny shrub of the southern dry zone. *A. Jacquemonti*, Bth.; Hook. Fl. Ind. ii. 293; Brandis 183. Vern. *Hauza*, Afg.; *Kikar, babúl, bamúl*, Pb.; *Murmutti*, Berar; *Ratabauli*, Guz., is a small, bushy, thorny shrub of the arid and northern dry zones, ascending in the Suliman Range and Hazara to 3,200 feet; it is used for fodder, and the bark of the root in the distillation of spirits. *A. Senegal*, Willd.; Hook. Fl. Ind. ii. 295 (*A. rupestris*, Stocks; Brandis 184) Vern. *Khor*, Sind; *Kúmta*, Rajputana, is a small thorny tree of the arid and northern dry zones, chiefly found in Sind and Ajmere. Brandis says, "Bark smooth, yellowish grey; wood light yellow, heavy and hard, with small irregular masses of black heartwood in the centre; it takes a beautiful polish, and is used for weavers' shuttles." It gives a gum which is collected and sold in Sind with that of *A. arabica*. *A. lenticularis*, Ham.; Hook. Fl. Ind. ii. 296; Brandis 186. Vern. *Khin*, Kumaun, is a small tree of the Siwaliks, of Kumaun and the Rajmehal hills in Bengal. *A. Suma*, Kurz; Hook. Fl. Ind. ii. 294; Brandis 187; Kurz i. 421 (*A. Catechu*, Bth.; Beddome t. 49, *Mimosa Suma*, Roxb. Fl. Ind. ii. 563.) Vern. *Saikanta*, Beng.; *Mügli*, Kan.; *Kumtia*, Pertabgarh; *Dhaula khejra*, Banswara; *Son kairi*, Dangs, is a tree of Bengal, South India, parts of the Central Provinces and Guzerat. It is recognised from *A. Catechu* by its having white bark, while that species has a black-coloured bark. It gives cutch, and the bark is used for tanning. *A. planifrons*, W. and A.; Hook. Fl. Ind. ii. 293; Beddome xcv.; Brandis 575. The Umbrella Thorn. Vern. *Salé, sal*, Tel., is a small gregarious tree of South India with a strong wood used for agricultural implements and fuel. *A. concinna*, DC.; Hook. Fl. Ind. ii. 296; Beddome xcv.; Brandis 188; Kurz i. 423; Gamble 33. (*Mimosa concinna*, Roxb. Fl. Ind. ii. 565). Vern. *Aila, rassaul*, Oudh; *Banritha*, Beng.; *Sikekai*, Dekkan; *Gogu, chikai*, Tel.; *Sigé*, Kan.; *Soopwotnway*, Burm., is an extremely thorny scandent shrub of most parts of India and Burma, except the arid zone. Its thick fleshy pods are used for washing the hair, and the acid leaves are eaten. *A. pruinescens*, Kurz i. 424, is a climber of the forests of Pegu.

The true gum arabic is the produce of *A. vera*, Willd., a tree of Egypt, Arabia and Northern Africa. "Sabicu" is the wood of *A. formosa*, a tree of the West Indies (W = 57; P = 994, Laslett).

The character of the Indian species of *Acacia* is to have sharp, prominent, medullary rays, which are short in *A. Catechu, ferruginea* and *modesta*, but long in the others; as a rule, they are not well marked on a radial section, but *A. leucophlœa* and *arabica* form an exception. The pores are, as a rule, uniform in size, but in *A. eburnea* they vary from small to large. With regard to their distribution, two series may be distinguished. In the first series the pores are isolated and enclosed in very narrow rings of softer tissue, and do not form concentric bands; to this section belong *A. arabica, modesta* and *ferruginea*. In the species of the second series, the pores are enclosed in elongated patches of softer tissue, which are frequently confluent and form distinct, though often irregular, concentric bands. This section includes *A. leucophlœa, eburnea, pennata* and *Catechu*. The Australian species have a different structure, and are all marked by short medullary rays.

1. **A. Farnesiana**, Willd.; Hook. Fl. Ind. ii. 293; Beddome t. 52; Brandis 180; Kurz i. 420. *Mimosa Farnesiana*, Linn.; Roxb. Fl. Ind. ii. 557. Vern. *Vilayati kikar, vilayati babúl, pissi babul, gú-kikar*, Hind.; *Gúya babula*, Beng.; *Vedda vala*, Tam.; *Kusturi, piktúmi, oda sale, murki tumma*, Tel.; *Jáli*, Kan.

A thorny shrub. Wood white, hard, close-grained. Pores moderate-sized, in oblique and concentric interrupted bands of soft texture. Medullary rays fine, numerous.

Indigenous to America, now cultivated all over India. The gum is collected in Sind. It has yellow, extremely fragrant flowers, from which a perfume is made. It makes a good fence.

Weight, 49 lbs. per cubic foot.

		lbs.
P 3076.	Sabathu, Punjab	49

2. A. arabica, Willd.; Hook. Fl. Ind. ii. 293; Beddome t. 47; Brandis 180. *Mimosa arabica*, Roxb. Fl. Ind. ii. 557. Vern. *Kikar*, Pb.; *Babbar*, Sind; *Babúl, babúr*, Hind.; *Karúvelum*, Tam.; *Túma, nella túma*, Tel.; *Gobli, karrijáli*, Kan.

A moderate-sized or large tree, seldom leafless, with dark brown rough bark. Sapwood large, whitish; heartwood pinkish white, turning reddish brown on exposure, hard, mottled with dark streaks. Pores moderate-sized, sometimes large, oval and subdivided. Medullary rays fine and moderately broad, short, numerous, unequally distributed, conspicuous on a radial section. The wood consists of darker and lighter coloured bands of an equal width.

Cultivated or self-sown throughout the greater part of India, except in the most humid tracts near the coast. Wild probably in Sind, Rajputana, Guzerat, and the Northern Dekkan.

Brandis says: "In the Punjab it attains a girth of 2½ feet in about 12 and 5 feet in about 30 years. In the forests of Lower and Middle Sind, the average growth has been ascertained to be:—

At 35 years 4 feet girth, at 4 feet from the ground.
" 55 " 6 " " " "

At Jacobabad it has reached 50 to 60 feet high with a girth of 6 to 8 feet in less than 30 years." These measurements would give from 2 to 5 rings per inch of radius, which would indicate a quick rate of growth. In Minniken's Report on the Delhi Bela plantation in 1878, the following data are recorded regarding *kikar*:—

			Age.	No. of tree.	Mean girth, inches.	Height, feet.
Compartment	1.	Chandrawál . . .	7½	4	23·5	25·30
"	3.	Kudsia . . .	6	4	13·5	25
"	4.	Jáffar Khan . . .	6	7	17	18 to 25

Chandrawál is probably on better soil than the others, as the rate of growth is 2 rings per inch as against 2·2 and 2·8 in Nos. 3 and 4 respectively.

Weight: Cunningham gives 54 lbs.; Skinner, No. 3, 54 lbs.; J. L. Stewart, 48 lbs.; our specimens give an average of 54 lbs. Cunningham's five Gwalior experiments with bars 2′ × 1″ × 1″ gave P = 875; Skinner gives 884. The wood is very durable if well seasoned. It is used extensively for wheels, well curbs, sugar and oil presses, rice-pounders, agricultural implements and tool handles. In Sind it is largely used for boat-building, rafters and for fuel; also occasionally for railway sleepers. The gum, which is similar to gum arabic, is largely collected and used in native medicine, and in dyeing and cloth printing. In Sind and Guzerat large quantities of lac are collected on it. The bark is used for dyeing and tanning, and is a powerful astringent; a decoction of it may be used as a substitute for soap. The pods also, when unripe, are astringent, and are used to make ink, and in Africa for tanning; they are given as fodder to cattle, sheep and goats.

It is largely cultivated in the Punjab and Sind, but it suffers much from frost. It comes up well self-sown, coppices well, and may be grown from cuttings. It sends down a very long taproot.

		lbs.
P 1198.	Madhopúr, Punjab	58
P 890.	Multán	49
P 1379.	Miani Forest, Sind	56
P 440.	Ajmere	...
C 843.	Amraoti, Berar	56
D 1051.	Salem, Madras	56
No. 1.	Salem Collection	50

3. A. eburnea, Willd.; Hook. Fl. Ind. ii. 293; Beddome xcv.; Brandis 183. *Mimosa eburnea*, Roxb. Fl. Ind. ii. 558. Vern. *Marmati*, Dekkan.

A short or small deciduous tree, with rough, dark-grey bark. Wood hard, yellowish white, extremely hard, splits in drying. Pores moderate-sized and large, often oval and subdivided into compartments enclosed in wavy and irregular concentric bands of softer tissue, which are frequently interrupted. Medullary rays fine and moderately broad, wavy, prominent in the bands of darker and finer tissue, which alternate with those of soft texture.

Sind, Suliman range, Berar, Dekkan and South India.
Weight, 52 lbs. per cubic foot.

		lbs.
C 844.	Amraoti Reserve, Berar	52

4. A. leucophlœa, Willd.; Hook. Fl. Ind. ii. 294; Beddome t. 48; Brandis 184; Kurz i. 421. *Mimosa leucophlœa*, Roxb. Fl. Ind. ii. 558. Vern. *Rerú, raunj, karír, nimbar, ringa, rinj, rohani, jhind, safed kikar*, Hind.; *Arinj*, Rajputana; *Raundra, runjra*, Banswara; *Renuja*, Bijeragogarh; *Tumma*, Gondi; *Hewar*, Mar.; *Velvaylam, vel-vaghe*, Tam.; *Tella-túma, harwar*, Tel.; *Bili jáli, topal, naibela*, Kan.; *Katu andara*, Cingh.; *Tanoung*, Burm.

A moderate-sized or large deciduous tree. Bark ⅓ inch thick; colour varying with age, grey and smooth when young, dark brown, almost black, and rough when old, exfoliating irregularly in patches and strips. Sapwood large; heartwood reddish brown with lighter and darker streaks, extremely hard. Pores moderate-sized, uniformly distributed in patches or short irregular concentric belts of white tissue which are prominent in, and alternate with, the dark-coloured firm tissue which separates the medullary rays. The latter are white, fine and moderate, and often slightly bent.

Plains of the Punjab from Lahore to Delhi, and in all forest tracts of Central and South India and Burma.

Weight, Skinner, No. 5, gives 55 lbs.; R. Thompson, 58 lbs.; and Central Provinces List of 1873, 45 lbs.; our specimens give 50 and 59 lbs. Skinner gives P = 861. It seasons well and takes a good polish; is strong and tough, but often eaten by insects. It gives an excellent fuel. The bark is eaten in times of scarcity; it is used in preparing spirits from sugar and palm juice, to precipitate by the tannin it contains the albuminous substances in the juice. It gives a fibre used for nets and coarse cordage. The young pods and seeds are eaten, and the gum is used in native medicine.

		lbs.
P 947.	Lahore	50
C 1118.	Ahiri Reserve, Central Provinces	59

5. A. modesta, Wall.; Hook. Fl. Ind. ii. 296; Brandis 185. *Mimosa dumosa*, Roxb. Fl. Ind. ii. 559, and probably *M. obovata*, Roxb. *l. c.* 561. Vern. *Palosa*, Afg.; *Phulahi*, Pb.

A thorny, moderate-sized, deciduous tree. Bark rough, with a multitude of narrow irregular cracks. Sapwood large, white, perishable; heartwood dark brown, with black streaks, extremely hard, harder than that of *A. Catechu*. Pores moderate-sized, sometimes joined by narrow bands of white tissue. Medullary rays fine, white, short.

Suliman and Salt Ranges, Sub-Himalayan tract between the Indus and the Sutlej, and the northern part of the Punjab plains.

Growth slow. Weight, according to J. L. Stewart, 55 lbs.; our specimens vary from 67 to 72; average 69 lbs. A most beautiful wood, strong and durable; valuable for cart-wheels, sugarcane crushers, Persian water-wheels and agricultural implements.

It gives a gum, used in native medicine. The leaves and fallen blossoms are collected for cattle fodder.

		lbs.
P 164.	Hoshiarpur (J. L. Stewart, 1866)	72
P 944.	Gujerat	68
P 945.	Multán	67

6. A. ferruginea, DC.; Hook. Fl. Ind. ii. 295; Beddome t. 51; Brandis 185; Kurz i. 423; Gamble 32. *Mimosa ferruginea,* Roxb. Fl. Ind. ii. 561. Vern. *Khour,* Nep.; *Kaiger,* Panch Mehals; *Son khair,* Berar; *Kar khair,* Gondi; *Phandra khair,* Mar.; *Teóri khair,* Bhíl; *Banni,* Kan.; *Velvelam,* Tam.; *Ansandra, tella tuma, wúni,* Tel.

A large deciduous tree. Bark ½ inch thick, rough. Sapwood large; heartwood olive brown, extremely hard, harder than *A. Catechu.* Pores moderate-sized, generally single, in small rounded patches of softer tissue, which are often confluent and joined into short interrupted concentric bands. Medullary rays short, white, fine, numerous.

Northern Bengal, Central and South India, Guzerat.

Weight, according to Skinner, No. 4, 60 lbs.; our specimens give 70 lbs. Skinner gives P = 798. A fine timber, but little used. Beddome says it is used for building, carts and agricultural implements. It gives a good gum, similar to gum arabic.

		lbs.
C 872.	Bairagarh Reserve, Berar	70
E 2357.	Bamunpokri, Darjeeling Terai	67
D 1081.	North Arcot	73

A piece of red wood, B 2529 (57 lbs.), collected in Burma in 1862 and marked *Sha,* has large and moderate-sized pores filled with resin; they are often subdivided and their transverse diameter is greater than the distance between the fine, closely packed and prominent medullary rays. It evidently belongs to a species of Acacia, and in structure resembles *A. ferruginea,* which has not yet been described from Burma.

7. A. Catechu, Willd.; Hook. Fl. Ind. ii. 295; Brandis 186; Kurz i. 422; Gamble 32. *A. Sundra,* Beddome t. 50. *Mimosa Sundra,* Roxb. Fl. Ind. ii. 562. Vern. *Khair,* Hind.; *Khoira, koir,* Ass.; *Khoiru,* Uriya; *Karangalli, bágá,* Tam.; *Sandra, nalla sandra,* Tel.; *Kagli,* Kan.; *Rat kihiri,* Cingh.; *Sha,* Burm.

A moderate-sized, gregarious, thorny, deciduous tree. Bark dark grey or greyish brown, rough, exfoliating in long narrow strips. Sapwood yellowish white; heartwood either dark or light red, extremely hard. The wood grown in the Himalayan valleys shews the annual rings marked by a whitish line and by a larger number of pores in the spring wood. Pores moderate-sized and large, often subdivided occasionally in radial groups of 2 or 3, and surrounded by narrow rings of softer tissue which are often joined and form interrupted concentric bands. Pores frequently filled with a white substance, uniformly distributed except that they are more numerous in the innermost part of each annual ring, distinctly marked on a longitudinal section. Medullary rays short, moderately broad, numerous, bent where they touch the pores, which are often larger than the space between two medullary rays.

Common in most parts of India and Burma, extending in the Sub-Himalayan tract westwards to the Indus.

The growth of the Himalayan trees, whose rings it is possible to count, is moderate, being 5 rings per inch of radius. The tree grows quickly when young, and its reproduction on newly formed sandbanks is sometimes very remarkable. A specimen in the Bengal Forest Museum, from the Mahanadi Forest, shews 24 well-marked rings on a mean radius of 6¼ inches, or 3·8 rings per inch, which is fast.

Weight: the confusion between this tree and *A. Suma* and the fact of this tree having two varieties has caused some uncertainty in the weight. Skinner describes two woods, *viz.*—

		Weight.	Value of P.
No. 10, P. 32.	*A. Suma* (*Tella sandra*, Tel.) . . .	77 lbs.	801
No. 11, P. 33.	*A. Sundra* (*Nalla sandra*, Tel.) . . .	81 „	915

The latter is probably our *A. Catechu*; the former *A. Suma*. Cunningham's experiments with bars of wood 2′ × 1″ × 1″ from Gwalior gave weight 70 lbs. P = 779. Brandis, in his Burma List of 1862, gives two varieties—

	lbs.
No. 29, Var. A.	56
No. 30, Var. B.	70

both of which are probably *A. Catechu*, and both here described, the ordinary red-wooded *A. Catechu* being Var. B. R. Thompson gives 75 lbs., while the Central Provinces List of 1873 gives 79 lbs.; ou rspecimens of Var. B. vary from 48 lbs. to 64 lbs., while our specimens of Var. A. give an average of 67 lbs. The wood seasons well, takes a fine polish and is extremely durable. It is not attacked by white ants or by teredo. It is used for rice pestles, oil and sugarcane crushers, agricultural implements, bows, spear and sword handles and wheelwrights' work. In Burma it is used for house posts, and very largely used as firewood for the steamers of the Irrawaddy Flotilla. In Northern India it is used for charcoal, and is one of the best woods for that purpose. It has been found good for railway sleepers, and it is probably only the smallness of the tree and the consequent waste in cutting up that has prevented its more general use. A number of sleepers were cut for the Northern Bengal State Railway in 1876, but no report has yet been made of their quality. The chief product of the tree is Catechu (cutch or *Katha*), which is obtained by boiling down the wood cut into chips. It is extensively manufactured in Kumaun, Oudh and in Burma, but not in Northern Bengal or Assam. Cutch is used by natives in India to chew with the betel-leaf, and is largely exported to Europe for dyeing and tanning. Medicinally it is used as an astringent for fevers and in other maladies.

			lbs.
H	938.	Hazara, Punjab	...
P	604.	Kangra, „	54
P	1196.	Madhopur, Punjab	63
P	98.	Sutlej Valley, Punjab	63
P	455.	Ajmere	...
O	255.	Garhwal (1868)	53
C	2758.	Moharli Reserve, Central Provinces	64
E	663.	Rakti Forest, Darjeeling Terai	59
E	2356.	Mahanadi Forest, Darjeeling Terai	48

The variety of *A. Catechu* with darker coloured wood, which probably corresponds to the variety A. of Brandis' Burma List of 1862, is found in the Central Provinces, Darjeeling Terai and Burma. There is some uncertainty regarding its identification, but apparently it is only a variety of *A. Catechu*, with darker coloured, less heavy and less hard heartwood, and a slightly different structure as above. The wood is not quite so hard as that of the ordinary form, and in structure it differs by having larger pores, and finer and more pronounced medullary rays. To this form belong—

			lbs.
C	189.	Mandla, Central Provinces (1866)	59
C	203.	„ „	63
E	625.	Bamunpokri, Darjeeling Terai (locally, *kankar*)	59
F	2355.	„ „ „ „ . . .	70
B	1454.	Prome, Burma	75
No.	2.	Salem Collection	76

C. 1308 (75 lbs.) and C. 1310 (76 lbs.), called *Khoiru* and *Seme*, from Gumsúr, differ from *A. Catechu* by smaller and more numerous pores, and finer and more numerous medullary rays. They may very probably belong to *A. Suma*, Buch.

8. A. Intsia, Willd.; Hook. Fl. Ind. ii. 297; Kurz i. 423. *A. cæsia,* W. and A.; Beddome xcv.; Brandis 189; Kurz i. 425; Gamble 33. *Mimosa cæsia,* Roxb. Fl. Ind. ii. 565. Vern. *Arhai-ka-bél,* Sutlej; *Katrar,* Kumaun; *Harrari,* Nep.; *Payir rik, ngraem rik,* Lepcha; *Korinta,* Tel.; *Jarri, chilor,* Mar.

A large climbing shrub with reddish grey bark, with usually five fluted, spirally-twisted grooves; wood white, soft, porous. Pores small and large, enclosed in irregular concentric bands which run into each other, and which separate the narrow belts of firmer and darker-coloured tissue in which the white, fine, medullary rays are prominent.

Sub-Himalayan tract from the Chenab eastwards, ascending to 4,000 feet, throughout India and Burma.

The bark is used by Lepchas in Sikkim as a substitute for soap in washing the hair.

E 478. Rakti Forest, Darjeeling Terai.
E 2379. Chunbati, Darjeeling, 2,000 ft.

9. A. pennata, Willd.; Hook. Fl. Ind. ii. 297; Beddome xcv.; Brandis 189; Kurz i. 424; Gamble 33. *Mimosa pennata,* Roxb. Fl. Ind. ii. 565. Vern. *Agla, awal,* Kumaun; *Biswúl,* Hind.; *Arfu,* Nep.; *Tol rik,* Lepcha; *Sooyit,* Burm.

A large climbing shrub. Bark reddish brown, ¼ inch thick, with horizontal cracks. Wood porous, moderately hard. Pores oval or oblong, occasionally subdivided into 2 or 3 compartments, from small to extremely large and very numerous, surrounded or enclosed in an irregular net-work of white tissue, which separates the patches of darker-coloured and firmer tissue, in which the white, moderately broad medullary rays are distinctly visible.

Oudh, Kumaun, Nepal, Eastern Bengal, Burma and South India.

Weight, 50 lbs. per cubic foot. Growth fast, 3 to 4 rings per inch of radius.

		lbs.
E 476.	Balasun Forest, Darjeeling Terai	...
E 2358.	Sivoke " " "	50

10. A. dealbata, Link.; Benth. Fl. Austr. ii. 415; Brandis 180. The Silver Wattle.

A tree spreading rapidly by numerous root-suckers. The wood is moderately hard, light brown, but warps considerably. Pores small, often in short linear groups. Medullary rays short, fine and moderately broad, well marked on a radial section.

Indigenous in New South Wales, Victoria and Tasmania. Introduced on the Nilgiris, and now naturalised since 1840.

The wood is extensively used in Australia for timber, and the bark for tanning. It is being tried in plantations in the hills of the Punjab, North-Western Provinces and Sikkim. Our specimen was cut from a tree 11 years old and 46 feet high, and was about 12 inches in diameter. Colonel Beddome, in his Report on the Nilgiri plantations of April 1878, says that this Wattle grows very readily from the stool, but comes up in a dense mass of small twig-like stems, so that it can only be depended on for very small firewood.

W 1099. Nilgiri Hills.

11. A. melanoxylon, R. Br.; Benth. Fl. Austr. ii. 415.; Brandis 180. Australian Blackwood.

A large tree with hard and durable wood; heartwood dark brown and beautifully mottled, soft, shining, even-grained; pores mostly oval, moderate-sized and divided into compartments conspicuously marked on a vertical section. Medullary rays short and fine.

New South Wales, Victoria, Tasmania and South Australia. Introduced on the Nilgiris since 1840 and now completely naturalised. Also being grown in the hills of the Punjab, Kumaun and Sikkim.

With regard to its rate of growth, Colonel Beddome, in his Report of April 1878 on the Nilgiri plantations, says that in the Bleakhouse plantation, Wellington, the average girth of the trees in the portion which is 21 to 22 years old, taken from the measurement of 30 trees as they came, was 35 inches at 6 feet from the ground (about 4 rings per inch of radius), the girth of some of the largest trees being 56, 55, 50, 46 and 44 inches. Our specimen was cut from a tree 20 years old and 90 feet high; it gave a plank 2 feet broad. The wood seems to be regarded on the Nilgiris as very inferior to that of *Eucalyptus Globulus*, either for timber or firewood; its growth is much slower and it is attacked by species of *Loranthus*, which parasites in time kill the tree. It does not coppice well, unless cut very young.

Weight, according to Mr. Newbery (Timbers of Victoria, 1877), 41 to 48 lbs. per cubic foot; our specimen gives 36 lbs.

It is used in Australia for cabinet work, coach-building, railway carriages and agricultural implements; on the Nilgiris chiefly for firewood. Its bark is used for tanning.

	lbs.
W 1100. Nilgiri Hills	36

Besides *A. melanoxylon* and *A. dealbata*, there are several other species of Wattle, some of which are cultivated in India. *A. decurrens*, Willd., the "Common" or "Black" Wattle, is a small or medium-sized tree; larger in moist localities. According to Mr. Newbery, the wood weighs 45 to 48 lbs. per cubic foot. It is being grown in several places in India. *A. pycnantha*, Bth., the "Golden" or "Broad-leaf" Wattle, is the most valuable species for tanner's bark and gum. Its wood weighs 51·5 lbs. per cubic foot. *A. homalophylla*, A. Cunn., is the Myallwood, a small tree with a hard, dark wood with the scent of violets.

Wattles grow in almost any soil, but their growth is best in loose, sandy places or where the surface has been broken for agricultural or other purposes. It is well, before sowing the seed, to soak it for a short time in warm water; this moistens the outer shell and induces more speedy germination. The seeds generally germinate in from 7 to 10 days, and are apt to damp off if too carelessly watered.

29. ALBIZZIA, Durazzini.

Contains 10 Indian species, most of which are common large trees found over the greater part of India, and are here described. *A. myriophylla*, Bl.; Hook. Fl. Ind. ii. 300; Kurz i. 426, (*Mimosa microphylla*, Roxb. Fl. Ind. ii. 549) Vern. *Tetúliya*, Sylhet, is a small evergreen tree of Sikkim, the Khasia Hills, Eastern Bengal and Tenasserim. *A. elegans*, Kurz i. 427, is a large evergreen tree of the tropical forests of the Pegu Yomas; while *A. lophantha*, Bth. Fl. Austr. ii. 421; Brandis 174, is an Australian tree of rapid growth, which has now been completely naturalised on the Nilgiri Hills. Baron von Müller says that it seeds profusely and germinates most easily, and is very valuable for re-clothing desert tracts, where it is important quickly to create shade, shelter and copious vegetation. The bark may be used for tanning. A new species has lately been discovered in the Chanda district, Central Provinces, by Mr. R. Thompson, called *Silari*. It is a large tree with short trunk, spreading branches and large fruit.

The structure of *Albizzia* is characterised by large or moderate-sized not very numerous pores, which are exceedingly prominent on a vertical section, the pores of successive concentric strata being not parallel, but running obliquely into each other. The medullary rays are not generally prominent, and the wood is softer than that of most species of *Acacia*.

1. A. Lebbek, Benth.; Hook. Fl. Ind. ii. 298; Beddome t. 53; Brandis 176; Kurz i. 427. *Mimosa Sirissa*, Roxb. Fl. Ind. ii. 544. The Siris Tree. Vern. *Siris, sirín, sirái, kalsis, tantia, garso,* Hind.; *Sirisha,* Beng.; *Harreri,* Panch Mehals; *Vaghe, kat vaghe,* Tam.;

Dirasan, darshana, kat vage, pedda duchirram, Tel.; *Kal baghi, bengha*, Kan.; *Chichola*, Mar.; *Kokoh*, Burm.; *Beymadá, gachodá*, And.

A large deciduous tree. Bark grey or brownish grey, rough, with numerous, short, irregular cracks. Sapwood large, white; heartwood dark brown, hard, shining, mottled, with deeper coloured, longitudinal streaks. The annual rings in trees grown in the Punjab are marked by a distinct line. Pores large, not numerous, often subdivided and enclosed in patches of softer whitish tissue, which are frequently arranged in short bands. Pores prominent on a longitudinal section. Medullary rays fine, very numerous.

Sub-Himalayan tract from the Indus eastwards, ascending to 5,000 feet; Bengal, Burma, Central and South India.

Growth exceedingly rapid during the first year. Brandis says that trees in the Punjab have 2¾ feet girth in 12 years 4½ feet in 30 years, and that trees at Sakhar in Sind 17 years old have reached 5 to 6 feet in girth. This would give from 1 to 3 rings per inch of radius, which is very fast.

The weight and transverse strength have been determined from the following experiments:—

Experiment by whom conducted.	Year.	Wood whence procured.	Weight.	No. of experiments.	Size of bar.	Value of P.
					Ft. In. In.	
Puckle	1859	Mysore	57	2	2 × 1 × 1	1052
„	„	„	61	4	„ „ „	959
„	„	„	56	4	„ „ „	1068
Cunningham	1854	Gwalior . . .	50	2	„ „ „	480
Baker	1820	Junagarh . . .	55	4	7 × 2 × 2	526
Skinner, No. 7	1862	South India . . .	50	...	......	793
„ „ 8	„	Burma	46	...	......	855
(List)	„	Mysore . . .	50	...	......	......
Brandis, No. 40	1862	Burma	48	...	......	......
A. Mendis	1855	Ceylon	42	...	......	......
Smythies	1878	Punjab	48·5	4	......	......
		South India . . .	45	3	......	......
		Burma . . .	45·5	2	......	......

It seasons, works and polishes well, and is fairly durable. It is used for sugarcane crushers, oil-mills, furniture, well curbs and wheel-work; in South India for boats. In the Andamans where trees of large size are procurable, it is used for building, but more usually for house-posts. It is often grown as an avenue tree, but its roots do not penetrate very deep. It grows easily from cuttings. It gives a gum which is not soluble in water, but merely forms a jelly. The leaves and twigs are given as fodder to camels.

			lbs.
P	1193.	Madhopur, Punjab	47
P	96.	Bhajji, Sutlej Valley, 3,000 feet	43
P	881.	Multán	49
P	468.	Ajmere	55
W	728.	South Kanara	41
W	748.	„ „	51
W	751.	„ „	44
B	1453.	Prome, Burma	48
B	2208.	Andaman Islands	43
No.	81.	Ceylon Collection (marked *Acacia speciosa*)	42

2. A. odoratissima, Benth.; Hook. Fl. Ind. ii. 299; Beddome t. 54; Brandis 175; Kurz i. 427; Gamble 33. *Mimosa odoratissima,* Roxb. Fl. Ind. ii. 546. Vern. *Lasrin, karambru, polach,* Pb.; *Siris, siran, bhandír, bersa, bás, bassein, bansa,* Hind.; *Chichwa, chichola, yerjoohetta,* Gondi; *Chichora,* Kurku; *Kali harreri,* Panch Mehals; *Tedong,* Lepcha; *Jati-koroi,* Ass.; *Moroi,* Cachar; *Kal-thuringi, kar vaghe, bilwara, solomanim, sela vanjai,* Tam.; *Shinduga, chindu, telsu, yerjuchinta, karu vage,* Tel.; *Pullibaghi, billawar,* Kan.; *Borhi, chichua, chichanda,* Mar.; *Iloore mara,* Cingh.; *Thitmagyi,* Burm.

A large deciduous tree. Bark ¼ inch thick, grey, with irregular cracks and patches of darker colour. Sapwood large, white; heartwood dark brown with darker streaks, very hard. Dark, narrow, concentric bands (annual rings?), alternating with bands of lighter colour. Pores large, often double, uniformly distributed, enclosed in very narrow rings of soft tissue and sometimes arranged in interrupted lines, very prominent on a longitudinal section. Medullary rays fine, wavy, short, indistinct. This species is characterised among common *Albizzias* by its greater hardness and short and less prominent medullary rays.

Sub-Himalayan tract from the Indus eastwards, ascending to 3,000 feet; Bengal, Burma, Central and South India.

Growth rapid, 4 rings per inch of radius. Weight, Wallich gives 45 lbs.; Kyd, 40 lbs.; Skinner, No. 6, 46 lbs.; Brandis, 52 lbs.; our specimens give an average of 54 lbs. Kyd's experiments with Assam wood with bars 2′ × 1″ × 1″ gave P = 547; Brandis found P = 984; and Skinner 800. The wood seasons, works and polishes well, and is fairly durable. It is used for wheels, oil-mills and furniture. It gives a dark-brown gum. The leaves and twigs are lopped for cattle fodder.

			lbs.
P	3223.	Nagpahar Forest, Ajmere	...
O	205.	Garhwal (1868)	43
O	219.	" "	...
C	184.	Mandla, Central Provinces (1870)	...
C	1122.	Ahiri Reserve, Central Provinces	60
C	2748.	Moharli Reserve, Central Provinces	...
E	2360.	Bamunpokri, Darjeeling Terai	59
W	725.	South Kanara	59
W	1189.	" "	42
D	1084.	North Arcot	52
B	290.	Burma (1867)	53
B	3121.	" (1862)	57
B	1427.	"	57
B	2231.	Andamans (1866)	56
No.	8.	Salem Collection	52

3. A. procera, Benth.; Hook. Fl. Ind. ii. 299; Beddome xcvi.; Brandis 175; Kurz i. 428; Gamble 33. *Mimosa elata,* Roxb. Fl. Ind. ii. 546. Vern. *Safed siris, gurar, karra, karo, karanji, gurbári, gurkur, baro, karolu, garso,* Hind.; *Karallu, kini, kilai, kili, tikiri,* Bombay; *Takmur,* Lepcha; *Koroi,* Beng., Ass.; *Kili,* Gáro; *Sarapatri,* Uriya; *Passerginni,* Gondi; *Kinni,* Bhíl; *Gurar,* Mar.; *Konda vaghe,* Tam.; *Pedda patseru, tella sopara, tella chindagu,* Tel.; *Chikul,* Kan.; *Choi,* Magh; *Seet,* Burm.; *Búrdá,* And.

A large, deciduous, fast-growing tree. Bark ½ inch thick, yellowish or greenish white or grey, smooth, with horizontal lines. Sapwood large, yellowish white, not durable; heartwood hard, brown, shining, with alternate belts of darker and lighter colour. Pores moderate-sized and large, enclosed in narrow rings of softer tissue, uniformly distributed, very prominent on a longitudinal section. Medullary rays fine. The difference in structure between *A. Lebbek* and the woods of *A. procera* is very slight.

Sub-Himalayan tract from the Jumna eastwards, Bengal, Satpura Range in the Central Provinces, Guzerat, South India and Burma.

Growth very rapid. Brandis says that it attains in 12 years 3 to 4 feet, and in 30 years 4 to 6 feet girth. This would give about 2 rings per inch of radius, which is very rapid. Our specimens are of somewhat slower growth, 6 rings per inch.

Weight, according to Skinner, No. 3, 39 lbs.; Brandis, No. 28, 48 lbs.; our specimens give an average of 46 lbs. Skinner gives P = 884; Brandis 750. The wood is straight and even-grained, seasons well, and the heartwood is durable. It is used for sugarcane crushers, rice-pounders, wheels, agricultural implements, bridges and house posts. It is used by tea planters for stakes for laying out tea gardens, as it is found to split well, and occasionally for tea boxes and for charcoal, for which it is found to be very good. It gives a copious gum.

		lbs.
O 220.	Garhwal (1868)	41
O 3004.	„ (1873)	44
C 2740.	Jamui Forest, Berar (sapwood)	26
E 2361.	Bamunpokri, Darjeeling Terai	37
E 949.	Eastern Dúars, Assam	51
E 1263.	Tezpúr, Assam	58
E 2194.	Nowgong, Assam	42
E 1955.	Chittagong	43
B 329.	Burma (1867)	39
B 811.	„	60
B 2527.	„ (1862)	41
B 506.	Andaman Islands	53
B 518.	„ „	46
B 2247.	„ „ (1866)	41

4. **A. lucida,** Benth.; Hook. Fl. Ind. ii. 299; Brandis 174; Kurz i. 429; Gamble 33. *Mimosa lucida*, Roxb. Fl. Ind. ii. 544. Vern. *Sil koroi*, Beng.; *Tapria-siris*, Nep.; *Ngraem*, Lepcha; *Mess-guch*, Ass.; *Gunhi*, Magh; *Thanthat*, Burm.

A large deciduous tree. Heartwood hard, brown, with dark streaks and alternating dark and light coloured, concentric bands. Pores moderate-sized, numerous, enclosed in round patches of soft tissue. Medullary rays fine and very numerous.

Eastern Bengal, Burma.

Weight, average of our specimens, 50 lbs. per cubic foot. Wood hard and good, but not used. Lac is obtained on it in Assam.

		lbs.
E 660.	Bamunpokri, Darjeeling Terai	55
E 677.	„ „ „	61

5. **A. Julibrissin,** Boivin; Hook. Fl. Ind. i. 300; Brandis 177. *Mimosa Kalkora*, Roxb. Fl. Ind. ii. 547 (?). Pink Siris. Vern. *Sirín, kurmru, surangru, shirsh, shishi, búna, tandái, mathirshi, brind*, Pb.; *Lal siris, baraulia, barau, bhokra*, Hind.; *Kalkora* (?), Beng.

A moderate-sized deciduous tree. Bark dark grey, with long horizontal wrinkles. Sapwood large; heartwood dark brown, almost black in old trees, beautifully mottled, shining. Annual rings distinctly marked by a sharp line. Pores large, often double, very prominent on a longitudinal section. Medullary rays fine, short, red, appearing as narrow, dark, straight bands on a radial section.

Himalaya, from the Indus to Sikkim, ascending to 5,000 feet.

Growth rapid, 3 to 4 rings per inch of radius (*Brandis*); our specimens give 5 rings.

Weight, 43 to 52 lbs. per cubic foot. The wood is used to make furniture. The tree is extremely handsome when in flower, with its innumerable pink tassels of delicate silky blossoms, from which it derives its name *guláb-resham*, rose silk.

		lbs.
H 97.	Sutlej Valley, Simla, 4,000 feet	52
H 152.	Sainj, Simla, 4,000 feet	43

6. A. stipulata, Boivin; Hook. Fl. Ind. ii. 300; Beddome t. Fl.; Brandis 178; Kurz i. 426; Gamble 34. *Mimosa stipulacea*, Roxb. 55, Ind. ii. 549. Vern. *Oi, oë, sirín, shirsha, kasír*, Pb.; *Siran, kanujer a. pattia, samsundra*, Hind.; *Kala siris*, Nep.; *Singriang*, Lepcha; *Sow*, Ass.; *Selcho*, Garo; *Chakua, amluki*, Beng.; *Kat turanji*, Tam.; *Konda chiragu, chindaga*, Tel.; *Kal baghi, hote baghi*, Kan.; *Kabal*, Cingh.; *Pokoh*, Magh; *Boomaiza*, Burm.

A large, deciduous, fast-growing tree. Bark grey, with numerous short, vertical wrinkles and a few larger horizontal furrows, with prominent edges, darker when old. Sapwood large, white; heartwood brown, generally not durable, soft, shining. Annual rings distinctly marked. Pores large, often oval and subdivided, very prominent on a longitudinal section. Medullary rays fine, short, reddish, not very distinct.

Sub-Himalayan tract from the Indus eastwards, ascending to 4,000 feet; Oudh, Bengal, Burma, South India.

Growth very rapid. Roxburgh says that a tree he planted in the Botanic Garden at Calcutta measured 48·5 inches in girth at 4 feet above the ground when 7 years old; this would give a rate of growth of slightly less than 1 ring per inch of radius. Stewart, in "Punjab Plants, p. 56," says that a tree in the Saharanpur Gardens was 7 feet in girth at about 17 years of age, which gives rather over 1 ring per inch of radius. Our specimens give 3 to 4 rings per inch of radius. A round in the Bengal Forest Museum from a young tree, shews 11 rings on a mean radius of 6 inches or 1·8 rings per inch of radius. The growth may be taken therefore at 1 to 4 rings per inch of radius, which is very rapid. Weight, according to Skinner, No. 9, 55 lbs.; according to Brandis' Burma List of 1862, No. 27, 66 lbs.; our specimens give only 33 lbs.; and Kyd (*Acacia marginata*, Ham.) 28 lbs. Kyd gives P = 222; and Skinner gives P = 823; but it is doubtful if his experiments were really from wood of *A. stipulata*. The wood is said by Beddome, probably quoting Skinner, to be used for building and for naves of wheels. Kurz says it is good for cabinet work, furniture and similar purposes. Brandis' Burma List, 1862, No. 27, says it is prized for cart-wheels and for the bells of cattle. In Bengal it has been tried for tea-boxes, for which purpose it will probably suit well; also for charcoal. It gives a gum which exudes copiously from the stem, and is used by Nepalese for sizing their "Daphne" paper. The branches are lopped for cattle fodder.

		lbs.
H 603.	Kangra, Punjab	29
O 217.	Garhwal (1868)	28
C 2989.	Jubbulpore, Central Provinces (1863)	39
E 647.	Bamunpokri, Darjeeling Terai	26
E 2362.	" " "	29
E 788.	Kamrúp, Assam	40
E 1956.	Chittagong	25
B 809.	Burma	36
B 2528.	" (1866)	33
B 2221.	Andaman Islands (1866)	45

7. A. amara, Boivin; Hook. Fl. Ind. ii. 301; Brandis 178. *A. amara* and *A. Wightii*, Grah.; Beddome t. 61, xcvi. *Mimosa amara* and *M. pulchella*, Roxb. Fl. Ind. ii. 548. Vern. *Lallei*, Dekkan; *Thuringi, wúnja, suranji, shekram*, Tam.; *Nallarenga, shekrani, sikkai, narlingi*, Tel.; *Bel-khambi*, Kan.; *Kadsige*, Coorg; *Oosulay*, Mal.

A moderate-sized deciduous tree. Sapwood large; heartwood purplish-brown, beautifully mottled, extremely hard, with alternate, concentric, light and dark bands. Pores small, in patches of white tissue, which are frequently joined, forming concentric bands. Medullary rays very fine, very numerous.

South India and Dekkan.

Skinner, No. 1, gives the weight at 70 lbs.; our specimens weigh 61 to 62 lbs. Skinner also gives P = 1284, and says, "The wood is strong, fibrous and stiff, close-grained, hard and durable, superior to sál and teak in transverse strength and direct cohesive power;" also that it is used for the beams of native houses and carts, the wood of the crooked branches for ploughs, and the leaves for washing the hair. Beddome says it is a good fuel, and is extensively used for the locomotives at Salem and Bangalore.

		lbs.
D 1052.	Salem, Madras	61
No. 6.	Salem Collection	62

B 2705 (59 lbs.) from Tavoy (Wallich, 1828) is a dark-red specimen of a heavy brown wood of *Albizzia* structure, which cannot be identified.

ORDER XII. ROSACEÆ.

Contains 20 genera of Indian trees, shrubs or climbers, chiefly found in the colder regions of the Himalaya and other mountain ranges. It is divided into 7 Tribes, *viz.*—

Tribe	I.—Chrysobalaneæ	*Parinarium* and *Parastemon.*
„	II.—Pruneæ	*Prunus, Maddenia, Pygeum* and *Prinsepia.*
„	III.—Spiræeæ	*Spiræa* and *Neillia.*
„	IV.—Rubeæ	*Rubus.*
„	V.—Potentilleæ	*Potentilla.*
„	VI.—Roseæ	*Rosa.*
„	VII.—Pomeæ	*Cydonia, Docynia, Eriobotrya, Pyrus, Photinia, Pourthiæa, Stranvæsia, Cratægus* and *Cotoneaster.*

Parinarium contains 3 species: *P. Griffithianum*, Bth.; Hook. Fl. Ind. ii. 310, is a tree of Tenasserim and the Andaman Islands; *P. indicum*, Beddome t. 191, is a tree of the forests of the Wynaad, between 2,000 and 3,000 feet; and *P. travancoricum*, Beddome, is a tree of the hills about Courtallum. *Parastemon urophyllum*, A. DC.; Hook. Fl. Ind. ii. 312, is a shrub or small tree of Tenasserim and the Andamans. *Maddenia* contains two species: *M. himalaica*, Hook. f. and Th.; Hook. Fl. Ind. ii. 318, a small tree of the Sikkim and Bhutan Himalaya from 8,000 to 10,000 feet; and *M. pedicellata*, Hook. f., of the Mishmi Hills. *Neillia thyrsiflora*, Don; Gamble 35, is a common shrub of the Sikkim Hills. *Potentilla* can scarcely be said to contain woody species, though *P. fruticosa*, Linn.; Hook. Fl. Ind. ii. 347; Gamble 36 (misspelt *frutescens*), is a small shrub common on rocks at high elevations from Kashmir to Bhutan, with a hard wood and annual rings marked by a line of very small pores; and *P. Salessovii*, Steph.; Hook. Fl. Ind. ii. 348, occurs as a small shrub above 11,000 feet in Lahoul and Northern Kashmir.

Cydonia vulgaris, Pers.; Hook. Fl. Ind. ii. 369 (*Pyrus Cydonia*, Linn.; Brandis 205). The Quince. Vern. *Bihi*, Hind.; *Bamtsúnt, bamsútu*, Kashmir, is cultivated in Afghanistan and the North-West Himalayas up to 5,500 feet. *Docynia* contains 2 species: *D. indica*, Dcne; Hook. Fl. Ind. ii. 369 (*Pyrus indica*, Wall.; Roxb. Fl. Ind. ii. 511; Kurz i. 441; Gamble 37). Vern. *Mehul, passy*, Nep.; *Likúng*, Lepcha; *Sopho*, Khasia, is a tree of the hills of Sikkim, Bhutan and Assam, with a yellow, edible, though harsh-tasting fruit; and, according to Aikin's description of Wallich's specimens, a compact, moderately hard, fine-grained wood; and *D. Hookeriana*, Dcne; Hook. Fl. Ind. ii. 369, of the Khasia Hills. *Photinia* contains 5 species as re-arranged in the Flora Indica; *P. Lindleyana*, Wight and Arn.; Hook. Fl. Ind. ii. 380; Beddome xcviii., is a small tree of the Nilgiris; *P. Notoniana*, Wight and Arn.; Beddome t. 192 (*Eriobotrya integrifolia*, Kurz i. 442) Vern. *Kaddi bikki*, Burghers, is a small tree of Eastern Bengal, South India and Burma; *P. integrifolia*, Lindl.; *P. Griffithii*, Dcne; and *P. mollis*, Hook. f., are trees of the North-East Himalaya. *Pourthiæa arguta*, Dcne; Hook. Fl. Ind. ii. 382, is a small tree of the Khasia Hills and Sikkim Terai.

Wood close and even grained; that of most species apt to warp. Pores small to extremely small. Medullary rays generally fine to extremely fine.

1. PRUNUS, Linn.

Contains 18 species including the Almond, Peach, Apricot, Plum and Cherry. *P. prostrata*, Labill.; Hook. Fl. Ind. ii. 313; Brandis 193. Vern. *Tára, ter, talle*, Pb., is a small shrub of rocky places in Afghanistan and the arid parts of the North-West Himalaya, generally above 7,000 feet. *P. Mahaleb*, Linn.; Brandis 195, is cultivated at Khelat. *P. rufa*, Wall.; Hook. Fl. Ind. ii. 314 (*P. sp.*, Gamble 35) Vern. *Kamki*, Bhutia, is a tree of the inner Sikkim Himalaya above 10,000 feet. *P. punctata*, Hook. f. and Th., is a small tree of the Khasia Hills; and *P. Jenkinsii*, Hook. f. and Th., a small tree of Upper Assam. *P. tomentosa*, Thunb.; Hook. Fl. Ind. ii. 314, is a shrub of Kashmir; and *P. Jacquemontii*, Hook. f., a shrub of the inner North-West Himalaya in Kunawar and Garhwal.

P. Amygdalus, Baillon; Brandis 190. (*Amygdalus communis*, Willd.; Roxb. Fl. Ind. ii. 500.) The Almond. Vern. *Badám*, is cultivated in Afghanistan, Persia, Kashmir and the Punjab. *P. Cerasus*, Linn.; Brandis 193. The Cherry. Vern. *Alú balú*, Pers.; *Kerasyo*, Arab.; *Gilás, olchi, krusbal*, Pb., is generally cultivated in the North-West Himalaya between 5,000 and 8,000 feet. *P. Persica*, Bth. and Hk. f.; Hook. Fl. Ind. ii. 313; Brandis 191; Kurz i. 433; Gamble 34. (*Amygdalus persica*, Willd.; Roxb. Fl. Ind. ii. 500). The Peach. Vern. *Ghwareshtái*, Afg.; *Shúft alú*, Pers.; *Aru, aor, chinannu, beinni, beimu, rek*, Pb.; *Aru*, Hind.; *Takpo*, Lepcha, is commonly cultivated everywhere throughout the Himalaya and in Upper Burma.

The species here described have a distinct heartwood; the pores are small or very small. The medullary rays are generally of two classes, fine and moderately broad. The annual rings are marked either by a continuous line of pores or by more numerous pores in the spring wood.

1. P. armeniaca, Linn.; Hook. Fl. Ind. ii. 313; Brandis 191; Roxb. Fl. Ind. ii. 501. The Apricot. Vern. *Hári, gardalu, jaldaru, shíran, cheroli, cher kúsh, serkuji, shari*, Pb.; *Iser*, Kashmir; *Chúari, zardalu, khoobani*, Hind.; *Mishmish*, Pers.

A moderate-sized deciduous tree. Bark dark brown, rough, with narrow longitudinal clefts. Sapwood white; heartwood greyish brown, mottled with dark-brown streaks, moderately hard. Annual rings marked by a narrow continuous belt of pores, which are larger than the very small scattered pores in the outer portion of the ring. Medullary rays of two classes, numerous; very fine rays between fewer moderately broad ones.

Cultivated in the North-West Himalaya. Growth moderate, 4 to 8 rings per inch of radius.

Weight, 49 lbs. per cubic foot; Mathieu, Fl. For. p. 131, gives 58 lbs. Wood handsome, used for various purposes in the Punjab Hills. In Lahoul and Upper Kanawar it is the chief firewood. The fruit, fresh or dried, is extensively used for food, and an oil is extracted from the kernels which is used to burn, in cooking and for the hair.

			lbs.
II	781.	Bathri, Chamba, 3,000 feet	49
II	20.	Madhan, Simla, 6,000 feet	49
II	2876.	Matiyána, Simla, 7,000 feet	...

2. P. communis, Huds.; Hook. Fl. Ind. ii. 315; Brandis 192. The Plum. Vern. *Alúcha, olchi, er, aor, gardalu*, Pb.

A moderate-sized tree. Wood reddish brown, hard, very close-grained, warps and splits. Annual rings marked by a belt of small, closely packed pores. Pores in the main portion of the annual ring extremely small, in groups. Medullary rays of two classes, moderately broad, numerous, with very fine rays between them.

Cultivated (or indigenous, Hook. Fl. Ind.) from Garhwal to Kashmir in the Western Himalaya, from 5,000 to 7,000 feet.

Growth fast, 2 to 3 rings per inch of radius. Weight, 52 lbs. per cubic foot. The wood is smooth to work, and is used in Kashmir for the skeleton of the so-called papier-maché boxes.

		lbs.
H 151.	Giri Valley, Simla, 4,000 feet	52

3. P. Puddum, Roxb.; Hook. Fl. Ind. ii. 314; Brandis 194; Kurz i. 434.; Gamble 34. Vern. *Chamiári, amalgúch, pája, pajia,* Pb.; *Paddam, páya,* Hind.; *Kongki,* Lepcha.

A moderate-sized (in Sikkim, a large) deciduous tree. Bark peeling off in thin, horizontal, shining layers. Sapwood large, greenish white. Heartwood reddish, beautifully mottled on a radial section by narrow, wavy, shining, medullary rays, moderately hard. Annual rings distinctly marked by an irregular and not continuous belt of numerous pores. Pores small; those of the spring wood very small, frequently arranged in oblique lines intersecting the medullary rays at an angle. Medullary rays of two classes; numerous, very fine rays alternating with fewer, short, moderately broad rays, which are broader than those of *P. Padus.* Scent pleasant, resembling that of *P. Mahaleb.*

Wild in the Himalaya, from the Indus to Assam, between 2,500 and 7,000 feet; Khasia Hills.

Growth variable, from 4 to 22 rings per inch of radius, the average being 12.

Weight, the average of our specimens give 44 lbs. per cubic foot. Gamble says 40 to 45 lbs.

The wood is used in the Punjab Himalaya for walking-sticks; in Darjeeling occasionally for furniture. It deserves to be better known, and to be more extensively used, as, at any rate in Sikkim, it is common and reaches a large size. It gives an abundant gum, not used.

			lbs.
H	46.	Nagkanda, Simla, 7,000 feet	52
H	234.	Garhwal Hills (1868)	46
E	683.	Sepoydura Forest, Darjeeling, 6,000 feet	42
E	2363.	Kurseong, Darjeeling, 5,000 feet	41
E	2364.	Tukdah Forest, Darjeeling, 5,000 feet	48
E	1447.	Mishmi Hills (Griffith, 1836)	37

4. P. Padus, Linn.; Hook. Fl. Ind. ii. 315; Brandis 194; Gamble 35. The Bird Cherry. Vern. *Páras, kalakat, gidar-dák, bart, zúm, zam, zambu, jamu, chúle, dúdla, krún,* Pb.; *Jamana,* Hind.; *Likh-aru, arupatti,* Nep.; *Hlo sa hlot-kúng,* Lepcha.

A moderate-sized deciduous tree, with dark, rough bark. Sapwood large, whitish. Heartwood reddish brown, with an unpleasant smell, beautifully mottled on a radial section by the shining medullary rays, moderately hard. Annual rings distinctly marked by a narrow belt of continuous, closely arranged pores. Pores small, in irregularly shaped groups, which are uniformly distributed. Medullary rays short, moderately broad.

Himalaya, from the Indus to Sikkim, between 4,000 and 10,000 feet.

Growth, varying from 4 to 30 rings per inch of radius; the average of our specimens gave 13 rings. Average weight 41 lbs. per cubic foot, Mathieu Fl. For. p. 128, gives an average of 41·5 lbs. The wood has often a very handsome grain and deserves to be better known; it is scarcely ever used.

			lbs.
H	916.	Hazara, 7,000 feet	38
H	22.	Matiyána, Simla, 7,000 feet	42
H	58.	Nagkanda, Simla, 8,000 feet	43
E	696.	Rangbúl Forest, Darjeeling, 7,000 feet	41
E	2369.	" " "	42

The two Darjeeling specimens are perhaps *P. nepalensis*, Ser.; Hook. Fl. Ind. 316.

5. P. acuminata, Wall.; Hook. Fl. Ind. ii. 317; Gamble 35 (*wrongly* Roxb.).

A tree with thin dark bark. Wood reddish brown. Pores small, sometimes in groups or radial lines; medullary rays of two classes; numerous, very fine rays, alternating with fewer, short, broad ones.

Eastern Himalaya and Khasia Hills from 4,000 to 7,000 ft.

E 3309. Sureil, Darjeeling, 6,000 feet.

6. P. martabanica, Wall.; Hook. Fl. Ind. ii. 316; Kurz i. 434. Vern. *Thitmanku*, Burm.

No. B 1975, collected by Kurz in the Andamans in 1866, bears this name. It is a heavy, cross-grained, red wood, with moderate-sized pores, often subdivided, and fine, closely packed, uniform medullary rays.

2. PYGEUM, Gaertn.

No. 28, Adrian Mendis' Ceylon Collection, marked *Cryptocarya floribunda*, and *Galmorre*, Cingh., is a close-grained yellow wood with a structure resembling that of *Eriobotrya*. It is probably *Pygeum zeylanicum*, Gaertn.; Hook. Fl. Ind. ii. 321; Thwaites Enum. Fl. Zeyl. 102. Vern. *Galmora*, Cingh. (Weight 65 lbs. per cubic foot.) A large tree of South India and Ceylon, which gives a good firewood for burning bricks or lime. There are 8 other species of this genus. *P. acuminatum*, Colebr.; Hook. Fl. Ind. ii. 318; Kurz i. 435; Gamble 35, is a tree of the North-East Himalaya, Khasia Hills, Eastern Bengal and Chittagong, in which regions are also found *P. glaberrimum*, Hook. f.; and *P. montanum*, Hook. f. *P. Andersoni*, Hook. f., has been found on the summit of Parasnáth in Behar at 4,000 ft.; *P. Wightianum*, Bl. (*P. ceylanicum*, Beddome t. 59) and *P. Gardneri*, Hook. f., are large trees of South India; while *P. arboreum*, Endl., and two other species are found in the forests of Burma, chiefly in Tenasserim.

3. PRINSEPIA, Royle.

1. P. utilis, Royle; Hook. Fl. Ind. ii. 323; Brandis 196. Vern. *Bhekal, bekkra, karanga, cherara, dhatela, jhatela*, Hind.; *Gurinda*, Hazara; *Talúa, phulwara*, Rajaori; *Jinti*, Chenab; *Bekling*, Kanawar.

A deciduous, thorny shrub, with thin brown bark, peeling off in small vertical flakes. Sapwood white; heartwood red, very hard and compact, close and even grained, but much liable to split. Annual rings marked by a narrow continuous belt or line of larger pores; the pores outside this belt are small. The pores are sometimes filled with a white substance. Medullary rays very fine and numerous.

Outer Himalaya, from Hazara to Bhutan between 2,000 and 9,000 feet. Khasia Hills.

Growth slow, 12 rings per inch of radius. Weight, 69 lbs. per cubic foot. The wood is only used for fuel and occasionally for walking-sticks. An oil is expressed from the seeds which is used for food and for burning.

		lbs.
H 49.	Nagkanda, Simla, 8,000 feet	69
H 2868.	" " "	...

4. SPIRÆA, Linn.

Contains 11 species found in the Himalaya, chiefly at elevations above 6,000 feet. They contain both herbs, such as the "Meadow Sweet" found in Kashmir; and shrubs, few of which attain any size. The two described are the most important.

1. S. sorbifolia, Linn.; Hook. Fl. Ind. ii. 324. *S. Lindleyana,* DC. Vern. *Sarbashtai, kikri, batu,* Pb.

A shrub, with reddish grey bark. Wood hard, compact, even-grained. Annual rings distinctly marked by a belt of more numerous pores. Pores small, scanty in the outer part of each annual ring. Medullary rays moderately broad.

North-West Himalaya, from the Sutlej to Kumaun, above 7,000 feet.

Growth moderate, 12 rings per inch of radius. The largest growing species. Recognised by its pinnate leaves from the other shrubby species. It is chiefly found in shady damp woods.

		lbs.
H 82.	Simla, 7,000 feet	49
H 3014.	Hattu Forest, Simla, 8,000 feet	...

2. S. canescens, Don.; Hook. Fl. Ind. ii. 325. Vern. *Chaku, taku,* Simla.

Structure similar to that of *S. sorbifolia.*

North-West Himalaya, from Murree to Kumaun.

Growth moderate, 12 rings per inch of radius. Found chiefly on open hill-sides as a stiff bush. Very handsome in flower in the spring.

		lbs.
H 159.	Simla, 7,000 feet	47
H 2827.	Mahasu, Simla, 8,000 feet	...

5. RUBUS, Linn.

Contains 40 species of erect, trailing or climbing, generally thorny shrubs. Many species are known on account of their edible fruits, the best of which is perhaps *R. ellipticus. R. fruticosus,* Linn.; Hook. Fl. Ind. ii. 337; Brandis 197. The Blackberry or Bramble. Vern. *Ankri, alish, kanachi, chench, pakhána,* Pb., is found in Afghanistan, the Salt Range and the Punjab Himalaya as far east as the Ravi. *R. rosæfolius,* Sm.; Hook. Fl. Ind. ii. 341.; Kurz i. 439 (*R. Sikkimensis,* O. Kze; Gamble 36), is a small shrub found in the Himalaya from Kumaun to Sikkim, in the Khasia Hills and in the hills of Burma. It has a large, red, edible fruit, which is sold in the bazar in Darjeeling. *R. paniculatus,* Sm.; Hook. Fl. Ind. ii. 329; Brandis 196; Gamble 36. Vern. *Kala akhi,* Kangra; *Anchu, pattarola, kala hisalu,* Hind.; *Numing rik,* Lepcha, is a simple leaved species with leaves covered beneath with dense white tomentum, common throughout the Himalaya. *R. biflorus,* Buch.; Hook. Fl. Ind. i. 338; Brandis 198. Vern. *Chánch, kantauch, khaniára,* Kashmir; *Karer, akhreri, akhe,* Ravi; *Dher,* Simla, is a white-stemmed shrub of the Himalaya from Hazara to Bhutan. *R. niveus,* Wall.; Hook. Fl. Ind. ii. 335; Brandis 199; Gamble 35. Vern. *Kalga,* Sutlej, has the same distribution. *R. moluccanus,* Linn.; Hook. Fl. Ind. ii. 330; Kurz i. 439; Gamble 39. Vern. *Bipemkanta,* Nep.; *Sufok-ji,* Lepcha, is a large shrub, with simple, rugose leaves, and red edible fruit, found in the North-East Himalaya and down to Burma. *R. racemosus,* Roxb., and two other species occur on the Nilgiris. There are many other interesting species, but too small and too numerous for mention here.

1. R. ellipticus, Smith; Hook. Fl. Ind. ii. 336. *R. flavus*, Ham., Brandis 197; Kurz i. 438; Gamble 35. *R. Gowreephul*, Roxb. Fl. Ind. ii. 517. Vern. *Akhi, ankri, kunáchi, guracha, pukana*, Pb.; *Esar, hishalu, hisalu*, Kumaun; *Tolu aselu, escalu, cesi*, Nep.; *Kashyem*, Lepcha.

A large thorny shrub with brown bark and moderately hard, light-brown wood. Pores small; medullary rays short, very broad and moderately broad.

Himalaya, from the Indus to Bhutan, between 1,500 and 8,000 feet; Khasia Hills and Assam.

The fruit is yellow and with the flavour of the raspberry; it is commonly eaten and made into preserves in the Himalaya, and is certainly one of the best of the wild fruits of India.

E 2367. Tukdah Forest, Darjeeling, 5,000 feet.

2. R. lasiocarpus, Smith; Hook. Fl. Ind. ii. 339; Brandis 198; Kurz i. 439; Gamble 36. Vern. *Gunacha, pukana*, Hazara; *Kandiári, kharmuch, súrganch*, Kashmir; *Túlanch*, Chenab; *Niú, kalliachi*, Beas; *Klenchu, galka*, Simla; *Kalga*, Sutlej; *Kalawar, kala hisalu*, Kumaun; *Kala aselu*, Nep.; *Kajutalam*, Lepcha.

Bark smooth. Structure similar to that of *R. ellipticus*.

Himalaya, Khasia Hills, Burma, South India and Ceylon.

The fruit has a glaucous blue-black colour; it is small, but of good flavour.

E 2368. Tukdah Forest, Darjeeling, 5,000 feet.

3. R. lineatus, Reinw.; Hook. Fl. Ind. ii. 333; Gamble 36. Vern. *Gempé aselu*, Nep.

A large thornless shrub with red bark peeling off in papery flakes. Wood yellowish brown, in structure resembling that of *R. ellipticus*.

Sikkim Himalaya, 6,000 to 9,000 feet.

Stems used to make fences. Fruit red, edible.

E 3307. Darjeeling 7,000 feet.

6. ROSA, Linn.

Contains 9 species without including those cultivated in India, full account of which is given in Brandis' Forest Flora, and referred to in the Flora Indica ii. 363. *Rosa involucrata*, Roxb. Fl. Ind. ii. 513, is a sub-scandent shrub of the banks of streams in the Gangetic plain, westward to Mount Aboo and eastward to Burma. *R. Eglanteria*, Linn.; Hook. Fl. Ind. ii. 366 (*R. lutea*, Mill.; Brandis 201), is a shrub of the arid parts of the inner Himalaya, with yellow flowers. *R. Webbiana*, Wall; Hook. Fl. Ind. ii. 366; Brandis 202. Vern. *Kantián, shingári*, Hazara; *Shikand, shawali, manayar, brazen*, Chenab; *Chúa*, Lahoul; *Sia*, Ladak, Piti; *Ringyal*, Kanawar, is a pink-flowered erect shrub of the same region. *R. anserinæfolia*, Boiss.; Hook. Fl. Ind. ii. 365, is a common, wild and cultivated, white-flowered rose of Afghanistan. *R. longicuspis*, Bertol.; Hook. Fl. Ind. ii. 367, is a climber of the Khasia Hills from 2,000 to 5,000 feet; and *R. Leschenaultiana*, W. and A.; Hook. Fl. Ind. ii. 368, a climber of the Nilgiri and Pulney Hills.

1. R. moschata, Mill.; Hook. Fl. Ind. ii. 367; Brandis 201. Vern. *Kuji, kajei, karer, kwia, kwiala*, Hind.; *Phulwara, chal*, Kashmir.

A large, thorny, climbing shrub. Bark greyish brown. Wood moderately hard, porous. Annual rings marked by a continuous line of large pores in the spring wood, the pores in the autumn wood being scanty and small. Medullary rays broad to very broad.

North-West Himalaya, from Afghanistan to Nepal, ascending to 11,000 feet.

A tall climber, very sweet scented, and very ornamental when in flower in May and June. Flowers white. Growth slow, 15 rings per inch of radius.

H 115. Bhajji, Simla, 5,000 feet.

2. **R. sericea,** Lindl.; Hook. Fl. Ind. ii. 367; Brandis 202; Gamble 36.

A thorny shrub with greyish brown bark, peeling off in papery flakes. Wood very hard, darkening on exposure. Annual rings marked by a continuous line of very small pores in the spring wood, the pores in the autumn wood being extremely small. Medullary rays short, moderately broad to broad, prominent.

Himalaya, from the Sutlej to Bhutan, from 9,000 to 14,000 feet.

Growth slow, 18 rings per inch of radius. Flowers white or pink.

E 2366. Suburkum, Darjeeling, 11,000 feet.

3. **R. macrophylla,** Lindl.; Hook. Fl. Ind. ii. 366; Brandis 203. Vern. *Guláb, ban-guláb,* Hind.; *Tikjik,* Chenab; *Akhiari,* Ravi; *Breri, bankoi,* Simla.

A thorny shrub. Bark blackish brown, peeling off in thin flakes. Wood hard and compact; annual rings marked by a belt of numerous small pores in the spring wood; pores in the rest of the wood extremely small. Medullary rays moderately broad to broad, prominent.

Himalaya, from the Indus to Sikkim, between 3,500 and 10,000 feet.

Growth slow, 13 rings per inch of radius. Weight, 57 lbs. per cubic foot. Flowers pink. It makes good hedges.

		lbs.
H 50.	Nagkanda, Simla, 8,000 feet	...
H 2872.	„ „ „	55
H 2847.	Mahasu, Simla „	59

7. ERIOBOTRYA, Lindl.

Contains 9 species. *E. japonica,* Lindl.; Hook. Fl. Ind. ii. 372; Brandis 575 (*Mespilus japonica,* Banks; Roxb. Fl. Ind. ii. 510). The Loquat, is cultivated in most parts of India (Weight 46 lbs., Wallich). *E. petiolata,* Hook. f.; Hook. Fl. Ind. ii. 370, is a tree of Sikkim and Bhutan at 5,000 to 9,000 feet. *E. bengalensis,* Hook. f.; Hook. Fl. Ind. ii. 371 (*E. dubia,* Kurz i. 443. *Mespilus bengalensis,* Roxb. Fl. Ind. ii. 510) is an evergreen tree of Northern and Eastern Bengal and Burma. The remainder are shrubs or small trees.

1. **E. dubia,** Dcne; Hook. Fl. Ind. ii. 371. *Photinia dubia,* Lindl. Gamble 37. Vern. *Berkúng,* Lepcha.

A small tree. Bark light brown, $\frac{1}{6}$ inch thick. Wood white, soft, even grained. Pores very small. Medullary rays of two classes, numerous very fine rays closely packed between fewer moderately broad rays.

North-East Himalaya, from 5,000 to 6,000 feet.

Weight, 46 lbs. per cubic foot.

E 2365. Rangbúl, Darjeeling, 7,000 feet.

2. **E. elliptica,** Lindl.; Hook. Fl. Ind. ii. 372. *Photinia sp.* Gamble 37. Vern. *Mihul, mya,* Nep.; *Yelnyo,* Lepcha.

A moderate-sized evergreen tree. Bark greyish brown, $\frac{1}{6}$ inch thick. Wood reddish brown, compact, hard, apt to warp slightly. Pores small and very small. Medullary rays fine and very fine, very numerous, prominent on a radial section.

Sikkim and Bhutan Himalaya, from 6,500 to 8,000 feet.

Growth moderate. Aikin, describing Wallich's specimens gives 8·4 rings; our specimens shew 10 rings per inch of radius. Weight, 57·5 lbs. per cubic foot. Wood good, but not used.

		lbs.
E 366.	Rangbúl, Darjeeling, 7,000 feet	58
E 3109.	Darjeeling, 7,000 feet	57

8. PYRUS, Linn.

Contains 22 species, all found in the Himalaya and Khasia Hills, one only extending southward to Burma. The genus is divided into 5 sections: *Malus*, 3 species; *Pyrus*, 4 species; *Aria*, 2 species; *Sorbus*, 5 species; and *Micromelus*, 8 species.

In the section *Malus*, besides *P. baccata*, Linn., *P. Malus*, Linn.; Hook. Fl. Ind. ii. 373; Roxb. Fl. Ind. ii. 511; Brandis 205. The Apple. Vern. *Shewa*, Afg.; *Shu, sun, chúnt, khajir, bisír, palu*, Pb.; *Kúshú*, Ladak; *Seo, seb*, Hind., is apparently wild and commonly cultivated in the North-West Himalaya. It is also cultivated in gardens in Berar, Central India, the Punjab and Sind. *P. sikkimensis*, Hook. f.; Hook. Fl. Ind. ii. 373, is found in the Sikkim Himalaya.

In the section *Pyrus*, besides *P. Pashia*, Ham., *P. communis*, Linn.; Hook. Fl. Ind. ii. 374; Roxb. Fl. Ind. ii. 510; Brandis 203. The Pear. Vern. *Tang, batang, nák, bo, sunkeint, charkeint, lí*, Pb. Hills; *Náshpáti, nák*, Pb. Plains; *Amrúd*, Arab. is apparently wild in Kashmir and cultivated in the Himalaya. The fruit is generally hard, but good for baking and preserves. *P. Kumaoni*, Dcne; Hook. Fl. Ind. ii. 374; Brandis 204, and *P. Jacquemontiana*, Dcne; Hook. Fl. Ind. ii. 374; Brandis 205, are found in the North-West Himalaya; they much resemble *P. Pashia*.

In the section *Aria*, two species only occur; they are here described.

In the section *Sorbus*, besides *P. foliolosa*, *P. Aucuparia*, Gaertn.; Hook. Fl. Ind. ii. 375, the Mountain Ash, is found in the North-West Himalaya from 11,500 feet to 13,000 feet from Kashmir to Kumaun; and *P. microphylla*, Wall., *P. Wallichii*, Hook. f., and *P. insignis*, Hook. f., in the Sikkim Himalaya.

In the section *Micromelus*, *P. Griffithii*, Dcne.; *P. rhamnoides*, Dcne; and *P. Thomsoni*, King, are described from high elevations in the Sikkim Himalaya; *P. ferruginea*, Hook. f., from Bhutan; and 4 species: *P. khasiana*, Dcne, *P. granulosa*, Bertol. (Vern. *Dingsopha*, Khasia), *P. polycarpa*, Hook. f., and *P. cuspidata*, Bertol., from the Khasia Hills.

Wood compact and close-grained, marked by very small pores and fine medullary rays. The wood of the Pears (sections *Pyrus* and *Malus*) warps and cracks, whereas that of the sections *Sorbus* and *Aria* seasons better.

1. P. baccata, Linn.; Hook. Fl. Ind. ii. 373; Brandis 205. The Siberian Crab. Vern. *Ban mehal, gwálam*, Hind.; *Baror, liú, lhijo, líwar*, Pb.

A small tree with grey bark. Wood white, with pale-brown heartwood, warps considerably. Structure similar to that of *P. Pashia*, but medullary rays slightly broader.

Himalaya, from the Indus to Bhutan, between 6,000 and 11,000 feet; Khasia Hills.

Growth slow, 12 rings per inch of radius. Weight, 53 lbs. per cubic foot. Fruit edible.

		lbs.
E 967.	Chumbi Valley, Tibet, about 10,000 feet	53

2. P. Pashia, Ham.; Hook. Fl. Ind. ii. 374; Kurz i. 441. *P. variolosa*, Wall.; Brandis 204, 575; Gamble 36. Vern. *Tang, batangi, keint, shindar, katári, kíthu, ku, shegul*, Pb.; *Mehal, mol*, Hind.; *Passi*, Nep.; *Li*, Lepcha.

A moderate-sized deciduous tree. Bark dark brown, exfoliating in small rectangular scales. Heartwood light reddish brown, hard, close and even-grained, cracks and warps. Annual rings marked by a dark line. Pores very small. Medullary rays very fine and very numerous, uniform and equidistant.

Outer Himalaya, from the Indus to Bhutan, between 2,500 and 8,000 feet.
Growth moderate, 8 rings per inch of radius. Weight, 47 lbs. per cubic foot. The wood is used for walking-sticks, combs, tobacco pipes and various other purposes. The fruit is only eaten when half rotten, like the Medlar, but even then is not sweet.

		lbs.
H 3185.	Dungagalli, Hazara, 7,000 feet	...
H 23.	Madhan, Simla, 6,000 feet	47
H 236.	Garhwal Hills (1868)	...

3. P. lanata, Don; Hook. Fl. Ind. ii. 375. *P. Aria*, Ehrh.; Brandis 206. Vern. *Gún palos*, Afg.; *Doda, chola, chilana, maila, paltu, ban pála, kanghi, thánki, morphal, marpol*, Pb.; *Galion, mánli, paltu, ban palti*, Hind.

A moderate-sized deciduous tree with dark-brown bark. Wood white, moderately hard, close and even-grained, seasons well. Annual rings marked by a narrow belt without pores, on the outside of each ring. Pores very small, most numerous in the spring wood. Medullary rays fine.

Himalaya, from the Indus to Bhutan, between 5,000 and 10,000 feet.
Growth slow, 22 rings per inch of radius. Weight, 40 to 47 lbs. per cubic foot; Mathieu gives 46 to 58 lbs. It might be useful for boxes and other purposes for which a close and even-grained wood is required. Fruit large, eaten when half rotten, like that of the Medlar (*P. germanica*, Ldl.).

		lbs.
H 64.	Nagkanda, Simla, 8,000 feet	47
H 2887.	Nagkanda, Simla, 8,000 feet	40
H 3186.	Dungagalli, Hazara, 7,000 feet	...

4. P. vestita, Wall.; Hook. Fl. Ind. ii. 375. *P. lanata*, Don; Gamble 37. Vern. *Mayhell, gúhor*, Nep.; *Singka*, Bhutia.

A deciduous tree. Wood reddish with brown streaks, moderately hard. Annual rings distinct. Pores very small. Medullary rays fine, numerous, not distinct.

Eastern Himalaya, between 8,000 and 10,000 feet.
Growth slow, 20 rings per inch of radius. Weight, 44 lbs. per cubic foot. Fruit edible.

		lbs.
E 380.	Tonglo, Darjeeling, 10,000 feet	44

5. P. foliolosa, Wall.; Hook. Fl. Ind. ii. 376; Brandis 207; Gamble 37. Vern. *Kharsani*, Nep.

A shrub or small tree. Wood white, with small, darker coloured heartwood. Annual rings distinct. Pores very small, more numerous in the spring wood. Medullary rays fine, very numerous.

Eastern Himalaya, between 7,000 and 10,000 feet.
Growth slow, 23 rings per inch of radius. Weight, 45 lbs. per cubic foot.

		lbs.
E 378.	Tonglo, Darjeeling, 10,000 feet	45

6. P. ursina, Wall.; Brandis 206. *P. foliolosa*, Wall.; Hook. Fl. Ind. ii. 376 (in part). Vern. *Súlia, húlia*, Pb.; *Wampu litsi*, Lahoul.

A small tree with smooth, reddish grey bark, peeling off in horizontal papery strips. Wood white, with a small, brown heartwood. Structure similar to that of *P. foliolosa.*

Himalaya, from the Indus to Sikkim, between 6,000 and 12,000 feet.
Growth slow, 32 rings per inch of radius. Weight, 54 lbs. per cubic foot.

		lbs.
H 134.	Lahoul, 10,000 feet	...
H 3020.	Hattu, Simla, 10,000 feet	54

9. STRANVÆSIA, Lindl.

1. S. glaucescens, Lindl.; Hook. Fl. Ind. ii. 382; Brandis 210. Vern. *Garmehal, súnd,* Kumaun.

A small evergreen tree. Bark ½ inch thick, rough, dark coloured. Wood light coloured when fresh cut, turning reddish brown on exposure, fine and even grained; annual rings marked by a thin line. Pores very small, numerous. Medullary rays numerous, uniform, very fine, equidistant.

Central Himalaya, Kumaun and Garhwal from 3,000 to 8,000 feet, Nepal, Khasia Hills.
Growth moderate, 7 rings per inch of radius. Weight, 48 lbs. per cubic foot.

		lbs.
H 2970.	Naini Tál, 6,000 feet	48

10. CRATÆGUS, Linn.

Contains 3 species. *C. Oxyacantha,* Linn.; Hook. Fl. Ind. ii. 383; Brandis 207; Gamble 37. The Hawthorn. Vern. *Ring, ramnia, pingyat, phindák, patakhan,* Pb.; *Ban-sanjli, súr sinjli,* Jhelam, is a small tree of Afghanistan and the Western Himalaya, from the Indus to the Ravi; elsewhere cultivated. *C. Clarkei,* Hook. f.; Hook. Fl. Ind. ii. 383, is a small tree of Kashmir.

1. C. crenulata, Roxb. Fl. Ind. ii. 509; Hook. Fl. Ind. ii. 384. *C. Pyracantha,* Persoon; Brandis 208. Vern. *Gingaru, gianru,* Hind.

A large spinescent shrub. Wood white, hard, very close and even grained. Annual rings marked by a belt of harder and darker-coloured wood on the outer edge of each ring. Pores very small, numerous. Medullary rays very fine, numerous.

Himalaya, from the Sutlej to Bhutan, from 5,000 to 7,000 feet, descending in Kumaun to 2,500 feet.

		lbs.
H 2967.	Naini Tál	48

11. COTONEASTER, Linn.

Contains 10 or 11 species, many of which are merely small prostrate shrubs. They are all Himalayan, one only extending to the Nilgiris and one (doubtfully) to the Khasia Hills. *C. frigida,* Wall.; Hook. Fl. Ind. ii. 385; Brandis 209, is a small tree of the Central and Eastern Himalaya. *C. buxifolia,* Wall.; Hook. Fl. Ind. ii. 387; Beddome xcvii.; Brandis 210. Vern. *Húrúnay,* Nilgiris, is a rigid shrub or small tree of the Nilgiri and Pulney Hills, with a dense elastic wood used by the Todas to make clubs. The remaining species not here described are all small.

Wood harder and more compact than that of *Pyrus;* also marked by extremely small pores.

1. C. bacillaris, Wall.; Hook. Fl. Ind. ii. 384; Brandis 208. Vern. *Rí, riu, lin, lún, ráu, reúsh, rish*, Pb. Hills; *Ruinsh*, Jaunsar Bawur.

A small deciduous tree with bluish grey, nearly smooth bark. Wood white, turning light red towards the centre, smooth, very hard, close and even grained, but splits and warps much. Annual rings marked by the darker colour of the outer portion of each ring. Pores extremely small, uniformly distributed. Medullary rays very fine, very numerous.

Salt Range above 1,500 feet, North-West Himalaya, from the Indus to the Sarda, between 5,000 and 10,000 feet, Sikkim and Bhutan.

Growth moderate, 11 rings per inch of radius. Weight, on an average, 57 lbs. per cubic foot. The wood is used for making walking-sticks: the "alpenstocks" sold at Simla are usually made of it.

			lbs.
H	55.	Nagkanda, Simla, 8,000 feet	61
H	2890.	" " "	...
H	26.	Madhan, Simla, 6,000 feet	58
H	124.	Kulu, about 7,000 feet	52
H	925.	Hazara " "	56
H	3177.	Dungagalli, Hazara, 7,000 feet	...

2. C. acuminata, Lindl.; Hook. Fl. Ind. ii. 385; Brandis 209. Vern. *Riú, ráuns, riús, ruinsh*, Hind.

A deciduous shrub. Wood hard, structure like that of *C. bacillaris.*

Himalaya, from the Beas to Sikkim, between 4,500 and 10,000 feet.

Growth slow, 15 rings per inch of radius. Weight, 54 lbs. per cubic foot. Wood used to make walking-sticks, like that of *C. bacillaris.*

			lbs.
H	120.	Jalaori Pass, Kulu, 9,000 feet	54
H	2889.	} Nagkanda, Simla, 8,000 feet	...
H	3013.	}	

3. C. microphylla, Wall.; Hook. Fl. Ind. ii. 387; Brandis 209; Gamble 37. Vern. *Kháriz, lúni*, Kashmir; *Garri*, Kumaun.

A small procumbent shrub. Wood hard, similar to that of *C. bacillaris*, but with slightly larger pores.

Himalaya, from Kashmir to Bhutan, from 4,000 to 8,000 feet in the North-West and above 10,000 feet in Sikkim. Often planted for ornament in England.

Growth slow, 24 rings per inch of radius.

H 2823. Simla, 7,000 feet.

ORDER XLII. SAXIFRAGEÆ.

An Order of about 8 Indian arboraceous genera, chiefly Himalayan. It is divided into 3 tribes of woody plants, *viz.*,—

Tribe I.—Hydrangeæ	*Hydrangea, Pileostegia, Dichroa, Deutzia* and *Philadelphus.*
" II.—Escallonieæ	*Itea* and *Polyosma.*
" III.—Ribesieæ	*Ribes.*

Five of these genera are here described. *Pileostegia viburnoides*, Hook. f. and Th.; Hook. Fl. Ind. ii. 405, is a shrub of the Khasia Hills. *Itea* contains three species of shrubs or small trees of the Himalaya and Khasia Hills, of which *I. nutans*, Royle; Hook. Fl. Ind. ii. 408; Brandis 213. Vern. *Lelar*, Kaghan; *Garkath*, Kumaun, is a small tree of the North-Western Himalaya from the Indus to Nepal, between 3,000 and 6,000 feet. *I. macrophylla*, Wall.; Hook. Fl. Ind. ii. 408; Gamble 38. Vern. *Teturldumm*, Lepcha is a small tree of the valleys round Darjeeling and in the Khasia Hills. *I. Chinensis*, Hook. and Arn.; Hook. Fl. Ind. ii. 408, is a small tree of the Khasia Hills between 4,000 and 6,000 feet. *Polyosma integrifolia*, Bl.; Hook. Fl. Ind. ii. 409. (*P. Wallichii*, Bennett; Kurz 444) is a small tree of the Khasia Hills, found also in the Andaman Islands.

Pores small to extremely small. Medullary rays often of two classes, moderately broad and very fine.

1. HYDRANGEA, Linn.

Contains 5 Indian species. Besides those described, the chief is *H. altissima*, Wall.; Brandis 211; Gamble 38. Vern. *Sema*, Lepcha, a large climbing or erect shrub of the Himalaya from the Sutlej to Bhutan above 5,000 feet; its bark is used as a substitute for paper. *H. aspera*, Don, and *H. stylosa*, Hook. f. and Th., are small trees of the Sikkim Himalaya. The Garden Hydrangea, or Chinese Guelder Rose, so commonly cultivated as an ornamental shrub in the Hills, is *H. Hortensia*, DC.

1. H. vestita, Wall.; Hook. Fl. Ind. ii. 405; Brandis 211; Gamble 38. Vern. *Kulain*, Bhutia; *Pokuttia*, Nep.

A small deciduous tree with light brown, rather corky bark. Wood pinkish white, moderately hard; annual rings indistinct. Pores extremely small. Medullary rays very fine.

Himalaya, from Kumaun to Sikkim between 5,000 and 11,000 feet.
Weight, 45 lbs. per cubic foot.

	lbs.
E 373. Tonglo, Darjeeling, 10,000 feet	45

2. H. robusta, Hook. f. and Th.; Hook. Fl. Ind. ii. 404; Gamble 38. Vern. *Bogoti*, Nep.

A small, handsome, deciduous tree, with thin, brown, papery bark, peeling off in large flakes. Wood white, moderately hard, close-grained. Pores very small. Medullary rays of two sizes, moderately broad, short and very fine, prominent.

Eastern Himalaya, Sikkim, from 5,000 to 7,000 feet, generally as undergrowth in the oak forests.
Weight, 42 lbs. per cubic foot.

	lbs.
E 2370. Rangbúl, Darjeeling, 7,000 feet	42

2. DICHROA, Lour.

1. D. febrifuga, Lour.; Hook. Fl. Ind. ii. 406; Gamble 38. *Adamia cyanea*, Wall. t. 213. Vern. *Basak, bansúk*, Nep.; *Gebokanak*, Lepcha; *Singnamúk*, Bhutia.

An evergreen shrub, with yellow bark peeling off in flakes. Wood white, moderately hard, with small pores and moderately broad to very fine medullary rays.

Common in the forests of the Eastern Himalaya, from Nepal to Bhutan and in the Khasia Hills, above 4,000 feet.

The shoots and bark of the roots are made into a decoction and used as a febrifuge by the Nepalese. It is a very handsome shrub, with blue flowers and bright blue berries, coming up on clearings in the oak forests.

	lbs.
E 2371. Darjeeling, 7,000 feet	41

3. DEUTZIA, Thunb.

Contains 3 species. *D. macrantha,* Hook. f. and Th. is a shrub of the Kumaun Hills above 5,500 feet.

1. D. corymbosa, Brown; Hook. Fl. Ind. ii. 406; Brandis 212. Vern. *Dalontchi, deutsch, bhujru,* Simla.

A shrub. Outer bark yellowish grey, peeling off in long thin papery rolls, leaving the smooth, thin, greenish brown inner bark exposed. Wood, white, soft, even-grained. Pores small, very numerous. Medullary rays moderately broad, alternating with numerous very fine rays.

Himalaya, from the Sutlej to Bhutan, from 6,000 to 10,000 feet.

		lbs.
H 2850.	Mahasu, Simla, 7,000 feet	46
H 2898.	Nagkanda, Simla, 8,000 feet	...

2. D. staminea, Brown; Hook. Fl. Ind. ii. 407; Brandis 212. Vern. *Muneti,* Kumaun; *Deutsch,* Simla.

A shrub. Bark grey, soft, peeling off in small strips, but to a less degree than in *D. corymbosa.* Wood white, soft; structure similar to that of *D. corymbosa.*

Himalaya, from Kashmir to Bhutan, from 5,000 to 8,000 feet.

		lbs.
H 2836. H 2819.	} Simla, 6,000 feet	43

4. PHILADELPHUS, Linn.

1. P. coronarius, Linn.; Hook. Fl. Ind. ii. 407; Brandis 212. Vern. *Dalunchi, bhoj,* Simla.

A shrub with soft, light grey bark. Wood soft, white, with large pith. Pores small and very small, more numerous near the inner edge of each annual ring. Medullary rays of two classes, very fine and moderately broad. The structure of the wood of the Indian shrub is the same as that of the European shrub, the "Syringa" of gardens.

Himalaya, from Kishtwar to Sikkim, from 6,000 to 10,000 feet. Often planted for ornament.

		lbs.
H 3038.	Nagkanda, Simla, 7,000 feet	44

5. RIBES, Linn.

Contains about 8 species of Himalayan shrubs. *R. Grossularia,* Linn.; Hook. Fl. Ind. ii. 410; Brandis 213. The Gooseberry. Vern. *Pilsa, pilikcha, kánsi, teila, amlanch,* Upper Chenab and Lahoul, is indigenous to the arid parts of the North-West Himalaya above 8,000 feet, and is cultivated in the hills. *R. nigrum,* Linn. The Black Currant. Vern. *Papar,* Kumaun, is found in Kashmir, Kunawar, Garhwal and Kumaun above 6,000 feet. *R. rubrum,* Linn. The Red Currant. Vern. *Niangha,* Lahoul, occurs in the Himalaya between 5,000 and 12,000 feet. *R. orientale,* Poiret; Brandis 214. Vern. *Gwaldokh, kaghak,* Kághan; *Nangke, nyái, phulanch,* Chenab; *Askúta,* Ladak; *Yange,* Piti, is a shrub of the Safedkoh and arid tracts of the Inner Himalaya. *R. desmocarpum,* Hook. f. and Th., *R. luridum,* Hook. f. and Th., and *R. Griffithii,* Hook. f. and Th. are all shrubs of the Sikkim and Bhutan Himalaya.

1. R. glaciale, Wall.; Hook. Fl. Ind. ii. 410; Brandis 214; Gamble 38. Vern. *Robhay,* Bhutia.

A small shrub with shining bark, peeling off in papery flakes. Wood white, compact, moderately hard. Pores extremely small, in narrow interrupted wavy, concentric lines. Medullary rays scanty, short, broad and very broad.

Himalaya, from Kashmir to Bhutan, between 7,000 and 11,000 feet.
Weight, 58 to 63lbs.

			lbs.
H 3021.	H 3022.	Hattu, Simla, 10,000 feet	63
H 2908.	H 2912.	Nagkanda, Simla, 9,000 feet	...
H 3025.		Matiyána, Simla, 9,000 feet	...
E 973.		Chumbi Valley, Tibet, about 10,000 feet	58

ORDER XLIII. HAMAMELIDEÆ.

Contains 7 genera of Indian trees or shrubs. *Distylium indicum*, Bth., *Sycopsis Griffithiana*, Oliv., and *Loropetalum chinense*, Oliv., are all shrubs of the Khasia Hills; while *Corylopsis himalayana*, Griff.; Hook. Fl. Ind. ii. 427, is found in the Eastern Himalaya and Khasia Hills, between 5,000 and 6,000 feet. *Liquidambar orientale*, Miller, a tree of Asia Minor, yields the fragrant resin "Storax" used in medicine.

Wood close-grained. Pores small and very small, numerous and uniformly distributed. Medullary rays numerous, fine and very fine.

1. PARROTIA, C. A. Meyer.

Besides the species described, *P. persica*, C. A. Meyer, is a shrub of the low forests on the south coast of the Caspian Sea.

1. P. Jacquemontiana, Decaisne; Hook. Fl. Ind. ii. 426; Brandis 216. Vern. *Páser, peshora, po, kilár, kirru*, Punjab.

A large deciduous shrub or small tree, with thin, grey bark. Wood light pinkish red, hard, heavy, very close-grained. Pores extremely small. Medullary rays fine, numerous.

North-West Himalaya from the Indus to the Ravi, between 2,800 and 8,500 feet.

Growth slow 12 to 16 rings per inch (*Brandis*). Weight, 56 lbs. per cubic foot. Wood highly esteemed for walking-sticks, tent pegs, charpoys and rice pestles, also for native bows for throwing pellets. But its chief use is in basket-work and in the making of bridges over the Himalayan rivers. The twigs are very tough and flexible, and are twisted together into thick ropes, often 300 feet long. The bridges consist of one large rope to walk on and two smaller side ropes, one for each hand, with smaller ropes connecting the hand ropes with the foot rope. (P 1000 was a fine specimen sent to the Paris Exhibition of 1878 from the Ravi.)

		lbs.
H 3178.	Dungagalli, Hazara, 6,000 feet	...
H 933.	Hazara, Punjab, 6,000 feet	56
H 905.	Upper Chenab, Punjab	...

2. BUCKLANDIA, R. Brown.

1. B. populnea, R. Br.; Hook. Fl. Ind. ii. 429; Kurz i. 445; Gamble 38. Vern. *Pipli*, Nep.; *Singliang*, Lepcha; *Dingdah*, Khasia.

A large evergreen tree with rough, brown bark. Wood greyish brown, rough, moderately hard, close-grained, durable. Pores small. Medullary rays fine, very numerous, uniform and equidistant.

Eastern Himalaya, Khasia Hills and hills of Martaban, from 3,000 to 8,000 feet. Growth moderately fast, 6 to 7 rings per inch of radius. Weight, on an average, 45 lbs. per cubic foot. Is very much used in Darjeeling for planking and door and window frames, and is in great demand. It is a very ornamental tree with tough poplar-like leaves, and thick, fleshy stipules. It is easily grown from seed, but the young plants are rather delicate.

		lbs.
E 699.	Sepoydura Forest, Darjeeling, 5,500 feet	41
E 2372.	Raugbúl " " 7,000 "	49
E 2373.	" " " " "	46

3. ALTINGIA, Noronha.

1. **A. excelsa,** Noronha; Hook. Fl. Ind. ii. 429; Kurz i. 446. Vern. *Jutili*, Ass.; *Nantayop*, Burm.

A lofty deciduous tree. Bark smooth, light grey, exfoliating in large thin flakes. Wood soft, reddish grey with lighter streaks. Annual rings marked by a narrow belt of firm wood without pores. Pores small, uniform and uniformly distributed in lines between the medullary rays. Medullary rays fine, equidistant, prominent on a radial section.

Assam and Tenasserim.
Growth moderate, 6 rings per inch of radius. Weight, 46 lbs. per cubic foot. Wood used in Assam for building and ordinary domestic purposes.

		lbs.
E 1269.	Lakhimpúr, Assam	46
B 2704.	Brought from Tavoy by Dr. Wallich in 1828. Resembles this in structure	48

ORDER XLIV. RHIZOPHOREÆ.

Contains seven Indian genera of trees, chiefly coast plants and known by the general name of "Mangroves." They form forests, binding together the mud, in the estuaries of the Indus, Ganges and Irrawaddi, as well as along the coasts of Malabar, Arracan, Tenasserim and the Andaman Islands. The Order is divided into 2 Tribes, *viz.*,—

Tribe I.—Rhizophoreæ . . . . . *Rhizophora, Ceriops, Kandelia* and *Bruguiera.*
" II.—Legnotideæ . . . . . . *Carallia, Gynotroches, Weihea* and *Blepharistemma.*

Blepharistemma corymbosum, Wall.; Hook. Fl. Ind. ii. 441; Beddome ci. is a small tree of the hills of Tellicherry and Coorg; *Gynotroches axillaris*, Bl.; Hook. Fl. Ind. ii. 440; Kurz. i. 451, is a small tree of Upper Tenasserim; and *Weihea ceylanica*, Baill.; Hook. Fl. Ind. ii. 441; Beddome t. 194, a small tree of Mysore and the Carnatic. The remaining genera are here described.

Rhizophora, Ceriops and *Bruguiera* have small pores and equidistant, fine or moderately broad rays. The pores are sometimes joined by interrupted concentric bands. The structure of *Kandelia* is different. *Carallia* and *Anisophyllea* differ by having two classes of medullary rays: numerous very fine rays between fewer moderately broad rays.

1. RHIZOPHORA, Linn.

The Mangroves. Two species. *R. conjugata,* Linn.; Hook. Fl. Ind. ii. 436; Beddome xcix.; Brandis 218; Kurz i. 447 is a small tree usually associated with that here described.

1. R. mucronata, Lamk.; Hook. Fl. Ind. ii. 435; Beddome xcix.; Brandis 217; Kurz i. 447. *R. Mangle,* Roxb. Fl. Ind. ii. 459. Vern. *Bhara,* Beng.; *Kamo,* Sind; *Upoo-poma,* Tel.; *Byoo, byooma,* Burm.; *Bairada, jumuda,* And.; *Kadol,* Cingh.

A small evergreen tree. Sapwood light red; heartwood dark red, extremely hard, splits and warps a little in seasoning. Pores small, numerous, uniformly distributed; each pore surrounded by a narrow ring of soft tissue. Medullary rays fine, wavy, numerous, uniform, equidistant; the distance between the rays equal to about twice the transverse diameter of the pores.

Muddy shores and tidal creeks of India, Burma and the Andaman Islands.

Weight, 70·5 per cubic foot. The wood is good, but is rarely used. It is durable, *e.g.* B 2721 has been kept 50 years in Calcutta and is still quite sound. The bark is used for tanning, and the fruit is said to be edible. Of the quick germination of the Mangroves, Roxburgh says, "The great length of the seed gives in a very short time a young tree; for if the apex from which the root issues is only stuck a little way into a wet soil or mud, the leaves quickly unfold at the opposite end." The seeds often germinate while yet on the tree and drop as young plants into the mud. The roots also progress and form constantly fresh stems supported by the buttressed roots standing out of the mud.

		lbs.
B 2721.	Tavoy (Wallich, 1828)	69
B 502.	Andaman Islands	67
B 2240.	" ". (1866)	73
B 2273.	" " "	73
No. 9.	Ceylon Collection (*Rhizophora* sp., *Caddol*)	65
No. 36.	" " (*Rhizophora* sp., *Hiri Kaddol*)	49

2. CERIOPS, Arn.

Contains two species. *C. Roxburghiana,* Arnott; Hook. Fl. Ind. ii. 436; Kurz i. 448. Vern. *Kapyaing,* Burm. is a large shrub of the coast forests from Chittagong to Tenasserim. Weight 46 lbs. (Wallich, No. 173, *Rhizophora decandra*).

1. C. Candolleana, Arnott; Hook. Fl. Ind. ii. 436; Beddome xcix.; Brandis 218; Kurz i. 448. Vern. *Kirrari, chauri,* Sind; *Goran,* Beng.; *Madá,* And.

A small evergreen tree, with dark red bark; wood red, hard. Pores very small. Medullary rays fine, slightly wavy, uniform and equidistant. Pores joined by fine, wavy, interrupted concentric bands.

Muddy shores and tidal creeks of India and the Andaman Islands.

Wood used in Sind for the knees of boats and other purposes; in Lower Bengal for house-posts and for firewood. The bark is used for tanning. Weight, 63 lbs. per cubic foot.

		lbs.
B 1985.	Andaman Islands (Kurz, 1866)	63

3. KANDELIA, Wight and Arn.

1. K. Rheedii, W. and A.; Hook. Fl. Ind. ii. 437; Beddome c.; Brandis 218; Kurz i. 449. Vern. *Guria,* Beng.

An evergreen shrub or small tree. Wood soft, close-grained. Pores very small, very numerous. Medullary rays very short, moderately broad, prominently marked on a radial section; the distance between the medullary rays being many times broader than the transverse diameter of the pores.

Muddy shores and tidal creeks of Bengal, Burma, and the Western Coast.
Weight, 38 lbs. per cubic foot. Wood used only for firewood. Bark used in Tavoy in dyeing red, probably as a mordant.

		lbs.
E 407.	Sundarbans	38

4. BRUGUIERA, Lam.

Contains five species. *B. eriopetala*, W. and A., *B. malabarica*, Arn., *B. caryophylloides*, and *B. parviflora*, W. and A., are all trees of the shores of Malabar, Bengal, Arracan, Tenasserim and the Andamans, the last species being also found at Masulipatam on the Coromandel Coast, and in the Sundarbans.

1. B. gymnorhiza, Lam.; Hook. Fl. Ind. ii. 437; Brandis 219; Kurz i. 450. *B. Rheedii*, Bl.; Beddome c. *Rhizophora gymnorhiza*, Roxb. Fl. Ind. ii. 460. Vern. *Kakra, kankra*, Beng.; *Byoo-bo*, Burm.

An evergreen tree, heartwood small, red, extremely hard. Pores small, oval, and subdivided; medullary rays moderately broad, fine, very numerous.

Muddy shores and tidal creeks of India, Burma, and the Andaman Islands.
Weight, 54 lbs. per cubic foot. The wood is used for firewood, house-posts, planks and articles of native furniture.

		lbs.
E 412.	Sundarbans	54

B 2217 (62 lbs.) and B 2222 (60 lbs.) are specimens which were received in 1866 from the Andamans under the respective names of *Garcinia* and *Mallotus*, but they are probably the wood of another species of *Bruguiera*. The pores are moderate-sized, oval and subdivided and the medullary rays are moderately broad and fine, nearly equidistant and prominent on a radial section. The pores are joined by narrow, interrupted, concentric lines.

5. CARALLIA, Roxb.

Contains two Indian trees. *C. lanceæfolia*, Roxb. Fl. Ind. ii. 481; Hook. Fl. Ind. ii. 439, is an evergreen tree of the forests of Upper Tenasserim.

1. C. integerrima, DC.; Hook. Fl. Ind. i. 439; Beddome t. 193; Brandis 219; Gamble 39. *C. lucida*, Roxb. Fl. Ind. ii. 481; Kurz i. 451. Vern. *Kierpa*, Beng.; *Palamkat*, Nep.; *Kujitekra*, Ass.; *Karalli*, Tel.; *Andipunar*, Kan.; *Punschi*, Bombay; *Dawata*, Cingh.; *Bya*, Arracan; *Maneioga*, Burm.

An evergreen tree with thin, dark-grey bark. Sapwood perishable; heartwood red, very hard, durable, works and polishes well. Pores moderate-sized to large, often subdivided. Medullary rays long, of two classes, extremely broad and fine, numerous fine rays between each pair of broad ones, marked on a radial section as broad, irregular, shining plates. Fine bars of soft tissue across the rays.

Eastern and Western moist zones, Eastern Himalaya, Bengal, Burma, South India and the Andamans.

Weight, according to Benson and Skinner, No. 37, 44 lbs ; A. Mendis, 42 lbs.; Brandis' Burma List, 1862, No. 106, 60 lbs.; our specimens give an average of 47 lbs. Benson's experiments with bars 3 feet × 1·4 inch × 1·4 inch, gave P = 797 ; Skinner gives P = 656.

Wood used in South Kanara for furniture and cabinet-making and in Burma for planking, furniture and rice-pounders.

		lbs.
W 743.	South Kanara	42
B 308.	Burma (1867)	47
B 816.	Burma	51
B 2530.	Burma (1862)	47
B 2210.	Andaman Islands (1866)	47
B 1500.	Burma	...
No. 19.	Ceylon Collection (marked *C. zeylanica*)	42

---

2. No. 90. Adrian Mendis, Ceylon Collection, weight 51 lbs. P = 464. Vern. *Ukbeiriye,* Cingh., is probably *C. calycina,* Bth.; Thwaites Enum. 121; Hook. Fl. Ind. ii. 439. The wood is brick-red; in structure it resembles that of *C. integerrima,* but the pores are fewer, and the broad rays are narrower and at regular distances.

6. ANISOPHYLLEA, Br.

1. A. zeylanica, Bth.; Hook. Fl. Ind. ii. 442; Thw. Enum. 119; Beddome t. 195. *Tetracrypta cinnamomoides,* Gard. and Ch. Vern. *Wellipiyanne,* Cingh.

A tree. Wood greyish brown, moderately hard. Pores moderate-sized and large, filled with a white substance, prominent on a vertical section as white streaks. Medullary rays of two classes, numerous but indistinct, fine, between fewer moderately broad rays. Bars of soft texture and the same width as the rays crossing these and dividing the wood into numerous rectangular unequal figures.

		lbs.
No. 96.	Ceylon Collection	35

ORDER XLV. COMBRETACEÆ.

An Order containing 8 Indian Genera of trees, shrubs or climbers, containing some of the most important of the timber trees of the Indian forests. It is divided into 2 Tribes:—

Tribe I.—Combreteæ . . . . . . *Terminalia, Calycopteris, Anogeissus, Lumnitzera, Combretum* and *Quisqualis.*

„ II.—Gyrocarpeæ . . . . . . *Illigera* and *Gyrocarpus.*

Four of these genera are here described, most of the remainder contain climbing shrubs. *Lumnitzera* contains two small evergreen trees. *L. racemosa,* Willd.; Hook. Fl. Ind. ii. 452; Beddome ciii.; Brandis 221; Kurz i. 468 (*Petaloma alternifolia,* Roxb. Fl. Ind. ii. 372) Vern. *Kripa, Kirpa,* Beng.; *Baireya,* Cingh.; *Yengyé,* Burm., is a tree of the muddy creeks and tidal forests of the Sundarbans, Malabar, Arracan, Tenasserim and the Andamans, also found by Beddome at Balasore. It has a strong and durable wood used for house-posts, and in Calcutta for fuel (Roxburgh). *L. coccinea,*

W. and A.; Hook. Fl. Ind. ii. 452. (*L. littorea*, Voigt; Kurz i. 169), is a small tree of the mangrove swamps of Tenasserim. *Combretum* comprises 16 large shrubs, generally climbing, found in the moist zones of India and Burma, of which the most common is *C. decandrum*, Roxb. Fl. Ind. ii. 232; Hook. Fl. Ind. ii. 452; Brandis 221; Kurz i. 460; Gamble 40. Vern. *Punk, pharsia, dhobela*, Hind.; *Kalilara*, Nep.; *Pindik*, Lepcha; *Arikota*, Tel.; *Thama-ka-nway*, Burm., an evergreen scandent shrub, with whitish-yellow floral leaves, climbing to the summits of the highest trees, and found in the intermediate and moist zones of India and Burma. It has a whitish grey bark, and soft light-brown wood, having large pores and moderate-sized, evenly distributed medullary rays (E 3301, Darjeeling Terai). *Quisqualis indica*, Roxb. Fl. Ind. ii. 427, is the "Rangoon Creeper," Vern. *Dawaihmine*, Burm., a climbing shrub with red flowers, indigenous in Tenasserim and cultivated in gardens in other parts of India.

Illigera contains 3 species: *I. Coryzadenia*, Meissn.; Hook. Fl. Ind. ii. 460 (*I. appendiculata*, Bl.; Kurz i. 469) of Tenasserim and the Andamans; *I. Kurzii*, C. B. Clarke, of Burma and the Khasia Hills; and *I. khasiana*, C. B. Clarke, of the Khasia Hills: all scandent shrubs.

Wood moderately hard to very hard, with a distinct dark-coloured heartwood in some, but not in all species. Pores varying in size. Medullary rays uniform, equidistant, fine or very fine, very numerous, the distance between the rays less than the diameter of the pores. The wood of *Gyrocarpus* is anomalous.

1. TERMINALIA, Linn.

Contains about 12 Indian trees, mostly of very large size, and furnishing valuable timber as well as other products. *T. procera*, Roxb. Fl. Ind. ii. 429; Hook. Fl. Ind. ii. 444; Kurz i. 454 is a lofty tree of the Andaman Islands. *T. fœtidissima*, Griff.; Hook. Fl. Ind. ii. 445, is a tree of Mergui. *T. pyrifolia*, Kurz i. 457; Hook. Fl. Ind. ii. 448. Vern. *Leinben*, Burm., is a Burmese deciduous tree, with wood weighing 39 lbs. per cubic foot.

Wood moderately hard to very hard. A distinct, dark-coloured, very hard heartwood in *T. tomentosa, Arjuna, myriocarpa*, and *paniculata;* dark-coloured, but not well-defined wood near the centre in *T. Chebula* and *citrina;* no heartwood in the remaining species. Pores moderate-sized to large, prominent on a vertical section. Medullary rays fine, numerous, uniform and equidistant, the distance between two rays being less than the transverse diameter of the pores. Concentric bands of soft texture continuous in *T. belerica, bi-alata, alata* and *Catappa;* interrupted and sometimes wanting in the other species.

1. T. belerica, Roxb. Fl. Ind. ii. 431; Hook. Fl. Ind. ii. 445; Beddome t. 19; Brandis 222; Kurz i. 455; Gamble 39. Vern. *Babela, beleyleh*, Pers.; *Bahera, bhaira, behara*, Hind.; *Bohera*, Beng.; *Baheri*, Rajbanshi; *Kanom*, Lepcha; *Chiroræ*, Gáro; *Hulluch, bauri*, Ass.; *Thara*, Uriya; *Tani, kattu elupay*, Tam.; *Tani, tandi, toandi, thandra*, Tel.; *Ahera, jhera*, Hyderabad; *Santi*, Kan.; *Bherda, bahera*, Mar.; *Balra, balda*, Dekkan; *Behedo*, Mandevi; *Tahaka, taka, banjir*, Gondi; *Yehera*, Bhíl; *Búlú*, Cingh.; *Sacheng*, Magh; *Thitsein*, Burm.

A large deciduous tree; bark ½ inch thick, bluish grey, with numerous fine vertical cracks. Wood yellowish grey, hard, no heartwood, not durable; readily attacked by insects; annual rings indistinct. Pores of two sizes, large and small; the large ones frequently subdivided, joined by irregular, wavy, concentric bands of softer tissue, which contain the small pores. Fine, uniform and equidistant medullary rays are distinctly visible in the harder and darker portions between the bands, and on the radial section.

This wood distantly resembles in structure that of *Ougeinia dalbergioides*, but the bands of soft tissue are more continuous, and the medullary rays are less prominent.

Sub-Himalayan tract from near the Indus eastwards, forests of India and Burma. Growth moderate to rapid, 3 to 7 rings per inch of radius. Weight, according to Kyd's Assam experiments, 43 lbs. per cubic foot; Central Provinces List, 39 lbs.; Brandis' Burma List, 1862, No. 47, 40 lbs.; the average of our specimens gives 48 lbs. Kyd gives P = 378. The wood is used for planking, packing cases, canoes, and in the North-Western Provinces for house-building after steeping in water which has the effect of making it more durable. In the Central Provinces it is used for plough shafts and carts when *bijasál* is not available. In South India it is used for packing-cases, coffee-boxes, catamarans, and grain measures. The fruit is one of the myrabolans, and is exported to Europe to be used in dyeing cloth and leather and in tanning. Native ink is made of it, and it is used in medicine as a purgative and for other purposes. The kernels of the fruit are eaten, but are said to produce intoxication if eaten in excess (Hunter's Statistical Account of Bengal, xvi. p. 51), and an oil is obtained from them which is used for the hair. The fruit is eaten by monkeys, deer, goats, sheep, and cattle. The tree gives a copious gum, which does not seem to be of much use. The leaves according to the Indore Forest Report of 1876-77 have been used as an antiseptic to impregnate sleepers of *Salei* (see under *Boswellia thurifera*, p. 66), which are said, after soaking for five months in a tank filled with Bahera leaves and water, to have been rendered durable.

		lbs.
P 1190.	Madhopúr, Punjab	35
O 534.	Dehra Dún	58
O 2995.	Garhwal (1874)	59
O 349.	Gorakhpur (1868)	52
C 176.	Mandla, Central Provinces (1870)	...
C 1125.	Ahiri Reserve, Central Provinces	42
C 2737.	Moharli Reserve, Central Provinces	44
C 2773.	Melghát, Berar	...
E 663.	Bamunpokri, Darjeeling Terai	46
W 1188.	South Kanara	44
B 2532.	Burma (1862)	...
No. 53.	Salem Collection (marked *Wrightia antidysenterica*)	52

2. T. Chebula, Retzius; Hook. Fl. Ind. ii. 446; Roxb. Fl. Ind. ii. 433; Beddome t. 27; Brandis 223; Kurz i. 456; Gamble 39. Vern. *Harra, har, harara,* Hind.; *Hilikha,* Ass.; *Haritáki,* Beng.; *Silim,* Lepcha; *Karedha,* Uriya; *Halra, harla,* Dekkan; *Karka, hir, harro, mahoka,* Gondi; *Kadakai,* Tam.; *Karaka, kadukar,* Tel.; *Heerda,* Kan., Mar.; *Alalé,* Mysore; *Kajo,* Magh; *Pangah,* Burm.; *Aalu,* Cingh.

A large deciduous tree. Bark ¼ inch thick, dark brown, with numerous generally shallow vertical cracks. Wood very hard, brownish grey, with a greenish or yellowish tinge, fairly smooth and close-grained, fairly durable, seasons well. No regular heartwood, but frequently irregular masses of dark purple wood near the centre. Annual rings indistinct. Pores small and moderate-sized, uniformly distributed, often subdivided; each pore or group of pores surrounded by a narrow ring of soft tissue. Medullary rays very fine, uniform, equidistant, very numerous, distinctly visible on a radial section. The structure of the wood differs from that of *T. tomentosa*, chiefly by smaller pores.

Sub-Himalayan tract from the Sutlej eastwards, ascending to 5,000 feet; Bengal, Assam, Chittagong, Central and South India.

Growth moderate, 6 to 10 rings per inch of radius. The weight and transverse strength have been determined by the following experiments:—

Name of person conducting experiment.	Year.	Wood whence procured.	Number of experiments.	Size of bar.	Weight.	Value of P.	
				Ft. In. In.			
Benson	......	Burma . .	......	3 × 1·4 × 1·4	58	1033	
R. Thompson .	1868	Satpuras. .	......	......	63	......	
Brandis . . .	1864	India . .	3	3 × 1 × 1	66	1090	
„ No. 48 . .	1862	Burma . .	......	......	53	......	
Skinner, No. 129 . .	1862	„ . .	......	Various	60	1032	
„ No. 126 . .	1872	South India .	......	......	54	825	
Wallich . . .	......	India . .	......	......	42	......	
Smythies . . .	1878	See list below .	10	......	63	......	
Kyd	1831	Goalpara .	1	2 × 1 × 1	56	850	(*T. Hilkha.*

The wood takes a good polish and is fairly durable; it is used for furniture, carts, agricultural implements and house-building. Beddome says it is cross-grained and difficult to work. It is being tried for sleepers in Bengal. The bark is used for tanning and dyeing. The fruit gives the black myrabolans, which are of a rather better quality than those of *T. belerica.* They are largely exported from Bombay to Europe. So valuable is this trade in the Southern Circle of Bombay that the Forest Department of that Circle clear annually at least Rs. 50,000 clear profit from it alone. In 1877-78 the net profit was Rs. 77,000, in future years it is expected to average a lakh. The unripe fruit is used for tanning, dyeing, and in medicine (*Balhar zengi, zangihar, kalchar,* Hind; *Koki,* Nep.). The fruits give with alum a yellow dye, and with iron-clay give a good sort of ink. Astringent galls form on the young twigs, which are also used for ink and in dyeing and tanning. The kernel gives a transparent oil.

		lbs.
O 213.	Garhwal (1868)	56
O 528.	Dehra Dún	66
O 336.	Gorakhpur (1868)	60
C 181.	Mandla, Central Provinces	57
C 1159.	Ahiri Reserve, Central Provinces (1870)	66
C 842.	Bairagarh Reserve, Berar	68
C 1247.	Gumsúr, Madras	60
E 671.	Bamunpokri, Darjeeling Terai	67
E 2374.	„ „ „	63
D 1074.	North Arcot, Madras	...
No. 50.	Salem Collection	62

3. **T. citrina,** Roxb. Fl. Ind. ii. 435; Hook. Fl. Ind. ii. 446; Kurz i. 456. Vern. *Haritaki,* Beng.; *Hilika, silikka,* Ass.; *Hortucki,* Cachar; *Kyoo,* Burm.

A large deciduous tree. Bark light grey, exfoliating with few large irregular flakes Wood grey, darker towards the centre, hard. Structure similar to that of *T. Chebula.*

Assam, Eastern Bengal, Burma and Andamans.

Weight, Wallich gives 60; our specimens 49 lbs. per cubic foot. Used for planks and general purposes of building in Assam; also as a dye-plant.

		lbs.
E 2198.	Nowgong, Assam	49
B 1982.	Andaman Islands (Kurz 1866)	...

4. T. Catappa, Linn.; Hook. Fl. Ind. ii. 444; Roxb. Fl. Ind. ii. 430; Beddome t. 20; Kurz i. 454. The Indian Almond. Vern. *Badam*, Beng.; *Taree*, Kan.; *Nat vadom*, Tam.; *Vedam*, Tel.; *Adamarram*, Mal.; *Catappa*, Malay.

A large deciduous tree, with whorled branches, leaves turning red in the cold season. Wood red, with lighter-coloured sapwood, hard. Pores moderate-sized, scanty, joined by wavy, short and concentric bands of soft texture. Medullary rays fine.

Beach forests of the Andaman Islands; cultivated in most parts of India and Burma.

Weight, according to Skinner, No. 125, 32 lbs. per cubic foot. P = 470. Wallich also gives 32, while our specimen gives 41 lbs. Beddome says the wood is used for various purposes in Madras. The kernels of the nuts are eaten at dessert; they are remarkable for the spiral folds of the cotyledons; the bark and leaves give a black dye. It is one of the trees on the leaves of which the "Tasar" or "Katkura" silkworm (*Antheræa Paphia*) is fed.

		lbs.
E 3005.	Calcutta	...
B 1983.	Andaman Islands (Kurz, 1866)	41

5. T. paniculata, W. and A.; Hook. Fl. Ind. ii. 448; Beddome t. 20; Brandis 226. *Pentaptera paniculata*, Roxb. Fl. Ind. ii. 442. Vern. *Pe-karakai*, Tam.; *Neemeeri*, Tel.; *Kinjal, kindal*, Mar.; *Honal, huluvá, hulvé*, Kan.; *Poo mardá, pillai mardá*, Anamalais.

A large deciduous tree. Wood grey, with dark heartwood, very hard. Pores large and moderate-sized, oval, numerous. Medullary rays very fine, uniform and equidistant, wavy, very numerous; the transverse diameter of the pores many times larger than the distance between two medullary rays. Pores surrounded by faintly marked patches of soft tissue, often arranged in oblique and wavy lines.

Western moist zone; forests of the western coast from Bombay southwards.

Weight, 61 lbs. per cubic foot. Wood valuable, though not quite as good as that of *T. tomentosa*. It is improved by being kept under water. It is fairly durable. It makes good planking and is used for the handles of ploughs in Ratnaghiri.

		lbs.
W 1221.	North Kanara	57
D 1280.	Anamalai Hills	65

6. T. bialata, Wall.; Hook. Fl. Ind. ii. 449; Kurz i. 456. *Pentaptera bialata*, Roxb. Fl. Ind. ii. 441. Vern. *Leinben*, Burm.

A large deciduous tree. Wood grey, beautifully mottled, moderately hard. Structure the same as that of *T. belerica*.

Burma and the Andaman Islands.

Weight, Brandis' Burma List, 1862, No. 49, gives 39; our specimens give 48 lbs. per cubic foot. Skinner No. 121 gives weight 64 lbs., and P = 1012, but there may have been some mistake.

		lbs.
B 1417.	Tharrawaddi, Burma	48

7. T. tomentosa, W. and A.; Hook. Fl. Ind. ii. 447; Beddome t. 17; Brandis 225; Kurz i. 458; Gamble 39. *Pentaptera crenulata, coriacea* and *tomentosa*, Roxb. Fl. Ind. ii. 438-440. Vern. *Saj, sein, asan, assain, assaina, asna, sadri*, Hind.; *Piasal, usan*, Beng.; *Jhau*, Rajbanshi; *Amari*, Ass.; *Taksor*, Lepcha; *Saháju, kala sahdju*, Uriya; *Barsaj*, Bijeragogarh; *Karra marda, karú marúthú, anemúi*, Tam.; *Maddi, halla maddi, nella-madu*, Tel.; *Matti, kari matti, banapu*, Kan.

Murada, kali maruthai, Arcot; *Karkaya, sadora, holda, dudi maddi,* Hyderabad; *Ain, madat, yén,* Mar.; *Saja,* Baigas; *Maru,* Gondi; *Madge,* Bhîl; *Toukkyan,* Burm.; *Chouchong,* Taleing; *Kúmbúk,* Cingh.

A large deciduous tree. Bark one inch thick, grey to black, with long, broad, deep, longitudinal fissures, and short, shallow, transverse cracks; inner substance red when fresh. Sapwood reddish white, heartwood dark brown, hard, beautifully variegated with streaks of darker colour, shewing on a radial section as dark streaks which are generally wavy or undulating, durable, seasons well and takes a good polish. Numerous concentric wavy lines unequally distributed. Pores moderate-sized and large, uniformly distributed, each pore enclosed in an irregularly shaped and generally elongated patch of soft tissue; these patches are often arranged in concentric lines and frequently joined by thin, white, wavy, concentric bands. Medullary rays not distinct, very fine, numerous, uniform, equidistant, often wavy, the transverse diameter of the pores many times larger than the distance between the rays. In the sapwood the patches of soft tissue enclosing the pores are more distinct, and the medullary rays more prominent.

Sub-Himalayan tract from the Ravi eastwards, ascending to 4,000 feet in places: Bengal, Central and South India and Burma.

The weight and transverse strength have been determined by the following experiments:—

Experiment by whom conducted.	Year.	Wood whence procured.	Number of experiments.	Size of scantling.	Weight.	Value of P.
				Ft. In. In.		
Puckle	1859	Mysore	3	2 × 1 × 1	56	1,010
(List)	1863	"	...	...	57	...
(List) Paris Exhibition	1862	Central Provinces.	...	...	50	...
R. Thompson	1869	" "	...	...	55	...
Skinner, * No. 127	1862	South India	...	Various	60	860
" †No. 128	1863	" "	...	"	55	840
Baker	1829	Jynaghur	4	7 × 2 × 2	62	677
French	1861	South India at Erode.	...	15 × 1 × 1	50	862
Balfour	...	...	3	7 × 2 × 2	66	675
Benson	...	Burma	...	3 ×1·4×1·4	71	1,001
Brandis, No. 50	1862	"	...	...	58	...
"	1864	"	3	3 × 1 × 1	56	903
Smythies	1878	See list below.	16	...	61	...

* T. coriacea, Skinner, p. 148. † T. glabra, Skinner, p. 150.

Its durability is uncertain; in Burma the heartwood decays rapidly, in North India beams are sometimes found to last well, at other times to perish from dry rot or be eaten by insects. The wood is largely used for house-building, carts, rice-pounders, ship and boat building. It has been tried for railway sleepers. Five sleepers laid down on the Oudh and Rohilkhand Railway in 1870 were reported in 1875 to be in capital preservation, but having been cut from small trees the sapwood has been eaten and the experiment cannot be considered as good as if the sleeper had been from large trees and without sapwood. In 1876, 720 sleepers were cut in the Sukna forests, Darjeeling, and laid down on the Northern Bengal State Railway, the result of the experiment will be very useful. The wood splits, however, very much, unless thoroughly seasoned. The wood is an excellent fuel and makes good charcoal. The bark is used for tanning and for dyeing black, and the ashes of the bark give a kind of lime which is eaten by the natives with betel leaf. The "tasar" silkworm (*Antheræa Paphia*) feeds on its leaves, and lac is occasionally gathered from its branches. It gives a brown gum.

			lbs.
O	207.	Garhwal (1868)	52
O	2996.	„ (1874)	65
O	874.	Kumaun Bhabar	53
O	389.	Oudh	...
O	391.	Oudh	54
O	393.	Oudh	56
C	332.	Gorakhpur (1868)	53
C	174.	Mandla, Central Provinces (1870)	61
C	2924.	Seoni, Central Provinces	70
C	1104.	Ahiri Reserve, Central Provinces	67
C	2743.	Moharli Reserve, Central Provinces (sapwood)	48
C	1241.	Gumsúr, Madras	64
E	662.	Bamunpokri, Darjeeling Terai	49
E	2375.	Sukna, Darjeeling Terai	56
W	755.	South Kanara	60
D	1059.	South Arcot	...
D	1077.	North Arcot	64
D	1281.	Anamalai Hills	69
B	2531.	Burma (1862)	59

Terminalia alata, Roth., is synonymous with *T. tomentosa*, W. and A.; but the wood sent under this name from the Andamans (B 522, 46 lbs.) is evidently, judging from its structure, a different species. Wood brown, with dark purple streaks, very hard, smooth. Annual rings doubtful. Pores small, uniformly distributed. Medullary rays short, prominent, moderately broad and fine, joined by numerous, very fine, white, transverse lines. Medullary rays distinctly visible on a radial section as long shining plates. The wood of this specimen differs from that of *T. tomentosa*, chiefly by the transverse bars and the small pores.

8. T. Arjuna, Beddome t. 28; Hook. Fl. Ind. ii. 447; Brandis 224. *T. crenulata*, Roth.; Kurz i. 458. *Pentaptera Arjuna* and *glabra*, Roxb. Fl. Ind. ii. 438, 440. Vern. *Anjan, arjún, arjúna, anjani, arjan, jamla, koha, kowa, kahúa* Hind.; *Arjún*, Beng.; *Hanjal*, Cuttack; *Vella marda, vella matti, vella marúthú*, Tam.; *Arjun, anjan, sadura*, Mar.; *Maddi, billi matti*, Mysore; *Yermaddi, érra maddi, tella madu*, Tel.; *Kahu*, Baigas; *Mangi, koha*, Gondi; *Toukkyan*, Burm.

A large deciduous tree. Bark ⅓ inch thick, smooth, pinkish grey, the old layers peeling off in thin flakes. Sapwood reddish white; heartwood brown, variegated with darker coloured streaks, very hard. Annual rings doubtful. Pores moderate-sized and large, sometimes very large, uniformly distributed, more numerous and larger than in *T. tomentosa*, often subdivided into 2 to 4 compartments, each pore surrounded by a ring of soft tissue. Numerous thin, wavy, concentric lines, which frequently anastomose. Medullary rays very fine, very numerous. Pores prominent on a longitudinal section.

Sub-Himalayan tract (not common), Oudh, Bengal, Burma, Central and South India.

Weight, Skinner's experiments, Nos. 123, 103, give 48 and 54 lbs.; the Central Provinces List 47 lbs.; while the average of our specimens is 57 lbs. Skinner gives P = 806 and 820. The wood is apt to split in seasoning and is not easy to work. It is used for carts, agricultural implements, boats and for building. It gives a brown transparent gum. The bark is used as a tonic and to heal wounds.

		lbs.
C 179.	Mandla, Central Provinces (1870)	54
C 1111.	Ahiri Reserve, Central Provinces	60
C 2760.	Moharli Reserve, Central Provinces	...

9. **T. myriocarpa,** Heurck and Muell. Arg.; Hook. Fl. Ind. ii. 447; Kurz i. 455. *T. myriopteron,* Kurz; Gamble 39. Vern. *Panisaj,* Nep.; *Sungloch,* Lepcha; *Hollock,* Ass.

A very large evergreen tree. Bark greyish brown, rough, peeling off in vertical flakes. Sapwood white, not broad; heartwood brown, beautifully mottled with dark streaks. Structure that of *T. tomentosa.*

Eastern Himalaya and Assam, in Sikkim up to 5,000 feet.

Growth moderate, 6 to 7 rings per inch of radius. Weight, 51 to 54 lbs. per cubic foot. Used for building and tea-boxes, also for charcoal.

		lbs.
E 500.	Khookloong Forest, Darjeeling Terai	54
E 2376.	Bamunpokri, Darjeeling Terai	51

E 2315 cut from a log of wood which had been lying for many years in the bed of the Chauwá Jhora, near Sivoke, in the Darjeeling Terai, and is now perfectly black, may be this species.

2. CALICOPTERIS, Lamck.

Contains two climbing shrubs. *C. nutans,* Kurz i. 468 (*Getonia nutans,* Roxb. Fl. Ind. ii. 428). Vern. *Kywotnay nway,* Burm., is a large scandent shrub of Burma.

1. **C. floribunda,** Lam.; Hook. Fl. Ind. ii. 449; Brandis 220. *Getonia floribunda,* Roxb. Fl. Ind. ii. 428. Vern. *Kokoranj,* C. P.; *Bandi murududu,* Tel.; *Marsada boli,* Mysore.

A large climbing shrub. Wood yellowish white, moderately hard. Pores small to large, numerous. Medullary rays very fine, very numerous, uniform and equidistant; the distance between the rays being less than the transverse diameter of the pores. Numerous broad medullary patches of soft, pith-like texture.

Central and Southern India.

Weight, 45 lbs. per cubic foot.

		lbs.
C 2755.	Moharli Reserve, Central Provinces	45

3. ANOGEISSUS, Wall.

Contains 4 Indian trees. *A. phillyreæfolia,* Heurck and Müll. Arg.; Hook. Fl. Ind. ii. 451, is a small tree of Burma.

Pores small. Medullary rays fine, uniform, sharply defined, equidistant, the transverse diameter of the pores equal to, or slightly larger than, the distance between the rays.

1. **A. latifolia,** Wall.; Hook. Fl. Ind. ii. 450; Beddome t. 15; Brandis 227. *Conocarpus latifolia,* Roxb. Fl. Ind. ii. 442. Vern. *Dhaura, dhauri, dhau, dháwa, dhauta, dohu, bakla, bakli,* Hind.; *Gólra, goldia, dhaukra, dhokri, dau,* Rajputana; *Khardháwa,* Banda; *Vellay naga, namme, veckali,* Tam.; *Chirimán, sheriman, yettama, tirman, yella maddi,* Tel.; *Dohu, dhobu,* Uriya; *Dháori, dhamora, dhaunda, dandua, dhavada,* Mar.;

Dinduga, dindlu, bejalu, dindal, Kan.; *Arma, yerma*, Gondi; *Dhawa*, Baigao; *Dhaundak*, Bhíl; *Dhaura*, Kurku; *Daawoo*, Cingh.

A large tree with smooth, whitish grey bark, ⅛ inch thick, with shallow, irregular depressions, caused by exfoliation. Wood grey, hard, shining, smooth, with a small purplish brown, irregularly shaped, extremely hard heartwood. Sapwood in young trees and branches yellow. Annual rings marked by darker lines. Pores small, very numerous, uniformly distributed, often subdivided. Medullary rays very fine, extremely numerous, uniform, equidistant, distinctly visible on a radial section, often giving the wood a mottled appearance. The transverse diameter of the pores equal to the distance between the medullary rays.

Sub-Himalayan tract from the Ravi eastwards ascending to 3,000 feet, Central and South India.

Growth moderate, 7 rings per inch of radius. Weight, 65 lbs. (Puckle and Skinner, No. 51); 61 (R. Thompson); 64 (Central Provinces List); 75 to 80 lbs. when green; our specimens give an average of 62 lbs. Skinner gives P = 1220, while French of the Madras Railway gives 752 and Puckle from 3 experiments with bars 2′ × 1″ × 1″, 870. The wood is highly valued on account of its great strength and toughness, but it splits in seasoning and unless kept dry is not very durable. It is used for axe handles, poles for carrying loads, axles in the construction of furniture, agricultural implements and in ship-building. It has been recommended for sleepers. Out of 18 sleepers which had lain 7 to 8 years on the Mysore State Railway there were found, when taken up, 4 good, 10 still serviceable and 4 bad. It gives a good fuel and an excellent charcoal. It gives a gum which is extensively sold for use in cloth-printing. The leaves are used for tanning.

		lbs.
P 446.	Ajmere	...
O 233.	Garhwal (1868)	68
O 2997.	„ (1874)	64
O 531.	Dehra Dún	62
O 394.	Oudh	62
C 2776.	Melghát, Berar	59
C 190.	Mandla, Central Provinces (1870)	58
C 1121.	Ahiri Reserve, Central Provinces	65
C 2744.	Moharli Reserve, Central Provinces	55
C 1244.	Gumsúr, Madras	66
D 1282.	Anamalai Hills, Madras	56
No. 21.	Salem Collection	69

2. A. acuminata, Wall.; Hook. Fl. Ind. ii. 450; Beddome t. 16; Brandis 228; Kurz i. 466. *Conocarpus acuminata*, Roxb. Fl. Ind. ii. 443. Vern. *Chakwa*, Beng.; *Panchi, pasi*, Uriya; *Numma*, Tam.; *Páchi mánu, panchman, paunchinan, bucha karum, pashi, pansi*, Tel.; *Phás*, Mar.; *Saikamehhia, thekri napay*, Magh; *Yung, sehoong*, Arracan; *Yungben*, Burm.; *Phassi*, Mar.

A large deciduous tree. Bark ½ inch thick, dark grey, rough, granulated when old. Wood grey, sometimes yellowish grey with a greenish tinge, shining, in structure moderately hard, resembling that of *Anogeissus latifolia*, but the pores considerably larger and the transverse diameter of the pores greater than the distance between two rays.

Chanda District, South India, Chittagong and Burma.

Weight, according to Skinner, No. 50, 59 lbs., 53 lbs. (Brandis' Burma List, 1862, No. 51). Our specimen gave 57 lbs. Skinner gives P = 880. The wood warps and cracks in seasoning, and is not very durable especially where exposed to water. Used in Burma and in Madras for building. Roxburgh says it is durable if kept dry, but soon decays if exposed to wet. The leaves are used for tanning in Gumsúr.

		lbs.
C 1143.	Ahiri Reserve, Central Provinces	57
B 3204.	Burma (1862)	...
B 3095.	Prome, Burma	...

The Central Provinces and Burma woods correspond exactly in structure.

3. A. pendula, Edgw.; Hook. Fl. Ind. ii. 451; Brandis 229. *Conocarpus myrtifolia,* Wall. Vern. *Dhau, dhaukra, kala dhaukra,* Meywar; *Kardahi,* Hind.

A small gregarious tree with pendulous branches, leaves turning copper-coloured in the cold season. Wood hard, yellowish white, with a small, irregular, blackish-purple heartwood. Annual rings indistinct. Pores very small and extremely small, often in groups between the very fine, very numerous, uniform and equidistant medullary rays.

Arid and northern dry zones, Rajputana, Malwa Plateau as far as the Nerbudda in Nimar, Mandla District on the Nerbudda (?)

Cunningham's 5 experiments made at Gwalior with bars 2′ × 1″ × 1″, give the weight at 59 lbs. per cubic foot and P = 837, the average of the 5 experiments which ranged from 697 to 1,034. It coppices well, but the wood is not in general use.

P 454. Ajmere.

4. GYROCARPUS, Jacq.

1. G. Jacquini, Roxb. Fl. Ind. i. 445; Hook. Fl. Ind. ii. 461; Beddome t. 196; Kurz i. 470. Vern. *Zaitun,* Hind.; *Tanaku, kumar pulki,* Tel.; *Pinlay thitkouk,* Burm.

A deciduous tree. Wood grey, soft. Pores large and moderate-sized, often subdivided, uniformly distributed, well marked on a longitudinal section. Medullary rays very short, moderately broad, the distance between them greater than the transverse diameter of the pores.

South India, Tenasserim and Andaman Islands.

Weight, 23 lbs. per cubic foot. Wood used in South India to make boxes and toys. It is preferred to all others for catamarans. The seeds are made into rosaries and necklaces.

		lbs.
D 1079.	North Arcot, Madras	23

ORDER XLVI. MYRTACEÆ.

An Order containing 11 Indian Genera, including *Eucalyptus,* some species of which are now almost naturalised. The Indian Genera belong to 3 Tribes:—

Tribe I.—Leptospermeæ	*Melaleuca, Eucalyptus* and *Tristania.*
„ II.—Myrteæ	*Psidium, Rhodomyrtus, Rhodamnia, Decaspermum* and *Eugenia.*
„ III.—Lecythideæ	*Barringtonia, Careya* and *Planchonia.*

Of these genera, 7 are here described. *Tristania* contains 3 trees of Tenasserim; one only, *T. burmanica,* Griff.; Hook. Fl. Ind. ii. 466; Kurz i. 474. Vern. *Toungyohpyeezeng,* Burm., extending northwards to Martaban and the Eng forests of the Pegu Yomas.

Rhodomyrtus tomentosa, DC.; Hook. Fl. Ind. ii. 469; Beddome cvi. Vern. *Thaontay,* Burghers, is a large shrub, abundant in the higher ranges of the

Nilgiris, said by Beddome to have a white soft wood, with a pink heartwood and to be used for turning. Its fruit is edible, and is made into preserves. *Rhodamnia trinervia*, Bl., Hook. Fl. Ind. ii. 468; Kurz i. 475, is a shrub of Tenasserim; while *Decaspermum paniculatum*, Kurz i. 475; Hook. Fl. Ind. ii. 470, is an evergreen tree which is said by Kurz to spring up on deserted hill toungyas at 3,000 to 4,000 feet elevation in Martaban and Tenasserim. The Myrtle (*Myrtus communis*, Linn.) is cultivated in India.

The flower-buds of *Caryophyllus aromaticus*, Linn., of the Moluccas give the Cloves of commerce, and *Pimenta officinalis*, Ldl., of the West Indies, Pimento or Allspice.

Pores small and moderate-sized. Medullary rays numerous, fine, rarely broad. Concentric bands of soft tissue not common.

1. MELALEUCA, Linn.

1. M. Leucadendron, Linn.; Hook. Fl. Ind. ii. 465; Kurz i. 472. *M Cajuputi*, Roxb. Fl. Ind. iii. 394.

An evergreen tree. Bark white, thick, spongy, peeling off in papery flakes. Wood reddish brown, hard. Pores moderate-sized, scanty. Medullary rays very fine, extremely numerous.

Tenasserim.

The leaves give the Cajuput oil of commerce, which is largely exported from the Malay Archipelago and is used in medicine as a stimulant and diaphoretic.

O 3270. Saharanpur Gardens.

2. EUCALYPTUS, L'Her.

Numerous species of this genus of trees have been introduced into India from Australia, where they have the general name of "Gum trees;" but their success has been very variable. *E. Globulus*, Lab., here described, and *E. obliqua*, L'Her., have been almost completely naturalised on the Nilgiris. The latter species is known by the name of "Stringy Bark," and in Victoria, South Australia and Tasmania is an immense tree, reaching occasionally to 300 feet in height, with a girth of 100 feet (Brandis, 231). It has also been tried at Changa Manga, but has failed at Lucknow. At Lucknow, however, the cultivation of *E. saligna*, Smith, "The White or Grey Gum" of New South Wales, has succeeded well in the Wingfield Park, and that of *E. rostrata*, Schlect, in the Horticultural Gardens. At Changa Manga Plantation several species have been found to grow well, and at Abbottabad *E. Globulus*, Lab., *E. Stuartiana*, F. Müll., *E. tereticornis*, Sm., *E. viminalis*, Lab., and *E. leucoxylon*, F. Müll., have succeeded admirably. The seeds of numerous other species have been sown at different places in the plains and valleys of the Punjab, as well as at the Botanic Gardens at Saharanpur, the Horticultural Gardens at Lahore and Lucknow, and many places in the Central Provinces, Berar and Central India; and there is no doubt that when it has been determined which species are most suited to the very different climates and soils of the various parts of India, the cultivation of the species of Eucalyptus which possess so many valuable properties, such as their quick growth, useful timber, and the numerous products to be obtained from their leaves and bark, their cultivation should be encouraged and their growth fostered.

1. E. Globulus, Labillardière; Brandis 231. The Blue Gum. Vern. *Kurpoora maram*, Madras.

A lofty tree with fibrous deciduous outer bark. In Australia the wood is brown, hard, tough, durable. The wood of a tree grown on the Nilgiris, 18 years old and 95 feet high, is grey, with darker streaks and moderately hard. Pores moderate-sized, round, frequently arranged in groups or in radial or oblique lines. Medullary rays fine, very numerous, the intervals between the rays smaller than the diameter of the pores. Pores marked on a longitudinal section, and medullary rays visible as narrow bands on a radial section.

Gregarious in Victoria and the south of Tasmania. Introduced on the Nilgiris, and now completely naturalised.

Of the *Eucalyptus Globulus* several successful plantations have been established on the Nilgiri Hills. There are 22 plantations in all, but some of them are exclusively of "Wattles" or Australian *Acacia;* others contain only a small proportion of *Eucalyptus,* while others have not been successful owing to bad locality or other reasons. The chief good plantations are—

Near Ootacamund—

1. Aramby	38 acres planted	1863-65
2. Governor's Shola	80 „ „	1870-72

(part, however, is *Acacia Melanoxylon*).

3. Norwood	26 „ „	1872-73
4. Cally	14 „ „	1870
5. Arnikal	11 „ „	1873
6. Baikie	33 „ „	1874

Near Wellington—

7. Newman	35 „ „	1870-71
8. Old Forest	200 „ „	1872-73

or, including smaller ones, about 500 acres altogether. Colonel Beddome in his Report of 12th June 1876, from which the above is taken, says that in Aramby the growth is very unequal, some being 30 to 40 inches in circumference, others only 3 to 4 inches; that about 504 were then found per acre. Measurements of 15 of the largest trees, made by Mr. Gass, gave an average girth of 34 inches, height 85 feet, and average contents 23 cubic feet, but these cannot be taken for an average.

Mr. Gass found in the Newman plantation, then 5 to 6 years old, an amount of material of 152 tons per acre, and Colonel Beddome is of opinion (Report of 20th July 1878) that the best treatment of *Eucalyptus* plantations, so as to get the greatest profit, will be to cut for coppice every 5 or 6 years, obtaining at the cuttings at least 100 tons per acre. The growth of Eucalyptus is sometimes very fast. Captain Campbell Walker in his paper on the "Plantations and Firewood Reserves in the Madras Presidency," read at the Forest Conference of 1875, says that the growth is often 1 foot per month during the first few years; and Colonel Beddome in his Report of July 1878 says that a *Eucalyptus* tree 12 years old, recently felled at Ootacamund, gave 144 cubic feet, which amounts to 1 foot per month, which is the same as was stated by Captain Campbell Walker. It would be extremely useful, however, before definitely basing the working plans of the Nilgiri Eucalyptus plantations on simple coppice with a 5 or 6 years' rotation to make further and careful measurements of the amount of material per acre at different ages.

The *Eucalyptus Globulus* has been tried at numerous places all over India, chiefly on account of the reports that it would prevent malaria, and that it was valuable in reclaiming marshy land. Whatever may be the truth about these questions, the tree has almost universally failed in the plains, and in the Himalaya it has only succeeded in a few localities. At Simla, whether from frost or for what reason, it seems to die down yearly, sending up vigorous shoots to replace the dead stem; at Darjeeling its growth has been slow, and the trees formed merely thin poles, probably the effect of too much damp; while its chief success has been at Ranikhet and Abbottabad. At Shillong, in the Khasia Hills, it had been said to be a failure, but in his review of the Assam Forest Report for 1876-77, Colonel Keatinge called attention to the fact that the *E. Globulus,* though a failure at the Shillong plantation, had yet grown well in other situations in that station, and that several self-sown seedlings were thriving under the old trees.

The seeds of *Eucalyptus* are usually very small, those of *E. Globulus* being perhaps the largest of the species usually tried in India; the seed, if good, germinates well usually, and the plants at once begin to grow fast, but they are very tender of transplanting, so that that operation has to be very carefully done. On the subject of the transplanting of Eucalyptus, the following memorandum was drawn up by Colonel H. R. Morgan, Deputy Conservator of Forests, Madras :—

"The seed, which should be procured in January or February, should be placed in beds in rows 6 inches apart. When the plants are 6 inches high, they should be taken up and placed 6 inches apart in beds; the roots should be shortened to 4 inches. When 3 feet in height, the plants are taken up with a ball of earth round their roots, moss is bound tightly round the ball, and the plants are left in beds well earthed up about the roots, and watered till the young rootlets show through. They may then be put out. April is the best month for planting, as the plants are then able to make strong roots before the monsoon. When moss is not available, bamboo pots may be used, taking care to keep the large end of the joint for the top of the pot; the hole at the bottom to be plugged with grass. The plants should be placed in the pots when 8 inches in height, and left till they are 2 feet high and the roots show through; then thrust the roots through, and the plant comes out with a ball of earth attached to the roots. Pits should be 18 inches cube."

Weight, Mr. Newbery's "Descriptive Catalogue of the Specimens in the Museum at Melbourne, illustrating the economic woods of Victoria," gives 44 lbs. on an average; our specimen gave 43 lbs. The weight and value of P., calculated from the average of the six experiments given at page 203 of Laslett's "Timber and Timber Trees," were W = 64 and P = 534. Wood strong and tenacious, durable, extensively used in Australia for beams, railway sleepers, piers and bridges; also for ship-building. The wood from the Nilgiri plantations has scarcely been used, except for firewood or charcoal. The leaves give an essential oil used in medicine, and paper has been made of the bark.

		lbs.
W 1094.	Nilgiri Hills, 7,400 feet age 18 years, height 95 feet . .	43
W 1095-7.	" " 6,000 " " 2, 3, 4 " " 42, 43, and 60 feet ...	

3. PSIDIUM, Linn.

1. P. Guava, Raddi; Hook. Fl. Ind. ii. 468; Brandis 232; Kurz i. 476; Gamble 40. *P. pomiferum* and *P. pyriferum,* Willd.; Roxb. Fl. Ind. ii. 480. The Guava Tree. Vern. *Amrút, amrúd, safri-ám,* Hind.; *Peyara,* Beng.; *Amuk,* Nep.; *Modhuriam,* Ass.; *Piyara,* Beng.; *Segapu, koaya,* Tam.; *Jama, coya,* Tel.; *Pela,* Mal.; *Sebe,* Kan.; *Malaka beng,* Burm.

A small evergreen tree, with smooth and thin greenish grey bark, peeling off in thin flakes. Wood whitish, moderately hard, even-grained. Pores small, numerous. Medullary rays moderately broad, short, the distance between them many times greater than the transverse diameter of the pores.

Introduced from America and now cultivated and occasionally semi-wild allover India.

Weight, Wallich gives 44 lbs.; our specimen 42 lbs.; Skinner 47 lbs. and P = 618. Cultivated for its fruit. The bark is used in medicine as an astringent, and (or the leaves) for dyeing in Assam. Skinner says that the wood works well and smoothly, that it is used for wood-engraving and for spear handles and instruments.

		lbs.
O 1371.	Gonda, Oudh	42

4. EUGENIA, Linn.

One of the largest of the Indian genera of trees. It contains about 77 trees, chiefly found in the moist zones of North-East and South India and Burma; 33 occur in South India, and 30 to 40 in Burma, 4 in the North-West and Central India, and a large number in Eastern Bengal. Few of them are, however, of very great importance; and besides those here described, it will suffice to mention only one or two of the most common. A list taken from Mr. Duthie's description in Volume II. of the Flora Indica, pages 471 to 506, is, however, given for the sake of the references :—

SECTION I.—JAMBOSA.

1.	*E. formosa*, Wall.	North-East Himalaya down to Burma.
2.	*E. amplexicaulis*, Roxb. Fl. Ind. ii. 483; Kurz i. 493.	Chittagong.
3.	*E. malaccensis*, Linn.	(Cultivated).
4.	*E. polypetala*, Wight; Kurz i. 493 (*E. angustifolia*, Roxb. Fl. Ind. ii. 490).	Khasia Hills, Eastern Bengal, Chittagong.
5.	*E. diospyrifolia*, Wall.	Khasia Hills, Sylhet.
6.	*E. Munronii*, Wight; Beddome cix. . . .	Khasia Hills, Western Ghâts.
7.	*E. aquea*, Burm.; Roxb. Fl. Ind. ii. 492; Beddome cix; Kurz i. 494.	Chittagong, Burma, Ceylon.
8.	*E. Jambos*, Linn.; Roxb. Fl. Ind. ii. 494; Beddome cix.; Brandis 233; Kurz i. 495; Gamble 40.	(Cultivated).
9.	*E. macrocarpa*, Roxb. Fl. Ind. ii. 497; Kurz i. 492.	Eastern Bengal, Burma.
10.	*E. javanica*, Lamk.; Kurz i. 494 (*E. alba*, Roxb. Fl. Ind. ii. 493).	Andaman Islands.
11.	*E. Wallichii*, Wight.	North-East Himalaya down to Burma.
Var.	*E. lanceæfolia*, Roxb. Fl. Ind. ii. 494; Gamble 40	North and East Bengal.
12.	*E. grandis*, Wight	Eastern Bengal, Burma.
13.	*E. lepidocarpa*, Wall.; Kurz i. 490 (under *E. grandis*).	Burma.
14.	*E. Beddomei*, Duthie	Tinnevelly.
15.	*E. pachyphylla*, Kurz i. 490	Tenasserim.
16.	*E. tristis*, Kurz i. 490	Ditto.
17.	*E. hemisphærica*, Wight; Beddome t. 203 .	Western Ghâts, Ceylon.
18.	*E. lanceolaria*, Roxb. Fl. Ind. ii. 494 . . .	Sylhet.
19.	*E. bifaria*, Wall. (*E. laurifolia*, Roxb. Fl. Ind. ii. 489).	Ditto.
20.	*E. Kurzii*, Duthie	North-East Himalaya to Burma.
21.	*E. albiflora*, Duthie; Kurz i. 491	Burma.
22.	*E. læta*, Ham. (*E. Wightii*, Beddome cix.) . .	Western Ghâts.
23.	*E. ramosissima*, Wall.; Gamble 40	North-East Himalaya to Sylhet.
24.	*E. Helferi*, Duthie	Mergui.
25.	*E. mangifolia*, Wall.	Assam, Eastern Bengal.
26.	*E. inophylla*, Roxb. Fl. Ind. ii. 496	Eastern Bengal, Burma.

SECTION II.—SYZYGIUM.

27.	*E. Thumra*, Roxb. Fl. Ind. ii. 495; Kurz i. 488 .	Burma.
28.	*E. rubens*, Roxb. Fl. Ind. ii. 496; Kurz i. 488 .	Chittagong, Burma.
29.	*E. cymosa*, Lam.; Kurz i. 486	Eastern Bengal, Burma.
30.	*E. toddalioides*, Wight [*E. toddaliæfolia*, Wight; Gamble 41 (*Misprint*)].	Sikkim, Mergui.
31.	*E. myrtifolia*, Roxb. Fl. Ind. ii. 490; Kurz i. 486	Eastern Bengal, Burma.
32.	*E. acuminatissima*, Kurz i. 487	Mergui.
33.	*E. Arnottiana*, Wight; Beddome cvii. Vern. *Nawal*.	Western Ghâts.
34.	*E. claviflora*, Roxb. Fl. Ind. ii. 488; Kurz i. 480; Gamble 41.	North-East Himalaya down to Burma, Andamans.
35.	*E. leptantha*, Wight; Kurz i. 480	Sikkim, Burma, Andamans.

36.	*E. Wightiana*, Wight; Beddome (*E. lanceolata*, Wight; Beddome cx).	Western Ghâts, Ceylon.
37.	*E. pellucida*, Duthie (*E. contracta*, Kurz i. 481)	Burma.
38.	*E. zeylanica*, Wight; Kurz i. 481 (*E. spicata*, Lam.; Beddome t. 202. *E. glandulifera*, Roxb. Fl. Ind. ii. 496).	Eastern Bengal, Burma, Andamans, Western Ghâts.
39.	*E. grata*, Wall.; Kurz i. 480	Assam, Khasia Hills, Burma.
40.	*E. rubricaulis*, Miq.	Tenasserim.
41.	*E. montana*, Wight; Beddome cvii. . . .	Nilgiris.
42.	*E. bracteolata*, Wight; Kurz i. 482 . . .	Tenasserim.
43.	*E. lissophylla*, Thwaites; Beddome cviii. . .	Western Ghâts, Ceylon.
44.	*E. venusta*, Roxb. Fl. Ind. ii. 491; Kurz i. 487 ..	Tipperah, Burma.
45.	*E. Gardneri*, Thw.; Beddome cviii. . . .	Western Ghâts, Ceylon.
46.	*E. caryophyllæa*, Wight; Beddome cviii. . .	Ditto, ditto.
47.	*E. frondosa*, Wall.	Nepal.
48.	*E. areolata*, DC.	Ditto.
49.	*E. khasiana*, Duthie	Khasia Hills.
50.	*E. revoluta*, Wight; Beddome cvii. . . .	Nilgiris.
51.	*E. oblata*, Roxb. Fl. Ind. ii. 493; Kurz i. 488 .	Assam down to Burma.
52.	*E. calophyllifolia*, Wight; Beddome cvii. . .	Nilgiris.
53.	*E. rubicunda*, Wight; Beddome cviii. . .	Tinnevelly.
54.	*E. cuneata*, Wall.	Khasia Hills, Eastern Bengal.
55.	*E. brachiata*, Roxb. Fl. Ind. ii. 488 (*E. cinerea*, Kurz i. 483).	Burma.
56.	*E. polyantha*, Wight	Ditto.
57.	*E. malabarica*, Beddome t. 199	Wynaad.
58.	*E. alternifolia*, Wight; Beddome t. 198 . .	Assam, Carnatic.
59.	*E. tetragona*, Wight	Sikkim, Khasia Hills, Sylhet.
60.	*E. occlusa*, Miq.	Nicobar Islands.
61.	*E. operculata*, Roxb.	Sub-Himalaya, Eastern Bengal, South India, Burma.
Var.	*E. Paniala*, Roxb. Fl. Ind. ii. 489 . . .	Eastern Bengal, Burma.
Var.	*E. obovata*, Wall.	Northern Bengal, Burma.
62.	*E. Stocksii*, Duthie	Concan, Wynaad.
63.	*E. balsamea*, Wight; Kurz i. 485; Gamble 41 .	Sikkim, Eastern Bengal, Burma.
64.	*E. fruticosa*, Roxb. Fl. Ind. ii. 487; Kurz i. 485	Sylhet to Burma.
65.	*E. Jambolana*, Lam.	Throughout India.
Var.	*E. caryophyllæfolia*, Roxb. Fl. Ind. ii. 486 . .	
Var.	*E. obtusifolia*, Roxb. Fl. Ind. ii. 485 . . .	
65.	*E. Heyneana*, Wall.	Central India, Western Ghâts.

SECTION III.—EUGENIA.

66.	*E. Jossinia*, Duthie (*E. cuneata*, Beddome) .	Western Ghâts.
67.	*E. floccosa*, Beddome t. 200	Tinnevelly.
68.	*E. codyensis*, Munro	Nilgiris, Coorg.
69.	*E. macrosepala*, Duthie	Northern Kanara.
70.	*E. calcadensis*, Beddome cx.	Tinnevelly.
71.	*E. bracteata*, Roxb. Fl. Ind. ii. 490; Beddome cx.	Eastern Bengal, South India, Western Ghâts.
72.	*E. Rottleriana*, W. and A.; Beddome cx. . .	Southern India.
73.	*E. argentea*, Beddome cx.	Wynaad.
74.	*E. Mooniana*, Wight; Beddome cx. . . .	Southern India, Western Ghâts.
75.	*E. microphylla*, Beddome cx.	Travancore.
76.	*E. singampattiana*, Beddome t. 273 . . .	Tinnevelly.
77.	*E. wynadensis*, Beddome cx.	Wynaad.

E. Jambos, Linn. Vern. *Guláb jaman*, Hind.; *Malle nerale*, Coorg; is the "Rose Apple" cultivated for ornament and for its fruit. *E. Arnottiana*, Wight. Vern. *Nawal*, Tam., is a large tree on the hills of South India at above 4,000 feet elevation. *E. alternifolia*, Wight; Vern. *Manchi moyadi*, Tel., is a large tree of the forests of the hills in the Cuddapah and North Arcot Districts of Madras. *E. aquea*, Rumph., is an evergreen tree of South India and Burma. *E. fruticosa*, Roxb. Vern. *Moungzebri*, Magh; *Thabyaynee*, Burm., is an evergreen tree of the forests of Chittagong and Burma; while *E. ramosissima*, Wall. and *E. lanceæfolia*, Roxb., are handsome trees of the Eastern Himalaya and Sub-Himalayan tract.

Wood rough, hard and moderately hard, seasons well. Some species have concentric bands of softer tissue and others have not. The pores are from small to moderate-sized.

1. **E. formosa,** Wall.; Hook. Fl. Ind. ii. 471; Kurz i. 492; Gamble 40. *E. ternifolia*, Roxb. Fl. Ind. ii. 489. Vern. *Bara jaman*, Nep.; *Bunkonkri*, Mechi; *Bolsobak*, Gáro; *Famsikól*, Lepcha.

A moderate-sized evergreen tree. Bark greyish white, smooth, thin. Wood grey, hard. Pores moderate-sized. Medullary rays fine, and very fine, numerous, prominent.

Eastern Himalaya and Sub-Himalayan tract, near streams; Chittagong and Tenasserim.

Weight, 61 lbs. per cubic foot. Has large, very handsome flowers and large fruit.

		lbs.
E 2956.	Tista Valley, Darjeeling	61

2. **E. malaccensis,** Linn.: Hook. Fl. Ind. ii. 471; Roxb. Fl. Ind. ii. 483; Kurz i. 493. Vern. *Thabyoo-thabyay*, Burm.

A moderate-sized evergreen tree. Wood reddish grey, rough, soft. Pores moderate-sized and large. Medullary rays broad or moderately broad, visible on a radial section.

Cultivated in Bengal and Burma for its fruit.

Weight, Wallich gives 30, our specimen 38 lbs. per cubic foot.

		lbs.
B 309.	Burma (1867)	38

3. **E. grandis,** Wight; Hook. Fl. Ind. ii. 475; Beddome cvii.; Kurz i. 489. *E. cymosa*, Roxb. Fl. Ind. ii. 492. Vern. *Jam*, Beng.; *Batti jamb*, Sylhet; *Zebri*, Magh; *Toung thabyay*, Burm.

An evergreen tree. Wood red, rough, hard. Pores small, joined by fine, wavy, concentric lines. Medullary rays fine, wavy, numerous, uniform and equidistant.

Eastern Bengal, Burma and the Andaman Islands.

Weight, 51 to 52 lbs.

		lbs.
B 314.	Burma (1867)	51
B 2256.	Andaman Islands (1866)	52

B 2713, 48 lbs., brought from Tavoy by Dr. Wallich in 1828, has a structure similar to that of *E. grandis*.

4. **E. Kurzii,** Duthie; Hook. Fl. Ind. ii. 478; Kurz i. 491, *E. cerasiflora*, Kurz; Gamble 41. Vern. *Jámun*, Nep.; *Sunom*, Lepcha.

A large evergreen tree. Bark $\frac{1}{3}$ inch thick, whitish grey. Wood reddish grey, moderately hard, rough. Pores moderate-sized, numerous, often subdivided. Medullary rays fine and moderately broad.

Hills of Bengal and Burma, from 3,000 to 6,000 feet.
Weight, 37 to 56 lbs. per cubic foot.

		lbs.
E 701.	Sepoydura Forest, Darjeeling, 5,500 feet.	56
E 2955.	Tukdah Forest, Darjeeling, 5,000 feet (young tree) . .	37

5. **E. tetragona,** Wight; Hook. Fl. Ind. ii. 497: Kurz i. 484. *E. præcox,* Roxb.; Gamble 41. Vern. *Kemma, chamlani,* Nep.; *Sunóm,* Lepcha.

A large evergreen tree. Wood brownish or olive grey, shining, hard. Pores moderate-sized, numerous, uniformly distributed, oval and subdivided. Medullary rays fine, visible on a radial section.

Hills of Northern Bengal up to 6,000 feet, Chittagong.
Weight, 47 lbs. per cubic foot. Wood used occasionally for building and for the handles of tools and for charcoal.

		lbs.
E 682.	Sepoydura Forest, 5,500 feet, Darjeeling	46
E 1446.	Mishmi Hills (Griffith, 1836)	48

6. **E. operculata,** Roxb. Fl. Ind. ii. 486; Brandis 234; Kurz i. 482. *E. nervosa,* DC.; Beddome cvi. Vern. *Rai jáman, paiman, jamawa, dúgdúgia,* Hind.; *Yethabyay,* Burm.

A moderate-sized evergreen tree, leaves turning red in the cold season. Bark grey or dark brown, rough, with irregular hard scales, leaving cavities when they exfoliate. Wood reddish grey, hard. Pores small, often in radial lines. Medullary rays very fine, closely packed, extremely numerous.

Sub-Himalayan tract from the Jumna to Assam, Chittagong, Burma, Western Ghâts and Ceylon.
Weight, 47 lbs. per cubic foot. Used for building and agricultural implements. The fruit is eaten.

		lbs.
O 334.	Gorakhpur (1868)	51
B 305.	Burma (1867)	43

7. **E. obovata,** Wall.; Gamble 40. *E. operculata,* Roxb. var. *obovata;* Hook. Fl. Ind. ii. 498; Kurz i. 482. Vern. *Kiamoni,* Nep.; *Jungsong,* Lepcha; *Boda-jam,* Mechi.

An evergreen tree, leaves turning red in the cold season. Bark white, smooth. Wood grey, rough, moderately hard. Pores moderate-sized, very numerous, joined by faint, concentric bands. Medullary rays fine.

Savannah forests of Bengal and Burma.
Weight, 51 lbs. per cubic foot. Fruit eaten.

		lbs.
E 584.	Khookloong Forest, Darjeeling Terai	51

8. **E. Jambolana,** Lam.; Hook. Fl. Ind. ii. 499 Roxb. Fl. Ind. ii. 484; Beddome t. 197; Brandis 233; Kurz i. 485; Gamble 40. Vern. *Jáman, jam, phalinda, jamni, phaláni, pharenda, phaunda, paiman,* Hind.; *Jam,* Beng.; *Jamo,* Uriya; *Phoberkúng,* Lepcha; *Chambu,* Gáro; *Kor-jam,* Mechi; *Jamu,* Ass.; *Naval, navvel, nawar, naga,* Tam.; *Nerale,* Mysore; *Narala,* Kan.; *Nasedu, nairuri, nareyr,* Tel.; *Naindi,* Gondi; *Jambúl,* Mar.; *Mahadan,* Cingh.; *Zebri, chaku, kau,* Magh; *Thabyai-pyoo,* Burm.

An evergreen tree. Bark ¼ inch thick, light grey, with large patches of darker colour, smooth, with shallow depressions caused by exfoliation.

Wood reddish grey, rough, moderately hard, darker near the centre, no distinct heartwood. Pores moderate-sized and small, numerous, frequently oval, elongated and subdivided. Medullary rays fine, numerous; the interval between the rays less than the diameter of the pores. Faint, fine, concentric bands of softer tissue.

Sub-Himalayan tract from the Indus eastwards, ascending to 5,000 feet in Kumaun; throughout India and Burma.

Weight, according to Skinner, No. 120, 48 lbs. per cubic foot; according to Kyd. (*Saljam ?*) 45 lbs.; the average of our 23 specimens gives 49 lbs. Skinner gives P = 600 and Kyd 577. Wood fairly durable. Five sleepers of it were laid down in 1870 on the Oudh and Rohilkhand Railway, and taken up in 1875, when they were reported to be fairly sound and not touched by white ants.

Used for building, agricultural implements and carts, also for well-work, as it resists the action of water well. The bark is used for dyeing and tanning, and is astringent and used in medicine for cases of dysentery. The fruit is eaten. It is one of the trees on which the "tasar" silkworm is fed.

		lbs.
P 1192.	Madhopur, Punjab	40
P 452.	Ajmere	44
O 209.	Garhwal (1868)	51
O 210.	" "	47
O 211.	" "	49
O 224.	" "	44
O 239.	" "	40
O 2993.	" (1874)	47
O 527.	Dehra Dún	59
O 535.	" "	64
O 875.	Mohun Forest, Kumaun Bhabar	58
O 337.	Gorakhpur (1868)	51
O 338.	" "	42
C 195.	Mandla, Central Provinces (1870)	52
C 1135.	Ahiri Reserve, Central Provinces (with a slightly different structure)	56
C 2761.	Moharli Reserve, Central Provinces	43
C 1251.	Gumsúr, Madras	57
E 664.	Rakti Forest, Darjeeling Terai	54
E 2377.	Sivoke Forest " "	44
E 1396.	Chittagong	48
E 1958.	"	48
E 413.	Sundarbans	...
B 3065.	Burma (1862)	52
No. 51.	Ceylon Collection	36

E 2199 (43 lbs.) received from Assam under the name of *E. mangifolia*, Wall. Hook. Fl. Ind. ii. 480, resembles in structure *E. Jambolana*.

B 2292 (56 lbs.) received from the Andamans in 1866 under the name of *Eugenia* sp. has a moderately hard, compact, grey wood, with the structure similar to that of *E. Jambolana*, which is not yet known to grow in the Andamans.

No. 1 of Adrian Mendis' Ceylon Collection (49 lbs.) is *E. sylvestris*, Wight; Hook. Fl. Ind. ii. 493; Beddome cvii. (*Syzygium sylvestre*, Thwaites Enum. 116. Vern. *Alubo*, Cingh.) In structure it resembles *E. Jambolana*.

9. E. Heyneana, Wall.; Hook. Fl. Ind. ii. 500, *E. salicifolia*, Wight; Beddome cix.; Brandis 234. Vern. *Panjam-búl* Mar.; *Hendi*, Gondi; *Gambu*, Kurku.

A large shrub or small tree with grey bark. Wood similar to that of *E. Jambolana*, but pores smaller.

Bombay Ghâts, Berar and Central Provinces.

		lbs.
C 2786.	Melghât, Berar	38

10. E. *sp.* Vern. *Thabyay*, Burm.

A tree with hard, close-grained, red wood. Pores small, in irregular patches of soft tissue, joined by wavy, concentric lines. Medullary rays fine, numerous.

		lbs.
B 316.	Burma (1867)	55

5. BARRINGTONIA, Forst.

Contains about 8 Indian species chiefly from Burma. *B. speciosa*, Forst.; Hook. Fl. Ind. ii. 507; Roxb. Fl. Ind. ii. 636; Beddome cxii.; Kurz i. 496. Vern. *Kyaigyee*, Burm.; *Doddá*, Andamans, is an evergreen tree of the sea-shore of the Andamans. *B. pterocarpa*, Kurz i. 498; Hook. Fl. Ind. ii. 509. Vern. *Kyaitha*, Burm., is an evergreen tree of the tropical forests of Pegu and Martaban. Four other species are described as found in Tenasserim, *viz.*, *B. conoidea*, Griff., *B. augusta*, Kurz, *B. Helferi*, C. B. Clarke, and *B. macrostachya*, Kurz (including *B. pendula*, Kurz).

Wood soft or moderately hard. Pores small, in short radial lines between the numerous broad, or moderately broad, medullary rays. Numerous transverse bars between the rays.

1. B. acutangula, Gaertn.; Hook. Fl. Ind. ii. 508; Roxb. Fl. Ind. ii. 635; Beddome t. 204; Brandis 235; Kurz i. 497. Vern. *Ijál, samundar phúl, panniári, ingar*, Hind.; *Hijál, samundar*, Beng.; *Kinjolo*, Uriya; *Hendol*, Ass.; *Kanapa, batta, kurpá, kadamic*, Tel.; *Piwar*, Mar.; *Kyaitha, kyainee*, Burm.

A moderate-sized evergreen tree. Bark ½ inch thick, dark brown, rough. Wood white, shining, warps in seasoning, moderately hard, even-grained. Pores small, in radial groups between the broad and very broad, rarely fine and moderately broad, long medullary rays, which form the greater part of the wood. The space between the medullary rays, where not occupied by the pores, consists of narrow bands of firm tissue with fine transverse bars of lighter colour. The radial section is beautifully mottled with the medullary rays, which appear as irregular plates.

Sub-Himalayan tract from the Jumna eastwards, Oudh, Bengal, Central and South India, Burma.

Weight, Skinner, No. 20, gives 56 lbs.; while Kyd's experiments (*Stravadium acutangulum*) give only 39·3 lbs. Our specimen weighed 46 lbs. per cubic foot. Benson's experiments with bars of Burma wood 3 feet × 1 ·4 inch × 1 ·4 inch gave P = 648; Skinner P = 863, while Kyd's experiments on Assam wood in bars 2 feet × 1 inch × 1 inch gave P = 315. Said to be durable.

The wood is used for boat-building, well-work, carts, rice-pounders and by cabinet-makers. The bark is used to intoxicate fish, also for tanning; and, as well as the leaves and fruit, in native medicine. Beddome says the wood turns black when buried in mud.

		lbs.
C 1132.	Ahiri Reserve, Central Provinces	...
B 814.	Burma	46

2. B. racemosa, Blume; Hook. Fl. Ind. ii. 507; Roxb. Fl. Ind. ii. 634; Beddome cxii.; Kurz i. 496. Vern. *Samudra, cuddapah*, Tam., Mal.; *Kyai-beng*, Burm.

A moderate-sized evergreen tree. Wood white, very soft, porous. Pores small and moderate-sized, numerous, uniformly distributed. Medullary rays moderately broad, long, equidistant.

Western Coast, Andaman Islands and Ceylon. It is mentioned from Assam by G. Mann in Assam Forest Report, 1874-75. Vern. *Kumringah*, Ass., but *B. acutangula* may be meant.

Skinner, No. 21, gives weight 53 lbs. (?) per cubic foot and P = 819; he also says it is used for house and cart building, and that it has been tried for railway sleepers.

	lbs.
B 1993. Andaman Islands (Kurz, 1866)	27

6. CAREYA, Roxb.

Besides the species described; *C. sphærica*, Roxb. Fl. Ind. ii. 636; Hook. Fl. Ind. ii. 511; Kurz i. 500, is a large deciduous tree of the Chittagong Hills; and *C. herbacea*, Roxb. Fl. Ind. ii. 638; Hook. Fl. Ind. ii. 510; Brandis 237; Gamble 41. Vern. *Bhooi dalim*, Beng.; *Chuwa*, Nep., is a small undershrub of grass lands in Bengal, Oudh and the Central Provinces, generally bringing out its beautiful pink flowers in April and best after the grass has been burnt by jungle fires.

1. C. arborea, Roxb. Fl. Ind. ii. 638; Hook. Fl. Ind. ii. 511; Beddome t. 205; Brandis 236; Kurz i. 499; Gamble 41. Vern. *Kumbi, Kumbh, khumbi*, Hind.; *Pilu*, Banda; *Gumar*, Mandla, Balaghát; *Kumri*, Chhindwara; *Gummar*, Gondi; *Boktok*, Lepcha; *Dambel*, Gáro; *Ayma, pailae, poota-tammi*, Tam.; *Budá-durmi, buda darini, dudippi*, Tel.; *Gavuldu*, Mysore; *Bambway*, Burm.; *Kabooay*, Taleing; *Tagooyi*, Karen; *Kahatte*, Cingh.

A large deciduous tree, leaves turning red in the cold season. Bark ½ inch thick, dark grey, with vertical and diagonal cracks, exfoliating in narrow flakes; inner substance reddish, fibrous. Sapwood whitish, large; heartwood dull red, sometimes claret-coloured, very dark in old trees, even-grained, beautifully mottled, seasons well, very durable, moderately hard. Pores oval, small and moderate-sized, subdivided. Medullary rays numerous, fine, equidistant and uniform; the space between two consecutive rays equal to the diameter of the pores. The medullary rays are visible on a radial section as narrow bands.

Sub-Himalayan tract from the Jumna eastwards, Bengal, Burma, Central and South India. Growth fast, a round in the Bengal Fruit Museum gave 4 rings per inch of radius.

The weight and transverse strength have been determined by the following experiments:—

Experiment by whom conducted.	Year.	Wood whence procured.	Number of experiments.	Size of scantling.	Weight.	Value of P.
				Ft. In. In.	lbs.	
Wallich	...	Goalpara	...	......	43	......
Adrian Mendis . .	1855	Ceylon	...	......	38	......
R. Thompson . . .	1869	Central Provinces . .	...	......	60	......
Skinner, No. 38 . .	1862	South India . . .	...	Various.	50	870
Benson	...	Burma	...	3 × 1·4 × 1·4	47	929
Brandis, Nos. 52, 53 .	1862	„	...	......	55	......
„	1864	„	4	3 × 1 × 1	60	880
„	„	„	5	2 × × 1	51	655
Kyd	1831	Assam	1	2 × 1 × 1	61	670
Commt. Dept. . . .	...	Moulmein. . .	...	......	50	950
Smythies	1878	See list below . .	12	......	54·5	......

Wood durable; the specimens brought by Dr. Wallich from Tavoy in 1828, and that brought from the Mishmi Hills by Dr. Griffith in 1836, were quite sound on being cut up, though they had been stored for 50 years in Calcutta. The wood is little used except for agricultural implements. It is being tried for railway sleepers on the Eastern Bengal and Northern Bengal State Railways, but the result of the experiment is not yet known. Kurz says it is used in Burma for gun-stocks, house-posts, planking, carts, furniture and cabinet-work. It stands well under water. Fuzes made from its bark are used to make slow matches. Its bark gives a good fibre for coarse, strong cordage, and is used in native medicine as an astringent.

		lbs.
O 208.	Garhwal (1868)	53
O 228.	„ „	53
O 1479.	Kheri, Oudh	59
C 1131.	Ahiri Reserve, Central Provinces	58
C 2747.	Moharli Reserve „ „ (sapwood)	37
E 624.	Rakti Forest, Darjeeling Terai	48
E 2378.	Sivoke „ „ „	51
E 1441.	Mishmi Hills (Griffith, 1836)	56
B 2703.	Tavoy (Wallich, 1822)	59
B 2685.	„ „ „	56
B 2710.	„ „ „	51
B 2228.	Andaman Islands (1866)	55
B 3147.	„ „ (Home, 1874)	56
No. 41.	Ceylon Collection	38

7. PLANCHONIA, Bl.

1. P. littoralis, Van Houtte; Hook. Fl. Ind. ii. 511. *P. valida*, Blume; Kurz i. 500. Vern. *Bambway nee*, Burm.; *Baila dá*, And.

An evergreen tree. Wood reddish brown, with yellow specks, very hard, close-grained. Pores moderate-sized and large, often subdivided, in rounded and elongated patches, which are sometimes joined by narrow, undulating bands of softer tissue. Medullary rays very fine, numerous, bending. The pores are frequently filled by a yellow substance, and are prominent on a vertical section.

Evergreen coast forests of the Andaman Islands.

Weight, our specimens give 61 to 64 lbs. per cubic foot; Bennett gives 56 lbs. and P = 600. A valuable wood, which should be better known; it seasons well and takes a fine polish.

		lbs.
B 514.	Andaman Islands	64
B 2495.	„ „ (Home, 1874, No. 7, *Youaygyee*)	61

ORDER XLVII. MELASTOMACEÆ.

An Order containing 13 Indian Genera of shrubs or small trees. They are chiefly found in South India or Tenasserim. They belong to 5 Tribes, *viz.*,—

Tribe I.—Osbeckieæ	*Osbeckia, Otanthera* and *Melastoma.*
„ II.—Oxysporeæ	*Oxyspora, Kendrickia, Allomorphia, Blastus, Ochthocharis* and *Anerincleistus.*
„ III.—Medinilleæ	*Anplectrum, Medinilla.*
„ IV.—Astronieæ	*Pternandra.*
„ V.—Memecyleæ	*Memecylon.*

Oxyspora paniculata, DC.; Hook. Fl. Ind. ii. 525; Gamble 41 is a large handsome shrub of the Eastern Himalaya and Khasia Hills. *Memecylon* contains about

20 species of shrubs or small trees. *M. umbellatum*, Burm.; Beddome t. 206; Kurz i. 516. Vern. *Udatulli*, Kan., is a small tree of the hills of South India, Arracan and the Andamans, whose wood is said by Beddome to be like boxwood and by VanSomeren to be durable. *M. edule*, Roxb.; Beddome cxiii.; Kurz i. 512. Vern. *Alli*, Tel.; *Anjan, kurpá*, Bombay, is a small tree of the Eastern Gháts of South India, Tenasserim and the Andamans, with a strong, hard wood and edible fruit, while *M. amabile*, Bedd. and *M. gracile*, Bedd. are small trees of the Western Gháts. The remaining genera contain shrubs or climbers of little forest interest.

1. OSBECKIA, Linn.

Contains a number of handsome-flowering herbs and shrubs of little importance.

1. O. crinita, Benth.; Hook. Fl. Ind. ii. 517. *O. stellata*, Don; Gamble 41. Vern. *Number*, Lepcha.

A shrub. Bark greyish brown, smooth. Wood light brown, moderately hard. Annual rings marked by a white line and more numerous pores. Pores moderate-sized, scanty. Medullary rays crooked, fine, the distance between the rays equal to the diameter of the pores.

Eastern Himalaya and Khasia Hills from 4,000 to 8,000 feet.
A very pretty shrub, common about Darjeeling.

E 3310. Darjeeling, 6,500 feet.

2. MELASTOMA, Linn.

Four Indian species.

1. M. Malabathricum, Linn.; Hook. Fl. Ind. ii. 523; Roxb. Fl. Ind. ii. 405; Kurz i. 503; Gamble 41. The Indian Rhododendron. Vern. *Choulisy*, Nep.; *Tungbram*, Lepcha; *Shapti, tunka*, Mechi; *Myetpyai*, Burm.

A large shrub. Back reddish brown, thin, smooth. Wood moderately hard, light brown, with medullary patches. Pores moderate-sized, often in concentric groups, and surrounded with white tissue. Medullary rays short, fine to moderately broad, numerous, unequally distributed. Concentric bands of soft tissue often joining the pores.

Throughout India up to 6,000 feet, chiefly near watercourses.
This is probably the *Lutki* bush on which, according to Mr. Brownlow of Cachar (Journal of the Agri-Horticultural Society of Calcutta), the silkworm *Atlacus Atlas* is often found, and fed on which it gives a very white silk.

E 3275. Borojhar Reserve, W. Dúars.

ORDER XLVIII. LYTHRARIEÆ.

Contains 8 Indian Genera of trees or shrubs all belonging to the tribe Lythreæ. Of these, 6 Genera are here described. *Pemphis acidula*, Forst.; Hook. Fl. Ind. ii. 573; Beddome cxvii.; Kurz i. 518, is an evergreen shrub of the sea-coast of Malabar, Tenasserim and the Andamans, while *Crypteronia paniculata*, Bl.; Kurz i. 519. (*C. pubescens* Bl. and *C. glabra*, Bl. in Hook. Fl. Ind. ii. 574.) Vern. *Ananpho*, Burm., is an evergreen tree of the upper tropical and moist forests of Chittagong and Burma. Brandis in his Burma List, 1862, No. 113, says it has a reddish, close but not straight-grained wood, used occasionally for cart-wheels, but more usually for burning.

Medullary rays fine or very fine and very numerous.

1. WOODFORDIA, Salisbury.

1. **W. floribunda,** Salisb.; Hook. Fl. Ind. ii. 572; Brandis 238; Gamble 42. *W. tomentosa,* Beddome cxvii. *W. fruticosa,* Kurz i. 518. *Grislea tomentosa,* Roxb. Fl. Ind. ii. 233. Vern. *Dáwi, thawi, sautha, dhaula,* Hind.; *Gul daur,* Kangra; *Dhai,* Kumaun; *Dhewti,* Oudh; *Dhuvi, surtári,* C.P.; *Pitta, petisurali, surteyli,* Gondi; *Khinni, dhi,* Kurku; *Dahiri, laldairo,* Nep.; *Chungkyek dum,* Lepcha; *Jatiko,* Uriya; *Jargi,* Tel.; *Phulsatti,* Mar.; *Datli,* Bhîl.

A large shrub with smooth bark, marked by longitudinal raised lines or protuberances, peeling off in thin scales. Wood reddish white, hard, close-grained. Pores small, uniformly distributed, sometimes in radial lines, medullary rays fine and very fine, closely packed.

Common throughout India, ascending to 5,000 feet in the Himalayas.

Cunningham gives weight 58 lbs., P = 730; our specimen weighs 46 lbs. The flowers give a red dye, which is used to dye silks.

		lbs.
C 2794.	Melghát, Berar	46
E 876.	Chenga Forest, Darjeeling Terai	...

2. LAWSONIA, Linn.

1. **L. alba,** Lam.; Hook. Fl. Ind. ii. 573; Beddome cxviii.; Brandis 238; Gamble 42. *L. inermis,* Linn.; Roxb. Fl. Ind. ii. 258; Kurz i. 519. The Henna Plant of Egypt. Vern. *Mehndi,* Hind.; *Dan,* Burm.; *Manghati,* Uriya; *Marithondi,* Tam.; *Gorantlu,* Kan.

A shrub with thin, greyish-brown bark. Wood grey, hard, close-grained; alternate bands of tissue, with fewer and more numerous pores, which may possibly be annual rings. Pores small and joined by faint, short, interrupted concentric bands. Medullary rays fine.

Wild in Beluchistan, on the Coromandel coast and perhaps in Central India.

Cultivated throughout India as a hedge plant and for its leaves, which, powdered and made into a paste, give the "henna" dye which is used to dye the nails, skin and beard.

C 2000. Nimar, Central Provinces.

3. LAGERSTRÖMIA, Linn.

Contains 11 Indian species, dispersed principally over South India and Burma, while a few extend to North-East India and Assam, and one to North-West and Central India. *L. indica,* Linn.; Hook. Fl. Ind. ii. 575; Roxb. Fl. Ind. ii. 505; Kurz i. 521 Vern. *Telinga-china,* Hind., is a handsome shrub, with pink flowers, cultivated in gardens in most parts of India. *L. calyculata,* Kurz i. 522. Vern. *Pymmahpyoo,* Burm., is an evergreen tree of the Martaban Hills. *L. floribunda,* Jack., a small tree of Tenasserim and *L. villosa,* Wall.; Kurz i. 524. Vern. *Young kalay,* a deciduous tree of the forests of the Pegu Yoma and Martaban.

The pores are of different sizes, the small pores being arranged in narrow, concentric bands, which join the lines of large pores. Medullary rays uniform, equidistant, fine and numerous.

1. **L. parviflora,** Hook. Fl. Ind. ii. 575; Roxb. Fl. Ind. ii. 505; Beddome t. 31; Brandis 239; Kurz i. 521; Gamble 42. Vern. *Bákli, kat dhaura, dhaura, lendya, seina, sida, asid,* Hind.; *Sida,* Beng., Mechi, Ass.; *Borderi, bordengri,* Nep.; *Kanhil,* Lepcha; *Shida,* Gáro; *Shej,*

Banda; *Seji*, Bijeragogarh; *Kakria*, Guz.; *Sahine*, Chanda; *Chinangi*, Tel.; *Chungi, pilúgu*, Hyderabad; *Nana, bondara, nandi, bellinandi, sína, lendi*, Mar.; *Ventaku, cheninge*, Kan.; *Lendya*, Baigas; *Sina, nelli, leria*, Gondi; *Chekerey*, Kurku; *Tsambelay*, Burm.

A large deciduous tree with light brown, thin bark, exfoliating in long, thin, woody scales. Wood very hard, grey or greyish brown, often with a reddish tinge, darker coloured near the centre, hard. No annual rings. Pores moderate-sized and large, often subdivided, uniformly distributed and frequently joined by narrow, irregular, wavy bands and lines of softer texture, distinctly visible on a longitudinal section. Medullary rays fine, numerous.

Sub-Himalayan Tract from the Jumna eastwards, Oudh, Bengal, Assam, Central and South India.

The weight and transverse strength have been given by the following experiments:—

	Ft. In. In.		Weight.	Value of P.
Kyd in 1831 specimens from Assam in bars	2 × 1 × 1	found	52	757
Skinner, No. 86 from South India	various	„	40	467
Brandis, No. 63 „ Burma, 1862		„	40	...
Smythies in 1878, average of 9 specimens . . .		„	52	...

Wood tough, elastic, seasons well, works freely and is fairly durable. It coppices well. Ten sleepers laid down on the Oudh and Rohilkhand Railway in 1870 were reported, on being examined in 1875, to be quite sound. A number of sleepers are being tried on the Northern Bengal State Railway, but the result is not yet known. It is used for ploughs and other agricultural implements, for construction, for buggy shafts and axe handles. It gives a very good charcoal. It gives a sweet gum from wounds in the bark. The bark is used for tanning. It is one of the trees on which the "tasar" silkworm is fed.

		lbs.
O 232.	Garhwal (1868)	45
O 2999.	„ (1874)	51
O 339.	Gorakhpur (1868)	54
C 196.	Mandla, Central Provinces (1870)	49
C 2735. C 2749.	} Moharli Reserve, Central Provinces	50
C 1140.	Ahiri Reserve, Central Provinces	60
C 2768.	Melghát, Berar	54
E 666.	Bamunpokri, Darjeeling Terai	52
E 2379.	Sukna Forest „ „	54
E 785.	Kámrúp, Assam	...

2. **L. lanceolata**, Beddome t. 32; Brandis 240. *L. parviflora*, Roxb. *var. majuscula*, C. B. Clarke; Hook. Fl. Ind. i. 575. Vern. *Bandára, nandi*, Kan.; *Nána, sokutia*, Mar.; *Boda, bondaga*, Dekkan.

A large tree, with leaves bluish white beneath. Inner wood red, moderately hard. Pores large and moderate-sized, joined by wavy concentric bands of soft texture, which are often interrupted. Medullary rays fine, numerous, uniform, equidistant.

Forests of the Western Ghâts as far north as Khandeish, Mysore and Courtallum.

Growth moderate, 10 rings per inch of radius. Weight, 57 lbs. per cubic foot.

		lbs.
C 956.	Guzerat, Bombay	...
W 1220.	North Kanara	57

3. **L. microcarpa**, Wight; Beddome t. 30; *L. lanceolata*, Wall.; Hook. Fl. Ind. ii. 576; Brandis 240. Vern. *Benteak, venteak*, Tam.;

Ventaku, Tel.; *Bolundúr, billi nandi*, Kan.; *Nandi*, Coorg; *Nanah*, Mar.

A large tree with smooth white bark, peeling off in thin flakes. Wood red, moderately hard. Pores large and small, often subdivided and frequently joined by narrow, irregular, wavy bands and lines of softer texture. Medullary rays extremely fine, very numerous. Distinct white concentric lines, which probably indicate the annual rings. Pores marked on a longitudinal section and medullary rays visible on a radial section as numerous narrow plates.

Western forests of the Madras Presidency.

Growth moderately fast, 6 to 8 rings per inch of radius. The weight and transverse strength have been determined as follows:

Experiment by whom conducted.	Year.	Whence procured.	Number of experiments.	Size of bar.	Weight.	Value of P.
				Ft. In. In.		
Skinner No. 85	1862	......	......	Various	41	619
Puckle	1859	Mysore	5	2×1×1	41	939
List	1863	„	......	......	39	......
Balfour	...	Malabar	3	7×2×2	49	542
Smythies	1878	South Kanara	2	......	48	......

Much used in construction and for ship-building, also for coffee-cases, and for furniture.

		lbs.
W 765.	South Kanara	48
W 862.	„ „	48

4. L. Reginæ, Roxb. Fl. Ind. ii. 505; Beddome t. 29; Brandis 240. *L. Flos-Reginæ*, Retz; Hook. Fl. Ind. ii. 577; Kurz i. 524. Vern. *Jarúl*, Beng.; *Ajhar*, Ass.; *Bolashari*, Gáro; *Kadali*, Tam.; *Challá*, Kan.; *Adamboe*, Mal.; *Taman, mota bondara*, Mar.; *Kamaung*, Magh; *Pymma*, Burm.; *Murute*, Cingh.

A large deciduous tree. Bark smooth, grey to cream-coloured. Wood shining, light red, hard; annual rings marked by a belt of large pores. Pores of all sizes from extremely small to large, the latter often subdivided, joined by narrow, wavy and often anastomosing concentric bands of soft tissue, which contain the smaller pores. Medullary rays very or extremely fine, often indistinct. The wood in Burma is frequently very porous with an abundance of large pores.

Eastern Bengal, Assam, Burma and Western Coast, extending north to Ratnagiri.

Growth moderate; our specimens show 7 rings per inch of radius. In 1876 Mr. Fisher measured 5 trees in the Sidli Forest, Goalpara district, Assam. The results were, on an average—

	In.	In.	In.	In.	In.
On a length of radius equivalent to a girth of	18	36	54	72	90
No. of rings	15	25	39	51	66

On an average, therefore, the number of rings per inch of radius is 4·6; and the tree appears to add a cubit to its girth every 13 years on an average. The weight and transverse strength have been determined by the following experiments.

Experiment by whom conducted.	Year.	Wood whence procured.	Number of experiments.	Size of bar.	Weight.	Value of P.
				Ft. In. In.	lbs.	
Wallich	...	India	...	...	46·5	...
Adrian Mendis	1855	Ceylon	...	...	42	...
Baker	1829	Bengal	11	2 × 1 × 1	...	850
Skinner, No. 87	1862	South India	...	...	40	637
Kyd	1831	Assam	...	2 × 1 × 1	37	407 ?
"	"	"	...	...	38	633
"	"	"	...	...	38	383 ?
Benson	...	Burma	...	3 × 1·4 × 1·4	38	849
Forbes Watson	...	"	...	3 × 1·5 × 1·5	36	651
Brandis, Nos. 61, 62	1862	"	...	...	40·5*	...
" " "	1864	"	4	7 × 2 × 2	47	680
Commissariat Department	...	Moulmein	...	...	38	822
Smythies	1878	As below	10	...	43	...

* Average of 37 and 44.

The most valuable timber of Sylhet, Cachar and Chittagong, and in Burma the most valuable after teak. It is used in ship-building and for boats and canoes, all kinds of construction, timber and carts. The Ordnance Department use it for many parts of their gun-carriages. In South India it is used for building and in Ceylon for casks. It gives a resin. It is cultivated for ornament all over the hotter parts of India and even as far north as Lahore.

		lbs.
E 620.	Eastern Dúars, Assam	48
E 1228.	Sibságar, Assam	40
E 2188.	Nowgong, Assam	40
E 1272.	Cachar	38·5
E 410.	Sundarbans	47
E 710.	Chittagong	47
W 726.	South Kanara	46
B 808.	Pegu	39
B 3067.	Burma (1862)	40
B 2717.	Tavoy (Wallich, 1828)	42

5. **L. macrocarpa,** Wall.; Kurz i. 524. *L. Flos-Reginæ,* Retz; Hook. Fl. Ind. ii. 577. Vern. *Jarúl,* Beng.; *Koonpymmah,* Burm.

A moderate-sized deciduous tree. Wood red, moderately hard, in structure resembling that of *L. Reginæ,* but the bands of white tissue more prominent and large pores fewer.

Burma in Pegu and Martaban.
Weight, 45 to 48 lbs. per cubic foot.

		lbs
B 296.	Burma (1867)	48
B 3068.	" (1862)	45

6. **L. hypoleuca,** Kurz i. 523; Hook. Fl. Ind. ii. 577. Vern. *Pymmah,* Burm.; *Pábdá,* And.

A large deciduous tree with thin whitish bark. Wood red, hard. Pores very small to very large, in fine, wavy, concentric, anastomosing, but sometimes interrupted lines of softer tissue, alternating with darker wood of firmer texture, in which the very fine medullary rays are distinctly visible.

Andaman Islands.
Growth slow, 10-18 rings per inch of radius. Weight, 41 to 50 lbs. according to

Major Prothero; our specimens give an average of 39 to 40 lbs.; Bennett gives 41 lbs. and P = 570. The wood is used largely in the Andamans for building, shingles and other purposes.

		lbs.
B 510.	Andaman Islands	...
B 2202.	" " (1866)	45
B 2274.	" " "	38
B 2283.	" " "	34
B 2496.	" " (Home, 1874, No. 2)	44

7. L. tomentosa, Presl; Hook. Fl. Ind. ii. 578; Kurz i. 522. Vern. *Laiza,* Burm.

A large deciduous tree. Bark ⅛ inch thick, grey. Wood grey or greyish brown, close-grained, moderately hard. Pores from very small to very large, the latter often subdivided, joined by numerous concentric lines, alternating with broad bands of firmer tissue, in which the fine medullary rays are prominent.

Burma. Frequent in Pegu and Martaban.

Weight, according to Brandis' Catalogue, 1862, No. 59 (*L. pubescens*, Wall.), 53 lbs.; Brandis' 3 experiments in 1864 with bars 3 ft. × 1 inch × 1 inch gave: Weight 38 lbs. and P = 588. Our specimens give 46 and 53 lbs. The timber is valued for bows and spear handles, and is also used for canoes and cart-wheels.

		lbs.
B 572.	Prome	46
B 2533.	Burma (1862)	53

4. DUABANGA, Ham.

1. D. sonneratioides, Buch.; Kurz i. 525; Gamble 42. *Lagerströmia grandiflora*, Roxb. Fl. Ind. ii. 503. Vern. *Bandorhulla,* Beng.; *Lampatia,* Nep.; *Dúr,* Lepcha; *Kochan, kokan,* Ass.; *Jarúl-jhalna,* Cachar; *Bondorkella, bolchim,* Gáro; *Baichua,* Magh; *Myoukgnau,* Burm.

A lofty deciduous tree, with light-brown bark, peeling off in thin flakes. Wood grey, often streaked with yellow, soft, seasons well, neither warps nor splits. Pores large and moderate-sized, often oval and subdivided, uniformly distributed. Medullary rays fine, very numerous, wavy. Pores well marked on a longitudinal section.

Eastern Bengal ascending to 3,000 foot, Assam and Burma.

Growth fast, 5 rings per inch of radius. Weight, according to Brandis' Burma List of 1862, No. 64, 30 lbs. per cubic foot; our specimens give an average of 32 lbs. The wood does not warp or split, and canoes cut out of it green are at once used, even when liable alternately to wet and the heat of the sun. Is used in Northern Bengal and Assam very extensively for tea-boxes, for which purpose it is admirably fitted. It is also made into canoes and cattle troughs. The seeds are extremely small and the seedlings very minute at first, but the growth is very fast. Seedlings at the Bamunpokri Plantation in Bengal, which had come up on the sites of old charcoal kilns (see "Indian Forester," Vol. iv. page 345), attained a height of 10 feet in two years, with proportionate girth and fine spreading branches.

		lbs.
E 652.	Rakti Forest, Darjeeling Terai	32
E 2380.	Sukna Forest, Darjeeling Terai	32
E 950.	Eastern Dúars, Assam	32
E 1230.	Sibságar, Assam	36
E 1436.	Assam	29
E 1285.	Cachar	32
E 1499.	Sylhet	...
E 713.	Chittagong	31
B 807.	Pegu	30
B 1995.	Andamans (Kurz, 1866) (young tree)	21

5. SONNERATIA, Linn. f.

Contains 4 Indian trees found in the coast forests of Sind, Bengal, Malabar, Arracan, Pegu, Tenasserim and the Andamans. Besides the two described: *S. alba.* Sm.; Hook. Fl. Ind. ii. 580; Kurz i. 526, is found in the shore forests of the Andamans and *S. Griffithii*, Kurz i. 527. Vern. *Tapyoo*, in those of Burma.

1. S. acida, Linn. f.; Hook. Fl. Ind. ii. 579; Roxb. Fl. Ind. ii. 506; Beddome cxviii.; Brandis 242; Kurz i. 526. Vern. *Orcha, archaká*, Beng.; *Tapoo, tamoo*, Burm.

A small evergreen tree. Wood grey, soft, even-grained. Pores small, oval and subdivided, very numerous, uniformly distributed. Medullary rays very fine, very numerous.

Tidal creeks and littoral forests of India, Burma, and the Andamans.

Weight, 31 lbs. per cubic foot. The wood is said by Beddome to be used for models, and in Ceylon to be a good substitute for coal in steamers. The fruit is eaten in the Sundarbans.

		lbs.
E 395.	Sundarbans	31

2. S. apetala, Buch.; Hook. Fl. Ind. ii. 579; Roxb. Fl. Ind. ii. 506; Beddome cxviii.; Kurz i. 527. Vern. *Keowra*, Beng.; *Kanpala*, Burm.

A moderate-sized evergreen tree. Sapwood grey; heartwood reddish brown, moderately hard. Pores small, numerous, oval and subdivided. Medullary rays fine, very numerous.

Tidal creeks and littoral forests of Bengal and Burma.

Weight, 44 lbs. per cubic foot. The wood is said by Kurz to be good for house-building, packing-boxes, etc.

		lbs.
E 399.	Sundarbans	44

6. PUNICA, Linn.

1. P. Granatum, Linn.; Hook. Fl. Ind. ii. 581; Roxb. Fl. Ind. ii. 499; Beddome cxix.; Brandis 241; Kurz i. 528; Gamble 42. The Pomegranate. Vern. *Anár, dárim, damú*, Hindi; *Dálim*, Kumaun; *Dalimbe*, Kan.; *Thalé*, Burm.

A shrub or small tree. Wood light yellow, with a small, darker coloured, irregularly shaped heartwood, compact and close-grained. Pores very small, uniformly distributed. Medullary rays fine, very numerous. Medullary patches common.

Wild in the Suliman Range, between 3,500 and 6,000 feet, Salt Range and North-West Himalaya. Cultivated in many parts of India and Burma.

Growth slow, 18 rings per inch of radius (Brandis). Weight, Mathieu Fl. For., p. 169, gives 52 to 63 lbs.; one specimen weighs 57 lbs. per cubic foot. Wood not used, but might be tried as a substitute for boxwood. The fruit is generally eaten, but the best kinds come from Afghanistan. The flowers are very handsome, bright scarlet, and give a light-red dye; the bark and the rind of the fruit are used for tanning and for dyeing morocco leather, and the root-bark is an effectual anthelmintic.

		lbs.
P 106.	Sutlej Valley, Punjab	57

ORDER XLIX. SAMYDACEÆ.

Contains two genera, *Casearia* and *Homalium*.

1. CASEARIA, Jacq.

Nine Indian species. *C. Vareca,* Roxb. Fl. Ind. ii. 418; Hook. Fl. Ind. ii. 593; Kurz i. 530; Gamble 43, is an evergreen shrub of the banks of streams in Northern and Eastern Bengal. *C. esculenta,* Roxb., *C. rubescens,* Dalz.; Beddome t. 41, and *C. wynaadensis,* Beddome cxx., are small trees of the forests of the Western Ghâts. *C. Kurzii,* C. B. Clarke; Hook. Fl. Ind. ii. 594, is a tree of Chittagong.

Wood yellowish white, moderately hard, rough. Medullary rays fine, numerous. Pores small or very small, often in radial groups or lines.

1. C. tomentosa, Roxb. Fl. Ind. ii. 421; Hook. Fl. Ind. ii. 593; Beddome cxix.; Brandis 243. Vern. *Chilla, chilara, bairi, bhari,* Hind.; *Maun,* Manbhúm; *Men, wasa, gamgudu,* Tel.; *Lainja, massei, karei,* Mar.; *Girari,* Uriya; *Thundri,* Gondi; *Khesa,* Kurku.

A small tree. Bark ⅓ inch thick, brittle, exfoliating in more or less square flakes. Wood yellowish white, moderately hard, rough, close-grained. Pores small and very small, sometimes in radial lines. Medullary rays fine and very fine, wavy, equidistant, very numerous.

Sub-Himalayan tract from the Indus eastwards, Oudh, Eastern Bengal, Central and South India.

Weight, 41 lbs. per cubic foot. Wood used to make combs. The bark is bitter; it is used for adulterating the "Kamela" powder and the pounded fruit for poisoning fish.

		lbs.
O 1393.	Gonda, Oudh	41
O 3085.	" "	...
O 3089.	Kheri, Oudh	...
C 1183.	Ahiri Reserve, Central Provinces	41
C 2802.	Melghát, Berar (young)	38

2. C. graveolens, Dalzell; Hook. Fl. Ind. ii. 592; Brandis 243. Vern. *Chilla, náro, kathera, pimpri,* Hind.; *Girchi,* Gondi; *Rewat,* Kurku.

A small deciduous tree. Bark dark grey, with a few longitudinal wrinkles. Wood light yellow, moderately hard, rough, even-grained. Pores small, often oval and subdivided. Medullary rays fine, equidistant, very numerous, visible as shining plates on a radial section.

Sub-Himalayan tract from the Chenab eastwards, Oudh, Central India.

Weight, 40 to 50 lbs. Wood not used; the fruit is used to poison fish.

		lbs.
O 240.	Garhwal (1868)	42
O 271.	" "	40
O 1456.	Bahraich, Oudh	49
O 3090.	Kheri, Oudh	...

3. C. glomerata, Roxb. Fl. Ind. ii. 419; Hook. Fl. Ind. ii. 591; Kurz i. 530; Gamble 42. Vern. *Lúrjúr,* Sylhet; *Burgonli,* Nep.; *Sugvat,* Lepcha.

A large evergreen tree. Wood yellowish white, moderately hard, rough. Pores small, in radial lines. Medullary rays of two sizes; numerous very fine rays between fewer moderately broad, giving on a radial section a beautifully mottled appearance.

Eastern Bengal ascending to 6,000 feet, Chittagong.

Weight, 45 to 48 lbs. per cubic foot. Wood used for building, charcoal and occasionally for tea-boxes.

		lbs.
E 691.	Chuttockpur Forest, Darjeeling, 6,000 feet	48
E 2381.	" " " "	45

2. HOMALIUM, Jacq.

Contains eight trees, chiefly Burmese. *H. zeylanicum*, Bth., Hook. Fl. Ind. ii. 596; Beddome t. 210, and *H. travancoricum*, Beddome t. 211, are large trees of the Western Ghâts. *H. minutiflorum*, Kurz i. 532, *H. propinquum*, C. B. Clarke; Hook. Fl. Ind. ii. 597, and *H. Griffithianum*, Kurz i. 531, are small trees of Burma. *H. Schlichii*, Kurz i. 532, is an evergreen tree of the tropical forests of Chittagong; and *H. nepalense*, Bth., is found in Nepal.

1. H. tomentosum, Bth.; Hook. Fl. Ind. ii. 596; Brandis 243; Kurz i. 531. *Blackwellia tomentosa*, Vent.; Brandis' Burma Catalogue, 1862, No. 58. Vern. *Myoukshaw*, Burm.

A large deciduous tree with thin, very smooth, white or greyish white bark. Wood brown, with dark-coloured heartwood, very hard, heavy and close-grained, splits in seasoning. Pores small, in radial lines between the closely-packed and fine medullary rays, which are bent outwards where they touch the pores. The distance between the rays is less than the transverse diameter of the pores.

Chittagong and Burma.

Weight, Brandis in Burma List, 1862, No. 58, gives 56 lbs. His experiments made in 1864 were as follows:

No.	Size of bar.	Weight.	Value of P.
2	3′ × 1″ × 1″	53	880
3	2′ × 1″ × 1″	54	868

Our specimens give an average of 58 lbs. This may be the wood experimented on by Skinner, No. 53 (see also under *Dalbergia lanceolaria*, p. 128) Weight 62 lbs., P = 1003. He calls it "Moulmein lancewood" and *Moukshow*. The wood is durable and is used for the teeth of harrows and for furniture.

		lbs.
B 331.	Burma (1866)	63
B 2534.	" (1862)	50
B 2692.	Tavoy (Wallich, 1828)	61
B 2699.	" " "	64
B 2702.	" " "	55

ORDER L. PASSIFLOREÆ.

Only one species. *Carica Papaya*, Linn.; Roxb. Fl. Ind. iii. 824; Brandis 244; Kurz i. 533; Gamble 43. The Papaw Tree. Vern. *Papaya*, Hind,; *Perinji* Kan.; *Thimbawthee*, Burm., is a small, soft-wooded, fast-growing tree which was introduced from South America, and is now cultivated all over India for its fruit. The tree has the property of rendering meat tender by its being soaked it in its juice or by suspending the joint under it. The Passion Flowers, *Passiflora*, herbaceous or perennial climbers, belong to this family.

ORDER LI. DATISCEÆ.

Two Genera. *Datisca cannabina*, Linn.; Hook. Fl. Ind. ii. 656. Vern. *Akalbir, bhang jalá*, Hind., is a tall, erect herb resembling hemp and found in the Punjab Himalaya. It gives a red or yellow dye.

1. TETRAMELES, R. Br.

1. T. nudiflora, R. Br.; Hook. Fl. Ind. ii. 657; Beddome t. 212; Brandis 245; Kurz i. 535; Gamble 43. Vern. *Mainakat,* Nep.; *Payomko,* Lepcha; *Bolong,* Gáro; *Sandugaza,* Beng.; *Tseikpoban,* Magh; *Thitpouk,* Burm.; *Bolur,* Kan.

A very large deciduous tree, with cylindrical, often much-buttressed stem. Bark grey-brown, brinkled. Wood white, very light, soft. Annual rings marked by a belt of closer pores. Wood cells large. Pores large, often in short, zigzag, transverse lines. Medullary rays fine to moderately broad, clearly marked, the distance between the rays equal to the diameter of the pores.

Sikkim, Gáro Hills, Chittagong, Western Gháts, Burma and the Andamans. Growth very fast. The wood may be found useful for tea-boxes.

E 3288. Rinkheong Reserve, Chittagong.

ORDER LII. CACTEÆ.

Contains only the Prickly Pear, *Opuntia Dillenii,* Haw.; Hook. Fl. Ind. ii. 657; Brandis 245 (*Cactus indicus,* Roxb. Fl. Ind. ii. 475.) Vern. *Nágphana, nágphansi,* Hind.; *Pápásh kalli,* Kan.; *Chaffal send,* Dekkan. An erect, fleshy, thorny shrub common all over the arid and dry zones of India and often planted as a hedge. The stems have been used in time of scarcity as fodder. It was originally brought from America.

ORDER LIII. ARALIACEÆ.

Contains 16 Genera of usually small, soft-wooded trees or shrubs, erect or climbing. They are divided into four Tribes, *viz.,*—

Tribe	I.—Araliеæ	*Aralia* and *Pentapanax.*
,,	II.—Panaceæ	*Acanthopanax, Helwingia, Polyscias, Heptapleurum, Trevesia, Brassaia* and *Dendropanax.*
,,	III.—Hedereæ	*Arthrophyllum, Heteropanax, Brassaiopsis, Macropanax, Hedera* and *Gamblea.*
,,	IV.—Plerandreæ	*Tupidanthus.*

Aralia contains 6 shrubs or small trees, the chief of which are *A. foliolosa,* Seem., and *A. armata,* Seem. Vern. *Somri,* Nep.; *Kajyang,* Lepcha, small trees of the hills of the N.E. Himalaya with large 2-3 pinnate leaves, prickly stems and the general aspect of tree ferns. *A. cachemirica,* Dcne.; Brandis 248, is a shrub of the higher elevations of the Himalaya from Kashmir to Sikkim. *Pentapanax* contains 4 species of usually climbing epiphytic shrubs: *P. Leschenaultii,* Seem., *P. subcordatum,* Seem., and *P. racemosum,* Seem., are large climbers of the Sikkim Hills. *Acanthopanax aculeatum,* Seem., is a shrub of the Khasia Hills. *Polyscias acuminata,* Wight; Beddome t. 213, is a tree of the hills of South India above 4,000 feet elevation. *Trevesia palmata,* Vis.; Hook. Fl. Ind. ii. 732; Kurz. i. 539; Gamble 44. (*Gastonia palmata,* Roxb. Fl. Ind. ii. 407.) Vern. *Kajpati,* Nep.; *Suntong,* Lepcha; *Baw,* Burm., is an evergreen palm-like tree with large palmate leaves and big fruit, found in the Eastern Himalaya, Eastern Bengal and Burma. *Brassaia capitata,* C. B. Clarke; Hook. Fl. Ind. ii. 732, is a tree of the Nilgiri Hills. *Arthrophyllum diversifolium,* Bl.; Hook. Fl. Ind. ii. 733. (*A. javanicum,* Bl.; Kurz i. 540), is an evergreen palm-like tree of the Andamans. *Heteropanax fragrans,*

Seem.; Hook. Fl. Ind. ii, 731; Brandis 249; Kurz 541; Gamble 44. Vern. *Lal totilla*, Nep.; *Siriokhtem*, Lepcha; *Kesseru*, Assam; *Hona*, Cachar; *Tachunsa*, Burm., is a small tree of the sub-Himalayan tract from Kumaun to Assam, Eastern Bengal, Chittagong and Burma. It is important as being a tree upon whose leaves, as well as on those of the Castor Oil plant, the "Eri" silkworm of Assam (*Attacus Ricini*) is fed. *Tupidanthus calyptratus*, H. f. and Th., is an evergreen scandent tree of the eastern slopes of the Arracan Yoma.

The Chinese rice-paper is the pith of *Aralia papyrifera*, Hk., a tree of Formosa.

Wood white, generally soft. Pores small, often arranged in concentric bands. Medullary rays distant, broad or moderately broad, generally several lines of pores between two rays.

1. HELWINGIA, Willd.

1. H. himalaica, Hook. f. and Th.; Hook. Fl. Ind. ii. 726; Gamble 44. Vern. *Lubbor*, Lepcha.

A large shrub. Wood white, moderately hard, pith large. Pores very small, arranged in groups or short concentric lines. Medullary rays short, fine to moderately broad.

Eastern Himalaya, above 7,000 feet, Khasia Hills.

A curious shrub with simple leaves and flowers in umbels from the centre of the leaves, like those of *Ruscus*.

E 3342. Darjeeling, 7,000 feet.

2. HEPTAPLEURUM, Gaertn.

Contains about 10 trees or climbers, among which 6 species occur in South India, 2 in Burma and 4 in the Sikkim Himalaya. *H. impressum*, C. B. Clarke; Hook. Fl. Ind. ii. 728. (*H. tomentosum*, Ham.; Gamble 44). Vern. *Baloo chinia*, Nep.; *Suntong*, Lepcha, is a handsome tree of the North-East Himalaya, from Kumaun to Bhutan, common in the forests from 6,000 to 10,000 feet, and recognised by its woolly leaves. It has a white, soft wood. *H. glaucum*, C. B. Clarke; Hook. Fl. Ind. ii. 728; Gamble 44. Vern. *Chinia*, Nep.; *Hloprongzam*, Lepcha, is a tree of North-East Himalaya and the Khasia Hills, in which latter locality, as well as in Burma, is also found *H. hypoleucum*, Kurz i. 539, a small branched tree, and *H. Khasianum*, C. B. Clarke. *H. racemosum*, Beddome t. 214, is a large tree of the Western Ghâts and Ceylon. *H. rostratum*, Beddome cxxii., and *H. Wallichianum*, C. B. Clarke, are trees of the Western Ghâts. *H. venulosum*, Seem.; Brandis 249; Kurz i. 538; Gamble 44 (*Aralia digitata*, Roxb. Fl. Ind. ii. 107) Vern. *Dain*, Hind.; *Singhata*, Nep., is a climbing shrub or small tree of most parts of India.

1. H. elatum, C. B. Clarke; Hook. Fl. Ind. ii. 728; Gamble 44. Vern. *Chinia*, Nep.; *Prongzam*, Lepcha.

A tree. Bark ¼ in thick, greyish brown. Wood white, soft. Structure similar to that of *Macropanax undulatum*.

Himalaya, from Kumaun to Bhutan, between 5,000 and 7,000 feet.

E 3326. Rangirúm, Darjeeling, 6,000 feet.

3. BRASSAIOPSIS, Dcne. and Planch.

Contains several small palm-like trees of the Eastern Himalaya, Eastern Bengal and Burma. *B. palmata*, Kurz i. 537, is found in the forests of Chittagong and the Andamans, and *B. Hainla*, Seem.; Hook. Fl. Ind. ii. 735; Gamble 44. Vern. *Tilhetter*, Nep.; *Suntong*, Lepcha, is a common small tree in the forests of the outer Sikkim Himalaya.

1. B. mitis, C. B. Clarke; Hook. Fl. Ind. ii. 736. *B.* sp.; Gamble 44. Vern. *Moqchini*, Nep.; *Suntong*, Lepcha.

A small tree with thin grey bark, and soft, white, spongy wood. Pores small, in groups and undulating lines. Medullary rays short, broad and very fine, marked on a radial section as shining plates.

Sikkim Himalaya, above 5,000 feet, common at Darjeeling.
Growth moderately fast, 5 rings per inch of radius. Weight, 24 lbs. per cubic feet.

		lbs.
E 2382.	Rangbúl Forest, Darjeeling, 7,000 feet	24

4. MACROPANAX, Miq.

Besides the species described, *M. oreophilum*, Miq.; Kurz i. 541, is an evergreen tree of the forests of the Martaban Hills above 5,000 feet.

1. M. undulatum, Seem.; Gamble 45. Vern. *Chinia*, Nep.; *Prongzam*, Lepcha.

A moderate-sized evergreen tree; wood soft, yellowish white, even-grained. Pores small, numerous. Medullary rays broad, often with a few fine rays intervening, prominent on a radial section as shining plates giving the wood an elegant reticulate appearance. The distance between the rays is many times larger than the diameter of the pores, there being many lines of pores between each pair of rays.

Eastern Himalaya, up to 5,000 feet.
Weight, 30 lbs. per cubic foot.

		lbs.
E 688.	Chuttockpur Forest, Darjeeling, 6,000 feet	30

5. HEDERA, Linn.

1. H. Helix, Linn.; Brandis 248; Gamble 45. The Ivy. Vern. *Halbambar, arbambal*, Jhelum; *Karmora, mandia*, Kashmir; *Kurol*, Chenab; *Kuri, karúr*, Ravi; *Brúmbrúm, dakári*, Beas; *Karbaru, kaniúri, kadeoli*, Sutlej; *Bánda*, Kumaun; *Dudela*, Nep.

A large woody climber. Wood white, soft, porous. Annual rings marked by a broad belt of pores and by less numerous pores in the autumn wood. Pores small, very numerous. Medullary rays short, moderately broad.

Himalaya from the Indus to Bhutan, between 3,000 and 9,000 feet; Khasia Hills.
Growth slow, 22 rings per inch of radius. Weight, our specimen gives 34 lbs.; Mathieu Fl. For. p. 174, gives 27 to 44 lbs.

		lbs.
H 69.	Mashobra, Simla, 7,000 feet	...
H 3010.	Kotgarh, Simla, 7,500 feet	34

ORDER LIV. CORNACEÆ.

Contains 7 Genera of Indian trees or shrubs. They are generally dispersed over India, but are chiefly found in the Himalayas. They may be divided into two sections—

Section I.—With hermaphrodite flowers . *Alangium, Marlea, Cornus* and *Mastixia*.
" II.—With diœcious flowers . . *Aucuba, Nyssa* and *Torricellia*.

Mastixia arborea, Wight; Beddome t. 216, is a tree of the forests of the Western Ghâts, between 2,000 and 7,000 feet. *Torricellia tiliæfolia*, DC.; Gamble 45, is a small tree of the Eastern Himalaya between 6,000 and 10,000 feet. *Nyssa sessiliflora*, Hook. f. and Th., is found in the Eastern Himalaya and Khasia Hills.

Wood close-grained, apt to warp. Pores generally small or very small. Medullary rays fine and numerous.

1. ALANGIUM, Lam.

Contains two species, one of which is here described. *A. Sundanum*, Miq. Vern. *Agnara*, And., is an evergreen climbing shrub of the tropical forests of the Andamans.

1. A. Lamarckii, Thwaites; Beddome t. 215; Brandis 250. *A. hexapetalum*, Roxb. Fl. Ind. ii. 502. *A. decapetalum*, Lam.; Kurz i. 543. Vern. *Akola, thaila*, Hind.; *Akar-kanta, bagh ankurá*, Beng.; *Alangi*, Tam.; *Urgu, udagu*, Tel.; *Ankola*, Kan.; *Uru*, Gondi.

A deciduous shrub or small tree. Bark ⅓ inch thick, grey. Sapwood light yellow; heartwood brown, hard, close and even-grained. Pores small, scanty, in radial lines between the fine, closely packed medullary rays, which often bend outwards; the transverse diameter of the pores being slightly larger than the distance between the rays.

Sub-Himalayan tract from the Ganges eastwards, Oudh, Bengal, Central and South India.

Growth moderately slow, 5 rings per inch of radius. Weight, according to Skinner, No. 13, 49 lbs. per cubic foot; our specimens give 49-56 lbs. Skinner gives P = 875. The wood is used for pestles, for oil-mills, wooden cattle-bells, and other purposes, and is valuable for fuel. It coppices well. The fruit is eaten, and the bark used in native medicine.

		lbs.
C 3116.	Chanda, Central Provinces	56
D 1082.	North Arcot, Madras	49

2. MARLEA, Roxb.

Besides the species here described, *M. tomentosa*, Endl.; Kurz i. 545. Vern. *Gorapongse*, Burm., is a large evergreen tree of the tropical forests of Martaban, said by Kurz to have a pale brown, close-grained wood with a silvery lustre.

1. M. begoniæfolia, Roxb. Fl. Ind. ii. 261; Brandis 251; Kurz i. 544; Gamble 45. Vern. *Garkum, budhal, túmbri*, North-Western Provinces; *Bodara*, Beas; *Siálu*, Chenab; *Prot*, Kashmir; *Tilpattra, chitpattra, kurkui*, Jhelum; *Tumri*, Kumaun; *Timil*, Nep.; *Palet*, Lepcha; *Tapuya*, Burm.; *Marlea, marliza*, Sylhet.

A small tree, with smooth, thin, grey bark. Wood white, soft, even-grained. Annual rings marked by a belt of numerous pores. Pores moderate-sized and large, small in the outer portion of each ring. Medullary rays short, wavy, fine and moderately broad, prominent on a radial section.

Outer Himalaya from the Indus to Bhutan, ascending in the North-West to 6,000 feet, and in Sikkim to 9,000 feet; Khasia Hills, Eastern Bengal, Chittagong and Martaban.

Growth moderately fast, 5 rings per inch of radius. Weight, 42 lbs. per cubic foot.

The wood is used for native houses in Sylhet. The leaves are sometimes given as fodder to cattle.

		lbs.
H 2831.	The Glen, Simla, 6,000 feet	42

3. CORNUS, Linn.

Besides the three species here described, *C. sanguinea*, Linn.; Brandis 253, the Dogwood, was found by Dr. Stewart in the Punjab Himalaya at 7,000 feet.

Numerous small pores and numerous fine medullary rays, often of different width.

1. C. macrophylla, Wall.; Brandis 252; Gamble 45. Vern. *Kasír, kachír, haleo, allian, haddú, harru, nang, kandara, kaksh, kachúr, kochan, kágsha, rúchia,* Hind.; *Patmoro,* Nep.

A small tree, with rough, brown bark, splitting into small squares. Wood pinkish white, hard, close-grained, warps badly and has an unpleasant scent. Annual rings marked by a narrow line without pores, on the outer edge of each ring. Pores small, numerous. Medullary rays short, moderately broad, with fewer fine rays, giving the wood on a radial section a beautifully mottled appearance.

Himalaya from the Indus to Bhutan, between 3,000 and 8,000 feet.

Growth moderate, 8 to 9 rings per inch of radius (Brandis); our specimens had 15 rings. Weight, 44 lbs. per cubic foot. The wood gives good gunpowder charcoal. The fruit is eaten and the leaves given as fodder to goats.

		lbs.
H 84.	The Glen, Simla, 6,000 feet	45
H 924.	Hazara, 6,000 feet	43

2. C. oblonga, Wall.; Brandis 253; Kurz i. 545. Vern. *Kagshi,* Sutlej; *Dab,* Kunawar; *Kasmol, bakár, ban-bakúr, halá,* Hind.

A small tree, with reddish brown, rough bark. Wood pinkish white, hard, even-grained, warps and has an unpleasant scent. Annual rings marked by a belt without pores at the outer edge of each ring. Pores small, numerous. Medullary rays fine, very numerous, with a few slightly broader ones.

Outer Himalaya from the Indus to Bhutan, between 3,000 and 6,000 feet; Martaban Hills in Burma, between 4,000 and 7,000 feet (Kurz).

Growth moderate, 10 rings per inch of radius. Weight, 48 lbs. per cubic foot.

		lbs.
H 150.	Sainj, Giri Valley, 4,000 feet	46
H 3094.	Tarwa Forest, Julung, Simla, 4,000 feet	50

3. C. capitata, Wall.; Brandis 253; Gamble 45. *Benthamia fragifera,* Lindley. Vern. *Thammal, tharbal, tharwar, thesi, bamaur, bamora,* Hind.; *Tumbúk,* Lepcha.

A small deciduous tree, with thin, greyish brown bark. Wood whitish, with reddish brown heartwood, warps in seasoning, very hard, close-grained. Pores very small. Medullary rays numerous, moderate-sized and fine.

Himalaya from the Beas to Bhutan, between 3,500 and 8,000 feet; Khasia Hills.

Growth slow, 16 rings per inch of radius. Weight, 45 lbs. per cubic foot. The wood is used only for firewood. This is probably the *Cornus, sp.,* of whose wood 5 maunds were sent to the Ishapore Gunpowder Agency in 1865 (Bengal Forest Report, 1865-66, page 2), of the result of which experiment we have no record. The fruit is red, strawberry-like, and is eaten and made into preserves. The tree is very handsome when in flower with its large cream-coloured involucre.

		lbs.
H 78.	Mashobra, Simla, 7,000 feet	...
H 94.	Simla, 6,000 feet	45

4. AUCUBA, Thunb.

Contains one large shrub or small tree of the Eastern Himalaya. *A. japonica*, Thunb. is a well-known shrub of English gardens, recognised by its shining leaves, blotched with yellow.

1. A. himalaica, Hook. f. and Th.; Brandis 254; Gamble 45. Vern. *Phul amphi*, Nep.; *Singna, tapathyer*, Lepcha.

A small evergreen tree, with thin, smooth, dark-grey bark. Wood black when fresh cut, becoming lighter-coloured on exposure, hard and close-grained. Pores extremely small. Medullary rays of two classes, numerous fine rays between fewer broad or very broad ones, visible on a radial section as irregular plates and bands.

Sikkim Himalaya between 5,000 and 9,000 feet.

Growth slow, 20 rings per inch of radius (Gamble); one specimen, E 3327, shews 10 rings. Weight, 55 lbs. per cubic foot.

		lbs.
E 2383.	Rangbúl Forest, Darjeeling, 7,000 feet	55
E 3327.	Rangirúm „ „ 6,000 „	...

ORDER LV. CAPRIFOLIACEÆ.

Contains 6 genera belonging to the two following tribes :—

Tribe I.—Sambuceæ	*Sambucus* and *Viburnum*.
„ II.—Lonicereæ	*Abelia, Lonicera, Leycesteria* and *Pentapyxis*.

Wood close-grained. Pores very small or extremely small, uniformly distributed. Medullary rays fine to extremely fine, numerous.

1. SAMBUCUS, Linn.

Contains 3 Indian species. *S. Ebulus*, Linn.; Brandis 260. The Dwarf Elder. Vern. *Richh kas, mushkiára, ganhúla*, Jhelum; *Gandal, gwandish, siske tásar*, Chenab, is a herbaceous plant from a perennial root stock, found in the valleys of the Jhelum and Upper Chenab. *S. adnata*, Wall.; Brandis 576; Gamble 46. Vern. *Chiriya-baug*, Nep., is an undershrub of Nepal and Sikkim found from 6,000 to 10,000 feet. Kurz gives *S. Thunbergiana*, Bl., as an undershrub of Ava and the Kakhyen Hills.

1. S. javanica, Reinw.; Gamble 46. Vern. *Galeni*, Nep.

A small tree. Bark light brown, rather corky. Wood white, soft. Pores small, in groups. Medullary rays distant, fine to broad. Pith large, about ½ inch in diameter.

Eastern Himalaya from 4,000 to 8,000 feet, Khasia Hills. Chiefly found in second-growth forest.

E 3133. Mangwa Forest, Darjeeling, 5,000 feet.

2. VIBURNUM, Linn.

Contains about 15 species, mostly Himalayan. Three species occur in the Nilgiris, seven in the North-West Himalaya, and about twelve in the Eastern Himalaya and Khasia Hills.

V. corylifolium, Hook. f. and Th.; Gamble 46, is a small tree of Sikkim and the Khasia Hills. *V. nervosum*, Don; Brandis 259. Vern. *Ambre, amrola, ari*, Ravi; *Ris, dáb*, Beas; *Thilkain, thalein*, Sutlej, is a shrub of the Himalaya above 7,000 feet, from Kumaun to Sikkim. *V. cordifolium*, Wall. and *V. punctatum*, Ham.; Beddome t. 217; Brandis 260; Gamble 46, are shrubs of the Outer Himalaya from Kumaun to Bhutan, the latter occurring also in the Western Ghâts. *V. involucratum*, Wall.; Gamble 46, Vern. *Gorakuri*, Nep., is a shrub of the Himalaya, chiefly eastern. *V. fœtidum*, Wall., *V. odoratissimum*, Ker, and *V. Simonsii*, Hook. f. and Th., are all from the Khasia Hills. *V. hebanthum*, W. and A.; Beddome cxxiv., is a small tree of the Western Ghâts and Ceylon.

The Guelder Rose, cultivated in gardens in Europe, is *V. Opulus*, Linn., and the Laurustinus is *V. Tinus*, Linn., indigenous in the Mediterranean region.

Bark thin. Wood hard and close-grained, characterised by very numerous, very fine medullary rays and very small pores. Annual rings indistinctly marked, generally by a narrow line of firmer wood. The wood of *V. lutescens* is softer, the pores larger, and the annual rings not visible.

All species here described, with the exception of *V. erubescens* and *V. lutescens*, are marked by distinct and numerous medullary patches, visible on the horizontal and vertical sections. The European species, both those with deciduous leaves, *V. Opulus* and *V. Lantana*, and the evergreen *V. Tinus* have no medullary patches.

1. V. cotinifolium, Don; Brandis 258. Vern. *Mar ghwalawa*, Trans-Indus; *Rich úklu, bankúnch*, Jhelum; *Richabi, kilmich, gúch*, Kashmir; *Bathor, pápat kalam, khímor, rájal, tumma*, Chenab; *Kátonda*, Ravi; *Jawa, khatip, túslús, sússú*, Sutlej; *Gwia, guya*, Kumaun.

A large deciduous shrub, with greyish brown bark, $\frac{1}{6}$ inch thick. Wood white, hard to very hard, close-grained. Pores very small, uniformly distributed. Medullary rays fine and very fine, extremely numerous. On a horizontal section are seen linear, concentric, but short and interrupted patches of soft tissue, which shew on a vertical section as undulating lines of darker colour and of varying length.

Suliman Range, North-West Himalaya, between 4,000 and 11,000 feet.
The ripe fruit is eaten.

H 52. }
H 2869. } Nagkanda, Simla, 8,000 feet.
H 76. Mashobra, „ 7,000 „

2. V. Mullaha, Ham.; Brandis 258, 576. *V. stellulatum*, Wall. Vern. *Jal bágú*, Jhelum; *Amliacha, phulsel*, Kashmir; *Lal titmaliya*, Kumaun; *Eri, ira*, Simla.

A shrub. Bark dark grey, reticulate. Wood white, moderately hard; structure the same as that of *V. cotinifolium*.

North-West Himalaya from 6,000 to 10,000 feet. Fruit eaten.

H 2834. The Glen, Simla, 6,000 feet.
H 2866. Nagkanda, „ 8,000 „

3. V. coriaceum, Bl.; Brandis 259; Gamble 46. Vern. *Kala titmaliya*, Kumaun; *Bara gorakuri*, Nep.

A large shrub or small tree. Bark grey brown, rather corky. Wood similar to that of *V. cotinifolium;* but the pores larger and the medullary rays slightly broader.

Himalaya from the Sutlej to Bhutan at 4,000 to 8,000 feet, Khasia Hills, Nilgiris and Ceylon.

Weight, 50 lbs. per cubic foot. The Nepalese are said to extract from the seeds an oil which they use for food and for burning.

		lbs.
H 2835.	The Glen, Simla, 6,000 feet	50

4. V. erubescens, Wall.; Beddome cxxiv.; Brandis 258; Gamble 46. Vern. *Ganné,* Nep.; *Kancha,* Lepcha; *Damshing,* Bhutia.

A small tree, with thin grey bark. Wood very hard, reddish, close and even-grained. Pores very small. Medullary rays undulating, fine and very fine, very numerous. No medullary patches.

Himalaya from Kumaun to Bhutan, between 5,000 and 11,000 feet; Nilgiris and Ceylon.

Weight, 59 lbs. per cubic foot. The wood might do as a substitute for boxwood and for carving. Used for house-posts in Sikkim. It grows well and quickly from cuttings.

		lbs.
E 2384.	Rangbúl, Darjeeling, 7,000 feet	59

5. V. lutescens, Bl.; Kurz ii. 2; Gamble 46.

A large shrub. Bark greyish brown, thin. Wood reddish, soft. Pores moderate-sized, very numerous. Medullary rays fine, very numerous. Annual rings not visible.

Terai and Lower Hills of Sikkim, Assam, Khasia Hills, in damp evergreen forests.

E 3273. Múraghát Reserve, W. Dúars.

6. V. fœtens, Decaisne; Brandis 259. Vern. *Gúch, úklu, kúnch,* Jhelum; *Kilmich, gúch, kwillim, kulára, jamára,* Kashmir; *Tilhanj, púlmu, tiláts, túin,* Chenab; *Talhang, tandei, túndhe, tunáni zenáni,* Ravi; *Talhang, thelain, tselain, thilkain,* Sutlej; *Gúya,* Kumaun.

A large shrub with grey bark. Wood white, hard to very hard, close-grained. Wood similar in appearance and structure to that of *V. cotinifolium.*

North-West Himalaya, from 5,000 to 11,000 feet.

Weight, 53 lbs. per cubic foot. Fruit eaten.

			lbs.
H	53.	Nagkanda, Simla, 8,000 feet	53
H	2886.	" " "	...
H	3015.	Matiyána " "	...
E	975.	Chumbi Valley, Tibet, 10,000 feet	...

3. ABELIA, Brown.

1. A. triflora, R. Brown; Brandis 257. Vern. *Adei, paktawar,* Trans-Indus; *Cheta búta,* Jhelum; *Ban bakharu, salanker,* Chenab; *Dalúng, kút sái,* Ravi; *Zbang, matzbang, peni,* Sutlej; *Munri, gogatti, kumki,* Kumaun.

A large shrub. Bark grey, with longitudinal fissures. Wood greyish or bluish white, hard, close and even-grained. Pores extremely small, except those at the edge of each annual ring, which are small and continuous. Medullary rays very numerous, moderately broad and very fine, the former short.

Safedkoh and Suliman Range, North-West Himalaya, between 4,000 and 10,000 feet.

Has very pretty flowers, but the wood is not used. Weight, 65 lbs. per cubic foot.

		lbs.
H 2937.	Naldehra, Simla, 7,500 feet	65

4. LONICERA, Linn.

Contains 26 species, 21 of which are erect and 5 climbing. They are mostly small shrubs of the Himalaya, 2 only being found in the Nilgiris and Western Gháts. The Himalayan species are mostly from high altitudes, some occurring only in Tibet. *L. spinosa*, Jacquemont; Brandis 255, is a small rigid shrub of the inner arid Himalaya. *L. hypoleuca*, Decaisne, Brandis 256. Vern. *Kharmo, kodi*, Chenab; *Zhiko, rapesho*, Sutlej, is a small shrub of the Inner Himalaya. *L. Myrtillus*, Hook. f. and Th., is a shrub of the Inner Himalaya from the Indus to Sikkim, from 9,000 to 12,000 feet. *L. ligustrina*, Wall.; Beddome cxxiv., is a shrub, common on the Nilgiris, where it is used as a hedge-plant: it is also found in the Himalaya. Of the climbing species, *L. japonica*, Thunb.; Gamble 46. Vern. *Duari lara*, Nep.; and *L. glabrata*, Wall.; Gamble 45. Vern. *Betlara*, Nep. (No. E 2863, Tukdah, Darjeeling, with a soft brown wood, large pores and the structure of a climber) come from the Eastern Himalaya; while *L. Leschenaultii*, Wall., grows in the Malabar hills from 5,000 to 7,000 feet. The European Honeysuckle is *L. Periclymenum*, Linn.

1. L. quinquelocularis, Hardwicke; Roxb. Fl. Ind. i. 537; Brandis 255. Vern. *Jarlangei, adei*, Trans-Indus; *Phút*, Jhelam; *Tila bateri, pákhur*, Kashmir; *Bakhru*, Chenab; *Khúm, sái*, Ravi; *Dendra*, Beas; *Kliunti, kraunti, takla, zbang, razbam, bhajra, bhijaul, bijgai*, Sutlej; *Bet kukri, bhat kukra, cheraya, kurmali*, Kumaun.

A large deciduous shrub. Bark thin, grey, with longitudinal fissures, peeling off in long shreds. Wood white, with a brown centre, very hard and close-grained. Annual rings marked by a narrow continuous belt of pores; in the remainder of the annual ring the pores are extremely small. Medullary rays short, fine, numerous.

Suliman Range, North-West Himalaya, between 2,500 and 9,000 feet.

Used only for firewood. Cattle are fed on the leaves. Weight, 52 lbs. per cubic foot.

		lbs.
H 81.	Mashobra, Simla, 7,000 feet	...
H 2874.	Nagkanda, „ 8,000 feet	52
H 3180.	Dungagalli, Hazara, 7,000 feet	...

2. L. orientalis, Lamarck; Brandis 256.

A shrub. Bark peeling off in thin flakes. Wood white, with a darker centre, moderately hard. Structure the same as that of *L. quinquelocularis*.

North-West Himalaya, from Kashmir to Kumaun, 8,000 to 10,000 feet.

H 2909. Nagkanda, Simla, 8,000 feet.
H 3017. Hattu, Simla, 10,000 feet.

3. L. angustifolia, Wall.; Brandis 255. Vern. *Geang,* Jaunsar; *Pílru, philku,* Sutlej.

A small shrub, with smooth, grey bark, exfoliating in broad flakes. Wood white, very close-grained. Structure similar to that of *L. quinquelocularis,* but pores much smaller.

Himalaya from the Indus to Sikkim, 6,000 to 10,000 feet. Fruits eaten. Weight, 60 lbs. per cubic foot.

		lbs.
H 2843.	Mahasu, Simla, 8,500 feet	60
H 2875.	Nagkanda, Simla, 8,000 feet	...

4. L. alpigena, Linn.; Brandis 256.

A shrub. Bark grey brown, peeling off in irregular papery flakes. Wood moderately hard, structure similar to that of *L. quinquelocularis.*

North-West Himalaya from Kashmir to Kumaun, 8,000 to 10,000 feet.

H 2912. Nagkanda, Simla, 8,000 feet.
H 3016. Hattu, Simla, 10,000 feet.

5. LEYCESTERIA, Wall.

1. L. formosa, Wall.; Brandis 256; Gamble 46. Vern. *Malkarr, saunjla, nalkaru, karnaliya,* Kumaun; *Tunguk,* Lepcha.

An erect shrub with hollow, generally herbaceous, stems. Bark grey, shining. Wood resembling in structure that of *Lonicera,* but with slightly broader medullary rays.

Throughout the Himalaya from the Sutlej to Bhutan, from 5,000 to 10,000 feet.
H 2849. Mahasu, Simla, 8,000 feet.

6. PENTAPYXIS, Hook. f.

Contains 2 species. P. *glaucophylla,* Hook. f., is a shrub of the Sikkim Himalaya, from 5,000 to 9,000 feet.

1. P. stipulata, Hook. f; Gamble 45. *Lonicera stipulata,* Hook. f. and Th. in Journ. Linn. Soc. ii. 165. Vern. *Berikuru,* Nep.

A large shrub, with greyish brown bark. Wood white, soft. Pores extremely small. Medullary rays fine and very fine. No annual rings.

Sikkim Himalaya, from 6,000 to 10,000 feet, very common on hill-sides cleared of forest, around Darjeeling.

E 2866. Rangbúl, Darjeeling, 7,000 feet.

ORDER LVI. RUBIACEÆ.

A large and very important forest Order containing many trees which are valuable for their timber, besides plants which have valuable properties, chiefly as medicines and dyes. It contains 44 Genera, divided into 13 Tribes, *viz.,*—

Tribe I.—Naucleeæ	*Sarcocephalus, Anthocephalus, Cephalanthus, Adina, Stephegyne, Nauclea* and *Uncaria.*

Tribe	II.—Cinchoneæ	*Cinchona, Hymenopogon, Hymenodictyon* and *Luculia.*
„	III.—Rondeletieæ	*Wendlandia.*
„	IV.—Hedyotideæ	*Hedyotis.*
„	V.—Mussændeæ	*Mussænda, Adenosacme, Myrioneuron* and *Urophyllum.*
„	VI.—Gardenieæ	*Byrsophyllum, Webera, Randia, Gardenia, Hypobathrum, Petunga, Morindopsis, Hyptianthera* and *Diplospora.*
„	VII.—Retiniphylleæ	*Scyphiphora.*
„	VIII.—Guettardeæ	*Guettarda* and *Timonius.*
„	IX.—Vanguerieæ	*Plectronia* and *Vangueria.*
„	X.—Ixoreæ	*Ixora, Pavetta* and *Coffea.*
„	XI.—Morindeæ	*Morinda* and *Gynochthodes.*
„	XII.—Psychotrieæ	*Psychotria, Chasalia, Lasianthus, Saprosma* and *Hydnophytum.*
„	XIII.—Pæderieæ	*Pæderia, Hamiltonia* and *Leptodermis.*

Sarcocephalus cordatus, Miq.; Beddome t. 318; Kurz ii. 63 (*Nauclea cordata*, Roxb. Fl. Ind. i. 508). Vern. *Maoolet-tan-shay*, Burm.; *Bakmi*, Cingh., is a deciduous tree of Burma and Ceylon, with a light, soft, perishable wood, weighing 23 to 34 lbs. per cubic foot. Beddome says it is used for sandals, common furniture, doors and other purposes. *Cephalanthus naucleoides*, DC.; Kurz ii. 68, is a small tree of Upper Burma. *Uncaria* contains several scandent shrubs, *U. pilosa*, Roxb. Fl. Ind. i. 520; Kurz. ii. 70; Gamble 47. Vern. *Baisi kara*, Nep.; *Kahukrik*, Lepcha, is a straggling shrub of Sikkim, Eastern Bengal and Burma, with large hooked sterile peduncles of the shape of a buffalo's horn, and handsome globular flower heads. *U. sessilifructus*, Roxb. Fl. Ind. i. 520; Kurz ii. 71; Gamble 47. Vern. *Pinri*, Lepcha, is a climber of Sikkim, Eastern Bengal, Chittagong and Burma. Kurz gives also *U. ferruginea*, DC., *U. sessilifolia*, Roxb., and *U. lævigata*, Wall., as climbing shrubs of Burma; while *U. Gambier*, Hunter; Roxb. Fl. Ind. i. 517; Beddome cxxix., is a scandent shrub of Ceylon and the Malay Archipelago, whose leaves produce the astringent extract called "Gambier," or "Terra japonica," which is used for chewing with pán leaves and areca nut in the same way as cutch in India, and of which large quantities are prepared and used throughout the Malay Archipelago.

Hymenopogon parasiticus, Wall.; Kurz ii. 73; Gamble 47. Vern. *Kursimla*, Nep., is an epiphytic shrub of the North-East Himalaya and Burma. *Luculia gratissima*, Sweet. Kurz ii. 71; Gamble 47. Vern. *Dowari*, Nep.; *Simbrangrip*, Lepcha, is a large shrub with handsome long-tubed pink flowers, found in the hills of Sikkim and in Upper Burma. Its leaves are used in dyeing. Weight 23 lbs. (Wallich, No. 43).

Hedyotis contains only small climbing shrubs. They are very numerous, and many of the species are used in dyeing.

Mussænda contains about 7 large shrubs remarkable for having one of the lobes of the calyx enlarged into a membranous, usually white leaf. *M. frondosa*, Linn.; Roxb. Fl. Ind. i. 557; Beddome cxxi.; Gamble 48. Vern. *Asari*, Nep.; *Tumberh*, Lepcha; *Maasenda*, Cingh., is a handsome shrub of the North-East Himalaya, Bengal, South India and Burma, with yellow flowers and large white calycine leaf, often cultivated in gardens. *M. macrophylla*, Wall.; Kurz ii. 57; Gamble 48, is a small tree of second growth forest in the Sikkim Himalaya; also found in the Andamans. Kurz mentions 5 other species as occurring in Burma. *Adenosacme longifolia*, Wall.; Kurz ii. 54; Gamble 48. Vern. *Pitamari*, Nep., is a shrub of the North-East Himalaya and Burma, remarkable for its pretty snow-white berries. *Myrioneuron nutans*, R. Br.; Kurz ii. 55, is a shrub of Chittagong. *Urophyllum* contains 3 shrubs or small trees of Martaban and Tenasserim and 2 small trees of Ceylon.

Byrsophyllum tetrandrum, Beddome t. 326, is a small tree of the hills of Travancore. *Hypobathrum racemosum*, Kurz ii. 51 (*Randia racemosa*, Roxb. Fl. Ind. i. 525) Vern. *Peetunga*, Beng., is a shrub of Eastern Bengal and of the swamp forests of Pegu and Arracan. *Petunga Roxburghii*, DC. Vern. *Jhijir*, Beng., is a small tree of the Sundarbans with hard white wood; and *Morindopsis capillaris*, Kurz, a tree of Pegu, Martaban and Tenasserim. *Hyptianthera stricta*, W. and A.; Brandis 274 (*Hypobathrum strictum*, Kurz ii. 50, *Randia stricta*, Roxb. Fl. Ind. i. 526), is an evergreen shrub of Oudh, Northern Bengal, Chittagong and Burma. *Diplospora singularis*, Korth.; Kurz ii. 56 (? No. B 1998, Andamans. Vern. *Thittoo*, with white wood, rough, with numerous prominent medullary rays; weight 36 lbs.), is a tree of Burma and the Andaman Islands.

Scyphiphora hydrophyllacea, Gaertn.; Beddome cxxxiv. 3; Kurz ii. 4, is a small simple-stemmed shrub of the coast forests of the Andamans and Ceylon.

Timonius flavescens (*Polyphragmon flavescens*), Kurz ii. 38 (? No. B. 1987, Andamans. Vern. *Tinlwonbeng*, Burm., with a hard, light-brown wood; weight, 48 lbs.), is a small tree of the tropical forests of the Andamans.

Vangueria contains 3 species. *V. edulis*, Vahl.; Kurz ii. 33. Vern. *Voa vanga*, is a thorny shrub of Madagascar, cultivated in Bengal for its edible fruit. Kyd calls it *Moyen*, and gives weight 43 lbs., P = 430. *V. spinosa*, Roxb. Fl. Ind. i. 526; Kurz ii. 34; Gamble 49. Vern. *Hsay-ma-kyee*, Burm., is a thorny small tree of Bengal and Burma; and *V pubescens*, Kurz ii. 34, a tree of the Eng and dry forests of Burma.

Gynochthodes macrophylla, Kurz, is a scandent shrub of the coasts of South Andaman.

Psychotria and *Lasianthus* contain a large number of small evergreen shrubs of Bengal, Burma and South India. *Chasalia curviflora*, Thw.; Kurz ii. 14; Gamble 49. Vern. *Antabi*, Lepcha, is a small shrub of the hills of Northern Bengal, Burma and Ceylon. *Saprosma* contains 4 shrubs of South India and 2 of Burma. *Hydnophytum formicarum*, Jack; Kurz ii. 8, is a small epiphytic shrub with an enlarged tuber-like trunk found on trees in the swamp forests of the Andamans.

Pæderia contains several shrubs or climbers. *P. lanuginosa*, Wall.; Kurz ii. 76, is a large climber of the forests of Burma; and *P. fœtida*, Wild.; Roxb. Fl. Ind. i. 683; Gamble 49. Vern. *Gundha badhuli*, Beng.; *Gundali*, Hind.; *Padebiri*, Nep.; *Takpædrik*, Lepcha, is a thin climber of Bengal and Burma, with handsome flowers, and fruit which is said to be used in Sikkim by Nepalese and Lepchas to blacken the teeth, and prevent toothache. *Hamiltonia suaveolens*, Roxb. Fl. Ind. i. 554; Beddome cxxxiv. 12; Brandis 278; Gamble 49. Vern. *Muskei, kantalu, fisauni*, Chenab; *Niggi, tulenni phúl, gohinla*, Ravi; *Kanera, pudári*, Beas; *Phillu*, Sutlej; *Padera*, Kumaun; *Bainchampa*, Nep., is a shrub of the North-West Himalaya, Sikkim (rare), Behar, Central and South India, with handsome lilac flowers; the wood is said by Brandis to be used in Chamba to make gunpowder charcoal.

Besides the genera described from India, which include such important ones as *Cinchona*, *Coffea* and *Morinda*, many genera contain plants of economic use. *Cephaëlis Ipecacuanha*, Rich., is the Ipecacuanha plant which has been largely propagated in India, but which has proved very difficult to naturalise or grow in such a way as to make its cultivation pay. "Madder" is given by *Rubia cordifolia*, Linn., the *Manjít* plant, common all over the Himalayas and largely exported; while many other genera are cultivated in gardens for the beauty of their flowers, and among the commonest of these are *Serissa*, *Catesbœa* and *Hamelia*, besides the numerous *Ixoras* and *Gardenias*, some species of which are described herein.

Wood white, yellow, or rarely red, close-grained, generally soft or moderately hard; no heartwood. Pores small or very small; in *Anthocephalus Cadamba* and a few other species, moderate-sized. Medullary rays uniform, equidistant, fine or very fine, very numerous, often closely packed.

The species which were formerly united under the old genus *Nauclea*, genera Nos. 1 to 4, have an exceedingly uniform structure. The wood seasons well, is soft, but close and even-grained. Pores numerous, small to moderate-sized. Medullary rays fine, very numerous.

1. ANTHOCEPHALUS, A. Richard.

1. A. Cadamba, Bth. and Hook f.; Brandis 261; Gamble 46. *Nauclea Cadamba*, Roxb. Fl. Ind. i. 512; Beddome t. 35. *Sarcocephalus*

Cadamba, Kurz ii. 63. Vern. *Kaddam, karam*, Hind., Beng.; *Bol-kadam*, Chittagong; *Pandúr*, Lepcha; *Kodum*, Mechi; *Roghu*, Ass.; *Kadambo*, Uriya; *Vella cadamba*, Tam.; *Kadambe, rudrak-shamba*, Tel.; *Heltega, arsanalega*, Mysore; *Kadam*, Mar.; *Kadda vailu, kadaga, kadwal*, Kan.; *Halamba*, Cingh.; *Maoo, sanyepang*, Magh; *Maoo, maookadoon*, Burm.

A large deciduous tree. Bark grey, with numerous regular, longitudinal fissures. Wood white, with a yellowish tinge (an old specimen from Burma, yellowish grey), soft, even-grained. Pores large, oval, elongated, subdivided, sometimes in short radial lines. Medullary rays fine, numerous, close together, bent outwards where they touch the pores.

Wild in Northern and Eastern Bengal, Pegu and the Western Coast; cultivated in Northern India.

Growth variable, 5 to 15 rings per inch of radius, average moderate, 9 rings per inch. The weight and transverse strength have been determined by the following experiments:—

Experiment by whom made.	Year.	Wood whence procured.	Weight.	Number of experiments.	Size of scantling.	Value of P.
			lbs.		Ft. In. In.	
Puckle, No. 19	1859	Mysore	43	2	2 × 1 × 1	616
Kyd	1831	Assam	36	...	2 × 1 × 1	560
Cunningham	1854	Gwalior	47	5	2 × 1 × 1	618
Brandis, No. 67	1862	Burma	37	...	......	......
Wallich	...	Travancore	38	...	......	......
Smythies	1878	Bengal	40	2	......	......
"	"	Assam	32	1	......	......

Wood used for building; in Assam, Cachar and occasionally in Darjeeling for tea-boxes. Cunningham (1854) says that it is used for beams and rafters on account of its cheapness and lightness, and that it is good for joiner's work, but that it is a brittle wood. The flowers are offered at Hindu shrines and the fruit eaten. It is often cultivated for ornament, and is very much used as an avenue tree in Bengal. Kurz, evidently quoting Brandis' 1862 List, No. 67, says "wood, a deep yellow;" this is not, however, the case with our specimens, and it may be suggested for investigation whether the Burma wood has not a more yellow colour than the Indian.

		lbs.
E 650.	Rakti Forest, Darjeeling Terai	40
E 3153.	Pankabari, Darjeeling (damp)	50
E 3144.	Julpigori, Bengal	40
E 1435.	Assam	32
B 2535.	Burma (1862)	32

2. ADINA, Salisbury.

Contains 3 Indian species. *A. polycephala*, Hook. f. and Bth. (*Nauclea polycephala*, Wall.; Kurz ii. 65), is a small evergreen tree of Chittagong and Tenasserim.

1. A. cordifolia, Hook. f. and Bth.; Brandis 263; Gamble 46. *Nauclea cordifolia*, Roxb. Fl. Ind. i. 514; Beddome t. 33; Kurz ii. 66. Vern. *Haldu, hardu, karam*, Hind.; *Bangka, keli-kadam, petpuria, da-kôm*, Beng.; *Karam*, Nep.; *Tikkoe*, Bahraich and Gonda; *Hardu, paspu, kurmi*, Gondi; *Holonda*, Uriya; *Shangdong*, Gáro; *Roghu*, Ass.; *Manja-kadambe*, Tam.; *Bandaru, dúdagú, paspu kadambe*, Tel.; *Hedde, yettéga, pettega, arsanaléga, yettada, ahnau*, Kan.; *Hedu*, Mar.; *Kolong*, Cingh.; *Thaing*, Magh; *Hnanbeng*, Burm.

A large deciduous tree. Bark soft, ½ inch thick, grey, rough. Wood yellow, moderately hard, even-grained. No heartwood, no annual rings.

Pores small, numerous, uniformly distributed, more numerous and more closely packed than in *Stephegyne parvifolia*. Medullary rays very fine, of uniform width, not prominent, numerous, distinctly visible on a radial section, finer and more uniform in width than those of *S. parvifolia*.

Sub-Himalayan tract from the Jumna eastwards, ascending to 3,000 feet, throughout the moister regions of India, Burma.

The weight and transverse strength have been determined by the following experiments:—

Experiment by whom made.	Year.	Wood whence procured.	Weight.	Number of experiments.	Size of bar.	Value of P.
			lbs.		Ft. In. In.	
Puckle, No. 26	1859	Mysore	36	4	2 × 1 × 1	464
Skinner, No. 99	1862	South India	42	...	......	604
Cunningham	1854	Gwalior	49	2	2 × 1 × 1	586
Brandis	1864	Burma	43	7	3 × 1 × 1	760
Brandis, No. 65	1862	„	42	...	......	...
R. Thompson	1868	Central Provinces	47	...	......	...
C. P. List	1873	„ „	42	...	......	...
Smythies	1878	Different Provinces	45	11	......	...

The wood seasons well, takes a good polish, and is durable, but somewhat liable to warp and crack. It is good for turning, and is extensively employed in construction, for furniture, agricultural implements, opium boxes, writing tablets, gun-stocks, combs and occasionally for dug-out canoes.

		lbs.
O 215.	Garhwal (1868)	43
O 2994.	„ (1874)	46
O 1491.	Kheri, Oudh	48
O 340.	Gorakhpur	41
C 825.	Bairagarh Reserve, Berar	48
C 2988.	Jubbulpore (1863)	43
C 1136.	Ahiri Reserve, Central Provinces	44
C 1245.	Gumsúr, Madras	49
E 2387.	Bamunpokri, Darjeeling Terai	50
B 2538.	Burma (1862)	43
No. 35.	Salem Collection	40

2. A. sessilifolia, Hook. f. and Bth.; Brandis 264. *Nauclea sessilifolia*, Roxb. Fl. Ind. i. 515; Kurz ii. 65. *Nauclea sericea*, Wall. Vern. *Kúm*, Beng.; *Kúmkoi*, Chakma; *Thaing*, Magh; *Teingala*, *thitpayoung*, Burm.

Wood yellowish brown, hard. Pores very numerous, moderate-sized, oval and subdivided, transverse diameter greater than the interval between the closely packed, fine, and uniform medullary rays.

Chittagong and Burma.

Weight, according to Brandis' Burma List of 1862, No. 70, 43 to 56 lbs.; our specimens give 55 lbs. as an average of three. The wood is used in Chittagong for building purposes and firewood. In Chittagong it is perhaps the only gregarious tree, being commonly found on flat places on the banks of rivers.

		lbs.
E 1391.	Chittagong	53
B 2537.	Burma (1862)	56
B 3069.	„ „	56

3. STEPHEGYNE, Korth.

Contains about 4 species of Indian trees. *S. diversifolia*, Hook. f. and Bth. (*Nauclea diversifolia*, Wall., placed by Kurz under *N. parvifolia*). Vern. *Bingah*, Burm., is a tree of Burma (weight, 45 lbs., Brandis' Burma List, 1862, No. 66), and *S. tubulosa*, Hook. f. and Bth.; Beddome cxxviii., is a tree of Ceylon.

1. S. parvifolia, Hook. f. and Bth.; Brandis 262. *Nauclea parvifolia*, Roxb. Fl. Ind i. 513; Beddome t. 34; Kurz ii 66. Vern, *Kaddam, kallam, keim, kangei*, Hind.; *Phaldu*, Kumaun; *Mundi*, Gondi, Baigas; *Kutebi*, Kurku; *Buta-kadambe*, Tam.; *Nir-kadambe, karmi, bataganapu*, Tel.; *Congú, hedu, yetega, kadwar, kadani*, Kan.; *Kadamb, karamb, kalam*, Mar.; *Tamák*, Bhíl; *Helembé*, Cingh.; *Kumra*, Banswara; *Hteinthay*, Burm.

A large deciduous tree. Bark ½ inch thick, light grey, smooth, with shallow depressions left by exfoliating scales. Wood light pinkish brown, moderately hard, generally harder than that of *Adina cordifolia.* No heartwood. Annual rings visible. Pores small, numerous, uniformly distributed. Medullary rays very fine, numerous, not quite uniform in width.

Throughout India and Burma.

Growth moderate, 5 to 15, averaging 9 rings per inch of radius. The weight and transverse strength have been determined by the following experiments:—

Experiment by whom made.	Year.	Wood whence procured.	Weight.	Number of experiments.	Size of bar.	Value of P.
			lbs.		Ft. In. In.	
Cunningham	1854	Gwalior	35	2	2 × 1 × 1	586
Skinner, No. 100	1862	South India	39	...	.. ...	683
Brandis, No. 69	1862	Burma	43	...	......	...
R. Thompson	1868	Central Provinces	47	...	......	...
Smythies	1878	As below	42·7	11	. ...	...
A. Mendis, No. 35	1855	Ceylon	42	...	......	...

The wood is easily worked and polishes well; it is durable, if not exposed to wet. It is used for building, furniture, agricultural implements, combs, cups, spoons and platters, and for turned and carved articles.

			lbs.
P	458.	Ajmere	...
O	269.	Garhwal (1868)	45
O	529.	Dehra Dún	41
O	344.	Gorakhpur	42
O	1481.	Kheri, Oudh	44
C	178.	Mandla, Central Provinces (1870)	42
C	186.	" " "	46
C	1120.	Ahiri Reserve, Central Provinces	44
C	2783.	Melghát, Berar	44
B	561.	Prome	40
B	2539.	Burma (1862)	38
No.	36.	Salem Collection	44
No.	35.	Ceylon Collection	42

W 1225 (42 lbs.; growth moderate, 8 rings per inch of radius), received from North Kanara under the name of *Anthocephalus Cadamba*, is in structure similar to *S. parvifolia*, but has red heartwood, with darker streaks. It is probably *Nauclea elliptica*, Dalzell, Bomb. Fl. 118; Beddome cxxix. Vern. *Ahnau*, Kan.

2. S. *Sp.* Gamble 46. Vern. *Kalé, kalikat*, Nep.

A large tree. Bark brownish white. Heartwood orange yellow, sapwood reddish. Wood moderately hard. Pores large and moderate-sized, very numerous, filled with a gummy substance. Medullary rays fine, very numerous, undulating.

Weight, 44 lbs. per cubic foot. Used for building.

		lbs.
E 2385.	Chenga Forest, Darjeeling	44

4. NAUCLEA, Linn.

Contains 3 or 4 Indian trees. *N. elliptica*, Dalz., a large tree of the Western Coast, has been referred to above. *N. purpurea*, Roxb.; Beddome cxxix., is a tree of the Eastern Ghâts of South India. Kurz gives *N. excelsa*, Bl., as a large evergreen tree of Pegu.

1. N. rotundifolia, Roxb. Fl. Ind. i. 516; Kurz ii. 67. Vern. *Bingah*, Burm.

Wood yellowish brown, moderately hard, close and even-grained. Pores small and moderate-sized. Medullary rays fine, uniform, very closely packed, the transverse diameter of the pores being greater than the interval between two successive rays.

Burma and the Andaman Islands.
Weight, 47 lbs. per cubic foot. Wood not used, but likely to be of value.

		lbs.
B 2536.	Burma (1862)	51
B 2288.	Andamans (1866)	44

B 2233 (47 lbs.), sent from the Andamans in 1866 under the name *Htainbyoo* resembles in structure *N. rotundifolia*, except that it has slightly larger pores.

5. CINCHONA, Linn.

A genus of about 36 species of trees or shrubs found in a narrow belt along the Andes of South America, between 2,300 and 8,000 feet elevation. Several species give the Peruvian bark or Cinchona of commerce, the value of which depends upon the presence of certain alkaloids which are known as "quinine," "cinchonine," "cinchonidine," &c., and which are so valuable as febrifuges.

The Cinchona trees were first brought to India in 1860, chiefly through the labours of Mr. C. R. Markham, C.B., who was sent by the Secretary of State in 1859 to Peru to collect plants and seeds of the different kinds. The plants he brought did not live, but the seeds were sown and the trees planted in the Nilgiri Hills. In 1862 Dr. T. Anderson instituted the plantations at Rangbi in Sikkim with plants and seeds brought by him from Java. There are 4 principal species cultivated in the Indian plantations: *viz.*, *C. succirubra*, *Calisaya*, *officinalis* and *micrantha*.

1. C. succirubra, Pavon; Brandis 265; Gamble 47. Red Bark.

Wood yellow, moderately hard. Pores small, in radial lines. Medullary rays closely packed, fine and very fine.

Cultivated on the Nilgiris and other hills of South India, at the plantations of Rangbi and Poomong in Sikkim, on the hills east of Toungoo in Burma and in parts of the Satpura Range in Central India. This species thrives at a lower elevation than the others, but is comparatively poor in quinine, though rich in cinchonine and cinchonidine. From this species is chiefly derived the "Cinchona Alkaloid," which is now largely manufactured at the Government Plantation of Rangbi.

E 1357.
E 3157. } Rangbi, Darjeeling, 3,700 feet.

2. C. Calisaya, Weddell; Brandis 266; Gamble 47. Yellow Bark.

Wood reddish-grey, moderately hard, even-grained. Pores small, in short radial lines. Medullary rays fine, closely packed.

Cultivated in Sikkim at moderate elevations.

It yields perhaps the most valuable of the Cinchona barks, rich in alkaloids, among which quinine forms ½ to ⅘ths.

E 1358.
E 3158. } Rangbi, Darjeeling, 3,700 feet.

3. C. officinalis, Linn.; Brandis 266; Gamble 47. Loxa or Crown Bark.

Wood yellowish grey, similar in structure to that of *C. Calisaya*.

Cultivated at high elevations on the Nilgiris, in Ceylon and in Sikkim, but not extensively.

Its bark is rich in alkaloids, of which more than one-half is quinine.

E 1356.
E 3159. } Rangbi, Darjeeling, 3,700 feet.

6. HYMENODICTYON, Wall.

Contains about 4 species. *H. flaccidum*, Wall.; Brandis 268; Gamble 47, is a tree of the hills of Eastern Bengal and the outer Himalaya as far west as the Jumna. *H. obovatum*, Wall.; Beddome t. 219; Brandis 268. Vern. *Yella malla kai*, Tam.; *Mallay tanák*, Madura; *Karwai*, Bombay, is a large tree of the Western Ghâts.

1. H. excelsum, Wall.; Beddome cxxx.; Brandis 267. *Cinchona excelsa*, Roxb. Fl. Ind. i. 529. Vern. *Bartu, barthoa*, Pb.; *Bhaulan, bhalena, bhamína, dhauli, kúkúrkat, bhúrkúı, phaldu, bhohár, potúr*, Hind.; *Dondru, dandelo*, Panch Mehals; *Bhoursál*, Mar.; *Sagapu*, Tam.; *Dudiyetta, dudippa, chetippa, burja, bandara*, Tel.; *Bodoka*, Uriya; *Manabina*, Karnúl.

A large deciduous tree. Bark soft, ½ to ¾ inch thick, grey, exfoliating in irregularly shaped, softish scales. Wood brownish grey, soft. Annual rings indistinctly marked. Pores moderate-sized, uniformly distributed, often in short radial lines. Medullary rays fine, very numerous, visible on a radial section. Numerous faint, white, transverse bars joining the medullary rays.

Sub-Himalayan tract from the Punjab to Oudh, ascending to 5,500 feet; Central and South India.

Growth moderate, 6 to 7 rings per inch of radius. Average weight of our specimens 31·5 lbs. per cubic foot. Wood used for agricultural implements, scabbards, grain measures, palanquins, toys and similar articles. The inner bark is bitter and astringent, and is used as a febrifuge, and for tanning; the leaves are used as cattle fodder.

		lbs.
O 216.	Garhwal (1868)	28
O 350.	Gorakhpur (1868)	...
O 1462.	Bharaich, Oudh	32
O 1482.	Kheri, Oudh	34
C 1127.	Ahiri Reserve, Central Provinces	32

2. H. thyrsiflorum, Wall.; Kurz ii. 72; Gamble 47. *Cinchona thyrsiflora,* Roxb. Fl. Ind. i. 530. Vern. *Purgur,* Hind.; *Khoozan,* Burm.

A deciduous tree. Bark 1 inch thick, grey, with corky flakes. Wood white or grey, soft. Annual rings indistinctly marked. Structure the same as that of *H. excelsum.*

Northern and Eastern Bengal and Burma.

Growth moderate, 10 rings per inch of radius. Weight, according to Brandis' Burma List of 1862, No. 104, 28 lbs.; our specimens give an average of 33 lbs. Used for black-boards and packing-cases.

		lbs.
E 1231.	Sibságar, Assam	26
E 1286.	Cachar	34
B 279.	Burma (1867)	31
B 3070.	„ (1862)	38
B 559.	Prome, Burma	33
B 2287.	Andaman Islands	34

7. WENDLANDIA, Bartling.

Contains about 12 Indian species. *W. tinctoria,* DC.; Beddome cxxx.; Brandis 269; Kurz ii. 74 (*Rondeletia tinctoria,* Roxb. Fl. Ind. i. 522; *Wendlandia* sp. Gamble 48.) Vern. *Túla-lodh,* Bengal.; *Kangi,* Nep.; *Singnok,* Lepcha; *Telli,* Uriya; *Tamayoke,* Burm., is a small tree of the forests of Kumaun, Oudh, Behar, Bengal and Burma, whose bark is used in Bengal as a mordant in dyeing. Several other species are found in the North-East Himalaya and several in Burma, chiefly Tenasserim, but they are unimportant. One or two are climbers.

1. W. exserta, DC.; Beddome cxxx.; Brandis 268; Gamble 48. *W. cinerea,* DC.; Gamble 47. *Rondeletia exserta,* Roxb. Fl. Ind. i. 523. Vern. *Chaulai, chila, chilkiya, tíla, birsa, tilki, tilai,* Hind.; *Kangi, tilki, mimri,* Nep.; *Kúrsi,* Seoni; *Marria,* Gondi; *Tilliah,* Baigas in Mandla.

A small deciduous tree with brown bark. Wood reddish brown, hard, close-grained. Pores small, medullary rays moderately broad and fine, the former short. Annual rings marked by firmer wood on the outer and more porous wood on the inner edge of each ring.

Sub-Himalayan tract from the Chenab eastwards, Oudh, Bengal Central and Southern India.

Growth fast, 4-5 rings per inch of radius. Weight, 47 lbs. Wood used for building and agricultural implements and used for house-posts in the Sikkim Terai.

		lbs.
O 1370.	Gonda, Oudh	47
E 589.	Khookloong Forest, Darjeeling Terai	...

2. W. Notoniana, Wall.; Beddome t. 224; Thwaites Enum. 159. Vern. *Rameneidelle,* Cingh.

A small tree of South India and Ceylon, with a red wood, having a similar structure to that of *W. exserta.*

	lbs.
No. 74. Ceylon Collection (marked *W. bicuspidata*)	48

8. WEBERA, Schreb.

Contains about 10 species of small trees, shrubs or climbers from Eastern Bengal, South India and Burma.

W. oppositifolia, Roxb. Fl. Ind. i. 698; Kurz ii. 47 is a small tree of Chittagong and Burma, said by Kurz to have a yellowish white, heavy, close-grained wood. *W. glomeriflora*, Kurz ii. 47, is a small tree of the Pegu Yomas. *W. myrtifolia*, Kurz ii. 49, is a small tree of the swamp forests of Burma and *W. monosperma*, W. and A.; Beddome cxxxiv., is a shrub of the Nilgiri Hills and Wynaad. Kurz also describes 4 scandent shrubs from Chittagong and Burma. Roxburgh gives *W. scandens*, Roxb. Fl. Ind. i. 698. Vern. *Gajer kota*, Beng., as a climber; and *W. odorata*, Roxb. Fl. Ind. i. 699. Vern. *Patagrúja*, Beng., as a small tree, of the forests of Sylhet.

1. W. asiatica, Linn.; Beddome cxxxiii. *W. corymbosa*, Willd.; Roxb. Fl. Ind. i. 697. *Stylocoryne Webera*, A. Rich.; Thwaites Enum. 158. Vern. *Kankra*, Beng.; *Kachuria chàll*, Cuttack; *Komi*, Tel.; *Tarana*, Cingh.

A large shrub or small tree. Wood yellowish white, hard, close-grained. Pores small, very numerous, uniformly distributed. Medullary rays short, fine and extremely fine.

Bengal, South India and Ceylon.

Weight, 57 lbs. per cubic foot. The wood is said by A. Mendis to be used in Ceylon for fishing-boats.

	lbs.
No. 84. Ceylon Collection	57

9. RANDIA, Linn.

Contains 10 to 12 species of shrubs or small trees, generally armed with strong axillary thorns. *R. rigida*, DC.; Brandis 273; Gamble 48, is a shrub found in the forests of the Eastern Himalaya, Nepal and probably Kumaun. *R. fragrans*, Beddome cxxxii. (*Posoqueria fragrans*, Kön.; Roxb. Fl. Ind. i. 717). Vern. *Pedalli*, Tel., is a shrub of South India, used to make hedges. *R. Gardneri*, Thw.; Beddome cxxxii., is a small tree of the South Tinnevelly hills and Ceylon; *R. dekkanensis*, Beddome cxxxiii., is a small tree of the Anamalais; and *R. speciosa*, Beddome cxxxii., a climbing shrub of the Western Ghâts, with sweet-scented flowers. *R. nutans*, DC.; Kurz ii., 45 is a shrub of the forests of Pegu.

Wood smooth, close-grained, hard. Pores small or very small. Medullary rays fine and very fine.

1. R. uliginosa, DC.; Beddome cxxxii.; Brandis 273; Kurz ii. 44; Gamble 48. *Posoqueria uliginosa*, Roxb. Fl. Ind. i. 712. Vern. *Pindálu, pindar, panár, paniah, bharani, katúl*, Hind.; *Piralo*, Beng.; *Maidal*, Nep.; *Kaurio*, Panch Mehals; *Pendra*, Uriya; *Katil, pender*, Gondi; *Gangru, gangáru*, Kurku; *Nallaika, nalla kakisha*, Tel.; *Wagatta*, Tam.; *Karé, pendri*, Kan.; *Telphetru, panelra, phetra, pindra*, Mar.; *Tapkél*, Bhíl; *Mhaniben, mhanpyoo*, Burm.

A small deciduous tree. Bark $\frac{1}{3}$ inch thick, reddish brown, exfoliating in thin flakes. Wood whitish grey, close-grained, hard, no heartwood. Annual rings marked by a narrow belt without pores. Pores small and very small, numerous, uniformly distributed. Medullary rays fine and very fine, very numerous, distinctly visible on a radial section.

Sub-Himalayan tract from the Jumna eastwards, Oudh, Bengal, Burma, Central and South India.

Growth moderate, 6 to 7 rings per inch of radius. Weight, the average of our specimens gives 48 lbs. per cubic foot; Brandis says 41 lbs. The fruit is eaten.

		lbs.
O 542.	Dehra Dún	48
O 1458.	Bahraich, Oudh	47
O 1487.	Kheri, Oudh	51
C 2782.	Melghát, Berar	...
C 1186.	Ahiri Reserve, Central Provinces	...
C 2756.	Moharli Reserve, Central Provinces	48
W 992.	North Kanara	46

2. R. dumetorum, Lam.; Beddome cxxxii.; Brandis 273; Gamble 48. *Posoqueria dumetorum,* Willd.; Roxb. Fl. Ind. i. 713. Vern. *Mindla, mandkolla, arara,* Pb.; *Mainphal, manyúl, karhar, main, mainhúri, manneul, arar,* Hind.; *Maidal, amuki,* Nep.; *Gundrow,* Mechi; *Guról,* Rajbanshi; *Panji,* Lepcha; *Pativa,* Uriya; *Madu karray,* Tam.; *Manda,* Tel.; *Gera, galay,* Mar.; *Kuay, katúl,* Gondi; *Bhita,* Kurku; *Karé,* Kan.

A deciduous thorny shrub or small tree, with grey bark. Wood white or light brown, compact, hard. Structure the same as that of *R. uliginosa.*

Throughout India, extending in the North-West Outer Himalaya as far as the Beas.

Growth moderate, 7 rings per inch of radius, according to our specimens; Brandis says slow: that "a section of a tree known to be 65 years old, 4-inch radius, hollow inside, shewed 54 annual rings on 2 inches of the radius near the circumference." Weight, 55 lbs. per cubic foot. Wood used for agricultural implements, fences and fuel. The bark of the root and stem and the fruit are used in native medicine, the latter as an emetic. The fruit is also used to poison fish, and when ripe is roasted and eaten.

		lbs.
O 262.	Garhwal (1868)	54
O 1366.	Gonda, Oudh	50
O 1461.	Bahraich, Oudh	62
O 1488.	Kheri, Oudh	54
C 2750.	Moharli Reserve, Central Provinces (young)	45
C 2799.	Melghát, Berar (young)	48
E 481. } E 493. }	Khookloong forest, Darjeeling Terai	...
E 2386.	Bamunpokri, Darjeeling Terai	...

3. R. tetrasperma, Bth. and Hook. f.; Brandis 272. *Gardenia tetrasperma,* Roxb. Fl. Ind. i. 709. Vern. *Bara garri, batya gingaru,* Kumaun.

A small procumbent shrub with grey bark. Wood white, very hard. Pores very small. Medullary rays very fine, very numerous. Medullary patches numerous and prominent, of a slightly bluish colour.

Himalaya, from the Indus to Bhutan, ascending to 6,000 feet.

Weight, 56 lbs. per cubic foot.

		lbs.
H 157.	Simla, 6,000 feet	56
H 2821.	„ 5,000 „	...

10. GARDENIA, Linn.

Contains 12 to 15 Indian species of shrubs or trees. *G. gummifera*, Linn.; Roxb. Fl. Ind. i. 708; Beddome cxxxiv. 1; Brandis 270. Vern. *Dekámáli, kamarri*, Hind.; *Chitta matta, chitnityal, gaggaru*, Tel.; *Chitta, bikke, kambi*, Kan., is a large shrub of Central and South India, with a white hard wood, and giving a yellow gum resin. *G. montana*, Roxb. Fl. Ind. i. 709. Vern. *Teliga, tella kakisha*, Tel., is a small tree of South India. *G. coronaria*, Ham.; Kurz ii. 43, is a tree of Chittagong and Burma, with a heavy, close-grained wood. *G. sessiliflora*, Wall.; Kurz ii. 40. Vern. *Majeebouk*, Burm., is a tree of the hills of Burma. Kurz describes several other Chittagong and Burma species of less importance. *G. florida*, Linn., of Indian gardens, is an introduction from China.

Wood smooth, close-grained, hard. Pores small to extremely small, numerous, uniformly distributed. Medullary rays very fine to moderately broad.

1. G. turgida, Roxb. Fl. Ind. i. 711; Beddome cxxxiv. 1.; Brandis 270; Kurz ii. 41. Vern. *Thanella, khúrrúr, khuriari, ghúrga, mhaner*, Hind.; *Karhár*, Banda; *Panjra, pendra*, Gondi; *Phurpata*, Kurku; *Khurphendra, pendri, phanda, phetra*, Mar.; *Phetrak*, Bhíl; *Bamemia*, Uriya; *Manjúnda, telél*, Tel.; *Bongeri*, Kan.; *Thamengsanee*, Burm.

A small deciduous tree. Bark smooth, bluish grey, $\frac{1}{5}$ inch thick, compact. Wood close-grained, hard, white with a purplish tinge, no heartwood. Annual rings indistinct. Pores very small. Medullary rays fine and very fine, very numerous.

Sub-Himalayan tract from Nepal to the Jumna, ascending to 4,000 feet; Rajputana, Burma, Central and South India.

Growth slow, 13 rings per inch of radius. Weight, according to R. Thompson 56·5 lbs. per cubic foot; our specimens give 54 lbs. Wood good, but splits and cracks in seasoning.

			lbs.
O	541.	Dehra Dún	...
O	1377.	Gonda, Oudh	60
O	1463.	Bahraich, Oudh	...
O	1489.	Kheri, Oudh	50
C	826.	Bairagarh Reserve, Berar	54
C	2779.	Melghát, Berar	58
C	1142.	Ahiri Reserve, Central Provinces	54
W	993.	North Kanara	48

Nos. C 1248 and C 1309 (61 and 63 lbs.) sent from Gumsúr under the name *Gorahadu*, have the same structure as, and probably are, this species.

2. G. lucida, Roxb. Fl. Ind. i. 707; Beddome cxxxiv.; Brandis 271. *G. resinifera*, Roth.; Kurz ii. 42. Vern. *Dikamali*, Hind., Guz.; *Konda manga, kokkita, tetta manga*, C.P.; *Papar*, Bijeragogarh; *Karinga, karaingi, tella-manga*, Tel.; *Kumbi*, Tam.

A small deciduous tree. Bark $\frac{1}{3}$ inch thick, greenish grey, exfoliating in irregular flakes. Wood yellowish white, close-grained, hard, no heartwood, no annual rings. Pores extremely small. Medullary rays very fine.

Central and South India, Chittagong.

Weight, 39 lbs. per cubic foot. Wood useful for turning; it is made into combs. It gives a gum resin from wounds in the bark. This gum is hard, opaque, yellow, greenish or brown, with a strong smell, and is used in the treatment of cutaneous diseases and to keep off flies and worms.

			lbs.
C	1185.	Ahiri Reserve, Central Provinces	39

3. G. latifolia, Aiton; Roxb. Fl. Ind. i. 706 (? *cf.* Brandis 272); Beddome cxxxiv. 1.; Brandis 271. Vern. *Pápra, páphar, pepero, ban pindálu,* Hind.; *Pannia bhil, gúngat, bhandara, geggar,* Gondi; *Phiphar, mali,* Baigas; *Kumbay,* Tam.; *Pedda karinga, pureea, bikki, gaiger,* Tel.; *Kota-ranga,* Uriya; *Ghogar, gogarli,* Mar.; *Gogar,* Bhíl.

A small deciduous tree. Bark ¼ inch thick, greenish grey, exfoliating and leaving smooth, conchoidal, rounded depressions. Wood light-yellowish brown, close and even-grained, hard, handsomely mottled, neither warps nor splits. No heartwood. Marked concentric annual rings. Pores extremely small, numerous. Medullary rays fine, short.

Sub-Himalayan tract from the Jumna eastwards, Bengal, Central and South India.

Growth moderate, 8 rings per inch of radius. Weight, 50 to 53 lbs. per cubic foot. The wood is easy to work, durable, and is recommended to be tried as a substitute for boxwood; it is likely to be very good for engraving and turning. Combs are made of it.

		lbs.
B 1173.	Ahiri Reserve, Central Provinces	53
B 2733.	Moharli Reserve, Central Provinces	50

4. G. obtusifolia, Roxb.; Kurz ii. 42. Vern. *Yengkhat,* Burm.

A small deciduous tree with thin, grey bark. Wood white, moderately hard, even-grained. Pores small. Medullary rays moderately broad, and a large number of very fine rays, which are not very distinct.

Burma.

Weight, 55 lbs. per cubic foot. It yields a yellow pellucid resin.

		lbs.
B 817.	Rangoon Division, Burma	55

5. G. costata, Roxb. Fl. Ind. i. 704. *G. coronaria,* Ham.; Kurz ii. 43. Vern. *Yengkhat, tsaythambyah.*

A small deciduous tree, with smooth, grey bark; wood light brown, hard, close-grained. Annual rings indistinct. Pores small. Medullary rays fine, scanty, distinctly visible on a radial section as long horizontal plates.

Chittagong and Burma.

Growth slow, 14 rings per inch of radius. Weight, 51 lbs. per cubic foot (Kurz identifies *G. lucida,* No. 72 of Brandis' Burma List of 1862 with this. Weight, 49 lbs.) Used for making combs and for turning, but liable to crack.

		lbs.
B 284.	Burma (1867)	50
B 2540.	„ (1862)	52

11. GUETTARDA, Linn.

1. G. speciosa, Linn.; Roxb. Fl. Ind. i. 686; Beddome cxxxiv. 4; Kurz ii. 37. Vern. *Domdomah,* And.; *Nil piteha,* Cingh.

A moderate-sized evergreen tree, with thin grey bark. Wood yellow, with a tinge of red. Pores small, often in radial lines. Medullary rays, moderately broad and very fine.

Tidal forests along the shores of the Andaman Islands and Ceylon.

		lbs.
B 1971.	Andaman Islands (Kurz, 1866)	49

12. PLECTRONIA, Linn.

Contains 10 to 12 shrubs, part of which are found in South India and Ceylon, and part in Burma and the Andamans. *P. parviflora*, Roxb.; Beddome cxxxiv. 5; (*Canthium parviflorum*, Roxb. Fl. Ind. i. 534) Vern. *Balsu*, Tel., is a thorny shrub of South India, whose wood is hard and used for turning, and whose leaves are eaten in curries.

1. P. didyma, Bth. and Hook. f.; Kurz ii. 35. *Canthium didymum*, Gaertn.; Roxb. Fl. Ind. i. 535; Beddome t. 221; Brandis 276. Vern. *Tolan*, Uriya; *Neckanie, nalla balsu*, Tam., Tel.; *Abalu*, Kan.; *Arsúl*, Bombay; *Poruwa*, Cingh.

A large shrub. Wood grey, hard. Pores very small, numerous, uniformly distributed. Medullary rays fine and very fine, numerous.

South India, Ceylon and Tenasserim.
Weight, 57 lbs. per cubic foot. Wood used for agricultural purposes.

	lbs.
No. 16. Salem Collection	57

13. IXORA, Linn.

A large genus containing some 30 or more Indian and Burmese shrubs or small trees. Beddome describes 7 species from South India, and Kurz 24 (excluding *Pavetta*) from Burma, while many species come from Eastern Bengal and Assam. *I. coccinea*, Linn.; Roxb. Fl. Ind. i. 375; Beddome cxxxiv. 7; Kurz ii. 26 (*I. Bandhuca*, Roxb. Fl. Ind. ii. 376). Vern. *Rangun, rajana*, Beng.; *Bandhuka*, Sans., is a well-known scarlet-flowered shrub called the "Flame of the Woods," indigenous in South India, Chittagong and Burma and cultivated in gardens all over India. *I. stricta*, Roxb. Fl. Ind. i. 379; Kurz ii. 26, is another scarlet-flowered species from Tenasserim. *I. acuminata*, Roxb. Fl. Ind. i. 383; Gamble 48. Vern. *Churipat*, Nep., is a handsome shrub of Sikkim, Assam and Eastern Bengal with large, crowded corymbs of scented white flowers. *I. undulata*, Roxb. Fl. Ind. i. 385; Gamble 48. Vern. *Palukajui*, Beng.; *Pari*, Nep.; *Takchirnyok*, Lepcha, is a small tree of Bengal, and *I. villosa*, Roxb. Fl. Ind. i. 383. Vern. *Chunari*, Beng., of Sylhet. *I. barbata*, Roxb., and *I. polyantha*, Wight; Beddome cxxxiv. 7, are small trees of the Western Ghâts.

1. I. parviflora, Vahl.; Roxb. Fl. Ind. i. 383; Beddome t. 222; Brandis 275; Kurz ii. 21. The Torch Tree. Vern. *Kota gandhal*, Hind.; *Rangan*, Beng.; *Disti*, Gondi; *Kúrat, lokandi*, Mar.; *Shulundu kora*, Tam.; *Karipal, kachipadél, tadda pallu*, Tel.; *Kori*, Gondi; *Korgi*, Kan.; *Tellu kurwan*, Uriya; *Maha ratambala*, Cingh.

An evergreen shrub or small tree. Bark ¼ inch thick, dark brown, exfoliating in irregular rounded scales. Wood light brown, smooth, very hard, close-grained. No heartwood. Annual rings indistinct. Pores very small. Medullary rays very fine and very numerous.

Bengal, Burma, Central and South India.
Growth moderate, 10 rings per inch of radius. Weight according to Skinner, No. 84 66 lbs.; our specimen gives 57 lbs. Skinner gives P = 717. The wood is well suited for turning and might do for engraving. Beddome says it is used for furniture and building purposes. The green branches are used for torches.

	lbs.
C 1156. Ahiri Reserve, Central Provinces	57

14. PAVETTA, Linn.

Contains 6 to 8 species of Indian shrubs or small trees. *P. indica*, Linn.; Beddome cxxxiv. 7; Brandis 275 (*Ixora Pavetta*, Roxb. Fl. Ind. i. 385; Kurz ii. 18.) Vern.

Kúkúra chúra, Beng.; *Pavetti*, Tam.; *Núni-papúta, tapra*, Tel.; *Pawetta*, Cingh., *Meenaban*, Burm., is a common shrub of Bengal, South and parts of Central India and the Andaman Islands. *P. breviflora*, DC.; Beddome cxxxiv. 7, is a shrub of the higher ranges of the Nilgiris. Kurz, under *Ixora*, describes 4 other species, viz.: *I. compactiflora*, and *I. naucleiflora*, from Upper Tenasserim; *I. weberæfolia*, from the Andamans; and *I. recurva* (*Pæderia recurva*, Roxb. Fl. Ind. i. 684), from Chittagong.

1. P. tomentosa, Smith; Beddome cxxxiv. 7.; Brandis 275. *Ixora tomentosa*, Roxb. Fl. Ind. i. 386; Kurz ii. 19; Gamble 48. Vern. *Padera*, Kumaun; *Júi*, Beng.; *Sundók*, Lepcha; *Papiri, papatta, nam-papúta*, Tel.

A large shrub with thin, smooth, brownish grey bark. Wood light brown, hard, close-grained. Pores extremely small. Medullary rays short, numerous, fine and very fine.

Sub-Himalayan tract from the Ganges eastwards, ascending to 4,000 feet, Bengal, South India and Burma.

		lbs.
O 3086.	Gonda, Oudh	59

15. COFFEA, Linn.

C. bengalensis, Roxb. Fl. Ind. i. 540; Beddome cxxxiv. 8; Brandis 277; Kurz ii. 28; Gamble 49. Vern. *Kath-jahi*, Hind.; *Kundrudi*, Mechi, is a small shrub found in most parts of the moister regions of India. The berries are used as coffee by Mechis and Rajbanshis in Northern Bengal, but the coffee is of inferior quality.

1. C. arabica, Linn.; Roxb. Fl. Ind. i. 539; Beddome cxxxiv. 8; Brandis 276; Kurz ii. 27; Gamble 49. Vern. *Bun* (the berry), *Kahwa* (the same roasted and ground).

A shrub with thin grey bark. Wood white, moderately hard, close-grained. Pores very fine and extremely fine. Medullary rays very fine, numerous.

Indigenous in Abyssinia and Soudan, cultivated since the fifteenth century in Arabia and introduced thence to India. It has been cultivated in many pasts of India, but on a large scale only in Mysore, Coorg, the Western Ghâts and Ceylon. It is occasionally found running wild in the forests. Growth moderate.

P 3150. Coorg (20-25 years old).

Prismatomeris tetrandra, Hook. f. and Bth. Genera Pl. ii. 119 (*Coffea tetrandra*, Roxb.; Kurz ii. 28) is an evergreen tree of the forests of Chittagong, the Martaban Hills and Andaman Islands up to 3,000 feet elevation.

16. MORINDA, Linn.

A genus of Indian and Burmese trees and shrubs, mostly giving a red or yellow dye from the root bark. Roxburgh Fl. Ind. i. 541 to 548, describes 7 species; and Brandis p. 278, says that 5 out of these species "cannot well be specifically distinguished" and that "it will be more convenient to consider them as one under the name *M. citrifolia*, Roxb." The names of Roxburgh's 5 species are (1.) *M. citrifolia*, Roxb., from Pegu; (2.) *M. tinctoria*, Roxb., cultivated; (3.) *M. bracteata*, Roxb., from Ganjam; (4.) *M. exserta*, Roxb., of Bengal; and (5.) *M. multiflora*, Roxb., from Nagpore and Berar. We will, however, retain the name *M. exserta* for our specimens at present.

M. angustifolia, Roxb. Fl. Ind. i. 547; Brandis 278; Kurz ii. 61. Vern. *Asugach*, Ass.; *Kchai tun*, Phekial; *Chenung, chengrung*, Gáro; *Yaiyo*, Burm., is an evergreen tree of Bengal and Burma, whose bark and wood give a yellow dye. *M. umbellata*, Linn.; Beddome cxxxiv. 9; Kurz ii. 62. *M. scandens*, Roxb. Fl. Ind. i. 548, is an evergreen scandent shrub of the Western Ghâts, Tenasserim and Ceylon. Kurz describes 5 other species from Burma.

1. M. exserta, Roxb. Fl. Ind. i. 545; Beddome cxxxiv.; Brandis 277; Kurz ii. 59. Vern. *Al, ach,* Hind.; *Alleri, alládi,* Panch Mehals; *Hardi,* Nep.; *Noona,* Tam.; *Toghur, togara mogali, mogali, manja pavatti,* Tel.; *Achu,* Uriya; *Nyau,* Burm.; *Ali,* Gondi.

A moderate-sized deciduous tree. Bark corky, brittle, brown or grey, with numerous deep, longitudinal cracks. Wood red, often yellow, with red streaks, or brown, moderately hard, close-grained. Annual rings faintly marked. Pores small, scanty, generally in radial lines between the numerous, fine and moderately broad medullary rays.

Bengal, Burma, Guzerat, South India.

Growth moderate, 7 rings per inch of radius. Weight, according to Skinner, No. 97 (*M. citrifolia*) 30 lbs. per cubic foot; Wallich 29 lbs.; our specimens give 41 lbs. Skinner gives P = 410. The wood is durable: Wallich's specimen (No. B 2690), cut in Burma in 1828, was quite sound when cut up after 50 years in Calcutta. It is used for plates and dishes. The bark of the root is largely used for dyeing red and yellow.

		lbs.
C 1130.	Ahiri Reserve, Central Provinces	36
C 1307.	Gumsúr, Madras	42
C 1246.	" "	47
B 2690.	Tavoy (Wallich 1828)	41
No. 34.	Salem Collection	40

17. LEPTODERMIS, Wall.

1. L. lanceolata, Wall.; Brandis 279. Vern. *Jogia padera,* Kumaun.

A small shrub of the North-Western Himalaya, generally on rocks between 5,000 and 10,000 feet. Bark thin, grey. Wood hard, white. Pores very small, scanty. Medullary rays fine and moderately broad.

		lbs.
H 2822.	Simla, 6,000 feet	48

ORDER LVII. COMPOSITÆ.

The largest Order of plants not only in India, but in the world. With very few exceptions, all the species are herbaceous. There are, however, genera containing shrubs or small trees. They belong to the following Tribes:—

Tribe I.—Vernonieæ	*Vernonia.*
" II.—Asteroideæ	*Microglossa.*
" III.—Inuloideæ	*Blumea, Pluchea* and *Inula.*
" IV.—Anthemideæ	*Artemisia.*
" V.—Mutisiaceæ	*Leucomeris.*

Microglossa volubilis, DC.; Kurz ii. 82, is a large climber of the hills of Martaban and Tenasserim, found in second-growth forests. *Blumea balsamifera,* DC.; Kurz ii. 82 (*Conyza balsamifera,* Roxb. Fl. Ind. iii. 427; Gamble 50) Vern. *Poungma-theing,* Burm., is a shrub which comes up freely on old cultivated lands in Northern and Eastern Bengal and Burma. *Pluchea indica,* Less.; Kurz ii. 83. Vern. *Kayu,* Burm., is a large evergreen shrub of tidal forests on the coasts of Chittagong, Burma and the Andamans. *Inula eupatorioides,* DC., and *Inula Cappa,* DC., are small shrubs of the Himalaya. *Leucomeris* contains two species: *L. spectabilis,* Don. Vern. *Panwa,* Kumaun; *Bhoea, phusrae,* Nep., a small tree of Nepal, also found in Garhwal; and *L. decora,* Kurz ii. 78, a deciduous tree of the Eng forests of Prome.

1. VERNONIA, Schreb.

About 7 species of small trees or climbers. *V. Wightiana*, Blth. and Hook. f. (*Monosis Wightiana*, Beddome t. 226), is a tree of the Nilgiri Hills. *V. Kurzii*, C. B. Clarke; Kurz ii. 80, is a small tree of the toungyas in the Martaban Hills; and V. *arborea*, Ham., is found in Tenasserim. The other three species are Burmese climbers.

1. V. volkameriæfolia, DC.; Beddome t. 225; Gamble 50. *V. acuminata*, DC.; Kurz ii. 79.

A small tree. Bark brown. Wood whitish, turning pale brown, moderately hard. Pores moderate-sized, often in short radial lines. Medullary rays numerous, fine and moderately broad. Pith large.

Eastern Himalaya, South India and Burma.

Weight, 31·5 lbs. This is probably Kyd's *Vernonia* (*major*)—Weight 31·5 lbs. P = 383.

E. 3312. Pankabari, Darjeeling, 3,000 feet.

2. ARTEMISIA, Linn.

Contains the "Wormwoods," only one of which reaches the size of a small shrub. The leaves of many species are used as a febrifuge and in the preparation of "absinthe."

1. A. vulgaris, Linn.; Roxb. Fl. Ind. iii. 420; Gamble 50. Vern. *Naga, naga dona, dona*, Hind., Beng.; *Titapat*, Nep.

Bark thin, with longitudinal fissures. Wood grey, hard. Pores very small; in short radial lines between the distant, fine and moderately broad medullary rays.

A gregarious shrub, coming up on old cultivations between 3,000 and 6,000 feet in the Sikkim Hills, and often covering large tracts of land until killed down by the tree growth which succeeds it. This is probably the *Nagdana* of Cachar, said by Mr. Brownlow to be one of the plants on which the *Attacus Atlas* silkworm is fed.

Its ashes when burnt are considered to give a good manure for cultivation.

E 2857. Tukdah Forest, Darjeeling, 5,000 feet.

ORDER LVIII. GOODENOVIEÆ.

Scævola Königii, Vahl.; Kurz ii. 84 (*S. Taccada*, Roxb. Fl. Ind. i. 527.) Vern. *Penglai htan*, Burm., placed by Kurz under *Campanulaceæ*, but in this Order by Bentham and Hooker in the Genera Plantarum II. 538, is an evergreen large shrub, common in the tidal forests of Tenasserim and the Andamans. It has a soft, spongy pith, and coarse, milky, fibrous wood.

ORDER LIX. VACCINIACEÆ.

An Order of small trees or shrubs, erect or epiphytic, of the mountains of Eastern and Southern India. It contains 4 genera: *Agapetes, Pentapterygium, Vaccinium* and *Corallobotrys*. *Agapetes* contains about 16 species, mostly epiphytical. *A. variegata*, G. Don (*Thibandia variegata*, Wall.; Royle t. 79, *Ceratostema variegata*, Roxb. Fl. Ind. ii. 413, *Vaccinium variegatum*, Kurz ii. 88) Vern. *Jalamút*, Gáro, is a shrub, often epiphytic, of the Khasia and Gáro Hills, Sylhet, Chittagong and Tenasserim. *A. obovata*, Don (*Vaccinium obovatum*, Wight; Gamble 50) Vern. *Ratay*, Nep., is a common shrub of the hill forests of Sikkim and Bhutan. *A. saligna*, Bth. and Hook. f.; Gamble 50, is a large epiphytic shrub of the Sikkim Hills from 1,000 to 5,000 feet, whose leaves are said by Hooker to be used as a substitute for tea. *A. Wallichiana*, Wight, and *A. hirsuta*, Wight, are shrubs of Sylhet; *A. verticillata*, Wight, and *A. odontocera*, Wight, of the Khasia Hills and Burma; and *A. auriculata*, Griff., is an epiphytic shrub of Burma.

Pentapterygium contains 3 species, among which *P. serpens*, Bth.; Gamble 50. Vern. *Kali hurchu*, Nep.; *Kúmbuten*, Lepcha, is a handsome epiphytic shrub common on trees and banks about Darjeeling.

Corallobotrys acuminata, Hook. f. and Bth. (*Vaccinium acuminatum*, Kurz ii. 90), is an evergreen shrub of Eastern Bengal and Burma.

1. VACCINIUM, Linn.

About 12 species, of which 4 occur on the Nilgiris and the rest in Eastern Bengal and Burma. *V. Leschenaultii*, Wight; Beddome t. 227. Vern. *Andúvan*, Nilgiris, is a pretty tree with an edible fruit, said by Beddome to have a fine-grained rose-coloured wood. *V. rotundifolium*, Wight, and *V. neilgherrense*, Wight; Beddome cxxxvi., are also small trees of the hills of South India. *V. Donianum*, Wight; Kurz ii. 91, is a large shrub of Burma and the Khasia Hills. *V. Dunalianum*, Wight, is an epiphytic shrub of Sikkim, Bhutan and the Khasia Hills.

1. V. serratum, Wight; Gamble 50. Vern. *Charu*, Nep.

A shrub, often epiphytic. Bark brown with white lenticels. Wood white. Pores extremely small. Medullary rays broad, wavy.

Sikkim, Bhutan and the Khasia Hills, from 4,000 to 8,000 feet.

E 3296. Babookhola, Darjeeling, 4,000 feet.

ORDER LX. ERICACEÆ.

Contains about 6 Genera of usually handsome-flowered Indian trees or shrubs; some of these, however, especially the genera *Cassiope* and *Diplarche*, contain merely small prostrate heath-like plants, found in the Inner Himalaya. The Genera belong to 2 Tribes, *viz.*:—

Tribe I.—Andromedeæ	*Gaultheria*, *Cassiope*, *Pieris* and *Enkianthus*.
„ II.—Rhodoreæ	*Diplarche* and *Rhododendron*.

Gaultheria contains about 5 species. *G. fragrantissima*, Wall.; Beddome cxxxvi. Vern. *Kappúrú*, Cingh., is a common shrub of the Nilgiri and Pulney Hills and Ceylon. *G. punctata*, Bl.; Kurz ii. 92 (in this he includes *G. fragrantissima*) is an evergreen shrub of the hill forests of Martaban at 6,000 to 7,000 feet; and *G. Griffithiana*, Wight; Gamble 51, is a small shrub of the hills of Sikkim and Bhutan from 7,000 to 9,000 feet. *Cassiope fastigiata*, Don, Vern. *Chhota lewar*, Beas; *Seeru*, Chor; *Kamba*, Kumaun, is the "Himalayan Heather" of travellers in the North-West Himalaya; it often covers large areas like the European heather. It was also found by Hooker in Sikkim at Mon Lepcha. The common "Heather" or "Ling" of Europe is *Calluna vulgaris*, Linn.

Bark generally thin. Wood compact, even-grained. Pores uniform and uniformly distributed, small or very small, numerous. Annual rings generally marked by belt of porous wood. Medullary rays short, generally fine or very fine.

1. PIERIS, Don.

P. lanceolata, Don, is a small tree of the Khasia Hills, and *P. formosa*, Don (*Andromeda formosa*, Wall.; Brandis 280. Vern. *Sheaboge*, Nep.), an evergreen tree of the Himalaya from Kumaun to Bhutan.

1. P. ovalifolia, Don. *Andromeda ovalifolia*, Wall.; Brandis 280; Kurz ii. 92; Gamble 50. Vern. *Ayatta, eilan, ellal, arur, arwân, aira, rattankat, erana, yarta*, Pb.; *Ayár*, Hind.; *Anjir, angiar, aigiri, jagguchal*, Nep.; *Piazay*, Bhutia; *Kangshior*, Lepcha.

A small deciduous tree. Bark brown, peeling off in long narrow strips, deeply cleft, the clefts often extending spirally round the stem. Wood light reddish brown, moderately hard. Annual rings marked by numerous larger pores in the spring wood. Pores small in the spring wood, very small in the autumn wood. Medullary rays fine, short, marked on a radial section as long narrow bands.

Outer Himalaya from the Indus to Assam, usually between 4,000 and 8,000 feet, Khasia Hills, and hills of Martaban from 5,000 to 7,000 feet.

Growth slow. Brandis says 34 rings per inch; our specimens gave 18 rings per inch for the Simla and 6 rings for the Darjeeling specimen. Weight, 41 lbs. per cubic foot. Wood not durable, warps and shrinks very badly in seasoning, is only used for fuel and charcoal. The young leaves and buds are poisonous to goats; they are used to kill insects, and an infusion of them is applied in cutaneous diseases. The bark of the Darjeeling tree is not so characteristically thick ast hat of the North-West tree.

		lbs.
H 17.	Simla, 7,000 feet	41
E 3328.	Darjeeling, 6,500 feet	...

2. ENKIANTHUS, Lour.

1. E. himalaicus, Hook. f. and Th.; Gamble 50. Vern. *Chothu*, Nep.

A small tree with thin grey bark. Wood white, moderately hard, even-grained. Annual rings marked by a belt of more numerous pores. Pores very small and extremely small. Medullary rays moderately broad and fine. Numerous, wavy, fine, concentric bands of soft tissue.

Sikkim Himalaya, 10,000 to 12,000 feet.
Growth slow, 40 rings per inch of radius.

E 976. Chumbi Valley, Tibet, about 10,000 feet.

3. RHODODENDRON, Linn.

Contains about 50 species, found chiefly and in great abundance and of great beauty in the inner Sikkim Himalaya. Four species extend to the North-West Himalaya, three to the hills ot Burma, and one to the Nilgiris. Some species are epiphytic, and among these are found two which are perhaps the finest and largest flowering, *viz.*: *R. Dalhousiæ*, Hook. f.; Gamble 52. Vern. *Guras*, Nep. and *R. Edgeworthii*, Hook. f.; Gamble 52, both of Sikkim, the first with very large cream coloured scented flowers, the second with woolly leaves and pure white flowers, having the odour of cinnamon. Some species are only small heath-like bushes found on the rocks at high elevations; among these are *R. Anthopogon*, Don; Brandis 282. Vern. *Nichni rattankát, nera*, Jhelum; *Tazak-tsum*, Kashmir; *Káizabán, morúa, talísa*, Ravi; *Talisri*, Beas; *Talsir*, Sutlej; *Talisfar*, Kumaun; *Palu*, Bhutia, found in the Himalaya from Kashmir to Sikkim above 11,000 feet, and on the Chor and Kedarkanta, with white or pale yellow flowers; *R. setosum*, Dòn. Vern. *Tsalu*, Bhutia, a red-flowered shrub of Sikkim which, with the last, gives a very strong and somewhat unpleasant aromatic scent; and *R. lepidotum*, Wall.; Brandis 282; Gamble 52. Vern. *Tsaluma, tsuma*, Bhutia, with reddish flowers. *R. formosum*, Wall.; Kurz ii. 94, is a small shrub of the Khasia and Nattoung Hills, above 7,000 feet. *R. moulmeinense*, Hook.; Kurz ii. 94, an evergreen tree of the hills of Martaban and Tenasserim above 4,000 feet. *R. Hodgsoni*, Hook. f.; Gamble 5, is a small tree of Sikkim from the wood of which the Tibetan yak saddles are frequently made, and whose leaves are used for plates and lining baskets. *R. nivale*, Hook. f., found at 17,500 to 18,000 feet altitude in the Sikkim Himalaya, is a small shrub which probably attains the highest elevation of any known woody plant.

The Indian rhododendrons are all characterised by even-grained wood, soft or moderately hard; by very fine and extremely fine pores, more numerous in the spring wood; and by fine, generally short medullary rays. The wood is apt to warp, with the exception of that of *R. argenteum* and *R. Falconeri*.

1. R. arboreum, Sm.; Beddome t. 228; Brandis 281; Kurz ii. 93; Gamble 51. *R. puniceum*, Roxb. Fl. Ind. ii. 409. Vern. *Chhán*, Hazara; *Ardáwal*, Jhelum; *Mandál*, Chenab; *Chiu, áru*, Ravi; *Brás, broa, búrans, búrúnsh*, Beas to the Sarda River; *Brus*, Kumaun; *Bhoráns, gurás, ghonás, toggú, lal gurás*, Nep.; *Etok*, Bhutia, Lepcha; *Billi, poomaram*, Nilgiris; *Ma-ratmal*, Cingh.

A small evergreen tree. Bark 1 inch thick, reddish brown, peeling off in small flakes. Wood soft, reddish white or reddish brown, close and even-grained, apt to warp and shrink. Annual rings marked by a belt of slightly larger pores in the spring wood. Pores very small and extremely small, uniformly distributed. Medullary rays fine and moderately broad, short, visible on a radial section.

Outer Himalaya from the Indus to Bhutan between 3,000 and 11,000 feet, hills of Southern India and Ceylon, Karennee Hills in Burma.

Growth slow: according to Brandis 14 rings per inch of radius; our specimens give 12 rings for the North-West specimens, and 22 to 36 rings for those from Sikkim.

Weight, 41·4 lbs. per cubic foot on an average of 5 specimens, the Sikkim ones weighing 39, while the Simla specimens give 45 lbs. The wood seasons very badly, and is chiefly used for fuel and charcoal, but is also sometimes employed for building and for making dishes, in Sikkim for "kukri" handles, boxes and other small articles, and on the Nilgiris for gun-stocks and posts. The flowers are eaten and are made into preserves; they are commonly offered in temples.

			lbs.
H	3171.	Dungagalli, Hazara, 7,000 feet	...
H	14.	Simla, 7,000 feet	45
H	73.	Mashobra, Simla, 7,000 feet	45
E	371.	Senchul forest, Darjeeling, 7,500 feet	39
E	383. } 2388. }	Tonglo, Darjeeling, 10,000 feet	39

The two last are the species *R. Campbelliæ*, Hook. f.; Gamble 51, distinguished from *R. arboreum*, Sm., by the ferruginous tomentum and cordate base of the leaf, but probably only a variety.

2. R. argenteum, Hook. f.; Gamble 51. Vern. *Kali gurás, putlinga*, Nep.; *Etok-amal*, Lepcha.

An evergreen tree. Bark reddish brown, peeling off in small scales. Wood yellowish, with darker heartwood, shining, soft, close and even-grained. Pores very small, somewhat more numerous in the spring wood.

Medullary rays of two sizes, very fine and very numerous between fewer short and moderately broad rays.

Hills of Sikkim, common on the outer ranges round Darjeeling and Dumsong, from 6,000 to 10,000 feet.

Growth slow, 27 rings per inch of radius. Weight, 39 lbs. per cubic foot. The wood warps less than that of *R. arboreum*. Flowers pure white, with a purple throat.

		lbs.
E 372.	Tonglo, Darjeeling, 9,000 feet	39

3. R. Falconeri, Hook. f.; Gamble 51. Vern. *Kurlinga,* Nep.; *Kégu,* Bhutia.

A moderate-sized evergreen tree. Bark reddish brown, peeling off in flakes; inner bark purple red. Wood reddish white, shining with a beautiful satiny lustre, takes a beautiful polish, hard. Annual rings marked by more numerous pores in the spring wood. Pores very small and extremely small. Medullary rays fine and moderately broad, short.

Hills of Sikkim, especially the summit of Tonglo, at 10,000 feet.

Growth slow, 17 rings per inch of radius. Weight, 39 lbs. per cubic foot. Does not warp. Flowers cream-coloured.

		lbs.
E 369.	Tonglo, Darjeeling, 10,000 feet	39

4. R. barbatum, Wall.; Gamble 51. Vern *Gurás, chimal,* Nep.; *Kému,* Bhutia.

A small evergreen tree. Wood light pinkish red, shining. Annual rings marked by a belt of more numerous and larger pores. Pores very small and extremely small. Medullary rays fine and very fine, numerous.

Eastern Himalaya, from 8,000 to 11,000 feet.

Growth slow, 35 rings per inch of radius. Weight, 39 lbs. per cubic foot. Flowers deep crimson.

		lbs.
E 375.	Tonglo, Darjeeling, 10,000 feet	39

5. R. campanulatum, Don; Brandis 281; Gamble 52. Vern. *Gaggar, yurmi,* Kashmir; *Sarngar, shinwala,* Ravi; *Shargar,* Beas; *Simrung,* Sutlej; *Chimul,* Kumaun; *Cheriala, teotosa,* Nep.

An evergreen shrub with thin grey bark. Wood light pinkish red, moderately hard. Annual rings distinctly marked by more numerous pores in the spring wood. Pores very small and extremely small. Medullary rays fine, very short.

Inner Himalaya from the Indus to Nepal, between 9,500 and 14,000 feet. Outer ranges on Chor and Kedarkanta. Sikkim at 11,000 feet (C. B. Clarke).

Growth moderate to slow. Our specimens shew 28 rings per inch of radius; while Aikin with Wallich's specimens found 8·4 rings per inch, very distinctly marked. Weight, 39 lbs. per cubic foot. Flowers light pink, lilac or mauve.

		lbs.
H 121.	Jalari Pass, Seoraj, Kulu, 10,000 feet	39
H 128.	Rotang Pass, Kulu, 13,000 feet	...

6. R. fulgens, Hook. f.; Gamble 51. Vern. *Chimal,* Nep.

A small tree or large shrub. Wood grey, darker in the centre, moderately hard, even-grained. Annual rings marked by more porous wood at the inner edge. Pores very small. Medullary rays short, fine, very numerous.

Sikkim Himalaya, from 12,000 to 14,000 feet.

Growth slow, 25 rings per inch of radius. Weight, 36 lbs. per cubic foot. Flowers deep crimson.

	lbs.
E 2957. Sandúkpho, Darjeeling, 12,000 feet	36

7. R. cinnabarinum, Hook. f.; Gamble 51. Vern. *Búlú*, Nep.; *Kema kechoong*, Lepcha.

A large shrub with thin grey bark. Wood grey, moderately hard, even-grained, warps. Annual rings not visible. Pores very small. Medullary rays short, fine.

Sikkim Himalaya above 12,000 feet.

Weight, 42 lbs. per cubic foot. The leaves are poisonous and the smoke of the wood causes inflammation of the face and eyes, according to Hooker. Flowers scarlet.

	lbs.
E 2958. Sandúkpho, Darjeeling, 12,000 feet	42

ORDER LXI. EPACRIDEÆ.

An Australian Order, of which one species only extends north to Tenasserim, *viz. Leucopogon malayanus*, Jack; Kurz ii. 95, an evergreen, small, rigid shrub.

ORDER LXII. PLUMBAGINEÆ.

An Order containing only one Indian species. *Ægialitis annulata*, R. Br.; Kurz ii. 96 (*Æ. rotundifolia*, Roxb. Fl. Ind. ii. 111), is a small evergreen treelet with a conically thickened trunk, found in the tidal forests of the Sundarbans, Chittagong, Arracan, Burma and the Andaman Islands.

ORDER LXIII. MYRSINEÆ.

Contains 6 Genera of Indian trees, shrubs, or climbers, belonging to the following Tribes:—

Tribe I.—Mæseæ	*Mæsa.*
„ II.—Eumyrsineæ	*Myrsine, Samara, Ardisia* and *Ægiceras.*
„ III.—Theophrasteæ	*Reptonia.*

Wood compact, close-grained. Pores very small or extremely small, often in groups and radial or oblique lines. Medullary rays distant, broad.

1. MÆSA, Forskal.

Contains 10 to 12 species of shrubs or trees. *M. indica* A. DC.; Beddome cxxxvii.; Brandis 283; Kurz ii. 99; Gamble 52 (*Bæobotrys indica*, Roxb. Fl. Ind. i. 557) Vern. *Kalsis*, Kumaun; *Atki*, Bombay; *Bilauni*, Nep.; *Phadupjoh*, Mechi; *Ramjani*, Beng.; *Tamomban*, Magh, is a shrub of the Sub-Himalayan tract from the Ganges to Assam, Bengal, South India and Burma. *M. argentea*, Wall.; Brandis

283. Vern. *Phusera, gogsa,* Hind., is a large shrub of the outer Himalaya, in Kumaun and Nepal. *M. macrophylla,* Wall.; Gamble 52. Vern. *Phusera,* Kumaun; *Bogoti,* Nep.; *Tugom,* Lepcha, is a common small tree of the North-East Himalaya, especially in second-growth forest. *M. ramentacea,* Wall.; Kurz ii. 99. Vern. *Malmúriya,* Sylhet, is a small tree of Eastern Bengal, Chittagong, Burma and the Andamans, also of second-growth forest, and said by Kurz to have a brown, heavy, close-grained, brittle wood.

1. M. montana, A. DC.; under *M. indica,* A. DC. in Brandis 283; Gamble 52. Vern. *Bilauni,* Nep.; *Purmo,* Lepcha.

An evergreen, gregarious shrub or small tree. Bark thin, reddish brown. Wood soft. Pores small, scanty, uniformly distributed. Medullary rays moderately broad, numerous.

North-East Himalaya from Nepal eastwards, Eastern Bengal and Burma (var. *B. elongata* = *M. paniculata,* A. DC.; Kurz ii. 99) often forming coppice-like dense second-growth forests at elevations from 3,000 to 6,000 feet on the Sikkim and Bhutan Hills.

Growth rather fast, 6 rings per inch of radius; used only for fuel and rough house-posts.

E 2389. Tukdah Forest, Darjeeling, 6,000 feet.

2. MYRSINE, Linn.

Contains 3 to 5 species. *M. capitellata,* Wall.; Beddome t. 234; Brandis 286 (*M. avenis,* DC.; Kurz ii. 105), is a small tree of Eastern Bengal, South India, Ceylon and Burma, said by Beddome to have a hard and durable timber. Weight, 22 lbs. (Wallich).

1. M. semiserrata, Wall.; Brandis 285; Kurz ii. 105; Gamble 52. Vern. *Parwana, kúngkúng, gogsa, bamora, gaunta,* Hind.; *Chupra,* Kumaun; *Bilsi, beresi, kalikatha, bilauni,* Nep.; *Tungcheong,* Lepcha.

A shrub, small or middling sized tree. Bark ash-coloured, dark, nearly black, with prominent dots. Wood red, hard. Pores extremely small, in small patches between the distant, broad medullary rays.

Outer Himalaya from the Beas to Bhutan, from 3,000 to 9,000 feet, Nattoung Hills of Martaban.

Wallich says the wood is chocolate-coloured, heavy, hard, handsome and used in Nepal for carpenters' work. It splits rather and is usually too small for anything but firewood.

		lbs.
H 2830.	The Glen, Simla, 6,000 feet	51
E 3322.	Darjeeling, 6,500 feet	...

2. M. africana, Linn.; Brandis 286. Vern. *Bebrang, kakhum, kokhúri, karuk, gugul, jutru, chachri, pratshu, branchu, khúshin, pápri, bandáru, bínsín, atuljan,* Pb.; *Guvaini, pahari cha, chúpra,* North-Western Provinces.

A small, evergreen shrub. Wood white, moderately hard. Pores extremely small, often in short radial lines, between the distant, fine medullary rays.

Afghanistan, Salt Range and Outer Himalaya as far as Nepal.

Fruit used as an anthelminthic, sold under the name of *Bebrang,* and often used as a substitute for that of *Samara Ribes.* The shrub might be useful for hedges.

		lbs.
H 2829.	Simla, 6,000 feet	49

3. SAMARA, Linn.

Contains about 10 species of shrubs or climbers, of which most are found in Eastern Bengal, South India and Burma. *S. Ribes*, Benth. and Hook. f. (*Embelia Ribes*, Burm.; Roxb. Fl. Ind. i. 586; Beddome cxxxviii.; Brandis 284; Kurz ii. 101; Gamble 53). Vern. *Bebrang*, Sylhet; *Himalcheri*, Nep.; *Kárkannie*, Bombay, is a large climber of Eastern and Northern Bengal, South India, Ceylon and Burma. The berries are used as an anthelminthic, and are used to adulterate black pepper. *S. floribunda*, Bth. and Hook. f. (*Embelia floribunda*, Wall.; Kurz ii. 102; Gamble 53). Vern. *Himalcheri*, Nep.; *Payong*, Lepcha, is a large climber of the hills of Sikkim and of Nattoung in Burma. It has a pinkish-white wood with very broad medullary rays and large regular pores, sometimes subdivided and often in concentric lines. (E 3294, Sepoydura, Darjeeling, 6,000 feet.) *S. frondosa*, King; Gamble 52. Vern. *Amili*, Nep.; *Monkyourik*, Lepcha, is a common climber of the Darjeeling forests.

1. S. robusta, Benth. and Hook. f. *Embelia robusta*, Roxb. Fl. Ind. i. 587; Beddome cxxxvii.; Brandis 284; Kurz ii. 102; Gamble 53. Vern. *Amti, ambat, barbatti, byebering*, Bombay; *Bebrang*, Oudh; *Kopadalli*, Gondi; *Bharangeli*, Kurku; *Kalay bogoti*, Nep.; *Aipmwaynway*, Burm.

A large shrub or small tree. Bark ¼ inch thick, brown, with horizontal cracks. Wood reddish. Pores small, often in groups or short radial lines, the transverse diameter many times smaller than the distance between the extremely broad medullary rays. Yellow spots shewing in the middle of the rays.

Sub-Himalayan tract from the Jumna eastwards, Bengal, Behar, Western India and Burma.

		lbs.
O 2478.	Gonda, Oudh	37.

2. S. undulata, Benth. and Hook. f. *Choripetalum undulatum*, A. DC.; Gamble 53. Vern. *Amilpati*, Nep.

A climbing shrub. Bark brown, with prominent lenticels. Wood yellowish white, moderately hard. Pores moderate-sized, more numerous in the inner part of each annual ring. Medullary rays moderately broad to broad, short, well defined.

North-East Himalaya, 3,000 to 6,000 feet.

E 3302. Tukdah, Darjeeling, 5,000 feet.

4. ARDISIA, Sw.

Shrubs or small trees. Brandis describes 2 from the North-Western Himalaya; Beddome 9 species from South India and Ceylon; and Kurz 20 from Burma and the Andamans; while a large number occur in the North-Eastern Himalaya and Eastern Bengal. *A. humilis*, Vahl.; Beddome cxxxix.; Brandis 287; Kurz ii. 110; Gamble 53 (*A. solanancea*, Roxb. Fl. Ind. i. 580), Vern. *Ban-jam*, Beng.; *Kadna*, Cuttack; *Conda-mayúr*, Tel.; *Kantena, maya rawa*, C. Prov.; *Bodina gidda*, Mysore; *Gyengmaope*, Burm., is a large shrub of the moister zones of India and Burma, extending as far to the north-west as the Jumna. *A. floribunda*, Wall.; Brandis 287; Gamble 53, is a small tree of the Sub-Himalayan tract from the Jumna to Assam. *A. pauciflora*, Heyne, *A. paniculata*, Roxb., *A. rhomboidea*, Wight, and *A. elliptica*, Thunb.; Beddome cxxxviii., are common small trees of South India and Ceylon.

1. A. crispa, DC.; Kurz ii. 113. *A. crenulata*, Vent.; Gamble 53. Vern. *Chamlani*, Nep.; *Denyok*, Lepcha.

A small erect shrub. Wood white, moderately hard. Pores extremely small. Medullary rays short, broad.

Eastern Himalaya, from 4,000 to 8,000 feet. Martaban at similar elevations.

Has pretty wax-like flowers and bright red berries, which ripen in winter. Very commom undergrowth in the hill forests.

E 3315. Pugraingbong, Darjeeling, 6,000 feet.

5. ÆGICERAS, Gaertn.

1. Æ. corniculata, Blanco; Kurz ii. 114. *Æ. majus,* Gaertn.; Beddome cxxxix.; Roxb. Fl. Ind. iii. 130. Vern. *Halsi, khalshi,* Beng.; *Bootayet,* Burm.

A small evergreen tree. Bark grey, ¼ inch thick. Wood hard, close-grained. No annual rings. Pores small, uniformly distributed. Medullary rays short, scanty, between moderately broad and broad.

Coast forests and tidal creeks of the Western Coast, Bengal, Burma and the Andaman Islands.

Weight, 40 lbs. per cubic foot. Wood used for firewood and for native huts in Jessore.

		lbs.
E 406.	Sundarbans	40

5. REPTONIA, A. DC.

1. R. buxifolia, A. DC.; Brandis 287. Vern. *Garar,* Afg.; *Gúrgúra,* Punjab.

A large evergreen shrub or small tree. Bark thin, dark grey, tesselated by deep longitudinal and transverse cracks. Wood light brown, with irregular purplish-brown heartwood, very hard, heavy, close and even-grained. Annual rings indistinct. Pores very small, arranged in wavy, radial, branching and anastomosing narrow white belts, of varying width, joined by fine, wavy, concentric lines which divide the firmer and darker tissue into irregularly-shaped figures, in which the white, fine, numerous and regularly distributed medullary rays are distinctly visible.

Salt Range and hills Trans-Indus.

Weight, 71 lbs. per cubic foot. Wood worthy of attention. The fruit is eaten, and the seeds are strung in rosaries.

		lbs.
P 169.	Kohat	71
P 912.	Salt Range	...

ORDER LXIV. SAPOTACEÆ.

Contains 9 genera of trees, sometimes of very large size, and chiefly found in the moist zones. These genera are *Chrysophyllum, Sarcosperma, Sideroxylon, Achras, Isonandra, Dichopsis, Bassia, Payena* and *Mimusops*.

Sideroxylon contains 4 species, the chief of which are *S. tomentosum*, Roxb., Fl. Ind. i. 602; Kurz ii. 116 (*Achras tomentosa*, Beddome cxlii.). Vern. *Hoodigolla*, Kan.; *Thitcho*, Burm., an evergreen tree of Western Mysore and the Prome district in Burma; and *S. elengioides*, Bth. and Hook. f. (*Achras elengioides*, DC.; Beddome t. 235) Vern. *Pálá*, Tam.; *Holay*, Burghers, a common tree of the Western Gháts, whose wood is said by Beddome to be dull red, straight-grained, dense, and to be used for house beams and carpenters' planes; and whose fruit is made into pickles and curries.

Achras Sapota, Linn.; Roxb. Fl. Ind. ii. 181; Beddome cxlii.; Brandis 288, Kurz ii. 118. The Sapota, Sapodilla, Bully Tree or Neesberry. Vern. *Simi, elupai,* Tam.; *Sima, ippa,* Tel.; *Twottapat,* Burm., is a tree of American origin, which is grown in gardens in India as far north as Saharanpur for its fine, good-flavoured fruit. *Isonandra Wightiana*, DC.; Beddome cxli., is a common tree of the Western Ghâts and Ceylon. *I. obovata*, Griff.; Kurz ii. 120 (probably *Dichopsis*), is an evergreen tree of Tenasserim yielding a sort of gutta-percha (B 2687, Tavoy, from Wallich, 1828, is perhaps this).

The *Argan* tree of Morocco which is found growing gregariously in forests in the Atlas Mountains is *Argania Sideroxylon*, R. S. Its leaves and fruit are used for fodder and an oil resembling olive oil is extracted from the seeds.

Wood hard, smooth, durable. Heartwood dark-coloured, generally red. Pores small and moderate-sized, in short, wavy, radial lines, which are frequently oblique. Medullary rays numerous, fine, equidistant, joined by fine, transverse bars or concentric lines of softer texture.

1. CHRYSOPHYLLUM, Linn.

1. C. Roxburghii, G. Don; Beddome t. 236; Thwaites Enum. 174; Kurz ii. 118. *C. acuminatum*, Roxb. Fl. Ind. i. 599. The Star Apple. Vern. *Petakara*, Beng.; *Pithogarkh*, Ass.; *Hali*, Kan.; *Tarsi*, Mar.; *Lawúlú*, Cingh.; *Thankya*, Burm.

An evergreen tree. Wood white, close-grained, moderately hard. Pores small, in short radial lines between the numerous, very fine medullary rays.

Bengal, Burma, Western Ghâts and Ceylon.

Weight, according to A. Mendis, 39 lbs. per cubic foot; Kyd gives weight 40·5 lbs. and P = 710. Wood used for building. Fruit edible.

	lbs.
No. 48. Ceylon Collection (called *Sideroxylon* sp.)	39

2. SARCOSPERMA, Hook. f.

Two trees of the Eastern Himalaya: *S. Griffithii*, Hook. f., and *S. arborea* Hook. f. (*Sideroxylon arboreum*, Ham.; Kurz in Trans. As. Soc. Beng. xlvi. ii. 229; Gamble 53). Vern. *Pahar lampati*, Nep.; *Kulyatzo*, Lepcha, a large tree of the Eastern Himalaya which is used in Sikkim to make canoes.

No. E 3316 from Chenga Forest, Darjeeling Terai, is probably this. Bark light-reddish brown, thin; wood pink, moderately hard, rather light (30·5 lbs. per cubic foot). Pores moderate-sized, in long wavy, radial lines. Medullary rays very numerous, fine, equidistant, the distance between two rays much less than the diameter of the pores. Concentric lines very indistinct.

3. DICHOPSIS, Thw.

About 3 species: *D. elliptica*, Benth. and Hook. f. (*Bassia elliptica*, Dalz.; Beddome t. 43). Vern. *Panchoti pala*, Tam.; *Panchonta*, Kan., is a very large tree of the Western Ghâts, affording a good timber and an inferior description of gutta-percha. *D. calonenra*, Bth. and Hook. f. (*Isonandra caloneura*, Kurz ii. 119), is a tree of the Andaman Islands. *D. Gutta*, Bth. and Hook. f. (*Isonandra Gutta*, Hook.), is the tree which yields the "Gutta-Percha" of commerce, of which large quantities are exported to Europe from Singapore and the Malay Archipelago, where the tree is indigenous.

1. D. polyantha, Benth. and Hook. f. in Gen. Plant. ii. 658. *Bassia polyantha*, Wall. *Isonandra polyantha*, Kurz ii. 119. Vern. *Tali*, Beng.; *Sill-kurta*, Cachar; *Thainban*, Magh.

A moderate-sized evergreen tree. Wood red, hard. Pores moderate-sized, in wavy radial lines, sometimes slightly oblique. Medullary rays very fine, not prominent. Fine, wavy, parallel and equidistant concentric lines.

Cachar, Chittagong and Arracan.

Weight, 53 lbs. per cubic foot. Much valued in Cachar and Chittagong. Mann says it does not float, but he must refer to green wood. Kurz says it yields a good quality of gutta-percha in large quantity. Major Lewin says it is used in Chittagong for making beds, tools, &c., and is sawn into boards for the Calcutta market.

		lbs.
E 1274.	Cachar	53
E 1494.	Sylhet	...
E 1952.	Chittagong	53
E 3285.	Rinkheong Reserve, Chittagong	...

4. BASSIA, Kön.

Contains 3 species of Indian trees with milky juice, useful for their timber as well as for many other products.

Wood moderately hard, heartwood red. Pores moderate-sized, in short radial lines. Medullary rays equidistant, the distance between the rays less than the transverse diameter of the pores.

1. B. latifolia, Roxb. Fl. Ind. ii. 526; Beddome t. 41; Brandis 289. Vern. *Mahwa, mowa, mahúa,* Hind.; *Mahwa, mahúla, maul,* Beng.; *Moha,* Uriya; *Illupi, elupa, kat illipi,* Tam.; *Ippi, yeppa,* Tel.; *Mahu,* Baigas; *Irúp, irrip, irhu,* Gondi; *Mohu,* Kurku; *Moho,* Mar.; *Ilonge,* Kan.; *Poonam,* Mal.; *Quindah* (the oil).

A large deciduous tree. Bark ½ inch thick, grey, with vertical cracks, exfoliating in thin scales. Sapwood large; heartwood reddish brown, from hard to very hard. Annual rings indistinct. Pores moderate-sized, not numerous, in short, sometimes oblique, radial, wavy lines between the numerous, fine, medullary rays, which are joined by numerous parallel, fine, transverse bars.

Indigenous in the forests of Central India. Cultivated and self-sown throughout India.

The weight and transverse strength have been determined by the following experiments:—

Experiment by whom made.	Year.	Wood whence procured.	Weight.	Number of experiments.	Size of bar.	Value of P.
					Ft. In. In.	
Cunningham .	1854	Gwalior . . .	68	1	2 × 1 × 1	715
Skinner, No. 22 .	1862	South India . . .	66	...	......	760
Fowke . .	1859	......	63	...	......	585
R. Thompson .	1868	Central Provinces .	53	...	......	...
List . .	1873	" "	66	...	......	...
Smythies . .	1878	As below . . .	64	9	......	...

The wood is not much used, as the tree is so prized for its flowers that it is rarely felled; it has been tried for railway sleepers in the Central Provinces, and Beddome says it is used for the naves of wheels, for door and window frames and panels, for furniture and country vessels. The flowers are an important article of food in many parts of India; they are eaten raw or cooked, or made into sweetmeats. They are also distilled into a coarse spirit. Mr. V. Ball, quoted in Dr. Hunter's Statistical Account of Bengal, Vol. XVI., page 48, has described the collection and use of the *Mahua* flowers in Chota Nagpore. He says that first class trees often yield about 30 maunds. The right of collection is usually sold both in the Government forests and by private owners, at a rate per tree varying from 4 annas to 2 or 3 rupees. The *mahua* flowers are usually eaten mixed with *sál* seeds or leaves of other plants. Full description of the collection in Palamow is given by Mr. L. R. Forbes quoted at page 243 of the same Volume. In that description he says that in the Palamow Sub-division there are nearly 114,000 *mahwa* bearing trees. He says the average yield of a tree is about 2¼ maunds, and that the flowers sell at about 12 annas per maund. The fruit, ripe or unripe, is eaten; it has two envelopes, the outer two of which are eaten raw or cooked as a vegetable, and the inner one is dried and ground into meal. From the kernel a greenish yellow oil is obtained, which is eaten by the Gonds and other Central Indian tribes, and is used to adulterate ghee and in soap-making. It solidifies at a low temperature, but melts at a temperature of 110°; and though it keeps well in a cold climate, in a hot one it soon becomes rancid and separates into two parts, a clear fluid oil above, and a thick brown substance below. One seer of oil is obtained from 4 seers of kernels.

		lbs.
O 266.	Garhwal (1868)	60
O 1493.	Kheri, Oudh	65
H 2969.	Kumaun, 5,000 feet	66
C 827.	Bairagarh Reserve, Berar	69
C 2771.	Melghát, Berar	...
C 1116.	Ahiri Reserve, Central Provinces	60
C 2731.	Moharli Reserve, Central Provinces (young)	52
C 1243.	Gumsúr, Madras	63

2. B. longifolia, Willd.; Roxb. Fl. Ind. ii. 523; Beddome t. 42; Brandis 290. Vern. *Kat illupi, elupa,* Tam.; *Ippi, yeppa, pinna,* Tel.; *Hippe,* Kan.; *Ellupi,* Mal.; *Mee,* Cingh.

A large evergreen tree. Heartwood red, moderately hard, close-grained. Pores moderate-sized, prominent on a vertical section, in short radial lines between the uniform, equidistant, numerous, fine medullary rays which are joined by fine transverse bars.

South India and Ceylon.

Weight, according to Skinner, No. 23, 60 lbs.; Adrian Mendis 61 lbs. Skinner, gives P = 730, Mendis 724. Beddome says it is very flexible and durable; that it is valued for ship's keels, for trenails and for planking below the water line; and that it is used for carts, furniture and bridge construction. The flowers are eaten in the same way as those of *B. latifolia,* and an oil is expressed from the ripe fruit, which is yellow, semi-solid and used for burning, for soap, and to adulterate ghee. It is also used medicinally, as well as the leaves, bark and the juice of the bark and young fruit.

		lbs.
No. 53.	Ceylon Collection	61

3. B. butyracea, Roxb. Fl. Ind. ii. 527; Brandis 290; Gamble 53. Vern. *Chiúra, chaiúra, phulel,* Kumaun; *Cheuli,* Oudh; *Phalwara,* Hind.; *Chúri,* Nep.; *Yel, yel pote,* Lepcha.

A deciduous tree. Bark ½ inch thick, dark grey, wood light brown, hard. Annual rings marked by a dark line. Pores moderate-sized, somewhat smaller than those of *B. latifolia,* in radial lines of different length between the numerous equidistant, fine medullary rays, which are joined by fine transverse bars.

Sub-Himalayan tract from Kumaun to Bhutan, between 1,500 and 4,500 feet.

Growth fast, 3 to 4 rings per inch of radius. Weight, 52 lbs. per cubic foot. The pulp of the fruit is eaten, and from the seeds a vegetable butter is extracted, of the consistence of fine lard and of a white colour. It does not melt under 120° and keeps a long time without deteriorating. It makes good soap, and is useful for candles as it is said to burn without smoke or unpleasant smell. When perfumed, it is used as an ointment and as an external application for rheumatism. The flowers are not eaten. The bark is used in Sikkim to poison fish.

		lbs.
E 622.	Bamunpokri, Darjeeling	52

5. PAYENA, A. DC.

Two species. *P. paralleloneura,* Kurz ii. 121, is an evergreen tree of the tropical forests of Martaban and Tenasserim.

1. P. lucida, DC.; Kurz. ii. 121. *Ceratophorus Wightii,* Hassk. *Isonandra polyandra,* Wight Icon. t. 1589. Vern. *Dolu-kurta,* Cachar.

An evergreen tree. Wood red, hard. Pores moderate-sized, in short radial lines. Medullary rays very fine, very numerous, uniform, equidistant. Numerous parallel, wavy, concentric lines, not very prominent.

Cachar, Tenasserim (?).
Weight, 45 lbs. per cubic foot. The wood is used for planking.

		lbs.
E 1275.	Cachar	45

6. MIMUSOPS, Linn.

Contains 4 Indian species. *M. Roxburghiana,* Wight; Beddome cxlii.; Brandis 293 Vern. *Kanu pala,* Tam.; *Renga,* Kan., is a common tree of the forests of the Western Ghâts. Beddome, evidently quoting Skinner's No. 96, *M. indica,* Vern. *Palava,* Tam., gives weight = 48 lbs. and P = 845; and says that the wood is reddish brown, rather coarse-grained, but strong, fibrous, durable and easily worked; Brandis, however, doubts whether this is a species of *Mimusops.* It is used for house-building and for gun-stocks.

Evergreen trees. Heartwood red, very hard. Pores small, in oblique lines. The distance between the rays equal to, or larger than, the transverse diameter of the pores. Numerous wavy, concentric lines.

1. M. Elengi, Linn.; Roxb. Fl. Ind. ii. 236; Beddome t. 40; Brandis 293; Kurz ii. 123. Vern. *Bukal, bohl,* Beng., Mar.; *Mulsári, maulser,* Hind.; *Magadam,* Tam.; *Pogada,* Tel.; *Bokal, boklu, mugali,* Kan.; *Barsoli,* Meywar; *Vavoli, ovalli,* Mar.; *Elengi,* Mal.; *Khaya,* Burm.; *Moonemal,* Cingh.

A large evergreen tree. Bark dark grey, rough, deeply cracked with vertical and transverse fissures. Sapwood large, whitish, very hard. Heartwood red. Pores small, in short lines, which are generally radial, but often irregular. Medullary rays very fine, very numerous, uniform and equidistant. Many parallel, wavy, concentric bands.

Wild on the Western Ghâts as far north as Khandalla, Northern Circars, Burma, Andaman Islands and Ceylon. Cultivated throughout India.

Weight, according to Skinner, No. 94, 61 lbs.; Wallich 46 lbs.; Adrian Mendis, 61 lbs.; our specimens give 60 lbs., leaving out the Salem specimen, which is extraordinarily heavy. Skinner gives P = 632. Beddome says the wood is used for house building, carts and cabinet work. Its fragrant star-shaped flowers are used for garlands and are distilled to make a perfume. The fruit is eaten, and the seeds give an oil. The bark is astringent and is used as a febrifuge and tonic.

		lbs.
W 1223.	North Kanara	62
D 1073.	„ Arcot	...
B 2224.	Andaman Islands	60
B 2241.	„	58
No. 56.	Ceylon Collection	61
No. 13.	Salem Collection (marked *Bassia longifolia*)	87

2. M. indica, A. DC.; Brandis 291. *M. hexandra*, Roxb. Fl. Ind. ii. 238.; Beddome cxli. Vern. *Khir, khirni*, Hind.; *Rain*, Meywar; *Palla, kannu palle*, Tam.; *Palle panlo, palla pandu*, Tel.; *Khirni*, Mar.; *Raini*, Gondi; *Palú*, Cingh.

A large evergreen tree. Heartwood red, very hard. Pores small, in wavy, radial and oblique lines. Medullary rays fine, uniform, equidistant, very numerous. Concentric wavy lines irregularly distributed and less prominent than in *M. Elengi*.

Mountains of South India extending in Central India to the sandstone hills of Pachmarhi, north of the Godavari. It is only found on sandstone, and frequently associated with *Buchanania angustifolia* and *Hardwickia binata*.

Weight, Skinner, No. 95, gives 70 lbs.; A. Mendis 68 lbs.; our specimen gives only 60 lbs. per cubic foot. Skinner gives P = 944, Mendis 1,052. The wood is tough, even-grained and durable; it is used for sugar-mill beams, oil-presses, house-posts and for turning. The fruit is eaten.

		lbs.
D 1283.	Anamalai Hills	60
No. 65.	Ceylon Collection	68

3. M. littoralis, Kurz ii. 123. *M. indica*, Kurz, And. Report; Brandis 292. Andaman Bullet Wood. Vern. *Kappali*, Burm.; *Dogola*, And.

A large evergreen tree with thin, smooth, dark-brown bark. Wood red, smooth, very hard and close-grained. Pores extremely small, elongated, subdivided, often in radial lines. Medullary rays very fine, very numerous, uniform and equidistant. Numerous parallel, equidistant, fine, wavy, concentric lines.

Coast forests of the Andaman Islands and Tenasserim, in the Andamans, forming nearly pure forests on the level lands behind the beach and the mangrove swamps.

The weight and transverse strength have been determined by the following experiments:—

Experiment by whom conducted.	Year.	Wood whence procured.	Weight.	Number of experiments.	Size of bar used.	Value of P.
					Ft. In. In.	
Brandis . .	1864	Andamans . . .	67	7	6 × 2 × 2	748
„ . . .	„	„ . . .	66	7	6 × 2 × 1½	963
„ . . .	„	„ . . .	68	11	2 × 1 × ¾	1,091
„ . . .	„	„ . . .	71	5	2 × 1 × 1	779
„ . . .	1865-66	„ . . .	65	3	6 × 2 × 2	931
„ . . .	„	„ . . .	64	1	6 × 2 × 1½	1,090
„ . . .	„	„ . . .	68	8	2 × 1 × ¾	1,266
Bennett . .	1872	„ . . .	66	...	......	1,128
Smythies . .	1878	„ . . .	72	3	......	......

The wood is handsome, it is close-grained and durable, but apt to split. It is used in the Andamans for bridges and house-posts, and Major Ford (1866) said it had been sent to Calcutta to be tried for sleepers. He also says the bark is used to give a red dye.

		lbs.
B 513.	Andaman Islands	41
B 2212.	„ „ (1866)	75
B 2497.	„ „ (Home, 1874, No. 6)	72

ORDER LXV. EBENACEÆ.

Containing 2 Indian Genera of trees or shrubs, *Maba* and *Diospyros*. A full description of all the species of this Order is found in Mr. W. P. Hiern's "Monograph of the Ebenaceæ," Cambridge Phil. Soc. Trans. xii. 1873.

Maba contains 5 species. *M. nigrescens*, Dalz. and Gibs. Bombay Flora, p. 142. Vern. *Raktrúra*, Kan., is a small tree of the Western Ghâts. *M. buxifolia*, Pers.; Beddome cxlviii.; Kurz ii. 139 (*Ferriola buxifolia*, Willd.; Roxb. Fl. Ind. iii. 790.) Vern. *Iramballi, eruvalli, humbilli*, Tam.; *Nella maddi, alli, pishinna*, Tel.; *Kalu-habaraleya*, Cingh.; *Mépyoung*, Burm., is a small evergreen tree of South India and Tenasserim; it is said to have a dark-coloured, hard and durable wood, weighing according to Skinner, No. 89, 58 lbs.; P = 875. *M. micrantha*, Hiern. (*Holochilus micranthus*, Dalz.; Beddome cxlvii.), is a tree of the Sahyádri hills of the Bombay Ghâts. *M. merguiensis*, Hiern; Kurz ii. 139, is a small tree of the Mergui Archipelago. *M. andamanica*, Kurz ii. 140, is an evergreen shrub of the Andaman Islands (*see page 253*).

1. DIOSPYROS, Linn.

Contains 41 or 42 species. From the list given below, which has been taken from Mr. Hiern's Monograph, it will be seen that 4 species are found in Northern India, 15 each in Burma and South India, 9 in Eastern Bengal and 6 in the Andamans; most of the Ceylon species have been omitted:—

Section I. MELONIA—

1. *D. insignis*, Thw. . . . . . S. India, Ceylon.
2. *D. Tupru*, Buch. . . . . . N. India.
3. *D. Melanoxylon*, Roxb. . . . . S. India.
4. *D. sylvatica*, Roxb. . . . . . S. India, Ceylon.
5. *D. Kurzii*, Hiern. . . . . . Andamans.
6. *D. ehretioides*, Wall. . . . . . Burma.
7. *D. hirsuta*, Linn. f. . . . . . S. India, Ceylon.
8. *D. burmanica*, Kurz . . . . . Burma.
9. *D. densiflora*, Wall. . . . . . Burma.

Section II. EBENUS—

10. *D. oocarpa*, Thw. . . . . . S. India, Ceylon.
11. *D. quæsita*, Thw. . . . . . Ceylon.

Section III. NOLTIA—

12. *D. Brandisiana*, Kurz . . . . Burma.
13. *D. pruriens*, Dalz. . . . . . S. India, Ceylon.

Section IV. GUNISANTHUS—

14. *D. foliolosa*, Wall. . . . . . S. India.
15. *D. pilosula*, Wall. . . . . . E. Bengal, Burma, Andamans.
16. *D. paniculata*, Dalz. . . . . S. India.

Section V. GUIACANA—

17. *D. Horsfieldii*, Hiern . . . . Burma.

Section VII. ERMELINUS—

18. *D. stricta*, Roxb. . . . . . E. Bengal.
19. *D. variegata*, Kurz . . . . . Burma.
20. *D. dasyphylla*, Kurz . . . . . Burma.
21. *D. oleifolia*, Wall. . . . . . Burma.
22. *D. flavicans*, Hiern . . . . . Burma, Andamans.
23. *D. sapotoides*, Kurz . . . . . Burma.
24. *D. nigricans*, Wall. . . . . . E. Bengal.
25. *D. Ebenum*, Kön. . . . . . S. India, Ceylon.

Section VIII. PATONIA—

26.	*D. lanceæfolia*, Roxb.	E. Bengal.
27.	*D. undulata*, Wall.	Burma, Andamans.

Section IX. LEUCOXYLON—

28.	*D. buxifolia*, Hiern	S. India.

Section X. DANZLERIA—

29.	{ *D. montana*, Roxb. / *D. cordifolia*, Roxb. }	N. India, S. India, and E. Bengal.
30.	*D. Lotus*, Linn.	N. India.
31.	*D. Kaki*, Linn.	E. Bengal.
32.	*D. chartacea*, Wall.	Burma.
33.	*D. vaccinioides*, Ldl.	Andamans.
34.	*D. Chloroxylon*, Roxb. . . .	S. India.

Section XI. PARALEA—

35.	*D. ramiflora*, Roxb.	E. Bengal.
36.	*D. ovalifolia*, Wight	S. India, Ceylon.

Section XIV. CAVANILLEA—

37.	*D. Embryopteris*, Pers. . . .	N. India, E. Bengal, S. India, Burma, and Ceylon.

Section XV. AMUXIS—

38.	*D. Toposia*, Ham.	E. Bengal, Ceylon.

Unclassified—

39.	*D. grata*, Wall.	Nepal.
40.	*D. orixensis*, Wight	S. India.
41.	*D. pyrrhocarpa*, Miq.	Andamans.

D. insignis, Thw.; Beddome cxlv., is a large tree of the Anamalai Hills and Ceylon. *D. sylvatica*, Roxb. Fl. Ind. ii. 537; Beddome cxliii. Vern. *Tella gada*, Tel. *Kaka suroli*, Kan., is a common tree of the Western Ghâts, with a white, strong wood. *D. burmanica*, Kurz ii. 133. Vern. *Tai-beng*, Burm., is a large tree of Burma, chiefly found in the Eng forests. *D. pruriens*, Dalz.; Beddome cxliv., is a small tree of the Western Ghâts of Bombay, Mysore, Malabar and Ceylon, whose fruit is covered with stinging hairs. *D. pilosula*, Wall. (*Gunisanthus pilosulus*, DC.; Kurz ii. 125), is a tree of the hills of Sylhet, the Pegu Yoma and the Andaman Islands. *D. stricta*, Roxb. Fl. Ind. ii. 539, is a tall tree of Eastern Bengal and Chittagong. *D. nigricans*, Wall., is a tree of the Khasia Hills and Sylhet. *D. lanceæfolia*, Roxb. Fl. Ind. ii. 537; Brandis 297; Kurz ii. 136. Vern. *Ardinia*, Kumaun; *Gulal*, Beng.; *Soilo*, Khasia or Cachar, is an evergreen tree of Eastern Bengal and Tenasserim, extending westwards to Kumaun, and said by Roxburgh to have a hard, durable timber. *D. buxifolia*, Hiern (*D. microphylla*, Beddome cxlv.), is a large tree of the Anamalai Hills, Wynaad and S. Kanara. *D. Kaki*, Linn.; Roxb. Fl. Ind. ii. 527, is a fruit tree of China and Japan found by Hooker in the Khasia Hills, and said by Roxburgh to grow in Nepal. It is cultivated in India and called "*Wilayati gâb.*" *D. Chloroxylon*, Roxb. Fl. Ind. ii. 538; Beddome clxiii.; Brandis 297. Vern. *Ninai*, Bombay; *Illinda, aulanche, nella ulemira*, Tel.; *Andúli* Gondi, is a tree or large shrub of Southern India from Guzerat and Orissa southwards, having a hard and durable yellow wood. *D. ramiflora*, Roxb. Fl. Ind. ii. 535. Vern. *Gulal, uri gâb*, Beng., is a large tree of Eastern Bengal with a strong hard wood. *D. Toposia*, Ham.; Kurz ii. 128. (*D. racemosa*, Roxb. Fl. Ind. ii. 536.) Vern. *Toposi, gulal*, Beng.; *Kahakaala*, Cingh., is a tree of the mountains of E. Bengal and of Ceylon, with an edible fruit.

The structure of the wood of the different species of *Diospyros* is very uniform, and is distinguished by small pores, often in radial lines, and fine, very numerous, uniform and equidistant medullary rays, often closely packed. In most species there are numerous wavy, concentric lines across the rays. In several respects the structure of the ebonies resembles the structure of *Sapotaceæ*.

1. D. Melanoxylon, Roxb. Fl. Ind. ii. 530; Brandis 294. *D. Wightiana,* Beddome t. 67. (Including *D. Tupru,* Buch., *D. exsculpta,* Ham.; Beddome t. 66, and *D. tomentosa,* Roxb. Fl. Ind. ii. 532.) Vern. *Tendu, kendu, temru, abnús* Hind.; *Kend, kyou,* Beng.; *Tumri, tummer, tumki,* Gondi; *Tendù,* Baigas; *Tumri, temru, timburni,* Mar.; *Tumbi, tumbali, karunthumbi,* Tam.; *Tumi, tumki, tumida, timmurri, damádi,* Tel.; *Kendhu,* Uriya; *Balai,* Kan.

A moderate-sized tree. Bark ½ inch thick, greyish black; the inner substance black and charcoal-like, with numerous transverse and longitudinal cracks exfoliating in regular oblong scales. Wood hard, of a light pink colour, with irregular-shaped masses of black ebony in the centre. No annual rings. Pores small, scanty, generally in radial lines. Medullary rays very fine, very numerous, equidistant and uniform, visible on a radial section. Numerous fine, wavy, concentric lines visible in the sapwood. The ebony is jet black with purple streaks, extremely hard, pores and medullary rays difficult to distinguish.

Throughout India, but not in Burma.

The weight and transverse strength have been determined by the following experiments:—

Puckle, in 1859, in Mysore, with bars 2′ × 1″ × 1″	found W = 75	...	...
Skinner, in 1862, No. 62	„ W = 80;	P =	1180
Cunningham, in 1854, in Gwalior, with bars 2′ × 1″ × 1″	„ W = 77;	P =	862
The Central Provinces List of 1873	gives W = 85	...	...

Kyd found W = 49·5, P = 547; R. Thompson 49·6: this was probably the outer wood; Wallich gives 61; Smythies' measurements of our specimens give: outer wood 54 lbs., ebony 72 lbs., but the good specimens with only ebony weigh 77, which is the best weight to take, and which accords with Brandis' statement that the weight per cubic foot varies from 75 to 80 lbs. Besides Skinner's and Cunningham's values for P, Fowke gives P = 756. The wood is used for building, shoulder-poles and carriage shafts, and the ebony for all purposes of fancy work and carving. The fruit is edible.

		lbs.
P 170.	Hoshiarpur, Punjab (Stewart, 1866), the specimen referred to at p. 137 of the "Punjab Plants"	69
P 469.	Ajmere	59
O 1492.	Kheri, Oudh	55
O 2981.	Bahraich, Oudh	48
C 828.	Bairagarh Reserve, Berar	53
C 1113.	Ahiri Reserve, Central Provinces	...
C 2754.	Moharli Reserve, Central Provinces	...
C 1237.	Gumsúr, Madras	65
C 1301.	„ „	77
C 1302.	„ „	68
D 2008.	Mysore	73
D 2045.	„	70
No. 26.	Salem Collection	82

2. D. Kurzii, Hiern; Kurz ii. 131. Andamanese Marble Wood. Vern. *Teakah, thitkya,* Burm.; *Pecha-da,* And.

An evergreen tree, with very thin, smooth, grey bark. Wood handsome, streaked with black and grey; the grey wood hard; the black wood very hard, with alternate streaks of black ebony and grey wood. The mass of ebony occupying the centre of the tree is large and very irregular in outline, and frequently encloses interrupted concentric belts of light-coloured wood. Pores small and very small, often oval and subdivided, between the very fine and extremely numerous, uniform and equidistant, wavy, medullary rays. Numerous, very fine transverse bars across the rays.

Andaman Islands.
Weight of the ebony 80 lbs. per cubic foot; the specimens partly ebony, partly grey wood, give 57 to 62 lbs. Brandis in his Memo. of August 25th, 1874, gives 70 lbs. The wood is used for cabinet work and should be better known, as a substitute for the Ceylon Calamander wood, which it resembles in appearance. It is said by Major Ford to be used in the Andamans for handles and sheaths of blades, and for furniture. Home's surveys gave 224 trees or 1 tree per acre; so it is pretty common.

		lbs.
B 2203.	Andaman Islands (1866)	57
B 2498.	„ „ (Home, 1874, No. 15)	80
B 521.	„ „	62

3. D. ehretioides, Wall.; Kurz ii. 129. Vern. *Ouk-chingza*, Burm.
A large tree with dark-grey bark. Wood dark grey, with darker streaks, moderately hard, even-grained. Pores moderate-sized, scanty, often oval and subdivided. Medullary rays fine, numerous. Numerous fine, wavy, concentric lines across the rays.

Burma.
Weight, according to Brandis' List of 1862, No. 73, 41 lbs.; our specimens give 53 lbs. The wood is used for house-posts.

		lbs.
B 1422.	Tharrawaddi, Burma	54
B 2542.	Burma (1862)	52

4. D. oocarpa, Thw. Enum. 180. Vern. *Kadoembaireya*, Cingh.
Wood purplish brown, with black streaks, moderately hard. Pores moderate-sized. Medullary rays very fine, very numerous. Numerous fine, wavy, concentric lines.

Concan, Mysore and Ceylon.
A handsome wood. Weight, 45 lbs. per cubic foot.

	lbs.
No. 40. Ceylon Collection (marked *Diospyros sp.*)	45

5. D. quæsita, Thwaites Enum. 179; Beddome cxlv.; Brandis 296. Calamander Wood. Vern. *Kaloomidereya*, Cingh.

A large tree. Wood hard, consisting of irregular alternate layers of black ebony and greyish brown wood. Pores scanty, moderate-sized, in short radial lines. Medullary rays fine, numerous, equidistant, traversed by innumerable wavy concentric lines.

Ceylon.
Weight, according to Adrian Mendis' List, 57 lbs. per cubic foot; Skinner, No. 62, 60 lbs.; our specimen gives 53 lbs. Skinner gives P = 751.
The most valuable ornamental wood in Ceylon; it is now scarce, but is much in demand.

		lbs.
D 2923.	S. India or Ceylon	53
No. 12.	Ceylon Collection (*D. hirsuta*)	57

6. **D. Ebenum,** König; Roxb. Fl. Ind. ii. 529; Beddome t. 65; Brandis 296; Thwaites Enum. 179. Ebony. Vern. *Ebans, abnús, tendu,* Hind.; *Kendhu,* Uriya; *Acha, tumbi, shengútan, kaka-tati, tai,* Tam.; *Tuki,* Tel.; *Karemara,* Kan.; *Tai, tendu, abnús,* Mar.; *Mallali,* Manjarabad; *Kalúwara,* Cing.

A large tree. Wood grey, with irregularly-shaped masses of jet-black ebony near the centre, frequently with lighter-coloured streaks. Structure of the wood similar to that of *D. Melanoxylon,* but pores slightly larger, oval and subdivided, not in radial lines. The structure of the ebony is exceedingly indistinct.

South India and Ceylon.

Weight, according to Beddome 81 lbs.; Adrian Mendis, 71 lbs.; our specimens give 61 to 70 lbs.; A. Mendis gives P = 720. The wood is used for inlaying and ornamental turnery, but the demand for it is not very great.

		lbs.
W 731.	South Kanara	61
W 750.	" "	70
No. 13.	Ceylon Collection (marked *Diospyros* sp.)	71

7. **D. montana,** Roxb. Fl. Ind. ii. 538; Beddome cxliii.; Brandis 296. Vern. *Hirek, keindu, temru, pasendu,* Pb.; *Tendu, dasáundu, lohari, bistênd,* Hind.; *Makar-tendi,* Banda; *Pasend,* Bhurtpur; *Temru,* Meywar; *Ambia,* Banswara; *Hádru,* Panch Mehals; *Kanchan, kadal, pattewar, patwan,* C.P.; *Muchi tanki, yerragoda, micha-tummurra,* Tel.; *Timru, timbúrni,* Mar.; *Goindú, kala goindu, balkuniki, jagalagante,* Kan.

A moderate-sized tree, with thin, pinkish grey, smooth bark, when old exfoliating in thick irregular flakes. Wood yellowish grey, soft, no heartwood, no annual rings. Pores numerous, small, in radial lines between the closely-packed medullary rays, which are very fine, and on a radial section distinctly visible as horizontal plates. White streaks parallel to the medullary rays.

Most parts of India except Sindh, the Northern Punjab and Burma.

Weight, 45·5 lbs. per cubic foot. The wood is durable and would be good for furniture.

		lbs.
C 192.	Mandla, Central Provinces (1870)	47
C 1167.	Ahiri Reserve, Central Provinces	44

8. **D. cordifolia,** Willd.; Roxb. Fl. Ind. ii. 538; Beddome cxliii.; Kurz ii. 130. *D. montana,* Roxb. (part); Brandis 296. Vern. *Bangáb,* Beng.; *Vackana, kaka ulimera,* Tel.; *Gyútbeng,* Burm.

Wood reddish, moderately hard. Pores small, often oval and subdivided. Medullary rays very fine and very numerous, with fine, wavy, transverse lines across.

Bengal, South India and Burma.

Weight, 47 lbs. per cubic foot; Kurz (evidently quoting Brandis' List of 1862, No. 74) gives 49 lbs.; Skinner, No. 60, gives 70 lbs. P = 1017, but this may be a mistake for some other species.

Wood useful for cabinet-work.

		lbs.
E 715.	Chittagong (*Moishkanda,* Beng.; *Chapraka,* Magh) . .	45
B 2541.	Burma (1862).	49

9. D. Lotus, Linn.; Brandis 297. Vern. *Amlúk, malúk,* Pb.

A middle-sized tree with dark-brown or black tesselated bark. Wood grey, moderately hard, close-grained. Pores small, in radial groups. Medullary rays very fine, closely packed. No concentric lines.

Punjab Himalaya, in Hazara and Kashmir, from 2,500 to 6,000 feet; Afghanistan, Beluchistan, extending to Southern Europe (*Mathieu,* Fl. For. p. 205).

Growth slow, 10 rings per inch of radius (*Brandis*). The fruit is sweetish and is eaten fresh or dried, by the Afghans; Mathieu says that in Southern France it is eaten when half-rotten like the Medlar.

H 3183. Dungagalli, Hazara, 5,000 feet.

10. D. Embryopteris, Pers.; Beddome t. 69; Brandis 298; Kurz ii. 128. *D. glutinosa,* Roxb. Fl. Ind. ii. 533. *Embryopteris glutinifera,* Roxb. Vern. *Gáb, makur-kendi,* Beng., Hind.; *Kúsi,* Banda; *Kendu,* Ass.; *Gusvakendhu,* Uriya; *Tumbika, pani-chika,* Tam.; *Tumil, tumika,* Tel.; *Holle-tupra,* Coorg; *Kusharta,* Kan.; *Timberee,* Cingh.

An evergreen shrub or small tree, with dark-green foliage and long shining leaves. Bark smooth, dark grey, almost black, with a greenish tinge. Wood white, moderately hard, close-grained. Pores small, scanty, in short radial lines. Medullary rays very fine, very numerous, uniform and equidistant.

Throughout India and Burma, except the arid and dry zones in the Punjab and Sindh.

Growth moderate, 7-8 rings per inch of radius (*Brandis*). Weight, our specimen gives 53 lbs. per cubic foot. Wood used in building, in Ceylon for masts and yards.

The fruit is large, reddish; it contains a viscid pulp, which is used as gum in bookbinding, and in place of tar for paying the seams of fishing-boats. Its use for "gabing" boats is general throughout the rivers of Lower Bengal and Assam. An infusion is used to render fishing-nets durable. It is full of tannin and is used in medicine as an astringent. The oil extracted from the seeds is used in native medicine.

		lbs.
O 3161.	Dehra Dún	52

11. D. pyrrhocarpa, Miq.; Kurz ii. 136. Vern. *Tay,* Burm.

An evergreen tree. Wood reddish brown, moderately hard to hard. Pores small, in short radial lines. Medullary rays very fine, closely packed, with fine transverse lines across them.

Andaman Islands.

Weight, 52 lbs. per cubic foot. Major Ford says the fruit is eaten by the Burmese and is used as a red dye for linen; that Chinese umbrellas are dyed with the juice, which also has the property of rendering them waterproof.

		lbs.
B 1991.	Andaman Islands (Kurz, 1866)	50
B 2244.	" " (1866)	54

12. D. *sp.* from the Andamans (B 2232, 61 lbs.) Vern. *Moong,* Burm., has very small scanty pores, often in short radial lines between the closely-packed, very fine, uniform, medullary rays. No concentric lines; white streaks parallel to the medullary rays.

Major Ford says that " the wood is hard, compact and close-grained, dark-purplish grey with narrow streaks of jet black ebony. The bark and fruit of this tree produce a beautiful black dye. The Burmese use the wood for flutes and other wind instruments, for earrings, carved images, tool handles, picture frames, &c. The black heartwood of large trees has a diameter of about 4 or 5 inches." It may possibly be *D. pilosula*, Wall.

---

13. B 1997 collected on the Andamans by Kurz in 1866 and marked *D. undulata* (Hingado) is a large tree with small black wood in the centre of large trees. Wood purplish grey. Pores, small, sometimes in short radial lines between the closely-packed, very fine, undulating, medullary rays. Weight, 49 lbs. Numerous wavy concentric lines.

B 2472 from Andamans (*Kurz*, 1866) marked *Maba andamanica*, with bluish-grey wood, is similar in structure to the preceding number. Weight, 49 lbs. per cubic foot.

ORDER LXVI. STYRACEÆ.

Contains two Genera of Indian trees or shrubs, *Symplocos* and *Styrax*. *Styrax* contains about 3 or 4 Indian species. *S. serrulatum*, Roxb. Fl. Ind. ii. 415; Kurz ii. 142; Gamble 54. Vern. *Kúm-jameva*, Beng.; *Chamo*, Lepcha, is a small evergreen tree of Sikkim, Eastern Bengal and Chittagong. *S. virgatum*, Wall.; Kurz ii. 142 is a small evergreen tree of Eastern Bengal. Both these species yield a kind of gum benjamin or benzoin of inferior quality. *S. rugosum*, Kurz ii. 141, is an evergreen tree of the Martaban Hills. *S. Benzoin* of the Malay Archipelago yields the true "Gum Benzoin," which is used in medicine, in perfumery, and to make incense. *S. officinale* of the Levant yields the gum known as "Storax," used in medicine and perfumery.

E 3320, Darjeeling, 6,500 feet, probably *S. virgatum*, Wall., has a thin bark; white, close-grained moderately hard wood with faint white, regular, concentric bands. The pores are scanty, usually subdivided; and the medullary rays short, fine, very numerous.

1. SYMPLOCOS, Linn.

Contains 25 to 30 species of Indian trees, generally small. *S. spicata*, Roxb. Fl. Ind. ii. 541; Beddome cxlix.; Brandis 300; Kurz ii. 146; Gamble 54. Vern. *Lodh*, Hind.; *Lodh bholia, búri*, Beng.; *Palyok*, Lepcha; *Boothgani*, Burghers, is a tree of the North-East Himalaya, Western Ghâts and Tenasserim, whose leaves are used in dyeing and whose seeds are strung as beads and hung round children's necks to prevent evil. *S. racemosa*, Roxb. Fl. Ind. ii. 539; Brandis 300; Kurz ii. 144; Gamble 53. Vern. *Lodh*, Beng.; *Chamlani*, Nep.; *Palyok*, Lepcha; *Kaiday*, Mechi; *Singyan*, Bhutia, is a common small tree of the plains and lower hills of Bengal and Burma, chiefly in dry forests. The leaves and bark are used in dyeing. *S. Gardneriana*, Wight; Beddome t. 237, is a handsome tree of the Western Ghâts. Mr. Mann says that *S. grandiflora*, Vern. *Bumroti*, Ass.; *Moat soom*, Phekial, is used to feed silkworms (the Muga worm, *Antheræa Assama*) and as a dye in Assam.

Wood white, close-grained, apt to warp and split. Pores very small. Medullary rays very fine.

1. S. cratægoides, Hamilton; Brandis 298; Kurz ii. 147. Vern. *Lú, lándar, loj, losh*, Pb.; *Lodh*, Kumaun; *Loja*, Sutlej.

A large shrub or small tree. Bark light grey, corky, with long vertical cracks. Wood white, hard, close-grained, splits and twists in seasoning. Pores small and very small, uniformly distributed. Medullary rays numerous, fine and very fine. Annual rings visible.

Himalaya from the Indus to Assam, between 3,000 and 8,000 feet; Khasia Hills; Hills of Martaban.

Growth slow, 15 rings per inch of radius. Weight, 45 to 54 lbs. per cubic foot. Wood durable, has been recommended for turning and would do for carvings, if properly seasoned. The leaves and bark give a yellow dye. This may be the *Lood* tree on which, according to Mr. Brownlow of Cachar, the silkworms *Attacus Atlas* and *A. Canningi* are fed.

		lbs.
H 54.	Nagkanda, Simla, 7,000 feet	54
H 2880.	" " " "	...
H 3018.	Kotgarh, " " "	...
H 429.	Kuruwa Forest, Jaunsar, 6,000 feet	45

2. S. lucida, Wall.; Kurz ii. 143; Gamble 54. Vern. *Kharani*, Nep.; *Chashing*, Bhutia.

A small evergreen tree. Bark thin, brown. Wood white, soft. Annual rings distinctly marked by a continuous line of pores. Pores very small, numerous. Medullary rays fine and very fine, numerous.

Sikkim Himalaya and hills of Martaban.

Growth moderate, 6 to 11 rings per inch of radius. Weight, 36 lbs. per cubic foot. Used for fuel and rough house-posts.

		lbs.
E 2390.	Rangbúl Forest, Darjeeling	36

3. S. ramosissima, Wall.; Brandis 299; Gamble 54. Vern. *Lodh*, Hind.; *Kala kharani, silingi*, Nep ; *Tungchong*, Lepcha.

A small evergreen tree with dark red bark. Wood white, soft, even-grained. Pores numerous, very small. Medullary rays fine and very fine, unequally distributed. Annual rings visible.

Himalaya from the Jumna to Bhutan ascending to 7,500 feet, Khasia Hills.

Growth moderate, 6 to 9 rings per inch of radius. Weight, 37 lbs. per cubic foot. Brandis says that in Sikkim the yellow silkworm is fed on its leaves.

		lbs.
E 367.	Rangbúl, Darjeeling, 7,000 feet	37
E 3336.	Rangirúm, Darjeeling, 6,000 feet	...

4. S. sp.; Gamble 54. Vern. *Lal chandan*, Nep.

Wood white, soft, close-grained. Annual rings marked by a white line. Pores extremely small. Medullary rays fine, numerous. Wood with vertical streaks of bright red colour; the red wood, which is most abundant in the root, is pounded and used for caste marks by Nepalese.

		lbs.
E 370.	Kalapokri, Darjeeling, 9,000 feet	45
E 2391.	Thosum La, Dumsong, 8,000 feet	...

(It is possible that this may prove to be *Daphniphyllum himalayense*, Müll. Arg.)

ORDER LXVII. OLEACEÆ.

Contains 10 Indian Genera, belonging to 4 Tribes, *viz.*:—

Tribe	I.—Jasmineæ	*Jasminum* and *Nyctanthes.*
"	II.—Syringeæ	*Schrebera* and *Syringa.*
"	III.—Fraxineæ	*Fraxinus.*
"	IV.—Oleineæ	*Osmanthus, Linociera, Olea, Ligustrum* and *Myxopyrum.*

Nyctanthes Arbor-tristis, Linn.; Roxb. Fl. Ind. i. 86; Beddome t. 240; Brandis 314; Kurz ii. 155. Vern. *Har, siháru, harsinghar, saherwa, seoli, nibari*, Hind.; *Harsinghar, sephálikà*, Beng.; *Pakúra, ladúri, kúri*, Pb.; *Shálí*, Meywar;

Kirsahár, Baigas; *Khersári*, Gondi; *Gongo seoli*, Uriya; *Khúrasli*, Mar.; *Karassi*, Bhíl; *Manja-pu, paghala*, Tam.; *Poghada, karchiá*, Tel.; *Hursing*, Kan.; *Tsaybeeloo*, Burm., is a large shrub of the Sub-Himalayan forests from the Chenab to the Sarda, Oudh, Bengal, Central India and Burma, with a brown, close-grained wood, used only for fuel. The leaves are used for polishing wood, and the flowers give an orange dye. It is often cultivated for ornament. *Myxopyrum smilacifolium*, Bl.; Kurz ii. 160, is a climbing shrub of the Darjeeling Terai, Eastern Bengal, Chittagong and Martaban.

Wood with few exceptions light-coloured, moderately hard or hard, most species without heartwood. In the genera *Fraxinus, Jasminum, Syringa* and *Ligustrum*, the annual rings are marked by continuous lines or belts of pores. In the other genera the pores are small and uniformly distributed, except in *Osmanthus*, where they are in reticulate tails. Medullary rays sharply defined.

1. JASMINUM, Linn.

Contains a large number of Indian shrubs, erect or climbing, of little importance. *J. Sambac*, Aiton; Roxb. Fl. Ind. i. 88; Brandis 311. Vern. *Chamba, múgra, bél*, Hind.; *Mallikaphal*, Beng.; *Sapai, mali*, Burm., is a fragrant climbing shrub cultivated throughout India. *J. hirsutum*, Willd.; Brandis 312; Kurz ii. 154. (*J. pubescens*, Roxb. Fl. Ind. i. 91; Gamble 55). Vern. *Kunda*, Hind.; *Parirajhar*, Nep., is a common shrub of the Sub-Himalayan tract from the Jumna eastwards, Bengal and the Central Provinces.

1. J. revolutum, Sims; Brandis 313. Vern. *Chamba, juari, tsonu, tsuman, summun, kuja*, Pb.; *Sonajáhi*, Kumaun.

A small shrub with soft, thin, grey bark. Wood white, moderately hard, even-grained. Annual rings marked by a narrow continuous belt of pores, which are small, while the pores in the outer part of the ring are extremely small. Medullary rays extremely fine, very numerous.

Afghanistan, Salt Range, Himalaya from the Indus to Nepal, Nilgiris and Ceylon. Growth slow, 25 to 40 rings per inch of radius.

		lbs.
H 2891, H 3027.	Nagkanda, Simla, 7,000 feet	45

2. 3. *J. grandiflorum*, Linn.; Roxb. Fl. Ind. i. 100; Brandis 313; Kurz ii. 150. Vern. *Chambel, jati*, Hind.; *Myablay*, Burm. found in the Himalaya and often cultivated (No. H 3026, Nagkanda, 8,000 feet) and *J. officinale*, Linn.; Brandis 313. Vern. *Chamba, chirichog, kiri*, Kashmir; *Bansú, kwer, dumni*, Chenab; *Dassi, samsem*, Ravi; *Suni, somun*, Sutlej; *Chambeli*, Kumaun, a climber of the Salt Range and Himalaya from the Indus to the Sarda (No. H 2879, Nagkanda, 8,000 feet) have white woods with a structure resembling that of *J. revolutum*.

2. SCHREBERA, Roxb.

1. S. swietenioides, Roxb. Fl. Ind. i. 109; Beddome t. 248; Brandis 305; Kurz ii. 156. Vern. *Moka, góki, ghant, gantha*, Hind.; *Patali, ghanta patali*, Bandelkhand; *Jantia*, Uriya; *Makkam, mokob*, Tel.; *Mogalinga*, Tam.; *Ghatlár*, Baigas; *Karindi, mokha, dhakka*, Gondi; *Jhán*, Kurku; *Mokkak*, Bhíl; *Kalgante*, Coorg; *Thitswaylway*, Burm.

A deciduous tree with grey bark, $\frac{1}{6}$ inch thick, exfoliating in thin irregular scales. Wood brownish grey, hard, close-grained, polishes well. No heartwood, but irregular masses of purple or claret-coloured wood in the centre, and scattered throughout the tree. Annual rings indistinct. Pores small, uniformly distributed, often in radial groups,

Medullary rays fine, numerous, uniform and at equal distances, conspicuous on a radial section as narrow plates.

Kumaun, Burma, Central and South India.

Weight, 56 lbs. per cubic foot; Brandis says 50 lbs. The wood is durable, works freely and does not warp or split. It is used for combs, weavers' beams and turning.

		lbs.
C 829.	Bairagarh Reserve, Berar	59
C 2772.	Melghát, Berar	...
C 193.	Mandla, Central Provinces (1870)	51
C 1108.	Ahiri Reserve, Central Provinces	...
C 1410.	Moharli „ „	...
B 1413.	Burma	59
B 3149.	„ (1862)	54

3. SYRINGA, Linn.

Contains 2 species. *S. persica*, Linn.; Brandis 306. Vern. *Hiásmin*, Kashmir, is a glabrous shrub found wild by Dr. Stewart at 8,000 feet on the Suliman Range and cultivated in the Punjab and Kashmir. *S. vulgaris*, Linn., is the "Lilac" so much prized in European gardens and occasionally cultivated in the Himalaya.

1. S. Emodi, Wall.; Brandis 306. Vern. *Ban phúnt, ban dakhúr, banchír, razli, juari, rangkrún, kehimu, lolti, leila, shafri, shapri, duden, chilanghati*, Pb.; *Ghia*, Kumaun.

A large shrub with grey bark, $\frac{1}{10}$ inch thick. Wood smooth, hard, with a small, dark-coloured heartwood. Annual rings well marked by a narrow porous belt. Pores small in the spring wood, extremely small and arranged in irregular groups in the autumn wood. Medullary rays fine, numerous.

Safed-koh, North-West Himalaya from the Indus to the Sarda, ascending to 11,000 feet.

Growth slow, 20 rings per inch of radius. Weight, 59 lbs. per cubic foot.

		lbs.
H 2911.	Nagkanda, Simla, 8,000 feet	...
H 3023.	„ „ 9,000 „	59

4. FRAXINUS, Tournef.

Contains 3 Indian species found in the North-West Himalaya. *F. excelsior*, Linn.; Brandis 303. Vern. *Súm, kúm*, Pb. The Ash, is found in the valleys of the Jhelum, Chenab and Ravi between 4,000 and 6,000 feet. *F. Moorcroftiana*, Wall.; Brandis 301. Vern. *Shang*, Afg.; *Hanúz, núch, shilli, chúj, siju, chúm, thúm, sandal, shangal, butru*, Pb.; *Auga, gaha*, North-Western Provinces, is a large shrub or small tree of Afghanistan, the Trans-Indus and the North-West Himalaya from the Jhelum to Kumaun. It is often gregarious, has a slow growth (20 rings per inch of radius) and a light-brown, heavy, hard, close-grained wood which is used for tool handles and makes good fuel.

Wood moderately hard, white in some species; with a brown heartwood. Pores large and numerous in the spring wood; small, scanty and often arranged in groups in the autumn wood. Medullary rays fine, uniform, equidistant. In *F. floribunda, excelsior*, and other species the wood consists of alternate layers of soft porous spring wood, and hard, compact, autumn wood.

1. F. floribunda, Wall.; Brandis 302. Vern. *Banárish*, Afg.; *Súm, súnnu, shún, húm, hamu, túnnú*, Pb.; *Angan, angu, dakkúri*, North-Western Provinces; *Kangu, tahási*, Nep.

A large deciduous tree. Bark grey, corky, with longitudinal furrows. Wood white, with a light red tinge, no heartwood, soft to moderately hard. Annual rings marked by an almost continuous line of large pores, the layers cutting differently under the knife. Pores in the outer part of the annual ring smaller. The large pores of the annual rings are well defined on a longitudinal section. Medullary rays fine, numerous, giving the wood a mottled appearance on a radial section.

Himalaya, from the Indus to Sikkim, between 5,000 and 8,500 feet.

Growth slow to moderately fast, averaging 13 rings per inch of radius for our specimens; Wallich says 8 rings (*Brandis*). Weight, 48 lbs. per cubic foot. The wood is tough and hard, and is used for oars, jampan poles, ploughs and other purposes.

		lbs.
H 612.	Parbatti Valley, Kulu, 7,000 feet	47
H 904.	Upper Chenab, 8,000 feet	...
H 2971.	Naini Tál	49
H 3190.	Dungagalli, Hazara, 7,000 feet	...

The structure is exceedingly similar to that of *F. excelsior*, the European Ash (No. 2974), but that species has a distinct brown heartwood.

5. OSMANTHUS, Lour.

Contains 2 or 3 species. *O. fragrans*, Lour.; Gamble 54. (*Olea fragrans*, Thunb.; Roxb. Fl. Ind. i. 105; Brandis 309.) Vern. *Shilling*, *silang*, Kumaun; *Tungrung*, Lepcha, is a small tree of the Himalaya from Kumaun to Bhutan, sometimes gregarious, but more often planted for the sake of its very sweet-scented flowers. The wood is whitish, mottled with brown; the flowers are used to keep insects away from clothes in Kumaun, and in China to flavour tea.

1. O. nov. sp. Vern. *Silingi*, Nep.; *Chashing*, Bhutia.

A small tree, with grey bark, white twigs, and opposite coriaceous leaves. Wood white, hard, close-grained, seasons well, mottled on vertical sections. Pores very small and extremely small, arranged in wavy, irregular, anastomosing oblique bands, which form a most elegant network on a horizontal section. Medullary rays fine, uniform, equidistant, numerous, traversed by parallel concentric lines of soft texture.

Tonglo, Darjeeling, 10,000 feet.

The structure of the flowers shews it to be a species of *Osmanthus*. The leaves are opposite, small, about 1 inch long, serrated; the flowers white, the berries purple, resembling small plums, and the bark of the twigs yellowish white, with raised specks.

		lbs.
E 379.	Tonglo, Darjeeling, 10,000 feet	53

6. OLEA, Linn.

Contains 6 to 8 species of Indian trees. *O. dioica*, Roxb. Fl. Ind. i. 106; Beddome cliii; Kurz ii. 157; Gamble 54. Vern. *Atta-jam*, Beng.; *Kala kiamoni*, Nep.; *Timber nyok*, Lepcha; *Koli*, Tam.; *Parjamb*, *burra-nuge*, *mudla*, Kan.; *Karambu*, Mar., is a tree of the forests of Northern and Eastern Bengal, Chittagong and South Kanara; giving, according to Beddome, a valuable strong timber. *O. dentata*, Wall; Kurz ii. 157, is an evergreen tree of the Burma forests. *O. europœa*, Linn., the Olive, has been introduced on the Himalaya and the Nilgiris.

Wood hard, with a distinct heartwood in a few species. Pores small, numerous, subdivided or in short radial groups. Medullary rays uniform, equidistant, fine or very fine.

1. O. ferruginea, Royle; Brandis 576. *O. cuspidata,* Wall.; Brandis 307. Vern. *Khwan, shwan,* Trans.-Indus; *Zaitún,* Afg.; *Ko, kohú, káo, kau,* Pb.; *Kau,* Hind.; *Khau,* Sind.

A moderate-sized deciduous tree. Bark grey, thin, smooth when young, when old exfoliating in large narrow strips. Sapwood whitish; heartwood large, regularly shaped, from light brown or olive brown to nearly black, smooth, extremely hard. Annual rings distinctly marked by a belt of closely-packed pores. Pores in the rest of the annual ring extremely small, in irregular patches of soft tissue. Medullary rays fine, uniform, very numerous, equidistant.

Sind, Suliman Range, Salt Range, North-West Himalaya, extending as far as the Jumna eastwards, and ascending to 6,000 feet.

Weight, 65 to 82 lbs. per cubic foot, averaging 73 lbs. Brandis says that Sind wood weighs 65 lbs., but his specimen from the Sind hills reaches 82 lbs. The wood polishes well and is highly prized for turning, for combs, agricultural implements and fuel. The fruit is eaten, but is rarely found on the trees owing to the fondness of crows for it. Oil has been extracted from it, but only in small quantity though of good quality. The wood is worth trying as a substitute for boxwood or for the wood of the European olive and for inlaying work, as it is often prettily marbled.

			lbs.
H	162.	Shahpur (Stewart, 1866)	65
H	118.	Vaziri-Rupi, 4,000 feet	73
H	779.	Chamba, 3,500 feet	71
H	425.	Koti Forest, Jaunsar, 6,000 feet	75
P	2729.	Hills of Sind	82

2. O. glandulifera, Wall.: Beddome t. 238; Brandis 309. *O. paniculata,* Roxb. Fl. Ind. i. 105, not *paniculata,* R. Brown (an Australian species). Vern. *Gúlíli, raban, síra, phalsh,* Pb.; *Gair, galdu, garúr,* Kumaun.

A moderate-sized tree. Bark ⅛ inch thick, grey, uneven, exfoliating in brittle scales. Wood reddish grey, hard. Annual rings marked by a distinct line. Pores moderate-sized, oval, subdivided, uniformly distributed. Medullary rays fine, numerous, prominent on a radial section.

Outer Himalaya from the Indus to Nepal, between 2,500 and 6,000 feet. Nilgiris and Anamalai Hills in South India.

A section of a tree 43 years old, in the Botanic Gardens, Calcutta, shewed 43 rings on a radius of 10 inches (*Brandis*); this would give 4·3 rings per inch or fast growth: our specimens give 12 to 33 rings per inch of radius. Weight, on an average, 54·5 lbs. per cubic foot. The wood is durable, takes a good polish and is not liable to be eaten by insects.

			lbs.
H	928.	Hazara, 3,000 feet	59
H	2940.	Suni, Simla, 3,000 feet	55
H	222.	Garhwal Hills (1868)	50

7. LIGUSTRUM, Linn.

Contains about 6 species of shrubs or small trees. *L. robustum,* Hook. f. and Th.; Beddome cliii.; Brandis 310; Gamble 54 (*Phillyrea robusta,* Roxb. Fl. Ind. i. 101. *Olea robusta,* Kurz ii. 158) Vern. *Keri, banpatara,* Hind.; *Jamu,* Nep., is a small tree of the outer Himalaya from Kumaun eastwards, Bengal, Southern India and Burma, with a hard durable wood. *L. nepalense,* Wall.; Roxb. Fl. Ind. i. 149; Brandis 310. Vern. *Gúmgacha,* Nep.; and *L. bracteolatum,* Don; Brandis 310, are small trees of Kumaun and Nepal. *L. microphyllum,* Beddome cliv., is a shrub of Coorg. The European Privet is *L. vulgare,* Linn.

1. L. compactum, Hook. f. and Th.; Brandis 310.

A large shrub. Bark grey, $\frac{1}{12}$ inch thick. Wood white, moderately hard. Annual rings marked by a narrow porous belt. Pores small in the spring wood, extremely small in the autumn wood. Medullary rays fine and very fine, numerous.

North-West Himalaya from the Beas to the Sarda, at 3,500 to 6,000 feet. Growth slow, 17 rings per inch of radius. Weight, 64 lbs. per cubic foot.

	lbs.
H 3059. Koti, Simla, 6,000 feet	64

8. LINOCIERA, Swartz.

Contains about 6 species. *L. intermedia*, Wight. (*Chionanthus intermedia*, Beddome t. 239) and *L. malabarica*, Wall. (*C. malabarica*, Beddome cliv.) are large trees of the Western Ghâts, while Kurz under *Chionanthus* describes 4 species from Burma and the Andamans.

No. 3211 is *L. macrophylla* (*Chionanthus macrophyllus*, Kurz ii. 159) from a cultivated tree in the Saharanpur Gardens; it has a brown bark, $\frac{1}{8}$ inch thick; pinkish white wood; pores small, arranged in radial lines or groups; and medullary rays fine, bent where they touch the pores.

ORDER LXVIII. SALVADORACEÆ.

Contains 2 genera, *Salvadora* and *Azima*. *Azima tetracantha*, Lamk.; Kurz ii. 161, is a straggling, diœcious, thorny shrub of South India and Burma. It is very common, and the leaves and bark are used in native medicine as an expectorant. (Wight Ill. t. 152, p. 156.)

1. SALVADORA, Linn.

1. S. persica, Linn.; Roxb. Fl. Ind. i. 389; Brandis 315. *S. Wightiana*, Beddome t. 247. The Tooth-brush Tree. Vern. *Arák, irak*, Arab.; *Kabbar, kharidjar, pilu*, Sind; *Jhál*, Rajputana; *Kauri ván, kauri-jal, jhár, jhit*, Pb.; *Opa, ughai*, Tam.; *Waragu-wenki, ghunia*, Tel.; *Pílu*, Mar.

A small evergreen tree, with thin grey bark. Wood white, soft. Pores small, in short radial lines, but enclosed in oval patches of soft tissue. Numerous fine concentric bands of soft tissue, separating broader bands of firm texture, in which the fine and numerous medullary rays are distinctly visible.

Wild in Sind, Rajputana, Guzerat, Konkan and the Circars.

The tree is generally small, but in favourable circumstances attains 30 to 40 feet, with a short trunk, often crooked and fluted, 8-10 feet long and 4-5 feet in girth. Specimens have been seen as much as 14 feet 9 inches in girth. Weight, 40·5 lbs. (Dalzell); 46 lbs. (Fenner); our specimen gives 38 lbs. It is very little used and is not even a good fuel. The twigs are used as tooth-cleaners; the root bark is very acrid and acts on the skin like a blister; the shoots and leaves are pungent, but are considered as an antidote to poison, they are eaten as salad and given as fodder to camels; the fruit also is pungent, bitter and aromatic, and is used medicinally.

	bs.
P 1381. Sind	38

2. S. oleoides, Linn.; Brandis 316. Vern. *Kabbar, jhár, diár, mithidiár,* Sind; *Jál, ván, váni, mithi van,* Pb.; *Jhal,* Hind.; *Ughai, koku,* Tam.; *Pílu,* Mar.

A large evergreen shrub or tree. Bark ¼ inch thick, whitish grey, tesselated. Wood light red, moderately hard, with small, irregular, purple heartwood. Pores large and small, oval, often subdivided into irregular patches of soft tissue, which are joined by wavy, irregular zigzag bands. Medullary rays fine, numerous, distinct, at unequal distances.

Arid zone. Sind and Punjab, often forming the greater part of the vegetation of the desert; ascends to 3,000 feet in the Trans-Indus hills and to 2,400 feet in the Salt Range.

Weight, 49 lbs. (Brandis); our specimens give 54 lbs. (Punjab) and 38 lbs. (Sind). Wood sometimes used for building and agricultural implements, Persian wheels and the knee timbers of boats. Is a bad fuel and leaves a great deal of ash. The fruit is sweet and is eaten.

		lbs.
P 942.	Multán (with heartwood)	54
P 1382.	Sind (no heartwood)	38

Order LXIX. APOCYNEÆ.

A large Order containing 33 genera, only a few of which are of any importance. They belong to 3 Tribes, *viz.*—

Tribe I.—Carisseæ	*Allamanda, Willoughbeia, Chilocarpus, Melodinus, Winchia* and *Carissa.*
„ II.—Plumerieæ	*Rauwolfia, Alyxia, Hunteria, Thevetia, Cerbera, Ochrosia, Kopsia, Rhazya, Vinca, Plumeria, Ellertonia, Alstonia, Tabernæmontana* and *Holarrhena.*
„ III.—Echitideæ	*Vallaris, Parsonsia, Pottsia, Wrightia, Nerium, Strophanthus, Parameria, Urceola, Ichnocarpus, Epigynum, Anodendron, Chonemorpha* and *Beaumontia.*

Among these genera, however, four contain only introduced plants. *Allamanda cathartica,* Linn.; Kurz ii. 164, is a large yellow-flowered shrub from America, much cultivated in India and run wild in tidal backwaters of the Western Coast (*Beddome*). *Thevetia neriifolia,* Juss.; Kurz ii. 168. Vern. *Zard kunél,* Hind.; *Hpayoungban,* Burm., is a handsome yellow-flowered small tree, much cultivated in Bengal and Burma. It has long narrow leaves and a hemispherical drupe, from the seeds of which a bright yellow oil can be obtained. *Vinca rosea,* Linn., the Madagascar Periwinkle, is a small pink-flowered shrub commonly planted in India and Burma. *Plumeria acutifolia,* Poiret; Brandis 323; Kurz ii. 179; Gamble 55. Vern. *Gul achin, golainchi, chameli,* Hind.; *Khair champa,* Bombay; *Champa pungár,* Gondi; *Kanagala,* Kan.; *Tayopsagah,* Burm., is a gouty-branched tree with large, yellowish white, fragrant flowers, commonly found in gardens in India and Burma. Van Someren calls it the "Pagoda tree."

Seventeen other genera contain only climbing shrubs. *Willoughbeia* contains 2 species. *W. edulis,* Roxb. Fl. Ind. ii. 57; Kurz ii. 165. Vern. *Luti-ám,* Beng., is a large climber of Chittagong with edible fruit. It yields a kind of caoutchouc, as does also *W. martabanica,* Wall.; Kurz ii. 165. Vern. *Thit kyouknway,* Burm., of Tenasserim.

Beaumontia grandiflora, Wall.; Kurz ii. 179; Gamble 56. (*Echites grandiflora*, Roxb. Fl. Ind. ii. 14). Vern. *Barbari*, Nep., is a large climber of Northern and Eastern Bengal, with a large trumpet-shaped flower. *Chonemorpha macrophylla*, G. Don; Brandis 328; Kurz ii. 187; Gamble 56 (*Echites macrophylla*, Roxb. Fl. Ind. ii. 13). Vern. *Gar badero*, Hind.; *Yokchounrik*, Lepcha; *Harki*, Sylhet, is a large milky climbing shrub of Northern and Eastern Bengal and the Andaman Islands, with broad leaves, beautiful large white flowers, and long fruit, yielding a kind of caoutchouc. *Vallaris dichotoma*, Wall.; Brandis 327; Kurz ii. 181 (*Echites dichotoma*, Roxb. Fl. Ind. 19). Vern. *Dudhi*, Kumaun; *Happur-mali*, Beng., is a large twining shrub of the Sub-Himalayan tract from the Ganges eastwards, Central and South India and Burma (C 2921 Central Provinces). *Urceola esculenta*, Bth.; Kurz. ii. 184 (*Chavannesia esculenta*, DC.), is a climber of Tenasserim, said by Mr. G. W. Strettell to be common all over Pegu and to yield a superior kind of caoutchouc (to this genus also belongs *U. elastica*, Roxb., giving the Borneo rubber). The remaining genera of climbers, *Chilocarpus, Melodinus, Winchia, Alyxia, Ellertonia* (South India), *Parsonsia, Pottsia, Strophanthus, Parameria, Ichnocarpus* (Northern and Eastern India), *Epigynum*, and *Anodendron*, are chiefly Burmese, but contain few species of any forest importance.

Rauwolfia serpentina, Bth.; Kurz ii. 171 (*Ophioxylon serpentinum*, Willd.; Roxb. Fl. Ind. i. 694; Beddome clvi.; Gamble 55.) Vern. *Chandra*, Beng.; *Patalgani*, Tel. is a small undershrub of Bengal, Burma and South India; and *R. densiflora*, Bth.; Beddome clvi., an erect shrub of the Western Ghâts and Ceylon. *Hunteria Roxburghiana*, Wight; Beddome clviii., is a shrub of the Tinnevelly Ghâts. *Ochrosia* contains 2 small trees: *O. salubris*, Bl.; Kurz ii. 172, of the tidal forests of the Andamans, and *O. Borbonica*, Gmel.; Beddome clviii., of similar localities in Ceylon and probably Travancore. *Kopsia fruticosa*, DC. (*Calpicarpum Roxburghii*, G. Don; Kurz ii. 178.) Vern. *Salap* Burm., is an evergreen large shrub of Burma, often planted. *Rhazya stricta*, Decaisne; Brandis 322. Vern. *Vena*, Salt Range; *Gandera*, Trans-Indus; *Sewar, sihar, ishwarg*, Sind, is a shrub of the arid zone of the Punjab, Sind and Afghanistan; its wood is used for fuel, and the fruit and leaves in native medicine.

Wood white, soft (hard in *Carissa*), without heartwood. Pores small or very small. Medullary rays very fine, very numerous. *Alstonia* is anomalous in having moderate-sized pores, distant rays and concentric lines of soft texture.

1. CARISSA, Linn.

Contains 4 species. *C. Carandas*, Linn.; Beddome clvi.; Brandis 320; Kurz ii. 169; Roxb Fl. Ind. i. 687. Vern. *Karaunda, karúnda, garinga, karroná, timukhia, gotho*, Hind.; *Kurumia, bainchi*, Beng.; *Karekai, heggarjige*, Kan., is a small tree cultivated, for its fruit in many parts of India, and wild in Oudh, Bengal and South India. *C. Dalzellii*, Beddome clvii., is a small tree of Coorg, S. Kanara and the Bombay Ghâts.

1. C. diffusa, Roxb. Fl. Ind. i. 689; Beddome clvii.; Brandis 321; Kurz ii. 169. Vern. *Karaunda*, Hind.; *Gán, garna, garinda*, Pb.; *San karunda*, Uriya; *Wakoilu*, Tel.

A small, thorny, evergreen shrub, with light grey bark. Wood hard, smooth, close-grained, said when very old (in Kangra) to be black and fragrant (Brandis). Annual rings marked by an interrupted line of pores. Pores very small and extremely small. Medullary rays very fine, very numerous.

Wild in most parts of India, especially in the drier zones as in the plains of the Punjab, the Sub-Himalayan tract up to 4,000 feet, and in Trans-Indus territory; also on the coast of South Andaman (Kurz).

It is generally gregarious, often forming undergrowth in forests of *Pinus longifolia*, bamboo, and occasionally teak. It spreads rapidly in clearings, coppices freely, and gives an excellent fuel. It is used for turning and combs, and to make dry fences. Growth slow, 15 rings per inch of radius.

P 112. Bhajji, Simla, 4,000 feet.

2. CERBERA, Linn.

1. C. Odollam, Gaertn.; Roxb. Fl. Ind. i. 692; Beddome clvii.; Brandis 322; Kurz ii. 171. Vern. *Dabúr, dhakur,* Beng.; *Kada má, katarali,* Tam.; *Gon-kadura,* Cingh.; *Ka-lwah,* Burm.

A moderate-sized evergreen tree. Wood grey, very soft, spongy. Annual rings marked by a sharp line. Pores small, in short radial lines. Medullary rays indistinct.

Coast forests of India and Burma.

Growth fast, 5 to 7 rings per inch of radius. Weight, 21 lbs. per cubic foot. The wood is only occasionally used for firewood. The seeds give an oil which is used for burning.

		lbs.
E 400.	Sundarbans	21

3. ALSTONIA, R. Brown.

Contains about 3 species. *A. venenata,* R. Br.; Beddome clx.; Gamble 55. Vern. *Chatwa,* Nep.; *Parbo,* Lepcha, is a shrub of Sikkim and the Nilgiris. *A. spectabilis,* R. Br.; Kurz ii. 183, is a large evergreen tree of the Andamans.

1. A. scholaris, R. Brown; Beddome t. 242; Brandis 325; Kurz ii. 183; Gamble 55. Vern. *Chatwan, chatinn,* Beng.; *Satiún, chatiún, satwín, satní,* Hind.; *Chatiwan,* Nep.; *Purbo,* Lepcha; *Satiana,* Ass.; *Satwin,* Mar.; *Sattni,* Cachar; *Pala, wodrase,* Tam.; *Eda-kula, pala garuda,* Tel.; *Mukampala,* Mal.; *Janthalla,* Kan; *Rookattana,* Cingh.; *Chaile, chalain,* Magh; *Let-top, toungmayobeng,* Burm.

A tall evergreen tree with dark grey bark and whorled branches. Wood white, soft, even-grained, seasons badly, and soon gets mouldy and discoloured. Pores moderate-sized, oval, subdivided. Medullary rays fine, wavy, irregularly distributed, with numerous intermediate extremely fine rays. Numerous, fine, wavy concentric lines at unequal distances.

Sub-Himalayan tract from the Jumna eastwards ascending to 3,000 feet, Bengal, Burma, South India.

Weight, 28 lbs. per cubic foot, according to our specimens; Brandis gives 40 lbs., and Kyd (*Echites scholaris*) 40·5 lbs. and P = 710. It is not durable, but is easily worked. The wood is used for boxes, furniture, scabbards, coffins and other purposes, and is made into blackboards in Burma. It is used occasionally in Darjeeling, Assam and Cachar for tea-boxes. The wood and bark are bitter; the latter is used as a tonic, anthelmintic and antiperiodic. The tree is readily recognised by its branches and leaves in whorls, the leaves are smooth, shining, parallel veined, milky.

		lbs.
E 577.	Khookloong Forest, Darjeeling Terai	28
E 718.	Chittagong	28
E 1270.	Lakhimpur, Assam	31
W 863.	South Kanara	28
No. 75.	Ceylon Collection	26

4. TABERNÆMONTANA, Plum.

Contains about 12 species of shrubs or rarely small trees found in Eastern Bengal, South India and Burma. Several species are cultivated for ornament. *T. recurva,* Roxb.; Kurz ii. 174. Vern. *Tau-sa-lap,* Burm., is a shrub of Chittagong and Burma, with handsome white flowers. *T. dichotoma,* Roxb., *T. crispa,* Roxb., and *T. verticellata,* Beddome clix., are shrubs of the Western Ghâts and Ceylon.

1. T. coronaria, Willd.; Roxb. Fl. Ind. ii. 23; Beddome clix.; Brandis 322; Gamble 55. Vern. *Chandni, taggai, taggar,* Hind.; *Asuru,* Nep.; *Krim,* Lepcha.

An evergreen shrub with silvery grey bark. Wood white, moderately hard, close-grained. Pores very small. Medullary rays fine, numerous.

Kumaun, Eastern Bengal, Konkan. Cultivated throughout India.

Growth fast, 5 rings per inch of radius. Weight, 47 lbs. per cubic foot. The fruit has a red pulp, which may give a dye.

		lbs.
E 2392.	Sivoke Forest, Darjeeling Terai	47

5. HOLARRHENA, R. Brown.

1. H. antidysenterica, Wall.; Beddome clx.; Brandis 326; Kurz ii. 182; Gamble 55. Vern. *Karra, kaura, kora, kúra, kúar, kari, karchi, dhúdi,* Hind.; *Kogar, kiam,* Pb.; *Kachri,* Oudh; *Samoka, girchi,* Gondi; *Kurakat,* Kurku; *Ankhria,* Bhil; *Dhowda,* Guz.; *Kirra, karingi,* Nep.; *Dudhali, dudhkuri,* Mechi; *Dudcory,* Ass.; *Madmandi,* Gáro; *Patrukurwan,* Uriya; *Vepali,* Tam.; *Pala, kodaga,* Tel.; *Kurra,* Mar.; *Lettoukgyee,* Burm.

A small deciduous tree. Bark ¼ inch thick, brown, rough, exfoliating in small irregular flakes. Wood white, soft, even-grained. Annual rings marked by a faint line. Pores very small, very numerous, often in radial lines. Medullary rays fine and very fine, very numerous.

Sub-Himalayan tract from the Chenab eastwards ascending to 3,500 feet, Oudh, Bengal, Burma, Central and South India.

Growth moderate, 7 to 8 rings per inch of radius. The weight and transverse strength have been determined by the following experiments:—

		Weight.	P=
Kyd (1831) in Assam with bars 2 feet × 1 in. × 1 in. found . .	(*H. antidysenterica*)	47	417
	(*H. pubescens*)	34	523
Skinner (1862) in South India, No. 134, found		38	562
Smythies in 1878 with our six specimens „		38	...

The wood is largely used for carvings, especially at Saharanpur and Dehra Dún; in Assam for furniture; in South India for turning. The bark, leaves, fruit and seeds are used medicinally, the bark as a tonic and febrifuge and in dysentery. Hamilton in Aikin's List of Wallich's specimens says beads are made of the wood in Assam to be worn round the neck as a medicine.

		lbs.
O 258.	Garhwal (1868)	33
O 263.	„ „	34
O 3083.	Gonda, Oudh	...
C 2801.	Melghát, Berar	36
C 1158.	Ahiri Reserve, Central Provinces	...
C 2734.	Moharli „ „ „	44
C 957.	Guzerat	41
No. 52.	Salem Collection (marked *Wrightia tinctoria*) . . .	39

2. H. mitis, R. Br.; Beddome clxi.; Thwaites Enum. 194. Vern. *Kiriwalla,* Cingh.

A tree. Wood white, close-grained, soft, in structure resembling that of *H. antidysenterica.*

Ceylon.

		lbs.
No. 46.	Ceylon Collection (*Echites lanceolata*)	35

6. WRIGHTIA, R. Brown.

Contains 4 to 6 species. *W. Wallichii*, DC.; Beddome clx., is a small tree of the Western Ghâts. *W. coccinea*, Sims; Kurz ii. 193. (*Nerium coccineum.* Roxb. Fl. Ind. ii. 2.) Vern. *Pallam*, Beng., is a small tree of Northern and Eastern Bengal and Chittagong.

1. W. tomentosa, Röm. and Sch.; Beddome clix; Brandis 323; Gamble 55. *W. mollissima*, Wall.; Kurz ii. 192. *Nerium tomentosum*, Roxb. Fl. Ind. ii. 6. Vern. *Keor, kiláwa*, Pb.; *Dudhi, dharauli, daira*, Hind.; *Karingi, kirra*, Nep.; *Selemnyok*, Lepcha; *Pal kurwán*, Uriya; *Harido*, Cuttack; *Tella pal, koila-mukri*, Tel.; *Kala inderjan*, Mar.; *Atkuri*, Ass.; *Lettouk thein*, Burm.

A small deciduous tree. Bark ½ inch thick, grey, corky. Wood yellowish white, moderately hard, close-grained. Annual rings marked by an interrupted line of pores. Pores very small, in short radial lines. Medullary rays very fine and extremely fine, very numerous, closely packed.

Sub-Himalayan tract from the Beas eastwards, Oudh, Bengal, Burma, Central and South India.

Growth moderate, 8 rings per inch of radius. Weight, according to Kyd 34 lbs. per cubic foot; our specimens give 44·5 lbs. Kyd gives P = 523. The wood is used for turning and carved work. The bark of the stem and roots are given as an antidote to snake-bite. Mr. Manson says the milky juice is used to stop bleeding by the Nepalese.

		lbs.
C 830.	Bairagarh Reserve, Berar	41
W 998.	Poona	48
W 994.	Sahyadri Ghâts, Ahmednagar	49
E 623.	Rakti Forest, Darjeeling Terai	40

2. W. tinctoria, R. Br.; Beddome t. 241; Brandis 324; Kurz ii. 193. *Nerium tinctorium*, Roxb. Fl. Ind. ii. 4. Vern. *Dudhi*, Banda; *Khirni*, Meywar; *Pálá, veypalé*, Tam.; *Tedlapál*, Tel.; *Kala kúdú*, Mar.

A small deciduous tree. Wood moderately hard, close-grained. Pores scanty, very small, in short radial lines. Medullary rays extremely fine and numerous.

Rajputana, Central and South India.

Growth moderate, 7 rings per inch of radius. Weight, Wallich gives 40, our specimen 49 lbs. per cubic foot. Wood used for carving and turning. The leaves are used for dyeing.

		lbs.
P 456.	Ajmere	49
P 3222.	Nagpahar, Ajmere	...

7. NERIUM, Linn.

N. Oleander, Linn.; Brandis 329, is the Oleander Tree of the Mediterranean, often cultivated in India.

1. N. odorum, Solander; Roxb. Fl. Ind. ii. 2; Brandis 328. Vern. *Kanira, kaner, ganhira*, Pb.; *Kanyúr*, Kumaun.

A large shrub. Wood greyish white, soft. Pores very small, in radial lines. Medullary rays very fine, very numerous.

South-West and Central India, Sind, Afghanistan, Outer Himalaya to 5,500 feet. Often cultivated.

The bark and root are poisonous, and the leaves used in native medicine.

		lbs.
H 3057.	Murree Hills, 5,000 feet	37

ORDER LXX. ASCLEPIADEÆ.

A large Order of shrubs or undershrubs, generally scandent. It contains about 11 genera with woody stems, divided into 5 tribes, *viz.*,—

Tribe I.—Periploceæ	*Cryptolepis*, *Finlaysonia*, *Streptocaulon* and *Periploca*.
„ II.—Secamoneæ	*Toxocarpus*.
„ III.—Cynancheæ	*Calotropis* and *Raphistemma*.
„ IV.—Marsdenieæ	*Gymnema*, *Marsdenia* and *Pergularia*.
„ V.—Ceropegieæ	*Leptadenia*

Cryptolepis Buchanani, Roem. and Sch.; Brandis 330; Kurz ii. 199 (*Nerium reticulatum*, Roxb. Fl. Ind. ii. 8). Vern. *Karanta*, Hind., is a twining shrub of most parts of India, rare in Burma. *Finlaysonia obovata*, Wall.; Kurz ii. 197, is a climber of the tidal forests of Burma. *Streptocaulon tomentosum*, Wight, and *S. extensum*, Wight; Kurz ii. 198, are climbers: the first of the Eng forests, the second of the lower mixed forests of Burma. *Periploca* contains 2 species. *P. aphylla*, Decaisne; Brandis 330. Vern. *Barrarra*, *bane*, Trans-Indus; *Báta*, Jhelum and Chenab, is a shrub of the arid and northern dry zones in the Punjab and Sind; and *P. calophylla*, Falc.; Brandis 330; Gamble 56. Vern. *Maslara*, Nep.; *Pargín*, Lepcha, a small shrub of the Outer Himalaya from the Jumna to Bhutan ascending to 6,000 feet, and of the Khasia Hills.

Toxocarpus laurifolius, Wight, Kurz ii. 199, is a large climber of the forests of the Pegu Yomah.

Calotropis contains 2 species. *C. gigantea*, R. Br.; Brandis 331; Kurz ii. 200; Gamble 56. (*Asclepias gigantea*, Roxb. Fl. Ind. ii. 30) Vern. *Madár*, *safed-ak*, Hind.; *Uk*, Sind; *Akand*, *swetakand*, Beng.; *Auk*, Nep.; *Yercum*, Tam; *Yekka*, Kan.; *Kadráti*, Gondi; *Mayo-beng*, Burm., is a large shrub found almost all over India chiefly in waste land. Its inner bark gives a valuable fibre of fine silky texture, which is very strong, and is used for bow strings, fishing nets and lines, and is found to be durable in water. The seeds are surrounded by silky hair, which is said to be made into thread in Borneo. It is difficult to spin, but mixed with one-fifth of cotton it gave, in experiments made by Mr. Monckton in Madras, a good wearing cloth, capable of being washed and dyed. It is well suited for stuffing pillows. The fibre of the stems was found to bear 552 lbs., against 407 borne by Sunn hemp, (*Crotalaria juncea*) and 224 lbs. borne by "coir" (Royle, Fibrous Plants of India, pp. 306 to 310) The wood is made into gunpowder charcoal in Kattiawar and the Dekhan, and the powdered root is used in medicine as an alterative, tonic and emetic. The acrid milky juice is also used for various medicinal purposes. *C. procera*, R. Br.; Brandis 331; Kurz ii. 200. Vern. *Spalwakka*, Afg.; *Ak*, *mudár*, Hind., is a shrub smaller than the preceding, but found in drier parts of India than it. It is chiefly found in the Sub-Himalayan tract from the Indus to the Jhelum, Oudh, Central India and the Dekkan. The fibre, wood, silk from the seeds, and root, are used in the same way as those of *C. gigantea*. *Raphistemma pulchellum*, Wall.; Gamble 56. Vern. *Chonfibrik*, Lepcha, is a handsome climber of the North-East Himalaya.

Gymnema tingens, W. and A.; Gamble 56, occurs in Sikkim Hills; and *G. acuminatum*, Wall.; Kurz ii. 202, in Chittagong and Tenasserim. *Marsdenia* contains 4 species, most of which give a strong fibre. *M. tinctoria*, R. Br.; Brandis 332; Kurz ii. 201; Gamble 56 (*Asclepias tinctoria*, Roxb., Fl. Ind. ii. 43) Vern. *Kali lara*, Nep.; *Ryóm*, Lepcha, of the North-East Himalaya and Burma, is a climbing shrub from whose leaves a black or blue dye resembling indigo is obtained. *M. tenacissima*, W. and A.; Brandis 333; Kurz ii. 201 (*Asclepias tenacissima*, Roxb. Fl. Ind. ii. 51), a climber of Kumaun, Oudh and Behar extending to Chittagong and Ava, gives a beautiful, strong, silky fibre called "Rajmahal fibre" used for bow-strings. Roxburgh states that a line of it broke with a weight of 248 lbs. when dry and 343 lbs. when wet, while common hemp only withstood 158 and 190 lbs. Royle says that a rope (1½ inch) broke with 903 lbs., strong European rope breaking with 1,203 lbs. *M. Roylei,* Wight; Brandis 333. Vern. *Pathor*, Chenab; *Tar, veri,* Salt Range; *Kurang,* Simla (H 3194. Naldehra, Simla, 6,000 feet, with a white porous wood and annual rings marked by large pores), and *M. lucida,* Edgew.; Brandis 333. Vern. *Dudhi,* Kumaun, are small climbers of the North-West Himalaya. *Pergularia* contains 2 species: *P. pallida,* W. and A.; Brandis 334; Kurz ii. 202. Vern. *Surkila,* Kumaun, of Northern India; and *P. odoratissima,* Linn.; Brandis 334; Kurz ii. 203; Gamble 56. Vern. *Kanja lúta, kunjalt,* Beng.; *Simpletbuk,* Lepcha, of Bengal, Burma and the North-West Himalaya as far as the Jumna, often cultivated.

Leptadenia viminea; Bth. and Hook. f. (*Orthanthera viminea,* Wight; Brandis 335) Vern. *Mowa, lanebár,* Trans-Indus; *Matti,* Beas; *Khip,* Delhi; *Kip,* Sind; *Chapkia,* Kumaun; *Mahúr,* Hind., is a glabrous shrub of the arid and northern dry region from Sind to Oudh. The flower-buds are eaten as a vegetable, and a rope is made of the fibre. *Hemidesmus indicus,* R. Br. (*Asclepias Pseudo-sarsa,* Roxb. Fl. Ind. ii. 39,) Vern. *Anantamul,* Beng., is a climber whose roots are used as a substitute for sarsaparilla. There are also numerous small climbers of other genera found in the Indian forests, but none sufficiently large to be worth mention.

ORDER LXXI. LOGANIACEÆ.

Contains 4 Indian genera, *Buddleia, Fagræa, Strychnos* and *Gardneria. Gaertnera,* Beddome clxiv, contains only Ceylon plants. *Gardneria ovata,* Wall.; Kurz ii. 227; Gamble 57. Vern. *Banjahi,* Kumaun; *Takpadik,* Lepcha, is a climber of the North-East Himalaya and Eastern Bengal. Kurz has divided this Order among several neighbouring ones, placing *Strychnos* in Apocyneæ; *Fagræa* in Gentianeæ; *Buddleia* in Pedalineæ; and *Gardneria* in Solaneæ; we have, however, considered it better to follow Bentham and Hooker, and retain the Order, although the diverse structure of the wood of the different genera would seem to accord with Kurz's views.

The structure of *Strychnos* and *Fagræa* is similar in having scattered, large, ramified pores (intercellular ducts?) and small pores in concentric bands or irregular patches; and very sharply marked medullary rays in the firmer tissue intervening between the irregular patches. The structure of *Buddleia* is altogether different.

1. BUDDLEIA, Linn.

Contains 4 or 5 species. *B. macrostachya,* Bth., is a shrub of the Himalaya from Simla eastwards, the Khasia Hills and Sylhet.

Wood soft or moderately hard, no heartwood. Annual rings distinctly marked by a belt of numerous pores, the pores in the outer wood being smaller and often arranged in groups or concentric lines.

1. B. asiatica, Lour.; Beddome clxiii; Brandis 318; Kurz ii. 250; Gamble 56. *B. Neemda,* Roxb. Fl. Ind. i. 396. Vern. *Bhati, dhaula, shiúntra,* Kumaun; *Bana,* Simla; *Newarpati,* Nep.; *Pondám,* Lepcha; *Nimda, budhbola,* Chittagong; *Kyoungmee koo,* Burm.

A large evergreen shrub. Bark thin, grey. Wood grey, moderately hard. Annual rings distinctly marked by a belt of closely-packed pores in the spring wood. Pores small, not all of equal size, scanty except along the annual rings. Medullary rays fine, numerous.

Sub-Himalayan tract from the Indus eastwards, ascending to 4,000 ft., Bengal, Burma, South India; chiefly found in second growth forests, deserted village sites and savannahs.

Growth fast, 4½ rings per inch of radius. Weight, 44 lbs. per cubic foot. It has white, long, tomentose leaves and long spikes of fragrant white flowers. It is very ornamental and is often grown in gardens.

		lbs.
H 110.	Sutlej Valley, Simla, 4,000 feet	44

2. B. paniculata, Wall.; Brandis 318; Kurz ii. 251; Gamble 56. *B. crispa,* Bth. Vern. *Spera wuna,* Afg.; *Dholtu, ghúttia, sodhera, sudhari,* North-Western Himalaya; *Sinna,* Nep.

A large evergreen shrub. Bark thin, light grey, peeling off in long strips. Wood white, moderately hard, close-grained. Annual rings marked by a belt of small pores. Pores in the autumn wood very small, in groups and in oblique lines. Medullary rays fine.

Himalaya, from the Indus to Bhutan, ascending to 7,000 ft.
Growth moderate, 11 rings per inch of radius. Weight, 41 lbs. per cubic foot.

		lbs.
H 158.	Simla, 7,000 ft.	41
H 2882.	Nagkanda, Simla, 7,000 feet	...

3. B. Colvillei, Hook. f. and Th.; Gamble 56. Vern. *Puri singbatti,* Nep.; *Pya-shing,* Bhutia.

A small tree. Wood reddish brown, soft. Pores of two sizes: large near the annual rings, smaller in the autumn wood, these latter grouped, the groups being enclosed in patches of soft tissue, which are arranged in interrupted concentric bands. Medullary rays fine.

Eastern Himalaya, 9,000 to 12,000 feet.
Growth slow, 13 rings per inch of radius. Weight, 35 lbs. per cubic foot. An extremely handsome tree with masses of dark crimson flowers, which appear in August and make the tree very conspicuous in its habitat on the summit of Mount Tonglo.

		lbs.
E 2393.	Tonglo, Darjeeling, 10,000 feet	35

2. FAGRÆA, Thunb.

Contains about 6 species. *F. coromandelina,* Wight; Beddome t. 244. Vern. *Ginnuna,* Kan., is a small handsome flowered tree of the Eastern Ghâts of South India. *F. auricularia,* Jack. and *F. carnosa,* Jack; Kurz ii. 204, are large shrubs of Tenasserim.

1. F. fragrans, Roxb. Fl. Ind. i. 461; Kurz ii. 205. Vern. *Anan,* Burm.

An evergreen tree. Wood hard, brown, close-grained, beautifully mottled. Pores of two classes, large ones scanty, often subdivided, small ones in narrow, wavy, concentric bands, which alternate with broader bands of firm and dark-coloured tissue in which the numerous fine medullary rays are distinctly visible. The large pores (vessels or intercellular ducts) are prominent on a vertical section.

Burma.
Weight, according to Baker, 70 lbs.; Wallich, 52·5 lbs.; Simpson, 57 lbs.; Major Seaton 60 lbs.; our specimens vary from 53 to 65 lbs. Baker's four experiments with Tavoy wood, with bars 7′ × 2″ × 2″ gave P = 553; Simpson's gave 387, but the wood was a bad specimen. The wood is very durable, and is not liable to the attacks of "Teredo." It is one of the most important of the reserved trees of Burma,

especially in Tavoy; and is used for house-building, bridge and wharf piles, boat-anchors and other purposes.

		lbs.
B 289.	Burma (1867)	53
B 550.	Martaban	65
B 3073.	Burma (1862)	57

2. F. racemosa, Jack; Kurz ii. 205. Vern. *Thit-hpaloo,* Burm.

A moderate-sized evergreen tree. Wood moderately hard, greasy to the touch and with a scent like that of India-rubber. Pores of two sizes: moderate-sized pores scattered, often oval and subdivided, and extremely small pores in narrow, wavy, concentric bands, alternating with broader bands of firmer tissue, in which the fine, numerous medullary rays are distinctly visible.

Andaman Islands.

Weight, 50 lbs. per cubic foot. Major Ford says it is strong and durable, that the wood is used for house-posts, and the root bark as a cure for fever.

		lbs.
B 1990.	Andamans (Kurz, 1866)	52
B 2294.	„ (Ford, 1866)	48

---

3. E 1450. (56 lbs) brought by Dr. Griffith from the Mishmi Hills in 1836, has the structure of *Fagræa*. It is probably *F. obovata,* Wall.; Beddome clxiv; Kurz ii. 205; Gamble 56. Vern. *Sunakhari,* Nep.; *Longsoma,* Magh; *Nyoungkyap,* Burman evergreen tree, often scandent or stem clasping, found in the forests of Northern and Eastern Bengal, Chittagong and Burma.

3. STRYCHNOS, Linn.

Contains 6 to 8 species of Indian trees or climbing shrubs. *S. Wallichiana,* Steud.; Kurz ii. 167, is an evergreen tree of the forests of the Pegu Yomah. *S. cinnamomifolia,* Thw. and *S. colubrina,* Linn.; Beddome clxiii are gigantic climbers of the Western Ghâts, while *S. laurina,* Wall. and *S. acuminata,* Wall.; Kurz ii. 166, are large evergreen climbers of Tenasserim, the latter also occurring on the coasts of South Andaman.

1. S. potatorum, Linn. fil.; Roxb. Fl. Ind. i. 576; Beddome clxiii; Brandis 317; Kurz ii. 167. The Clearing Nut Tree. Vern. *Nirmali, nel mal,* Hind.; *Kotaku,* Uriya; *Ustumri,* Gondi; *Tettancottai, tettian,* Tam.; *Chilla, indupa, induga, katakamu, judapa,* Tel.; *Nirmali, chilbinj,* Mar.; *Ustumri,* Gondi; *Tettam-parel,* Mal.; *Chillu,* Kan.; *Ingini,* Cingh.

A moderate-sized evergreen tree. Bark $\frac{1}{10}$th inch thick, greyish brown and sometimes almost black, with numerous small angular, exfoliating scales. Wood white when fresh cut, turning yellowish grey on exposure, hard, close-grained, seasons well. No heartwood, no annual rings. Pores of two classes: large pores scanty, very small pores numerous, arranged in irregularly ramified patches, which are extremely variable in shape, giving the wood a remarkably fantastic pattern on a cross section. These patches are joined by white concentric lines which may possibly be annual rings. Medullary rays white, fine and moderately broad, numerous, sharply defined in the darker tissue. The large pores, which are prominent on a radial section, are filled with a white shining substance and are often ramified. They are probably not vessels, but large intercellular ducts.

Bengal, Central and South India.

Weight, 57 lbs. per cubic foot. Wood durable, used for building, carts and agricultural implements. The pulp of the fruit is eaten, and the ripe seeds are used to clear muddy water by merely rubbing the inside of the jar with the seed.

		lbs.
C 1101.	Ahiri Reserve, Central Provinces	55
C 2979.	Bijeragogarh, Central Provinces	...
D 1060.	South Arcot	61
No. 44.	Salem Collection	56

2. **S. Nux-vomica,** Linn.; Roxb. Fl. Ind. i. 575; Beddome t. 243; Brandis 317; Kurz ii. 166. The Snake Wood, Nux-vomica or Strychnine Tree. Vern. *Kuchla, kajra,* Hind.; *Kuchila,* Beng.; *Kerra, korra,* Uriya *Yetti,* Tam.; *Mushti, musadi,* Tel.; *Kasaraka, kujarra, khasca, kasaragadde,* Kan.; *Kara, jhar katchura,* Mar.; *Kanjaram,* Travancore; *Goda kadúru,* Cingh.; *Khaboung,* Burm.

A moderate-sized evergreen tree, with dark grey bark. Wood brownish grey, hard, close-grained, splits and warps. Pores of two classes: very large pores (intercellular ducts) scanty, filled with a white substance, very prominent on a vertical section, where they are often branching; and small pores in irregularly shaped, ramified patches, which are joined by concentric and oblique white lines. Medullary rays fine and moderately broad, prominent in the firm, shining, hard tissue intervening between the patches above described.

Bengal, Burma and South India.

Weight, according to Skinner, No. 119, 56 lbs. (P = 1160); Brandis' experiments (3) made in 1864 with Burma wood in bars 3 ft. × 1 inch × 1 inch gave weight 49 lbs.; P = 623; his list of Burma woods of 1862, No. 75, gave 52 lbs.; our specimens give an average of 57 lbs. The wood is used in Burma for carts, agricultural implements, and fancy cabinet-work. The seeds contain 0·28 to 0·53 per cent. of strychnia mixed with brucia, poisonous alkaloids. The pulp of the fruit is eaten by birds.

		lbs.
W 1224.	North Kanara	65
W 727.	South ,,	59
B 3072.	Burma (1862)	49

ORDER LXXII. BORAGINEÆ.

Contains 4 genera belonging to 3 tribes, *viz.*,—

Tribe I.—Cordieæ	*Cordia.*
,, II.—Ehreticæ	*Ehretia* and *Rhabdia.*
,, III.—Heliotropieæ	*Tournefortia.*

Rhabdia viminea, Dalzell; Brandis 341, 577; Kurz ii. 211, is a small shrub of sandy and shingly river beds in Kumaun, Bengal, South India and Burma.

Tournefortia viridiflora, Wall.; Gamble 57. Vern. *Ampati,* Nep.; *Tungrong,* Lepcha, is a climbing shrub of the North-East Himalaya, with soft brown wood having the anual rings marked by darker lines, and large pores (E 3299, Chunbati, Darjeeling, 3,000 feet). The Heliotrope, *Heliotropium peruvianum,* Linn., in some places in the hills and especially on the Nilgiris, reaches to the size of a shrub, and may be used for hedges.

Pores small or moderate-sized, the transverse diameter generally less than the distance between the rays, which are uniform and equidistant, generally short, either fine or moderately broad. *Cordia* has concentric bands of soft texture which are wanting in *Ehretia.*

1. CORDIA, Linn.

Contains 13 Indian species. *C. Wallichii*, G. Don; Beddome t. 245. Vern. *Chandle*, Kan., is a tree of the Western Ghâts, Mysore and Bombay, with woolly leaves. *C. grandis*, Roxb.; Kurz ii. 208; Gamble 57; Roxb. Fl. Ind. i. 593. Vern. *Asari*, Nep.; *Thanat*, Burm.; is an evergreen tree of Northern and Eastern Bengal and Chittagong. *C. octandra*, DC.; Beddome clxvi. (*C. serrata*, Roxb. Fl. Ind. i. 591.) Vern. *Gadgondori*, Hind., is a small tree of Travancore. *C. monoica*, Roxb. Fl. Ind. i. 592; Beddome clxvi. Vern. *Pida*, Hind.; *Panugeri*, Tel., is a small poor-looking tree of the barren parts of the Circar forests. *C. polygama*, Roxb. Fl. Ind. i. 594; Beddome clxvi.; Kurz ii. 207. Vern. *Bottukuru, patcha*, Tel., is a small tree of the mountains on the Coromandel Coast and the Eng forests of Martaban. *C. Perottetii*, DC.; and *C. fulvosa*, Wight, are small trees of the Western Ghâts. The above are white-flowered species. *C. subcordata*, Lamk.; Kurz ii. 209 (*C. campanulata*, Roxb. Fl. Ind. i. 593) is a handsome large shrub of the Andamans and Tenasserim, with red flowers, often cultivated. *C. speciosa*, Willd., and *C. tectonifolia*, Wall., are small trees with handsome scarlet flowers, cultivated in gardens, but introduced from the West Indies.

Numerous concentric lines of soft tissue, which sometimes are interrupted, but generally with the medullary rays divide the wood into oblongs or squares. Medullary rays prominent on a radial section.

1. C. Myxa, Linn.; Roxb. Fl. Ind. i. 590; Beddome clxv.; Brandis 336; Kurz ii. 208; Gamble 57. Vern. *Lasora, bhokar, gondi*, Hind.; *Laswara*, Pb.; *Lesúri, gidúri*, Sind; *Borla, baurala*, Kumaun; *Bohari, buhal*, Beng.; *Boeri*, Nep.; *Nimat*, Lepcha; *Dobakari*, Mechi; *Gondi*, Uriya; *Vidi, verasu*, Tam.; *Pedda boku, virgi, nakkera, irki, iriki*, Tel.; *Semar, goden, gondan*, Mar.; *Chotte*, Kan.; *Selte*, Gondi; *Silu*, Kurku; *Lasséri*, Baigas; *Lolú*, Cingh.; *Chaine*, Magh; *Thanat, toung thanat*, Burm.

A moderate-sized deciduous tree. Bark ½ to ¾ inch thick, grey or brown, rough with shallow longitudinal wrinkles and furrows. Wood grey, moderately hard. Pores of two sizes, a few moderate-sized or large, uniformly scattered and frequently double, the rest very small in narrow continuous concentric belts of soft tissue. Medullary rays alternately fine and broad, the rays with the white concentric lines dividing the wood into marked squares or oblong compartments. Medullary rays prominent on a radial section as rough horizontal plates, having a mottled appearance.

Salt Range, Sub-Himalayan tract from the Chenab to Assam ascending to 5,000 feet, Khasia Hills, Bengal, Burma, Central and South India.

Growth moderately fast, 3 to 9 rings per inch of radius (*Brandis*); our specimens do not shew the rings well, with the exception of two, which give 1 to 2 rings per inch, which must be called very fast. The weight is very variable. Brandis in Burma List of 1862, No. 82, gives 33 lbs. per cubic foot; our specimens vary from 23 to 42 lbs., but the average is 33 lbs. Brandis in For. Fl., p. 337, says 33 to 49 lbs. The wood, in spite of its softness, is fairly strong, and seasons well, but is readily attacked by insects. It is used for boat-building, well-curbs, gun-stocks and agricultural implements, in Bengal for canoes. It might be tried for tea-boxes. It is an excellent fuel. The bark is made into ropes and the fibre is used for caulking boats. The leaves are used as plates and in Pegu to cover Burmese cheroots. The fruit (*Sebestan*) is eaten, it is very mucilaginous and is used in native medicine. The viscid pulp is used as birdlime. The kernel is eaten and is used for marking linen, but the mark is fugacious.

			lbs.
O	250.	Garhwal (1868)	42
O	1376.	Gonda, Oudh	38
C	1149.	Ahiri Reserve, Central Provinces	37
E	642.	Rakti Forest, Darjeeling Terai	28

		lbs.
E 2394.	Bamunpokri, Darjeeling Terai	28
E 714.	Chittagong	23
B 2543.	Burma (1862)	36
No. 42.	Salem Collection (marked *Spondias mangifera*) . . .	32

2. **C. Macleodii,** Hook. f. and Th.; Brandis 337. Vern. *Dhengan, dháman, dháian, dewan, dahi, dahipalás, dihgan,* Hind.; *Dhaiwan,* Sattara; *Daiwas, dhaim, bhoti,* Mar.; *Bot,* Gondi; *Lauri kassamár,* Kurku; *Gadru,* Ajmere.

A middling-sized deciduous tree, with thick, grey, soft, corky bark. Heartwood light brown, beautifully mottled with darker veins, even-grained, very hard, strong, tough and elastic, seasons well and works easily. Pores small, in irregular concentric belts of white tissue, often joined by white lines without pores. Medullary rays white, fine and moderately broad, prominent.

Central and South India, Dekkan.

Weight, 40 to 50 lbs. (*Brandis*); our specimens give 49 to 53, average 51 lbs. The wood is used for furniture, picture frames and other ornamental work; also for fishing-rods, which are said to be excellent. It deserves to be better known and more in use.

		lbs.
P 3219.	Nagpahar, Ajmere	...
C 180.	Mandla, Central Provinces (1870)	53
C 2985.	Jubbulpore (1863)	50
C 831.	Bairagarh Reserve, Berar	49

3. **C. vestita,** Hook. f. and Th.; Brandis 338. *Gynaion vestitum,* A. DC. Vern. *Kúmbi, karúk,* Pb.; *Kúm paimán, pín, indak, chinta, ajánta, bairula, berula,* Hind.

A small deciduous tree. Bark ½ inch thick, dark grey, exfoliating when old in large woody scales. The wood has the same structure and appearance as that of *C. Macleodii,* except that the concentric lines are occasionally interrupted.

Sub-Himalayan tract, from the Jhelum to the Sarda River, Oudh.

Weight, 52 to 53 lbs. per cubic foot. Wood strong, used for wheel and well work. The fruit is eaten, it is preferred to that of *C. Myxa.*

		lbs.
O 231.	Garhwal (1868)	52
O 2998.	,, (1874)	53
O 3232.	Dehra Dún	...

4. **C. fragrantissima,** Kurz ii. 207. Vern. *Toungkalamet,* Burm.

A deciduous tree. Wood moderately hard, reddish brown with darker streaks, beautifully mottled, has a fragrant scent. Pores small, in roundish patches, which are joined by fine, concentric lines. Medullary rays short, moderately broad, distinctly marked on a vertical section.

Burma, chiefly in the hills of Martaban and Tenasserim.

Weight, 48 to 51 lbs. per cubic foot. It is a beautiful wood and should be better known. It has a handsome grain, and its fresh, fragrant odour makes it very pleasant to use. Pieces sent to London for sale in 1878 realized £4-10 per ton.

		lbs.
B 285.	Burma (1867)	48
B 1428.	Tharrawaddy, Burma	51

5. **C. Rothii,** Röm. and Schultes; Brandis 338. *C. angustifolia,* Roxb. Fl. Ind. i. 595. Vern. *Gondi, gondni, gundi,* Hind.; *Liár, liái,* Sind; *Narvilli,* Tam.

A small tree. Bark grey or brownish grey, with deep longitudinal furrows. Wood grey, compact, hard. Pores small, often subdivided. Medullary rays fine and moderate-sized. Numerous fine bands of softer tissue which on a transverse section divide the wood between the medullary rays into small squares.

Dry zones of North-West and South India.

Growth moderate, 10 rings per inch of radius. Weight, 42 to 52 lbs. per cubic foot (*Brandis*); our specimen gives 46 lbs. Used for fuel, in Sind for building, and in Cutch for agricultural implements. The bark when wounded gives a gum, and the liber is made into ropes. The pulp of the fruit is eaten.

		lbs.
P 449.	Ajmere	46

2. EHRETIA, Linn.

Species about 8. *E. serrata*, Roxb. Fl. Ind. i. 596; Brandis 339; Kurz ii. 210; Gamble 57. Vern. *Pursan, kalthaun*, Pb.; *Púnyan, púnjlawái, panden, koda, kúrkúna, arjún*, Hind.; *Narra*, Garhwal; *Shaursi*, Kumaun; *Rend*, Kurku; *Ridi*, Baigas; *Nalshuna, chillay*, Nep.; *Bual*, Ass.; *Kala-aja*, Beng., is a tree of the Sub-Himalayan tract from the Indus to Bhutan ascending to 5,000 feet, Eastern Bengal, and Chittagong. Brandis says "the wood is light brown, with white specks, fairly even and compact, soft, not heavy, easily worked, made into scabbards, sword-hilts, gun-stocks, and employed for building and agricultural implements." Aikin in Wallich's List of 1831 gives 3·3 rings per inch of radius for the rate of growth. Kyd gives for the weight, 37 lbs. per cubic foot, and P = 530. The fruit is eaten. *E. aspera*, Roxb. Fl. Ind. i. 598; Beddome clxvi. Vern. *Tella júvi*, Tel., is a small bushy tree of dry barren places in South India; as is also *E. buxifolia*, Roxb. Fl. Ind. i. 598; Beddome clxvi. Vern. *Bapana-búri*, Tel. *E. ovalifolia*, Wight; Beddome clxvi., is a small tree of Coimbatore, Madura and Tinnevelly up to 2,000 feet, and *E. Wightiana*, Wall.; Beddome clxvi., a small tree of the Tinnevelly Ghâts.

1. E. lævis, Roxb. Fl. Ind. i. 597; Beddome t. 246; Brandis 340; Kurz ii. 210. Vern. *Chamrúr, kóda, darar, datranga*, Hind.; *Tamboli*, Banda; *Mosonea*, Uriya; *Dotti, disti, gilchi*, Gondi; *Datranga*, Mar.; *Paldatam, redda pul-mera, seregad*, Tel.; *Kappura*, Kan.

A moderate-sized tree. Bark ⅛ inch thick, grey. Wood greyish white, hard. Annual rings indistinctly marked. Pores small, grouped in small clusters or radial lines. Medullary rays fine, short, numerous, distinctly visible on a radial section.

Suliman Range, Punjab, Sub-Himalayan tract, Oudh, Bengal, Burma and the Andaman Islands, Central and South India.

Growth moderate, 5 to 8 rings per inch of radius. Weight, 33 to 38 lbs. per cubic foot. Wood tough, durable, used for agricultural implements and building. The fruit is eaten, as is also the inner bark in times of famine.

		lbs.
O 257.	Garhwal (1868)	33
C 1155.	Ahiri Reserve, Central Provinces	38

2. E. obtusifolia, Hochstetter; Brandis 340.

A small shrub. Bark grey, thin. Wood resembling in structure that of *E. lævis*.

Salt Range in the Punjab, Sind and Rajputana.

P 3245. Ajmere.

3. E. Wallichiana, Hook. f. and Th.; Gamble 57. Vern. *Boeri, dowari*, Nep.; *Kalet*, Lepcha.

A large tree, sometimes gregarious. Wood grey, moderately hard. Annual rings marked by light-coloured belts. Pores small and moderate-sized, in scattered groups and short radial lines. Medullary rays short, fine, uniform, distinctly marked on a radial section.

Darjeeling Forests, from 2,000 to 7,000 feet.

Growth moderate, 7 rings per inch of radius. Weight, 33 lbs. per cubic foot. The wood is used for building, for charcoal, and occasionally for making tea-boxes.

	lbs.
E 690. Sepoydura Forest, Darjeeling, 5,500 feet	33

ORDER LXXIII. CONVOLVULACEÆ.

Contains 7 genera of Indian shrubs or climbers, *viz.*, *Erycibe*, *Rivea*, *Argyreia*, *Lettsomia*, *Ipomæa*, *Porana* and *Neuropeltis*.

With few exceptions such as the erect-growing *Erycibe glomerata*, Wall.; Kurz ii. 213, of Tenasserim, they are all large climbers, often with showy flowers, but of very little forest interest. *Argyreia speciosa*, Sweet.; Brandis 343, is the well-known "Elephant Creeper."

ORDER LXXIV. SOLANEÆ.

An Order of no special forest interest, though of considerable economic importance producing the potato, capsicum, tomato, tobacco, datura and Cape gooseberry. It contains 2 genera of Indian shrubs or small trees, *Lycium* and *Solanum*. *Lycium europæum*, Linn.; Brandis 345. Vern. *Ganger, kangu, chirchitta, niral*, Pb., is a thorny shrub of the Punjab, Sind and Guzerat, whose fruit is eaten. It is used as fuel, and the branches are made into wattled frames for the walls of huts. *Solanum* contains several shrubs, many of them occurring in waste places. The largest is perhaps, *S. verbascifolium*, Linn.; Kurz ii. 225; Gamble 58. Vern. *Dursul*, Nep.; *Sivor*, Lepcha, a small tree or large shrub of Northern and Eastern Bengal and Burma. It has a grey bark and light yellow soft wood with scanty, moderate-sized, often subdivided pores and numerous short, medullary rays. The annual rings are marked by a line of larger pores. (E 3344. Kalimpung, Darjeeling, 4,000 feet.)

ORDER LXXV. SCROPHULARINEÆ.

Contains only very few genera of woody plants, such as *Brandisia* and *Wightia*. *Brandisia* contains two species, one from Bhutan, the other, *B. discolor*, Hook. f. and Th.; Kurz ii. 250, from the hill forests of Martaban at 2,000 to 3,000 feet elevation.

The *Paulownia*, *P. imperialis*, Bth., a handsome-flowered tree often cultivated for ornament, belongs to this Order.

1. WIGHTIA, Wall.

1. W. gigantea, Wall.; Gamble 581. Vern. *Lakori*, Nep.; *Bop*, Lepcha.

Bark grey, smooth, of unequal thickness, on the outside ½ inch thick, much thinner where it touches the stem of the supporting tree. Wood white, moderately soft, porous. Pores large, often subdivided, equally distributed. Medullary rays moderately broad, uniform, not equidistant.

Hill forests of Sikkim and Bhutan, from 3,000 to 7,000 feet.

A huge epiphytic tree which climbs by sending out horizontal, stem-clasping, aërial roots round the stem of the tree on which it grows, often shewing its masses of pink flowers above the summit of the latter.

The wood is used to make Buddhist idols; it is light and very soft, but does not warp. The stem is often 3 to 4 feet in girth.

E 3323. Rangirúm, Darjeeling, 6,000 feet.

ORDER LXXVI. GESNERACEÆ.

An Order scarcely worth mentioning, as it contains but one shrubby plant, the rest being mostly handsome-flowered, herbaceous plants of the damp zones.

1. LEPTOBŒA, Bth.

1. L. multiflora, Bth.; Gamble 58. *Championia multiflora,* C. B. Clarke. Vern. *Tungrangmook,* Lepcha.

A small shrub. Bark grey, peeling off in papery lakes. Wood yellowish white, hard, close and even-grained. Pores very small but distinct, in short radial lines. Annual rings marked by closer pores. Medullary rays extremely fine.

Hills of N. E. Himalaya up to 3,000 feet.

E 3314. Pankabari, Darjeeling, 2,000 feet.

ORDER LXXVII. BIGNONIACEÆ.

Contains 8 genera of Indian trees, belonging to 2 tribes, *viz.,*—

Tribe I.—Bignonieæ	*Millingtonia* and *Oroxylum.*
„ II.—Tecomeæ	*Tecoma, Dolichandrone, Heterophragma, Stereospermum,* and *Pajanelia.*

Mayodendron igneum, Kurz Prel. Report of Pegu, Appendix D; Burma For. Fl. ii. 233, is a handsome tree with scarlet flowers found in the Martaban Hills up to 2,000 feet.

To this family belong *Amphicome arguta,* Royle, a herb with large perennial rootstock, found on rocks in the North-West Himalaya; the Catalpa, *C. bignonioides,* an American tree with a greyish, handsomely-marked, very durable wood, often planted in Europe and now largely cultivated in America, and said to be good for sleepers; and numerous other large American trees with fine timber.

With few exceptions, this Order is characterised by irregular concentric bands of soft texture. The pores are moderate-sized and frequently filled with resin, and the medullary rays fine, the distance between the rays being generally equal to the transverse diameter of the pores.

1. MILLINGTONIA, Linn. fil.

1. M. hortensis, Linn.; Beddome t. 249; Brandis 347; Kurz ii. 238. *Bignonia suberosa,* Roxb. Fl. Ind. iii. 111. The Indian Cork Tree. Vern. *Nimi chambeli, akas-nim,* Hind.; *Aykayet,* Burm.; *Kát malli,* Tam.

A large tree. Wood soft, yellowish white. Pores small, numerous. Medullary rays fine, the distance between the rays somewhat larger than the transverse diameter of the pores. The specimen from the Saharanpur gardens shews distinct annual rings marked by more numerous and larger pores in the spring wood.

Cultivated in avenues and gardens in most parts of India, believed to be indigenous in Burma and the Malay Archipelago. Kurz says it is rather rare in the tropical forests from Martaban down to Tenasserim.

Weight, 42 lbs. per cubic foot (Skinner, No. 27); P = 610. Our specimen gives 40 lbs. Growth fast, 4 to 5 rings per inch of radius, as far as we can judge from our young specimen.

		lbs.
O 3160.	Saharanpur Gardens	40

2. OROXYLUM, Vent.

1. O. indicum, Bth.; Kurz ii, 237. *Calosanthes indica,* Bl.; Brandis 347; Gamble 59. *Bignonia indica,* Roxb. Fl. Ind. iii. 110; Beddome clxviii. Vern. *Mulín, mirianga, sori, tálpalang, tálmorang,* Pb.; *Ullu, arlu, kharkath, pharkath, sanna, assar sauna, shyona,* Hind.; *Tattunúa,* C.P.; *Totilla, karamkanda,* Nep.; *Kering,* Gáro; *Cherpong,* Mechi; *Sozong,* Rajbanshi; *Pomponia,* Uriya; *Pana, vanga, achi,* Tam.; *Pamania, pampana, dundillam, dondlup,* Tel.; *Dhatte,* Gondi; *Tetu,* Mar.; *Totilla,* Cingh.; *Kyoungyabeng,* Burm.; *Baladah,* And.

A small tree. Bark ¼ inch thick, light-brownish grey, soft, yields a green juice when cut. Wood yellowish white, soft; no heartwood. Pores moderate-sized, uniformly distributed. Annual rings marked by more numerous pores. Medullary rays fine to moderately broad, prominent on a radial section.

Sub-Himalayan tract from the Jumna eastwards ascending to 3,500 feet, Bengal Burma, Central and South India, Andamans.

Growth fast, 2½ to 4 rings per inch of radius. Weight 30 lbs. per cubic foot. The bark and fruit are used in tanning and dyeing; the seeds are used to line hats and, between two layers of wickerwork, to make umbrellas; they may be seen in Buddhist temples in Sikkim, hung up in strings or made into ornaments to suspend from the roof. The tree is remarkable for its long, flat, sword-like capsule and large dull-coloured flowers. Mr. Manson says that the ground-up bark mixed with "hardi" is used to cure sore backs in horses.

		lbs.
P 111.	Sutlej Valley	...
C 1179.	Ahiri Reserve, Central Provinces	27
E 582.	Khookloong Forest, Darjeeling Terai	32
E 2396.	Bamunpokri, Darjeeling Forest	31

3. TECOMA, Juss.

1. T. undulata, G. Don; Brandis 352. *Bignonia undulata,* Roxb. Fl. Ind. iii. 101. Vern. *Reodána, rebdán,* Trans-Indus; *Lahúra, lúar, roír, rahíra,* Pb.; *Lohúri, lohéro,* Sind; *Roira,* Mhairwarra; *Rakht reora,* Mar.

An evergreen shrub or small tree. Bark ¼ inch thick, corky, reddish brown. Heartwood greyish or yellowish brown, close-grained, mottled with lighter streaks, takes a fine polish. Pores small and moderate-sized, often subdivided, enclosed in small rounded patches, which are frequently arranged in concentric lines. Medullary rays short, fine and moderately broad, very prominent on a radial section as long, smooth plates.

Suliman and Salt Ranges, Punjab plains, Rajputana, Guzerat.

Weight, 44 lbs. per cubic foot (*Brandis*); our specimen gives 64 lbs. The wood is tough, strong and durable, works and polishes well. It is highly prized for furniture, carving work and agricultural implements. The flowers are bright orange and very handsome.

		lbs.
P 943.	Salt Range, Punjab	64

4. DOLICHANDRONE, Fenzl.

Contains 5 Indian trees. *D. arcuata,* Hook. f. and Bth. Gen. Plant. ii. 1046 (*Spathodea arcuata,* Wight; Beddome clxix.) Vern. *Ran-palai,* Tam.; *Mersinghi,* Mar., is a tree of the Palghát and Coimbatore forests. *D. crispa,* Seem. (*Spathodea crispa,* Wall.; Beddome clxviii.; Brandis 350. *Bignonia crispa,* Buch.; Roxb. Fl. Ind. iii. 103) Vern. *Pumbadri,* Tam., is a handsome, white-flowered tree of South India, especially Cuddapah and North Arcot, and probably the Central Provinces.

D. falcata and *D. Rheedii* have white, soft wood, without heartwood. Medullary rays very fine. Concentric bands of soft tissue very numerous. *D. stipulata* has hard, orange-coloured heartwood, and no concentric bands.

1. D. stipulata, Seem.; Bth. and Hook. f. Gen. Plant. ii. 1046. *Spathodea stipulata,* Wall.; Kurz ii. 234. *Bignonia stipulata,* Roxb. Fl. Ind. iii. 108. Vern. *Petthan, malwa,* Burm.

A moderate-sized deciduous tree. Heartwood orange-red, beautifully mottled, hard, close-grained. Pores numerous, small, enclosed in round patches of soft tissue which are often arranged in wavy, concentric lines. Medullary rays prominent, very fine, very numerous, generally filled with a yellow substance.

Burma and Andaman Islands.

Weight, Brandis' Burma List, 1862, No. 77, gives 48 lbs.; Skinner, No. 26, gives weight 64 lbs., P = 1386; our specimens give 56 lbs. per cubic foot. Wood used for bows, spear handles, oars and paddles. Major Ford says it is a durable wood for house-posts and makes good furniture. Flowers orange-yellow.

		lbs.
B 2544.	Burma (1862)	58
B 2261.	Andaman Islands (1866)	54

2. D. falcata, Seem.; Benth. and Hook. f. Gen. Plant. ii. 1046. *Spathodea falcata,* Wall.; Beddome t. 71; Brandis 350. *Bignonia spathacea,* Roxb. Fl. Ind. iii. 103. Vern. *Háwar,* Oudh; *Kanséri,* Meywar; *Mendal, manehingi,* Banswara; *Mersingi,* Mar.; *Udda, wodi,* Tel.; *Mersingh,* Bhíl; *Karanjelo,* Kurku; *Nir pongilam,* Mal.

A small deciduous tree. Bark ⅛ inch thick, bluish grey, exfoliating in irregular woody scales. Wood whitish, hard, close and even-grained, seasons well, shining and glossy; no heartwood. Annual rings indistinct. Pores small, oval and subdivided, arranged in wavy, narrow, concentric bands. Medullary rays very fine, very numerous.

Oudh, Rajputana, Central and South India.

Growth moderate, 7 to 8 rings per inch of radius. Weight, 42 to 43 lbs. per cubic foot. Wood used for building and agricultural purposes. Flowers white, leaves small.

		lbs.
C 1139.	Ahiri Reserve, Central Provinces	42
W 995.	Sahyádri Ghâts, Ahmednagar	43

3. D. Rheedii, Seem.; Bth. and Hook. f. Gen. Pl. ii. 1046. *Spathodea Rheedii,* Wall.; Beddome clxviii.; Kurz ii. 234. Vern. *Deyadanga,* Cingh.; *Thakootma,* Burm.

Wood white, soft. Structure similar to that of *D. falcata,* but medullary rays very prominent on a vertical section.

Burma, Malabar, Ceylon and the Andamans.

Growth moderate, 7 to 13 rings per inch of radius. Weight, 23 lbs. (Adrian Mendis); our specimens give 32 to 39 lbs.; Brandis' Burma List, 1862, No. 79, gives 35 lbs. Flowers white.

		lbs.
B 2545.	Burma (1862)	32
B 2252.	Andaman Islands (1866)	39
No. 18.	Ceylon Collection	23

5. HETEROPHRAGMA, DC.

Wood soft, no heartwood. Pores moderate-sized. Medullary rays fine, the distance between the rays being equal to the transverse diameter of the pores. No distinct concentric bands.

1. H. Roxburghii, DC.; Beddome clxix. *Spathodea Roxburghii,* Sprengel; Brandis 350. *Bignonia quadrilocularis,* Roxb. Fl. Ind. iii. 107. Vern. *Baro-kala-goru,* Tam.; *Bondgu,* Tel.; *Pullung, warras,* Mar.

A large tree. Bark ½ inch thick, dark brown, exfoliating in small angular scales. Wood grey, rough, moderately hard. No heartwood, no annual rings. Pores moderate-sized, uniformly distributed. Medullary rays fine, visible on a radial section as long narrow plates.

Chanda District, Godavari Forests and Western Coast.

Growth moderate, 7 rings per inch of radius. Weight, 40 lbs. per cubic foot. Flowers rose-coloured.

		lbs.
C. 1106.	Ahiri Reserve, Central Provinces	40

2. H. adenophylla, Seem.; Bth. and Hook. f. Gen. Pl. ii. 1047; Kurz ii. 236. Vern. *Petthan,* Burm.

A moderate-sized deciduous tree. Wood yellowish white, moderately hard. Pores moderate-sized, often subdivided, uniformly distributed. Medullary rays fine, numerous.

Burma and Andaman Islands.

Weight, 41 lbs. per cubic foot. Flowers large, dull brown.

		lbs.
B 1421.	Tharrawaddy, Burma	42

3. H. sulfurea, Kurz ii. 235. Vern. *Thitlinda,* Burm.

A deciduous tree. Wood dark grey, soft, even-grained, in structure resembling that of *H. Roxburghii.*

Burma, chiefly in Prome District.

Brandis' Burma List, 1862, No. 78, gives weight, 63 lbs.; the specimen now weighs 42 lbs. Flowers yellow.

		lbs.
B 2547.	Burma (1862)	42

6. STEREOSPERMUM, Chamisso.

Contains 5 to 6 species. *S. amœnum,* Benth. and Hook. f. (*Spathodea amœna,* A. DC; Brandis 349. *Radermachera amœna,* Seem.; Kurz ii. 232) is a tree introduced from the Mauritius, but wild in Ava; it is cultivated in gardens. *S. neuranthum,* Kurz ii. 230. Vern. *Thanday,* with pale lilac flowers, is found in the forests of the Pegu Yoma; the wood weighs 33 to 36 lbs. and is reddish brown, close-grained, but little used.

Wood rough. Heartwood small, brown, sometimes wanting. Pores moderate-sized, often joined by concentric bands or lines of soft texture, which are sometimes interrupted. Medullary rays fine; the distance between the rays equal to the transverse diameter of the pores.

1. S. chelonoides, DC.; Beddome t. 72; Brandis 352; Kurz ii. 230; Gamble 58. *Bignonia chelonoides*, Linn.; Roxb. Fl. Ind. iii. 106. Vern. *Pader, padri, parral*, Hind.; *Parari*, Nep.; *Singyen*, Lepcha; *Sirpang*, Mechi; *Bolzel*, Gáro; *Parolli*, Ass.; *Pareya-auwal*, Cachar; *Dharmara, atcapali*, Beng.; *Tsaingtsa*, Magh; *Padri, pon-padira, pathiri, vela-padri*, Tam.; *Tagada, thágu, kala gorú, moka-yapa, pisúl*, Tel.; *Taitu*, Berar; *Pamphunia*, Uriya; *Kirsel, tuatuka, padul*, Mar.; *Padurni*, Bhíl; *Nai-udi, mallali*, Coorg; *Kall-udi*, Kan.; *Lúnú-madala*, Cingh.; *Thakooppo*, Burm.

A large deciduous tree. Bark brown, varying in thickness up to ½ inch, outer bark corky. Wood hard, grey, no heartwood. Pores moderate-sized and large, joined by narrow, irregular, wavy, interrupted belts and lines of soft tissue. Pores frequently filled with a white substance of a resinous nature, which is prominent on a vertical section. Medullary rays short, wavy, moderately broad, numerous, prominent on a radial section as long, narrow, horizontal bands.

Bengal, Burma, Central and South India.

Growth moderate, about 7 rings per inch of radius. Weight, 45 lbs. (Kyd); 42·5 lbs. (Wallich); 48 lbs. (Skinner, No. 25); our specimens give 47 lbs. Kyd gives P = 710; Skinner 642. The wood is moderately durable, elastic, easy to work; it is used for building and is good for furniture. It is used for canoes and building in Assam, and for tea-boxes in Cachar. The roots, leaves and flowers are used medicinally.

			lbs.
C	1164.	Ahiri Reserve, Central Provinces	40
C	1172.	" " " "	38
C	1411.	Moharli " " "	46
C	833.	Bairagarh Reserve, Berar	...
E	659.	Khookloong Forest, Darjeeling Terai	51
E	673.	Bamunpokri Forest " "	48
E	632.	Eastern Dúars, Assam	40
E	1398.	Chittagong	59
D	1070.	North Arcot	50
B	2546.	Burma (1862)	52

2. S. suaveolens, DC.; Beddome clxix.; Brandis 351; Kurz ii. 231; Gamble 59. *Bignonia suaveolens*, Roxb. Fl. Ind. iii. 104. Vern. *Paral padal, padiála, padaria, parur*, Hind.; *Pandri*, C.P.; *Phalgataitu*, Melghát; *Parari*, Nep.; *Singyen*, Lepcha; *Parúl*, Beng.; *Patúli*, Uriya; *Padri*, Tam.; *Kala-goru, kuberakashi, padari, patali*, Tel.; *Hooday, billa*, Kan.; *Ūnt katar, padar*, Gondi; *Padar*, Kurku; *Pandan*, Bhíl; *Parúl, kalagori*, Mar.

A large deciduous tree. Bark ¼ inch thick, grey, exfoliating in large, irregularly shaped, flat scales. Sapwood large, grey, hard. Heartwood small, yellowish brown, beautifully mottled with darker streaks, very hard, seasons and polishes well. Pores moderate-sized, enclosed in long, wavy, concentric, interrupted bands of softer tissue. The pores are frequently filled with a white shining substance, which becomes yellow in the heartwood. Medullary rays fine, sharply defined, numerous, wavy, equidistant, prominent on a radial section.

Sub-Himalayan tract from the Jhelum eastwards, ascending to 4,000 feet, Bengal, Burma, Central and South India.

Weight, 44 lbs. per cubic foot (*Brandis*); our specimens give 46 lbs. The wood is fairly durable, and easy to work; it is much valued for building and makes excellent charcoal. The root and bark are used in native medicine.

		lbs.
O 243.	Garhwal (1868)	41
O 341.	Gorakhpúr (1868)	49
C 197.	Mandla, Central Provinces (1869)	40
C 1114.	Ahiri Reserve, Central Provinces	46
C 2745.	Moharli " " "	50
C 832.	Bairagarh Reserve, Berar	...
E 1959.	Chittagong	51
B 307.	Burma (1867)	44

3. S. xylocarpum, Bth. and Hook. f. Gen. Pl. ii. 1047. *Spathodea xylocarpa,* T. And.; Brandis 349. *Bignonia xylocarpa,* Roxb. Fl. Ind. iii. 108; Beddome t. 70. Vern. *Kharsing, bersinge,* Mar.; *Jai-mangal, sondar-padal,* Mandla; *Dhóla mara, dhotte,* Gondi; *Teto,* Kurku; *Vadencarni,* Tam.; *Ghansing,* Kan.

A deciduous tree. Bark ¼ inch thick, light grey. Sapwood large, grey; heartwood very hard, brown. Annual rings marked by an irregular belt of numerous pores. Pores small and moderate-sized, often subdivided, each pore or group of pores in a small patch of soft tissue; these patches are frequently grouped in zig-zag and more or less concentric lines. In the heartwood the pores are generally filled with a yellow substance. Medullary rays short, fine.

Satpura Range, Khandeish and South India.
Growth moderate, 7 to 8 rings per inch of radius. Weight, 47 lbs. per cubic foot. Wood tough and elastic, close-grained; used for cabinet work.

		lbs.
C 2810.	Melghát, Berar (sapwood)	36
C 958.	Guzerat	47
W 996.	Sahyádri Gháts, Ahmednagar	47

4. S. fimbriatum, DC.; Kurz ii. 231. Vern. *Thanthat,* Burm.

A deciduous tree. Heartwood small, dark brown. Sapwood light brown. Wood very hard in structure similar to that of *S. suaveolens.*

Martaban and Tenasserim in Burma.
Weight, 54 lbs. per cubic foot.

		lbs.
B 2696.	Tavoy (Wallich, 1828)	54

Nos. E 719 (52 lbs.) from Chittagong; D. 1284 (54 lbs.) from the Anamalai Hills; B. 2355 (52 lbs.) and B. 2234 (56 lbs.), from the Andamans, probably belong to this genus.

Wood rough, yellowish grey, moderately hard, with a small heartwood; in structure resembling *S. suaveolens.*

7. PAJANELIA, DC.

1. P. multijuga, DC.; Kurz ii. 237. Vern. *Kyoungdouk, kingalun,* Burm.; *Kaukonda,* And.

A large evergreen tree. Bark ¼ inch thick, dark grey, rough. Wood orange-brown, very hard, close-grained. Pores large, occasionally filled with yellow resin; each pore surrounded by a narrow ring of soft tissue, uniformly distributed. Medullary rays fine, very numerous, uniform and nearly equidistant, prominent. Wood very similar to that of *Planchonia valida*, but differs by more prominent medullary rays, and larger pores, which are not arranged in bands, but isolated.

Burma and Andaman Islands.

Weight, 52 lbs. per cubic foot. Used for canoes by the Andamanese. A fine wood.

		lbs.
B 503.	Andaman Islands	52

Order LXXVIII. PEDALINEÆ.

Contains no woody plants; the genera placed by Kurz under this Order have already been described under Loganiaceæ and Scrophulariaceæ *Sesamum indicum*, Linn. Vern. *Til*, is the plant which yields the Sesamum or Gingelly oil, and is commonly cultivated in India.

Order LXXIX. ACANTHACEÆ.

Contains a large number of Indian genera, most of which are herbaceous. About 10, however, produce shrubs or climbers, and these are divided into four tribes, *viz.*,—

Tribe I.—Thunbergieæ	*Thunbergia*.
„ II.—Ruellieæ	*Dædalacanthus, Strobilanthes* and *Æchmanthera*.
„ III.—Acantheæ	*Acanthus*.
„ IV.—Justicieæ	*Barleria, Asystasia, Phlogacanthus, Justicia* and *Adhatoda*.

Thunbergia contains several large climbers. *T. grandiflora*, Roxb. iii. 34.; Kurz ii. 240; Gamble 59. Vern. *Mullúta*, Hind., Beng., is a large handsome climber of the forests of Northern and Eastern Bengal down to Chittagong, with pale blue flowers. *T. coccinea*, Wall.; Gamble 59, is a large climber of the North-East Himalaya, with long clusters of pendulous scarlet flowers. *T. laurifolia*, Ldl.; Kurz ii. 240, Vern. *Nwaycho*, Burm., is a lofty climber of Burma and the Andamans. *Dædalacanthus* contains about 14 species, the commonest of which are *D. splendens*, T. And.; Gamble 59. Vern. *Shechin*, Nep., a handsome shrub, with long spikes of pink flowers, common in the undergrowth of the sál forests of the North-East Himalaya and Terai; and *D. nervosus*, T. And.; Gamble 59. Vern. *Shechin*, Nep.; *Tepatnyok*, Lepcha, a beautiful shrub with brilliant blue flowers, found in the damp forests of the sub-Himalayan tract from Dehra Dún to Assam. *Strobilanthes* contains over 100 Indian species of handsome-flowered herbs or shrubs. Kurz says that *S. flaccidifolius*, Nees, is cultivated by the Karens for its blue dye; Anderson* says that it is also cultivated in Assam and the Mishmi Hills, and is called "*Room*" and Fortune that it is similarly cultivated in China. Mann, in the Assam Forest Administration Report for 1876-77, paragraph 135, gives *S. flaccidus* (probably this species). Vern. *Rampat*, Ass.; *Hom*, Phekial, as a dye-producing plant. *S. flava*, Kurz. Vern. *Mya naban*, Burm.; *S. Simonsii*, T. And.; *S. lamioides*, T. And.; *S. fimbriata*, Nees; and *S. Neesii*, Kurz, are all large shrubs described by Kurz ii. 243-245 from Burma. *Æchmanthera Wallichii*, Nees; Gamble 60. Vern. *Patrang, Ban marua*, Pb., is a small shrub of the Himalaya from Simla to Bhutan. *Acanthus* contains 5 species. *A. ilicifolius*, Linn.; Roxb. Fl. Ind. iii. 32; Kurz ii. 241. Vern. *Kentki*, Beng.; *Khaya*, Burm., is a common shrub of the Sundarbans and the coast forests of Chittagong, Burma and the Andamans; *A. ebracteatus*, Vahl; Kurz ii. 242, is a shrub of those of the Andamans and Tenasserim; while *A. volubilis*, Wall., is a climbing

---

* An Enumeration of the Indian species of Acanthaceæ, Journal Linn.; Soc. Vol. IX, No. 40, 1867, by Dr. T. Anderson, Supdt. Royal Botanic Gardens, Calcutta.

shrub in similar places and *A. carduaceus*, Griff., a climber of Bhutan. *Barleria* and *Asystasia* both contain handsome-flowered shrubs. *Justicia Gendarussa*, Linn.; Kurz ii. 247; Gamble 60; Roxb. Fl. Ind. i. 128. Vern. *Jagat-madan*, Beng.; *Jatrasigi*, Mechi; *Bawanek*, Burm., is a shrub of the beds of streams in Bengal and Burma.

1. PHLOGACANTHUS, Nees.

Contains 11 species. *P. insignis*, Kurz ii. 246, is an evergreen shrub of the Pegu Yomas. *P. pubinervis*, T. And.; Gamble 60, is a shrub of the Sikkim Hills. The remaining species are found, 5 in the North-East Himalaya and Khasia Hills, 2 in Burma and 1 in Coorg.

1. P. thyrsiflorus, Nees; Kurz ii. 246; Gamble 60. Vern. *Sua, shechin*, Nep.; *Sumcker*, Lepcha; *Bashkah*, Mechi.

A large evergreen shrub. Bark grey. Wood white, moderately hard, close-grained. Pores small, scanty, often in short radial lines. Medullary rays numerous, moderately broad and fine.

Sub-Himalayan tract from Kumaun to Assam, Khasia Hills and Burma.

Weight, 37 lbs. per cubic foot. Often cultivated, as it is a very handsome shrub with long spikes of flame-coloured flowers.

		lbs.
E 2410.	Bamunpokri, Darjeeling Terai	37

2. ADHATODA, Nees.

1. A. Vasica, Nees; Gamble 60. *Justicia Adhatoda*, Linn.; Roxb. Fl. Ind. i. 126; Kurz ii. 248. Vern. *Bakas, vasúka*, Beng.; *Bhekkar*, Jhelum; *Basúti*, Beas; *Bekkar*, Salt Range; *Tora bujja*, Trans-Indus; *Bashang arús*, Kumaun; *Kath, alesi*, Nep.

A small shrub with white, moderately hard wood. Pores very small, uniformly distributed. Medullary rays fine and very fine, numerous.

Common in the Sub-Himalayan tract from Nepal westwards, up to 4,000 feet, elsewhere cultivated; sometimes gregarious.

The wood is used for gunpowder charcoal and for brick-burning. The leaves are used as a cattle medicine, and the flowers for ophthalmia. The shrub is not eaten down, even by goats.

H 2943. Sutlej Valley, Simla, 3,000 feet.

ORDER LXXX. VERBENACEÆ.

A large and important Order containing 15 genera belonging to 5 Tribes: *viz.*,

Tribe	I.—Verbeneæ	containing . . .	*Lantana.*
„	II.—Viticeæ	„	*Callicarpa, Tectona, Premna, Gmelina, Vitex, Clerodendron* and *Holmskioldia.*
„	III.—Caryopterideæ	„	*Caryopteris, Glossocarya* and *Hymenopyramis.*
„	IV.—Symphoremeæ	„	*Symphorema, Sphenodesma* and *Congea.*
„	V.—Avicennieæ	„	*Avicennia.*

Lantana alba, Miller; Brandis 369; Kurz ii. 253 (*L. dubia*, Roxb. Fl. Ind. ii 89) is a shrub of the Punjab, Sind, the North-West Sub-Himalayan tract up to 3,000 feet, the Dekkan and South India.

Holmskioldia sanguinea, Retz; Brandis 370; Kurz ii. 256; Gamble 62. (*Hastingia coccinea*, König; Roxb. Fl. Ind. iii. 65.) Vern. *Kub-tolia*, Kumaun; *Sarputtia*, Nep.; *Sivettachim*, Lepcha, is a large straggling shrub with showy scarlet flowers in a scarlet membranous calyx, common in the outer Himalaya from the Sutlej to Assam up to 3,000 feet, and in the Prome district of Burma.

Glossocarya mollis, Wall.; Kurz ii. 257, is a shrub of Tenasserim. *Hymenopyramis brachiata*, Wall.; Kurz ii. 258, is an evergreen climber of the Prome forests.

Symphorema contains 2 climbers of South India: *S. polyandrum*, Wight, from near Madras, and *S. involucratum*, Roxb. Fl. Ind. ii. 262; Kurz ii. 254. Vern. *Súrúdú*, Tel.; *Nwaysat*, Burm., of the forests of the Coromandel Coast and Burma. *Sphenodesma* contains 5 species, among which *S. Wallichiana*, Schauer (*Symphorema pentandrum*, Kurz ii. 255) is a climber of Eastern Bengal and Tenasserim; and *S. unguiculata*, Schauer (*Symphorema unguiculatum*, Kurz ii. 255.) Vern. *Ka-nway*, Burm., is a climber of Burma and the Andaman Islands. *Congea tomentosa*, Roxb.; Kurz ii. 256. Vern. *Tha-ma-ka-nway*, Burm., is a large climbing shrub of South India, Chittagong and Burma, with beautiful pink, lilac or white bracted flowers.

With the exception of teak, the trees of this Order have no dark-coloured heartwood. The annual rings are generally well marked. The pores are small or moderate-sized, rarely large. Medullary rays generally fine and equidistant. The wood of *Avicennia* is anomalous.

1. CALLICARPA, Linn.

Contains about 7 species. *C. macrophylla*, Vahl.; Roxb. Fl. Ind. i. 393 (also *C. incana*, Roxb.) Brandis 368; Kurz ii. 274. Vern. *Pattharman*, *bá-pattra*, *baunu*, Jhelum; *Súmáli*, Chenab; *Denthar*, *drúss*, Ravi; *Daya*, *shiwali*, Kumaun; *Mathara*, *mattranja*, Beng., is a tall shrub of Northern India, found as far north as Hazara, and up to 6,000 feet. *C. lanata*, Linn.; Beddome clxxiii; Roxb. Fl. Ind. i. 391, is a tree of the hills of Western and South India. *C. rubella*, Ldl.; Kurz ii. 274; Gamble 60. Vern. *Sugroomook*, Lepcha, is a small tree of the North-East Himalaya and the hills of Martaban. *C. longifolia*, Lamk.; Kurz ii. 275, is a shrub of Eastern Bengal and Burma.

1. C. arborea, Roxb. Fl. Ind. i. 390; Brandis 368; Kurz ii. 274; Gamble 60. Vern. *Ghiwala*, *dera*, *shiwali*, Kumaun; *Bormala*, Beng.; *Goehlo*, Nep.; *Kodo*, *kozo*, Mechi; *Súng-a*, Lepcha; *Doika*, Rajbanshi; *Khoja*, Ass.; *Makanchi*, Gáro; *Turmong*, Magh; *Doung-sap-pya*, Burm.

A moderate-sized tree with brownish, rough grey bark. Wood grey, moderately hard, even-grained. Annual rings visible. Pores small to large, oval and often elongated, subdivided into numerous compartments, often in radial lines. Medullary rays broad, short, with numerous fine rays between them, well marked on a radial section; the distance between the rays greater than the transverse diameter of the pores.

Kumaun, Oudh, Eastern Bengal and Burma; chiefly in second-growth forest.

Growth fast, 5 rings per inch of radius. Weight, our specimens give 32 to 35 lbs. per cubic foot; Kyd gives only 22 to 25, but there was probably some mistake. The wood is not used except for charcoal.

		lbs.
E 597.	Khookloong Forest, Darjeeling Terai	32
E 2397. } E 2398. }	Bamunpokri, Darjeeling Terai	35

2. C. cana, Linn.; Gamble 60.

A shrub. Bark thin, grey-brown. Wood white, soft. Annual rings marked by a line of closer pores. Pores moderate-sized, sometimes subdivided. Medullary rays moderately broad, the distance between them greater than the transverse diameter of the pores.

Bengal.

Common in forests and along roadsides in the Terai and Dúars, extending probably southwards to the Ganges. It has pretty pink flowers.

E 3276. Dainah Reserve, W. Dúars.

2. TECTONA, Linn. fil.

1. T. grandis, Linn. fil.; Roxb. Fl. Ind. i. 600; Beddome t. 250; Brandis 354; Kurz ii. 259; Gamble 60. The Teak Tree. Vern. *Sáj*, Arab.; *Sáj, sál*, Pers.; *Ságun*, Hind.; *Singuru*, Uriya; *Ság, ságwan*, Mar.; *Teka*, Gondi; *Ság*, Bhíl; *Tekku, tek*, Tam.; *Teku*, Tel.; *Jádi, sagwani, téga*, Kan.; *Tekka*, Cingh.; *Kyún*, Burm.; *Jati*, Malay.

A large deciduous tree. Bark ⅓ inch thick, grey, fibrous, with shallow longitudinal wrinkles, peeling off in long thin flakes. The sapwood is white and small; the heartwood when cut green has a pleasant and strong aromatic fragrance and a beautiful dark golden yellow colour, which on seasoning soon darkens into brown mottled with darker streaks. The timber retains its fragrance to a great age, the characteristic odour being apparent whenever a fresh cut is made. It is moderately hard, exceedingly durable and strong, does not split, crack, warp, shrink, or alter its shape when once seasoned, works easily and takes a good polish. The annual rings are distinctly marked by larger and more numerous pores in the spring wood. The pores are mostly single, but sometimes subdivided, those of the inner layer of each annual ring are large, while those of the outer portion are moderate-sized and small. The medullary rays are short, moderately broad, equidistant; the distance between the rays about equal to the transverse diameter of the larger pores. The pores are well marked on a longitudinal section, and the medullary rays give the wood a beautifully mottled appearance. The pores are sometimes filled with a white substance. The pith is large and quadrangular.

The Teak tree is found in Central and South India and Burma. Its northern limit may be defined by a line passing from the mouth of the Nerbudda up that river, and across to and down the Mahanadi; but in some places it extends farther north, and it is found as far as Jhansi and Banda. It is cultivated in Assam, Bengal, and the Sub-Himalaya as far north as Saharanpur. It seems to require an annual rainfall of 30 inches, but to thrive best with from 50 inches to 120 inches mean annual rainfall.

Annual rings.—It is now established beyond doubt that the concentric rings which are so marked in the wood of Teak correspond each to one year's growth. The following statement exhibits the rings counted on sections of trees grown in the Nilambur plantations. These sections were cut in 1877, and were taken from the base of the stem; and, with a few exceptions, the number of rings agrees with the age of the tree. The average diameter is the mean of three diameters. The statement shews the gradual increase of the heartwood as the tree grows older, and it also exhibits the number of rings on one inch of average radius in the wood of trees of different ages. But it must be borne in mind that these sections do not represent the average of each year's plantation, but were selected from among the dominant trees.

They therefore exhibit a more rapid rate of growth than average specimens would do.

Year of plantation.	Number of rings counted.	Average diameter of section (wood only).	Average diameter of heartwood.	Rings per inch of average radius.
		Inches.	Inches.	
1844	33	20·8	19·3	3·17
1845	31	21·1	18·7	2·95
1846	31	20·	17·7	3·10
1847	30	23·8	21·5	2·52
1848	28	16·7	15·4	3·34
1849	28	18·1	16·2	3·09
1850	27	14·	12·5	3·85
1851	25	15·2	13·4	3·28
1852	32*	15·2	13·5	Omitted.
1853	24	15·1	12·	3·17
1854	24	17·3	15·2	2·77
1855	23	12·4	10·5	3·71
1856	21	15·2	12·6	2·76
1857	20	12·2	10·6	3·27
1858	19	14·	11·3	2·71
1859	18	14·	10·6	2·57
1860	17	12·9	10·4	2·63
1861	16	13·1	10·5	2·44
1862	15	11·7	9·	2·56
1863	14	13·6	10·4	2·06
1864	13	12·5	9·4	2·08
1865	12	9·4	6·9	2·55
1866	11	10·4	7·3	2·11
1867	10	11·8	8·3	1·69
1868	9	10·5	7·6	1·71
1869	8	7·4	4·8	2·16
1870	7	7·4	4·5	1·89
1871	7	7·7	4·3	1·81
1872	5	6·5	2·6	1·53
				Average 2·62 rings per inch of average radius.

* There is evidently a mistake here. The tree which yielded this section must have been an older tree standing in the plantation of 1852.

The sections ranged in age from 5 to 33 years. Dividing them into three groups, two of 10 years each, and the third of 9 years, we obtain the following as the mean diameter in inches of these three groups:—

	Inches.
Mean diameter of trees 5—14 years old	9·72
15—24 „	13·79
25—33 „	18·71

The following statement shews the measurements made by Mr. Popert in some of the plantations of the Tharrawaddy Division in Burma; the results have been obtained by taking the average of some 5 to 10 trees in each :—

Name of plantation.	Age.	Year of plantation.	No. of rings counted.	Average diameter of section (wood only).	Average diameter of heartwood.	Height of tree in feet.	Girth at breast height in inches.	Rings per inch of average radius.	Remarks.
	Years.			Inches.	Inches.				
Thongzai . . .	15	1863	15	6·4	4·5	61	20	4·7	Burnt yearly.
Myodwin . . .	15	1863	15	6·2	4·8	65	17·5	4·8	Protected.
Kangyee . . .	13	1865	14	4·8	3·0	44	14	5·8	Burnt yearly.
Choungwah . .	12	1866	12	5·8	4·0	46	16·5	4·1	Protected.
Ditto . .	10	1868	10	5·0	2·1	42	14	4·0	Do.
Ditto . .	8	1870	8	4·8	2·4	38	13·71	3·3	Do.
Quaymakeing . .	11	1867	11	5·9	3·5	53	18·75	3·7	Do.
Ditto . .	9	1869	9	4·4	2·6	49	13·6	4·1	Do.
Ditto (private	10	1869	10	7·5	5·2	53	23	2·6	Burnt yearly.

A section sent from the Thinganneenoung plantation in Burma, cut from a tree 21 years old, planted in 1856, gave 21 rings on a mean diameter of 16·3″, the heartwood of which occupied 14·5″. This section shewed 2·57 rings per inch of average radius.

From other plantations, also, sections of Teak trees of known age were sent for the Paris Exhibition, but apparently they were not in all cases cut from the base of the stem; they are, however, instructive as shewing the rate of growth and the number of rings on one inch of mean radius.

Year of plantation.	Number of rings counted.	Average diameter of section in inches.		Rings per inch of average radius.
		Wood.	Heartwood.	
South Kanara (Parappa plantation).				
Not known . . .	10	9·	4·9	2·22
Ditto . . .	5	5·5	2·5	1·81
North Kanara (Kalanadi valley).				
Sulageri, 18 years old	18	8·	6·	4·5
	17	8·8	7·5	3·9
	17	9·	7·	3·7
Murdi, 12 years old	8	7·5	Heartwood not distinct.	2·1
	11	6·		3·7
	11	5·7		3·8
Kadra, 10 years old	8	6·5	...	2·5
	8	7·5	5·	2·1
	7	7·	4·	2·
Bengal (Bamunpokri).				
1868	8	6·5	2·5	2·5 measured 1877.
1871	6	6·	1·	2· „ „
1872	4	5·	1·	1·6 „ „
Andamans (Port Blair).				
1873	6*	10·1	6·	1·2 „ „
Burma (Tenasserim).				
Shoaygoon, 1856 .	22	5·3	3·5	8·3 „ 1878.
Koloon „ .	22	4·6	3·	9·6 „ „
Thingameenoung „ .	21	7·6	4·5	5·5 „ 1877.

* The tree was probably older.

It will be noticed that as far as the data go, which are furnished by the sections received, South Kanara, North Kanara and Bamunpokri exhibit an increase of diameter similar to that of Nilambur; while in the samples from Burma the annual rings are much narrower and the specimen from Port Blair shewed an extremely rapid rate of growth.

Girth and height at different ages.—The following measurements illustrate the rate of growth of Teak in plantations in different provinces as nearly as possible from 5 to 5 years. The Nilambur plantation again furnishes the largest amount of information:—

Age.	Mean girth at breast high.	Total height of tree.
	Nilambur plantation.—Alluvial soil.	
3—7 years	12 inches	29 feet.
8—12 "	17 "	63 "
13—17 "	23 "	68 "
18—22 "	25 "	71 "
23—27 "	27 "	77 "
29 "	34 "	87 "
30 "	35 "	85 "
31 "	32 "	75 "
32 "	34 "	92 "
33 "	37 "	95 "
	Nilambur plantation.—Gneiss and laterite.	
7 years	13 inches	30 feet.
16 "	14 "	50 "
20 "	21 "	50 "
24—26 "	22 "	52 "
30 "	24 "	50 "

These figures are taken from that portion of Colonel Beddome's report (paragraphs 11—44) which contains his notes on each year's plantation, and the data recorded are stated to be average figures.

In another part of his report (paragraph 81), however, he gives data which would seem to shew that the average size of the trees in the older plantations (all on alluvial soil) is considerably greater. He there states the dimensions of the largest, smallest and medium sized trees in four plantations, the results being as follows:—

Age.	Mean girth (probably breast high).			Length of bole.		
	Largest.	Medium.	Smallest.	Largest.	Medium.	Smallest.
	Inches.	Inches.	Inches.	Feet.	Feet.	Feet.
30 years	67	47	29	79	65	50
31 "	69	49	30	80	65	50
32 "	63	46	30	83	67	50
33 "	68	56	43	86	68	50

The first three lines shew the average of 6 trees in each case, and the last line the average of 8 trees each. It is distinctly stated that the length is that of the bole, and not of the entire tree.

The plantations made on gneiss and laterite shew a much slower rate of growth than those on alluvial soil; the difference being considerable in height, and much less in girth.

In 1878 Col. Beddome measured 10 trees in the plantation of 1844, the first five *outside*, the remainder *inside*, trees of the plantation, in order to obtain information regarding the ratio of decrease in passing from breast height to half height. The results were that the *outside* trees shewed a decrease of 24 per cent., while the *inside* trees shewed 18·5 per cent. only, a difference such as might have been expected. The measurements of the trees cut for the Paris exhibition shew an average decrease of 20 per cent., which may be approximately taken.

Up to 10 years of age, the growth in length of teak on alluvial soil at Nilambur is at the rate of about 6 feet a year, and later on it is at the rate of only about 1 foot a year. On page 358 of the Forest Flora of North-West and Central India, it is stated that "it is probable that, as a rule, teak attains half its length with a girth of 2—3 feet." This assumption is borne out by the present figures. The trees grown upon alluvial soil in girth between 25 and 34 inches are from 77 to 87 feet high; and from all that is known regarding the growth of Teak in similar localities, it is probable that, unless damaged by storms, disease, insects, or other causes, they will attain a height of 150 feet in soil of this description, and in the climate of Nilambur.

From Burma, we have the following data. The figures from Pegu represent averages of plantations in the Rangoon, Toungoo and Tharrawaddi districts, brought together on page 358 of the Forest Flora of North-West and Central India.

	Age, in years.	Mean girth, breast high, in inches.	Total height of tree, in feet.
Pegu	4	5—9	15—27
	10	15	40—45
	15	23	...
Thinganeenoung	21	27	50—60
Garden—Moulmein	22	40	...

The fourth line is the average of 150 trees in the Thinganneenoung plantation in the Attaran district of Tenasserim, given in paragraph 146 of the report for 1876-77 of the Tenasserim forests. Major Seaton gives the average height at 30—40 feet, but this probably means the height to the first branch. The maximum girth was 55½ inches. The average rate of growth of the present plantations in Burma is somewhat less rapid than that of the alluvial portion of Nilambur. The last line gives the average of 15 trees measured in 1856 in a private garden at Moulmein. An instance of extremely rapid growth was the tree already mentioned, a section of which was sent from Port Blair for the Paris Exhibition, probably 6 years old (said to have been planted in 1873, but 6 rings were counted), with a girth of 36 inches and a height of 44 feet.

For the Lakvalli plantation in Mysore, the following data are given in Captain VanSomeren's report for 1875-76. Age 13—15 years, mean girth 14 inches, height 32 feet. This is a remarkably slow rate of growth, considering that the soil is good, and the climate moist, though of course not so forcing as the climate of Nilambur.

The plantations in the Central Provinces and Berar have given the following:—

Plantation.	Age, in years.	Mean girth, breast high, in inches.	Total height of tree, in feet.
Machna, Central Provinces	6	7	15—22
Pili, Berar	6	4	10
Sakata, Central Provinces	7	11	20—25
Pili, Berar	8	8	20
Sonawani, Central Provinces	9	12	30—40
Machna, Central Provinces	8—10	9	17—30

Compared with Malabar and Burma, the rate of growth is slow, as may be expected in a dry climate and near the northern limit of the tree.

Outside the range of the natural growth of teak, the following data, regarding its rate of growth, are available:—

Plantation.	Age, in years.	Mean girth, breast high, in inches.	Total height of tree, in feet.
Bamunpokri (Sikkim)	5	5·5	12—15
Hoolingamara (Chittagong)	5	11	20—25
	4	6	10—15
Rampahar (Chittagong) 3 specimens	7	17	20—30
Kulsi (Assam)	5	11	29
Makúm "	4	9	18
" "	5	11	27
" "	7	16	31

The growth at that early age is fairly good; but it does not follow from these figures that teak in Bengal and Assam will attain a great age, and produce good timber.

The following instances of older trees of known age in Assam and Bengal are on record:—

Locality.	Number of trees measured.	Age, in years.	Mean girth, in inches.
Gauhati, banks of the Brahmaputra	15	37	85
Royal Botanical Gardens, Calcutta	19	6	16
Ditto ditto	8	70	79
Garden at Mohesh, Serampore	27	50	52

The trees at Gauhati were on an average 30—50 feet high.

The trees in the Botanical Garden, Calcutta, were measured in January 1856. The older trees have since been blown down by the cyclones of 1864 and 1867.

On the banks of the Hooghly at Mohesh, below Serampore, stands a grove of teak trees planted in 1828. Their mean girth, breast high, taken by measuring 27 average-sized trees, was 52 inches. The trees were measured in January 1878, and were therefore 50 years old. They are from 40—50 feet high.

In paragraphs 177 and 183 of Dr. Schlich's report for 1872-73, the dimensions of a large number of Teak trees at different stations of Lower Bengal are given; but unfortunately no trustworthy information regarding their age is available.

Cubic contents of trees at different ages.—In paragraph 4 of Colonel Beddome's report a statement is given exhibiting the dimensions of the trees, sections of which were sent to the Paris Exhibition. As already stated, these trees were selected as samples of the dominant trees, *viz.*, of those which will eventually be selected to remain on the ground as the ultimate crop; but, with few exceptions, they were not selected from among the largest individuals which had much outrun their neighbours. Arranging them in groups from 10 to 10 years, the following results are obtained:—

Age.	Height of tree, in feet.	Girth at base, in inches.	Length of bole, in feet.	Mean cubic contents, in cubic feet.
4—13 years	48—75	21—60	32—56	10·6
14—23 "	65—110	51—69	40—70	23·8
24—33 "	70—110	60—105	41—72	51·3

This gives us the cubic contents at different ages as follows :—

Mean age.	Cubic contents, in cubic feet.	Periodical annual increment, in cubic feet.
9	10·6	1·1 to 9 years.
19	23·8	1·3 from 9 to 19 years.
29	51·3	2·8 from 19 to 29 years.

The annual increment increases steadily to the age of 30 years, and probably continues increasing for a considerable time beyond it.

Number of trees and cubic contents of growing stock per acre.—Regarding the number of trees and the growing stock per acre at different ages, we depend almost entirely upon Nilambur for our data. Sample areas of half an acre each were selected in each of seven plantations; each tree was measured, the cubic contents determined, and the following is the result. It is not expressly stated, but it is probable, that these sample areas were all selected on alluvial soil* :—

Name and year of plantation.	Age of plantation, in years.	Number of trees, per acre.	Average length of bole, in feet.	Mean quarter girth of trees, in inches.	CUBICAL CONTENTS IN CUBIC FEET.		AVERAGE ANNUAL INCREMENT, IN CUBIC FEET.	
					Per tree.	Per acre.	Per tree.	Per acre.
Iravelly Kava . . . 1844	33	120	59	9·7	41	4,879	1·2	148
Elanjerry . . . 1845	32	158	61	7·9	30	4,742	·9	148
" . . . 1846	31	156	60	7·4	27	4,204	·9	136
Moolathamanoo . . 1847	30	140	62	7·5	27	3,713	·9	124
" . . 1848	29	156	60	6·8	21	3,243	·7	112
Elanjerry . . . 1858	19	270	45	5·0	8	2,203	·4	116
Wallashary . . . 1868	9	750	40	3·4	3	2,491	·4	277

Colonel Beddome estimates that on alluvial soil, the Teak at Nilambur will reach maturity at from 60 to 80 years; that fellings will be spread in each plantation over 50 years; and that at the time of cutting (say at 85 years of age) the mean quarter girth will be 2 feet, the length of bole will be 70 feet, and the mean cubic contents of each tree 280 cubic feet. He also estimates that at that age, there will only be 60 trees to the acre, making the cubic contents per acre 16,800 cubic feet.

No safe speculations can be formed regarding the future of a pure Teak forest like that of Nilambur. In its natural state Teak does not grow alone, but is associated with bamboos and a variety of other trees; and it is impossible to foresee the risk of damage by storms, insects, disease, or other causes to which pure Teak forests may be exposed. It may be doubted whether, even on the best alluvial soil, the average mean girth of trees 85 years of age will be as much as 8 feet. On the other hand, it is not impossible that the bole will be longer than 70 feet, and it is probable that it will be advantageous to allow more than 60 trees per acre. On page 155 of the Attaran Report of 1860, a plot in the Tsintsway forests (Yoonzaleen) is described measuring 3,833 square feet, and stocked with 8 Teak trees with clear stems to the

* The length of stem to the top of sale measurement, where the head begins, of every tree in the plantations of 1844 to 1848, both inclusive, was measured by sending up a climber with a tape. In the plantations of 1858 and 1868 a large number of felled saplings were available, of which the average was taken.

The mean quarter girth was determined in the following manner. Ten saplings were measured breast high, and in the middle of the stem at half its length, and this gave ⅚ as the reducing factor. Those trees 30 inches in girth breast high were found to have a girth of 25 inches in the middle of the bole.

first branch of 50 feet, the girth between 4′ 6″ and 6′ 5″; this would give 91 trees to the acre. Full stocked forests of Oak and Beech in Europe 130—180 years old under favourable conditions contain 120—140 trees per acre, with a cubic contents (including tops and branches) of about 11,000 cubic feet. A forest of silver fir in the Jura, 180 years old, was found to contain 94 trees per acre, with a cubic contents of 16,000 feet.

The total area now stocked at Nilambur is 3,436 acres, of which 1,787 are stocked with a full crop on alluvial soil, the rest not being expected to yield a full crop. In his estimate of the future value of the plantations, Colonel Beddome only assumes 6,000 cubic feet as the full crop expected on alluvial soil.

Mr. Carter reports from Burma that at Magayee and Kyekpyoogan in each plantation the trees upon ¼ acre were measured. A breadth of 24 feet and a length of 454 feet was given to this area, so as by extending over a greater portion of the plantation, to avoid the experiment being confined to a small spot on which the growth was particularly good. But this strip was not taken in a part of the plantation which contained many blanks, but rather in a part which was well stocked without choosing the very finest parts of the plantation. These measurements then do not profess to shew the exact state of the plantations, but to give data which are nearly normal. In the 1873 and 1872 plantations—after the deduction of the mean girth, 3 sample trees in each were felled and the contents calculated by sections, the length of which were taken at 2 feet. In the 1875, 1874, 1869 and 1870 plantations only one sample tree in each was cut; and in those of 1876 and 1871 no trees were cut, enough data being to hand as to the reducing factor to enable the contents of an average tree to be calculated without its being felled. In the 1871 plantation only were the heights and girths so divergent as to render the separation of the trees into two classes with a sample tree for each necessary. The plantation of 1868 at Kyekpyoogan is so poorly-stocked and so badly grown that no measurements were taken as they would have been valueless for comparison.

The results, as might be expected from plantations with only an interval of one year, diverge very widely.

The plantations of 3 and 4 years shew an abnormally high annual increment; those of a 8, 9 and 10 years an abnormally low one, attributable to their increase for the last 3 years being almost nil, due most probably to fire and in part also to caterpillars consuming the first growth of leaves.

Name and year of plantation.		Age.	Number of trees per acre.	Average height.	Average girth at breast height.
		Years.		Feet.	Inches.
Magayee,	1876 . . .	3	1,059	10	6 (3—9)
	1875 . . .	4	1,048	22	8 (3—12)
	1874 . . .	5	952	10	6 (2—10)
	1873 . . .	6	1,084	18	8 (4—14)
	1872 . . .	7	1,100	26·6	10 (4—17)
Kyekpyoogan,	1871 . . .	8	876	20	8½ (2—16)
	1870 . . .	9	800	30	9½ (6—17)
	1869 . . .	10	848	30	10 (6—18)

In natural forests, where Teak is associated with bamboos and other trees, the number of first and second class Teak trees (above 4′ 6″ in girth) rarely attains 10 trees per acre over large areas. The following are instances of forests exceptionally well stocked with Teak :—

Date of survey.	Forest.	Area.	NUMBER PER ACRE. Class. Girth above 6 feet.	Girth 4½ to 6 feet.	Total.
1876 . .	Bimaram (Central Provinces)	50 acres . .	4	4·3	8·3
1870-71 .	Pegu (Prome District) . .	17 square miles	3·6	3·0	6·6

The weight and transverse strength have been determined by the following experiments :—

Experiment by whom conducted.	Year.	Wood whence obtained.	Weight.	Number of experiments.	Size of bar.	Value of P.
					Ft. in. in.	
Wallich . . .	...	Ceylon	47	...	......	...
„ . . .	...	Travancore	42	...	......	...
„ . . .	...	Malabar	37	...	......	...
„ . . .	...	Moulmein	31·5	...	......	...
A. Mendis, No. 85 .	1855	Ceylon	55	...	}	810
„ No. 86 .	„	Cochin	44	...	2 × 1 × 1	672
„ No. 87 .	„	Moulmein	42	...	}	640
Bennett, No. 12 .	1872	„	42	3	3 × 1½ × 1½	747
French (Erode) .	1861	South India	...	3	1 × 1 × 1	467
Cunningham . .	1854	Vindhyan hills	44·5	1	2 × 1 × 1	953
Puckle . . .	1859	Mysore	43	4	2 × 1 × 1	730
Couch (Plymouth) .	...	India	38·5	2	......	...
Simpson . . .	...	Thoungyeen and Zimmee { Good timber girdled .	43·5	13	}	478
„ . . .	...	Young timber girdled .	42	4	3 × 1½ × 1½	660
„ . . .	...	Large timber girdled .	38	8	}	591
„ . . .	...	Dead timber not girdled	39·5	6	}	631
Skinner, No. 122 .	1862	Malabar	45	...	}	814
„ . . .	„	Moulmein	43	...	......	809
„ . . .	„	Pegu.	37	...	}	786
Fowke . . .	1859	Nagpore	41	4	......	472
Kyd . . .	1831	Burma	38	1	2 × 1 × 1	663
Campbell . . .	1831	„ (unseasoned) . .	47	4	}	634
„ . . .	„	„ „ . . .	42	2	}	604
„ . . .	„	Java	43	1	6 × 2 × 2	693
„ . . .	„	Bombay	41	2	}	537
„ . . .	„	Malabar	48	1	}	468
Maitland . . .	1802	Burma	41	...	3 × 1½ × 1½	589 to 839
Baker . . .	1829	Rangoon . } Received at Cossipore, April 1825.	43	5	6 × 2 × 2	658
„ . . .	„	Bombay . }	43	6	„ „ „	652
„ . . .	„	Pegu . }	46	3	}	602
„ . . .	„	Malabar . }	45	3	}	782
„ . . .	„	Burma { Received at Cossipore, April 1826.	43	3	}	756
„ . . .	„	Malabar {	48·5	3	5½ × 2 × 2	689
„ . . .	„	Malabar { Received at Cossipore, April 1827.	46·5	2	}	683
„ . . .	„	Bengal {	...	12	3 × 1½ × 1	693
„ . . .	„	Bengal	...	14	2 × 1 × 1	666
„ . . .	„	„ very old, taken from a Dutch house at Cossipore	41·5	6	7 × 2 × 2	631
„ . . .	„	„ „	46·5	6	„ „ „	731
Russell . . .	1862	„ „	41	3	1½ × 1 × 1	836

Experiment by whom conducted.	Year.	Wood whence obtained.	Weight.	Number of experiment.	Size of bar.	Value of P.
					Ft. in. in.	
Brandis	1862	Burma (No. 86)	40 to 51	...	4 × 1 × 1	570 to 867
„	1864	„	40·5	12	6 × 2 × 2	563
„	„	„	40	6	6 × 2 × 1½	577
„	„	„ Half seasoned	45	10	6 × 2 × 2	534
„	„	„ Half seasoned	43	9	6 × 2 × 1½	584
„	„	„ Half seasoned	46	20	6 × 2 × 2	598
„	1865-66	„	38	4	„ „ „	617
„	„	„	38	9	6 × 2 × 1½	670
„	„	„	40·5	5	3 × 1 × 1	812
„	„	„	38	11	2 × 1 × 1	649
„	„	„	37	17	2 × 1 × ½	612
Laslett, p. 125	1875	Moulmein, No. 1	48·5	6	7 × 2 × 2	684
„ „	„	„ No. 2	50	6	7 × 2 × 2	637
„ p. 126	„	„	49·5	6	......	...
Dundas	1877	Moulmein	34	12	10 × 4 × 6	467
„	„	„	34	12	2 × 1 × 1	791
Warth	1878	Central India	43·5	5	......	...
„	„	Malabar	42	3	......	...
„	„	Burma	40	4	......	...

The weight may, therefore, for practical purposes, be taken approximately at 40 lbs. per cubic foot, and the value of P. at 600, on an average. Molesworth, however, in 'Graphic Diagrams for strength of teak beams' gives: Weight 45 lbs., P = 800, E = 5,000. Captain J. C. Dundas, V. C., R. E., in his report on experiments (see above) made at Lucknow in 1877 and 1878 (Roorkee Professional Papers April 1879, Vol. VIII, No. 32), in which he gives the weight at 34 lbs., P = 470 and E. = 2,200 as an average, says that logs as received at Lucknow shew a weight of nearly 50 lbs. per cubic foot, but that after being well dried and sawn into scantlings, the weight falls to 34 or 35 lbs. His value for P. is a reliable one, for it is based on experiments made with beams of the large size of 10 feet × 4 in. × 6 in.

Teak wood does not split, crack, warp or alter its shape when once seasoned, it does not suffer in contact with iron, and is rarely, if ever, attacked by white ants. Its durability is probably due to the aromatic oil contained in the wood.

It is the chief timber of India and Burma; it is exported largely for ship-building and the construction of railway carriages. In India it is used for all purposes of house and ship-building, for bridges, sleepers, furniture, and most other purposes.

The leaves give a red dye; they are very large and are used as plates, for packing and for thatching. The oil is extracted from the wood in Burma and is used medicinally, as a substitute for linseed oil and as a varnish.

		lbs.
C 1408.	Jagmandal Reserve, Central Provinces	...
C 1409.	Ahiri Reserve, Central Provinces	38
C 2933.	Sonawani, Satpura Reserve, Central Provinces (Tree planted in 1867, cut down in 1876, 10-inch girth.)	...
C 2983.	(White Teak, *Dudhia Sagun*) — Jubbulpore, Central Provinces, 1863.	41
C 2982.	(Black „ *Telia Sagun* or oil teak) — Jubbulpore, Central Provinces, 1863.	48
C 2987.	(Stone „ *Pattharee Sagun*.) — Jubbulpore, Central Provinces, 1863.	44

(Black Teak is rather darker coloured, but otherwise there is no difference in structure, and very little in appearance between these three specimens.)

		lbs.
C 834.	Bairagarh Reserve, Berar	46
C 2809.	Melghát, Berar (sapwood)	38
E 1202.	Bamunpokri Plantation, Darjeeling Terai, Bengal	...
	Specimens from compartment I. 1 planted 1868	...
	„ „ „ II. 1 „ 1871	...
	„ „ „ I. 1 „ „	...
	„ „ „ I. 3 b „ 1872	...

E 3290–291.	Hoolingamara Block, Sitapahar Plantations, Chittagong, 1873 and 1875.	
E 3386–88.	Rampahar Block, Sitapahar Plantation, Chittagong, 1873.	
W 1216.	North Kanara Plantation, Bombay. Specimen from { Sulageri, 18 years old. Murdi 12 „ „ Kadra 10 „ „	

		lbs.
W 1217.	North Kanara, Bombay	39
W 730.	South Kanara, Madras	46
W 753.	„ „ „	42
W 1206.	Parappa Teak Plantation, South Kanara, Madras. Saplings of 5 and 10 years' growth	...
W 2959.	Nilambur Plantation, Malabar. Specimens cut by Mr. Brandis in 1864, Nos. 1, 2 and 4 aged 5, 10 and 20 years, and measuring 16, 19 and 25 inches in girth respectively .	...
W 1203.	Nilambur Plantation, Malabar. Series, Nos. 1 to 33, aged 33 years to 1 year respectively	...
B 2551.	Burma (1862)	44
B 801.	Pegu	40
B 1385.	Thinganneenoung Plantation, Martaban . . . . . Tree 54 feet high, 30 feet to first branch, planted in 1856.	34
B 2709.	Tavoy (Wallich, 1828)	42
B 1346.	Andaman Islands . . . . Tree planted at Dhunee Valley, Leaf Creek, Port Blair, in 1873. Height 44 feet: girth at 5 feet, 36 inches; at 21½ feet, 17 inches; at 28½ feet, 10 inches.	...

		lbs.
No. 85.	Ceylon Collection (Ceylon wood)	44
„ 86.	„ „ (Cochin wood)	40
„ 87.	„ „ (Moulmein wood)	44
„ 47.	Salem Collection	40

2. T. Hamiltoniana, Wall.; Kurz ii. 259. **Vern.** ***Tanap,*** **Burm.**

A deciduous tree. Wood light brown, hard, close-grained. Pores small. Medullary rays fine, the distance between them equal to the transverse diameter of the pores. Annual rings marked by a continuous line of somewhat larger pores.

Prome district and Upper Burma.

Growth moderate, 9 to 10 rings per inch of radius. Weight, 64 lbs. per cubic foot. A good wood, and likely to be useful.

		lbs.
B 3126.	Prome, Burma	64

3. PREMNA, Linn.

Contains about 20 to 25 species of Indian trees, shrubs or climbers. Besides those here described, most of the species are small shrubs, climbers, or at most small trees, chiefly of South India and Burma. *P. barbata*, Wall.; Brandis 367; Gamble 61, Vern. *Ganhila*, Pb.; *Lammar*, Hind.; *Michapnok*, Lepcha, is a small tree of the North-East Himalaya and Sub-Himalayan tract. *P. viburnoides* is a small deciduous tree of the forests of Prome; and *P. sambucina*, Wall., an evergreen small tree of Arracan and Tenasserim. *P. scandens*, Roxb. Fl. Ind. iii. 82; Brandis 367; Kurz ii. 263; Gamble 61. Vern. *Sindri*, Nep.; *Monkakrik*, Lepcha, is a climbing shrub of Eastern Bengal and Burma; and *P. interrupta*, Wall.; Gamble 61, a common climber of the forests of the Sikkim Hills. The latter has a soft, white wood with the structure of a climber; large pores and uniform moderately broad medullary rays, the distance between which is usually equal to the diameter of the pores (E 3395, Darjeeling, 7,000 feet).

The structure of the wood is similar to that of *Vitex* (p. 296), but rather lighter and softer.

1. P. tomentosa, Willd.; Roxb. Fl. Ind. iii. 76; Beddome t. 251; Brandis 367; Kurz 260. Vern. *Nagal, naoru, naura,* Tel.; *Chambara,* Mar.; *Ije,* Kan.; *Boosairu,* Cingh.; *Kyunnalin,* Burm.

A moderate-sized deciduous tree with grey bark similar to that of teak. Wood smooth, light brown, the colour of teak but lighter (hence the Burmese name), moderately hard, smooth, close and even grained, seasons well. Pores moderate-sized, sometimes small, sometimes subdivided, very numerous, uniformly distributed, except that they are a little more numerous near the inner edge of the annual rings, which are fairly well marked. Medullary rays numerous, short, moderately broad, very prominent on a radial section.

South India and Burma.

Growth rather fast, 4 to 8 rings per inch of radius. Weight: Brandis' Burma List, 1862, No. 85, gives 52 lbs.; our specimens vary from 40 to 54 lbs. per cubic foot. Brandis' four experiments in 1864 gave, with bars 3′ × 1″ × 1″, Weight = 43 lbs., P. = 670. The wood polishes well, and is used for weaving shuttles in Burma. It would do for turning and fancy work.

		lbs.
B 317.	Burma (1867)	54
B 2718.	Tavoy (Wallich, 1828)	53
B 2548.	Burma (1862)	51
B 1424.	Burma	40

(Wood rough, grey, and lighter than the other specimens of *P. tomentosa.*)

2. P. longifolia, Roxb. Fl. Ind. iii. 79. *P. tomentosa,* Willd.; Gamble 61. Vern. *Gwyheli,* Nep.; *Sungna,* Lepcha; *Dhaoli,* Mechi; *Gohora,* Ass.

An evergreen tree with thin white bark and indented stem. Wood greyish brown, hard, close-grained. Annual rings well marked by a belt of darker and firmer wood on the outer edge of each ring. Pores small, often subdivided. Medullary rays fine and moderately broad, wavy.

Eastern Sub-Himalayan tract of Bengal and Assam.

Growth fast, 3 to 5 rings per inch of radius. Weight, 47 to 50 lbs. per cubic foot. Wood used for house-posts in Assam.

		lbs.
E 2400.	Sivoke, Darjeeling Terai	47
E 1267.	Lakhimpur, Assam	50

3. P. latifolia, Roxb. Fl. Ind. iii. 76; Beddome clxxii.; Brandis 366; Gamble 61. Vern. *Gineri,* Nep.; *Michapgong,* Lepcha; *Dauli,* Rajbanshi; *Pedda-nella-kura,* Tel.; *Gondhona,* Uriya; *Middi,* Cingh.

A small deciduous tree with greyish white bark. Wood grey with yellow, green, and purple streaks. Annual rings marked by a faint line. Pores between small and moderate-sized, often oval and subdivided. Medullary rays numerous, uniform, equidistant, moderately broad, marked on a radial section. Distinguished from *P. tomentosa* by softer wood, by the medullary rays being closer together, and by smaller pores.

Sub-Himalayan tract from Kumaun eastwards, South India.

Growth moderate, 4 to 9 rings per inch of radius. Weight 38 to 43 lbs. per cubic foot. Used to obtain fire by the hill tribes of Sikkim. The leaves are said by Beddome to be eaten in curries: they are sometimes given as fodder to cattle.

		lbs.
E 621.	Rakti Forest, Darjeeling Terai	38
E 2399.	Bamunpokri, " "	43

4. P. integrifolia, Linn.; Brandis 366; Gamble 60. *P. serratifolia,* Linn.; Roxb. Fl. Ind. iii. 77; Beddome clxxii.; Kurz ii. 262. Vern. *Bakarcha,* Garhwal; *Ganniari,* Oudh; *Bhut-bhiravi,* Beng.; *Gineri,* Nep.; *Munnay,* Tam.; *Ghebu-nelli, pinna-nelli,* Tel.; *Chamari,* Mar.; *Appel,* Mal.

A small deciduous tree, the stem and branches often armed with stout woody spines. Wood white with purple streaks, moderately hard, close-grained; structure similar to that of *P. latifolia,* from which it is probably not specifically distinct.

Oudh, Northern Bengal, South India, Ceylon, Tenasserim, and the Andaman Islands. Weight 35 lbs. per cubic foot. The wood is used for firewood, the leaves for feeding cattle. The fresh felled wood exudes a green coloured sap.

		lbs.
O 3082.	Gonda, Oudh	35
O 3092.	Kheri, „	...

5. P. mucronata, Roxb. Fl. Ind. iii. 80; Brandis 366; Gamble 61, Vern. *Bankhar, gián,* Pb.; *Bakar, bakarcha, basóla, agniún, tumari, jhatela,* Hind.; *Agniú,* Kumaun.

A small tree with grey bark. Wood moderately hard, light purple, structure the same as that of *P. integrifolia.*

Sub-Himalayan tract from the Chenab eastwards. Wood a good fuel, used to obtain fire by friction.

O 3091. Kheri, Oudh.

4. GMELINA, Linn.

Contains 3 species. *G. asiatica,* Linn.; Roxb. Fl. Ind. iii. 87; Beddome clxxii.; Brandis 365; Kurz ii. 265. Vern. *Gumudu,* Tel., is a large branching shrub or small tree of swamp forests in South India, Burma and Ceylon. *G. Hystrix,* Schult; Kurz ii. 265, is a large scandent shrub of Tenasserim.

1. G. arborea, Roxb. Fl. Ind. iii. 84; Beddome t. 253; Brandis 364; Kurz ii. 264; Gamble 61. Vern. *Gumhár, khammara, kambhar, kúmár, gambari, sewan, shewan,* Hind.; *Gúmár, gúmbar,* Beng.; *Gambari,* Nep., Uriya; *Gomari,* Ass.; *Numbor,* Lepcha; *Gumai,* Cachar; *Bolkobak,* Gáro; *Gumadi, cummi,* Tam.; *Gúmar-tek, peddagomru, tagumúda, gumudu,* Tel.; *Shewney, kuli,* Kan.; *Shewan,* Mar.; *Chimman, sag,* Bhíl; *Kumbulu,* Mal.; *Kurse,* Gondi; *Kássamar,* Kurku; *Al-demmata,* Cingh.; *Ramani,* Magh; *Yamaney,* Burm.

A moderate-sized or large deciduous tree. Bark ¼ inch thick, smooth, white or whitish grey. Wood yellowish, greyish or reddish white, with a glossy lustre, close and even-grained, soft, light and strong, durable, does not warp or crack. Annual rings marked either by a white line or by more numerous pores in the spring wood. Pores large and moderate-sized, often subdivided, rather prominent on a vertical section. Medullary rays short, moderately broad, prominent, visible on a radial section as irregular horizontal bands, giving the wood a mottled appearance.

Sub-Himalayan tract from the Chenab eastwards and throughout India, Burma and the Andaman Islands.

Growth fast, our specimens shew about 4 rings per inch of radius; a small round in the Bengal Forest Museum shews 10 rings for a mean diameter of 10½ inches or rather less than 2 rings per inch of radius; another shewed 27 rings with a diameter of 14 inches or nearly 4 rings per inch. The weight and transverse strength have been determined by the following experiments :—

Experiment by whom made.	Year.	Wood whence procured.	Weight.	Number of experiments.	Size of bar.	Value of P.
					Ft. In. In.	
Wallich	...	India . .	32	...	...	...
Kyd	1831	Assam . .	38	...	2 × 1 × 1	675
Baker	1829	Bengal . .	29	3	7 × 2 × 2	375
"	"	" . .	28	4	6 × 2 × 2	398
"	"	Junagarh. .	50? wet	4	7 × 2 × 2	324
Brandis, No. 87 . .	1862	Burma . .	35	...	...	...
Warth	1878	as below	36	18	...	...

The wood is easily worked and readily takes paint or varnish ; it is very durable under water. It is highly esteemed for planking, furniture, door panels, carriages and palanquins, well-work, boats, toys, packing cases and all ornamental work ; it is used in Burma for carving images, clogs and canoes. It would probably be a valuable wood for tea-boxes. It is the chief furniture wood of Chittagong and is in some demand in Calcutta. Writing in May 1829, in 'Gleanings in Science,' Captain Baker, the Superintendent of Suspension Chain Bridges, spoke of *Gumbhar* wood as "well calculated for light planking, panelling, blinds and venetians, and of much estimation for picture frames, organ pipes, sounding boards and other such work where shrinkage is to be avoided," so that it has evidently been long known in the Calcutta market. The fruit is eaten by Gonds, and, as well as the bark and root, is used in native medicine. It is now being planted at Sitapahar and Jamguri in Bengal, and, if not eaten down by deer who are very fond of it, it grows very fast. Seedlings in the Jamguri Nursery, Buxa Reserve, in 1879 reached a height of nearly 4 feet in 6 months.

			lbs.
O	325.	Garhwal (1868)	33
O	343.	Gorakhpur (1868)	32
O	1372.	Gonda, Oudh	40
O	1457.	Bahraich, Oudh	38
O	1483.	Kheri, Oudh	39
C	182.	Mandla, Central Provinces (1870)	35
C	1129.	Ahiri Reserve, Central Provinces	...
C	835.	Bairagarh Reserve, Berar	45
C	2775.	Melghát, Berar	38
C	959.	Guzerat, Bombay	34
E	676.	Bamunpokri, Darjeeling Terai	41
E	2396.	Sivoke Forest, " "	35
E	948.	Eastern Dúars, Assam	36
E	2193.	Nowgong, Assam	39
E	2303.	Kámrúp, "	37
E	1435.	Assam	31
E	1390.	Chittagong	33
B	295.	Burma (1867)	28
B	1425.	Tharrawaddy, Burma	35

5. VITEX, Linn.

Contains 10 to 12 species of Indian trees. *V. trifolia*, Linn.; Roxb. Fl. Ind. iii. 69; Beddome clxxii.; Brandis 370; Gamble 61 (*V. Agnus-castus*, Linn.; Kurz ii. 269) Vern. *Nishinda*, Hind.; *Pajpati*, Nep.; *Nir-nochi*, Tam.; *Vavili*, Tel.; *Karanuchi*, Kan., is a small tree or shrub of Bengal, South India and Burma. *V. heterophylla*, Roxb. Fl. Ind. iii. 75; Kurz ii. 270; Gamble 61. Vern. *Neri*, Nep.; *Murkut*, Lepcha, is a large tree of Northern and Eastern Bengal and Burma. *V. canescens*, and *V. limonifolia*, Kurz ii. 270, 271, are deciduous trees of the forests of Prome. *V. Wimberleyi*, Kurz ii. 271, is a small evergreen tree of the Andaman Islands.

Wood between 40 and 55 lbs. in weight, hard, close-grained. Annual rings distinct. Pores small or moderate-sized. Medullary rays fine, uniform, numerous, equidistant.

1. **V. Negundo,** Linn.; Roxb. Fl. Ind. iii. 70; Beddome clxxi. Brandis 369. Vern. *Marwan, moráun, máura, mora, wana, banna, torban, binna,* Pb.; *Shiwari, shawáli, nengar, mewri, nisinda,* Hind.; *Beygúna,* Uriya; *Nirgunda, nirgúr,* Mar.; *Nirgiri,* Gondi; *Nirgudi,* Kurku; *Vella-nuchi,* Tam.; *Veyala,* Tel.; *Lakki,* Kan.; *Súdú nika,* Cingh.

A deciduous shrub, with thin grey bark. Wood greyish white, hard. Annual rings marked by a narrow belt of more numerous and larger pores at the inner edge. Pores small and moderate-sized. Medullary rays numerous fine, uniform, equidistant.

Common in the drier parts of India, and ascending to 5,000 feet in the North-West Himalaya.

Growth moderate, 7 rings per inch of radius. Weight 41 to 42 lbs. per cubic foot. The branches are used for wattle-work; the root is employed as a febrifuge and the leaves to cure headache.

		lbs.
H 3044.	Kumharsen, Sutlej Valley	42
C 2789.	Melghát, Berar	41

2. **V. altissima,** Linn.; Roxb. Fl. Ind. iii. 71; Beddome t. 252, Brandis 370; Gamble 61. Vern. *Ahay,* Ass.; *Maila,* Tam.; *Myrole, balgay, nauladi, sampaga-pala,* Kan.; *Banalgay,* Mar.; *Miliila,* Cingh.

A large tree. Bark ⅛ inch thick, grey, fibrous. Wood grey with a tinge of olive brown, hard, close-grained, polishes well. Annual rings distinctly marked by a belt of firmer wood on the outer edge. Pores small, scanty. Medullary rays fine, numerous, wavy.

Bengal, South India and Ceylon.

Growth moderate, 8 to 9 rings per inch of radius. Weight 50 to 53 lbs. per cubic foot (South Kanara specimens); 49 and 56 lbs. (Adrian Mendis' Ceylon specimens); Skinner, No. 145, gives 63 lbs. for Kanara specimens. A. Mendis gives P = 788, Skinner P = 557. Molesworth in 'Graphic diagrams for strength of teak beams' gives: Weight 56 lbs. P = 722, E = 4700. The wood is used for building and for carts, and deserves attention.

		lbs.
W 724.	South Kanara	53
W 757.	" "	50
Nos. 54 (56 lbs.) and 78 (49 lbs.), Ceylon Collection		...

3. **V. pubescens,** Vahl.; Beddome clxxi.; Kurz ii. 271. *V. arborea,* Roxb. Fl. Ind. iii. 73. Vern. *Nowli eragu, búsi,* Tel.; *Myladi,* Tam.; *Kyet-yoh,* Burm.

A large tree. Wood smooth, grey with an olive-brown tinge, very hard, close-grained. Annual rings marked by a more or less sharp line and by a broad belt of firmer wood on the outer edge. Pores small, uniformly distributed. Medullary rays fine and very fine, numerous, equidistant; the distance between the rays equal to the transverse diameter of the pores.

South India, Burma and the Andaman Islands.

Growth moderate, 8 to 10 rings per cubic foot. Weight, according to Brandis' Burma List of 1862, No. 83, 45 lbs., but his specimen now weighs 51 lbs.; A. Mendis gives

56 lbs.; our specimens give 55 lbs. Mendis gives P = 770. The wood is durable and is used for various purposes in South India.

		lbs.
D 1058.	South Arcot, Madras	51
D 1063.	Cuddapah „	59
B 1429.	Tharrawaddi, Burma	56
B 2550.	Burma (1862)	51
No. 10.	Ceylon Collection [marked *V. altissima* (*Caha milille*)]	56

4. V. alata, Roxb. Fl. Ind. iii. 72; Kurz ii. 272. *V. peduncularis*, Wall. in DC. Prod. xi. 687. Vern. *Osai*, Ass.; *Boruna, goda*, Beng.; *Krawru*, Magh; *Hila auwal*, Cachar; *Shelangri*, Gáro; *Kyetyo*, Burm.

A tree. Bark thick. Wood purplish or reddish grey, heavy, hard, close-grained. Annual rings distinctly marked by a white line. Pores small, moderate-sized, sometimes filled with a yellowish substance. Medullary rays fine, very numerous.

Assam, Chittagong and Burma.
Growth moderate, 6 to 8 rings per inch of radius. Weight, 60 lbs. per cubic foot. Used in Cachar for posts and beams, in the Gáro Hills for sugarcane crushers.

		lbs.
E 784.	Kámrúp, Assam	...
E 1393.	Chittagong	60
B 1423.	Tharrawaddi, Burma	60

5. V. leucoxylon, Linn. f.; Roxb. Fl. Ind. iii. 74; Beddome clxxi.; Brandis 370; Kurz ii. 273. *V. saligna*, Roxb. l. c. 75. Vern. *Goda, horina, ashwal*, Beng.; *Luki, neva-ledi*, Tel.; *Sengeni, karril*, Kan.; *Tokra*, Magh; *Longarbi thiras*, Mar.; *Htouksha*, Burm.

A very large deciduous tree. Wood grey with a satiny lustre, hard, close-grained, durable. Annual rings marked by a prominent line. Pores small, often oval and subdivided, numerous. Medullary rays short, moderately broad and broad, marked as long shining bands on a radial section.

Chittagong, Burma, Andaman Islands and South India.
Growth moderate to fast, 3 to 12 rings per inch of radius, averaging 6 rings. The following experiments have been made to determine the weight and transverse strength:—

	Weight.	P.
1831, Kyd, with Assam wood, bars 2′ × 1″ × 1″	40	337
1864, Brandis, „ Burma „ „ 3′ × 1″ × 1″	39	763
„ „ „ „ „ „ 2′ × 1″ × 1″	39	508
1878, Warth, with Chittagong and Burma wood (below)	41	...
1862, Brandis, with Burma wood, No. 84	42	...

The wood is used for cart-wheels, and deserves attention for furniture and other purposes. The fruit is eaten by Burmese in the Andamans, and the bark and root used as an astringent (Major Ford).

		lbs.
E 1392.	Chittagong	45
B 330.	Burma (1867)	40
B 2549.	„ (1862)	40
B 2711.	Tavoy (Wallich, 1828)	36
B 2218.	Andaman Islands (1866)	41

6. CLERODENDRON, Linn.

Contains about 12 to 18 species of Indian shrubs or small trees. *C. phlomoides*, Linn.; Roxb. Fl. Ind. iii. 57; Beddome clxxxiv.; Brandis 363. Vern. *Urni*, Hind.; *Irun, arni*, Guz.; *Telaki*, Tel., is a tall white-flowered shrub of the arid and northern and southern dry zones. *C. infortunatum*, Linn.; Beddome clxxiii.; Brandis 363; Kurz ii. 267; Gamble 62 (*Volkameria infortunata*, Roxb. Fl. Ind. iii. 59) Vern. *Bhânt, bhat*, Hind.; *Chitu*, Nep.; *Kadung*, Lepcha; *Lukunah*, Mechi; *Khaoung-gyce*, Burm., is a pinkish-white-flowered shrub common in undergrowth of forests, especially of sál, and in waste places in the greater part of India and Burma. *C. inerme*, Gaertn.; Roxb. Fl. Ind. iii. 58; Beddome clxxiv.; Brandis 363; Kurz ii. 266. Vern. *Ban-jamat, batraj*, Beng., is an evergreen shrub with white flowers, common in tidal forests in Bengal, Burma and the Andamans. *C. serratum*, Spreng.; Brandis 364; Kurz ii. 267; Gamble 61 (*Volkameria serrata*, Roxb. Fl. Ind. iii. 62) Vern. *Barangi*, Hind.; *Chúa*, Nep.; *Yi*, Lepcha; *Bebya, baikyo*, Burm., is a blue-flowered shrub common in the Sub-Himalayan tract and outer Himalaya from the Sutlej eastwards, the Khasia Hills, South India and Burma. *C. Siphonanthus*, R. Br.; Brandis 364; Gamble 62 (*Siphonanthus indica*, Linn.; Roxb. Fl. Ind. iii. 67) Vern. *Barangi*, Hind.; *Bamauhatti*, Beng., is a large shrub with red calyx, white flowers and blue berries, found in Kumaun, Bengal and South India. Home says the wood is tied round the neck by Bengalis and used as a charm against various ailments, in the Sundarbans. *C. nutans*, Wall.; Kurz ii. 268.; Gamble 62. Vern. *Baichua*, Nep.; *Tongsor*, Lepcha, is a white-flowered shrub of evergreen forests in Northern and Eastern Bengal. *C. bracteatum*, Wall.; Gamble 62. Vern. *Chitu*, Nep.; *Kadung*, Lepcha, is a small tree of the Sikkim Hills. *C. villosum*, Bl.; Kurz ii. 268, is an evergreen shrub of the Martaban Hills, chiefly found in deserted toungyas.

1. C. Colebrookianum, Walp.; Gamble 62. Vern. *Kadungbi*, Lepcha.

A small evergreen tree with silvery grey bark. Wood grey, soft. Pores large and moderate-sized, often subdivided, the large pores arranged in interrupted concentric lines, and all pores, especially the smaller ones, joined by irregular concentric bands of softer tissue. Medullary rays moderately broad and fine, irregularly distributed.

Sikkim and Khasia Hills, 3,000 to 6,000 feet.

Weight, 29 lbs. per cubic foot. The whole plant has a strong disagreeable smell; the young leaves are eaten by Lepchas.

		lbs.
E 2401.	Tukdah Forest, Darjeeling, 5,000 feet	29

7. CARYOPTERIS, Bunge.

1. C. Wallichiana, Schauer; Brandis 370; Gamble 62. Vern. *Moni, moháni*, Kumaun; *Shechin*, Nep.; *Malet*, Lepcha.

A large shrub with thin grey papery bark, peeling off in vertical strips. Wood dark grey, moderately hard, with the scent of cherry wood. Pores very small, often in groups, uniformly distributed. Medullary rays moderately broad, the distance between them much greater than the transverse diameter of the pores.

Outer Himalaya, from the Indus to Bhutan, ascending to 3,000 feet.

Growth rapid, 5 rings per inch of radius. Weight, 44 lbs. per cubic foot. Has handsome lilac flowers.

		lbs.
E 2402.	Chunbati, Darjeeling, 2,000 feet	44

8. AVICENNIA, Linn.

1. A. officinalis, Linn.; Beddome clxxiv.; Brandis 371; Kurz ii. 275. Vern. *Bani*, Beng.; *Mada, nalla mada*, Tel.; *Thamé*, Burm.

A shrub or small tree. Wood grey, with a darker heartwood, hard, heavy, consisting of numerous, narrow, well-marked, concentric layers; the inner portion of each layer is firm, with moderate-sized pores which are often in short radial or oblique lines; the outer irregular narrower portion of each layer consists of soft tissue, with a few larger pores. Medullary rays fine, numerous, prominent in the inner layer of each ring.

Salt marshes, coast and tidal forests of India, Burma, and the Andaman Islands.

Weight, 58 lbs. per cubic foot. Wood very brittle, used only for firewood. Major Ford says it is used for mills for husking paddy, rice-pounders, and oil-mills in the Andamans.

		lbs.
E 398.	Sundarbans	58
B 2284.	Andaman Islands	58

Order LXXXI. LABIATÆ.

Contains a large number of herbaceous genera, a few only reaching the size of small shrubs or trees. There are about 7 Indian genera with woody species belonging to 5 tribes:—

Tribe	I.—Ocimoideæ	*Plectranthus.*
„	II.—Satureineæ	*Colebrookia* and *Elsholtzia.*
„	III.—Monardeæ	*Meriandra.*
„	IV.—Stachydeæ	*Colquhounia* and *Roylea.*
„	V.—Ajugoideæ	*Teucrium.*

Colquhounia elegans, Wall.; Kurz ii. 278, is a scandent shrub of the hill forests of Martaban at 4,000 to 5,000 feet. *C. coccinea*, Wall., and *C. vestita*, Wall., are scandent shrubs of Nepal and the Eastern Himalaya.

Wood light-coloured, hard. Pores small or very small, generally in groups. Medullary rays moderately broad, distant.

1. PLECTRANTHUS, L'Hér.

1. P. rugosus, Wall. Vern. *Khwangere,* Trans-Indus; *Itsit,* Salt Range; *Búi,* Jhelam; *Solei,* Kashmir; *Piúmar, chúgú,* Chenab; *Kot, siringri,* Ravi; *Pek, rosbang, chichri,* Sutlej.

A small shrub with brown bark. Wood grey, hard. Pores small and very small. Medullary rays moderately broad. Annual rings marked by a narrow belt of more numerous pores.

Common on dry hill-sides and rocks in the North-West Himalaya and Salt Range above 3,000 feet.

H 2840. Simla, 7,000 feet.

2. COLEBROOKIA, Sm.

C. ternifolia, Roxb., is a shrub of the hills of the Carnatic.

1. C. oppositifolia, Sm.; Kurz ii. 277; Gamble 63. Vern. *Shakardana,* Trans-Indus; *Phiis bekkar,* Salt Range; *Dúss, sampni,* Jhelam; *Súáli,* Chenab; *Dúss,* Ravi; *Briali, basuti,* Beas; *Barmera,* Sutlej; *Dulshat,* Kumaun; *Dosúl,* Nep.

A shrub with grey bark. Wood greyish white, moderately hard, close-grained. Pores very small, in groups. Medullary rays moderately broad; the distance between the rays several times larger than the transverse diameter of the pores.

Outer Himalaya, from the Indus to Bhutan, ascending to 4,000 feet.

Weight, 46 lbs. per cubic foot. The wood is used for gunpowder charcoal, and the leaves applied to wounds and sores (*Stewart*).

		lbs.
H 3046.	Below Komharsen, Sutlej Valley, 2,500 feet	46

3. ELSCHOLTZIA, Willd.

1. E. polystachya, Benth. Vern. *Rangchari, mehndi,* Jhelam; *Garúdar, tappaddar,* Chenab; *Dúss,* Ravi; *Pothi,* Sutlej; *Bhangria,* Kumaun.

A shrub with grey, fibrous bark, peeling off in thin, longitudinal strips. Wood grey, moderately hard, splits and cracks, and in seasoning separates into concentric masses. Annual rings distinctly marked by a belt of numerous and larger pores in the spring wood. Pores small and very small, often subdivided, those in the outer belt of the annual ring arranged in groups. Medullary rays moderately broad; the distance between the rays larger than the transverse diameter of the pores.

North-Western Himalaya, from the Jhelam eastwards, and the Khasia Hills, from 6,000 to 10,000 feet.

Growth slow, 15 rings per inch of radius. Weight, 42 lbs. per cubic foot. Common in forest undergrowth, growing often to 10 or 12 feet high.

		lbs.
H 2841. H 2936.	} Mahasu, Simla, 7,000 feet	42

4. MERIANDRA, Benth.

M. bengalensis, Bth., is often cultivated in Indian gardens as a substitute for sage.

1. M. strobilifera, Benth.

A small shrub with grey bark. Wood white, hard. Pores small and very small. Medullary rays fine, numerous. Annual rings marked by an interrupted line of larger pores on the inner edge, and a narrow belt of firmer wood on the outer edge of each ring.

North-West Himalaya, about 6,000 feet.

The leaves are very aromatic, having the scent of sage; they are distinguished from those of *Elsholtzia polystachya* by being sagittate. The shrub is chiefly found on dry rocks, especially limestone.

H 2839. Simla, 6,500 feet.

5. ROYLEA, Wall.

1. R. elegans, Wall. Vern. *Kaur, kauri,* Pb.; *Titpáti,* Kumaun; *Patkarru,* Hind.

A shrub with grey bark. Wood white, hard. Pores small and very small, in groups and short tails. Medullary rays moderately broad, unequally distributed.

North-West Himalaya, from the Ravi to Nepal, up to 3,000 feet.

A handsome shrub. Weight, 52 lbs. per cubic foot.

		lbs.
H 3045.	Komharsen, Sutlej Valley, 4,000 feet	52

6. TEUCRIUM, Linn.

1. T. macrostachyum, Wall.; Gamble 62. Vern. *Matsola, gurupis,* Nep.; *Chúng,* Lepcha.

A small evergreen tree. Bark thin, corky. Wood yellowish white, moderately hard, close and even-grained. Pores small, in groups. Medullary rays moderately broad, numerous. Annual rings indistinctly marked.

Eastern Himalaya from Nepal eastwards, Khasia Hills and Sylhet, from 5,000 to 8,000 feet.

Growth rapid, 3 to 5 rings per inch of radius. Weight, 38 to 41 lbs. per cubic foot. A common tree in second growth forests in the Sikkim Hills, and easily recognised by its greyish foliage and long erect spikes of dirty white flowers with long-exserted stamens. Its wood is a fair fuel. It coppices well and strikes easily from cuttings.

		lbs.
E 2411.	Rangbúl, Darjeeling, 7,000 feet	41
E 3376.	Darjeeling, 6,500 feet.	38

ORDER LXXXIII. NYCTAGINEÆ.

Contains one genus of Indian trees—*Pisonia aculeata,* Linn.; Beddome clxxv.; Kurz ii. 279, is a large straggling climber of Southern India and of the coast forests of Burma and the Andaman Islands. *P. alba,* Span, and *P. umbellifera,* Seem.; Kurz ii. 279, 280, are evergreen trees of the coast forests of the Andamans. To this family belong the beautiful *Bougainvilleas,* common in gardens, and the Marvel of Peru, *Mirabilis Jalapa,* cultivated or run wild over the greater part of India.

ORDER LXXXIV. AMARANTACEÆ.

A large genus of herbaceous plants containing only 2 or 3 genera of Indian shrubs. *Deeringia baccata,* Moq.; Gamble 63 (*D. celosioides,* R. Br.; Roxb. Fl. Ind. i. 682) Vern. *Gola mohani,* Beng.; *Kala loári,* Kumaun; *Latman,* Hind., is a common climber of Northern India, climbing over bushes and covering them in the cold season with its long branches covered with bright crimson berries.

1. RODETIA, Moquin-Tandon.

1. R. amherstiana, Moq. *Deeringia Amherstiana,* Wall. Vern. *Bilga,* Koti.

A large straggling shrub, with thin, brown, rough bark. Wood grey, soft, divided by concentric and anastomosing bands of cellular tissue into irregular, narrow, concentric belts, which are subdivided into oblong porous areas by short medullary rays varying in breadth, which often gradually widen where they join the concentric bands of cellular tissue. Pores moderate-sized, numerous.

North-west Himalaya and Burma.

Weight, our specimen gives 41 lbs. per cubic foot. It seems to be often grown as a hedge; the young shoots are eaten fried in ghee, and a black dye is obtained from the leaves. The berries, which are bright crimson, resembling those of *Deeringia,* are also eaten.

		lbs.
H 3097.	Koti, near Simla, 6,000 feet	41

ORDER LXXXV. POLYGONEÆ.

A large Order of herbaceous plants, containing only 3 genera which have woody plants indigenous in India, *viz.*, *Calligonum*, *Polygonum* and *Rumex*.

1. CALLIGONUM, Linn.

1. C. polygonoides, Linn.; Brandis 372. Vern. *Balanja, berwaja, tatúke,* Trans-Indus; *Phók, phóg,* Pb.

A slow-growing shrub. Bark reddish grey, rough, peeling off in long thin flakes; inner substance red. Most old stems are hollow. Heartwood reddish brown, very hard. Annual rings distinctly marked by a continuous belt of moderate-sized and large pores; in the outer portion of each annual ring the pores are small, in groups, scanty, often joined by wavy lines of soft tissue. Medullary rays fine, numercus.

Arid zone of Sind, the Punjab and Rajputana, Afghanistan and Western Asia.

It is chiefly used for fuel, but twigs and branches are sometimes employed for the walls and roofs of huts. The abortive flowers are swept up and eaten, either made into bread or cooked with ghee.

P 889. Multán.

2. POLYGONUM, Linn.

Contains several shrubs of the Himalaya, some with very handsome flowers, but none of any importance, except the one described. Besides the shrubs there are a large number of herbaceous plants belonging to this genus, many of them very common.

1. P. molle, Don; Gamble 63. Vern. *Totnye, tuknu, patu-swa,* Nep.

A large trailing shrub, with thin, dark grey bark and hollow stems. Wood reddish white. Annual rings marked by a belt of moderate-sized pores; in the outer portion of each ring the pores are small, scanty, often in groups. Medullary rays moderately broad, often in pairs, irregularly distributed.

Hills of Sikkim and Bhutan, from 5,000 to 8,000 feet.

An extremely common, often almost gregarious, and scandent or straggling shrub. The young shoots are pleasantly acid and are eaten like rhubarb. There is some doubt about the name of this very common plant, but it is probably *Coccoloba Totnea,* Ham., in Don. Prodr. Fl. Nep. 74. It has the enlarged succulent calyx of *Coccoloba* round the fruit.

E 2412. Rangbi, Darjeeling, 5,000 feet.

3. RUMEX, Linn.

1. R. hastatus, Don. Vern. *Katambal, khattimal,* Jhelam; *Ami,* Chenab, Ravi; *Malorigha, amla,* Beas; *Amlora,* Sutlej; *Almora,* Kumaun.

Generally an undershrub, sometimes a shrub. Woodl ight red, moderately hard. Pores small, more numerous at the inner edge of the annual rings. Medullary rays broad and very broad.

North-West Himalaya from 2,500 to 9,000 feet, chiefly on rocks and dry hill-sides. The leaves are acid and are eaten as sorrel.

H 3018. Kot, Sutlej Valley, 2,500 feet.

Atraphaxis spinosa, Linn.; Brandis 373, is a thorny shrub of the hills of Afghanistan and Beluchistan belonging to this family.

ORDER LXXXV. LAURACEÆ.

A large Order containing 17 genera of Indian trees, many of which are important. These genera belong to 4 tribes, *viz.*—

Tribe I.—Perseaceæ	*Cinnamomum, Alseodaphne, Phœbe, Machilus, Haasia, Beilschmiedia* and *Apollonias.*
„ II.—Cryptocaryeæ . . .	*Cryptocarya.*
„ III.—Litsæaceæ	*Tetranthera, Cylicodaphne, Dodecadenia, Actinodaphne, Litsæa, Daphnidium, Aperula* and *Lindera.*
„ IV.—Hernandieæ . . .	*Hernandia.*

Nectandra and *Sassafras* belong to the Sub-Order Oreodaphneæ, *Persea* to Perseaceæ and *Laurus* to Litsæaceæ. The identification of many of the species of the Order is very difficult, and few Orders more require further and careful investigation.

Haasia Wightii, Nees; Beddome t. 298, is a tree of the Anamalai Hills and the Ghâts of Tinnevelly and Travancore. *Apollonias Arnottii,* Nees; Beddome t. 291; Brandis 377, is a tree of the Tinnevelly and Travancore Ghâts and Malabar.

Cryptocarya contains about 6 species. *C. Wightiana,* Thw.; Beddome t. 299, is a large tree of the Western Ghâts and Ceylon. *C. Stocksii,* Meissn., is a tree of Kanara; and *C. Neilgherrensis,* Meissn., of the Nilgiri Hills. *C. floribunda,* Nees, and *C. amygdalina,* Nees; Gamble 64. Vern. *Patmaro,* Nep.; *Kaledzo,* Lepcha, are trees of the outer Sikkim Himalaya and Eastern Bengal. *C. ferrea,* Bl.; and *C. Griffithiana,* Wight; Kurz ii. 295, are trees of Tenasserim.

Cylicodaphne contains about 8 species placed by Beddome and Kurz under *Tetranthera,* but separated by Meissner in DC. Prodromus, Vol. XV. *C. nitida,* Meissn. (*Tetranthera nitida,* Roxb.; Kurz ii. 302. Vern. *Kotoloah* Ass.) is a large tree of Eastern Bengal and Burma upon whose leaves the "Muga" silkworm (*Antheræa Assama*) is sometimes fed. *C. Wightiana,* Nees, is a tree of Assam, South India and Ceylon. *Dodecadenia grandiflora,* Nees; Brandis 381; Kurz ii. 304, is an evergreen tree of the Himalaya from Kumaun eastwards. *Actinodaphne* contains about 9 species. *A. angustifolia,* Nees; Beddome clxxxvi.; Brandis 381 (*Litsæa angustifolia*); Kurz ii. 305. Vern. *Samkoh,* Ass., *Boltanaro,* Gâro; *Tabongdeing,* Magh, is a large evergreen tree of Eastern Bengal, South India and Burma. *A. salicina,* DC.; Beddome t. 295, Kurz ii. 305, is a tree of the Western Ghâts and Ceylon. *A. Hookeri,* Meissn.; Beddome t. 296; Brandis 381, is a small tree of Sikkim and the Eastern and Western Ghâts of South India. *A. obovata,* Hook. f. and Th.; Gamble 65. Vern. *Muslindi,* Nep.; *Pohor,* Lepcha; *Laiphanzeh,* Mechi; *Cherritinga,* Ass., is a large evergreen tree of the outer Sikkim Himalaya, Assam, Khasia Hills and Sylhet, with large 3-nerved leaves, generally in whorls. *Aperula* contains 2 trees: *A. assamica,* Meissn. (*Lindera assamica,* Kurz ii. 308), of Sikkim, Assam and the Martaban Hills; and *A. Neesiana,* Bl.; Brandis 383. (*Lindera Neesiana,* Kurz ii. 309) Vern. *Karaway,* Burm., of Nepal, Sikkim and Burma, yielding, according to Kurz, excellent sassafras. *Lindera* contains about 5 species, chiefly of Sikkim and Bhutan, the chief among which is *L. heterophylla,* Meissn., of the hills of Sikkim at 8,900 to 9,000 feet. *Hernandia peltata,* Meissn.; Beddome t. 300; Kurz ii. 309. Vern. *Uparanthi* Mysore; *Palati,* Cingh., is an evergreen tree with peltate leaves found in the coast forests of the Andamans and Ceylon. Beddome says that the wood is very light and takes fire readily, that the juice is a powerful depilatory, removing the hair without pain, and that the seed and young leaves are cathartic. *Persea gratissima* is the fruit tree, the Avocado Pear, cultivated in India. The bay laurel is *Laurus nobilis.*

The wood of the Indian laurels is generally light-coloured, soft or moderately hard, without heartwood, even-grained, seasoning well without splitting. They have, with few exceptions, an exceedingly uniform structure. Pores small or moderate-sized, uniformly distributed. Medullary rays fine, uniform and equidistant. Annual rings distinctly marked in most species either by a sharp line, or by a firmer belt of wood in the outer portion of the ring.

1. CINNAMOMUM, Burman.

According to Meissner this genus contains 16 Indian species, 5 of which from South India Beddome considers should only be varieties of one species. It contains 2 sections: *Malabathrum* with 3 to 5-nerved leaves, and *Camphora* usually with penni-veined leaves. The first section contains 10 species. *C. Wightii*, Meissn.; Beddome t. 262, is a tree of the Nilgiri Hills and Ceylon. *C. sulphuratum*, Nees; Kurz ii. 288, is a species with yellow pubescent leaves, from the Western Ghâts and Tenasserim. *C. iners*, Rwdt.; Brandis 375; Kurz ii. 287. Vern. *Looleng-kyau*, Burm., is a tree of Eastern Bengal, South India and Burma. *C. Perrottetii*, Meissn., is a Nilgiri tree. *C. impressinervium*, Meissn.; Gamble 64, is a large tree of Sikkim. *C. caudatum*, Nees; Kurz ii. 289; Gamble 63. Vern. *Kharsoni*, Nep.; *Sanging*, Lepcha, is a round-leaved large tree of Nepal, Sikkim and Upper Burma. *C. Zeylanicum*, Breyn.; Beddome clxxxiv.; Brandis 375; Kurz ii. 287. Vern. *Dalchini*, Hind.; *Karruwa*, Tam.; *Sanalinga*, Tel.; *Rassu kúrúndu*, Cingh.; *Loolengkyau*, Burm., is the true Cinnamon. The cinnamon is the bark of the tree, the leaves also are aromatic, giving oil of clove. The root yields camphor and the liber oil of cinnamon. The tree is indigenous in the Ceylon forests up to 8,000 feet, and is largely grown in that island in coppice woods.

To the second section belong *C. inunctum*, Meissn., and *C. Parthenoxylon*, Meissn.; Kurz ii. 289, of South Tenasserim, the latter being said by Kurz to be the Martaban Camphor Wood. *C. pseudo-Sassafras*, Meissn., is a tree of Mergui. *C. Cecidodaphne*, Meissn. Vern. *Buddai Soom*, Ass., is a tree of Sylhet. *C. Camphora*, Nees and Eberm.; Brandis 376, is the Japan Camphor Tree, from whose wood camphor is obtained.

Wood soft, seasons well, and does not warp or crack. Pores well marked on a longitudinal section. Medullary rays uniform and equidistant. The leaves and bark, as well as the wood of many species, are aromatic.

1. C. obtusifolium, Nees; Brandis 375; Kurz ii. 287; Gamble 63. *Laurus obtusifolia*, Roxb. Fl. Ind. ii. 302. Vern. *Tezpat, ramtezpat, linton*, Beng.; *Bara singoli*, Nep.; *Nupsor*, Lepcha; *Patichanda*, Ass.; *Dupatti*, Mechi; *Krowai*, Magh; *Loolengkyau*, Burm.

An evergreen tree, with grey aromatic bark ¼ inch thick. Wood reddish grey, moderately hard, shining, mottled on a vertical section by the medullary rays, the pores containing a gummy substance which exudes copiously on the wood being wetted. Annual rings very indistinctly marked. Pores moderate-sized, often subdivided, uniformly distributed in frequently grouped oblique lines. Medullary rays moderately broad, slightly undulating, prominent on a radial section as long narrow plates. The wood has a kind of lustre, and the bark of the roots is highly aromatic.

Outer North-East Himalaya to 7,000 feet, Eastern Bengal, Burma, and Andaman Islands.

Growth moderate, our specimens shew 10 to 12 rings per inch of radius; a tree examined by Mr. McDonell near Darjeeling gave 15½ rings per inch of radius. Weight, 41 lbs. per cubic foot. The leaves are aromatic, and the bark, especially that of the roots, resembles cinnamon. The "Muga" silkworm (*Antheræa Assama*) sometimes feeds on its leaves.

		lbs.
E 498.	Sukna Forest, Darjeeling Terai	44
E 693.	Sepoydura Forest, Darjeeling, 5,500 feet	38

2. C. pauciflorum, Nees. Vern. *Dinglatterdop*, Khasia.

Wood light red, very aromatic, beautifully mottled on a radial section by the medullary rays, rough, hard. Pores moderate-sized, often in radial lines. Medullary rays moderately broad, numerous.

Assam Valley, Khasia Hills and Sylhet.

Growth fast, 4 rings per inch of radius. Weight, 39 lbs. per cubic foot.

		lbs.
E 798.	Khasia Hills, 5,000 feet	39

3. C. Tamala, Nees; Brandis 374; Gamble 63. *C. albiflorum*, Nees; Wight Ic. t. 140. *C. Cassia*, Bl.; Kurz ii. 288. *Laurus Cassia*, Roxb. Fl. Ind. ii. 297. Cassia Cinnamon. Vern. *Dálchíni, kirkiria; kikra, sinkami, silkanti*, Hind.; *Chota sinkoli*, Nep.; *Nupsor*, Lepcha; *Dopatti*, Ass.

A moderate-sized evergreen tree. Bark thin, compact, brown, wrinkled, with an aromatic taste. Wood reddish grey, splits and warps, moderately hard, close-grained, slightly scented. Annual rings distinctly marked by a narrow belt of firmer wood on the outer edge with fewer pores. Pores small to moderate-sized. Medullary rays fine, numerous, equidistant.

Himalaya, sparingly from the Indus to the Sutlej, common thence eastwards between 3,000 and 7,800 feet, Eastern Bengal, Khasia Hills and Burma.

Growth moderate, the Darjeeling specimen shewing 6 rings, that from Jaunsar 7, and the Hazara one 10 rings per inch of radius. Weight, 39 lbs. per cubic foot. The wood is not used. The bark is largely collected and sold under the name of *Taj*. The leaves are also much sold under the names *Tezpat, tajpat*.

		lbs.
H 937.	Hazara, 4,000 feet	40
H 3162.	Dungagalli, Hazara, 4,000 feet	...
H 427.	Bagiyar Forest, Jaunsar, 4,000 feet	35
E 575.	Sukna Forest, Darjeeling Terai	42

4. C. glanduliferum, Meissn.; Brandis 376; Gamble 64. The Nepal Camphor Wood. Vern. *Malligiri, marisgiri*, Nep.; *Rohu*, Lepcha; *Gunserai*, Mechi, Ass.; *Gundroi*, Cachar.

A large tree. Bark 1 to 2 inches thick, dark grey, uneven, outside corky, highly scented. Wood rough, pale brown, highly scented with a strong smell of camphor when fresh cut, has a certain lustre. The wood distantly resembles that of an *Albizzia* on a vertical section, but is rougher; it is soft to moderately hard, even-grained. Annual rings marked by a distinct line. Pores between moderate-sized and large, uniformly distributed, often oval and subdivided and filled with a glittering resinous substance. Medullary rays short, numerous, uniformly distributed, fine or moderately broad, the distance between the rays generally less than the transverse diameter of the pores. Pores distinctly marked on a vertical section.

South Himalaya from Kumaun eastwards, Assam, Khasia Hills and Sylhet.

Growth fast, 2 to 3 rings per inch of radius. Weight, 38·5 lbs. per cubic foot. Wood durable, easily worked, is not touched by insects. It is used in Assam for canoes and boat-building; in Sikkim for boxes, almirahs and other articles, also for planking. It is being tried for sleepers.

		lbs.
E 670.	Dulka Jhar, Darjeeling Terai	38
E 2413.	Tista Valley, Darjeeling	37
E 628.	Eastern Dúars, Assam	39
E 639.	Kámrúp, Assam	34
E 2304.	" "	40
E 2187.	Nowgong, "	41

5. C. sp. (perhaps *C. Parthenoxylon*, Meissn.; Kurz ii. 289, or *Aperula Neesiana*, Bl.; see Brandis 383). Vern. *Karaway*, Burm.

Wood orange-brown, scented, moderately hard, oily to the touch. Pores moderate-sized and large, often subdivided, filled with resin, the transverse diameter often equal to, or slightly larger than, the distance between the fine, prominent, medullary rays. It resembles the wood of *C. glanduliferum* in structure.

South Tenasserim.

Weight, 43 to 46 lbs. per cubic foot. Wood durable, used for house-building and shingles.

		lbs.
B 1945.	Tavoy	43
B 2483.	„	46

6. C. sp. Vern. *Hmanthin*, Burm.

Wood white with a pink tinge, shining, moderately hard, highly scented. Pores moderate-sized, often subdivided, frequently filled with resin, their transverse diameter generally equal to the distance between the short, fine, prominent medullary rays. In structure the wood most resembles that of *C. obtusifolium*.

South Tenasserim.

Weight, 36 to 43 lbs. per cubic foot. The wood is plentiful at Tavoy and Mergui, where it is used for building.

		lbs.
B 1946.	Tavoy	43
B 2482.	„	36

7. C. sp. Vern. *Sinkozi*, Burm.

Wood red, soft, strongly scented. Pores moderate-sized, often subdivided, their transverse diameter generally equal to, or less than, the distance between the short and fine medullary rays. Somewhat resembles in structure the wood of *C. parviflorum*.

South Tenassserim.

Weight, 41 lbs. Found by the late Mr. Lee in Mergui, but rather scarce.

		lbs.
B 1387.	Tavoy	41

Nos. B 298, Burma (1867), 24 lbs.; B 2691 (40 lbs.); B 2695 (39 lbs.); B 2719 (36 lbs.), Tavoy (Wallich, 1828), are all evidently Lauraceæ and probably *Cinnamomum*. They have a light, soft, aromatic wood. Pores moderate-sized, generally subdivided. Medullary rays fine, equidistant, numerous.

2. ALSEODAPHNE, Nees.

A. semecarpifolia, Nees; Beddome t. 297. Vern. *Wiwarana*, Cingh., is a large tree of the Western Ghâts and Ceylon, where it is known as a valuable timber of a yellow colour, which resists the attacks of "teredo" and is used for building and boats. *A. grandis*, Nees; Kurz ii. 293, is an evergreen tree of Burma with a yellowish wood.

1. A. sp. Vern. *Dowki poma*, Assam.

Wood soft, red, even-grained. Pores small, in radial lines. Medullary rays fine, red, equidistant, visible on a radial section.

Assam.

Weight, 32 lbs. per cubic foot. Used for boats, furniture and building.

		lbs.
E 633.	Eastern Dúars, Assam	32

3. PHŒBE, Nees.

Contains about 7 species. *P. pallida*, Nees; Brandis 377. Vern. *Kanwál*, Kumaun, is a small tree of the Himalaya from Kumaun eastwards and Burma. *P. paniculata*, Nees; Brandis 377 [*P. villosa*, Wight, and *P. pubescens*, Nees, Kurz ii. 290. *P. Wightii*, Meissn.; Beddome t. 292 (probably). *Laurus villosa* Roxb. Fl. Ind. ii. 310 (probably)] Vern. *Kumara*, Burghers; *Kapua kanwál* Kumaun; *Boltigachu*, Gáro; *Chekio*, Magh, is a tree of the Eastern Himalaya, Eastern Bengal, Burma and South India, with, according to Beddome, a good wood of a light red colour. *P. angustifolia*, Nees, is a tree of the Khasia Hills. *P. glaucescens*, Nees; Gamble 64. Vern. *Surúl*, Nep., is a tree of the Eastern Himalaya and Eastern Bengal.

1. P. lanceolata, Nees; Brandis 377; Kurz ii. 290; Gamble 64. *Laurus lanceolaria*, Roxb. Fl. Ind. ii. 309. Vern. *Chan, chandra, badror, shalanghi*, Pb.; *Haulia, dandorla, káwal, sún kawal, bilphari*, Hind.; *Dupatti*, Mechi; *Nuni ajhar*, Gáro; *Sun kanwál*, Kumaun.

A small evergreen tree. Wood white, hard, close-grained. Annual rings marked by a distinct line. Pores moderate-sized, often oval and subdivided, or in short radial lines, uniformly distributed. Medullary rays fine, equidistant. The wood turns brown on exposure, and varies in colour in different localities.

Outer Himalaya from the Jumna to Bhutan, ascending to 6,000 feet, Khasia Hills, Sylhet, Burma and the mountains of South India.

Growth fast, 3 to 4 rings per inch of radius. Weight, 46 to 55 lbs. per cubic foot.

			lbs.
H	91.	Bhajji, Simla, 4,000 feet	46
E	2415.	Chunbati, Darjeeling, 2,500 feet	55

2. P. attenuata, Nees; Gamble 64. Vern. *Dudri*, Nep.; *Lepchaphal*, Darjeeling; *Phani*, Lepcha.

A large evergreen tree. Wood grey, turning darker on exposure, hard, even-grained. Annual rings marked by a distinct line. Pores large and moderate-sized, uniformly distributed, frequently oval and subdivided. Medullary rays fine, equidistant.

Sikkim and Bhutan, from 4,000 to 8,000 feet, hills of Eastern Bengal.

Growth moderate, 5 to 9 rings per inch of radius. Weight, 39 to 44 lbs. per cubic foot. Much used at Darjeeling for building, for tea-boxes and other purposes. The fruit is large, when ripe the size of a green walnut; it is eaten by Lepchas. (The identity of this species requires further investigation; it is a very handsome tree with long, narrow leaves.)

			lbs.
E	363.	Rangbúl, Darjeeling, 7,000 feet	44
E	2416.	Chuttockpur Forest, Darjeeling, 6,000 feet	39

4. MACHILUS, Rumphius.

Contains about 9 species. *M. macrantha*, Nees; Beddome t. 264. Vern. *Kromá*, Burghers; *Iruli*, Kaders; *Kurma*, Kan.; *Ullalu*, Cingh., is a large tree of the Western Gháts and Ceylon, with a soft, light, even-grained wood, used for building. *M. rimosa*, Bl., *M. fruticosa*, Kurz, and *M. tavoyana*, Meissn.; Kurz ii. 292, are trees of Tenasserim. *M. khasyana*, Meissn., is a tree of the Khasia Hills.

1. M. odoratissima, Nees; Brandis 378; Gamble 64. *M. indica*, Lour.; Kurz ii. 291. Vern. *Dalchini, mith-patta, prora, badror, leddil*, Pb.; *Kawala*, Hind.; *Kawala, lali, jagrikat*, Nep.; *Phamlet*, Lepcha; *Soom*, Ass.; *Dingpingwait*, Khasia.

A large tree. Wood grey, darkening and turning red on exposure, soft to moderately hard, even-grained. Pores moderate-sized, often oval and subdivided, their transverse diameter equal to the distance between the uniformly distributed fine medullary rays. Annual rings very indistinct.

Outer Himalaya ascending to 8,000 feet, Khasia Hills, Burma.

Growth moderate to fast, 2 to 11, averaging 7 rings per inch of radius; a tree examined by Mr. McDonell in the Park, Darjeeling, shewed 6 rings per inch. Weight 40 lbs. per cubic foot. Used in Darjeeling, where it is very common, for building, chiefly for native houses. In Assam it grows gregariously in large forests, which are used for feeding the silkworms (*Antheræa Assama*) which give the "Muga" or "Moonga" silk. This silk, which is chiefly produced on the *Soom* tree, is also produced on *Cinnamomum obtusifolium, Tetranthera polyantha, glauca* and *monopetala, Cylicodaphne nitida* and *Symplocos grandiflora*. For an account of its production see "Indian Forester," Vol. V, p. 35, an article entitled "The Muga Silk Industry in the Sibságar District, Assam," by Dr. Brandis.

			lbs.
H	92.	The Glen, Simla, 6,000 feet	37
H	929.	Hazara, Punjab	39
E	435.	Rangbúl Forest, Darjeeling, 7,000 feet	43
E	2414.	" " " "	36
E	592.	Khookloong Forest, Darjeeling Terai	43
E	1271.	Lakhimpúr, Assam	43

5. BEILSCHMIEDIA, Nees.

Contains about 4 species. *B. fagifolia*, Nees; Beddome t. 263; Brandis 379, is a large tree of the Western Gháts with a good timber used for building. *B. macrophylla*, Meissn., is a tree of Mergui. *B. assamica*, Meissn., is a tree of Assam, and *B. globularia*, Kurz, a tree of the hill forests of Martaban.

1. B. Roxburghiana, Nees; Brandis 378; Kurz ii. 293; Gamble 64. *Laurus bilocularis*, Roxb. Fl. Ind. ii. 311. Vern. *Konháiah*, Oudh; *Tarsing*, Nep.; *Kanyu*, Lepcha; *Tapchi*, Gáro; *Serai-guti*, Ass.; *Shatoobeng*, Burm.

An evergreen tree. Wood white, moderately hard, even-grained; heartwood with red and green streaks. Annual rings marked by sharp lines. Pores moderate-sized, scanty, oval and subdivided. Medullary rays fine and very fine, numerous.

Eastern Himalaya up to 8,000 feet, Eastern Bengal, Burma and the Andaman Islands.

Growth moderate, 5 to 9 rings per inch of radius. Weight, 36·5 lbs. per cubic foot. Wood used in Assam for boats; in Darjeeling for building, tea-boxes and other purposes.

			lbs.
E	1258.	Tezpur, Assam	36
E	1264.	" "	39
E	700.	Chuttockpur Forest, Darjeeling, 6,000 feet	35
E	2419.	Rangbúl " " 7,000 "	36

These two last have less numerous pores.

6. TETRANTHERA, Jacq.

About 26 species are described in the "Prodromus" as occurring in India and Burma. *T. amara*, Nees; Kurz ii. 299; Gamble 65. Vern. *Likh paieli*, Nep.; *Safednyok*, Lepcha, is an evergreen tree of the Eastern Himalaya, Burma and the Andamans, with a pale brown wood. *T. polyantha*, Wall.; Kurz ii. 301; Gamble 45. Vern. *Siltimber*, Nep.; *Terhilsok*, Lepcha; *Adakuri, edenkuri, mezenkuri*, Ass., is a small tree of the Eastern Himalaya, Assam and the Khasia Hills, generally of old cultivated land. In Assam the leaves are used to feed the silkworms which produce the "muga" silk (*Antheræa Assama*). *T. grandis*, Wall.; Kurz ii. 299, is an evergreen tree of the forests of Burma, having, according to Kurz, a handsome yellow wood with a fine lustre. *T. Wightiana*, Wall.; Beddome t. 293. Vern. *Keyngee*, Burghers'; *Hammadi*, Kan. is a tree of the forests of the Western Ghâts from 2,000 to 8,000 feet, having a handsome yellow wood, which is used for building. *T. glauca*, Wall.; Kurz ii. 300; Gamble 65. Vern. *Sempat*, Nep.; *Diglilati*, Mechi; *Diglotti*, Ass., is an evergreen tree of the outer Eastern Himalaya and Eastern Bengal on the leaves of which in Assam the Muga silkworms are sometimes fed.

1. T. laurifolia, Jacq.; Brandis 379; Kurz ii. 297; Gamble 65. *T. apetala*, Roxb. Fl. Ind. iii. 819. Vern. *Maida, meda, gwá, rián, chandra*, Pb.; *Garbijaur, singrauf, medh, ménda*, Hind.; *Suppatnyok*, Lepcha; *Kukúr chita*, Beng.; *Narra alagi*, Tel.; *Ungdung*, Burm.

A moderate-sized evergreen tree. Bark 1 inch thick. Wood greyish brown or olive grey, moderately hard, shining, close and even-grained, seasons well, durable, is not attacked by insects. Annual rings indistinctly marked by a white line. Pores small and moderate-sized, often subdivided, uniformly distributed. Medullary rays fine and moderately broad.

Kumaun, Garhwal, Bengal, Burma, Central and South India.

Growth moderate, 6-7 rings per inch of radius. Weight, 47 lbs. per cubic foot A fine wood worth notice. The bark is used medicinally for external application bruised and mixed with goat's milk, for sprains and bruises.

		lbs.
O 253.	Garhwal (1868)	48
O 1378.	Gonda, Oudh	45
O 1484.	Kheri „	48
D 1087.	Madura, Madras	46
B 2286.	Andaman Islands (1866)	47

2. T. monopetala, Roxb. Fl. Ind. iii. 821; Brandis 380; Kurz ii. 299; Gamble 65. Vern. *Meda, gwa, singraf, sangran, marda, kat marra, kakúri, kerauli, patoia, katmoria, papria, katmedh, kari, randkari*, Hind.; *Mendah, kari, kjera, toska, leja*, Gondi; *Leinja*, Kurku; *Ratmanti, kadmero*, Nep.; *Suphut*, Lepcha; *Bút, mogasong*, Mechi; *Sualu*, Ass.; *Huara*, Cachar; *Bolbek*, Gáro; *Ranamba*, Mar.; *Ungdung*, Burm.

A moderate-sized evergreen tree. Bark dark grey, smooth, when old exfoliating in corky scales. Wood olive grey, soft, not durable, is readily attacked by insects. Annual rings indistinct. Pores moderate-sized, uniformly distributed, often oval and subdivided. Medullary rays short, fine. The wood is very similar to that of *T. laurifolia*, but is softer, not durable, and the annual rings are not well marked.

Sub-Himalayan tract from the Ravi eastwards, Kumaun, Garhwal, Bengal, Burma, Central and South India.

Growth moderate to fast, 2 to 6 rings per inch of radius. Weight, 38 lbs. per cubic foot. The wood is used for agricultural implements. The leaves are used in Assam to feed the "muga" silkworms *Antheræa Assama*; they have a cinnamon-like smell when bruised.

		lbs.
O 246.	Garhwâl (1868)	38
O 1367.	Gonda, Oudh	38

3. T. tomentosa, Roxb., Kurz ii. 297; Gamble 65. Vern. *Phusri*, Nep.; *Phane*, Lepcha.

A tree. Bark light brown, thin. Wood soft greyish-yellow with an unpleasant odour when fresh cut. Pores small, uniformly distributed. Medullary rays fine, numerous. Annual rings marked by a faint line.

Himalaya, from Sirmur (Wallich) eastwards, common in the Sikhim Hills from 6,000 to 8,000 feet, South India and Burma.

E 3374. Darjeeling, 6,000 ft.

4. **T. angustifolia**, Wall. T. *saligna*, Nees. Vern. *Risapaing*, Beng.; *Shealbuk*, Magh.

A large shrub. Bark brown, thin. Wood soft, light brown or nearly white. Pores moderate-sized, uniformly distributed.

Medullary rays short, fine to moderately broad.

River banks in Chittagong, where it forms the most characteristic vegetation.

It has long, narrow, willow-like leaves. In Dr. Schlich's list of 1874 it is marked *Homonoya*, and indeed in leaves and in habit it resembles *H. riparia*.

E 3283. Rinkheong Valley, Chittagong Hill Tracts.

E 717 (34 lbs.) from Chittagong, a light olive-coloured wood sent under the name of "*Hooria*," is not an *Excœcaria* (see Roxb., Fl. Ind. iii. 692), but rather resembles *Tetranthera*. Wood soft. Pores moderate-sized, uniformly distributed. Medullary rays short, broad.

7. LITSÆA, Juss.

Contains, according to Meissner, about 8 species, but most of these have been latterly joined under one species, *viz.*, *L. zeylanica*.

Wood soft or moderately hard. Pores small, often in groups. Medullary rays fine, equidistant.

1. **L. zeylanica**, Nees; Beddome t. 294; Brandis 382. *L. foliosa*, Nees. *L. umbrosa*, Nees. *L. scrobiculata*, Nees in DC. Prodr. xv. Vern. *Chimdi, shalanglu, rauli, chilotu, charkhu, kaderu, narki, thirmal, zopru*, Pb.; *Kanwal, titbora, sara, jhatela, chirara, chirchira*, Hind.; *Belori*, Burghers; *Dawal kúrúndú*, Cingh.

A moderate-sized evergreen tree. Wood reddish white, with darker heartwood, moderately hard. Annual rings distinctly marked by a stratum of firmer wood on the outside of each ring, where the pores are often arranged in oblique lines. Pores small, uniformly distributed. Medullary rays fine, numerous.

North-West Himalaya, between 2,000 and 8,000 feet, Eastern Bengal, Burma and South India.

Growth slow, 13 rings per inch of radius. Weight, 36 to 38 lbs. per cubic foot. The wood is used for house-building in South India. An oil is extracted from the fruit which is used for burning.

		lbs.
H 63.	Nagkanda, Simla, 8,000 feet	36
H 3055.	Mahasu, Simla, 7,000 feet	38

No. 20 of Adrian Mendis' Ceylon Collection (51 lbs.) marked *L. zeylanica*, of Ceylon, has a shining wood with the same structure, but more close-grained than that of the tree of the North-West Himalaya.

2. **L. consimilis**, Nees; Gamble 65. *L. zeylanica*, Nees; Brandis 382 (part). Vern. *Chirira, chir chira*, Kumaun; *Pooteli*, Nep.

A small evergreen tree with thin grey bark. Wood yellow, moderately hard, close-grained. Pores small, uniformly distributed. Medullary rays short, fine and moderately broad, the distance between the rays greater than the transverse diameter of the pores.

Himalaya from Simla eastwards.
Weight, 43 lbs. per cubic foot. A good wood. An oil is extracted from the fruit, and used for burning.

		lbs.
E 2420.	Hoom Linding, Darjeeling, 5,000 feet	43

3. L. lanuginosa, Nees; Brandis 382. Vern. *Kálban,* Pb.; *Kokra,* Hind.

A moderate-sized tree. Bark brown. Wood yellow, when fresh cut. Pores small, arranged in radial groups and oblique lines. Medullary rays short, fine, numerous.

Outer Himalaya, from the Indus eastwards up to 6,000 feet.

H 2948. Sutlej Valley, 3,000 feet.

8. DAPHNIDIUM, Nees.

Contains about 6 species. *D. bifarium,* Nees; Brandis 383, is an evergreen shrub or tree of the Himalaya from Kumaun eastwards. *D. venosum,* Meissn., is from Bhutan. *D. argenteum,* Kurz ii. 307, is a deciduous tree of the low and Eng forests of Pegu and Martaban, said by Kurz to have a yellowish close-grained wood. These three, with *D. elongatum,* form the section with penniveined leaves. The section, with tri-nerved leaves contains, besides *D. pulcherrimum, D. melastomaceum,* Nees, of Assam, the Khasia Hills and Sylhet, and *D. caudatum,* Nees, Kurz ii. 307, an evergreen tree of the Khasia Hills, Eastern Bengal and the hills of Martaban and Tenasserim above 4,000 feet.

1. D. elongatum, Nees; Gamble 65. Vern. *Paieli, pooalay, phusri,* Nep.; *Phamlet,* Lepcha.

A large evergreen tree. Wood yellow, turning olive grey on exposure, moderately hard, even-grained. Pores small, occasionally in groups, uniformly distributed. Annual rings marked by firmer wood on the outside of each ring. Medullary rays fine, uniform and equidistant; the distance between them slightly greater than the transverse diameter of the pores.

Sikkim and Bhutan Himalaya, from 6,000 to 8,000 feet, Khasia Hills.
Growth moderate to slow, 10 to 22 rings per inch of radius. Weight, 34 to 41 lbs. per cubic foot. A very pretty wood, worthy of attention. Wood used for building, chiefly planking.

		lbs.
E 362.	Rangbúl, Darjeeling, 7,000 feet	34
E 2418.	" "	41

2. D. pulcherrimum, Nees; Brandis 383; Kurz ii. 306; Gamble 65. Vern. *Dadia,* Hind.; *Sisi,* Nep.; *Nupsor,* Lepcha; *Dingpingwai,* Khasia.

A large evergreen tree with thin bark. Wood reddish white, moderately hard, even-grained. Structure similar to that of *D. elongatum.*

Kumaun, Nepal and Sikkim Himalaya between 4,000 and 9,000 feet, Khasia Hills, Burma.

Growth moderate, 4 to 12 rings per inch of radius. A round in the Bengal Forest Museum shews 5 rings per inch of radius. Weight, 33 to 40 lbs. per cubic foot. Wood used for building, cattle yokes and occasionally tea-boxes. The leaves are aromatic.

		lbs.
E 368.	Rangbúl, Darjeeling, 7,000 feet	33
E 2417.	„ „ „ „	40

3. D. *nov. sp.* Vern. *Siltimber*, Nep.

A small evergreen tree. Wood grey, moderately hard. Annual rings marked by firmer tissue on the outside of each ring. Pores small, uniformly distributed. Medullary rays fine, uniform.

Higher Darjeeling Hills, above 9,000 feet.
Growth slow, 18 rings per inch of radius. Weight, 42 lbs.

		lbs.
E 384.	Tonglo, Darjeeling, 10,000 feet	42

Sassafras officinale, Nees, No. 2962, from North America, is the "Sassafras" wood, which is there largely used in medicine and as a dye. The wood is soft, porous, highly scented, preserving its odour a long time. Pores large to small. Medullary rays moderately broad, undulating; the transverse diameter of the pores being greater than the distance between the rays.

Nectandra Rodiæi, Rob. Schomb., No. 2961, from Demerara, weighing, our specimen, 68 lbs., according to Laslett 72 lbs. (specific gravity = 1·15) per cubic foot, is the "Greenheart," largely used in shipbuilding. The wood is dark brown, very hard and heavy, with the centre almost black. Pores moderate-sized, often filled with yellow resin. Medullary rays fine, uniform, equidistant, the distance between the rays being equal to the transverse diameter of the pores. According to Laslett P = 1,000.

Persea Nan-muh, Oliv., No. 3259, received from Japan by the kindness of Mr. G. Takeda, is the "Nan-muh" tree of which the expensive coffins used in China by persons of wealth and quality are made. The wood is soft to moderately hard, with a pleasant aromatic scent when fresh cut, even-grained, of a dark olive-brown colour, shining with a beautiful lustre. Pores small to moderate-sized, uniformly distributed, often subdivided, distinctly visible on a longitudinal section. Medullary rays fine, uniform and equidistant. Annual rings marked by a band of darker coloured autumn wood.

Weight, 34 to 35 lbs. per cubic foot.

Nos. E 1290. Vern. *Dumbail*, 31 lbs., and E 1292. Vern. *Raun dolu*, 32 lbs., from Cachar, have the structure of *Lauraceæ*. The pores are larger than in *Beilschmiedia*, which they otherwise most resemble.

ORDER LXXXVI. MYRISTICACEÆ.

1. MYRISTICA, Linn.

Contains about 12 to 14 species of Indian trees. Five species are found in Northern and Eastern Bengal, four in Burma, six in Bombay and South India, and four in the Andamans. *M. moschata*, Willd.; Roxb. Fl. Ind. iii. 843. Vern. *Jaiphal* (nutmeg), *jati, jauntari* (mace), is the tree whose fruit gives the spices known as "nutmeg" and "mace," the former is the hard albumen and the latter the aril of the seed. The tree is cultivated in many parts of India, in Ceylon and in the Malay Archipelago. *M. elliptica*, Wall.; Kurz ii. 282, is an evergreen tree of the Andamans. *M. laurifolia*, Hook f. and Th., is a common large tree of the Western Ghâts and Ceylon. *M. Farquhariana*, Wall.; Beddome t. 270. Vern. *Pindi*, Kan., is a common tree of the evergreen forests of Kanara. *M. glabra*, Bl., is a tree of Sylhet. *M. amygdalina*, Wall.; Kurz ii. 283. Vern. *Toungsaga*, Burm., is an evergreen tree of Burma and the Andaman Islands. *M. longifolia*, Wall.; Kurz ii. 283; Gamble 67. (*M. linifolia*, Roxb. Fl. Ind. iii. 847) Vern. *Gurmungban*, Magh; *Zadeip-hpo*, Burm., is an evergreen tree of Northern and Eastern Bengal and Burma. *M. erratica*, Hook. f. and Th., and *M. gibbosa*, Hook. f. and Th., are trees of the Khasia Hills. *M. attenuata*. Wall.; Beddome clxxvi., is a tall tree of the Concan Ghâts of Bombay. *M. corticosa* Hook. f. and Th.; Beddome t. 271; Kurz ii. 284; Gamble 68 (*M. angustifolia*, Roxb. Fl. Ind. iii. 847), is an evergreen tree of the forests of Northern and Eastern Bengal, Burma, South India and the Andaman Islands. *M. magnifica*, Beddome t. 268, Vern. *Ramanadike*, Kan., is a very large tree of Travancore.

1. M. malabarica, Lamk.; Beddome t. 269. Vern. *Kánagi*, Kan., *Pindi-kai* (seeds).

A small evergreen tree. Wood reddish grey, moderately hard. Annual rings (?) marked by concentric lines. Pores moderate-sized, oval, not numerous, uniformly distributed. Medullary rays fine, not prominent.

South Kanara and Malabar.

Weight, 32 lbs. per cubic foot. Wood used for building. The seeds give an oil which is used for burning and as an ointment for sores.

	lbs.
W 736. South Kanara	39

2. M. Irya, Gaertn.; Beddome clxxvi.; Kurz ii. 282. Vern. *Maloh*, Burm.; *Mutwindá, chooglum*, And.

A moderate-sized evergreen tree. Wood dark olive grey, hard, close-grained. Annual rings marked by distinct lines. Pores moderate-sized and large, oval and subdivided, uniformly distributed. Medullary rays numerous, very fine, wavy, bent outwards where they touch the pores, prominent on a radial section; the distance between the rays smaller than the transverse diameter of the pores.

Burma, Andaman Islands and Ceylon.

Weight, 52 lbs. per cubic foot. A handsome wood and worthy of attention; it seasons well and takes a good polish.

	lbs.
B 509. Andaman Islands	52

ORDER LXXXVII. THYMELACEÆ.

Contains 6 Indian genera belonging to 2 tribes, *viz.*,—

Tribe I.—Thymeleæ	*Daphne, Edgeworthia, Wikströmia, Lasiosiphon* and *Linostoma*.
„ II.—Aquilarineæ	*Aquilaria*.

Edgeworthia Gardneri, Meissn.; Brandis 386; Gamble 67. Vern. *Kaghuti, aryili*, Nep., is a large shrub of Nepal, Sikkim and Bhutan, from 4,000 to 7,000 feet, with a white, thick, fibrous bark. Wood grey, light, soft with little lustre. It is the chief species used in the manufacture of the Nepal paper, and it gives the whitest kind. The paper is very tough, and large quantities are made in Nepal and Sikkim *Wikströmia virgata*, Meissn.; Beddome clxxviii; Brandis 386. Vern. *Bhatniggi, thilak*, Pb.; *Chamlia*, Kumaun, is a small shrub of the Himalaya from the Indus eastwards, the Khasia Hills and Ceylon, between 5,000 and 7,000 feet. An inferior sort of paper and rope is made of its bark in Kumaun. *Lasiosiphon eriocephalus*, Dcne; Beddome clxxix. Vern. *Naha*, Cingh.. is a large shrub of Bengal and South India. A fibre is obtained from its bark, which is, besides, used for poisoning fish in Ceylon. *Linostoma* contains 4 species: *L. pauciflorum*, Griff.; Kurz ii. 334, is an evergreen shrub of the Martaban Hills at 3,000 to 4,000 feet; *L. decandrum*, Wall., Kurz ii. 334, a shrub of Chittagong; *L. scandens*, Kurz ii. 334, a shrub of Tenasserim; and *L. siamense*, Kurz ii. 335, a shrub of the *Eng* forests of Prome. *Gyrinops Walla*, Gaertn.; Beddome t. 303. Vern. *Walla*, Cingh., is a handsome small tree found in Ceylon. *Lagetta lintearia*, Lamk. is the Lacebark tree of Jamaica, whose liber is made into cloth, paper, lace, ropes, whips and other articles.

1. DAPHNE, Linn.

Contains about 7 species. *D. cachemiriana*, Meissn., from the Pirpanjal, and *D. oleoides*, Schreber, are described by Brandis, p. 385, under *D. mucronata*. *D. pendula*, Sm.; Kurz ii. 333, is an evergreen shrub of the Martaban Hills at 5,000 to 6,000 feet elevation. *D. Wallichii*, Meissn. Vern. *Chhota argili*, Nep., and *D. longifolia*, Meissn. Vern. *Shedbarwa*, Nep., are shrubs of the Eastern Himalaya, Khasia Hills and Eastern Bengal, whose bark is used in the manufacture of paper, the latter species yielding the commoner coarse kind. *D. Mezereum*, Linn., the "Mezereum" with deciduous leaves, and *D. Laureola*, Linn., the "Spurge Laurel," with evergreen leaves, are well-known European shrubs.

Pores very small, arranged in oblique tails or irregular patches (*D. Mezereum*). Medullary rays fine or very fine.

1. D. mucronata, Royle; Brandis 384. Vern. *Laghúne*, Afg.; *Pech*, Sind; *Kútilál, kanthan, gandalún, shalangri, zosho, shing, mashúr, swána, jikri, dona, channi niggi, kágsari, sind, kansian, sonái*, Pb.

A small evergreen shrub. Wood white, soft. Pores very small and extremely small, arranged in oblique tails. Medullary rays numerous, very fine. Numerous faint concentric lines across the rays.

Suliman Range from 3,000 to 7,000 feet, Himalaya from 2,300 to 9,000 feet.

The wood is used in Chamba to make gunpowder charcoal. The bark and leaves are used in native medicine. The berries are eaten, but are said to cause nausea and vomiting; on the Sutlej a spirit is distilled from them (Brandis).

H 2826. Cheog Forest, Simla, 7,000 feet.
H 2828. Simla, 7,000 feet.

2. D. papyracea, Wall.; Brandis 386; Gamble 67. Vern. *Niggi*, Pb.; *Set barúwa, satpúra*, Hind.; *Balwa*, Kumaun; *Gande, kaghuti*, Nep.; *Dayshing*, Bhutia.

A large shrub. Bark grey, smooth, liber well developed and yielding a very strong fibre which is used for the manufacture of ropes and paper. Wood white, moderately hard. Pores extremely small in long narrow oblique and bending tails of soft tissue. Medullary rays fine, numerous.

Himalaya from near the Indus to Bhutan, between 3,000 and 9,000 feet, Khasia Hills.

Growth moderate, 9 rings per inch of radius. Weight, 34 lbs per cubic foot. Flowers very sweet scented. Bark used to make Nepal and Bhutia paper, the commoner thin kind; also to make ropes for various purposes such as carrying loads.

	lbs.
E 2408. Darjeeling, 7,000 feet.	34

2. AQUILARIA, Lam.

Two species only of this genus are known from India, *viz.*, *A. Agallocha*, here described, and *A. malaccensis*, Lamk.; Kurz ii. 336, from Tenasserim, which, according to Meissner, is the "Garo de Malacca" or Malacca Eaglewood. There is still some doubt about the identification of the species of *Aquilaria* which yields the Eaglewood of commerce. Roxburgh says the *A. Agallocha* is an immense tree, a native of the mountains east and south-east of Sylhet between 24° and 25° north latitude. "There can be little doubt that this is the tree which furnishes the real Calambac or Agallochum of the ancients, and there seems more reason to think that it was carried to China from our eastern frontier than to suppose it was carried from Cochin China or any other country in the vicinity of China, where it has always been in great demand. Small quantities are sometimes imported into Calcutta by sea from the eastward; but such is always deemed inferior to that of Sylhet." Kurz seems to consider the Sylhet and the Tenasserim tree as the same species, and as the structure of the wood of both is identical, there is a strong probability of his view being correct. Further investigation, however, is necessary to ascertain if the species described by Roxburgh as growing in Assam and Sylhet (*A. Agallocha*) is identical with the tree furnishing the *Akyau* wood of Burma. As far as our account is concerned, we shall only speak of one species.

1. A. Agallocha, Roxb. Fl. Ind. 422; Brandis 387; Kurz ii. 335. Lign Aloes or Eaglewood. Vern. *Ugúr*, Hind., Beng.; *Sasi*, Ass.; *Akyau*, Burm.; *Kayu garu*, Malay; *Nwahmi*, Siam; *Nyaw-chah*, Chinese; *Kihay*, *sinnah*, Cingh.

A large evergreen tree. Wood white, soft, even-grained, scented when fresh cut. In the interior of old trees are found irregular masses of harder and darker coloured wood, which constitute the famous Eaglewood of commerce, called *Kaya garu* by the Malays, and *Akyau* by the Burmese. Pores small and moderate-sized, in short radial lines. Medullary rays fine, numerous; the distance between two consecutive rays less than the transverse diameter of the pores. Numerous short transverse bands of pores and intercellular ducts filled with a brownish substance.

Eastern Bengal, Burma, Malay Peninsula and Archipelago.

Growth moderate, 8 rings per inch of radius. Weight, Kyd gives 20 lbs.; our specimen 25 lbs. per cubic foot. Kyd gives P = 203. A description of Eaglewood and its method of collection is given in extracts from Mr. Lee's reports given at p. 80 of the Burma Forest Report for 1875-76, and at p. 19 of the Burma Forest Report for 1876-77. From these it appears that the Akyau is the most important forest produce of the forests of South Tenasserim and the Mergui Archipelago. It is found in fragments of various shapes and sizes in the centre of the tree, and usually, if not always, where some former injury has been received. To collect it the trees are felled and allowed to rot for about three years in the forest, when they are again visited, the tree cut into fragments, and the odoriferous wood cut out. Mr. Lee says that most usually the Akyau is found in the sapwood.

		lbs.
E 951.	Golaghát, Assam	24
B 1948.	Tavoy	23
B 2485.	„	29

ORDER LXXXVIII. ELÆAGNEÆ.

Contains 2 genera only, *Elæagnus* and *Hippophaë*.

Pores small and moderate-sized. Annual rings distinctly marked by a belt of larger pores. *Hippophaë* has numerous uniform and fine medullary rays, while *Elæagnus* has short rays of different width, which in some species are broad.

1. HIPPOPHAË, Linn.

Contains 2 species, distinguished by the scales or hairs on the under surface of the leaf. *H. salicifolia*, Don; Brandis 387. Vern. *Ashúk*, Nep.; *Dúr chuk*, Kumaun; *Súrch*, Bassahir, is a large shrub, the under surface of the leaves having a dense tomentum of rust-coloured hairs. It is found in the Upper Sutlej Valley and from thence eastwards to Bhutan.

1. H. rhamnoides, Linn.; Brandis 388. Vern. *Tsarap, tsarma, sirma, tsúk, tarru, niechak, tserkar, tsermang*, Ladak, Piti and Lahoul.

A large thorny shrub, sometimes a small tree. Bark grey, rough, with vertical furrows. Heartwood yellowish brown, mottled, moderately hard, close-grained. Annual rings distinctly marked by the inner or spring wood being porous and mainly composed of numerous moderate-sized pores, the outer or autumn wood being more compact, with fewer and smaller pores. Medullary rays numerous, very fine, equidistant. The wood of the shrub from Lahoul has the same structure as the European one.

Inner tract of the North-West Himalaya, chiefly in moist, gravelly stream beds, from 5,000 to 10,000 feet.

Growth fast, 5 rings per inch of radius. Weight, 44 lbs. per cubic foot, according to Mathieu, Fl. For., p. 245, 38 lbs. to 54 lbs. It is used for fuel and charcoal, and the dry branches for hedges. It is very valuable in the dry, almost treeless tracts of the Inner Himalaya. The fruit is eaten, but is very acid; it is made into a preserve. The leaves are covered with silvery scales.

		lbs.
H 135.	Lahoul, 10,000 feet	44
H 3063.	Kunawar, 8,000 „	...

2. ELÆAGNUS, Linn.

Contains about 4 species of Indian trees or shrubs.

E. hortensis, M. Bieb.; Brandis 389 (*E. Moorcroftii*, Wall., *E. angustifolia*, Linn.) Vern. *Sanjít*, Afg.; *Sirshing*, Tibet; *Shiúlik*, N.-W. P., is a middling-sized tree of Ladak and Baltistan, Afghanistan and westwards to the Mediterranean region. Brandis says: "The tree is deciduous, but the withered leaves remain attached to the tree instead of falling off at the end of autumn. Attains 25 feet with an erect, straight trunk, 5 to 6 feet girth, and a rounded, close, handsome crown. Bark thick, fibrous, smooth, light grey, between deep, longitudinal, rugged, dark brown furrows. Sapwood narrow; heartwood dark brown, porous and soft. Medullary rays numerous. Wood used for fuel." It gives a transparent gum. The fruit is eaten, and in Yarkand a spirit is distilled from it. It weighs, according to Mathieu Fl. For., p. 245, 36 lbs. to 41 lbs. per cubic foot. It is often planted. *E. arborea*, Roxb. Fl. Ind. i. 441; Brandis 390; Kurz ii. 331. Vern. *Sheashong*, Gáro; *Mingu*, Burm., is an evergreen tree of Nepal, the Eastern Himalaya, Gáro Hills and Burma.

1. E. latifolia, Linn.; Beddome clxxx.; Brandis 390; Gamble 67. *E. conferta*, Roxb. Fl. Ind. i. 440; Kurz ii. 331. Vern. *Ghiwáin, mijhaula*, Kumaun; *Jarila*, Nep.; *Guara*, Beng.; *Kamboong*, Magh.

A straggling evergreen shrub or small tree. Wood white, soft. Pores moderate-sized and small, in irregular, concentric belts, which, however, do not appear to be annual rings; between the belts the pores are smaller and scanty. Medullary rays fine and broad.

Himalaya, from Kumaun to Bhutan, Khasia Hills, Eastern Bengal and South India.

Weight, 45 lbs. per cubic foot. Fruit eaten; it is acid and somewhat astringent. Beddome says it makes good tarts.

		lbs.
E 2407.	Tukdah, Darjeeling, 5,000 feet	45

2. E. umbellata, Thunberg; Brandis 390. Vern. *Ghiwâin, ghain, kankoli, bammewa,* Pb.

A thorny, deciduous shrub, with silvery grey leaves. Bark grey. Wood white, hard, even-grained, warps in seasoning. Annual rings distinctly marked by a narrow continuous belt of moderate-sized pores; in the rest of the wood the pores are very small and uniformly distributed, but occasionally intermediate bands of larger pores are found. Medullary rays short, fine and broad.

Himalaya, from near the Indus to Bhutan, between 3,000 and 10,000 feet.
Growth moderate, 10 rings per inch of radius. Weight, 45 lbs. per cubic foot. The fruit is eaten.

	lbs.
H 71. Mashobra, Simla, 7,000 feet	45

ORDER LXXXIX. PROTEACEÆ.

A large Order of plants, chiefly Australian and South African, containing only one Indian genus, *Helicia*. Many of the species are cultivated on account of the beauty of their flowers or foliage; such are the species of *Hakea, Banksia* and *Grevillea,* the best known of which is *Grevillea robusta,* the 'Silk Oak,' a large tree of New South Wales, which has become quite established in gardens in Bengal and South India. It grows well in Calcutta, where a fine avenue of it may be seen at the Botanic Gardens.

Pores in concentric bands. Medullary rays very broad and prominent.

1. HELICIA, Lour.

Contains about 7 Indian species. *H. Cochin-Chinensis,* Lour.; Kurz ii. 311; Gamble 66, is an evergreen tree of the hills of Sikkim, Assam, and Martaban in Burma. *H. excelsa,* Bl.; Kurz ii. 312 (*Rhopala excelsa*; Roxb. Fl. Ind. i. 362), is a large tree of Chittagong and Tenasserim. *H. nilagirica,* Beddome clxxviii., is a shrub of the western slopes of the Nilgiris at an elevation of 3,000 to 4,000 feet. *H. pyrrobotrya,* Kurz ii. 312, is a tree of the Martaban Hills. *H. salicifolia,* Presl.; Kurz ii. 312, is a tree of Tenasserim; and *H. attenuata,* Bl. (*Rhopala moluccana,* Roxb. Fl. Ind. i. 364), a tree of the Khasia Hills.

1. H. robusta, Wall.; Beddome t. 301; Kurz ii. 311; Gamble 66. Vern. *Joweea,* Sylhet; *Tegala mugu,* Kan.; *Donkya beng,* Burm.

A small evergreen tree. Bark grey, ¼ inch thick. Wood pinkish grey, moderately hard. Pores small, in numerous, narrow concentric bands of softer tissue, interrupted by the broad and very broad medullary rays, which are prominent on a radial section.

Hills of Bengal, Burma, and Southern India.
Weight, 44 lbs. per cubic foot. Has very pretty flowers.

	lbs.
E 2409. Sumbong, Darjeeling, 2,000 feet	44

Grevillea robusta has a rough bark, 3-16ths inch thick. Wood hard, light reddish brown, sapwood greyish white. Pores moderate-sized, scanty, in concentric patches of white tissue. These concentric patches are interrupted by the medullary rays and bend outward where they meet the rays, so that the concentric bands have a wavy outline. Medullary rays broad and very broad, very prominent on a radial section, shewing a beautiful silver grain. The heartwood seems durable, but the sapwood decays quickly. It would be a handsome furniture wood. (O 3263, Saharanpur.)

ORDER XC. LORANTHACEÆ.

Contains 4 Indian genera of evergreen parasitic shrubs, living on the stems, branches or roots of other shrubs or trees. These genera are *Viscum, Arceuthobium, Loranthus* and *Ginalloa.*

Viscum contains about 6 species, which may be divided into 2 sections, those with and those without leaves. To the first section belongs the Mistletoe, *V. album,* Linn.; Brandis 392; Kurz ii. 323; Gamble 66. Vern. *Túrapáni,* Afg.; *Bhangra, bánda, bambal, kahbang, ahalu, wahal, rini, reori, reng, jerra,* Pb.; *Bán, bánda,* Hind.; *Hurchu,* Nep., a parasitic shrub found in the Suliman Range, Himalaya and hills of Martaban above 3,500 feet, chiefly on Rosaceæ, the Walnut, Elm, Willow, Alder, Maple, Poplar, Olive and Mulberry. In Lahoul it is used medicinally, and in Europe it is used for birdlime. *V. monoicum,* Roxb. Fl. Ind. iii. 763; Brandis 393; Kurz ii. 324, is a shrub, parasitic on *Elæodendron* and other trees in the Sub-Himalayan tract, Bengal and Burma. *V. ovalifolium,* Wall.; Kurz ii. 325, is a shrub of Tenasserim; and *V. orientale,* Willd.; Brandis 393; Kurz ii. 324 (*V. verticillatum,* Roxb. Fl. Ind. iii. 764), a shrub of Bengal and South India.

To the second section belong *V. articulatum,* Brown; Brandis 393; Kurz ii. 325 (also *V. moniliforme,* W. and A.; Kurz ii. 325) Vern. *Pand,* Hind., a parasitic shrub of the Himalaya, Khasia Hills, South India and Burma, found chiefly on Oaks, Rhododendron and Apricot. *V. attenuatum,* DC.; Brandis 394; Gamble 66. Vern. *Púdú, pand,* Pb.; *Patha,* Banda; *Bánda,* C. P.; *Hurchu,* Nep., is a parasitic shrub of the Outer Himalaya and Sub-Himalayan tract from the Indus to Assam, ascending to 7,000 feet, Khasia Hills, South India and Ceylon. In Sikkim it is found on Maple and Chestnut especially, in Simla on Oaks, and *Cornus* (No. H 3081 on *C. capitata*).

Arceuthobium Oxycedri, M. Bieb.; Brandis 394. Vern. *Shúk, sái,* Lahoul, is a small parasite found on *Juniperus excelsa* in Lahoul at elevations from 9,000 to 11,000 feet. It grows by spreading its roots between the bark and the wood of the Juniper, often killing the branch on which it grows. It occurs also westward to the south of France. *Ginalloa* contains two parasitic shrubs: *G. Helferi,* Kurz ii. 326, of Tenasserim, and *G. andamanica,* Kurz ii. 326, found on "*Artocarpus Chaplasha*" in the Andamans.

1. LORANTHUS, Linn.

Contains 20 to 30 or more species of parasitical shrubs, some of them with very handsome flowers. *L. ligustrinus,* Wall.; Brandis 396, is found in the outer Himalaya from the Jumna to Sikkim, ascending to 4,000 feet, chiefly on *Albizzia, Olea* and *Litsæa. L. pulverulentus,* Wall.; Brandis 396; Kurz ii. 318. Vern. *Parand,* Kumaun; *Bánda,* C. P., is a woody parasite found in the Sub-Himalayan tract from Kumaun eastwards, Central and Western India, often on *Butea. L. cordifolius,* Wall. and *L. umbellifer,* Schultes, are Himalayan parasitic shrubs, the first often found on *Platanus,* the second on *Rhododendron, Andromeda* and *Salix. L. farinosus,* Desr., *L. viridiflorus,* Wall., and *L. globosus,* Roxb.; Gamble 66, are common on Sál in Northern Bengal. Kurz describes 17 species from Burma. Numerous species also occur in South India; and on the Nilgiris they are reported to have done such damage to the plantations of Australian *Acacia* as to have necessitated those plantations being given up. In his "Report on Neilgherry Loranthaceous Parasitical Plants," Madras, 1874, Dr. G. Bidie describes 8 species as attacking peaches, pears, Australian acacias and other trees about Ootacamund. The species described are *L. obtusatus,* Wall., *L. Neilgherrensis,* W. and A., *L. loniceroides,* Linn., *L. amplexifolius,* DC., *L. tomentosus,* Heyn., *L. cuneatus,* Heyn., *L. Candolleanus,* W. and A., and *L. capitellatus,* W. and A. Of the trees attacked, *Acacia Melanoxylon* has most suffered, owing to its rough bark, while the smooth-barked *A. dealbata* has been but little injured. *Eucalyptus Globulus* does not appear to have been attacked.

Most species are called *Pand* in Hindi, *Ajeru* in Nepalese and *Khyee-poung* in Burmese.

1. L. vestitus, Wall.; Brandis 396. Vern. *Pand*, Hind.

A parasitic shrub. Wood reddish white, compact, close-grained, moderately hard. Pores very small, arranged in rounded groups or patches, which are uniformly distributed. Medullary rays short, fine to broad; the distance between the rays several times larger than the transverse diameter of the pores.

North-West Himalaya from the Ravi to Sikkim up to 7,000 feet, Khasia Hills. Growth slow, about 14 rings per inch of radius. Weight, 51 lbs. per cubic foot. It grows often to a large size, and is extremely common in some parts of the Himalaya, especially on the Oaks, *Q. incana* and *Q. dilatata*. It is also found on *Odina, Schleichera, Randia, Machilus* and other trees.

		lbs.
H 3033.	Theog, Simla, 7,000 feet (on *Q. dilatata*)	...
H 2938.	Below Naldehra, Simla, 5,000 feet (on *Q. incana*) . .	51

2. L. longiflorus, Desr.; Brandis 397; Kurz ii. 321; Gamble 66. *L. bicolor*, Roxb. Fl. Ind. i. 548. Vern. *Pand, amút*, Pb.; *Bánda*, C. P.; *Patha*, Banda; *Bara manda*, Beng.; *Proosti*, Lepcha; *Ajeru*, Nep.; *Yelinga wadinika*, Tel.; *Kaurak*, Bhîl.

A parasitical shrub. Wood reddish, moderately hard. Pores very small, very numerous. Medullary rays short, fine to very broad.

Outer Himalaya from the Jhelam eastwards, ascending to 7,500 feet, Bengal, Central and South India, Burma, Andaman Islands and Ceylon.

The commonest species. It has large, handsome, scarlet flowers. It grows on most trees; in North India on *Melia, Bauhinia, Albizzia, Mallotus*, the Mango, Peach and Pear; in Oudh on *Bassia, Buchanania, Diospyros;* in Sikkim on Sál and *Albizzia;* in the North-West Himalaya on Oak.

H 3061. Koti, Simla, 6,000 feet (on *Q. dilatata*).

ORDER XCI. SANTALACEÆ.

Contains 4 genera of Indian trees or shrubs: *viz.—Pyrularia, Henslowia, Osyris* and *Santalum*.

Henslowia heterantha, Hook. f.; Kurz ii. 328; Gamble 67. Vern. *Ajeru*, Nep., is a large mistletoe-like shrub, sometimes parasitic, sometimes terrestrial, of the North-East Himalaya and the hills of Martaban. *Osyris arborea*, Wall.; Beddome clxxxi.; Brandis 399 (*O. Wightiana*, Wall.) Vern. *Bakardharra, bakarja*, Kumaun; *Popli*, Belgaum; *Jhuri*, Nep., is a shrub of the Himalaya from Simla to Bhutan ascending to 7,000 feet, Western Ghâts and Ceylon, said by Aikin in Wallich's List to have a red-brown, hard, compact and fine-grained wood.

1. PYRULARIA, Mich.

Contains 2 species. *P. Wallichiana*, Meissn.; Beddome t. 304. Vern. *Benduga*, Kan., is a small tree of Coorg, the Wynaad and Ceylon, with a light-coloured, curiously-grained wood.

1. P. edulis, A. DC.; Gamble 66. Vern. *Amphi*, Nep.; *Safhyi*, Lepcha.

A small or moderate-sized thorny tree. Bark thin, grey. Wood white, moderately hard, close-grained. Pores small and very small, in oblique bands of softer tissue. Medullary rays fine and broad, numerous, prominently reticulated on a radial section.

Nepal, Sikkim and the Khasia Hills, from 4,000 to 5,000 feet.

Growth moderate, about 8 rings per inch of radius. Weight, 47 to 50 lbs. per cubic foot. Wood used by Bhutias for butter-making implements. Fruit eaten.

		lbs.
E 2406.	Tukdah, Darjeeling, 5,000 feet	47
E 698.	Rangbúl, Darjeeling, 7,000 feet	50

2. SANTALUM, Linn.

1. S. album, Linn.; Roxb. Fl. Ind. i. 442; Beddome t. 256; Brandis 398; Kurz ii. 329. Sandalwood. Vern. *Chandan, chandal, sandal,* Hind.; *Gandha,* Kan.; *San-ta-ku,* Burm.

A small evergreen tree, rarely exceeding 4 feet in girth and 30 feet in height. Bark dark grey, nearly black, rough, with short vertical cracks, inner substance dark red. Sapwood white, scentless; heartwood yellowish brown, strongly scented, very hard, very close-grained and oily. Annual rings distinctly marked by more numerous and slightly larger pores in the spring wood. Pores small, circular, numerous. Medullary rays short, fine, numerous, uniform and equidistant.

Dry region of South India. It grows naturally in the drier parts of Mysore, Coimbatore and Salem districts, extending south to Madura and north to Kolhapúr, generally at an elevation of from 2,000 to 3,000 feet, in poor soils and seeking the protection of hedgerows and scrub jungles.

Regarding the rate of growth, not much information is available. The specimens in our collection shew a growth of 5 to 7 rings per inch of radius. A tree in the Saharanpur Botanic Gardens, said to be 36 years old, measured 3 feet 4 inches in girth, giving 5·6 rings per inch of radius,

In Colonel Beddome's report on the forests of Northern Coimbatore, July 1876, the following data are given:—

		Age.	Height.	Girth.
Talle Mally Plantation commenced 1863-64.	Trees in unfavourable locality.	14	5 to 6 feet	3 to 4 inches,
	Trees in favourable locality.	14	30 „	15 „
Bylur Plantation commenced 1870.	Planted 1870 . .	6	10 to 15 „	8 to 11 „
	„ 1872 . .	4	7 to 8 „	5 to 9 „

The first of these gives 25, the rest 6, 4 and 3·5 rings per inch of radius respectively.

In his report of the 3rd March 1877 on the Salem forests, Colonel Beddome states that the largest of 3 sandal trees which were growing under shade in favourable conditions in the Denkincottah plantation on the Mailgherry hills had a height of 16 feet and a girth of 8 inches. As the trees were planted in 1874 and were consequently only 3 years old at the time of measurement, their growth has been very fast.

Again, in his report on plantations and fuel reserves of 28th May 1878, Colonel Beddome gives the following average measurements of trees in different plantations—

	Age.	Height.	Girth.	
1. North Coimbatore, Talle Mally Plantation, 3,000 feet altitude.	14 years	30 feet	15 in.	But only where there is shade.
2. North Coimbatore, Bylur Plantation, 3,200 feet altitude.	7 „	8 to 15 „	8 to 11 „	
	4 „	8 to 8 „	5 to 6 „	
3. Nilgiris, Segur Plantation, 3,000 feet altitude.	6 „	12 to 15		

or 6, 4·5 and 4·5 rings per inch of radius respectively.

In this plantation Colonel Beddome expects a yield per acre, when the plantation is mature, in 25 years, of at least 150 maunds of heartwood. There are 23 acres with about 21,000 trees. The growth in the Coimbatore plantations varies from 2 to 6 rings per inch, averaging 4½ rings; but the locality in each case was favourable.

In an article in the "Indian Forester" for April 1878, Vol. iii., No. 4, entitled "Notes on Sandal," 8 trees or groups of trees in Mysore are mentioned, of whose approximate age there is some evidence. In some cases the girth was taken at the base; in others the mean girth is given.

The following are the measurements given in that paper:—

No. of trees.	Place.	Age (probable).	Girth.	No. of rings of radius.	Height of bole.	Total height.	
		Years.	Inches.		Feet.	Feet.	
1	Mudagerri	55	20	17	9	...	Mean girth.
1	"	44	27	10	12	50	Girth at base.
1	"	43	35	8	...	17	Ditto.
1	"	64	48	9	...	30	Ditto.
1	Ijapûr	45	40	7	...	30	Mean girth.
1	"	30	40	5	5	...	Ditto.
1	Bobagalli	96	27	11	20	...	Girth at base.
7	"	75	33	7	...	27½	Girth at 6 feet.

These measurements give an average of 9·2 rings per inch of radius. It will be seen that no approximately correct generalisation as to the usual rate of growth can be obtained. In good conditions it seems probable that 5 to 6 rings per inch is about the average rate, while in unfavourable places the average growth cannot be taken at much less than 10 rings per inch.

The weight of sandalwood is given by Fowke at 55 lbs.; by Skinner, No. 113, at 58 lbs.; our specimens average 61·5 lbs. per cubic foot. Fowke gives P = 878; Skinner 874. The heartwood is used for carving, for incense and perfume. It is an important article of trade in India, and is largely exported to China and Arabia. It has been found to be well suited for engraving. Sandalwood oil is distilled from the wood.

It is chiefly spread through the agency of birds, and comes up in hedges and under the shade of shrubs. It is very impatient of mutilation, is difficult to transplant, and suffers greatly from wounds in the bark. Plantations of sandal have been established in Mysore and Madras.

		lbs.
E 2489.	Botanic Gardens, Calcutta (from a tree which was blown down in the Cyclone of 1864)	56
D 1209.	Mysore	71
D 2307.	"	60
D 3140.	"	60
D 1360.	Salem, Madras	61
No. 41.	Salem Collection	61

B 1950, 62 lbs., was sent from Tavoy under the name of *Kalamet*. The specimen is evidently very old, of a brown colour, like that of the heartwood of sandal, and in structure it differs only in having more prominent medullary rays, which are broader than in sandal, uniform and equidistant. The wood is scented, resembling that of sandalwood, and it may possibly be another species of *Santalum*.

ORDER XCII. URTICACEÆ.

A large Order remarkable for many useful products, chiefly fibres, given by species belonging to it. The chief fibrous plants are the nettles, the 'Rhea,' the 'Puya,' the Paper Mulberry, *Antiaris* and *Sponia*. Fruits are given by the mulberries, figs and species of *Artocarpus*. India-rubber is produced by several species of *Ficus*, especially *F. elastica*; while valuable timber is obtained from the Elms, Mulberries, *Artocarpus*, and other genera. The Order is divided into 4 Sub-Orders, and these into 12 tribes containing 25 genera—

SUB-ORDER 1. **URTICACEÆ**—

Tribe	I.—Ureres	*Laportea* and *Girardinia*.
"	II.—Böhmerieæ	*Böhmeria*, *Pouzolzia*, *Sarcochlamys*, *Villebrunea*, *Debregeasia* and *Maoutia*.

SUB-ORDER 2. **MORACEÆ**—

Tribe	III.—Strebleæ	*Phyllochlamys*, *Streblus* and *Pseudostreblus*.
"	IV.—Broussonetieæ	*Malaisia*, *Broussonetia* and *Plecospermum*.
"	V.—Moreæ	*Morus*.
"	VI.—Dorstenieæ	*Dorstenia*.

SUB-ORDER 3. **ARTOCARPEÆ**—

Tribe	VII.—Conocephaleæ	*Conocephalus*.
"	VIII.—Artocarpeæ	*Artocarpus* and *Cudrania*.
"	IX.—Ocmedieæ	*Antiaris*.
"	X.—Ficeæ	*Ficus*.

SUB-ORDER 4. **ULMEÆ**—

Tribe	XI.—Ulmeæ	*Ulmus*.
"	XII.—Celtideæ	*Celtis*, *Sponia* and *Gironniera*.

Laportea crenulata, Gaudich.; Beddome t. 306; Brandis 404; Kurz ii. 421; Gamble 77. (*Urtica crenulata*, Roxb. Fl. Ind. iii. 591). Vern. *Chorpatta, surat*, Beng.; *Moringi*, Nep.; *Mealum-ma, sunkrong*, Lepcha; *Phetya-kyee*, Burm.; *Maúsa*, Cingh., is a small tree of Sikkim, Assam, Eastern Bengal, the Western Coast, Ceylon and Burma, with glossy, broad leaves and minute, stinging hairs, the effects of which are extremely painful and often very lasting. The fibre is good and can be made into ropes and coarse cloth, but the preparation has a poisonous effect. *Girardinia heterophylla*, Dcne.; Brandis 404 (*Urtica heterophylla*, Roxb. Fl. Ind. iii. 586; Gamble 77) Vern. *Keri, kingi, ein, sanoli, au, ján, kal, kárla, bhabar*, Pb.; *Awa, alla, chichru, bichua*, Hind.; *Ullo*, Nep.; *Kazu*, Lepcha; *Horu surat*, Ass.; *Serpa, herpa*, Bhutia, is an extremely common, large, annual forest weed, with long stinging bristles. It affords a fine silky fibre, which is used in Sikkim for ropes, twine, and coarse cloth like gunny. It is common throughout most of the hilly districts of India and Burma, but especially in the Himalaya.

Sarcochlamys pulcherrima, Gaudich.; Brandis 405; Kurz ii. 426 (*Urtica pulcherrima*, Roxb. Fl. Ind. iii. 588). Vern. *Tsatya, sapsha*, Burm., is a large handsome shrub with tri-nerved leaves, grey beneath, common in Eastern Bengal and Burma, especially in deserted cultivation. The liber gives a good fibre for ropes. *Maoutia Puya*, Wedd.; Brandis 406; Kurz ii. 429; Gamble 77. Vern, *Pói, púa*, Hind.; *Puya*, Nep.; *Kyinki*, Lepcha; *Yenki*, Limbu (*Urtica frutescens*, Thunb.; Roxb. Fl. Ind. iii. 588), is a shrub with leaves very white beneath, found in the Himalaya from Garhwal eastwards, the Khasia Hills and Burma, chiefly in old cultivations and up to 4,000 feet. The fibre is very good and strong, and is used to make fishing nets, net bags, twine and cloth.

Phyllochlamys spinosa, Bureau; Brandis 411 (*Trophis spinosa*, Roxb. Fl. Ind. iii. 762. *Taxotrophis Roxburghii*, Beddome ccxxi.) Vern. *Sukali*, Tel.; *Sheora*, Beng.; *Sahadra*, Uriya; *Kurrera*, Mar., is a small tree of the hills of the Coromandel Coast, Madras and Ceylon. *Pseudostreblus indica*, Bureau, is a small tree of the Khasia Hills.

Malaisia tortuosa, Blanco; Kurz ii. 466, is a large deciduous scandent shrub of Burma. *Broussonetia papyrifera*, Vent.; Brandis 410; Kurz ii. 467, is the "Paper Mulberry," a small tree wild in the Martaban Hills. The inner bark gives the *Tapa* cloth of the South Sea Islands. In Japan it is made into paper; and in Siam and Burma into the thick blackened cardboards called "palabeiks," which are used like slates in Europe for writing on.

Dorstenia Griffithiana, Kurz ii. 462, is an evergreen low shrub of Tenasserim.

Conocephalus suaveolens, Bl.; Kurz ii. 430; Gamble 77, is a large climber of Northern and Eastern Bengal and Burma.

Cudrania javanensis, Trecul; Brandis 425; Gamble 73 (*Cudranus Rumphii*, Thw.; Beddome ccxx., *C. amboinensis*, Rumph.; Kurz ii. 434) Vern. *Manda, mandei, kangu*, Hind., is a straggling shrub of the Sub-Himalayan tract, Eastern Bengal and Ceylon. The bark is yellowish brown, smooth, and the wood used for fuel. *C. fruticosa*, Wight, and *C. frutescens*, Trecul; Kurz ii. 434, 435, are scandent Burmese shrubs.

Gironniera contains 4 to 5 trees. *G. reticulata*, Thw.; Beddome t. 313 (*G. cuspidata*, Planch.; Kurz ii. 470), is a large tree of the Western Ghâts and Burma, said to have a valuable timber. *G. nervosa*, Planch.; Kurz ii. 469, is a large tree of Chittagong and Burma. *G. lucida*, Kurz ii. 470, is a tree of the Andaman Islands; and *G. Thomsoni*, King; Gamble 73, a large tree of the Sikkim hills.

As regards structure, the following three types may be distinguished:—

1st.—Artocarpus type. Distinct dark-coloured heartwood (excepting *Antiaris, Sponia, Debregeasia* and *Pouzolzia*). Pores isolated, sometimes in groups, but not in concentric or oblique lines; sometimes enclosed in a ring. The species of a temperate climate have annual rings, which are generally marked by a belt of larger pores. To this belong the arborescent Urticeæ, *Böhmeria, Pouzolzia*, and *Debregeasia*; of Moreæ, *Morus* and *Broussonetia*; of Artocarpeæ, *Antiaris* and *Artocarpus*; and of Ulmeæ, *Sponia*.

2nd.—Ulmus type. Pores united by concentric narrow bands of softer texture; in the temperate species the annual rings are marked by a porous belt of large pores. To this belong: of Ulmaceæ, *Celtis* and *Ulmus*.

3rd.—Ficus type. Wood soft, no heartwood, consisting of alternate bands of soft and firm texture, the small or moderate-sized pores being generally included in the former. To this belong: of Moreæ, *Streblus*; and of Artocarpeæ, *Ficus*.

The only character which the species of the Order *Urticaceæ* may be said to have in common is that the medullary rays are prominent, fine, rarely moderately broad.

1. BÖHMERIA, Jacq.

Contains about 10 to 12 species. *B. macrophylla*, Don; Brandis 403; Kurz ii. 424; Gamble 76. Vern. *Saochála, golka*, Kumaun; *Kamli*, Nep., is a handsome long-leaved shrub of the outer Himalaya from Kumaun eastwards up to 4,000 feet, and the Khasia Hills. It gives a good fibre, used to make ropes and fishing lines. *B. travancorica*, Beddome ccxxv., is a small tree of the Wynaad, South Kanara Ghâts and Travancore hills up to 4,500 feet. *B. malabarica*, Wedd.; Kurz ii. 422; Gamble 76. Vern. *Takbret*, Lepcha; and *B. Hamiltoniana*, Wedd.; Kurz ii. 424; Gamble 76. Vern. *Taksur*, Lepcha; *Kanaitscik*, Magh; *Sapsha*, Burm., are common undershrubs which give a strong fibre. The first is found in the moister zones of India and Burma, the second in Northern and Eastern Bengal and Burma. *B. nivea*, Hook. and Arn.; Brandis 402 (*Urtica tenacissima*, Roxb. Fl. Ind. iii. 590), is the "China Grass" or "Rhea" plant, cultivated in Assam, Bengal and parts of North-West India for its fibre, which is one of the finest produced in the world. It is a finer fibre than jute, and the plant would be still more largely grown and exported were it not for its requiring a richer soil, and being more difficult of preparation.

1. B. rugulosa, Wedd.; Brandis 403; Gamble 76. Vern. *Geti, gainti*, Hind.; *Dar*, Nep.; *Sedeng*, Lepcha.

A small tree. Wood red, moderately hard, even-grained, seasons well. Pores scanty, moderate-sized, often subdivided. Medullary rays fine to broad, short, the distance between the rays as large as or larger than the transverse diameter of the pores. The medullary rays shew on a radial section, giving the wood a mottled appearance.

Garhwal, Kumaun, Nepal, Sikkim and Bhutan.

Growth fast, 2 to 5 rings per inch of radius. Weight, 41 lbs. per cubic foot. It is a nice wood, easy to cut and work, and is used in Kumaun and Nepal for making bowls; in Sikkim for milk pails, churns and other dairy utensils. The Lepchas make cups, bowls and tobacco-boxes of it.

		lbs.
O 324.	Garhwal (1868)	35
O 3005.	„ (1874)	44
E 600.	Khookloong Forest, Darjeeling Terai	46
E 2443.	Mangwa, Tista Valley, Darjeeling, 3,000 feet	39

2. **B. platyphylla,** Don; Brandis 403; Gamble 76. Vern. *Gargela,* Hind.; *Kamli,* Nep. This is var. *rotundifolia,* Wedd.

A large shrub or small tree. Bark thin, greyish brown, longitudinally striated. Wood moderately hard, reddish-brown with occasional concentric bands of darker and lighter colour. Pores moderate-sized, scanty. Medullary rays moderately broad, the distance between them greater than the transverse diameter of the pores.

Outer Himalaya up to 7,000 feet, Khasia Hills, E. Bengal, S. India and Ceylon.

E 3377. Darjeeling, 6,500 feet.

2. POUZOLZIA, Gaudichaud.

Includes several Indian herbs or undershrubs.

1. **P. viminea,** Wedd.; Brandis 405; Kurz ii. 425; Gamble 77. Vern. *Chhota kúail,* Nep.; *Kyingbi,* Lepcha.

A shrub or small tree with thin, grey bark. Wood light reddish brown, hard, apt to warp. Pores small and moderate-sized, often subdivided, uniformly distributed. Medullary rays moderately broad, numerous, uniform and equidistant.

Kumaun, Nepal, Sikkim, Eastern Bengal, Assam, and Chittagong, ascending to 5,000 feet.

Weight, 37 lbs. per cubic foot. Growth very fast. The leaves are eaten by Lepchas. The bark is used to make ropes.

		lbs.
E 2447.	Latpanchor, Darjeeling, 4,500 feet	37

3. VILLEBRUNEA, Gaudichaud.

Three species. *V. appendiculata,* Wedd.; Gamble 77 (*Oreocnide acuminata,* Kurz ii. 427. *Urtica acuminata,* Roxb. Fl. Ind. iii. 592) Vern. *Lipic, lipiah,* Nep.; *Kaphitki,* Lepcha; *Bun rhea,* Ass., is a small tree of the North-East Himalaya, Khasia Hills and Chittagong, whose fibre, which is brown in colour, strong and flexible, is made, in Sikkim and Assam, into ropes, nets and coarse cloth. The tree is of quick growth and coppices easily, and the fibre is likely to prove valuable. *V. sylvatica,* Bl. (*Oreocnide sylvatica,* Miq.; Beddome ccxxv.; Kurz ii. 427), is a small tree of the Western Gháts, Ceylon and the Martaban Hills, chiefly in deserted clearings.

1. **V. frutescens,** Bl.; Brandis 406; Gamble 77. *Urtica frutescens,* Thumb.; Roxb. Fl. Ind. iii. 589. Vern. *Gar tashiára, poidhaula, kagshi,* Kumaun; *Kirma,* Nep.; *Takbret,* Lepcha.

A shrub or small tree with a rough, dark grey bark. Wood brown moderately hard. Pores small. Medullary rays fine and broad, equidistant, the distance between the rays equal to the transverse diameter of the pores.

Himalaya, from Simla eastwards, Sikkim, Bhutan and Assam, ascending to 5,000 feet.

The fibre is used for ropes.

H 3130. Simla, 5,000 feet.

4. DEBREGEASIA, Gaudichaud.

1. **D. bicolor,** Wedd.; Brandis 405. *Urtica bicolor*, Roxb. Fl. Ind., iii. 589. Vern. *Kharwala, shakai*, Afg.; *Chainchar, chainjli, amrer, sandári*, Jhelum; *Sansaru, súss*, Chenab; *Siaru, talsiari*, Ravi; *Pincho, prin*, Sutlej; *Tashiári*, Kumaun.

A large shrub. Bark thin, grey. Wood soft, grey. Pores small and moderate-sized, uniformly distributed. Medullary rays moderately broad, uniform and equidistant.

Salt Range, North-West Himalaya, ascending to 5,000 feet.

Growth fast, 3 to 4 rings per inch of radius. Weight, 27 lbs. per cubic foot. The fibre is made into twine and ropes.

	lbs.
H 88. Bhajji, Simla, 4,000 feet	27

2. **D. longifolia,** Wedd.; Brandis 405; Gamble 77. *Morocarpus longifolius*, Bl.; Beddome ccxxvi.; Kurz ii. 428. Vern. *Tashiari*, Nep.; *Kamhyem*, Lepcha; *Capsee*, Kan.; *Pwot-chau-beng*, Burm.

A small tree. Bark thin, greyish-brown, rough. Heartwood reddish brown, hard; sapwood white. Pores moderate-sized, scanty; annual rings marked by a line of closer pores. Medullary rays moderately broad, uniform, the distance between them equal to, or greater than, the transverse diameter of the pores.

North-East Himalaya up to 7,000 feet, Khasia Hills, South India and Burma. Common on old cultivations.

Growth fast, 4 rings per inch of radius. The fibre of the bark is occasionally used for ropes and to make fishing nets.

E 3328. Darjeeling, 6,500 feet.

3. **D. leucophylla,** Wedd. *Morocarpus Wallichianus*, Miq.; Kurz ii. 428. Vern. *Púrúni*, Nep.; *Senén*, Lepcha.

A small tree, erect or epiphytic. Bark brown fibrous, peeling off in small vertical papery flakes. Annual rings distinctly marked by a white line. Pores large, scanty, medullary rays fine to moderately broad, often bent where they touch the pores.

North-East Himalaya up to 7,000 feet, Khasia Hills and down to the upper forests of the Pegu Yoma.

Growth moderate, 5 rings per inch of radius. A very pretty plant with round leaves of the purest white beneath. Fibre used sometimes for cordage.

E 3329. Darjeeling, 6,000 feet.

5. STREBLUS, Loureiro.

1. **S. asper,** Lour.; Beddome ccxxi.; Brandis 410; Kurz 464; Gamble 73. *Trophis aspera*, Retz; Roxb. Fl. Ind. iii. 761. Vern.

Jindi, Pb.; *Siora, karchanua, rúsa*, Hind.; *Sheora*, Beng.; *Sahada*, Uriya; *Baranki, barinka, pakki*, Tel.; *Karera, kharaoli*, Mar.; *Karasni*, Gondi; *Milli*, Kan.; *Ungnai*, Magh; *Opnai*, Burm.; *Gattao nitlúl*, Cingh.

A small evergreen tree. Bark ⅛ inch thick, soft, light grey, irregularly ribbed. Wood white, moderately hard, no heartwood, no annual rings. Pores small, in irregular concentric belts of soft tissue which contain the greater number of the pores and alternate with broader belts of firm tissue, in which a few pores are scattered. Medullary rays fine, numerous, equidistant.

Sub-Himalayan tract from the Beas eastwards, Bengal, Central and South India, Burma and the Andaman Islands.

Weight, Skinner, No. 66 (*Epicarpurus orientalis*), 45 lbs.; Kyd 42 to 75 lbs.; our specimens give 39 to 40 lbs. Kyd gives P = 570; Skinner P = 604. The wood is tough and elastic. In South India it is sometimes used for cart-wheels. It is good for hedges, coppices well, and has been recommended for fuel. The twigs are used as tooth-brushes, and the rough leaves to polish wood and ivory. The milky juice is used medicinally.

		lbs.
O 1478.	Gonda, Oudh	40
C 1165.	Ahiri Reserve, Central Provinces	39

6. PLECOSPERMUM, Trecul.

1. P. spinosum, Trecul; Beddome ccxx.; Brandis 401. *Batis spinosa*, Roxb. Fl. Ind. iii. 762. Vern. *Mainakat-lara, maidal-lara*, Nep.; *Gumbengfong*, Mechi (?); *Koriti*, Tel.

A large thorny shrub. Bark thin, orange-coloured, peeling off in thin brittle flakes. Wood greyish white, with a small bright orange-yellow heartwood, which is very hard. Pores from small to large, joined by wavy, more or less concentric, bands or lines of soft and often interrupted tissue, which alternate with shining bands of firmer texture of about the same width. In the heartwood the pores are filled with a yellow resinous substance. Medullary rays fine and very fine, wavy.

Salt Range (rare on mountains at 3,000 feet), Rohilkhand, Nepal, Sikkim, South India and Ceylon.

Growth slow, 12 rings per inch of radius. Weight, 50 lbs. per cubic foot. The wood is used in the Darjeeling Terai to give a yellow dye.

		lbs.
O 3134.	Dehra Dún	56
E 487.	Khookloong Forest, Darjeeling Terai	45
E 2308.	Darjeeling Terai	52
E 2448.	Tukdah Forest, Darjeeling, 5,000 feet	47

7. MORUS, Linn.

Contains 6 species which are all referred to one, *M. alba*, by Bureau in DC. Prodr., Vol. xvii.

M. alba, Linn.; Roxb. Fl. Ind. iii. 594; Brandis 407. Vern. *Tút, túl, túlklu, chínni, chún*, Hind., is the Mulberry, cultivated in Afghanistan and the plains and hills of the Punjab. The wood is good and is used for building, boats, furniture and agricultural implements. It weighs 38 to 56 lbs. Its chief use is, however, for feeding the silkworm, especially in Kashmir, with its leaves; and for its fruit for which it is largely grown and which is eaten either fresh or dried. *M. lævigata*, Wall.; Brandis 409. Kurz ii. 467. Vern. *Tút*, Hind.; *Malaing*, Burm., is a tree, wild and cultivated in the Himalaya from the Indus to Assam up to 4,000 feet, in Bengal and

Burma. Its fruit is long, cylindrical, sweet, but insipid. *M. atropurpurea*, Roxb. Fl. Ind. iii. 595, is a kind which was introduced from China and is now cultivated in many parts of India.

Wood hard, even-grained, seasons well, with yellow or brown heartwood. Annual rings distinctly marked generally by a belt of larger pores. Medullary rays fine, uniform.

1. M. indica, Linn.; Roxb. Fl. Ind. iii. 596; Brandis 408; Kurz ii. 468; Gamble 77. Vern. *Túl*, Pb.; *Tutri*, Hind.; *Shahtút*, Kumaun; *Tút*, Beng.; *Chhota kimbu*, Nep.; *Mekrap*, Lepcha; *Nuni*, Ass.; *Posa*, Burm.

A moderate-sized deciduous tree. Wood yellow with darker streaks of various colours, hard. Annual rings distinctly marked by a belt of closely packed, moderate-sized and large pores which are generally subdivided. The pores in the outer portion of the annual ring are very small, in small, irregular patches, uniformly distributed. Medullary rays moderately broad, short. The structure of this wood is very similar to that of *Morus alba* of Europe and Japan, but the medullary rays are broader and further apart.

Sub-Himalayan tract ascending to 5,000 feet, Sikkim valleys up to 4,000 feet. Cultivated throughout North India.

Growth, the specimen received from Multán had very little more than one ring per inch of radius; that from Madhopur shewed 5 rings; its growth must therefore be considered very fast.

Weight, our specimens gave, the Multán one, 42; the Madhopur one 47 lbs. per cubic foot. It is largely cultivated for its leaves, which are used to feed silkworms. In Assam, the silk of the 'Pat' worm (*Bombyx Textor* and *B. Crœsi*) is produced on this mulberry.

		lbs.
P 891.	Multán	42
P 1195.	Madhopur	47

2. M. serrata, Roxb. Fl. Ind. iii. 596; Brandis 409. Vern. *Karún, tút, káura, túlúkúl, soá, án, shta, chimu, kimu*, Pb.; *Kimu, himu*, Hind.

A large deciduous tree. Bark greyish brown. Sapwood small, white; heartwood yellow or brown, with a slight lustre, moderately hard. Annual rings distinctly marked by a line or irregular belt of moderate-sized and large pores. Pores frequently subdivided, filled with gum. In the outer portion of each annual ring the pores are small and moderate-sized, scanty, often arranged in groups. Medullary rays moderately broad.

North-West Himalaya between 4,000 and 9,000 feet.

Growth moderate, our specimens averaging 8 rings per inch of radius. Weight, 35 to 36 lbs. per cubic foot. It is often of very large size. Dr. Stewart noted several trees of 20 feet girth, and one at the Hindu temple at Barmaor, Chamba 7,000 feet, of 28 feet girth. It works well, does not warp, and takes a beautiful polish, shewing a golden lustre. It is used for troughs, agricultural implements and for cabinet-work. It is much esteemed by the Simla wood-carvers.

		lbs.
H 3174.	Dungagalli, Hazara, 7,000 feet	...
H 10.	Julung, Simla, 4,000 feet	36
H 28.	Madhan, Simla, 5,000 „	35
H 95.	Simla, 6,000 feet	36

3. M. cuspidata, Wall. *M. serrata*, Roxb.; Gamble 77. Vern. *Kimbu*, Nep.; *Nambyong*, Lepcha; *Singtok*, Bhutia; *Bola*, Ass.

A tall tree. Wood yellow, with yellowish brown heartwood, hard, close-grained, with a beautiful lustre. Annual rings marked by a white line and sometimes by a continuous string of pores. Pores uniformly distributed, moderate-sized to large, often oval and subdivided, each pore in a narrow ring of soft tissue, prominent on a vertical section. Medullary rays fine and moderately broad; the distance between the rays generally equal to, or larger than, the transverse diameter of the pores. Medullary rays prominent on a radial section, giving the wood a markedly mottled appearance.

Valleys of the Outer Eastern Himalaya, from Sikkim to Assam.

Growth moderate, averaging 7 rings per inch of radius. Weight, our specimens average 45·6 lbs. per cubic foot. It often reaches a very large size; trees of over 100 feet in height are not uncommon in the valleys of the Teesta and Great Rangít. The wood is used in Assam for boat oars and furniture; it does not seem to have been much used for tea-boxes, but would be extremely suitable. It resembles that of *M. serrata*, and would be good for planking, furniture and cabinet-work.

		lbs.
E 706.	Great Rangít Valley, Darjeeling, 3,500 feet	42
E 3376.	" " " " 1,000 "	44
E 656.	Bamunpokri, Darjeeling	48
E 2306.	Eastern Dúars, Assam	47
E 2196.	Nowgong, Assam	42
E 2305.	Kamrúp, "	49

No. 2965 is the "Fustic" *Maclura tinctoria*, D. Don, from the West Indies, Central and South America, whose wood is used for dyeing different shades of yellow, brown and green. The wood is orange-yellow, hard. Pores moderate-sized to large, often subdivided and filled with resin. The medullary rays are fine, prominent, uniform, wavy, the distance between the rays being less than the transverse diameter of the pores. Weight of our specimen, 53 lbs. per cubic foot. *M. aurantiaca*, Nuttall, is the "Osage Orange" of North America.

8. ARTOCARPUS, Linn.

About 8 Indian species. *A. calophylla*, Kurz, *A. rufescens*, Miq., *A. Gomeziana*, Wall., and *A. rigida*, Bl. (*A. echinata*, Roxb. Fl. Ind. iii. 527), are all trees described in Kurz ii. 431 to 433 from Tenasserim. The last species has a light white wood and gives a kind of Caoutchouc. *A. incisa*, Linn.; Beddome ccxx.; Brandis 426, is the "Bread Fruit" Tree of the South Sea Islands; it is cultivated in Southern India, Ceylon and Burma, and there bears fruit; but does not stand the cold season in Bengal.

The wood of the species of *Artocarpus* here described is very uniform in character. Heartwood moderately hard to hard, sometimes yellow, seasons well, weighs between 30 and 50 lbs. Pores moderate-sized to large, often in circular light-coloured rings of softer tissue, prominent on a longitudinal section. Medullary rays fine to moderately broad, very distinct, the distance between the rays generally about equal to the transverse diameter of the pores.

1. A. integrifolia, Linn.; Roxb. Fl. Ind. iii. 522; Beddome ccxix.; Brandis 425; Kurz ii. 432; Gamble 73. The Jack Tree. Vern. *Kanthal, kathal*, Hind., Beng.; *Panasa*, Uriya, Tel.; *Phanás*, Mar.; *Pilla*, Tam.; *Halsu, heb-helsu, halsina*, Kan.; *Teprong*, Gáro; *Peingnai*, Burm.; *Cos*, Cingh.

A large tree. Bark thick, blackish, deeply cracked. Heartwood yellow or rich yellowish brown, darkening on exposure, compact, even-grained, moderately hard, seasons well and takes a fine polish. Pores often oval and subdivided, moderate-sized to large, in irregular patches of soft tissue, which are often arranged in short oblique lines or groups, sometimes filled with a white substance which is visible on a vertical section. Pores prominent on a vertical section. Medullary rays numerous, fine and moderately broad.

Cultivated throughout India, except in the northernmost part. Wild in the mountain forests of the Western Gháts, ascending to 4,000 feet (Beddome).

The growth appears to be very fast, but the rings are indistinct and difficult to count. The following experiments have been made to determine the weight and transverse strength:—

	Weight.	P=
Puckle in 1859 in Mysore (4 experiments), with bars 2′ × 1″ × 1″ found	42 lbs.	562
Skinner, No. 17, in 1862 in South India	„ 44 „	788
Adrian Mendis, No. 16, in 1855, in Ceylon, with bars 2′ × 1″ × 1″	„ 42 „	712
Wallich	„ 42 „	...
„ in 1862 in Travancore	„ 35 „	...
Warth in 1878 with specimens below given	„ 40 „	...

The wood is largely used for carpentry, boxes and furniture, and is exported to Europe for cabinet work, turning and brush-backs. The wood yields a yellow dye used in Burma to dye the yellow clothes worn by "phoongies." The tenacious milky juice is used as birdlime. The fruit is very largely used all over India for food, but, except the seeds, rarely by Europeans. It has an unpleasant smell when ripe. The fruit in young trees is borne on the branches, in older trees on the trunk, and in very old trees near the root.

		lbs.
E 598.	Darjeeling Terai (young tree)	38
E 2444.	Siliguri, Bengal	41
W 756.	South Kanara	43
B 806.	Tharrawaddi, Burma	30
No. 9.	Salem Collection	42
No. 16.	Ceylon „	44

2. A. Lakoocha, Roxb. Fl. Ind. iii. 524; Beddome ccxix.; Brandis 426; Kurz ii. 433; Gamble 73. Vern. *Tiún, dheu, daheo,* Pb.; *Dahu, dhau, barhal, lakúch,* Hind.; *Dháo,* Kumaun; *Dephúl, dehua,* Beng.; *Dowa, chama, chamba,* Ass.; *Dawa,* Cachar; *Kamma regu, laku-chamma, nakka-renu,* Tel.; *Myouklouk,* Burm.; *Cauna-gona,* Cingh.

A large tree. Bark ⅓ inch thick, dark grey, rough. Sapwood large, white, soft, perishable. Heartwood yellow, hard. Pores large, enclosed in rings of light coloured, soft tissue, uniformly distributed. Medullary rays fine and moderately broad, very distinct, prominent on a radial section.

Outer Hills of Kumaun, Sikkim, Eastern Bengal, Burma, evergreen forests of Western Gháts and Ceylon.

Growth fast, 3 to 4 rings per inch of radius. Weight, our specimens give on an average, 39·5 lbs. per cubic foot; Brandis in his Burma List of 1862, No. 92, gave 40 lbs. The wood seasons well, takes a good polish and is used for furniture and canoes. Mann says the bark is chewed in Assam. The male flower-heads are pickled and the fruit is eaten.

		lbs.
E 2445.	Siliguri, Bengal	48
E 794.	Kámrúp, Assam	36
E 1402.	Chittagong	43
W 740.	South Kanara	47
B 810.	Rangoon Division, Burma	30
B 2553.	Burma (1862)	39
No. 67.	Ceylon Collection (marked *Artocarpus* sp. Vern. *Patta-del*)	34

3. A. Chaplasha, Roxb. Fl. Ind. iii. 525; Brandis 426; Kurz ii. 432; Gamble 73. Vern. *Chaplash, chaplis,* Beng.; *Lut-ter,* Nep.; *Chram,* Gáro; *Sam,* Ass.; *Cham,* Cachar; *Pani, toponi,* Magh; *Toungpeingnai,* Burm.; *Kaila-dá,* And.

A lofty deciduous tree. Bark of young trees smooth, light grey with dark blotches; of old trees dark brown, tuberculate, ⅛ inch thick. Wood yellow to brown, moderately hard, even-grained, rough, durable, seasons well. Pores large and moderate-sized, uniformly distributed. Medullary rays short, fine and moderately broad. Pores frequently filled with a white substance.

Eastern Bengal, Burma and the Andaman Islands.

Growth rather fast, 5 to 6 rings per inch of radius. Weight, 36·8 for the average of our 14 specimens; Brandis' Burma List of 1862, No. 91 gives 39 lbs.; No. 92 gives 30 lbs. No. 15, Skinner (1862) (*Artocarpus echinatus*, Vern. *Toungpeingnai*), gives: Weight = 63 lbs., P = 672. Bennett (1872) gives: Weight = 32 lbs.; P = 459 for Andaman wood. The wood seems to get harder and heavier as it gets older; two of our specimens from the Andaman Islands cut in 1866 and stored since then in Calcutta give respectively 46 and 52 lbs., and Skinner gives 63 lbs., but this is probably a mistake. It is much used for canoes; in Sikkim and Assam for planking, tea-boxes and furniture. Kurz says it gives a tenacious milky caoutchouc. The leaves of young plants are pinnatifid, resembling a gigantic hairy leaf of *Quercus Robur;* those of old trees are oblong, entire.

			lbs.
E	587.	Khookloong Forest, Darjeeling Terai (young)	30
E	629.	Eastern Dúars, Assam	32
E	2301.	Kámrúp, Assam	33
E	2186.	Nowgong, „	35
E	721.	Chittagong	33
B	2554.	Burma (1862)	39
B	2693.	Tavoy (Wallich, 1828)	37
B	2683.	„ („ „)	32
B	2204.	Andaman Islands, (1866)	52
B	2211.	„ „ „	33
B	2289.	„ „ „	46
B	512.	„ „ „	34
B	2499.	„ „ (Home, 1874, Nos. 4 and 5)	{ 31 48

4. A. hirsuta, Lamk.; Roxb. Fl. Ind. iii. 521; Beddome t. 308; Brandis 426. Vern. *Ayni, anjalli, aiyanepela,* Tam.; *Aini, ansjeni,* Mal.; *Hebalsu, heb halasu, hesswa, hessain,* Kan.; *Hebalsu, pat-phanas, ran-phanas,* Mar.

A lofty evergreen tree. Heartwood hard to very hard, yellowish brown, durable, seasons well. Pores moderate-sized to large, enclosed in narrow rings of soft tissue, often filled with a white substance. Medullary rays fine to moderately broad, wavy, very distinct.

Evergreen forests of the Western Ghâts, ascending to 4,000 feet.

Growth appears fast, but the rings are too indistinct for proper counting. Weight, Skinner, No. 16, gives 40 lbs.; Wallich, 37 lbs.; our three specimens average 34 lbs. Skinner gives P = 744. The wood is much used on the western coast for house and ship building, furniture and other purposes.

			lbs.
D	1090.	Madura, Madras	32
W	1219.	North Kanara	31
W	744.	South „	39
W	755.	„ „	41

(This last specimen differs by having very short, moderately broad, medullary rays and pores in irregular patches of soft texture; it may possibly be *A. Lakoocha.*)

5. A. nobilis, Thw. Enum. 262; Beddome t. 309. Vern. *Del, aludel,* Cingh.

A large tree. Heartwood shining, moderately hard. Pores large, filled with a white substance, prominent on a vertical section, and thereby giving the wood an elegant mottled appearance. Medullary rays short, moderately broad; the distance between the rays being equal to the transverse diameter of the pores.

Ceylon.

Weight, Adrian Mendis' two experiments made in 1855 with bars 2 feet × 1 inch × 1 inch gave: No. 2, weight 51 lbs., P = 712; No. 21, weight 40 lbs., P = 528. The specimens, now again weighed, give 40 and 49 lbs. respectively. Wood used for canoes and furniture. The seeds are roasted and eaten by the Cinghalese.

		lbs.
No. 2.	Ceylon Collection marked *A. pubescens*	51
No. 21.	" " " "	40

9. ANTIARIS, Lesch.

1. **A. toxicaria, Lesch.**; Kurz ii. 462. *A. innoxia*, Bl.; Beddome t. 307; Brandis 427. *A. saccidora*, Dalz. The Upas Tree. Vern. *Alli, nelavil*, Tam.; *Jazúgri, karwat, jagúri*, Kan.; *Jasúnd*, Bombay; *Arayaangely*, Mal.; *Riti*, Cingh.; *Myah-seik*, Burm.

A gigantic evergreen tree attaining a height of 250 feet, with thick grey bark. Wood white, soft, even-grained. Annual rings faintly marked. Pores large and moderate-sized, often subdivided. Medullary rays moderately broad, undulating, uniform and equidistant; the distance between two rays generally equal to the transverse diameter of the pores, which are prominent on a vertical section.

Evergreen forests of Burma, the Western Ghâts and Ceylon.

Growth fast, 4 to 6 rings per inch of radius. Weight, 25 lbs. per cubic foot. Beddome says it is the largest tree in the forests of the western coast, and that it reaches 250 feet in height, with an enormous girth. It exudes a white poisonous resin used for poisoning arrows. The inner bark gives a good fibre which makes strong cordage; it is also stripped off whole from a branch or young tree to form sacks which are used to carry rice.

		lbs.
B 813.	Rangoon Division, Burma	25

Nos. E 408 from the Sundarbans, E 1294 from Cachar, and W 729 from South Kanara resemble this in structure.

10. FICUS, Linn.

A large genus containing more than 80 Indian species. They are trees or shrubs often climbing, but more often epiphytic, and some species are of enormous size. *F. tomentosa*, Willd.; Roxb. Fl. Ind. iii. 550; Beddome ccxxiii.; Brandis 414. Vern. *Petta-mari*, Tel., is a large tree of Banda, Behar, Central and Southern India. *F. Wightiana*, Wall.; Beddome ccxxii.; Brandis 414, is a large tree of Southern India. *F. mysorensis*, Roth.; Brandis 414; Kurz ii. 440; Gamble 73. Vern. *Sunkong*, Lepcha; *Goni*, Kan. is a large epiphytic tree of Sikkim, Martaban, Mysore and the Western Ghâts. *F. laccifera*, Roxb. Fl. Ind. iii. 545; Beddome ccxxiii.; Kurz ii. 441; Gamble 74. Vern. *Yokdúng*, Lepcha; *Prab, phegran*, Gáro; *Bur*, Ass.; *Nyoungben*, Burma, is a large epiphytic tree of the North-East Himalaya, Eastern Bengal, Burma, South India and the Andamans, giving India-rubber, but more sparingly and of not such good quality as that of *F. elastica*. *F. obtusifolia*, Roxb. Fl. Ind. iii. 546; Kurz ii. 443; Gamble 74. Vern. *Krapchi*, Mechi; *Nyoung-kyap*, Burm.; *Date*, Magh, is a small-leaved epiphytic tree of Northern and Eastern Bengal and Burma, also yielding a moderately good variety of caoutchouc. *F. triloba*, Ham.; Brandis 423 (*F. hirsuta, F. hirta*, Roxb. Fl. Ind. iii. 528-531. *F. Roxburghii*, Miq.; Gamble 75) Vern. *Dungra, khura dumúr*, Beng.; *Kasreto*, Nep.; *Gyasay*, Lepcha; *Mhow, man*, Ass., is a handsome small tree of

Northern and Eastern Bengal with hairy, large leaves and large golden pubescent edible fruit. *F. Chittagonga,* Miq.; Kurz ii. 458; Gamble 76. Vern. *Yogona,* Beng.; *Saphai,* Magh; *Tha-hpan-ben,* Burm., is a tree of the savannah forests of Pegu and Chittagong.

F. Carica, Linn.; Brandis 418. The Fig. Vern. *Anjír,* Hind.; *Kimri, fagu, fagúri, fagári,* Pb., is cultivated in the plains of North-West India and hills up to 5,000 feet, but the produce is generally poor. Mathieu Fl. For., page 251, gives the weight of the wood at 34 to 45 lbs. per cubic foot. The wood is soft, white with a yellowish tinge, and full of milky juice.

Those here given are only a few of the most important among the very numerous species. There are many more which are common enough, but few of any very great forest interest.

The structure of all species of *Ficus* is exceedingly uniform. Wood generally soft, marked by alternate bands of soft and firm tissue; no heartwood. Pores small to large, scanty, except in the wood of the scandent species, which is porous as usual in the case of climbers. Medullary rays generally of two classes, fine and moderately broad. As far as the materials at our disposal permit us to venture upon a classification, we should be inclined to say that there are two types which differ more in the general appearance of the wood than in structure. *Ficus religiosa, elastica, retusa, Cunia, nemoralis* and *virgata* have wood of plain, smooth appearance, which, though the medullary rays are apparent on a radial section, is not mottled and streaked as in the other species. The species with rough, mottled and streaked wood are *Ficus bengalensis, infectoria, cordifolia, comosa, regia, glomerata* and *Roxburghii*. *Ficus virgata* differs from all the rest by having white, more compact wood. *F. parasitica* has the large pores of a climber.

1. F. bengalensis, Linn.; Beddome ccxxii.; Brandis 412; Kurz ii. 440; Gamble 73. *F. indica,* Roxb. Fl. Ind. iii. 539. The Banyan. Vern. *Bor, bar, ber, bargat,* Hind.; *Bur, but,* Beng.; *Boru,* Uriya; *Borhar,* Nep.; *Kangji,* Lepcha; *Ranket,* Gáro; *Bot,* Ass.; *Barelli,* Gondi; *Wóra,* Kurku; *Ala,* Tam.; *Mári, peddi-mari,* Tel.; *Ahlada, aladamara, ala,* Kan.; *Peralu,* Mal.; *War, vada,* Mar.; *Maha-núga,* Cingh.; *Pyee-nyoung,* Burm.

A large evergreen tree, throwing down numerous aërial roots from the branches. Bark ½ inch thick, greyish white, smooth, exfoliating in small irregular plates. Wood grey, moderately hard; no heartwood. Pores scanty, moderate-sized, joined by narrow, wavy, concentric bands of soft tissue alternating with broader bands of firmer tissue and darker colour. Medullary rays fine, equidistant, prominent. On a radial section pores and medullary rays distinctly marked, giving the wood a mottled appearance.

Planted by Hindoos throughout India up to 4,000 feet; wild in the Sub-Himalayan tract, Bengal and Central India.

The rate of growth is not distinguishable by means of the annual rings, but it is known that it is very fast. The tree sends down aërial roots from the branches, these root in the ground and grow into separate trunks which serve as supports for the branches and as feedeers for the tree, which thus largely increases in spread of foliage. Roxburgh states that he saw some trees with fully 500 yards circumference round the spread of branches and about 100 feet high. Brandis says that many specimens may be seen in Bengal with the crown 200 to 300 feet in diameter. In Bengal the aërial roots and long branches are usually more developed than in Northern India, but the trunk in the latter drier region attains a larger girth, often 25 to 30 feet. In the forest it does not seem to spread so widely as in the open or as the India-rubber Fig (*F. elastica*) does. Roxburgh says the largest trees are to be found about the villages situated in fertile valleys among the mountains. Balfour says that Marsden mentions a tree near Patna having a diameter of 363 to 375 feet of spread, circumference of shadow 1,116 feet, with 50 to 60 principal stems. The well-known tree in the Botanic Gardens, Calcutta, which was ascertained by Falconer to have grown in 1782 from a seed deposited in the crown of a date palm, and which is consequently now 98 years old, measured when examined by Falconer in 1834, Hooker in 1847, and Balfour in 1863, 300 feet in diameter of spread and 80 feet in height. It has since suffered severely in the cyclones of 1864 and 1867. Brandis met with a tree at Chicholi in Hoshungabad district, Central Provinces, 85 feet high with a diameter of 275 feet, and occupying an area of 1½ acres. Its aërial roots were not, as usual in cultivaiion, assisted by bamboos, but small mounds of earth were heaped up to meet and receive them.

Weight, Skinner (No. 70) gives 36 lbs.; our specimens weigh 38 and 39 lbs. per cubic foot. Skinner gives P = 600.

The wood is of little value, but is durable under water, and therefore used for well curbs. It is sometimes used for boxes and door panels. The wood of the drops is stronger and is used for tent poles, cart yokes and banghy poles. The bark and small root drops give a coarse fibre for rope-making. Five specimens were sent to the 1878 Paris Exhibition from Berar (No. C 981). The milky juice is made into birdlime, the leaves are used as plates, and the fibre is used for slow matches by the Sikhs. Lac is sometimes collected on it, the leaves are used to cure bruises, the bark in native medicine, and the fruit is sometimes eaten. It is a common avenue tree, and being evergreen, fast-growing and easily propagated by large cuttings is very useful for planting on road-sides. Cuttings, 8 to 10 feet long, planted in July, succeed well. The *Gori* or *Deomuga* silkworm (*Bombyx religiosa*) feeds on its leaves in Assam. It is one of the epiphytic species of *Ficus*, which do so much harm to valuable timber trees in the forests, and which often has to be cut.

		lbs.
C 1150.	Ahiri Reserve, Central Provinces	38
C 836.	Bairagarh Reserve, Berar	39
C 2813.	Melghát, Berar	...

2. **F. infectoria,** Willd.; Roxb. Fl. Ind. iii. 551; Beddome ccxxii., Brandis 414; Kurz ii. 446; Gamble 75. *F. venosa*, Ham. Vern. *War, batbar, jangli pipli, palakh, trimbal*, Pb.; *Pilkhan, kahimmal, ramanjír, pákhar, pakri, keol, kaim, khabar*, Hind.; *Pákar*, Beng.; *Safed kabra*, Nep.; *Kangji*, Lepcha; *Prab*, Gáro; *Serilli*, Gondi; *Pepere*, Kurku; *Jovi, kall-alun*, Tam.; *Jewi, yuri*, Tel.; *Tsjakela*, Mal.; *Bassari*, Tel.; *Kari basri, bassari*, Kan.; *Nyoungchin*, Burm.

A large tree. Bark ½ inch thick, greenish grey, smooth, exfoliating irregularly in flakes and patches. Wood grey, moderately hard. Pores scanty, large, often subdivided, joined by narrow concentric bands of soft tissue, which alternate with broader bands of firmer texture. Medullary rays uniform, moderately broad, equidistant, prominent on a radial section.

Suliman and Salt Ranges, Outer Himalaya ascending to 5,000 feet, Bengal, Burma, Central India, Western Coast and Ceylon.

Growth rapid. Weight: according to Brandis 30 lbs.; our specimens give an average of 34 lbs. It is often found as an epiphyte on other trees, but does not send down numerous roots like the Banyan, though it often has one or two aërial roots. It is often planted in avenues. It is common in the forests; but the wood is not durable. It is used in Assam and Cachar to make charcoal. The young shoots are eaten in curries, and the leaves make good elephant fodder. The bark gives a fibre good for rope. (No. C 982 from Berar was a fine specimen.)

		lbs.
P 911.	Salt Range	31
C 1166.	Ahiri Reserve, Central Provinces	37
C 838.	Bairagarh Reserve, Berar	34
C 2808.	Melghát, Berar	...

3. **F. religiosa,** Linn.; Roxb. Fl. Ind. iii. 547; Beddome t. 314;

Brandis 415; Kurz ii. 448; Gamble 75. The Peepul. Vern. *Pipal*, Hind.; *Aswat*, *asúd*, Beng.; *Pipli*, Nep.; *Bor-bur*, Cachar; *Arasa*, Tam.; *Rái*, *raiga*, *ragi*, *ravi*, Tel.; *Ali*, Gondi; *Pipri*, Kurku; *Rangi*, *basri*, Kan.; *Bo*, Cingh.; *Nyoungbandi*, Burm.

A large tree. Bark grey, nearly ½ inch thick, exfoliating in rounded irregular flakes of varying size, often leaving rounded depressions. Wood greyish white, moderately hard. Pores moderate-sized to large, often subdivided, joined by narrow bands of soft tissue, which alternate with broader bands of firmer substance. Medullary rays uniform and equidistant, moderately broad, visible on a radial section, but not giving the wood a markedly mottled appearance.

Wild in the Sub-Himalayan tract, Bengal and Central India.

Growth very fast. It is often planted as an avenue tree, for which it is very suitable; it grows well and quickly, either from cuttings or seedlings. The weight and transverse strength have been determined by the following experiments:—

		Weight.	P.
Cunningham at Gwalior in 1854 in two experiments with bars 2'× 1"×1"	found	44	458
Skinner in Madras in 1862 (No. 72)	„	34	584
Warth with our six specimens in 1878	„	34·7	...

The tree being sacred is rarely felled; the wood is used for fuel, for packing cases and in Cachar for charcoal. The leaves and branches are good elephant fodder; the young leaf buds are eaten in Central India in famine time; the leaves, bark and fruit are used in native medicine, and the bark gives a tenacious milky juice which hardens into a substance resembling gutta-percha. It is usually epiphytic and is most destructive to buildings, walls, and other trees. The *Gori* or *Deomuga* silkworm feeds on its leaves in Assam.

			lbs.
P	893.	Multán	45
O	533.	Dehra Dún	31
O	538.	„ „	31
O	543.	„ „	23
C	1168.	Abiri Reserve, Central Provinces	44
C	837.	Bairagarh Reserve, Central Provinces	34
C	2814.	Melghát, Berar	...

4. **F. cordifolia**, Roxb. Fl. Ind. iii. 548; Brandis 416; Gamble 75. *F. Rumphii*, Kurz ii. 448. Vern. *Rúmbal*, *palák*, *badha*, *pilkhan*, Pb.; *Kabar*, *gajiún*, *gajna*, *pipal*, *gagjaira*, *pakar*, *khabar*, Hind.; *Kabai pipal*, Kumaun; *Gai aswát*, Beng.; *Pakar*, Nep.; *Pakri*, Ass.; *Sat-bur*, Cachar; *Prab*, Gáro; *Parás pipal*, Ajmere; *Pair*, Mar.; *Nyoungpyoo*, Burm.

A large deciduous tree. Bark smooth, ½ inch thick. Wood very soft, spongy. Pores oval, arranged in wavy, concentric bands, alternating with bands of firmer texture and of the same width. Medullary rays fine, uniform, equidistant, very marked on a radial section, giving the wood a beautifully mottled appearance.

Outer Himalaya, from the Chenab eastwards ascending to 5,000 feet, Bengal, Central India and Burma.

Weight, 27 lbs. per cubic foot. Wood used in Cachar for charcoal for tea manufacture. It is generally epiphytic and is then very destructive to timber trees. In Assam the lac insect is reared on it (Mann). The fruit is eaten and the leaves and branches used for cattle fodder.

			lbs.
H	605.	Chitul Forest, Kangra	27
P	3224.	Nagpahar, Ajmere	...

E 586, 20 lbs., sent from the Darjeeling Terai under the name of "*Niwaro*" and, E 716 (27 lbs.) sent from Chittagong under those of *Hijalya*, Beng.; *Choupaha*, Magh, resemble this species in structure.

5. F. retusa, Linn.; Beddome ccxxiii.; Brandis 417; Kurz ii. 445; Gamble 75. *F. nitida*, Thunb.; Wight Ic. t. 642. *F. Benjamina*, Willd.; Roxb. Fl. Ind. iii. 550. Vern. *Kamrup, zir*, Beng.; *Jamu*, Nep.; *Sitnyok*, Lepcha; *Yerra juvi*, Tel.; *Pilála*, Kan.; *Nyoungop, nyoungthabyeh*, Burm.

A large evergreen tree. Wood light reddish grey, close-grained, moderately hard, beautifully mottled. Pores moderate-sized, often subdivided, scanty. Medullary rays short, moderately broad. Numerous narrow, wavy, red, concentric bands of soft tissue alternating with broader bands of firmer texture.

Kumaun, Bengal, South India, Burma and the Andaman Islands.

Weight, 40 lbs. per cubic foot. Wood used for fuel, but as it is very prettily grained it might be found valuable for tables, door panels and other purposes. It is often planted as an avenue tree, and for this, from its dense shade, it is very suitable. It is often epiphytic.

		lbs.
E 404.	Sundarbans	40
B 2278.	Andaman Islands	40
No. 45.	Ceylon Collection (*Ficus* sp., *Kiripelle*, Cingh.) . . .	42

6. F. elastica, Bl.; Roxb. Fl. Ind. iii. 541; Brandis 417; Kurz ii. 444; Gamble 74. The India-rubber Fig or Caoutchouc Tree. *Bor, attah bar*, Beng., Ass.; *Kagiri, kasmir*, Khasia; *Lesu*, Nep.; *Yok*, Lepcha; *Rauket*, Gáro.

A large evergreen tree, throwing down numerous aërial roots from the branches. Bark grey or reddish brown, smooth. Wood white or light brown. Pores moderate-sized, scanty; narrow belts of soft tissue alternating with broad belts of firmer texture and darker colour. Medullary rays fine and very fine, numerous, unequally distributed.

Outer North-East Himalaya from the Mechi river eastwards, Assam, Cachar, mountains east of Bengal and Arracan. It is found in the vicinity of the Irrawaddy river as far south as 25° north latitude, but it will probably be found further south on hills east of Arracan.

Weight, 43 lbs. per cubic foot. The wood is not used.

The tree is usually epiphytic, the seeds generally germinating at the summit of tall forest trees, where the seedlings can get light. It is often of very great height, trees 100 to 120 feet high being not unusual. It sends down innumerable aërial roots which have a reddish-brown bark, peeling off in small thin narrow strips or flakes; and these roots often extend considerable distances, giving a great spread to the tree. In Brandis' Forest Flora the measurements of a tree described by Griffith (1838) are given; these are:

Height, 100 feet.
Circumference of main trunk, 74 feet.
" of supports, 120 feet.
" of area covered by the branches, 610 feet.

Mann in his report of 1875 gives the following measurements for a tree at Tezpur aged 32 years, and having over 100 aerial roots:

Height 110 feet.
Diameter of crown 140 feet.
Circumference of stem with central supports 70 feet.

The tree is tapped by means of slanting notches made in the stem, aërial roots and roots about 12 inches apart. The milk is allowed to collect and coagulate in these notches for two or three days, after which time the hard India-rubber in each notch is easily collected by being pulled out in a strip. The tree will not bear yearly tapping, once in three years is as much as it will stand; if tapped yearly, it is liable to die off, as did many of the trees in Darjeeling after heavy tapping in 1871, 1872 and 1873. Those which then survived have not yet (1880) recovered sufficiently to be fit for tapping again.

It is easily propagated from seed in small beds thatched over and fenced round to keep out the sun, and provided with small trenches filled with water. By these means a constant hot moist atmosphere is secured and seedlings do well, but the soil should be good and contain plenty of "humus."

The following extracts from Mr. Mann's and Dr. Schlich's reports will explain in more detail the systems used in Assam and Bengal. Mr. Mann says:

"To give the raising of rubber plants from seed a fair trial, about 30 seers of seed, or rather fruit, were collected and sown in three different ways both at the Kulsi plantation in the Gauhati subdivision and the Charduar plantation in the Tezpur subdivision. The different modes used were the following:—

"*First.*—On beds covered with broken bricks, half of which was sown with entire fruit of figs, and the other half with the fruit broken up or rubbed into powder between the hands.

"*Secondly.*—Sown like the above, but on broken charcoal.

"*Thirdly.*—Sown like the above, but on earth only.

"The seed was sown in the middle of January, and germinated in the middle of April. Germination took place best on the broken bricks, next best on the charcoal and least on the earth. The seedlings on the charcoal stood the heavy rains best, those on the broken bricks next, whilst those on the soil nearly all perished. They require no shading, and grow all the stronger by exposure to the light and sun; but as a matter of course they will require a great deal more care and attention than cuttings, and for several years, whilst cuttings can be transplanted before they are a year old.

"The artificial shading over these seeds-beds caused drip and excessive moisture, which proved fatal to many of the seedlings before the cause of the mischief was recognised.

"The number saved amounted, however, to about 1,200, which were on an average of the undermentioned sizes as they grew:—

On the 27th June 1874, $\frac{2}{10}$ths of an inch.
„ 12th August 1874, $1\frac{3}{10}$ths inch.
„ 10th September 1874, $5\frac{7}{10}$ths inches.
„ 21st April 1875, 2 feet 10 inches.

"It should here be mentioned that the last of these was a seedling which has been left undisturbed in the seed-bed, and was exceptionally vigorous in growth."

And Dr. Schlich says: "At Bamunpokri nine nursery beds were prepared, three with common garden soil, three with broken bricks, and three with charcoal, and all intersected by irrigation trenches, thus keeping the soil thoroughly moist by percolation. The seed was collected in September 1874, and sown in that month and in October partly in whole figs, and partly crumbled up by the hand. The beds were then shaded by thatch, raised 2 feet above the ground on the south, and 3 feet on the north, and the sides were closed in with mats which could be removed at will.

"From four to six weeks after sowing the seeds germinated profusely, best of all in the garden soil, next best on the broken bricks, and last, though still pretty well, on the charcoal; they have thriven well, and are now up to 5 inches high, with leaves up to 2 inches long." *

The propagation by cuttings is still easier, but the cuttings must be from young fleshy shoots, such as are obtained by pollarding several branches of an old tree and allowing them to send out shoots. In Sikkim and Assam plants grown from seedlings or cuttings have succeeded either planted directly in the ground or in baskets of mould tied to the upper branches of trees. In Assam plantations are formed by cutting lines at some distance apart through the forest, and planting the rooted cuttings or seedlings at intervals. The following extracts from Mr. Mann's memorandum of 1875 will best explain the method of plantation:—

"The method of planting adopted in the Kulsi caoutchouc plantation is the following:—

"Lines 20 feet in width and 50 feet apart are opened out in mixed plain and savannah forest, and the trees are planted out on these lines at distances of 25 feet.

"The plants were examined by me on the 26th of April, and the countings shewed 2 per cent. of failures, which were filled up the same day. Nothing could surpass the healthiness and vigour of the young trees, whose only enemies are the deer, which has made fencing necessary; but the plants will soon have grown beyond the reach of them.

"The method of planting adopted in the Charduar plantation was the following:—

"Lines of 20 feet in width and 100 feet apart were opened out through lower hill

* Many of these trees are now (1880) 15 to 20 feet high, have many aërial roots, and a considerable girth of main stem. The plantation made of them is so dense as to be almost impenetrable and to exclude all other vegetation.

forest, and trees were planted out on these lines at distances of 50 feet. The width of lines proved insufficient as soon as the rains set in, and the excessive shade and drip from the trees on either side of the line proved injurious and in many cases fatal to the plants. The planting on split stumps of trees and in earthenware rings, placed with the widest opening on stumps was suggested by the Chief Commissioner and proved very successful in low situations, counteracting the excessive wet on the ground; but vigorous growth was not insured until more light was admitted. All the lines of last year's plantation were therefore opened to 40 feet in width, and the effect on the young trees has already been most beneficial, so that, although it is only the commencement of the growing season, nothing could surpass the vigour and healthy appearance of the trees, and so far as the planting on lines opened out through the forest goes it certainly is a perfect success. The ground on these lines was not cleared except just around the plants, but the opening out of bridle-paths has become necessary to save time in going over the plants, since frequent inspection is the only way to prevent any vacancies remaining in the plantation."

		lbs.
E 2449.	Chawa Jhora, Sivoke, Darjeeling	43

7. **F. comosa,** Roxb. Fl. Ind. iii. 552; Beddome ccxxiii.; Gamble 74 *F. Benjamina,* Linn. var. *comosa,* Kurz ii. 446. Vern. *Kabra,* Nep.; *Kunhip,* Lepcha; *Juri pakri,* Ass.; *Putra-juvi,* Tel.

A moderate-sized, evergreen, often epiphytic tree with thin grey bark. Wood grey, beautifully mottled, moderately hard. Pores large, often subdivided, scanty. Medullary rays fine, numerous. Numerous concentric bands of soft tissue alternating with broader bands of firmer texture.

Bengal, Burma, mountains of the eastern side of the peninsula, Tinnevelly.

A very pretty small-leaved fig. Weight, 34 lbs. per cubic foot. Lac is produced on it in Assam (Mann).

		lbs.
E 588.	Bamunpokri, Darjeeling	34

8. **F. virgata,** Roxb. Fl. Ind. iii. 530; Brandis 419. *F. caricoides,* Roxb. Fl. Ind. iii. 529. Vern. *Anjir, inzar,* Afg.; *Fagu, fagóra, dudhi, dhura, phedu, kak, daholia* (Hills), *fagwara, thapur* (Plains), Pb.; *Gúlar, khabára, anjiri, beru, bedu,* Hind.

A moderate-sized tree. Bark grey, smooth. Wood white, close and even-grained, moderately hard. Pores small and moderate-sized, often oval and subdivided. Numerous wavy concentric bands of soft tissue, alternating with bands of equal width of firmer tissue. Medullary rays fine and moderately broad, unequally distributed. The distance between the rays is generally less than the transverse diameter of the pores.

Suliman and Salt Ranges, Outer Himalaya eastward to Nepal, ascending to 6,000 feet.

Weight, 39 lbs. per cubic foot. It often grows to a tolerably large size, reaching to 10 feet in girth. The leaves are lopped for cattle fodder, and the fruit is eaten in the Punjab hills.

		lbs.
P 910.	Salt Range	41
H 607.	Chitul Forest, Kangra	38
H 156.	Bhajji, Simla, 3,000 feet	39

9. **F. nemoralis,** Wall.; Brandis 424.

A moderate-sized tree with smooth grey bark. Wood white, moderately hard, close-grained. Pores small and moderate-sized, in groups and short radial lines. Medullary rays fine and moderately broad. Narrow white wavy bands of soft texture alternating with belts of firmer wood.

Outer Himalaya from the Jhelum to Sikkim, ascending to 7,000 feet.
Weight, 38 lbs. per cubic foot. The leaves are lopped for cattle fodder.

		lbs.
H 3080.	Gowai, Simla, 6,000 feet	38

10. F. foveolata, Wall.; Brandis 423; Gamble 75. Vern. *Grelu*, Simla; *Makreru*, Kunawar; *Dudíla*, Nep.; *Taksot*, Lepcha. (It is probably *F. reticulata*, Miq., of Stewart's Punjab Plants.)

An evergreen scandent shrub. Wood light brown, soft, very porous. Pores small to very large, very numerous. Medullary rays fine, bending, the distance between the rays being less than the transverse diameter of the pores. Numerous concentric bands of soft texture between the pores.

Himalaya, from the Sutlej to Bhutan, Khasia Hills.
Weight, 38 lbs. per cubic foot.

		lbs.
H 2833.	The Glen, Simla, 6,000 feet	38

11. F. Cunia, Buch.; Roxb. Fl. Ind. iii. 561; Beddome ccxxiv.; Brandis 421; Kurz ii. 461; Gamble 76. Vern. *Khewnau, khurhur kassæ, ghwi*, Hind.; *Kunia*, Kumaun; *Kanhya*, Nep.; *Kanai, palkai, taikrau*, Mechi; *Sangji*, Lepcha; *Dumbur, jagya-domur*, Beng.; *Jonua, sodoi*, Magh; *Ye-kha-ong*, Burm.

A moderate-sized tree. Wood rough, moderately hard, greyish brown. Pores small and moderate-sized, joined by narrow concentric bands which alternate with broader bands of firmer texture, over which a portion of the pores are scattered. Medullary rays fine, equidistant.

Sub-Himalayan tract from the Chenab eastwards, ascending to 4,000 feet, Bengal, Burma, mountains on the east side of the peninsula.

Weight 31 lbs. per cubic foot. Wood not used. The bark is used to tie the rafters of natives houses; the fruit is eaten, and is good, though somewhat insipid; the leaves are rough, and are said to be used for polishing wood. This species is easily recognised by the long rough leaves, which are very unequal sided.

		lbs.
O 1365.	Gonda, Oudh	36
E 583.	Bamunpokri, Darjeeling Terai	36
E 1953.	Chittagong	22

12. F. glomerata, Roxb. Fl. Ind. iii. 558; Beddome ccxxiv.; Brandis 422; Kurz ii. 458; Gamble 76. Vern. *Kathgúlar, krumbal, kakammal, dadhúri*, Pb.; *Gúlar, paroa, lelka, umar, umrái, tue*, Hind.; *Dumri*, Nep.; *Tchongtay*, Lepcha; *Jagya dumar*, Beng.; *Dimeri*, Uriya; *Thoja*, Gondi; *Alawa*, Kurku; *Atti*, Tam.; *Moydi, atti, bodda, paidi, mari*, Tel.; *Kulla-kith*, Kan.; *Atteeka*, Cingh.; *Ye-tha-pan*, Burm.

A large tree. Bark ⅓ inch thick, smooth, reddish brown, with a few large cracks. Wood grey, soft. Pores large, joined by narrow concentric bands of soft tissue, which alternate with bands of firmer tissue and darker colour. Medullary rays moderately broad, equidistant. Wood mottled on a longitudinal section.

Salt Range, Sub-Himalayan Tract, Bengal, Central and South India, Burma.

Weight, Cunningham gives 36 lbs.; our specimens 25 lbs. Cunningham's two experiments with bars of Gwalior wood 2′ × 1″ × 1″ gave P = 458. This may be the *F. racemosa* of Skinner No. 71, the weight of which is given at 40 lbs. and P = 583. The wood is not durable, though it lasts well under water, and is consequently used for well-frames. Birdlime is made of the milky juice; the leaves are used for cattle and elephant fodder. The leaves, bark, and fruit are used in native medicine, and the ripe fruit is eaten and is good either raw or stewed.

		lbs.
C 1138.	Ahiri Reserve, Central Provinces	...
C 839.	Bairagarh Reserve, Berar	25
C 2796.	Melghát, Berar	...
E 643.	Bamunpokri, Darjeeling Terai	25

13. F. Roxburghii, Wall.; Brandis 422; Kurz ii. 460. *F. macrophylla,* Roxb. Fl. Ind. iii. 556; Gamble 75. Vern. *Urbúl; urmúl, barbaru, túsi, trimbal, tirmal, trímal, tirmi, tiamle,* Pb.; *Trimmal, timal, timla,* Hind.; *Kasrekan,* Nep.; *Kundoung,* Lepcha; *Demúr,* Beng.; *Sapai,* Magh; *Sin-tha-hpan,* Burm.

A moderate-sized tree with grey warty bark. Wood reddish grey, moderately hard. Pores moderate-sized and large, often subdivided, joined by broad bands of soft tissue, alternating with darker bands of firmer texture, and of the same width, in which a few pores are found scattered. Medullary rays fine to broad, short, very prominent on a radial section, giving the wood a handsome mottled appearance.

Outer Himalaya from the Indus eastward, ascending to 6,000 feet, Sylhet, Chittagong, and Burma.

Weight, 34 lbs. The fruit is eaten and is good. The leaves are used for fodder.

		lbs.
H 606.	Chital Forest, Kangra	34

P 149 from Sainj, near Simla, 4,000 feet, Vern. *Dudela* (*Ficus glomerata*), resembles this species most. Weight, 34 lbs.

14. F. regia, Miq.; Kurz ii. 459; Gamble 76. Vern. *Neverra,* Nep.

An evergreen tree with grey bark. Wood soft, spongy. Pores scanty, moderate-sized. Narrow bands of soft tissue alternating with broader bands of firm texture. Medullary rays short, moderately broad, very prominent on a radial section, giving the wood a mottled appearance.

North-East Himalaya and Burma.

		lbs.
E 689.	Sepoydura Forest, Darjeeling, 5,500 feet	29

15. F. hispida, Linn. f.; Beddome ccxxiv.; Brandis 423; Kurz ii. 460; Gamble 76. *F. oppositifolia,* Roxb. Fl. Ind. iii. 561. *F. dæmona;* König; Roxb. lc. 562. Vern. *Dadúri, degar, rúmbal,* Pb.; *Kagsha, gobla, totmila, kat gularia, konea dumbar,* Hind.; *Dhedu mera,* Panch Mehals; *Kharwa,* Nep.; *Taksot,* Lepcha; *Dumar, kako-dumar,* Beng.; *Poksha,* Mechi; *Khoskadumar,* Ass.; *Shakab,* Gáro; *Boda-mamadi, bummarri, bamári,* Tel.; *Katumer, bomair,* Gondi; *Koreh,* Kurku; *Maiu-lok,* Magh; *Kadot,* Burm.

A moderate-sized tree. Bark $\frac{1}{8}$ inch thick, grey, peeling off in irregular flakes, with slight horizontal ribs encircling the tree. Wood soft, dirty grey, no heartwood, no annual rings. Pores scanty, moderate-sized, often oval and subdivided. The pores are mostly contained in regular concentric bands of soft tissue, which alternate with firmer bands of equal width and darker colour. Medullary rays moderately broad and fine, prominent as long narrow bands on a radial section.

Outer Himalaya from the Chenab eastwards, ascending to 3,500 feet, Bengal, Central and South India, Burma and the Andaman Islands.

Growth fast, a round in the Bengal Forest Museum shews 3 rings per inch of radius. Weight, Kyd's Assam experiments give 25 lbs.; our specimen weighs 35 lbs. Kyd gives P = 360. The leaves are lopped for cattle fodder. This species is easily recognised by its opposite leaves.

		lbs.
C 1180.	Ahiri Reserve, Central Provinces	...
C 2803.	Melghát, Berar	...
E 2450.	Bamunpokri, Darjeeling Terai	35

11. ULMUS, Linn.

About six Indian species. *U. parvifolia*, Jacq.; Brandis 434. (*U. virgata*, Roxb. Fl. Ind. ii. 67), is a small tree of the Himalaya from Kumaun to Bhutan between 4,000 and 5,000 feet. *U. Hookeriana*, Planch., is found in Sikkim at 4,500 feet. The European Elms are *U. campestris*, Sm.; the Common Elm; *U. montana*, Sm.; the Wych Elm (No. 2075 from Germany); and *U. effusa*, Willd., which are all described in Brandis, pp. 431 to 433.

Heartwood grey. Annual rings consisting of an inner porous belt with numerous large pores, and an outer belt of firm texture with small pores arranged in wavy concentric or oblique lines. Medullary rays moderately broad. Pores marked on a longitudinal section. The wood of *U. lancifolia* and *U. integrifolia* differs from that of the European and North-West Indian elms.

1. U. Wallichiana, Planch.; Brandis 432. Vern. *Káin, bren, brera, bránkul, amrái, marári, marrún, marazh, makshári, manderung, maldung, shko, kummar, hembra*, Pb.; *Mored, pabúna, chambar máya*, Hind.

A large deciduous tree. Bark grey, rough, with diagonal cracks, exfoliating in diamond-shaped scales. Heartwood greyish brown, moderately hard. Annual rings marked by a soft porous belt in the spring wood, the outer part of the annual ring consisting of firm and very hard tissue. Pores in spring wood moderate-sized and large, closely packed, in the autumn wood small and very small, arranged in oblique, undulating, concentric lines. Medullary rays fine and moderately broad, marked on a radial section as long narrow bands.

North-West Himalaya, from the Indus to Nepal, between 3,500 and 10,000 feet. Growth slow; countings on our three specimens gave: H 59, 15 rings; H 122, 10½ rings; and H 917, 25½ rings per inch of radius; the average of the three is therefore about 17 rings per inch of radius. The tree often reaches a large size, 80 to 90 feet in height, with a girth of 16 to 24 feet. The average weight of our three specimens is 36 lbs. per cubic foot. The wood is used locally in places where deodar is not available and *Pinus excelsa* not very abundant, such as in Hazara, where it finds a ready sale at from Rs. 3 to Rs. 5 per tree. It certainly seems worthy of more attention. The bark contains a strong fibre which is made into cordage, sandals and slow matches. The leaves are lopped for cattle fodder.

		lbs.
H 59.	Nagkanda, Simla, 8,000 feet	40
H 122.	Manali, Kulu, 7,000 feet	35
H 917.	Hazara, 7,000 feet	32
H 3175.	Dungagalli, Hazara, 7,000 feet	...

2. U. sp.; Brandis 433 (note under *U. campestris*) Vern. *Yúmbok*, Ladak; *Brán, brahmi, kái, morún, marál, maúru, mannu, mandu, mamji, marn, meru, merinu, bhamji, bhamni, chipál*, Pb.

(On specimens of this tree sent to Kew lately, Prof. Oliver reported: "This Elm is the *U. pedunculata*, Fouq., of the Herbarium Hooker fil. and Thomson. I think it is *not* the *U. pedunculata*, Fouq., of Central Europe and Asia, but probably a distinct species near to *U. campestris*.")

A shrub or small tree. Bark brown, surface whitish, between deep, dark-coloured, longitudinal, regular furrows, running diagonally into each other. Wood grey with darker streaks, hard, otherwise the structure is the same as that of *U. Wallichiana.*

Kulu and Hazara.

Growth, our specimens shewed a slightly faster rate than those of *U. Wallichiana.* No. H 123 gave 16 and H 918, 9 rings per inch of radius. Weight, 34 to 37 lbs. per cubic foot. Wood not used, but considered better than that of *U. Wallichiana;* our specimens, however, do not shew this superiority.

		lbs.
H 123.	Manali, Kulu, 7,000 feet	37
H 918.	Hazara, 7,000 feet	34
H 3164.	Dungagalli, Hazara, 7,000 feet	...

3. **U. lancifolia,** Roxb. Fl. Ind. ii. 66; Kurz ii. 473; Gamble 72. Vern. *Lapi,* Nep.; *Thalai,* Burm.

A large tree. Bark brown, thick. Wood light red, hard. Pores small, usually surrounded by white tissue and joined by white concentric lines which are sometimes broken. Medullary rays fine to moderately broad, the distance between them about equal to the transverse diameter of the pores.

North-East Himalaya from Sikkim to Assam, Chittagong and Burma.

E 3343. Singtam, Darjeeling, 1,500 feet.

4. **U. integrifolia,** Roxb. Fl. Ind. ii. 68; Beddome t. 310; Brandis 431; Kurz ii. 473. *Holoptelea integrifolia,* Planch.; DC. Prodr. xvii. 164; Wight Ic., t. 1968. Vern. *Papri, khulen, arján, rajáin, kachám,* Pb.; *Papar, kanju,* Kumaun; *Papri, dhamna, kúnj, karanji, chilbil, chilmil, kúmba, kúnja náli, kandru, begana,* Hind.; *Chilla* Banda; *Karinji,* Gondi; *Karanjel,* Kurku; *Aya,* Tam.; *Namli, navili, nali, pedda-nowli-eragu,* Tel.; *Wawali,* Mar.; *Ras bija,* Kan.; *Thapsi,* Mysore, Coorg; *Kaládri,* Hassan; *Dadahirilla,* Cingh.; *Myoukseit,* Burm.

A large deciduous tree. Bark ½ inch thick, whitish grey, exfoliating in long, irregular flakes, soft, with an offensive smell when fresh, like the leaves and branchlets. Wood light yellowish grey, moderately hard, no heartwood. Annual rings indistinct. Pores small, uniformly distributed, joined by very fine and often faint lines of soft texture, frequently filled with a snow-white substance, marked on a vertical section. Medullary rays fine, undulating, uniform, equidistant, visible on a radial section; the distance between the rays equal to the transverse diameter of the pores.

Sub-Himalayan tract from the Beas eastwards, Central and South India, Burma.

Growth moderately fast, averaging 6 rings per inch of radius, some specimens shewing as little as 2 rings. Weight, 39 lbs. per cubic foot. The wood is used for building, carts, and carving. The leaves are lopped for cattle fodder. An oil is extracted from the seed in the Melghát.

		lbs.
P 445.	Ajmere	42
O 264.	Garhwal (1868)	46
O 3002.	„ (1874)	41
O 392.	Oudh	34
C 1148.	Ahiri Reserve, Central Provinces	37
C 1181.	„ „ „	37
B 1416.	Tharrawaddi, Burma	42
B 1410.	„ „	41

12. CELTIS, Tournefort.

Contains about 8 species, which are very difficult to distinguish, cf. Brandis, p. 429. A rough key to the general characters of the leaves is, however, given; it may be useful in ascertaining the species.

Leaves evergreen, entire	*C. Wightii.*
Leaves semi-deciduous, serrate	*C. cinnamomea.*
Leaves deciduous, serrate—	
Leaves lanceolate, long-acuminate	*C. eriocarpa.*
Leaves oblong, lanceolate, cuspidate	*C. Hamiltonii.*
Leaves ovate or ovate-oblong—	
Leaves penniveined—	
Leaves of perigonium obtuse . .	*C. australis.*
Leaves of perigonium acute . .	*C. tetrandra.*
Leaves with 3 nerves—	
Leaves sub-cordate at base . .	*C. Roxburghii.*
Leaves rhomboid	*C. caucasica.*

C. cinnamomea, Ldl.; Kurz ii. 472 is a tree of Northern and Eastern Bengal, Chittagong and Burma, the leaves semi-deciduous at the time of flowering. *C. eriocarpa*, Dcne.; Brandis 429. Vern. *Tagha*, Afg.; *Batkar, bat-taman*, Pb.; *Ákata, katáia*, Hind., is a tree of the Punjab Hills, Kumaun, Oudh and Nepal. *C. Hamiltonii*, Planch.; Kurz ii. 472, is a tree of the Khasia Hills and Tenasserim. *C. Roxburghii*, Beddome ccxviii. t. 312; Brandis 429 (*C. trinervia*, Roxb. Fl. Ind. ii. 65; Gamble 72). Vern. *Kharak, batkar, brúmaj, brúndu*, Pb.; *Cheri chara, kathuniar*, C.P.; *Sedongtagla*, Lepcha, is a tree of Eastern Bengal, Central and South India.

Wood light-coloured, moderately hard, no heartwood, seasons well. Annual rings in the species of Europe, Northern India and Bengal, distinctly marked by belts of large pores. The pores in the outer portion of the annual ring small, and generally arranged in groups or oblique tails.

1. C. Wightii, Planchon; Beddome ccxviii; Wight Ic. t. 1969. *Solenostigma Wightii*, Bl.; Kurz ii. 471. Vern. *Vella-thorasay*, Tam.; *Tella-káká-mushti*, Tel.

A small evergreen tree. Wood greyish white, very hard, close-grained. Annual rings indistinctly marked by a narrow belt without pores. Pores small, enclosed in narrow, undulating, concentric, interrupted lines of soft tissue. Medullary rays fine, numerous, uniform and equidistant.

Mountains of South India, Andaman Islands.
Weight, 53 lbs. per cubic foot.

	lbs.
D 1089. Madura, Madras	53

2. C. australis, Linn.; Brandis 428. Vern. *Kharak*, Simla, Kumaun; *Tagho, takhúm*, Afg.;

A moderate-sized deciduous tree. Bark bluish grey. Wood grey or yellowish grey, with irregular streaks of darker colour. Annual rings marked by an irregular belt of moderate-sized and large pores. Pores moderate-sized and large, gradually getting smaller towards the outer limit of each annual ring, where they are very small and arranged in wavy, interrupted, concentric lines. Medullary rays moderately broad and fine.

Suliman and Salt Ranges, Himalaya from the Indus to Bhutan ascending to 8,500 feet, Khasia Hills.

Growth moderate, 8 to 9 rings per inch of radius. Weight, 47 lbs. per cubic foot; Mathieu Fl. For., p. 257, gives 37 to 50 lbs. The wood is tough and strong, and is used for oars, whip handles and for other purposes requiring toughness and elasticity. The tree is largely planted about villages in the North-West Himalaya for shade and fodder.

		lbs.
H 36.	Julung, Simla, 5,000 feet	47

3. C. tetrandra, Roxb. Fl. Ind. ii. 63; Brandis 429; Kurz ii. 472; Gamble 72. *C. serotina,* Planch.; Beddome ccxviii. Vern. *Kúmsúm, sungsúm,* Lepcha; *Haktapatia,* Ass.

A tall tree. Wood greyish white, moderately hard. Pores numerous, frequently subdivided, those of the inner edge of each annual ring large, forming a narrow, porous belt; those of the outer portion moderate-sized and arranged in oblique wavy lines. Medullary rays moderately broad and fine, prominent on a radial section as long, narrow plates.

Outer Himalaya, from Kumaun eastwards, Western Ghâts.

Growth moderate, 5 to 10 rings per inch of radius. Weight, 36 to 37 lbs. per cubic foot. Used in Assam for planking and canoes.

		lbs.
E 669.	Bamunpokri Forest, Darjeeling Terai	36
E 707.	Great Rangit Valley, Darjeeling	37

4. C. caucasica, Willd.; Brandis 429. Vern. *Batker,* Pb.

A moderate-sized tree, with grey bark ¼ inch thick. Wood light yellow, hard to very hard. Structure resembling that of *C. australis,* but the pores on the inner edge of each annual ring are very large, and consequently very prominent on a vertical section. Medullary rays broader and further apart than in *C. australis.*

Afghanistan, Beluchistan, Salt Range, Hazara, Kashmir.

Growth moderate, 10 rings per inch of radius. Weight, 44 lbs. per cubic foot.

		lbs.
H 932.	Hazara	44
H 3169.	Dungagalli, Hazara	...

13. SPONIA, Comm.

Wood light-coloured, no heartwood, soft or moderately hard. Pores small or moderate-sized. Medullary rays fine and moderately broad.

1. S. orientalis, Planchon; Beddome ccxix.; Brandis 430; Gamble 72. *Celtis orientalis,* Linn.; Roxb. Fl. Ind. ii. 65. *Trema orientalis,* Bl.; Kurz ii. 468. *S. Wightii,* Planch.; Beddome t. 311, and *S. amboinensis,* Dcne (*S. velutina,* Planch.), are probably not specifically distinct. Indian Nettle Tree. Vern. *Badu manu,* C.P.; *Kooail,* Nep.; *Tugla,* Lepcha; *Param,* Mechi; *Jupong, phakram, jigini, sapong, sempak, amphak, opang* (see Agri-Horticultural Society of India Proceedings for November 1877), Ass.; *Mini,* Tam.; *Gada-nelli,* Tel.; *Gorklu,* Kan.; *Gol,* Mar.; *Rukni,* Baigas.

A small fast-growing and short-lived tree. Bark thin, greyish brown, with numerous lenticels. Wood light reddish grey, soft. Pores moderate-sized, often subdivided, uniformly distributed. Medullary rays fine, numerous, uniform, very prominent on a radial section, the distance between the rays generally equal to or greater than the transverse diameter of the pores.

Himalaya from Nepal eastwards, Bengal, Burma, Central and Southern India.

Growth extremely fast. The tree from which our specimen was cut, and which was growing in front of the Sivoke Forest House, had attained in five years a height of 25 feet and about 40 inches in girth, equivalent to less than one ring per inch of radius. Weight, 28 lbs. per cubic foot. The wood is used for charcoal, which is good for gunpowder manufacture. The bark gives a fibre which is used to tie the rafters of native houses and for carrying loads; and in Assam for making the coarse *Amphak* cloth. VanSomeren says it is often allowed to grow for shade in the Mysore and Coorg coffee plantations, and is there called the 'Charcoal Tree.' Brandis says the same has been done in Wynaad. It comes up self-sown in forest clearings and waste places, often in great profusion, and may be much utilized in plantations to help to keep down the grass jungle.

	lbs.
E 2446. Sivoke, Darjeeling Terai	28

2. S. politoria, Planch.; Brandis 430; Gamble 72. Vern. *Bantamman, kanglu, khúri,* Pb.; *Jáún, khasaroa, márni, bátu, banharria,* Hind.; *Kháoi, khάksi, kooail,* Nep.; *Tuksat,* Lepcha.

A small evergreen tree. Bark smooth, or with longitudinal wrinkles, inner bark red. Wood white, moderately hard, splits and cracks in seasoning. Annual rings marked by a belt of firmer tissue on the outer edge of each ring. Pores small, often subdivided, uniformly distributed. Medullary rays fine and moderately broad.

Salt Range, Outer Himalaya, Oudh, Sikkim.

Growth very fast, 2 rings per inch of radius. Weight, 36 lbs. per cubic foot. Wood and bark used in a similar way to those of *S. orientalis.* The leaves are used to polish wood and horn.

	lbs.
O 1369. Gonda, Oudh	36

ORDER XCIII. PLATANEÆ.

1. PLATANUS, Tourn.

P. occidentalis, Linn., is the American Plane, which differs according to Mathieu and Brandis by less deeply lobed leaves, which are pubescent when full grown and by slightly smaller fruit-heads. Mathieu Fl. For., p. 377, gives its weight at 41 lbs. per cubic foot.

1. P. orientalis, Linn.; Brandis 434. Vern. *Chinár,* Pers., Afgh.; *Búin, búna, boin,* Kashmir.

A large deciduous tree. Bark $\frac{1}{8}$ inch thick, smooth, light or dark grey, peeling off in large thin scales. Wood white, hard, with a faint tinge of yellow or red. Annual rings marked by a band of firm texture with few pores on the outer edge of each ring. Pores very small, uniform, and uniformly distributed except in the outer band of the autumn wood. Medullary rays broad, equidistant, shewing on a radial section as glossy, irregular, wavy, shining plates.

Cultivated in the North-West Himalaya east to the Sutlej, ascending to 8,300 feet in Ladak. Indigenous in Greece, Macedonia, Armenia and Northern Persia.

Growth rather fast, our specimen shewed 6 rings per inch of radius. Mathieu, Fl. For., p. 374, gives measurement of a tree in the garden of the Forest School at Nancy, which had 88¼ feet in height with a girth of 12·3 feet at the age of 1·30 years; this would be equivalent to 5¼ rings per inch of radius. Measurements of several large trees in Persia, Kashmir and Chamba are given by Brandis, p. 435.

Weight, our specimen gives 41 lbs. per cubic foot; experiments made in 1879 at Kandahar by Captain Call, R.E. (Indian Forester, vol. v., p. 478), with bars 1 ft. × 1 in. × 1 in. gave an average weight of 38·8 lbs., P = 587. Mathieu gives 41 to

49 lbs. It is used in Kashmir for boxes, trays, pen-cases and other articles, which are lacquered and painted. It has a pretty grain and may be recommended for cabinet-work.

	lbs.
H 922. Hazara	41

ORDER XCIV. CASUARINACEÆ.

One genus, containing chiefly Australian trees, one species only extending northwards to India. Several other species, however, have been introduced and grown in India.

1. CASUARINA, Linn.

1. C. equisetifolia, Forster; Beddome ccxxvi.; Brandis 435; Kurz ii. 494. *C. muricata,* Roxb. Fl. Ind. iii. 519. The Beefwood of Australia. Vern. *Chouk,* Tam.; *Serva,* Tel.; *Kásrike,* Mysore; *Tinyu,* Burm.; *Aru,* Malay.

A large evergreen tree, with leafless drooping branches, and branchlets which are deciduous and perform the functions of leaves. Wood white, brown near the centre, very hard, cracks and splits. Pores moderate-sized, in radial and oblique lines. Medullary rays very fine, uniform, equidistant. Numerous wavy, concentric lines, composed of soft tissue and minute pores.

Coasts of Chittagong, Burma, the Malay Archipelago, North Australia and Queensland. Cultivated all over India, except in the North-Western portion of the Punjab.

The growth is fast, our specimen shews 3 to 4 rings per inch of radius. From Colonel Beddome's Report on the plantations in the North Arcot District, dated December 30th, 1876, the measurements of trees in two plantations were—

	Age.	Height.	Girth.
Veeringapuram plantation . . .	4 years	32 feet	24 inches at 3 feet.
Trivellam „ . . .	6 „	70-80 „	36-48 „ „

which would shew an average growth of 1 ring per inch of radius, or a girth of 6 feet at 22 years of age.

The wood is hard and heavy, and difficult to cut, and according to Skinner, No. 42 weighs 55 lbs. per cubic foot; our specimen gives 62 lbs. M. Sebert in 'Notice sur les Bois de la Nouvelle Caledonie' gives 63 lbs. Skinner gives P = 920. It has been largely planted in North Arcot, South Arcot, Madras and other districts of the Madras Presidency for fuel, for which it is excellent, but it requires to be near the sea-coast and to have water at the roots, at least 10 feet from the surface of the ground. Trees planted in sandy soil often suffer much from drought the first two or three years, the taproot then finds its way down to about 10 feet and reaching water the tree begins to thrive. It is of course best near the sea, but fine trees may be seen in places in Northern India, especially at Saharanpur and Umballa. Casuarina seems to coppice well, and undoubtedly is, in suitable localities, and considering its extremely quick growth and the qualities of its wood, one of the most important trees we have for fuel and other plantations.

	lbs.
E 2465. Calcutta	62

ORDER XCV. EUPHORBIACEÆ.

We shall here follow the nomenclature used in Müller's and Boissier's Monographs of this large Order in the Prodromus of DeCandolle, but adding as Sub-Orders the two separate Orders described in Vol. XVI, *viz., Daphniphyllaceæ* and *Buxaceæ.*

The Order then contains 57 genera belonging to 9 tribes. It contains many important species, though with the exception of *Bischoffia* and *Briedelia* and, of course, Boxwood, few are specially remarkable for their timber. Oils are given by *Ricinus*, *Croton* and *Aleurites*. *Mallotus philippinensis* gives a red dye. *Phyllanthus Emblica* gives a fruit which is one of the myrabolams used in tanning, while several species in other parts of the world furnish India-rubber.

SUB-ORDER I. EUPHORBIACEÆ.

Tribe I.—Phyllantheæ . . .	*Actephila, Andrachne, Sauropus, Antidesma, Phyllanthus, Melanthesopsis, Breynia, Putranjiva, Securinega, Baccaurea, Aporosa, Hymenocardia, Bischoffia, Cyclostemon, Hemicyclia.*
„ II.—Bridelieæ . . .	*Briedelia, Cleistanthus, Lebedieropsis.*
„ III.—Crotoneæ . . .	*Croton.*
„ IV.—Acalypheæ . . .	*Aleurites, Agrostistachys, Sarcoclinium, Sumbavia, Cœlodiscus, Cœlodepas, Cephalocroton, Symphyllia, Claoxylon, Acalypha, Alchornea, Cnesmone, Tragia, Trewia, Mallotus, Cleidion, Macaranga, Ricinus, Homonoya.*
„ V.—Hippomaneæ . .	*Bennettia, Microdesmis, Manihot, Jatropha, Trigonostemon, Givotia, Ostodes, Codiæum, Chætocarpus, Mischodon, Baliospermum, Gelonium, Excæcaria.*
„ VI.—Dalechampieæ . .	*Dalechampia.*
„ VII.—Euphorbieæ . . .	*Pedilanthus, Euphorbia*

SUB-ORDER II. DAPHNIPHYLLACEÆ.

Tribe VIII.—Daphniphylleæ . .	*Daphniphyllum.*

SUB-ORDER III. BUXACEÆ.

Tribe IX.—Buxeæ . . .	*Buxus, Sarcococca.*

Actephila contains 4 or 5 large shrubs or small trees. *A. excelsa*, Dalz.; Beddome clxxxix., is a small tree of the Western Ghâts. *A. Thomsoni*, Müll. Arg.; Beddome cxc., is a shrub of Mysore and the Carnatic. *A. Javanica*, Miq., and *A puberula*, Kurz ii. 340-1, are shrubs of the Andaman Islands. *Sauropus* contains 6 species, the most important of which is *S. albicans*, Bl.; Kurz ii. 349; Gamble 69. Vern. *Yoma hinyo*, Burm.; *Sentungrung*, Lepcha, a common undershrub of forests in Bengal and Burma. *Melanthesopsis patens*, Müll. Arg.; Beddome cxcvi.; Brandis 455; Kurz ii. 348; Gamble 68 (*Phyllanthus patens*, Roxb. Fl. Ind. iii. 667) Vern. *Ikti*, Lepcha, is a shrub of Bengal, South India and Burma; and *M. fruticosa*, Müll. Arg.; Kurz ii. 349 (*Phyllanthus reclinatus*, Roxb. Fl. Ind. iii. 669), is a small shrub of the Martaban Hills. *Breynia rhamnoides*, Müll. Arg.; Beddome cxcvi.; Brandis 456; Kurz ii. 350 (*Phyllanthus vitis-idæa*, Roxb. Fl. Ind. iii. 665) Vern. *Tikhar*, Hind.; *Kamkata Juli*, Beng.; *Yerra púrúgúdú*, Tel.; *Gong-nyin-ya*, Burm., is a small tree of Oudh, Bengal, South India, Arracan and the Andamans, with a white, hard, durable wood. *Hymenocardia Wallichii*, Tul.; Kurz ii. 394. Vern. *Ye-kin*, Burm.; and *H. plicata*, Kurz ii. 395. Vern. *Ye-chin*, Burm., are trees of the swamp forests in Burma. *Cyclostemon* contains 5 species: *C. indicus*, Müll. Arg.; Beddome cxcix., is a tree of Sikkim, the Khasia Hills and South India; *C. macrophyllus*, Bl.; Beddome t. 278; Kurz ii. 364, a tree of the Western Ghâts and the Andaman Islands; *C. eglandulosus*, Kurz ii. 364, is an evergreen tree of Arracan; *C. malabaricus*, Bedd., of the Tinnevelly Ghâts, and *C. subsessilis*, Kurz ii. 364; Gamble 69. Vern. *Ban bokul*, Beng.; *Bway champ*, *asura*, Nep., a small tree of Sikkim, Eastern Bengal and Burma, with a brown close-grained wood. *Hemicyclia* contains 5 species: *H. elata*, Beddome, t. 279, is a large, and *H. venusta*, Wight, a small, tree of the Western Ghâts; *H. sumatrana*, Müll. Arg.; Kurz ii. 365, is a tree of Burma, and *H. andamanica*, Kurz, of the Andaman Islands; while *H. sepiaria*, W. and A., is a tree of Southern India and Ceylon.

Aleurites moluccana, Willd.; Beddome t. 276; Kurz ii. 377 (*A. triloba*, Forst.; Roxb. Fl. Ind. iii. 629) Vern. *Akrot*, is a handsome tree introduced from the Malay Archipelago and now found in cultivation or run wild in many parts of South India.

It is called the 'Belgaum Walnut,' and is so called from the nuts resembling the walnut in flavour. These nuts contain about 50 per cent of oil, which is extracted and used for food and for burning. In M. Sebert's 'Notice sur les bois de la Nouvelle Calédonie,' the wood is said to be white, soft, light and of bad quality, and to have a mean weight of 38 lbs. per cubic foot. *A. cordata*, Müll. Arg., is found in Nepal. *Agrostistachys indica*, Dalz.; Beddome ccv. (*A. longifolia*, Kurz ii. 377) is a small evergreen tree of the Western Gháts, Ceylon, Burma and the Andamans. *Sarcoclinium longifolium*, Wight; Beddome ccv., is a small tree of the Nilgiri Hills and Ceylon, from 4,000 to 6,000 feet. *Sumbavia macrophylla*, Müll. Arg, Kurz ii. 376, is an evergreen tree of the tropical forests of Burma. Of *Cœlodiscus*, Kurz describes 5 new species from Burma, all shrubs. *Cœlodepas calycinum*, Beddome ccvii. t. 320. Vern. *Kátpira*, is a small hard-wooded tree of the Tinnevelly Hills. *Cephalocroton* contains 2 species: *C. leucocephalus*, Baill.; Beddome ccvi., of the Nilgiris; and *C. indicus*, Beddome t. 261, a moderate-sized tree of the Western Gháts, said to give a good building timber. Of *Symphyllia* 2 species are found: *S. mallotiformis*, Müll. Arg.; Beddome ccvii., in the Nilgiris; and *S. silhetana*, Baill.; Kurz ii. 378, in the Khasia Hills, Eastern Bengal and Tenasserim. *Claoxylon* contains 3 and *Acalypha* 1 (*A. fruticosa*, Forsk.) shrub of the forests of Burma. *Tragia* contains 2 and *Cnesmone* 1 (*C. javanica*, Bl.) climbing shrubs of Burma. *Alchornea* contains 3 shrubs: *A. mollis*, Müll. Arg., of Nepal; *A. rugosa*, Müll. Arg., of Tenasserim and the Andamans, and *A. tiliæfolia*, Müll. Arg.; Kurz ii. 386; Gamble 71, of Sikkim, the Khasia Hills, Sylhet, Tenasserim and the Andamans. *Cleidion Javanicum*, Bl.; Beddome t. 272; Kurz ii. 390; Gamble 70, is a tree of Northern and Eastern Bengal, South India and Burma.

Bennettia Wallichii, R. Br. (*Galearia Wallichii*, Kurz ii. 407) and *Microdesmis caseariæfolia*, Planch.; Kurz ii. 408, are small trees of the forests of Tenasserim. *Manihot utilissima*, Pohl.; Kurz ii. 408. Vern. *Pulu pinan myouk*, Burm., is a shrub of tropical America, introduced and cultivated in Burma. It yields 'the manioc', or 'cassava' meal and 'tapioca.' *Trigonostemon* contains about 6 species, the chief of which is *T. Lawianus*, Nimmo; Beddome t. 273, a small tree of the Western Gháts and Ceylon. *Codiæum* contains 4 species: *C. umbellatum*, Müll. Arg.; Beddome ccxiii. of the Western Gháts, one species in Burma and two in the Andaman Islands. This genus gives the ornamental variegated-leaved plants called 'Crotons,' now so much cultivated in Indian gardens. *Mischodon zeylanicus*, Thw.; Beddome t. 290. Vern. *Tamana*, Cingh., is a handsome large tree of Ceylon, with good timber; it has been found by Beddome in Tinnevelly. *Baliospermum* contains 3 undershrubs of Northern and Eastern Bengal, the commonest of which, *B. montanum*, Müll. Arg. (*Croton polyandrum*, Roxb. Fl. Ind. iii. 682; Gamble 70). Vern. *Hakún*, Hind.; *Konda-amadum*, Tel; *Poguntig*, Lepcha, extends to South India and Burma.

Dalechampia scandens, Linn.; Kurz ii. 400, is a climbing shrub of Burma, *Pedilanthus tithymaloides*, Poir.; Kurz ii. 418, is a short rather fleshy shrub often cultivated in Burma. *Daphniphyllum glaucescens*, Bl.; Beddome ccxvii. t. 288. Vern. *Nir-chappay*, Burghers, is a handsome tree of the Western Gháts; and *D. himalayense*, Müll. Arg. Vern. *Raktchandan, rakt anglia*, Kumaun, is a tree of the Himalaya from Kumaun eastwards and the Khasia Hills found above 5,000 feet altitude.

Several exotic trees belonging to this family have been introduced, and an attempt made at their cultivation in India *Hevea braziliensis*, Müll. Arg.; and other species of *Hevea* give the Brazilian caoutchouc. That named is the Para rubber, and is now being grown for distribution in the Botanic Gardens, Calcutta, from plants received in 1877. The 'Ceara' caoutchouc, a species of *Manihot*, probably *M. Glaziovii*, is also being grown. The very interesting account of their collection by Mr. Cross may be found at vol. iv, No. 1, p. 5 of the 'Indian Forester' for 1878, and an account of their state on arrival in India in Dr. King's annual report of the Botanic Gardens at Calcutta for the year 1877-78.

The great majority of the woody Euphorbiaceæ the wood of which is here described, belonging to the following genera—*Antidesma, Baccaurea, Bischoffia, Cleistanthus, Excæcaria, Homonoya, Jatropha, Lebidieropsis, Macaranga, Mallotus, Ostodes, Putranjiva, Trewia*—may, as regards the structure of their wood, be said to belong to one type, which is characterised as follows:

Very fine, or extremely fine, and closely packed medullary rays. Pores small or very small, often in radial lines.

The genera *Phyllanthus* and *Briedelia* differ by having their medullary rays broader and further apart.

The genera *Securinega, Andrachne, Buxus* and *Sarcococca* have very small or extremely small pores, and fine to extremely fine medullary rays.

Croton and *Chætocarpus* have extremely fine and closely packed medullary rays, but the wood is marked by wavy concentric lines, which are wanting in other genera of Euphorbiaceæ.

Givotia has scanty pores and short distant medullary rays.

Of these genera only *Lebidieropsis* and *Bischoffia* have a distinct heartwood, some of the others have darker coloured wood near the centre.

1. ANDRACHNE, Linn.

Two shrubs. *A. telephioides*, Linn.; Brandis 457, is a small undershrub of the Punjab Salt Range.

1. A. cordifolia, Müll. Arg.; Brandis 456. Vern. *Kúrkni, gúrgúli,* Jhelam; *Bersu,* Chenab; *Barotri, madáre,* Ravi; *Mútkar, chírmútti, pín,* Beas; *Tsátin,* Sutlej.

A small shrub. Wood white, moderately hard, close-grained. Pores very small and extremely small, larger and more numerous in the inner belt of the annual rings. Medullary rays extremely fine, very numerous.

North-West Himalaya, from the Indus to Nepal, ascending to 8,000 feet.
Weight, 45 lbs.

	lbs.
H 2945. Jander, Sutlej Valley, 3,500 feet	45

2. ANTIDESMA, Burm.

About 14 species. *A. refractum*, Müll. Arg., is a small tree of Sikkim, at about 2,000 feet. *A. nigricans*, Tul.. and *A. simile*, Müll Arg., are small trees of Sylhet and *A. oblongatum*, Müll. Arg., of the Khasia Hills. *A. martabanicum*, Presl., and *A. molle*, Müll. Arg. (*A. velutinosum*, Bl.; Kurz ii. 359) are small trees of Tenasserim. *A. velutinum*, Tul.; Kurz ii. 359. Vern. *Kin-pa-lin,* Burm., is a small evergreen tree of river banks in Burma; and *A. fruticulosum*, Kurz ii. 359, of tidal forests in Pegu. *A. lanceolatum*, Tul.; Beddome cci., is a small tree of the Nilgiri Hills.

Wood hard, smooth, apt to split and warp. Pores small, numerous. Medullary rays of two classes, very fine, and moderately broad.

1. A. Ghæsembilla, Gaertn.; Beddome cc.; Brandis 446; Kurz ii. 358. *A. pubescens,* Willd., and *A. paniculatum,* Roxb. Fl. Ind. iii. 769, 770. Vern. *Khúdi jamb, limtoá,* Beng.; *Umtoá,* Hazaribagh; *Pulsur, polari, jana-pa-laseru, pollai,* Tel.; *Jondri,* Mar.; *Byaitsin,* Burm.; *Boo-ambilla,* Cingh.

A small deciduous tree, with grey or pale brown bark, $\frac{1}{6}$ inch thick, with a few deciduous scales. Wood red, with darker coloured heartwood, smooth, hard, close and even grained. Annual rings indistinctly marked by concentric lines. Pores small and moderate-sized, uniformly distributed. Medullary rays of two sizes, few moderately broad rays with numerous fine rays between them, prominent on a radial section.

Nepal, Oudh, Bengal, Burma, Chanda district and South India.
Weight, 49 lbs. per cubic foot. The leaves are eaten in Bengal.

		lbs.
C 1161.	Ahiri Reserve, Central Provinces	46
B 2246.	Andaman Islands (1866)	52

2. E 2430 (46 lbs.) from the Chenga Forest, Darjeeling, has a similar structure. It is marked *A. Bunias*, Spr.; Beddome cc.; Kurz. ii. 358; Gamble 69. Vern. *Himalcheri*, Nep.; *Kantjer*, Lepcha. A small tree of Northern and Eastern Bengal, South India and Tenasserim.

3. A. Menasu, Müll. Arg.; Kurz ii. 360; Gamble 69. Vern. *Kumbyúng, tungcher*, Lepcha; *Kin-pa-lin*, Burm.

A small tree. Bark thin. Wood red, structure similar to that of *A. Ghæsembilla*, but the pores smaller and the medullary rays finer.

Sikkim, Khasia Hills, Burma and the Andaman Islands.
Weight, 52 lbs. per cubic foot. Fruit eaten.

		lbs.
E 2431.	Chenga Forest, Darjeeling	52

4. A. diandrum, Tulasne; Beddome cci.; Brandis 447; Kurz ii. 360; Gamble 69. *Stilago diandra*, Roxb. Fl. Ind. iii. 759. Vern. *Amli, amári, sarshoti, gúr mussureya, ban mussureya, dhakki*, Hind.; *Mutta*, Beng.; *Patimil*, Nep.; *Kantjer*, Lepcha; *Nuniári*, Uriya; *Pellagumudu*, Tel.; *Masúr bauri*, Gondi; *Kin-pa-lin*, Burm.

A small tree with smooth grey bark; inner bark pale red, fibrous. Wood pinkish grey, hard, close-grained. Pores small and very small, uniformly distributed. Medullary rays of two sizes, moderately broad and very fine, wavy. Annual rings marked by a fine line.

Garhwal, Kumaun, Oudh, Bengal, South India and Burma.
Weight, 41 lbs. per cubic foot. The leaves are acid and are eaten; they resemble sorrel and are made into chutni. The fruit is eaten.

		lbs.
O 1368.	Gonda, Oudh	42
O 1464.	Bahraich, Oudh	40

3. PHYLLANTHUS, Linn.

A large genus formed by the grouping together of several genera or sections, such as *Glochidion, Phyllanthus, Emblica*, etc. It contains 43 Indian species of trees or shrubs, which are thus arranged by Müller:—

SECTION I. EUGLOCHIDION.

P. multilocularis, Müll. Arg.	Bengal, Burma.
(*P. calocarpus*, Kurz)	Andamans.
P. coccineus, Müll. Arg.	Bengal, Burma.
P. zeylanicus, Müll. Arg.	South India, Andamans.
(*P. andamanicus*, Kurz)	Andamans.
P. nitidus, Müll. Arg.	South India.
P. lanceolarius, Müll. Arg.	North India, Bengal, Burma.
P. tomentosus, Müll. Arg.	South India.
P. canaranus, Müll. Arg.	Ditto.
P. Helferi, Müll. Arg.	Burma, Andamans.
P. subscandens, Müll. Arg.	Burma.

SECTION II. HEMIGLOCHIDION.

P. Hohenackeri, Müll. Arg.	South India.
P. fagifolius, Müll. Arg.	Bengal, Burma, South India.
P. nepalensis, Müll. Arg.	North India, Bengal.

P. Thomsoni, Müll. Arg.	Bengal.
P. sphærogynus, Müll. Arg.	Burma.
P. asperus, Müll. Arg.	South India.
P. sylheticus, Müll. Arg.	Bengal.
P. assamicus, Müll. Arg.	Ditto.
P. glaucifolius, Müll. Arg.	Burma.
P. neilgherrensis, Müll. Arg.	South India.
P. arboreus, Müll. Arg.	Ditto.
P. stellatus, Retz.	Bengal.
P. malabaricus, Müll. Arg.	South India.
P. Perrottetianus, Müll. Arg.	Ditto.
P. velutinus, Müll. Arg.	Bengal, South India.
P. Daltoni, Müll. Arg.	Bengal, Burma, South India.
P. Heyneanus, Müll. Arg.	South India.
P. bicolor, Müll. Arg.	Bengal.
P. khasicus, Müll. Arg	Ditto.
(*P. dasystylus*, Kurz)	Burma.
(*P. leiostylus*, Kurz)	Ditto.

SECTION III. KIRGANELIA.

P. reticulatus, Müll. Arg.	All India and Burma.

SECTION IV. EMBLICA.

P. Emblica, Linn.	All India and Burma.
P. polyphyllus, Willd.	South India.
P. bæobotryoides, Müll. Arg.	Bengal, Burma.
P. columnaris, Müll. Arg.	Burma.

SECTION V. PARAPHYLLANTHUS.

P. juniperinoides, Müll. Arg.	South India.

SECTION VI. CICCA.

P. distichus, Müll. Arg.	India, Burma, Andamans.
P. cyanospermus, Müll. Arg.	South India.
P. indicus, Müll. Arg.	Ditto.
(*P. albizzioides*, Kurz)	Burma.
(*P. macrocarpus*, Kurz)	Ditto.

Thus it will be seen that 4 species are found in North-West India, 16 in Northern and Eastern Bengal, 21 in South India, 18 in Burma, and 5 in the Andaman Islands. Few of them are of much importance. *P. lanceolarius*, Müll. Arg.; Brandis 453; Gamble 68 (*Glochidion lanceolarium*, Dalz.; Beddome cxcii.; Kurz 343. *Bradleia lanceolaria*, Roxb. Fl. Ind. iii. 697) Vern. *Anguti*, *bhauri*, Beng.; *Bangikat*, Nep.; *Fagiri*, Lepcha; *Tsekoban*, Magh; *Bhoma*, Bombay, is a small tree of the Sub-Himalayan tract, from Kumaun eastwards, Eastern Bengal, South India and Burma, with a hard, durable wood. *P. nepalensis*, Müll. Arg.; Brandis 452; Gamble 68 (*G. nepalense*, Kurz ii. 344). Vern. *Gol kamela*, *sama*, *chamar kas*, *amblu*, *kodmil*, Pb.; *Mowa*, *bakalwa*, *kari*, *koria*, Hind.; *Katmowa*, Garhwal; *Gubermowa*, *bair mao* Kumaun; *Latikat*, Nep., is a small tree of the Outer Himalaya and Sub-Himalayan tract from the Indus eastwards. It has a brownish-white wood, and the bark is used for tanning. *P. polyphyllus*, Willd.; Beddome cxc., is a small tree of South India, distinguished from *P. Emblica* by having a dry instead of a fleshy fruit. *P. distichus*, Müll. Arg.; Beddome cxci. (*P. longifolius*, Roxb. Fl. Ind. iii. 672. *Cicca disticha*, Linn.; Kurz ii. 353) Vern. *Loda*, *nori*, Beng.; *Harfaruri*, *chalmeri*, Hind.; *Russa-usareki*, Tel. *Arunelli*, Tam.; *Kirnelli*, Mysore; *Thin-bo-zi-pyoo*, Burm., is a small tree, cultivated in South India, Burma and the Andaman Islands for the sake of its fruit.

Wood red, splits and warps. No heartwood. Pores moderate-sized, subdivided. Medullary rays moderately broad, distant, prominent on a vertical section, giving the wood a mottled appearance.

1. **P. Emblica,** Linn.; Roxb. Fl. Ind. iii. 671; Beddome t. 258;

Brandis 454; Gamble 68. *Cicca Emblica*, Kurz ii. 352. Vern. *Ambal, ambli*, Pb.; *Daula, amla, amlika, aura, aola, aunra*, Hind.; *Aunla*, Nep.; *Suom*, Lepcha; *Amla, ambolati, amulati*, Beng.; *Ambari*, Gáro; *Amluki*, Ass.; *Alá thanda*, Cuttack; *Nilli, milli, nalli, aunri, usir, lulla*, Gondi; *Aunre*, Kurku; *Nelli, nellekai*, Tam.; *Osirka, usri, asereki*, Tel.; *Nelli, nilika*, Kan.; *Ohalu, gondhona*, Uriya; *Aonli*, Mar.; *Nelli*, Cingh.; *Shabju, tasha*, Burm.

A moderate-sized deciduous tree. Bark somewhat less than ⅛ inch thick, grey, exfoliating in small irregular patches, inner substance red. Wood red, hard, close-grained, warps and splits in seasoning. No heartwood, annual rings not distinct. Pores small and moderate-sized, uniformly distributed, often subdivided or in short radial lines. Medullary rays moderately broad and broad, the distance between two rays generally greater than the transverse diameter of the pores. Medullary rays very prominent on a radial section, giving the wood a handsome mottled appearance.

Dry forests of India and Burma.

The annual rings are not sufficiently distinct in our specimens for counting. Aikin in Wallich's list gives 2·7 rings per inch of radius.

The weight and transverse strength have been determined by the following experiments:—

Experiment by whom made.	Year.	Wood whence procured.	Weight.	No. of experiments.	Size of bar used.	Value of P.
					Ft. in. in.	
Puckle	1859	Mysore	67	2	2 × 1 × 1	975 (?)
Kyd	1831	Assam	45	...	......	617
Skinner, No. 105	1862	South India	46	...	......	562
Cunningham	1864	Gwalior	46	2	2 × 1 × 1	559
R. Thompson	1868	Central Provinces	45	...	......	...
A. Mendis	1855	Ceylon	49	...	......	...
Brandis (No. 98)	1862	Burma	35	...	......	...
Warth	1878	Different Provs.	51	8	......	...

The wood is durable under water, and is used for well-work; also for agricultural implements, building and furniture.

The bark is used for tanning and in medicine; chips of the wood are said to clear muddy water. The fruit is the Emblic Myrobolam, and is used as a medicine, for dyeing, tanning, and for food and preserves. It gives a gum, which is not used.

			lbs.
P	104.	Bhajji, Simla, 3,000 feet	56
P	438.	Ajmere	...
O	252.	Garhwal (1868)	49
O	539.	Dehra Dún	48
E	580.	Khookloong Forest, Darjeeling Terai	56
E	2432.	Bamunpokri, Darjeeling Terai	48
C	1126.	Ahiri Reserve, Central Provinces	51
C	2738.	Moharli Reserve, Central Provinces	56
C	841.	Bairagarh Reserve, Berar	45
C	2774.	Melghát, Berar	...
No.	61.	Ceylon Collection	56

2. P. Thomsoni, Müll. Arg.; Gamble 68. Vern. *Latikat*, Nep.
A small tree. Wood red, structure the same as that of *P. Emblica*.

Sikkim and the Khasia Hills.
Weight, 42 lbs. per cubic foot.

		lbs.
E 2434.	Bamunpokri, Darjeeling Terai	42

3. **P. bicolor**, Müll. Arg.; Brandis 453; Gamble 68. Vern. *Latikat, lakrikat*, Nep.; *Kair, tetrikair*, Lepcha.

An evergreen tree, with thin, grey bark. Wood red or reddish grey, hard. Pores small and moderate-sized, uniformly distributed. Medullary rays fine and moderately broad, numerous, very prominent on a radial section, giving the wood a mottled appearance.

Nepal, Sikkim, and Khasia Hills, ascending to 7,000 feet.
Growth moderate, 8 rings per inch of radius.
Weight, 37 to 47 lbs. per cubic foot.

		lbs.
E 685.	Sepoydura forest, Darjeeling, 5,500 feet	37
E 2433.	Tukdah Forest, Darjeeling, 6,000 feet	47

4. **P. reticulatus**, Poiret; Beddome exc.; Brandis 453; Gamble 68. *P. multiflorus*, Roxb. Fl. Ind. iii. 664. *Cicca reticulata*, Kurz ii. 354. Vern. *Panjúle, mákhi*, Hind.; *Nella púrúdúdú, phulsar*, Tel.; *Welkyla*, Cingh.

A straggling shrub. Bark brown, thin. Wood white or greyish white, hard, close-grained. Pores small, scanty, more numerous in the spring wood, marking thus the annual rings. Medullary rays fine, numerous, wavy.

Common in most parts of India and Burma, especially along river banks.

E 3362. Dhupguri, W. Dúars.

4. PUTRANJIVA, Wall.

1. **P. Roxburghii**, Wall.; Beddome t. 275; Brandis 451; Kurz ii. 366. *Nageia Putranjiva*, Roxb. Fl. Ind. iii. 766. Vern. *Putájan*, Pb.; *Jia puta, joti, júti, pútra-jiva, patji, jivputrak, patigia*, Hind.; *Karupale*, Tam.; *Kadrajuvi*, Tel.; *Pongalam*, Mal.; *Jewan-putr*, Mar.; *Toukyap*, Burm.

A moderate-sized evergreen tree with pendent branches. Bark dark grey. Wood grey, shining, moderately hard, close-grained. Annual rings marked by prominent concentric lines. Pores small to moderate-sized, in radial lines, between closely packed, uniform, fine, medullary rays. Very numerous, very fine transverse bars.

Sub-Himalayan tract from the Chenab eastwards, Oudh, Bengal, Burma and South India.

Growth fast, 4½ rings per inch of radius. Weight, 36·6 lbs. according to Wallich; our specimens give 48 to 49 lbs. The wood is sometimes used for tools and turning. The seeds are strung in rosaries and children's necklaces. The leaves are lopped for fodder.

		lbs.
O 1459.	Bahraich, Oudh	48
O 1477.	Gonda, Oudh	49
E 5469.	Calcutta	48

5. SECURINEGA, Juss.

Three species. *S. grisea*, Müll. Arg., is a shrub of the Khasia Hills.

1. S. obovata, Müll. Arg.; Beddome cxcvii.; Brandis 455; Gamble 68. *Phyllanthus retusus* and *virosus*, Roxb. Fl. Ind. iii. 657, 659. *Cicca obovata*, Kurz ii. 354. Vern. *Dalme, dhâni, bakarcha, ghari, gwala, darim*, Hind.; *Iktibi*, Lepcha; *Ukieng, thaka*, Mechi; *Kodarsi*, Mar.; *Korchi*, Gondi; *Yae-chinya*, Burm.

A small tree. Bark rusty or reddish brown. Wood reddish yellow, close-grained. Annual rings marked by a white line. Pores small, numerous, uniformly distributed. Medullary rays fine, the distance between the rays greater than the transverse diameter of the pores.

Suliman Range, Sub-Himalayan tract and Outer Himalaya ascending to 5,000 feet, Eastern Bengal, Central and South India and Burma.

Growth slow, 14 to 16 rings per inch of radius. Weight, 52 lbs. per cubic foot. Wood durable, used for agricultural implements. Bark astringent, used to intoxicate fish.

		lbs.
H 2941.	Jander, Sutlej Valley, 3,000 feet	52
P. 3247.	Ajmere	...

2. S. Leucopyrus, Müll. Arg.; Beddome cxcvii.; Brandis 456; Gamble 68. *Phyllanthus Leucopyrus*, Roxb. Fl. Ind. iii. 658. *Cicca Leucopyrus*, Kurz ii. 353. Vern. *Pera pastawane*, Afg.; *Kakún, rithei, girthan, gargas, bhâthi, bata, vanúthi, girk*, Pb.; *Hartho, aintha*, North-Western Provinces; *Kiran*, Sind; *Challa manta, sále manta*, Central Provinces; *Achal*, Nep.

A large shrub or small tree. Bark smooth, reddish brown, with few vertical cracks. Wood pink, hard, close-grained. Pores small, often subdivided or in short radial lines, numerous, uniformly distributed. Medullary rays very fine and fine, numerous, bent where they touch the pores.

Outer Himalaya, ascending to 5,000 feet, throughout India and Burma.
Wood only used as fuel.

E 3319. Pankabari, Darjeeling, 2,000 feet.
E 3282. Sitapahar Reserve, Chittagong.

6. BACCAUREA, Lour.

Müller describes 6 species: *B. affinis*, Müll. Arg. and *B. parviflora*, Müll. Arg.; Kurz ii. 357, from South Tenasserim; *B. propinqua*, Müll. Arg., from Sylhet; *B. courtallensis*, Müll. Arg., and *B. flaccida*, Müll. Arg., from South India.

1. B. sapida, Müll. Arg.; Beddome t. 280; Kurz ii. 356; Gamble 69. *Pierardia sapida*, Roxb. Fl. Ind. ii. 254. Vern. *Lutco*, Hind.; *Kala bogoti*, Nep.; *Sumbling*, Lepcha; *Latecku*, Ass.; *Koli kuki*, Kan.; *Kanaizu*, Magh; *Kanazo*, Burm.

A moderate-sized evergreen tree, with thin grey corky bark. Wood greyish brown, soft, liable to split badly. Pores small, in short radial lines. Medullary rays moderately broad to broad, the distance between the rays being from one to three times the transverse diameter of the pores. Wood cells very large, arranged in transverse lines which have the appearance of innumerable short fine bars across the rays.

Bengal, Assam, Burma, and Andaman Islands.

Weight, according to Brandis' Burma List of 1862, No. 97, 61 lbs.; Wallich, No. 154, 38 lbs.; our specimens average 42 lbs. The wood is not used. The fruit is much eaten, it is acid and pleasant, and is called '*Lutqua.*' The leaves are used in Northern Bengal and Assam for dyeing.

		lbs.
E 1265.	Tezpur, Assam	42
B 2552.	Burma (1862)	44
B 3145. ♂	Magayee, Burma	42
B 3146. ♀	" "	43
B 2686.	Tavoy (Wallich, 1828)	41
B 2720.	" "	41

7. APOROSA, Bl.

Contains eight species. *A. villosa*, Baill.; Kurz ii. 361. Vern. *Ye-mein*, Burm., is a tree of Burma whose bark is used for dyeing red, and which gives a red resin. *A. macrophylla*, Müll. Arg.; Kurz ii. 361. Vern. *In-jin*, Burm., *A. villosula*, Kurz ii. 362. Vern. *Thitsap*, Burm., and *A. microstachya*, Müll. Arg.; Kurz ii. 363, are evergreen trees of Burma. *A. oblonga*, Müll. Arg. and *A. lanceolata*, Thw.; Beddome cxcix.; Kurz ii. 363, are trees of Tenasserim. *A. Lindleyana*, Wight; Beddome t. 286; Gamble 69. Vern. *Sulla, surroli*, Kan.; *Kagbhalai*, Nep., is a tree of Sikkim and the Western Ghâts with a good timber. *A. dioica*, Müll. Arg.; Gamble 69 (*A. Roxburghii*, Baill.; Kurz ii. 362. *Alnus dioica*, Roxb. Fl. Ind. iii. 580. *Lepidostachys Roxburghii*, Wall.) Vern. *Kokra*, Beng.; *Sanpalu*, Gáro; *Tauprengjan*, Magh, is a tree of Northern and Eastern Bengal and Burma.

This last has been identified with the tree producing the 'Coco-wood' of commerce, generally supposed to come from the West Indies.

No. 2925 is the Coco-wood. It has a dark-brown, very hard, close-grained wood, with white sapwood, and resembles that of *Homonoya* (see page 364) in structure. It weighs 79 lbs. per cubic foot.

The wood of *Aporosa dioica* should be carefully examined to prove that the Indian tree gives a timber similar to Coco-wood.

8. BISCHOFFIA, Bl.

1. B. javanica, Bl.; Beddome t. 259; Brandis 446; Kurz ii. 355; Gamble 69. *Andrachne trifoliata*, Roxb. Fl. Ind. iii. 728. Vern. *Kein, korsa, irum*, Hind.; *Kainjal*, Nep.; *Sinong*, Lepcha; *Taisoh, urúm*, Mechi; *Uriam*, Ass.; *Bolzuru*, Gáro; *Joki*, Cachar; *Boke*, Bombay; *Thondi*, Tam.; *Govarnellu*, Hassan; *Modagerri vembu*, Tinnevelly.

A deciduous tree. Bark rough, dark grey with a brown tinge, exfoliating in angular scales. Wood red, rough, moderately hard, with a small darker-coloured heartwood. Pores moderate-sized, in short radial lines. Medullary rays moderately broad and very fine, the distance between the broad rays being from one to three times the transverse diameter of the pores.

Kumaun, Garhwal, Oudh, Gorakhpur, Bengal, South India and Burma.

Growth fast, some of our specimens shewed 4 rings per inch of radius. Weight, the average of our specimens gave, heartwood 47·5 lbs., sapwood 36 lbs. per cubic foot. Kyd gives: Weight 43 lbs., P = 617. Kurz evidently identifies with this, No. 99 of Brandis' list of 1862. Vern. *Yagine*, Burm. Weight 35 lbs. In Assam it is esteemed one of the best timbers and used for bridges and other works of construction. Beddome says it is used by planters in the Nilgiris for building, and is sometimes called 'Red Cedar.'

		lbs.
O 1374.	Gonda, Oudh	44
E 654.	Bamunpokri, Darjeeling Terai	53
E 1257.	Tezpur, Assam	47
E 2191.	Nowgong, Assam	46
E 2467.	Calcutta (sapwood)	36

9. BRIEDELIA, Willd.

About 7 species. *B. ovata*, Dcne; Kurz ii. 368, is a small tree of Tenasserim and the Andamans. *B. Hamiltoniana*, Müll. Arg., is a small tree with two varieties, one found in Behar, the other on the Bombay Ghâts. *B. stipularis*, Bl.; Beddome cci.; Brandis 449; Kurz ii. 369; Gamble 69 (*B. scandens*, Roxb. Fl. Ind. iii. 736) Vern. *Madlatáh, undergúpa*, Oudh; *Lilima*, Nep.; *Dúnkibúra*, Tel.; *Kihur, kohi*, Ass.; *Harinhara*, Beng; *Sin-ma-no-pyin*, Burm., is a large climbing shrub of most parts of India and Burma, with a dark heartwood; it is used for fuel in the Sundarbans. *B. dasycalyx*, Kurz ii. 369, is a climber of the forests of Burma.

Heartwood grey or olive brown, seasons well. Pores small to moderate-sized. Medullary rays fine or moderately broad.

1. B. retusa, Sprengel; Beddome t. 260; Brandis 449; Kurz ii. 368; Gamble 69. *B. crenulata*, Roxb., and *B. spinosa*, Willd.; Roxb. Fl. Ind. iii. 734, 735. Vern. *Pathor, mark*, Pb., *Khaja, kassi, gauli*, Hind.; *Lamkana*, Ajmere; *Angnera*, Banswara; *Asana*, Mar.; *Geio*, Nep.; *Pengji*, Lepcha; *Nanda*, Rajbanshi; *Katakuchi*, Mechi; *Kashi*, Gâro; *Kamkúi*, Chittagong; *Kosi*, Uriya; *Mulu-vengay, kamanji*, Tam.; *Koramau, dudi máddi, koramadi, duriamadi*, Tel.; *Kassei*, Gondi; *Karka*, Kurku; *Gúnjan, kati ain*, Mar., Bhíl; *Asuna, gojé*, Kan.; *Adamarathu*, Tinnevelly; *Tseichyee*, Burm., *Katta kaala*, Cingh.

A large deciduous tree, with thorns on the bark of young stems. Bark ¼ inch thick, grey or brown, rough with longitudinal cracks and exfoliating in long irregular plates. Sapwood small; heartwood grey to olive brown, close-grained, seasons well, moderately hard, the annual rings marked by concentric lines. Pores uniformly distributed, moderate-sized, often in short radial lines. Medullary rays numerous, uniform and equidistant, moderately broad, visible on a radial section as rough, narrow plates; the distance between two rays equal to, or less than, the transverse diameter of the pores. This wood has a mottled grain and takes a beautiful polish.

Sub-Himalayan tract, from the Chenab eastwards, ascending to 3,600 feet, Oudh, Bengal, Central and South India, Burma.

Growth fast, our specimens shewed an average of 5-6 rings per inch of radius. Weight, Skinner, No. 291, gives 60 lbs.; R. Thompson, 54 lbs.; Brandis, No. 23, Burma List, 1862, 66 lbs.; the average of our specimens is 50 lbs. according to Dr. Warth's weighings of specimens. Skinner gives P = 892. This is, probably, Kyd's *B. stipularis*, Vern. *Kohi*, Ass., weight 64 lbs., P = 525. Wood durable, used for cattle-yokes, agricultural implements, carts and building. It stands well under water. The bark is used for tanning, the fruit eaten, and the leaves cut to feed cattle.

		lbs.
P 461.	Ajmere	48
O 259.	Garhwal (1868)	45
O 3001.	„ (1874)	43
O 1480.	Kheri, Oudh	61
O 347.	Gorakhpur (1868)	47
C 1174.	Ahiri Reserve, Central Provinces	55

		lbs.
C 840.	Bairagarh Reserve, Berar	63
C 2765.	Melghát, Berar	45
E 645.	Sepoydura, Darjeeling, 5,000 feet	53
E 619.	Bamunpokri, Darjeeling Terai	56
E 2428.	" " "	46
B 3074.	Burma (1862)	46
B 1431.	Tharrawaddy Division, Burma	56
No. 43.	Ceylon Collection	44
No. 68.	" "	38

2. B. montana, Willd.; Roxb. Fl. Ind. iii. 735; Beddome ccii.; Brandis 450; Gamble 70. Vern. *Kargnalia, khaja, geia, kusi,* Hind.; *Geio,* Nep.; *Kaisho,* Ass.; *Patenga,* Tel.

A moderate-sized deciduous tree. Wood grey, beautifully mottled; annual rings distinctly marked by darker and firmer wood on the outside of each ring. Pores small and moderate-sized, often in radial lines; the transverse diameter of the pores being generally less than the distance between the fine and uniformly distributed medullary rays, which are prominent on a radial section.

Sub-Himalayan tract from the Jhelam eastwards, ascending to 4,000 feet, Oudh, Bengal.

Growth fast, 4 rings per inch of radius. Weight, 46 to 59 lbs. per cubic foot, but the heavier specimen was perhaps not sufficiently seasoned. Wood very similar to that of *B. retusa* and might be used for the same purposes. The leaves are lopped for cattle fodder.

		lbs.
O 1375.	Gonda, Oudh	59
C 199.	Mandla, Central Provinces (1870)	46

3. B. tomentosa, Bl.; Kurz ii. 367; Gamble 70. *B. lanceæfolia,* Roxb. Fl. Ind. iii. 737. Vern. *Sibri,* Nep.; *Mantet,* Lepcha; *Sirai, mindri,* Beng.

A small evergreen tree. Wood light olive brown, hard, close-grained. Pores small, often subdivided, enclosed in rounded patches of soft tissue, which are generally arranged in oblique, undulating lines; the transverse diameter is greater than the distance between the very fine, very numerous, uniform and equidistant medullary rays.

North-East Himalaya, ascending to 2,000 feet, Eastern Bengal and Burma.

Weight, 64 lbs. per cubic foot.

		lbs.
E 1397.	Chittagong	64

10. CLEISTANTHUS, Hook. f.

About 7 species. *C. patulus,* Müll. Arg., *C. malabaricus,* Müll. Arg., and *C. stipularis,* Müll. Arg., are small trees of South India. *C. oblongifolius,* Müll. Arg., and *C. chartaceus,* Müll. Arg., trees of Eastern Bengal, the first extending northwards to Sikkim. *C. stenophyllus,* Kurz, and *C. myrianthus,* Kurz, are trees of Burma and the Andaman Islands.

1. C. myrianthus, Kurz ii. 370. Vern. *Mo-man-tha,* Burm.

A moderate-sized evergreen tree. Wood moderately hard, reddish grey. Pores small, numerous, often subdivided. Medullary rays fine, very numerous, closely packed.

Tropical forests of Burma and the Andaman Islands.

		lbs.
B 2474.	Andamans (Kurz, 1866)	41

11. LEBEDIEROPSIS, Müll. Arg.

1. L. orbicularis, Müll. Arg.; Beddome cciii.; Brandis 450. *Cluytia collina,* Roxb. Fl. Ind. iii. 732. Vern. *Garrar, garári,* Hind.; *Karada,* Uriya; *Korsi, wodesha, kadishen, korshe,* Tel.; *Wodayu, waddan,* Tam.; *Garari,* Mar.; *Madara,* Cingh.

A small deciduous tree. Bark ¼ inch thick, dark brown, almost black, often with a reddish tinge, rough with numerous cracks, exfoliating in rectangular woody scales. Wood red, tough, moderately hard to hard, close and even-grained, warps in seasoning. Heartwood dark red, small; sapwood lighter coloured. Pores small, arranged in radial lines between the very fine and very numerous equidistant medullary rays.

Bandelkhand, Satpura Range and forests southwards to the Godavari mountains of South India.

Weight, 54 to 55 lbs. per cubic foot. Beddome says the wood is much used in India. It coppices readily and in great abundance; it may, therefore, be specially recommended where fuel has to be produced in tropical parts of India, but it is also recommended as a useful wood for turning. The outer crust of the capsule is said to be poisonous.

		lbs.
C 1175.	Ahiri Reserve, Central Provinces	54
C 1252.	Gumsúr, Madras	55
C 1306.	" "	54

This wood resembles that of *Eugenia operculata* in outward appearance and in structure, but differs by the absence of concentric lines. It is almost identical with that of *Flacourtia Ramontchi,* and if it were not for the great difference in the bark which in *Lebedieropsis* is darkcoloured, almost black and deeply fissured, and in *Flacourtia* light coloured, smooth, with short narrow horizontal cracks, one might be inclined to suspect a mistake in the specimens. The only difference that can be seen under the glass is that the medullary rays in *Flacourtia* are slightly wavy, while those of *Lebedieropsis* are straight.

12. CROTON, Linn.

A large genus of trees and shrubs, erect or straggling, with about 19 Indian species. The following list has been extracted from Müller's Monograph in DeCandolle's Prodromus, Vol. xv. 2, those newly added by Beddome and Kurz being given in brackets:—

SECTION I. ELUTERIA.

C. Joufra, Roxb.	Eastern Bengal, Burma.

SECTION II. EUCROTON.

C. argyratus, Bl.	Burma, Andamans.
C. oblongifolius, Roxb.	North and South India, Bengal, Burma.
C. reticulatus, Müll. Arg.	South India.
C. lacciferus, Linn.	Ditto.
C. aromaticus, Linn.	Ditto.
C. chlorocalyx, Müll. Arg.	Eastern Bengal.
C. rhodostachyus, Müll. Arg.	Burma.
C. caudatus, Müll. Arg.	Eastern Bengal, Burma, South India.
C. Tiglium, Linn.	Bengal, Burma, South India.
C. birmanicus, Müll. Arg.	Burma.
C. lævifolius, Bl.	Eastern Bengal.
C. Wallichii, Müll. Arg.	Burma.

(*C. scabiosus*, Beddome)	South India.
(*C. malabaricus*, Beddome)	Ditto.
(*C. robustus*, Kurz)	Burma.
(*C. sublyratus*, Kurz)	Andamans.
(*C. flocculosus*, Kurz)	Burma.
(*C. calococcus*, Kurz)	Ditto.

C. Joufra, Roxb. Fl. Ind. iii. 685; Kurz ii. 373. Vern. *Joufra*, Beng., is a tree of Eastern Bengal and Burma. *C. oblongifolius*, Roxb. Fl. Ind. iii. 688; Beddome cciv.; Brandis 439; Kurz ii. 373; Gamble 70. Vern. *Arjunna*, Oudh; *Ach*, Nep.; *Burma*, *parokupi*, Ass.; *Bhutankusam*, Tel.; *Thityin*, Burm., is a small tree found in the Sub-Himalayan tract from Oudh eastwards, South India, Burma, and Ceylon. Bark 1 inch thick, grey or brownish, inner bark red. Wood white, close-grained, moderately hard, cracks in seasoning; the seeds give an oil. *C. Tiglium*, Linn.; Roxb. Fl. Ind. iii. 682; Brandis 440; Kurz ii. 374. The Purging Croton. Vern. *Jaipál*, *jamal-gota*, Hind.; *Kanakho*, Burm., is a small tree, cultivated in many parts of India and Burma, the seeds are a powerful purgative, and the yellow oil is a valuable medicine.

C. scabiosus, Beddome t. 283, and *C. malabaricus*, Beddome cciv., are trees of the Western Ghâts with silvery leaves.

1. C. argyratus, Bl.; Kurz ii. 372. Vern. *Chonoo*, Burm.; *Talibdá*, And.

A moderate-sized or small evergreen tree. Bark thin, grey. Wood hard, yellow, close and even-grained, seasons well. Pores large and very large, scanty, circular, very prominent on a vertical section. Medullary rays extremely fine, very numerous. Numerous wavy concentric lines (of darker colour?).

Martaban, Tenasserim and the Andaman Islands.
Weight, 46 to 48 lbs. per cubic foot. Wood worthy of notice.

		lbs.
B 501.	Andaman Islands	48
B 515.	" "	46

2. C. caudatus, Müll. Arg.; Kurz ii. 375; Gamble 70. *C. drupaceum*, Roxb. Fl. Ind. iii. 683. Vern. *Nan bhantúr*, Beng.; *Takchabrik*, Lepcha.

A large straggling shrub. Bark thin, grey. Wood white or yellowish white, hard, close-grained. Pores large, scanty, sometimes subdivided, prominent on a vertical section. Medullary rays very fine to extremely fine, very numerous. Numerous wavy concentric lines of white tissue often interrupting the rays.

Bengal, Assam, Burma and South India, chiefly on the banks of streams.
Home says the wood is used for fuel and the leaves applied as poultices to sprains.
E 3298. Sivoke, Darjeeling Terai.

B 3201. Burma (1862) *Thityinkat*, supposed to be *Croton oblongifolius*, has a white wood similar in structure to *C. argyratus*, except that the fine, wavy concentric bands are more prominent and the pores are smaller.

13. TREWIA, Linn.

1. T. nudiflora, Linn.; Roxb. Fl. Ind. iii. 837; Beddome t. 281; Brandis 443; Kurz ii. 379; Gamble 70. Vern. *Túmri*, *khamara*, *bhillaura*, Hind.; *Pitali*, Beng.; *Garum*, *gamari*, Nep.; *Tungflam*, Lepcha;

Pitari, Mar.; *Kat kumbla*, Kan.; *Hruprukban*, Magh; *Thitmycke, ye-myot*, Burm.

A deciduous tree. Bark smooth, grey. Wood white, soft, not durable. Pores moderate-sized, subdivided and often elongated, the transverse diameter several times greater than the distance between the closely packed uniform, fine medullary rays.

Sub-Himalayan tract from the Jumna eastwards, ascending to 3,000 feet, Bengal, Burma, South India.

Weight, 28 to 29 lbs. Used for native drums and agricultural implements. Recognised by its opposite leaves, which resemble those of *Gmelina arborea*.

		lbs.
E 2468.	Calcutta	29
B 311.	Burma (1867)	28

14. MALLOTUS, Loureiro.

A genus of trees or shrubs with large, often peltate, leaves. Most of them are of no importance, and only a few are common. The following list is taken from the Prodromus, from Dr. Müller's Monograph, wherein 22 Indian species are described:—

SECTION I. BLUMEODENDRON.

M. Tokbrai, Mül. Arg. (*B. Tokbrai*, Kurz ii. 391) .	Andamans.

SECTION II. ROTTLEROPSIS.

M. lappaceus, Müll. Arg.	Burma.

SECTION III. MELANOLEPIS.

M. barbatus, Müll. Arg.	Western Ghâts, Burma.
M. moluccanus, Müll. Arg. Beddome ccviii. (*Ricinus dicoccus*, Roxb. Fl. Ind. iii. 690)	North Arcot.

SECTION IV. EUMALLOTUS.

M. Roxburghianus, Müll. Arg.	Sikkim, Eastern Bengal, Burma.
M. ricinoides, Müll. Arg.	Tenasserim.
M. oreophilus, Müll. Arg.	Sikkim, Khasia.
M. nepalensis, Müll. Arg.	Nepal.
M. albus, Müll. Arg.	Sikkim, Eastern Bengal, South India.
M. paniculatus, Müll. Arg.	Burma.
M. acuminatus, Müll. Arg.	Andamans.
M. Helferi, Müll. Arg.	Sikkim, Burma, Andamans.
M. muricatus, Müll. Arg.	Western Ghâts, Andamans.
M. stenanthus, Müll. Arg.	Bombay Ghâts.
M. aureo-punctatus, Müll. Arg.	Western Ghâts.
M. Lawii, Müll. Arg.	West Coast.
M. distans, Müll. Arg.	Tinnevelly.
M. decipiens, Müll. Arg.	Tenasserim.
M. atrovirens, Müll. Arg.	Tinnevelly.
M. rhamnifolius, Müll. Arg.	South India.
M. philippinensis, Müll. Arg.	All India.
M. repandus, Müll Arg. (*Rottlera dicocca*, Roxb. Fl. Ind. iii. 829)	Eastern Bengal, South India, Burma.

Fine, uniform, closely packed medullary rays; pores small, in radial lines, in some species numerous faint transverse bars.

1. M. philippinensis, Müll. Arg.; Beddome t. 289; Brandis 444; Kurz ii. 381; Gamble 70. *Rottlera tinctoria,* Roxb. Fl. Ind. iii. 827. Vern. *Kamela, kamal, kambal, kúmila,* Pb.; *Rúen, riúna, roli,* Kumaun; *Rohni,* Oudh; *Reoni,* Banda; *Rauni, rori,* C. P.; *Púnag, túng, kishur,* Beng.; *Sinduria,* Nep.; *Puroa, tukla,* Lepcha; *Baraiburi, sindurpong,* Mechi; *Chinderpang, machugan,* Gáro; *Gangai, puddum,* Ass.; *Kumala, sundragundi,* Uriya; *Kapli, kapila,* Tam.; *Kúmkuma, vassuntagunda, chendra, sinduri,* Tel.; *Koku,* Gōndi; *Kurku, corunga-manje, saruakasari, hulichellu,* Kan.; *Shendri,* Mar.; *Ponnagam,* Mal.; *Ilamparandella,* Cingh.; *Tau-theedin,* Burm.

A small tree. Bark ¼ inch thick, grey, inner substance red, marked by irregular cracks. Wood smooth, grey to light red, hard, close-grained, no heartwood. Annual rings indistinct. Pores small, uniformly distributed, scanty, often subdivided. Medullary rays uniform, very fine, very numerous, equidistant, the distance between them less than the diameter of the pores. Faint indications of transverse bars.

Sub-Himalayan tract from the Indus eastwards, ascending to 4,500 feet, Bengal, Central and South India, Burma and the Andaman Islands.

Weight, 48 lbs. per cubic foot. Wood warps and shrinks, used only for fuel. The bark is used for tanning. The crimson powder which covers the ripe fruit is used for dyeing silk, and as a purgative and anthelmintic. Dr. Bidie states in his Paris Exhibition List of 1878 that he described the structure of the grains of Kamela in the *Madras Quarterly Journal of Medical Science.* He says that they consist of a red substance enclosed in a membranous sac, which is not acted on by water, though soluble in alcohol or an alkaline solution.

			lbs.
P	109.	Sutlej Valley, 3,000 feet	50
C	1178.	Ahiri Reserve, Central Provinces	43
E	599.	Bamunpokri, Darjeeling Terai	51
E	2421.	" " "	49

2. M. albus, Müll. Arg.; Beddome ccviii.; Brandis 444; Gamble 70; *M. tetracoccus,* Kurz ii. 382. *Rottlera alba* and *tetracocca,* Roxb. Fl. Ind. iii. 829, 826. Vern. *Marleya,* Sylhet; *Jogi mallata,* Nep.; *Numbong,* Lepcha.

A small evergreen tree with thin brownish grey bark. Wood soft, white. Pores moderate-sized and large, often subdivided. Medullary rays as in *M. philippinensis.*

Sikkim, Eastern Bengal, Chittagong, Western Gháts, Mysore and Ceylon.

Weight, 31 lbs. per cubic foot. Leaves covered beneath with dense white tomentum.

			lbs.
E	2422.	Sivoke, Darjeeling Terai	31

3. M. Roxburghianus, Müll. Arg.; Kurz ii. 383; Gamble 70. *Rottlera peltata,* Roxb. Fl. Ind. iii. 828. Vern. *Kamli mallata, phusri mallata,* Nep.; *Ním pooteli,* Beng.; *Sírgúllum,* Sylhet.

A small evergreen tree. Wood white, moderately hard, close-grained. Pores small, often in radial lines, uniformly distributed. Medullary rays uniform, fine, very numerous, equidistant. Faint transverse bars.

Sikkim, Assam, Khasia Hills, Eastern Bengal and Burma.
Weight, 46 lbs. per cubic foot.

		lbs.
E 2423.	Chenga Forest, Darjeeling Terai	46

4. M. muricatus, Müll. Arg.; Beddome ccviii.; Kurz ii. 384. Vern. *Ouk-mouk,* Burm.

A large evergreen shrub. Wood grey, moderately hard. Pores very small, often in radial lines. Medullary rays very fine, very numerous, equidistant. Numerous very fine transverse bars.

Western Ghâts and Andaman Islands.
Weight, 57 lbs. per cubic foot.

		lbs.
B 2476.	Andaman Islands (Kurz, 1874)	57

5. M. oreophilus, Müll. Arg.; Gamble 70. Vern. *Numboongkor,* Lepcha; *Safed mallata,* Nep.

A small tree. Bark ⅛th inch thick, light brown, with corky lenticels. Wood white, soft. Pores moderate-sized and large, rather scanty, often subdivided or in short radial lines. Medullary rays very fine, very numerous, equidistant, the distance between them less than the transverse diameter of the pores.

Sikkim 5,000 to 7,000 feet, Khasia Hills.
Growth moderately fast, 5 rings per inch of radius. A common tree about Darjeeling, chiefly in second-growth forest.

E 3397. The Park, Darjeeling, 6,500 feet.

15. MACARANGA, Pet. Thouars.

A genus of about 12 species of Indian trees or shrubs. They have large often peltate leaves, are fast growing, and chiefly found in old clearings, where they often come up gregariously. The following list gives Dr. Müller's species, those since described by Kurz being given in brackets:—

SECTION I. MAPPA.

M. Tanarius, Müll. Arg.	Andamans.
M. gummiflua, Müll. Arg.	Sikkim, Eastern Bengal.
M. denticulata, Müll. Arg.	Sikkim, Burma.
M. Helferi, Müll. Arg.	Burma, Andamans.
M. populifolia, Müll. Arg.	Andamans.

SECTION II. EUMACARANGA.

M. indica, R. Wight	Sikkim, Khasia Hills, Western Ghâts, Andamans.
M. flexuosa, R. Wight	Tinnevelly.
M. tomentosa, R. Wight	Western Ghâts.
M. peltata, Müll. Arg.	Eastern Ghâts.
M. minutiflora, Müll. Arg.	Tenasserim.
(*M. andamanica,* Kurz)	Andamans.
(*M. membranacea,* Kurz)	Martaban Hills, 4,000 to 6,000 feet.

M. tomentosa, R. Wight; Beddome t. 287. Vern. *Vatte kanni*, Tam.; *Upligi, upalkai, kanchupranthi*, Kan.; *Chenthakanni*, Mysore; *Chanda*, Bombay; *Kanda*, Cingh., is a rapid growing small tree of the Western Ghâts, usually of old clearings; it gives a gum which is used medicinally and for taking impressions.

Wood soft, spongy. Pores moderate-sized to large. Medullary rays uniform, very fine, closely packed.

1. M. indica, Wight; Beddome ccxi.; Kurz ii. 387; Gamble 71. Vern. *Dagdakti*, Mechi; *Lal mallata*, Nep.; *Laikezau*, Mechi; *Boura*, Beng.; *Modala*, Ass. (*M. pudica* of Mr. Mann's list is probably this.)

A small evergreen tree. Bark grey, thin, smooth. Wood greyish red, moderately hard. Pores moderate-sized to large, oval, elongated and subdivided. Medullary rays faint, uniform, very fine, very numerous, equidistant.

Sikkim up to 3,000 feet, Khasia Hills, Western Ghâts and Andaman Islands. Growth very fast. Weight, 33 lbs. per cubic foot. It gives a red resin.

		lbs
E 2424.	Chunbati, Darjeeling, 2,000 feet	33
B 2475.	Andaman Islands (Kurz, 1874)	...

2. M. denticulata, Müll. Arg.; Kurz ii. 387; Gamble 71. Vern. *Mallata*, Nep.; *Numro*, Lepcha; *Toung-hpek-wan*, Burm.

A small tree, often gregarious. Bark grey, smooth. Wood soft, greyish red, structure similar to that of *M. indica*.

Sikkim Hills, from 3,000 to 6,000 feet, chiefly on old clearings, Burma

Growth fast, our specimen shewed 2 rings per inch of radius; Gamble says it reaches in 10 years a height of 40 feet with a girth of 3 feet. Weight, 29 lbs. per cubic foot. It is much used for fencing and temporary huts. It gives a gum, but scanty. The botanical determination of this and the next species is not quite certain.

		lbs.
E 2425.	Tukdah Forest, Darjeeling, 5,000 feet	29

3. M. gummiflua, Müll. Arg.; Gamble 70. Vern. *Jogi mallata*, Nep.; *Chakro*, Gáro; *Burua*, Chittagong; *Pawaing*, Magh.

A small tree, often gregarious. Bark grey, smooth. Wood greyish red, soft, in structure similar to that of *M. indica*.

Sikkim, from 3,000 to 6,000 feet, Eastern Bengal.

Growth fast, our specimen shewed 3 rings per inch of radius. Weight, 22 lbs. per cubic foot. Wood used for similar purposes to that of *M. denticulata*.

		lbs.
E 2426.	Pugraingbong, Darjeeling, 5,000 feet	22

16. RICINUS, Linn.

1. R. communis, Linn.; Roxb. Fl. Ind. iii. 689; Brandis 445; Kurz ii. 400; Gamble 71. The Castor Oil Plant or Palma Christi. Vern. *Rand, arand, arendi, ind*, Hind.; *Aneru*, Chenab; *Harnauli*, Salt Range; *Ind-rendi*, Kumaun; *Orer*, Nep.; *Raklop*, Lepcha; *Sittamunuk*, Tam.; *Amadum, amdi, sittamindi*, Tel.; *Nerinda*, Gondi; *Haralu*, Kan.; *Kyeksu*, Burm.

A large shrub or small tree. Bark thin, light greyish brown. Wood white, soft, light, with large central pith. Pores moderate-sized, scanty, uniformly distributed, often subdivided. Medullary rays numerous, fine to moderately broad.

Indigenous in Arabia and North Africa, cultivated throughout India and often found run wild.

Usually cultivated for the oil which is expressed from its seeds, and which is so largely used for burning, for lubricating machinery and in medicine.

It is also grown for its leaves, which are used for feeding silkworms. The 'Eri' silk of Assam produced by *Attacus Ricini* fed on the leaves of the castor oil plant, gives a beautiful fine silk, used to make wearing apparel by the Assamese and Mechis.

E 3277. Naltanpara, Western Dúars.

17. HOMONOYA, Loureiro.

Three species. *H. retusa*, Müll. Arg.; Beddome ccxii.; Brandis 445, is a small shrub of river banks in South India.

1. H. symphylliæfolia, Kurz; Gamble 71. Vern. *Bajadanti*, Nep.; *Ching*, Lepcha.

A moderate-sized evergreen tree. Bark very thin, white or light grey, peels off in thin flakes. Wood yellowish white, hard, smooth, close-grained. Annual rings indistinct. Pores very small, numerous, uniformly distributed, sometimes in radial lines. Medullary rays very fine, very numerous. Few concentric lines (?).

Damp forests of the lower Darjeeling Hills.

Weight, 54 to 59 lbs. per cubic foot. The section of the stem is very irregular, presenting deep sinuosities. The wood is hard and tough, and is used for punting poles by the Tista boatmen. It is recommended for trial as a substitute for boxwood.

		lbs.
E 496.	Khookloong Forest, Darjeeling	54
E 2429.	Tista Valley, near Sivoke, Darjeeling	59

2. H. riparia, Lour.; Beddome ccxii.; Brandis 445; Kurz ii. 401; Gamble 71. *Adelia neriifolia*, Roxb. Fl. Ind. iii. 849. Vern. *Kandágar*, Kumaun; *Khola ruis*, Nep.; *Mongthel*, Lepcha; *Taniki*, Tel.; *Sundeh*, Gondi; *Jeljambu*, Kurku; *Kat-alluri*, Mal.; *Momakha, yay-tagyeeben*, Burm.

A small shrub. Bark brown. Wood grey or greyish brown, moderately hard, close-grained. Pores scanty, moderately large, often subdivided. Medullary rays of two classes: few moderately broad and short, and numerous long, fine rays, which, as a thin section, appear as a succession of small black cells.

Rocky and stony river beds throughout India.

Weight, 40 lbs. per cubic foot.

		lbs.
E 3303.	Sivoke, Darjeeling Terai	40

18. JATROPHA, Linn.

About 4 species: *J. Wightiana*, Müll. Arg., is a small shrub of South India. *J. nana*, Dalz., is an undershrub of stony places in the Dekkan. *J. glandulifera*, Roxb. Fl. Ind. iii. 688; Kurz ii. 403 (*Addalay*, Tam.; *Nela-amida*, Tel.) is a shrub common near villages in Bengal and Burma. The seeds give an oil which is used in medicine. *J. multifida*, Linn., the Coral Plant, is much grown in gardens for its handsome scarlet flowers and deeply-cut leaves.

1. **J. Curcas,** Linn.; Roxb. Fl. Ind. iii. 686; Brandis 442; Kurz ii. 403; Gamble 71. The Physic Nut. Vern. *Bagberenda, safed ind,* Hind., Beng.; *Kadam,* Nep.; *Kaat-amunak,* Tam.; *Nepalam,* Tel.; *Maranarulle, maraharalu,* Kan.; *Kaak-avenako,* Mal.; *Thinbau-kyeksu,* Burm.

A soft, wooded evergreen shrub. Bark greenish white, smooth, peeling off in thin flakes. Wood white, very soft. Pores small, scanty; often subdivided. Medullary rays extremely fine, very numerous.

Indigenous in America, cultivated in most parts of India.

Weight, 25 lbs. per cubic foot. Often used for hedges and planted near villages. The juice of the leaves forms a lather like soap. The seeds give an oil which is used for burning, in medicine as a purgative and emetic, and as an application in cutaneous diseases.

	lbs.
E 2427. Manjha, Darjeeling Terai	25

19. GIVOTIA, Griff.

1. **G. rottleriformis,** Griff.; Beddome t. 285; Brandis 442. Vern. *Vendale, butalli, bulali,* Tam.; *Tella púnki,* Tel.

A middle-sized tree. Wood white, exceedingly light, very soft but even-grained. Pores moderate-sized, scanty, very prominent on a vertical section, often in concentric lines; annual rings marked by a line of larger, more numerous pores. Medullary rays uniform, fine, short, the distance between the rays greater than the transverse diameter of the pores.

Dekkan, Mysore, Eastern Ghâts and Ceylon.

Growth very fast, our specimen shews 1½ rings per inch, but the annual rings are somewhat doubtful. Weight, 14 lbs. per cubic foot. The wood is used to carve figures, for toys, imitation fruit and other fancy articles, which are lacquered and painted; also for catamarans. The seed give an oil which is valuable for lubricating fine machinery.

	lbs.
D 3152. Cuddapah, Madras	14

20. OSTODES, Bl.

Three species. *O. Zeylanicus,* Müll. Arg.; Beddome t. 274. Vern. *Sotege,* Hassan; *Walkakoona,* Cingh., is a very large tree of the Western Ghâts and Ceylon. *O. Helferi,* Müll. Arg. Kurz ii. 404, is a tree of Upper Tenasserim, in the plains round Moulmein.

1. **O. paniculata,** Bl.; Kurz ii. 404; Gamble 72. Vern. *Bepari,* Nep.; *Palok,* Lepcha.

A large evergreen tree. Bark light grey. Wood white, soft. Pores scanty, small to large, subdivided. Medullary rays very fine, uniform, closely packed.

Forests of Sikkim from 2,000 to 6,000 feet, Khasia Hills and the Hills of Martaban.

Growth moderate, 8 to 9 rings per inch of radius. Weight, 26 lbs. per cubic foot. It gives a gum which is used as size in the manufacture of paper.

	lbs.
E 3110. Darjeeling, 6,000 feet	26

21. CHÆTOCARPUS, Thw.

1. **C. castaneæcarpus,** Thw. Enum. 275; Beddome t. 284; Kurz ii. 409. Vern. *Búlkokra*, Beng.; *Haddoka*, Cingh.

A moderate-sized tree. Wood light red, moderately hard, close-grained. Pores small, numerous. Medullary rays very fine, very numerous, traversed by narrow wavy concentric bands.

Khasia Hills, Eastern Bengal, Burma, Andaman Islands and Ceylon. Weight, 58 lbs. per cubic foot. Wood used in Ceylon for building.

	lbs.
No. 34. Ceylon Collection (*C. pungens*)	58

22. EXCÆCARIA, Linn.

The following list of species is taken from the 'Prodromus' of DeCandolle:—

SECTION I. TRIADICA.

E. sebifera, Müll. Arg.	Cultivated, Northern India.
E. baccata, Müll. Arg.	Sikkim, Eastern Bengal, Burma.

SECTION II. FALCONERIA.

E. insignis, Müll. Arg.	North India, South India, Burma.

SECTION III. SCLEROCROTON.

E. cochinchinensis, Lour.	South India.
E. virgata, Miq.	Martaban.
E. indica, Müll. Arg.	Sundarbans, Tenasserim.

SECTION IV. EUEXCÆCARIA.

E. oppositifolia, Jack.	Malabar, Mysore, Tenasserim.
E. Agallocha, Willd.	Bengal, South India, Burma, Andamans.
E. acerifolia, F. Didrichs	Kumaun, Nepal, Khasia Hills.
(*E. holophylla*, Kurz)	Martaban and Tenasserim.

E. acerifolia, F. Didrichs; Brandis 441. Vern. *Pútkiá*, Kumaun, is a large milky shrub, whose root is used as a cathartic.

Wood soft, spongy. Pores moderate-sized to large. Medullary rays very fine, uniform, closely packed. Faint concentric lines.

1. **E. sebifera,** Müll. Arg.; Brandis, 441; Gamble ii. *Carumbium sebiferum*, Kurz ii. 412. *Sapium sebiferum*, Roxb. Fl. Ind. iii. 693. The Chinese Tallow-tree. Vern. *Mom-china*, Beng.

A moderate-sized tree. Bark grey, with shallow, vertical cracks. Wood white, moderately hard. Pores small to large, often subdivided. Medullary rays very fine, very numerous, the distance between the rays less than the transverse diameter of the pores; the rays are traversed by numerous fine, wavy, concentric lines.

Indigenous and cultivated in China and Japan. Introduced and cultivated throughout Northern India.

Growth rather fast, 6 rings per inch of radius (our specimen). Weight, 32 lbs. per cubic foot. The white pulp round the seeds gives the Chinese tallow, which is separated by boiling in water. It is used in China and Japan for candles. Roxburgh says it is bad for burning, that it only remains firm at a cool temperature, and that it easily becomes rancid. It melts at 104°. The seeds give an oil, and the leaves a black dye. It is a handsome tree, somewhat like Sissú in foliage, and often planted for ornament.

		lbs.
O 3114.	Dehra Dún	32

2. E. baccata, Müll. Arg.; Brandis 441; Gamble 72. *Carumbium baccatum,* Kurz ii. 412. *Sapium baccatum,* Roxb. Fl. Ind. iii. 694. Vern. *Pudlikat, lal kainjal,* Nep.; *Adamsali,* Ass.; *Billa,* Sylhet; *Linhlún,* Burm.

To this species probably belongs E 1962 from Chittagong, a soft grey wood, in structure resembling that of *E. indica*; as well as E 3340 from Assam, called there *Tarsing,* Nep.; *Selling,* Chota Nagpur coolies; *Larrna,* Assamese.

A large evergreen tree of Northern and Eastern Bengal, Chittagong and Burma. Weight, 28 lbs. per cubic foot. The bark is chewed by natives in Assam.

3. E. insignis, Müll. Arg.; Beddome ccxiv.; Brandis 442. *Carumbium insigne,* Kurz ii. 412. *Falconeria insignis,* Royle. Vern. *Dúdla, bilodar, biloja, karállo, ledra,* Pb.; *Khinna, khina lienda, lendwa,* Hind.; *Garpa shola,* Anamalais.

A small deciduous tree. Bark grey, smooth, shining, with large, broad, longitudinal wrinkles. Wood grey, very soft, spongy. Annual rings faintly marked. Pores moderate-sized and large, subdivided, and often in short radial lines. Medullary rays very fine, indistinct.

Sub-Himalayan tract from the Beas eastwards, ascending to 4,000 feet, Chittagong, Burma, and Western Gháts as far north as Násik.

Growth rather fast, 4·7 rings per inch of radius. Weight, 23 to 29 lbs. per cubic foot. Wood used for the cylinders of native drums. The whole tree is full of an acrid milk said to be poisonous.

		lbs.
H 103.	Bhajji, Simla, 4,000 feet	29
H 615.	Kulu, 5,000 feet	23

4. E. indica, Müll. Arg.; Beddome ccxv.; Brandis 441; Kurz ii. 413. *Sapium indicum,* Roxb. Fl. Ind. iii. 692. Vern. *Húruá, batúl,* Beng.; *Kirri makalu,* Cingh.

A small evergreen tree, with smooth, grey bark. Wood soft, white, with small brown heartwood. Pores moderate-sized and large, oval, often subdivided. Medullary rays equally distributed, very fine, closely packed. The transverse diameter of the pores is greater than the distance between the rays.

Sundarbans and tidal forests of Tenasserim and Ceylon.

Weight, 29 lbs. per cubic foot. The wood is used in the Sundarbans for fuel. The juice of the tree is very poisonous and the seeds are used to poison fish.

		lbs.
E 409.	Sundarbans	29

5. E. Agallocha, Willd.; Roxb. Fl. Ind. iii. 686; Beddome ccxv.; Brandis 442; Kurz ii. 414. Vern. *Gangwa, geor, uguru, geria,* Beng.; *Tayan, kayan,* Burm.; *Yekin,* Burm. in the Andamans.

A small evergreen tree which exudes poisonous milk. Wood very soft, spongy. Pores small, scanty, sometimes in radial lines. Medullary rays very numerous, extremely fine.

Coast and tidal forests of India, Burma and the Andaman Islands.

Weight, 26 lbs. per cubic foot. Home in his Sundarbans List of 1874 says: "Grows occasionally to 5 feet in girth and 40 feet in height, though generally cut for posts when of small girth. It is a useful wood for general carpentering purposes, such as toys, bedsteads, tables, &c., a white timber; the juice which exudes from the bark when green is very poisonous." Roxburgh says it is only used for charcoal and firewood.

		lbs.
E 396.	Sundarbans	24
B 2477.	Andaman Islands (Kurz, 1866)	28

23. EUPHORBIA, Linn.

About 11 species of Indian small trees or shrubs usually with thick, fleshy, angular branches and short gouty stems. *E. sessiliflora,* Roxb. Fl. Ind. ii. 471; Kurz ii. 415, is a fleshy undershrub of Pegu. *E. neriifolia,* Linn.; Beddome ccxvi.; Brandis 439; Kurz ii. 416; Gamble 72 (*E. ligularia,* Roxb. Fl. Ind. ii. 465). Vern. *Mausa sij,* Beng.; *Gangichú,* Pb.; *Thor,* Bombay; *Shasoung,* Burm., is a small tree with cylindric stem and 5-angled, spirally twisted stem, cultivated near villages in most parts of India. It is considered a sacred tree by the Mechis of the Sikkim Terai and Bhutan Dúars, and is consequently often found on deserted village sites. The milk is used in native medicine and the root to cure snake-bite. *E. Nivulia,* Ham.; Beddome ccxvi.; Brandis 439; Kurz ii. 417 (*E. neriifolia,* Roxb. Fl. Ind. ii. 467) Vern. *Sij,* Beng.; *Newrang,* Mar.; *Sha-soung,* Burm., is a shrub of dry and rocky sites in Garhwal, Sind, the Dekkan and Burma, with round branches. *E. antiquorum,* Linn.; Roxb. Fl. Ind. ii. 468; Beddome ccxvi.; Brandis 438; Kurz ii. 416. Vern. *Nara sij, tekata sij,* Beng.; *Tidhara,* Hind.; *Shidu,* Mechi; *Shasoung-pya-thal,* Burm.; *Dalúk,* Cingh., is a shrub with 3-angled branches, common on dry hills in Bengal and the Peninsula. *E. trigona,* Roxb. Fl. Ind. ii. 468; Beddome ccxvi; Brandis 438, is a small tree with 3-angled stems found on arid hills in Coimbatore. *E. tortilis,* Rottler; Beddome ccxvi.; Brandis 439, is a small tree of dry hills in South India, with 3-angled, spirally twisted branches. *E. Cattimandoo,* Elliot, Beddome ccxvi.; Brandis 438. Vern. *Katti mandu,* Tel., is a small tree with 5-angled branches common in Vizagapatam district, and yielding a copious milk, which is used as a cement. *E. Tirucalli,* Linn.; Roxb. Fl. Ind. ii. 470; Beddome ccxvii.; Brandis 439; Kurz ii. 417. Vern. *Lanka sij,* Beng.; *Sehnd,* Hind.; *Tiru kalli,* Mal.; *Sha-soung-leknyo,* Burm., is a small tree with round stems and smooth green branches, cultivated throughout India and used as hedges. The wood is strong and used for veneering and toys; the milk is very acrid. Skinner, No. 69, gives the weight 36 lbs., P = 618. He says that twigs thrown into a tank when the water is low intoxicate and kill the fish. *E. epiphylloides,* Kurz ii. 416, is a small tree of the Andamans. The well-known *E. pulcherrima,* Willd. or *Poinsettia pulcherrima* is a garden shrub with large crimson floral leaves, introduced from Mexico, and cultivated in gardens in most parts of India.

1. E. Royleana, Boissier; Brandis 438. *E. pentagona,* Royle. Vern. *Thor,* Punjab; *Sali,* Jhelam; *Chúla,* Chenab; *Chún,* Ravi; *Chú, chúnga, súrs,* Beas; *Súro, tsui,* Sutlej; *Sohúnd,* Kumaun.

A large, milky shrub. Wood spongy. Pores small, subdivided, scanty. Medullary rays extremely fine.

North-Western Himalaya, ascending to 6,000 feet.

It reaches 15-16 feet in height, the stems having 2-3, and often even 5-6 feet in girth.

It is often planted as a hedge and grows readily from cuttings, even on the driest soil.

P 3075. Sabathu, Punjab.

24. BUXUS, Tournefort.

1. B. sempervirens, Linn.; Brandis 447. *B. Wallichiana,* Baillon. Vern. *Shanda laghúne,* Afg.; *Chikri,* Kashmir; *Papri, papar, paprang, shamshád, shumaj,* Pb.

An evergreen shrub or small tree. Bark grey, soft, corky, cut into small plates by deep irregular cracks. Wood yellowish white, hard, smooth, very close and even-grained. Annual rings distinctly marked by a narrow line without pores. Pores extremely small, very numerous, uniform and uniformly distributed. Medullary rays fine to extremely fine, very numerous.

Suliman and Salt Ranges, North-West Himalaya between 4,000 and 8,000 feet, Bhutan about 6,000 to 7,000 feet; but scattered in different parts of the Himalaya, chiefly on a calcareous soil and often in remote localities. From recent reports on the localities of boxwood in the North-West Himalaya, the following appear to be the chief:—

In the Punjab.—

Rawul Pindi Division . .	Occasional in ravines of the Margulla Syudpore Range, but of small size, the largest being 6 inches and the average 4 inches in girth.
Fuel Reserve, North . .	Scattered trees in the Talagang and Khusha forests.
Beas Division	1. On the Grán-Nála, a tributary of the Parbatti; about 500 poles, 20 feet high and 4 to 12 inches in diameter below the Grán village and a few trees higher up, the largest of which is 15 inches in diameter. (Kulu Report, 1877, paragraph 24.) 2. On the Brahmganga River. 3. On two tributaries of the Sainj River. 4. A locality in Seoraj, Kulu. 5. A locality in Balhan Koti.
Sutlej Division . . .	Trees and groups of trees between Wangtu and Kilba. A small forest to the north of the Shali Range.
In the North-West Provinces.—	About 3,400 trees were counted in the forests of the Garhwal State. The finest trees were in the Kelso Valley near the village of Alyora, where trees 6 feet in girth were seen with fine straight stems.

It is estimated that the cost per cubic foot of boxwood delivered at Saharanpur from the Kelso forest would be Re. 1-8; its further cost by rail from Saharanpur to Bombay would be at least Re. 1-8 or total Rs. 3 per cubic foot. Considering 1 cubic foot as weighing 60 lbs., we have the cost per ton as Rs. 112, which could only be just covered by receipts if the very best description of wood were sent down. There is consequently little likelihood of much trade in boxwood from the Himalayan forests. Growth very slow: Brandis says, 15 to 20 rings per inch of radius. In Holtzappfel's "Descriptive Catalogue of Woods" English boxwood is said only to attain a diameter of

1½ to 2 inches in 20 to 25 years. An examination of the specimens received by us shewed that the growth is extremely variable. We found—

H 990.	75 rings per inch of radius	Average of 8 specimens 33·5 rings per inch of radius.
H 424.	41 ,, ,, ,,	
H 930.	40 ,, ,, ,,	
H 614.	30 ,, ,, ,,	
H 2914.	27 ,, ,, ,,	
H 165.	25 ,, ,, ,,	
H 38.	16 ,, ,, ,,	
H 77.	14 ,, ,, ,,	

Weight, Brandis says, 60 to 65 lbs. per cubic foot; Mathieu, Fl. For., p. 268, gives 56 to 72 lbs.; our specimens average 57 lbs.

The uses of boxwood are well known. In Europe it is used for engraving, turning, carving and mathematical instruments. In the Himalaya small boxes to contain butter, honey, tinder, snuff, &c., are made of it, and it is carved into combs. The leaves are poisonous to cattle, only goats eat them sparingly with impunity; they are used in the south of France as manure for vineyards. The boxwood to be used for engraving requires very careful and lengthened seasoning; on this subject and on the other requisite characters of boxwood for commercial purposes, the following extract from a letter of Messrs. J. Gardner and Sons, of Liverpool, to the Inspector-General of Forests, dated April 3rd, 1877, will give information:—

"The value of boxwood at Bombay of suitable texture for the English market, of which latter we can judge from a few sample pieces, will depend principally upon the quality.

"Wood from 2 to 4 inches diameter is required to be free from splits or cracks, otherwise, however free from knots and straight and round it may be, the value would not exceed £1 to £2 per ton, whilst if free from splits, round and straight and with—

not exceeding one knot per foot in length	the value would probably be	£10 per ton,
exceeding 1 knot and not exceeding 2 knots		£7-10*s*. ,,
,, 2 knots ,, ,, 3 ,,		£5 ,,

all knots or holes, counted as such, however small.

"Wood 4 inches and upwards in diameter is preferred with one split rather than sound or with more than one split, any splits after the first reducing the value on account of the additional waste in working the same.

		Averaging per foot in length. 1 knot.	2 knots.	3 knots.
		£	£	£
The value of round and straight (1 split) averaging.	4 to 5 inches diameter	6	4-10*s*.	3
	5 to 6 ,,	9	6	3
	6 inches and upwards diameter	12	9	4-10*s*.

"If the splits are twisted more than 1 inch to the foot if small, 2 inches if medium size, and 3 inches to the foot length if large, the value is reduced one-half.

"The above values will, of course, vary in accordance with the supply and demand for the various sizes and qualities.

"The most suitable texture of wood will be found growing upon the sides of mountains. If grown in the plains, the growth is usually too quick, and consequently the grain is too coarse; the wood of best texture being of slow growth and very fine in the grain.

"It should be cut down in the winter, and, if possible, stored at once in airy wooden sheds, well protected from sun and rain, and not to have too much air through the sides of the shed, more especially for the wood under 4 inches diameter.

"The boxwood also must not be piled upon the ground, but be well skidded under, so as to be kept quite free from the effects of any damp from the soil.

"After the trees are cut down, the longer they are left exposed the more danger is there afterwards of the wood splitting more than is absolutely necessary during the necessary seasoning before shipment to this country.

"If shipped green there is great danger of the wood sweating and becoming mildewed during transit, which causes the wood afterwards to dry light and of a defective colour, and in fact rendering it of little value for commercial purposes.

"There is no occasion to strip the bark off, or to put cowdung or anything else upon the ends of the pieces to prevent their splitting.

"Boxwood is the nearest approach to ivory of any wood known, and will therefore probably gradually increase in value, as it, as well as ivory, become scarcer. It is now used very considerably in manufacturing concerns, but on account of its gradual advance in price during the past few years, cheaper woods are in some instances being substituted.

"Small wood under 4 inches is used principally by flax-spinners for rollers and by turners for various purposes, rollers for rink skates, &c., &c., and if free from splits is of equal value with the larger wood. It is imported here as small as 1½ inches in diameter, but the most useful sizes are from 2½ to 3½ inches, and would, therefore, we suppose, be from 15 to 30 or 40 years in growing, whilst larger wood would require 50 years and upwards at least, perhaps we ought to say 100 years and upwards. It is used principally for shuttles for weaving silk, linen and cotton, and also for rule-making and wood engraving. *Punch, The Illustrated London News, The Graphic,* and all the first class pictorial papers use large quantities of boxwood."

Messrs. Churchill and Sim, reporting on some boxwood sent to them for sale in 1880, and which fetched 21 shillings per cwt., equivalent at 60 lbs. per cubic foot to 11*s.* 1*d.* or about Rs. 6 per cubic foot say :—

"The pieces of boxwood were remarkably fine specimens, equal in quality to the best Abasia, and fetched a very high price, equivalent to £21 per ton. These logs were depreciated in value for ordinary purposes, owing to their having been squared, which was a mistake, as in that operation much valuable wood had been wasted, and when the bark is removed, a good protection to the log is destroyed. In the present state of the boxwood trade, and considering the fact that the supplies which have been coming forward for some time past are deteriorating in quality, from the action of the Turkish Govenment in closing the forests and from other causes, the probability of a supply of this wood from India is a matter of considerable importance. The usual run of this wood would not, however, fetch the high price of this picked sample. The price realized cannot, however, be taken as any criterion, for whether supplies can be sent to this market, and sold at prices which will cover transit and freight, and then leave a profit, is very doubtful. Could this wood be regularly placed on the market at a moderate figure, there is no reason why a trade should not be developed in it."

			lbs.
H	930.	Hazara, 7,000 feet	59
H	165.	Kangra (Stewart, 1866)	58
H	168.	Shahpur " "	...
H	614.	Kulu, 7,000 feet	56
H	954.	Kunawar	...
H	990.	"	54
H	38.	Kandru, Simla, 8,000 feet	60
H	77.	Shali, Simla, 7,000 feet	57
H	2914.	" " " "	...
H	424.	Darua block, Deoban, North-Western Provinces, 6,800 feet	55

25. SARCOCOCCA, Lindl.

Two species, *S. saligna*, Müll. Arg., with tri-nerved and *S. Hookeriana*, Baill., with penniveined leaves. The latter is a shrub of the hills of Sikkim.

1. S. saligna, Müll. Arg.; Beddome ccxvii.; Brandis 448; Gamble 72. Vern. *Sukat sing,* Kumaun; *Chilikat,* Nep.

A small evergreen shrub. Wood white, moderately hard. Pores very small and extremely small. Medullary rays fine and moderately broad.

Afghanistan, Himalaya at 4,000 to 7,000 feet, ascending in Sikkim to 9,000 feet, Khasia Hills, Nilgiris and Western Coast.

Wood sometimes used for walking-sticks.

H 2832. Simla, 7,000 feet.

ORDER XCVI. BETULACEÆ.

Two genera, *Betula* and *Alnus*. Himalayan trees, with similar qualities to the Birches and Alders of Europe.

Wood soft, tough to cut. Pores small, uniformly distributed. No distinct heartwood.

1. BETULA, Tournefort.

Three Indian species. The common European Birch is *B. alba*, Linn., and the American Paper Birch, of which the light, portable canoes are made in Canada, is *B. papyracea*, Willd.

Wood tough, close-grained, moderately hard. Pores small, not numerous. Medullary rays fine. Medullary patches scanty.

1. B. Bhojpattra, Wall.; Brandis 457; Gamble 79. *B. Jacquemontii*, Spach. Vern. *Búrj, burzal, bhúj, phurz*, Pb.; *Shák, pád, phatak, takpa*, Ladak, Lahoul, Piti, Kanawar; *Takpa*, Bhutia; *Bhújpattra*, Hind.; *Phuspat*, Nep.

A moderate-sized deciduous tree. Bark smooth, shining, with white oblong lenticels, the outer bark consisting of numerous distinct, thin, papery layers, peeling off in broad horizontal rolls. Wood white with a pinkish tinge, tough, even-grained, moderately hard. Pores small, not numerous, uniform and uniformly distributed except that sometimes they are arranged in interrupted lines along the edges of the annual rings. Medullary rays fine and very fine, numerous, prominent on a radial section.

Higher ranges of the Himalaya, forming the upper edge of arborescent vegetation and ascending to 14,000 feet.

Growth slow, the countings taken from our specimens were very uniform, 5 specimens varying only from 13 to 18 rings, giving an average of 15 rings per inch of radius. Aikin, in Wallich's List, gives 3·4 rings per inch. In weight, also, the experiments of Dr. Warth on six specimens gave only a variation from 42 to 46 lbs. with an average of 44 lbs.; Wallich gave 35·5 lbs. per cubic foot.

The wood is extensively used in the inner arid Himalaya for building; it is elastic, seasons well and does not warp. The bark is very valuable; it is used as paper for writing and packing, for umbrellas, hooka tubes, and for roofing houses. The branches are made into twig bridges, and the leaves are lopped for cattle fodder.

			lbs.
H	909.	Upper Chenab, 10,000 feet	45
H	610.	Lahoul, 10,000 feet	44
H	126.	Rotang Pass, Kulu, 9,000 feet	42
H	127.	Monali, Kulu, 8,000 feet	46
E	381.	Tonglo, Darjeeling, 10,000 feet	44
E	2404.	" " "	43

2. B. acuminata, Wall.; Brandis 458; Kurz ii. 476; Gamble 79. Vern. *Púya udish, hambar máya, makshéri, sheori, shag*, Pb.; *Bhújpattra, háur, shául*, Hind.; *Haoul*, Kumaun; *Shakshin*, Tibet; *Saver, sauer, payong, útis*, Nep.; *Hlosungli*, Lepcha; *Dingleen*, Khasia.

A large tree. Bark grey, peeling off in horizontal rolls. Wood white, moderately hard, close-grained. Pores small and very small, often subdivided; numerous in the inner part of each annual ring, scanty and smaller in the outer half. Medullary rays fine.

Himalaya, from 6,000 to 8,000 feet, Khasia hills, and hills of Martaban.

Growth moderate, our specimens shew 10 rings per inch of radius; a round in the Bengal Forest Museum shews 6·5 rings per inch. Weight 41 lbs. per cubic foot. The wood is very little used, but Wallich says it is hard and esteemed in Nepal for all purposes where strength and durability are required.

		lbs.
H 611.	Parbatti Valley, Kulu, 8,000 feet	41
H 2914.	Nagkanda, Simla, 8,000 feet	41
E 2405.	Darjeeling, 7,000 feet	...

3. B. cylindrostachys, Wall.; Gamble 80. Under *B. acuminata*, Wall. in Brandis For. Flora 458; Kurz ii. 476. Vern. *Shaoul*, Kumaun; *Sauer*, Nep.; *Sungli*, Lepcha.

A tall deciduous tree. Bark pink, peeling off in large vertical flakes, giving the stem a shaggy appearance. Wood red, hard, heavy. Annual rings indistinct. Pores scanty, small, often subdivided, uniformly distributed. Medullary rays fine, numerous, the distance between the rays larger than the transverse diameter of the pores.

Kumaun, Nepal, Darjeeling Hills from the Terai up to 6,000 feet.

Growth fast, 5½ rings per inch of radius. Weight, 52 lbs. per cubic foot. The wood is strong and seasons well, but is not used except for firewood and charcoal, for which purposes it is very good. It is an extremely handsome tree with drooping branches.

		lbs.
E 678.	Bamunpokri, Darjeeling Terai	52

2. ALNUS, Tournefort.

Two species. The chief European Alders are *A. glutinosa*, Linn., with glutinous leaves, and *A. incana*, Willd., with pubescent leaves.

Pores small, uniformly distributed, often in radial lines. Medullary rays of two classes, the broad rays composed of numerous fine rays. Medullary patches scanty (common in some of the European species).

1. A. nitida, Endl.; Brandis 460. Vern. *Gíra*, Afg.; *Shrol, saroli, sawáli, rikunra, chámb, chápu, piák, kúnsa, kúndash, niú, kosh, raján*, Pb.; *Paya udesh*, Kumaun.

A large tree. Bark brown, rough with deep furrows. Wood reddish white, soft, close-and even-grained, tough to cut; annual rings distinctly marked by harder wood near the inner edge of each ring. Pores small, numerous, uniformly distributed, arranged in radial lines. Medullary rays of two classes, a few broad rays at considerable intervals with numerous fine rays between them; the broad rays, which consits of a large number of small, closely-packed rays, are marked as irregular shining plates on a radial section. Medullary patches scanty.

Punjab, Himalaya, ascending to 9,000 feet.

Growth fast, our specimens shew 3 rings per inch of radius. Weight, 28 to 31 lbs. per cubic foot. The wood is used for bedsteads and for the hooked sticks of rope bridges. Twigs are used for tying loads and for rope bridges. The bark is used for dyeing and tanning.

		lbs.
H 119.	Vaziri Rupi, 6,000 feet	28
H 147.	Sainj, Simla, 4,000 feet	31

2. A. nepalensis, D. Don; Brandis 460; Kurz ii. 476; Gamble 80. Vern. *Kohi*, Pb.; *Udesh*, Kumaun; *Udis, utis*, Nep.; *Kowal*, Lepcha.

A large deciduous tree. Bark thick, outside silvery grey, resembling that of the birch. Wood similar to that of *A. nitida*, but the pores are fewer and somewhat larger, and the broad medullary rays are very broad and very numerous. No medullary patches.

Himalaya, from the Ravi eastwards, between 3,000 and 9,000 feet, Khasia Hills.

Growth fast, our specimens shew 3·6 rings per inch of radius; a round in the Bengal Forest Museum shews 2·4 rings. Aikin, in Wallich's List, mentions 2 specimens, one giving 11·8 rings, the other 2·7 rings per inch. Weight, 27 to 28 lbs. per cubic foot. The wood is not used, but as the tree is common and grows to a large size in the East Himalaya it might be used for tea-boxes. The bark is used for dyeing and tanning.

		lbs.
H 83.	The Glen, Simla, 6,000 feet	28
E 356.	Tukdah Forest, Darjeeling, 5,000 feet	27
E 2406.	" " " "	...

ORDER XCVII. SALICINEÆ.

Two genera, *Salix* and *Populus*. With one or two exceptions, all Himalayan trees.

Wood soft, even-grained. Pores small, numerous. Medullary rays fine.

1. SALIX, Tournef.

About 33 species, with very few exceptions confined to the Himalaya. They are mostly small, often prostrate shrubs, but in the arid regions of the inner Himalaya are of great use for firewood, bridges, basket-work and other purposes, and are often planted, as their quick growth and ready reproduction, either by cuttings or in coppice, ensures a constant supply of wood. The following list of the Indian species has been extracted from N. J. Anderson's Monograph in vol. xvi., p. 2, of DeCandolle's Prodromus.

The European species of willow, which are very numerous, belong to two sections, the "Sallows," the type of which is *S. Caprea*, and the "Osiers," the type of which is *S. alba*. They are largely cultivated, and are in great use for all purposes, and especially for the protection of river banks and for basket-work.

SECTION I. PLEIANDRÆ.

(*Stamens 3 or more, free.*)

S. tetrasperma, Roxb.	All India.
S. pyrina, Wall.	Nepal.
S. calostachya, And.	Hazara.
S. urophylla, Lindl.	Oudh.
S. populifolia, And.	India (?)
S. acmophylla, Boiss. (Brandis 463. Vern. *Bed*, Afg.; *Bada, bisu*, Pb.)	Afghanistan, Sind, Punjab.
S. fragilis, Linn.	Lahoul, Ladak.
S. alba, Linn.	Ladak, Kashmir.
S. babylonica, Linn.	Suliman Range, elsewhere cultivated.

SECTION II. DIANDRÆ.

(*Stamens 2, free.*)

S. Caprea, Linn. (Brandis 467. Vern. *Bedmushk*, Pb. The leaves are used for sherbet) . .	Northern India, cultivated.
S. Wallichiana, And.	Himalaya.
S. sclerophylla, And.	Ladak, Dras.

S. elegans, Wall.	North-Western Himalaya.
S. hastata, Linn. (Brandis 467)	Kashmir to Kunawar, 9,000 to 15,000 feet.
S. daphnoides, Vill.	North-Western Himalaya.
S. insignis, And. (Brandis 470. Vern. *Bitsu*, Pb.; *Gir*, Kashmir.)	Kashmir, Piti, 5,000 to 12,000 feet.
S. viminalis, Linn.	Inner Himalaya.
S. obscura, And.	Sikkim, 9,000 to 14,000 feet.
S. Sikkimensis, And.	" " "
S. Daltoniana, And.	" " "
S. eriophylla, And.	Khasia Hills, 4,000 to 5,000 feet.
S. eriostachya, Wall.	Nepal.
S. longiflora, Wall	Sikkim, 9,000 feet.
S. serphyllum, And.	Sikkim, 10,000 to 14,000 feet.
S. flabellaris, And. (Brandis 471. A small procumbent shrub.)	Dras, Lahoul, Kunawar, 11,000 to 15,000 feet.
S. Lindleyana, Wall. (Brandis 471. A small procumbent shrub.)	Kumaun, Nepal, Sikkim, 11,000 to 16,000 feet.
S. calyculata, Hook. f.	Sikkim, 14,000 to 15,000 feet.
S. oreophila, Hook. f.	Sikkim, 15,000 to 16,000.
S. Thomsoniana, And.	Sikkim, 10,000 feet.

SECTION III. SYNANDREÆ.

(*Filaments connate.*)

S. pycnostachya, And. (Brandis 470. Cultivated in Ladak. Vern. *Changma*, Thibet.)	Zanskar, Ladak, 13,000 feet.
S. oxycarpa, And. (Brandis 471)	Kashmir, Kistwar, 6,000 to 11,000 feet.
S. divergens, And.	Kistwar, Zanskar, 12,000 feet.
S. angustifolia, Wild. (Brandis 47)	Afghanistan, Kashmir, Zanskar, 7,000 to 12,000 feet.

S. Caprea, Linn., is grown in Northern India, usually from cuttings, as in the gardens at Lahore. Brandis gives 27 to 39 lbs. per cubic foot as the weight according to Nordlinger; Mathieu, Fl. For., p. 405, gives 27 to 45 lbs., while the experiments made by Captain Call, R.E., at Kandahar, give, if the determination of the species is correct, with bars 1 ft. × 1 in. × 1 in., Weight 32·2 lbs., P = 641 (Indian Forester, Vol. v. p. 480).

S. alba is also cultivated in the Western Himalaya. Brandis says the wood is soft, white near the circumference, yellow or brown towards the centre; the medullary rays are fine and numerous; the pores very numerous, fine and uniformly distributed, the annual rings distinctly marked by a dark line. He gives the weight as 26 to 33 lbs.; Mathieu, Fl. For., p. 393, gives 24 to 38 lbs., while Captain Call's experiments, if the species is correctly determined, give 27·7 lbs., P = 602.

Wood soft, even-grained, white or light red. Pores small, numerous, rarely subdivided, uniform and uniformly distributed, except that in most species they are more numerous in the inner belt of the annual ring. Medullary rays numerous, fine, uniform. Medullary patches frequent. The species can hardly be distinguished by the structure of their wood.

1. **S. tetrasperma**, Roxb. Fl. Ind. iii. 753; Beddome t. 302; Brandis 462; Kurz ii. 493; Gamble 81. Vern. *Bed, bent, baishi*, Hind.; *Laila, bains*, North-Western India; *Bis, beis, bitsa, bín, bídu, bakshel,*

magsher, safedar, badha, Pb.; *Yír*, Kashmir; *Bilsa*, Oudh; *Pani jama*, Beng.; *Bhesh*, Gáro; *Bhi*, Ass.; *Wallunj, bacha*, Bombay; *Niranji*, Kan.; *Momakha*, Burm.

A moderate-sized deciduous tree. Bark rough, with deep vertical, rough, shining fissures. Heartwood red, soft, porous, even-grained. Annual rings indistinctly marked by concentric lines. Pores small, very numerous, uniformly distributed, sometimes subdivided. Medullary rays fine, numerous, not distinct.

Throughout India, on river banks and in moist places, and in the Himalayan valleys ascending to 6,000 feet.

Growth fast. In Minniken's report on the Delhi Bela Plantation the following measurements are given :—

		Trees.	Mean girth.	Height.	Age.
Compt. 3.	Kudsia . .	3	18 in.	25 ft.	6 years
„ 4.	Jaffar Khan .	3	15 in.	...	6 „

or 2 to 2½ rings per inch of radius; our specimens shew 2 to 6 rings per inch of radius. Weight, Brandis' Burma List of 1862, No. 89, gave 37 lbs.; our specimens give 31 to 35 lbs. The wood is rarely used; it has been used for gunpowder charcoal; Mann says that in Assam it is used for posts and planks. The twigs are made into baskets and the leaves lopped for cattle fodder. The bark is said by Kurz to be used for tanning, and by Dalzell to be used as a febrifuge.

			lbs.
H	155.	Sainj, Giri Valley	35
H	99.	Bhajji, Sutlej Valley	32
O	1485.	Kheri, Oudh	32
O	1465.	Gonda, Oudh	35
C	2818.	Melghát, Berar	31
E	1256.	Tezpur, Assam	35

2. S. fragilis, Linn.; Brandis 466. Vern. *Tilchang*, Lahoul.

A tree with grey, deeply fissured bark. Wood with reddish heartwood. Annual rings marked by concentric lines.

H 141, from Lahoul, is probably this species. It is cultivated in Lahoul and Ladak. Growth moderate, 11 rings per inch of radius, but the growth is fast while young, and gradually gets slower as the tree ages. Our specimen was 50 years old, and had a girth of 30 inches. Weight, 28 lbs. per cubic foot.

3. S. babylonica, Linn.; Roxb. Fl. Ind. iii. 754; Brandis 465; Gamble 81. The Weeping Willow. Vern. *Bísa, bada, bed, katíra, majnún*, Pb.; *Giúr*, Kashmir; *Tissi, bhosi*, Nep.

A tree with pendent branches. Bark grey, ¼ to ½ inch thick. Wood white, annual rings marked by a belt of more numerous pores in the spring wood.

Commonly cultivated in North India. Said by Stewart to be indigenous in the Suliman Range.

Growth fast, our small specimen shews 5 rings per inch of radius; Stewart records 4 to 5 rings per inch of radius, and a girth of 4 feet as the average of 6 trees, 10 years planted out. The branches are made into baskets, and are used for weirs and the protection of canal banks. It is very commonly grown for ornament, and is readily reproduced by cuttings.

H 3060. Koti, Simla, 7,000 feet.

4. S. Wallichiana, And.; Brandis 468. Vern. *Bwir*, Pb.; *Bhains, bhangli, kalgúli*, North-Western Provinces.

A large shrub with greenish grey bark. Wood white or pinkish white, structure that of the genus.

Afghanistan, Kashmir, Himalaya eastwards to Bhutan, ascending to 9,000 feet.

Growth fast, 6 rings per inch of radius. Weight, 32 lbs. per cubic foot. The branches are made into baskets.

		lbs.
H 2910.	Nagkanda, Simla, 8,000 feet	32
H 3035	„ „	...

5. S. elegans, Wall.; Brandis 466. Vern. *Bail, blail, bhains,* Simla.

A small shrub with pinkish wood. Annual rings marked by a porous spring wood and by an autumn wood of firmer texture.

North-West Himalaya, from 7,000 to 10,000 feet, as far east as Nepal, Lahoul, Kunawar, as high as 11,500 feet.

Growth slow, 15 rings per inch of radius. Weight, 33 lbs. per cubic foot. Used for fodder for cattle and goats. The leaves of this and *S. daphnoides* are often attacked by a brilliant orange-coloured fungus, which is *Lecythea salicina,* Lev.

		lbs.
H 2842.	Mahasu, Simla, 8,000 feet	33
H 2906.	Nagkanda, Simla, 9,000 feet	...

6. S. daphnoides, Vill.; Brandis 469. Vern. *Bed, bidái, betsa, beli, bushan, bashal, bhail, bhéul, mudanu, shún, tháil,* Pb.; *Yúr,* Kashmir; *Changma, chámma, malchang, kalchang,* West Tibet; *Richang, roangching, changkar,* Lahoul.

A shrub or tree with smooth bark. Heartwood red, shining. Annual rings marked by more numerous pores in the spring wood.

North-West Himalaya, both on the outer ranges and in the inner arid tract. It extends to the Alps and the mountains of Central Europe.

Growth variable: the Lahoul specimen shewed a rate of 4 rings per inch; the rest gave from 10 to 15 rings. Weight, our specimens average 33·5 lbs. per cubic foot; Mathieu, Fl. For. p. 397, gives 32·7 lbs. The wood is used in the arid inner valleys for building, pails, tubs and tools. The twigs are used for baskets, twig bridges in Piti, Zanskar and Ladak, and for building (willow wattle and daub) in Ladak. It is much grown in Lahoul, from cuttings 9 to 12 feet long; the trees are pollarded every third or fourth year, and the branches and leaves used for cattle-fodder and litter.

		lbs.
H 2854.	Mahasu, Simla, 7,000 feet	...
H 47.	Kalashi, Simla, 7,000 „	30
H 66.	Nagkanda, Simla, 8,000 feet	34
H 2905.	„ „ 9,000 „	...
H 3034.	„ „ 8,000 „	37
H 3036.	„ „ 8,000 „	33
H 142.	Lahoul, about 9,000 feet	34

7. S. viminalis, Linn.; Brandis 470. Vern. *Bítsu,* Pb.; *Kumanta,* Lahoul.

A shrub with shining, grey, slightly-cracked bark, and white wood, with the structure of the genus.

Inner arid Himalaya from the Jhelam to Sikkim (*S. Smithiana,* Willd.), from 5,000 to 9,000 feet, cultivated in Lahoul, Dras and Kunawar. Common throughout Europe in osier beds.

H 143. Lahoul, about 9,000 feet.

8. S. sp. (It may be near *viminalis.*)

A deciduous shrub with smooth dark-coloured bark and lanceolate leaves, covered beneath with white tomentum. Wood soft, close-grained, heartwood red. Annual rings distinctly marked by an irregular belt of numerous pores in the spring wood. Pores small and numerous in the spring wood, very small and scanty in the autumn wood. Medullary rays very fine, very numerous, uniform and equidistant.

Growth moderately slow, 13 rings per inch of radius.
Weight, 31 lbs. per cubic foot.

		lbs.
E 966.	Chumbi Valley, Tibet, about 8,000 feet	31

2. POPULUS, Tournef.

Five species. *P. nigra*, Linn.; Brandis 472. The Black or Lombardy Poplar. Vern. *Suféda*, Pb.; *Frast*, Kashmir; *Prost, farsh, makkal*, Chenab; *Kramali, biúns, do*, Sutlej; *Yarpa, yúlatt, kabúl*, Ladak, is a large tree commonly planted in Afghanistan, Kashmir, the plains and hills of the Punjab, up to 12,500 feet in Ladak. Both varieties are fast growers, the Black Poplar attaining 80 feet in height with a diameter of 2 feet in 50 years. Both grow well from cuttings, and the leaves are lopped for cattle fodder. Mathieu, Fl. For. p. 428, gives the weight as 25 to 36 lbs. per cubic foot. *P. alba*, Linn.; Brandis 473. The Abele or White Poplar. Vern. *Sperdor, spelda*, Afg.; *Chitta bagnu, safedar, janali frast, fras, prist, rikkan, sannún, chanún, mál*, Pb., is a large tree, wild and cultivated in the North-West Himalaya up to 10,000 feet, and extending to Afghanistan, Beluchistan and on into Europe. It is generally raised from cuttings, and the growth is very fast, reaching a diameter of 2 to 3 feet in 50 years. The wood of this and of *P. nigra* is used for the Afghan grape-boxes. Mathieu, Fl. For. p. 422, gives the weight as 28 to 44 lbs. per cubic foot. *P. tremula*, Linn.; Brandis 474, is the Aspen Poplar of Europe.

Wood soft, even-grained. Pores small, numerous, often subdivided, uniformly distributed, except that they are scanty and generally somewhat smaller in the autumn wood. Medullary rays very fine, uniform. Medullary patches scanty.

1. P. euphratica, Olivier; Brandis 474. Vern. *Bahan*, Sind, Pb.; *Patki*, Brahui; *Hodung*, Ladak.

A large deciduous tree. Bark thick, with irregular, vertical furrows. Sapwood white, heartwood red, often nearly black near the centre, moderately hard, compact, even-grained. Annual rings marked by a very narrow belt with fewer pores. Pores small, very numerous, uniformly distributed, often subdivided. Medullary rays very fine, uniform, equidistant, the distance between the rays equal to the transverse diameter of the pores.

Banks of the Indus in Sind, the Upper Valley of the Indus, and its tributaries in Tibet.

Growth rapid: Brandis says 3 to 4 rings per inch of radius; our specimens are evidently fast grown, but the rings very difficult to distinguish, they seem to shew about 4 to 6 per inch. Weight, our specimens shew 32 to 37 lbs. per cubic foot, some experiments made at Kandahar by Captain Call, R.E., with bars 1 ft. × 1 in. × 1 in. gave the weight 27·2 lbs. and 427 for the value of P (Indian Forester, Vol. v. p. 480.) The wood is largely used in Sind for building, turnery, lacquered boxes, but not for fuel for the river steamers, as its heating powers are not great. On the Euphrates and Tigris it is used for planking and boat-building, and in the Punjab for the lining of walls. The inner bark is made into gun-match in Sind, and the bark given as a vermifuge. The leaves are used for fodder for goats and cattle. In Ladak it is much prized for fuel. It coppices well and bears pollarding long; coppice shoots are often used as rafters in Sind.

		lbs.
P 883.	Múltan	32
P 1384.	Indus bank, Central Sind	37

2. P. ciliata, Wall.; Brandis 475; Gamble 81. Vern. *Safeda, bagnu, phalja, phlassu, falís, palúch, phalsh, ban phrastu, dud phras, asán, suáli, ríkkan, saki, pábe, chanún, krammal, krambal, pahari pipal,* Pb.; *Chelaun, chelún,* Simla; *Garpipal,* Kumaun; *Bangikat,* Nep.; *Sungribong,* Lepcha.

A large deciduous tree. Bark smooth when young, with deep, vertical fissures when old. Wood grey or brownish grey, shining, soft. Annual rings marked by a belt of firm wood with scanty pores near the outer edge of each ring. Pores small, numerous, often subdivided, and arranged in short, radial lines. Medullary rays uniform, very fine, very numerous.

Himalaya from the Indus to Bhutan, between 4,000 and 10,000 feet.

Growth variable, the measurements of our specimens gave, H 34, 12 rings; H 770, 7 rings; E 970 8 rings; average 9 rings per inch of radius, which is moderate. Weight, on an average, 29·5 lbs. per cubic foot. The wood is used for water troughs, and the leaves as fodder for goats. The leaves are often attacked in autumn by a fungus which turns them white, and gives to a group of trees a curious appearance. This fungus is *Erysiphe Martii,* Lev.

		lbs.
H 3138.	Dungagalli, Hazara	...
H 34.	Matiyana, Simla, 7,000 feet	35
H 2884.	Nagkanda, „ 8,000 „	30
H 770.	Kalatop, Dalhousie, 7,000 feet	26
E 970.	Chumbi Valley, Tibet, about 8,000 feet	27

3. P. balsamifera, Linn.; Brandis 476. Vern. *Phalsh, makkal, pakhshu, pakh, bút, kramal,* Pb.; *Berfa, changma, yarpa, magkal, máhal,* W. Tibet.

A large tree. Bark grey, thick, rough, with longitudinal fissures. Wood light grey, soft to moderately hard. Annual rings distinctly marked. Pores very small and numerous in the spring wood, extremely small, scanty, and in short radial and oblique lines in the firmer autumn wood. Medullary rays very fine, uniform, numerous.

Inner arid Himalaya and Tibet, 8,000 to 14,000 feet. Extends to Afghanistan, Northern Asia and North America.

Growth, our specimen shews only a slow rate, 30 rings per inch of radius. It gives a weight of 32 lbs. per cubic foot. The wood is grown for fuel in the inner arid Himalaya, the branches are lopped for cattle fodder. The leaves and branches are full of balsamic juice, which also exudes on a fresh cut between the bark and the wood.

		lbs.
H 136.	Lahoul, about 9,000 feet	32

H 138, received from Lahoul, is a tree with smooth, greenish grey bark, similar to that of *P. tremula,* the Aspen. Wood light grey, soft, in structure resembling that of *P. balsamifera.* Our specimen had a girth of 32 inches, and was 22 years old, shewing thus 4 to 6 rings per inch of radius, which is very fast. The wood weighed 30 lbs. per cubic foot.

ORDER XCVIII. CUPULIFERÆ.

Four Indian genera: *Quercus, Castanopsis, Carpinus* and *Corylus.* Four other genera are found in the world, three of which, *Castanea, Fagus* and *Ostrya,* contain European species, and one, *Distegocarpus,* Japanese trees allied to *Carpinus. Castanea vulgaris,* Lam.; Brandis 491 (*C. Vesca,* Gaertn.), is the 'Sweet Chestnut' or 'Spanish Chestnut' of the south of Europe, largely cultivated either as coppice for hop poles and vine stakes or in high forest for its fruit. It has been introduced in the Himalaya and grown in various localities, and especially in a large number of places in the Punjab and the hills of the North-West Provinces, in Darjeeling and in the Khasia Hills. The experiment is as yet quite recent, and results are not sufficiently certain yet; but considering the large number of plants now growing and many favourable reports, it is probable that the experiments will be successful in some localities. *Fagus sylvatica*, Linn., is the 'Beech' Tree of Europe; and *Ostrya carpinifolia*, Scop., the 'Hop Hornbeam' of the Mediterranean region.

Pores generally arranged in radial lines or tails (not in *Fagus sylvatica*, *Castanea Vulgaris* and *Corylus Colurna*); medullary rays generally of two classes, broad and fine (not in *Castanea Vesca*, *Castanopsis* and four species of Indian Oaks). Most species have a distinct heartwood, exceptions are *Corylus* and *Carpinus*.

1. QUERCUS, Linn.

A large genus, one of the most important, not only in India and Europe, but also largely represented in America, Japan, and other parts of the world. It contains nearly 300 known species, of which 30 to 40 are probably Indian. The following list is taken from Alphonse De Candolle's Monograph in the Prodromus, Vol. xvi., those lately described by Kurz being given in brackets:—

SECTION I. LEPIDOBALANUS.

Q. Griffithii, Hook. f. and Th.	Khasia Hills, 5,000 to 6,000 feet.
Q. semecarpifolia, Sm.	North-West Himalaya, Nepal.
Q. Ilex, Linn.	North-West Himalaya, Afghanistan.
Q. dilatata, Lindl.	North-West Himalaya, Afghanistan.
Q. serrata, Thunb.	Nepal, Khasia Hills.
Q. lanuginosa, Don.	Kumaun, Nepal.
Q. incana, Roxb.	Outer North-West Himalaya.

SECTION II. PASANIA.

Q. Amherstiana, Wall.; Kurz ii. 484. Wood used for boat building. Weight 58 lbs. (Wallich)	Upper Tenasserim.
[*Q. Falconeri*, Kurz, in Journ. As. Soc. Bengal xliv. p. 197; Burma For. Fl. ii. 485]	Assam, Tenasserim.
Q. mixta, Alph. DC.	Upper Tenasserim.
Q. fenestrata, Roxb.	Sikkim, Khasia Hills, Eastern Bengal, Tenasserim.
Q. dealbata, Hook. f. and Th. Vern. *Dingir*, Khasia	Nepal, Khasia, Hills, Eastern Bengal.
Q. spicata, Sm.	North-East Himalaya, Eastern Bengal, Burma.
[*Q. pachyphylla*, Kurz]	Sikkim.
Q. lappacea, Roxb.	Assam, Eastern Bengal, Burma.
Q. acuminata, Roxb.	Sikkim, Eastern Bengal, Burma.

SECTION III. CYCLOBALANUS.

Q. Thomsoniana, Alph. DC.	Sikkim, 5,000 to 8,000 feet.
Q. oxyodon, Miq.	Khasia Hills, 5,000 feet.
Q. velutina, Lindl.; Kurz ii. 487	Chittagong, Burma.
Q. semiserrata, Roxb.; Brandis 488; Kurz ii. 488. Vern. *Thitkya*, Burm. Weight, 48 lbs.	Sylhet, Burma.

Q. annulata, Sm.	Himalaya, Khasia Hills.
Q. lamellosa, Sm.	Nepal, Sikkim, Bhutan, 6,000 to 9,000 feet.
Q. mespilifolia, Wall.; Kurz ii. 488	Ava, Prome, Arracan Hills, 4,000 to 5,000 feet.
[*Q. Brandisiana*, Kurz ii. 488]	Martaban, to 4,000 feet.

SECTION IV. CHLAMYDOBALANUS.

Q. lanceæfolia, Roxb.	Sikkim, Assam, Eastern Bengal.

[*Q. xylocarpa*, Kurz in Journ. As. Soc. Beng. xliv. 196]	Arracan.
[*Q. eumorpha*, Kurz ii. 487]	Martaban Hills, 6,000 to 7,000 feet.
[*Q. bancana*, Scheff.; Kurz ii. 485]	Martaban Hills, 3,000 to 5,000 feet.
[*Q. Olla*, Kurz in Journ. As. Soc. Beng. xliv. 197] .	Assam.
Q. nov. sp. Vern. *Dingwa*	Khasia Hills.

The most important of the non-Indian Oaks are described in Brandis For. Fl. pp. 483 to 487, and in other works such as Mathieu's Flore Forestière; we need, therefore, merely say that the British Oaks are *Q. pedunculata*, Ehrh., and *Q. sessiliflora*, Sm., usually united by botanists under the name *Q. Robur*, Linn. The Cork Oak is *Q. Suber*, Linn., found throughout the Mediterranean region; and cork is also produced by *Q. occidentalis*, Gay, of Spain, Portugal and Western France. The Vallonea Oak of Syria and Asia Minor, whose acorns are so largely used for tanning and dyeing, is *Q. Ægilops*, Linn.

Wood brown, very hard to extremely hard, heavy, generally with a distinct, darker coloured heartwood. Pores small to large, arranged in irregular radial lines, or elongated patches. Annual rings very indistinct, and not marked as in the case of European oaks by a belt of larger pores in the spring wood (*Q. Griffithii* and *Q. serrata* are an exception to this). As regards the medullary rays, two types may be distinguished. In the first type (*Q. pachyphylla, fenestrata* and *lappacea*), there is only one class of medullary rays, all being very fine, very numerous, uniform and equidistant. All other species have two classes, namely, besides the very fine rays already described, a small number of broad, or very broad, rays.

First group.—All medullary rays very fine, very numerous, uniform and equidistant. Wood seasons well, does not warp or crack.

Second group.—Medullary rays of two classes, very fine and broad, the latter very prominent on a vertical section, giving rise to that appearance which is generally known as "silver grain." The wood of most Indian species warps and splits in seasoning.

1. Q. Griffithii, Hook. f. and Th. Vern. *Dingim*, Khasia.

A large deciduous tree. Bark black, with deep vertical fissures. Wood brown, very hard. Annual rings marked by a belt of large pores in the spring wood. Pores small to moderate-sized, large in the spring wood, gradually decreasing outwards, enclosed in patches or radial wavy groups of soft tissue. Medullary rays of two classes: numerous, fine, uniform and equidistant rays and few broad to very broad rays. Very numerous, fine, parallel, wavy, transverse lines. The wood of this oak more resembles that of the English oak than any other we have examined.

Khasia Hills at 5,000 to 6,000 feet.

Growth fast, judging from our small specimen, and from the size attained by planted trees at Mongpu, Darjeeling. The timber is much used in the Khasia Hills for building and other purposes.

E 3337. Shillong, Khasia Hills, 5,000 feet.

2. Q. semecarpifolia, Smith; Brandis 479. Vern. *Barchar, jangal ka parúngi,* Jhelam; *Kreu, khareu, krúi,* Chenab, Ravi; *Karshu, karsúi, karzu, sáuj,* Sutlej to Sarda; *Ghesi, kasru,* Nep.

A large evergreen tree with dark grey bark, often with protuberances arranged in horizontal lines. Heartwood grey, often with a reddish tinge, very hard. Annual rings marked by few somewhat larger pores in the spring wood. Pores small and very small, in long, narrow, wavy, radial bands. Medullary rays of two classes: very numerous, very fine, uniform, and equidistant rays; and very few, broad ones, not very prominent on a longitudinal section. Numerous faint, wavy, concentric bands.

Afghanistan, North-west Himalaya between 8,000 and 10,000 feet, Nepal, Bhutan.

Growth difficult to distinguish, but from our specimens it appears to be moderate. Brandis says, 10 to 15 rings per inch of radius, and Aikin, describing Wallich's specimens, gives 14·5 rings per inch. The rate of growth in the Deoban Forest was ascertained by counting the annual rings on 15 stumps of large trees. The result may be expressed as follows:—

Girth at five feet from the ground.		Corresponding radius (of wood only).	No. of rings.	No. of rings per inch of radius.
ft.	in.	inches.		
1	6	2·9	40	13·8
3	0	5·7	86	15·1
4	6	8·6	138	16
6	0	11·5	192	16·7

This shews an increase of nearly 3 inches of radius every 50 years after the first 40, and an average growth of 15·4 rings per inch of radius.

The examination of *coppice* poles at an elevation of 9,000 feet in the same forest gave:

	Poles.	Average diameter. Inches.	No. of rings.
Jadi Block	27	4·7	32·8
Mohna	103	4·8	34·4

or a general average for 130 poles of 4·8 inches average diameter to 34 rings or 10·4 rings per inch of radius.

Weight, our specimens give 53 to 54 lbs. per cubic foot. The tree often grows to large size, and has a fine, straight stem, but the wood, though probably better than that of the other North-West Himalayan oaks, is not exported, and only but little locally used. It is used for building, door-frames, bedsteads, carrying poles, helves and ploughs, is a good firewood, and yields good charcoal. The leaves are stored as winter fodder for cattle. It coppices well and reproduces well from seed, and is often gregarious, forming considerable extents of almost pure forest.

			lbs.
H	39.	Mahasu, Simla, 9,000 feet	54
H	72.	Nagkanda, Simla, 9,000 feet	53
H	2893.	Nagkanda, Simla, 9,000 feet	...

No. E 2464, sent by Dr. Schlich from the Valley of Chumbi, Tibet, between Sikkim and Bhutan, is a tree, the leaves of which resemble those of *Q. semecarpifolia*, but are smaller and less tomentose beneath. The wood is light coloured, the pores small, surrounded by soft tissue, in long, radial anastomosing bands. The wood resembles that of *Q. Ilex*, which or near which species it probably is.

3. Q. Ilex, Linn.; Brandis 480. *Q. Baloot*, Griff. *Q. Ballota*, Desf. The Holm Oak. Vern. *Charrei, serei, balúl*, Afg.; *Spercherei, pargái, kharanja*, Trans-Indus; *Chúr, keharsu, kharen irri, yúru, heru, ban, bré, brekche*, Pb.

A moderate-sized evergreen tree. Bark ¼ inch thick, dark grey, tesselated, and cut into quadrangular plates. Heartwood red or reddish brown, very hard, durable. Pores small, uniform, in irregular anastomosing, radial bands. Medullary rays of two classes, numerous, very fine, uniform and equidistant rays, and fewer broad and very broad rays, the latter consisting of an agglomeration of finer rays; numerous fine, wavy, concentric rings of softer texture.

Afghanistan, Suliman Range, arid tracts of the Inner Himalaya, generally between 3,000 and 8,500 feet. Westwards to Southern Europe.

Growth slow, rings uncertain; if the concentric lines in No. H 1406 are annual rings the growth of that specimen was 70 rings in 4 inches of radius. In 1880 in a small forest in the Spingawai Pass in the Kuram Valley, Mr. Bagshawe counted the rings of 8 trees. These trees averaged 85 inches in girth with an average number of 270 rings, or nearly 20 rings per inch of radius. Weight, that of the European tree varies between 60 and 69 lbs. per cubic foot; our three specimens give an average of 61 lbs., but the third was old wood, having been cut in 1867. Mathieu, Fl. For. p. 325, gives the weight as varying from 55 to 74 lbs. per cubic foot. The wood warps and twists, but when well seasoned it works admirably and takes a fine polish. It is largely used for tool handles, and pieces are brought from the Suliman Range for that purpose. It is used for agricultural implements, and yields good fuel and charcoal. The branches with prickly leaves are used for fencing, and those without prickles are stored for winter cattle-fodder. The acorns are eaten in France, and the bark is considered of good quality for tanning.

			lbs.
H	903.	Upper Sutlej Valley, 8,000 feet	62
H	953.	Upper Sutlej Valley, 8,000 feet	68
H	1406.	Suliman Range (Stewart, 1867)	54
	2978.	Dalmatia	...

4. Q. dilatata, Lindl.; Brandis 482.; Vern. *Záih*, Kafiristan; *Bún, banji, banchar, barachar, baráin, banni, parúngi, chora, káli ring, máru, máur, moru, marghang, karsh*, Pb.; *Moru, tilangsa, kilonj, tilonj, timsha*, N.-W. P.

A large tree, changing its leaves yearly in spring at the time of flowering, but not quite deciduous. Bark dark grey, almost black, often with horizontal cracks, peeling off in longitudinal scales. Heartwood reddish grey, with darker streaks, very hard, seasons well and does not warp much, faintly but elegantly marked on longitudinal sections by the medullary rays. Pores small and very small, in groups, patches and irregular radial lines. Medullary rays of two classes, the broad rays more frequent, but narrower than those of *Q. incana*; the others are very fine, very numerous, uniform and equidistant. Fine, wavy, concentric bands irregularly distributed.

Afghanistan, Suliman Range, North-West Himalaya, between 7,000 and 9,000 feet.

Growth moderate at first, probably slow afterwards; the annual rings are not sufficiently marked for counting. Weight, 61 lbs. per cubic foot. Major Lang gives

P. = 670. The wood is durable, and is used for building, for agricultural implements and jampan poles. The leaves are much lopped for fodder for sheep and goats, and unlopped forests are rare. Near Simla, the chief localities where forests, pure or almost pure, of this tree are seen, are at Mahasu and on the east side of the ridge between Theog and Matiyana. The latter forest contains fine trees, and is very interesting.

The tree coppices well, and reproduces abundantly naturally, but the seedlings, when once established, require light to be let in, or they die off.

		lbs.
H 935.	Hazara, 8,000 feet	61
H 4.	Mahasu, Simla, 8,000 feet	56
H 40.	Mahasu, Simla, 8,000 feet	69
H 2845.	Mahasu, Simla, 8,000 feet	58
H 2873.	Nagkanda, Simla, 9,000 feet	...

5. **Q. serrata,** Thunb.; Brandis 486. *Q. polyantha,* Ldl. Vern. *Dingrittiang,* Khasia.

A moderate-sized deciduous tree. Bark dark grey, rough when old, light silver grey and shining when young, deeply cleft with vertical fissures. Wood brown, very hard. Annual rings marked by a belt of large, sometimes very large, pores in the spring wood. Pores small to moderate-sized, increasing gradually to large and very large to the edge of the spring wood, enclosed in patches or radial wavy groups of soft tissue. Medullary rays of two classes: numerous fine, uniform and equidistant rays and fewer broad, very short rays. Very numerous fine, parallel, wavy, transverse lines. This much resembles *Q. Griffithii* in structure and also comes near that of the English oak. A Japanese specimen has the same structure, but the annual rings much more distinctly marked.

North-East Himalaya and Khasia Hills, from 3,000 to 5,000 feet.

Growth, our specimen shews 9 rings per inch of radius. Wood used in Assam for building. In Japan the "*Yamamai*" silkworm is raised on its leaves.

E 3339. Shillong, Assam, 5,000 feet.

6. **Q. lanuginosa,** Don; Brandis 481. *Q. lanata,* Wall. Vern. *Ranj, rianj, rai banj,* Kumaun; *Banga,* Nep.

A large, evergreen tree. Bark ¼ inch thick. Wood greyish brown, very hard, warps and splits. Pores moderate-sized, in radial bands. Medullary rays of two classes, the broad rays prominent on a vertical section, giving the wood a handsome, mottled appearance. Numerous wavy, concentric lines.

Naini Tál and a few other places in Kumaun, between 6,000 and 7,500 feet. Gregarious, or associated with *Q. incana.*

Growth, annual rings not sufficiently recognizable for certainty, but if the lines on our specimen are annual rings, the growth was moderate, 7 rings per inch of radius. Weight, our specimen gives 55 lbs. per cubic foot. Wood used for firewood, the leaves for cattle fodder.

		lbs.
H 2968.	Naini Tál, 7,000 feet	55

7. **Q. incana,** Roxb. Fl. Ind. iii. 642; Brandis 482. Vern. *Vari,* Salt Range; *Rhin,* Hazara; *Rinj, rín,* Jhelam; *Bán, banj,* Pb.; *Banj,* Kumaun.

A large evergreen tree. Bark dark coloured, rough, with cracks and fissures. Heartwood very hard, reddish brown, warps and splits. Annual rings indistinct. Pores small and moderate-sized, surrounded by soft tissue and arranged in irregular patches and groups, and radial belts. Medullary rays of two classes: numerous, very fine, uniform, and equidistant rays, and fewer very broad rays, visible on a radial section as high, narrow, tapering, shining plates. Numerous faint, interrupted, wavy, thin, concentric lines.

Outer Himalaya from the Indus to Nepal, between 3,000 and 8,000 feet; it can be grown in the Panjab plains. It is gregarious, or often associated with *Rhododendron* and *Pieris*, and a few other species, such as *Cornus capitata* and deodar. Growth not recognisable from the specimens. Weight, 64 lbs. per cubic foot, average of our 4 specimens; Major Lang gives P. = 491. The wood is very difficult to season, it is used for building, for ploughs, is a good fuel and makes good charcoal. The acorns are greedily eaten by bears and monkeys, which may to some extent account for its bad natural reproduction in spite of profuse seeding.

			lbs.
H	899.	Murree, 7,000 feet	62
H	171.	Kangra, 6,000 „ (Stewart, 1867)	...
H	1.	Simla, 7,000 feet	67
H	24.	„ „ „	66
H	2867.	„ „ „	...
H	2.	Mahasu, Simla, 7,000 feet	60

8. Q. fenestrata, Roxb. Fl. Ind. iii. 633; Brandis 489; Kurz ii. 483; Gamble 78. Vern. *Kala chakma*, Beng.; *Patlé katús*, Nep., *Kashiendúng*, Lepcha; *Dingjing*, Khasia; *Thitkya*, Burm.

A moderate-sized tree. Bark ½ inch thick, rough, greyish brown, deeply fissured into small rectangular plates. Heartwood red, very hard. Pores large, arranged in groups, and short or oblique belts. Medullary rays very numerous, very fine, uniform and equidistant. Numerous wavy, concentric bands.

Eastern Himalaya, between 5,000 and 8,000 feet, Khasia Hills, Eastern Bengal and hills of Martaban and Upper Tenasserim.

Growth, the annual rings are doubtful, but our Burma specimen seems to shew 7 rings per inch of radius. Weight, Major Seaton says 48 lbs. per cubic foot (probably mistaken for *Q. semiserrata*, 48 lbs. in Brandis' Burma List of 1862, No. 88, also called *Thitkya*), Wallich gives 47, and our specimen 56 lbs. Used for building and farm purposes in the Khasia Hills.

			lbs.
E	3338.	Shillong, Khasia Hills, 5,000 feet	...
B	552.	Martaban Hills	56

9. Q. spicata, Smith; Brandis 489; Kurz ii. 486; Gamble 78. *Q. squamata*, Roxb. Fl. Ind. iii. 638. Vern. *Danwa singali, phaco singali, arkaula*, Nep.; *Bara chakma*, Beng.; *Kacheeng*, Lepcha; *Sahu hingori*, Ass.; *Dingjing*, Khasia; *Thitcha*, Burm.

A large, evergreen tree. Wood red, very hard. Bark grey, smooth. Pores moderate-sized and large, enclosed in soft tissue in groups, patches and radial belts. Medullary rays of two classes: numerous very fine, uniform and equidistant rays, and fewer broad and very broad ones; the silver grain being very prominent on a radial section. Very numerous fine, parallel, wavy, transverse lines.

Nepal, Sikkim up to 5,000 feet, Eastern Bengal, Burma and Indian Archipelago.

Growth, annual rings not recognisable. Weight, 58 lbs. per cubic foot. The wood is used for building in Assam and for charcoal in Darjeeling. It coppices very freely and is often almost gregarious or mixed with chestnut, *Engelhardtia* and *Schima*. It is very durable and does not warp.

		lbs.
E 595.	Khookloong Forest, Darjeeling Terai	56
E 1444.	Mishmi Hills (Griffith, 1836)	59
E 1445.	" " (" ")	55
B 545.	Martaban Hills	63

Q. turbinata, Roxb. Fl. Ind. iii. 636 (*Q. Thomsoni*, Miq.; Kurz ii. 486) from Chittagong (Vern. *Bansúa batana*) is probably only a narrow-leaved variety of this.

10. Q. pachyphylla, Kurz in Journ. As. Soc. Bengal, vol. xliv. 197, 1875; Gamble 78. Vern. *Bara katús*, Nep.; *Hlosiri*, Lepcha.

A large evergreen tree. Wood grey, very hard, seasons well, does not warp or split, is more durable under exposure to damp than that of *Q. lamellosa* and *annulata*. Annual rings faintly marked by concentric lines. Pores moderate-sized, isolated or in short, irregular, radial, oblique and branching belts. Medullary rays very fine, numerous, uniform and equidistant. Numerous, wavy, interrupted, concentric bands of soft tissue. Medullary rays very prominent on a radial section as numerous, long, narrow bands, the groups of pores also prominent, giving the wood a beautifully mottled appearance.

Higher ranges of the Sikkim Himalaya, above 7,000 feet, the common oak of the forests between 8,000 and 10,000 feet.

Growth apparently moderate, but the annual rings are not clearly distinguishable. Weight, 50 lbs. per cubic foot. The wood is largely used in Darjeeling for planking, palings, shingles and other purposes. The leaves are smooth, longacuminate, greyish green, and the acorns large, deeply-bedded in scaly cups, generally in compact masses, containing each 3 nuts.

		lbs.
E 364.	Rangbúl Forest, Darjeeling, 7,500 feet	51
E 2454.	" " "	48
E 2455.	Rangirúm " " "	51

11. Q. lappacea, Roxb. Fl. Ind. iii. 637; Brandis 489; Kurz ii. 484. Vern. *Oolu chakma*, Beng.; *Thitcha*, Burm.

An evergreen tree. Sapwood light brown or yellow. Heartwood very hard, reddish. Pores large, uniform, isolated, sometimes arranged in radial groups. Medullary rays very fine, very numerous, uniform, equidistant, with innumerable, fine, transverse bars across the rays.

Khasia Hills, Eastern Bengal and Tenasserim.

Weight, Wallich gives 51, our specimens 56 lbs. per cubic foot. The acorns have a cup composed of imbricate, soft tomentose scales.

		lbs.
B 553.	Upper Tenasserim	56
B 2715.	Brought by Wallich from Tavoy in 1828, has a structure most resembling this species	45

12. Q. acuminata, Roxb. Fl. Ind. iii. 636; Kurz ii. 484; Gamble 78. Vern. *Sanu arkaula*, Nep.; *Kanta gola batana*, Chittagong.

An evergreen tree. Bark thin, grey to greyish black, smooth. Wood light red, very hard. Pores scanty, moderate-sized, arranged in short irregular branching lines, which rarely go beyond the spring wood. Annual rings marked by the larger pores in the spring wood. Medullary rays of two classes: numerous, uniform and equidistant very fine rays and very few broad ones.

Eastern Himalaya, Khasia Hills and down to Chittagong, ascending to 6,000 feet.

Growth fast, $3\frac{1}{3}$ rings per inch of radius. Weight of our specimen, 43 to 55 lbs. per cubic foot, but this is probably low. The tree coppices well and is very good for firewood.

		lbs.
E 2456.	Tukdah Forest, Darjeeling, 5,500 feet	43
E 3333.	Birch Hill Park, Darjeeling, 6,500 feet	55

13. Q. annulata, Smith; Brandis 487; Gamble 78. *Q. Phullata,* Don. Vern. *Brán, brén, barín, banni, imbri, indri,* Pb.; *Pharonj, phanát, phaliant, inai,* N.-W. P.; *Phalat,* Nep.; *Siri,* Lepcha.

A large evergreen tree. Bark $\frac{1}{6}$ inch thick, grey, smooth when young, rough with short deep transverse fissures when old. Wood grey or greyish brown, very hard, warps and cracks; a handsome, markedly mottled wood, polishes well. Pores moderate-sized and small, surrounded by soft tissue and arranged in groups, patches, and irregular radial lines. Medullary rays of two classes: numerous, very fine, uniform, equidistant rays, and fewer broad and extremely broad ones. Numerous, fine, wavy, concentric bands across the rays. The medullary rays appear as broad irregular plates, sometimes one inch high, and shew a silver grain on a radial section.

Valleys of the outer Himalaya, ascending to 6,000 feet, Garhwal, Kumaun, Nepal, Sikkim (6,000 to 9,000 feet), Bhutan, Khasia Hills.

Growth: of all our specimens, only one, No. H 90, shews any sign of annual rings, and these appear to be 8 per inch of radius. Weight, 60 lbs. per cubic foot, the average of 7 specimens. The wood is not much esteemed in the North-West Himalaya; in Darjeeling it is used for the same purposes as *Q. lamellosa,* but is not considered so good as that species. The acorns have small cups with 4 to 8 narrow, velvety belts.

			lbs.
H	927.	Hazara, 6,000 feet	55
H	90.	Bhajji, Simla, 4,000 feet	62
H	423.	Raulagrad, Chakrata, 6,500 feet	57
E	433.	Rangbúl, Darjeeling, 7,000 „	60
E	2451.	„ „ „ „	69
E	1439.	Mishmi Hills (Griffith, 1836)	59
E	1443.	„ „ „ „	58

14. Q. lamellosa, Smith; Brandis 488; Gamble 78. *Q. paucilamellosa,* Alph. DC. *Q. lamellata,* Roxb. Fl. Ind. iii. 641 (from Penang). *Q. imbricata,* Don. Vern. *Shalshi, pharat-singhali, budgrat,* Nep.; *Búk,* Lepcha.

A very large tree. Bark greyish brown, $\frac{1}{3}$ to $\frac{1}{2}$ inch thick. Heartwood greyish brown, shewing a beautiful silver grain on a radial section; does not warp to the same extent as *Q incana* and *Q. annulata.* Pores small to large, surrounded by soft tissue, in loose radial strings. Medullary rays of two classes: numerous, very fine, uniform, equidistant rays; and fewer broad to extremely broad ones, shewing on a radial section as high, irregularly-shaped, shining plates. Numerous, wavy, concentric lines.

Nepal, Sikkim, Bhutan, between 5,000 and 9,000 feet.

Growth, probably moderate, but the annual rings are too difficult to distinguish to be readily counted. Attempts to count rings have been frequently made in Darjeeling, but with very little success. Its growth is, however, slow. Weight, 59 lbs. per cubic foot, the average of 5 specimens. The wood is durable if not much exposed to wet; it is used for beams and posts in the construction of houses and bridges, and for door-posts, window-frames, rafters and other house-building purposes. In Darjeeling the bark is used for tanning. It often attains 100 to 120 feet in height, with a girth of 20 to 30 feet, but old trees are very frequently hollow. The acorns are very large, the cups often 2 to 3 inches in diameter, and composed of broad, annular rings. The leaves are large, parallel-veined, sharply serrated, grey underneath; they are renewed every 2 or 3 years. It is grown easily from seed, if the seed is good, but it is very liable to be found eaten by grubs. It often takes a long time to germinate, and instances of more than one year being taken are common. It is being largely grown by planting in the Darjeeling Forests, where it is the principal and most important tree.

		lbs.
E 434.	Rangbúl Forest, Darjeeling, 7,500 feet	63
E 2452.	„ „ „ „ „	59
E 2453.	„ „ „ „ „	57
E 1438.	Mishmi Hills (Griffith, 1836)	57
E 1448.	„ „ „ „	59

15. **Q. lanceæfolia,** Roxb. Fl. Ind. iii. 634; Brandis 489; Gamble 79. *Castanea lanceæfolia,* Kurz ii. 482. Vern. *Patlé katús,* Nep.; *Siri,* Lepcha; *Shingra, chauko,* Gáro; *Bucklai,* Ass.; *Hingori,* Cachar; *Dingsning,* Khasia.

A small evergreen tree. Wood greyish white, hard. Pores large, enclosed in soft tissue and arranged in wavy, radial and oblique lines. Medullary rays of two classes: numerous, very fine, uniform and equidistant rays, and few broad rays. Numerous, fine, wavy, concentric lines.

Sub-Himalayan tract, in Bengal and Chittagong, ascending to 4,000 feet.

Weight, 42 lbs. per cubic foot (Wallich and our specimens). Wood used for building in Assam. The acorns have thin, broad, ringed cups, which are set sideways on the branch; they have ruminate albumen.

		lbs.
E 1262.	Tezpur, Assam	42

2. CASTANOPSIS, Spach.

About 9 to 11 species. *C. javanica,* Alph. DC. (*Castanea javanica,* Bl.; Kurz ii. 479) is an evergreen tree of Burma. *C. Hystrix,* Alph. DC. Vern. *Dingsning,* Khasia, is a tree of the Khasia hills. *C. argentea,* Alph. DC.; Gamble 79 (*Castanea argentea,* Bl.; Kurz ii. 479.) Vern. *Hingori,* Ass., is an evergreen tree of Sikkim, Assam and Burma. *C. echidnocarpa,* Alph., DC., is a tree of the Khasia hills from 3,000 to 5,000 feet. *Castanea diversifolia,* Kurz ii. 479. Vern. *Kyanya,* Burm., is a tree of the Martaban hills, from 3,500 to 5,000 feet, and *C. Roxburghii,* Ldl.; Kurz ii. 480, is a large evergreen tree of Chittagong. *Castanea rhamnifolia,* Kurz and *C inermis,* Lindl.; Kurz ii. 481, are Burmese trees nearly allied to *Quercus lanceæfolia.*

The species of *Castanopsis* have a uniform structure which resembles that of the oaks with one class of medullary rays. Wood grey, moderately hard to hard, does not split or warp, seasons well, durable. Pores large, in wavy, radial bands, and lines very prominent on a vertical section. Medullary rays of one class, very fine, uniform and equidistant. Numerous, wavy, concentric lines.

1. **C. indica,** Alph. DC.; Brandis 490; Gamble 79. *Castanea indica,* Roxb. Fl. Ind. iii. 643; Kurz ii. 478. *Quercus serrata,* Roxb. l. c. 641 (probably) Vern. *Banj katús,* Nep.; *Kashiorón,* Lepcha; *Serang,* Ass.; *Charang,* Gáro; *Tailo,* Cachar; *Nikari, gol-shingra,* Sylhet.

A moderate-sized, evergreen tree. Bark silvery grey, ¼ inch thick, with regular equidistant longitudinal fissures. Wood grey, hard. Pores small to very large, arranged in wavy, interrupted, radial lines; the largest pores being often in the middle of each line. Medullary rays extremely fine, uniform, equidistant, very numerous. Numerous, fine, concentric lines of soft tissue.

Nepal, Eastern Bengal, Assam and Chittagong, ascending to 5,000 feet.

Growth apparently fast, about 4 to 6 rings per inch of radius. Weight, Wallich gives 39, our specimens 44 lbs. per cubic foot. Skinner, No. 40, gives W = 35 lbs., P = 404, but as he gives *Theethkaya* for the Burmese name and this species is not described from Burma, he may refer to some other species. The wood splits well, and is very largely used for shingles in Darjeeling. It coppices freely, and is often pollarded and the branches burnt for manure. The fruit is eaten; it much resembles the filbert, both in shape and in flavour, but has a thinner shell. It is enclosed in a very prickly cup.

			lbs.
E 494.	Dalka Jhar,	Darjeeling Terai	43
E 681.	Khookloong Forest,	„ „	45
E 1254.	Tezpur, Assam		44

2. C. tribuloides, Alph. DC.; Brandis 490; Gamble 79. *Castanea tribuloides,* Kurz ii. 480. *Quercus ferox* and *Q. armata,* Roxb. Fl. Ind. iii. 639, 640. Vern. *Túmari, katonj,* Kumaun; *Musré katús, kotur, chisi, maku, shingali,* Nep.; *Bar hingorí, kanta singar,* Ass.; *Dingsaot,* Khasia; *Singhara,* Tipperah; *Kanta lal batana,* Chittagong; *Kyansa,* Burm.

An evergreen tree. Wood grey, moderately hard. Annual rings marked by darker lines. Pores moderate-sized and large, in long wavy radial lines and bands. Medullary rays numerous, very fine, uniform and equidistant. Numerous fine, wavy, concentric lines.

South-East Kumaun, Nepal, Eastern Bengal, ascending from the plains to 6,000 feet. Chittagong and hills in Burma, above 3,000 feet.

Growth, apparently very fast, 2 to 3 rings per inch of radius, but the rings are doubtful. Weight, Kyd gives weight 43 lbs., P = 483, our specimens give 32 to 39 lbs. per cubic foot. Wallich gives 62, which is much too great unless quite fresh, damp wood were weighed. The wood is used for planking, and is good and durable; also for shingles. The fruit is eaten; it is similar to that of *C. indica*, but is enclosed in a cup armed with strong, distant, branching prickles. The tree coppices admirably, and with *C. indica, Quercus spicata* and *Engelhardtia* should be grown wherever firewood and charcoal forests are required, as they often are by planters.

			lbs.
E 626.	Dulka Jhar,	Darjeeling Terai	32
E 495.	Khookloong Forest,	„ „	39

3. C. rufescens, Hook. f. and Th.; Gamble 79. Vern. *Dalné katús,* Nep.; *Sirikishu,* Lepcha; *Hingori,* Ass.

A very large evergreen tree. Wood grey, hard. Annual rings marked by narrow belts of firmer texture. Pores moderate-sized and large, enclosed in soft tissue, arranged in irregular, radial bands and lines. Medullary rays very fine, very numerous, uniform and equidistant, with numerous short, fine, transverse bars.

Sikkim Himalaya, from 6,000 to 9,000 feet.

Growth moderate, 8 rings per inch of radius. Weight, 46 lbs. per cubic foot. The wood is used in Darjeeling for house-building and other purposes, exactly as that of *Quercus pachyphylla*, which it very closely resembles. It gives excellent shingles, and is more valuable as planking and posts wherever exposed to wet than other species of this genus. The fruit is small, but edible and of good flavour; it is enclosed in a large cup with long needle-like prickles, longer than those of *C. indica.*

		lbs.
E 354.	Rangbúl Forest, Darjeeling, 7,000 feet	47
E 2457.	„ „ „ „	45

3. CARPINUS, Tournef.

Two Indian species. *C. faginea*, Lindl.; Brandis 492. Vern. *Shirásh, imar, bijauwi*, Pb.; *Gish*, North-Western Provinces, is a moderate-sized tree of the Himalaya, from the Beas eastward, from 4,000 to 7,000 feet. The Hornbeam of Europe is *C. Betulus*, Linn., generally found in forests of Oak and Beech throughout the greater part of Europe and eastward to Asterabad, south of the Caspian Sea.

Slow-growing trees, with white wood, without heartwood. Pores small, often in radial lines. Medullary rays fine and broad, the latter consisting of a number of fine rays closely packed.

1. C. viminea, Wall.; Brandis 492; Kurz ii. 477. Vern. *Charkhri, kái*, Pb.; *Pumne, goria, chamkharak*, North-Western Provinces; *Chukissi, konikath*, Nep.;

A moderate-sized tree, with grey, compact bark, ⅓ inch thick. Wood white, shining, no heartwood, warps in seasoning. Pores small, sometimes in short radial lines. Medullary rays of two apparent classes: very numerous, very fine rays; and broad rays, composed of numerous closely packed, very fine rays.

Himalaya, from the Ravi eastwards, from 5,000 to 7,000 feet, often near water. Martaban Hills at 5,000 to 6,000 feet.

Growth moderately slow, Brandis says 10 rings per inch, our specimen shews the same. Weight, 50 lbs. per cubic foot. The stem is irregular in section like that of the European Hornbeam, which it much resembles both in bark and wood, and in general appearance.

	lbs.
H 3098. Sipi, Simla, 6,500 feet	50

4. CORYLUS, Tournef.

Two Indian species. The European Hazel is *C. Avellana*, Linn., found in England, France and eastwards to the Caucasus and Asia Minor.

Wood soft, even-grained, light-coloured. Pores very small. Medullary rays of two classes, the broad rays being composed of numerous fine rays.

1. C. ferox, Wall.; Brandis 494; Gamble 79. Vern. *Curri*, Nep.; *Langura*, Bhutia.

A small tree. Wood pinkish white, moderately hard, even-grained. Pores very small, generally in short, radial lines, not very numerous. Medullary rays of two classes: fine and very broad, the broad ones numerous and, as in *C. Colurna*, composed of an agglomeration of fine rays.

Nepal, Sikkim, 8,000 to 10,000 feet.

Growth slow, 18 rings per inch of radius. Weight, 38 lbs. per cubic foot. The fruit is covered with a very prickly cup, the kernel is edible.

	lbs.
E 376. Tonglo, Darjeeling, 9,000 feet	38

2. C. Colurna, Linn.; Brandis 494. *C. lacera*, Wall. Vern. *Urni*, Jhelam; *Wínri, wiri, warawi, wúriya, thangi, thankoli*, Kashmir and Chamba; *Jangi*, Chenab; *Shurli, sharoli, ban pálu, geh, ban dilla*, Sutlej; *Kapasi, bhotia badám*, Kumaun.

A moderate-sized tree, with thin, dark-grey bark. Wood pinkish white, moderately hard. Annual rings distinctly marked by narrow belt of firm wood, with few pores inside the outer edge of each ring

Pores very small, numerous, uniformly distributed, sometimes in short radial lines. Medullary rays fine, numerous, with few broader rays, which consist of an agglomeration of fine rays.

North-West Himalaya, between 5,500 and 10,000 feet.

Growth moderate, our specimens shew about 10 rings per inch of radius. Weight, 33 to 37 lbs. per cubic foot. The wood is only used locally, but it is well grained and does not warp, and deserves to be better known, especially as many specimens shew a fine shining grain resembling Birds'-eye Maple. The fruit is as good as that of the English Hazel, and is largely eaten.

			lbs.
H	57.	Nagkanda, Simla, 80,000 feet	37
H	908.	Upper Chenab	33
H	3179.	Dungagalli, Hazara	...

ORDER XCIX. MYRICACEÆ.

1. MYRICA, Linn.

In DeCandolle's Prodromus, Vol. xvi, two species are given from India: viz., *M. sapida*, Wall., and *M. integrifolia*, Roxb. For the differences between these and *M. Nagi*, Thunb. of Japan, see Brandis, p. 496, where the conclusion is arrived at that they will eventually be all placed under one species *M. Nagi*, Thunb., with the wide range from the Punjab to China and Japan, and to the sea-coast of Singapore and Borneo. *M. integrifolia*, Roxb. Fl. Ind. iii. 765. Vern. *Sophi*, Beng., is described as a large shrub of the Khasia Hills and Sylhet. *M. Gale*, Linn., is the Sweet Gale or Bog Myrtle of Europe. Vegetable wax is given by *M. cerifera*, Linn., the Bayberry of North America, which is also a valuable sand-binding plant; by *M. cordifolia*, Linn., *M. quercifolia*, Linn., and *M. serrata*, Lamk., of South Africa, and by *M. arguta*, Kunth, of South America.

1. M. sapida, Wall.; Brandis 495. *M. Nagi*, Thunb.; Kurz ii. 475. Vern. *Kaphal, kaiphal*, North-Western Himalaya; *Kobusi*, Nep.; *Dingsolir*, Khasia.

A moderate-sized evergreen tree. Bark grey or brownish grey, rough, with deep vertical wrinkles. Wood purplish grey, hard, close-grained, apt to warp. Annual rings marked by a belt of firmer texture without pores in the autumn wood. Pores very small, uniformly distributed, but somewhat less numerous near the outer edge of each annual ring. Medullary rays fine and very fine, numerous.

Outer Himalaya, from 3,000 to 6,000 feet, Khasia Hills, hills of Burma between 4,000 and 6,000 feet.

Weight, 48 lbs. per cubic foot. The bark is exported to the plains; it is used as an aromatic stimulant and externally as a plaster against rheumatism. In the Khasia Hills it is used to poison fish. The fruit is edible.

			lbs.
H	87.	Sutlej Valley, 5,000 feet	46
H	426.	Ghite Forest, Jaunsar, 5,500 feet	45
E	799.	Khasia Hills, about 5,000 feet	52

ORDER C. JUGLANDEÆ.

Two Indian genera. The Hickories of America are species of *Carya*. Among these, the chief are: *C. alba*, Nuttall, the Shellbark; *C. glabra*, Torrey, the Hognut, and *C. oliviformis*, Nuttall, the Pear nut. The wood of all is very strong and elastic, and is used for building, but is not durable (von Mueller).

Wood moderately hard, shining. Pores moderate-sized, uniformly distributed, prominent on a vertical section. Medullary rays fine or very fine.

1. JUGLANS, Linn.

The Black Walnut wood of America is given by *J. nigra*, Linn.; and the Butternut tree of Canada is *J. cinerea*, Linn.

1. J. regia, Linn.; Roxb. Fl. Ind. iii. 631; Brandis 497; Kurz ii. 490; Gamble 80. The Walnut. Vern. *Charmaghz*, Pers.; *Ughz, waghz*, Afg.; *Akhor, krot, dún*, Kashmir; *Kabotang, thanka*, Pb.; *Starga*, Ladak; *Ká*, Kunawar; *Akhor, kharot*, Kumaun; *Akhrot*, Hind.; *Akrút*, Beng.; *Kowal*, Lepcha; *Tagashing*, Bhutia.

A large tree with grey bark, characteristically marked by deep vertical parallel fissures, ½ inch to 2 inches thick. Heartwood greyish brown with darker streaks, often beautifully mottled, moderately hard, even-grained, seasons and polishes well. Annual rings marked by a sharp line. Pores moderate-sized, not very numerous, sometimes oval and subdivided, uniformly distributed, but somewhat more numerous in the spring wood. Medullary rays short, very fine. Numerous regular, fine, wavy, concentric lines. Pores visible on a longitudinal section.

Wild in the North-West and Sikkim Himalaya. Cultivated largely throughout the hills, especially in Afghanistan and Kashmir.

Growth variable; our specimens gave the following per inch of radius:—

H 9. 14 rings; H 15. 14 rings; H 125. 19 rings;
H 29. 3 rings; (young tree).
E 357. 9 rings; E 2441-a, 3 rings; b, 7 rings; E 2440, 4 rings.

So that the wood from the North-West Himalaya, omitting the specimen cut from a young tree, shews an average of 15 rings, and that from Sikkim an average of 6 rings per inch of radius.

Weight: European Walnut weighs 40 to 48 lbs. per cubic foot; our specimens give, North-West Himalaya 41 lbs., Sikkim 33 lbs. on an average. The tree reaches a very large size. Brandis describes trees up to 28 feet in girth and 100 feet high from the North-West Himalaya; in Sikkim it often reaches 100 to 120 feet in height with a girth of 12 feet or more. It is being grown in plantation at Rangbúl and other places near Darjeeling. The wood is extensively used for furniture throughout the Himalaya, and its principal use is for gun-stocks. In Darjeeling it is occasionally used for shingles by the Bhutias, but is not so good as chestnut. Before it became scarce in the forests it was largely used for house-fittings, and many of the older houses in Darjeeling have their doors and windows and other fittings almost entirely of Walnut. The bark is used as a dye and in medicine; and is exported to the plains for cleaning the teeth. The twigs and leaves are used for fodder. It is commonly cultivated for its fruit throughout the Himalaya; the wild tree has a thick shell and small kernel, and is rarely eaten; the cultivated trees are of numerous kinds, one of the best being the thin-shelled or *Kaghazi* variety. A clear, good description of oil is made from the fruit, and the rind is used for tanning and dyeing.

			lbs.
H	3163.	Dungagalli, Hazara, 7,000 feet	...
H	9.	Matiyana, Simla, 7,000 feet	38
H	29.	” ” ” ”	43
H	15.	Jubal, 4,000 feet	33
H	41.	Madhan, 6,000 feet	41
H	780.	Chamba, 4,000 feet	46
H	125.	Ralla, Kulu, 6,000 feet	42

		lbs.
H 428.	Durani block, Deoban, Jaunsar, 6,000 feet	43
E 357.	Tukdah Forest, Darjeeling, 5,000 feet	28
E 2440.	Darjeeling, 6,000 feet	37
E 2441.	Rangirúm Forest, Darjeeling, 5,000 feet	33

2. ENGELHARDTIA, Lesch.

Three species, though Brandis, p. 500, thinks that the two described are probably varieties only of one and the same, *viz.*, *E. spicata*. *E. villosa*, Kurz ii. 491, is a tree of the *Eng* forests of Martaban and Tenasserim.

1. E. Colebrookiana, Lindl.; Brandis 499. Vern. *Tímar rákh,* Pb.; *Mowa, gobar mowa, bodal mowa, mao,* Kumaun; *Khusam,* Banda.

A small deciduous tree. Bark grey. Wood grey with a reddish tinge, moderately hard, even-grained, seasons and polishes well, but is not durable. Annual rings faintly marked. Pores moderate-sized and large, mostly oval and subdivided, uniformly distributed. Medullary rays fine, uniform, equidistant, numerous. Pores marked on a longitudinal section.

Outer North-West Himalaya ascending to 6,500 feet, often gregarious.

Growth, our specimen shews 5 rings per inch of radius. Weight, 33 lbs. per cubic foot.

		lbs.
H 241.	Garhwal Hills (1868)	33

2. E. spicata, Bl.; Brandis 500; Gamble 81. *E. Roxburghiana,* Lindl. *Juglans pterococca,* Roxb. Fl. Ind. iii. 631. Vern. *Silapoma,* Hind.; *Mowa, mahua,* Nep.; *Suviak,* Lepcha; *Bolas,* Beng.; *Rumgach,* Ass.; *Bor-patta-jam,* Cachar; *Dinglaba,* Khasia; *Vakru,* Gáro.

A large, handsome, deciduous tree. Character and structure of the wood similar to that of *E. Colebrookiana,* shewing a beautiful grain on a radial section. Faint concentric lines joining the pores.

Terai and outer hills of Eastern Himalaya up to 6,000 feet, Chittagong and Burma.

Growth fast, 3 to 5 rings per inch of radius. Weight, Wallich gives 40, our specimens 33 lbs. per cubic foot. The wood is used in Sikkim for tea-boxes and building; in the Khasia Hills and Cachar for planking and spoons. It does not warp. The tree coppices very freely, and coppice woods almost pure or mixed with oak and chestnut, are not uncommon near Darjeeling.

		lbs.
E 653.	Bamunpokri, Darjeeling Terai	30
E 687.	Sepoydura Forest, Darjeeling, 5,000 feet	33
E 2442.	Chuttockpur Forest, Darjeeling, 6,000 feet	36

ORDER CI. GNETACEÆ.

Two genera, *Gnetum* and *Ephedra;* the first containing 5 species, chiefly of the moist zones; the latter 2, of the arid zone and inner arid Himalaya.

Gnetum scandens, Roxb. Fl. Ind. iii. 518; Brandis 502. (*G. edule,* Bl.; Kurz ii. 495) Vern. *Kúmbal, úmbli,* Bombay; *Nanu-witi,* Sylhet; *Gyootnway,* Burm., is a large climbing shrub of Sikkim, the Khasia Hills, Eastern Bengal, Western Gháts, Burma and the Andamans, whose fruit is eaten. *G. funiculare,* Bl.; Kurz ii. 496. Vern. *Gyootnway,* Burm., is a large scandent shrub of Chittagong and Burma, *G. neglectum,* Bl., is a climber of Arracan and South Tenasserim; and *G. Gnemon,*

Linn.; Kurz ii. 497; Roxb. Fl. Ind. iii. 518, is an evergreen tree of the forests of south Tenasserim, whose bark is made into strong cords, and whose leaves are eaten as spinach.

The wood consists of a large number of distinct wedge-shaped ligneous masses which are arranged in concentric circles and separated by cellular tissue. It resembles the wood of Menispermaceæ. (Brandis.)

Ephedra vulgaris, Rich.; Brandis 501. Vern. *Asmánia, búdshúr, chewa*, Pb.; *Khanda, khanna*, Kunawar; *Tse, tsapatt, trano*, Ladak, is a small rigid shrub of the inner arid, North-West Himalaya, with a fibrous tough wood and red fruit, which is sometimes eaten. *E. Alte*, C. A. Meyer; Brandis 501. Vern. *Alte*, Arab.; *Kuchan, nikki kúrkan, bratta, tandala, lastúk, mangarwal*, Pb., is a gregarious shrub of the arid zone, in stony places in the Punjab and Sind.

ORDER CII. CONIFERÆ.

An Order containing many very important forest trees. It is found throughout the world, but chiefly in temperate and cold regions; and in India, with few exceptions, the species are confined to the Himalaya. The following list which is taken from Parlatore's Monograph in DeCandolle's Prodromus, gives the five tribes and the most important genera, those found in India being given in italics; the others are added in consequence of their being universally planted for ornament or for timber:—

Tribe	I.—Araucarieæ	*Araucaria, Dammara.*
„	II.—Abietineæ	*Pinus, Cedrus, Abies, Larix.*
„	III.—Taxodieæ	*Cunninghamia, Sequoia, Cryptomeria, Taxodium.*
„	IV.—Cupressineæ	*Callitris, Thuya, Biota, Cupressus, Juniperus.*
„	V.—Taxineæ	*Dacrydium, Taxus, Ginkgo, Podocarpus.*

Araucaria contains about seven species, most of which have been introduced and cultivated in gardens in India. *A. imbricata*, Pavon (Brandis 503) from the mountains of Chili, is well known in Europe; it is much grown in England and is hardy, though sometimes liable to be injured by frost. *A. excelsa*, R. Br., from Norfolk Island, is much planted in Calcutta, where also may be seen *A. Cunninghamii*, Ait., of Queensland, *A. Cookii*, R. Br., of New Caledonia, and *A. Bidwilli*, Hook., the Bunya-Bunya Pine of North-East Australia. *Dammara australis*, Lamb, is the Kauri Pine of New Zealand, which, though much cut, still forms forest occasionally and gives a valuable timber. *D. alba*, Rumph, of the Moluccas, yields the resin called Dammar.

Cunninghamia sinensis, R. Br. is a large tree of Southern China. *Sequoia* contains two Californian species: *S. gigantea*, Torrey, the *Wellingtonia* or Mammoth Tree, which reaches over 300 feet in height, with a girth of 80 to 100 feet; and *S. sempervirens*, Endl., the Redwood, which reaches to 300 feet in height, with a girth of 55 feet (see Brandis 504). *Taxodium distichum*, Rich., is the Cypress of the swamps of the Southern States of North America.

Callitris quadrivalvis, Vent.; Brandis 535; Mathieu Fl. For. 453, is a large tree of the forests of Algeria. Of *Thuya* or Arbor Vitæ trees, three species occur in North America, giving a light, soft but durable, building timber. *Biota orientalis*, Endl. (Brandis 531) is the Arbor-Vitæ of China and Japan, occasionally cultivated in India.

Dacrydium contains several fine trees of Australia and New Zealand, and Kurz gives *D. elatum*, Wall., from Tenasserim, while *Ginkgo biloba*, Linn., with leaves like those of the Maiden Hair Fern, and thence commonly known by the name of *Salisburia adiantifolia*, is a deciduous tree of China and Japan, now much planted for ornament in Europe.

The wood of Coniferous trees is without vessels, hence, on a horizontal section, without pores. It consists of medullary rays and long wood cells tapering at the ends; in the case of most species these wood cells are large and visible under the lens. The annual rings are, as a rule, distinctly marked by a belt of thick-walled wood-cells in the outer (autumn) wood and a belt of larger and thin-walled wood cells in the inner (spring) wood.

In the case of the Juniper, Cypress, Yew and *Podocarpus*, the firmer belt of autumn wood is narrow, and the whole structure of the wood, therefore, is homogeneous. On the other hand, in the case of the Pines, Firs, Cedar and Larch the wood consists of alternate layers of soft spring wood and firm autumn wood.

The turpentine (resin) is secreted in large, branching, intercellular ducts, lined by thin-walled cells. These cavities are called 'resinous ducts,' and they are of two classes; *vertical*, running with the wood-cells parallel to the axis of the stem, and *horizontal* ducts, running with the medullary rays. The horizontal ducts can, as a rule, only be seen under the microscope; they will, therefore, not be generally noted in the following descriptions. The vertical ducts appear on a cross section as scattered pores varying in size. Resin is also found in parenchymatic cells with straight ends, which are found mixed with ordinary wood cells: this is the case in Cypress.

The timber is homogeneous in the case of Cupressineæ and Taxineæ, but, as explained, in the case of Abietineæ it consists of alternate layers of soft spring wood and hard autumn wood. The value of the timber of Abietineæ for building purposes depends in a great measure upon the greater or less proportion of the firmer belt of autumn wood and also upon the more or less spongy nature of the spring wood. Under certain circumstances, for instance, the timber of Deodar has an extremely soft and spongy spring wood, and a comparatively narrow belt of autumn wood. Such timber is probably less durable and not as strong as timber grown under other circumstances, which has a less spongy spring wood and a larger proportion of firm autumn wood. Similar variations in the structure may be noticed in the case of *Pinus longifolia* and other coniferous trees, and it is a subject worth careful enquiry how far durability and strength are effected by these characters, and to determine the conditions of growth under which the wood of coniferous trees exhibits the varieties of structure here adverted to. It is generally supposed that slow-grown timber of coniferous trees is heavier and more durable than timber of the same species which had grown more rapidly. This, however, is not always the case. The following are instances of a light weight in the case of slow-grown timbers:—

				lbs.
Pinus excelsa	H	140.	(22 rings)	26
Cedrus Deodara	H	902.	(34 „	32 „

Logs which contain much resin are heavier than those which contain little resin.

With few exceptions the wood of coniferous trees seasons well. The woods are light, the weight per cubic foot ranging between 20 and 40 lbs., with few exceptions, such as Taxus, which weighs over 40 lbs.

1. PINUS, Linn.

Five Indian species; the whole genus according to Parlatore in DeCandolle's

Prodromus (Subgenus I. *Pinus*) containing 66 species, and according to Gordon's 'Pinetum' 92 species. The European species are, many of them, very important:—

P. sylvestris, Linn. is the Scotch Fir, which gives the timber known as Red Memel, Dantzic Fir and Red Deal of the Baltic. *P. Pinaster*, Soland. (*P. maritima*, Lamk.) is the Maritime or Cluster Pine so largely used in reclothing sandy wastes on the sea-shore, like the 'Landes' of Gascony, and for the production of resin. *P. halepensis*, Mill., is the Aleppo Pine found throughout the Mediterranean region, chiefly on limestone. *P. Laricio*, Poiret, gives two varieties, called respectively the Corsican Pine and Austrian Pine, which are also used for the production of resin and for replanting barren soils. *P. Pinea*, Linn. is the Stone Pine of Italy, with edible fruits, and *P. Cembra*, Linn., the 'Arolle' of the mountains of Central Europe.

Of the American Pines the most important is the *P. Strobus*, Linn., the White Pine or Weymouth Pine, whose wood is extensively used in America and is exported to Europe from the forests of Canada.

The species indigenous in India may thus be recognized by the characters of their leaves and cones:—

Leaves in pairs . . . . *P. Merkusii.*
„ in threes
Scales of cone beaked.
Leaves long . . . . *P. longifolia.*
„ short . . . . *P. Gerardiana.*
Scales of cone obtuse . . . . . . *P. Kasya.*
Leaves in fives . . . . *P. excelsa.*

Wood generally very resinous, not homogeneous, consisting of alternate layers of soft and often spongy spring wood, and of hard and darker coloured autumn wood. Vertical resinous ducts large and numerous, in most species visible on horizontal and vertical sections. The Indian species have a distinct heartwood.

1. P. longifolia, Roxb. Fl. Ind. iii. 651; Brandis 506; Gamble 81 Vern. *Nakhtar*, Afg.; *Chíl, chír, dráb chir*, Pb.; *Gúlo, thansa*, Kangra; *Anander*, Jhelam; *Saral*, Jaunsar; *Chír, salla, sapin, kolon, kolan, kolain*, Garhwal and Kumaun; *Dhúp*, Oudh; *Dhúp, sala dhúp, sula*, Nep.; *Gniet*, Lepcha; *Teadong*, Bhutia.

A large tree. Bark 1 to 2 inches thick, reddish brown, inner substance dark red, cut by deep fissures into large plates of irregular shape. The bark of the Sikkim tree is thinner and the plates smaller. Heartwood small, soft, reddish. Annual rings well marked, consisting of an inner belt of soft and spongy tissue, and an outer hard, compact and darker coloured belt, the inner soft belt generally occupying half to two-thirds or more of the ring. Medullary rays fine and extremely fine, numerous, prominent as narrow lines on a radial section. Vertical resinous ducts large and numerous, irregularly distributed, prominent on a vertical section.

Afghanistan, Outer North-West Himalaya ascending to 7,500 feet, Sikkim and Bhutan ascending to 4,000 feet, though scarce above 3,000 feet.

P. longifolia generally shows a moderate or slow rate of growth as far as our experience goes. Its growth, other circumstances being equal, is most rapid in the North-West Himalaya at elevations between 4,000 and 7,000 feet, less rapid at lower and higher elevations. On this subject, however, as well as on the rate of growth of *P. longifolia* generally, systematic observations are much wanted.

The rates of growth shown by our small specimens are, per inch of radius—

	rings.		rings.
H. 13	14	E. 704 (large round, 2 ft. diameter)	11·7
H. 93	5·6	E. 2135	23
H. 602	5·5	E. 2136 (planted tree about 20 years old.)	4·5
O. 3803	18		

which would seem to indicate that the growth in Sikkim is slower than in the North-West Himalaya. From a paper by Mr. Smythies in the Indian Forester, Vol. VI, p. 13, a list of countings of 153 trees made by a Forest Guard under his supervision is given, the result being an average rate of growth of 12 rings per inch of radius. This would give 138 years as the average age at which 6 feet girth is reached, though Mr. Smythies gives 104 years, or, excluding suppressed trees, 86 years. Brandis gives four to five rings as the rate, and probably five rings per inch is the proper rate for well-grown trees at a tolerably high elevation such as that where H 93 and H 602 were cut. The growth in height is undoubtedly fast at first, as the leading shoot often reaches 18 to 24 inches yearly, and the growth in diameter appears to be equally great in well-grown trees.

Regarding the weight and transverse strength of Chír the following experiments have been made :—

Captain Jones at Almora in 1844—

	Weight.	P =
15 experiments, unseasoned wood, 4 ft. × 2 in. × 2 in., gave	39 lbs.,	626
5 „ seasoned „ „ „	27 „	555

Experiments at Roorkee in 1858 on Garhwal wood by Colonel Maclagan, R. E.

	Weight.	P =
3 experiments, with bars 22 ft. × 1 in. × 1 in.,	gave 27 lbs.	906
4 „ „ „ 34 „ × 1 „ × 1 „	„ 27 „	961
4 „ „ „ 34 „ × 2 „ × 1 „	„ 27 „	916

Dr. Warth's weighings of our specimens shewed that the weight varied from 37 to 45 lbs., averaging 41 lbs., the Sikkim wood being rather heavier, as well as darker coloured, and more filled with resin. The wood is not durable; it is attacked by insects and decays rapidly when exposed to wet; it is, however, easy to work and is extensively used in some localities in the hills for building, shingles, tea boxes and the bottoms of boats. It gives large quantities of resin, more than any of the other Himalayan Pines, but the process is exhaustive. Brandis says, "The yield of an ordinary tree is 10 to 20 lbs. of resin the first, and about one-third of the quantity the second year, after which the tree either dies or is blown down." Tar is also extracted from it, and turpentine is distilled from the tar. The bark is used for tanning and as fuel for iron-smelting. The wood is often made into charcoal, and the charcoal of the leaves mixed with rice-water is used as ink.

Chír requires much light and seedlings do not spring up under shade; but the natural reproduction is good and should present no difficulty if fire and cattle are excluded from the cuttings.

			lbs.
H	602.	Tuttul Forest, Kangra	37
H	13.	Simla, 6,000 feet	39
H	93,	„ „ „	39
O	3003.	Garhwal (1874)	45
E	704.	Badamtam Forest, Darjeeling, 2,500 feet	45
E	2435.	Great Rangít Valley „ 2,000 feet	42
E	2436.	Darjeeling, 7,000 feet (planted).	

2. P. Kasya, Royle; Brandis 508; Kurz ii. 499. Vern. *Dingsa*, Khasia; *Tinyu-ben*, Burm.

Bark thick, with deep cracks and fissures. Wood very resinous, heartwood red. Inner layer of annual ring soft and spongy, outer layer moderately hard. Resinous ducts moderate-sized, numerous in the outer and middle belt of each annual ring, very prominent on a vertical section.

Khasia Hills above 2,000 feet, higher hills of Chittagong and mountains between the Sittang and the Salween rivers in Burma above 3,000 feet.

Growth, our specimen shows a moderately fast growth, 6 rings per inch of radius; the weight is 38 lbs. per cubic foot. In an account of the firs of the Khasia Hills by Captain Jones of the Quarter Master General's Department in "Gleanings of Science," vol. i., p. 202, 1829, the weight determined by Captain Baker, but with small bars 15″ × 0·8″ × 0·9″ is given as 37 lbs. and the value of P. 522. The wood is extensively used in the Khasia Hills for building and other purposes. It is very rich in resin.

		lbs.
E 797.	Khasia Hills	38

3. P. Merkusii, Jungh.; Kurz ii. 499. Vern. *Tinyu-ben*, Burm.

A large tree with thick, rough bark. Heartwood yellowish brown with dark streaks, moderately hard, exceedingly resinous. Structure similar to that of *P. Kasya.*

Tropical forests of Burma on the Thoungyeen river, associated with *Dipterocarpus tuberculatus.*

Our specimen shews a moderate growth, 11 rings per inch of radius; its weight is 51 lbs. per cubic foot. Major Seaton gives 54 lbs. The wood is sometimes brought to Moulmein for mast pieces, but the difficulties of land and water transport are very great, almost preventing its extraction at a profit. Splinters are extensively used for torches.

		lbs.
B 547.	Thoungyeen, Burma	51

4. P. Gerardiana, Wall.; Brandis 508. Vern. *Chilghoza, jalghoza,* Afg.; *Chiri, prita, mirri, galboja, galgoja,* Chenab; *Kashti,* Ravi; *Ri, rhi,* Kunawar; *Kannuchi, koniúnchi, kaninchi, shangti,* W. Tibet; the seeds, *neoza.*

A moderate-sized tree, with very thin, smooth, grey bark, exfoliating in large thin scales, leaving shallow, rounded depressions; cracked only in very old trees. Heartwood yellowish-brown, hard, durable, very resinous. Resinous ducts scattered, similar in size to those of *P. excelsa,* prominent on a vertical section.

Inner dry and arid North-West Himalaya, found in isolated areas of no great extent, generally between 6,000 and 10,000 feet, mountains of North Afghanistan and Kafiristan.

Growth, specimen H 991 gives 24 rings, but appears to have been cut from a branch; H 1405, of old heartwood, gives 13 rings. Weight, 44 to 47 lbs. per cubic foot. The wood is rarely used, as the tree is valued for its edible seeds; it is, however, sometimes hollowed out for watercourses, and is used for the hook which attaches the seat to the rope in a single-rope swing-bridge.

The seeds are a staple article of food in Kunawar, and other parts of the Himalaya; they are largely brought into India from Afghanistan. They are oily, with a slight turpentine flavour, and are generally roasted and eaten at dessert.

		lbs.
H 991.	Kunawar, Punjab, 9,000 feet	44
H 1405.	Chenab, „ „ (Stewart, 1867.) . . .	47

5. P. excelsa, Wall.; Brandis 510; Gamble 82. Vern. *Piuni,* Afg.; *Biár,* Hazara; *Chíl, chír, chíltu, chítu, chiú,* Kashmir to Jaunsar; *Chíla,* Garhwal; *Kail,* Beas, Sutlej; *Lím,* Chamba, Kunawar; *Yara, yúr, yiro,* Kashmir; *Shomshing, limshing,* Lahoul; *Raisalla, lamshing, byans,* Kumaun; *Tongschí,* Bhutan.

A large tree with greyish brown bark, cut into small, rather regular plates by shallow fissures ¼ inch thick. Heartwood distinct, red, moderately hard. Annual rings distinctly marked by a narrow outer belt or line of compact wood, inner belt not spongy. Medullary rays very fine and very numerous, prominent on a radial section. Vertical resinous ducts scattered, smaller than those of *P. longifolia,* very numerous and prominent on a vertical section.

Himalaya, between 6,000 and 10,000 feet, occasionally found as low as 5,000 feet and as high as 12,500 feet from the Indus to Bhutan, extending into the inner arid tract. Mountains of Afghanistan and South Macedonia.

The wood is more durable than that of *P. longifolia*, but less so than Deodar. As far as our knowledge goes at present the tree grows most rapidly up to a certain age at low elevations. In the outer Himalaya it has a moderate, and in the inner arid Himalaya a slow, rate of growth. When young the tree is supposed to grow more rapidly than Deodar. The following are the rates shewn by our specimens:—

	Rings.
H 901	6·7
H 1403α	7·8
H 27	8
H 923	9·5
H 1407	11
H 609	13
H 1404	14·5
H 140	22
H 1403β	27
E 2463	6·5

leaving out the three last, *viz.*, those giving 22, 27 and 6·5 rings respectively, we have an average of 10 rings per inch of radius; but more information is much required.

In paragraph 41 of the Kulu Report of 1877 the following measurements of Kail trees in Jangarkaláon and Deoban Reserves are given:—

	Mean radius.	Age.	Rings per inch.
No. 1	10·5	49 years	4·7
„ 2	9·5	55 „	5·8
„ 3	10·75	65 „	6·0

or an average growth of 5·5 rings per inch of radius.

Dr. Warth's weighings of our specimens shewed a variation of only from 26 to 33 lbs., and an average of 30 lbs., per cubic foot.

In durability Kail wood ranks next to Deodar, and is preferred to that of Chíl or the Firs. It is used for house-building, shingles, water channels, wooden spades and other implements. It gives an excellent charcoal for iron-smelting. The wood is very resinous and gives turpentine, but it is not usually extracted, as is that of *P. longifolia*. Very resinous wood is used for torches, the bark is used to roof huts in the forest, and the leaves are largely lopped for litter.

The seedlings like light, and natural reproduction is very good even on hill sides bare of trees, if grazing and fires are prevented. It seems to prefer to grow on sandy or clayey soils, and not to be partial to limestone.

		lbs.
H 923.	Hazara, (7,000 feet)	29
H 901.	„ „	30
H 140.	Lahoul (about 10,000 feet)	26
H 609.	„ „ „ „	27
H 37.	Mashobra, Simla, 7,000 feet	33
H 2871.	Nagkanda, „ , 8,000 „	...
H 1403α	Punjab Hills, Dr. Stewart (1867	32
H 1403β	„	32
H 1404.	„	33
H 1407.	„	28
E 2463.	Chumbi Valley, Tibet, about 10,000 feet	30

2. CEDRUS, Link.

The Lebanon and Atlas Cedars are *C. Libani*, Barr. and *C. atlantica*, Manetti; they are joined into one species by Parlatore in DeCandolle's Prodromus, but kept separate from *C. Deodara*. It is not, however, possible to separate the three by any constant specific characters. On this subject see Brandis, page 324. A fourth variety has lately been discovered in Cyprus.

Wood resinous, with a distinct heartwood, somewhat more homogeneous than that of *Pinus* and *Abies*, but consisting of alternate layers of softer spring wood, and harder autumn wood. The resin is found in parenchymatic wood cells with horizontal ends.

1. **C. Deodara**, Loudon; Brandis 516. *Pinus Deodara*, Roxb. Fl. Ind. iii. 651. Deodar, Himalayan Cedar. Vern. *Nakhtar, lmanza*, Afg.; *Diár, deodár, dedwar, dadár*, Hazara, Kashmir, Garhwal, Kumaun; *Palúdar*, Hazara; *Kelu, keoli, kilar, kilei*, Chenab to Jumna; *Kelmang*, Kunawar; *Giam*, Tibet.

A very large and tall tree. Bark greyish brown, with numerous shallow, vertical fissures, which run into each other and present a reticulate appearance. Heartwood light yellowish brown, scented, moderately hard. In each annual ring the outer belt of firmer and darker coloured tissue is generally narrow, and the inner belt is not very soft, but in exceptional cases and under certain conditions, which have not yet been studied, the inner belt is soft and spongy (*e.g.* H 617). This peculiarity has nothing to do with the rate of growth or with the altitude, as fast-grown trees possess hard tissue in the spring wood. Medullary rays fine and very fine, unequal in width. No vertical resinous ducts, as in *Pinus*, but the resin exudes from cells which are not visible to the naked eye. On the edge of certain annual rings are frequently found concentric strings of dark-coloured pores or intercellular ducts, which are prominent on a vertical section as dark lines, and in the vicinity of which the wood is sometimes more resinous.

North-West Himalaya, between 4,000 and 10,000 feet, extending east to the Dauli river, a tributary of the Alaknanda below the Niti Pass. Mountains of Afghanistan and North Beluchistan.

In common with most species of the Order, the Deodar has well marked annual rings which, there is little, if any, reason to doubt, each represent the growth of a year. More information has, perhaps, been collected on the subject of the rate of growth of Deodar than of any other species of Indian tree, though we have as yet no such complete series of trees of known age to deal with as were available at Nilambur for the question of the rate of growth of Teak. The geographical range of Deodar, especially in altitude, is very wide, and this circumstance, considering that some specimens may be obtained from sheltered places in comparatively warm valleys, while others come from exposed and high situations, makes it doubtful whether much value can be attached to general deductions from data collected from many quarters, and whether it should not usually be the practice to take only for use in any forests, the experiments made on trees in that or neighbouring localities. But the experience we have hitherto gained is very valuable, and it will be best to put together the items of information available. In Brandis' Forest Flora of North-West and Central India, pp. 520 to 524, a large amount of information is collected, to which reference can be made. It is there stated that the Deodar forests may be classified in three great divisions, *viz.*:—

1st.—Those in a dry climate in the vicinity of the arid zone of the inner Himalaya, having usually the age of trees 6 feet in girth above 140 years.

2nd.—Those in the intermediate ranges and valleys, having 6 feet in girth for an age of between 110 and 140 years.

3rd.—Those in the outer ranges under the full influence of the monsoon and having the age of trees 6 feet in girth usually below 110 years.

This is exemplified by an important table given at page 9 of the "Report on the Deodar Forests of Bussahir, 1865," which is here reproduced, and which gives the information collected by Messrs. Brandis, Stewart and Wood in their travels of that year in the Sutlej Valley.

Statement showing the average age of 1st and 2nd class Deodars examined in the different Forests of Kunawur, and some of the adjoining Forests.

FOREST.	No. of trees examined.	Age of 1st class trees.	Age of 2nd class trees.	Diff.	REMARKS.
		Years.	Years.		
1. Bhagarati { Exd. by Dr. Brandis	4	229	143	86	Forests with a slow rate of growth Age of 1st class trees above 140 years. Age of 2nd class trees above 100 years.
1. Bhagarati { Exd. by Mr. A. D. Campbell	18	169	148	48	
2. Cabul River	13	214	158	56	
3. Skyamdangdang, Sutlej	3	189	142	47	
4. Yolinge (upper part of Forest), S.	2	177	133	44	
5. Barunalang, S.	7	160	119	41	
6. Swat River	10	156	112	44	
7. Phinla, Kiuden, S.	7	154	110	44	
8. Manda (Jangi), S.	2	153	115	38	
9. Chini, S.	6	152	91	61	
10. Nachar, S.	30	149	112	37	
11. Poari, Purbani, Akpa, measured at Rupar, S.	9	145	106	39	
12. Kilba, S.	5	138	100	38	
13. Sleepers from Chenab at Lahore Railway Station.	50	134	97	37	Forests with an average rate of growth. Age of 1st class trees between 110 and 140 years.
14. Ravi timber, slow growth	4	134	93	41	
15. Serinche, (steep slope), S.	4	132	98	34	
16. Drift timber, examined at Rupar, S.	4	130	96	34	
17. Tinala (Teedong), S.	7	130	91	39	
18. Rakcham, S.	3	125	80	45	
19. Chenab, measured at Wazirabad	39	124	88	36	
20. Rogi, S.	15	119	86	33	
21. Dippi, S.	2	117	88	29	
22. Yak Bursari, S.	3	116	87	29	
23. Topan and Kashang, S.	5	113	85	28	
24. Mebar, S.	7	113	83	30	
25. Chaog	5	110	87	23	
26. Simla (north side, young trees)	23	99	73	26	Forests with a rapid rate of growth. Age of 1st class trees below 110 years. Age of 2nd class trees below 80 years.
27. Jhelam	4	97	71	26	
28. Kadelli (between Matiyana and Nagkanda).	1	94	85	9	
29. Simla (south side)	9	91	67	24	
30. Kumkumee, Shoang, S.	10	91	66	25	
31. Ravi timber, good growth	4	91	62	29	
32. Kilba, Dippi, Kusthal (Rupar), S.	8	90	66	24	
33. Janee, S.	3	80	56	24	
34. Yolinge (lower part of forests), S.	2	76	57	19	
35. Jaunsar Bawur	17	71	53	18	
36. Simla, (north side, large trees)	7	71	52	19	
37. Taranda	4	67	49	18	
38. Chasoo Limsantang, S.	6	65	47	18	
39. Serinche (level ground), S.	10	62	44	18	
40. Nagadar	8	50	34	16	
TOTAL	380	...	...	...	

NOTE.—The Sutlej Forests are marked S.

In 'Notes on Deodar Localities near Simla, 1867,' by Dr. Brandis, the following measurements are recorded :—

	No.	Rings.	Radius.	Rings per inch.
Dewra (Naldehra) Forest, altitude about 7,000 feet	1	86	11 in.	7·82
	2	128	12 in.	10·66

	No.	Rings.	Radius.	Rings per inch.

the first giving 90, the second 122 years to a girth of 6 feet.

	No.	Rings.	Radius.	Rings per inch.
Gund Forest (Giri Valley) a *deota* forest, low	1	117	11	11·54
	2	155	11·5	13·47

averaging 12·5 rings, or an age of 140 years at 6 feet; the great age being accounted for by their having evidently grown up in a close thicket when young.

		Rings.	Radius.	Rings per inch.
Cheog forest, 7,000 feet, 9 trees averaging		106	13·5	8

or by calculation 90 years for a girth of 6 feet.

For the "Valuation of the Water-catchment Area at Mahasu near Simla, 1877" (Indian Forester, vol. v., p. 139), the following measurements of Deodar stumps and poles were made:—

Locality.	No.	Soil, elevation, etc.	No. of rings.	Average radius.	Height.	Rings per inch of radius.
Stumps.				inches		
Block I, Compt. *b.* .	1	soil deep, slope 15° . .	54	9	Stumps.	6·00
" " *c.* .	2	" " , " 35° . .	77	9		8·55
" " .	3		89	9		9·88
Block IV, " *k.* .	4	isolated, ground flat and stony	84	9		9·33
" " .	5		79	9		8·78
" " *l.* .	6	soil rich, rocky . . .	104	9		11·55
" " .	7	" good, on ridge . .	101	9		11·22
" " .	8	" deep	119	9		13·22
Block V, " *n.* .	0	ground rocky, easy slope .	82	9		9·11
" " .	10		77	9		8·55
Block VII, " *s.* .	11	slope 25°-30°, good soil .	81	9		9·00
" " .	12		79	9		8·78
" " .	13		72	9		8·00
Block VIII, " *u.* .	14	rocky, good soil . .	73	9		8·11
" " .	15		89	9		9·88
Block IX, " *x.* .	16	very stony, slope 20°-25° .	105	9		11·67
" " .	17		111	9		12·33
		Average	...	...	...	9·64
Poles.						
Block I, Compt. *b.* .	3	soil deep, slope 25° . .	18	2·71	31	6·65
" " *c.* .	6	" " , " 35° . .	20·5	3·02	33	6·77
Block II, " *d.* .	6	" rocky, " 40° . .	22	2·71	25	8·13
" " *e.* .	3	" good, " 15° . .	32	2·86	29	5·24
Block III, " *h.* .	3	" rocky, " 20° , .	28	2·07	23	13·53
" " *j.* .	3	" poor, " 25° . .	15	2·23	23	8·51
Block IV, " *l.* .	10	" deep, " 25°-35° .	34	4·77	43	7·12
" " .	10	" " , " 30° . .	32	3·10	30	10·31
" " .	5	" stony, " 35° . .	31	2·71	29	11·45
" " *m.* .	7	" " , " " . .	31	2·86	32	10·81
Block V, " *n.* .	6	" deep, " 20° . .	25·5	2·86	26	8·87
Block VII, " *s.* .	4	" " , " 30° . .	28·5	3·50	30·5	8·13
Block VIII, " *u.* .	5	" good, " 20° . .	28	2·71	27	5·18
Block IX, " *x.* .	6	" stony . .	33	4·08	50	8·29
" " .	5	" very stony . .	35	2·71	29	12·93
		Average	...	...	...	8·08

The stumps, it will be seen, gave an average of 9·67 rings per inch of radius, the countings being made in a radius of 9 inches. This gave 87 years as the age of a tree 4⅓ feet in girth at base, or, allowing for bark, about 4¼ feet girth breast high. On the same calculation 6 feet girth trees would be 111 years old. This is a slower rate than in the neighbouring forests of Simla and Cheog, but the difference is explained by the Mahasu trees being at least 500 feet higher in altitude than those localities. The 82 poles gave an average of 8·8 rings per inch of radius for an average age of

29 years. At this rate of growth they would reach 4½ feet in girth in 76 years, and 6 feet in 99 years.

In "Suggestions regarding the Demarcation and Management of the Forests in Kulu, 1876" a large number of observations are recorded. The Danabiál plantation was commenced in 1864, and trees planted in that year and 1866 were examined with the following result:—

	No.	Age.	Girth (average).	Height.	Rings per inch.
		Years.	Inches.	Feet.	
Planted in 1864	2	12	25·5	25 to 30	3
„ „ 1866	5	10	13·4	16 to 25	4·7

—a fast rate of growth.

In the Kulu forests the following measurements were made:—

	No.	Mean radius. Inches.	No. of rings.	Rings per inch of radius.
Aliobiál Forest	1	5	60	12
	2	7	70	10
	3	10¼	137	13
	4	6	85	14
		Average		12¼
Deoban Forest	1	6	35	5·8
	2	5	48	0·6
	3	5	26	5·2
	4	22·5	88	3·9
		Average		6·1
Súm Forest (poor soil)	1	8	65	8·1
	2	6·5	67	10·3
	3	9	67	7·4
	4	10·75	83	7·7
		Average		8·4
Betarjir (good soil)	1	14·75	94	6·4
	2	17·5	103	5·9
	3	23·75	99	4·2
		Average		5·5
Sandhar Forest, 6,500 feet elevation, soil good, a succession of terraces, with steep slopes between.	1	150	17·25	8·69
	2	100	14·00	7·14
	3	196	17·25	11·36
	4	175	20	8·75
	5	175	14	12:50
	6	120	13·50	8·88
	7	195	17	11·46
	8	175	25	7
	9	400	37·50	10·60
	10	175	18	9·72
	11	190	23·50	8·08
		Average		9·47

	1	135	24	5·62
	2	196	21·5	9·11
	3	215	21	10·24
	4	172	20·75	8·29
	5	249	26	9·58
	6	276	19	14·53
	7	200	20·75	9·64
	8	236	18·75	12·58
	9	230	23·75	9·68
Phulga Forest, 7,000 feet, forest very fine, soil good, a succession of terraces. Rock granite.	10	236	23·75	9·93
	11	269	21·75	12·36
	12	293	13	22·38
	13	190	25	7·60
	14	90	7	12·85
	15	166	18	9·22
	16	154	24	6·42
	17	190	50	3·80
	18	190	17	11·18
	19	196	20	9·80
	20	260	29	8·96
	21	259	25	10·36
	22	298	16	18·62
			Average .	10·53

The average result of the measurements of these 48 trees is 9·5 rings per inch of radius, shewing that in the forests of Kulu it may be expected that Deodar reaches 4½ feet in girth at an age of 82, and 6 feet in girth at an age of 109 years, which is good growth for forests which must be looked on as in the second category.

In the just published 'Memorandum on the Forests of the Kuram Assigned Districts' by Mr. C. Bagshawe (Indian Forester, vol. vi., p. 28) a few measurements on sample areas of 2 acres each are recorded as follows:—

	No. of trees.	Mean radius.	Mean No. of rings.	No. per inch of radius.
Peiwar Forest—				
(1) S.-E. aspect, 8,600 feet . . .	6	7·5 inches	191	25·5
(2) E. to N.-E. aspect, 8,500 feet .	20	9·4 „	191	20·3
(3) N.-W. aspect, 8,700 feet . .	7	10· „	223	22·3
(4) S. aspect, 8,660 feet	5	12·2 „	148	14·5

The average of these measurements gives nearly 21 rings per inch of radius, equivalent to an age of 241 years corresponding to 6 feet in girth. This is entirely in accordance with Dr. Brandis' division of the Deodar forests, for such forests as those of Afghanistan will naturally come into the first category. We may, therefore, say that there is nothing to be obtained from measurements made since the publication of the 'Forest Flora of N.-W. and Central India' to alter materially the statement therein made that the average ages of 6-ft. girth trees are—

1st Division	above	140 years.
2nd Division	from 110 to 140	„
3rd Division	under	110 „

Girth and height at different ages.—The proportion between the height and girth naturally depends, to a very great extent, on the condition of the forest in which the trees are found; isolated trees will naturally increase in girth more than in height, while trees grown in dense forest will run up fast in height at the same time that the increase in girth is slow. The pole forests examined at Mahasu, whose measurements are given on page 402, shewed trees which varied in age from 15 to 35 years, in radius from 13 to 30 inches, and in height from 23 to 50 feet. When young Deodar grows slowly, Brandis says it attains 12 to 20 inches only during the first 3 to 4 years. But further information regarding the increase in height of Deodar at different ages is much wanted.

Crop of timber per acre.—Little information on this point has been collected since the publication of the 'Forest Flora of N.-W. and Central India,' where the subject is discussed at pp. 521-522.

The results of surveys given in the Bussahir Report are there quoted and here reproduced; they give—

No.		Locality.	Area surveyed.	Age of forest.	Trees per acre.	Crop per acre.
			Acres.	Yrs.		C. ft.
1	Jaunsar.	Mayshak Forest	0·69	70	54	2,464
2	Jaunsar.	Khattowa „	0·46	84	69	3,604
3	Jaunsar.	Chilara „	0·34	83	70	4,323
4	Kunawar.	Kiuden „	1·60	180	56	5,512
5	Kunawar.	„ „	0·33	180	90	8,972
6	Kunawar.	Nachar „	2·30	250	62	12,300

In para. 21 of the Mahasu Report it is stated that the probable expectation in that locality would be, at 80 years of age, 20 trees of $4\frac{1}{2}$ ft. girth and upwards.

The valuations made in the Kuram Forests by Mr. Bagshawe give as follows:—

No.	Acres.	Under 4'6"	4' 6" to 6."	above 6.'	Total.	Per acre.
1	2	66	30	26	122	61
2	2	48	58	62	168	84
3	2	41	37	20	98	49
4	2	23	17	37	77	39·5
Average	.	44·5	35·5	36·25	116·25	58·1
Per acre	.	22·25	17·75	18·1	58·1	...

Thus, the Jaunsar and Kunawar data would give, as far as the information we have goes, about the following:—

	No. of trees of 2 higher classes.	Cubic contents.
Forest 80 years old	64	3,464
„ 180 „ „	73	7,242
„ 250 „ „	62	12,300

while the Kuram countings give, for forests which lie between 180 and 250 years, in all probability, 36 trees of the two higher classes per acre.

With regard to the weight of Deodar and its transverse strength, the following experiments are available:—

Experiment by whom made.	Year.	Wood whence procured.	No. of experiments.	Size of bar.	Weight.	Value of P.
				Ft. In. In.		
Col. Maclagan, R.E. .	1858	Punjab . . .	1	2 × 1 × 1	23·05	554
„ „ .	„	„ . . .	4	3 × 1 × 1		580
„ „ .	„	„ . . .	4	3 × 1 × 2		602
„ „ .	„	Garhwal . .	1	2 × 1 × 1	24·65	630
„ „ .	„	„ . . .	3	3 × 1 × 1		637
„ „ .	„	„ . . .	4	3 × 1 × 2		550
Major Robertson and Captain Henderson.	1856	Punjab . ..	10	various	...	538
Major Cunningham .	1854	......	20	2 × 1 × 1	...	656
„ „ .	„	......	12	various	36·70	340
Captain W. Jones . .	1844	Kumaun .	10	......	38	443, unseasoned.
			10	......	40	560, seasoned.

Experiment by whom made.	Year.	Wood whence procured.	No. of experiments.	Size of bar.	Weight.	Value of P.
				Ft. In. In.		
Rai Kanhya Lal* . .	1876	Punjab { Ravi .	4	12 × 6 × 4	38	331
,, . .	,,	Ujh .	4	,,	35	304
,, . .	,,	Chenab .	4	,,	33	346
,, . .	,,	Sutlej .	4	,	34	215
,, . .	,,	Ravi .	8	8 × 5 × 3	34	367
,, . .	,,	Ujh .	8	,,	38	387
,, . .	,,	Chenab .	8	,,	34	341
,, . .	,,	Sutlej .	8	,,	33	315
Ganga Ram . . .	,,	Chamba . .	2	12 × 3 × 3	32	351
,, . . .	,,	,, . .	1	12 × 2·9 × 2·9	34	330
,, . . .	,,	,, . .	1	12 × 2·8 × 2·8	35	302
Dr. Warth . . .	,,	Punjab, different localities.	8	......	36·5	...

NOTE.—The Roorkee experiments gave a mean of 587 as the value of P. for Punjab timber, and 592 for Garhwal timber. It has since been proved that these values were too high, and the experiments of Rai Kanhya Lal, who operated on larger pieces give a mean of 334. The working value of P. as taken by the Department Public Works in the Punjab is now 300.

Deodar wood is extremely durable, being by far the most durable of the woods of the Himalayan Conifers. It is the chief timber of North-West India and is used for all purposes of construction, for railway sleepers, bridges, and even for furniture and shingles. An oil is obtained from the wood by destructive distillation; it is dark-coloured, thick, and resembles crude turpentine. It is used for anointing the inflated skins which are used for crossing rivers; and as a remedy for ulcers and eruptions for mange in horses and sore feet in cattle.

Rings per inch of radius.			lbs.
......	H 940.	Chenab Forests	34
34 rings.	H 902.	Siúl Valley, Chumba	32
23 ,,	H 900.	Ravi Forests	36
11 ,,	H 616.	Beas Forests (Kulu)	42
7·5 ,,	H 617.	Sutlej Forests (Bussahir)	31
18 ,,	H 16.	Cheog Forest, Simla, 7,000 feet . . .	41
7 ,,	H 42.	Mahasu Forest, Simla, 8,000 feet . . .	35
	H 3058.	,, ,, ,, ,, ...	...
10 ,,	H 3096.	,, ,, ,, ,, ...	42

3. ABIES, Tournef.

Three Indian species. The Spruce Fir of Europe is *A. excelsa*, DC.; Brandis 526, and is nearly allied to, and much resembles, the Himalayan *A. Smithiana*. The Silver Fir of Europe is *A. pectinata*, DC.; Brandis 528, which is similarly related to *A. Webbiana* of the Himalaya; while the Himalayan *A. dumosa* finds its counterpart in the Hemlock Spruce of Canada, *A. canadensis*, Michaux (Brandis 527). Nearly related to this last is the Douglas Spruce, *A. Douglasii*, Lindl., a tree which forms extensive forests in North-West America, attaining a height of 300 feet and more, and furnishing a valuable strong timber. It is extremely fast grown and has succeeded admirably in Great Britain. Many other species of *Abies* are in cultivation in Europe.

Wood generally not resinous (the resin being usually found in the bark), light-coloured, almost white, no heartwood, not homogeneous, consisting of alternate layers of soft spring wood and hard autumn wood. Vertical resinous ducts scanty.

Cones at the ends of branches, drooping or horizontal,
scales persistent.
Cones 4-6 inches long, leaves green . . . *A. Smithiana.*
Cones 1 inch ,, ,, white beneath . *A. dumosa.*
Cones lateral erect, scales deciduous . . . *A. Webbiana.*

* Experiments made at Lahore between May 10 and August 5, 1876 and published in Circular No. 44 of November 30, 1877 of the Government of the Punjab, Public Works Department.

1. A. Smithiana, Forbes; Brandis 525; Gamble 82. *A. Khutrow,* Loudon. The Himalayan Spruce. Vern. *Wesha, bajúr,* Afg.; *Kachal, kachan,* Hazara, Kashmir; *Rewari, ban lúdar, sangal, salla, sarei, káuli, roi, rág, ráo, bang re, krok,* Pb. Himalaya; *Tos,* Ravi; *Rau, raiang, re,* Sutlej; *Rai,* Jaunsar; *Kandre, re, rhái, ráo, khutrau, riálla, rágha, morinda, kail, kilu,* Garhwal, Kumaun; *Sehshing,* Bhutia.

A lofty tree, with rough greyish-brown bark, cut into small quadrangular plates by shallow furrows. Wood white, with a reddish or brown tinge, a little harder than that of *A. Webbiana.* The inner belt of annual rings soft and spongy. Vertical resinous-ducts scanty, visible on a vertical section. Medullary rays fine and extremely fine, very numerous, prominent on a radial section.

North-West Himalaya between 7,000 and 11,000 feet, Sikkim and Bhutan in the inner valleys between 7,800 and 10,000 feet, mountains of Afghanistan, Kafiristan and Gilgit.

Regarding the rate of growth of Spruce, very little information has yet been collected. In Mr. Ribbentrop's "Working Plan of the Kalatóp Forest, 1873," the measurement of 10 trees are given thus:—

No.	Locality.	Girth at base.	Height.	Age.	No. of rings per inch.
1.	Bindrabán	68 inches	108 feet	125	11·6
2.	„	69 „	104 „	112	10·2
3.	Kalatóp	65 „	90 „	70	6·7
4.	„	64 „	98 „	74	7·2
5.	Jagrota	89 „	82 „	80	5·6
6.	Near house	69 „	114 „	70	6·3
7.	„ „	90 „	— „	237	16·5
8.	Dainkúnd	102 „	142 „	310	19·1
9.	„	87 „	125 „	202	14·6
10.	„	90 „	125 „	183	12·8

giving an average growth of 11 rings per inch of radius, and 125 years of age to a girth of 6 feet. In Appendix II to the "Preliminary Report on the Deoban Working Circle, 1875" the measurements of 67 trees, 17 in the Kanjátra and 50 in the Thona Block, gave an average radius of 9·9 inches and average age of 105·6 years; this would shew a mean rate of growth of 10·67 rings per inch of radius. Up to 6 inches, which is as far as the averages can be taken for all the trees counted, we have as follows:—

Radius.	0—2 inches.	2—4 inches.	4—6 inches.
Average number of rings	16·3	19·4	22·5
or, per inch	8·15	9·7	11·25

shewing that the growth in Deoban Forest seems to get slower as the tree gets older. The figures further shew that the following are the average ages for different girths:—

Girth.	Radius.	Age.
18 inches	2·9 inches	20
36 „	5·7 „	39
54 „	8·6 „	63
72 „	11·2 „	91

Our small specimens shew an average rate of growth of 12 rings per inch of radius.

The weight given by our specimens varies from 26 to 32, giving an average of 30 lbs. per cubic foot, which is slightly heavier than the wood of *A. Webbiana.* The wood is extensively used locally, *e. g.,* in Simla, for packing-cases, rough furniture and planking, and sometimes for shingles. It crackles and sends out sparks in burning, besides burning away very quickly, but it is much used for charcoal. The bark is used for roofing shepherd's huts, and to make water-troughs; and the leaves and twigs are used for litter and manure.

It comes up well naturally in tolerably moist localities, where it has not too much shade, and it generally makes very quick growth the first year, yearly shoots 18 to 24 inches being not uncommon.

		lbs.
H 3165.	Dungagalli, Hazara, 7,000 feet	...
H 775.	Kalatóp Forest, Dalhousie, 7,000 feet	31
H 3.	Mahasu Forest, Simla, 8,000 feet	28
H 12.	" " " " "	32
H 43.	" " " " "	32
H 2898.	Nagkanda, Simla, 9,000 feet	...
H 3032.	Hattu Forest, Simla, 9,000 feet (young tree)	39
H 420.	Mohna Block, Deoban Forest, 8,000 feet	26

E 965 sent by Dr. Schlich from the Chumbi Valley, Tibet, between Sikkim and Bhutan, from about 9,000 to 10,000 feet, is a species of *Abies* closely allied to *A. Smithiana*, but with shorter needles and smaller cones. It is probably undescribed. The structure of the wood is identical with that of *A. Smithiana*.

2. **A. dumosa**, Loudon; Brandis 527; Gamble 83. *Pinus Brunoniana*, Wall. The Indian Hemlock Spruce. Vern. *Changathasi dhúp, thingia, thingáni súla*, Nep.; *Tangshing*, Bhutia; *Semadung, chemdang*, Lepcha.

A large tree, with thick, rough bark. Wood white, soft, with a slight pinkish tinge. Resinous ducts scanty.

North-East Kumaun, Nepal, Sikkim between 8,000 and 10,500 feet.

Growth, our specimens shew the following:— E 377, 17·5 rings; E 968, 11·5 rings, average 14·5 rings per inch of radius. Weight, 27 to 29 lbs. per cubic foot. The wood is used in Sikkim for shingles. The bark is also used for roofing.

		lbs.
E 377.	Phallaloong ridge, Darjeeling, 10,000 feet	27
E 968.	Chumbi Valley, Tibet, about 10,000 feet	29

3. **A. Webbiana**, Lindl.; Brandis 528; Gamble 82. *A. Pindrow*, Royle. The Himalayan Silver Fir. Vern. *Palúdar, rewari*, Jhelam; *Búdar, búdar, túng*, Kashmir; *Dhúnu, rág, rail, pe, re, salle, sara*, Chamba; *Tos*, Kulu; *Spun, pun, krok, kalrei*, Kunawar; *Bharda; thanera*, Shali; *Burla, pindrau, pindrai*, Hattu; *Kúdrom*, Matiyana; *Burúl, búrra, búldu*, Bhajji; *Kalrai, satrai, chúr*, Kotkai; *Raho, row, chilrow, kilaunta*, Chor; *Morinda*, Jaunsar; *Ragha, rao ragha, ransla, raisalla*, Kumaun; *Wúman*, Byans; *Gobria sulah*, Nep.; *Dumshing*, Bhutia.

A lofty evergreen tree. Bark smooth, silvery on young stems, on old stems brown, cut into long, narrow scales by anastomosing spiral clefts, rough, ¼ inch thick. Wood white, soft. The inner zone of each annual ring is soft and spongy. Medullary rays very fine and exceedingly fine, very numerous, not prominent on a vertical section. Vertical resinous ducts very rare.

Himalaya, from the Indus to Bhutan; in the North-West Himalaya between 7,000 and 13,000 feet; in the inner ranges of Sikkim and Bhutan, between 9,000 and 13,000 feet; in the outer ranges it does not descend below 10,000 feet.

Not much more information is available regarding the rate of growth of Silver Fir than there is that of Spruce. The Kalatóp Working Plan and Deoban Report again afford most of the information. The measurements of 10 trees in Kalatóp are given thus:—

No.	Locality.	Girth at base.	Height.	Age.	No. of rings per inch.
1.	Bindrabán	78 inches	110 feet	170	13·7
2.	"	56 "	106 "	170	19·1
3.	Kalatóp	67 "	97 "	85	7·9
4.	"	67 "	93 "	72	6·7

No.	Locality.	Girth at base.	Height.	Age.	No. of rings per inch.
5.	Jagrota	72 inches	90 inches	73	6·4
6.	„	55 „	90 „	73	8·3
7.	Dainkúnd	82 „	120 „	248	19·0
8.	„	77 „	103 „	192	15·7
9.	„	72 „	120 „	195	17·0
10.	„	80 „	108 „	223	17·5

giving an average growth of 13 rings per inch of radius, or nearly 150 years of age to a girth of 6 feet. Appendix III of the 'Preliminary Report on the Deoban Working Circle, 1875' gives the measurements of 8 trees in the Kanjátra Block. These give an average radius of 10·1 inches and an average age of 97·8 years; this would shew a mean rate of growth of 9·7 rings per inch of radius. Up to 6 inches radius we have as follows:—

Radius.	0—2 inches.	2—6 inches.	4—6 inches.
Average number of rings	16·7	19·2	17·3
or, per inch	8·35	9·6	8·6

or a tolerably uniform rate of growth. The Kanjátra figures further shew that the following are the average ages for different girths:—

Girth.	Radius.	Age.
18 inches	2·9 inches	25
36 „	5·7 „	50
54 „	8·6 „	81
72 „	11·5 „	113

Our small specimens appear to have all come from slow-grown trees, as they shew an average of 16·8 rings per inch.

With regard to the weight and transverse strength the following is all the information available. Captain Jones' ten experiments in 1844 gave: Weight 31 lbs., P = 440; Wallich gave the weight at 21 lbs., while our specimens, weighed by Dr. Warth, gave an average of 29 lbs.

The wood is not durable when exposed to the weather, but seems to last well as shingles in Sikkim, whence it is sometimes exported to Tibet for roofing. At Murree shingles are said to last eight to ten years, and in Kulu three to six. In Kunawar and Lahoul it is much used for construction. In the North-West Himalaya the bark is used for roofing shepherds' huts; in Sikkim it is used for troughs for the salt which is given to sheep grazing on the higher hills. On the Jhelum the twigs and leaves are cut and stored for winter use as fodder and litter for cattle.

			lbs.
H	934.	Hazara, 7,000 feet	29
H	774.	Kalatóp Forest, Dalhousie, 7,500 feet	...
H	2895.	Hattu, Simla, 9,000 feet	...
H	3031.		
H	65.	Nagkanda, Simla, 9,000 feet	29
H	421.	Thona Block, Deoban Forest, 8,000 feet	30
E	359.	Sandakpho, Darjeeling, 11,500 feet	27
E	2437.	„ „ „	...
E	964.	Chumbi Valley, Tibet, 10,000 feet	29

4. LARIX, Tournef.

One Indian species. The European Larch is *L. europæa*, DC.; Brandis 531, found in the Alps of France, Switzerland, Austria and Bavaria, and in the Carpathians. The Siberian Larch, *L. sibirica*, Led., forms large forests in Russia, Siberia and the Ural and Altai mountains.

Wood resinous, with a distinct red heartwood, not homogeneous, consisting of alternate layers of soft spring wood, and hard autumn wood. Large vertical resinous ducts.

1. L. Griffithii, Hook. f. and Th.; Brandis 531; Gamble 83. Vern. *Boargasella,* Nep.; *Sah, saar,* Sikkim.

A deciduous tree, with reddish brown bark, ½ inch thick. Heartwood red. Inner zone of each annual ring soft and spongy, outer zone narrower, firm and shining. Resinous ducts scanty, large. Medullary rays fine and extremely fine, numerous, prominent on a radial section.

Nepal, Sikkim and Bhutan, between 8,000 and 12,000 feet.

Growth, our specimen shews 21 rings per inch of radius; its weight is 32 lbs. per cubic foot. The wood is considered durable, and is exported from Sikkim into Tibet. Hooker in Himalayan Journals, ii, p. 44, says that he never saw the wood to be red but always white and soft. Our specimen, however, is red and closely resembles the wood of the European Larch.

		lbs.
E 969.	Chumbi Valley, Tibet, about 10,000 feet	32

5. CUPRESSUS, Linn.

One indigenous Indian species, three others generally cultivated. *C. glauca,* Lam. Brandis 534, is cultivated in gardens in Western India above Ghát.

Wood homogeneous, fragrant, the firm belt of autumn wood very narrow. Resin is found in parenchymatic cells with horizontal ends.

1. C. torulosa, Don; Brandis 533. The Himalayan Cypress. Vern. *Devi-diár,* Ravi; *Deodar,* Kulu, Bhajji; *Gulla, gulrai, kallain,* Simla; *Leauri,* Jaunsar; *Raisalla, sarai,* Kumaun; *Sarrú, súrah-vyu,* Tibet.

A large tree. Bark ½ inch thick, brown, the outer layer peeling off in numerous long, narrow, thin strips, inner substance reddish brown. Heartwood light brown with darker streaks, very fragrant, moderately hard. Annual rings distinctly marked by a narrow, firm and dark coloured belt on the inner edge. Numerous intermediate, deceptive but not continuous, rings. Medullary rays very fine and extremely fine, very numerous. No vertical resinous ducts similar to those in pines; the resin is here contained in parenchymatic wood cells similar to those which form the tissue of the wood.

Outer ranges of North-West Himalaya, from Chamba to Nepal, scattered and in numerous isolated localities of greater or less extent, chiefly on limestone, between 5,500 and 9,000 feet.

Growth slow. Stewart records twelve to eighteen rings per inch of radius; our specimens shew: H 613 nine rings, H 61 thirteen rings and H 771 fourteen rings per inch of radius. The average weight of our specimens is 39 lbs. per cubic foot. The wood has been much used at Naini Tál for building, and is sometimes used for beams on the Ravi and Sutlej. In Kulu it is made into images, and is used for the poles which carry the sacred ark. It is often burnt as incense in temples.

		lbs.
H 36.	Tika, Simla, 8,000 feet	34
H 61.	Kandru, Simla, 8,000 feet	42
H 771.	Belj, near Bassú, Chamba, 7,000 feet	36
H 613.	Kulu, 7,000 feet	44

2. C. funebris, Endl.; Brandis 534; Gamble 83. Vern. *Chandang, tchenden,* Bhutia.

A handsome tree with pendulous branches, and a fibrous brown bark, often planted in Nepal, Sikkim and Bhutan near temples and monasteries, and in China. Structure similar to that of *C. torulosa.*

		lbs.
E 972.	Darjeeling Hills, about 5,500 feet	34

3. C. sempervirens, Linn.; Brandis 533. Vern. *Sara, sarús*, North-West India.

A tall tree. Bark thin, light brown, fibrous, peeling off in thin strips. Wood light brown, moderately hard to hard. Annual rings distinctly marked by the dark, narrow, firm belt of autumn wood. Medullary rays fine, brown, very numerous. Resin-cells as in C. *torulosa*.

Cultivated in gardens in Afghanistan and North-West India, sometimes reaching 6 to 9 feet in girth, with 70 to 100 feet in height.

		lbs.
O 3267.	Saharanpur Gardens	37

E 697 from Rungbee, Darjeeling, 5,500 feet (21 lbs. per cubic foot), is the wood of *Cryptomeria japonica*, Don; Gamble 83. This is a large tree of China and Japan, the seeds of which were originally brought to India by Mr. Fortune. It is now very largely cultivated throughout the district of Darjeeling and occasionally in other hill districts. Its growth is extremely rapid: our specimen shews an average of 1·2 ring per inch of radius, and many of the rings are over one inch wide. It grows best at an elevation of from 3,000 to 6,000 feet, but very fine specimens planted in 1847 or 1848, are to be seen in Darjeeling at 7,000 feet. It is, however, brittle, and the tops and branches are easily broken by high winds. It seeds abundantly, and the seedlings are very easily raised in boxes or sheltered beds.

Bark brown, fibrous, peeling off in narrow strips. Wood soft, very uniform, with narrow bands of darker and firmer tissue at the edge of each annual ring. Medullary rays short, fine and very fine, extremely numerous.

6. JUNIPERUS, Linn.

Four Indian species. Among exotic junipers the most important are *J. virginiana*, Linn., of the Atlantic coast of North America, and *J. bermudiana*, Linn., of the Bermudas, West Indies and Florida, which species mainly yields the wood of which pencils are made. *J. drupacea*, Labill.; Brandis 539, is a diœcious shrub with edible fruit, found in the mountains of Asia Minor and Syria, and cultivated in England.

Wood homogeneous, fragrant, generally of slow growth, the ring of firmer wood at the outside of each annual ring very narrow.

1. J. communis, Linn.; Brandis 535. The Juniper. Vern. *Núch, páma, pethra, bentha, betar*, Kashmir, Chamba and Kulu; *Lang shúr, thelu, lewar*, Kunawar; *Chúni, shúpa*, Piti; *Sbama*, Lahoul; *Chichia*, Kumaun.

A large shrub, with thin, reddish brown, fibrous bark. Wood white, moderately hard, fragrant, with a small mass of darker wood near the centre. Wood cells large, visible under the lens. Medullary rays very fine, somewhat unequal in width.

North-West Himalaya ascending to 14,000 feet, extending eastward to Kumaun. Mountains of Western Asia and Europe.

In the Himalaya it rarely attains more than 6 to 7 feet in height, often with a disproportionately thick stem, 18 to 24 inches in girth. Growth extremely slow, our specimens shew: one 35, the other 50 rings per inch of radius. Weight, according to Mathieu, Fl. For., p. 448, 34 lbs.; our specimen gives 33 lbs. per cubic foot. The wood is used for fuel, and, as well as the leaves and twigs, is burnt as incense (*dhúp*). The fruit is sweet, aromatic and resinous; it is sold in the bazars of North India as a medicine (*abhúl, húber*) and is administered in decoctions as a stimulant and diuretic. In Europe the berries are used to flavour gin.

		lbs.
H 137.	Lahoul, about 10,000 feet	33
H 907.	Upper Chenab "	...

2. J. excelsa, M. Bieb.; Brandis 538. The Himalayan Pencil Cedar. Vern. *Apúrs*, Beluchistan; *Chalai*, Jhelam; *Shúkpa, shúr, shúrgu, lewar*, Chenab and Sutlej; *Luir*, Ravi; *Shúrbúta, shúrgú, shúkpa*, Tibet; *Dhup, padám, padmak, súrgi*, N-W. P.; *Dhúpi, dhúpri chandan, shúkpa*, Nepal.

A moderate-sized tree, with thin, reddish brown, fibrous bark, peeling off in thin, longitudinal flakes. Sapwood white, heartwood red, very fragrant, often with a purplish tinge. Annual rings marked by a narrow belt of darker coloured and firm wood on the outer edge. Medullary rays of two classes, extremely fine and fine, the latter very short.

Arid tract of the North-West Himalaya and Western Tibet, extending eastward to Nepal, mountains of Afghanistan and North Beluchistan.

Growth slow, Stewart records sections shewing 24, 40 and 44 rings per inch respectively. Our specimens vary exceedingly: of the two from Lahoul, H 608 shews only 10, while H 139 shews as many as 59 rings; of the remainder, H 163 from Hazara shews 20, H 772, 15 and H 906 43 rings; the last, however, was evidently cut from a small, much stunted, tree. Weight, Brandis gives 25 to 37 lbs. per cubic foot, Wallich 34·5, our specimens average 32 lbs. The wood is used in Quetta and Khelat for house-building, also mixed with stone for the walls of houses in Lahoul. Some of the temples in Kunawar are built of it, and it is there made into drinking cups and walking sticks. At Leh it is largely used as fuel, and is sometimes made into charcoal. It is burnt for incense in Kunawar, and is sometimes exported for that purpose.

		lbs.
H 163.	Hazara, 7,000 feet	32
H 772.	Barmúr, Ravi, 7,000 feet	34
H 906.	Upper Chenab Valley, 8,000 feet	...
H 139.	Lahoul, about 8,000 feet	34
H 608.	„ „ „	29

3. J. recurva, Ham.; Brandis 536; Gamble 83. The Weeping Blue Juniper. Vern. *Wetyar, bettar, chúch, thelu, phulu*, Pb.; *Bettir, bhedára, bidelganj, thelu, phulu, jhora, gúggal, bil, úrú, agáni*, N.-W. P.; *Tupi*, Nep.; *Páma*, Tibet; *Deschú, chakbu*, Sikkim.

A moderate-sized tree. Bark thin, peeling off in long fibrous strips. Sapwood white, heartwood light red, very fragrant. Structure similar to that of *J. excelsa*, except that the short broader medullary rays are wanting.

Sikkim and Bhutan, 9,000 to 12,000 feet.

Growth slow. No. E 2438 was cut from a log which shewed 167 rings with a mean diameter of 18½ inches, or 18 rings per inch of radius; No. E 374 shews 27 rings. Weight, 38 to 42 lbs. per cubic foot. The wood is used for fuel at high elevations, and the twigs and leaves are largely exported from Sikkim to be used as incense to burn in temples.

		lbs.
E 374.	Sandukpho, Darjeeling, 12,000 feet	38
E 2438.	„ „ „	42

H 144. Lahoul, is what is generally called *J. recurva* in the North-West Himalaya; a low procumbent shrub, covering large slopes in the inner arid Himalaya. Heartwood small, reddish, structure similar to that of the Blue Juniper of Sikkim. Weight, 47 lbs. per cubic foot.

4. J. Wallichiana, Hook f. and Th.; Brandis 537. The Black Juniper. Vern. *Tchokpo*, Sikkim.

In the North-West a large shrub, in Sikkim a tree. Bark brown smooth, exfoliating in large flakes. Wood resembling that of *J. excelsa*.

Himalaya from 9,000 to 15,000 feet from the Indus to Sikkim.

H 127. Rotang Pass, Lahoul, 12,000 feet.

7. TAXUS, Tournef.

Heartwood distinct. Wood hard, nearly homogeneous, with a narrow band of firm autumn wood and softer spring wood.

1. T. baccata, Linn.; Brandis 539; Gamble 83. *T. nucifera,* Wall. *T. Wallichiana,* Zucc. The Yew. Vern. *Saráp, badar,* Afg.; *Birmi, barma, barini, túng, thúnu, sungal, püstül, chogu, chatúng,* Kashmir, Chamba; *Rakhal,* Beas; *Barmi,* Shali; *Thúna,* Hattu; *Yamdal, rikaling,* Kunawar; *Thúner, geli, gallu, túst,* N.-W. P.; *Nhare,* Tibet; *Pung-cha, sungcha,* Ladak; *Tcheiray sulah,* Nep.; *Tingschi, tsashing,* Bhutia; *Cheongbu,* Lepcha; *Dingsableh,* Khasia.

A large evergreen tree. Bark purplish-grey, thin, fibrous, peeling off in longitudinal flakes. Sapwood white, heartwood red or orange-red, hard, close-grained, smooth, works and polishes well. Annual rings wavy, marked by a narrow belt of firm and dark-coloured wood. Medullary rays fine and extremely fine, very numerous. No vertical resinous ducts.

Himalaya, from the Indus to Bhutan, generally between 6,000 and 10,000 feet, and in the Khasia Hills. Europe, North Africa, Western Asia, Japan, and North America.

The tree sometimes reaches a very large size. Madden records a tree at Gangutri 100 feet high and 15 feet in girth; 5 to 6 feet in girth is, however, the usual size in the North-West Himalaya, though trees 8 to 9 feet have been found in Hazara. The writer measured two trees on Tonglo in Sikkim, which gave—

No. 1.	Height 30 feet . .	to first branch 10 feet . .	girth 20 feet.
No. 2.	„ 70 „ . . .	„ 30 „ . . .	„ 16 „

and there are many in the same locality of similar dimensions. The growth is slow, our specimens shewing the following:—

H 56 . . .	12 rings.	H 161 . . .	18 rings.
H 116 . . .	12 „	H 18 . . .	19 „
H 422 . . .	13 „	H 921 . . .	20 „
H 895 . . .	13 „	H 773 . . .	44 „
E 796 . . .	14 „	E 382 . . .	55 „

Brandis says. 20 to 32 rings per inch of radius.

Weight, according to Brandis, 46 to 59 lbs. per cubic foot; Mathieu Fl., For., p. 445, gives 42 to 55 lbs., the average of our specimens gives 44 lbs. The wood is used for bows, carrying poles and native furniture, and deserves to be better known and more extensively used, as it is very strong and elastic, and works and polishes beautifully. In some parts of the Himalaya and the Khasia Hills it is held in great veneration and called *Deodár* (God's tree); the wood is burnt as incense, the branches are carried in religious processions in Kumaun, and in Nepal the twigs are used to decorate houses at religious festivals. The bark is used in Kunawar as a substitute for, or mixed with, tea; the berries are eaten and the leaves are exported to the plains and used as a medicine. In Europe they are considered poisonous, but are not always so, as goats, rabbits and sheep eat them with impunity.

The young plant requires shelter and thrives in deep shade; it consequently will not reproduce where the forest has been cleared. It flowers in spring; the young leaves appear almost immediately after, and the fruit ripens in autumn.

			lbs.
H	161.	Hazara, 8,000 feet	41
H	921.	„ „	43
H	895.	Murree, „	40
H	116.	Jagatru, Kulu, 8,000 feet	41
H	773.	Chanota, Ravi, 7,500 „	43
H	18.	Matiyana, Simla, 9,000 feet	46
H	56.	Hattu, Simla, 9,500 feet	50
H	2865.	„ „ „	47
H	422.	Mohna Block, Deoban, 8,000 feet	43
E	382.	Tonglo, Darjeeling, 9,000 feet	46

This specimen shews cracks in the wood, which are filled with a white substance, probably carbonate of lime or magnesia. It turns an orange colour with dilute sulphuric acid.

		lbs.
E 796.	Khasia Hills, 5,000 feet	45

This last has been identified by specimens to be undoubtedly *Taxus baccata*. The structure is identical with that of our other specimens, but the colour of the heartwood is not red like the rest of the specimens, but brownish white.

8. PODOCARPUS, L'Hér.

Three species. *P. neriifolia*, Don; Brandis 541; Gamble 83. Vern. *Gúnsi*, Nep.; *Dingsableh*, Khasia, referred by Kurz to *P. bracteata*, Bl., but kept separate by Parlatore, is an evergreen tree of Nepal, Sikkim and the Khasia Hills, up to 3,000 feet. The wood is considered to be superior and is held sacred in the Khasia Hills.

Wood homogeneous. Wood cells large, easily visible under the lens. Annual rings generally indistinct. No vertical resinous ducts. Wood very durable, not resinous.

1. P. bracteata, Bl. *Nageia bracteata*, Kurz ii. 500. Vern. *Jinari*, Cachar; *Thitmin* (Prince of Woods), Burm.; *Welimadá*, And.

A large evergreen tree. Bark grey-brown, thin, fibrous, peeling off in narrow flakes. Wood grey, moderately hard, of very uniform grain and texture throughout. The annual rings are faintly marked by darker lines, but the texture of the different belts of one ring is uniform. Medullary rays extremely fine, closely packed. No vertical resinous ducts.

Khasia Hills, Burma, and the Andaman Islands.

Growth slow, our specimens average 15 rings per inch of radius. Weight, according to Brandis (*P. neriifolia, Thitmin*, No. 94 of Burma List of 1862), 50 lbs. per cubic foot, according to Bennett 34 lbs., our specimens give an average of 39 lbs. Bennett gives $P = 588$. The wood is used for oars, masts of boats, and for planking It is greatly esteemed by the Burmese. Dr. Mason says, "It is used by carpenters for various purposes, and the Burmese have a superstition that the beams of balances should be made of it." Major Berdmore says it is used to avert evil by driving a peg of it into a house-post or boat.

		lbs.
E 1277.	Cachar	38
B 508.	Andaman Islands	37
B 2265.	„ „ (Major Ford, 1866)	39
B 2556.	„ „ (Home, 1874, No. 10)	41

2. P. latifolia, Wall.; Beddome t. 257. *Nageia latifolia*, Kurz ii. 500. Vern. *Soplong*, Khasia; *Nirambali*, Tinnevelly; *Thitmin*, Burm.

A large evergreen tree, with grey aromatic wood, and structure similar to that of *P. bracteata*.

Tropical forests of Martaban and Tenasserim Hills; Hills of Tinnevelly, at 3,000 to 5,000 feet (Beddome); Khasia Hills and Eastern Bengal (Parlatore).

Weight, our specimen gives 33 lbs. The wood is used for similar purposes to that of *P. bracteata*.

		lbs.
B 569.	Tonghoo, Burma	33

E 3414 from a planted tree at Darjeeling is *Biota orientalis*, Endl. Bark thin, brown, peeling off in papery flakes, and with numerous resin-cells. Wood moderately hard, close-grained; heartwood dark reddish-brown, the annual rings marked by darker colour. Medullary rays numerous, fine, very short.

ORDER CIII. CYCADACEÆ.

One genus, *Cycas*, including four Indian species. *C. Rumphii*, Miq.; Beddome ccxxvii; Kurz ii. 502. (*C. circinalis*, Willd.; Roxb Fl. Ind. iii. 744). Vern. *Mongtain*, Burm., is an evergreen palm-like tree, with a thick, cylindrical, simple or branched trunk, found in the coast forests of South Tenasserim and the Andamans and often cultivated in South India. The wood yields a quantity of sago or starch, and the stem exudes a resin which is used to cure ulcers. *C. circinalis*, Linn.; Beddome ccxxvii. (*C. sphærica*, Roxb. Fl. Ind. iii. 747). Vern. *Orasmaro*, Cuttack, is found in South India and Ceylon. The seeds are ground into flour and used for food in time of scarcity. *C. siamensis*, Mid.; Kurz ii. 503, is a low stemless, palm-like tree, common in the *Eng* and dry forests of Prome, and yielding a whitish gum.

1. C. pectinata, Griff.; Kurz ii. 503; Gamble 84. Vern. *Thakal*, Nep.

An evergreen, simple-stemmed, palm-like tree. Bark in horizontal folds, with diagonal clefts, making diamond-shaped bosses. Wood yellowish white, in narrow wedge-shaped plates, arranged in nearly concentric rings and separated by white tissue, which, like the central pith, is full of starchy granules.

Sikkim, Eastern Bengal and Burma, often in sál or eng or pine forests.

It yields a coarse sago, which, with the fruits, is eaten by the hill people in Sikkim.

There is some doubt about the identification of this species, which may prove to be new.

		lbs.
E 2439.	Chenga Forest, Darjeeling, 1,000 feet	54
E 877.	Balasun Forest, Darjeeling Terai	...

II. MONOCOTYLEDONS.

ORDER CIV. ZINGIBERACEÆ.

An Order scarcely containing any woody plants with the exception of *Ravenala madagascariensis*, Sonn.; Kurz ii. 504, an evergreen tree, allied to the plantains, with a thick woody stem and distichous plantain-like leaves—cultivated in gardens in Bengal and Burma. To this Order belong the Plantains, of which there are many wild forest species; the Ginger (*Zingiber officinale*, Roscoe) and the Cardamoms plant (*Elettaria Cardamomum*, Maton.)

ORDER CV. PALMÆ.

A large and very important Order of trees, shrubs or climbers, found almost all over India from the most moist to the most arid zones and containing many of the most important economic plants.

They belong to 7 Tribes, *viz.*—

Tribe I.—Borassineæ	*Borassus.*
„ II.—Coryphineæ	*Corypha, Chamærops, Livistona, Licuala.*
„ III.—Phœnicineæ	*Phœnix.*
„ IV.—Arecineæ	*Wallichia, Caryota, Areca, Bentinckia, Arenga.*
„ V.—Cocoineæ	*Cocos.*
„ VI.—Lepidocaryineæ	*Calamus, Plectocomia, Korthalsia, Zalacca.*
„ VII.—Nipineæ	*Nipa.*

Besides these, several species from other countries are to be seen, cultivated, in India. The magnificent *Oreodoxa regia* from Brazil may be seen in Calcutta, where avenues of it have been planted in the Botanic Gardens, and isolated plants in the gardens of many houses.

The wood and bark are not distinct, but the stem generally consists of an inner softer, and an outer harder portion. The stem consists of a large number of scattered fibro-vascular bundles, embedded in soft cellular tissue. On a horizontal section the vascular bundles appear most numerous near the circumference of the stem; here they are small, very hard, and often nearly confluent, so as to form a hard rind. In the centre of the stem, the bundles are less numerous and generally not so hard as near the circumference. Consequently, the central portion of the stem is chiefly composed of cellular tissue which often decays, so that the centre of old palms is frequently hollow.

On a vertical section the fibro-vascular bundles appear like long wavy lines, which do not run parallel to each other. On a radial section the vascular bundles cross each other, and they can be traced from the base of the leaf, where they terminate, bending inwards to the centre of the stem and then outwards again towards the circumference.

The structure of each bundle is different in its upper and lower parts. In its upper part it contains *firstly*, vessels varying in size, which on a horizontal section appear as pores; *secondly*, elongated or polygonous cells, generally forming a mass of softer tissue immediately surrounding the vessels; *thirdly*, a mass of long, thick-walled fibres, of which the hard horny portion of the bundle is composed. In the lower part, the bundle is composed almost entirely of fibres without any vessels or cells.

A horizontal section shews the bundles near the circumference in their lower part; these therefore only consist of fibre, while towards the centre the upper part of the bundles is cut through and shews fibres, vessels and cells. It must not be forgotten that on a cross section the upper portion of the bundles is cut through near the circumference where they enter the leaf stalk, but these are cut through obliquely, are easily recognised, and there are few of them.

1. BORASSUS, Linn.

1. B. flabelliformis, Linn.; Roxb. Fl. Ind. iii. 790; Brandis 544; Kurz ii. 529. The Palmyra Tree. Vern. *Tál, tála, tár*, Hind.; *Tál*, Beng.; *Polu tádi* ♀, *penti tádi*, ♀ Tel.; *Panam, pannie*, Tam.; *Pana* Mal.; *Tali, talé*, Kan.; *Tad*, Guz.; *Tál*, Cingh.; *Htan*, Burm.

A large tree with tall cylindric stem, surmounted by a terminal crown of fan-shaped leaves. The young stems are covered with dry leaves or the lower part of petioles, while the old stems are marked with the hard, black, long and narrow scars of the fallen petioles.

Centre soft, but not often hollow. Fibro-vascular bundles black, crowded in the outer portion of the stem; if cut through at right angles, they are oblong, generally with one large pore and a mass of cells at one end. Outer wood hard, heavy, and durable.

Cultivated throughout tropical India and beyond the tropics in Bengal, and the southern part of the North-Western Provinces.

The following experiments have been made on the weight and transverse strength of the timber:—

		Weight.	Value of P.
A. Mendis, Ceylon, No. 83, bars 2'×1"×1"	. .	found 65 lbs.	814
Skinner, Madras, No. 30, 1862	. . . . .	„ 65 „	944
Warth in 1878, No. W. 2922	. . . . . .	„ 63 „	...
„ „ Salem, No. 15	. . . . .	„ 72 „	...

The weights of all our pieces are given below, but Nos. W. 2922 and Salem 15 were the only ones consisting entirely of the outer, harder wood. The average of all our specimens gives 49 to 50 lbs., which may be taken as the average weight of pieces containing partly outside, partly inside wood. The hollowed out stems are used as water pipes; and, split in half, for gutters and open water channels. The hard, outer wood is used for posts, rafters and other purposes. The leaves are used for thatch, mats and basket work, and for writing on. The pulp of the fruit is eaten, and in Ceylon is made into a preserve. Seemann says that the Dutch, when they had possession of Ceylon, considered the preserved pulp or *Punatoo* such a dainty that large quantities of it, preserved in sugar, were exported to Holland and Java. The chief product, however, of the Palmyra Tree "is the sweet sap which runs from the peduncles cut before flowering and collected in bamboo tubes or earthen pots tied to the cut peduncle," *Brandis*. Seemann says that in Ceylon the spathes are tied up from end to end with thongs, and then beaten and crushed between wooden battens for three successive mornings, that on each of the following four a thin slice is cut from the points of the spathes, while on the eighth day the sweet, clear sap begins to exude, and is caught in earthen pots or bamboos. The sap is fermented into toddy, is distilled, or is made into sugar, known as 'jaggery.' The tree generally reaches 40 to 60, and occasionally 100, feet high, and often measures 18 to 24 inches in diameter above the usually thick base.

			lbs.
C	960.	Guzerat, Bombay	42
E	418.	Jessore, Bengal	46
W	767.	South Kanara	51
W	869.	„ „	...
W	2922.	Malabar	63
D	1475.	Salem, Madras	25
B	563.	Prome, Burma	49
B	2458.	Myanoung, Burma	31
No.	15.	Salem Collection	72
No.	83.	Ceylon Collection	65

2. CORYPHA, Linn.

Five species: *C. Taliera*, Roxb. Fl. Ind. ii. 174; Brandis 549. Vern. *Tara, talier. tarít*, Beng., is found in Bengal, as is also *C. elata*, Roxb. Fl Ind. ii. 176; Brandis 549. Vern. *Bajúr, bajúr-batúl*, Beng., a handsome palm, whose stem is marked with spiral furrows. *C. Gebanga*, Bl.; Kurz ii. 525, the *Gebang* palm of Java, is occasionally found in Burma, *e. g.*, round Tonghoo. *C. macropoda*, Kurz ii. 525. Vern. *Dondah*, And. is a large stemless palm found in the bamboo jungles of the western side of South Andaman. The *Corypha* palms flower but once, and then die.

1. C. umbraculifera, Linn.; Roxb. Fl. Ind. ii. 177; Brandis 549; Kurz ii. 524. The Talipat Palm. Vern. *Conda-pani*, Tam.; *Biné*, Kan.; *Tala*, Cingh.; *Pe-beng*, Burm.

A tall tree, with terminal flowers, which dies after seeding. Wood soft, with a hard rind composed of black vascular bundles. The vascular bundles in the centre of the stem are soft.

Ceylon and the Malabar Coast. Cultivated in Bengal and Burma.

The tree often grows to a great size before flowering; one whose measurements were given in the Indian Agriculturist for November 1878 as flowering at Peradeniya,

Ceylon, measured: height of stem 84 feet, of flower panicle 21 feet, total 105 feet; girth at 3 feet from the ground round the persistent bases of the leaves 13 feet 9 inches, at 21 feet from the ground 8 feet 3 inches; age about 40 years. The leaves are very large, often 10 feet in diameter; they are made into fans, mats and umbrellas, and are used for writing on, as also are those of *C. Taliera.* A kind of sago is yielded by the pith.

W 867. South Kanara.

Kurz joins *C. Taliera* with this and *C. elata* with *C. Gebanga.*

3. CHAMÆROPS, Linn.

Of *Chamærops*, two or three species occur in India. *C. Martiana*, Wall. Brandis 546. Vern. *Jhaugra, jhaggar, tal,* Kumaun; *Taggu,* Nep., is a tall, handsome palm, found on the Thakil mountain in East Kumaun, at from 6,500 to 7,800 feet elevation, in damp, shady glens, with a north-west aspect. It is also found in one or two minor localities in Kumaun and in Nepal, and is, besides, considered to be probably the same as *C. khasyana*, Griff.; Kurz i. 527. Vern. *Pakha,* found in the Khasia Hills and on the hills of Martaban at 4,000 to 6,500 feet. The writer has once found small plants of what is probably this palm on Rissoom, near Dumsong, beyond Darjeeling, at 6,500 feet elevation. *C. Ritchieana*, Griff.; Brandis 547. Vern. *Mazri, nozarái,* Trans-Indus; *Kilu, kaliún,* Salt Range; *Pfis, pesh, pease, pharra,* Sind, Beluch., is a generally stemless, gregarious shrub, peculiar to the arid zone of Sind, Trans-Indus, the Punjab, Afghanistan and Beluchistan. Its leaves are used to make matting, fans, sandals, baskets, hats and other articles; its leaves and leafstalks give a fibre which is made into ropes, and its seeds are pierced and made into rosaries, and for sale for that purpose are exported from the Beluchi port of Gwadur to Mecca. (A beautiful collection of the products of this palm [P 1779] was sent to the Paris Exhibition of 1878 from the Punjab, chiefly from the Salt Range.)

4. LIVISTONA, R. Br.

Livistona Jenkinsiana, Griff.; Gamble 86. Vern. *Talainyom, tulac-myom, purbong,* Lepcha; *Toko pat,* Ass., is an extremely handsome fan-leaved palm found in the forests of the Sivoke Hills in Sikkim and eastwards to Assam, where it is commonest in Nowgong and the Naga Hills. The leaves are largely used by Lepchas for thatching and for umbrellas, in Assam for the roofs of huts, boats and doolies, and for the large Naga hats (often 3 to 4 feet in diameter, and called *jhapies*), and umbrellas (Nos. E 1728 to 1731, Assam). The tree reaches 30 feet in height, the wood is very soft, with white fibro-vascular bundles (No. E 2461, Sivoke Hills, Darjeeling). *L. speciosa*, Kurz, Journal As. Soc. Beng., xliii. ii., p. 204; For. Fl. ii. 526. Vern. *Thalu,* Magh; *Tuu-htam,* Burm., is an evergreen, lofty palm of the forests of Chittagong the Pegu Yoma and Upper Tenasserim. Its leaves are sometimes used for thatching in Chittagong, instead of those of *Licuala.*

5. LICUALA, Rumph.

Licuala contains three Indian species. *L. paludosa*, Griff.; Kurz ii. 528, is an evergreen, gregarious palm of the tidal swamps of the Andamans. *L. peltata*, Roxb. Fl. Ind. ii. 179; Kurz ii. 527. Vern. *Patti, chattah-pat,* Ass.; *Kurud, kurkuti,* Beng.; *Sa-lu,* Burm., *Kápadah,* And. is a peltate-leaved palm of the forests of Assam, Eastern Bengal, Chittagong, Burma and the Andamans, said to extend westward as far as Sikkim. It is used in Assam for umbrellas, and in the Andamans for thatching (B 1046, Andamans). In Chittagong it forms a great part of the undergowth in some of the forests, notably the Kasalong Reserve, and its leaves, under the name of *Kuruchhpat* are universally used in the inner Hill Tracts for thatching and when grass is scarce are largely exported to the plains. The stems are about 9 to 12 inches in girth, and 5 to 15 feet high; the wood is rather soft, and the vascular bundles evenly distributed, and dark coloured (E 3366 Kasalong Reserve, Chittagong). *L. longipes*, Griff.; Kurz ii. 528, is found in Mergui. The well-known walking sticks called 'Penang Lawyers' are the young trunks of *L. acutifida*, Mart., a very small palm of the Malay Peninsula.

6. PHŒNIX, Linn.

Six to seven Indian species. *P. dactylifera,* Linn.; Roxb. Fl. Ind. iii. 786; Brandis 552. Vern. *Khajúr, khaji,* is the Date Palm, cultivated and self-sown in Sind and the Southern Punjab, and producing the well-known fruit. *P. acaulis,* Roxb. Fl. Ind. iii. 783; Brandis 555; Kurz ii. 535; Gamble 86. Vern. *Khajuri, pind khajúr, jangli khajúr,* Hind.; *Schap,* Lepcha; *Boichind,* Mar.; *Chindi, hindi, jhari sindi,* Gondi; *Juno,* Kurku; *Thinboung,* Burm., is a low palm with a thick, short, bulbous-looking stem, found in the Sub-Himalayan tract from the Jumna eastwards, and up to 2,500 feet, also in Central India, Behar, and Burma. It chiefly grows in forests of Sál or Chíl pine in India and Eng in Burma. The fruit is eaten by Lepchas, and a kind of sago is obtained from the centre of the tree in Chota Nagpur. Brandis refers to this species two species described by Griffith, *viz., P. Ouseleyana* from Chota Nagpur and Assam, and *P. pedunculata* from the Nilgiris. *P. farinifera,* Willd.; Roxb. Fl. Ind. iii. 785; Brandis 556. Vern. *Chilta-eita,* Tel.; *Ichal,* Kan., is a small, almost stemless palm of sandy lands near the sea at Coringa, whose leaves are used for making mats, and whose trunk gives a quantity of farinaceous substance, used for food, especially in times of scarcity. *P. paludosa,* Roxb. Fl. Ind. iii. 789; Brandis 556; Kurz ii. 536. Vern. *Hintal, hital, golpatta,* Beng.; *Thinboung,* Burm., is a soboliferous, often gregarious, palm of the Sundarbans, Burma and Andaman Islands; its leaves are used in the Sundarbans to make rough ropes for tying boats and logs, and for thatching. *P. rupicola,* T. And. in Journal Linn. Soc. xi. 49, p. 13, 1869; Gamble 86. Vern. *Schiap,* Lepcha, is a beautiful palm of the lower hills of Darjeeling and Bhutan, generally growing on rocks, often to a height of 20 feet. The interior of the stem is often eaten by Lepchas.

1. P. sylvestris, Roxb. Fl. Ind. iii. 787; Brandis 554; Kurz ii. 535. The Wild Date Palm. Vern. *Khajúr, khaji, salma, thalma, thakil,* Hind.; *Pedda eita,* Tel.; *Peria-eetcham,* Tam.; *Ichal, kullu,* Kan.; *Seindi,* Berar; *Boichand,* Mar.; *Sindi,* Gondi.

A tree with ashy grey foliage, 30 to 40 feet high. Stem rough, with the prominent scars of fallen petioles. Wood light brown, the outer portion hard and durable. Vascular bundles less numerous than in *Borasssus,* brown, horny, on a horizontal section circular or slightly oval, the fibrous portion uniform, enclosing the cells and vessels.

Wild and cultivated throughout India.

The following experiments have been made to determine the weight and transverse strength of the wood:—

	Weight.	P. =
Skinner in Madras, No. 104, found	39 lbs.	512
Warth in 1878 found our specimen give	45 „	...

The wood is sometimes used for building, water tubes and other purposes; the leaves are made into mats, ropes and baskets; but the chief produce of the tree is the sweet sap which is collected in the cold season by cutting a notch in the tree at the base of the lower leaves; the sap then flows for some time, and a thin slice is daily cut off the surface of the wound. A tree is usually fit to tap at 10 years old and remains yielding for about 20 years. The juice is either fermented or boiled down into sugar.

			lbs.
E	416.	Sundarbans	45
P	887.	Multán	...

7. WALLICHIA, Roxb.

Contains 4 or 5 Indian species. *W. densiflora,* Martius, Brandis 540; Kurz, ii. 532; Gamble 84 (*Harina oblongifolia,* Griff.) Vern. *Kala aunsa, gor aunsa*

Kumaun; *Ooh*, Lepcha; *Takosu*, Nep.; *Zanoung*, Burm., is a small stemless palm, common in the outer Himalaya, from Kumaun eastwards, up to 4,000 feet, and in Eastern Bengal and Chittagong. In Kumaun the leaves are used for thatch and in Darjeeling for fodder for ponies. *W. caryotoides*, Roxb.; Brandis 550; Kurz ii. 532 (*Wrightea caryotoides*, Roxb. Fl. Ind. iii. 621) Vern. *Chilpatta, belpatta*, Chittagong; *Mochooma*, Magh; *Zanoung*, Burm., is a small palm of Chittagong and Burma. (Kurz refers to *W. caryotoides*, the *W. densiflora* of Brandis: this genus then requires further investigation). *W. nana*, Griff., is described as a small palm found near Gauhati in Assam. *W. disticha*, T. And. in Linn. Soc. Journal xi. 49, p. 6; Gamble 84. Vern. *Katong*, Lepcha, is a handsome palm of the outer hills of Sikkim, found by Brandis as far west as Kumaun in 1874. It grows to a height of 20 feet, and has distichous leaves joined at the base by a network of dark fibres. The Lepchas fell it to eat the pith of the stem near the summit of the tree. Anderson says the berries, and perhaps the leaves, irritate the skin. The wood is soft, the stem almost hollow in the centre, and the fibrovascular bundles dark brown coloured (E 878, E 2460, Darjeeling). *W. Yomæ*, Kurz ii. 533. Vern. *Zanoung*, Burm., is an arborescent species of the Pegu Yoma, with longer pinnæ and the leaves spirally arranged.

8. CARYOTA, Linn.

Two, or perhaps three, species. *C. sobolifera*, Wall.; Kurz ii. 530. Vern. *Baratahdah*, And., said by Mr. Homfray to be called the 'Sago Palm' (No. B 1045, Andamans), is a soboliferous palm of the tropical forests of Arracan, Martaban and the Andaman Islands. Griffith describes a *C. obtusa* from the Mishmi Hills resembling *C. urens*, but having more obtuse pinnules.

1. C. urens, Linn.; Roxb. Fl. Ind. iii. 625; Brandis 550; Kurz ii. 530; Gamble 84. Vern. *Rungbong, simong*, Lepcha; *Bara flawar*, Ass.; *Salopa*, Uriya; *Mhár, mardi, mari, jirúgú*, Tel.; *Conda-panna, erim-panna, utali-panna*, Tam.; *Bhyni, beina, bagni*, Kan.; *Berli*, Mar.; *Shunda pana*, Mal.; *Kittúl, nepora*, Cingh.; *Hlyamban*, Magh; *Minbo*, Burm.

A beautiful tree, with smooth annulate stem, large bipinnate leaves and wedge-shaped leaflets. The outer part of the stem is hard and durable and the vascular bundles crowded, black, very large.

Evergreen forests of western and eastern moist zone of India. On the Western Ghâts it extends to near Mahableshwar. It is common in Burma, Bengal, and Orissa, ascending in Sikkim up to 5,000 feet.

A. Mendis gives the weight at 71 lbs. per cubic foot, our specimen weighs 45 lbs. only, but perhaps contains more of the softer inner wood. The wood is strong and durable; it is used for agricultural purposes, water conduits and buckets. The leaves give the '*Kittul*' fibre, which is very strong, and is made into ropes, brushes, brooms, baskets and other articles; the fibre from the sheathing petioles and the peduncle is made into ropes and fishing lines, which are very strong. The interior of the stem is filled with a sago-like starch which is made into bread or boiled into gruel. Seemann says it is good and very nutritious. From the cut spadix large quantities of toddy are obtained, which is either fermented or boiled down into sugar. With regard to the length of life of the tree, Seemann says (*Popular History of Palms*, p. 135):—

"The *Caryotas* flower only once during their course of existence. The first spadix appears at the top of the tree; as soon as that has done flowering, others (latent buds) issuing from the axils, or former axils, of the leaves, make their appearance; this process, being of a downward tendency, is repeated until the last spadix, which may be looked upon as the death-knell of the plant, shews itself at the foot of the trunk, proclaiming that the hour of departure from life is at hand."

			lbs.
E	2459.	Chawa Jhora, Sivoke, Darjeeling	45
No.	44.	Ceylon Collection	71

9. ARECA, Linn.

Four to eight Indian species. *A. triandra,* Roxb. Fl. Ind. iii. 617; Kurz ii. 537. Vern. *Bangúa, ramgua, runi supari,* Beng.; *Tau-kwam-thee,* Burm.; *Abaradah,* And., is a stoloniferous or simple-stemmed palm, found in Chittagong, Burma and the Andamans. *A. gracilis,* Roxb. Fl. Ind. iii. 619; Gamble 84 (*Pinanga gracilis,* Kurz ii. 538). Vern. *Gua supari, ramgua,* Beng.; *Khur,* Lepcha; *Ranga,* Ass., is a small slender-stemmed, often gregarious, palm of the undergrowth in damp forests in Sikkim, Assam, Eastern Bengal and Burma; it is used for native huts and roofing in Assam. The outer portion is hard, with closely-packed fibro-vascular bundles, the inner part is so soft that the cane shrinks in drying (E 3425 Dalingkote, Br. Bhutan.) *A. hexasticha,* Kurz in Journal, As. Soc. Beng. xliii. ii., p. 201, For. Flora, British Burma, ii. 539, is a small palm of Burma, and *A. costata,* Bl.; Kurz ii. 538, a palm of the Andamans. Griffith describes several other species, such as *A. laxa,* Buch., from the Andamans (placed by Kurz under *A. triandra,* see above); *A. nagensis,* Griff. Vern. *Tál pát,* Naga; *Tougtaw,* Singpho, of the Naga Hills; *A. Dicksoni,* Roxb. Fl. Ind. iii. 617, of Malabar; and *A. disticha,* Roxb. Fl. Ind. iii. 620, from the Khasia Hills.

1. A. Catechu, Linn.; Roxb. Fl. Ind. iii. 615; Brandis 551; Kurz ii. 536; Gamble 84. The Areca Nut or Betel Palm. Vern. *Supari,* Hind.; *Gua,* Beng.; *Poka, oka, vaka,* Tel.; *Camugu, paku,* Tam.; *Adike,* Kan.; *Adaka, cavugu,* Mal.; *Puwak,* Cingh.; *Kwam-thee-beng,* Burm.; *Ah-búddah, ah-pur-rud-dah,* And.

A tall tree, attaining 100 feet in height, with a slender, cylindrical, annulate stem, the inner part of which is generally hollow. Vascular bundles brown, forming a hard rind on the outside of the stem.

Cultivated throughout Tropical India.

A. Mendis gives the weight per cubic foot at 57 lbs. The wood is used for furniture pins, bows, spear handles, and for scaffolding poles in Ceylon. The sheaths of the leaves are used to wrap up articles and as paper to write upon; the seeds are used in turning for necklaces, the knobs of walking sticks, and other small articles, on account of the reticulated appearance formed by the ruminate lines in the albumen of the nut. These nuts are the well-known betel nut, so universally chewed by natives of India, especially Bengal and Burma. For the production of the nut large groves of betel palms are formed, and these groves form often an extremely handsome object in tropical scenery. Most villages in Bengal, Burma and South India have their few betel trees.

			lbs.
E	419.	Sundarbans	...
W	769.	South Kanara	...
No.	73.	Ceylon Collection	57

10. ENTINOKIA CODDA PANNA, Berry; Roxb. Fl. Ind. iii. 621. Vern. *Codda panna,* Tel., is a slender palm, about 20 feet high, found in the Travancore Hills.

11. ARENGA, Lab.

A. saccharifera, Labill.; Brandis 550; Kurz ii. 533 (*Saguerus Rumphii,* Roxb. Fl. Ind. iii. 626). Vern. *Toung-ong,* Burm., is a common Malayan palm, very commonly cultivated in India, and said by Kurz to be wild in the forests of Burma. The heart of the stem contains large quantities of sago, and the cut flower stalks yield a sugary sap, made into sugar and palm wine. The horse-hair-like fibre found at the base of the petioles is similar in its uses to cocoanut fibre and is valuable for cordage. The palm dies after ripening its whole crop of fruit, and the stems are then useful for troughs and water-channels, lasting well underground. Roxburgh was so impressed with its general utility that he recommended its being largely cultivated in India. Griffith mentions another species, *A. Wightii,* from the hills about Coimbatore.

12. COCOS, Linn.

1. **C nucifera,** Linn.; Roxb. Fl. Ind. iii. 614; Brandis 556; Kurz ii. 540; Gamble 86. The Cocoanut Tree. Vern. *Narel, nariyal,* Hind.; *Narikel,* Beng.; *Tenna, tenga,* Tam.; *Nari kadam, tenkaia, kobbari,* Tel.; *Thenpinna, kinghena, tengina,* Kan.; *Tenga,* Mal.; *Pol,* Cingh.; *Ong,* Burm.; *Jadhirdah,* And.

A pinnate-leaved palm, with annulate, often curved stem. Outer wood close-grained, hard and heavy. Vascular bundles black or dark purple, closely packed in the outer part of the stem on horizontal section, circular or uniform, enclosing vessels and cells.

Cultivated throughout Tropical India, particularly near the sea-coast.

The following experiments have been made to determine the weight and transverse strength.

	Weight. lbs.	Value of P.
Skinner in 1862, No. 49, with Madras wood, found . . .	70	608
Puckle, 4 experiments in Mysore, bars 2 feet × 1 inch × 1 in. .	47	562
A. Mendis, Ceylon, No. 72, found . .	70	...
Warth, in 1878, the average of our 3 specimens, found .	49	...

The wood is commercially known as 'Porcupine wood;' it is used for rafters and ridge poles, house posts and other building purposes; for spear handles, walking sticks and fancy work. The leaves are used for thatching, and the net of fibres at the base of the petioles is made into bags and paper, and is used in Ceylon for toddy straining. The cut flower stalks yield toddy which is fermented or made into sugar; the kernels of the nuts are eaten, and the sweet fluid of the young nut is a pleasant drink; the thick fibrous rind of the fruit is the 'Coir' fibre, used for ropes, mats, and other articles; the shell of the nut is made into spoons and cups and other utensils; while the oil obtained from the fruit is an important article of trade and is used for burning, for cooking and in the manufacture of candles and soap. In fact, the uses of the cocoanut tree are innumerable, and much has been written about them.

			lbs.
E	417.	Sundarbans	40
W	768.	South Kanara	55
W	868.	" "	...
B	562.	Burma	52
No.	72.	Ceylon Collection	70

13, 14, 15. CALAMUS, PLECTOCOMIA, KORTHALSIA.

Perhaps no genera of Indian forest plants are so little known as these, even those comparatively accessible, like the canes of Dehra Dún and Darjeeling, being of very uncertain nomenclature. When the collection of specimens for the Paris Exhibition of 1878 was going on, large numbers of canes were received from Burma, Assam and elsewhere, accompanied by merely native names; and being, of course, stripped of their leaves, sheaths and flowers, and tied up in the bundles in which they are sold, they had to be rejected, as the principle was not to exhibit anything whose scientific name was not known.

As far as regards the canes of Burma and the Andamans, Kurz's Forest Flora and his 'Enumeration' of Burmese Palms in Vol. xliii. of the Journal of the Asiatic Society of Bengal, 1874, are of great help; the canes of Sikkim are tolerably well known from Dr. T. Anderson's 'Enumeration of the Palms of Sikkim' in the Linnean Society's Journal, Vol. xi., 1869; those of Assam, Eastern Bengal and Chittagong are given in Griffith's 'Palms of British East India' and the 'Flora Indica' of Roxburgh; but the whole nomenclature is confused, and the difficulties in the determination of species are very great. The following list has been drawn up giving the Indian species described in those books which have been accessible, but it should be understood that the list is merely compiled, and that no opinion whatever is given as to the value of the specific names :—

13. CALAMUS.

SECTION I.—COLEOSPATHES.

A.—Erect.

1. *C. collinus*, Griff. No. 2	Khasia Hills, Upper Assam.
2. *C. macrocarpus*, Griff. No. 3 (under *C. erectus*, Roxb.; Kurz ii. 516, Enum. 32).	Bhutan Dúars.
3. *C. schizospathus*, Griff. No. 4; T. And. 1; Gamble 85. Vern. *Rong*, Lepcha.	Sikkim, Khasia Hills.

E. 3377 from the Sivoke Hills, Darjeeling, is this species. It has a stem of about 2 inches in diameter, with hard wood and closely packed fibro-vascular bundles, very close, as usual, towards the edge.

4. *C. arborescens*, Griff. No. 5; Kurz ii. 516, Enum. 31. Vern. *Danoung*, *kyenbankyen*, Burm. (B 1026 Toungoo, Burma).	Pegu.
5. *C. erectus*, Roxb. Fl. Ind. iii. 774; Kurz ii. 516. Enum. 32. Vern *Sungotta*, Sylhet; *Theing*, Burm.	Sylhet, Chittagong, Pegu.
6. *C. humilis*, Roxb. Fl. Ind. iii. 773.	Chittagong.

B.—Scandent.

7. *C. flagellum*, Griff. No. 8; T. And. 2; Gamble 85. Vern. *Rabi bet*, Nep.; *Reem*, Lepcha; *Nagagola bet*, Assam.	Sikkim, Assam.
8. *C. acanthospathus*, Griff. No. 9	Khasia Hills.
9. *C. Royleanus*, Griff. No. 11 (under *C. Rotang*, Linn.; Brandis 559; Gamble 85).	Dehra Dún, Northern Bengal.
10. *C. Rotang*, Roxb. Fl. Ind. iii. 777; Brandis 559 (*C. Roxburghii*, Griff. No. 12). The common Rattan. Vern. *Bet*, *chachi bet*, Beng., Hind.; *Pepa*, *prabba*, Central Provinces (O 1038, Dehra Dún).	Northern India from the Jumna eastwards, Central, Western and South India, and Ceylon.
11. *C. tenuis*, Roxb. Fl. Ind. iii. 780; Griff. No. 13; Kurz ii. 520, Enum. 37; Brandis 559. Vern. *Bandhari bet*, Chittagong; *Kring*, Magh; *Jalla bet*, Ass.	Assam, Sylhet, Chittagong and Pegu.
12. *C. polygamus*, Roxb. Fl. Ind. iii. 780. Vern. *Húdúm*, Chittagong.	Chittagong.
13. *C. leptospadix*, Griff. No. 14; T. And. 3; Gamble 85. Vern. *Dangri bet*, Nep.; *Lat*, Lepcha.	Sikkim, Khasia Hills.
14. *C. fasciculatus*, Roxb. Fl. Ind. iii. 779; Griff. No. 15; Kurz ii. 517, Enum. 33; Brandis 559. Vern. *Bara bet*, Beng.; *Kyeing-kha*, Burm.	Bengal, Orissa, Chittagong, Burma, Andamans.
15. *C. gracilis*, Roxb. Fl. Ind. iii. 781; Griff. No. 16; Kurz ii. 520, Enum. 38. Vern. *Mapuri bet*, Beng.; *Kraipang*, Magh; *Hundi bet*, Ass.	Assam, Chittagong.
16. *C. mishmiensis*, Griff. No. 17	Mishmi Hills.
17. *C. floribundus*, Griff. No. 18	Upper Assam.
18. *C. latifolius*, Roxb. Fl. Ind. iii. 775; Griff. No. 19; Kurz ii. 518, Enum. 34; Brandis 560. Vern. *Korak bet*, Chittagong; *Sain*, Magh; *Yamatha*, Burm. (B 1001, 1003, 1027, Burma. E 1004, Chittagong).	Chittagong, Burma, Andamans.
19. *C. palustris*, Griff. No. 22 (under *C. latifolius*, Kurz ii. 518, Enum. 34).	Mergui.

20. *C. extensus*, Roxb. Fl. Ind. iii. 777. Vern. *Dengullar*, Sylhet.	Sylhet.
21. *C. quinquenervius*, Roxb. Fl. Ind. iii. 777. Vern. *Hurnur-gullar*, Sylhet.	„
22. *C. montanus*, T. And. 4; Gamble 85. Vern. *Gouri bet*, Nep.; *Rue*, Lepcha.	Sikkim, Bhutan.
23. *C. macracanthus*, T. And. 5; Gamble 85. Vern. *Phekori bet*, Nep.; *Ruebee, greem*, Lepcha (E 1017, Darjeeling).	„ „
24. *C. inermis*, T. And. 6; Gamble. Vern. *Dangri bet*, Nep.; *Brool*, Lepcha (E 1016, Darjeeling).	„ „
25. *C. andamanicus*, Kurz ii. 519, Enum. 35. Vern. *Chowdah*, And.	Andamans.
26. *C. tigrinus*, Kurz ii. 519, Enum. 36. Vern. *Lémé*, Burm.; *Amdah*, And. (B 1042, Andamans).	Burma, Andamans.
27. *C. Helferianus*, Kurz ii. 521, Enum. 39 . .	Tenasserim or Andamans.
28. *C. paradoxus*, Kurz ii. 521, Enum. 40 . .	Martaban.
29. *C. Guruba*, Mart.; Kurz ii. 522, Enum. 41. Vern. *Kyeingnee*, Burm. (B 1031, Toungoo).	Chittagong and Burma.
(Four other species are given by Martius as occurring in Tenasserim, called *C. platyspathus*; *C. concinnus*; *C. nitidus*, and *C. melanacanthus*).	
30. *C. Mastersianus*, Griff. No. 29, under *C. Guruba*, Kurz ii. 522, Enum. 41). Vern. *Sundi-bet, quabi-bet*, Ass.	Assam.

SECTION II.—CYMBOSPATHES.

31. *C. nutantiflorus*, Griff. No. 31	Assam.
32. *C. Jenkinsianus*, Griff. No. 32; T. And 7. (*Cymbospathes Jenkinsianus* Gamble 85.) Vern. *Gola bet*, Ass. (E 1018, Darjeeling).	Sikkim Terai, Dúars and Assam.
33. *C. grandis*, Griff. No. 33; Kurz 523. (*Dæmonorops grandis*, Kurz Enum. 30).	Andamans.
34. *C. hypoleucus*, Kurz ii. 523 (*Dæmonorops hypoleucus*, Kurz Enum. 29).	Tenasserim.

Of these canes, *C. Rotang* is largely used in North-West India for chairs, blind and basket work. *C. latifolius* is much used in Burma for tying timber in rafts, and making the cables which stretch across the river at the Salween rope station. *C. montanus* is the best cane for suspension bridges and dragging logs in Sikkim, and *C. inermis* furnishes the finest 'alpenstocks.' No. E 1007 from the Sundarbans. Vern. *Gola bet*, has been pronounced by Dr. King to be a species new to India, which he has identified with *C. longipes*, Griff. No. 26, hiherto only known from Malacca.

14. PLECTOCOMIA.

1. *P. khasyana*, Griff. 106	Khasia.
2. *P. assamica*, Griff. 107	Upper Assam.
T. Anderson joins these two in one species.	
3. *P. himalayana*, Griff. 108; T. And. p. 11; Gamble 86. Vern. *Takri bet*, Nep.; *Runool*, Lepcha.	Hills of Sikkim, 4,000 to 7,000 feet.
4. *P. macrostachya*, Kurz ii. 514, Enum. 28 . .	Tenasserim Hills.

15. KORTHALSIA.

1. *K. scaphigera*, Mart.; Kurz ii. 513, Enum. 25. (*Calamosagus scaphiger*, Griff. 29). Vern. *Bordah, paridah*, And. (B 1041, Andamans).	Andamans.
2. *K. laciniosa*, Mart.; Kurz ii. 513, Enum. 26, (*Calamosagus laciniosus*, Griff. 27).	Tenasserim.

It may be useful to give the vernacular names of the canes sent from different localities for the Paris Exhibition, which it was impossible to name, as those who have opportunities of doing so may be able to identify them. From Chittagong were received *Kerak, jayat* and *golak*; the first is probably *C. latifolius*; from Assam *Riphin, ringer, risan, raidang, bent, sowka bent, rangi, pakhori, howka, charainari, lijai;* from Cachar, *Jali, soondi,* and *gallah*; from Burma, *Theinkyeng, dyauthaukyeng, engkyeng, toungkyeng, kyengbot, zanoung, khaboung*; from South Kanara *Betha* and *nagabetha,* and from the Andamans *Boledah, jobetahdah, jobetah,* and a palm called *chardah.*

16. ZALACCA WALLICHIANA, Mart.; Kurz ii. 511. Vern. *Yingan,* Burm., is an almost stemless palm of the tropical forests of Burma.

17. NIPA FRUTICANS, Wurmb.; Roxb. Fl. Ind. iii. 650; Kurz ii. 541. Vern. *Gúlga, gabna,* Beng.; *Da-ne,* Burm.; *Poothadah,* And. (*Golphal* [fruits] Beng.), is a large soboliferous palm of the river estuaries and tidal forests of the Sundarbans, Chittagong, Burma and the Andamans. The leaves are used for thatching, and toddy is obtained from the spathe. The inside of the large fruit is, when young, edible; when old it is hard like ivory, but transparent (E. 1530 Sundarbans).

ORDER CVI. PANDANEÆ.

Two genera, *Pandanus* and *Freycinetia.* Of *Pandanus,* the Screw Pines, there are about seven Indian species, all Burmese or Andaman plants, a few of which extend to Northern and Eastern Bengal and to South India. *P. fœtidus,* Roxb. Fl. Ind. iii. 742; Kurz ii. 506; Gamble 86. Vern. *Keurkanta,* Hind.; *Kea kanta,* Beng.; *Thaky-et,* Burm., is a common stemless shrub of the undergrowth in swamp forests in Bengal and Burma. *P. furcatus,* Roxb. Fl. Ind. iii. 744; Beddome ccxxviii.; Kurz ii. 507: Gamble 86. Vern. *Jarika,* Nep.; *Bor,* Lepcha; *O-kaiyeya,* Cingh., is a palm-like tree of Northern and Eastern Bengal, Burma and the Western Coast. Stems grey, with a distinct bark, wood resembling that of the palms, outer wood moderately hard, containing satiny-white vascular bundles; inner wood soft, spongy (E 473, E 2462, Darjeeling Hills, 30 lbs. per cubic foot). *P. odoratissimus,* Willd.; Roxb. Fl. Ind. iii. 738; Beddome ccxxviii; Kurz ii. 508. Vern. *Keura,* Hind.; *Kea, ketuki, keori,* Beng.; *Mugalik,* Tel.; *Thalay, talum,* Tam.; *Kaida, thala,* Mal.; *Mudu-kaiyeya,* Cingh.; *Tsat-tha-pu,* Burm., is a common much branched shrub frequently planted on account of the powerful fragrance of the flowers, but wild on the coasts of South India, Burma and the Andamans. *P. Leram,* Jones, and *P. Andamanensium,* Kurz, are trees of the Andaman Islands. *P. graminifolius,* Kurz, and *P. lævis,* Rumph., are screw pines of Burma, the latter only cultivated. *Freycinetia insignis,* Bl.; Kurz ii. 509, is a scandent shrub of the tropical forests of the Andamans and Ceylon.

ORDER CVII. LILIACEÆ.

Two genera of shrubs or small trees, *viz., Dracæna* and *Cordyline.* Kurz describes seven species of *Dracæna,* four of which are from the Andamans and the other three from the forests of Burma; they are almost all small undershrubs, with rather large, linear or elliptical leaves, but *D. angustifolia,* Roxb. Fl. Ind. ii. 155; Kurz ii. 543. Vern. *Kwam-lin-nek,* Burm., of the Andamans, and *D. spicata,* Roxb. Fl. Ind. ii. 157; Kurz ii. 545, also from the Andamans, but found in Chittagong as well, reach the size of small trees. *D. terniflora,* Roxb. Fl. Ind. ii. 159. Vern. *Bunamtol,* Beng., and *D. atropurpurea,* Roxb. Fl. Ind. ii. 160, are shrubs of the forests of Sylhet.

Cordyline terminalis, Kth.; Kurz ii. 546 (*Dracæna terminalis,* Roxb. Fl. Ind. ii. 156), is a large shrub from the Moluccas, now extensively grown in gardens in Bengal and Burma.

To this Order also belong *Sanseviera zeylanica,* Willd.; Roxb. Fl. Ind. ii. 161. The Bowstring Hemp. Vern. *Múrba, murahara, murgali,* Beng.; *Mallai mauji,* Salem;

Ishamacoda nar, Tel., a small perennial plant with a strong, silky fibre; and the Aloe *Agave americana*, Linn. (*A. cantula*, Roxb. Fl. Ind. ii. 167.) Vern. *Cantula, banskeora*, Hind.; *Pachakathalai*, Salem, commonly run wild or planted in all the drier zones in India and yielding a strong and useful fibre; the New Zealand Flax (*Phormium tenax*) and other fibre-producing plants.

ORDER CVIII. GRAMINEÆ.

The grasses constitute one of the largest and most important families of the vegetable kingdom, containing plants of every size from the tiny herbs of the meadows to the giant bamboos of the forests of Burma. In most forest regions of India, tall grasses cover the greater part of such land as is not too densely shaded with trees to prevent their growth; these tall grasses are found, like the species of *Arundo* and *Saccharum*, near the banks of streams; or, like the *Anthistiria* and *Androscepia*, in drier localities, covering sometimes large extents of land and rendering it liable to the evil effects of jungle fires. Such grasses have, however, many uses, and chief among them that of providing material for thatching, for in some countries in India not only the roofs but even the walls of all village houses are made of grass. The chief species used for thatch are *Saccharum cylindricum*, Linn. and *S. spontaneum*, Linn.

The tribe with which we have chiefly to deal, however, is that of the *Bambuseæ* or bamboos, which are tree-grasses, sometimes attaining enormous dimensions, sometimes scarcely more than an inch in diameter. The *Bambuseæ* have been described by Colonel Munro in the Transactions of the Linnean Society of London, Vol. xxvi, 1870, and many details are given of them by Brandis, Beddome, Kurz and other writers on Indian forests and their flora. For us it will be sufficient to give merely a list of genera taken from Munro and of such species as are described therein, as well as in other books. According to Munro, then, bamboos are divided as follows:—

Section I.	Triglosseæ	*Arundinaria, Thamnocalamus, Phyllostachys.*
„ II.	Bambuseæ	*Bambusa, Gigantochloa, Oxytenanthera.*
„ III.	Bacciferæ	*Melocanna, Cephalostachyum, Pseudostachyum, Beesha, Dendrocalamus, Dinochloa.*

The names given in Kurz's Forest Flora differ often from those given by Munro. Munro's names, have, therefore, been given, Kurz's names being added as synonyms and his new species quoted in the genera in which he had placed them.

GENUS I—ARUNDINARIA.

1.	*A. racemosa*, Munro. 17. Vern. *Pummoon*, Lepcha; *Pat-hioo, maling*, Nep.; *Myooma*, Bhutia, 2 to 4 feet high, with bluish, rough internodes, probably the common '*Maling*' bamboo of Darjeeling. It is very common all over the Sikkim Hills above 7,000 feet, sometimes growing to a large size (1½ to 2 inch diameter), and is extensively used for making mats for roofing, for fodder and other purposes.	Sikkim and Nepal, above 6,000 feet. (E 1354, Darjeeling).
2.	*A. Wightiana*, Nees; Munro 19; Beddome ccxxx.; Brandis 563, 6 to 12 feet high.	Nilgiris.
3.	*A. Griffithiana*, Munro 20, 4 to 6 feet high, internodes woolly, sometimes prickly.	Khasia Hills.
4.	*A. falcata*, Nees; Munro 26; Brandis 562; Gamble 86. (*A. utilis*, Cleghorn.) Vern. *Nirgal, nigál, ringal, nagre, narri, garri, gero*, Hind.; *Spiág, gurwa, spikso, pitso*,	Himalaya, from the Ravi to Bhutan, above 4,500 feet in the western, but descending nearly to the

Kunawar; *Kwei*, Tibet; *Prong*, N.-W. P.; *Titi nigala*, Nep.; *Prongnok*, Lepcha. Stems 6 to 10 feet high, strong, annual; leaves narrow, without transverse veins. Used for roofing and baskets. — plains in the Eastern Himalaya, Khasia Hills (H 132, Kulu; E 1339, E 3427, Darjeeling).

5. *A. khasiana*, Munro 28. Vern. *Namlang*, Khasia, stem 8 to 12 feet. — Khasia Hills.

6. *A. intermedia*, Munro 28. Stem about 6 to 8 feet. — Sikkim, 7,000 to 8,000 feet.

7. *A. Hookeriana*, Munro 29. Vern. *Praong, prong*, Lepcha; *Singhani*, Nep.; stems 12 to 15 feet. This bamboo is common about Dumsong, and has handsome glaucous green stems, the nodes marked by a bluish ring. The seeds are edible. The leaves have conspicuous transverse veins. — Sikkim, at 4,000 to 6,800 feet.

8. *A. elegans*, Kurz ii. 549. Stems 12 to 20 feet . — Martaban Hills.

GENUS II—THAMNOCALAMUS.

1. *T. Falconeri*, Hook. f.; Munro 34; Brandis 563. — Kumaun and Nepal, at 8,000 feet.

2. *T. spathiflorus*, Munro 34; Brandis 563, Gamble 87. Vern. *Ringall*, Jaunsar; *Purmiok*, Lepcha; *Myoosay*, Bhutia. The common small bamboo of Hattu and Deoban. The hard yellow-stemmed red-branched bamboo from Tonglo and the Singalila Range of Sikkim is probably this species. Transverse veins prominent. — Himalaya, from the Sutlej to Bhutan, above 8,000 feet. (H 131, Kulu E 3426, Tonglo, Darjeeling 10,000 ft.).

GENUS III—PHYLLOSTACHYS.

1. *P. bambusoides*, Sieb. and Zucc.; Munro 36 . — Mishmi Hills.

GENUS IV—BAMBUSA.

1. *B. Tulda*, Roxb. Fl. Ind. ii. 193; Munro 91; Brandis 566; Kurz ii. 552. Vern. *Peka*, Hind.; *Tulda, jowa, mitenga, matela*, Beng.; *Wahghi*, Gâro; *Madaewah*, Magh; *Theiwa, thoukwa*, Burm. The common Bamboo of Bengal. The wood is strong and the halms are used for roofing, and scaffolding, mats, and other purposes. — Bengal and Burma (E. 1333, Sundarbans; E. 1329, Chittagong; B. 1321, Toungoo.)

2. *B. nutans*, Wall.; Munro 92; Brandis 567; Gamble 87. Vern. *Mahlbans*, Nep.; *Mahlu*, Lepcha; *Jiushing*, Bhutia; *Bidhuli, mukial*, Ass.; *Pichle*, Sylhet. A most beautiful species largely planted near villages in Sikkim and Bhutan. — Nepal, Sikkim and Khasia Hills. (O 1338: Dehra Dún ?).

3. *B. affinis*, Munro 93; Kurz 551. Vern. *Theeshe, thaikwa*, Burm. Said by Munro to be scandent, by Kurz to be small and tufted, and 15 to 20 feet high. — Martaban.

4. *B. teres*, Ham.; Munro 95 . . . . . — Bengal and Assam.

5. *B. Falconeri*, Munro 95; Brandis 568. Vern. *Chye, kag*. — North-West Himalaya.

6. *B. pallida*, Munro 97. Vern. *Burwal, bakhal*, Cachar; *Usken*, Khasia. Stem 50 feet. — Eastern Bengal and Assam.

7. *B. Khasiana*, Munro 97. Vern. *Tumar*, Khasia — Khasia Hills.

8. *B. polymorpha*, Munro 97; Kurz ii. 553. Vern. *Kya-thoungwa*, Burm. — Burma (B. 1316, Toungoo).

9. ***B. Balcooa***, Roxb. Fl. Ind. ii. 196; Munro 100; Brandis 567. Vern. *Balku*, Beng.; *Betwa*, Cachar; *Bara baluka*, Ass. Stems 50 to 70 feet. The best Bengal species for building and scaffolding. It differs from *B. Tulda* by its larger leaves, not pubescent beneath, and having distinct transverse veins, which are not found in *B. Tulda*. — Bengal and Assam. (E 1332, Sundarbans).

10. ***B. arundinacea***, Retz; Munro 103; Beddome, ccxxxi, t. 321; Roxb Fl. Ind. ii. 191; Brandis 564; Kurz ii. 554. Vern. *Magar, nál*, Pb.; *Bans, kattang*, Hind.; *Wahkantek*, Gáro; *Bariála*, Chittagong; *Mándgay*, Bombay; *Kati wadúr*, Gondi; *Mangil*, Tam.; *Vedru*, Tel.; *Bidungulu*, Kan.; *Wa-nah*, Magh; *Kya-kat-wa*, Burm. Stems 70 to 90 feet, spinescent. Leaves small. This bamboo is of good quality and strong, and is used for all purposes. The stems contain much tabasheer, which is used in native medicine. As a rule all the clumps in one district flower simultaneously, but isolated flowering clumps are occasionally found. Flowering years in 1804, 1836 and 1868 are recorded on the western coast, but a flowering took place also in Kanara in 1864. (On this subject see Brandis, pages 565 and 566.) — Central and South India, Burma. (O 1337, Dehra Dún; B 1319, Toungoo; W 1330, South Kanara.)

11. ***B. spinosa***, Roxb. Fl. Ind. ii. 198; Munro 104; Beddome ccxxxi; Brandis 566, Vern. *Behor*, Beng.; *Koto*, Ass.; *Kinkoit*, Cachar; *Yakatwa*, Burm. (not given by Kurz, or rather, united with *B. arundinacea*, probably; a view in which Brandis concurs). — Bengal, Assam, Burma.

12. ***B. orientalis***, Nees; Munro 105; Beddome ccxxxi. — South India.

13. ***B. vulgaris***, Wendl.; Munro 106; Beddome ccxxxii; Brandis 568. Vern. *Kulluk*, Bombay; *Una*, Cingh. Stems 20 to 50 feet, yellow or striped yellow and green. The leaves have well marked transverse veins. — Cultivated in India.

14. ***B. Brandisii***, Munro 109. (*Dendrocalamus Brandisii*, Kurz ii. 560.) Vern. *Ora*, Beng.; *Turgu-wah*, Magh; *Kyellowa, wabo*, Burm. A gigantic species, up to 120 feet high, stems often 30 inches in circumference. Flowered in Chittagong in 1879. — Chittagong and Burma, up to 4,000 feet. (E 3428 Chittagong Hill Tracts; B 1313, 1314, Toungoo.)

GENUS V—GIGANTOCHLOA.

1. ***G. andamanica***, Kurz ii. 556. Vern. *Podáh*, And. Stems 20 to 30 feet, thin, tufted; leaves used for thatching. — Andamans (B 1331).

2. ***G. auriculata***, Kurz ii. 557. Vern. *Ta-la-kuwa*, Burm. Stems 30 to 40 feet. — Chittagong, Arracan, Pegu.

3. ***G. macrostachya***, Kurz ii. 557. Vern. *Madi*, Magh; *Wa-net*, Burm. Stems 30 to 50 feet. — Chittagong and Burma, (B 1314, Toungoo).

GENUS VI—OXYTENANTHERA.

1. ***O. nigro-ciliata***, Munro 128. Beddome ccxxxiii. (*Bambusa gracilis*, Wall.) Stems 30 to 40 feet. — Western Ghâts, Chittagong, Burma, Andamans.

2.	*O. albo-ciliata*, Munro 129. (*Gigantochloa albo-ciliata*, Kurz ii. 555.) Vern. *Wa-pyoo-galay*, Burm. Stems 20 to 30 feet.	Burma.
3.	*O. Thwaitesii*, Munro 129; Beddome ccxxxii, t. 322. Vern. *Watte*, Anamalais. Stem 10 to 12 feet, 1 inch diam.	Western Ghâts.
4.	*O. Stocksii*, Munro 130; Beddome ccxxxiii .	Concan.
5.	*O. monostigma*, Beddome ccxxxiii . . .	Anamalais.

Genus VII—Melocanna.

1.	*M. bambusoides*, Trin.; Munro 132; Kurz ii. 569, (*Bambusa baccifera*, Roxb. Fl. Ind. ii. 197.) Vern. *Múli*, *metunga*, *bish*, Beng.; *Kayoung-wa*, Magh. Stems 50 to 70 feet long, 12 to 13 inches girth. Fruit large, pear-shaped, 3 to 5 inches long, edible. The common, gregarious, not cæspitose, bamboo of the Chittagong Hills. It is of good quality, durable, straight and with straight knots, and is very largely cut and exported for house-building, mats and other purposes.	Eastern Bengal, Chittagong, Arracan and Tenasserim. (E 1325, Chittagong).
2.	*M. Kurzii*, Munro 134 (*Cephalostachyum schizostachyoides*, Kurz ii. 565.) Stems 20 to 30 feet.	Andamans.
3.	*M. humilis*, Kurz ii. 569. Stems 8 to 15 feet .	Arracan, Pegu.

Genus VIII—Cephalostachyum.

1.	*C. capitatum*, Munro 139; Gamble 87. Vern. *Gobia*, *gopi*, Nep.; *Payong*, Lepcha; *Silli*, *sullea*, Khasia. Stems 12 to 30 feet, thin, yellow, semi-scandent, strong, with long internodes of about 2½ feet, used for bows and arrows by Lepchas. The leaves are good fodder. It is often gregarious. This bamboo flowered and died down in Sikkim in 1874.	Sikkim and Khasia Hills. (E 1353, E 3429, Damsong, Darjeeling).
2.	*C. pallidum*, Munro 139; Kurz ii. 563. Vern. *Beti*. Stems shrubby.	Mishmi Hills, Ava.
3.	*C. latifolium*, Munro 140. Leaves large . .	Bhutan.
4.	*C. pergracile*, Munro 141; Kurz ii. 564. Vern. *Tinwa*, *kengwa*, Burm. Stems 30 to 50 feet. Common in upper mixed forests; often gregarious.	Burma (B 1317, Toungoo.)

Genus IX—Pseudostachyum.

1.	*P. polymorphum*, Munro 142. Vern. *Purphiok*, *paphok*, Lepcha; *Filing*, Nep. Stems green, soft, used for baskets, mats, and for tying houses.	Sikkim at 4,000 to 6,000 feet, Assam (E 1340, Darjeeling Terai).
2.	*P. compactiflorum*, Kurz ii. 567. Stems 15 to 25 feet.	Martaban Hills, 4,000 to 6,000 feet.
3.	*P. Helferi*, Kurz ii. 568. Vern. *Watha bo-wa*, Burm. Stems 20 to 25 feet, gregarious.	Hills of Burma, up to 3,000 feet. (B 1318 Toungoo.)

Genus X—Beesha.

1.	*B. Rheedii*, Kunth; Munro 144; Beddome ccxxxiv. Stems 16 feet high.	Malabar, Cochin.
2.	*B. stridula*, Munro 145; Beddome ccxxxiv. Vern. *Batta*, Cingh. Stems 6 to 18 feet.	Bombay, Ceylon.

3. *B. Travancorica*, Beddome ccxxxiv, t. 324. Vern. *Irúl*, Travancore. Stems 6 to 8 feet. Stems densely gregarious. — Hills of Tinnevelly and Travancore, 3,000 to 5,500 feet.

Genus XI—Dendrocalamus.

1. *D. strictus*, Nees; Munro 147; Beddome ccxxxv, t. 325; Brandis 569; Kurz ii. 558. (*Bambusa stricta*, Roxb. Fl. Ind. ii. 193.) Male Bamboo. Vern. *Bans, bans kaban, bans khúrd, kopar* (stem), Hind.; *Karail* (stem), Beng.; *Bás, udha*, Bombay; *Halpa, veddar, vadúr*, Gondi; *Indo*, Kurku; *Bhiru*, Baigas; *Kark*, Pandratola; *Kauka*, Tel.; *Myinwa*, Burm. Leaves often deciduous. The stems are strong, elastic, nearly solid, 20 to 40 and up to even 100 feet high, used for spear handles, and all purposes of building and basket work. — India and Burma.

This species occasionally flowers gregariously, but generally single stems only or single clumps are found in flower.

Mr. Greig, Conservator of Forests, North-Western Provinces, writing in January 1879, reports the following interesting points regarding the flower of this bamboo in the outer valleys of the Garhwal Hills:—

"We have a wonderful crop of bamboos this year, I have been observing our bamboos a good deal lately, and I have observed numbers with one or two stems of a clump in flower, in some places as many as 5 per cent. of the clumps have flowering stems, and in others I have only found ten clumps with flowering stems out of several thousands examined. Between Kohdwara and Haldu Khata whole clumps over large areas have seeded and died, and the ground is now a dense thicket of young clumps of from 10 to 30 feet high. The seeding commenced here in 1869 or 1870, and has been going on ever since. Many of the few remaining *old* clumps are now seeding, not one or two stems, but *every stem of the clump*, and not one single instance did I see in that forest of only one or two stems in seed. These remarks apply to the forests below Gorighát and along the *base of the hills* between the Ganges and Ramganga rivers. I hope to see the bamboos of the Palim, Kansore, &c., this year, whole areas in those valleys seeded and died in 1877-78."

2. *D. sericeus*, Munro 148. Flowered in 1858 . — Parasnáth in Chota Nagpore.

3. *D. Parishii*, Munro 149; Brandis 570 . . — Panjab. (P. 114, Sutlej.)

4. *D. membranaceus*, Munro 149; Kurz ii. 560. Vern. *Wa-yai*, Burm. Stems 40 to 50 feet. — Martaban (B 1315, Toungoo.)

5. *D. giganteus*, Munro 150. (*Bambusa gigantea*, Wall.) Vern. *Waklé, waya*, Burm. Stems very tall, often 26 inches in girth. — Tenasserim (B 1329, Moulmein.)

6. *D. Hookeri*, Munro 151; Brandis 570. Vern. *Ussey, assey denga, ukotang*, Ass. Stems 50 feet. — Assam.

7. *D. Hamiltonii*, Nees and Arnott; Munro 151; Brandis 570; Gamble 87. Vern. *Tama*, Nep.; *Pao*, Lepcha; *Pa-shing*, Bhutia *Kokwa*, Beng.; *Wah*, Mechi *Wahnok*, Gáro. The common bamboo of the Eastern Himalaya. The halms are large, 3 to 6 inches diameter, rather hollow and not always straight, but they are used for every variety of purpose. This bamboo grows gregariously, on hill-sides, up to 3,000 feet, and the stems are 40 to 60 feet high. They often grow low and tangled, instead of straight, and the bamboo may often be recognised by this — Sikkim, Bhutan, Assam (E 1341, Bamunpokri.)

character and by the very thick shoots which grow out at the nodes. The young shoots are eaten.

8. *D. criticus*, Kurz ii. 559. Stems 15 to 30 feet. — Pegu, Yoma, at 3,000 feet.
9. *D. longispathus*, Kurz ii. 561. Vern. *Waya*, Burm. Stems 40 to 60 feet. — Burma (B 1324, Toungoo).

Genus XII—Dinochloa.

1. *D. andamanica*, Kurz ii. 576. Stems scandent, up to 100 feet high. — Andamans.
2. *D. Maclellandii*, Kurz ii. 571. (*Bambusa Maclellandii*, Munro 114.) Vern. *Wa-nway*. Stems 60 to 100 feet, scandent. — Chittagong, Burma. (B 1320, Toungoo.)

The identification of the different species of Indian and Burmese bamboos is still very obscure and requires considerable research to settle accurately. The large-leaved bamboo of Dehra Dún, the one known as *Dendrocalamus Parishii* from the Punjab, *Bambusa spinosa*, Roxb. and other species are mentioned by Brandis as still doubtful. Munro gives long lists of doubtful species, many of which are Indian, while numbers of species are known only by vernacular names. The following, of which Lepcha names are given, have been collected in Sikkim by Mr. E. Fuchs: *Pugriang*, a magnificent species with large thick leaves and stems having a diameter of 5 inches and internodes 18 inches long; *Pogslo*, a species with light hollow stem, 2½ to 3 inches in diameter and from 3 to 4 feet between the nodes; *Podiam, pshi, pugjiok, pobong, pati, posong*, and *bongshing*. Lewin, in his account of the Hill tracts of Chittagong, gives the following Bengali names for bamboos, the species of which has not yet been definitely settled. *Paia, dolu, kullai, boodoom, lota, kata, burria, turras*, while Assam, Cachar, the Khasia, Jaintie and Gáro Hills produce many more whose identification is uncertain.

Section III. CRYPTOGAMIÆ.

Order CIX. FILICES.

Tree Ferns are found in the whole of the Eastern and Western moist zones and principally in the Eastern Himalaya, Khasia Hills, Eastern Bengal, Burma and on the Western Coast. One species extends to Central India. The Burmese species are described by Kurz; those from Ceylon are given in Thwaites' 'Enumeratio,' while the species from Northern India are to be found in the newly published 'Revision of the Ferns of Northern India' by C. B. Clarke in the 'Transactions of the Linnean Society 1880, p. 425.' Of true tree ferns there are 4 genera: viz., *Cyathea, Hemitelia, Alsophila* and *Brainea*.

Cyathea contains only one species from the Indian Peninsula, viz.: *C. spinulosa*, Wall.; Kurz ii. 572, Clarke p. 429, a small tree of Nepal, the Kkasia Hills, Tenasserim and South India, attaining 30 feet in height. In Ceylon, however, two or three other species occur, of no great size, the most remarkable of which is the beautiful *C. sinuata*, Hook. and Grev., with undivided fronds.

Hemitelia contains, according to Clarke, two species. *H. decipiens*, J. Scott, Clarke 430, Gamble 83, is a common species in the Khasia Hills, and the Hills of Sikkim, up to 6,000 feet. Numbers of fine specimens may be seen about Kurseong, and some reach a height of 30 feet, with a rather thin, prickly stem. (E. 3423, Balasun Valley, Darjeeling, 5,000 feet; E 3424, Dumsong, Darjeeling, 5,000 feet). *H. Brunoniana*, C. B. Clarke 430 (*Alsophila Brunoniana*, Wall., *A. latebrosa*, Hook. (part) Vern. *Unyo, pakpa*, Nep.; *Pashien*, Lepcha, is a tall, thick-stemmed, handsome tree fern of Sikkim (4,000 to 7,500 feet) and the Khasia Hills (3,000 to 5,000 feet). It is the common species at Darjeeling, and often reaches 40 feet in height.

In *Alsophila*, there are, as far as is yet known, seven Indian species, most of which are found in the Eastern Himalaya. *A. latebrosa*, Hook. (part); Kurz ii. 573; Clarke 431, is found in Burma, while a variety of it (*A. Schmidiana*. Kze.) occurs in the Hills of Sikkim. *A glauca*, J. Sm.; Clarke 432 (*A. contaminans*, Wall.; Kurz ii. 573; Gamble 88) Vern. *Pakjik, paludúm*, Lepcha, is a splendid tree fern of the lower hills of Sikkim, Eastern Bengal and Burma. It is probably the largest Indian species, reaching a height of 50 feet, with a stem of considerable girth at the base, smaller above but widening again beneath the fronds. These fronds are very large, often reaching 10 to 12 feet in length, and the fern is easily recognized by its smooth rachis and leaves glaucous beneath. *A. ornata*, J. Scott, Clarke 432, and *A. Andersoni*, J. Scott, Clarke 433, are Sikkim species, which are very rare and but little known. They were collected first by the late Mr. Scott, in the Cinchona plantation at Rangbi, at an elevation of 2,500 feet. *A. Oldhami*, Bedd.; Clarke 433 (*A. Scottiana*, Baker; Gamble 88) is a very pretty tree fern, not uncommon about Darjeeling, and usually gregarious and branching. *A. glabra*, Hook.; Clarke 433; Kurz ii. 573; Gamble 88, is the common species of the plains. It is found in damp forests in the Sub-Himalayan tract and Eastern Bengal, from Nepal down to Chittagong and Tenasserim, Central and Southern India, and Ceylon (*A. gigantea*, Hook.; Thw. Enum. 396). It is, however, rather a small species, rarely reaching to more than 15 feet, though Clarke says it occasionally attains 50 feet. *A. crinita*, Hook., is a tree fern of South India and Ceylon reaching 20 feet in height and remarkable for its being densely covered with shaggy scales. None of these species are used in India, except that the inner part of the stems of Sikkim species is sometimes eaten by Lepchas.

Brainea insignis, Hook.; Kurz ii. 574; Clarke 571, is a tree fern of the pine forests of the Martaban Hills, at 4,000 to 6,000 feet elevation. It has a stem only 3 to 5 feet high.

Among other species of ferns, which, though not exactly arborescent, are yet remarkable and of interest in the Indian forests, may be mentioned *Angiopteris evecta*, Hoffm., a thick fleshy fern of most of the moister regions of India, with a huge fleshy root-stock and leaves which often reach 6 feet in length. *Acrostichum aureum*, Linn. Vern. *Dhekwa*, Beng. is a handsome fern, used occasionally for thatching in the Sundarbans. On the hillsides and in the forests of most of the mountainous regions of India is found the Bracken, *Pteris equilina*, Linn. *Asplenium polypodioides*, Mett. is a common large-leaved fern of the Himalaya, which has often a distinct stem of a few feet in height, and may almost be ranked as a tree fern.

The structure of the stems of tree ferns presents a great difference from that of either Dicotyledonous or Monocotyledonous trees. The appearance of the stem is usually that of a dark brown cylinder, marked above by regular scars, the bases of fallen leaves, and below by an entangled mass of fibres formed by the interlacement of roots. The inner structure is shewn by a horizontal section to consist mainly of three portions: *First*, the outer layer formed by the bases of fallen leaves and interlacing rootlets; *secondly*, the cellular tissue which occupies the greater part of the interior; and, *thirdly*, the vascular bundles which form an irregular and cylindrically arranged ring inside the cortical layer. These vascular bundles present the appearance of a closed mass of curved, usually crescent-shaped, outline, having on the outside a hard black layer of woody fibres, and inside two light-coloured layers of soft tissue, chiefly containing scalariform vessels. When dry, the cellular tissue which fills the interior contracts, leaving usually a hollow space, the ring of vascular bundles then showing a wavy pattern of alternately light and dark layers.

INDEX TO EUROPEAN NAMES.

INDEX TO VERNACULAR NAMES.

B.

D.

E.

F.

G.

H.

M.

O.

P.

U.

V.

INDEX TO NUMBERS OF WOOD SPECIMENS.

No.	Name.	Page.	No.	Name.	Page.
O 219	Albizzia odoratissima	158	B 291	Dalbergia nigrescens	129
O 220	Albizzia procera	159	B 292	Dipterocarpus lævis	32
O 221	Acer oblongum	99	B 293	Dipterocarpus turbinatus	32
H 222	Olea glandulifera	258	B 294	Mangifera caloneura	107
O 224	Eugenia Jambolana	195	B 295	Gmelina arborea	296
O 225	Garuga pinnata	67	B 296	Lagerströmia macrocarpa	203
O 226	Odina Wodier	111	B 298	Cinnamomum	307
H 227	Pistacia integerrima	107	B 299	Schima Noronhæ	30
O 228	Careya arborea	198	B 301	Cassia marginata	138
O 229	Bauhinia purpurea	140	B 302	Dillenia pentagyna	3
O 230	" "	140	B 303	" "	3
O 231	Cordia vestita	271	B 305	Eugenia operculata	194
O 232	Lagerstrœmia parviflora	201	B 306	Dipterocarpus tuberculatus	33
O 233	Anogeissus latifolia	186	B 307	Stereospermum suaveolens	279
H 234	Prunus Puddum	163	B 308	Carallia integerrima	178
O 235	Elæodendron Roxburghii	88	B 309	Eugenia malaccensis	193
H 236	Pyrus Pashia	169	B 311	Trewia nudiflora	360
O 237	Butea frondosa	123	B 312	Cratoxylon neriifolium	21
O 239	Eugenia Jambolana	195	B 313	Bursera serrata	68
O 240	Casearia graveolens	206	B 314	Eugenia grandis	193
H 241	Engelhardtia Colebrookiana	393	B 315	Afzelia bijuga	142
O 243	Stereospermum suaveolens	279	B 316	Eugenia	196
O 244	Cassia Fistula	137	B 317	Premna tomentosa	294
O 245	Buchanania latifolia	110	B 319	Schleichera trijuga	96
O 246	Tetranthera monopetala	310	O 324	Böhmeria rugulosa	325
O 247	Bauhinia racemosa	140	O 325	Gmelina arborea	296
O 248	Aegle Marmelos	63	B 326	Eriolæna Candollei	51
O 250	Cordia Myxa	270	B 327	Berrya Ammonilla	53
O 252	Phyllanthus Emblica	352	B 329	Albizzia procera	159
O 253	Tetranthera laurifolia	310	B 330	Vitex leucoxylon	298
O 255	Acacia Catechu	154	B 331	Homalium tomentosum	207
H 256	Ilex odorata	83	O 332	Terminalia tomentosa	184
O 257	Ehretia lævis	272	O 333	Cassia Fistula	137
O 258	Holarrhena antidysenterica	263	O 334	Eugenia operculata	194
O 259	Briedelia retusa	356	O 335	Bauhinia racemosa	140
O 260	Flacourtia Ramontchi	18	O 336	Terminalia Chebula	181
O 262	Randia dumetorum	227	O 337	Eugenia Jambolana	195
O 263	Holarrhena antidysenterica	263	O 338	" "	195
O 264	Ulmus integrifolia	342	O 339	Lagerströmia parviflora	201
O 265	Zizyphus Jujuba	89	O 340	Adina cordifolia	221
O 266	Bassia latifolia	244	O 341	Stereospermum suaveolens	279
O 268	Aegle Marmelos	63	O 342	Saccopetalum tomentosum	10
O 269	Stephegyne parvifolia	222	O 343	Gmelina arborea	296
O 270	Cratæva religiosa	16	O 344	Stephegyne parvifolia	222
O 271	Casearia graveolens	206	O 346	Garuga pinnata	67
B 272	Cedrela Toona	79	O 347	Briedelia retusa	356
B 273	(Anonaceæ)	11	O 348	Dillenia pentagyna	3
B 274	Hopea odorata	40	O 349	Terminalia belerica	180
B 276	(Anonaceæ)	ii	O 350	Hymenodictyon excelsum	225
B 278	Lophopetalum littorale	85	E 354	Castanopsis rufescens	389
B 279	Hymenodictyon thyrsiflorum	225	E 355	Ilex insignis	83
B 281	Pentace burmanica	52	E 356	Alnus nepalensis	374
B 282	Hopea odorata	40	E 357	Juglans regia	393
B 283	Shorea obtusa	39	E 358	Elæocarpus lanceæfolius	57
B 284	Gardenia costata	229	E 359	Abies Webbiana	409
B 285	Cordia fragrantissima	271	E 360	Cedrela Toona	79
B 286	Eriolæna Candollei	51	E 361	Meliosma Wallichii	103
B 287	Lophopetalum littorale	85	E 362	Daphnidium elongatum	312
B 288	Berrya Ammonilla	53	E 363	Phœbe attenuata	308
B 289	Fagræa fragrans	268	E 364	Quercus pachyphylla	386
B 290	Albizzia odoratissima	158	E 365	Magnolia Campbellii	5

No.	Name.	Page.
E 495	Castanopsis tribuloides	389
E 496	Homonoya symphylliæfolia	364
E 497	Shorea robusta	38
E 498	Cinnamomum obtusifolium	305
E 499	Spondias mangifera	113
E 500	Terminalia myriocarpa	185
B 501	Croton argyratus	359
B 502	Rhizophora mucronata	176
B 503	Pajanelia multijuga	280
B 504	Garcinia speciosa	23
B 505	(Meliaceæ)	79
B 506	Albizzia procera	159
B 507	Melia	71
B 508	Podocarpus bracteata	414
B 509	Myristica Irya	314
B 510	Lagerströmia hypoleuca	204
B 511	Hopea odorata	40
B 512	Artocarpus Chaplasha	331
B 513	Mimusops littoralis	246
B 514	Planchonia littoralis	198
B 515	Croton argyratus	359
B 516	Odina Wodier	111
B 517	Heritiera littoralis	48
B 518	Albizzia procera	159
B 519	Murraya exotica	62
B 520	Mesua ferrea	27
B 521	Diospyros Kurzii	250
B 522	Terminalia alata	184
B 523	Adenanthera pavonina	146
B 524	Afzelia bijuga	142
B 525	Calophyllum spectabile	25
O 526	Pterocarpus indicus	130
O 527	Eugenia Jambolana	195
O 528	Terminalia Chebula	181
O 529	Stephegyne parvifolia	222
O 530	Erythrina suberosa	122
O 531	Anogeissus latifolia	186
O 532	Bauhinia retusa	141
O 533	Ficus religiosa	335
O 534	Terminalia belerica	180
O 535	Eugenia Jambolana	195
O 536	Schleichera trijuga	96
O 537	Dalbergia Sissoo	126
O 538	Ficus religiosa	335
O 539	Phyllanthus Emblica	352
O 541	Gardenia turgida	228
O 542	Randia uliginosa	227
O 543	Ficus religiosa	335
O 544	Bauhinia Vahlii	139
B 545	Quercus spicata	386
B 546	Hopea odorata	40
B 547	Pinus Merkusii	398
B 548	Pterocarpus indicus	xvii
B 549	Garcinia Cowa	24
B 550	Fagræa fragrans	268
B 551	Melanorrhœa usitata	110
B 552	Quercus fenestrata	385
B 553	„ lappacea	386
B 554	Mesua ferrea	27
B 555	Shorea obtusa	39
B 556	„ „	39
B 557	Dillenia pentagyna	3
B 559	Hymenodictyon thyrsiflorum	225
B 560	Spondias mangifera	113
B 561	Stephegyne parvifolia	222
B 562	Cocos nucifera	422
B 563	Borassus flabelliformis	417
B 564	Aegle Marmelos	63
B 565	Cratæva religiosa	16
B 569	Podocarpus latifolia	414
B 572	Lagerströmia tomentosa	204
E 573	Sterculia coccinea	47
E 574	Dalbergia stipulata	129
E 575	Cinnamomum Tamala	306
E 576	Michelia Champaca	6
E 577	Alstonia scholaris	262
E 578	Semecarpus Anacardium	112
E 579	Cassia Fistula	137
E 580	Phyllanthus Emblica	352
E 581	Elæocarpus robustus	57
E 582	Oroxylum indicum	275
E 583	Ficus Cunia	339
E 584	Eugenia obovata	194
E 585	Bauhinia purpurea	141
E 586	Ficus	335
E 587	Artocarpus Chaplasha	331
E 588	Ficus comosa	338
E 589	Wendlandia exserta	225
E 590	Bauhinia malabarica	139
E 591	„ variegata	141
E 592	Machilus odoratissima	309
E 593	Pterospermum acerifolium	49
E 594	Mangifera sylvatica	108
E 595	Quercus spicata	386
E 596	Dillenia indica	3
E 597	Callicarpa arborea	282
E 598	Artocarpus integrifolia	330
E 599	Mallotus philippinensis	361
E 600	Böhmeria rugulosa	325
E 601	Ougeinia dalbergioides	120
H 602	Pinus longifolia	397
H 603	Albizzia stipulata	160
P 604	Acacia Catechu	153
H 605	Ficus cordifolia	335
H 606	„ Roxburghii	340
H 607	„ virgata	338
H 608	Juniperus excelsa	412
H 609	Pinus excelsa	399
H 610	Betula Bhojpattra	372
H 611	„ acuminata	373
H 612	Fraxinus floribunda	257
H 613	Cupressus torulosa	410
H 614	Buxus sempervirens	371
H 615	Excæcaria insignis	367
H 616	Cedrus Deodara	406
H 617	„ „	406
E 618	Dalbergia lanceolaria	129
E 619	Briedelia retusa	357
E 620	Sterculia villosa	46
E 621	Premna latifolia	294
E 622	Bassia butyracea	244
E 623	Wrightia tomentosa	264

No.	Name.	Page.	No.	Name.	Page.
W 753	Tectona grandis	293	C 823	Bauhinia variegata	141
W 754	Xylia dolabriformis	149	C 824	Stephegyne parvifolia	xxiii
W 755	Terminalia tomentosa	184	C 825	Adina cordifolia	221
W 756	Artocarpus Lakoocha	330	C 826	Gardenia turgida	228
W 757	Vitex altissima	297	C 827	Bassia latifolia	244
W 758	Artocarpus hirsuta	xxvii	C 828	Diospyros Melanoxylon	249
W 759	Hopea parviflora	41	C 829	Schrebera swietenioides	256
W 761	Xylia dolabriformis	149	C 830	Wrightia tomentosa	261
W 762	Calophyllum tomentosum	26	C 831	Cordia Macleodii	271
W 763	Cedrela Toona	79	C 832	Stereospermum suaveolens	279
W 764	Chickrassia tabularis	76	C 833	Stereospermum chelonoides	278
W 765	Lagerströmia microcarpa	202	C 834	Tectona grandis	292
W 767	Borassus flabelliformis	417	C 835	Gmelina arborea	296
W 768	Cocos nucifera	422	C 836	Ficus bengalensis	334
W 769	Areca Catechu	421	C 837	„ religiosa	336
H 770	Populus ciliata	379	C 838	„ infectoria	334
H 771	Cupressus torulosa	410	C 839	„ glomerata	340
H 772	Juniperus excelsa	412	C 840	Briedelia retusa	357
H 773	Taxus baccata	413	C 841	Phyllanthus Emblica	352
H 774	Abies Webbiana	409	C 842	Terminalia Chebula	181
H 775	„ Smithiana	408	C 843	Acacia arabica	151
H 776	Æsculus indica	95	C 844	„ eburnea	152
H 777	Quercus dilatata	xxix	W 845	Garcinia Cambogia	24
H 778	Euonymus Hamiltonianus	84	W 847	Sterculia villosa	46
H 779	Olea ferruginea	258	W 850	Pterocarpus Marsupium	133
H 780	Juglans regia	392	W 853	Lophopetalum Wightianum	86
H 781	Prunus armeniaca	162	W 855	Dalbergia latifolia	128
H 782	Cedrela serrata	79	W 857	Xylia dolabriformis	149
E 783	Cassia Fistula	137	W 861	Calophyllum Wightianum	26
E 784	Vitex alata	297	W 862	Lagerströmia microcarpa	202
E 785	Lagerströmia parviflora	201	W 863	Alstonia scholaris	262
E 786	Derris robusta	134	W 864	Cassia Fistula	137
E 788	Albizzia stipulata	160	W 867	Corypha umbraculifera	418
E 793	Mesua ferrea	27	W 868	Cocos nucifera	422
E 794	Artocarpus Lakoocha	330	W 869	Borassus flabelliformis	417
E 796	Taxus baccata	413	C 870	Sesbania ægyptiaca	118
E 797	Pinus Kasya	398	E 871	„ grandiflora	119
E 798	Cinnamomum pauciflorum	306	E 872	Acacia ferruginea	153
E 799	Myrica sapida	391	O 873	Shorea robusta	38
C 800	Hardwickia binata	143	O 874	Terminalia tomentosa	184
B 801	Tectona grandis	283	O 875	Eugenia Jambolana	195
B 802	Pentace burmanica	52	E 876	Woodfordia floribunda	200
B 803	Cedrela Toona	79	E 877	Cycas pectinata	415
B 804	Sandoricum indicum	72	E 878	Wallichia disticha	420
B 805	Xylia dolabriformis	149	E 879	Leea robusta	93
B 806	Artocarpus integrifolia	330	E 880	Leea sambucina	xv
B 807	Duabanga sonneratioides	204	P 881	Albizzia Lebbek	157
B 808	Lagerströmia Reginæ	203	P 882	Prosopis spicigera	147
B 809	Albizzia stipulata	160	P 883	Populus euphratica	378
B 810	Artocarpus Lakoocha	330	P 884	Dalbergia Sissoo	126
B 811	Albizzia procera	159	P 885	Zizyphus flexuosa	89
B 812	Garuga pinnata	67	P 886	Tamarix articulata	20
B 813	Antiaris toxicaria	332	P 887	Phœnix sylvestris	419
B 814	Barringtonia acutangula	196	P 888	Tamarix dioica	20
B 815	Pentace burmanica	52	P 889	Calligonum polygonoides	303
B 816	Carallia integerrima	178	P 890	Acacia arabica	151
B 817	Gardenia obtusifolia	229	P 891	Morus indica	328
B 818	Dipterocarpus alatus	33	P 892	Capparis aphylla	15
C 820	Erythrina indica	122	P 893	Ficus religiosa	335
C 821	Bauhinia malabarica	139	P 894	Dodonæa viscosa	101
C 822	„ purpurea	140	H 895	Taxus baccata	413

No.	Name.	Page.	No.	Name.	Page.
D 1059	Terminalia tomentosa . .	184	C 1122	Albizzia odoratissima . .	158
D 1060	Strychnos potatorum . .	269	C 1123	Soymida febrifuga . .	76
D 1061	Pterocarpus Marsupium .	133	C 1124	Buchanania latifolia . .	110
D 1062	Shorea Tumbuggaia . .	39	C 1125	Terminalia belerica . .	180
D 1063	Vitex pubescens . . .	298	C 1126	Phyllanthus Emblica . .	532
D 1064	Hardwickia pinnata . .	144	C 1127	Hymenodictyon excelsum .	225
D 1065	Gluta travancorica . .	100	C 1128	Zizyphus Jujuba . . .	89
D 1066	Heritiera Papilio . . .	48	C 1129	Gmelina arborea . . .	296
D 1069	Chloroxylon Swietenia . .	77	C 1130	Morinda exserta . . .	232
D 1070	Stereospermum chelonoides .	278	C 1131	Careya arborea . . .	198
D 1071	Zizyphus Jujuba . . .	89	C 1132	Barringtonia acutangula .	196
D 1072	Dalbergia latifolia . .	128	C 1133	Pongamia glabra . . .	133
D 1073	Mimusops Elengi . .	245	C 1134	Capparis grandis . . .	15
D 1074	Terminalia Chebula . .	181	C 1135	Eugenia Jambolana . .	195
D 1075	Pterocarpus santalinus .	132	C 1136	Adina cordifolia . . .	221
D 1076	Cassia Fistula . . .	137	C 1137	Bauhinia malabarica . .	139
D 1077	Terminalia tomentosa . .	184	C 1138	Ficus glomerata . . .	340
D 1078	Shorea Tumbuggaia . .	39	C 1139	Dolichandrone falcata . .	276
D 1079	Gyrocarpus Jacquini . .	187	C 1140	Lagerströmia parviflora .	201
D 1080	Cassia siamea . . .	138	C 1141	Cochlospermum Gossypium .	17
D 1081	Acacia ferruginea . .	153	C 1142	Gardenia turgida . . .	228
D 1082	Alangium Lamarckii . .	211	C 1143	Anogeissus acuminata . .	187
D 1083	Erythroxylon monogynum .	58	C 1144	Dalbergia lanceolaria . .	129
D 1084	Albizzia odoratissima . .	158	C 1145	Erythrina suberosa . .	122
D 1085	Acrocarpus fraxinifolius .	136	C 1146	Dalbergia latifolia . .	127
D 1086	Pterocarpus Marsupium .	133	C 1147	Hardwickia binata . .	143
D 1087	Tetranthera laurifolia . .	310	C 1148	Ulmus integrifolia . .	342
D 1088	Sterculia urens . . .	46	C 1149	Cordia Myxa . . .	270
D 1089	Celtis Wightii . . .	343	C 1150	Ficus bengalensis . .	334
D 1090	Artocarpus hirsuta . .	331	C 1151	Xylia dolabriformis . .	149
D 1091	Erythroxylon monogynum .	58	C 1152	Ougeinia dalbergioides .	120
D 1092	Shorea Talura . . .	34	C 1153	Chloroxylon Swietenia . .	77
D 1093	Melia dubia . . .	71	C 1154	Cassia Fistula . . .	137
W 1094	Eucalyptus Globulus . .	190	C 1155	Ehretia lævis . . .	272
W 1095	" " . .	190	C 1156	Ixora parviflora . . .	230
W 1096	" " . .	190	C 1157	Semecarpus Anacardium .	112
W 1097	" " . .	190	C 1158	Holarrhena antidysenterica .	263
W 1098	" " . .	190	C 1159	Terminalia Chebula . .	181
W 1099	Acacia dealbata . . .	155	C 1160	Bauhinia retusa . . .	141
W 1100	" melanoxylon . .	156	C 1161	Antidesma Ghæsembilla .	350
C 1101	Strychnos potatorum . .	269	C 1162	Celastrus senegalensis . .	87
C 1102	Sterculia urens . . .	46	C 1163	Kydia calycina . . .	44
C 1103	Odina Wodier . . .	111	C 1164	Stereospermum chelonoides .	278
C 1104	Terminalia tomentosa . .	184	C 1165	Streblus asper . . .	326
C 1105	Pterocarpus Marsupium .	133	C 1166	Ficus infectoria . . .	334
C 1106	Heterophragma Roxburghii .	277	C 1167	Diospyros montana . .	251
C 1107	Garuga pinnata . . .	67	C 1168	Ficus religiosa . . .	335
C 1108	Schrebera swietenioides . .	255	C 1169	Grewia tiliæfolia . . .	54
C 1109	Saccopetalum tomentosum .	10	C 1170	Bauhinia racemosa . .	140
C 1110	Schleichera trijuga . .	96	C 1171	Balanites Roxburghii . .	65
C 1111	Terminalia Arjuna . .	185	C 1172	Stereospermum chelonoides .	278
C 1112	Boswellia thurifera . .	66	C 1173	Gardenia latifolia . .	229
C 1113	Diospyros Melanoxylon .	249	C 1174	Briedelia retusa . . .	357
C 1114	Stereospermum suaveolens .	279	C 1175	Lebedieropsis orbicularis .	358
C 1115	Dalbergia paniculata . .	129	C 1176	Aegle Marmelos . . .	63
C 1116	Bassia latifolia . . .	244	C 1177	Kydia calycina . . .	44
C 1117	Bombax malabaricum . .	44	C 1178	Mallotus philippinensis .	361
C 1118	Acacia leucophlœa . .	152	C 1179	Oroxylum indicum . .	275
C 1119	Butea frondosa . . .	123	C 1180	Ficus hispida . . .	341
C 1120	Stephegyne parvifolia . .	222	C 1181	Ulmus integrifolia . .	342
C 1121	Anogeissus latifolia . .	186	C 1182	Elæodendron Roxburghii .	88

No.	Name.	Page.	No.	Name.	Page.
B 1317	Cephalostachyum pergracile	429	E 1394	Sterculia colorata	47
B 1318	Pseudostachyum Helferi	429	E 1395	Dillenia indica	3
B 1319	Bambusa arundinacea	428	E 1396	Eugenia Jambolana	195
B 1320	Dinochloa Maclellandii	431	E 1397	Briedelia tomentosa	357
B 1321	Bambusa Tulda	427	E 1398	Stereospermum chelonoides	278
B 1322	Dendrocalamus strictus	430	E 1399	Odina Wodier	111
B 1324	„ longispathus	431	E 1400	Calophyllum polyanthum	26
E 1325	Melocanna bambusoides	429	E 1401	Chickrassia tabularis	76
E 1327	Bambusa Brandisii	428	E 1402	Artocarpus Lakoocha	330
E 1328	„ Tulda	427	H 1403	Pinus excelsa	399
B 1329	Dendrocalamus giganteus	430	H 1404	„ „	399
W 1330	Bambusa arundinacea	428	H 1405	„ Gerardiana	398
B 1331	Gigantochloa andamanica	428	H 1406	Quercus Ilex	383
E 1332	Bambusa Balcooa	428	H 1407	Pinus excelsa	399
E 1333	„ Tulda	427	C 1408	Tectona grandis	292
O 1337	„ arundinacea	428	C 1409	„ „	292
O 1338	„ nutans	427	C 1410	Schrebera swietenioides	255
E 1339	Arundinaria falcata	427	C 1411	Stereospermum chelonoides	278
E 1340	Pseudostachyum polymor-		C 1412	Chloroxylon Swietenia	77
	phum	429	B 1413	Schrebera swietenioides	255
E 1341	Dendrocalamus Hamiltonii	430	B 1414	Odina Wodier	111
B 1346	Tectona grandis	393	B 1416	Ulmus integrifolia	342
P 1347	Dalbergia Sissoo	126	B 1417	Terminalia bialata	182
E 1351	Arundinaria racemosa	426	B 1418	Pterospermum	50
P 1352	Dendrocalamus strictus	430	B 1419	Ulmus integrifolia	342
E 1353	Cephalostachyum capitatum	429	B 1420	Berrya Ammonilla	53
E 1354	Arundinaria racemosa	426	B 1421	Heterophragma adenophylla	277
E 1356	Cinchona officinalis	224	B 1422	Diospyros ehretioides	250
E 1357	„ succirubra	224	B 1423	Vitex alata	298
E 1358	„ Calisaya	224	B 1424	Premna tomentosa	294
D 1360	Santalum album	322	B 1425	Gmelina arborea	296
E 1361	Swietenia Mahagoni	75	B 1427	Albizzia odoratissima	158
O 1362	Amoora Rohituka	73	B 1428	Cordia fragrantissima	271
O 1363	Casearia tomentosa	206	B 1429	Vitex pubescens	298
O 1365	Ficus Cunia	339	B 1431	Briedelia retusa	357
O 1366	Randia dumetorum	227	E 1432	Bombax malabaricum	44
O 1367	Tetranthera monopetala	310	E 1433	Anthocephalus Cadamba	219
O 1368	Antidesma diandrum	350	E 1434	Dysoxylum procerum	72
O 1369	Sponia politoria	345	E 1435	Gmelina arborea	296
O 1370	Wendlandia exserta	225	E 1436	Duabanga sonneratioides	204
O 1371	Psidium Guava	190	E 1437	Michelia Champaca	6
O 1372	Gmelina arborea	296	E 1438	Quercus lamellosa	388
O 1373	Tetranthera laurifolia	310	E 1439	„ annulata	387
O 1374	Bischoffia javanica	356	E 1440	Shorea robusta	38
O 1375	Briedelia montana	357	E 1441	Careya arborea	198
O 1376	Cordia Myxa	270	E 1442	Michelia excelsa	7
O 1377	Gardenia turgida	228	E 1443	Quercus annulata	387
P 1379	Acacia arabica	151	E 1444	„ spicata	386
P 1380	Prosopis spicigera	147	E 1445	„ „	386
P 1381	Salvadora persica	259	E 1446	Eugenia tetragona	194
P 1382	„ oleoides	260	E 1447	Prunus Puddum	163
P 1384	Populus euphratica	378	E 1448	Quercus lamellosa	388
B 1385	Tectona grandis	293	E 1449	Schima Wallichii	30
B 1386	Pentace burmanica	52	E 1450	Fagræa obovata	268
B 1387	Cinnamomum	307	B 1451	Xylia dolabriformis	149
P 1388	Tamarix dioica	20	B 1452	Berrya Ammonilla	53
E 1389	Garuga pinnata	67	B 1453	Albizzia Lebbek	157
E 1390	Gmelina arborea	296	B 1454	Acacia Catechu	154
E 1391	Adina sessilifolia	221	B 1455	Eriolæna Candollei	51
E 1392	Vitex leucoxylon	298	O 1456	Casearia graveolens	206
E 1393	„ alata	298	O 1457	Gmelina arborea	296

No.	Name.	Page.
B 2227	Anacardium occidentale	108
B 2228	Careya arborea	198
B 2229	Anacardium occidentale	108
B 2230	Dalbergia purpurea	128
B 2231	Albizzia odoratissima	158
B 2232	Diospyros	252
B 2233	Nauclea rotundifolia	223
B 2234	Stereospermum	279
B 2235	,,	279
B 2236	(Anonaceæ)	11
B 2238	Mesua ferrea	27
B 2239	Carapa moluccensis	74
B 2240	Rhizophora mucronata	176
B 3241	Mimusops Elengi	245
B 2243	Dipterocarpus alatus	33
B 2244	Diospyros pyrrhocarpa	252
B 2245	Dillenia pilosa	4
B 2246	Antidesma Ghœsembilla	350
B 2247	Albizzia procera	159
B 2248	Lophopetalum Wallichii	86
B 2249	Millettia	118
B 2250	Dysoxylum	72
B 2251	(Anonaceæ)	11
B 2252	Dolichandrone Rheedii	277
B 2253	Dillenia aurea	4
B 2255	Dysoxylum	72
B 2256	Eugenia grandis	193
B 2257	Calophyllum inophyllum	25
B 2258	,, ,,	52
B 2259	Sapindus	96
B 2260	Cassia	138
B 2261	Dolichandrone stipulata	276
B 2263	Calophyllum inophyllum	25
B 2265	Podocarpus bracteata	414
B 2273	Rhizophora mucronata	176
B 2274	Lagerströmia hypoleuca	204
B 2275	Dillenia pilosa	4
B 2278	Ficus retusa	336
B 2281	Polyalthia Jenkinsii	10
B 2282	Vatica lanceæfolia	34
B 2283	Lagerströmia hypoleuca	204
B 2284	Avicennia officinalis	300
B 2285	Heritiera littoralis	48
B 2286	Tetranthera laurifolia	310
B 2287	Hymenodictyon thyrsiflorum	225
B 2288	Nauclea rotundifolia	223
B 2289	Artocarpus Chaplasha	331
B 2292	Eugenia	195
B 2294	Fagræa racemosa	268
B 2295	Cassia	138
B 2300	Lophopetalum littorale	85
B 2301	Artocarpus Chaplasha	331
B 2302	Mangifera indica	107
E 2303	Gmelina arborea	296
E 2304	Cinnamomum glanduliferum	306
E 2305	Morus cuspidata	328
E 2306	,, ,,	328
D 2307	Santalum album	322
E 2308	Plecospermum spinosum	327
E 2309	Mesua ferrea	27
E 2310	Dillenia indica	3

No.	Name.	Page.
E 2311	Dillenia pentagyna	3
E 2312	Michelia excelsa	7
E 2313	,, Champaca	6
E 2314	,, Cathcartii	6
E 2315	Terminalia myriocarpa	185
E 2316	Miliusa Roxburghiana	10
B 2317	Anona squamosa	9
E 2318	Berberis nepalensis	13
E 2319	Eurya symplocina	28
E 2320	,, acuminata	29
E 2321	Saurauja napaulensis	29
E 2322	Shorea robusta	38
E 2323	Bombax malabaricum	44
E 2324	Sterculia villosa	46
E 2325	Grewia vestita	56
E 2326	Eriolæna Wallichii	50
E 2327	Grewia multiflora	56
E 2329	Zanthoxylum alatum	61, viii
E 2330	Skimmia Laureola	61
E 2331	Amoora Rohituka	73
E 2332	Cedrela Toona	79
E 2333	,, ,,	79
E 2334	Celastrus paniculatus	86
E 2335	Elæodendron Roxburghii	88
E 2336	Zizyphus rugosa	90
E 2337	Acer Campbellii	101
E 2338	,, Hookeri	99
E 2339	Meliosma simplicifolia	103
E 2340	Rhus semialata	105
E 2341	Semecarpus Anacardium	112
E 2342	Odina Wodier	110
E 2343	Erythrina indica	122
E 2344	,, stricta	122
E 2345	Butea frondosa	123
E 2346	Dalbergia lanceolaria	129
E 2347	,, Sissoo	127
E 2348	,, latifolia	127
E 2349	,, stipulata	129
E 2350	Bauhinia malabarica	139
E 2351	,, variegata	141
E 2352	Cassia Fistula	136
E 2353	Tamarindus indica	143
E 2354	Mimosa rubicaulis	148
E 2355	Acacia Catechu	154
E 2356	,, ,,	154
E 2357	,, ferruginea	153
E 2358	,, pinnata	155
E 2359	,, Intsia	155, xix
E 2360	Albizzia odoratissima	158
E 2361	,, procera	159
E 2362	,, stipulata	160
E 2363	Prunus Puddum	163
E 2364	,, ,,	163
E 2365	Eriobotrya dubia	167
E 2366	Rosa sericea	167
E 2367	Rubus ellipticus	166
E 2368	,, lasiocarpus	166
E 2369	Prunus Padus	164
E 2370	Hydrangea robusta	172

No.	Name.	Page.
B 2491	Mesua ferrea	27
B 2492	Garcinia speciosa	23
B 2493	„	23
B 2494	Pterocarpus indicus	130
B 2495	Planchonia littoralis	198
B 2496	Lagerströmia hypoleuca	204
B 2497	Mimusops littoralis	246
B 2498	Diospyros Kurzii	250
B 2499	Artocarpus Chaplasha	331
B 2500	Garcinia	23
B 2501	Dillenia indica	3
B 2502	„ aurea	4
B 2504	Mesua ferrea	27
B 2505	Dipterocarpus tuberculatus	33
B 2506	„ lævis	32
B 2507	Shorea siamensis	39
B 2508	Vatica lanceæfolia	34
B 2509	Hopea odorata	40
B 2510	Pterospermum acerifolium	49
B 2511	„ semi-sagittatum	50
B 2512	Eriolæna Candollei	51
B 2513	Lophopetalum littorale	85
B 2514	Carapa moluccensis	74
B 2515	Schleichera trijuga	96
B 2516	Chickrassia tabularis	76
B 2517	Odina Wodier	111
B 2518	Melanorrhœa usitata	110
B 2519	Mangifera caloneura	107
B 2520	Millettia pendula	118
B 2521	Dalbergia cultrata	128
B 2522	„ nigrescens	129
B 2523	„ purpurea	128
B 2524	Pterocarpus indicus	130
B 2525	Cassia Fistula	136
B 2526	„ siamea	138
B 2527	Albizzia procera	159
B 2528	„ stipulata	160
B 2529	Acacia	153
B 2530	Carallia integerrima	178
B 2531	Terminalia tomentosa	184
B 2532	„ belerica	180
B 2533	Lagerströmia tomentosa	204
B 2534	Homalium tomentosum	207
B 2525	Anthocephalus Cadamba	220
B 2536	Nauclea rotundifolia	223
B 2537	Adina sessilifolia	221
B 2538	„ cordifolia	221
B 2539	Stephegyne parvifolia	222
B 2540	Gardenia costata	229
B 2541	Diospyros cordifolia	251
B 2542	„ ehretioides	250
B 2543	Cordia Myxa	271
B 2544	Dolichandrone stipulata	279
B 2545	„ Rheedii	277
B 2546	Stereospermum chelonoides	278
B 2547	Heterophragma sulfurea	277
B 2548	Premna tomentosa	294
B 2549	Vitex leucoxylon	298
B 2550	Vitex pubescens	298
B 2551	Tectona grandis	293
B 2552	Baccaurea sapida	355
B 2553	Artocarpus Lakoocha	330
B 2554	„ Chaplasha	331
B 2555	Dipterocarpus turbinatus	32
B 2556	Podocarpus bracteata	414
B 2683	Artocarpus Chaplasha	331
B 2685	Careya arborea	198
B 2686	Baccaurea sapida	355
B 2687	Isonandra obovata	242
B 2690	Morinda exserta	232
B 2691	Cinnamomum	307
B 2692	Homalium tomentosum	207
B 2693	Artocarpus Chaplasha	331
B 2695	Cinnamomum	307
B 2696	Stereospermum xylocarpum	279
B 2697	Dalbergia cultrata	128
B 2698	Hopea odorata	40
B 2699	Homalium tomentosum	207
B 2700	Mesua ferrea	27
B 2702	Homalium tomentosum	207
B 2703	Careya arborea	198
B 2704	Altingia excelsa	175
B 2705	Albizzia	161
B 2706	Pterospermum semi-sagittatum	50
B 2708	Pterocarpus indicus	130
B 2709	Tectona grandis	293
B 2710	Careya arborea	197
B 2711	Vitex leucoxylon	298
B 2712	Cassia siamea	138
B 2713	Eugenia grandis	193
B 2714	Hopea odorata	40
B 2715	Quercus lappacea	86
B 2716	Hopea odorata	340
B 2717	Lagerströmia Reginæ	203
B 2718	Premna tomentosa	294
R 2719	Cinnamomum	307
B 2720	Baccaurea sapida	355
B 2721	Rhizophora mucronata	176
B 2722	Berrya Ammonilla	53
B 2728	Dalbergia cultrata	128
P 2729	Olea ferruginea	258
C 2731	Bassia latifolia	244
C 2732	Dalbergia latifolia	127
C 2733	Gardenia latifolia	229
C 2734	Holarrhena antidysenterica	263
C 2735	Lagerströmia parviflora	201
C 2736	Zizyphus xylopyra	90
C 2737	Terminalia belerica	180
C 2738	Phyllanthus Emblica	352
C 2739	Flacourtia Ramontchi	18
C 2740	Albizzia procera	159
C 2741	Pterocarpus Marsupium	133
C 2742	Chloroxylon Swietenia	77
C 2743	Terminalia tomentosa	184
C 2744	Anogeissus latifolia	186
C 2745	Stereospermum suaveolens	279
C 2746	Semecarpus Anacardium	112
C 2747	Careya arborea	198
C 2748	Albizzia odoratissima	158
C 2749	Lagerströmia parviflora	201

No.	Name.	Page.	No.	Name.	Page.
H 2886	Viburnum fœtens	215	H 2946	Sageretia theezans	92
H 2887	Pyrus lanata	169	H 2947	Zizyphus oxyphylla	89
H 2888	Berberis aristata	13	H 2948	Litsæa lanuginosa	312
H 2889	Cotoneaster acuminata	171	H 2949	Xylosma longifolium	18
H 2890	„ bacillaris	171	H 2950	Celastrus spinosus	xiii
H 2891	Jasminum revolutum	255	H 2951	Sageretia theezans	92
H 2892	Meliosma dilleniæfolia	103	H 2952	Rhamnus procumbens	92
H 2893	Quercus semecarpifolia	382	E 2953	Calophyllum polyanthum	26
H 2894	Berberis coriacea	14	E 2954	Bauhinia Vahlii	139
H 2895	Abies Webbiana	408	E 2955	Eugenia Kurzii	194
H 2896	„ Smithiana	407	E 2956	„ formosa	193
		xxx	E 2957	Rhododendron fulgens	238
H 2897	Euonymus Hamiltonianus	84	E 2958	„ cinnabarinum	238
H 2898	Deutzia corymbosa	173	W 2959	Tectona grandis	293
H 2899	Acer villosum	100	2961	Nectandra Rodiæi	313
H 2900	Staphylea Emodi	102	2962	Sassafras officinale	313
H 2901	Acer cæsium	100	2963	Cæsalpinia crista	135
H 2903	Rhamnus triquetrus	92	2964	„ echinata	135
H 2904	Betula acuminata	373	2965	Maclura tinctoria	328
		xxix	2966	Hæmatoxylon Campechianum	135
H 2905	Salix daphnoides	377	H 2967	Cratægus crenulata	170
H 2906	„ elegans	377	H 2968	Quercus lanuginosa	384
H 2907	Rhus succedanea	106	H 2969	Bassia latifolia	244
H 2908	Ribes glaciale	174	H 2970	Stranvæsia glaucescens	170
H 2909	Lonicera orientalis	216	H 2971	Fraxinus floribunda	257
H 2910	Salix Wallichiana	377	B 2972	Shorea siamensis	39
H 2911	Syringa Emodi	256	B 2973	„ obtusa	39
H 2912	Lonicera alpigena	217	2974	Fraxinus excelsior	257
H 2913	Vitis himalayana	93	2975	Ulmus montana	341
H 2914	Buxus sempervirens	371			xxviii
B 2915	Pentace burmanica	vii	2978	Quercus Ilex	383
E 2916	Heritiera littoralis	48	C 2979	Strychnos potatorum	269
D 2917	Pterocarpus Marsupium	132	O 2980	Shorea robusta	38
C 2918	„ „	133	O 2981	Diospyros Melanoxylon	249
P 2919	Balsamodendron Mukul	67	C 2982	Tectona grandis	292
C 2920	Ventilago maderaspatana	91	C 2983	„ „	292
C 2921	Vallaris dichotoma	261	C 2984	Dalbergia latifolia	127
W 2922	Borassus flabelliformis	417	C 2985	Cordia Macleodii	271
D 2923	Diospyros quæsita	250	C 2986	Hardwickia binata	143
C 2924	Terminalia tomentosa	184	C 2987	Tectona grandis	292
2925	Aporosa dioica	355	C 2988	Adina cordifolia	221
D 2926	Chloroxylon Swietenia	xii	C 2989	Albizzia stipulata	160
C 2927	Spatholobus Roxburghii	122	C 2990	Shorea robusta	38
C 2928	Dalbergia paniculata	129	O 2991	Elæodendron Roxburghii	38
C 2929	Hardwickia binata	143	O 2992	Odina Wodier	111
H 2930	Pistacia integerrima	107	O 2993	Eugenia Jambolana	195
P 2931	Zizyphus nummularia	89	O 2994	Adina cordifolia	221
P 2932	Celastrus spinosus	87	O 2995	Terminalia belerica	180
C 2933	Tectona grandis	292	O 2996	„ tomentosa	184
H 2934	Desmodium tiliæfolium	120	O 2997	Anogeissus latifolia	186
H 2935	Indigofera heterantha	117	O 2998	Cordia vestita	271
H 2936	Elscholtzia polystachya	301	O 2999	Lagerströmia parviflora	201
H 2937	Abelia triflora	216	O 3000	Böhmeria rugulosa	325
H 2938	Loranthus vestitus	320	O 3001	Briedelia retusa	356
H 2939	Cocculus laurifolius	12	O 3002	Ulmus integrifolia	342
H 2940	Olea glandulifera	258	O 3003	Pinus longifolia	396
H 2941	Securinega obovata	354	O 3004	Albizzia procera	159
H 2942	Rhus semialata	105	E 3005	Terminalia Catappa	182
H 2943	Adhatoda Vasica	281	H 3006	Acer villosum	100
H 2944	Acer oblongum	99	H 3007	Acer caudatum	100
H 2945	Andrachne cordifolia	349	H 3008	„ pictum	101

No.	Name.	Page.	No.	Name.	Page
E 3138	Shorea robusta	38	E 3211	Linociera macrophylla	259
E 3139	Æsculus punduana	95	E 3214	Moringa pterygosperma	114
D 3140	Santalum album	322	P 3215	Boswellia thurifera	66
B 3141	Millettia	118	P 3216	Bauhinia racemosa	140
O 3143	Camellia Thea	30	P 3217	Cratæva religiosa	16
E 3144	Anthocephalus Cadamba	220	P 3218	Grewia asiatica	55
B 3145	Baccaurea sapida ♂	355	P 3219	Cordia Macleodii	271
B 3146	„ „ ♀	355	P 3220	Sterculia urens	46
B 3147	Careya arborea	198	P 3221	Flacourtia Ramontchi	18
B 3148	Garcinia Cowa	24	P 3222	Wrightia tinctoria	264
B 3149	Schrebera swietenioides	256	P 3223	Albizzia odoratissima	158
W 3150	Coffea arabica	231	P 3224	Ficus cordifolia	335
D 3151	Pterocarpus santalinus	132	P 3225	Odina Wodier	111
D 3152	Givotia rottleriformis	365	P 3226	Moringa concanensis	114
E 3153	Anthocephalus Cadamba	220	P 3227	Grewia salvifolia	55
O 3154	Kydia calycina	44	P 3228	„ populifolia	54
D 3155	Gluta travanorica	109	P 3229	Dichrostachys cinerea	148
H 3156	Clematis barbellata	1	P 3230	Grewia pilosa	56
E 3157	Cinchona succirubra	224	P 3231	Rhus mysorensis	105
E 3158	„ Calisaya	224	O 3232	Cordia vestita	271
E 3159	„ officinalis	224	P 3235	Grewia asiatica	55
O 3160	Millingtonia hortensis	275	P 3237	„ salvifolia	55
O 3161	Diospyros Embryopteris	252	P 3238	Balsamodendron Mukul	67
H 3162	Cinnamomum Tamala	306	P 3239	Dichrostachys cinerea	148
H 3163	Juglans regia	392	P 3242	Capparis sepiaria	iii
H 3164	Ulmus	342	P 3244	„ horrida	ii
H 3165	Abies Smithiana	409	P 3245	Ehretia obtusifolia	272
H 3167	Rhus succedanea	106	P 3247	Securinega obovata	354
H 3168	Rhamnus virgatus	91	P 3248	Rhus mysorensis	105
H 3169	Celtis caucasica	344	P 3256	Grewia pilosa	56
H 3170	Rhus punjabensis	105	P 3259	Persea Nanmuh	313
H 3171	Rhododendron arboreum	236	O 3260	Nephelium Litchi	97
H 3173	Euonymus Hamiltonianus	84	O 3263	Grevillea robusta	318
H 3174	Morus serrata	328	O 3264	Parkia Roxburghii	145
H 3175	Ulmus Wallichiana	341	O 3265	Murraya Kœnigii	ix
H 3177	Cotoneaster bacillaris	171	O 3266	Ceratonia siliqua	145
H 3178	Parrotia Jacquemontiana	174	O 3267	Cupressus sempervirens	411
H 3179	Corylus Colurna	391	O 3270	Melaleuca leucadendron	188
H 3180	Lonicera quinquelocularis	216	E 3271	Saurauja Roxburghii	v
H 3181	Cedrela serrata	79	E 3272	Sapindus attenuatus	97
H 3182	Rhus Cotinus	104	E 3273	Viburnum lutescens	215
H 3183	Diospyros Lotus	252	E 3274	Dalbergia foliacea	130
H 3184	Desmodium tiliæfolium	120	E 3275	Melastoma malabathricum	199
H 3185	Pyrus Pashia	169	E 3276	Callicarpa cana	283
H 3186	„ lanata	169	E 3277	Ricinus communis	364
H 3187	Euonymus lacerus	84	E 3278	Leea gigantea	93
H 3188	Populus ciliata	379	E 3279	Flemingia semialata	123
		xxix	E 3281	Desmodium Cephalotes	121
H 3189	Staphylea Emodi	102	E 3282	Securinega Leucopyrus	354
H 3190	Fraxinus floribunda	257	E 3283	Tetranthera angustifolia	311
C 3191	Eriolæna Hookeriana	51	E 3284	Glycosmis pentaphylla	x
		vii	E 3285	Dichopsis polyantha	243
H 3192	Lespedeza eriocarpa	119	E 3286	Hyptianthera stricta	xxiii
H 3194	Marsdenia Roylei	266	E 3287	Holigarna longifolia	112
B 3195	Murraya exotica	62	E 3288	Tetranthera nudiflora	208
B 3197	Calophyllum spectabile	25	E 3289	Hibiscus macrophyllus	vi
B 3198	Alsodeia	16	E 3290	Tectona grandis	293
B 3201	Croton oblongifolius	359	E 3291	„ „	293
B 3203	Bauhinia malabarica	139	E 3293	Skimmia Laureola	ix
B 3204	Anogeissus acuminata	187	E 3294	Samara floribunda	240
D 3209	Sapindus emarginatus	96	E 3295	Paramignya monophylla	x

No.	Name.	Page.	No.	Name.	Page.
C 3432	Desmodium pulchellum .	xvi	C 3496	Thevetia neriifolia . .	xxvi
C 3433	Zizyphus xylopyra . .	xiv	C 3497	Eryeibe paniculata . .	xxvi
C 3434	Shorea robusta . . .	vi	C 3498	Briedelia tomentosa . .	xxviii
C 3435	Gardenia turgida . . .	xxiii	C 3499	Cipadessa fruticosa . .	xi
C 3436	Sterculia urens . . .	vii	C 3500	Strychnos potatorum . .	xxvi
C 3437	Eriolæna Hookeriana . .	vii	C 3501	Phyllanthus lanceolarius .	xxviii
C 3438	Embelia robusta . . .	xxiv	C 3502	Maba buxifolia . . .	xxv
C 3439	Eugenia Heyneana . .	xx	C 3503	Briedelia stipularis . .	xxix
C 3440	Shorea robusta . . .	vi	C 3504	Sideroxylon tomentosum .	xxiv
C 3441	" " . . .	vi	C 3506	Acacia leucophlœa . .	xviii
C 3442	Heptapleurum venulosum .	xxii	C 3507	Pisonia aculeata . . .	xxvii
C 3443	Chloroxylon Swietenia .	xii	C 3508	Zizyphus xylopyra . .	xiv
C 3444	Shorea robusta . . .	vi	C 3509	Euphorbia Tirucalli . .	xxix
C 3445	Callicarpa arborea . .	xxvii	C 3511	Carissa Carandas . . .	xxv
C 3446	Calotropis gigantea . .	xxvi	C 3512	Calotropis gigantea . .	xxvi
C 3447	Indigofera pulchella . .	xvi	C 3513	Ochrocarpus longifolius .	iv
C 3448	Celastrus paniculata . .	xiii	C 3514	Xylia dolabriformis . .	xviii
C 3449	Ailanthus excelsa . .	x	C 3515	Atalantia monophylla . .	x
C 3450	Dalbergia volubilis . .	xvii	C 3516	Shorea robusta . . .	vi
C 3451	Breynia rhamnoides . .	xxviii	C 3517	Gyrocarpus Jacquinii . .	xx
C 3452	Lebedicropsis orbicularis .	xxix	C 3518	Carissa diffusa . . .	xxv
C 3453	Flacourtia Ramontchi . .	iii	C 3519	Flacourtia sepiaria . .	iii
C 3454	Schrebera swietenioides .	xxv	C 3520	Webera aciatica . . .	xxiii
C 3455	Cordia Macleodii . . .	xxvi	C 3521	Celastrus emarginatus . .	xiv
C 3456	Dalbergia latifolia . .	xvii	C 3522	Dalbergia latifolia . .	xvii
C 3457	Grewia salvifolia . .	vii	C 3523	Pterospermum suberifolium .	vii
C 3458	Croton oblongifolius . .	xxix	C 3524	Ochrocarpus longifolius .	iv
C 3459	Heynea trijuga . . .	xi	C 3526	Acacia Catechu . . .	xviii
C 3460	Cæsalpinia sepiaria . .	xvii	C 3527	Casearia tomentosa . .	xxi
C 3461	Terminalia Arjuna . .	xx	C 3528	Embelia robusta . . .	xxiv
C 3462	Anogeissus acuminata . .	xx	C 3529	Odina Wodier . . .	xv
C 3463	Ardisia solanacea . . .	xxiv	C 3530	Limonia acidissima . .	x
C 3464	Ixora parviflora . . .	xxiii	C 3531	Terminalia Chebula . .	xx
C 3465	Gardenia gummifera . .	xxiii	C 3532	Buchanania latifolia . .	xv
C 3466	Alangium Lamarckii . .	xxii	C 3533	Schleichera trijuga . .	xiv
C 3467	Olax scandens . . .	xiii	C 3534	Pterospermum suberifolium .	vii
C 3468	Acacia Intsia . . .	xix	C 3535	Morinda tinctoria . .	xxiv
C 3470	Barringtonia acutangula .	xxi	C 3536	Saccopetalum tomentosum .	ii
C 3471	Saccopetalum tomentosum .	ii	C 3537	Strychnos Nux-vomica . .	xxvi
C 3472	Shorea robusta . . .	vi	C 3538	" " . .	xxvi
C 3473	" " . . .	vi	C 3539	Phyllanthus Emblica . .	xxviii
C 3474	Diospyros Embryopteris .	xxv	C 3541	Ochna squarrosa . . .	x
C 3475	Rhabdia viminea . . .	xxvi	C 3542	Pterocarpus Marsupium .	xvii
C 3476	Cedrela Toona . . .	xii	C 3543	Adina cordifolia . . .	xxiii
C 3477	Ougeinia dalbergioides . .	xvi	C 3544	Cassia Fistula . . .	xviii
C 3478	Shorea robusta . . .	vi	C 3545	Cedrela Toona . . .	xii
C 3479	" " . . .	vi	C 3546	Xylia dolabriformis . .	xviii
C 3480	" " . . .	vi	C 3547	Lagerströmia parviflora .	xxi
C 3481	Plectronia didyma . .	xxiii	C 3548	Gelonium lanceolatum . .	xxix
C 3482	Carallia integerrima . .	xx	C 3549	Gmelina arborea . . .	xxvi
C 3483	Polyalthia suberosa . .	i	C 3550	Vitex pubescens . . .	xxvii
C 3484	Ventilago calyculata . .	xiv	C 3551	Mimusops indica . . .	xxiv
C 3485	Phyllanthus lanceolarius .	xxviii	C 3553	Phyllanthus lanceolarius .	xxviii
C 3486	Linociera dichotoma . .	xxv	C 3556	Shorea robusta . . .	vi
C 3488	Flacourtia Ramontchi . .	iii	C 3558	Holarrhena antidysenterica .	xxvi
C 3490	Shorea robusta . . .	vi	C 3559	Zizyphus xylopyra . .	xiv
C 3491	Symplocos racemosa . .	xxv	C 3560	Albizzia Lebbek . . .	xix
C 3492	Nyctanthes Arbor-tristis .	xxv	C 3561	Memecylon umbellatum . .	xxi
C 3493	Diospyros Melanoxylon .	xxiv	C 3562	Anogeissus latifolia . .	xx
C 3494	Olax scandens . . .	xiii	C 3564	Alangium Lamarckii . .	xxii
C 3495	Murraya exotica . . .	x	C 3565	Hymenodictyon excelsum .	xxiii

INDEX TO SCIENTIFIC NAMES.

C.

D.